NOTABLE
TWENTIETH-CENTURY
SCIENTISTS

NOTABLE
TWENTIETH-CENTURY
SCIENTISTS

VOLUME 4 S-Z/INDEXES

Emily J. McMurray, Editor

Jane Kelly Kosek and Roger M. Valade III, Associate Editors

 **Gale Research Inc.**

An International Thomson Publishing Company

I(T)P

NEW YORK • LONDON • BONN • BOSTON • DETROIT • MADRID
MELBOURNE • MEXICO CITY • PARIS • SINGAPORE • TOKYO
TORONTO • WASHINGTON • ALBANY NY • BELMONT CA • CINCINNATI OH

Editor
Emily J. McMurray

Production Editor
Donna Olendorf

Associate Editors
Joanna Brod
Pamela S. Dear
Kathleen J. Edgar
Marie Ellavich
David M. Galens
Jeff Hill
Denise E. Kasinec
Thomas F. McMahon
Jane Kelly Kosek
Mark F. Mikula
Mary L. Onorato
Scot Peacock
Terrie M. Rooney
Deborah A. Stanley
Aarti Dhawan Stephens
Brandon Trenz
Roger M. Valade III
Polly A. Vedder
Thomas Wiloch

Assistant Editors
John Jorgenson
Margaret Mazurkiewicz
Geri J. Speace
Linda Tidrick
Kathleen Wilson

Senior Editor
James G. Lesniak

Picture Permissions Supervisor
Margaret A. Chamberlain

Picture Permissions Assistant
Susan Brohman

Front Matter Design
Paul Lewon

Art Director
Cynthia Baldwin

Cover Design
Mark Howell

Copyright © 1995
Gale Research Inc.
835 Penobscot Building
Detroit, MI 48226-4094

ISBN 0-8103-9181-3 (Set)
ISBN 0-8103-9185-6 (Volume 4)

Printed in the United States of America.
Published simultaneously in the United Kingdom by Gale Research International Limited (An affiliated company of Gale Research Inc.)

I(T)P ™ Gale Research Inc., an International Thomson Publishing Company.
ITP logo is a trademark under license.

Library of Congress Cataloging-in-Publication Data

Notable twentieth century scientists / Emily J. McMurray, editor.
    p. cm.
    Includes bibliographical references and index
    ISBN 0-8103-9181-3 (set)
    1. Scientists—Biography—Dictionaries. 2. Engineers-
-Biography—Dictionaries. I. McMurray, Emily J., 1959- .
Q141.N73 1995
509.2′2—dc20
[B]   94-5263
                                                                CIP

10 9 8 7 6 5 4 3

Contents

Introduction

Over the past several years, Gale Research Inc. has received numerous requests from librarians for a source providing biographies of scientists. *Notable Twentieth-Century Scientists* has been designed specifically to fill that niche. The four-volume set provides students, educators, librarians, researchers, and general readers with an affordable and comprehensive source of biographical information on approximately 1,300 scientists active in this century in all of the natural, physical, and applied sciences, including the traditionally studied subjects of astronomy, biology, botany, chemistry, earth science, mathematics, medicine, physics, technology, and zoology, as well as the more recently established and as yet sparsely covered fields of computer science, ecology, engineering, and environmental science. International in scope, *Notable Twentieth-Century Scientists* coverage ranges from the well-known scientific giants of the early century to contemporary scientists working at the cutting edge of discovery and knowledge.

Superior Coverage of Women, Minority and Non-Western Scientists

Addressing the growing interest in and demand for biographical information on women, minority and non-Western scientists, *Notable Twentieth-Century Scientists* also seeks to bring to light the achievements of more than 225 women scientists, almost 150 Asian American, African American, Hispanic American, and Native American scientists, and nearly 75 scientists from countries outside North America and Western Europe. The scarcity of published information on scientists representing these groups became evident during the compilation of this volume; as a result, information for many of the sketches on these listees has been obtained through telephone interviews and correspondence with the scientists themselves or with their universities, companies, laboratories, or families.

Though we have made every attempt to include key figures, we make no claim to having isolated the "most notable" women, minority, or non-Western scientists—an impossible goal. We are pleased that the majority of the biographies we wanted to feature are included; however, time constraints, space limitations, and research and interview availability prevented us from listing more scientists deserving of inclusion. Our hope is that in presenting these entries, we are providing a basis for future research on the lives and contributions of these important and historically marginalized segments of the scientific community.

Inclusion Criteria

A preliminary list of scientists was compiled from a wide variety of sources, including established reference works such as the *Dictionary of Scientific Biography,* history of science indexes, science periodicals, awards lists, and suggestions from organizations and associations. The advisory board, made up of librarians, academics, and individuals from scientific associations, evaluated the names and made suggestions for inclusion. Final selection of names to include was made by the editors on the basis of the following criteria:

- Discoveries, inventions, overall contributions, influence, and/or impact on scientific progress in the twentieth century
- Receipt of a major science award; all Nobel Prize winners in Physics, Chemistry, and Physiology or Medicine are found here, as are selected recipients of numerous other awards, including the Fields Medal (mathematics), Albert Lasker awards (medicine), the Tyler Prize (environmental science), the National Medal of Science, and the National Medal of Technology
- Involvement or influence in education, organizational leadership, or public policy
- Familiarity to the general public
- Notable "first" achievements, including degrees earned, positions held, or organizations founded; several listees involved in the first space flights are also included

Entries Provide Easy Access to Information

Entries are arranged alphabetically by surname. The typical *Notable Twentieth-Century Scientists* entry provides the following information:

- **Entry head**—offers an at-a-glance information: name, birth/death dates, nationality and primary field(s) of specialization.

- **Biographical essay**—ranges from 400 to 2500 words and provides basic biographical information [including date and place of birth, parents names and occupations, name(s) of spouse(s) and children, educational background and degrees earned, career positions, awards and honors earned] and scientific endeavors and achievements explained in prose accessible to high school students and readers without a scientific background. Intratextual headings within the essays highlight the significant events in the listee's life and career, allowing readers to find information they seek quickly and easily. In addition, **bold-faced** names in entries direct readers to entries on scientists' colleagues, predecessors, or contemporaries also found in *Notable Twentieth-Century Scientists*.

- **Selected Writings** by the Scientist section—lists representative publications, including important papers, textbooks, research works, autobiographies, lectures, etc.

- **Sources** section—provides citations of biographies, interviews, periodicals, obituaries, and other sources about the listee for readers seeking additional information.

Indexes Provide Numerous Points of Access

In addition to the complete list of scientists found at the beginning of each volume, readers seeking the names of additional individuals of a given country, heritage, gender, or profession can consult the following indexes at the end of volume 4 for additional listings:

- **Field of Specialization Index**—groups listees according to the scientific fields to which they have contributed
- **Gender Index**—provides lists of the women and men covered
- **Nationality/Ethnicity Index**—arranges listees by country of birth and/or citizenship and/or ethnic heritage
- Comprehensive **Subject Index**—provides volume and page references for scientists and scientific terms used in the text. Includes cross references.

Photos

Individuals in *Notable Twentieth-Century Scientists* come to life in the 394 photos of the scientists.

Acknowledgments

The editors would like to thank, in addition to the advisory board, the following individuals for their assistance with various aspects of the production of *Notable Twentieth-Century Scientists*: Bruce Seely, Secretary of the Society for the History of Technology and Professor at Michigan Technological University, Houghton, Michigan for his assistance in identifying notable engineers; Nancy Anderson, librarian at University of Illinois at Urbana Champaign Mathematics Library for assistance with mathematicians; Arthur Norberg, former director of the Charles Babbage Institute Center for the History of Information Processing at the University of Minnesota, Minneapolis, for assistance with computer scientists; and Kathleen Prestwidge for much assistance in identifying and providing information about minority and women scientists. Special acknowledgment is also due to Jim Kamp and Roger Valade for their technical assistance and to Denise Kasinec for her administrative assistance in the preparation of these volumes.

Advisory Board

Contributors

Russell Aiuto, Ethan E. Allen, Julie Anderson, Olga K. Anderson, Denise Adams Arnold, Nancy E. Bard, Dorothy Barnhouse, Jeffery Bass, Matthew A. Bille, Maurice Bleifeld, Michael Boersma, Barbara A. Branca, Hovey Brock, Valerie Brown, Leonard C. Bruno, Raymond E. Bullock, Marjorie Burgess, Gerard J. Buskes, Joseph Cain, Jill Carpenter, Dennis W. Cheek, Kim A. Cheek, Tom Chen, Miyoko Chu, Jane Stewart Cook, Kelly Otter Cooper, G. Scott Crawford, Tom Crawford, Karin Deck, Margaret DiCanio, Mindi Dickstein, Rowan L. Dordick, John Henry Dreyfuss, Thomas Drucker, Kala Dwarakanath, Marianne Fedunkiw, Martin R. Feldman, Eliseo Fernandez, George A. Ferrance, Jerome P. Ferrance, William T. Fletcher, David N. Ford, Karyn Hede George, Chris Hables Gray, Loretta Hall, Betsy Hanson, Robert M. Hawthorne, Jr., Elizabeth Henry, T. A. Heppenheimer, Frank Hertle, J. D. Hunley, Roger Jaffe, Jessica Jahiel, Jeanne Spriter James, J. Sydney Jones, D. George Joseph, Mark J. Kaiser, Lee Katterman, Sandra Katzman, Janet Kieffer Kelley, Evelyn B. Kelly, Karen S. Kelly, James Klockow, Susan E. Kolmer, Geeta Kothari, Jennifer Kramer, Marc Kusinitz, Roger D. Launius, Penelope Lawbaugh, Benedict A. Leerburger, Jeanne M. Lesinski, Linda Lewin, John E. Little, Pamela O. Long, C. D. Lord, Laura Mangan-Grenier, Gail B. C. Marsella, Liz Marshall, Renee D. Mastrocco, Patricia M. McAdams, William M. McBride, Mike McClure, Avril McDonald, Christopher McGrail, Kimberlyn McGrail, Donald J. McGraw, William J. McPeak, Carla Mecoli-Kamp, Leslie Mertz, Robert Messer, Philip Metcalfe, Fei Fei Wang Metzler, George A. Milite, Carol L. Moberg, Sally M. Moite, Patrick Moore, Paula M. Morin, M. C. Nagel, Margo Nash, Laura Newman, David E. Newton, F. C. Nicholson, Joan Oleck, Donna Olshansky, Nicholas Pease, Daniel Pendick, David Petechuk, Tom K. Phares, Devera Pine, Karl Preuss, Rayma Prince, Barbara J. Proujan, Amy M. Punke, Lewis Pyenson, Susan Sheets Pyenson, Jeff Raines, Mary Raum, Leslie Reinherz, Jordan P. Richman, Vita Richman, Francis Rogers, Terrie M. Romano, Daniel Rooney, Shari Rudavsky, Kathy Sammis, Karen Sands, Neeraja Sankaran, Joel Schwarz, Philip Duhan Segal, Alan R. Shepherd, Joel Simon, Michael Sims, Julian A. Smith, Linda Wasmer Smith, Lawrence Souder, Dorothy Spencer, John Spizzirri, David Sprinkle, Darwin H. Stapleton, Sharon F. Suer, Maureen L. Tan, Peter H. Taylor, Melinda Jardon Thach, Sebastian Thaler, R. F. Trimble, Cynthia Washam, Wallace Mack White, C. A. Williams, Katherine Williams, Nicholas S. Williamson, Philip K. Wilson, Rodolfo A. Windhausen, Karen Wilhelm, Karen Withem, Alexandra Witze, Cathleen M. Zucco.

Photo Credits

Photographs appearing in *Notable Twentieth-Century Scientists* were received from the following sources:

AP/Wide World Photos: **pp. 1, 31, 36, 38, 45, 48, 75, 98, 108, 112, 129, 150, 166, 169, 172, 174, 186, 192, 195, 198, 202, 203, 207, 211, 219, 221, 231, 234, 241, 278, 285, 295, 297, 299, 310, 313, 315, 321, 322, 326, 331, 341, 344, 348, 358, 373, 377, 388, 390, 397, 401, 402, 414, 417, 424, 434, 437, 441, 456, 476, 481, 484, 496, 503, 507, 516, 518, 529, 539, 541, 544, 550, 556, 565, 568, 573, 597, 613, 624, 628, 649, 657, 660, 668, 671, 675, 685, 702, 707, 709, 713, 722, 725, 744, 746, 756, 761, 763, 768, 771, 774, 778, 803, 806, 833, 835, 842, 853, 855, 877, 885, 890, 900, 932, 939, 949, 951, 959, 970, 986, 990, 1023, 1045, 1057, 1060, 1062, 1084, 1090, 1125, 1134, 1137, 1160, 1163, 1172, 1184, 1185, 1188, 1191, 1202, 1203, 1206, 1211, 1216, 1219, 1234, 1236, 1240, 1246, 1253, 1261, 1271, 1281, 1284, 1313, 1339, 1346, 1354, 1357, 1386, 1392, 1405, 1410, 1414, 1420, 1429, 1436, 1444, 1455, 1465, 1475, 1483, 1493, 1499, 1507, 1513, 1516, 1525, 1536, 1549, 1568, 1573, 1591, 1600, 1618, 1643, 1654, 1666, 1678, 1680, 1683, 1714, 1720, 1724, 1733, 1741, 1751, 1762, 1767, 1777, 1781, 1800, 1802, 1803, 1808, 1818, 1832, 1849, 1865, 1877, 1891, 1894, 1898, 1908, 1917, 1961, 1970, 1975, 2005, 2016, 2029, 2034, 2039, 2041, 2049, 2064, 2072, 2101, 2106, 2112, 2122, 2125, 2128, 2153, 2158, 2161, 2168, 2170, 2176, 2200, 2208, 2227, 2236, 2245, 2266, 2273, 2302, 2305;** The Bettmann Archive: **pp. 12, 426, 739, 925, 1037;** Courtesy of Keiiti Aki: **p. 14;** UPI/Bettmann: **pp. 58, 511, 546, 583, 751, 945, 1003, 1016;** Courtesy of Francisco Jose Ayala: **p. 80;** UPI/Bettmann Newsphotos: **pp. 83;** Archive Photos: **pp. 102, 523, 1040, 1210, 1769, 1990, 2132, 2276;** Courtesy of George Keith Batchelor: **pp. 124;** Photograph by Ingbert Gruttner, Courtesy of Arnold Beckman: **pp. 131;** Courtesy of Robert Arbuckle Berner: **p. 160;** Courtesy of Yvonne Brill: **p. 255;** Courtesy of Lester Brown: **p. 266;** Courtesy of Glenn W. Burton: **p. 283;** Courtesy of John R. Cairns: **p. 291;** The Granger Collection, New York: **pp. 304, 469, 652, 655, 1050, 1086, 1168, 1480, 1588, 1754, 1796, 2019, 2054;** New York University Medical Center Archives: **p. 355;** Courtesy of Stanley N. Cohen: **p. 379;** Courtesy of Rita R. Colwell: **p. 386;** Courtesy of Francisco Dallmeier: **p. 445;** Courtesy of Michael Ellis DeBakey: **p. 466;** Courtesy of Dennis Jack: **p. 489;** Courtesy of Nance K. Dicciani: **p. 495;** Courtesy of Theodor O. Diener: **p. 499;** Courtesy of Edsgar Dijkstra: **p. 501;** Archive/DPA: **pp. 513, 839, 1958;** Courtesy of Mildred Dresselhaus: **p. 521;** Courtesy of Cecile Hoover Edwards: **p. 559;** Courtesy of Helen T. Edwards: **p. 561;** Courtesy of the estate of Philo T. Farnsworth: **p. 609;** Courtesy of Lloyd Ferguson: **p. 622;** Courtesy of Solomon Fuller: **p. 710;** Courtesy of William Gates: **p. 733;** Courtesy of Adele Jean Goldberg: **p. 781;** Courtesy of Mary L. Good: **p. 796;** © Michael K. Nichols/Magnum Photos: **p. 798;** Courtesy of Govindjee: **p. 809;** Courtesy of Evelyn Granville: **p. 812;** Photograph by Washington University Photographic Services, Courtesy of Viktor Hamburger: **p. 851;** Courtesy of Wesley L. Harris, Sr.: **p. 868;** Courtesy of William Hewlett: **p. 918;** Photograph by Bradford Bachrach, Courtesy of Gladys Hobby: **p. 935;** Archive/Express Newspapers: **pp. 937, 961;** Courtesy of Phillip G. Hubbard: **p. 967;** Courtesy of Russell Hulse: **p. 978;** Courtesy of Keiichi Itakura: **p. 998;** Courtesy of Frank B. Jewett: **p. 1021;** Courtesy of Barbara Crawford Johnson: **p. 1026;** Courtesy of Marvin M. Johnson: **p. 1032;** Courtesy of Harold S. Johnston: **p. 1036;** Courtesy of Yuet Wai Kan: **p. 1056;** Courtesy of Motoo Kimura: **p. 1097;** Courtesy of Georges Köhler: **p. 1117;** Courtesy of Thomas E. Kurtz: **p. 1147;** Courtesy of Raymond Kurzweil: **p. 1149;** Mary Evans Picture Library: **pp. 1178, 1462, 1637, 1829, 2027, 2119, 2138, 2250;** The Granger Collection: **p. 1197, 1640, 1737;** Courtesy of Susan E. Leeman: **p. 1213;** Courtesy of Carroll Leevy: **p. 1214;** © Leonard Freed/Magnum Photos: **p. 1222;** Courtesy of Aldo Leopold: **p. 1226;** Courtesy of Julian H. Lewis: **p. 1239;** Courtesy of Irene D. Long: **p. 1270;** © Dennis Stock/Magnum Photos: **p. 1277;** Courtesy of Stanford University Visual Services: **p. 1350;** Courtesy of Evangelia Micheli-Tzanakou: **p. 1370;** Courtesy of Elizabeth and James Miller: **p. 1376;** Courtesy of Stanley L. Miller: **p. 1379;** Courtesy of Beatrice Mintz: **p. 1394;** Courtesy of Russell Mittermeier: **p. 1397;** Courtesy of Robert N. Noyce: **p. 1491;** Courtesy of NASA: **p. 1497;** Courtesy of David Packard: **p. 1523;** Courtesy of Jennie Patrick: **p. 1535;** Brown Brothers, Sterling, Pa.: **pp. 1542, 1708, 1871, 1998,**

Entry List

A

Abelson, Philip Hauge
Adams, Roger
Adams, Walter Sydney
Adamson, Joy
Adrian, Edgar Douglas
Ahlfors, Lars V.
Aiken, Howard
Aki, Keiiti
Alcala, Jose
Alcorn, George Edward
Alder, Kurt
Aleksandrov, Pavel S.
Alexander, Archie Alphonso
Alexander, Hattie
Alexanderson, Ernst F. W.
Alfvén, Hannes Olof Gösta
Alikhanov, Abram Isaakovich
Allen, Jr., William E.
Altman, Sidney
Alvarez, Luis
Alvariño, Angeles
Amdahl, Gene M.
Ames, Bruce N.
Ammann, Othmar Hermann
Anders, Edward
Andersen, Dorothy
Anderson, Carl David
Anderson, Gloria L.
Anderson, Philip Warren
Anderson, W. French
Anfinsen, Christian Boehmer
Appleton, Edward
Arber, Agnes
Arber, Werner
Armstrong, Edwin Howard
Armstrong, Neil
Arrhenius, Svante August
Artin, Emil
Astbury, William
Aston, Francis W.
Atanasoff, John
Atiyah, Michael Francis
Auerbach, Charlotte
Avery, Oswald Theodore
Axelrod, Julius
Ayala, Francisco J.

Ayrton, Hertha

B

Baade, Walter
Bachrach, Howard L.
Backus, John
Baeyer, Johann Friedrich Wilhelm
   Adolf von
Baez, Albert V.
Bailey, Florence Merriam
Baird, John Logie
Baker, Alan
Baker, Sara Josephine
Baltimore, David
Banach, Stefan
Banks, Harvey Washington
Banting, Frederick G.
Bárány, Robert
Barber, Jr., Jesse B.
Bardeen, John
Barkla, Charles Glover
Barnard, Christiaan Neethling
Barnes, William Harry
Barr, Murray Llewellyn
Bartlett, Neil
Barton, Derek H. R.
Bascom, Florence
Basov, Nikolai
Batchelor, George
Bateson, William
Bayliss, William Maddock
Beadle, George Wells
Beckman, Arnold
Becquerel, Antoine-Henri
Bednorz, J. Georg
Begay, Fred
Behring, Emil von
Békésy, Georg von
Bell, Gordon
Bell Burnell, Jocelyn Susan
Beltrán, Enrique
Benacerraf, Baruj
Benzer, Seymour
Berg, Paul
Berger, Hans
Bergius, Friedrich

Bergström, Sune Karl
Berkowitz, Joan B.
Bernays, Paul
Berner, Robert A.
Bernstein, Dorothy Lewis
Berry, Leonidas Harris
Bers, Lipman
Best, Charles Herbert
Bethe, Hans
Bhabha, Homi Jehangir
Binnig, Gerd
Birkhoff, George David
Bishop, Alfred A.
Bishop, J. Michael
Bishop, Katharine Scott
Bjerknes, Jacob
Bjerknes, Vilhelm
Black, Davidson
Black, James
Blackburn, Elizabeth H.
Blackett, Patrick Maynard Stuart
Blackwell, David
Bloch, Felix
Bloch, Konrad
Blodgett, Katharine Burr
Bloembergen, Nicolaas
Bluford, Guion S.
Blumberg, Baruch Samuel
Bohr, Aage
Bohr, Niels
Bolin, Bert
Bondi, Hermann
Booker, Walter M.
Bordet, Jules
Borel, Émile
Borlaug, Norman
Born, Max
Bosch, Karl
Bose, Satyendranath
Bothe, Walther
Bott, Raoul
Bovet, Daniel
Bowie, William
Boyer, Herbert W.
Boykin, Otis
Brady, St. Elmo
Bragg, William Henry
Bragg, William Lawrence

Branson, Herman
Brattain, Walter Houser
Braun, Karl Ferdinand
Breit, Gregory
Brenner, Sydney
Bressani, Ricardo
Bridgman, Percy Williams
Brill, Yvonne Claeys
Bronk, Detlev Wulf
Brønsted, Johannes Nicolaus
Brooks, Ronald E.
Brouwer, Luitzen Egbertus Jan
Brown, Herbert C.
Brown, Lester R.
Brown, Michael S.
Brown, Rachel Fuller
Browne, Marjorie Lee
Bucher, Walter Herman
Buchner, Eduard
Bullard, Edward
Bundy, Robert F.
Burbidge, E. Margaret
Burbidge, Geoffrey
Burnet, Frank Macfarlane
Burton, Glenn W.
Bush, Vannevar
Butenandt, Adolf

C

Cairns, Jr., John
Calderón, Alberto P.
Caldicott, Helen
Callender, Clive O.
Calvin, Melvin
Cambra, Jessie G.
Canady, Alexa I.
Cannon, Annie Jump
Cantor, Georg
Cardona, Manuel
Cardozo, W. Warrick
Cardús, David
Carlson, Chester
Carothers, Wallace Hume
Carrel, Alexis
Carrier, Willis
Carruthers, George R.
Carson, Benjamin S.
Carson, Rachel
Carver, George Washington
Castro, George
Cech, Thomas R.
Chadwick, James
Chain, Ernst Boris
Chamberlain, Owen
Chamberlin, Thomas Chrowder
Chance, Britton
Chandrasekhar, Subrahmanyan
Chang, Min-Chueh
Chargaff, Erwin

Charpak, Georges
Chaudhari, Praveen
Cherenkov, Pavel A.
Chestnut, Harold
Chew, Geoffrey Foucar
Child, Charles Manning
Chinn, May Edward
Cho, Alfred Y.
Chu, Paul Ching-Wu
Church, Alonzo
Clarke, Edith
Claude, Albert
Claude, Georges
Clay, Jacob
Clay-Jolles, Tettje Clasina
Cloud, Preston
Cobb, Jewel Plummer
Cobb, William Montague
Cockcroft, John D.
Cohen, Paul
Cohen, Stanley
Cohen, Stanley N.
Cohn, Mildred
Cohn, Zanvil
Colmenares, Margarita
Colwell, Rita R.
Commoner, Barry
Compton, Arthur Holly
Conway, Lynn Ann
Conwell, Esther Marly
Cooke, Lloyd M.
Coolidge, William D.
Cooper, Leon
Corey, Elias James
Cori, Carl Ferdinand
Cori, Gerty T.
Cormack, Allan M.
Cornforth, John
Coulomb, Jean
Courant, Richard
Cournand, André F.
Cousteau, Jacques
Cowings, Patricia S.
Cox, Elbert Frank
Cox, Geraldine V.
Cox, Gertrude Mary
Cram, Donald J.
Cray, Seymour
Crick, Francis
Cronin, James W.
Crosby, Elizabeth Caroline
Crosthwait Jr., David Nelson
Curie, Marie
Curie, Pierre

D

Dale, Henry Hallett
Dalén, Nils
Dallmeier, Francisco

Dalrymple, G. Brent
Daly, Marie M.
Daly, Reginald Aldworth
Dam, Henrik
Daniels, Walter T.
Dantzig, George Bernard
Darden, Christine
Dart, Raymond A.
Dausset, Jean
Davis, Margaret B.
Davis, Marguerite
Davis, Jr., Raymond
Davisson, Clinton
DeBakey, Michael Ellis
de Broglie, Louis Victor
Debye, Peter
de Duvé, Christian
de Forest, Lee
de Gennes, Pierre-Gilles
Dehmelt, Hans
Deisenhofer, Johann
Delbrück, Max
Deligné, Pierre
Dennis, Jack B.
de Sitter, Willem
d'Hérelle, Félix
Diaz, Henry F.
Dicciani, Nance K.
Diels, Otto
Diener, Theodor Otto
Dijkstra, Edsger W.
Dirac, Paul
Djerassi, Carl
Dobzhansky, Theodosius
Doisy, Edward A.
Dole, Vincent P.
Domagk, Gerhard
Donaldson, Simon
Douglas, Donald W.
Draper, Charles Stark
Dresselhaus, Mildred S.
Drew, Charles R.
Drucker, Daniel Charles
Dubois, Eugène
Dubos, René
Dulbecco, Renato
Durand, William F.
Durrell, Gerald
du Vigneaud, Vincent
Dyson, Freeman J.

E

Earle, Sylvia A.
Eccles, John C.
Eckert, J. Presper
Eddington, Arthur Stanley
Edelman, Gerald M.
Edgerton, Harold
Edinger, Tilly

Edison, Thomas Alva
Edwards, Cecile Hoover
Edwards, Helen T.
Ehrenfest, Paul
Ehrenfest-Afanaseva, Tatiana
Ehrlich, Paul
Ehrlich, Paul R.
Eigen, Manfred
Eijkman, Christiaan
Einstein, Albert
Einthoven, Willem
Eisner, Thomas
Eldredge, Niles
Elion, Gertrude Belle
El-Sayed, Mostafa Amr
Elton, Charles
Emerson, Gladys Anderson
Enders, John F.
Engler, Adolph Gustav Heinrich
Enskog, David
Erlanger, Joseph
Ernst, Richard R.
Esaki, Leo
Esau, Katherine
Estrin, Thelma
Euler, Ulf von
Euler-Chelpin, Hans von
Evans, Alice
Evans, James C.

F

Faber, Sandra M.
Farnsworth, Philo T.
Farquhar, Marilyn G.
Farr, Wanda K.
Fauci, Anthony S.
Favaloro, René Geronimo
Fedoroff, Nina V.
Feigenbaum, Edward A.
Feigenbaum, Mitchell
Fell, Honor Bridget
Ferguson, Lloyd N.
Fermi, Enrico
Fersman, Aleksandr Evgenievich
Feynman, Richard P.
Fibiger, Johannes
Fieser, Louis
Fieser, Mary Peters
Fischer, Edmond H.
Fischer, Emil
Fischer, Ernst Otto
Fischer, Hans
Fisher, Elizabeth F.
Fisher, Ronald A.
Fitch, Val Logsdon
Fitzroy, Nancy D.
Fleming, Alexander
Fleming, John Ambrose
Flexner, Simon

Florey, Howard Walter
Flory, Paul
Flügge-Lotz, Irmgard
Fokker, Anthony H. G.
Forbush, Scott Ellsworth
Ford, Henry
Forrester, Jay W.
Forssmann, Werner
Fossey, Dian
Fowler, William A.
Fox, Sidney W.
Fraenkel, Abraham Adolf
Fraenkel-Conrat, Heinz
Franck, James
Frank, Il'ya
Franklin, Rosalind Elsie
Fraser-Reid, Bertram Oliver
Fréchet, Maurice
Freedman, Michael H.
Frenkel, Yakov Ilyich
Friedman, Jerome
Friedmann, Aleksandr A.
Friend, Charlotte
Frisch, Karl von
Frisch, Otto Robert
Fujita, Tetsuya Theodore
Fukui, Kenichi
Fuller, Solomon

G

Gabor, Dennis
Gadgil, Madhav
Gadgil, Sulochana
Gagarin, Yuri A.
Gajdusek, D. Carleton
Gallo, Robert C.
Gamow, George
Gardner, Julia Anna
Garrod, Archibald
Gasser, Herbert Spencer
Gates, Bill
Gates, Jr., Sylvester James
Gaviola, Enrique
Gayle, Helene Doris
Geiger, Hans
Geiringer, Hilda
Geller, Margaret Joan
Gell-Mann, Murray
Ghiorso, Albert
Giacconi, Riccardo
Giaever, Ivar
Giauque, William F.
Gibbs, William Francis
Giblett, Eloise R.
Gilbert, Walter
Gilbreth, Frank
Gilbreth, Lillian
Glaser, Donald
Glashow, Sheldon Lee

Glenn, Jr., John H.
Goddard, Robert H.
Gödel, Kurt Friedrich
Goeppert-Mayer, Maria
Goethals, George W.
Gold, Thomas
Goldberg, Adele
Goldmark, Peter Carl
Goldring, Winifred
Goldschmidt, Richard B.
Goldschmidt, Victor
Goldstein, Avram
Goldstein, Joseph L.
Golgi, Camillo
Good, Mary L.
Goodall, Jane
Goudsmit, Samuel A.
Gould, Stephen Jay
Gourdine, Meredith Charles
Gourneau, Dwight
Govindjee
Granit, Ragnar Arthur
Granville, Evelyn Boyd
Greatbatch, Wilson
Greenewalt, Crawford H.
Griffith, Frederick
Grignard, François Auguste Victor
Gross, Carol
Grothendieck, Alexander
Groves, Leslie Richard
Guillaume, Charles-Edouard
Guillemin, Roger
Gullstrand, Allvar
Gutenberg, Beno
Guth, Alan
Gutierrez, Orlando A.

H

Haagen-Smit, A. J.
Haber, Fritz
Hadamard, Jacques
Hahn, Otto
Haldane, John Burdon Sanderson
Hale, George Ellery
Hall, Lloyd Augustus
Hamburger, Viktor
Hamilton, Alice
Hanafusa, Hidesaburo
Hannah, Marc R.
Hansen, James
Harden, Arthur
Hardy, Alister C.
Hardy, Godfrey Harold
Hardy, Harriet
Harmon, E'lise F.
Harris, Cyril
Harris, Wesley L.
Hartline, Haldan Keffer
Hassel, Odd

Hauptman, Herbert A.
Hausdorff, Felix
Hawking, Stephen
Hawkins, W. Lincoln
Haworth, Walter
Hay, Elizabeth D.
Hazen, Elizabeth Lee
Healy, Bernadine
Heimlich, Henry Jay
Heinkel, Ernst
Heisenberg, Werner Karl
Hench, Philip Showalter
Henderson, Cornelius Langston
Henry, John Edward
Henry, Warren Elliott
Herschbach, Dudley R.
Hershey, Alfred Day
Hertz, Gustav
Hertzsprung, Ejnar
Herzberg, Gerhard
Herzenberg, Caroline L.
Hess, Harry Hammond
Hess, Victor
Hess, Walter Rudolf
Hevesy, Georg von
Hewish, Antony
Hewlett, William
Heymans, Corneille Jean-François
Heyrovský, Jaroslav
Hicks, Beatrice
Hilbert, David
Hill, Archibald V.
Hill, Henry A.
Hinshelwood, Cyril N.
Hinton, William Augustus
Hitchings, George H.
Hobby, Gladys Lounsbury
Hodgkin, Alan Lloyd
Hodgkin, Dorothy Crowfoot
Hoffmann, Roald
Hofstadter, Robert
Hogg, Helen Sawyer
Holley, Robert William
Holmes, Arthur
Hopkins, Frederick Gowland
Hopper, Grace
Horn, Michael Hastings
Horstmann, Dorothy Millicent
Houdry, Eugene
Hounsfield, Godfrey
Houssay, Bernardo
Hoyle, Fred
Hrdlička, Aleš
Huang, Alice Shih-hou
Hubbard, Philip G.
Hubbert, M. King
Hubble, Edwin
Hubel, David H.
Huber, Robert
Huggins, Charles B.
Hulse, Russell A.
Humason, Milton L.

Hunsaker, Jerome C.
Hutchinson, G. Evelyn
Huxley, Andrew Fielding
Huxley, Julian
Hyde, Ida H.
Hyman, Libbie Henrietta

I

Imes, Elmer Samuel
Ioffe, Abram F.
Isaacs, Alick
Itakura, Keiichi
Iverson, F. Kenneth

J

Jackson, Shirley Ann
Jacob, François
Jansky, Karl
Janzen, Dan
Jarvik, Robert K.
Jason, Robert S.
Jeffreys, Harold
Jeffries, Zay
Jemison, Mae C.
Jensen, J. Hans D.
Jerne, Niels K.
Jewett, Frank Baldwin
Jobs, Steven
Johannsen, Wilhelm Ludvig
Johnson, Barbara Crawford
Johnson, Clarence L.
Johnson, Jr., John B.
Johnson, Joseph Lealand
Johnson, Katherine Coleman
  Goble
Johnson, Marvin M.
Johnson, Virginia E.
Johnston, Harold S.
Joliot-Curie, Frédéric
Joliot-Curie, Irène
Jones, Fred
Jones, Mary Ellen
Josephson, Brian D.
Julian, Percy Lavon
Juran, Joseph M.
Just, Ernest Everett

K

Kamerlingh Onnes, Heike
Kan, Yuet Wai
Kapitsa, Pyotr
Kapitza, Pyotor Leonidovich
  See Kapitsa, Pyotr
Karle, Isabella
Karle, Jerome

Karlin, Samuel
Karrer, Paul
Kastler, Alfred
Kates, Robert W.
Kato, Tosio
Katz, Bernard
Katz, Donald L.
Kay, Alan C.
Keith, Arthur
Kelsey, Frances Oldham
Kemeny, John G.
Kendall, Edward C.
Kendall, Henry W.
Kendrew, John
Kettering, Charles Franklin
Kettlewell, Bernard
Khorana, Har Gobind
Khush, Gurdev S.
Kilburn, Thomas M.
Kilby, Jack St. Clair
Kimura, Motoo
Kinoshita, Toichiro
Kinsey, Alfred
Kirouac, Conrad
  See Marie-Victorin, Frère
Kishimoto, Tadamitsu
Kistiakowsky, George B.
Kittrell, Flemmie Pansy
Klug, Aaron
Knopf, Eleanora Bliss
Knudsen, William Claire
Knuth, Donald E.
Koch, Robert
Kocher, Theodor
Kodaira, Kunihiko
Kohler, Georges
Kolff, Willem Johan
Kolmogorov, Andrey Nikolayevich
Kolthoff, Izaak Maurits
Konishi, Masakazu
Kornberg, Arthur
Korolyov, Sergei
Kossel, Albrecht
Kountz, Samuel L.
Krebs, Edwin G.
Krebs, Hans Adolf
Krim, Mathilde
Krogh, August
Kuhlmann-Wilsdorf, Doris
Kuhn, Richard
Kuiper, Gerard Peter
Kurchatov, Igor
Kurtz, Thomas Eugene
Kurzweil, Raymond
Kusch, Polycarp

L

Ladd-Franklin, Christine
Lamb, Jr., Willis E.
Lancaster, Cleo

Lancefield, Rebecca Craighill
Land, Edwin H.
Landau, Lev Davidovich
Landsberg, Helmut E.
Landsteiner, Karl
Langevin, Paul
Langmuir, Irving
Latimer, Lewis H.
Lattes, C. M. G.
Laub, Jakob Johann
Laue, Max von
Lauterbur, Paul C.
Laveran, Alphonse
Lawless, Theodore K.
Lawrence, Ernest Orlando
Leakey, Louis
Leakey, Mary
Leakey, Richard E.
Leavitt, Henrietta
Le Beau, Désirée
Lebesgue, Henri
Le Cadet, Georges
Leder, Philip
Lederberg, Joshua
Lederman, Leon Max
Lee, Raphael C.
Lee, Tsung-Dao
Lee, Yuan T.
Leeman, Susan E.
Leevy, Carroll
Leffall, Jr., LaSalle D.
Lehmann, Inge
Lehn, Jean-Marie
Leloir, Luis F.
Lemaître, Georges
Lenard, Philipp E. A. von
Leopold, Aldo
Leopold, Estella Bergere
Leopold, Luna
Lester, Jr., William Alexander
Levi-Civita, Tullio
Levi-Montalcini, Rita
Lewis, Gilbert Newton
Lewis, Julian Herman
Lewis, Warren K.
Li, Ching Chun
Li, Choh Hao
Libby, Willard F.
Liepmann, Hans Wolfgang
Lillie, Frank Rattray
Lim, Robert K. S.
Lin, Chia-Chiao
Lipmann, Fritz
Lippmann, Gabriel
Lipscomb, Jr., William Nunn
Little, Arthur D.
Lizhi, Fang
Lloyd, Ruth Smith
Loeb, Jacques
Loewi, Otto
Logan, Myra A.
London, Fritz

Long, Irene D.
Lonsdale, Kathleen
Lord Rayleigh
    See Strutt, John William
Lorentz, Hendrik Antoon
Lorenz, Edward N.
Lorenz, Konrad
Lovelock, James E.
Luria, Salvador Edward
Lwoff, André
Lynen, Feodor
Lynk, Miles Vandahurst

M

Maathai, Wangari
MacArthur, Robert H.
Macdonald, Eleanor Josephine
MacDonald, Gordon
MacGill, Elsie Gregory
Mac Lane, Saunders
MacLeod, Colin Munro
Macleod, John James Rickard
Maillart, Robert
Maiman, Theodore
Maloney, Arnold Hamilton
Mandelbrot, Benoit B.
Mandel'shtam, Leonid Isaakovich
Manton, Sidnie Milana
Marchbanks, Jr., Vance H.
Marconi, Guglielmo
Marcus, Rudolph A.
Margulis, Gregori Aleksandrovitch
Margulis, Lynn
Marie-Victorin, Frère
Markov, Andrei Andreevich
Martin, A. J. P.
Massevitch, Alla G.
Massey, Walter E.
Massie, Samuel P.
Masters, William Howell
Matthews, Alva T.
Matuyama, Motonori
Mauchly, John William
Maunder, Annie Russell
Maury, Antonia
Maury, Carlotta Joaquina
Maynard Smith, John
Mayr, Ernst
McAfee, Walter S.
McCarthy, John
McCarty, Maclyn
McClintock, Barbara
McCollum, Elmer Verner
McConnell, Harden
McMillan, Edwin M.
Medawar, Peter Brian
Meitner, Lise
Mendenhall, Dorothy Reed
Merrifield, R. Bruce

Meselson, Matthew
Metchnikoff, Élie
Meyerhof, Otto
Michel, Hartmut
Micheli-Tzanakou, Evangelia
Michelson, Albert
Midgley, Jr., Thomas
Miller, Elizabeth C. and James A.
Miller, Stanley Lloyd
Millikan, Robert A.
Milne, Edward Arthur
Milnor, John
Milstein, César
Minkowski, Hermann
Minkowski, Rudolph
Minot, George Richards
Minsky, Marvin
Mintz, Beatrice
Mitchell, Peter D.
Mittermeier, Russell
Mohorovičić, Andrija
Moissan, Henri
Molina, Mario
Moniz, Egas
Monod, Jacques Lucien
Montagnier, Luc
Moore, Charlotte E.
Moore, Raymond Cecil
Moore, Ruth
Moore, Stanford
Morawetz, Cathleen Synge
Morgan, Arthur E.
Morgan, Garrett A.
Morgan, Thomas Hunt
Mori, Shigefumi
Morley, Edward Williams
Morrison, Philip
Moseley, Henry Gwyn Jeffreys
Mössbauer, Rudolf
Mott, Nevill Francis
Mottelson, Ben R.
Moulton, Forest Ray
Muller, Hermann Joseph
Müller, K. Alex
Müller, Paul
Mulliken, Robert S.
Mullis, Kary
Munk, Walter
Murphy, William P.
Murray, Joseph E.

N

Nabrit, Samuel Milton
Nagata, Takesi
Nambu, Yoichiro
Nathans, Daniel
Natta, Giulio
Neal, Homer Alfred
Néel, Louis

Neher, Erwin
Nernst, Walther
Neufeld, Elizabeth F.
Newell, Allen
Newell, Norman Dennis
Nice, Margaret Morse
Nichols, Roberta J.
Nicolle, Charles J. H.
Nier, Alfred O. C.
Nirenberg, Marshall Warren
Nishizawa, Jun-ichi
Nishizuka, Yasutomi
Noble, G. K.
Noddack, Ida Tacke
Noether, Emmy
Noguchi, Hideyo
Nomura, Masayasu
Norrish, Ronald G. W.
Northrop, John Howard
Novikov, Sergei
Noyce, Robert

O

Oberth, Hermann
Ocampo, Adriana C.
Ochoa, Ellen
Ochoa, Severo
Odum, Eugene Pleasants
Odum, Howard T.
Ogilvie, Ida H.
Olden, Kenneth
Oldham, Richard Dixon
Onnes, Heike Kamerlingh
    See Kamerlingh Onnes, Heike
Onsager, Lars
Oort, Jan Hendrik
Oparin, Aleksandr Ivanovich
Oppenheimer, J. Robert
Osborn, Mary J.
Osterbrock, Donald E.
Ostwald, Friedrich Wilhelm

P

Packard, David
Palade, George
Panajiotatou, Angeliki
Panofsky, Wolfgang K. H.
Papanicolaou, George
Pardue, Mary Lou
Parker, Charles Stewart
Parsons, John T.
Patrick, Jennie R.
Patrick, Ruth
Patterson, Claire
Patterson, Frederick Douglass
Paul, Wolfgang

Pauli, Wolfgang
Pauling, Linus
Pavlov, Ivan Petrovich
Payne-Gaposchkin, Cecilia
Peano, Giuseppe
Pearson, Karl
Peden, Irene Carswell
Pedersen, Charles John
Pellier, Laurence Delisle
Pennington, Mary Engle
Penrose, Roger
Penzias, Arno
Perey, Marguerite
Perrin, Jean Baptiste
Pert, Candace B.
Perutz, Max
Péter, Rózsa
Petermann, Mary Locke
Peterson, Edith R.
Piasecki, Frank
Piccard, Auguste
Pimentel, David
Pinchot, Gifford
Pincus, Gregory Goodwin
Planck, Max
Pogue, William Reid
Poincaré, Jules Henri
Poindexter, Hildrus A.
Polanyi, John C.
Polubarinova-Kochina, Pelageya
    Yakovlevna
Pólya, George
Ponnamperuma, Cyril
Porter, George
Porter, Rodney
Poulsen, Valdemar
Pound, Robert
Powell, Cecil Frank
Powless, David
Prandtl, Ludwig
Pregl, Fritz
Prelog, Vladimir
Pressman, Ada I.
Prichard, Diana García
Prigogine, Ilya
Prokhorov, Aleksandr
Punnett, R. C.
Purcell, Edward Mills

Q

Qöyawayma, Alfred H.
Quarterman, Lloyd Albert
Quimby, Edith H.
Quinland, William Samuel

R

Rabi, I. I.

Rainwater, James
Ramalingaswami, Vulimiri
Raman, C. V.
Ramanujan, S. I.
Ramart-Lucas, Pauline
Ramey, Estelle R.
Ramón y Cajal, Santiago
Ramsay, William
Ramsey, Frank Plumpton
Ramsey, Norman Foster
Randoin, Lucie
Rao, C. N. R.
Ratner, Sarah
Ray, Dixy Lee
Rayleigh, Lord
    See Strutt, John William
Reber, Grote
Reddy, Raj
Reed, Walter
Rees, Mina S.
Reichmanis, Elsa
Reichstein, Tadeus
Reid, Lonnie
Reines, Frederick
Revelle, Roger
Richards, Jr., Dickinson Woodruff
Richards, Ellen Swallow
Richards, Theodore William
Richardson, Lewis Fry
Richardson, Owen W.
Richet, Charles Robert
Richter, Burton
Richter, Charles F.
Rickover, Hyman G.
Ride, Sally
Rigas, Harriett B.
Risi, Joseph
Ritchie, Dennis
Robbins, Frederick
Roberts, Lawrence
Roberts, Richard J.
Robinson, Julia
Robinson, Robert
Rock, John
Rockwell, Mabel M.
Roelofs, Wendell L.
Rogers, Marguerite M.
Rohrer, Heinrich
Roman, Nancy Grace
Romer, Alfred Sherwood
Romero, Juan Carlos
Röntgen, Wilhelm Conrad
Ross, Mary G.
Ross, Ronald
Rossby, Carl-Gustaf
Rothschild, Miriam
Rous, Peyton
Rowland, F. Sherwood
Rowley, Janet D.
Rubbia, Carlo
Rubin, Vera Cooper
Runcorn, S. K.

Ruska, Ernst
Russell, Bertrand
Russell, Elizabeth Shull
Russell, Frederick Stratten
Russell, Henry Norris
Russell, Loris Shano
Rutherford, Ernest
Ružička, Leopold
Ryle, Martin

S

Sabatier, Paul
Sabin, Albert
Sabin, Florence Rena
Sagan, Carl
Sager, Ruth
Sakharov, Andrei
Sakmann, Bert
Salam, Abdus
Salk, Jonas
Samuelsson, Bengt
Sanchez, David A.
Sanchez, Pedro A.
Sandage, Allan R.
Sanger, Frederick
Satcher, David
Schaller, George
Schally, Andrew V.
Scharff Goldhaber, Gertrude
Scharrer, Berta
Schawlow, Arthur L.
Schneider, Stephen H.
Schou, Mogens
Schrieffer, J. Robert
Schrödinger, Erwin
Schultes, Richard Evans
Schwartz, Melvin
Schwinger, Julian
Seaborg, Glenn T.
Segrè, Emilio
Seibert, Florence B.
Seitz, Frederick
Semenov, Nikolai N.
Serre, Jean-Pierre
Shannon, Claude
Shapiro, Irwin
Shapley, Harlow
Sharp, Phillip A.
Sharp, Robert Phillip
Shaw, Mary
Sheldrake, Rupert
Shepard, Jr., Alan B.
Sherrington, Charles Scott
Shockley, Dolores Cooper
Shockley, William
Shoemaker, Eugene M.
Shokalsky, Yuly Mikhaylovich
Shtokman, Vladimir Borisovich
Shurney, Robert E.

Siegbahn, Kai M.
Siegbahn, Karl M. G.
Sikorsky, Igor I.
Simon, Dorothy Martin
Simon, Herbert A.
Simpson, George Gaylord
Singer, I. M.
Singer, Maxine
Sioui, Richard H.
Sitterly, Charlotte Moore
    See Moore, Charlotte E.
Skoog, Folke Karl
Slater, John Clarke
Slipher, Vesto M.
Slye, Maud
Smale, Stephen
Smith, Hamilton O.
Smith, Michael
Snell, George Davis
Soddy, Frederick
Solberg, Halvor
Solomon, Susan
Sommerfeld, Arnold
Sommerville, Duncan McLaren
    Young
Sorensen, Charles E.
Sørensen, Søren Peter Lauritz
Spaeth, Mary
Sparling, Rebecca H.
Spedding, Frank Harold
Spemann, Hans
Sperry, Elmer
Sperry, Roger W.
Spitzer, Jr., Lyman
Stahl, Franklin W.
Stanley, Wendell Meredith
Stark, Johannes
Starling, Ernest H.
Starr, Chauncey
Starzl, Thomas
Staudinger, Hermann
Stefanik, Milan Ratislav
Stein, William Howard
Steinberger, Jack
Steinman, David B.
Steinmetz, Charles P.
Steptoe, Patrick
Stern, Otto
Stevens, Nettie Maria
Stever, H. Guyford
Steward, Frederick Campion
Stewart, Thomas Dale
Stibitz, George R.
Stock, Alfred
Stoll, Alice M.
Stommel, Henry
Størmer, Fredrik
Strassmann, Fritz
Straus, Jr., William Levi
Strutt, John William
Strutt, Robert
Stubbe, JoAnne

Sturtevant, A. H.
Sumner, James B.
Suomi, Verner E.
Sutherland, Earl
Sutherland, Ivan
Sutton, Walter Stanborough
Svedberg, Theodor
Swaminathan, M. S.
Synge, Richard
Szent-Györgyi, Albert
Szilard, Leo

T

Tamm, Igor
Tan Jiazhen
Tapia, Richard A.
Tarski, Alfred
Tatum, Edward Lawrie
Taube, Henry
Taussig, Helen Brooke
Taylor, Frederick Winslow
Taylor, Jr., Joseph H.
Taylor, Moddie
Taylor, Richard E.
Taylor, Stuart
Telkes, Maria
Teller, Edward
Temin, Howard
Tereshkova, Valentina
Terman, Frederick
Terzaghi, Karl
Tesla, Nikola
Tesoro, Giuliana Cavaglieri
Tharp, Marie
Theiler, Max
Theorell, Axel Hugo Teodor
Thom, René Frédéric
Thomas, E. Donnall
Thomas, Martha Jane Bergin
Thompson, D'Arcy Wentworth
Thompson, Kenneth
Thomson, George Paget
Thomson, J. J.
Thurston, William
Tien, Ping King
Tildon, J. Tyson
Timoshenko, Stephen P.
Tinbergen, Nikolaas
Ting, Samuel C. C.
Tiselius, Arne
Tizard, Henry
Todd, Alexander
Tombaugh, Clyde W.
Tomonaga, Sin-Itiro
Tonegawa, Susumu
Townes, Charles H.
Trotter, Mildred
Trump, John G.
Tsao, George T.

Chronology of Scientific Advancement

1895 Scottish physicist *C. T. R. Wilson* invents the cloud chamber

French physicist *Jean Baptiste Perrin* confirms the nature of cathode rays

1896 American agricultural chemist *George Washington Carver* begins work at the Tuskegee Institute

1897 English physicist *J. J. Thomson* discovers the electron

1898 Polish-born French radiation chemist *Marie Curie* and French physicist *Pierre Curie* discover polonium and radium

1900 German physicist *Max Planck* develops Planck's Constant

1901 Austrian American immunologist *Karl Landsteiner* discovers A, B, and O blood types

German geneticist *Wilhelm Weinberg* outlines the "difference method" in his first important paper on heredity

1902 English geneticist *William Bateson* translates Austrian botanist Gregor Mendel's work

1903 Polish-born French radiation chemist *Marie Curie* becomes the first woman to be awarded the Nobel Prize

German chemist *Otto Diels* isolates molecular structure of cholesterol

1904 English electrical engineer *John Ambrose Fleming* develops the Fleming Valve

Russian physiologist *Ivan Petrovich Pavlov* receives the Nobel Prize for digestion research

1905 German-born American physicist *Albert Einstein* publishes the theory of relativity

German chemist *Fritz Haber* publishes *Thermodynamics of Technical Gas Reactions*

German chemist *Walther Nernst*'s research leads to the Third Law of Thermodynamics

1906 Danish physical chemist *Johannes Nicolaus Brønsted* publishes his first paper on affinity

English neurophysiologist *Charles Scott Sherrington* publishes *The Integrative Action of the Nervous System*

1907 Prussian-born American physicist *Albert Michelson* becomes the first American to receive the Nobel Prize for physics

1908 American astrophysicist *George Ellery Hale* discovers magnetic fields in sunspots

1909 German bacteriologist and immunologist *Paul Ehrlich* discovers a cure for syphilis

American engineer and inventor *Charles Franklin Kettering* successfully tests the first prototype of the electric automobile starter

1910 English American mathematician *Alfred North Whitehead* and English mathematician and philosopher *Bertrand Russell* publish the first volume of *Principia Mathematica*

American engineer and inventor *Lee De Forest* attempts the first live broadcast of radio

New Zealand-born English physicist *Ernest Rutherford* postulates the modern concept of the atom

 1911 English mathematician *Godfrey Harold Hardy* begins his collaboration with J. E. Littlewood

Polish-born French radiation chemist *Marie Curie* becomes the first scientist to win a second Nobel Prize

 1912 Danish physicist *Niels Bohr* develops a new theory of atomic structure

Austrian physicist *Victor Hess* discovers cosmic rays

English biochemist *Frederick Gowland Hopkins* publishes a groundbreaking work illustrating the nutritional importance of vitamins

German physicist *Max von Laue* discovers X-ray diffraction

Austrian physicist *Lise Meitner* becomes the first woman professor in Germany

German meteorologist and geophysicist *Alfred Wegener* proposes the theory of continental drift

1913 German bacteriologist and immunologist *Paul Ehrlich* gives an address explaining the future of chemotherapy

English physicist *Henry Gwyn Jeffreys Moseley* discovers atomic number

French physicist *Jean Baptiste Perrin* verifies German-born American physicist *Albert Einstein*'s calculations of Brownian Motion

American astronomer and astrophysicist *Henry Norris Russell* publishes Hertzsprung-Russell diagram

Russian-born American aeronautical engineer *Igor I. Sikorsky* designs *Ilya Mourometz* bomber

German chemist *Richard Willstätter* and Arthur Stoll publish their first studies of chlorophyll

American geneticist *A. H. Sturtevant* develops gene mapping

 1916 American chemist and physicist *Irving Langmuir* receives a patent for an energy-efficient, longer-lasting tungsten filament light bulb

American geneticist and embryologist *Thomas Hunt Morgan* publishes *A Critique of the Theory of Evolution*

German theoretical physicist *Arnold Sommerfeld* reworks Danish physicist *Niels Bohr*'s atomic theory

American anatomist *Florence Rena Sabin* publishes *The Origin and Development of the Lymphatic System*

1918 Danish physical chemist *Johannes Nicolaus Brønsted* publishes his thirteenth paper on affinity

1919 New Zealand-born English physicist *Ernest Rutherford* determines that alpha particles can split atoms

1920 American astronomer *Harlow Shapley* convinces the scientific community that the Milky Way is much larger than originally thought and the Earth's solar system is not its center

1921 Canadian physiologist *Frederick G. Banting* and Canadian physiologist *Charles Herbert Best* discover insulin

 1923 Danish physical chemist *Johannes Nicolaus Brønsted* redefines acids and bases

English astronomer *Arthur Stanley Eddington* publishes *Mathematical Theory of Relativity*

American astronomer *Edwin Hubble* confirms the existence of galaxies outside the Milky Way

American physicist *Robert A. Millikan* begins his study of cosmic rays

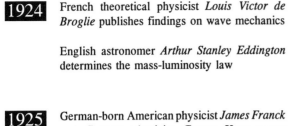

French theoretical physicist *Louis Victor de Broglie* publishes findings on wave mechanics

English astronomer *Arthur Stanley Eddington* determines the mass-luminosity law

 1925

German-born American physicist *James Franck* and German physicist *Gustav Hertz* prove Danish physicist *Niels Bohr*'s theory of the quantum atom

Italian-born American physicist *Enrico Fermi* publishes a paper explaining Austro-Hungarian-born Swiss physicist *Wolfgang Pauli*'s exclusion principle

English statistician and geneticist *Ronald A. Fisher* publishes *Statistical Methods for Research Workers*

 1926

German-born English physicist *Max Born* explains the wave function

American physicist and rocket pioneer *Robert H. Goddard* launches the first liquid-propellant rocket

American geneticist *Hermann Joseph Muller* confirms that X rays greatly increase the mutation rate in *Drosophila*

Austrian physicist *Erwin Schrödinger* publishes his wave equation

1927

American physicist *Arthur Holly Compton* receives the Nobel Prize for X-ray research

English physiologist *Henry Hallett Dale* identifies the chemical mediator involved in the transmission of nerve impulses

German chemist *Otto Diels* develops a successful dehydrogenating process

German physicist *Werner Karl Heisenberg* develops the Uncertainty Principle

Belgian astronomer *Georges Lemaître* formulates the big bang theory

Hungarian American mathematical physicist *Eugene Paul Wigner* develops the law of the conservation of parity

American astronomer *Edwin Hubble* puts together the theory of the expanding universe, or Hubble's Law

1928

German chemist *Otto Diels* and German chemist *Kurt Alder* develop the Diels-Alder Reaction

Scottish bacteriologist *Alexander Fleming* discovers penicillin

Austro-Hungarian-born German physicist *Hermann Oberth* publishes a book explaining the basic principles of space flight

Indian physicist *C. V. Raman* discovers the Raman Effect

 1929

American physicist *Robert Van de Graaff* constructs the first working model of his particle accelerator

Danish astronomer *Ejnar Hertzsprung* receives the Gold Medal Award for calculating the first intergalactic distance

Norwegian American chemist *Lars Onsager* develops the Law of Reciprocal Relations

German-born American mathematician *Hermann Weyl* develops a mathematical theory for the neutrino

Russian-born American physicist and engineer *Vladimir Zworykin* files his first patent for color television

1930

English statistician and geneticist *Ronald A. Fisher* publishes *The Genetical Theory of Natural Selection*

Austrian-born American mathematician *Kurt Friedrich Gödel* proves the incompleteness theorem

Austro-Hungarian-born Swiss physicist *Wolfgang Pauli* proposes the existence of the neutrino

 1931

American engineer *Vannevar Bush* develops the differential analyzer with colleagues

American chemist *Wallace Hume Carothers* founds the synthetic rubber manufacturing industry with his research

South African-born American virologist *Max Theiler*'s research leads to the production of the first yellow-fever vaccine

German biochemist *Otto Warburg* establishes the Kaiser Wilhelm Institute for Cell Physiology

 1936 German experimental physicist *Hans Geiger* perfects the Geiger-Mueller Counter

Russian biochemist *Aleksandr Ivanovich Oparin* publishes his origin of life theory

 1932 English atomic physicist *John Cockcroft* and Irish experimental physicist *Ernest Walton* split the atom

English mathematician *Alan Turing* publishes a paper detailing a machine that would serve as a model for the first working computer

American physicist *Carl David Anderson* discovers the positron

English-born Indian physiologist and geneticist *John Burdon Sanderson Haldane* publishes *The Causes of Evolution*

 1937 Russian-born American biologist *Theodosius Dobzhansky* writes *Genetics and the Origin of Species*

Australian English pathologist *Howard Walter Florey* discovers the growth potential of polymeric chains

American physicist *Ernest Orlando Lawrence* develops the cyclotron and disintegrates a lithium nucleus

German-born English biochemist *Hans Adolf Krebs* identifies the workings of the Krebs Cycle

 1933 Canadian-born American biologist and bacteriologist *Oswald Theodore Avery* identifies DNA as the basis of heredity

Hungarian American biochemist and molecular biologist *Albert Szent-Gyorgyi* receives the Nobel Prize for isolating vitamin C

English physicist *Paul Adrien Maurice Dirac* wins the Nobel Prize for his work on the wave equation

Italian-born American physicist *Enrico Fermi* proposes his beta decay theory

 1938 German chemist *Otto Hahn*, Austrian physicist *Lise Meitner*, and German chemist *Fritz Strassmann* discover nuclear fission

German inventor *Felix Wankel* successfully operates the first internal combustion, rotary engine

American physicist *Carl David Anderson* discovers the meson

 1934 French nuclear physicist *Frédéric Joliot-Curie* and French chemist and physicist *Irène Joliot-Curie* discover artificial radioactivity

1939 Swiss-born American physicist *Felix Bloch* measures the neutron's magnetic movement

American inventor *Edwin H. Land* develops a commercial method to polarize light

American chemist *Wallace Hume Carothers* founds the synthetic fiber industry with his research

New Zealand-born English physicist *Ernest Rutherford* achieves the first fusion reaction

French-born American microbiologist and ecologist *René Dubos* discovers tyrothricin

American chemist and physicist *Harold Urey* receives the Nobel Prize in chemistry for his discovery of deuterium, or heavy hydrogen

American chemist *Linus Pauling* develops the theory of complimentarity

Russian-born American aeronautical engineer *Igor I. Sikorsky* flies the first single-rotor helicopter

1935 American seismologist *Charles F. Richter* and German American seismologist *Beno Gutenberg* develop the Richter(-Gutenberg) Scale

1940 American physicist and inventor *Chester Carlson* receives a patent for his photocopying method

English physicist *James Chadwick* receives the Nobel Prize for the discovery of the neutron

English experimental physicist *George Paget Thomson* forms the Maud Committee

 1941 German-born English biochemist *Ernst Boris Chain* and Australian English pathologist *Howard Walter Florey* isolate penicillin

German-born American physicist *Hans Bethe* develops the Bethe Coupler

American biochemist *Fritz Lipmann* publishes "Metabolic Generation and Utilization of Phosphate Bond Energy"

 1942 Hungarian American physicist and biophysicist *Leo Szilard* and Italian-born American physicist *Enrico Fermi* set up the first nuclear chain reaction

German-born American biologist *Ernst Mayr* proposes the theory of geographic speciation

American physicist *J. Robert Oppenheimer* becomes the director of the Manhattan Project

1943 German-born American molecular biologist *Max Delbrück* and Italian-born American molecular biologist *Salvador Edward Luria* publish a milestone paper regarded as the beginning of bacterial genetics

English physicist *James Chadwick* leads the British contingent of the Manhattan Project

French oceanographer *Jacques-Yves Cousteau* patents the Aqualung

Italian-born American molecular biologist *Salvador Edward Luria* devises the fluctuation test

1944 German American rocket engineer *Wernher Von Braun* fires the first fully operational V-2 rocket

Austrian-born American biochemist *Erwin Chargaff* discovers the genetic role of DNA

American nuclear chemist *Glenn T. Seaborg* successfully isolates large amounts of plutonium and develops the actinide concept

American paleontologist *George Gaylord Simpson* publishes *Tempo and Mode in Evolution*

Russian-born American microbiologist *Selman Waksman* develops streptomycin

 1945 English physicist *James Chadwick* witnesses the first atomic bomb test

American biochemist *Fritz Lipmann* discovers coenzyme A

Hungarian American mathematician *Johann Von Neumann* publishes a report containing the first written description of the stored-program concept

American chemist *Linus Pauling* determines the cause of sickle-cell anemia

Austrian physicist *Erwin Schrödinger* publishes *What Is Life?*

1946 American geneticist *Joshua Lederberg* and American biochemist *Edward Lawrie Tatum* show that bacteria may reproduce sexually

English zoologist *Julian Huxley* becomes the first director-general of UNESCO

 1947 French oceanographer *Jacques-Yves Cousteau* breaks the free diving record using his Aqualung

Hungarian-born English physicist *Dennis Gabor* discovers holography

American inventor *Edwin H. Land* demonstrates the first instant camera

American mathematician *Norbert Wiener* creates the study of cybernetics

1948 American physicist *John Bardeen* develops the transistor

American chemist *Melvin Calvin* begins research on photosynthesis

Russian-born American physicist *George Gamow* publishes "Alpha-Beta-Gamma" paper

American zoologist and sex researcher *Alfred Kinsey* publishes *Sexual Behavior in the Human Male*

American biochemist *Wendell Meredith Stanley*

receives Presidential Certificate of Merit for developing an influenza vaccine

Swedish chemist *Arne Tiselius* receives the Nobel Prize for research in electrophoresis

 Hungarian-born American physicist *Edward Teller* begins developing the hydrogen bomb

American astronomer *Fred Lawrence Whipple* suggests the "dirty snowball" comet model

 American geneticist *Barbara McClintock* publishes the discovery of genetic transposition

1951 American chemist *Katharine Burr Blodgett* receives the Garvan Medal for women chemists

American biologist *Gregory Goodwin Pincus* begins work on the antifertility steroid the "pill"

Dutch-born English zoologist and ethologist *Nikolaas Tinbergen* publishes *The Study of Instinct*

1952 German-born American astronomer *Walter Baade* presents new measurements of the universe

French-born American microbiologist and ecologist *René Dubos* publishes a book linking tuberculosis with certain environmental conditions

American microbiologist *Alfred Day Hershey* conducts the "Blender Experiment" to demonstrate that DNA is the genetic material of life

Italian-born American molecular biologist *Salvador Edward Luria* discovers the phenomenon known as restriction and modification

American microbiologist *Jonas Salk* develops the first polio vaccine

English chemist *Alexander Todd* establishes the structure of flavin adenine dinucleotide (FAD)

1953 Russian theoretical physicist *Andrei Sakharov* and Russian physicist *Igor Tamm* develop the first Soviet hydrogen bomb

English molecular biologist *Francis Crick* and American molecular biologist *James D. Watson* develop the Watson-Crick model of DNA

English molecular biologist *Rosalind Elsie Franklin* provides evidence of DNA's double-helical structure

American physicist *Murray Gell-Mann* publishes a paper explaining the strangeness principle

American zoologist and sex researcher *Alfred Kinsey* publishes *Sexual Behavior in the Human Female*

French microbiologist *André Lwoff* proposes that "inducible lysogenic bacteria" can test cancerous and noncancerous cell activity

English biologist *Peter Brian Medawar* proves acquired immunological tolerance

American chemist *Stanley Lloyd Miller* publishes "A Production of Amino Acids under Possible Primitive Earth Conditions"

Austrian-born English crystallographer and biochemist *Max Perutz* develops method of isomorphous replacement

 English chemist *Alexander Todd* and English chemist and crystallographer *Dorothy Crowfoot Hodgkin* determine the structure of vitamin B12

American biochemist *Sidney W. Fox* begins identifying properties of microspheres

American microbiologist *Jonas Salk*'s polio vaccine pronounced safe and ninety-percent effective

English biochemist *Frederick Sanger* determines the total structure of the insulin molecule

 American biochemist *Stanley Cohen* extracts NGF from a mouse tumor

American experimental physicist *Leon Max Lederman* helps discover the "long-lived neutral kaon"

 American biochemist *Arthur Kornberg* and Spanish biochemist *Severo Ochoa* use DNA polymerase to synthesize DNA molecules

1958 American physicist *James Van Allen* discovers Van Allen radiation belts

American geneticist *George Wells Beadle* receives the Nobel Prize for the One Gene, One Enzyme Theory

American population biologist *Paul R. Ehrlich* makes his first statement regarding the problem of overpopulation

German physicist *Rudolf Mössbauer* discovers recoilless gamma ray release

 1959 American computer scientist *Grace Hopper* develops the COBOL computer language

German physicist *Rudolf Mössbauer* uses the Mössbauer Effect to test the theory of relativity

 1960 English physicist and biochemist *John Kendrew* and Austrian-born English crystallographer and biochemist *Max Perutz* formulate the first three-dimensional structure of the protein myoglobin

American Chemist *Willard F. Libby* receives the Nobel Prize for his development of radiocarbon dating

Russian-born American virologist *Albert Sabin*'s oral polio vaccine is approved for manufacture in the United States

 1961 French biologists *François Jacob* and *Jacques Monod* discover messenger ribonucleic acid (mRNA)

American chemist *Melvin Calvin* receives the Nobel Prize in his chemistry for research on photosynthesis

American biochemist *Marshall Warren Nirenberg* cracks the genetic code

 1962 American marine biologist *Rachel Carson* publishes *Silent Spring*

Russian theoretical physicist *Lev Davidovich Landau* receives the Nobel Prize for his research into theories of condensed matter

Hungarian-born American physicist *Edward Teller* becomes the first advocate of an "active defense system" to shoot down enemy missiles

New Zealand-born English biophysicist *Maurice Hugh Frederick Wilkins* shows the helical structure of RNA

 1963 German American physicist *Maria Goeppert-Mayer* becomes the first woman to receive the Nobel Prize for theoretical physics

American chemist *Linus Pauling* becomes the only person to receive two unshared Nobel Prizes

 1964 American psychobiologist *Roger W. Sperry* publishes the findings of his split-brain studies

 1965 American geneticist *A. H. Sturtevant* publishes *The History of Genetics*

 1967 English astrophysicist *Antony Hewish* and Irish astronomer *Jocelyn Susan Bell Burnell* discover pulsars

South African heart surgeon *Christiaan Neethling Barnard* performs the first human heart transplant

American primatologist *Dian Fossey* establishes a permanent research camp in Rwanda

 1968 American physicist *Luis Alvarez* wins the Nobel Prize for his bubble chamber work

1969 American astronaut *Neil Armstrong* becomes the first man to walk on the moon

1970 Indian-born American biochemist *Har Gobind Khorana* synthesizes the first artificial DNA

American biologist *Lynn Margulis* publishes *Origins of Life*

1971 English ethologist *Jane Goodall* publishes *In the Shadow of Man*

 1972 American evolutionary biologist *Stephen Jay Gould* and American paleontologist *Niles*

Eldredge introduce the concept of punctuated equilibrium

American physicist *John Bardeen* develops the BCS theory of superconductivity

American inventor *Edwin H. Land* reveals the first instant color camera

1973 American radio engineer *Karl Jansky* receives the honor of having the Jansky unit adopted as the unit of measure of radiowave intensity

Austrian zoologist and ethologist *Konrad Lorenz* receives the Nobel Prize for his behavioral research

American biochemist and geneticist *Maxine Singer* warns the public of gene-splicing risks

1974 English astrophysicist *Antony Hewish* receives the first Nobel Prize awarded to an astrophysicist

1975 French oceanographer *Jacques-Yves Cousteau* sees his Cousteau Society membership reach 120,000

American zoologist *Edward O. Wilson* publishes *Sociobiology: The New Synthesis*

1976 American computer engineer *Seymour Cray* introduces the CRAY-1 supercomputer

1977 Russian-born Belgian chemist *Ilya Prigogine* receives the Nobel Prize in chemistry for his work on nonequilibrium thermodynamics

1980 American biochemist *Paul Berg* receives the Nobel Prize for the biochemistry of nucleic acids

1981 American virologist *Robert C. Gallo* develops a blood test for the AIDS virus and discovers human T-cell leukemia virus

1982 American astronaut and physicist *Sally Ride* becomes the first American woman in space

1983 Indian-born American astrophysicist and applied mathematician *Subrahmanyan Chandrasekhar* receives the Nobel Prize for research on aged stars

American primatologist *Dian Fossey* publishes *Gorillas in the Mist*

French virologist *Luc Montagnier* discovers the human immunodeficiency virus (HIV)

American astronomer and exobiologist *Carl Sagan* publishes an article with others suggesting the possibility of a "nuclear winter"

1986 American physicist *Richard P. Feynman* explains why the space shuttle *Challenger* exploded

1987 Chinese American physicist *Paul Ching-Wu Chu* leads a team that discovers a method for higher temperature superconductivity

1987 American molecular biologist *Walter Gilbert* begins the human genome project to map DNA

1988 English theoretical physicist *Stephen Hawking* publishes *A Brief History of Time: From the Big Bang to Black Holes*

English pharmacologist *James Black* receives the Nobel Prize for his heart and ulcer medication work

1989 German-born American physicist *Hans Dehmelt* and German physicist *Wolfgang Paul* share the Nobel Prize for devising ion traps

1990 American physicists *Jerome Friedman, Henry W. Kendall,* and *Richard E. Taylor* are awarded the Nobel Prize for confirming the existence of quarks

American surgeon *Joseph E. Murray* receives the Nobel Prize for performing the first human kidney transplant

1991 German physician and cell physiologist *Bert Sakmann* and German biophysicist *Erwin Neher*

are awarded the Nobel Prize for inventing the patch clamp technique

1993   English biochemist *Richard J. Roberts* and American biologist *Phillip A. Sharp* share the Nobel Prize for their research on DNA structure

American astrophysicists *Russell A. Hulse* and *Joseph H. Taylor, Jr.* receive the Nobel Prize for their work on binary pulsars

NOTABLE
TWENTIETH-CENTURY
SCIENTISTS

Paul Sabatier
1854-1941
French chemist

Paul Sabatier, who shared the 1912 Nobel Prize in chemistry with his countryman **Victor Grignard**, spent thirty-two years of a fifty-year career studying heterogeneous catalysis, especially the catalytic hydrogenation of organic compounds over finely divided metals.

Born on November 5, 1854, in Carcassone, France, Sabatier attended school in Carcassone, where his uncle was a teacher. An older sister helped tutor him, taking Latin and mathematics for that purpose. When his uncle transferred to the Toulouse Lycée, Sabatier followed. While at Toulouse, he used his free time to attend a public course in physics and chemistry that gave him a taste for science.

Accepted at both the École Polytechnique and the École Normale Supérieure in 1874, he entered the latter and graduated at the head of his class in 1877. He worked as an instructor in Nîmes for a year, but teaching secondary school physics was not what he wanted, and he returned to Paris as an assistant to Marcellin Berthelot at the Collège de France. There, in 1880, he earned his doctoral degree with a thesis on metallic sulfides.

After a year of teaching physics at the Faculté des Sciences at Bordeaux, he returned to Toulouse in 1882 to teach physics at the Faculté des Sciences there. In 1883, his duties expanded to include chemistry, and in 1884, at the age of thirty, the earliest allowable, he was appointed Professor of Chemistry. He remained in that post for the rest of his career, refusing offers from the Sorbonne to succeed **Henri Moissan** and from the Collège de France to succeed Berthelot. He was chosen Dean of the Faculty of Science in 1905, an office which he held for over twenty-five years. In addition to his research and teaching during this period, he was instrumental in the creation of schools of chemistry, agriculture, and electrical engineering at Toulouse. Even after his official retirement in 1929, he continued, by special permission, to lecture until failing health forced him to stop in 1939. Sabatier died on August 14, 1941.

Sabatier was a man of great reserve, and there is little information available about his private life. His marriage to Mlle. Herail was ended by her death in 1898. He never remarried, and their four daughters were raised with the help of his older sisters.

After receiving the Nobel Prize in 1912, Sabatier was elected a year later the first member of the Academy of Sciences who did not reside in Paris. He had been a corresponding member since 1901, but the residency requirement kept him from full membership until a special class of six non-resident members was created, in part so that he could become a full member without having to move to Paris. He was made a Chevalier of the Légion d'Honneur in 1907 and named Commander in 1922. Among the many other honors bestowed on him by various organizations in different countries were the Davy Medal from the Royal Society in 1915 and the Franklin Medal from the Franklin Institute in Philadelphia in 1933. He received honorary doctoral degrees from the universities of Pennsylvania (in 1926, in conjunction with the Philadelphia Sesquicentennial celebration), Louvain, and Saragossa.

Switches from Inorganic to Organic Chemistry

For his doctoral research and during his first fifteen years at Toulouse, Sabatier worked in the area of inorganic chemistry. His early work on the sulfides, hydrogen sulfides, and polysulfides of alkali and alkaline earth metals helped to clarify a complicated area of chemistry. He prepared the first pure sample of dihydrogen disulfide and was the first to make silicon monosulfide and tetraboron monosulfide as well as boron and silicon selenides. He carried out a number of thermochemical studies of the hydration (addition of H_2O) of metal chlorides and chromates and various copper compounds and was a pioneer in the use of absorption spectroscopy to study chemical reactions. Absorption spectroscopy exploits the unique patterns of light absorption characteristic of chemical substances to identify them. Spectroscopes scatter the light with a prism so that the dark absorption lines become visible in the spectrum.

In the 1890s it occurred to Sabatier to see if nitric oxide would produce a compound with nickel analogous to the recently discovered compound of nickel and carbon monoxide. These experiments, conducted with the chemist Jean-Baptiste Senderens, were not very fruitful, though some nitrogen compounds of copper, cobalt, nickel, and iron were obtained by the reaction of nitrogen dioxide with the metal. Sabatier then thought to use acetylene, an organic compound, but learned that Moissan and François Moreau had passed acetylene over powdered nickel made by heating nickel oxide with hydrogen and reported the formation of only carbon, some liquid hydrocarbons, and a gas they thought to be hydrogen.

In 1897, after being assured that Moissan and Moreau had no plans to continue their acetylene studies further, Sabatier and Senderens tried the reaction using the gas ethylene, another hydrocarbon. The experiment was successful and thus solidified Sabatier's switch to organic (carbon-based) chemistry. The result was again the formation of carbon, liquid hydrocarbons, and a gas, but on analyzing the gas, they found it to be mostly ethane and only a little hydrogen. Appreciating that the ethane could only have arisen through the addition of hydrogen to the ethylene (hydrogenation), they tried passing a mixture of ethylene and hydrogen over finely divided nickel and found that the smooth hydrogenation of ethylene took place at only a little above room temperature (30–40°C). For the next thirty-two years, Sabatier and his students investigated the heterogeneous catalysis (a process in which a third substance, or catalyst, influences the rate of a chemical reaction) of a variety of organic reactions by metals and metal oxides.

On the basis of his studies, Sabatier explained the catalytic action by the formation of unstable intermediate compounds between the catalyst and the reactant(s). This view, opposed to an earlier theory that the effect was due only to local extremes of pressure and temperature in small pores of the catalyst, proved to be correct and revolutionized organic chemistry.

In 1912, Sabatier's work was recognized by the shared award of the Nobel Prize in chemistry. The following year, he summed up his fifteen years of work on catalysis and reviewed the accumulating literature in the field in the book *La Catalyse en chimie organique*. Although his pioneer work was basic to the development of important industrial processes such as the catalytic cracking of petroleum to increase the yield of gasoline and the hydrogenation of vegetable oils to make shortening, Sabatier did not interest himself in such practical applications, nor did he profit from them.

SELECTED WRITINGS BY SABATIER:

Books

La Catalyse en chimie organique, 2nd edition, 1920, translation by Emmet Reid published with revisions in Reid's *Catalysis Then and Now,* Franklin, 1965.

Periodicals

"How I Have Been Led to the Direct Hydrogenation Method by Metallic Catalysts," *Industrial and Engineering Chemistry,* Volume 18, number 10, 1926, pp. 1005–1008.

SOURCES:

Books

Nobel Lectures Including Presentation Speeches and Laureate's Biographies-Chemistry, 1901–1921, Elsevier, 1966, pp. 217–233.
Obituary Notices of Fellows of the Royal Society, Volume 4, Morrison & Gibb, 1942, pp. 62–66.
Partington, J. R., *A History of Chemistry,* Volume 4, Macmillan, 1964, pp. 858–859.

Periodicals

Camichel, Charles, Georges Champetier, and Gabriel Bertrand, "Commémoration du Centenaire de la Naissance de Paul Sabatier," *Bulletin de la Société Chimique,* 1955, pp. 465–475.
Taylor, Hugh S., "Paul Sabatier," *Journal of the American Chemical Society,* Volume 66, number 10, 1944, pp. 1615–1617.

—*Sketch by R. F. Trimble*

Albert Sabin
1906-1993
Russian-born American virologist

Albert Sabin, a noted virologist, developed an oral vaccine for polio that led to the once-dreaded disease's virtual extinction in the Western Hemisphere. Sabin's long and distinguished research career included many major contributions to virology, including work that led to the development of attenuated live-virus vaccines. During World War II, he developed effective vaccines against dengue fever and Japanese B encephalitis. The development of a live polio vaccine, however, was Sabin's crowning achievement.

Although Sabin's polio vaccine was not the first, it eventually proved to be the most effective and became the predominant mode of protection against polio throughout the Western world. In South America, "Sabin Sundays" were held twice a year to eradicate the disease. The race to produce the first effective vaccine against polio was marked by intense and often acrimonious competition between scientists and their supporters; in addition to the primary goal of saving children, fame and fortune were at stake. Sabin, however, allowed his vaccine to be used free of

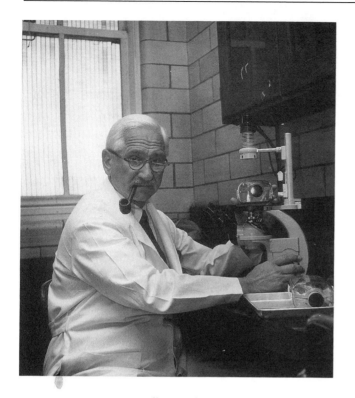

Albert Sabin

charge by any reputable organizations as long as they met his strict standards in developing the appropriate strains.

Albert Bruce Sabin was born in Bialystok, Russia (now Poland), on August 26, 1906. His parents, Jacob and Tillie Sabin, immigrated to the United States in 1921 to escape the extreme poverty suffered under the czarist regime. They settled in Paterson, New Jersey, and Sabin's father became involved in the silk and textile business. After Albert Sabin graduated from Paterson High School in 1923, one of his uncles offered to finance his college education if Sabin would agree to study dentistry. But during his dental education, Sabin read the *Microbe Hunters* by Paul deKruif and was drawn to the science of virology, as well as to the romantic and heroic vision of conquering epidemic diseases.

After two years in the New York University (NYU) dental school, Sabin switched to medicine and promptly lost his uncle's financial support. He paid for school by working at odd jobs—primarily as a lab technician—and through scholarships. He received his B.S. degree in 1928 and enrolled in NYU's College of Medicine. In medical school Sabin showed early promise as a researcher by developing a rapid and accurate system for typing (identifying) pneumococci, or the pneumonia viruses. After receiving his M.D. degree in 1931, he went on to complete his residency at Bellevue Hospital in New York City, where he gained training in pathology, surgery, and internal medicine. In 1932, during his internship, Sabin

isolated the B virus from a colleague who had died after being bitten by a monkey. Within two years, Sabin showed that the B virus's natural habitat is the monkey and that it is related to the human herpes simplex virus. In 1934 Sabin completed his internship and then conducted research at the Lister Institute of Preventive Medicine in London.

Begins Polio Research

In 1935 Sabin returned to the United States and accepted a fellowship at the Rockefeller Institute for Medical Research. There, he resumed in earnest his research of poliomyelitis (or polio), a paralytic disease that had reached epidemic proportions in the United States at the time of Sabin's graduation from medical school. By the early 1950s, polio afflicted 13,500 out of every 100 million Americans. In 1950 alone, more than 33,000 people contracted polio. The majority of them were children.

Ironically, polio was once an endemic disease (or one usually confined to a community, group, or region) propagated by poor sanitation. As a result, most children who lived in households without indoor plumbing were exposed early to the virus; the vast majority of them did not develop symptoms and eventually became immune to later exposures. But after the public health movement at the turn of the century began to improve sanitation and more and more families had indoor toilets, children were not exposed at an early age to the virus and thus did not develop a natural immunity. As a result, polio became an epidemic disease and spread quickly through communities to other children without immunity, regardless of race, creed, or social status. What made the disease so terrifying was that it caused partial or full paralysis by lodging in the brain stem and spinal cord and attacking the central nervous system. Often victims of polio would lose complete control of their muscles and had to be kept in a respirator, or what became known as an iron lung, to help them breathe.

In 1936, Sabin and Peter K. Olitsky used a test tube to grow some polio virus in the central nervous tissue of human embryos. Not a practical approach for developing the huge amounts of virus needed to produce a vaccine, this research nonetheless opened new avenues of investigation for other scientists. However, their discovery did reinforce the mistaken assumption that polio only affected nerve cells.

Although primarily interested in polio, Sabin was "never able to be a one-virus virologist," as he told Donald Robinson in an interview for Robinson's book *The Miracle Finders.* Sabin also studied how the immune system battled viruses and conducted basic research on how viruses affect the central nervous system. Other interests included investigations of toxoplasmosis, a usually benign viral disease that sometimes caused death or severe brain and eye damage in prenatal infections. These studies resulted in the development of rapid and sensitive serologic diagnostic tests for the virus.

During World War II Sabin served in the United States Army Medical Corps. He was stationed in the Pacific theater where he began his investigations into insect-borne encephalitis, sandfly fever, and dengue. He successfully developed a vaccine for dengue fever and conducted an intensive vaccination program on Okinawa using a vaccine he had developed at Children's Hospital of Cincinnati that protected more than 65,000 military personnel against Japanese encephalitis. Sabin eventually identified a number of antigenic (or immune response-promoting) types of sandfly fever and dengue viruses that led to the development of several attenuated (avirulent) live-virus vaccines.

After the war, Sabin returned to the University of Cincinnati College of Medicine, where he had previously accepted an appointment in 1937. With his new appointments as professor of research pediatrics and fellow of the Children's Hospital Research Foundation, Sabin plunged back into polio research. He and his colleagues began performing autopsies on everyone who had died from polio within a four-hundred-mile radius of Cincinnati, Ohio. At the same time, Sabin performed autopsies on monkeys. From these observations he found that the polio virus was present in humans in both the intestinal tract and the central nervous system. Sabin disproved the widely held belief that polio entered humans through the nose to the respiratory tract, showing that it first invaded the digestive tract before attacking nerve tissue. Sabin was also among the investigators who identified the three different strains of polio.

Sabin's discovery of polio in the digestive tract indicated that perhaps the polio virus could be grown in a test tube in non-nervous tissue as opposed to costly and difficult-to-work-with nerve tissue. In 1949 **John Franklin Enders**, Frederick Chapman Robbins, and Thomas Huckle Sweller grew the first polio virus in human and monkey nonnervous tissue cultures, a feat that would earn them a Nobel Prize. With the newfound ability to produce enough virus to conduct large scale research efforts, the race to develop an effective vaccine heated up.

Competes with Salk to Develop Vaccine

At the same time that Sabin began his work to develop a polio vaccine, a young scientist at the University of Pittsburgh—**Jonas Salk**—entered the race. Both men were enormously ambitious and committed to their own theory about which type of vaccine would work best against polio. While Salk committed his efforts to a killed polio virus, Sabin openly expressed his doubts about the safety of such a vaccine as well as its effectiveness in providing lasting protection. Sabin was convinced that an attenuated live-virus vaccine would provide the safe, long-term protection needed. Such a vaccine is made of living virus which is diluted, or weakened, so that it spurs the immune system to fight off the disease without actually causing the disease itself.

In 1953 Salk seemed to have won the battle when he announced the development of a dead virus vaccine made from cultured polio virus inactivated, or killed, with formaldehyde. While many clamored for immediate mass field trials, Sabin, Enders, and others cautioned against mass inoculation until further efficacy and safety studies were conducted. But Salk had won the entire moral and financial support of the National Foundation for Infantile Paralysis, and in 1954 a massive field trial of the vaccine was held. In 1955, to worldwide fanfare, the vaccine was pronounced effective and safe.

Church and town hall bells rang throughout the country, hailing the new vaccine and Salk. However, on April 26, just fourteen days after the announcement, five children in California contracted polio after taking the Salk vaccine. More cases began to occur, with eleven out of 204 people stricken eventually dying. The United States Public Health Service (PHS) ordered a halt to the vaccinations, and a virulent live virus was found to be in certain batches of the manufactured vaccine. After the installation of better safeguards in manufacturing, the Salk vaccine was again given to the public and greatly reduced the incidence of polio in the United States. But Sabin and Enders had been right about the dangers associated with a dead-virus vaccine; and Sabin continued to work toward a vaccine that he believed would be safe, long lasting, and orally administered without the need for injection like Salk's vaccine.

By orally administering the vaccine, Sabin wanted it to multiply in the intestinal tract. Sabin used Enders's technique to obtain the virus and tested individual virus particles on the central nervous system of monkeys to see whether the virus did any damage. According to various estimates, Sabin's meticulous experiments were performed on anywhere from nine to fifteen thousand monkeys and hundreds of chimpanzees. Eventually he diluted three mutant strains of polio that seemed to stimulate antibody production in chimpanzees. Sabin immediately tested the three strains on himself and his family, as well as research associates and volunteer prisoners from Chillicothe Penitentiary in Ohio.

Results of these tests showed that the viruses produced an immunity to polio with no harmful side effects. But by now the public and much of the scientific community were committed to the Salk vaccine. Two scientists working for Lederle Laboratories had also developed a live-virus vaccine. However, the Lederle vaccine was tested in Northern Ireland in

1956 and proved dangerous, as it sometimes reverted to a virulent state.

Although Sabin could not get backing for a large-scale clinical trial in the United States, he remained undaunted. He was able to convince the Health Ministry in the Soviet Union to try his vaccine in massive trials. At the time, the Soviets were mired in a polio epidemic that was claiming eighteen to twenty thousand victims a year. By this time Sabin was receiving the political backing of the World Health Organization in Geneva, Switzerland, which had previously been using Salk's vaccine to control the outbreak of polio around the world; they now believed that Sabin's approach would one day eradicate the disease. Sabin began giving his vaccine to Russian children in 1957, inoculating millions over the next several years. Not to be outdone by Salk's public relations expertise, Sabin began to travel extensively, promoting his vaccine through newspaper articles, issued statements, and scientific meetings. In 1960 the U.S. Public Health Service, finally convinced of Sabin's approach, approved his vaccine for manufacture in the United States. Still, the PHS would not order its use and the Salk vaccine remained the vaccine of choice until a pediatrician in Phoenix, Arizona, Richard Johns, organized a Sabin vaccine drive. The vaccine was supplied for free, and many physicians provided their services without a fee on a chosen Sunday. The success of this effort spread, and Sabin's vaccine soon became "the vaccine" to ward off polio.

The battle between Sabin and Salk persisted well into the 1970s, with Salk writing an op-ed piece for the *New York Times* in 1973 denouncing Sabin's vaccine as unsafe and urging people to use his vaccine once more. But, for the most part, Salk was ignored, and by 1993, health organizations began to report that polio was close to extinction in the Western Hemisphere.

Sabin's drive and commitment (some called it stubbornness) to his work served him well during the scientific turmoil and infighting of the 1950s that surrounded the development of a polio vaccine. Described socially as mild-mannered, quiet, and unassuming, Sabin was known by his colleagues to be egotistical and possessive about his own work. Sabin often insisted that his vaccine was totally safe, despite the evidence that in very rare cases it could cause paralytic poliomyelitis. He continued his virology research focusing on the role of viruses in cancer.

Sabin's personal life largely remained behind the scenes. He married his first wife, Sylvia Tregillus, in 1935, and they had two daughters. After Sylvia Sabin died in 1966, Sabin married Jane Warner; the two later divorced. In 1972, he married Heloisa Dunshee De Abranches, a newspaperwoman.

Sabin continued to work vigorously and tirelessly into his seventies, traveling to Brazil in 1980 to help with a new outbreak of polio. He antagonized Brazilian officials, however, by accusing the government bureaucracy of falsifying data concerning the serious threat that polio still presented in that country. He officially retired from the National Institutes of Health in 1986. Despite his retirement, Sabin continued to be outspoken, saying in 1992 that he doubted whether a vaccine against the human immunodeficiency virus, or HIV, was feasible. Sabin died from congestive heart failure at the Georgetown University Medical Center on March 3, 1993. In an obituary in the *Lancet,* Sabin was noted as the "architect" behind the eradication of polio from North and South America. Salk issued a statement praising Sabin's work to vanquish polio.

SELECTED WRITINGS BY SABIN:

Books

Viruses and Cancer: A Public Lecture in Conversational Style, University of Newcastle upon Tyne, 1965.

Periodicals

"Behavior of Chimpanzee-Avirulent Poliomyelitis Viruses in Experimentally Infected Human Volunteers," *American Journal of the Medical Sciences,* 1955, pp. 1–8.
"Recent Advances in Our Knowledge of Dengue and Sand Fly Fever," *American Journal of Tropical Medicine and Hygiene,* 1955, pp. 198–207.

SOURCES:

Books

Great Events from History II, Salem Press, 1991, pp. 1522–1526.
McGraw-Hill Modern Men of Science, McGraw-Hill, 1966, pp. 411–412.
Robinson, Donald, *The Miracle Finders,* David McKay, 1976, pp. 42–47.
Shorter, Edward, *The Health Century,* Doubleday, 1987, pp. 60–70.

Periodicals

Beale, John, *Lancet,* March 13, 1993, p. 685.
Schmeck, Harold M., Jr., "Albert Sabin, Polio Researcher, 86, Dies," *New York Times,* March 4, 1993, p. B8.

—Sketch by David Petechuk

Florence Rena Sabin
1871-1953
American anatomist

Florence Rena Sabin's studies of the central nervous system of newborn infants, the origin of the lymphatic system, and the immune system's responses to infections—especially by the bacterium that causes tuberculosis—carved an important niche for her in the annals of science. In addition to her research at Johns Hopkins School of Medicine and Rockefeller University, she taught new generations of scientists and thus extended her intellectual reach far beyond her own life. In addition, Sabin's later work as a public health administrator left a permanent imprint upon the communities in which she served. Some of the firsts achieved by Sabin include becoming the first woman faculty member at Johns Hopkins School of Medicine, as well as its first female full professor, and the first woman to be elected president of the American Association of Anatomists.

Sabin was born on November 9, 1871, in Central City, Colorado, to George Kimball Sabin, a mining engineer and son of a country doctor, and Serena Miner, a teacher. Her early life, like that of many in that era, was spare: the house where she lived with her parents and older sister Mary had no plumbing, no gas and no electricity. When Sabin was four, the family moved to Denver; three years later her mother died.

After attending Wolfe Hall boarding school for a year, the Sabin daughters moved with their father to Lake Forest, Illinois, where they lived with their father's brother, Albert Sabin. There the girls attended a private school for two years and spent their summer vacations at their grandfather Sabin's farm near Saxtons River, Vermont.

Sabin graduated from Vermont Academy boarding school in Saxtons River and joined her older sister at Smith College in Massachusetts, where they lived in a private house near the school. As a college student, Sabin was particularly interested in mathematics and science, and earned a bachelor of science in 1893. During her college years she tutored other students in mathematics, thus beginning her long career in teaching.

A course in zoology during her junior year at Smith ignited a passion for biology, which she made her specialty. Determined to demonstrate that, despite widespread opinion to the contrary, an educated woman was as competent as an educated man, Sabin proceeded to chose medicine as her career. This decision may have been influenced by events occurring in Baltimore at the time.

Florence Rena Sabin

The opening of Johns Hopkins Medical School in Baltimore was delayed for lack of funds until a group of prominent local women raised enough money to support the institution. In return for their efforts, they insisted that women be admitted to the school—a radical idea at a time when women who wanted to be physicians generally had to attend women's medical colleges.

Begins Medical Career at Johns Hopkins

In 1893 the Johns Hopkins School of Medicine welcomed its first class of medical students; but Sabin, lacking tuition for four years of medical school, moved to Denver to teach mathematics at Wolfe Hall, her old school. Two years later she became an assistant in the biology department at Smith College, and in the summer of 1896 she worked in the Marine Biological Laboratories at Woods Hole. In October of 1896 she was finally able to begin her first year at Johns Hopkins.

While at Johns Hopkins, Sabin began a long professional relationship with Dr. Franklin P. Mall, the school's professor of anatomy. During the four years she was a student there and the fifteen years she was on his staff, Mall exerted an enormous influence over her intellectual growth and development into prominent scientist and teacher. Years after Mall's death, Sabin paid tribute to her mentor by writing his biography, *Franklin Paine Mall: The Story of a Mind.*

Sabin thrived under Mall's tutelage, and while still a student she constructed models of the medulla and mid-brain from serial microscopic sections of a newborn baby's nervous system. For many years, several medical schools used reproductions of these models to instruct their students. A year after her graduation from medical school in 1900, Sabin published her first book based on this work, *An Atlas of the Medulla and Midbrain,* which became one of her major contributions to medical literature, according to many of her colleagues.

After medical school, Sabin was accepted as an intern at Johns Hopkins Hospital, a rare occurrence for a woman at that time. Nevertheless, she concluded during her internship that she preferred research and teaching to practicing medicine. However, her teaching ambitions were nearly foiled by the lack of available staff positions for women at Johns Hopkins. Fortunately, with the help of Mall and the women of Baltimore who had raised money to open the school, a fellowship was created in the department of anatomy for her. Thus began a long fruitful period of work in a new field of research, the embryologic development of the human lymphatic system.

Sabin began her studies of the lymphatic system to settle controversy over how it developed. Some researchers believed the vessels that made up the lymphatics formed independently from the vessels of the circulatory system, specifically the veins. However, a minority of scientists believed that the lymphatic vessels arose from the veins themselves, budding outward as continuous channels. The studies that supported this latter view were done on pig embryos that were already so large (about 90mm in length) that many researchers—Sabin included—pointed out that the embryos were already old enough to be considered an adult form, thus the results were inconclusive.

Embryo Research Yields Important Findings

The young Johns Hopkins researcher set out to settle the lymphatic argument by studying pig embryos as small as 23mm in length. Combining the painstaking techniques of injecting the microscopic vessels with dye or ink and reconstructing the three-dimensional system from two-dimensional cross sections, Sabin demonstrated that lymphatics did in fact arise from veins by sprouts of endothelium (the layer of cells lining the vessels). Furthermore, these sprouts connected with each other as they grew outward, so the lymphatic system eventually developed entirely from existing vessels. In addition, she demonstrated that the peripheral ends (those ends furthest away from the center of the body) of the lymphatic vessels were closed and, contrary to the prevailing opinion, were neither open to tissue spaces nor derived from them. Even after her results were confirmed by others they remained controversial. Nevertheless, Sabin

firmly defended her work in her book *The Origin and Development of the Lymphatic System.*

Sabin's first papers on the lymphatics won the 1903 prize of the Naples Table Association, an organization that maintained a research position for women at the Zoological Station in Naples, Italy. The prize was awarded to women who produced the best scientific thesis based on independent laboratory research.

Back at Hopkins from her year abroad, she continued her work in anatomy and became an associate professor of anatomy in 1905. Her work on lymphatics led her to studies of the development of blood vessels and blood cells. In 1917 she was appointed professor of histology, the first woman to be awarded full professorship at the medical school. During this period of her life, she enjoyed frequent trips to Europe to conduct research in major German university laboratories.

After returning to the United States from one of her trips abroad, she developed methods of staining living cells, enabling her to differentiate between various cells that had previously been indistinguishable. She also used the newly devised "hanging drop" technique to observe living cells in liquid preparations under the microscope. With these techniques she studied the development of blood vessels and blood cells in developing organisms—once she stayed up all night to watch the "birth" of the bloodstream in a developing chick embryo. Her diligent observation enabled her to witness the formation of blood vessels as well as the formation of stem cells from which all other red and white blood cells arose. During these observations, she also witnessed the heart make its first beat.

Sabin's technical expertise in the laboratory permitted her to distinguish between various blood cell types. She was particularly interested in white blood cells called monocytes, which attacked infectious bacteria, such as *Mycobacterium tuberculosis,* the organism that causes tuberculosis. Although this organism was discovered by the German microbiologist **Robert Koch** during the previous century, the disease was still a dreaded health menace in the early twentieth century. The National Tuberculosis Association acknowledged the importance of Sabin's research of the body's immune response to the tuberculosis organism by awarding her a grant to support her work in 1924.

In that same year, she was elected president of the American Association of Anatomists, and the following year Sabin became the first woman elected to membership in the National Academy of Sciences. These honors followed her 1921 speech to American women scientists at Carnegie Hall during a reception for Nobel Prize-winning physicist **Marie Curie**, an event that signified Sabin's recognized importance in the world of science.

Although her research garnered many honors, Sabin continued to relish her role as a professor at Johns Hopkins. The classes she taught in the department of anatomy enabled her to influence many first-year students—a significant number of whom participated in her research over the years. She also encouraged close teacher-student relationships and frequently hosted gatherings at her home for them.

One of her most cherished causes was the advancement of equal rights for women in education, employment, and society in general. Sabin considered herself equal to her male colleagues and frequently voiced her support for educational opportunities for women in the speeches she made upon receiving awards and honorary degrees. Her civic-mindedness extended to the political arena where she was an active suffragist and contributor to the Maryland *Suffrage News* in the 1920s.

Immune System Research Continues at Rockefeller Institute

Sabin's career at Johns Hopkins drew to a close in 1925, eight years after the death of her close friend and mentor Franklin Mall. She had been passed over for the position of professor of anatomy and head of the department, which was given to one of her former students. Thus, she stepped down from her position as professor of histology and left Baltimore.

In her next position, Sabin continued her study of the role of monocytes in the body's defense against the tubercle bacterium that causes tuberculosis. In the fall of 1925, Sabin assumed a position as full member of the scientific staff at the Rockefeller Institute for Medical Research (now Rockefeller University) in New York City at the invitation of the institute's director, **Simon Flexner**. At Rockefeller Sabin continued to study the role of monocytes and other white blood cells in the body's immune response to infections. She became a member of the Research Committee of the National Tuberculosis Association and aspired to popularize tuberculosis research throughout Rockefeller, various pharmaceutical companies, and other universities and research institutes. The discoveries that she and her colleagues made concerning the ways in which the immune system responded to tuberculosis led her to her final research project: the study of antibody formation.

During her years in New York, Sabin participated in the cultural life of the city, devoting her leisure time to the theater, the symphony, and chamber music concerts she sometimes presented in her home. She enjoyed reading nonfiction and philosophy, in which she found intellectual stimulation that complemented her enthusiasm for research. Indeed, one of

her co-workers was quoted in *Biographical Memoirs* as saying that Sabin possessed a "great joy and pleasure which she derived from her work . . . like a contagion among those around her so that all were stimulated in much the same manner that she was. . . . She was nearly always the first one at the laboratory, and greeted every one with a *joie de vivre* which started the day pleasantly for all of us."

Meanwhile, she continued to accrue honors. She received fourteen honorary doctorates of science from various universities, as well as a doctor of laws. *Good Housekeeping* magazine announced in 1931 that Sabin had been selected in their nationwide poll as one of the twelve most eminent women in the country. In 1935 she received the M. Carey Thomas prize in science, an award of $5,000 presented at the fiftieth anniversary of Bryn Mawr College. Among her many other awards was the Trudeau Medal of the National Tuberculosis Association (1945), the Lasker Award of the American Public Health Association (1951), and the dedication of the Florence R. Sabin Building for Research in Cellular Biology, at the University of Colorado Medical Center.

Plays Prominent Role in Denver's Public Health

In 1938 Sabin retired from Rockefeller and moved to Denver to live with her older sister, Mary, a retired high school mathematics teacher. She returned to New York at least once a year to fulfill her duties as a member of both the advisory board of the John Simon Guggenheim Memorial Foundation and the advisory committee of United China Relief.

Sabin quickly became active in public health issues in Denver and was appointed to the board of directors of the Children's Hospital in 1942 where she later served as vice president. During this time she became aware of the lack of proper enforcement of Colorado's primitive public health laws and began advocating for improved conditions. Governor John Vivian appointed her to his Post-War Planning Committee in 1945, and she assumed the chair of a subcommittee on public health called the Sabin Committee. In this capacity she fought for improved public health laws and construction of more health care facilities.

Two years later she was appointed manager of the Denver Department of Health and Welfare, donating her salary of $4,000 to the University of Colorado Medical School for Research. She became chair of Denver's newly formed Board of Health and Hospitals in 1951 and served for two years in that position. Her unflagging enthusiasm for public health issues bore significant fruit. A *Rocky Mountain News* reporter stated that "Dr. Sabin . . . was the force and spirit behind the Tri-County chest X-ray campaign" that contributed to cutting the death rate from tuberculosis by 50 percent in Denver in just two years.

But Sabin's enormous reserve of energy flagged under the strain of caring for her ailing sister. While recovering from her own illness, Sabin sat down to watch a World Series game on October 3, 1953, in which her favorite team, the Brooklyn Dodgers, were playing. She died of a heart attack before the game was over.

The state of Colorado gave Sabin a final posthumous honor by installing a bronze statue of her in the National Statuary Hall in the Capitol in Washington, D.C., where each state is permitted to honor two of its most revered citizens. Upon her death, as quoted in *Biographical Memoirs,* the Denver *Post* called her the "First Lady of American Science." Sabin's philosophy of life and work might be best summed up by words attributed to Leonardo da Vinci, with which she chose to represent herself on bookplates: "Thou, O God, dost sell unto us all good things at the price of labour."

SELECTED WRITINGS BY SABIN:

Books

An Atlas of the Medulla and Midbrain: A Laboratory Manual, Friedenwald Company, 1901.
The Origin and Development of the Lymphatic System, Johns Hopkins Press, 1916.
Franklin Paine Mall: The Story of a Mind, Johns Hopkins Press, 1934.

SOURCES:

Books

Bluemel, Elinor, *Florence Sabin: Colorado Woman of the Century,* University of Colorado Press, 1959.
Kronstadt, Janet, *Florence Sabin,* Chelsea House, 1990.
McMaster, Philip D. and Michael Heidelberger, "Florence Rena Sabin," *Biographical Memoirs,* Columbia University Press, 1960.
Yost, Edna, *American Women of Science,* Frederick A. Stokes, 1943.

Periodicals

Rocky Mountain News (Denver, CO), March 1, 1951.

—*Sketch by Marc Kusinitz*

Carl Sagan
1934-
American astronomer and exobiologist

One of the first scientists to take an active interest in the possibility that life exists elsewhere in the universe, and an astronomer who has been both a best-selling author and a popular television figure, Carl Sagan is one of the best-known living scientists in the world. He has made important contributions to studies of Venus and Mars, and he was extensively involved in planning NASA's Mariner missions. Regular appearances on the *Tonight Show* with Johnny Carson began a television career which culminated in the series Sagan hosted on public television called *Cosmos,* seen in sixty countries by over 400,000,000 people. He is also one of the authors of a paper that predicted drastic global cooling after a nuclear war; the concept of "nuclear winter" affected not only the scientific community but also national and international policy, as well as public opinion about nuclear weapons and the arms race. Although some scientists consider Sagan to be too interested in speculation and not sufficiently committed to detailed scientific inquiry, many concede his talent for explaining science and acknowledge the importance of the publicity he generates.

Sagan was born in Brooklyn, New York, on November 9, 1934, the son of Samuel Sagan, a Russian emigrant and a cutter in a clothing factory, and Rachel Gruber Sagan. He became fascinated with the stars as a young child and was an avid reader of science fiction, particularly the novels by Edgar Rice Burroughs about the exploration of Mars. By the age of five he was sure he wanted to be an astronomer, but, as he told Henry S. F. Cooper, Jr., of the *New Yorker,* he sadly assumed it was not a paying job; he expected he would have to work at "some job I was temperamentally unsuited for, like door-to-door salesman." When he found out a few years later that astronomers actually got paid, he was ecstatic: "That was a splendid day," he told Cooper.

Sagan's degrees, all of which he earned at the University of Chicago, consist of an A.B. in 1954, a B.S. in 1955, an M.S. in physics in 1956, and a doctorate in astronomy and astrophysics in 1960. As a graduate student, Sagan was deeply interested in the possibility of life on other planets, a discipline known as exobiology. This was an interest which was then considered beyond the realm of responsible scientific investigation, but he received important early support from scientists such as Nobel laureates **Hermann Joseph Muller** and **Joshua Lederberg**. He also worked with **Harold C. Urey**, who had won the 1934 Nobel Prize in chemistry and had been **Stanley Lloyd**

Carl Sagan

Miller's thesis adviser when he conducted his famous experiment on the origin of life. Sagan wrote his doctoral dissertation, "Physical Studies of the Planets," under **Gerard Peter Kuiper**, one of the few astronomers who was a planetologist at that time. It was during his graduate student days that Sagan met his first wife, Lynn Alexander, who was then studying biology. They were married on June 16, 1957, and would have two sons before their divorce in 1963.

From graduate school, Sagan moved to the University of California at Berkeley, where he was the Miller residential fellow in astronomy from 1960 to 1962. He then accepted a position at Harvard as an assistant professor from 1962 to 1968. On April 6, 1968, he married his second wife, the painter Linda Salzman; they would have one son before divorcing. From Harvard he went to Cornell University, where he was first an associate professor of astronomy at the Center for Radiophysics and Space Research. He was then promoted to professor and associate director at the center, serving in that capacity until 1977 when he became the David Duncan Professor of Astronomy and Space Science.

Suggestions About Mars and Venus Confirmed by Spacecrafts

Sagan's first important contributions to the understanding of Mars and Venus began as insights while he was still a graduate student. Color variations had long been observed on the planet Mars, and some believed these variations indicated the seasonal changes of some form of Martian plant life. Sagan, working at times with James Pollack, postulated that the changing colors were instead caused by Martian dust, shifting through the action of wind storms; this interpretation was confirmed by Mariner 9 in the early 1970s. Sagan also suggested that the surface of Venus was incredibly hot, since the Venusian atmosphere of carbon dioxide and water vapor held in the sun's heat, thus creating a version of the "greenhouse effect." This theory was also confirmed by an exploring spacecraft, the Soviet probe Venera IV, which transmitted data about the atmosphere of Venus back to Earth in 1967. Sagan also performed experiments based on the work of Stanley Lloyd Miller, studying the production of organic molecules in an artificial atmosphere meant to simulate that of a primitive Earth or contemporary Jupiter. This work eventually earned him a patent for a technique that used gaseous mixtures to produce amino acids.

Sagan first became involved with spaceflight in 1959, when Lederberg suggested he join a committee on the Space Science Board of the National Academy of Sciences. He became increasingly involved with NASA (National Aeronautics and Space Administration) during the 1960s and participated in many of their most important robotic missions. He developed experiments for the Mariner Venus mission and worked as a designer on the Mariner 9 and the Viking missions to Mars, as well as on the Pioneer 10, the Pioneer 11, and the Voyager spacecrafts. Both the Pioneer and the Voyager spacecrafts have left our solar system carrying plaques which Sagan designed with Frank Drake as messages to any extraterrestrials that find them; they have pictures of two humans, a man and a woman, as well as various astronomical information. The nude man and woman were drawn by Sagan's second wife, Linda Salzman, and they provoked many letters to Sagan denouncing him for sending "smut" into space. During this project Sagan met his third wife, Ann Druyan, who was the creative director. She is also a professional writer, as well as the secretary of the Federation of American Scientists. They have two children.

Sagan continued his involvement in space exploration in the 1980s and 1990s. The expertise he developed in biology and genetics while working with Muller, Lederberg, Urey, and others, is unusual for an astronomer, and he extensively researched the possibility that Jupiter's moon, Titan, which has an atmosphere, might also have some form of life. Sagan has been involved in less direct searches for life beyond Earth. He was one of the prime movers behind NASA's establishment of a radio astronomy search program that Sagan calls CETI, for Communication with Extra-Terrestrial Intelligence.

A colleague of Sagan's working on the Viking mission explained to Cooper of the *New Yorker* that this desire to find extraterrestrial life is the focus of all of Sagan's various scientific works. "Sagan desperately wants to find life someplace, anyplace—on Mars, on Titan, in the solar system or outside it. I don't know why, but if you read his papers or listen to his speeches, even though they are on a wide variety of seemingly unrelated topics, there is always the question 'Is this or that phenomenon related to life?' People say, 'What a varied career he has had,' but everything he has done has had this one underlying purpose." When Cooper asked Sagan why this was so, the scientist had a ready answer: "I think it's because human beings love to be alive, and we have an emotional resonance with something else alive, rather than with a molybdenum atom."

During the early 1970s Sagan began to make a number of brief appearances on television talk shows and news programs; Johnny Carson invited him on the *Tonight Show* for the first time in 1972, and Sagan soon was almost a regular there, returning to discuss science two or three times a year. But it was *Cosmos,* which Public Television began broadcasting in 1980, that made him into a media sensation. Sagan narrated the series, which he wrote with his third wife, Ann Druyan, and Steven Soter, and they used special effects to illustrate a wide range of astronomical phenomena such as black holes. In addition to being extremely popular, the series was widely praised both for its showmanship and its content, although some reviewers had reservations about Sagan's speculations as well as his tendency to claim as fact what most scientists considered only hypotheses.

Warns About the Possibility of Nuclear Winter

Sagan has long been involved in politics; as a graduate student he was arrested in Wisconsin for soliciting funds for the Democratic Party, and he was also involved in protests against the Vietnam War. In December, 1983, he published with Richard Turco, Brian Toon, Thomas Ackerman, and James Pollack an article about the possible consequences of nuclear war. They proposed that even a limited number of nuclear explosions could drastically change the world's climate by starting thousands of intense fires that would throw hundreds of thousands of tons of smoke and ash into the atmosphere, lowering the average temperature ten to twenty degrees and bringing on what they called a "nuclear winter." The authors happened upon this insight accidentally a few years earlier, while they were observing how dust storms on the planet Mars cooled the Martian surface and heated up the atmosphere. Their warning provoked a storm of controversy at first; their article was then followed by a number of studies on the effects of war and other human interventions on the world's climate. Sagan and his colleagues stressed that their predictions were only preliminary and were based on certain assumptions about nuclear weapons and large-scale fires and that their computations had been done on complex computer models of the imperfectly understood atmospheric system. However, despite numerous attempts to minimize the concept of a nuclear winter, the possibility that even a limited nuclear war might well lead to catastrophic environmental changes has been confirmed by later research.

The idea of nuclear winter not only led to the reconsideration of the implications of nuclear war by many countries, institutions, and individuals, but it also produced great advances in research on Earth's atmosphere. In 1991, when the oil fields in Kuwait were burning after the Persian Gulf War, Sagan and others made a similar prediction about the effect the smoke from these fires would have on the climate. Based on the prediction of nuclear winter and the historical examples of the effects of certain volcanic eruptions, these predictions have not turned out to be accurate, although the smoke from the oil fires represented about one percent of the volume of smoke that would be created by a full-scale nuclear war.

In 1978 Carl Sagan won a Pulitzer Prize for his book on evolution called *The Dragons of Eden.* He has also won the A. Calvert Smith Prize (1964), NASA's Apollo Achievement Award (1969), NASA's Exceptional Scientific Achievement Medal (1972), NASA's Medal for Distinguished Public Service (twice), the International Astronaut Prize (1973), the John W. Campbell Memorial Award (1974), the Joseph Priestly Award (1975), the Newcomb Cleveland Prize (1977), the Rittenhouse Medal (1980), the Ralph Coats Roe Medal from the American Society of Mechanical Engineers (1981), the Tsiolkovsky Medal of the Soviet Cosmonautics Federation (1987), the Kennan Peace Award from SANE/Freeze (1988), the Oersted Medal of the American Association of Physics Teachers (1990), the UCLA Medal (1991), and the Mazursky Award from the American Astronomical Association (1991). Sagan is a fellow of the American Association for the Advancement of Science, the American Academy of Arts and Sciences, the American Institute for Aeronautics and Astronautics, and the American Geophysical Union. Sagan was also the chairman of the Division for Planetary Sciences of the American Astronomical Society (from 1975 to 1976) and for twelve years was editor-in-chief of *Icarus,* a journal of planetary studies.

SELECTED WRITINGS BY SAGAN:

Books

The Cosmic Connection, Doubleday, 1973.
The Dragons of Eden: Speculations on the Evolution of Human Intelligence, Random House, 1977.
Broca's Brain: Reflections on the Romance of Science, Random House, 1979.

Cosmos, Random House, 1980.
(With Ann Druyan) *Comet,* Random House, 1985.
Contact: A Novel, Simon and Schuster, 1985.
(With Richard Turco) *A Path Where No Man Thought: Nuclear Winter and the End of the Arms Race,* Random House, 1990.
(With Ann Druyan) *Shadows of Forgotten Ancestors,* Random House, 1992.

Periodicals

"The Radiation Balance of Venus," *California Institute of Technology, Jet Propulsion Laboratory, Technical Report 32–34,* 1960.
"Comets and the Origin of Life," *Astronomy,* Volume 20, February, 1992, p. 20.

SOURCES:

Books

Contemporary Authors: New Revision Series, Volume 11, Gale, 1984.
Goodell, Rae, *The Visible Scientists,* Little, Brown, 1975.

Periodicals

Baur, Stuart, "Kneedeep in the Cosmic Overwhelm with Carl Sagan," *New York,* September 1, 1975, p. 28.
Cooper, Henry S. F., "A Resonance with Something Alive," *New Yorker,* June 21 and 28, 1976, pp. 39–80 and 29–57.
Hernbest, Nigel, "Organic Molecules from Space Rained Down on Early Earth," *New Scientist,* January 25, 1992, p. 27.
Hogan, A. R., "Carl Edward Sagan: Astronomer and Popularizer of Science," *Ad Astra,* Volume 3, 1991, p. 30.
Lewin, Roger, "Shadows of Forgotten Ancestors," *New Scientist,* Volume 137, January 16, 1993, p. 40.
Ridpath, Rian, "A Man Whose Time Has Come," *New Scientist,* Volume 63, July 4, 1974, p. 36.
Ruina, Jack, "A Path Where No Man Thought," *Nature,* Volume 352, August 29, 1991, p. 765.
Zimmer, Carl, "Ecowar," *Discover,* Volume 13, January, 1992, p. 37.

—*Sketch by Chris Hables Gray*

Ruth Sager
1918-
American biologist and geneticist

Ruth Sager has devoted her career to the study and teaching of genetics. She has conducted groundbreaking research in chromosomal theory, disproving nineteenth-century Austrian botanist Gregor Johann Mendel's once-prevalent law of inheritance—a principle stating that chromosomal genes found in a cell's nucleus control the transmission of inherited characteristics. Through her research beginning in the 1950s, Sager revealed that a second set of genes (nonchrosomomal in nature) also play a role in one's genetic composition. In addition to advancing the science of nonchromosomal genetics, she has worked to uncover various genetic mechanisms associated with cancer.

Born on February 7, 1918, in Chicago, Illinois, Ruth Sager was one of three girls in her family. Her father worked as an advertising executive, while her mother maintained an interest in academics and intellectual discourse. As a child, Sager did not display any particular interest in science. At the age of sixteen, she entered the University of Chicago, which required its students to take a diverse schedule of liberal arts classes. Sager happened into an undergraduate survey course on biology, sparking her interest in the field. In 1938, she graduated with a B.S. degree. After a brief vacation from education, Sager enrolled at Rutgers University and studied plant physiology, receiving an M.S. in 1944. Sager then continued her graduate work in genetics at Columbia University and in 1946 was awarded a fellowship to study with botanist Marcus Rhoades. In 1948 she received her Ph.D. from Columbia, and in 1949 she was named a Merck Fellow at the National Research Council.

Two years later, Sager joined the research staff at the Rockefeller Institute's biochemistry division as an assistant, working at first in conjunction with Yoshihiro Tsubo. There she began her work challenging the prevailing scientific idea that only the chromosomal genes played a significant role in genetics. Unlike many of her colleagues of the time, Sager speculated that genes which lay outside the chromosomes behave in a manner akin to that of chromosomal genes. In 1953 Sager uncovered hard data to support this theory. She had been studying heredity in Chlamydomonas, an alga found in muddy ponds, when she noted that a gene outside the chromosomes was necessary for the alga to survive in water containing streptomycin, an antimicrobial drug. Although the plant—which Sager nicknamed "Clammy"—normally reproduced asexually, Sager discovered that she could force it to reproduce sexually by withholding nitrogen from its environment. Using this tactic, Sager managed to cross male and females via sexual fertilization. If either of the parents had the streptomycin-resistant gene, Sager showed, the offspring exhibited it as well, providing definitive proof that this nonchromosomal trait was transmitted genetically.

During the time she studied "Clammy," Sager switched institutional affiliations, taking a post as a research associate in Columbia University's zoology department in 1955. The Public Health Service and National Science Foundations supported her work. In 1960 Sager publicized the results of her nonchromosomal genetics research in the first Gilbert Morgan Smith Memorial Lecture at Stanford University and a few months later in Philadelphia at the Society of American Bacteriologists. Toward the end of the year, her observations were published in *Science* magazine. As she continued her studies, she expanded her knowledge of the workings of nonchromosomal genes. Sager's further work showed that when the streptomycin-resistant alga mutated, these mutations occurred only in the non-chromosomal genes. She also theorized that nonchromosomal genes differed greatly from their chromosomal counterparts in the way they imparted hereditary information between generations. Her research has led her to speculate that nonchromosomal genes may evolve before the more common DNA chromosomes and that they may represent more closely early cellular life.

Sager continued announcing the results of her research at national and international gatherings of scientists. In the early 1960s Columbia University promoted her to the position of senior research associate, and she coauthored, along with Francis J. Ryan, a scientific textbook titled *Cell Heredity*. In 1963 she travelled to the Hague to talk about her work, and the following year she lectured in Edinburgh on nonchromosomal genes. In 1966 she accepted an offer to become a professor at Hunter College of the City University of New York. She remained in New York for nine years, spending the academic year of 1972 to 1973 abroad at the Imperial Cancer Research Fund Laboratory in London. The following year she married. Harvard University's Dana Farber Cancer Institute lured her away from Hunter in 1975 with an offer to become professor of cellular genetics and head the Institute's Division of Cancer Genetics.

In the past twenty years, Sager's work has centered on a variety of issues relating to cancer, such as tumor suppressor genes, breast cancer, and the genetic means by which cancer multiplies. Along with her colleagues at the Dana Farber Institute, Sager has been researching the means by which cancer multiplies and grows, in an attempt to understand and halt the mechanism of the deadly disease. She has likened the growth of cancer to Darwinian evolution in that cancer cells lose growth control and display chromo-

some instability. In 1983 she told reporter Anna Christensen that if researchers discover a way to prevent the chromosomal rearrangements, "we would have a potent weapon against cancer." More recently, she has speculated that tumor suppressor genes may be the secret to halting cancer growth.

Sager continues to publish and serves on numerous scientific panels. In 1992 she offered scientific testimony at hearings of the Breast Cancer Coalition. A member of the Genetics Society of America, the American Society of Bacteriologists, and the New York Academy of Sciences, Sager was appointed to the National Academy of Sciences in 1977. An avid collector of modern art, she is also a member of the American Academy of Arts and Sciences.

SELECTED WRITINGS BY SAGER:

Books

(With Francis J. Ryan) *Cell Heredity,* Wiley, 1961.

Periodicals

"Tumor Suppressor Genes: The Puzzle and the Promise," *Science,* December 15, 1989, pp. 1406–1412.

SOURCES:

Christensen, Anna, "Potential Weapon in War on Cancer," United Press International, February 7, 1983.

—*Sketch by Shari Rudavsky*

Andrei Sakharov
1921-1989
Russian theoretical physicist

Russian nuclear physicist Andrei Sakharov was as well known as a Soviet dissident and human rights advocate as he was for his role in the development of the hydrogen bomb. The so-called "father of the H-Bomb" won the 1975 Nobel Peace Prize for his calls for détente between the U.S.S.R. and the United States and for an end to the arms race. Once fully committed to the Soviet Union's development of a hydrogen bomb in the belief that nuclear parity

Andrei Sakharov

Andersen, Jules Verne, Charles Dickens, Mark Twain, H. G. Wells, Jack London, Leo Tolstoy, Jonathan Swift, Aleksander Pushkin, and Nikolai Gogol. He was educated primarily at home until he was about thirteen, in math and physics by his father and in geography, history, biology, chemistry, and Russian language and literature by private tutors. Late in 1934, he entered the Third Model School. At home, in the meantime, he carried out simple physics experiments in electrostatics and optics. He also became interested in photography, and built a crystal radio based on his father's design. His reading progressed to include science fiction and science books, including those of Yakov Perelman, Sir James Jean's *The Universe Around Us,* and Max Valier's *Space Travel as a Technical Possibility.*

Sakharov graduated from high school as one of only two honors students in his class. In 1938 he enrolled in Moscow State University's physics program. During his third year, Germany invaded the Soviet Union, and Sakharov's work became geared towards the war effort. He repaired radio equipment for the army and invented a magnetic device for locating shrapnel in injured horses. During his fourth year, the faculty was moved to Ashkhabad, capital of the Turkmen Republic in Central Asia. He graduated in 1942.

Joins War Effort after College

After finishing college, Sakharov was invited to remain on as a graduate student of theoretical physics. He refused the offer, preferring to join in the war effort. He was assigned to work at a cartridge factory in Ulyanovsk, a city on the Volga. Before long, he transferred to the central laboratory's metallurgical department, where he devised a novel method of testing the armor-piercing steel cores of 14.5 mm bullets for antitank guns.

November 10, 1942, the day he started work at the laboratory, was also the day he met his first wife, Klavdia (Klava) Vikhireva, a laboratory assistant in the chemical department. They were married on July 10 of the following year. They had three children—Tanya, Lyuba, and Dmitri.

In 1945, Sakharov was invited to join the staff of the P. N. Lebedev Institute of Physics of the Soviet Academy of Science. There, he worked closely with the Russian physicist **Igor Tamm**, who went on to win the 1958 Nobel Prize for Physics jointly with **Il'ya Frank** and **Pavel Cherenkov** for their work on Cherenkov radiation. Sakharov produced papers on the generation of a hard component of cosmic rays, on the interaction of electrons and positrons, and on the temperature of excitation in plasma of a gaseous discharge. He also lectured in nuclear physics, relativity theory, and electricity at the Moscow Energetics Institute for three semesters, and for half a year at the

between the superpowers would prevent a nuclear war, Sakharov had a change of heart and became active in the fight for nuclear disarmament. He was exiled to the city of Gorky in 1980 as a punishment for his outspokenness. With the rise to power of Mikhail Gorbachev and the introduction of *perestroika* (a policy of moderate political and economic "restructuring"), Sakharov and his wife Yelena Bonner were permitted to return to Moscow in 1986.

Andrei Dmitrievich Sakharov was born in Moscow on May 21, 1921, into a family of intellectuals. His father, Dmitri Sakharov, a physicist who wrote popular physics textbooks and taught at the Lenin Pedagogical Institute, was also a talented pianist. Andrei's mother, Ekaterina Sofiano, a teacher of gymnastics before her marriage, was the daughter of a professional soldier. Sakharov had one brother, Georgy, known to the family as Yura. The Sakharovs shared a communal apartment with five other families, including four sets of relatives. The immediate family shared two rooms, equal to 300 square feet, among its four members. Despite these straitened circumstances, by Soviet standards Sakharov's family was reasonably well off—they were able to rent rooms in a country house during the summer—thanks to the extra income generated by Dmitri's writing.

Sakharov taught himself to read when he was about four. His childhood favorites among the mostly pre–revolutionary books that filled his parents' and relatives' libraries were the works of Hans Christian

Kurchatov Institute's workers night school. In his *Memoirs,* Sakharov described the hardships of these years. He and his family were forced to move house every two months; "at one point, we found ourselves without money even to buy milk," he says. Even more frustrating were the restrictions on his professional freedom: his scientific and technical articles were censored, as was all published material. In 1947, at age twenty-six, he was awarded a Candidate of Doctor of Science degree—equivalent to an American doctorate—for his research into cosmic ray theory.

Disappears to Work on Hydrogen Bomb Project

Despite his straitened circumstances, Sakharov turned down an offer to work for the government and continued working with Tamm. In 1948, they jointly published a paper outlining a principle for the magnetic isolation of high temperature plasma which was to change the entire course of Soviet thermonuclear physics. That was the last the mainstream scientific establishment heard from either of them for the next twenty years, as the pair went underground to work on the hydrogen bomb project. Although Sakharov had no real choice in the matter, he later admitted that he had welcomed the opportunity to work on what he described as "superb physics" and that he had believed his work to be "essential." He firmly believed that strategic parity in the great powers' nuclear arsenals would prevent a war.

In June, 1948, Sakharov and the rest of the H-bomb team were transferred to the "Installation," a secret city where he spent the next eighteen years of his life. By 1950, he and Tamm had come up with a theoretical basis for controlled thermonuclear fusion, that is, a method of using thermonuclear power for peaceful means, such as the generation of electricity. But their work was also geared toward more belligerent ends. By 1953, they were in a position to carry out the first test explosion of a Soviet hydrogen bomb. Although the United States had tested an H-bomb the previous November, the Soviets were the first to explode a compact device deliverable by plane or rocket. Sakharov was credited with developing an essential triggering device that used a fission explosion to set off the process of hydrogen fusion that released the bomb's destructive energy.

Sakharov was richly rewarded for these services. He received the Stalin Prize and three orders of Socialist Labor, all in top secret. In 1953, he became the youngest man to be elected a full member of the Soviet Academy of Sciences. He was given the relatively enormous salary of 2,000 rubles a month (equivalent to about $27,000 a year at current exchange rates), privileged housing, a chauffeured car, access to black-market consumer goods, a bodyguard, and other perks.

Begins Speaking Out against Soviet Policies

By the end of the 1950s, however, Sakharov began to question the morality of some of his scientific work. He first publicly aired his opposition to the Soviet government in 1958, in an article published in *Pravda* jointly with **Yakov B. Zeldovich** on the subject of education. In it, he decried the Soviet educational system and called for reform. Some of his recommendations were adopted by the government. Soon afterwards, he unsuccessfully opposed the government's plan to resume nuclear testing, which it had briefly suspended. This experience changed him profoundly. He also joined with two agricultural scientists, V. P. Efroimson and F. D. Schhepotyev, to denounce the attacks being made on Mendelian genetics.

Sakharov's scientific interests shifted in the 1960s, from thermonuclear energy to the structure of the universe. He published a paper on the appearance of non-uniformity in the distribution of matter in 1965, and one on quarks in 1966. He continued to write on non-scientific subjects, including nuclear disarmament, intellectual freedom, and the need to establish civil liberties in the Soviet Union. His manifesto *Reflections on Progress, Coexistence, and Intellectual Freedom,* self-published in 1968 in the form of a *samizdat* (an illegal, typewritten book), brought Sakharov a wider audience. In it, he discussed various threats facing humankind, including widespread famine, wars, environmental catastrophe, and the danger of nuclear annihilation, and laid out his vision of a less frightening and threatening world based on convergence between socialism and capitalism and rapprochement between the U.S.S.R. and the United States. He called for disarmament, condemned repression in the Soviet Union, and castigated Stalin. The essay was widely circulated both in the U.S.S.R. and abroad; reportedly 18 million copies in all were published.

Sakharov's complete break with the military-industrial complex came in 1968 with the Soviet invasion of Czechoslovakia. Sakharov and some of his friends had seen the Czechoslovakia of the "Prague Spring" as a model of democratic socialism. Sakharov appealed directly to Soviet President Yuri Andropov to exercise leniency towards the people who had been arrested for demonstrating against the invasion in Red Square. Soon after, he was released from his official duties at the Installation. That year, his wife became seriously ill with gastric hemorrhages. In October, they both moved to the Council of Ministers' sanitarium in Zheleznovodsk. Doctors examining Sakharov found a cardiovascular disorder. In December, his wife was diagnosed with terminal stomach cancer. She died on March 8, 1969.

In 1970, Sakharov came further into conflict with the authorities when he joined other Soviet scientists in forming the Committee for Human Rights to promote the principles espoused in the Universal Declaration of Human Rights. His "Manifesto II" was also published that year in the form of an open address to President Leonid Brezhnev. Written with physicist Valentin F. Turchin and historian Roy A. Medvedev, it accused the government of having failed the people and of having failed to meet the challenges of the modern world. It urged the government to embark on an urgent course of democratization. As the 1970s advanced, Sakharov continued to publish controversial works on these themes, including *Sakharov Speaks* in 1974, *My Country and the World* in 1975, and *Alarm and Hope* in 1979. These writings won him universal acclaim. He was elected a foreign member of the American Academy of Arts and Sciences in 1969, and of the National Academy of Sciences in 1972. He received the Eleanor Roosevelt Peace Award from SANE (Committee for a Sane Nuclear Policy) in 1973; Chicago University's Cino del Duca Prize and Rheinhold Niebuhr Prize in 1974; and the Fritt Ord Prize in 1980. He became a foreign associate of the French Academy of Science in 1981.

In the meantime, Sakharov had remarried. He wed Yelena Bonner, an Armenian-Siberian Jewish dissident, on January 7, 1972. His bride's mother had spent sixteen years in Stalinist gulags. Bonner herself had served as a nurse's aide during World War II, being promoted to lieutenant in the medical corps. Afterwards, she had become a doctor and an activist. She was divorced, with two children.

Prevented from Accepting Nobel Peace Prize

Sakharov's outspokenness on a range of issues—from the exile of the Tartar people of the Crimea to the government's use of punitive psychiatry—brought him into increasing conflict with the government throughout the 1970s, and he was prevented from traveling to Norway to accept the 1975 Nobel Peace Prize. Sakharov was especially vocal in his opposition to the 1979 Soviet invasion of Afghanistan. In consequence, in January, 1980, he was stripped of his titles and honors and exiled to Gorky, a town of one million that is closed to foreigners. He was forbidden contact with foreigners and most other visitors and kept under constant surveillance. In addition, he was continually harassed. His apartment was repeatedly ransacked by the KGB, and twice he had important manuscripts and documents stolen. He eked out a precarious living on a pension provided by the Academy of Sciences. Sakharov's family also suffered; his stepdaughter was dismissed from Moscow University's journalism school, her husband lost his job, and Sakharov's stepson was denied admission to Moscow University.

On November 21, 1981, Sakharov and Bonner began a seventeen-day hunger strike to protest the Soviet government's refusal to issue an exit visa for Liza Alexeyeva, who wanted to join her fiancé, Bonner's son Alexi Semyonov, in the United States. Their protest attracted worldwide attention, and the Soviet government eventually capitulated. In 1984, Sakharov again staged a hunger strike when Bonner was convicted of "slandering the Soviet system," sentenced to internal exile, and prevented from traveling to Moscow. He was detained against his will in Gorky's Semashko Hospital and force-fed. He went on hunger strike again on July 25, 1985, to protest the government's refusal to allow Bonner an exit visa so that she could go to the United States for medical treatment and to visit her children. Once again he was taken to hospital and force-fed. He ended his strike only when his wife was finally given permission to leave in late October.

In February, 1986, Sakharov wrote to Gorbachev, calling for the release of prisoners of conscience. In October, he wrote yet again, asking that he and Bonner be released from Gorky. He told the General Secretary that he had been exiled illegally, and promised to cease speaking out on public affairs, except when "he could not remain silent." On December 16, 1986, the phone rang in the Sakharov apartment. Mikhail Gorbachev was on the line. He told Sakharov that he and Bonner were at last free to return to Moscow.

On November 6, 1988, Sakharov traveled abroad for the first time in his life. In the United States he met with President George Bush and British Prime Minister Margaret Thatcher. In France for the fortieth anniversary of the Universal Declaration of Human Rights, he met President François Mitterrand, Polish president Lech Walesa, and Javier Pérez de Cuéllar, the United Nations secretary general. In February, he and Yelena Bonner traveled to Italy, where they met with Bettino Craxi, the president of the Italian Socialist Party; Alessandro Pertini, the former president of Italy; and the Pope. Afterwards, they visited Canada. In the summer of 1989, shortly after addressing the first Congress of People's Deputies, Sakharov and Bonner traveled to the United States to visit Bonner's children. Sakharov died of a heart attack on December 14, 1989, in Moscow.

SELECTED WRITINGS BY SAKHAROV:

Books

Reflections on Progress, Peaceful Coexistence, and Intellectual Freedom, Self–published, 1968, published as *Progress, Peaceful Coexistence, and Intellectual Freedom,* Norton, 1968.
Sakharov Speaks, Knopf, 1974.
My Country and the World, Knopf, 1975.

Alarm and Hope, Knopf, 1979.
Collected Scientific Works, Dekker, 1982.
Memoirs, Knopf, 1990.
Moscow and Beyond, 1986 to 1989, Vintage Book, 1992.

SOURCES:

Books

Babyonyshev, Alexander, editor, *On Sakharov,* Knopf, 1982.
Bonner, Yelena, *Alone Together,* Knopf, 1986.
Contemporary Authors, Volume 128, Gale, 1990, pp. 355–358.
Medvedev, Zhores A., *Soviet Science,* Norton, 1978.
Parry, Albert, *The Russian Scientist,* Macmillan, 1973, p. 172.

Periodicals

Chicago Tribune, December 17, 1989.
Los Angeles Times, December 15, 1989.
New York Times, December 16, 1989; December 18, 1989; December 19, 1989.
Washington Post, December 16, 1989; December 18, 1989; December 19, 1989.

—*Sketch by Avril McDonald*

Bert Sakmann
1942-
German physician and cell physiologist

Bert Sakmann, along with physicist **Erwin Neher**, was awarded the 1991 Nobel Prize in physiology or medicine for inventing the patch clamp technique. The technique made it possible to realize a goal that had eluded scientists since the 1950s: to be able to examine individual ion channels—pore-forming proteins found in the outer membranes of virtually all cells that serve as conduits for electrical signals. Introduced in 1976, the patch clamp technique opened new paths in the study of membrane physiology. Since then, researchers throughout the world have adapted and refined patch clamping, contributing significantly to research on problems in medicine and neuroscience. The Nobel Committee credited Sakmann and Neher with having revolutionized modern biology.

Sakmann was born in Stuttgart, Germany, on June 12, 1942. His later education involved much time around the laboratory. From 1969 to 1970, he was a research assistant in the department of neurophysiology at the Max Planck Institute for Psychiatry in Munich. Between 1971 and 1973, Sakmann studied biophysics with Nobel Laureate **Bernard Katz** at University College in London as a British Council scholar. In 1974 he received his medical degree from the University of Göttingen. From that year until 1979 he was a research associate in the department of neurobiology at the Max Planck Institute for Biophysical Chemistry in Göttingen.

In the 1950s and 1960s, the existence of ion channels that allow for the transmission of electrical charges from one cell to another was inferred from research since no one had been able to actually locate the sites of these channels. Cell physiologists were being drawn to the question of how electrically charged ions control such biological functions as the transmission of nerve impulses, the contraction of muscles, vision, and the process of conception. Sakmann's early interest in ion channels was stimulated by two papers published in 1969 and 1970 that gave strong evidence for the existence of ion channels. As stronger evidence began to accumulate for their existence, it became clear to Sakmann and Neher, who were sharing laboratory space at the Max Planck Institute, that they would have to develop a fine instrument to be able to locate the actual sites of the ion channels on the cell membrane.

Innovation of Patch Clamp Wins Nobel Prize

Bedeviling efforts of researchers to that point was the electrical "noise" generated by the cell's membrane, which made it impossible to detect signals coming from individual channels. Sakmann and Neher set about to reduce the noise by shutting out most of the membrane. They applied a glass micropipette one micron wide and fitted with a recording electrode to a cell membrane and were able to measure the flow of current through a single channel. "It worked the first time," Sakmann recalled in *Science* magazine. The biophysical community was exultant.

Over the next few years, Sakmann and Neher refined their "patch clamp" technique, solving a residual noise problem caused by leaks in the seals between pipette and cell by applying suction with freshly made and fire-polished pipettes. The refinements made it possible to measure even very small currents, and established the patch clamp as a tremendously versatile tool in the field of cell biology. Patch clamping has been instrumental in studies of cystic fibrosis, hormone regulation, and insulin production in diabetes. The technique has also made possible the development of new drugs in the treatment of heart disease, epilepsy, and disorders affecting the nervous and muscle systems. In 1991 Sakmann and Neher won the 1991 Nobel Prize in physiology or medicine for their work on ion channels. The Nobel Awards citation congratulated the researchers for conclusively establishing the existence and function of the channels, and contributing immeasurably to the understanding of disease mechanisms.

Sakmann has continued to work with other research teams, altering the genes for identified ion channels in order to trace the molecules in the channel responsible for opening and closing the ion pore. Even though Sakmann expressed surprise at receiving the Noble Prize, given all the other important work going on in cell physiology, the opinion of many of his colleagues was that the award was long overdue. Sakmann is married to Christianne, an ophthalmologist; they have three children. He is described by friends as someone who enjoys playing tennis and soccer, having a good sense of humor, and someone who enjoys spending time with his family. In 1989 he moved from the Max Planck Institute in Göttingen to the University of Heidelberg as a professor on the medical faculty. Among his other awards are the Spencer and Louisa Gross-Horwitz Awards from Columbia University in 1983 and 1986, respectively.

SELECTED WRITINGS BY SAKMANN:

Periodicals

(With O. P. Hamill, A. Marty, E. Neher, and others) "Improved Patch-Clamp Techniques for High-Resolution Current Recording from Cells and Cell-Free Membrane Patches," *Pfluegers Archiv: European Journal of Physiology,* August, 1981, pp. 85–100.

(With F. A. Edwards, A. Konnerth, and T. Takahashi) "A Thin Slice Preparation for Patch Clamp Recordings from Neurons of the Mammalian Central Nervous System," *Pfluegers Archiv: European Journal of Physiology,* September, 1989, pp. 600–612.

(With Erwin Neher) "The Patch Clamp Technique," *Scientific American,* March, 1992, pp. 44–51.

"Elementary Steps in Synaptic Transmission Revealed by Currents through Single Ion Channels," *Science,* April 24, 1992, pp. 503–512.

SOURCES:

Periodicals

New York Times, October 13, 1991, pp. C1, C3.

Physics Today, January, 1992, pp. 17–18.
Science, Volume 254, 1991, p. 380.

—Sketch by Jordan Richman

Abdus Salam
1926-
Pakistani physicist

Abdus Salam's major field of interest in the 1950s and 1960s was the relationship between two of the four basic forces governing nature then known to scientists: the electromagnetic and weak forces. In 1968, Salam published a theory showing how these two forces may be considered as separate and distinct manifestations of a single more fundamental force, the electroweak force. Experiments conducted at the European Center for Nuclear Research (CERN) in 1973 provided the empirical evidence needed to substantiate Salam's theory. For this work, Salam shared the 1979 Nobel Prize in physics with physicists **Sheldon Glashow** and **Steven Weinberg**, who had each independently developed similar theories between 1960 and 1967. Salam's long-time concern for the status of science in Third World nations prompted him in 1964 to push for the establishment of the International Center for Theoretical Physics (ICTP) in Trieste, Italy. The Center provides the kind of instruction for Third World physicists that is generally not available in their own homelands.

Salam was born on January 29, 1926, in the small rural town of Jhang, Pakistan, to Hajira and Muhammed Hussain. Salam's father worked for the local department of education. At the age of sixteen, Abdus Salam entered the Government College at Punjab University in Lahore, and, in 1946, he was awarded his master's degree in mathematics. Salam then received a scholarship that allowed him to enroll at St. John's College at Cambridge University, where he was awarded a bachelor's degree in mathematics and physics, with highest honors, in 1949.

Attempts to Return to Pakistan

Salam remained at Cambridge as a graduate student for two years, but felt an obligation to return to Pakistan. Accepting a joint appointment as professor of mathematics at the Government College of Lahore and head of the department of mathematics at Punjab University, Salam soon discovered that he had no opportunity to conduct research. "To my dismay," he told Nina Hall for an article in the *New*

Abdus Salam

Scientist, "I learnt that I was the only practicing theoretical physicist in the entire nation. No one cared whether I did any research. Worse, I was expected to look after the college soccer team as my major duty besides teaching undergraduates."

As a result, Salam decided to return to Cambridge, from which he had received a Ph.D. in theoretical physics in 1952. He taught mathematics for two years at Cambridge and, in 1957, was appointed professor of theoretical physics at the Imperial College of Science and Technology in London. He has held that post ever since.

Attacks the Problem of Force Unification

Beginning in the mid–1950s, Salam turned his attention to one of the fundamental questions of modern physics, the unification of forces. Scientists recognize that there are four fundamental forces governing nature—the gravitational, electromagnetic, strong, and weak forces—and, that all four may be manifestations of a single basic force. The unity of forces would not actually be observable, they believe, except at energy levels much greater than those that exist in the everyday world, energy levels that currently exist only in cosmic radiation and in the most powerful of particle accelerators.

Attempts to prove unification theories are, to some extent, theoretical exercises involving esoteric mathematical formulations. In the 1960s, three physi-

cists, Salam, Steven Weinberg, and Sheldon Glashow, independently derived a mathematical theory that unifies two of the four basic forces, the electromagnetic and weak forces. A powerful point of confirmation in this work was the fact that essentially the same theory was produced starting from two very different beginning points and following two different lines of reasoning.

One of the predictions arising from the new electroweak theory was the existence of previously unknown weak "neutral currents," as anticipated by Salam and Weinberg. These currents were first observed in 1973 during experiments conducted at the CERN in Geneva, and later at the Fermi National Accelerator Laboratory in Batavia, Illinois. A second prediction, the existence of force-carrying particles designated as W^+, W^-, and Z^0 bosons was verified in a later series of experiments also carried out at CERN in 1983. By that time, Salam, Glashow, and Weinberg had been honored for their contributions to the electroweak theory with the 1979 Nobel Prize in physics.

Theoretical physics has been only one of Salam's two great passions in life. The other has been an ongoing concern for the status of theoretical physicists in Third World nations. His own experience in Pakistan has been a lifelong reminder of the need for encouragement, instruction, and assistance for others like himself growing up in developing nations. His concern drove Salam to recommend the establishment of a training center for such individuals. That dream was realized in 1964 with the formation of the ICTP in Trieste, Italy, which invites outstanding theoretical physicists to teach and lecture aspiring students on their own areas of expertise. In addition, the Center acts, according to *New Scientist*'s Nina Hall as a "sort of lonely scientist's club for Brazilians, Nigerians, Sri Lankans, or whoever feels the isolation resulting from lack of resources in their own country." Salam has also served as a member of Pakistan's Atomic Energy Commission (1958–1974) and its Science Council (1963–1975), as Chief Scientific Advisor to Pakistan's President (1961–1974) and as chairman of the country's Space and Upper Atmosphere Committee (1962–1963)

Salam, director of ICTP since its founding, has been involved in a host of other international activities linking scientists to each other and to a variety of governmental agencies. He was a member (1964–1975) and chairman (1971–1972) of the United Nations Advisory Committee on Science and Technology, vice president of the International Union of Pure and Applied Physics (1972–1978), and a member of the Scientific Council of the Stockholm International Peace Research Institute (1970—). Salam has been awarded more than two dozen honorary doctorates and has received more than a dozen major awards, including the Atoms for Peace Award for

1968, the Royal Medal of the Royal Society in 1978, the John Torrence Tate Medal of the American Institute of Physics in 1978, and the Lomonosov Gold Medal of the U.S.S.R. Academy of Sciences in 1983.

SELECTED WRITINGS BY SALAM:

Books

(Edited with E. P. Wigner), *Aspect of Quantum Mechanics,* Cambridge University Press, 1972.
Ideas and Realities: Selected Essays of Abdus Salam, World Scientific, 1987.

Periodicals

"The Electroweak Force, Grand Unification, and Superunification," *Physical Sciences,* Volume 20, 1979, pp. 227–34.

SOURCES:

Books

Nobel Prize Winners, H. W. Wilson, 1987, pp. 914–16.
Weber, Robert L., *Pioneers of Science: Nobel Prize Winners in Physics,* American Institute of Physics, 1980, pp. 263–64.
The Way of the Scientist, Simon & Schuster, 1962, pp. 67–76.

Periodicals

Coleman, Sidney, "The 1979 Nobel Prize in Physics," *Science,* December 14, 1979, pp. 1290–91.
Hall, Nina, "A Unifying Force for Third World Science," *New Scientist,* January 27, 1990, p. 31.
"Nobel Prizes: To Glashow, Salam and Weinberg for Physics . . .," *Physics Today,* December, 1979, pp. 17–19.
"Nobels for Getting It Together in Physics," *New Scientist,* October 18, 1979, pp. 163–64.

—Sketch by David E. Newton

Jonas Salk
1914-1995
American microbiologist

Jonas Salk is one of the United States's best known microbiologists, chiefly celebrated for his discovery of the polio vaccine. His greatest contribution to immunology has been the insight that a "killed virus" is capable of serving as an antigen, prompting the body's immune system to produce antibodies that will attack invading organisms. This realization enabled Salk to develop a polio vaccine composed of killed polio viruses, producing the necessary antibodies to help the body to ward off the disease without itself inducing polio.

The eldest son of Orthodox Jewish-Polish immigrants, Jonas Edward Salk was born in East Harlem, New York, on October 28, 1914. His father, Daniel B. Salk, was a garment worker, who designed lace collars and cuffs and enjoyed sketching in his spare time. He and his wife, Dora Press, encouraged their son's academic talents, sending him to Townsend Harris High School for the gifted. There, young Salk was both highly motivated and high achieving, graduating at the age of fifteen and proceeding to enroll in the legal faculty of the City College of New York. Ever curious, however, he attended some science courses and quickly decided to switch fields. Salk graduated with a bachelor's degree in science in 1933, at the age of nineteen, and went on to New York University's School of Medicine. Initially he scraped by on money his parents had borrowed for him; after the first year, however, scholarships and fellowships paid his way. In his senior year, Salk met the man with whom he would collaborate on some of the most important work of his career, Dr. Thomas Francis, Jr.

On June 7, 1939, Salk was awarded his M.D. The next day, he married Donna Lindsay, a Phi Beta Kappa psychology major who was employed as a social worker. The marriage would produce three sons: Peter, Darrell, and Jonathan. After graduation, Salk continued working with Francis, and concurrently began a two-year internship at Mount Sinai Hospital in New York. Upon completing his internship, Salk accepted a National Research Council fellowship and moved to the University of Michigan to join Dr. Francis, who had been heading up Michigan's department of epidemiology since the previous year. Working on behalf of the U.S. Army, the team strove to develop a flu vaccine. Their goal was a "killed-virus" vaccine—able to kill the live flu viruses in the body, while simultaneously producing antibodies that could fight off future invaders of the same type, thus producing immunity. By 1943, Salk and Francis had developed a formalin-killed-virus vaccine, effective

Jonas Salk

against both type A and B influenza viruses, and were in a position to begin clinical trials.

Gets Backing of National Foundation For Infantile Paralysis

In 1946, Salk was appointed assistant professor of epidemiology at Michigan. Around this time he extended his research to cover not only viruses and the body's reaction to them but also their epidemic effects in populations. The following year he accepted an invitation to move to the University of Pittsburgh School of Medicine's Virus Research Laboratory as an associate research professor of bacteriology. When Salk arrived at the Pittsburgh laboratory, what he encountered was not encouraging. The laboratory had no experience with the kind of basic research he was accustomed to, and it took considerable effort on his part to bring the lab up to par. However, Salk was not shy about seeking financial support for the laboratory from outside benefactors, and soon his laboratory represented the cutting edge of viral research.

In addition to building a respectable laboratory, Salk also devoted a considerable amount of his energies to writing scientific papers on a number of topics, including the polio virus. Some of these came to the attention of Daniel Basil O'Connor, the director of the National Foundation for Infantile Paralysis—an organization that had long been involved with the treatment and rehabilitation of polio victims. O'Connor eyed Salk as a possible recruit for the polio vaccine research his organization sponsored. When the two finally met, O'Connor was much taken by Salk—so much so, in fact, that he put almost all of the National Foundation's money behind Salk's vaccine research efforts.

Poliomyelitis, traceable back to ancient Egypt, causes permanent paralysis in those it strikes, or chronic shortness of breath often leading to death. Children, in particular, are especially vulnerable to the polio virus. The University of Pittsburgh was one of four universities engaged in trying to sort and classify the more than one hundred known varieties of polio virus. By 1951, Salk was able to assert with certainty that all polio viruses fell into one of three types, each having various strains; some of these were highly infectious, others barely so. Once he had established this, Salk was in a position to start work on developing a vaccine.

Salk's first challenge was to obtain enough of the virus to be able to develop a vaccine in doses large enough to have an impact; this was particularly difficult since viruses, unlike culture-grown bacteria, need living cells to grow. The breakthrough came when the team of **John F. Enders**, **Thomas Weller**, and **Frederick Robbins** found that the polio virus could be grown in embryonic tissue—a discovery that earned them a Nobel Prize in 1954.

Salk subsequently grew samples of all three varieties of polio virus in cultures of monkey kidney tissue, then killed the virus with formaldehyde. Salk believed that it was essential to use a killed polio virus (rather than a live virus) in the vaccine, as the live-virus vaccine would have a much higher chance of accidentally inducing polio in inoculated children. He therefore exposed the viruses to formaldehyde for nearly 13 days. Though after only three days he could detect no virulence in the sample, Salk wanted to establish a wide safety margin; after an additional ten days of exposure to the formaldehyde, he reckoned that there was only a one-in-a-trillion chance of there being a live virus particle in a single dose of his vaccine. Salk tested it on monkeys with positive results before proceeding to human clinical trials.

Despite Salk's confidence, many of his colleagues were skeptical, believing that a killed-virus vaccine could not possibly be effective. His dubious standing was further compounded by the fact that he was relatively new to polio vaccine research; some of his chief competitors in the race to develop the vaccine—most notably **Albert Sabin**, the chief proponent for a live-virus vaccine—had been at it for years and were somewhat irked by the presence of this upstart with his unorthodox ideas.

As the field narrowed, the division between the killed-virus and the live-virus camps widened, and what had once been a polite difference of opinion became a serious ideological conflict. Salk and his chief backer, the National Foundation for Infantile Paralysis, were fairly lonely in their corner. But Salk failed to let his position in the scientific wilderness dissuade him and he continued, undeterred, with his research. To test his vaccine's strength, in early 1952 Salk administered a type I vaccine to children who had already been infected with the polio virus. Afterwards, he measured their antibody levels. His results clearly indicated that the vaccine produced large amounts of antibodies. Buoyed by this success, the clinical trial was then extended to include children who had never had polio.

In May, 1952, Salk initiated preparations for a massive field trial in which over four hundred thousand children would be vaccinated. The largest medical experiment that had ever been carried out in the United States, the test finally got underway in April, 1954, under the direction of Dr. Francis and sponsored by the National Foundation for Infantile Paralysis. More than one million children between the ages of six and nine took part in the trial, each receiving a button that proclaimed them a "Polio Pioneer." A third of the children were given doses of the vaccine consisting of three injections—one for each of the types of polio virus—plus a booster shot. A control group of the same number of children was given a placebo, and a third group was given nothing.

At the beginning of 1953, while the trial was still at an early stage, Salk's encouraging results were made public in the *Journal of the American Medical Association.* Predictably, media and public interest were intense. Anxious to avoid sensationalized versions of his work, Salk agreed to comment on the results thus far during a scheduled radio and press appearance. However, this appearance did not mesh with accepted scientific protocol for making such announcements, and some of his fellow scientists accused him of being little more than a publicity hound. Salk, who claimed that he had been motivated only by the highest principles, was deeply hurt.

Despite the doomsayers, on April 12, 1955, the vaccine was officially pronounced effective, potent, and safe in almost 90 percent of cases. The meeting at which the announcement was made was attended by five hundred of the world's top scientists and doctors, 150 journalists, and sixteen television and movie crews.

Instant Celebrity

The success of the trial catapulted Salk to instant stardom. He was inundated with offers from Hollywood and with pleas from top manufacturers for him to endorse their products. He received a citation from President Eisenhower and addressed the nation from the White House Rose Garden. He was awarded a congressional medal for great achievement in the field of medicine and was nominated for a Nobel Prize but,

contrary to popular expectation, did not receive it. He was also turned down for membership in the National Academy of Sciences, most likely a reflection of the discomfort the scientific community still felt about the level of publicity he attracted and of continued disagreement with peers over his methods.

Wishing to escape from the glare of the limelight, Salk turned down the countless offers and tried to retreat into his laboratory. Unfortunately, a tragic mishap served to keep the attention of the world's media focused on him. Just two week after the announcement of the vaccine's discovery, eleven of the children who had received it developed polio; more cases soon followed. Altogether, about 200 children developed paralytic polio, eleven fatally. For a while, it appeared that the vaccination campaign would be railroaded. However, it was soon discovered that all of the rogue vaccines had originated from the same source, Cutter Laboratories in California. On May 7, the vaccination campaign was called to a halt by the Surgeon General. Following a thorough investigation, it was found that Cutter had used faulty batches of virus culture which were resistant to the formaldehyde. After furious debate and the adoption of standards that would prevent such a reoccurrence, the inoculation resumed. By the end of 1955, seven million children had received their shots, and over the course of the next two years more than 200 million doses of Salk's polio vaccine were administered, without a single instance of vaccine-induced paralysis. By the summer of 1961 there had been a 96 percent reduction in the number of cases of polio in the United States, compared to the five-year period prior to the vaccination campaign.

After the initial inoculation period ended in 1958, Salk's killed-virus vaccine was replaced by a live-virus vaccine developed by Sabin; use of this new vaccine was advantageous because it could be administered orally rather than intravenously, and because it required fewer "booster" inoculations. To this day, though, Salk remains known as the man who defeated polio.

Founds Institute for Biological Studies

In 1954, Salk took up a new position as professor of preventative medicine at Pittsburgh, and in 1957 he became professor of experimental medicine. The following year he began work on a vaccine to immunize against all viral diseases of the central nervous system. As part of this research, Salk performed studies of normal and malignant cells, studies that had some bearing on the problems encountered in cancer research. In 1960, he founded the Salk Institute for Biological Studies in La Jolla, California; heavily funded by the National Foundation for Infantile Paralysis (by then known as the March of Dimes), the institute attracted some of the brightest scientists in the world, all drawn by Salk's promise of full-time, uninterrupted biological research.

When his new institute finally opened in 1963, Salk became its director and devoted himself to the study of multiple sclerosis and cancer. He remained a driven man, thinking nothing of working sixteen to eighteen hours a day, six days a week. He made the headlines again in 1967 when he married Francis Gilot, Pablo Picasso's first wife and mother of two of the artist's children. During the 1970s Salk turned to writing, producing books about the philosophy of science and its social role. In 1977, he received the Presidential Medal of Freedom.

Despite the sense of expectancy that he seems to encourage, Jonas Salk takes his successes and failures in stride. In the early 1990s, many people looked to him as the one would might finally develop a vaccine against the HIV virus. But Salk, though continuing to strive toward scientific breakthroughs, seems content simply to work at his chosen craft. "I don't want to go from one crest to another," he once said, as quoted by Sarah K. Bolton in *Famous Men of Science.* "To a scientist, fame is neither an end nor even a means to an end. Do you recall what Emerson said?— 'The reward of a thing well done is the opportunity to do more.'" Salk died of heart failure in La Jolla, California on June 23, 1995.

SELECTED WRITINGS BY SALK:

Books

Man Unfolding, Harper, 1972.
Anatomy of Reality, Columbia University Press, 1973.
The Survival of the Wisest, Harper, 1973.
How Like an Angel, David and Charles, 1975.
World Population and Human Values, Harper, 1981.

SOURCES:

Books

Berger, Melvin, *Famous Men of Modern Biology,* Crowell, 1968, pp. 177.
Bolton, Sarah K., *Famous Men of Science,* Crowell, 1960, pp. 267.
Carter, Richard, *Breakthrough: The Saga of Jonas Salk,* Trident Press, 1966.
Curson, Majorie, *Jonas Salk,* Silver Burdett, 1990.
Hargrove, Jim, *The Story of Jonas Salk and the Discovery of the Polio Vaccine,* Children's Press, 1990.
Hendin, David, *The Life Givers,* Morrow, 1976.
McGraw-Hill Modern Men of Science, McGraw-Hill, 1966, pp. 413.
Robinson, Donald, *The Miracle Finders,* David McKay, 1976, pp. 39.
Rowland, John, *The Polio Man: The Story of Dr. Jonas Salk,* Roy Publishing, 1961.
Siemens, Pliny, *The Great Scientists,* Grolier, 1989, p. 137.

—*Sketch by Avril McDonald*

Bengt Samuelsson
1934-
Swedish biochemist

Bengt Samuelsson shared the 1982 Nobel Prize for physiology or medicine with his compatriot **Sune K. Bergström** and British biochemist **John R. Vane** "for their discoveries concerning prostaglandins and related biologically active substances." Because prostaglandins are involved in a diverse range of biochemical functions and processes, the research of Bergström, Samuelsson, and Vane opened up a new arena of medical research and pharmaceutical applications.

Bengt Ingemar Samuelsson was born on May 21, 1934, in Halmstad, Sweden, to Anders and Kristina Nilsson Samuelsson. Samuelsson entered medical school at the University of Lund, where he came under the mentorship of Sune K. Bergström. Called "the father of prostaglandin chemistry," Bergström was on the university faculty as professor of physiological chemistry. In 1958, Samuelsson followed Bergström to the prestigious Karolinska Institute in Stockholm, which is associated with the Nobel Prize awards. There, Samuelsson received his doctorate in medical science in 1960 and his medical degree in 1961, and he was subsequently appointed as an assistant professor of medical chemistry. In 1961, he served as a research fellow at Harvard University, and then in 1962 he rejoined Bergström at the Karolinska Institute, where he remained until 1966.

At the Karolinska Institute, Samuelsson worked with a group of researchers who were trying to characterize the structures of prostaglandins. Prostaglandins are hormone-like substances found throughout the body, which were so named in the 1930s on the erroneous assumption that they originated in the prostate. They play an important role in the circulatory system, and they help protect the body against sickness, infection, pain, and stress. Expanding on their earlier research, Bergström, Samuelsson, and other researchers discovered the role that arachidonic acid, an unsaturated fatty acid found in meats and vegetable oils, plays in the formation of prostaglandins. By developing synthetic methods of producing prostaglandins in the laboratory, this group made prostaglandins accessible for scientific research worldwide. It was Samuelsson who discovered the process through which arachidonic acid is converted into compounds he named endoperoxides, which are in turn converted into prostaglandins.

Prostaglandins have many veterinary and livestock breeding applications, and Samuelsson joined the faculty of the Royal Veterinary College in Stockholm in 1967. He returned to the Karolinska Institute as professor of medicine and physiological chemistry in 1972. Samuelsson served as the chair of the department of physiological chemistry from 1973 to 1983, and as dean of the medical faculty from 1978 to 1983, combining administrative duties with a rigorous research schedule. During 1976 and 1977, Samuelsson also served as a visiting professor at Harvard University and the Massachusetts Institute of Technology.

During these years, Samuelsson continued his investigation of prostaglandins and related compounds. In 1973, he discovered the prostaglandins which are involved in the clotting of the blood; he called these thromboxanes. Samuelsson subsequently discovered the compounds he called leukotrienes, which are found in white blood cells (or leukocytes). Leukotrienes are involved in asthma and in anaphylaxis, the shock or hypersensitivity that follows exposure to certain foreign substances, such as the toxins in an insect sting.

In the wake of such research, prostaglandins have been used to treat fertility problems, circulatory problems, asthma, arthritis, menstrual cramps, and ulcers. Prostaglandins have also been used medically to induce abortions. As noted by *New Scientist* magazine, the 1982 Nobel Prize shared by Bergström, Samuelsson, and Vane acknowledged that they had "carried prostaglandins from the backwaters of biochemical research to the frontier of medical applications." In 1983, succeeding Bergström, Samuelsson was appointed as president of the Karolinska Institute.

The importance of Samuelsson's research has been recognized by numerous awards and honors in addition to the Nobel Prize. Such acknowledgments include the A. Jahres Award in medicine from Oslo University in 1970; the Louisa Gross Horwitz Prize from Columbia University in 1975; the Albert Lasker Medical Research Award in 1977; the Ciba-Geigy Drew Award for biomedical research in 1980; the Gairdner Foundation Award in 1981; the Bror Holberg Medal of the Swedish Chemical Society in 1982; and the Abraham White Distinguished Scientist Award in 1991. Samuelsson has published widely on the biochemistry of prostaglandins, thromboxanes, and leukotrienes.

Samuelsson married Inga Karin Bergstein on August 19, 1958; they have three children.

SELECTED WRITINGS BY SAMUELSSON:

Books

Prostaglandins, Interscience Publishers, 1967.
Third Conference on Prostaglandins in Fertility Control, Karolinska Institute, 1972.

Periodicals

"Leukotrienes: Mediators of Immediate Hypersensitivity Reactions and Inflammation," *Science,* May 6, 1983, pp. 568–75.

SOURCES:

Books

Nobel Prize Winners, H. W. Wilson, 1987, pp. 919–21.

Periodicals

Miller, J. A., "Nobel Prize in Medicine for Prostaglandin Discoveries," *Science News,* October 16, 1982, p. 245.
New York Times, October 12, 1982.
Oates, John A., "The 1982 Nobel Prize in Physiology or Medicine," *Science,* November 19, 1982, pp. 765–68.
Sattaur, Omar, "On the Trail of Prostaglandins," *New Scientist,* October 14, 1982, pp. 82–83.
"Sharing the Nobel Prize," *Time,* October 25, 1982, p. 84.

—*Sketch by David Sprinkle*

David A. Sanchez
1933-
American mathematician

David A. Sanchez is a mathematics scholar with international teaching experience whose recent positions have led him into science administration and academic research program development.

Through his study of calculus during his early career, Sanchez developed a particular interest in using ordinary differential equations to create mathematical models for the study of population growth and competing populations. More recently, he has been actively interested in minority participation in academics, and as the vice chancellor for academic affairs of the Texas A & M University System, he provides leadership and coordination to a system of seven universities with an enrollment of over 75,000 students.

David Alan Sanchez was born in San Francisco, California, on January 13, 1933, to Cecilio and Concepcion Sanchez. After obtaining his bachelor of science degree in mathematics from the University of New Mexico in 1955, Sanchez entered the U.S. Marine Corps in 1956. In 1959 he left the Corps as a lieutenant to attend the University of Michigan, where he earned his M.S. in 1960 and his Ph.D. in 1964. During those graduate school years, he also worked as a research assistant in the Radar Laboratory of the university's Institute of Science and Technology, where he investigated signal processing and battlefield simulations for U.S. Army applications. In 1963 he accepted an instructor's position at the University of Chicago; he remained there until 1965 when he became a visiting professor for a year at Manchester University in Manchester, England. In 1966 he returned to the United States, becoming an assistant professor at the University of California at Los Angeles (UCLA). In 1970 he took another year as visiting assistant professor, this time at Brown University in Providence, Rhode Island, and then returned to UCLA as associate professor. After spending a school year during 1973 and 1974 as visiting associate professor at the University of Wisconsin's Mathematics Research Center, Sanchez became a full professor at UCLA in 1976. In 1977 he returned to his alma mater, accepting a professorship at the University of New Mexico. He remained there until 1986, serving as chair of the department of mathematics and statistics from 1983 to 1986. He took time during 1982 to teach at the University of Wales in Aberystwyth.

During this period, Sanchez developed an interest in biomathematics—math that can be applied to the study of biology. He began using mathematical models to study population growth and competing populations. In his study on an ordinary game bird, the sand hill crane, for instance, Sanchez used a mathematical model to predict the effect of an external force that reduces a population, in this case by hunting. He wanted to formulate a simple mathematical equation that could predict the point at which the crane population would face extinction because it was being hunted at a rate faster than it could reproduce and grow. In this and other research studies, Sanchez constructed mathematical models that have implications for the study of human populations.

In 1986, Sanchez made a career switch and accepted a position as vice president and provost at Lehigh University in Bethlehem, Pennsylvania. After four years of administrative experience there, he became the assistant director for mathematical and physical sciences for the National Science Foundation in Washington, D.C. In 1992 he changed from administering science funds to helping to run a federal laboratory, joining the Los Alamos National Laboratory in New Mexico as deputy associate director for research and education. On November 1, 1993, he became vice chancellor for academic affairs for the Texas A & M University System. This large state system, which is composed of seven universities and eight agencies, has an enrollment of over 75,000 students, employs more than 19,000 people, and has operations in each of the 254 counties in Texas. In a *Texas A & M Fortnightly* article, university chancellor William Mobley said that Sanchez's extensive experience with academic and research program development both at the university and at the federal level made him capable of providing the long-range academic planning and linkages needed by its vast university system.

Sanchez is a member of the American Mathematical Society, the Mathematical Association of America, the Society of Industrial and Applied Mathematics, and the Society for the Advancement of Chicanos and Native Americans in Science. A specialist in differential equations, he has published more than fifty articles in professional and technical journals and also is the author of three books on mathematics. He has served on several boards of governors, directors, advisory boards, and policy committees. Always interested in minority participation in academics, he served on the American Mathematical Society's Committee on Opportunities in Mathematics for Disadvantaged Groups, and the Committee on Minority Participation in Mathematics for the Mathematics Association of America.

Sanchez married Joan Patricia Thomas in 1957, and they have two children, Bruce and Christina. Besides mathematics and administration, Sanchez enjoys fishing, bridge, and fiction writing and has published articles in *Flyfishing News* and *The Steamboat Whistle.*

SELECTED WRITINGS BY SANCHEZ:

Books

Ordinary Differential Equations and Stability Theory: An Introduction, W. H. Freeman and Co., 1968.

(With William D. Lakin) *Topics in Ordinary Differential Equations: A Potpourri,* Prindle, Weber & Schmidt, 1970.

(With R. C. Allen and W. T. Kyner) *Differential Equations: An Introduction,* 2nd edition, Addison-Wesley, 1988.

Periodicals

Beaumont, Penny, "Vice Chancellor for Academic Affairs Chosen," *Texas A & M Fortnightly,* September 27, 1993.

Other

Sanchez, David A., interview with Donna Olendorf, April 20, 1994.

—Sketch by Leonard C. Bruno

Pedro A. Sanchez

Pedro A. Sanchez
1940-
Cuban-born American soil scientist

Pedro A. Sanchez has spent his career improving the management of tropical soils for sustained food production. He has focused on overcoming tropical deforestation, land depletion, and rural poverty through improved agroforestry. His research interests as a soil scientist also include nutrient cycling. Sanchez has served as director general of the International Centre for Research in Agroforestry in Nairobi, Kenya, since 1991.

Pedro Antonio Sanchez was born October 7, 1940, in Havana, Cuba, the oldest of four children of Georgina (San Martin) and Pedro Antonio Sanchez. His interest in agroforestry and soil science began early—Sanchez told contributor Marianne Fedunkiw in an interview that he travelled throughout Cuba with his father, who managed the family farm and fertilizer business. His mother was a pharmacist and high school teacher. After completing high school at the Colegio de la Salle in Havana, Sanchez travelled to the United States to study at Cornell University. He received his B.S. in agronomy in 1962; two years later he finished his master of science degree in soil science and in 1968 received his Ph.D., also in soil science. While studying for his doctorate, he was a graduate assistant in soil science in the University of the Philippines-Cornell Graduate Education Program in Los Baños, Philippines. He was both a researcher and a teacher of soil fertility courses at the university.

Having completed his education, Sanchez joined the faculty of North Carolina State University (NCSU) as an assistant professor of soil science in 1968, followed by a three-year stint as co-leader of the university's National Rice Program of Peru, an agricultural mission established by NCSU. In this capacity, he supervised a research and extension program aimed at helping Peruvians achieve self-sufficiency by improving and sustaining their rice production. Sanchez continued his work in South America from 1971 until 1983, first as the leader of the Tropical Soils Program responsible for field soil research projects in the Cerrado of Brazil, the Amazon of Peru, and in Central America (1971–1976); then as coordinator for the Beef-Tropical Pastures Program, Centro International de Agricultural Tropical (CIAT), in Cali, Colombia (1977–1979); and as chief of the North Carolina State University Mission to Lima, Peru (1982–1983). During these years, he was also promoted first to associate professor of soil science at NCSU in 1973 and then to full professor in 1979.

In 1984 Sanchez expanded his work into other parts of the world—for seven years he was coordinator of the Tropical Soils Program at NCSU, supervising activities throughout Bolivia, Indonesia, and Madagascar. Concurrently, from 1990 to 1991 he was also director of the Center for World Environment and Sustainable Development, a joint project sponsored by Duke University, North Carolina State University, and the University of North Carolina at Chapel Hill.

The year 1991 marked a time of change for Sanchez. He became professor emeritus of soil science and forestry at NCSU and moved to Nairobi, Kenya, to become the third director general at the International Centre for Research in Agroforestry. Sanchez married Cheryl Palm in 1990; she is also a soil scientist, and they have co-authored a number of articles. He was married previously in 1965 and has three children: Jennifer Sanchez Goebel, an environmental lawyer; Evan, who studies business administration and works in the music business in New York; and Juliana, a high school senior.

Sanchez, who is fluent in English, Spanish, and Portuguese, is the author of two books and has also edited or co-edited eight books and written or contributed to more than 125 articles. In recognition of his work, he received both the International Soil Science Award from the Soil Science Society of America, and the International Service in Agronomy Award from the America Society of Agronomy in 1993. His work has been noted in other countries as well: in 1984 the Peruvian government presented him with the Orden de Merito Agricola, which is seldom given to a non-Peruvian citizen, and in 1979 he received the Diploma de Honor from the Instituto Colombiano Agropecuario. Sanchez is a member of more than ten professional and honorary societies, including the American Society of Agronomy; the International Society of Soil Science; and the Asociación Latinoamericana de Ciencias Agrícolas.

SELECTED WRITINGS BY SANCHEZ:

Books

Properties and Management of Soils in the Tropics, John Wiley and Sons, 1976.

Periodicals

(With J. H. Villachica and D. E. Bandy) "Soil Fertility Dynamics after Clearing a Tropical Rainforest in Peru," *Soil Science Society of America Journal,* Volume 47, 1983, pp. 1171–1178.

(With J. R. Benites) "Low Input Cropping for Acid Soils of the Humid Tropics," *Science,* Volume 238, 1987, pp. 1521–1527.

SOURCES:

Sanchez, Pedro A., interview with Marianne Fedunkiw conducted March 4, 1994.

—*Sketch by Marianne Fedunkiw*

Allan R. Sandage
1926-
American astronomer

Allan R. Sandage has won international recognition for his telescopic discoveries at the Hale Observatories at Mount Wilson and Palomar Mountain in California. In 1960, Sandage became the first person to identify a quasar, the most luminous object in the universe, by optical means. Sandage's discovery led the way for the identification of other quasars. Radioastronomers, who study celestial and extragalactic objects according to the radio waves they emit, have used quasars to refine estimations of the age and evolution of the universe. Since quasars are considerably more luminous than other cosmological bodies, they are detectable at greater distances and thus make it possible, in effect, to look farther back in time. Sandage has also gained renown for his work in determining the age of stars or globular clusters of stars and the age and size of the universe. The worldwide scientific community recognized Sandage's achievements in 1991 by bestowing upon him the $260,000 Crafoord Prize, astronomy's equivalent of the Nobel Prize.

Allen Rex Sandage was born in Iowa City, Iowa, on June 18, 1926, the son of Charles Harold Sandage and Dorothy (Briggs) Sandage. He began college studies at Miami University in Ohio, where his father was a professor of advertising, was drafted into the U.S. Navy in 1945, and completed his baccalaureate degree at the University of Illinois in 1948. He pursued graduate studies as a member of the first class of astronomy students at the California Institute of Technology, where he received his Ph.D. in 1953. Sandage wrote his doctoral thesis on the stellar components of the globular cluster M3 (M for Charles Messier, the French astronomer who identified the nebulae or fuzzy clouds of light in our galaxy), a group of stars clustered together thousands of light-years away that appears to form a halo around the Milky Way. In 1952, Sandage had joined the Mount Wilson Observatory overlooking Pasadena, California, as a research assistant to the renowned astronomer **Edwin P. Hubble**. Sandage's outstanding efforts as a young astronomer were recognized with the Helen Warner Prize from the American Astronomical Society in 1958, for a lecture on problems in the extragalactic distance scale.

Although Sandage has maintained a research position at the Mount Wilson and Palomar Observatories (later known collectively as the Hale Observatories) since the early 1950s, visiting lectureships and fellowships have taken him around the world to universities including Cambridge (1957), Harvard

(1957), Haverford (1958 and 1966), the University of South Africa (1958), Australian National University (1968–1969), the University of Basel (1985), the University of California at San Diego (1985–86), the University of Hawaii (1986), and Johns Hopkins (1987–1989).

Observes Mysterious Quasi-Stellar Object

Using the large 200-inch diameter reflecting telescope at the Palomar Observatory, commonly believed to be the world's largest telescope, Sandage built his career by employing the methods of radioastronomers, who survey the traveling electromagnetic disturbances or radio waves whose frequency and wavelengths lie within the radio region of the electromagnetic spectrum. In particular, Sandage examined the spectra of light emitted from stars and star clusters in the radio sky. In late summer 1960, Sandage, together with the young radioastronomer Thomas Matthews, optically identified a distant star-like object in another galaxy as the source of radio waves being emitted from the same sky coordinates. Before this time, no individual star had been identified as a radio source. This mysterious object was soon to be labeled a quasi-stellar radio source or, more commonly, a quasar.

Sandage's identification spurred astronomical observatories around the world to hunt for additional quasars. Astronomers began to think of quasars as what Dennis Overbye, in *Lonely Hearts of the Cosmos,* calls "beacons from deep time and space." In 1965, Sandage thought he had uncovered a way to identify cosmological objects as quasars by the large quantities of either ultraviolet or blue wavelength radiation they emitted. Although his quickly reported findings proved to be erroneous, he did confirm that, unlike his initial find, most quasars did not emit radio waves. Quasars remain an enigma, as astronomers continue to dispute their nature.

Dating the Age of the Universe

Sandage has also worked toward an answer to one of the greatest questions addressed by science: What is the age and origin of the universe? Early in his career, Sandage attempted to date the age of the universe by studying globular clusters, using as his basis the findings of his mentor, Edwin Hubble, the "father of observational cosmology." Hubble had gathered spectrophotometric data demonstrating that the spectral lines of globular clusters in distant galaxies are diverted towards longer red wavelengths of the electromagnetic spectrum. These spectral patterns, called red-shifts, are indicative of objects which are moving away from us. Quantitatively, the larger the shift, the greater the velocity at which the object is receding. Hubble concluded that a galaxy's distance was proportional to its red-shift displacement (Hubble's law).

Sandage refined measurements of the cosmological constant known as the Hubble Constant or Hubble Parameter, a number which greatly affects determination of the age of the universe and of the speed at which the universe is expanding. Sandage attempted to fit his spectrophotometric analyses of globular clusters and quasars into Hubble's equation. From this work, Sandage depicted the universe in terms of diverse, dynamic galaxies that are receding from our own at velocities proportional to their distances. This pattern, according to Sandage, was most likely put into motion by a primordial "big bang": like Hubble and Einstein, Sandage considered the universe to have originated in a massive explosion, after which it is still expanding. Sandage described the dynamics of this expansion in terms of oscillation. Specifically, the rate of expansion appears to be decreasing; the universe will eventually cease expanding and begin an oscillatory phase of contraction. Sandage estimated that the universe is approximately 15 billion years old, and that the entire period of oscillation will be approximately 80 billion years.

Sandage's contributions have been recognized by professional societies throughout the world. He has received awards from England's Royal Astronomical Society (1963), the Pontifical Academy of Science (1966), the Franklin Institute (1973), the American Astronomical Society (1958 and 1973), the Astronomical Society of the Pacific (1975), and the Swiss Physics Society (1991). The award of greatest professional significance was the Royal Swedish Academy's Crafoord Prize, bestowed upon Sandage in 1991. As astronomy is a science not considered by the Swedish Academy's Nobel Prize committee, the Crafoord award ranks as astronomy's equivalent to a Nobel Prize.

While giving a series of guest lectures at Harvard in 1957, Sandage met Mary Lois Connelly, a University of Indiana and Radcliffe graduate, who was teaching at Mount Holyoke College. They were married on June 8, 1959, and have two children, David Allan and John Howard. Sandage resides in Pasadena, where in his spare time he enjoys gardening and cooking. A passionate opera fan, Sandage listened to operatic music on the countless cold nights he spent galaxy-gazing through Palomar's 200-inch telescope. According to Overbye, Sandage is a dedicated Christian who maintains that "life is not a dreary accident."

SELECTED WRITINGS BY SANDAGE:

Books

The Hubble Atlas of the Galaxies, Carnegie Institute, 1961.

(With G. A. Tammann) *A Revised Shapley-Ames Catalogue of the Bright Galaxies,* Carnegie Institute, 1981, 2nd edition, 1987.

(With John Bedke) *Atlas of Galaxies Useful for Measuring the Cosmological Distance Scale,* National Aeronautics and Space Administration, 1988.

Periodicals

"The Red-Shift," *Scientific American,* September 1956, pp. 170–182, reprinted in *New Frontiers in Astronomy: Readings from Scientific American,* edited by Owen Gingerich, W.H. Freeman, 1975, pp. 309–315.

"Cosmology: A Search for Two Numbers," *Physics Today,* February 1970, pp. 34–41.

"The Size and Shape of the Universe: the Quest for the Curvature of Space," *Endeavour,* 1990, pp. 104–111.

SOURCES:

Books

Overbye, Dennis, *Lonely Hearts of the Cosmos: The Story of the Scientific Quest for the Secret of the Universe,* HarperCollins, 1991.

Periodicals

Osmer, Patrick S., "Quasars as Probes of the Distant and Early Universe," *Scientific American,* February 1982, pp. 126–138.

—*Sketch by Philip K. Wilson*

Frederick Sanger

Frederick Sanger
1918-
English biochemist

Frederick Sanger's important work in biochemistry has been recognized by two Nobel Prizes for chemistry. In 1958 he received the award for determining the arrangement of the amino acids that make up insulin, becoming the first person to thusly identify a protein molecule. In 1980 Sanger shared the award with two other scientists, being cited for his work in determining the sequences of nucleic acids in deoxyribonucleic acid (DNA) molecules. This research has had important implications for genetic research, and taken in conjunction with Sanger's earlier work on the structure of insulin, represent considerable contributions to combatting a number of diseases.

Frederick Sanger was born in Rendcombe, Gloucestershire, England, on August 3, 1918. His father, also named Frederick, was a medical doctor, and his mother, Cicely Crewsdon Sanger, was the daughter of a prosperous cotton manufacturer. Young Frederick attended the Bryanston School in Blandford, Dorset, from 1932 to 1936 and was then accepted at St. John's College, Cambridge. By his own admission, Sanger was not a particularly apt student. Later in life he wrote in *Annual Review of Biochemistry* that "I was not academically brilliant. I never won scholarships and would probably not have been able to attend Cambridge University if my parents had not been fairly rich."

Upon arriving at Cambridge and laying out his schedule of courses, Sanger found that he needed one more half-course in science. In looking through the choices available, Sanger came across a subject of which he had never heard—biochemistry—but that sounded appealing to him. "The idea that biology could be explained in terms of chemistry," he later wrote in *Annual Review of Biochemistry,* "seemed an exciting one." He followed the introductory course with an advanced one and eventually earned a first–class degree in the subject.

Sanger rapidly discovered his strengths and weaknesses in science. Although he was not particularly interested in or skilled at theoretical analysis, he was a superb experimentalist. He found that, as he later observed in *Annual Review of Biochemistry,* he could "hold my own even with the most academically outstanding" in the laboratory. This observation was to be confirmed in the ingenious experiments that he was to complete in the next four decades of his career.

Graduate Studies Lead to Protein Research

After receiving his bachelor's degree from St. John's in 1939, Sanger decided to continue his work in biochemistry. Though World War II had just begun, Sanger avoided service in the English army because his strong Quaker pacifist beliefs qualified him as a conscientious objector. Instead, he began looking for a biochemistry laboratory where he could serve as an apprentice and begin work on his Ph.D. The first position he found was in the laboratory of protein specialist, N. W. Pirie. Pirie assigned Sanger a project involving the extraction of edible protein from grass. That project did not last long as Pirie left Cambridge, and Sanger was reassigned to Albert Neuberger. Neuberger changed Sanger's assignment to the study of lysine, an amino acid. By 1943, Sanger had completed his research and was awarded his Ph.D. for his study on the metabolism of lysine.

After receiving his degree, Sanger decided to stay on at Cambridge, where he was offered an opportunity to work in the laboratory of A. C. Chibnall, the new Professor of Biochemistry. Chibnall's special field of interest was the analysis of amino acids in protein, a subject in which Sanger also became involved. The structure of proteins had been a topic of considerable dispute among chemists for many years. On the one hand, some chemists were convinced that proteins consisted of some complex, amorphous material that could never be determined chemically. Conversely, other chemists believed that, while protein molecules might be complex, they did have a structure that could eventually be unraveled and understood.

Probably the most influential theory of protein structure at the time of Sanger's research was that of the German chemist **Emil Fischer**. In 1902, Fischer had suggested that proteins consist of long chains of amino acids, joined to each other head to tail. Since it was known that each amino acid has two reactive groups, an amino group and a carboxyl group, it made sense that amino acids might join to each other in a continuous chain. The task facing researchers like Sanger was to first determine what amino acids were present in any particular protein, and then to learn in what sequence those amino acids were arranged. The first of these steps was fairly simple and straightforward, achievable by conventional chemical means. The second was not.

The protein on which Sanger did his research was insulin. The reason for this choice was that insulin—used in the treatment of diabetes—was one of the most readily available of all proteins, and one that could be obtained in very high purity. Sanger's choice of insulin for study was a fortuitous one. As proteins go, insulin has a relatively simple structure. Had he, by chance, started with a more complex protein, his research would almost certainly have stretched far beyond the ten years it required.

New Techniques Yield Structure of Insulin

In 1945, Sanger made an important technological breakthrough that made possible his later sequencing work on amino acids. He discovered that the compound dinitrophenol (DNP) will bond tightly to one end of an amino acid and that this bond is stronger than the one formed by two amino acids bonding with one another. This fact made it possible for Sanger to use DNP to take apart the insulin molecule one amino acid at a time. Each amino acid could then be identified by the newly discovered process of paper chromatography. This was a slow process, requiring Sanger to examine the stains left by the amino acids after they were strained through paper filters, but the technique resulted in the eventual identification of all amino acid groups in the insulin molecule.

Sanger's next objective was to determine the sequence of the amino acids present in insulin, but this work was made more difficult by the fact that the insulin molecule actually consists of two separate chains of amino acids joined to each other at two points by sulfur-sulfur bonds. In addition, a third sulfur-sulfur bond occurs within the shorter of the two strands. Despite these difficulties, Sanger, in 1955, announced the results of his work: he had determined the total structure of insulin molecule, the first protein to be analyzed in this way. Sanger's work in this area was considered important because it involved proteins—"the most important substances in the human body," as Sanger described them in a *New York Times* report on his work. Proteins are integral elements in both the viruses and toxins that cause diseases and in the antibodies that prevent them. Sanger's research, in laying the groundwork for future work on proteins, greatly increased scientists' ability to combat diseases. For his important work on proteins, Sanger was awarded the Nobel Prize in chemistry in 1958.

Writing in *The Annual Review of Biochemistry,* Sanger referred to the decade after completion of the insulin work as the "'lean years' when there were no major successes." Part of this time was taken up with various research projects aimed at learning more about protein structure. In one series of experiments, for example, he explored the use of radioactive isotopes for sequencing. The work was not particularly productive, however, and Sanger soon undertook a new position and a new area of research.

In 1962 he joined the newly established Medical Research Council (MRC) Laboratory of Molecular Biology at Cambridge, a center for research that included such scientists as **Max Perutz, Francis Crick**, and **Sydney Brenner**. This move marked an important turning point in Sanger's career. The presence of his new colleagues—and Crick, in particular—sparked Sanger's interest in the subject of nucleic acids. Prior to joining the MRC lab, Sanger had had little interest in this subject, but he now became convinced of their importance. His work soon concentrated on the ways in which his protein-sequencing experiences might be used to determine the sequencing of nucleic acids.

The latter task was to be far more difficult than the former, however. While proteins may consist of as few as 50 amino acids, nucleic acids contain hundreds or thousands of basic units, called nucleotides. The first successful sequencing of a nucleic acid, a transfer RNA molecule known as alanine, was announced by **Robert William Holley** in 1965. Sanger had followed Holley's work and decided to try a somewhat different approach. In his method, Sanger broke apart a nucleic acid molecule in smaller parts, sequenced each part, and then determined the way in which the parts were attached to each other. In 1967, Sanger and his colleagues reported on the structure of an RNA molecule known as 5S using this technique.

Work on DNA Earns Second Nobel Prize

When Sanger went on to the even more challenging structures of DNA molecules, he invented yet another new sequencing technique. In this method, a single-stranded DNA molecule is allowed to replicate itself but stopped at various stages of replication. Depending on the chemical used to stop replication, the researcher can then determine the nucleotide present at the end of the molecule. Repeated applications of this process allowed Sanger to reconstruct the sequence of nucleotides present in a DNA molecule.

Successful application of the technique made it possible for Sanger and his colleagues to report on a 12 nucleotide sequence of DNA from bacteriophage λ in 1968. Ten years later, a similar approach was used to sequence a 5,386 nucleotide sequence of another form of bacteriophage. In recognition of his sequencing work on nucleic acids, Sanger was awarded his second Nobel Prize in chemistry in 1980, shares of which also went to **Walter Gilbert** and **Paul Berg**. Their work has been lauded for its application to the research of congenital defects and hereditary diseases and has proved vitally important in producing the artificial genes that go into the manufacture of insulin and interferon, two substances used to treat diseases.

In 1983, at the age of 65, Sanger retired from research. He was beginning to be concerned, he said in the *Annual Review of Biochemistry,* about "occupying space that could have been available to a younger person." He soon found that he very much enjoyed retirement, which allowed him to do many things for which he had never had time before. Among these were gardening and sailing. He also had more time to spend with his wife, the former Margaret Joan Howe, whom he had married in 1940, and his three children, Robin, Peter Frederick, and Sally Joan.

During his career, Sanger received many honors in addition to his two Nobel Prizes. In 1954, he was elected to the Royal Society and in 1963 he was made a Commander of the Order of the British Empire. He has been given the Corday-Morgan Medal and Prize of the British Chemical Society, the Alfred Benzons Prize, the Copley Medal of the Royal Society, and the Albert Lasker Basic Medical Research Award, among other honors.

SELECTED WRITINGS BY SANGER:

Periodicals

"Chemistry of Insulin," *Science,* May 12, 1959, pp. 1340–1345.
"Sequences, Sequences, and Sequences," *Annual Review of Biochemistry,* Volume 57, 1988, pp. 1–28.

SOURCES:

Books

Current Biography 1981, H. W. Wilson, 1981, pp. 354–356.
Nobel Prize Winners, H. W. Wilson, 1987, pp. 921–924.
Silverstein, A., *Frederick Sanger: The Man Who Mapped Out a Chemical of Life,* John Day, 1969.

Periodicals

Chemistry and Industry, December 13, 1958, pp. 1653–1654.
New York Times, October 29, 1958, p. 10.

—*Sketch by David E. Newton*

David Satcher
1941-
American medical geneticist

David Satcher has devoted his career to ensuring that all members of society receive the benefits of health care. Satcher, himself an educator and administrator, has made sure that minorities, women and children, and the impoverished are not locked out of the system. In addition to his efforts to improve the quality and availability of health care, Satcher has achieved fame in the medical community for his research on sickle cell anemia and his efforts in revitalizing Meharry Medical College, a historically African American medical school in Tennessee. Satcher's work has won him respect and several honors from the medical community.

Born in Anniston, Alabama, on March 2, 1941, David Satcher was one of nine children born to self-educated farmers. He credits his parents for his lifelong commitment to providing better health care for minorities. In an interview with Marlene Cimons, published in the *Los Angeles Times,* Satcher said, "I may have come from a poor family economically, but they were not poor in spirit." When he was two years old, Satcher came close to dying from whooping cough, and was saved only by his mother's ministrations and the efforts of a local black doctor—the only one who would come to serve the poor family. The story of his near-death became a family shibboleth, and by age eight, Satcher had determined that he would become a doctor and help those who were traditionally ignored by society: the poor and minorities.

Satcher, whose parents instilled in their children a love of learning and a respect for educators, did well in school. When it came time for college, he won scholarships in addition to working his way through Morehouse College, graduating Phi Beta Kappa in 1963. He went on to Case Western Reserve University in Cleveland, Ohio, where he earned an M.D. and then a Ph.D. in cytogenetics in 1970 with a dissertation on "The Effects of Iodine–131 and X-Radiation on the Chromosomes of Peripheral Blood Leukocytes." While he conducted genetic research, Satcher also became interested in community medicine and administration. In 1972 he was made director of the King-Drew Medical Center in Los Angeles, California, also serving as associate director of its Sickle Cell Center from 1973 to 1975. From 1975 to 1979, he was a professor and chair of the department of family medicine as well as acting dean of the Charles R. Drew Postgraduate Medical School in Los Angeles. At Drew, Satcher created a cooperative program with the University of California, Los Angeles, whereby medical students would study two years at each institution and also provide medical care to the people of Watts. In 1979 Satcher returned to his undergraduate alma mater, Morehouse College, as a professor and chair of the department of community medicine.

Helps Breathe Life into Meharry

Although he successfully continued his efforts in administrating and teaching at Morehouse, it was in 1982 that Satcher took on his most challenging position. Appointed the president of Meharry Medical College in Nashville, Tennessee, Satcher was faced with the unenviable task of reorganizing and revitalizing a university plagued by annual deficits and decreasing enrollment. By all accounts, Meharry was on the brink of collapse when Satcher arrived. Undaunted, Satcher worked with a team of faculty and administrators to turn Meharry around, and by 1986 the institution had hired 40 new faculty members, raised $25 million in gifts and pledges, organized a health maintenance organization (HMO) for Nashville employers, and was running with a balanced budget for the first time in years. Satcher, a popular and energetic administrator, also made it a priority to ensure that black medical students received the same quality education as their white counterparts. He stayed at Meharry until 1993 when President Bill Clinton appointed him director of the Centers for Disease Control and Prevention in Atlanta, Georgia. His priorities for the Center included prevention, women's health, education, and creating a sense of community to stop the violence in America. "That's why kids join gangs," Satcher said in his *Los Angeles Times* interview, "to try to have a family, a community."

Satcher married Nola Satcher, a poet, with whom he has four children: Gretchen, David, Daraka, and Daryl. A member of the American Academy of Family Physicians and the American Society of Human Genetics, Satcher was a Macy Foundation Faculty fellow in community medicine in 1972 and 1973. He was honored with the Outstanding Morehouse Alumnus Award in 1973, the Award for Medical Education for Sickle Cell Disease in 1973, and the Outstanding Alumnus award from Case Western Reserve University in 1980.

SELECTED WRITINGS BY SATCHER:

Books

Editor, *Sickle Cell Counseling,* National Foundation—March of Dimes, 1973.

Periodicals

"Does Race Interfere with the Doctor-Patient Relationship?" *Journal of the American Medical Association,* March, 26, 1973, pp. 1498–99.

"Study in Watts—Family Practice for the Inner City," *Urban Health,* October, 1976, p. 72.

(With T. Coleman) "Future Family Physicians Get Early Community Contact in Morehouse Curriculum," *Urban Health,* January, 1983, pp. 46–48.

"Introducing Preclinical Students to Primary Care through a Community Preceptorship Program," *Journal of Medical Education,* March, 1983, pp. 179–85.

"Crime—Sin or Disease: Drug Abuse and AIDS in the African-American Community," *Journal of Health Care for the Poor and Underserved,* fall, 1990, pp. 212–18.

(With M. L. Rivo) "Improving Access to Health Care through Physician Workforce Reform," *Journal of the American Medical Association,* September 1, 1993, pp. 1074–78.

(With P. Edelman) "Violence as a Public Health Priority," *Health Affairs,* winter, 1993, pp. 123–25.

George Schaller

SOURCES:

Periodicals

Applebome, Peter, "CDC's New Chief Worries as Much about Bullets as about Bacteria," *New York Times,* September 26, 1993, p. E7.

Cimons, Marlene, "To Heal a Nation," *Los Angeles Times,* March 1, 1994, p. E1.

Jet, March 17, 1986, p. 23; June 16, 1986, p. 37.

Journal of the National Medical Association, February, 1983, pp. 210, 213.

Martin, Thad, "Turnaround at Meharry," *Ebony,* March, 1986, pp. 42–50.

"Medical School Chief Named CDC Director," *Washington Post,* August 21, 1993, p. A3.

"Meharry Medical School Finds Its 8th President," *New York Times,* February 1, 1982, p. B12.

—*Sketch by J. Sydney Jones*

George Schaller
1933-

German-born American zoologist, naturalist, and conservationist

George Schaller, the widely-respected zoologist and author, has accomplished ground-breaking research on a variety of different animals by studying them in their natural habitats. Associated with the New York Zoological Society since 1966 (he was named the director of the Society's Animal Research and Conservation Center in 1979, and subsequently its Director for Science), Schaller has sought to inform—through his numerous published works—a public that has frequently misunderstood and exploited wildlife. In the *New York Times Book Review,* Schaller told Lynn Karpen that "there's a moral obligation to do more for conservation. If you only study, you might get to write a beautiful obituary but you're not helping to perpetuate the species."

George Beals Schaller was born on May 26, 1933, in Berlin, Germany, to Georg Ludwig and Bettina Byrd (Beals) Schaller. After World War II, he accompanied his mother to an uncle's home in Missouri, where he developed an interest in animals and the outdoors. This pursuit influenced Schaller's college choice, and he entered the University of Alaska to study wildlife and the wilderness with the idea of making these subjects his life's work. Shortly after his graduation in 1955 (he received a B.S. in zoology and a B.A. in anthropology), Schaller joined his first expedition.

Explores Brooks Range in Northern Alaska

Hired as an assistant to Olaus Murie—president of the Wilderness Society in 1956 and Schaller's lifelong role model—Schaller traveled to the last true wilderness in the United States: the Brooks Range in northeastern Alaska. The New York Zoological Society sponsored the expedition, which was the first biological survey of the region. Approximately thirty-four years later Schaller wrote about the experience in an article for *Wildlife Conservation:* "We traversed many mountains and nameless valleys to collect information. We pressed plants, made bird lists, examined places where grizzlies had turned sod in search of voles, and analyzed wolf and lynx droppings to determine what these predators had eaten. . . . Each of us received, in the words of Margaret Murie, 'the gift of personal satisfaction, the personal well-being purchased by striving.'"

Schaller was doing graduate work in bird behavior in 1957 at the University of Wisconsin when he was offered the opportunity to study gorillas in Africa. "Here is a creature, considered with the chimpanzee the nearest relative of man, and we know almost nothing about its life in the wild," Schaller noted in his introduction to *The Year of the Gorilla.* "Does it live in small family units or in large groups; how many males and females are there in each group; what do groups do when they meet; how far do they travel each day; how long are infants dependent on their mothers?" These questions, which were answered as he studied free-living gorillas in Uganda, formed the basis of all his future field studies of large mammals. (A preceding work, *The Mountain Gorilla,* received the Best Terrestrial Wildlife Publication Award from the Wildlife Society in 1965.)

No-Weapons Policy: Unarmed and Unharmed

In 1962 Schaller earned a Ph.D. from the University of Wisconsin and became a fellow at the Center for Advanced Study in the Behavioral Sciences at Stanford University. Then, under the auspices of Johns Hopkins University (where he was a research associate from 1963 to 1966), Schaller studied the tiger in central India. A year of field research led to the book *The Deer and the Tiger: A Study of Wildlife in India,* published in 1967. Meanwhile, Schaller had became a research associate at the Institute for Research in Animal Behavior at the New York Zoological Society. The institute, along with Rockefeller University, sponsored his study of lions in Tanzania's Serengeti Park. Schaller's findings on predator-prey relations were published in *The Serengeti Lion,* which won the National Book Award in 1973.

Schaller refuses to carry weapons in his field work because he is convinced that the sight of an armed person makes the animals hostile. Despite the dangers commonly associated with working with wild animals, Schaller has remained unharmed; in a *National Geographic* article, he described one close call on the Serengeti Plain: "The breathing of a drugged lioness faltered while I was tagging her. As I administered artificial respiration by pressing on her chest, another lioness charged. I had to dash to the safety of

my Land-Rover. Fortunately, the immobilized lioness survived—and so did I."

First Encounter with Pandas in the Wilderness

In all of his wildlife studies, Schaller attempts to enter the world of his subjects by sharing their lifestyle. During a cold January in 1980, Schaller trailed a male panda named Wei-Wei for five-and-a-half days through the snow-covered Wolong Natural Reserve in China's Sichuan province. "I learned that he averaged just over three-quarters of a mile of travel a day, surprisingly little for such a large animal, that he left his scent on forty-five trees, that he had nine lengthy rest periods, that he deposited an average of ninety-seven droppings per day. . . . I developed at least a more perceptive mind by following Wei's tracks and could appreciate even more the uniqueness of his personal world," Schaller wrote in his book *The Last Panda.*

According to Geoffrey C. Ward in the *New York Times Book Review,* "*The Last Panda* is really two books in one: a group portrait of the animals [Schaller] calls 'the most endearing creatures I have ever seen,' and a litany of human errors—of crimes against nature—that may already have insured the panda's disappearance from the wild." Among the various human factors that have impeded on the panda's survival are zoos which "'vie for status, publicity and profit' through 'rent a panda' deals," Schaller told Sharon Bagley in *Newsweek.* Bagley further explained that "panda rentals disrupt the breeding of a species that reproduces poorly in captivity even without transoceanic sabbaticals. When they take up long-term residence, any cubs they have rarely survive."

A Touch of the Poet

"No one else ever will have the chance to do what Schaller has done," William Conway told contributor Rayma Prince in an interview, referring to the range of his colleague's subjects: lions, tigers, jaguars, giant pandas, snow leopards, and mountain gorillas. Conway, who is general director of the New York Zoological Society/The Wildlife Conservation Society, worked with Schaller for thirty-five years. Conway commented, "George differs from most of the scientists in that he is an exceptionally shy and thoughtful person, with a bit of the poet in his soul and the way he looks at life, and I think this comes through in his writings." In *The Year of the Gorilla* Schaller wrote, "To see African wildlife in all its abundance and variety, living as it has always lived, was one of the most priceless experiences I have ever had."

The list of honors bestowed on Schaller is extensive: besides a 1971 Guggenheim fellowship, a 1971 gold medal from the San Diego Zoological

Society, and a 1980 gold medal from the World Wildlife Fund (among other honors), he has received the Order of the Golden Ark from Prince Bernhard of The Netherlands (1978) and, from West Germany, the 1985 Bruno H. Schubert Conservation Award. When Schaller was awarded the Explorers Medal by the Explorers Club in 1990, his name was added to a list of famous people that began with Admiral Peary, the first man to reach the North Pole.

Schaller married Kay Suzanne Morgan in 1957 and the couple has two sons, Eric and Mark. Kay Schaller, a trained anthropologist, went on many expeditions with her husband and often helped him with his books. William Weber, director of conservation operations at the Bronx facility, traced his interest in conservation to Schaller's influence. "When my wife Amy and I were working as Peace Corps volunteers in Zaire, we read his books," Weber told Rayma Prince in an interview. "The goal to save gorillas came from George's original work. He is certainly somebody who's inspired a lot of people to go out and carry on. In our case, it's quite something twenty years later to be working in the same organization with this person." Weber reported that Schaller, after thirty-five years, is probably going back out to do some more surveys on gorillas. "When Amy asked him how far he intended to walk, George said, 'Well, I think I've got a few hundred kilometers left in me.'"

SELECTED WRITINGS BY SCHALLER:

Books

The Mountain Gorilla, University of Chicago Press, 1963.
The Year of the Gorilla, University of Chicago Press, 1964.
The Deer and the Tiger, University of Chicago Press, 1967.
The Serengeti Lion, University of Chicago Press, 1972.
The Last Panda, University of Chicago Press, 1993.

Periodicals

"American Serengeti," *Wildlife Conservation,* November/December 1990, pp. 54–69.
"Life with the King of the Beasts," *National Geographic,* April, 1969, pp. 494–519.
"Pandas in the Wild," *National Geographic,* December, 1981, pp. 735–749.

SOURCES:

Periodicals

Bagley, Sharon, "Killed by Kindness," *Newsweek,* April 12, 1993, pp. 50–56.

Karpen, Lynn, "A Beautiful Obituary Won't Help," *New York Times Book Review,* March 28, 1993, p. 18.

Other

Conway, William, interview with Rayma Prince conducted August, 1993.
Weber, William, interview with Rayma Prince conducted August, 1993.

—*Sketch by Rayma Prince*

Andrew V. Schally
1926-
Polish-born American biochemist

Andrew V. Schally helped conduct pioneering research concerning hormones, identifying three brain hormones and greatly advancing scientists' understanding of the function and interaction of the brain with the rest of the body. His findings have proved useful in the treatment of diabetes and peptic ulcers, and in the diagnosis and treatment of hormone-deficiency diseases. Schally shared the 1977 Nobel Prize with French-born American endocrinologist **Roger Guillemin** and **Rosalyn Yalow** (an American scientist whose work in the discovery and development of radioimmunoassay, the use of radioactive substances to find and measure minute substances—especially hormones—in blood and tissue, helped Schally and Guillemin isolate and analyze peptide hormones).

Andrew Victor Schally was born on November 30, 1926, in Wilno, Poland, to Casimir Peter Schally and Maria Lacka Schally. His father served in the military on the side of the Allies during World War II, and Schally grew up during Nazi occupation of his homeland. The family later left Poland and immigrated to Scotland, where Schally entered the Bridge Allen School in Scotland. He studied chemistry at the University of London and obtained his first research position at London's highly regarded National Institute for Medical Research. Leaving London for Montreal, Canada, in 1952, Schally entered McGill University, where he studied endocrinology and conducted research on the adrenal and pituitary glands. He obtained his doctorate in biochemistry from McGill in 1957. Also in 1957, Schally became an assistant professor of physiology at Baylor University School of Medicine in Houston, Texas. There he was able to pursue his interest in the hormones produced by the hypothalamus.

Expands on Geoffrey Harris's Discoveries

Scientists had long thought that the hypothalamus, a part of the brain located just above the pituitary gland, regulated the endocrine system, which includes the pituitary, thyroid and adrenal glands, the pancreas, and the ovaries and testicles. They were, however, unsure of the way in which hypothalamic hormonal regulation occurred. In the 1930s British anatomist Geoffrey W. Harris theorized that hypothalamic regulation occurred by means of hormones, chemical substances secreted by glands and transported by the blood. Harris was able to support his hypothesis by conducting experiments that demonstrated altered pituitary function when the blood vessels between the hypothalamus and the pituitary were cut. Harris and others were unable to isolate or identify the hormones from the hypothalamus.

Schally devoted his work to identifying these hormones. He and Roger Guillemin, who also worked at Baylor University's School of Medicine, were engaged in research to unmask the chemical structure of corticotropin-releasing hormone (CRH). Their efforts, however, were unsuccessful—the structure was not determined until 1981. The two then focused their work, independently, on other hormones of the hypothalamus. Schally left Baylor in 1962, when he became director of the Endocrine and Polypeptide Laboratory at the Veterans Administration (VA) Hospital in New Orleans, Louisiana. Also that year, Schally became a U.S. citizen and took on the post of assistant professor of medicine at Tulane University Medical School.

Schally's first breakthrough came in 1966 when he and his research group isolated TRH, or thyrotropin-releasing hormone. In 1969 Schally and his VA team demonstrated that TRH is a peptide containing three amino acids. It was Guillemin, though, who first determined TRH's chemical structure. The success of this research made it possible to decipher the function of a second hormone, called luteinizing-hormone releasing factor (LHRH). Identified in 1971, LHRH is a decapeptide and controls reproductive functions in both males and females. The chemical makeup of the growth-releasing hormone (GRH) was also discovered by Schally's team in 1971. Schally was able to show that GRH, a peptide consisting of ten amino acids, causes the release of gonadotropins from the pituitary gland. These gonadotropins, in turn, cause male and female sex hormones to be released from the testicles and ovaries. In conjunction with this, Schally was able to identify a factor that inhibits the release of GRH in 1976. Guillemin, however, had determined its structure earlier and named it somatostatin. Subsequent studies by Schally showed that somatostatin serves multiple roles, some of which relate to insulin production and growth disorders. This led to speculation that the hormone could be useful for treating diabetes and acromegaly, a growth-disorder disease.

The hormone research done by Schally and his colleagues was tedious and expensive. Thousands of sheep and pig hypothalami were required to extract the smallest amount of hormone. These organs were solicited from many area slaughterhouses and required immediate dissection to prevent the hormones from degrading. Their accomplishment of isolating the first milligram of pure thyrotropin-releasing hormone, Guillemin stated, cost many times more than the NASA space mission that brought a kilogram of moon rock back to earth.

Schally's intense years of hard work and accomplishment were capped by the Nobel Prize, but he has also received many other awards and honors. In 1974 he was given the Charles Mickle Award of the University of Toronto, and the Gairdner Foundation International Award. He received the Borden Award in the Medical Sciences of the Association of American Medical Colleges in 1975 and, that same year, the Lasker Award and the Laude Award. He has held memberships in the National Academy of Sciences, the American Society of Biological Chemists, the American Physiology Society, the American Association for the Advancement of Science, and the Endocrine Society. In the years prior to receiving the Nobel Prize, Schally and his colleagues published more than 850 papers. Married to Brazilian endocrinologist, Ana Maria de Medeiros-Comaru, Schally often lectures in Latin America and Spain. He and his first wife, Margaret Rachel White, have two children.

SELECTED WRITINGS BY SCHALLY:

Books

(With W. Locke), *The Hypothalamus and Pituitary in Health and Disease,* Thomas Press, 1972.

Periodicals

(With others) "Isolation of Thyrotropin Releasing Factor (TRF) from Porcine Hypothalamus," *Biochemical and Biophysical Research Communications,* Volume 25, 1966, p. 165.

(With others) "Purification of Thyrotropic Hormone Releasing Factor from Bovine Hypothalamus," *Endocrinology,* Volume 78, 1966, p. 726.

(With others) "The Amino Acid Sequence of a Peptide with Growth Hormone Releasing Activity Isolated from Porcine Hypothalamus," *Journal of Biological Chemistry,* Volume 246, 1971, p. 6647.

SOURCES:

Periodicals

Meites, Joseph, "The 1977 Nobel Prize in Physiology or Medicine," *Science,* November 11, 1977, pp. 594–596.
New York Times, October 14, 1977, pp. A1, A18.

—*Sketch by Jane Stewart Cook*

Gertrude Scharff Goldhaber

Gertrude Scharff Goldhaber
1911-
German-born American physicist

Gertrude Scharff Goldhaber has been widely recognized both for her fundamental research on the characteristics of atomic nuclei and for her promotion of education and professional opportunities for women in science. She is also a proponent of precollege science education for both genders.

Gertrude Scharff was born on July 14, 1911, in Mannheim, Germany, the daughter of Otto Scharff, a businessman, and Nelly Steinharter Scharff. When Gertrude entered first grade, her mother told her how she would have loved to study at the university if only Germany had allowed girls to do so at that time. "I immediately made up my mind to attend the university at any cost," Scharff Goldhaber later said at a speech at the New York Academy of Sciences. Fortunately for her ambitions, a girls' gymnasium had recently been opened in Munich, and her parents enrolled her. The girl's study of English and chemistry at the gymnasium gave her entry to the universities of Freiburg, Zurich, and Berlin. She then pursued doctoral studies at the University of Munich, working under the experimental physicist Walther Gerlach, who suggested to her her thesis work on ferromagnetism. After Hitler came to Munich in 1933, Scharff Goldhaber was ostracized by most members of the Physics Institute because she was Jewish; Gerlach nevertheless promised to protect her until she had finished her thesis. After receiving her Ph.D. in 1935, Scharff Goldhaber quickly left Hitler's Germany for postdoctoral work with **George Thomson** at Imperial College in London, carrying out studies of surfaces by means of electron diffraction.

While in London, Scharff Goldhaber renewed her acquaintance with Maurice Goldhaber, who had been a fellow physics student with her in Berlin. Maruice Goldhaber had just received his Ph.D. and was working at Lord Rutherford's Cavendish Laboratory in Cambridge. In 1938 he accepted an assistant professorship at the University of Illinois in Champaign-Urbana. That same year, Scharff Goldhaber traveled to the United States, visiting various physics centers and stopping in Illinois to see Maurice Goldhaber. In May of 1939, Scharff Goldhaber married Maurice Goldhaber in London and returned with him to the United States. The University of Illinois gave Scharff Goldhaber a laboratory and graduate students, but not a paid staff position, explaining that this would violate its antinepotism policy. While working at Illinois, in 1942, Scharff Goldhaber discovered that neutrons are emitted in spontaneous fission (the splitting of an atomic nucleus); the discovery was classified top secret and was not published until 1946. Also in 1942, Scharff Goldhaber gave birth to her second son, Michael; his older brother Alfred had been born in 1940. (Both later became physicists.)

In 1948, the Brookhaven National Laboratory, a newly established federal nuclear laboratory on Long Island, New York, offered both Scharff Goldhaber and her husband jobs. The couple began to do some work at Brookhaven while also remaining with Illinois, which finally gave Scharff Goldhaber a paid staff position. In 1950, she and her husband moved permanently to Brookhaven, where they remained for the rest of their careers. Scharff Goldhaber—who was the first woman with a Ph.D. to join the laboratory's scientific staff—worked her way from associate physicist in 1950 to physicist in 1958 to senior physicist in

1962, a position she held until 1979. After her retirement, she continued her work at Brookhaven as a research collaborator.

In the early years, Scharff Goldhaber and her husband often worked together; in 1948 they established the identity of beta rays (a stream of high speed electrons) with atomic electrons. Independently, Scharff Goldhaber systematically studied energy levels and characteristics of a wide range of atomic nuclei and synthesized the understanding of these nuclear properties into far-ranging models. She developed the variable moment of inertia model, studied parity violation in electromagnetic transitions, investigated nuclear structure by using heavy ion projectiles, and experimentally examined high and low spin states.

In addition to her research, Scharff Goldhaber was deeply engaged in promoting physics education and the place of women in science. She states in the *Brookhaven Bulletin:* "The vicious cycle which was originally created by the overt exclusion of women from mathematics and science must be broken.... [I]t is of the utmost importance to give a girl at a very early age the conviction that girls are capable of becoming scientists." In 1958, Goldhaber started a training course at Brookhaven for precollege science teachers, in 1960 she founded the Brookhaven Lecture Series, and from 1978 to 1983 she worked on the National Research Council's committee on the education and employment of women in science and engineering. In 1979 she helped to found Brookhaven Women in Science (BWIS) and enthusiastically participated in its career days, introducing schoolgirls and their teachers to role models and career opportunities for women in science.

Goldhaber was elected a fellow of the American Physical Society (APS) in 1947 and to the National Academy of Sciences (NAS) in 1972. She served on many APS, NAS, and other professional society committees and published over one hundred articles in scientific journals. BWIS established a Gertrude S. Goldhaber Prize in 1992, to be awarded annually to a female graduate student in physics, and Boston University established a Gertrude and Maurice Goldhaber Prize for outstanding new graduate students in physics.

SELECTED WRITINGS BY SCHARFF GOLDHABER:

Books

"Isomeric Nuclei," *Encyclopedia of Physics,* R. G. Lerner and G. L. Trigg, editors, Dowden, Hutchinson & Ross, 1977.

Periodicals

"Spontaneous Emission of Neutrons from Uranium," *Physical Review,* Volume 70, 1946, p. 229.

"Identification of Beta Rays with Atomic Electrons," *Physical Review,* Volume 73, 1948, p. 1472.

SOURCES:

Books

Kass-Simon, G., and Patricia Faines, editors, *Women of Science: Righting the Record,* Indiana University Press, 1990.

Periodicals

"BNL's Fabulous Forty," *Brookhaven Bulletin,* March 27, 1987.

"Colloquium and Dinner to Honor Scharff-Goldhaber," *Brookhaven Bulletin,* September 18, 1987.

"Distinguished Physicists Manifest Lifelong Commitment to Succeed," *Burrelle's,* November 26, 1990.

"First Gertrude S. Goldhaber Prize Presented," *Brookhaven Bulletin,* October 16, 1992.

"Gertrude Scharff Goldhaber," *Science Teacher,* December 1973, p. 15.

"New Women's Physics Prize Honors Gertrude Goldhaber," *Brookhaven Bulletin,* March 27, 1992.

"Phi Beta Kappa Honors G. Goldhaber," *Brookhaven Bulletin,* March 30, 1984.

"Scharff-Goldhaber Saluted by N.Y. Academy of Sciences," *Brookhaven Bulletin,* March 23, 1990.

Other

Talk by Gertrude Scharff Goldhaber at presentation of prize by New York Academy of Sciences, June 14, 1990.

—*Sketch by Kathy Sammis*

Berta Scharrer
1906-
German-born American biologist

Berta Scharrer, together with her husband Ernst Scharrer, pioneered the field of neuroendocrinology—the interaction of the nervous and endocrine systems. Fighting against the then-accepted belief that nerve cells were only electrical conductors, as well as against the prejudice toward women in the sciences, Berta Scharrer established the concept of neurosecretion through her research with insects and other invertebrates. A highly respected educator, she was also among the founding faculty of the department of anatomy at the Albert Einstein College of Medicine in New York.

Berta Vogel Scharrer was born in Munich, Germany on December 1, 1906, the daughter of Karl Phillip and Johanna (Greis) Vogel. She developed an early interest in science, and attended the University of Munich, earning her Ph.D. in 1930 in biology for research into the correlation between sweetness and nutrition in various sugars. Upon graduation, Scharrer took a position as research associate in the Research Institute of Psychiatry in Munich, and in 1934 she was married to Ernst Albert Scharrer, a biologist. Together they formed an intellectual and domestic partnership that would last until Ernst Scharrer's death in 1965.

In 1928 Ernst Scharrer had discovered what he termed nerve-gland cells in a species of fish and made the rather startling hypothesis that some nerve cells actually were involved in secreting hormonal substances just as cells of the endocrine system do. It was a thesis sure to upset the more conservative members of the scientific community, as the synaptic function between neurons or nerve cells was then thought to be purely electrical. The idea of neurons having a dual function was looked on as something of a heresy: either cells secreted hormones, in which case they were endocrine cells belonging to the endocrine system, or they conducted electrical impulses, making them nerve cells, part of the nervous system. But what Ernst and Berta Scharrer demonstrated was that there existed an entire class of cells which performed both functions. The nerve-gland or neurosecretory cells are actually a channel between the nervous system and the endocrine system—an interface between an organism's environment and its glandular system. Some of the neurohormones secreted by neurosecretory cells actually control the release of other hormones via the anterior pituitary gland. To elucidate such action fully, the Scharrers divided up the animal kingdom between them: Ernst Scharrer took the vertebrates and Berta Scharrer the invertebrates.

Working as a research associate at the Neurological Institute of the University of Frankfurt, where her husband had been named director of the Edinger Institute for Brain Research, Berta Scharrer discovered other nerve-gland cells: in mollusks in 1935, in worms in 1936, and in insects beginning in 1937. But if research into neurosecretion was going well, life in Germany under Hitler was far from positive. The Scharrers decided, in 1937, to immigrate to the United States.

Introduce Neurosecretion to American Neuroscientists

The Scharrers travelled the long way to America, via the Pacific, collecting specimens for research along the way. They joined the Department of Anatomy at the University of Chicago for a year, and then moved on to New York where Ernst Scharrer was visiting investigator at the Rockefeller Institute from 1938 to 1940. Berta Scharrer continued her insect research in New York, and together the Scharrers prepared the results of their research for presentation at the 1940 meeting of the Association for Research in Nervous and Mental Diseases, the first presentation of the concept of neurosecretion in the United States, and one that was warmly received. That same year, Ernst Scharrer took a position as assistant professor in the anatomy department of Western Reserve University School of Medicine in Cleveland, Ohio, a post he would hold until 1946. Berta Scharrer was offered a fellowship assisting in the histology laboratory, which gave her research facilities, but scant professional standing. It was during these years that she accomplished some of her most important research into the localization of neurosecretory cells and their role in animal development, using the South American cockroach, *Leucophaea maderae*, as her research subject.

After the Second World War, Ernst Scharrer accepted a position at the University of Colorado Medical School in Denver, and Berta Scharrer won a Guggenheim Fellowship to continue her research, becoming an assistant professor in Denver in 1947. The next years were some of the Scharrers' most fruitful, as they loved the mountains, skiing, and horseback riding. Professionally these were also important times, for the theory of neurosecretion was beginning to be accepted around the world, especially after a German scientist was able to successfully stain neurosecretory granules—the packaging for neurohormones which some neurons secrete. Thus it became possible to study the fine structure of such granules and follow their course upon secretion. Neurosecretion became an accepted fact, in fact the cornerstone of the emerging field of neuroendocrinology. By 1950 it had also become an accepted fact that a chemical transmission took place at the synapse along with electrical charge. These advancements not only confirmed the Scharrers' work, but also paved the way for advances in their research. Berta Scharrer applied the new findings to her own work on the maturation of the ovarian systems of her South American cockroaches with results that verified earlier findings in the endocrinology of invertebrates.

Wins Full Professorship at Albert Einstein College

In 1955 the Scharrers were offered joint positions at the new Albert Einstein College of Medicine at Yeshiva University in New York: Ernst as department head of anatomy, and Berta as full professor in the same department. This was the first real professional recognition for Berta Scharrer, and the couple left Denver for New York. Here she taught histology —the microscopic structure of tissues—and continued with research into insect glands. Using the electron microscope, she was able to accomplish some of the earliest detailing of the insect nervous system and especially the neurosecretory system. Together with her husband, she published *Neuroendocrinology* in 1963, one of the basic texts in the new discipline. Tragically, her husband died in a swimming accident in Florida in 1965, but Berta Scharrer carried on with their research, acting as chair of the department for two years until a successor could be found. She also went on to elucidate the fine structure of the neurosecretory cell—composed of a cell body, projecting dendrites, the extending long axon, and synaptic contacts at one end, just as in other neurons or nerve cells. Additionally, neurosecretory cells have special fibers allowing for feedback, as well as neurohemal organs—the point at which the neurohormones pass into the blood stream. Neurosecretory cells, it was shown, can affect targets contiguous with them or distant, through the blood stream, as with other hormones. Scharrer also investigated the make-up of the secretory material, discovering that it was a peptide or polypeptide—a combination of amino acids. Scharrer's later research deals with the immunoregulatory property of neuropeptides, or the relationship between the immune and nervous systems in invertebrates.

Continuing with her research and instruction, as well as co-editing *Cell and Tissue Research*, Scharrer became an emeritus professor of anatomy and neuroscience at Albert Einstein College of Medicine in 1978. She was honored with a National Medal of Science in 1983, for her "pioneering contributions in establishing the concept of neurosecretion and neuropeptides in the integration of animal function and development." She has also won the F. C. Koch Award of the Endocrine Society in 1980, the Henry Gray Award of the American Association of Anatomists in 1982, and has been honored by her former country with the Kraepelin Gold Medal from the Max Planck Institute in Munich in 1978 and the Schleiden Medal in 1983. She is a member of the National

Academy of Sciences and holds honorary degrees from colleges and universities around the world, including Harvard and Northwestern. Reading and music are among Berta Scharrer's free-time activities, and she has continued scientific research well into her eighties.

SELECTED WRITINGS BY SCHARRER:

Books

(With Ernst A. Scharrer) *Neuroendocrinology,* Columbia University Press, 1963.
An Evolutionary Interpretation of the Phenomenon of Neurosecretion, American Museum of Natural History, 1978.

Periodicals

"Comparative Physiology of Invertebrate Endocrines," *Annual Review of Physiology,* Volume 25, 1953, pp. 456–472.
"The Fine Structure of the Neurosecretory System of the Insect Leucophaea Maderae," *Memoirs of the Society of Endocrinology,* Volume 12, 1962, pp. 89-97.
"Peptidergic Neurons: Facts and Trends," *General and Comparative Endocrinology,* January, 1978, pp. 50–62.
"Neurosecretion: Beginnings and New Directions in Neuropeptide Research," *Annual Review of Neuroscience,* Volume 10, 1987, pp. 1–17.
"Insects as Models of Neuroendocrine Research," *Annual Review of Entomology,* Volume 32, 1987, pp. 1–16.
"Recent Progress in Comparative Neuroimmunology," *Zoological Science,* December, 1992, pp. 1097–1100.

SOURCES:

Periodicals

"Honorary Degrees Given By Harvard," *New York Times,* October 16, 1982, p. 9.
"Medal of Science to Berta Scharrer," *Einstein,* Spring, 1985, p. 2.

Other

Palay, Sanford L., "Presentation of the Henry Gray Award to Professor Berta Scharrer at the Ninety-Fifth Meeting of the American Association of Anatomists" (speech), April 5, 1982.

—Sketch by J. Sydney Jones

Arthur L. Schawlow
1921-
American physicist

Arthur L. Schawlow's contribution to physics lies in his Nobel Prize-winning research regarding the use of laser and maser spectroscopy, which is the examination of spectra shown under the amplification of either a laser or a maser, in order to discover properties of the targeted material. Schawlow is also recognized as an important professor, lecturer, and highly visible member of the scientific community.

Arthur Leonard Schawlow was born on May 5, 1921, in Mount Vernon, New York. His father, Arthur Schawlow, was an insurance agent who had come to the United States from Latvia circa 1910, and his mother, the former Helen Mason, was a citizen of Canada. After the Schawlow family moved to Toronto, Canada, in 1924, young Arthur was educated at the Winchester Elementary School, the Normal Model School, and the Vaughan Road Collegiate Institute, all in Toronto.

After graduating from high school at the age of sixteen in 1937, Schawlow entered the University of Toronto. He had originally planned to major in radio engineering, but the only scholarship he was able to find was one in physics and mathematics. Thus, it was in these fields that he studied for his bachelor's degree, which he received in 1941. Schawlow also found time during his student days to pursue his favorite hobby, jazz music. A biographer, Boris P. Stoicheff, reports in *Science* that Schawlow "distinguished himself in certain Toronto circles as a clarinetist playing Dixieland jazz at a time when his idols were Benny Goodman and 'Jelly Roll' Morton.'"

Shortly after Schawlow received his bachelor's degree, Canada and the United States became involved in World War II. His assignment for the next three years was to teach physics to military personnel at the University of Toronto. At the same time, he was able to complete the work necessary for his M.A. degree, which he received in 1942. At the war's conclusion, Schawlow returned to his graduate studies full time. In 1949 he was awarded his Ph.D. in physics for research completed under the supervision of Malcolm F. Crawford.

Schawlow Begins Collaboration with Charles H. Townes

In 1941 Schawlow was awarded a Carbide and Carbon Chemicals scholarship that allowed him to spend two years as a postdoctoral researcher at Columbia University. While there, Schawlow met

Charles H. Townes, who was later to win the 1964 Nobel Prize in physics for his work on the development of the maser. A maser (microwave amplification by stimulated emission of radiation) is a device for amplifying microwave signals. Schawlow and Townes began a long and productive collaboration on the subjects of masers, lasers, and laser spectroscopy. One product of that collaboration was a book, *Microwave Spectroscopy,* published in 1955. Also, towards the end of his postdoctoral work at Columbia, on May 19, 1951, Schawlow married Townes's sister, Aurelia. The couple later had three children, Arthur Keith, Helen Aurelia, and Edith Ellen.

In 1951 Schawlow accepted a job as a research physicist at the Bell Telephone Laboratories in Murray Hill, New Jersey. He worked on a variety of topics there, including superconductivity and optical and microwave spectroscopy. But he also remained interested in a problem he and Townes had been investigating, an optical maser.

Schawlow and Townes Invent Method for Building a Laser

The first maser had been designed and built in the mid–1950s by Townes and two Russian physicists, **Nikolai Gennadiyenich Basov** and **Aleksandr Prokhorov**. Following that achievement, a number of physicists had explored the possibility of extending the maser principle to the optical region of the electromagnetic spectrum. After much discussion, Schawlow and Townes developed a proposal for building such an instrument, one that was later given the name laser, for light amplification by stimulated emission of radiation. They published their ideas in the December, 1958, issue of *Physical Review.*

Their next step was to attempt the actual construction of a laser. Unfortunately for Schawlow and Townes, they took a somewhat more difficult approach than was necessary and were to see their concept brought to reality by a fellow physicist, **Theodore Maiman**, who built the first successful laser in 1960. Schawlow and Townes were not far behind in constructing their own laser, however, and put the new device to use in a number of ways.

One of the most productive uses of laser technology has been in the area of laser spectroscopy, a field in which Schawlow has become one of the world's authorities. In laser spectroscopy, a laser beam is directed at a material to be studied. The wavelengths absorbed and then reemitted by the sample are determined by the electron energy levels and chemical bonds present in the material. By studying the spectra produced by laser analysis, a researcher can determine a number of fundamental properties of a material as well as the changes that take place within the material. For his contributions to the design of the laser and to its applications in laser spectroscopy, Schawlow (along with **Nicolaas Bloembergen** and **Kai M. Sieg-bahn**) was awarded a share of the 1981 Nobel Prize in physics.

In 1961 Schawlow left Bell Laboratories to accept a post as professor of physics at Stanford University. He served as chair of the department from 1966 to 1970 and in 1978 became J. G. Jackson-C.J. Wood Professor of Physics. Schawlow has been honored not only for his accomplishments as a researcher, but also for his skills as a teacher. Boris Stoicheff's report on the 1981 Nobel Prize in *Science* referred to Schawlow and fellow Nobel laureate Bloembergen as "celebrated teachers, possessed of a characteristic flair and combination of talents that have marked them as outstanding scientists and gifted lecturers."

Schawlow has been a highly visible scientist also, having appeared on Walter Cronkite's television series *The 21st Century,* Don Herbert's *Experiment* series, and on a variety of other U.S. and British educational programs. Among his many awards are the Ballantine Medal of the Franklin Institute (1962), the Thomas Young Medal and Prize of London's Physical Society and Institute of Physics (1963), the Morris Liebmann Memorial Award of the Institute of Electricians and Electrical Engineers, and the Frederick Ives Medal of the Optical Society of America (1976).

SELECTED WRITINGS BY SCHAWLOW:

Books

(With C. H. Townes) *Microwave Spectroscopy,* McGraw-Hill, 1955.

Periodicals

(With C. H. Townes) "Infrared and Optical Masers," *Physical Review,* Volume 112, December, 1958, pp. 1940–1949.
(With G. E. Devlin) "Simultaneous Optical Maser Action in Two Ruby Satellite Lines," *Physical Review Letters,* Volume 6, 1961, pp. 605–607.

SOURCES:

Books

Weber, Robert L., *Pioneers of Science: Nobel Prize Winners in Physics,* American Institute of Physics, 1980, pp. 275–276.
Yen, William M., and Marc D. Levenson, *Lasers, Spectroscopy, and New Ideas: A Tribute to Arthur L. Schawlow,* Springer-Verlag, 1987.

Periodicals

"Nobel Physics Prize to Bloembergen, Schawlow and Siegbahn," *Physics Today,* December, 1981, pp. 17–20.
Stoicheff, Boris P., "The 1981 Nobel Prize in Physics," *Science,* November 6, 1981, pp. 629–633.

—*Sketch by David E. Newton*

Stephen H. Schneider
1945-
American climatologist

Stephen H. Schneider, formerly a longtime senior scientist at the National Center for Atmospheric Research and later a professor in the department of biological sciences at the Institute for International Studies at Stanford University in California, is among the most respected scientists in the field of climatology. He has conducted research in many areas, including such publicized topics as nuclear winter and global warming, participated in numerous conferences, and published widely. Schneider is known outside the scientific community for his books and television appearances, in which he explains often difficult scientific concepts in a fashion understandable to the nonscientist.

Stephen Henry Schneider was born on February 11, 1945, in New York City to Samuel and Doris C. Swarte Schneider, both educators. He earned his undergraduate and graduate degrees in mechanical engineering from Columbia University, culminating his studies there with a doctorate in mechanical engineering and plasma physics in 1971. For the next year Schneider held a postdoctoral research associateship at the Goddard Institute for Space Studies in New York City. He followed this position with a yearlong fellowship at the National Center for Atmospheric Research in Boulder, Colorado, where he remained for the next twenty years, heading various research groups. During this time Schneider married Cheryl Kay Hatter. Their wedding was on August 19, 1978, and they have two children, Rebecca Eden and Adam William. In 1992 Schneider joined the faculty at Stanford University.

Conducts Vital Research

A tireless researcher, Schneider has received numerous grants to study the earth's climate. His work has touched on climate modeling, the climatic effects of a nuclear war (known as nuclear winter), climatic impact on society, and ecological implications of climate change, particularly of the phenomenon described as the greenhouse effect. Carbon dioxide and water in the earth's atmosphere help keep heat from escaping into space and enable life to flourish; deforestation and atmospheric pollution—in particular, high levels of carbon dioxide—are thought to increase the natural "greenhouse effect" of the atmosphere and thus increase global temperatures.

With grant support from the federal government in the 1980s, Schneider worked extensively on the theory of nuclear winter. This theory deals with the possible cooling of the atmosphere should the detonations of nuclear weapons spew tons of dust and debris into the atmosphere, blocking the sun's rays and adversely affecting plant growth. Schneider's later work involves history and climate models. Very interested in policy issues, Schneider deals not only with science but also with politics. He has been called many times to testify before congressional committees and was a member of the Defense Science Board Task Force on Atmospheric Obscuration, and he also served as a consultant to the administrations of presidents Richard Nixon and Jimmy Carter.

Adopts Activist Stance

Schneider's experiences in Washington led him to believe that many scientists' concerns about possible climate-related crises were being ignored by shortsighted government officials. To bring climatological issues directly to the public, Schneider embarked on the additional career of scientific activist. He has, like most scientists, made the results of his research known in numerous scientific publications. Yet he has gone a step further and written several books geared to the layperson, among them *The Coevolution of Climate and Life,* written with Randi Londer, and *Global Warming: Are We Entering the Greenhouse Century?*

In the preface to *Global Warming,* which he dedicated to his children, Schneider explained the rationale behind his forays from the ivory towers of scientific research: "I believe that scientists have the obligation to explain to those who pay our salaries what we have learned about complex issues: what we think we know well, what we don't know, what we might be able to learn, when we might learn it, how much it might cost to learn, and, most importantly, what it might mean for civilization." Schneider continued, "This means explaining issues in plain language, using appropriate but familiar metaphors, and holding back nothing—that is, letting the public decide whether a certain amount of uncertainty or knowledge is sufficient for action." Although Schneider has been the object of criticism from academic

colleagues for his efforts to popularize complicated and uncertain scientific concepts, he believes that his activist efforts are necessary. He has appeared on network nightly news programs, talk shows, and programs created by the Corporation for Public Broadcasting. He also acted as scientific adviser and script consultant for several episodes of the television series *Nova.* In addition, he has spread his message by editing the journal *Climatic Change* since 1975. As Schneider told *Contemporary Authors, New Revision Series,* "I intend to continue to study, write and speak on the urgent need for society to anticipate potential long-term consequences of its short-term policies with emphasis on issues with a technological component."

SELECTED WRITINGS BY SCHNEIDER:

Books

(With Lynne E. Mesirow) *The Genesis Strategy: Climate and Global Survival,* Plenum, 1976.
(With Lynne Morton) *The Primordial Bond: Exploring Connections between Man and Nature through the Humanities and Sciences,* Plenum, 1981.
(With Randi Londer) *The Coevolution of Climate and Life,* Sierra Club, 1984.
Global Warming: Are We Entering the Greenhouse Century?, Sierra Club, 1989.

SOURCES:

Books

Contemporary Authors New Revision Series, Volume 12, Gale, 1984.
Schneider, Stephen H., *Global Warming: Are We Entering the Greenhouse Century?,* Sierra Club, 1989.

Periodicals

Earth Science, spring, 1990, pp. 33–34.
New York Times, September 1, 1981.
Smil, Vaclav, "Heat, Little Light," *Bulletin of the Atomic Scientists,* June, 1990, p. 39.
Washington Post, July 18, 1981.

—*Sketch by Jeanne M. Lesinski*

Mogens Schou
1918-
Danish physician, psychiatrist, and psychopharmacologist

Mogens Schou is today's foremost exponent of lithium therapy in the treatment of manic-depressive disorder. Although the drug had been used to treat the manic, or "up" side of manic-depressive patients, it was Schou who insisted that the drug prevented recurrences of the depressive side as well, making it an optimum therapeutic solution for victims of the disease.

Mogens Abelin Schou, the second son of Dr. Hans Jacob Schou and Margrethe Brodersen, was born in Copenhagen on November 24, 1918. His father was medical superintendent of a large hospital for mental disorders and epilepsy in Dianalund. His mother was a pianist. After graduating from high school, Schou attended a Danish folk high school where he met his wife, Agnete Henriette Jessen. They married in 1943 and soon after began studies in their respective fields—medicine and teaching. Schou graduated from Copenhagen University Medical School in 1944 and undertook clinical training in psychiatry at Danish, Swedish, and Norwegian hospitals. He received further training at the Institute of Cytophysiology in Copenhagen and the Department of Psychiatry at Columbia University, New York, and was a research fellow at the New York State Psychiatric Institute. He also studied at the Institute of Physiology at Aarhus University in Denmark. From 1956 to 1988 he headed the Psychopharmacology Research Unit at the Aarhus Institute of Psychiatry at the Psychiatric Hospital in Risskov. From 1965 to 1988 he served as professor (from 1971 full professor) of pharmacology at Aarhus University. Schou and his wife have four children.

Joins Aarhus Department of Psychiatry

In 1953 Schou joined the Department of Psychiatry at Aarhus University Psychiatric Hospital as a research associate specializing in biological psychiatry. Soon after his arrival, Schou's superior, Professor Erik Strömgen, brought to his attention the claims of Australian doctor John Cade that the drug lithium could be used to treat manic symptoms. During the mid-nineteenth century, lithium salts had been used to treat mood disorders in Denmark, but the drug was considered dangerous and in need of further study. Strömgen urged Schou to pursue the anti-manic claims for lithium as a research topic, an investigation which would spark a renaissance of lithium therapy in Denmark.

Mogens Schou

Conducts Clinical Trial to Test Lithium Claim

To test lithium's possible anti-manic properties, Schou set up a clinical trial in collaboration with Strömgen and N. Juel-Nielsen and H. Voldby, who were psychiatrists at the hospital. Published in 1954, their report verified the findings from Australia. Lithium had beneficial effects against mania in a high number of cases, and a switch from lithium to a placebo, or dummy tablet, had clinical consequences which verified these findings. This was done through the use of what is believed to be the first double-blind trial in psychopharmacology, in which neither the psychiatrists nor the manic patients knew who was to receive lithium and who was to receive the placebo. "I sat in the laboratory and flipped a coin to decide whether lithium or placebo should be used for the next patient for the next period, but I did not see the patients or participate in the clinical assessment, so the trial remained fully blind throughout," writes Schou in *The Neurosciences: Paths of Discovery II.*

The study also gave Schou an idea of lithium concentrations in the blood, as he took pains during the trials to keep accurate measurements. Finally Schou paid especially close attention to matters of side effects and toxic reactions during the trial. Taking the findings into consideration, Schou concluded that lithium therapy was of value in some cases of mania, but that it was a treatment to be dealt with cautiously, requiring careful clinical and biochemical monitoring.

Schou and his associates increased their data on lithium therapy over the next few years and by 1955 they were able to report that of forty-eight patients treated with lithium alone, eighty-one percent showed significant clinical improvement. In 1959 he added an additional 119 patients to the total, of whom seventy-six percent had improved. Other research centers in France, Australia, England, Italy and Denmark were showing similar results. The combined improvement rate of these studies taken together was sixty-four percent, and although this was less than the result first presented by Schou, it indicated to him that lithium certainly had potential concerning anti-mania therapy. Working in a mental hospital, the Aarhus group, led by Mogens Schou, instituted a clinical approach with supporting animal work in the further study of lithium, particularly in lithium physiology.

Work in Anti-Manic Study Leads to Discovery Regarding Depression

Manic-depressive patients experience extreme mood swings, from mania to depression. Mania is characterized by easily aroused anger, increased mental speed, feelings of elation and sometimes violence, feelings of self-confidence and a lack of self-criticism. Patients often lack discrimination regarding their actions and may destroy their marriages and reputations and ruin themselves financially. The depressive side of the disease is marked by inhibition, extreme sadness, slow mental speed and a lack of self-confidence in which a patient may harbor such feelings of guilt and self-reproach that he or she considers or even commits suicide. This bipolar nature of the disease, together with an important factor of regular recurrence, is essential concerning its diagnosis.

Schou had verified that lithium therapy provided clinical improvement concerning the mania side of the disorder. At this point he took another look at the records of those treated with lithium over a two-year period and discovered that one of his patients had responded with not only a reduction in manic episodes, but with some dissipation of depressive episodes as well. He considered the possibility that although the symptoms of mania and depression were different, they often occurred together in the same patient and might have some factor in common regarding their control mechanisms. If, by acting on one of these mechanisms, lithium produced its therapeutic effect, then it was possible that the depression occurring in association with mania might also respond to lithium therapy. Schou then initiated another double-blind trial, but he later abandoned the study when, due to how it had been set up, it failed to show any clear evidence that depression responded to lithium.

Schou's interest in the treatment of manic-depression was due in large part to the fact that his younger brother suffered from the disorder on a regular basis, and from the age of twenty had experienced depressions every year. Electroconvulsive or "shock" therapy and anti-depressant drugs provided some temporary relief from current episodes, but did not stop the attacks, which came year after year, putting him out of work and devastating his family. Lithium therapy, started in the mid-sixties, freed Schou's brother from depressive episodes, in effect curing him of the disease.

Work with Lithium as Antidepressant Sparks Other Studies

Although Schou's test had failed to produce satisfactory results, two independent studies begun in 1957—one conducted by Poul Baastrup of Vordingborg, Denmark, the other by G. P. Hartigan of Canterbury, England—demonstrated that lithium had the potential to limit psychosis and block depression. When these results were brought to Schou's attention, he actively encouraged both scientists to bring these results to the attention of a wide public, as he had suspected that in some cases depressive states, as well as manic ones, might respond to lithium therapy. He began to work with Baastrup, who collected the clinical data and cooperated with Schou in interpreting it. This constituted a systematic, substantial study on lithium prophylaxis in which eighty-eight manic-depressive patients were observed for one to two years without lithium treatment and then given lithium continuously for one to five years. Baastrup and Schou found that the lithium treatment lessened the frequency and duration of both manic and depressive recurrences. The action of lithium blocked relapse in both states of the disease, and was called relapse-preventive, or prophylactic. Furthermore, they found lithium's prophylactic action effective also in patients who experienced depression only, without signs of mania.

The study, however, met with some criticism. A few psychiatrists felt that the study should have been conducted on a double-blind basis, in which Baastrup and Schou randomly administered a placebo to patients to find out if the lithium really worked, to eliminate the factors of chance or bias from the study. Yet the two scientists knew that this would mean the deliberate subjection of some patients to relapse, and, with a disease which often renders patients suicidal, the two were faced with a major ethical dilemma when contemplating a second study. This was especially difficult for Schou, whom the disease affected so personally. However, the two eventually decided to proceed with the double-blind study, but took extreme care in monitoring it. It showed conclusively that lithium, under strictly controlled circumstances, exerted a prophylactic action in patients with depression and with manic-depression.

In 1967 Baastrup and Schou drew on these findings as part of a detailed and thorough review of lithium usage which extended the use of lithium worldwide. Other clinical reports were published which confirmed Baastrup and Schou's findings. In 1987 Schou received the Albert Lasker Clinical Medical Research Award for his work on lithium treatment of manic-depressive illness, especially pertaining to the discovery of its relapse-preventive action. He has received innumerable other scientific awards and honors and has served in many honorary offices. He also has published numerous books and articles in many languages on the subject of lithium.

SELECTED WRITINGS BY SCHOU:

Books

"Phases in the Development of Lithium Treatment in Psychiatry," in *The Neurosciences: Paths of Discovery II,* edited by Fred Samson and George Adelman, Birkhauser, 1992, pp. 149-166.

Lithium Treatment of Manic-Depressive Illness: A Practical Guide, Karger, 5th ed., 1993.

Periodicals

(With Juel Nielsen, E. Strömgen and H. Voldby) "The Treatment of Manic Psychoses by the Administration of Lithium Salts," *Journal of Neurological Neurosurgical Psychiatry,* Volume 17, 1954, pp. 250–260.

"Normothymotics, 'Mood Normalizers': Are Lithium and the Imipramine Drugs Specific for Affective Disorders?," *British Journal of Psychiatry,* Volume 109, 1963, pp. 803–809.

(With Baastrup) "Lithium as Prophylactic Agent: Its Effect Against Recurrent Depressions and Manic-Depressive Psychosis," *Archives of General Psychiatry,* Volume 16, 1967, pp. 162–172.

(With P. C. Baastrup, J. C. Poulsen, K. Thomsen, and A. Amdisen) "Prophylactic Lithium: Double-Blind Discontinuation in Manic-Depressive and Recurrent Depressive Disorders," *Lancet,* Volume 2, 1970, pp. 326–330.

"Effects of Long-Term Lithium Treatment on Kidney Function: An Overview," *Journal of Psychiatric Resources,* Volume 22, 1988, pp. 287–296.

SOURCES:

Books

Johnson, F. Neil, *The History of Lithium Therapy,* Macmillan, 1984.

Periodicals

Baastrup, P.C., "The Use of Lithium in Manic-Depressive Psychosis," *Comprehensive Psychiatry,* Volume 5, 1964, pp. 396-408.

Blackwell, B., "Lithium: Prophylactic or Panacea?," *Medical Counterpoint.* November 1969, pp. 52–59.

Cade, J. F. J., "Lithium Salts in the Treatment of Psychotic Excitement," *Medical Journal of Australia,* Volume 36, 1949, pp. 349–352.

Hartigan, G. P., "The Use of Lithium Salts in Affective Disorder," *British Journal of Psychiatry,* Volume 109, 1963, pp. 810–814.

—*Sketch by Janet Kieffer Kelley*

J. Robert Schrieffer
1931-
American physicist

As a young doctoral student, J. Robert Schrieffer was working under Nobel laureate **John Bardeen** at the University of Illinois when, together with **Leon Cooper**, the three men developed a theory of the superconductivity of metals. Known as the BCS theory (the initials of their last names), it explains how certain metals and alloys lose all resistance to electrical current when chilled to extremely low temperatures. This means that once a superconducting magnet is set in motion, it will flow forever with no loss of power. This proved to be one of the major discoveries of twentieth-century physics, and the three shared the 1972 Nobel Prize in physics.

Known as an "unassuming man with a quip for any occasion," according to a *New York Times* profile written on the occasion of his winning the Nobel Prize, John Robert Schrieffer was born in Oak Park, Illinois, on May 31, 1931, to John and Louise Anderson Schrieffer. He received his B.S. in 1953 from the Massachusetts Institute of Technology and then went on to the University of Illinois, where he began his work with Bardeen and Cooper. He received his M.S. in 1954 and his Ph.D. in 1957.

The practical implications of the theoretical work Schrieffer did on superconductivity are numerous. "Superconductivity is a most accurate determinant of the measure of electrical potential, voltage," said Dr. Erik Rudberg, secretary of the Swedish Royal Academy of Sciences, when he announced the Nobel Prize. "The application of superconductivity is important not only for scientific instruments, but also for accelerators and motors." As a result of this theory, certain alloys have been developed that are superconductors at less extreme temperatures. These alloys can be used, for example, in underground cables to store and transmit electricity without the loss of power characteristic of overhead electrical wires.

Authors Work on Superconductivity Theory

Schrieffer began his teaching career as an assistant professor at the University of Chicago in 1957, returned to the University of Illinois as an associate professor from 1960 to 1962, and then moved to a position as full professor at the University of Pennsylvania. After publication in 1964 of his book, *Theory of Superconductivity,* he was named the Amanda Wood Professor of Physics at the University of Pennsylvania, a position he held until 1979. In 1980 Schrieffer took a position at the University of California in Santa Barbara, where he was named Essan Khashoggi Professor of Physics in 1985. He also was director of the Institute of Theoretical Physics there from 1984 to 1989. In 1992, he became a professor at Florida State University in Tallahassee and chief scientist at the National High Magnetic Field Laboratory.

Throughout these years he continued to focus his research on particle physics, metal impurities, spin fluctuations, and chemisorption. He has been honored with numerous awards besides the Nobel Prize, among them the Comstock Award from the National Academy of Sciences, which he received in 1968, and the National Medal of Science, which he received in 1984. He has been known to speak out on social and political issues. At the time he won the Nobel, he was critical of science's focus on the arms and space race. "The crying needs of society and of science itself can use the manpower and the money," he told the *New York Times.*

Schrieffer was married in 1960 to Anne Grete Thomsen. They have two daughters and a son.

SELECTED WRITINGS BY SCHRIEFFER:

Books

Theory of Superconductivity, W. A. Benjamin, 1964, revised edition, 1983.

Periodicals

(With L. N. Cooper and J. Bardeen) "Microscopic Theory of Superconductivity," in *Physical Review,* Volume 106, 1957, pp. 162–164.

"Recent Advances in the Theory of Superconductivity," in *Physica,* Volume 26, 1960, pp. S1-S16.

SOURCES:

Periodicals

New York Times, October 21, 1972, pp. 1, 14.

—*Sketch by Dorothy Barnhouse*

Erwin Schrödinger
1887-1961
Austrian physicist

Erwin Schrödinger shared the 1933 Nobel Prize for physics with English physicist **Paul Dirac** in recognition of his development of a wave equation describing the behavior of an electron in an atom. His theory was a consequence of French theoretical physicist **Louis Victor de Broglie**'s hypothesis that particles of matter might have properties that can be described by using wave functions. Schrödinger's wave equation provided a sound theoretical basis for the existence of electron orbitals (energy levels), which had been postulated on empirical grounds by Danish physicist **Niels Bohr** in 1913.

Schrödinger was born in Vienna, Austria, on August 12, 1887. His father, Rudolf Schrödinger, enjoyed a wide range of interests, including painting and botany, and owned a successful oil cloth factory. Schrödinger's mother was the daughter of Alexander Bauer, a professor at the Technische Hochschule. For the first eleven years of his life, Schrödinger was taught at home. Though a tutor came on a regular basis, Schrödinger's most important instructor was his father, whom he described as a "friend, teacher, and tireless partner in conversation," as Armin Hermann quoted in *Dictionary of Scientific Biography.* From his father he also developed a wide range of academic interests, including not only mathematics and science but also grammar and poetry. In 1898, he entered the Akademische Gymnasium in Vienna to complete his pre-college studies.

Hasenöhrl Inspires Early Interest in Physics

Having graduated from the Gymnasium in 1906, Schrödinger entered the University of Vienna. By all accounts, the most powerful influence on him there was Friedrich Hasenöhrl, a brilliant young physicist who was killed in World War I a decade later. Schrödinger was an avid student of Hasenöhrl's for the full five years he was enrolled at Vienna. He held his teacher in such high esteem that he was later to

Erwin Schrödinger

remark at the 1933 Nobel Prize ceremonies that, if Hasenöhrl had not been killed in the war, it would have been Hasenöhrl, not Schrödinger, being honored in Stockholm.

Schrödinger was awarded his Ph.D. in physics in 1910 and was immediately offered a position at the University's Second Physics Institute, where he carried out research on a number of problems involving, among other topics, magnetism and dielectrics. He held this post until the outbreak of World War I, at which time he became an artillery officer assigned to the Italian front. As the War drew to a close, Schrödinger looked forward to an appointment as professor of theoretical physics at the University of Czernowitz, located in modern-day Ukraine. However, those plans were foiled with the disintegration of the Austro-Hungarian Empire, and Schrödinger was forced to return to the Second Physics Institute.

During his second tenure at the Institute, on April 6, 1920, Schrödinger married Annemarie Bertel, whom he had met prior to the War. Not long after his marriage, Schrödinger accepted an appointment as assistant to Max Wien in Jena, but remained there only four months. He then moved on to the Technische Hochschule in Stuttgart. Once again, he stayed only briefly—a single semester—before resigning his post and going on to the University of Breslau. He received yet another opportunity to move after being at the University for only a short time: he was offered the chair in theoretical physics at the University of Zürich in late 1921.

Work at Zürich Results in Wave Equation

The six years that Schrödinger spend at Zürich were probably the most productive of his scientific career. At first, his work dealt with fairly traditional topics; one paper of particular practical interest reported his studies on the relationship between red-green and blue-yellow color blindness. Schrödinger's first interest in the problem of wave mechanics did not arise until 1925. A year earlier, de Broglie had announced his hypothesis of the existence of matter waves, a concept that few physicists were ready to accept. Schrödinger read about de Broglie's hypothesis in a footnote to a paper by American physicist **Albert Einstein**, one of the few scientists who did believe in de Broglie's ideas.

Schrödinger began to consider the possibility of expressing the movement of an electron in an atom in terms of a wave. He adopted the premise that an electron can travel around the nucleus only in a standing wave (that is, in a pattern described by a whole number of wavelengths). He looked for a mathematical equation that would describe the position of such "permitted" orbits. By January of 1926, he was ready to publish the first of four papers describing the results of this research. He had found a second order partial differential equation that met the conditions of his initial assumptions. The equation specified certain orbitals (energy levels) outside the nucleus where an electron wave with a whole number of wavelengths could be found. These orbitals corresponded precisely to the orbitals that Bohr had proposed on purely empirical grounds thirteen years earlier. The wave equation provided a sound theoretical basis for an atomic model that had originally been derived purely on the basis of experimental observations. In addition, the wave equation allowed the theoretical calculation of energy changes that occur when an electron moves from one permitted orbital to a higher or lower one. These energy changes conformed to those actually observed in spectroscopic measurements. The equation also explained why electrons cannot exist in regions between Bohr orbitals since only non-whole number wavelengths (and, therefore, non-permitted waves) can exist there.

After producing unsatisfactory results using relativistic corrections in his computations, Schrödinger decided to work with non-relativistic electron waves in his derivations. The results he obtained in this way agreed with experimental observations and he announced them in his early 1926 papers. The equation he published in these papers became known as "the Schrödinger wave equation" or simply "the wave equation." The wave equation was the second theoretical mechanism proposed for describing electrons in an atom, the first being German physicist **Werner Karl Heisenberg**'s matrix mechanics. For most physicists, Schrödinger's approach was preferable since it lent itself to a physical, rather than strictly mathematical, interpretation. As it turned out, Schrödinger was soon able to show that wave mechanics and matrix mechanics are mathematically identical.

Rise of Nazis Forces Schrödinger to Oxford and Dublin

In 1927, Schrödinger was presented with a difficult career choice. He was offered the prestigious chair of theoretical physics at the University of Berlin left open by German physicist **Max Planck**'s retirement. The position was arguably the most desirable in all of theoretical physics, at least in the German-speaking world; Berlin was the center of the newest and most exciting research in the field. Though Schrödinger disliked the hurried environment of a large city, preferring the peacefulness of his native Austrian Alps, he did accept the position.

Hermann quoted Schrödinger as calling the next six years a "very beautiful teaching and learning period." That period came to an ugly conclusion, however, with the rise of National Socialism in Germany. Having witnessed the dismissal of outstanding colleagues by the new regime, Schrödinger decided to leave Germany and accept an appointment at Magdalene College, Oxford, in England. In the same week he took up his new post he was notified that he had been awarded the 1933 Nobel Prize for physics with Dirac.

Schrödinger's stay at Oxford lasted only three years; then, he decided to take an opportunity to return to his native Austria and accept a position at the University of Graz. Unfortunately, he was dismissed from the University shortly after German leader Adolf Hitler's invasion of Austria in 1938, but Eamon de Valera, the Prime Minister of Eire and a mathematician, was able to have the University of Dublin establish a new Institute for Advanced Studies and secure an appointment for Schrödinger there.

In September, 1939, Schrödinger left Austria with few belongings and no money and immigrated to Ireland. He remained in Dublin for the next seventeen years, during which time he turned to philosophical questions such as the theoretical foundations of physics and the relationship between the physical and biological sciences. During this period, he wrote one of the most influential books in twentieth-century science, *What Is Life?* In this book, Schrödinger argued that the fundamental nature of living organisms could probably be studied and understood in terms of physical principles, particularly those of quantum mechanics. The book was later to be read by and become a powerful influence on the thought of the founders of modern molecular biology.

After World War II, Austria attempted to lure Schrödinger home. As long as the nation was under Soviet occupation, however, he resisted offers to return. Finally, in 1956, he accepted a special chair position at the University of Vienna and returned to the city of his birth. He became ill about a year after he settled in Vienna, however, and never fully recovered his health. He died on January 4, 1961, in the Alpine town of Alpbach, Austria, where he is buried.

Schrödinger received a number of honors and awards during his lifetime, including election into the Royal Society, the Prussian Academy of Sciences, the Austrian Academy of Sciences, and the Pontifical Academy of Sciences. He also retained his love for the arts throughout his life, becoming proficient in four modern languages in addition to Greek and Latin. He published a book of poetry and became skilled as a sculptor.

SELECTED WRITINGS BY SCHRÖDINGER:

Books

Abhandlungen zür Wellenmechanik, [Leipzig], 1927, second edition, 1928.
What Is Life?, Cambridge University Press, 1945.
Space-time Structure, Cambridge University Press, 1950.
Science and Humanism, Cambridge University Press, 1952.
Statistical Thermodynamics, Cambridge University Press, 1952.
Nature and the Greeks, Cambridge University Press, 1954.
Expanding Universes, Cambridge University Press, 1956.
Mind and Matter, Cambridge University Press, 1958.
Einstein, Lorentz, Briefe zur Wellenmechanik, [Vienna], 1963.

SOURCES:

Books

Biographical Memoirs of Fellows of the Royal Society, Volume 7, Royal Society (London), 1961, pp. 221–228.
Dictionary of Scientific Biography, Volume 12, Scribner, 1975, pp. 217–223.
Weber, Robert L., *Pioneers of Science: Nobel Prize Winners in Physics,* American Institute of Physics, 1980, pp. 99–100.

—Sketch by David E. Newton

Richard Evans Schultes
1915-
American ethnobotanist

Richard Evans Schultes is a pioneer in ethnobotany, the study of the relationship between people and their plant environment. He also contributed extensively to existing knowledge about the use of plants by humans, especially in the fields of medicine and narcotics, by combining a traditional background in botanical taxonomy with the growing field of economic botany.

Schultes was born January 12, 1915, in Boston, Massachusetts, to Otto Richard and Maude Beatrice (Bagley) Schultes. He attended Harvard University, receiving a bachelor of arts in 1937 with Phi Beta Kappa honors, a master's degree the next year, and a doctorate in 1941. On March 26, 1959, Schultes married Dorothy Crawford McNeil; together they had three children, Richard Evans II, and twins, Neil Parker and Alexandra Ames.

Upon receiving his doctorate, Schultes joined the staff of the Harvard Botanical Museum and would later become its director, a position he held from 1967 to 1985. At the museum, Schultes wrote and edited numerous leaflets on botanical subjects. While curator of the Orchid Herbarium of Oakes Ames at Harvard, he wrote *Generic Names of Orchids,* a book giving the etymological history of some 1,250 generic names of Orchidaceae, with morphological characteristics of each plant, along with its geographic distribution. Meanwhile, he served as a Harvard University professor from 1968 until his retirement in 1985. He has also worked in the taxonomy of rubber plants.

Investigation of Jungle Plants Leads to Discoveries

Schultes explored jungles of the northwest Amazon from 1941 to 1954 and acquired first-hand knowledge of the indigenous flora there. During this pivotal time in his career, he collected and taxonomically catalogued about 24,000 specimens. By enlisting the aid of the Makunas, Puinave, and Tanimuka Indians of the region, he investigated tropical rain forest areas in search of plants used by the natives as medicines, narcotics, and poisons. He gained the Indians' confidence by his serious devotion to plant collecting and by participating in dances and rituals. He even sampled their botanical preparations personally, and later wrote in *Lloydia* that on one occasion, after sampling a narcotic snuff prepared in the Amazon, he was "ill in [his] hammock for several days, so strong was the snuff."

Another time, despite serious leg ulcers resulting from exposure to flooded tropical forests, he forsook the clean accommodations of a Columbian river gunboat to accompany a native on a three-day journey upstream and through flooded swamp forest to search out an undescribed species known to the Indians as yoco, which was later shown to be rich in caffeine. In another incident, his respect for Indian customs enabled him to do what he called "fascinating detective work" in uncovering a plant source of curare, used by the natives in preparing their poison arrows.

During the 1960s, when drug use proliferated in American society, Schultes drew on his interest and experience in ethnobotany to make detailed studies of hallucinogens. He explained that his research in the Amazon showed that primitive societies used some plant species to induce visual, auditory and other hallucinations, which were considered to have religious significance. On the basis of their unearthly effects, these plants were considered sacred by the natives, who included them in their rituals. By contrast, as he read about the use, misuse and abuse of drugs in modern civilized society, he felt the time had come to consolidate existing knowledge about hallucinogens. Also, Schultes expected that scientific interest in these substances might lead to the discovery of drugs which could be useful in psychiatry and as possible tools in explaining some types of mental abnormalities. In 1969, the government of Colombia recognized Schultes's scientific contributions by bestowing upon him the Orden de la Victoria Regia.

Campaigns for Preservation of Rain Forests

In his analysis of psychoactive plant species, Schultes found they were concentrated mostly among fungi and angiosperms. He classified these species, mentioned their location, identified the biochemical nature of their compounds, and explained their physiological and psychological effects. He described two broad groups of organic substances having hallucinogenic properties, nitrogenous and non-nitrogenous. Nitrogenous species include fungi such as psychedelic mushrooms and plants which are used to produce mescaline and cocaine. As an example of one of the most important non-nitrogenous hallucinogens, he described in detail the Cannabis species (the source of marijuana) and other narcotic products. He wrote that of the total number of existing plant species, estimated as ranging from 400,000 to 800,000, only sixty are known to be sources of hallucinogens—twenty of which can be considered important—with most occurring in the New World. He stated that the destruction of tropical rain forests and the disappearance of primitive cultures were disturbing threats to our knowledge of yet-unknown hallucinogenic species. For his efforts in promoting tropical rain forest conservation by demonstrating, through ethnobotany, the value of tropical species to industry and medicine, he was awarded the Tyler Prize for Environmental Achievement from the University of Southern California in 1987.

Throughout his career, Schultes has pursued many fields of professional activity in addition to his positions at Harvard. Respected as an authority in economic botany, at various times he has served as a visiting professor and consultant in universities, symposia, and pharmaceutical companies with international itineraries. He has written a number of books expounding his knowledge of hallucinogenic drugs, economic botany, taxonomy of rubber plants, orchids, the Amazon tropical rain forest, and the Harvard Botanical Museum's collection of the famous Blaschka glass flowers. A contributor of over four hundred and fifty articles and reviews to various books and science journals, Schultes also served as editor of *Chronica Botanica* from 1947 to 1952 and *Economic Botany* from 1962 to 1979. He has also served as an editorial board member of *Lloydia, Journal of Psychedelic Drugs, Journal of Latin American Folklore, Altered States of Consciousness,* and other journals. In addition, Schultes was called upon to contribute to *Encyclopedia Britannica, Encyclopedia of Biological Sciences, Encyclopedia of Biochemistry, International Encyclopedia of Veterinary Medicine,* and the *McGraw-Hill Yearbook of Science and Technology.* He has been elected a member of scientific and academic societies throughout the world, and his travels have taken him to Brazil, Colombia, Switzerland, Hawaii, Berlin, Stockholm, Canada, India, Peru, England, Sri Lanka, Ecuador, Omen, Italy, and Malaysia.

In addition to his other recognitions, Schultes was named Distinguished Economic Botanist by the Society for Economic Botany in 1979. He has also received various honorary degrees, as well as the Lindbergh Award, 1981; the Cross of Boyaca from the Republic of Columbia, 1983; the Gold Medal of the World Wide Fund for Nature, 1984; the Gold Medal of Sigma Xi, 1985; the Botanical Society of America Merit Award, 1988; the Linnean Medal, 1992; and the Harvard University Medal, 1992.

SELECTED WRITINGS BY SCHULTES:

Books

(With P. A. Vestal) *Economic Botany of the Kiowa Indians,* Harvard University Botanical Museum, 1941, AMS Press, 1981.
Native Orchids of Trinidad and Tobago, Pergamon, 1960.
(With A. S. Pease) *Generic Names of Orchids—Their Origin and Meaning,* Academic Press, 1963.
(With Hoffmann) *The Botany and Chemistry of Hallucinogens,* Thomas, 1973, revised edition, 1980.

Hallucinogenic Plants, Western Publishing, 1976.
(With Albert Hoffmann) *Plants of the Gods: Origins of Hallucinogenic Use,* McGraw-Hill, 1979.
(With William A. Davis) *The Glass Flowers at Harvard,* Dutton, 1982.

Periodicals

"The Role of the Ethnobotanist in the Search for New Medicinal Plants," *Lloydia,* December, 1962, pp. 257–266.
"The Search for New Natural Hallucinogens," *Lloydia,* Volume 29, 1966, pp. 293–308.
"Hallucinogens of Plant Origin," *Science,* January, 1969, pp. 245–254.
"The Botanical and Chemical Distribution of Hallucinogens," *Annual Review of Plant Physiology,* 1970, pp. 571–598.

SOURCES:

Books

Contemporary Authors, New Revisions Series, Volume 25, Gale, 1989, pp. 397–399.

—*Sketch by Maurice Bleifeld*

Melvin Schwartz
1932-
American physicist

Melvin Schwartz's research and experimentation in the weak force of the four fundamental forces of nature resulted in the proof of the existence of the neutrino, a particle of zero-rest mass, and the Nobel Prize-winning discovery and definition of the two existing types of neutrinos, the electron neutrino, and the muon neutrino.

Schwartz was born in New York City on November 2, 1932, to Harry and Hannah Shulman Schwartz. Desperately poor as a result of the Great Depression, his parents "worked extraordinarily hard," Schwartz was later to say, as quoted in *Nobel Prize Winners Supplement,* to provide some level of "economic stability" in their lives. He entered the world-famous Bronx High School of Science in 1944, at the age of twelve, and graduated five years later. By that time, he had made up his mind to become a theoretical physicist. That decision having been made, his choice

Melvin Schwartz

for a college education was easy. At the time New York City's own Columbia University had, as Schwartz later characterized it, a physics department that was "unmatched by any in the world."

Schwartz Attacks the Problem of the Weak Force

Schwartz earned his bachelor's degree in mathematics and physics in 1953. That year, Schwartz was married to Marilyn Fenster, with whom he later had two daughters, Diane and Betty Lynne, and a son, David. He began his doctoral studies under the direction of **Jack Steinberger**, whom Schwartz has called "the best experimental physicist I have ever been associated with, and the best teacher," as quoted by Bertram Schwarzschild in *Physics Today*. It was from Steinberger that Schwartz gained his special interest in particle physics, an interest that was to dominate much of his research over the next four decades.

Schwartz was awarded his Ph.D. in physics in 1959 and then joined the faculty at Columbia. Within a year, an event was to take place that would dramatically alter Schwartz's future. During an afternoon coffee hour in November 1959, at Columbia's Pupin Laboratory, a group of physicists discussed the problems of studying the weak force, one of the four fundamental forces of nature (the others being gravitation, electromagnetism and the strong force). **Tsung-Dao Lee**, a theoretical physicist, challenged his colleagues to find a way to obtain additional empirical evidence on the weak force. The challenge at first seemed an enormous one since at atomic dimensions, the weak force is much weaker—and therefore much harder to observe—than are the electromagnetic and strong forces. According to Schwarzschild, Schwartz later described his feeling about Lee's challenge as one of "hopelessness. There seemed to be no decent way," he said, "of exploring the terribly small cross-sections characteristic of weak interactions." This feeling lasted less than twenty-four hours, as that evening, Schwartz suddenly had the answer. "It was incredibly simple," he decided. "All you had to do was use neutrinos."

Neutrinos turned out to be the perfect tool with which to study the weak force. Because these tiny particles are uncharged and have very small mass, they are essentially unaffected by electromagnetic or strong forces. When a beam of neutrinos passes through matter, the only interactions it undergoes are those involving the weak force.

Schwartz Confirms the Existence of Two Kinds of Neutrinos

To work out the details of the neutrino/weak force experiment, Schwartz met with his former doctoral advisor, Steinberger, and Columbia colleague Leon Max Lederman. The three devised a method for generating an intense beam of neutrinos using the Brookhaven National Laboratory's new 30 billion-electron-volt alternating gradient synchrotron (AGS). Proton beams from the AGS would be directed at a target of beryllium metal. The collision between beam and target would tear apart beryllium atoms and release an avalanche of subatomic particles, neutrinos among them. The neutrinos thus produced would then be directed through a block of steel where at least some would interact with atoms by means of the weak force.

One issue involved in the experiment was the nature of the neutrinos to be used, as relatively little was known about these particles. When the neutrino was discovered, physicists assumed that it existed in only one form, the form now known as the electron neutrino. For various theoretical reasons, however, Columbia theoretical physicist Gerald Feinberg posed the possibility in 1958 that a second neutrino, associated with mu mesons (muons), which are particles of a different weight, might also exist. The Schwartz-Steinberger-Lederman experiment was designed to determine also the validity of Feinberg's hypothesis.

By September 1961, the experiment was under way. Eight months later, an estimated 10^{14} neutrinos had been produced, of which fifty-one interactions with matter were observed. In every one of these cases, the interaction was such that it confirmed the existence of a muon neutrino distinct from the electron neutrino. Feinberg's hypothesis had been confirmed. The 1988 Nobel Prize awarded to Schwartz, Steinberger, and Lederman recognized not only the discovery of the muon neutrino, but also the development of a technique that, the Nobel committee said, promised to provide "entirely new opportunities for research into the innermost structure and dynamics of matter."

Schwartz resigned his post at Columbia in 1966 in order to take a position as professor of physics at Stanford University, where the new 2-mile long linear accelerator was available for his research. He remained at Stanford until 1979 when he decided to establish his own software development business, Digital Pathways, Inc. After dividing his time between Stanford and Digital for four years, he resigned the former post and became a full-time business man. In 1991 Schwartz returned to the academic world by accepting the post of associate director of high energy and nuclear physics at the Brookhaven National Laboratory. Schwartz is a member of the National Academy of Sciences and is a fellow of the American Physical Society, which awarded him the Hughes Prize in 1964.

SELECTED WRITINGS BY SCHWARTZ:

Books

Principles of Electrodynamics, McGraw-Hill, 1972.

Periodicals

"Observation of High-Energy Neutrino Reactions and the Existence of Two Kinds of Neutrinos," *Physical Review Letters,* Volume 9, 1961, p. 36.
"Search for Intermediate Bosons," *Physical Review Letters,* Volume 15, 1965, p. 42.

SOURCES:

Books

Nobel Prize Winners Supplement 1987–1991, H. W. Wilson, 1992, pp. 124–126.

Periodicals

Schwarzschild, Bertram, "Physics Nobel Prize to Lederman, Schwartz and Steinberger," *Physics Today,* January 1989, pp. 17–20.
Sutton, Christine, Ian Anderson, and Christopher Joyce, "When Particle Physics Was Still Fun," *New Scientist,* October 29, 1988, p. 30.

Waldrop, M. Mitchell, "A Nobel Prize for the Two-Neutrino Experiment," *Science,* November 4, 1988, pp. 669–670.

—Sketch by David E. Newton

Julian Schwinger
1918-1994
American physicist

American physicist Julian Schwinger worked primarily to develop a quantum theory of radiation. As a theorist, he produced mathematical frameworks that showed the relationships between charged particles and electromagnetic fields, and his equations eventually united relativity and quantum theory. In recognition of this work, Schwinger received the National Medal of Science in 1964 and the Nobel Prize for physics in 1965, which he shared with American theoretical physicist **Richard P. Feynman** and Japanese physicist **Sin-Itiro Tomonaga**.

Julian Seymour Schwinger was born on February 12, 1918, in the Jewish Harlem section of New York City. His father was Benjamin Schwinger, a garment manufacturer, and his mother was Belle (Rosenfeld) Schwinger. Julian was the younger of two brothers. As a child, Schwinger had an insatiable appetite for science. He became interested by reading popular scientific magazines. When he entered high school, he had already decided to study physics. He had read all that the *Encyclopedia Britannica* offered in physics, and he scoured the New York Public libraries for all the books he could find on mathematics and physics, starting at the uptown branches and methodically working his way down to the main branch. He also combed used book stores for texts in mathematics and physics.

Schwinger was known to be very shy, but he became a member of the world of adults at a very young age. He skipped three grades in high school and graduated at the age of 14. While he was still in high school, Schwinger studied scientific papers about quantum mechanics by the English physicist **Paul Dirac** as they appeared in the *Proceedings of the Royal Society of London.* Schwinger would later base his mathematical work in quantum electrodynamics on Dirac's theories.

Schwinger started his undergraduate studies at the College of the City of New York, where he began writing papers on theoretical physics. One of these papers was on quantum mechanics and was published

Julian Schwinger

in the *Physical Review.* It so impressed Isador Issac Rabi, a physicist at Columbia University, that he helped Schwinger to get a scholarship at Columbia. While at Columbia, Schwinger was interested almost solely in science to the neglect of his other classes, particularly English composition. Were it not for Rabi's intervention, Schwinger would have been expelled from Columbia. He excelled in physics, however, and often served as a substitute lecturer in quantum mechanics. Schwinger graduated from Columbia in 1936 at the age of 17. Three years later at Columbia he earned his Ph.D. degree.

Works on Atomic Bomb and Radar

After Columbia, Schwinger continued his research at the University of California under **J. Robert Oppenheimer**. In 1941 he joined Purdue University as an instructor and left there in 1943 as an assistant professor. In 1943 he went to the Metallurgical Laboratory at the University of Chicago to assist in developing the atomic bomb. In the same year he joined the radiation laboratory at the Massachusetts Institute of Technology, where he worked on microwave problems and helped to improve radar systems.

During these early years of moving from one position to another, his reputation for maintaining nocturnal working habits and sleeping until the afternoons preceded him. But it was rarely an issue. In 1945 he became an associate professor at Harvard University, and in 1947 he was made one of the

youngest full professors in the university's history. In addition to his research in theoretical physics, Schwinger also distinguished himself in his presentations in scientific journals and in lecture halls. His published papers were considered exemplars for the scientific community.

In the lecture hall Schwinger's presentations often drew applause, a rare response from a scientific audience. He gave his lectures extemporaneously, with little preparation, and without the use of notes. Jeremy Bernstein, in an article for the *American Scholar,* said of Schwinger's lecture, "It's like poetry." Schwinger was known for speaking with long measured periods delivered without pause. He took equal care in his accompanying board work; he rarely made mistakes with formulas. In addition, James Gleick in his biography of Richard Feynman, *Genius,* reports that Schwinger was ambidextrous and able to list on the board the steps for two equations simultaneously.

Since his high school days Julian Schwinger had shown a great respect for and faith in the work of Paul Dirac. Dirac's work was a mathematical account of the interaction between electric and magnetic forces inside the atom. It was a useful description of these forces, but physicists who studied radiation through observation began to find discrepancies between calculations based on the theory and their measurements in the laboratory. In particular, the theory required the electron to behave as though it were a particle with infinite mass. The unreal nature of this notion led William Laurence in a 1948 *New York Times* article to call it the "cosmic ghost".

Adjusts Dirac's "Cosmic Ghost" Theory

Because of this discrepancy, quantum physicists were anxious to discard Dirac's theory. But Schwinger believed that with some corrections this theory could still be an accurate account of observable phenomena. At a 1948 meeting of the American Physical Society Schwinger showed his colleagues how Dirac's theory could be corrected. Schwinger had found the terms in Dirac's work that produced the ghost of infinite mass and showed how to account for them in a way that both preserved Dirac's theory and kept it congruent with reality. With this work, Schwinger routed the cosmic ghost and eventually earned the Nobel Prize in 1965.

Almost all of Schwinger's writings are abstract and directed to a highly specialized audience of theoretical physicists. One of Schwinger's more recent books, however, *Einstein's Legacy: The Unity of Space and Time,* attempts to reach a general audience. In it, Schwinger explains in lay terms how **Albert Einstein**'s theories of special and general relativity are unified and what consequences they have for experiments.

Julian Schwinger and Clarice Carrol were married in 1947 and had no children. Outside of the lecture hall Schwinger was known for his reserved manner but firm convictions. He was one of the few scientists of his stature open to the possibility of achieving cold fusion. He died of cancer in Los Angeles on July 16, 1994.

SELECTED WRITINGS BY SCHWINGER:

Books

Discontinuities in Waveguides, Gordon & Breach, 1968.
Particles and Sources, Gordon & Breach, 1969.
Quantum Kinematics and Dynamics, W. A. Benjamin, 1970.
Einstein's Legacy: The Unity of Space and Time, Scientific American Library, 1986.

SOURCES:

Books

Current Biography, H. W. Wilson, 1967, pp. 379–381.
Gleick, James, *Genius: The Life and Science of Richard Feynman,* Pantheon, 1992.

Periodicals

Bernstein, Jeremy, "A Scientific Education," *American Scholar,* Volume 50, 1981, pp. 237–293.
Laurence, William L., "Schwinger States His Cosmic Theory," *New York Times,* June 25, 1948.

—*Sketch by Lawrence Souder*

Glenn T. Seaborg
1912-
American nuclear chemist

Glenn T. Seaborg is a pioneering nuclear chemist whose work with isotopes and transuranium elements contributed to the development of nuclear technology in medicine, power, and weapons. His early research on the identification of radioisotopes advanced radiological imaging techniques and radio-

Glenn T. Seaborg

therapy; he was the codiscoverer of technetium–99m, one of the most widely used radioisotopes in nuclear medicine. Seaborg's most significant accomplishments resulted from his discovery of a number of transuranic elements, including plutonium, which is used to build the atomic bomb. His contributions to the "atomic age" began during World War II with his work on the Manhattan Project to develop nuclear weapons. His impeccable reputation as a scientist and administrator earned him an appointment as chairman of the Atomic Energy Commission, where he was influential in the development and testing of nuclear energy and weapons and in the establishment of nuclear arms control agreements.

Glenn Theodore Seaborg was born in Ishpeming, Michigan, on April 19, 1912, to Swedish immigrants Herman Theodore Seaborg, a machinist, and Selma O. (Erickson). Both had come to the United States in 1904, entering through the historic landmark Ellis Island in New York City, and then traveling to Ishpeming. As a child Seaborg learned how to speak Swedish before English, and his early upbringing included the cultural traditions of his mother's homeland. His parents moved to southern California when he was ten, in part to seek better educational opportunities for him and his sister. He was educated in the multicultural Watts district of Los Angeles, where he gained the ability to deal effectively with people of different backgrounds, a skill that was useful to him in later life. Although his parents urged the young Seaborg to focus on commercial studies in high school, a dynamic chemistry teacher inspired his interest in science. After graduating as valedictorian of his class in 1929, Seaborg enrolled at the University of California, Los Angeles (UCLA), earning his tuition through a series of odd jobs, including stevedore and farm laborer. After graduating from UCLA in 1934 with a degree in chemistry, Seaborg pursued his graduate work at the University of California, Berkeley, which had renowned chemistry and physics departments. There he studied under chemist **Gilbert Newton Lewis** and physicist **Ernest Orlando Lawrence**, who had a twenty-seven inch cyclotron (a circular device that serves as an accelerator in which charged particles are propelled by an alternating electric field in a constant magnetic field). Seaborg often worked all night, conducting research with the cyclotron when it was not being used by Lawrence and his colleagues. He earned a Ph.D. in 1937 for his thesis concerning the interaction of "fast" neutrons with lead and was appointed to the faculty at Berkeley, where he worked as an assistant in Lewis's laboratory. Shortly thereafter, Seaborg met Lawrence's secretary, Helen L. Griggs, whom he married in 1942.

While still working on his Ph.D., Seaborg began to collaborate with physicist Jack Livingood on the chemical separations that occurred in the cyclotron to produce radioactive isotopes (different forms of the same element having the same atomic number but a different number of protons). Radioisotopes have vital applications in the field of radiology, both in radiotherapy and diagnosing disease with radiological imaging techniques. Seaborg, Livingood, and colleagues discovered iodine–131, iron–59, cobalt–60, and technetium–99m, one of the most widely used radioisotopes in nuclear medicine.

Embarks on Nobel Prize-winning Research

In 1934, physicist **Enrico Fermi** attempted to create new elements by irradiating uranium with neutrons. Uranium was the element with the "heaviest" nuclei on the periodic table, a chart that systematically groups together the elements with similar properties in order of increasing atomic number. In 1939 the German scientists **Otto Hahn** and **Fritz Strassmann** were able to split a uranium nucleus by bombarding it with neutrons, and this fission reaction produced a powerful release of energy. **Edwin M. McMillan** and **Philip Hauge Abelson**, working with the cyclotron at the Lawrence Radiation Laboratory at Berkeley, discovered the first transuranium element (elements with atomic number higher than 92), element 93. Although they also created nuclear fission with their experiments, McMillan and Abelson noticed that some of the nuclei bombarded by neutrons did not undergo fission but had decayed through electron emission, creating the new element. Since

uranium was named after Uranus, the seventh planet in our solar system, they named their new element neptunium, after Neptune, the eighth planet.

Seaborg soon took over the work of searching for element 94 when McMillan left Berkeley to conduct war research on the East Coast. Working with Joseph W. Kennedy and graduate student Arthur C. Wahl, Seaborg discovered the chemically unstable element 94 in 1941 by bombarding neptunium with deuterons, the nuclei of the hydrogen isotope deuterium, and named the new element plutonium–238, after the ninth planet, Pluto. During the course of these experiments, Seaborg and colleagues isolated the isotope plutonium–239, which was a fissionable isotope with potential for use in the development of nuclear weapons and nuclear power. The following year, Seaborg, John W. Gofman, and Raymond W. Stoughton identified the isotope uranium–233, which would lead to the use of thorium, an abundant element, as a source of nuclear fuel.

On April 19, 1942, Seaborg left Berkeley to work on the Manhattan Project in Chicago, a large-scale scientific effort supported by the government with the goal of creating an atomic bomb. He led a group of scientists, including B. B. Cunningham and L. B. Werner, in the difficult task of developing methods for chemically extracting plutonium–239 from uranium in amounts that could be used to produce nuclear energy. Seaborg later reflected on this work as being the most exciting efforts of his career as he and his colleagues worked feverishly to develop an atomic weapon before Germany.

Because of their nearly identical chemical makeup, separating plutonium from uranium was a difficult task. In the course of their work, Seaborg and colleagues pioneered ultramicrochemical analysis, a technique used in working with minute amounts of radioactive material, and discovered that minuscule amounts of plutonium existed in pitchblende and carnotite ores. Seaborg was a primary influence in the decision to use plutonium instead of uranium for the first atomic-bomb experiments. By 1944, Seaborg's group had achieved success in isolating large amounts of plutonium, which enabled the Manhattan Project scientists to construct two nuclear weapons.

After Seaborg met his primary responsibility of developing enough plutonium to construct atomic weapons, he returned his attention to the transuranium elements. In 1944, Seaborg postulated that the element actinium and the 14 elements heavier than it were similar in nature and should be placed in a separate group on the periodic table. Known as the actinide concept, this theory helped scientists to accurately predict the chemical properties of heavier elements in the periodic table, and was the most significant alteration to the table since it was devised by Dmitry Mendeleev in 1869. Interestingly, **Niels**

Bohr had predicted this alteration to the table many years earlier. Using his new actinide concept, Seaborg and colleagues began to predict the chemical makeup of other possible transuranics and, as a result, discovered element 95, americium, and element 96, curium. Seaborg applied for and received patents for these elements, the only person ever to do so for a chemical element.

When Seaborg returned to Berkeley in 1946, he began to assemble a premiere group of scientists (many of whom were colleagues on the Manhattan Project) to search for transuranium elements. From 1948 to 1959, under Seaborg's guidance as associate director of the university's Lawrence Radiation Laboratory, this group isolated and identified the transuranic elements berkelium (element 97), californium (element 98), einsteinium (element 99), fermium (element 100), mendelevium (element 101), and nobelium (element 102). In 1951, Seaborg shared the Nobel Prize for chemistry with McMillan for their groundbreaking work in discovering transuranic elements. In 1974, scientists working under Seaborg discovered element 106 (unnilhexium).

Becomes Involved in Politics and Policy

Patriotism required Seaborg and his colleagues on the Manhattan Project to contribute to the war effort, but once they achieved success in creating atomic weapons, they urged the government not to use this new-found means of mass destruction on the Japanese, who doggedly refused to surrender despite the fall of Germany. Seaborg and six others signed the Franck Report, which recommended that the government merely demonstrate the bomb's terrible power by inviting the Japanese to watch a detonation. Yet the bomb was used twice, and the enormous loss of human life that resulted from it inspired Seaborg and other scientists to crusade actively for the control of nuclear weapons. They realized that the creators of such weapons were morally obligated to contribute to the outcome of a debate that might determine the survival of life on earth.

Seaborg's accomplishments as an administrator at the University of California, Berkeley, were nearly as impressive as his scientific discoveries. In 1958 he became the second vice-chancellor at the university and helped guide the institution during a period of dynamic growth. There was an ambitious building program at Berkeley, and the College of Environmental Design and the Space Sciences Laboratory were established at this time. He was also the faculty representative from Berkeley to the panel that oversaw the development of the Pac Ten athletic conference, which aimed at resolving abuses and corruption in California's collegiate athletic system. During this period, Seaborg also contributed to national educational reform by chairing the steering committee that created a new chemistry curriculum to help improve science education in schools. This curriculum was, in part, a response to the Russia's first manned space flight, *Sputnik*, in 1957, which seemed to demonstrate the Soviet Union's superior scientific talent. Seaborg also served on the National Commission on Excellence in Education, which published *A Nation at Risk* (1983), a book that delineated the failings of the U.S. educational system.

Seaborg's knack for handling difficult issues was tested during his tenure as chairman of the Atomic Energy Commission (AEC) in the turbulent decade that stretched from 1961 to 1971. He entered the debate raging over society's concerns about nuclear power and its potential to harm the environment and produce mass destruction. Seaborg received this appointment during a conversation with President Kennedy in what he described in his book *Kennedy, Khrushchev and the Test Ban* as "the telephone call that changed my life." He continued, "Within a few days I accepted, and soon I was plunged into a new kind of chemistry, that of national and international events."

In 1961, Seaborg was a member the American delegation that signed the Limited Nuclear Test Ban Treaty, outlawing nuclear testing in the atmosphere, water, and space. He also contributed to the ratification of the Non-Proliferation Treaty of 1970 by developing safeguards for handling nuclear materials, and by ensuring that those products meant for industrial and medical technology would not be illegally diverted to weapons' manufacture. In spite of these victories, Seaborg was disappointed by the failure to develop a "*comprehensive* treaty to prohibit *any* nuclear weapons testing. . . . [D]espite some near misses," he wrote, "this glittering prize, which carried with it the opportunity to arrest the viciously spiraling arms race, eluded our grasp."

In 1971 he returned to the University of California at Berkeley as University Professor of Chemistry. He continued to foster international cooperation in science and arms control. He was one of the founders and in 1981 president of the International Organization for Chemical Sciences in Development (IOCD), an organization that seeks solutions to Third World problems through scientific collaboration. In the 1980s he also published two influential books, the first of which was *Kennedy, Khrushchev and the Test Ban* (1981). Based on his scrupulous memoirs, this book was an attempt "to contribute some facts and insights not previously published" about nuclear testing." Seaborg hoped that it might aid future negotiations by providing "a wider understanding of what is involved in the achievement of an important arms control agreement." He also wrote *Stemming the Tide: Arms Control in the Johnson Years,* which was published in 1987.

During the course of his career, Seaborg acquired many honors and appointments, including election to the American Association for the Advancement of Science and ten foreign national academies of science. Many of the younger scientists, however, disapproved of Seaborg, and suspicious of nuclear power, they opposed his appointment to the National Academy of Sciences. Outside of the political and scientific arenas, Seaborg is devoted to his family of four sons and two daughters. An outdoor enthusiast, he spends his rare free time playing golf, gardening, and hiking. He is also a passionate conservationist, who helped to establish the "Golden State Trail" in California and served as vice-president of the American Hiking Society.

SELECTED WRITINGS BY SEABORG:

Books

The Transuranium Elements, Yale University Press, 1958.
Education and the Atom, McGraw-Hill, 1964.
Man and Atom, W. R. Corliss, 1971.
(With Benjamin Loeb) *Kennedy, Khrushchev and the Test Ban,* University of California Press, 1981.
Stemming the Tide: Arms Control in the Johnson Years, Lexington Books, 1987.

SOURCES:

Books

Frank N. Magill, The Great Scientists, Grolier Educational Corporation, 1989.
McGraw-Hill Modern Men of Science, McGraw-Hill, 1966, p. 423.
The New Illustrated Science and Invention Encyclopedia, Stuttman, 1987, pp. 864–865.
Nobel Prize Winners, H. W. Wilson, 1987, pp. 945–948.

—*Sketch by David Petechuk*

Emilio Segrè
1905-1989
Italian-born American physicist

Emilio Segrè is credited as the co-discoverer of three chemical elements, technetium in 1937, astatine in 1940, and plutonium in 1941. In addition, he was codiscoverer, with his former student **Owen**

Chamberlain, of the antiproton in 1955, an achievement for which he shared the 1959 Nobel Prize in physics. Segrè's early academic career is closely intertwined with that of nuclear physicist **Enrico Fermi**, under whom he received his doctorate at the University of Rome in 1928. Segrè then continued his affiliation with that university for most of the next eight years. In 1936, he was appointed professor of physics at the University of Palermo, but was discharged two years later by the Fascist government of Benito Mussolini. Already in the United States at the time of his dismissal, Segrè accepted an appointment at the University of California at Berkeley, where he remained until his retirement in 1972. He returned to the University of Rome, where a special chair in physics had been created for him by the Italian government.

Emilio Gino Segrè was born on February 1, 1905 in Tivoli, Italy, one of three sons born to Giuseppe Segrè, a manufacturer, and the former Amelia Treves. Segrè attended the local elementary school in Tivoli and graduated in 1922 from the Liceo Mamiani in Rome. He subsequently entered the University of Rome, where he majored in engineering. Segrè eventually switched to physics, however, and completed his Ph.D. in that field in 1928. Biographers have conjectured that Segrè's decision to change majors was strongly influenced by his mentor, Enrico Fermi, on the Rome faculty. In any case, Segrè was Fermi's first doctoral student at Rome.

Discovers Technetium

After receiving his degree, Segrè spent a year in the Italian army and then returned to the University of Rome as an instructor in physics. From 1930 to 1932, he studied at Hamburg under Otto Stern and at Amsterdam under Pieter Zeeman. He returned to Rome as associate professor of physics, where he again collaborated with Fermi. At Fermi's suggestion, Segrè's early research into atomic spectroscopy, molecular beams, and X rays soon gave way to neutron physics, Fermi's own field of specialization. As part of Fermi's research team, Segrè was involved in the discovery which showed that slow neutrons are more effective in bringing about nuclear fission than are fast neutrons.

In 1936, Segrè was invited to become chairman of the department of physics at the University of Palermo. Shortly after accepting that position, he traveled to the United States to visit **Ernest Orlando Lawrence** and observe Lawrence's cyclotron at the University of California. During his visit, Segrè talked with Lawrence about a possible search for element number forty-three, one of the two elements known to exist that had not yet been discovered. The discovery of the element had been announced in the 1920s by German chemists Walter Noddack, Ida Tacke, and

Otto Berg, but had not been confirmed. Only its missing space in the periodic table was evidence that it existed.

Based on his earlier work with Fermi, Segrè reasoned that the bombardment of molybdenum (element forty-two) with neutrons should result in the production of an element with an atomic number one greater than that of molybdenum—the missing forty-three. When he left Berkeley to return to Italy, therefore, Segrè obtained from Lawrence a sample of molybdenum that had been bombarded with deuterons (in this case, the equivalent of neutrons). In the following year, in collaboration with a colleague, C. Perrier, Segrè was able to confirm chemically the presence of the anticipated element forty-three in the molybdenum sample. This was the first artificially produced new element in scientific history. Segrè and Perrier suggested the name *technetium* for the element from the Greek word *teknetos,* for "artificial."

Assists in the Discovery of Astatine and Plutonium 239

Segrè returned to the United States again in 1938 to work with Lawrence at Berkeley. While there, he designed an experiment by which he was convinced the last remaining missing element, number eighty-five, could be prepared. Working with Dale R. Corson and K. R. MacKenzie, Segrè bombarded a small sample of polonium (element eighty-four) with deuterons and obtained evidence for the existence of element eighty-five. The team suggested the name *astatine,* from the Greek *astatos,* for "unstable," since the element is a radioactive element without stable isotopes.

Segrè's planned return to Italy in the summer of 1938 was interrupted by an unexpected development. The Fascist government of Italy had instituted a purge of Jews similar to that which was carried out by the Nazis in Germany. Segrè, a Jew, was consequently expelled from his post at Palermo. Segrè's response to this snub, according to Isaac Asimov in *Asimov's Biographical Encyclopedia of Science and Technology,* was that he "shrugged and remained in the United States, becoming a citizen in 1944." Offered a research post at Berkeley, Segrè continued his work on neutron physics and artificial radioactivity. Two years later, he was involved in the discovery of yet another new element—plutonium—element number ninety-four. This line of research, along with Segrè's previous work on neutron physics, made him an invaluable asset during work on the development of the atomic bomb and, in 1943, he was appointed a group leader at the Los Alamos Scientific Laboratory of the Manhattan Project.

Discovers the Antiproton with Chamberlain

After the war, Segrè returned to Berkeley as professor of physics and began his collaboration with Owen Chamberlain on the search for the antiproton. In 1928, the English physicist **Paul Dirac** had predicted the existence of a particle identical to the electron in all respects except for its having a positive rather than a negative electrical charge. The discovery of the positron in 1932 by **Carl David Anderson** confirmed Dirac's prediction.

An extension of Dirac's original hypothesis suggested that all subatomic particles, not just the electron, should have their "anti-" counterparts. The search for the next antiparticle, a negatively-charged proton, was hampered by the fact that the particle was known to exist only at very high energies, such as the energy of cosmic radiation.

The construction of the 6.2 billion-electron-volt bevatron in the early 1950s provided another possible source of antiprotons. The accelerator had the potential to produce levels of energy at which the antiproton might be generated. Working with the bevatron, Segrè and Chamberlain finally discovered the hypothesized particle in 1955. For that discovery and the further confirmation it provided for Dirac's antimatter theory, Segrè and Chamberlain were awarded the 1959 Nobel Prize in physics.

Segrè was married to Elfriede Spiro on February 2, 1936. After she died in 1970, he married Rosa Mines. Segrè had three children, Claudio, Amelia, and Fausta, by his first wife. In addition to his Nobel Prize, Segrè was awarded the Hofmann Medal of the German Chemical Society in 1954, the Cannizzaro Medal of the Accademia Nazionale de Lincei in 1956, and honorary doctorates from the University of Palermo, Gustavus Adolphus College, and Tel Aviv University. Segrè died in Lafayette, California, on April 22, 1989, of a heart attack.

SELECTED WRITINGS BY SEGRÈ:

Books

Experimental Nuclear Physics, Wylie, 1953.
Nuclei and Particles, Benjamin Company, 1953.
Enrico Fermi, Physicist, University of Chicago Press, 1970.
From X-Rays to Quarks: Modern Physicists and Their Discoveries, W. H. Freeman, 1980.
From Falling Bodies to Radio Waves: Classical Physicists and Their Discoveries, W. H. Freeman, 1984.

Periodicals

(Contributor) "Observations of Antiprotons," *Physical Review,* Volume 100, 1955, pp. 947–950.
(Contributor) "Antiprotons," *Nature,* Volume 177, 1956, pp. 11–12.

SOURCES:

Books

Weber, Robert L., *Pioneers of Science: Nobel Prize Winners in Physics,* American Institute of Physics, 1980, pp. 177–178.

—*Sketch by David E. Newton*

Florence B. Seibert
1897-1991
American biochemist

Florence B. Seibert

A biochemist who received her Ph.D. from Yale University in 1923, Florence B. Seibert is best known for her research in the biochemistry of tuberculosis. She developed the protein substance used for the tuberculosis skin test. The substance was adopted as the standard in 1941 by the United States and a year later by the World Health Organization. In addition, in the early 1920s, Seibert discovered that the sudden fevers that sometimes occurred during intravenous injections were caused by bacteria in the distilled water that was used to make the protein solutions. She invented a distillation apparatus that prevented contamination. This research had great practical significance later when intravenous blood transfusions became widely used in surgery. Seibert authored or coauthored more than a hundred scientific papers. Her later research involved the study of bacteria associated with certain cancers. Her many honors include five honorary degrees, induction into the National Women's Hall of Fame in Seneca Falls, New York (1990), the Garvan Gold Medal of the American Chemical Society (1942), and the John Elliot Memorial Award of the American Association of Blood Banks (1962).

Florence Barbara Seibert was born on October 6, 1897, in Easton, Pennsylvania, the second of three children. She was the daughter of George Peter Seibert, a rug manufacturer and merchant, and Barbara (Memmert) Seibert. At the age of three she contracted polio. Despite her resultant handicaps, she completed high school, with the help of her highly supportive parents, and entered Goucher College in Baltimore, where she studied chemistry and zoology. She graduated in 1918, then worked under the direction of one of her chemistry teachers, Jessie E. Minor, at the Chemistry Laboratory of the Hammersley Paper Mill in Garfield, New Jersey. She and her professor, having responded to the call for women to fill positions vacated by men fighting in World War I, coauthored scientific papers on the chemistry of cellulose and wood pulps.

Although Seibert initially wanted to pursue a career in medicine, she was advised against it as it was "too rigorous" in view of her physical disabilities. She decided on biochemistry instead and began graduate studies at Yale University under Lafayette B. Mendel, one of the discoverers of Vitamin A. Her Ph.D. research involved an inquiry into the causes of "protein fevers"—fevers that developed in patients after they had been injected with protein solutions that contained distilled water. Seibert's assignment was to discover which proteins caused the fevers and why. What she discovered, however, was that the distilled water itself was contaminated—with bacteria. Consequently, Seibert invented a distilling apparatus that prevented the bacterial contamination.

Seibert earned her Ph.D. in 1923, then moved to Chicago to work as a post-graduate fellow under H. Gideon Wells at the University of Chicago. She continued her research on pyrogenic (fever causing) distilled water, and her work in this area acquired practical significance when intravenous blood transfusions became a standard part of many surgical procedures.

After her fellowship ended, she was employed part-time at the Otho S. A. Sprague Memorial Institute in Chicago, where Wells was the director. At the same time, she worked with Esmond R. Long, whom she had met through Wells's seminars at the University of Chicago. Supported by a grant from the National Tuberculosis Association, Long and Seibert would eventually spend thirty-one years collaborating on tuberculosis research. Another of Seibert's long-time associates was her younger sister, Mabel Seibert, who moved to Chicago to be with her in 1927. For the rest of their lives, with the exception of a year in Sweden, the sisters resided together, with Mabel providing assistance both in the research institutes (where she found employment as secretary and later research assistant) and at home. In 1932, when Long moved to the Henry Phipps Institute—a tuberculosis clinic and research facility associated with the University of Pennsylvania in Philadelphia—Seibert (and her sister) transferred as well. There, Seibert rose from assistant professor (1932–1937), to associate professor (1937–1955) to full professor of biochemistry (1955–1959). In 1959 she retired with emeritus status. Between 1937 and 1938 she was a Guggenheim fellow in the laboratory of **Theodor Svedberg** at the University of Upsala in Sweden. In 1926 Svedberg had received the Nobel prize for his protein research.

Works on Unknown Aspects of Tuberculosis

Seibert's tuberculosis research involved questions that had emerged from the late-nineteenth-century work of German bacteriologist **Robert Koch**. In 1882 Koch had discovered that the tubercle bacillus was the primary cause of tuberculosis. He also discovered that if the liquid on which the bacilli grew was injected under the skin, a small bite-like reaction would occur in people who had been infected with the disease. (Calling the liquid "old tuberculin," Kock produced it by cooking a culture and draining off the dead bacilli.) Although he had believed the active substance in the liquid was protein, it had not been proven.

Using precipitation and other methods of separation and testing, Seibert discovered that the active ingredient of the liquid was indeed protein. The next task was to isolate it, so that it could be used in pure form as a diagnostic tool for tuberculosis. Because proteins are highly complex organic molecules that are difficult to purify, this was a daunting task. Seibert finally succeeded by means of crystallization. The tiny amounts of crystal that she obtained, however, made them impractical for use in widespread skin tests. Thus, she changed the direction of her research and began working on larger amounts of active, but less pure protein. Her methods included precipitation through ultrafiltration (a method of filtering molecules). The result, after further purification procedures, was a dry powder called TPT (Tuberculin Protein Trichloracetic acid precipitated). This was the first substance that was able to be produced in sufficient quantities for widespread use as a tuberculosis skin test. For her work, Seibert

received the 1938 Trudeau Medal from the National Tuberculosis Association.

At the Henry Phipps Institute in Philadelphia, Seibert continued her study of tuberculin protein molecules and their use in the diagnosis of tuberculosis. Seibert began working on the "old tuberculin" that had been created by Koch and used by doctors for skin testing. As Seibert described it in her autobiography *Pebbles on the Hill of a Scientist,* old tuberculin "was really like a soup made by cooking up the live tubercle bacilli and extracting the protein substance from their bodies while they were being killed." Further purification of the substance led to the creation of PPD (Purified Protein Derivative). Soon large quantities of this substance were being made for tuberculosis testing. Seibert continued to study ways of further purifying and understanding the nature of the protein. Her study in Sweden with Svedberg aided this research. There she learned new techniques for the separation and identification of proteins in solution.

Upon her return from Sweden, Seibert brought the new techniques with her. She began work on the creation of a large batch of PPD to serve as the basis for a standard dosage. The creation of such a standard was critical for measuring the degree of sensitivity of individuals to the skin test. Degree of sensitivity constituted significant diagnostic information if it was based upon individual reaction, rather than upon differences in the testing substance itself. A large amount of substance was necessary to develop a standard that ideally would be used world-wide, so that the tuberculosis test would be comparable wherever it was given. Developing new methods of purification as she proceeded, Seibert and her colleagues created 107 grams of material, known as PPD-S (the S signifying "standard"). A portion was used in 1941 as the government standard for purified tuberculins. Eventually it was used as the standard all over the world.

In 1958 the Phipps Institute was moved to a new building at the University of Pennsylvania. In her memoirs, Seibert wrote that she did not believe that the conditions necessary for her continued work would be available. Consequently, she and Mabel, her long-time assistant and companion, retired to St. Petersburg, Florida. Florence Seibert continued her research, however, using for a time a small laboratory in the nearby Mound Park Hospital and another in her own home. In her retirement years she devoted herself to the study of bacteria that were associated with certain types of cancers. Her declining health in her last two years was attributed to complications from childhood polio. She died in St. Petersburg on August 23, 1991.

In 1968 Seibert published her memoirs, which reveal her many friendships, especially among others engaged in scientific research. She particularly enjoyed international travel as well as driving her car, which was especially equipped to compensate for her handicaps. She loved music and played the violin (privately, she was careful to note).

SELECTED WRITINGS BY SEIBERT:

Books

Pebbles on the Hill of a Scientist, self-published (printed by St. Petersburg Printing Co.), 1968.

SOURCES:

Periodicals

New York Times, August 31, 1991.

—*Sketch by Pamela O. Long*

Frederick Seitz
1911-
American physicist

Frederick Seitz, a physicist and science administrator, has made fundamental contributions to the theory of solids, nuclear physics, fluorescence, and crystals. He has also been a leader in the post-World War II scientific establishment in the United States. The honors presented to Seitz for his scientific contributions include the National Medal of Science in 1973, the NASA Distinguished Service Award in 1979, and the Department of Energy Award for Public Service in 1993. The University of Illinois dedicated the Frederick Seitz Materials Research Laboratory in 1993.

Seitz was born on July 4, 1911, in San Francisco, California, to Frederick and Elizabeth Hofman Seitz. His mother was a native of San Francisco while his father had emigrated as a child from Heidelberg, Germany. Seitz credits his father—a baker who had a deep interest in science—for the implicit assurance from childhood that he would go to college and become a scientist. In his youth Seitz was an avid reader of popular science and engineering magazines as well as science fiction. He attended Lick-Wilmerding high school in San Francisco because it had a level of science preparation acceptable to most colleges. Graduating at the end of 1928, Seitz entered Stanford

University in January, 1929, starting out as a biochemistry major on the advice of his father. Soon, however, he focused on mathematics and physics.

At Stanford (and at the California Institute of Technology, which he attended for the fall, 1930, semester), Seitz was able to meet and hear presentations by the world's leading mathematicians and physicists. He graduated from Stanford in three years with a degree in mathematics, then started doctoral studies in physics at Princeton University in 1932.

Develops Wigner-Seitz Method for Solid-State Wave Functions

Seitz's mentors at Princeton were professors Edward Uhler Condon and **Eugene Pauk Wigner**. Condon was among the new generation of American physicists whose contributions to the field first achieved parity with the accomplishments of physicists in Europe; he already had a reputation for leadership in wave theory by the time Seitz arrived at Princeton. Wigner, a student of physicist **Max Born**, was a German theoretician with a particular interest in the properties of metals. A few months after Seitz arrived at Princeton, Condon suggested to Seitz that he become Wigner's first doctoral student. Working in Wigner's laboratory late in 1932, Seitz developed the cellular method of deriving solid-state wave functions that became known as the Wigner-Seitz method. They illustrated its application in two studies of the energy bands of metallic sodium published in *Physical Review,* 1933–34. The widespread application of the Wigner-Seitz method to the understanding of metals usually is regarded as the catalyst for the formation of the field of solid-state physics in the United States.

Completing his doctorate in 1934, Seitz remained at Princeton for a year as a Proctor fellow. In 1935 he was appointed as an instructor at the University of Rochester, where he stayed for two years before working as a research physicist for the General Electric laboratories at Schenectady, New York, from 1937 to 1939.

Publishes Important Text on Physics

Seitz's partner in these moves was Elizabeth (Betty) K. Marshall, a graduate student in physics at Cornell University; he had met her in the fall of 1934 while she was teaching at Bryn Mawr College. They married in May, 1935, and in that same year teamed up to begin work on the publication *The Modern Theory of Solids.* Based on lectures Frederick presented at Rochester, Betty created a consistent and well-documented text that was finally published in 1940. Seitz later said that although the book was attributed to him alone, it should have appeared under joint authorship.

At General Electric, Seitz worked on fluorescent crystals and dyes both for illumination purposes and for coatings on cathode-ray tubes. At the same time he was publishing papers on the related topics of the constitution and magnetic properties of lithium and sodium. In 1939 Seitz moved to the University of Pennsylvania, first as assistant professor, then as an associate professor in the Morgan Laboratory of Physics. While there, he was a consultant at the U.S. Army's Frankford Arsenal in Philadelphia, Pennsylvania, where he studied metallurgical problems associated with armor-piercing bullets and cartridge casings. This was the first in a series of defense-related activities that stretched over the next thirty years.

Contributes to Military Application

The Carnegie Institute of Technology convinced Seitz to join its staff as professor of physics in 1942. His service there, however, was interrupted frequently by the demands of wartime. Wigner (working on reactor designs at the University of Chicago as part of the atomic bomb program), asked **Arthur Compton**, the head of the laboratory, to invite Seitz to assist with problems related to both the uranium fuel and the graphite moderator. Seitz worked at the facility from 1943 to 1945, regularly traveling back to Pittsburgh where his wife held a teaching appointment.

At the end of the war in Europe, Seitz served several months in the army's field intelligence agency as an interviewer of German scientists thought to have knowledge of nuclear physics. In 1946 Wigner persuaded Seitz to go to the atomic energy laboratory at Oak Ridge, Tennessee, to assist in establishing the Monsanto Company's "reactor school," a year-long series of lectures on atomic energy for civilian purposes.

At Chicago and Oak Ridge, Seitz came to know the key scientists in the postwar nuclear physics community, including **Robert Oppenheimer**, **Leo Szilard**, and **Edward Teller**. Seitz took a middle road in the debate regarding the public responsibilities of those physicists whose knowledge had created the atomic bomb that ended World War II and began the pursuit of more powerful and deadlier weapons. Seitz participated in the early Pugwash conferences intended to create international dialogue at the height of the Cold War, but he also spoke out supporting development of the hydrogen bomb as a countervailing force against what he saw as an expansionary Soviet Union. Later, during the Kennedy administration, he supported the resumption of nuclear tests in the atmosphere after the Soviet Union broke the voluntary moratorium on testing.

Seitz moved to the University of Illinois in 1949 to take an appointment as a professor of physics. While at Illinois he also served as the director and technical director of the Control Systems Laboratory from 1951 to 1957, head of the physics department from 1957 to 1964, and dean of the graduate college and vice president for research from 1964 to 1965. During the 1940s and 1950s Seitz's research focused on the theory and properties of crystals. His published work included studies of dislocations and imperfections in crystal structures, the effect of irradiation on crystals, and the process of diffusion (the movement of atoms or particles caused by random collision) in crystalline materials.

Moves into Administrative Role

Seitz's major scientific contributions ended in the late 1950s as administrative tasks fully claimed his time. Among his responsibilities were the chairmanship of the governing board of the American Institute of Physics, a year in Paris serving as science advisor to the secretary-general of the North Atlantic Treaty Organization, chairmanship of the Naval Research Advisory Committee, presidency of the American Physical Society, and membership on the President's Science Advisory Committee.

In 1962 Seitz was elected president of the National Academy of Sciences in Washington, D.C., a part-time role that nonetheless involved a considerable commitment. Seitz helped to restructure the presidency into a full-time role with a six-year term, and beginning in 1965 he was selected to be the first incumbent. During his years in Washington, he was an advocate for government support of basic science and was an ex officio member of several government councils. In 1964 Seitz was elected a trustee of Rockefeller University in New York City, and in 1968 he succeeded **Detlev Bronk** (who had been the president of the National Academy of Sciences prior to Seitz) as president of the university. Bronk had transformed Rockefeller—originally a biomedical research institution dependent wholly on the endowment created by philanthropist John D. Rockefeller—into a learning center which brought in federal research money; he persuaded the university's trustees to establish a Ph.D. program, and also expanded the faculty and constructed several new buildings.

From the beginning of Seitz's presidency it was clear that Bronk's expansionary program could not be sustained. The federal government was ending two decades of increased spending on the basic sciences, and many at Rockefeller believed that some of Bronk's innovations needed to be rolled back. These pressures set the tone for much of the Seitz administration, which was characterized by limits on faculty growth. The university's options also were shaped by the poor investment climate of the 1970s, which had a particularly negative effect on institutions such as Rockefeller which depended heavily on endowment income. Faced with a series of deficit budgets, Seitz nonetheless was able to see through a modest building program, which included a new animal research facility and a new faculty residence. He negotiated for the acquisition of air rights over the adjacent FDR Drive, which gave the university future opportunities for expansion, and he welcomed the opportunity to have the Rockefeller Archive Center, an institution housing the records of numerous Rockefeller family philanthropies, become a division of the university.

Retiring from the presidency of Rockefeller University in 1978, Seitz was subsequently appointed to a variety of consulting roles and directorships, including the chair of the Scientific and Technology Advisory Group to the premier of Taiwan, the chair of the Strategic Defense Initiative ("Star Wars") Organization Advisory Committee, and the boards of several corporations.

SELECTED WRITINGS BY SEITZ:

Books

The Modern Theory of Solids, McGraw, 1940.
The Physics of Metals, McGraw, 1943.
(With Rodney W. Nichols) *Research and Development and the Prospects for International Security,* Crane, 1973.
The Science Matrix: Past, Present, and Future, Springer-Verlag, 1991.

Periodicals

"Solid," *Physics Today,* Volume 2, 1949, pp. 18–22.
"The Government Science Administrator," *Physics Today,* Volume 14, 1961, pp. 36–38.
"Science and the Government," *Physics Today,* Volume 16, 1963, pp. 28–30, 32.
"Space Science and the Universities," *Science,* 1963, pp. 614–618.

SOURCES:

Books

Current Biography, H. W. Wilson, 1956, pp. 563–564.

Periodicals

New York Times, April 25, 1962.

Other

Frederick Seitz, oral history transcript, 1981–82, American Institute of Physics, College Park, Maryland.

Frederick Seitz's personal papers are at the Rockefeller Archive Center, North Tarrytown, New York, and the University of Illinois archives at Urbana.

—*Sketch by Darwin H. Stapleton*

Nikolai N. Semenov
1896-1986
Russian physical chemist and physicist

Nikolai N. Semenov was a physical chemist and physicist who was the first Soviet citizen living in Russia to win the Nobel Prize. His scientific work focused on chain reactions and their characteristic "explosiveness" during chemical transformations. This influenced the development of greater efficiency in automobile engines and other industrial applications where controlled combustion was involved, such as jet and rocket engines. Enjoying important academic success, he also played a significant role as a spokesperson for the Soviet scientific community. He was instrumental in establishing institutions where physical chemistry could be studied, and he collaborated in creating a journal dedicated to the field. In addition, he actively participated in scientific conferences dealing with physical chemistry.

Nikolai Nikolaevich Semenov was born on April 16, 1896, in Saratov, Russia, to Nikolai Alex and Elena (Dmitrieva) Semenov. He graduated from Petrograd University (later renamed Leningrad; now called St. Petersburg, its original name) in 1917, the year of revolution that led to the establishment of Communism in Russia. Semenov had shown an interest in science from the time he entered Petrograd University at age sixteen in 1913 to study physics and mathematics. He published his first paper at the age of twenty on the subject of the collision of molecules and electrons. After graduation from Petrograd, Semenov accepted a post in physics at the Siberian University of Tomsk, but in 1920, he returned to Petrograd where he was associated with the Leningrad Institute of Physics and Technology for eleven years. In 1928, Semenov organized the mathematics and physics departments at the Leningrad Polytechnical Institute. He became the head of the Institute of Physical Chemistry of the Soviet Academy of Sciences in 1931, where he remained for more than thirty years. In 1944, Semenov became the head of the department of chemical kinematics at the University of Moscow.

Kinetics Critical to Semenov's Research

The branch of physical chemistry concerned with the rates and conditions of chemical processes, called chemical kinetics, dominated Semenov's research from his earliest studies. His work led to the understanding of the sequence of chemical reactions and provided insight into the conversion of substances into products. Along with some of his colleagues, Semenov felt that physics held the key to understanding chemical transformations. The branch of science referred to as chemical balances was a consequence of their work.

Semenov was awarded the Nobel Prize in chemistry in 1956 with English chemist **Cyril Hinshelwood** for their researches into the mechanism of chemical reactions. Both scientists had worked independently for twenty-five years on chemical chain reactions and their importance in explosions. There is wide agreement in the scientific community that Semenov and Hinshelwood were responsible for the development of plastics and the improvement of the automobile engine. There remains some controversy over whether their work on chain reactions contributed to atomic research.

Other experiments by Semenov had culminated in his theory of thermal explosions of mixtures of gases. As a result of this research, he increased the understanding of free radicals—highly unstable atoms that contain a single, unpaired electron. Semenov demonstrated that when molecules disintegrate, energy-rich free radicals are formed. His extensive works on this subject were published first in Russian in the 1930s and later in English.

Chain Reaction Theory Holds Important Applications

In subsequent research, Semenov found that the walls of an exploding chamber can influence a chain reaction as well as the substances within the chamber. This concept was particularly beneficial in the development of the combustion engine in automobiles. Semenov's chemical chain reaction theory and his observations on the inflammable nature of gases informed the study of how flames spread, and had practical applications in the oil and chemical industries, in the process of combustion in jet and diesel engines, and in controlling explosions in mines. This work was based on Semenov's earlier investigations of condensation of steam on hard surfaces and its reaction under electric shock.

Semenov made substantial contributions to the development of Soviet scientific institutions and journals. He was active in the training of Soviet scientists and the organizing of important institutions for scientific research in physical chemistry. His long association with the Academy of Sciences of the U.S.S.R. earned him an appointment as a full member in 1932. When the Academy moved to Moscow in 1944, Semenov began teaching at Moscow University. Semenov's theories of combustion, explosion, and problems of chemical kinetics, along with a bibliography of his work by the Academy, were published during the 1940s and 1950s and helped secure his role in his field.

Semenov was not immune to the politics of his country. He became a member of the Communist Party in 1947, and he was the person who answered criticism of the Soviet Union from the *Bulletin of the Atomic Scientists,* a publication of the United States. The *Bulletin* challenged Soviet scientists to protest against Soviet restrictions on release of scientific publications from the country. Semenov replied that there were no such restrictions and accused the American scientists of ignoring their own government restrictions. It was discovered later that some Soviet publications had been arriving regularly at the Library of Congress in Washington, D.C.

In his own country, Semenov was highly regarded. He had received the Stalin Prize, the Order of the Red Banner of Labor, and the Order of Lenin, the latter seven times. He served his country in the political capacity of deputy in the Supreme Soviet in the years 1958, 1962, and 1966, and he was made an alternate to the Central Committee of the Communist Party in 1961. While he was a loyal Soviet citizen, he did work diligently for freedom in scientific experimentation.

On September 15, 1924, he married Natalia Nikolaevna Burtseva, who taught voice, and they had a son, Yurii Nikolaevich, and a daughter, Ludmilla Nikolaevna. Semenov enjoyed hunting, gardening, and architecture in his leisure time. He died in 1986.

SELECTED WRITINGS BY SEMENOV:

Books

Chain Reactions, Clarendon Press, 1935.
Chemical Kinetics and Chain Reactions, Clarendon Press, 1935.
Problems of Chemical Kinetics and Reactivity, Princeton University Press, 1958–1959.

Periodicals

Bulletin of the Atomic Scientists, February, 1953.

SOURCES:

Books

Prado and Seymour, *McGraw-Hill Encyclopedia of World Biography,* Jack Heraty & Associates, 1973, pp. 504–505.

Current Biography, H. W. Wilson, 1947, pp. 498–500.

—*Sketch by Jordan Richman*

Jean-Pierre Serre
1926-
French mathematician

Educated at the École Normale Supérieure in Paris, Jean-Pierre Serre received a Fields Medal for his work in topology, the study of geometric figures whose properties are unaffected by physical manipulation. The award, which was given to him in 1954, when he was only twenty-eight years old, is the equivalent in mathematics to the Nobel Prize in other fields of study. He has been professor of algebra and geometry at the Collège de France since 1956.

Serre was born in Bages, France, on September 15, 1926, to Jean and Adèle Serre. Both pharmacists, they instilled in their son an early interest in chemistry. That interest eventually gave way to mathematics, however, when Serre began reading his mother's calculus books. In a short time, he was teaching himself the fundamentals of derivatives, integrals, series, and other topics. During high school at the Lycée de Nîmes, Serre found a practical use for his mathematical talents. He told C. T. Chong and Y. K. Leong in *Mathematical Intelligencer* that some of the older students at the school had a tendency to bully him. "So to pacify them," he said, "I used to do their math homework. It was as good a training as any."

In 1945 Serre passed the entrance examination for the prestigious École Normale Supérieure in Paris. Soon after he enrolled at the institution, he decided to abandon his plans to become a high-school math teacher and to concentrate instead on research in mathematics. It was not until then, he later told Chong and Leong, that he realized he could earn a living as a research mathematician. Serre's earliest research at the École was in the field of topology. He was awarded his doctorate in this subject in 1952 for a dissertation on homotopy groups. For his work in this area, he was also awarded a 1954 Fields Medal from the International Congress of Mathematics.

Since receiving the Fields Medal, Serre has gone on to other topics in mathematics, including complex variables, cohomology and sheaves, algebraic geometry, and number fields. He explained to Chong and Leong that he finds it easy to move gradually from one topic to another, as he perceives their relationships to each other. In 1956 Serre was appointed professor of algebra and geometry at the Collège de France, a post he continues to hold.

Serre was married in 1948 to Josiane Heulot, a chemist. The couple has one daughter. Serre is a member of the French, Dutch, Swedish, and U.S. academies of science and has been made an honorary fellow of the Royal Society in London. In addition to the Fields Medal, he has been awarded the Prix Balzan in 1985 and the Médaille d'Or of the Centre National de la Recherche Scientifique.

SELECTED WRITINGS BY SERRE:

Books

Faiseaux algébriques cohérents, 1955.
Groupes algébriques et corps de classes, 1959.
Corps Locaux, 1962.
Cohomologie galoisienne, 1964.
Abelian l-adic representations, 1968
Cours d'arithmétique, 1970.
Représentations linéaires des groupes finis, 1971.

SOURCES:

Periodicals

Chong, C. T., and Y. K. Leong, "An Interview with Jean-Pierre Serre," *Mathematical Intelligencer,* Volume 8, 1986, pp. 8–12.

—*Sketch by David E. Newton*

Claude Shannon
1916-
American mathematician and information theorist

Claude Shannon is considered by many to be the father of the information sciences. At the Massachusetts Institute of Technology (MIT) in 1940, Shannon first applied Boolean algebra to electrical systems, laying the groundwork for both the computer industry and telecommunications. Later that same decade, while working at Bell Laboratories, he formulated a sweeping theory explaining the communication of information. By distinguishing between meaning and information and reconceptualizing information as all of the possible messages in a communication, he was able to quantify information for the first time. This made it possible to analyze mathematically various communication technologies. His general theory of information, however, is not restricted to the analysis of specific technologies; it has broad philosophical implications as well, and Shannon has also made major contributions to research on artificial intelligence.

Claude Elwood Shannon was born in Gaylord, Michigan, on April 30, 1916, to Claude Elwood and Mabel Wolf Shannon. He earned his B.S. degree from the University of Michigan in 1936; he then went on to MIT, where he studied both electrical engineering and mathematics, receiving a master's degree in the former and a doctorate in the latter. For his master's degree in electrical engineering, he applied George Boole's logical algebra to the problem of electrical switching. Boole's system for logically manipulating 0s and 1s was little known at the time, but it is now the nervous system of every computer in the world. For his Ph.D. dissertation, Shannon applied mathematics to genetics. He received both his master's degree and his doctorate in 1940. He was named a National Research Fellow and spent a year at Princeton's Institute for Advanced Study.

In 1941, Shannon joined Bell Laboratories as a research mathematician, and he spent most of World War II working in a top secret section of the laboratories on cryptanalysis and anti-aircraft gun directors. It was there that he met **Alan Turing**, the leader of the British team that was designing one of the first computers to crack Germany's secret codes. Shannon had been interested in computing since he was a graduate student at MIT, where he was in charge of **Vannevar Bush**'s differential analyzer, an analog computer. Turing was thrilled to meet Shannon, because they had both independently conceived of logical machines. After they had met, Turing—as quoted in *Alan Turing: The Enigma*—exclaimed in joy: "Shannon wants to feed not just *data* to a Brain, but *cultural* things! He wants to play *music* to it!"

Lays the Foundations for Information Science

In the late forties and early fifties, Shannon designed programs for chess playing machines and a maze-running mechanical mouse, and in 1956 he helped **John McCarthy** organize the very first conference on artificial intelligence at Dartmouth College. But his greatest contribution was a series of papers he wrote which established the field of information science—the theoretical and mathematical basis for the mechanical conveyance of information. As Howard Rheingold explains in *Tools for Thought,* Shannon "presented a set of theorems that were directly related to the economical and efficient transmission of messages on noisy media, and indirectly but still fundamentally related to the connection between energy and information." These theorems, endlessly elaborated and refined by engineers making color televisions, running telephone systems, establishing radio networks, and proliferating various types of computers, have had a tremendous impact on the late twentieth-century.

Like his friend Alan Turing, Shannon is much more interested in ideas than fame. In fact, he seems to loathe public accolades, and he even went out of his way to criticize the mania about information which swept the sciences in the 1950s, after his work became known. In an article called "Bandwagon," printed in the *IEEE Transactions on Information Theory,* he warned that the mania for information "has perhaps ballooned to an importance beyond its actual accomplishments ... Seldom do more than a few of nature's secrets give way at one time."

In addition to his work at Bell Laboratories, Shannon has spent many years teaching at MIT. He was a visiting professor of electrical communication in 1956, and then in 1957 he was named professor of communications sciences and mathematics. He was the Donner Professor of Science from 1958 to 1978, when he retired. Shannon has received many honors including the Morris Liebmann Memorial Award in 1949, the Ballantine Medal in 1955, and the Mervin J. Kelly Award of the American Institute of Electrical Engineers in 1962. He was awarded the National Medal of Science in 1966, as well as the Medal of Honor that same year from the Institute of Electrical and Electronics Engineers. He also received the Jaquard award in 1978, the John Fritz Medal in 1983, and the Kyoto Prize in Basic Science in 1985, as well as numerous other prizes and over a dozen honorary degrees. He is a member of the American Academy of Arts and Sciences, the National Academy of Sciences, the National Academy of Engineering, the American Philosophical Society, and the Royal Society of London.

On March 27, 1949, Shannon married Mary Elizabeth Moore; they had three children together. While he has lectured or published only intermittently since the early 1960s, he continues to research information in its many forms, from the stock market to the English language. He currently he lives in Winchester, Massachusetts.

SELECTED WRITINGS BY SHANNON:

Books

(With W. Weaver) *The Mathematical Theory of Communication,* University of Illinois Press, 1949.

(With John McCarthy and William Ross Ashby) *Automata Studies: Annals of Mathematics Studies Number 34,* Princeton University Press, 1956.

Periodicals

"The Mathematical Theory of Communication," *Bell System Technical Journal,* Volume 27, 1948, pp. 379–423 and 623–656.
"Communication in the Presence of Noise," *Proceedings of the IRE,* Volume 37, 1949, pp. 10–21.

SOURCES:

Books

Hodges, Andrew, *Alan Turing: The Enigma,* Simon and Schuster, 1983, pp. 250–251.
Rheingold, Howard, *Tools for Thought,* Simon and Schuster, 1985.

Periodicals

Aspray, William, "The Scientific Conceptualization of Information: A Survey," *Annals of the History of Computing,* Volume 7, April, 1985, pp. 117–140.

—Sketch by Chris Hables Gray

Irwin Shapiro
1929-
American radio astronomer and educator

Irwin Shapiro, a noted innovator of techniques in radar and radio astronomy, was appointed director of the Harvard-Smithsonian Center for Astrophysics (CfA) in January 1983. Respected as both teacher and physicist, Shapiro became the guiding force behind one of the largest astrophysical centers in the world. While continuing his own research, Shapiro found himself controlling a $40 million budget and the work of hundreds of CfA staff members. Besides radio and microwave astronomy, Shapiro has worked on geophysics, planetary physics, and tests of gravitation theories.

Irwin Ira Shapiro was born in New York City on October 10, 1929, to Samuel Shapiro, a civil engineer and teacher who had come to America from Russia at age two, and Esther Feinberg Shapiro, a schoolteacher. Becoming interested in science at six, Shapiro learned math from an uncle and was doing fractions by the second grade. As a teenager he commuted from his home in Far Rockaway, New York, to the elite Brooklyn Technical High School, an experience he found intellectually enriching. At fifteen Shapiro built a telescope in his attic, grinding the mirror himself and making its tube out of wood. Shapiro majored in math at Cornell University, receiving his bachelor's degree in three years.

After receiving a master's degree at Harvard University in 1951, Shapiro was appointed a member of the staff of the Lincoln Laboratory of the Massachusetts Institute of Technology (MIT) in Lexington in 1954; the following year he received a Ph.D. in physics from Harvard. At the Lincoln Laboratory, Shapiro worked on radar applications, writing a book on missile trajectory observations in 1958. On December 20, 1959, he married Marian Helen Kaplun, and the couple eventually had two children, Stephen and Nancy. A few years later Shapiro was involved with a controversial project intended to duplicate the radio-reflective properties of the Earth's ionosphere—a region of electrically-charged particles surrounding the planet—with millions of hairlike, man-made materials scattered through the upper atmosphere. The project, carried out in 1963, drew criticism from various sources; astronomers complained it would ruin their observations, and Soviets called it an imperialist scheme. Shapiro's predictions of the experiment's effectiveness and duration proved correct nonetheless, and the worried radio astronomers could not even locate the objects before they fell out of orbit. In another early experiment, Shapiro used radar and light to verify physicist **Albert Einstein**'s theory of general relativity, which includes the idea that although the speed of light in a vacuum is constant, the pull of gravity can affect it. Shapiro sent a light signal past the sun to reflect off a planet and measured with radar the extra delay in its return caused by the sun's gravitational pull.

Among First to Study Superluminal Motion

Shapiro was appointed professor of geophysics and physics at MIT in 1967, and four years later he headed a team of researchers that observed motion within the quasars 3C 273 and 3C 279. (A joint team led by Marshall Cohen and Kenneth Kellermann was studying these two objects at that time as well.) Quasars are mysterious, compact sources of tremendous amounts of radio emission, and Shapiro's team discovered that both quasars had a double structure. Four months later, his group noticed that the separation between the two parts of each double structure had widened, doing so at a velocity apparently exceeding that of light. This so-called superluminal motion—motion faster than light—observed by Shapiro in 1971 has been attributed to observing effects and the angle at which the quasars were seen. This apparent faster-than-light motion did not in fact contradict the theory of special relativity (which holds that the speed of light and the laws of physics are constant; therefore nothing can exceed light's speed), since no actual objects were moving that quickly. In order to detect these quasars' motions, Shapiro relied on a technique called very long baseline interferometry (VLBI), a form of radio astronomy using widely separated radio telescopes and combining the data from each in a computer.

Thrust into Spotlight as Head of Center for Astrophysics

After a series of academic appointments in the 1970s and 1980s at the California Institute of Technology, Harvard University, and MIT, Shapiro became a senior scientist at the Smithsonian Astrophysical Observatory in 1982. In January of 1983 Shapiro was chosen as director of the Center for Astrophysics. Originally formed by astronomer and Smithsonian Institute secretary Samuel Pierpont Langley in 1890, the CfA boasted about five hundred staff members, including 170 scientists, by the early 1980s. The CfA headquarters are located on Observatory Hill, about one mile from Harvard University, in Cambridge, Massachusetts, and about fifteen minutes away from Shapiro's home in Lexington, Massachusetts. With facilities in Massachusetts, Texas, and Arizona, the CfA sustains research on a wide variety of areas from theoretical astrophysics to the planetary sciences. Shapiro has tried to steer researchers into the most valuable lines of research. "I try to get the very best people I can—that's where the bright new ideas come from—and I attempt to provide researchers with world-unique facilities," Shapiro told *Smithsonian* writer Bruce Fellman in 1990. Discussing the Center's ongoing efforts to study a wide range of radio waves, he added, "Every time we've looked at the Universe in a new wavelength band, we've discovered something new."

Over the years, Shapiro has received many awards and honors, including the Benjamin Apthorp Gould prize of the National Academy of Sciences in 1979, a Guggenheim fellowship in 1982, and the Charles A. Whitten medal of the American Geophysical Union in 1991.

SELECTED WRITINGS BY SHAPIRO:

Books

The Prediction of Ballistic Missile Trajectories from Radar Observations, McGraw-Hill, 1958.

SOURCES:

Periodicals

Fellman, Bruce, "After 100 Years Discoveries Come Faster and Faster," *Smithsonian,* December, 1990, pp. 125–26, 128–38, 140, 142.
Park, Edwards, "Around the Mall and Beyond," *Smithsonian,* December, 1983, pp. 24, 26, 28–29.

—*Sketch by Sebastian Thaler*

Harlow Shapley
1885-1972
American astronomer

American astronomer Harlow Shapley was known for his accomplishments in astronomy, education, and humanitarian causes. Shapley, whose obituary in the *New York Times* described him as the "dean of American astronomers," was chiefly known for discovering that the Milky Way galaxy was much larger than originally thought and that Earth's solar system was not in fact at the center of the galaxy. For this achievement, he was compared to Nicolaus Copernicus, the Polish astronomer who in 1514 proposed that the Earth was not the center of the solar system. As an educator, Shapley helped make the Harvard Observatory the leading center for astronomy in the United States during his time. Finally, through his humanitarian efforts, Shapley helped save Jewish scientists from Nazi Germany; he also founded and supported international causes and organizations such as the United Nations Educational, Scientific and Cultural Organization (UNESCO).

Shapley was born on November 2, 1885, along with his twin brother, Horace, in Nashville, Missouri. The twins were later followed by a younger brother, John. Shapley's father was farmer and teacher Willis Shapley, and his mother was Sarah Stowell, whose ancestors were early settlers in Massachusetts. Shapley's youth was marked by the death of his father and by limited schooling: a mere five grades' worth of education in a local rural school. Shapley received his high school education from the Presbyterian Carthage Collegiate Institute, from which he graduated in two semesters. In addition, during this time Shapley worked as a reporter for the Chanute *Daily Sun* in Kansas; he was the paper's city editor by age twenty.

Shapley attended college beginning at age twenty, enrolling in the University of Missouri. He originally

Harlow Shapley

planned to study journalism but switched to astronomy when he found out that the university's journalism school was still a year away from opening. By his junior year at the university, Shapley was working as assistant to the director of the Laws Observatory, Frederick H. Seares. Shapley graduated in 1910 with a B.A. in mathematics and physics; the following year he received his M.A.

From the University of Missouri, Shapley went directly to Princeton Observatory as a recipient of the Thaw fellowship in astronomy. Under the guidance of **Henry Norris Russell**, director of the observatory, Shapley completed his graduate work, receiving his Ph.D. in 1913. In his dissertation, Shapley presented information about the properties of stars known as eclipsing binary (or double) stars. He eventually expanded and published his thesis; the resulting work, which analyzed ninety binaries, is considered a significant contribution to the field of astronomy.

In 1913 Shapley interviewed with **George Ellery Hale**, director of the Mount Wilson Observatory in Pasadena, California, about the possibility of obtaining a position there. Shapley got the post, but before moving to California he spent five months touring Europe with his brother John and then returned to Princeton for several months to complete his work there. In addition, on his way to California in 1914, Shapley married Martha Betz, a former classmate from Missouri. Shapley and his wife eventually had five children. Martha Betz Shapley was herself a

mathematician and astronomer, and she wrote several scientific papers with her husband.

The Center of the Galaxy

In his seven years at Mount Wilson, Shapley was to make some of his most significant discoveries. Shapley concentrated his efforts on studying stars known as Cepheid variables and on globular clusters —concentrated areas of stars. Shapley found that the Cepheid variables (named for the first star of this type to be discovered, Delta Cephei) were pulsating stars, whose size and brightness fluctuated regularly. Another Harvard astronomer, **Henrietta Leavitt**, had shown that the rate at which a Cepheid pulsed was directly related to its brightness. Using this information, Shapley could then determine the star's absolute brightness (or luminosity) and by comparing this to its observed brightness could calculate how far away the star was.

It was this measuring system that allowed Shapley to determine the placement of Earth's solar system in the Milky Way. Shapley charted the distance and location of the globular clusters and found that they were distributed almost symmetrically above and below the plane of the Milky Way. He then used this information as a guide to the general outline of the Milky Way and estimated that the center of the galaxy was located fifty thousand light-years from the sun, in the constellation Sagittarius. The Shapley Center, as it came to be known, is actually 33,000 light-years from the sun. Shapley also estimated the diameter of the Milky Way to be about 300,000 light-years, later revising that figure to 150,000 light-years.

At the time, Shapley's conclusions were almost revolutionary: his figures increased the then-estimated size of the Milky Way by a factor of ten and as a result, many astronomers believed he overestimated. In fact, Shapley's conclusions weren't fully accepted until he took part in a now-famous debate at the National Academy of Sciences in Washington in 1920 with Heber D. Curtis of the Lick Observatory. It is generally agreed that at this debate Shapley won his point about the size and structure of the Milky Way.

In addition to his work on the question of the center of the galaxy, Shapley also studied spiral nebulae while at Mount Wilson (in that era, the term "nebula" described anything not positively identified as a star). At the time, astronomers were not sure whether the nebulae were part of the Milky Way or were what was known as "island universes"—in modern terms, galaxies. Several new stars had been discovered in the nebulae, and Shapley, using information about the luminosity of the stars, estimated the distance to the Andromeda nebula (now known as the Andromeda galaxy) to be one million light-years. The theories of other scientists at the time caused

Shapley to withdraw this estimate; ironically, his figures turned out to be nearly correct.

Shapley also pursued scientific interests that went beyond astronomy at Mount Wilson. He discovered a relationship between temperature and the speed at which ants run, for instance, and published five scientific papers on ants. According to Shapley biographers, he was especially proud of his work in this area.

Made Harvard Observatory U.S. Leader

Shapley returned to Cambridge, Massachusetts, in 1921 to become director of the Harvard Observatory and Paine Professor of Practical Astronomy. At Harvard he concentrated his research on stars in the Magellanic Clouds (later revealed as two neighboring galaxies), working on a unique round desk that rotated. A few years into his tenure, in 1924, he was elected to the National Academy of Sciences, and he received that organization's Draper Medal in 1926. Among Shapley's scientific achievements in this period was, in the 1930s, the first discovery of two dwarf galaxies in the constellations of Sculptor and Fornax (in the southern hemisphere). Interestingly, he used the term "galaxy," while his fellow astronomer and rival of the period, **Edwin Hubble**, used the term "extragalactic nebulae." Shapley maintained that galaxies were distributed irregularly, in contrast to Hubble's view that the universe was more uniform. Shapley's work at Harvard also included overseeing group projects that cataloged tens of thousands of galaxies in both the northern and southern hemispheres (the Harvard Observatory had observatories in both hemispheres) and that worked on a catalog of the spectral classifications of stars (the light from a star, broken into its rainbow or spectrum of colors, reveals its chemical makeup).

Perhaps more significantly, Shapley helped make the Harvard Observatory the leading astronomy education center in the United States in the 1920s. He set up a graduate program in astronomy and attracted scientists from the international community as well as from across America. Among the scientists that Shapley brought to Harvard and the United States were refugees from Nazi Germany: Shapley personally led an effort to bring in Jewish scientists. According to Shapley biographer Bart J. Bok in an article for *Sky and Telescope,* "One of these who came to Harvard was Richard Prager of Berlin Observatory, who told me quietly and seriously that every night at least a thousand Jewish scientists must say a prayer of thanks for Harlow Shapley's humanitarian efforts to help save them and their families." His activities in the early 1940s also included serving as president of the American Academy of Arts and Sciences.

International Efforts

After World War II Shapley continued to focus on international affairs. He helped form the United Nations Educational, Scientific and Cultural Organization, serving as a U.S. representative in writing UNESCO's charter in 1945. Shapley lobbied the U.S. Government for the creation of the posts of Secretary of Peace and Welfare, Secretary of Education, and Secretary of Science and Technology after World War II. According to the *New York Times,* Shapley believed that peace should be the first concern of government. Eventually, only the Department of Health, Education, and Welfare was established.

After a visit to the Soviet Union in 1945 as the Harvard representative at the 220th anniversary of the Academy of Sciences in Moscow, Shapley became a supporter of scientific cooperation with the Soviets. He served as chairman of the Independent Citizens Committee of the Arts, Sciences, and Professions, a fund-raising group for liberal congressional candidates. In addition, he was the chairman of several meetings of left-wing groups that dared to invite Russian delegates. Shapley, who believed that the Soviet government's support of science would speed its development, urged the United States to give similar support to research in order to remain competitive. His views were not popular at the time, and in 1946 the House Committee on Un-American Activities subpoenaed Shapley to question him about his views. Shapley's obituary in the *New York Times* reported that Representative John E. Rankin, a Mississippi Democrat who had questioned Shapley as a one-man subcommittee, reported after the meeting, "I have never seen a witness treat a committee with more contempt." The paper reported that in return Shapley charged the committee with "Gestapo methods" and called for its elimination. The same year, Shapley was elected president of the American Association for the Advancement of Science, a move widely regarded as a show of support by the scientific community. Despite his encounter with reactionary politics, Shapley continued with his efforts against the committee, becoming, for example, acting chairman of the Committee of One Thousand, an organization geared toward protecting First Amendment rights. Physicist **Albert Einstein** and author-lecturer Helen Keller were also members. In March of 1950, Senator Joseph McCarthy "charged that Dr. Shapley had belonged to many Communist-front organizations," according to the *New York Times.* Later that year, a Senate subcommittee cleared him of the charges.

Shapley was director of the Harvard Observatory until 1952; he continued to teach courses there until 1956 and then traveled and lectured through his seventies, speaking on astronomy, religion, philosophy, and evolution. His many appearances during his career included one at the 1939 New York World's Fair, at which he gave the speech "Astronomy in the

World of Tomorrow." He also wrote extensively, publishing hundreds of scientific papers as well as newspaper and magazine articles and several popular books, including *Through Rugged Ways to the Stars.* At eighty-five Shapley moved to Boulder, Colorado, where one of his four sons lived; he died there in a nursing home at age eighty-six after a long battle with illness.

SELECTED WRITINGS BY SHAPLEY:

Books

Starlight, George H. Doran, 1926.
Flights from Chaos: A Survey of Material Systems from Atoms to Galaxies, McGraw, 1930.
Star Clusters (monograph), McGraw, 1930.
Of Stars and Men: The Human Response to an Expanding Universe, Beacon Press, 1958, revised edition, 1964.
The View from a Distant Star: Man's Future in the Universe, Basic Books, 1963.
Beyond the Observatory, Scribner, 1967.
Through Rugged Ways to the Stars, Scribner, 1969.

Periodicals

"Sixth Paper: On the Determination of the Distances of Globular Clusters" and "Seventh Paper: The Distances, Distribution in Space, and Dimensions of 69 Globular Clusters," both *Astrophysical Journal,* Volume 48, 1918, pp. 89–124, 154–81.
"Twelfth Paper: Remarks on the Sidereal Universe," *Astrophysical Journal,* Volume 49, 1919, pp. 311–36.
"The Scale of the Universe" (article includes material by Heber D. Curtis), *Bulletin of the National Research Council,* Volume 2, number 11, 1921.
"Two Stellar Systems of a New Kind," *Nature,* Volume 142, 1938, pp. 715–16.

SOURCES:

Books

Biographical Memoirs, The National Academy of Sciences, Volume 48, Columbia University Press, 1976.
Dictionary of Scientific Biography, Scribner, 1975, pp. 345–52.

Periodicals

Bok, Bart J., "Harlow Shapley—Cosmographer and Humanitarian," *Sky and Telescope,* December, 1972, pp. 354–57.

New York Times, October 21, 1972, p. 1.

—*Sketch by Devera Pine*

Phillip A. Sharp
1944-
American biologist

Phillip A. Sharp has conducted research into the structure of deoxyribonucleic acid (DNA—the chemical blueprint that synthesizes proteins) which has altered previous views on the mechanism of genetic change. For his work in this area, Sharp was presented with the 1993 Nobel Prize in medicine along with **Richard J. Roberts**. In addition to the Nobel Prize, Sharp has received honors from the American Cancer Society and the National Academy of Science, and is the recipient of the Howard Ricketts Award, the Alfred P. Sloan Jr. Prize, the Albert Lasker Basic Medical Research Award, and the Dickson Prize.

Born in Falmouth, Kentucky, on June 6, 1944, Sharp grew up on a small agricultural farm owned by his parents, Katherin Colvin and Joseph Walter Sharp. Earnings from tobacco land given to him by his parents allowed him to attend Union College in Barbourville, Kentucky, where he received a B.A. degree in chemistry and mathematics in 1966. Sharp earned his Ph.D. degree from the University of Illinois in 1969; he later received an honorary L.H.D. from Union College in 1991.

Sharp and Roberts discovered in 1977 that, in some higher organisms, genes may be comprised of more than one segment, separated by material which apparently plays no part in the creation of the proteins. Previously, most scientists believed that genes were continuous sections of DNA and that the string of coding information that makes up each gene was a single, linear unit. Sharp and Roberts, however, distinguished between the *exons,* the sequences that contain the vital information needed to create the protein, and the *introns,* incoherent biochemical information that interrupts the protein-manufacturing instructions. Each gene is apparently composed of fifteen to twenty exons, in between which introns may be located. During protein synthesis, exons are copied and spliced together, creating complete sequences, while the introns are ignored.

This discovery had not been made earlier largely because scientists had conducted most of their genetic research on prokaryotic organisms, such as bacteria, which do not have their genetic material located in clearly defined nuclei. Studies of bacteria had indicated that gene activity resulted in the transcription of double-stranded DNA into single-stranded messenger ribonucleic acid (mRNA); this is translated to the corresponding protein by ribosomes. Prokaryotic organisms have no introns, however, and therefore could not supply evidence for the existence, or the significance, of noncoding regions of DNA. Roberts and Sharp carried their research out on adenoviruses, the virus responsible for the common cold in humans. Although these are also prokaryotic organisms, Roberts and Sharp were able to take advantage of the fact that viruses reproduce themselves using the mechanisms of eukaryotic cells. Since their genome has some similarities to the genetic material in human cells, their protein synthesis was therefore relevant to the study of the cells of higher organisms.

In their experiments, Sharp's team created hybrid molecules in which they could observe mRNA strands binding to their complementary DNA strands. Electron micrographs allowed the scientists to identify which parts of the viral genomes had produced the mature mRNA molecules. What they discovered was that substantial sections of DNA were ignored in producing the final mRNA. This unexpected result gave evidence of a greater complexity of mRNA synthesis in eukaryotic organisms than in prokaryotic ones. Further research indicated that the mRNAs of eukaryotic organisms are synthesized as large mRNA precursor molecules; the introns are spliced out by means of enzyme activity to produce the mature mRNA that manufactures proteins. They found that a single gene could produce a variety of proteins—some defective—as a result of different splicing patterns.

Further research has indicated that the introns, rather than simply being "junk" DNA, contain some information that is necessary for the production of proteins, but the nature of this information is not yet understood.

It is now believed that many hereditary diseases are caused by imperfect splicing of the genetic material, leading to the creation of faulty proteins. This may occur if the copying and splicing of the exons is not carried out accurately. One such disease is beta-thalassemia, a form of anemia prevalent in some Mediterranean areas that is caused by a faulty protein responsible for the formation of hemoglobin. Because of the insight Sharp's and Roberts's research has produced into the mechanisms of cell reproduction, it has important ramifications for research on malignant tumors and the viruses responsible for their development. It has also led to an investigation of methods for stopping the replication of the human immunodeficiency virus type 1 (HIV–1), with potential benefits in the search for a treatment for AIDS.

Sharp and Roberts's work has also led to new theories on the nature of evolutionary change; rather than being the cumulative effect of genetic mutation over time, it is now believed that it may be the result of the shuffling of large segments of DNA into new combinations to produce new proteins.

In 1990, before his earlier work had led to his Nobel Prize, Sharp was offered, and accepted, the presidency of the Massachusetts Institute of Technology. A short time later, he decided not to accept the position in order to devote his time exclusively to research. He has remained active in the field of academic administration, however, and has lobbied for research funding. He has also been active in industry; he was one of the founders of Biogen, a corporation started in Switzerland and now operating in Cambridge, Massachusetts, that has employed techniques developed in genetic engineering to produce the drug interferon.

SELECTED WRITINGS BY SHARP:

Periodicals

"Splicing of Messenger RNA Precursors," *Science,* Volume 235, 1987, pp. 766–771.
"Five Easy Pieces," *Journal of the American Medical Association,* Volume 260, 1988, pp. 3035–3041.
(With David D. Chang) "Messenger RNA Transport and HIV Rev Regulation," *Science,* Volume 249, 1990, pp. 614–615.

SOURCES:

Periodicals

New York Times, October 12, 1993, p. C3.
Science, Volume 262, October 22, 1993, p. 506.
Science News, October 16, 1993, p. 245.

—*Sketch by Michael Sims*

Robert Phillip Sharp
1911-
American geologist and geomorphologist

Robert Phillip Sharp is primarily known for his investigations into the causes of landscape forms on the surface of the earth and other planets. He has employed techniques derived from the disciplines of geophysics and geochemistry to analyze the problems of landform development, and he isolated and observed the processes producing enough visible changes on a planet within a single human lifetime to allow for adequate research and conclusive results. His research topics have included glaciers and sand dunes, as well as oxygen isotopes in ice and the terrains and landforms on Mars.

Sharp was born June 24, 1911, in Oxnard, California, to Julian and Alice Darling Sharp. He attended Oxnard Union High School and then earned a B.S. from the California Institute of Technology in 1934, followed by an M.A. in 1935. He completed a Ph.D. in geology at Harvard University in 1938. He taught geology at the University of Illinois from 1938 until he entered military service in 1942 as a captain in the United States Air Force. He taught at the University of Minnesota from 1945 to 1947, and then he returned to the California Institute of Technology, where he taught until 1979, serving as chairman of the geology department from 1952 to 1967. Though he officially retired in 1979, Sharp continues as instructor of the introductory field course in geology at Cal Tech that he has taught for more than thirty years.

Sharp has participated in field explorations and expeditions which have yielded significant discoveries and stimulated further research. In 1937, he accompanied other researchers on an expedition by boat of the Grand Canyon; their findings contributed to the scientific understanding of erosion in the Precambrian era, the earliest geologic era. In 1941, Sharp participated in an expedition to the Ice Field Ranges in the Saint Elias mountains along the border between Alaska and Canada. This project served as the catalyst for comprehensive research on glaciers in Alaska, Canada, and the northwestern United States.

Discovers Causes of Desert Sand Dunes

While employed in the Midwest, Sharp investigated the contrasting characteristics of continental and mountain glaciation, and he identified patterns and formations in the soil created by frozen ground that lay outside of glaciers in Illinois. After moving to southern California, Sharp took the opportunity to study the various processes acting on the earth's surface in desert areas. He studied desert domes and sand dunes, in particular, and among his many findings are his discoveries about sand transport by wind, sandblasting of natural and artificial objects, dune movements, and the causes for the shapes and activities of sand dunes.

Sharp has provided a substantiated theory for how the five-hundred-foot Kelso Dunes of the Mojave Desert were developed; he explained why they were located in the middle of the valley instead of piled up against the mountains, as would be expected given the prevailing wind direction. Because the wind regime in that area is so complex, storm winds are able to cancel out the strong westerly winds. This scenario also explains the asymmetrical shape of sand dunes. His research into dune movement also led Sharp to the important, but as of yet unsubstantiated, projection that the large intradune flats of the Algodones Dunes chain in southeastern California are advancing southeasterly and will eventually jeopardize the All-American Canal. He also studied glacial deposits in the Sierra Nevada of California and distinguished the glacial deposits and features in the earth's surface created by separate episodes of ice advance. His investigations are responsible for expanding the accepted model of Sierra glaciation.

Appointed to Research Landforms on Mars

Sharp's knowledge of terrestrial landforms and processes earned him a position on the team analyzing the results of the various *Mariner* flights to Mars between 1965 and 1971. Sharp and his colleagues interpreted terrains and surface features from photographs of Mars taken from the spacecraft. The team was able to recognize various terrains, and they concluded that although Mars does not now have water, conditions of the planet's surface indicate it did at one time. He theorized that the large chasms in the surface of Mars were due to water trapped underground which froze and melted before it could reach the surface. There were forms on Earth which served as good models for terrestrial features on Mars, but the configuration and scale of these features represent processes that have not occurred here.

Sharp's honors and awards include the Kirk Bryan Award in 1964, the Exceptional Science Achievement Medal from NASA in 1971, and the Penrose Award from the Geology Society of America in 1977. He also received the National Medal of Science in 1989, and the Charles P. Daly Medal from the American Geographical Society in 1991.

In 1938 Sharp married Jean Prescott Todd, whom he met while she was at Radcliffe College. They have two adopted children, a daughter and a son. Sharp now has two grandchildren and he lives in California where he continues his association with the California Institute of Technology; in 1978 an endowed professorship in geology was created there in his name. His research continues to involve those processes that affect land surfaces and that are measurable, as well as forms on the earth's surface such as glaciers and volcanoes.

SELECTED WRITINGS BY SHARP:

Books

Glaciers, University of Oregon Press, 1960.

Geology Field Guide to Southern California, W. C. Brown, 1972.

Geology Field Guide to Coastal Southern California, Kendall Hunt, 1978.

(With A. F. Glazner) *Geology under Foot in Southern California,* Mountain Press, 1993.

SOURCES:

Sharp, Robert Phillip, interview with Kelly Otter Cooper conducted October 12, 1993.

—*Sketch by Kelly Otter Cooper*

Mary Shaw

Mary Shaw
1943-
American computer scientist

Professor of computer science and dean of professional programs at Carnegie-Mellon University in Pittsburgh, Pennsylvania, Mary Shaw has made major contributions to the analysis of computer algorithms, as well as to abstraction techniques for advanced programming methodologies, programming-language architecture, evaluation methods for software performance and reliability, and software engineering. She has also been involved in the development of computer-science education. She was elected to the Institute of Electrical and Electronic Engineers in 1990 and the American Association for the Advancement of Science in 1992; she received the Warnier Prize in 1993.

Mary M. Shaw was born in Washington, D.C., on September 30, 1943, to Eldon and Mary Holman Shaw. Her father was a civil engineer and an economist for the Department of Agriculture, and Shaw attended high school in Bethesda, Maryland, at the height of the Sputnik—the first artificial satellite— era, when the country was making a concerted effort to bolster science and mathematics education. Her father encouraged her interest in science with books and simple electronic kits when she was in the seventh and eighth grades, and her high-school years provided opportunities to delve more deeply into both computers and mathematics.

An International Business Machines (IBM) employee named George Heller from the Washington area participated in an after-school program which taught students about computers; he arranged for the students to visit an IBM facility and run a program on an IBM 709 computer. This was Shaw's introduction to computers. For two summers during high school, as well as during the summer after she graduated, she worked at the Research Analysis Corporation at the Johns Hopkins University Operation Research Office. This was part of a program begun by a woman named Jean Taylor to give advanced students a chance to explore fields outside the normal high school curriculum. "They would give us a system analysis problem and ask us to investigate," Shaw told contributor Rowan Dordick. Among the problems she worked on was a study of the feasibility of using irradiated foods to supply army units.

Shaw entered Rice University with the idea of becoming a topologist, having become enamored with Moebius strips and Klein bottles while in high school. She quickly changed her mind, however, after looking through a textbook on topology. Though there were no courses at that time in computer science, there was something called the Rice Computer Project, a group which had built a computer—the Rice I—under the leadership of an electrical engineering professor named Martin Graham. Shaw wandered into the project area one day and asked a question about the computer. By way of an answer, she was given a machine reference manual and was told to read it first and then come back. She surprised the project members by doing just that. It was a small group, consisting mostly of faculty and graduate students, and Shaw ended up working with the project part-time during her last three years, under the mentorship of Jane Jodeit, the head programmer. Shaw gained valuable experience on the Rice I; she worked on a programming language, wrote subroutines, and helped figure out ways to make the operating system run faster.

After her junior year, Shaw attended summer school at the University of Michigan, where she met Alan Perlis, a professor at Carnegie Mellon University. After receiving her B.A. *cum laude* in mathematics from Rice in 1965, she entered Carnegie Mellon, where Perlis became one of her advisors. She received her Ph.D. in 1971 in computer science, with a thesis on compilers—programs that translate language a human can easily understand into language that the computer understands. Shaw was invited to join the faculty after receiving her degree. One of her first notable accomplishments, in collaboration with Joseph Traub, was the development of what is known as the Shaw-Traub algorithm, an improved method for evaluating a polynomial which allows computers to compute faster. This effort was part of a general interest Shaw had in finding ways to formalize computations in order to make them more efficient.

Clarifies the Organization of Data in Programs

Shaw's focus on improved software design led her to pursue an approach to the organization of computer programs called abstract-data types. This approach is one of the foundations of object-oriented programming. Large programs are difficult to read or modify unless there is some intrinsic structure, and this is the problem abstract-data-type programming was designed to address. Abstract-data types is a method of organizing the data and computations used by a program so that related information is grouped together. For example, information about electronic details of a telephone-switching network would be grouped in one part of the program, whereas information about people and their telephone numbers would be grouped in another part.

Shaw's work in this area came to fruition in two ways. The first was in the creation of a programming language called Alphard that implemented abstract-data types; she developed this language with William A. Wulf and Ralph L. London between 1974 and 1978. The second, more theoretical result, was the clarification of abstractions in programming. Shaw made it easier to design programs that are more abstract—the word "abstract" in this context means that elements of the program are further removed from the details of how the computer works and closer to the language of the problem that a user is trying to solve. This work can be viewed as a continuation of the trend in programming languages, begun with FORTRAN, to write programs in a higher-order language that reflects the nature of the problem, as opposed to programming in the binary

machine language—ones and zeros—that the computer understands.

Charts a Future for Software Engineering

Shaw's concerns with abstraction proved a natural bridge to a more general issue, which she posed to herself as a question: What other ways are there of organizing programs? The answer emerged as Shaw came to realize that what she was really looking for was the organization of software engineering. In "Prospects for an Engineering Discipline of Software," she wrote: "The term 'software engineering' was coined in 1968 as a statement of aspiration—a sort of rallying cry." The problem, as she and others realized, was that the term was not so much the name of a discipline as a reminder that one did not yet exist.

Through historical study of the evolution of civil and chemical engineering, Shaw has developed a three-stage model for the maturation of a field into a complete engineering discipline. She has shown that an engineering discipline begins with a craft stage, characterized by the use of intuition and casually learned techniques by talented amateurs; it then proceeds through a commercial stage, in which large-scale manufacturing relies on skilled craftsmen using established techniques that are refined over time. Finally, as a scientific basis for the discipline emerges, the third stage evolves, in which educated professionals using analysis and theory create new applications and specialties and embody the knowledge of the discipline in treatises and handbooks. Shaw has concluded that contemporary software engineering lies somewhere between the craft and commercial stages, and this conclusion has led to an effort on her part first to promote an understanding of where software engineering should be headed and second to develop the scientific understanding needed to move the discipline into the third stage.

The transformation of a discipline proceeds through its practitioners, so it is natural that Shaw has devoted much of her career to improving computer-science education. She was a coauthor of the first undergraduate text to incorporate the concept of abstract-data structures, and she led a group that redesigned the undergraduate computer-science curriculum. She was also involved in the execution of an innovative Ph.D. program that has been widely adopted.

Shaw's accomplishments are not limited to computer science. She was the National Women's Canoe Poling Champion from 1975 to 1978, and she placed in the Whitewater Open Canoe National Championships in 1991. Her marriage to Roy R. Weil—a civil engineer, software engineer, and commercial balloon pilot—spurred an interest in aviation. She has become an instrument-rated pilot, a single-engine commercial glider pilot, and a Federal Aviation Administration (FAA) certified ground instructor.

SELECTED WRITINGS BY SHAW:

Books

(With W. A. Wulf, P. N. Hilfinger, and L. Flon) *Fundamental Structures of Computer Science,* Addison-Wesley, 1981.

Periodicals

(With J. F. Traub) "On the Number of Multiplications for the Evaluation of a Polynomial and Some of Its Derivatives," *Journal of the ACM,* January, 1974, pp. 161–67.

"An Introduction to the Construction and Verification of Alphard Programs," *IEEE Transactions on Software Engineering,* December, 1976, pp. 253–265.

"The Impact of Abstraction Concerns on Modern Programming Languages," *Proceedings of the IEEE,* September, 1980, pp. 1119–1130.

"Prospects for an Engineering Discipline of Software," *IEEE Software,* November, 1990, pp. 15–24.

Other

Shaw, Mary, interview with Rowan Dordick conducted on February 2, 1994.

—Sketch by Rowan L. Dordick

Rupert Sheldrake
1942-
English biochemist

Rupert Sheldrake, a British biochemist, is best known for his controversial hypothesis of "formative causation," or the idea that nature itself has memory. According to Sheldrake's theory, every system in the universe—molecules, cells, crystals, organisms, societies—reacts in similar or established patterns in response to invisible fields of influence. This is known as "morphic resonance." Sheldrake purports that the invisible field, known as a "morphic field," is where established patterns collect to influence a like activity that may be taking place contemporaneously. An example that he often uses to convey this idea more readily is that of crystallization; in his book *The Rebirth of Nature,* Sheldrake explained morphic resonance thus: "The development of crystals is shaped by morphogenetic fields with an inherent memory of previous crystals of the same kind. From this point of view, substances such as penicillin crystallize the way they do not because they are governed by timeless mathematical laws but because they have crystallized that way before; they are following habits established through repetition." Sheldrake further claims that morphic resonance transcends time and space.

Born Alfred Rupert Sheldrake on June 28, 1942, in Newark Notts, England, Sheldrake received his Ph.D. in biochemistry from Cambridge University. He was a research fellow of the Royal Society and a fellow of and director of studies in cell biology and biochemistry at Clare College at Cambridge. He studied philosophy at Harvard from 1963 to 1964 as Frank Knox Fellow in the special studies program. Beginning in 1974, Sheldrake conducted research on tropical plants at the International Research Institute in India, as well as in Malaysia. He is married to Jill Purce, has two sons, and lives in London. Sheldrake's father was an herbalist and pharmacist. Sheldrake credits his strong interest in plants and animals to both of his parents, who encouraged him in his studies.

Sheldrake developed the necessary emotional detachment required of one pursuing scientific study during his early years at Cambridge. He came to believe—as he was taught—that nature was, in fact, a lifeless mechanistic system without purpose. But a tension persisted between his scientific studies and his personal experiences. He felt the two bore little relationship to each other and were often irreconcilable. He later came to see this conflict as rooted in the mechanistic view of nature—nature as lifeless as opposed to nature as alive and evolving. Sheldrake's hypothesis of formative causation, with its morphic fields creating morphic resonance, subscribes to the latter view.

Sheldrake's books, *A New Science of Life* (1981), *The Presence of the Past* (1988), and *The Rebirth of Nature* (1991) address his theory of formative causation—one not openly embraced by the scientific community at large. Sheldrake's theory that nature has memory and is, therefore, alive challenges the basic foundations of modern science. According to Sheldrake, the conventional scientific approach has been unable to answer the questions relative to morphogenesis—how things come into being or take form—because of their mechanistic outlook.

Sheldrake's hypothesis has elicited much criticism from his contemporaries. Joseph Hannibal, writing for *Library Journal* on *The Rebirth of Nature,* stated, "This new work is even more unorthodox—some might say outrageous—as Sheldrake attempts to combine scientific, religious, and even mystical views." Critic Patrick H. Samway wrote in *America*, "Sheldrake's methodology parallels in many ways that of the Jesuit paleontologist Teilhard de Chardin, who formulated his view that the world in its entirety is developing toward the Omega Point."

Some of Sheldrake's contemporaries who do not subscribe to the theory of formative causation do, nonetheless, believe that science must be open to new possibilities. "Science is not threatened by the imaginative ideas of the Sheldrakes of the world," wrote fellow scientist **James Lovelock** in *Nature*, "but those who would censor them." Lovelock went on to say, "Sheldrake is a threat, but only to the established positions of those who teach and practice an authoritarian science. A healthy scientific community would accept or reject formative causation as the evidence appeared." Critic Theodore Roszak allowed in *New Science*, "If for no better reason than to exercise their wits against a first class polemic, his critics should value this work. Finding answers to his questions will fortify their ideology." And though terms such as "unrealistic," "fanciful," and "off-the-wall" have been used to describe Sheldrake's hypothesis of formative causation, his theory has indeed received significant attention from the scientific community.

SELECTED WRITINGS BY SHELDRAKE:

Books

A New Science of Life: The Hypothesis of Formative Causation, Blonds & Briggs, 1981.
The Presence of the Past: Morphic Resonance and the Habits of Nature, Times Books, 1988.
The Rebirth of Nature: The Greening of Science and God, Bantam, 1991.

Periodicals

"The Production of Auxin in Higher Plants," *Biological Reviews*, Volume 48, 1973, pp. 509–59.
"The Ageing, Growth and Death of Cells," *Nature*, Volume 250, 1974, pp. 381–85.

SOURCES:

Periodicals

Hannibal, Joseph, review of *The Rebirth of Nature*, *Library Journal*, December, 1990.
Lovelock, James E., "A Danger to Science?," *Nature*, Volume 348, December, 1990, p. 685.
Marbach, William D., "A New Theory of Causation," *Newsweek*, July 7, 1986, p. 64.
Raeburn, Paul, "Morphic Fancies," *Psychology Today*, July-August, 1988.

"The Rebirth of Nature: The Greening of Science and God, by Rupert Sheldrake," *Time*, December 3, 1990.
Roszak, Theodore, "The Greening of Rupert Sheldrake," *New Science*, January, 1991, p. 54.
Samway, Patrick H., review of *The Rebirth of Nature*, *America*, March 2, 1991.

—*Sketch by Paula M. Morin*

Alan B. Shepard, Jr.
1923-
American astronaut

One of the original seven American astronauts, Alan B. Shepard, Jr. became the first American to venture into space in a suborbital flight aboard the Mercury capsule, *Freedom 7*. His achievements—including his landmark *Freedom 7* flight on May 5, 1961—symbolized the beginning of a technological revolution in the 1960s and marked the onset of "new frontiers" in space. A decade later, he commanded the *Apollo 14* lunar mission, becoming the fifth man to step on the Moon's surface and the only one of the original astronauts to make a flight to the Moon. In addition to his space flight accomplishments, he served as Chief of the Astronaut Office and participated in the overall astronaut training program. He received the National Aeronautics Space Administration (NASA) Distinguished Service Medal from President John F. Kennedy for his Mercury flight. In 1971, appointed by President Nixon, he served as a delegate to the 26th United Nations General Assembly. He was promoted to rear admiral by the Navy in 1971, the first astronaut to achieve flag rank. In 1979, President Jimmy Carter awarded him the Medal of Honor for gallantry in the astronaut corps.

Alan Bartlett Shepard, Jr. was born on November 18, 1923, in East Derry, New Hampshire, and spent most of his formative years in this New England setting. The son of a career military man—his father was an Army colonel—Shepard showed a strong interest at an early age for mechanical things, disassembling motors and engines and building model airplanes. He attended primary school in East Derry and received his secondary education from Pinkerton Academy in Derry in 1940. During high school, he did odd jobs at the local airport hangar in exchange for a chance to take airplane rides. There was little doubt in the family that Shepard would pursue a military career, and after completing a year's study at Admiral Farragut Academy in New Jersey, he entered the U.S. Naval Academy, graduating in 1944 with a B.S. in science. Shepard married the former Louise Brewer of Kennett Square, Pennsylvania, and has two daughters, Laura and Julie.

Shepard's flying career began in 1947 after he served aboard the destroyer USS *Cogzwell* in the Pacific during the last year of World War II. He received flight training at both Corpus Christi, Texas, and Pensacola, Florida, receiving his wings in 1947. Between the years 1947 and 1950, he served with Fighter Squadron 42 at bases in Virginia and Florida, completing two cruises aboard carriers in the Mediterranean. In 1950 as a lieutenant, junior grade, he was selected to attend U.S. Navy Test Pilot School at Patuxent River in Maryland, serving two years in flight test work at that station. During those tours, he participated in high-altitude tests and experiments in the development of the Navy's in–flight refueling system. He was project test pilot on the FSD *Skylancer* and was involved in testing the first angled deck on a U.S. Navy carrier. During his second tour to Patuxent for flight test work, the navy sent him to the Naval War College in Newport, Rhode Island. Upon graduation he became a staff officer at Atlantic Fleet Headquarters in Norfolk, in charge of aircraft readiness for the fleet. Being skipper of an aircraft squadron was a goal of any career pilot in the Navy and one that was of interest to Shepard. About this same time, NASA was developing Project Mercury and was seeking astronauts for America's space program.

Making Space History

Knowing that he met the required qualifications of NASA's advertised program, Shepard eagerly applied for a chance to serve his country and meet the challenge of the race to space. On April 27, 1959, NASA announced that Shepard and six other astronauts were selected as the first class of astronauts. A rigorous and intensive training program followed as preparations were being made for the first manned space flight. With the Russian space program forging ahead, it was imperative that a U.S. astronaut follow cosmonaut **Yury Gagarin** into space as soon as possible. Three astronauts, Shepard, Virgil Grissom and **John Glenn**, were selected to make three suborbital "up-and-down" missions to ready Mercury for orbital flight. Interest in the first manned American space flight was keen, forcing NASA to keep Shepard's identity secret until three days before the launch. At 9:45 A.M. on May 5th, 1961, Shepard, enclosed in the tiny bell-shaped Mercury capsule named *Freedom 7,* was thrust into space by a Redstone rocket to a distance of 2300 miles and a height of 113 miles above the surface of the Earth. The flight lasted only 15 minutes and 22 seconds and travelled at a speed of 5,180 mph. According to *Space Almanac,* Shepard, reporting from space that everything was "AOK," was weightless just five minutes

before splashdown in the Atlantic Ocean. The USS *Lake Champlain* spotted his orange and white parachute 297 miles downrange from Cape Canaveral. Just before landing, the heat shield was dropped 4 feet, pulling out a rubberized landing bag designed to reduce shock. Shepard exclaimed "Boy what a ride," according to Tim Furniss in *Manned Spaceflight Log,* and with that successful, text-book perfect launch, NASA's space program gained support from the government and from people around the world.

Shepard's performance also showed the world the tradition of engineering excellence, professionalism and dedication that was evident in the subsequent missions. About ten weeks after this historic flight another Mercury-Redstone blasted Virgil Grissom's spacecraft for a similar flight. Shepard continued his training and space preparation and was selected for one of the early Gemini flights, but in early 1964 his career was sharply changed by an inner–ear ailment called Meniere's syndrome, which causes an imbalance and a gradual degradation of hearing. The Navy doctors would not let Shepard fly solo in jet planes, which forced NASA to ground him. The offer of a job as Chief of the Astronaut office with NASA came along about this time, and it helped allay some of the intense disappointment that Shepard experienced. As Chief, Shepard was in charge of all phases of the astronaut training program and played an influential role in the selection of crews for upcoming missions. Periodic checks on his condition during this time showed a continued loss of hearing on the left side, and in May, 1968, he submitted to an experimental operation to insert a plastic tube to relieve the pressure in his inner ear. After waiting six months for the final results of the operation, Shepard was declared by NASA officials and doctors fully fit to fly and to resume his role in the space flight program.

A Ride to the Moon

Shepard worked extremely hard and long to ready himself for his next space endeavor, *Apollo 14,* which would last nine days and send a crew of three to the moon. The crew for this flight, Shepard as mission commander, Stuart Roosa as Command module pilot, and Edgar Mitchell as pilot of the lunar excursion module, was chosen in August, 1969, just after the successful moon landing by *Apollo 11.* The mission was tentatively scheduled for an October, 1970, launch date, but the explosion of the oxygen tank aboard *Apollo 13* called for several alterations in the *Apollo 14* spacecraft. One of the goals of this flight was to explore the Fra Mauro region of the Moon, and Shepard and Mitchell each spent more than 300 hours walking in desert areas and using simulators that resembled the lunar surface. A Saturn V rocket launched the *Apollo 14* capsule at 4:03 p.m. on January 31, 1971. The astronauts had chosen the name *Kitty Hawk* as a tribute to the first manned powered flight in 1903 and named the lunar lander *Antares* for the star on which it would orient itself just before descending to the Fra Mauro landing site. *Apollo 14* entered lunar orbit on February 4, with touchdown in the uplands of the cone crater scheduled for the next day. Shepard and Mitchell departed from *Kitty Hawk* and *Antares* and descended smoothly to the surface, coming to rest on an 8 degree slope. Shepard descended the lander's ladder, stepping on the moon at 9:53 A.M., February 5, becoming the fifth man to walk on the moon. With much emotion, he reported to Houston, "I'm on the surface. It's been a long way, and I'm here," as quoted by Anthony J. Cipriano in *America's Journeys into Space*. He and Mitchell then collected 43 pounds of lunar samples and deployed TV, communications and scientific equipment in their first extra vehicular activity (EVA), which lasted 4 hours, 49 minutes. Their second EVA lasted 4 hours, 35 minutes, and the two astronauts used a Modularized Equipment Transporter for this landing. It was a rickshaw-like device in which they pulled their tools, cameras and samples with them across the moon. Shepard and Mitchell set off the first two moonquakes to be read by seismic monitors planted by earlier *Apollo* moonwalkers. As they prepared to leave the lunar surface in *Antares*, Shepard, an avid golfer, surprised his audience by making the first golf shot on the Moon, rigging a 6-iron club head to the end of a digging tool and hitting a ball hundreds of yards. On February 6, *Kitty Hawk* rocketed out of lunar orbit and headed for Earth. After nearly three days of coasting flight, *Apollo 14* splashed down in the Pacific Ocean, 4.6 miles from the recovery vessel *New Orleans*, on February 9—216 hours, 42 minutes after launch.

Return to Private Life

At Shepard's retirement from NASA and the U.S. Navy on August 1, 1974, Dr. James C. Fletcher, NASA Administrator, praised the astronaut's dedication and determination in a *NASA News* bulletin. "Al Shepard was the first American to make a space flight and his determination to overcome a physical ailment after his suborbital mission carried him to a highly successful manned lunar landing mission." Shepard joined the private sector as partner and chairman of the Marathon Construction Company of Houston, Texas. He has become an extremely successful businessman in Houston, pursuing interests as a commercial property developer, a venture capital group partner, and director of mutual fund companies. He also chairs the board of the Mercury Seven Foundation, created by the six living Mercury Seven astronauts and Grissom's widow to raise money for science and engineering scholarships. The Mercury capsule *Freedom 7* is on display at the National Air and Space Museum in Washington, D.C., and the *Apollo 14*

command module *Kitty Hawk* is displayed at the Los Angeles County Museum in California.

SELECTED WRITINGS BY SHEPARD:

Books

(With others) *We Seven*, Simon and Schuster, 1962.

SOURCES:

Books

Bell, Joseph N., *Seven into Space: The Story of the Mercury Astronauts*, University of Chicago Press, 1960.
Caiden, Martin, *The Astronauts: The Story of Project Mercury America's Man-in-Space Program*, Dutton, 1960.
Cipriano, Anthony J., *America's Journeys into Space: The Astronauts of the United States*, Messner, 1979, pp. 136–140.
Furniss, Tim, *Manned Spaceflight Log*, Jane's Publishing, 1983.
Kennedy, Gregory P., *The First Men in Space*, Chelsea House, 1991.
Research Guide to American Historical Biography, Volume 5, Beacham Pub., 1991.
Spangenburg, Ray and Diane Moser, *Space Exploration; Space People from A-Z*, Facts-on-File, 1990.
Westman, Paul, *Alan Shepard: The First American in Space*, Dillon Press, 1979.
Wolf, Tom, *The Right Stuff*, Farrar Straus, 1979.

Periodicals

Cole, Dandridge, "Alan B. Shepard, Jr.," *Ad Astra*, July/August, 1991, p. 60.
Hall, A. J., "Climb up Cone Crater," *National Geographic*, Volume 140, July, 1971, p. 136–148.
NASA News (bulletin), NASA, July 19, 1974, p. 2.
Wainwright, Louden, "The Old Pro Gets His Shot at the Moon," *Life*, July 31, 1970.

—Sketch by Nancy E. Bard

Charles Scott Sherrington
1857-1952
English neurophysiologist

Charles Scott Sherrington

Charles Scott Sherrington helped to found the discipline of neurophysiology by his research on how nerve impulses are transmitted between the central nervous system and muscles. Sherrington focused much of his career on understanding the structure and the function of the nervous system. Drawing on the research of Spanish neuroanatomist **Santiago Ramón y Cajal**, Sherrington proposed viewing nervous activity as part of an integrated and complex system. For his work on how the central nervous system elicits motor activity from muscles, Sherrington shared the 1932 Nobel Prize in physiology or medicine with **Edgar Douglas Adrian**.

Born November 27, 1857, in London, England, Sherrington was the son of James Norton and Anne (Brookes) Sherrington. James Sherrington died while his son was still very young, and later Sherrington's mother married Caleb Rose, Jr., a physician in Ipswich, England. Rose was broadly and classically educated, and his home served as a gathering place for artists, writers, and scholars. Exposure to these diverse arts influenced Sherrington and was reflected in his own broad interests in the humanities and the sciences. After attending Ipswich Grammar School, Sherrington began medical training in 1875 at St. Thomas's Hospital in London. In 1879 he enrolled in Caius College at Cambridge University. Two years later, Sherrington began work in the laboratory of Michael Foster, England's foremost physiologist. In Foster's laboratory, Sherrington also met John Newport Langley, Newell Martin, Walter Gaskell, and Sheridan Lea, individuals who would become important physiologists in their own right.

Proposes an Integrated Nervous System

After earning a bachelor's degree in medicine in 1884, Sherrington left Cambridge to pursue graduate studies in German laboratories. He remained abroad for three years, receiving training and conducting research in physiology, histology, and pathology, and working in the laboratories of Rudolf Virchow, **Robert Koch**, and Friedrich Goltz, with whom he studied the central nervous system. Upon returning to England, Sherrington assumed a post teaching systematic physiology to medical students at his training site, St. Thomas's Hospital in London. He left this position in 1891 to become professor and superintendent of the Brown Institute for Advanced Physiological and Pathological Research. A year later, Sherrington married Ethel Mary Wright; their only child, Charles E. R. Sherrington, was born in 1897.

Sherrington accepted the physiology chair at the University of Liverpool in 1895. Seeking to understand the structures and the mechanisms that operated the nervous system, Sherrington began to draw on the work of Ramón y Cajal. Prior to the latter scientist's work in the late 1880s, neurophysiologists believed that nerve fibers formed a continuous network or system through the body. This proposition was known as the reticular theory. Ramón y Cajal refuted the reticular theory by using a silver-based dye developed by the Italian anatomist **Camillo Golgi**. Golgi's preparation stained individual nerve cells a black color and demonstrated to neuroanatomists that nerve cells were discrete entities and not part of a nexus as was previously thought. The new theory that saw nerve cells as independent units was called the neuron theory, or popularly, the neuron doctrine. Although nerve cells were discrete units, neurons in a series could form pathways through which information can be transmitted. Nerves—consisting of a bundle of fibers—relay sensations (like touch and smell) and instructions on motor activity (like moving an arm or a leg) by electrical impulses. Sherrington became interested in understanding how nerves formed integrative pathways between the central nervous system and muscles. He considered some simple reflexive behavior, such as the knee-jerk, and attempted to explain the neurophysiology of the phenomena. Finding that he had an insufficient knowledge of neural anatomy to conduct the research, Sherrington stoically devoted the next decade to mapping the pathways between the central nervous system and muscle groups and to identifying the sensory nerves that innervated muscle tissue.

Sherrington's commitment to understanding the neural pathways proved to have an important impact. He came to realize that a particular reflexive behavior was not controlled by a single pathway or an isolated response to a single stimulus. Rather, a simple reflex was the product of a complex process that involved the inhibition and excitation of many nerve cells in many different pathways. Sherrington concluded that the central nervous system was an integrated whole that coordinated multiple pathways to produce any single action. His contributions on this point were not only theoretical but experimental. He introduced seminal research strategies for studying questions of the central nervous system. For example, the spinal animal, an animal with a transected spinal cord, and the decerebrate rigid animal, an animal partially paralyzed by the excision of the cerebral cortex, were introduced as important approaches to exploring the activity of the nervous system. Sherrington's analysis of the hind limb scratch of a dog helped to elucidate neuronal action.

Continues Explorations of the Central Nervous System

Sherrington's study of the scratch reflex in dogs elucidated other important principles of how the central nervous system is organized. He concluded that reflexes can have "reciprocal innervation" so that inhibitory and excitatory reflexes are coordinated simultaneously. Sherrington also concluded that there are two levels on which actions are controlled—higher level control by the brain and lower level control by the muscle nerves. His most important idea perhaps reflected in the integrative scheme is that there is a break between one nerve cell and another, between brain and muscles, between inhibitory and excitatory processes. To describe this break, Sherrington coined the term "synapse." The idea of a synapse became important for two reasons. First, it acknowledged that nerve cells were not organized in the reticular fashion as it was previously argued. Second, understanding how synapses were transcended became the next challenge for twentieth-century neurophysiologists. Sherrington lucidly offered these ideas about the nervous system in his seminal work, *The Integrative Action of the Nervous System,* published in 1906.

In 1913 Sherrington left the University of Liverpool after eighteen years of service to assume the Waynflete Professorship of Physiology at Oxford University. The post offered Sherrington the opportunity to continue his research on the central nervous system, but the entry of Great Britain into World War I in August, 1914, meant Sherrington had to postpone his studies for some time. He joined the war effort, serving as chair of the Industrial Fatigue Board. Not satisfied with merely reading about the conditions of war-time industrial workers, in 1915 Sherrington worked incognito in a shell factory to experience first-hand the hardships and long shifts faced by workers. Although he managed to complete a textbook of physiology during the war period, Sherrington did not return to his normal research work until the mid–1920s. He successfully recruited a number of promising assistants, including E. G. T. Liddell and **John Carew Eccles**. Eccles would go on to win the 1963 Nobel Prize in physiology or medicine for research that had its roots in his stint in Sherrington's Oxford laboratory. Eccles, Liddell, and Sherrington's other students grew in reputation as the "Sherrington school," and their assistance allowed Sherrington to complete a minimum of an experiment a week.

Sherrington's research at Oxford after the 1920s differed from the work that he had been doing prior to World War I. Rather than studying the nervous system as a whole, Sherrington focused his attention on specific mechanisms in the central nervous system. He developed with Eccles the idea of a "motor unit" —a nerve cell that coordinates many muscle fibers. He also concluded that neuronal excitation and inhibition were separate and distinct processes; one was not merely the absence of the other.

Leads an Active Life During Retirement

Although Sherrington retired in 1936, four years after being named a Nobel Prize-winner, he maintained an active life after his formal retirement. He cultivated many of the interests that he had as child in the eclectic home of his stepfather, including poetry, history, and philosophy. In 1925 Sherrington wrote and published a book of poems titled *The Assaying of Brabantius.* His deep interests in philosophy and history were reflected in two post-retirement publications, 1941's *Man on His Nature* and 1946's *The Endeavor of Jean Fernel.* In addition to being a popular and sought-after speaker, Sherrington was a trustee of the British Museum in London and served as governor of the Ipswich School from which he had graduated.

In addition to the Nobel Prize, Sherrington garnered virtually every honor that could be given to a British scientist. At the time of his death in 1952, he held memberships in more than forty scholarly societies and had been given honorary degrees from twenty-two universities. Most notably, Sherrington was a past president of the Royal Society of London (1920–1925), and recipient of the Knight Grand Cross of the British Empire in 1922 and the Order of Merit in 1924. He died on March 4, 1952, from heart failure.

SELECTED WRITINGS BY SHERRINGTON:

Books

The Integrative Action of the Nervous System, Yale University Press, 1906.
Reflex Activity of the Spinal Cord, Oxford University Press, 1932.
The Brain and Its Mechanism, Cambridge University Press, 1933.
Man on His Nature, Cambridge University Press, 1941.

SOURCES:

Books

Brazier, Mary, "The Historical Development of Neurophysiology," in *Handbook of Physiology, Section I: Neurophysiology,* edited by John Field, H. W. Magoun, and Volume E. Hall, American Physiological Society, 1959.
Fearing, Franklin, *Reflex Action: A Study in the History of Physiological Psychology,* Johns Hopkins University Press, 1930.
Swazey, Judith P., *Reflexes and Motor Integration: Sherrington's Concept of Integrative Action,* Harvard University Press, 1969.

Periodicals

Denny-Brown, Derek, "The Sherrington School of Physiology," *Journal of Neurophysiology,* Volume 20, 1957, pp. 543–48.
Fulton, John F., "Sir Charles Scott Sherrington, O. M.," *Journal of Neurophysiology,* Volume 15, 1952, pp. 167–90.
Penfield, Wilder, "Sir Charles Sherrington, Poet and Philosopher," *Brain,* Volume 80, 1957, pp. 402–10.

—Sketch by D. George Joseph

Dolores Cooper Shockley
1930-

American pharmacologist

Dolores Cooper Shockley is the first African American woman to earn a Ph.D. from Purdue University and the first African American woman in the United States to receive a Ph.D. in pharmacology.

In 1977 she became chair of the department of microbiology at Meharry Medical College.

Shockley was born in Clarksdale, Mississippi, on April 21, 1930. She enrolled at Louisiana State University in 1947, intending to pursue a major in pharmacy with the goal of eventually opening her own drug store. During her college years, however, Shockley's interests shifted from retail business to research. When she earned her bachelor of science degree in 1951, she decided to continue her education in the field of pharmacology at Purdue University in Lafayette, Indiana. She was awarded her M.S. at Purdue in 1953 and then her Ph.D. in pharmacology two years later. After graduation, Shockley used a Fulbright Fellowship to do postdoctoral research at the University of Copenhagen.

When Shockley returned to the United States, she accepted an appointment as assistant professor of pharmacology at Meharry Medical College in Nashville, Tennessee. She was greeted in her new job with a certain amount of suspicion, she later told an interviewer for *Ebony,* because "some men thought that I was just working temporarily." She soon put those doubts to rest and became a valued and respected member of the faculty. In 1967 Shockley was promoted to associate professor, and ten years later she became head of the college's department of microbiology. She has since served also as Meharry's foreign student advisor and its liaison for international activities to the Association of American Medical Colleges. Shockley's research interests have focused on the consequences of drug action on stress, the effects of hormones on connective tissue, the relationships between drugs and nutrition, and the measurement of non-narcotic analgesics (pain killers). She was visiting assistant professor at the Einstein College of Medicine in New York City from 1959 to 1962 and was a recipient of the Lederle Faculty Award from 1963 to 1966. Shockley is married and the mother of four children.

SOURCES:

Periodicals

"A Veteran at Meharry Medical College," *Ebony,* August, 1977, p. 116.

—Sketch by David E. Newton

William Shockley
1910-1989
American physicist

William Shockley was a physicist whose work in the development of the transistor led to a Nobel Prize. By the late 1950s, his company, the Shockley Transistor Corporation, was part of a rapidly growing industry created as a direct result of his contributions to the field. Shockley shared the 1956 Nobel Prize in physics with **John Bardeen** and **Walter Brattain**, both of whom collaborated with him on developing the point contact transistor. Later, Shockley became involved in a controversial topic for which he had no special training, but in which he became avidly interested: the genetic basis of intelligence. During the 1960s, he argued, in a series of articles and speeches, that people of African descent have a genetically inferior mental capacity when compared to those with Caucasian ancestry. This hypothesis became the subject of intense and acrimonious debate.

William Bradford Shockley was born in London, England, on February 13, 1910, to William Hillman Shockley, an American mining engineer, and May (Bradford) Shockley, a mineral surveyor. The Shockleys, living in London on a business assignment when William was born, returned to California in 1913. Shockley did not enter elementary school at the usual age, however, because, as he told *Men of Space* author Shirley Thomas, "My parents had the idea that the general educational process was not as good as would be done at home." As a result, he was not enrolled in public schools until he had reached the age of eight.

Shockley's interest in physics developed early, inspired in part by a neighbor who taught the subject at Stanford and by his own parents' coaching and encouragement. By the time he had completed his secondary education at Palo Alto Military Academy and Hollywood High School at the age of seventeen, Shockley had made his commitment to a career in physics. Shockley and his parents agreed that he should spend a year at the University of California at Los Angeles (UCLA) before attending the California Institute of Technology (Caltech), where he earned a bachelor's degree in physics in 1932. Offered a teaching fellowship at the Massachusetts Institute of Technology (MIT), Shockley taught while working on his doctoral dissertation, "Calculations of Wave Functions for Electrons in Sodium Chloride Crystals," for which he was awarded his Ph.D. in 1936. Shockley later told Thomas that this research in solid-state physics "led into my subsequent activities in the transistor field."

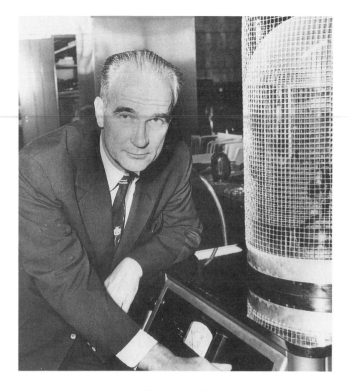

William Shockley

Begins Research on Semiconductors at Bell Labs

Upon graduation from MIT, Shockley accepted an offer to work at the Bell Telephone Laboratories in Murray Hill, New Jersey. An important factor in that decision was the opportunity it gave him to work with **Clinton Davisson**, who was to win the 1937 Nobel Prize in physics for proving **Louis Victor de Broglie**'s theory that electrons assumed the characteristics of waves. Shockley's first assignment at Bell was the development of a new type of vacuum tube that would serve as an amplifier. But, almost as soon as he had arrived at Bell, he began to think of a radically new approach to the transmission of electrical signals using solid-state components rather than conventional vacuum tubes. At that time, vacuum tubes constituted the core of communication devices such as the radio because they have the ability to rectify (create a unidirectional current) and multiply electronic signals. They have a number of serious practical disadvantages, however, as they are relatively fragile and expensive, and have relatively short life-spans.

As early as the mid–1930s, Bell scientists had begun to think about alternatives to vacuum tubes in communication systems, and by 1939, Shockley was experimenting with semiconducting materials to achieve that transition. Semiconductors are materials such as silicon and germanium that conduct an electrical current much less efficiently than do conductors like silver and copper, but more effectively than do insulators like glass and most kinds of plastic.

Shockley knew that one semiconductor, galena, had been used as a rectifier in early radio sets, and his experience in solid-state physics led him to believe that such materials might have even wider application in new kinds of communication devices.

World War II Interrupts Research

The limited research Shockley was able to complete on this concept of alternative conductors was unsuccessful, largely because the materials available to him at the time were not pure enough. In 1940, war was imminent, and Shockley soon became involved in military research. His first job involved the development of radar equipment at a Bell field station in Whippany, New Jersey. In 1942, he became research director of the U.S. Navy's Anti-Submarine Warfare Operations Research Group at Columbia University, and served as a consultant to the Secretary of War from 1944 to 1945.

In 1945, Shockley returned to Bell Labs as director of its research program on solid-state physics. Together with John Bardeen, a theoretical physicist, and Walter Brattain, an experimental physicist, Shockley returned to his study of semiconductors as a means of amplification. After more than a year of failed trials, Bardeen suggested that the movement of electric current was being hampered by electrons trapped within a semiconductor's surface layer. That suggestion caused Shockley's team to suspend temporarily its efforts to build an amplification device and to concentrate instead on improving their understanding of the nature of semiconductors.

Bardeen and Brattain Bring Shockley's Idea to Fruition

By 1947, Bardeen and Brattain had learned enough about semiconductors to make another attempt at building Shockley's device. This time they were successful. Their device consisted of a piece of germanium with two gold contacts on one side and a tungsten contact on the opposite side. When an electrical current was fed into one of the gold contacts, it appeared in a greatly amplified form on the other side. The device was given the name transistor (for *trans*fer re*sistor*). More specifically, it was referred to as a point contact transistor because of the three metal contacts used in it.

The first announcement of the transistor appeared in a short article in the July 1, 1948 edition of the *New York Times.* Few readers had the vaguest notion of the impact the fingernail-sized device would have on the world. A few months later, Shockley proposed a modification of the point contact transistor. He suggested using a thin layer of P-type semiconductor (in which the charge is carried by holes) sandwiched between two layers of N-type semiconductor (where the charge is carried by electrons). When Brattain built this device, now called the junction transistor, he found that it worked much better than did its point contact predecessor. In 1956, the Nobel Prize for physics was awarded jointly to Shockley, Bardeen, and Brattain for their development of the transistor.

Shockley left Bell Labs in 1954 (some sources say 1955). In the decade that followed, he served as director of research for the Weapons Systems Evaluation Group of the Department of Defense, and as visiting professor at Caltech in 1954–55. He then founded the Shockley Transistor Corporation to turn his work on the development of the transistor to commercial advantage. Shockley Transistor was later incorporated into Beckman Instruments, Inc., and then into Clevite Transistor in 1960. The company went out of business in 1968.

Studies the Genetic Basis of Intelligence

In 1963, Shockley embarked on a new career, accepting an appointment at Stanford University as its first Alexander M. Poniatoff Professor of Engineering and Applied Science. Here he became interested in genetics and the origins of human intelligence, in particular, the relationship between race and the Intelligence Quotient (IQ). Although he had no background in psychology, genetics, or any related field, Shockley began to read on these topics and formulate his own hypotheses. Using data taken primarily from U.S. Army pre-induction IQ tests, Shockley came to the conclusion that the genetic component of a person's intelligence was based on racial heritage. He proposed that people of African ancestry were inherently less intelligent than those of Caucasian lineage. He also surmised that the more "white genes" a person of African descent carried, the more closely her or his intelligence corresponded to that of the general white population. He ignited further controversy with his suggestion that inferior individuals (those whose IQ numbered below 100) be paid to undergo voluntary sterilization.

The social implications of Shockley's theories were and still are profound. Many scholars regarded Shockley's whole analysis as flawed, and they rejected his conclusions. Others were outraged that such views were even expressed publicly. Educators pointed out the significance of these theories for their field, a point pursued by Shockley himself when he argued that compensatory programs for blacks were doomed because of their inherent genetic inferiority. For a number of years, Shockley could count on the fact that his speeches would be interrupted by boos and catcalls, provided that they were allowed to go forward at all.

During his life, Shockley was awarded many honors, including the U.S. Medal of Merit in 1946, the Morris E. Liebmann Award of the Institute of Radio Engineers in 1951, the Comstock Prize of the National Academy of Sciences in 1954, and the Institute of Electrical and Electronics Gold Medal in 1972 and its Medal of Honor in 1980. He was named to the National Inventor's Hall of Fame in 1974. Shockley remained at Stanford until retirement in 1975, when he was appointed Emeritus Professor of Electrical Engineering. In 1933, Shockley had married Jean Alberta Bailey, with whom he had three children, Alison, William, and Richard. After their 1955 divorce, Shockley married Emily I. Lanning. He died in San Francisco on August 11, 1989, of prostate cancer.

SELECTED WRITINGS BY SHOCKLEY:

Books

Electrons and Holes in Semiconductors, with Applications to Transistor Electronics, Van Nostrand, 1950.
(Editor) *Imperfections of Nearly Perfect Crystals,* Wiley, 1952.
(With Walter A. Gong) *Mechanics,* C. E. Merrill, 1966.

Periodicals

(With Walter Brattain) "Density of Surface States on Silicon Deduced from Contact Potential Measurements," *Physical Review,* Volume 72, 1947, p. 345.
(With G. L. Pearson) "Modulation of Conductance of Thin Films of Semiconductors by Surface Charges," *Physical Review,* Volume 74, 1948, pp. 232–33.

SOURCES:

Books

McGraw-Hill Modern Scientists and Engineers, Volume 3, McGraw-Hill, 1980, pp. 111–12.
National Geographic Society, Special Publications Division, *Those Inventive Americans,* National Geographic Society, 1971, pp. 209–16.
Thomas, Shirley, *Men of Space,* Volume 4, Chilton Books, 1962, pp. 170–205.
Nobel Prize Winners, H. W. Wilson, 1987, pp. 962–64.

—*Sketch by David E. Newton*

Eugene M. Shoemaker
1928-
American geologist

Eugene M. Shoemaker is a geologist whose research interests and expertise range far beyond the Earth. Shoemaker has studied impact craters (craters created by the collision of an asteroid or comet and a planet) on both the Earth and the Moon, as well as searched for the comets and asteroids that could have caused the craters. He was a key figure in formulating the scientific exploration of the lunar surface during the 1960s. Intrigued by the study of craters in general, Shoemaker then turned his focus back to the planet Earth and has become a leader in studying the impact history of the planet.

Eugene Merle Shoemaker was born in Los Angeles on April 28, 1928, to George Estel and Muriel May Scott Shoemaker. His mother was a teacher, and his father at different times worked in teaching, business, farming and for motion picture studios. The family moved to Oregon, New York, Wyoming, and finally back to Los Angeles when Shoemaker was fourteen years old. He has one younger sister. Shoemaker's interest in geology coalesced early in his life. He began collecting rocks, minerals and fossils when he was seven. He took classes in mineralogy and geology at the science museum in Buffalo, New York, starting when he was nine. By the time he finished high school in Los Angeles he wanted to be a geologist. Shoemaker earned his bachelor's degree in geology from the California Institute of Technology in 1947 and his master's degree the next year.

In July 1948 he moved to Grand Junction, Colorado, to join the United States Geological Survey (U.S.G.S.) as a geologist. For two years he searched for uranium deposits and investigated salt structures in Colorado and Utah. During the early 1950s he concentrated on the geochemistry, volcanology, and structure of the rocks of the Colorado Plateau. He took a leave from the U.S.G.S. to study at Princeton University from 1950 to 1951 and 1953 to 1954, receiving his M.A. from Princeton in 1954. During the late 1950s Shoemaker became interested in craters, both those created by meteorite impacts and by nuclear explosions. His doctoral thesis was to draw the first detailed geological map of the huge Meteor Crater in Arizona, also known as the Barringer Crater. In 1960 Shoemaker and Edward C. T. Chao discovered the presence of the mineral coesite at Meteor Crater. Since coesite is a high-pressure form of silica that forms when quartz is squeezed at intense pressures, Shoemaker and Chao had essentially proven that the Barringer Crater was indeed formed by a meteorite striking the Earth, rather than by volcanic action as some scientists had thought. That year Shoemaker received his Ph.D. from Princeton.

From Arizona to the Moon

Shoemaker had begun working on Meteor Crater and other impact-related craters because of his interest in the Moon and its pocketed surface. "I got a bug in my ear in 1948, shortly after I went to work for the U.S. Geological Survey, that during my professional career human beings would go to the Moon. I made up my mind then that I was going to be the first scientist to get to the Moon," he told *Astronomy* in 1993. During the 1960s, the decade that astronauts did indeed walk on the moon, Shoemaker became heavily involved with the science of lunar exploration.

In 1960 Shoemaker established a lunar geological time scale and developed improved ways to map the Moon's surface. He then organized a U.S.G.S. unit on astrogeology at the Survey's office in Menlo Park, California, where he had been working. (The unit later became a full branch and moved to Flagstaff, Arizona, in 1965.) In 1962 and 1963 the U.S.G.S. loaned Shoemaker to the National Aeronautics and Space Administration (NASA) to help develop plans for exploring the Moon. For several months Shoemaker was acting director of NASA's Manned Space Sciences Division, which was charged with formulating the scientific objectives for the first astronauts to land on the moon.

While an administrator at NASA and the U.S.G.S., Shoemaker continued to work on terrestrial impact craters in addition to attempting to figure out what the lunar surface was like. He promoted using television systems to investigate the geology of other moons and planets. Shoemaker was in charge of the television experiments on Project Ranger and, later, Project Surveyor. (From 1979 to 1990 he was also co-investigator for the television set-up on the two *Voyager* probes that visited the outer planets of the solar system.) During the mid–1960s Shoemaker studied photographs of the lunar surface sent back by exploratory spacecraft to determine the nature of the surface. With photos from the Ranger 7 probe, Shoemaker used his method of "photoclinometry," which computed the steepness of craters' edges by the amount of shadow they threw onto the ground. He announced that the surface was quite smooth. With later photographs, Shoemaker determined that the Moon is predominantly gray and that it is covered with shallow, silty soil. (Before the *Surveyor* spacecraft landed on the surface, there was worry that a thick layer of dust might preclude a probe landing.) Shoemaker became the principal scientist for the geological field studies of the *Apollo* landings from 1965 to 1970.

In 1966 Shoemaker resigned as administrator of the U.S.G.S. astrogeology branch so that he could return to full-time research as chief scientist in Flagstaff. He began an association with the California Institute of Technology (Caltech), as a visiting professor in 1962 and 1987, and a full-time professor of geology from 1969 to 1985. He chaired Caltech's Division of Geological and Planetary Sciences from 1969 to 1972.

By this time Shoemaker's experience with Moon studies prompted him to consider the objects that create impact craters on the Earth as well. His research in the late 1960s shifted to Earth-crossing asteroids, those objects that one day might hit the earth and form another Meteor Crater. He decided to try to catalogue the asteroids, a task that would take assiduous sky-searching. At Caltech he hired the young geologist Eleanor Helin to begin an asteroid search program. He and Helin started in 1973 to use the 18-inch Schmidt telescope atop Palomar Mountain in California for the first-ever systematic asteroid search, named the Palomar Planet-Crossing Asteroid Survey. It took them six months to find their first asteroid, and two and a half years for the second one. Eventually they decided to step up their search and spend more nights at the telescope.

Shoemaker has continued to supervise the hunt for near-Earth asteroids. He calculated that about 1,000 to 1,500 asteroids at least half a mile across are on potential collision courses with the Earth. When Helin left the search in 1982, Shoemaker's wife Carolyn soon joined the hunt, renamed the Palomar Asteroid and Comet Survey. The two Shoemakers developed a stereoscopic technique for comparing pairs of film: one eye looks at one photograph, the other eye looks at a snapshot taken 45 minutes to an hour later, and any moving asteroid or comet appears to float above the combined image.

Mass Extinctions and Monster Collisions

Shoemaker also continued to work on the impact history of the Earth. In 1980, his line of research got a shot of excitement when a group led by the physicist **Luis Alvarez** suggested that a cataclysmic impact had struck the Earth 65 million years ago, triggering the chain of events that led to the death of the dinosaurs and many other species. Scientists had previously blamed the dinosaurs' demise on many other causes, from climate change to constipation. The Berkeley group offered as proof the thin layer of iridium appearing in 65-million-year-old sediments around the world. Iridium is a rare element on Earth, but extraterrestrial sources like meteorites are relatively rich in iridium. Thus, the Alvarez group suggested, a giant meteorite must have struck the Earth, kicking up a cloud of dust that covered the Earth, blocking the planet from sunlight and causing a massive extinction.

Soon after the Alvarez hypothesis, the hunt began for the giant scar that must have been left by such an impact. Scientists have identified the Chicxulub crater, buried under water and sediments off the coast of the Yucatan, as the most likely candidate for the impact's calling card, since it is at least 120 miles across. However, a smaller crater in Iowa—22 miles across—has been dated at roughly the same age of 65 million years. Shoemaker suggested that it was just too coincidental to have two large craters of the same age. He proposed instead that multiple impacts smashed the Earth, one right after another on the scale of geologic time. And since the probability of several huge meteorites coming at the same time is slim, Shoemaker suggested that perhaps a comet had broken up and shed its remains on our planet in a destructive repetition, leaving both the Mexican and the Iowa craters. Most scientists now believe that the Chicxulub crater is the scar of the primary impact that killed off the dinosaurs. The question of multiple impacts has not been resolved.

Shoemaker's career has been recognized with numerous honors, including honorary doctorates of science from Arizona State College, Temple University and the University of Arizona. He is a fellow of the American Academy of Arts and Sciences and a member of the National Academy of Sciences. Among other awards, he has received the NASA Medal for Scientific Achievement, the Kuiper Prize of the American Astronomical Society, and the National Medal of Science.

Shoemaker married Carolyn Jean Spellman in 1951. They have two daughters, Christine and Linda, and one son, Patrick. Carolyn Shoemaker, a former teacher, became involved with the Palomar asteroid search after her three children were grown. She has since discovered more comets than any other person in history except for the nineteenth-century observer Jean-Louis Pons. But only twenty-six comets bear Pons's name; that record was broken in 1992, as Carolyn Shoemaker found her twenty-seventh comet. The Shoemakers work at spotting asteroids for a week at Palomar every month. Gene uses the telescope to take the photographs; Carolyn searches the film for fuzzy objects that might have moved. Together they have discovered more than three-hundred asteroids, some of which are named after the Shoemakers' children and grandchildren.

One of the comets found by Carolyn Shoemaker became a once-in-a-lifetime chance for stargazers to witness a rare event. Comet Shoemaker-Levy 9, discovered in March 1993, collided with Jupiter in July 1994. Gene Shoemaker calculated that this sort of celestial collision happens once in a millennia, or once in a thousand years. "I've been hoping for many

decades that I would live long enough to see the impact of a significant object," he told Alexandra Witze in an interview. "I was thinking it might be something small on Earth. I never dreamed we would discover something to impact another planet."

SOURCES:

Periodicals

Astronomy, June, 1993, pp. 13–17.
Time, February 1, 1992, p. 58.

Other

Shoemaker, Eugene M., interview with Alexandra Witze conducted July 22, 1993.

—*Sketch by Alexandra Witze*

Yuly Mikhaylovich Shokalsky
1856-1940
Russian geographer and oceanographer

Yuly Mikhaylovich Shokalsky was a pioneering geographer and oceanographer whose career spanned the transition between Czarist Russia and the Soviet Union. Although the majority of his works have not been translated from Russian, he has influenced the fields of cartography, hydrography, and hydrometeorology. One of his most important accomplishments was the oceanographic exploration of the Black Sea. He also compiled a standard general map of Russia, and there are twelve geographic features in that country named in his honor, including Shokalsky Island in the Kara Sea.

Shokalsky was born in St. Petersburg, Russia, in October, 1856. He demonstrated an early interest in geography, and in 1873 he entered the Naval College in St. Petersburg. He graduated in 1877 and served briefly with the Russian fleet in the Baltic Sea. The duties of a naval officer, however, left little time for his scientific interests, and in 1878 he enrolled in the Naval Academy. He graduated in 1880, and in 1881 he was put in charge of the marine meteorology division at the Central Physics Observatory. Shokalsky also worked at the Main Hydrographic Administration, measuring and mapping surface waters for navigation. In 1882, he published his first scientific paper, "On Forecasting Weather and Storms."

Shokalsky began his teaching career at the Naval College in 1883, where he would teach geography and marine description until 1908. During this period, he also served in the Russian navy's department of hydrography. He was named director of the naval library in 1890, and in 1907 he was placed in charge of the hydrometeorological division. Hydrometeorology is the study of the effects of water in the atmosphere, such as hail, rain, or clouds.

In 1900, Shokalsky began designing an oceanographic project in the Arctic Ocean which was to last fifteen years. He played a key role in the preparations for the icebreaker expeditions which discovered Severnaja Zemlja, a group of islands off the northern coast of Russia near the North Pole. In 1908, Shokalsky moved to the Naval Academy, where he became the first professor of oceanography in Russia. He continued to teach physical geography and meteorology, and in 1908 he helped organize the Eleventh International Congress on Navigation in 1908, which was held in St. Petersburg.

Shokalsky published *Okeanografia* ("Oceanography") in 1917; this is his most famous work. Here, he argued that all marine phenomena are interdependent. Shokalsky saw all bodies of saltwater as being interconnected in some fashion, and he later maintained that there was a "worldwide ocean." This book also discussed the methodology and techniques for making scientific observations from a ship. *Okeanografia* was both popular and scientifically well respected, and it earned prizes for its author from the Russian Academy of Sciences in 1919 and the Paris Academy of Sciences in 1923.

Plans and Executes Exploration of the Black Sea

In 1909, the Hydrographic Administration commissioned Shokalsky to lead an oceanographic exploration of the Black Sea. He developed all aspects of the project from planning to methodology, designing the expedition to include the Kerchenskiy Proliv strait, the Bosporus and Dardanelles straits, as well as the Azov and Marmara seas. His plans, as it turned out, were long delayed; the outbreak of World War I, the collapse of Czarist Russia, and the Bolshevik Revolution made it impossible to conduct the first expedition until 1923. At first Shokalsky was only able to concentrate on the narrowest section of the Black Sea, near the Anatolian coast of Turkey. But by 1925, he had the resources to expand the survey, but it still took fifty-three voyages and twelve years to complete the project.

Shokalsky oversaw the extraction of over 1600 hydrological and 2000 soil and biological samples. Some of the most important accomplishments of this expedition were discoveries relating to the density of seawater. Scientific opinion had previously held that distinct layers of different chemical composition existed in relation to depth, but Shokalsky demonstrated a high level of mobility between the layers and perpetual intermingling. The expedition was also involved in studying the Northern Sea Route in the hope of developing it. The project drew to a close in 1935.

During this period, Shokalsky served in a variety of academic and official posts. He remained on the faculty at the Naval Academy until 1930, and he added teaching responsibilities at Leningrad State University in 1925. He was elected president of the Russian Geographic Society in 1914, and following the Soviet Revolution he served as president of the Geographic Society of the U.S.S.R. from 1917 to 1931. He had his hand in the compilation and editing of a number of geographic maps and atlases. He was responsible for a new topographical map of the North Polar region; he also produced what was to become the standard general map of Russia. Working with A. A. Tillo, he was able to calculate the surface of the Asiatic region of Russia and the lengths of the most prominent rivers.

At the age of seventy-six, Shokalsky showed no signs of slackening the pace of his scientific endeavors. He served on a commission to develop programs for the Second International Polar Year (1932–33), and he pressed for oceanographic studies to be included. In 1933, he sat on the organizing committee of the Fourth Hydrologic Conference of Baltic Nations. He was the Soviet delegate to the Fourteenth International Geographical Congress in Warsaw the following year.

Shokalsky continued to teach at Leningrad State University until the time of his death. This distinguished academic and field worker was a member of fifteen foreign geographic societies. A prolific writer, Shokalsky published over 1300 articles during his career. In 1929, the American Geographical Society bestowed on him their Cullum Geographical Medal. Presented to those "who distinguish themselves by geographical discoveries, or in the advancement of geographical science," it was the first awarding of the medal in four years. The Russian Geographic Society bestowed the title of "honored scientist" to his long list of accomplishments. Shokalsky died in Leningrad on March 26, 1940.

SELECTED WRITINGS BY SHOKALSKY:

Books

Okeanografia, [Petrograd], 1917.

Periodicals

"O predskazanii veroyatnoy pogody i shtormov," (title means "On Forecasting Weather and Storms"), *Morskoi sbornik,* Volume 192, 1882, pp. 87–125.

SOURCES:

Books

Gillespie, Charles, editor, *Dictionary of Scientific Biography,* Volume 12, Scribner's, 1975.
Prokhorov, A. M., editor, *Great Soviet Encyclopedia,* Volume 29, Macmillan, 1982.

Periodicals

"The Medal Awards of the American Geographical Society," *Science,* March 28, 1930, pp. 333–334.

—Sketch by Chris McGrail

Vladimir Borisovich Shtokman
1909-1968

Russian oceanographer

Recognized among Soviet scientists, Vladimir Borisovich Shtokman influenced the development of physical oceanography in the former Soviet Union as well as around the world. By focusing on the relationship between the overall wind field and current field—rather than looking at wind and current velocities at a given point—Shtokman led the way into a new era in understanding the overall dynamics of ocean currents. Shtokman also formulated important equations by which the total transport capability of ocean currents could be determined. In an article in the 1969 issue of *Oceanography,* fellow scientist A. D. Dobrovol'skiy called Shtokman "one of the greatest physical oceanologists of our country."

Shtokman was born on March 11, 1909, in Moscow, where his father was a mechanical and construction engineer. Shtokman attended the First Moscow University, where he joined the mathematics department of the physical mathematics faculty in 1929. There he decided to specialize in geophysics, finding his niche in oceanography and quickly gaining recognition for his work. During his tenure at the First Moscow University, the geophysics curriculum of the physical mathematics faculty split in two, becoming the Moscow Geological Exploration Institute and the Moscow Hydrometeorological Institute. Shtokman connected with the latter because it allowed him to work on the dynamics of the oceans, as well as to pursue his intense interest in mathematics and logic.

Rises to Prominence in the Scientific Community

During the early 1930s, Shtokman rose from senior lab assistant in the hydrological division of the State Oceanographic Institute, located in Yekaterininskaya Gavan', to a senior scientific position, which he acquired after successfully leading an expedition to Motovskiy Zaliv (Murman Peninsula). In 1934 he transferred to Baku to establish the All-Union Institute of Fisheries and Oceanography's physical oceanology laboratory, which he headed for approximately eight years. It was here that Shtokman's career began in earnest. His first professional journal article was published during this year, and he continued to write until his death in 1968, producing more than one hundred articles. According to Dobrovol'skiy, these publications became models of well-organized oceanographic research.

In 1938, Shtokman was awarded the degree of candidate of physical and mathematical science. A year later the USSR Academy of Sciences recognized his achievements in the field of oceanography by inviting him to join the staff of the Institute of Theoretical Geophysics. Shtokman accepted and began work in the sea physics division. Once settled as a researcher at the institute, he commenced his career as a teacher when, in addition to his full-time position at the institute, he began teaching oceanography at the Moscow Hydrometeorological Institute. His research and teaching duties, however, were soon interrupted by World War II.

In the early 1940s Shtokman joined the Arctic Research Institute in Krasnoyarsk because of his background investigations on the mixing of the Atlantic Ocean in the Arctic Basin. Two years later he transferred to the oceanology laboratory of the Academy of Sciences, also in Krasnoyarsk. Later that year he moved back to Moscow, where he remained for the rest of his life. In 1944 he received the degree of doctor of physical and mathematical science and two years later was appointed head of the physical oceanology division of the Institute of Oceanology of the Academy of Sciences. In 1947 he rose to the position of professor of geophysics.

According to Dobrovol'skiy in *Oceanography,* Shtokman dedicated himself to the study of the dynamics of ocean currents. "His first great achievement in this field," Dobrovol'skiy pointed out, "was his development of the idea of wind variations affecting these currents. He showed that if the wind direction is constant, but the speed not constant (transverse nonuniformity, as he called it), countercurrents will be created transversely on the sea surface, i.e., there will be currents flowing in the direction opposite to that of the wind.... The development of this idea subsequently led Shtokman to formulate the theory of oceanic equatorial countercurrents and then to interpret the features of current systems in straits and around islands."

A scientist, educator, writer, and participant in over fifteen ocean expeditions, Shtokman also made time for other pursuits. A naturalist, he especially enjoyed hiking through the woodlands around Moscow with his dog by his side. He loved dogs, and enjoyed a huge collection of pictures and statuettes of his favorite animal, as well as monographs on dog breeding and some rare dog magazines. In addition, he collected paintings, about which he was knowledgeable. He was married to Galina Vasil'yevna.

Shtokman had been diagnosed with heart disease when he was forty-eight, but he had been well and productive during most of the following eleven years. He passed away suddenly during a trip to the country on June 14, 1968. Upon his death, his colleagues named a research vessel in his honor. The *RV Shtokman* has completed more than twenty major expeditions—primarily in the Atlantic, Arctic, and Indian Oceans; the Baltic and Black Seas; and the Bering Strait—continuing the work of a scientist who influenced the development of physical oceanography for four decades.

SELECTED WRITINGS BY SHTOKMAN:

Periodicals

"Are Countercurrents Possible in an Unbounded Sea Due to Local Variations of Wind?," *Meteorologiya i Gidrologiya,* Number 5, 1947.
"On the Magnitude of the Deflection of Sea Currents Caused by Bottom Relief," *Meteorologiya i Gidrologiya,* Number 8, 1952.
"A Scientific Conference on Sea Currents," *Okeanologiya,* Volume 4, 1964.
"A Development of the Theory of Sea and Ocean Circulation over 50 Years in the USSR," *Okeanologiya,* Volume 7, 1967.

SOURCES:

Periodicals

Dobrovol'skiy, A. D., "Vladimir Borisovich Shtokman," *Oceanography,* Volume 9, 1969, pp. 1–8.

—*Sketch by Patricia M. McAdams*

Robert E. Shurney
American aeronautical engineer

Perhaps the most noteworthy of Robert E. Shurney's engineering accomplishments was the development of the wheels for the lunar roving vehicle (LRV) or "moon buggy" used by America's Apollo astronauts in the early 1970s. Shurney has also been active in doing tests under weightless conditions, and has logged over six hundred hours of weightlessness in tests aboard the weightless KC–135 aircraft.

Shurney obtained his physics degree from A & I State University in Nashville, Tennessee, before accepting a position as an aeronautical engineer at Alabama's Marshall Space Flight Center in 1962. Though his appointment came only through he direct urging of Attorney General Robert Kennedy, Shurney soon became something of an expert on microgravity, or weightlessness, spending a great deal of time in the weightless conditions created by the KC–135 Zero 9 aircraft. A converted Air Force tanker, the KC–135 describes a parabolic flight path; during the final 30 seconds of its flight the aircraft approaches free-fall, creating a condition similar to the weightlessness that affects free-falling spacecraft and their passengers. Much of Shurney's work in the KC–135 involved perfecting space toilets (or refuse disposal units) and other devices that had been proposed for use in space. Although Shurney had a hand in designing the toilets for the space shuttle, his most important work as a designer of space commodes went into NASA's Skylab.

Shurney's greatest contribution to the space program, however, was his design for the tires used on the Apollo moon buggy. The moon buggy required wheels that conformed to very strict standards: they had to be compact, yet strong enough to withstand sudden bumps and jolts; they had to be light-weight, so as not to add substantially to the payload of the Apollo rocket; and they could not kick up a great deal of the flour-like dust that covered the surface of the moon. Shurney's design, which prevailed over others under consideration, called for tires to be made from a spring-wire mesh; such a construction would be strong, light, had good traction, and would resist abrasion and other kinds of damage as they rolled over rocks and rough surfaces. In addition, wire would withstand the extreme temperatures found on the moon better than rubber. Commenting on the requirements for a moon tire, S. F. Morea, the LRV project manager at NASA, commented in *Machine Design* magazine that upon hitting a rock on the moon at ten or twelve miles per hour there was no way to know how high the wheel would bounce, hence the need for a tire with considerable resilience.

In addition to the moon tire, Shurney helped construct the Penitromiter, a device used by astronauts to measure the density and depth of the lunar "topsoil" as well as any vibrations present on the moon's surface. He also made improvements to the design of the spacecraft's solar panels, making it possible to retrieve and reuse the panels once they'd been deployed.

Shurney and his wife, the former Susie Flynt, have four children: Darrell, Glyndon, Glenn, and Ronald.

SOURCES:

Books

Blacks in Science & Medicine, Hemisphere, 1990, p. 213.
Van Sertima, Ivan, editor, *Blacks in Science: Ancient and Modern,* Transaction Books, 1984, pp. 249–251.

Periodicals

Machine Design, March 19, 1970, pp. 40–42.
Oakwood College Update, November, 1993, pp. 6–7.

—*Sketch by Karl Preuss*

Kai M. Siegbahn
1918-
Swedish physicist

Kai M. Siegbahn, the son of a Nobel physics laureate, himself won the Nobel Prize in physics for his development of electron spectroscopy for chemical analysis (ESCA). This reliable technique reveals many more details about the atomic and molecular structure of matter than was previously possible to determine. Siegbahn's electron spectroscopy soon became widely used around the world in scientific and industrial research labs.

Siegbahn was born to **Karl M. G. Siegbahn** and Karin Högbom Siegbahn on April 20, 1918, in Lund, Sweden. His father was a lecturer in physics at the University of Lund and the director of the Nobel Institute for Physics of the Royal Swedish Academy of Sciences for nearly thirty years. The elder Siegbahn's discoveries and research in X-ray spectroscopy

won him the 1924 Nobel Prize in physics. About growing up with such a role model, Kai Siegbahn was quoted in *Newsweek* as saying, "It's a decided advantage if you start discussing physics every day at the breakfast table."

The younger Siegbahn pursued his interests in mathematics, physics, and chemistry at the University of Uppsala, from which he earned his bachelor of science degree in 1939 and his master of science degree in 1942. He received his doctorate in 1944 from the University of Stockholm and worked as a researcher from 1942 to 1951 at the Nobel Institute of Physics. After a few years as a physics professor at the Royal Institute of Technology in Stockholm, Siegbahn left in 1954 to become professor and then head of the physics department at the University of Uppsala, where he remained and conducted his important research.

It was while he was pursuing his graduate degree that Siegbahn's interest in spectroscopy developed. Spectroscopy studies the frequencies, or wavelengths, at which particles of matter emit light or radiation. Since the frequencies are specific, or characteristic, of the matter being studied, they can yield valuable information about the atomic and molecular structure of that matter. Heinrich Hertz had discovered the photoelectric effect in 1883: objects struck by ultraviolet light release electrons, called photoelectrons. The nature of the effect was further examined by **Max Planck** and **Albert Einstein**, and researchers, hoping to advance scientific knowledge about the composition of matter, began attempting to use spectroscopy to analyze the photoelectrons. Electrons collide and scatter as they leave matter, losing unknown amounts of energy and creating spectra that are very difficult to read. Existing spectroscopes were inadequate to analyze the particles, but Siegbahn solved this problem.

Adaptations to Instrument Lead to ESCA

When he was in graduate school during the 1940s, Siegbahn studied electrons given off by radioactive nuclei, a process called beta decay. If he could measure the energies of these beta-ray electrons, he could learn much more about the nuclei. Existing instruments were of limited use for this purpose, so Siegbahn developed a mushroom-shaped magnet that allowed focusing in two directions. Siegbahn's high-resolution instrument increased the accuracy of measurements of these photoelectrons ten times. By the 1950s Siegbahn had turned his attention to electron spectroscopy—knocking electrons out of nonradioactive atoms with light or X rays—to determine the energies that bind electrons to atoms. Again, he found the spectroscopes he was using unable to produce accurate measurements. He decided to apply the double-focusing method he had developed for nuclear physics to the energy spectra of photoelectrons. The outcome was a double-focusing spectrometer with a high resolution that revealed previously unseen, narrow, but well-defined electron lines.

Siegbahn and his colleagues completed the first high-resolution, double-focusing spectrometer in 1954, and again it improved measurement accuracy tenfold. In 1957 the team recorded the first extremely sharp lines that allowed precise measurement of binding energies. In the 1960s the usefulness of the device was greatly extended when Siegbahn and two fellow researchers found that their electron spectrometer also revealed the chemical environment of the atoms that released the photoelectrons being studied, yielding details about chemical bonding as atoms combined into molecules. The technique now became known as electron spectroscopy for chemical analysis, or ESCA. Siegbahn and his team also adapted ESCA for the analysis of gases and liquids as well as solids.

Siegbahn's ESCA technique changed electron spectroscopy from a laboratory concept with a very limited application to a widely-used tool. ESCA provides high-resolution analysis of the atomic, molecular, and chemical characteristics of a nearly unlimited range of scientific, commercial, and industrial materials that includes atmospheric pollutants and surface corrosion. To acknowledge his contribution, Siegbahn was awarded the 1981 Nobel Prize in physics for his role in the development of a technique that provided a better understanding of the nature of matter.

SELECTED WRITINGS BY SIEGBAHN:

Books

ESCA-Atomic, Molecular, and Solid State Structure Studied by Means of Electron Spectroscopy, Almqvist & Wicksell (Uppsala, Sweden), 1967.
ESCA Applied to Free Molecules, North-Holland (Amsterdam, the Netherlands), 1969.

Periodicals

"Electron Spectroscopy for Atoms, Molecules, and Condensed Matter," *Review of Modern Physics* July, 1982, pp. 709–28.

Other

"Photoelectron Spectroscopy: Retrospects and Prospects," in *Royal Society Meeting on Studies of the Surfaces of Solids by Electron Spectroscopy: Recent Trends,* 1985.

SOURCES:

Books

Nobel Prize Winners, H. W. Wilson, 1987.

Nobel Prize Winners: Physics, Volume 3 (1968–88), Salem Press, 1989.

Periodicals

Begley, Sharon, "The Physics of Chemistry," *Newsweek,* November 2, 1981, p. 100.
New York Times, October 20, 1981, p. C2.
Science, November 6, 1981, pp. 629–631.
Scientific American, December, 1981, pp. 83–86.
Time, November 2, 1981, p. 52.

—Sketch by Kathy Sammis

Karl M. G. Siegbahn
1886-1978
Swedish physicist

Noted for modernizing Swedish physics, Karl M. G. Siegbahn contributed significantly to the field of X-ray spectroscopy begun in Germany and England. His design and application of equipment and techniques in this field vastly improved the accuracy of existing methods by which X-ray wavelengths were distinguished, and led to important discoveries about the nature of X rays (electromagnetic radiation invisible to the unaided human eye) and atomic structure. In recognition of his work, Siegbahn was awarded the 1924 Nobel Prize in physics. He became the first director of the Nobel Institute of Experimental Physics in 1937, and remained director of the institute until his retirement in 1964.

Karl Manne Georg Siegbahn was born in Örebro, Sweden, on December 3, 1886. His father was Nils Reinhold Georg Siegbahn, a station master for the Swedish national railway system, and his mother was the former Emma Sofia Mathilda Zetterberg. After his father's retirement, the family moved to Lund, Sweden, where Siegbahn entered the University of Lund in 1906. He studied astronomy, chemistry, mathematics, and physics there, eventually receiving his bachelor's degree in 1908, and his licentiate degree (comparable to a master's degree) in 1910. Studying electromagnetism as a research assistant to Johannes Rydberg, Siegbahn was awarded a doctorate in physics in 1911 for his dissertation on the measurement of magnetic fields. He spent the summer semesters of 1908 and 1909 studying at the universities of Göttingen and Münich respectively, and took up studies in Paris and Berlin during the summer of 1911.

Begins Studies on X rays

Upon receiving his doctorate, Siegbahn remained in his position as assistant to Rydberg, eventually assuming Rydberg's duties as lecturer when the older man was ill for long periods of time. When Rydberg died in 1920, Siegbahn succeeded him as professor of physics. Siegbahn's work under Rydberg had dealt primarily with studies of electrical and magnetic phenomena. By 1914, however, visits to research centers in Paris and Heidelberg turned his attentions toward the study of X-ray spectroscopy, a field to which he would devote the rest of his academic life.

Fundamental research on the properties of X rays had been carried out by the English physicist **Charles Barkla** in the first decade of the twentieth century. Barkla had found that X rays emitted from certain elements were of two types, "hard" or "K" X rays, and "soft" or "L" X rays, based on an element's atomic weight. Barkla's equipment was too primitive, however, to permit more detailed characterization of their wavelengths, or spectrums. In 1912, the German physicist **Max von Laue** developed a technique for revealing the spectral lines of X rays based on the diffraction grating technique used for visible light. But, because the wavelengths of X rays are much shorter than wavelengths of visible light, von Laue needed a finer grating or spacing device. He discovered that the regular spacing between atoms in a crystal would serve this purpose, so that X rays passed through an analyzing crystal, such as zinc sulfide, would separate into a series of spectral lines similar to those in an optical spectrum. The father-and-son team of physicists **William Henry Bragg** and **William Lawrence Bragg** refined the process and developed the first X-ray spectrometer shortly thereafter.

Perfects the Techniques of X-ray Spectroscopy

By 1914, Siegbahn had embarked on his research program in X-ray spectroscopy, one aspect of which involved the improvement of equipment used in the field. Over a period of more than three decades, Siegbahn designed improvements in the tubes, vacuum systems, and spectrometers used in X-ray spectroscopy, all with the objective of attaining more precise measurements of X-ray wavelengths. One of his first developments was the vacuum spectrometer, which enclosed the whole analytical system—X-ray tube, target, and spectroscopic and photographic plates—in a high vacuum, thus reducing the possibility of any extraneous interference. Siegbahn also designed more accurate spectrometers capable of reading specific wavelength regions.

Each improvement in technology achieved by Siegbahn was soon followed by new discoveries. He was able not only to confirm the existence of Barkla's K and L series of lines, for example, but also to discover two new series, which he named the M and N. He also found that the two K lines discovered by the English physicist **Henry Moseley** were actually doublets and, where Moseley had found four or five L lines, Siegbahn found as many as twenty-eight.

These discoveries were especially important because of the information they provided about atomic structure. Spectral lines are emitted when electrons move from one energy level to another in an atom. **Niels Bohr**'s 1913 model of the atom had offered a simplistic view of electron energy levels, one in which electrons were restricted to a small number of orbitals around the nucleus. With the discovery of elliptical orbitals, magnetic effects within the atom, and electron spin, however, this picture became much more complex. The number and type of electron transitions possible within an atom became much greater and Siegbahn's analysis of X-ray spectra provided invaluable keys to learning more about them. For both his discoveries and contributions to the improvement of X-ray spectroscopic technology, Siegbahn was awarded the 1924 Nobel Prize in physics. He also earned a number of other honors and awards throughout his life, including the Hughes (1934) and Rumford (1940) medals of the Royal Society, and the Duddel Medal of the London Physical Society, as well as honorary degrees from a number of universities throughout the world.

In 1923, Siegbahn was offered the position of professor of physics at the University of Uppsala, a post he held until 1937. He then became the first director of the newly created Nobel Institute of Experimental Physics in Stockholm. In addition to his continuing interest in X-ray spectroscopy, Siegbahn established a school of nuclear physics at the institute and, by 1938, had overseen the construction of Sweden's first particle accelerator. Siegbahn also served as president of the International Union of Pure and Applied Physics from 1938 to 1947.

Siegbahn's influence on the history of science goes beyond his own personal accomplishments. For most of his life, he maintained a strong commitment to the expansion and improvement of scientific facilities and programs of science education in Sweden. At both Uppsala and the Nobel Institute, he took facilities with poor or limited equipment and built them into first-class research institutions. Siegbahn was married to Karin Högbom in 1914. They had two sons, Bo Siegbahn and **Kai M. Siegbahn**, the latter a Nobel Laureate in physics himself in 1981. Karl M. G. Siegbahn died in Stockholm on September 26, 1978.

SELECTED WRITINGS BY SIEGBAHN:

Books

The Spectroscopy of X-rays, translation by George A. Lindsay, Oxford University Press, 1925.

On the Methods of Precision Measurements of X-ray Wavelengths, 1929.

SOURCES:

Books

Dictionary of Scientific Biography, Volume 12, Scribner, 1975, pp. 821–26.
Heathcote, Niels H. de V., *Nobel Prize Winners in Physics, 1901–1950,* Henry Schuman, 1953, pp. 218–28.
McGraw-Hill Modern Scientists and Engineers, Volume 10, McGraw-Hill, 1980, pp. 114–16.
Nobel Prize Winners, H. W. Wilson, 1987, pp. 969–71.

—*Sketch by David E. Newton*

Igor I. Sikorsky
1889-1972
Russian-born American aeronautical engineer

Igor I. Sikorsky was one of the most significant aeronautical engineers and aircraft designers of the twentieth century. He was a leader in the design of four-engine bombers in World War I and large passenger-carrying seaplanes in the interwar years, but he is best known for designing the first single-rotor helicopters. During and after World War II the Sikorsky Aircraft Division of United Aircraft Corporation became synonymous with a multitude of helicopter designs used for everything from military operations to forest firefighting.

In some respects, Sikorsky's career in the United States was a rags-to-riches story. After gaining a reputation for aeronautical design in Russia, he fled the country following the Bolshevik Revolution and arrived nearly penniless in New York City in 1919. Teaching mathematics to other Russian emigres to make ends meet, he soon obtained financial backers and formed an aeronautical engineering company on Long Island in 1923. Within a decade he had established a central place in the expanding American aviation industry, a place he maintained until his death in 1972.

Perhaps Sikorsky's fascination with helicopters throughout his long life is an appropriate metaphor for his own experience. The search for freedom, whether in flight or in his personal life, motivated much of Sikorsky's career. Sikorsky said he fled Russia for freedom's sake, and he founded his own company and pursued helicopter design for the same reason. According to *Air Force* magazine, in a speech Sikorsky gave in 1967 when he received the Wright Memorial Trophy for his contributions to aeronautics, he summarized his beliefs by emphasizing the importance of "individual initiative, individual work, and total freedom" in the accomplishment of great tasks.

Igor Ivan Sikorsky was born on May 25, 1889, in Kiev, Russia, the youngest of Ivan and Zinaida Temrouk-Tcherkoss Sikorsky's five children. His family was prominent in Tsarist Russia, where his father was a professor of psychology at St. Vladimir University in Kiev and his mother was a medical school graduate. Well educated, the young Sikorsky learned about and was fascinated by fifteenth-century Italian artist Leonardo da Vinci's aeronautical studies, especially his drawings of a helicopter-like flying machine.

At age fourteen Sikorsky entered the Imperial Naval College in St. Petersburg and after graduating in 1906 entered the Mechanical College of the Polytechnic Institute in Kiev. During his two years at the Mechanical College, he concentrated on the new science of aviation. There Sikorsky learned everything he could about early aviators **Wilbur** and **Orville Wright** and their experiments in the United States. He also studied the work of Count Ferdinand von Zeppelin, who developed lighter-than-air craft in Germany. In 1909 Sikorsky went to Paris, considered the mecca of aeronautics in Europe at the time, to study the latest design efforts.

Even during that early part of his career, Sikorsky was already studying the possibilities of building a helicopter. He purchased in Paris, for instance, a small 25-horsepower engine to power the rotor on his planned helicopter. For almost two years after his return to Russia, Sikorsky concentrated on designing and building helicopters, but the two prototypes he constructed were unable to lift their own weight. While the designs were sound, the engines needed to be more powerful. As a result, Sikorsky turned to more conventional, winged aircraft, on which a larger body of technical knowledge was available. In 1911 he produced the S–5 racer, which set a speed record of 70 miles per hour. The next year Sikorsky's S–6A design earned an award at a military competition and on the basis of these efforts the Russo-Baltic Railroad Car Works hired him to design a bomber for the Imperial Army.

Designs *Ilya Mourometz* Bomber

Sikorsky responded with a huge four-engine aircraft, the *Ilya Mourometz,* which first flew on May 13, 1913. Its four engines each generated from 100 to 220 horsepower, its crew of five had sleeping compartments in the rear fuselage, and it was protected from air attack by either three or four machine guns. The most advanced variant of the *Ilya Mourometz* could remain aloft for five hours at an altitude of approximately 9,000 feet and a speed of eighty-five miles per hour. It could carry a bomb load of between 992 and 1,543 pounds, depending on other operational factors. The aircraft also enjoyed a sixty percent bombs-on-target rating because of precise bombsights and excellent training of bombardiers.

During World War I, Russian Major-General M. V. Shidlovski, commanding the *Eskadra Vozdushnykh Korablei* (Squadron of Flying Ships), equipped his unit with the *Ilya Mourometz*. Formed specifically to exploit the weakness in the air of the Central Powers on the Eastern Front early in the war, Shidlovski made his squadron into a self-contained force with its own test operations, training, and other activities. He first employed it in combat on February 15, 1915, when it left from its base at Jablonna, Poland, and raided a German base in East Prussia. Between this time and November of 1917, Shidlovski's unit made more than 400 bombing raids over Germany and the Baltic states.

Sikorsky's *Ilya Mourometz* was a rugged airplane. Its only casualty from air attack occurred on September 12, 1916, but only after the aircraft's gunners had shot down three German fighters. Two other bombers were lost in crashes, but the force was not crippled until February of 1918, when thirty planes were destroyed by the Russians at Vinnitza to prevent capture by an advancing German army.

Immigrates to the United States

When the Bolshevik Revolution was successful in Russia in 1917, Sikorsky's career as the tsar's bomber designer came to an abrupt end. Not only was Sikorsky targeted as an enemy of Communist revolutionaries because of his family's prominence, but also because of his importance to the tsar as the designer of the *Ilya Mourometz*. Sikorsky abandoned his business and land holdings and went to France, where he was commissioned to build a bomber for the Allied forces still fighting in World War I. The aircraft had not yet progressed beyond the design stage when the Armistice was signed in 1918, and the French cancelled his contract. The next year he came to the United States and lived for a time in New York City, where he lived hand-to-mouth.

Soon after arriving in the United States, Sikorsky tried to obtain a military contract to produce an aircraft, but the War Department declined. It was not until four years later that he found sufficient financial backing to set up the Sikorsky Aero Engineering Corporation on a farm near Roosevelt Field, Long Island.

Builds Passenger Aircraft

Immediately after starting his own company, Sikorsky began work on an all-metal passenger monoplane. It became known as the S–29, a twin-engine, fourteen-passenger aircraft with a top speed of 115 miles per hour. In 1925 he organized the Sikorsky Manufacturing Corporation to build the S–29 and combined the engineering and manufacturing companies into the Sikorsky Aviation Corporation in 1928. A string of successful designs that reestablished Sikorsky as a leading aeronautical designer followed. The most important of his designs was the S–38, ten-passenger amphibian, sold to Juan Trippe's Pan American Airways. It was in this business arrangement that Sikorsky first met Charles A. Lindbergh, who had gained international fame for making a solo flight nonstop over the Atlantic in 1927. The two eventually became good friends and sometime business associates.

Sikorsky eventually turned out more than 100 S–38 seaplanes, and they were used extensively in opening the airline connections between North and South America. Because of this success, in 1929 Sikorsky was bought out by the United Aircraft Corporation, although he continued to direct his operation as a subsidiary. More advanced variations on the S–29 seaplane appeared throughout the 1930s, among them the S–40, called the *American Clipper,* a four-engine amphibian that became a standard vehicle for international flights in the 1930s.

Returns to the Helicopter Problem

By the mid–1930s Sikorsky had persuaded United Aircraft to allow him to develop a helicopter, and it invested a reported $300,000 in the effort. On September 14, 1939, he flew the first true single-rotor helicopter, the VS–300, a strange configuration of welded pipes and open-air cockpit powered by a seventy-five-horsepower engine that turned a three-bladed rotor by means of an automobile fanbelt. Sikorsky was elated when it flew. He wrote in his autobiography, *Recollections and Thoughts of a Pioneer,* "It is a dream to feel the machine lift you gently up in the air, float smoothly over one spot for indefinite periods, move up or down under good control, as well as move not only forward or backward but in any direction."

Recognizing that this new air vehicle had military potential, the U.S. Army purchased its first helicopter from Sikorsky in 1941. Two years later it ordered the production of the R–4 helicopter, a VS–300 variant. Several years elapsed before the helicopter became a military staple—few of them were used during World War II—but by the time of the Korean War (1950-1953) several different designs were being routinely used for observation, transportation of wounded, and movement of high priority cargo and passengers into areas without airfields. In acknowledgment of this use, American helicopter manufacturers received the 1951 Collier Trophy, given annually to the person or group making the most significant contribution to American aviation. U.S. President Harry S. Truman chose Sikorsky to accept the award on behalf of the industry. Since that time the military has found increasingly sophisticated uses for helicopters, including as gunships, transport vehicles for its "air cavalry" units, and rescue and recovery and commando craft.

Sikorsky was especially delighted with the business and humanitarian uses found for the helicopter during the same era. For instance, in January of 1944 his helicopters were called upon to carry vital blood plasma from New York to Sandy Hook, New Jersey, for the victims of a steamship explosion. Sikorsky recalled in his autobiography, "It was a source of great satisfaction to all the personnel of our organization, including myself, that the helicopter started its practical career by saving a number of lives and by helping man in need rather than by spreading death and destruction." In the latter 1940s other uses were found for Sikorsky's helicopter, including as an air mail carrier and as air buses transporting passengers from airports to the hearts of major cities. By the early 1960s they were also being routinely used for traffic observation, forest firefighting, crop dusting, rescue, and a host of other practical jobs.

The Sikorsky Aeronautical Division built a succession of helicopters for various purposes during the 1940s and 1950s. After the VS–300 and the R–4 military production model, Sikorsky's helicopters grew in size and complexity. The S–55 was the first certificated transport helicopter in the United States, while the twin-engine S–56 was capable of carrying 50 combat troops. An important breakthrough design was the economical S–58, which could carry twelve passengers and was excellent for moving people short distances. Subsequent incarnations of the helicopter included the S–62, an amphibious helicopter with a flying-boat hull, and the S–61 twin-turbine helicopter, used for antisubmarine warfare. Sikorsky also developed the giant S–64 "Skycrane" helicopter, which could haul cargoes of up to ten tons suspended from its belly.

Sikorsky retired from active involvement in aircraft design and production in 1957 but continued as a consultant to his company. Furthermore, after his retirement, Sikorsky enjoyed the role of aviation sage. He was in the spotlight on numerous public occasions, as when he received the National Medal of Science from U.S. President Lyndon B. Johnson in 1968. He also lectured widely on aeronautical development to government organizations, at universities, and within the industry. In every case, Sikorsky spoke of his quest for freedom and his commitment to both technological and personal excellence.

Sikorsky was a deeply religious man, a member of the Russian Orthodox Church and author of two books on Christianity—*The Message of the Lord's Prayer* and *The Invisible Encounter*. He died of a heart attack on October 26, 1972, at the age of 82 in his home in Easton, Connecticut. His second wife, Russian-born Elizabeth A. Semion, whom he married in 1924, survived him. Additionally, he had four sons and a daughter, some of whom followed him into the aviation business.

SELECTED WRITINGS BY SIKORSKY:

Books

Story of the Winged-S, Dodd, 1938.
The Message of the Lord's Prayer, Scribner, 1942.
The Invisible Encounter, Scribner, 1947.
Recollections and Thoughts of a Pioneer, 1964.

Periodicals

"Free Men Are the True Pioneers," *Air Force,* February, 1968, pp. 100–101.

SOURCES:

Books

Finne, K. N., *Igor Sikorsky: The Russian Years,* edited by Carl J. Bobrow and Von Hardesty, Smithsonian Institution Press, 1987.

Periodicals

Hughes, Albert D., "Pioneer of Flight Frontiers," *Christian Science Monitor,* September, 1963.
Witze, Claude, "A Tribute to Igor Sikorsky," *Air Force Magazine,* December, 1972, pp. 26–27.

Other

The Aviation Careers of Igor Sikorsky, exhibit at the National Air and Space Museum, Smithsonian Institution, Washington, DC, 1990.
Letter from Thurman H. Bane, Engineering Division, Air Service, to Jerome C. Hunsaker, Navy Department, U.S. War Department document, 1919.

—*Sketch by Roger D. Launius*

Dorothy Martin Simon
1919-
American chemist

Dorothy Martin Simon has been responsible for several significant advances in space engineering, particularly in the area of combustion. By relating the fundamental properties of flame to each other through the principles of heat and mass transfer and chemical reaction, she helped establish the present-day theory of flame propagation and quenching. She also contributed to the development of ablative coatings, which protect missiles from heat damage upon reentering the Earth's atmosphere. In recognition of these accomplishments, as well as her success in executive management and public speaking, the Society of Women Engineers presented Simon with their Achievement Award in 1966.

Simon was born Dorothy Martin on September 18, 1919, in Harwood, Missouri. Her parents were Robert William Martin, head of the chemistry department at Southwest Missouri State College, and Laudell Flynn Martin. Simon attended high school at Greenwood Laboratory School in Springfield, where she won the highest sports honor while also earning the highest grade-point average in the school's history. After graduation, she attended the college at which her father taught, where she received a bachelor's degree with honors in 1940. Once again, she was class valedictorian. From there, she went on to the University of Illinois, where her thesis research on active deposits from radon and thoron gas was among the earliest work on radioactive fallout. She obtained a Ph.D. in chemistry in 1945.

Upon completing college, Simon first spent a year as a chemist at the Du Pont Company in Buffalo, New York. During this time, she studied the chemical reactions involved in producing the synthetic fiber now known as Orlon. In 1946, she began working for the Atomic Energy Commission (AEC) at Oak Ridge Laboratory in Tennessee and the Argonne Laboratory in Illinois. Among her accomplishments while with the AEC was the isolation of a new isotope of calcium.

Advances the Understanding of Combustion

In 1949, Simon began six years with the National Advisory Committee for Aeronautics, the agency that evolved into NASA. These proved to be her most fruitful years as a researcher. During this period, her work elucidating the fundamental nature of flames was recognized with a Rockefeller Public Service Award. Simon used the stipend of $10,000 to visit university and technical laboratories in England, France, and the Netherlands. She studied at Cambridge University with **Ronald G. W. Norrish**, who later won the Nobel Prize in chemistry.

In 1955 she spent a year as group leader at the Magnolia Petroleum Company in Dallas. Then in 1956, Simon began a lengthy association with Avco Corporation, where her early work addressed the design problems of reentry vehicles for intercontinental ballistic missiles. Her research dealt with ablation cooling—a method of protecting the missile body from extreme heat while reentering the Earth's atmosphere by absorbing the heat in a shielding material that is changing phase. This was the topic of a Marie Curie Lecture that Simon delivered at Pennsylvania State University in 1962.

Soon Simon's interests turned toward management within the giant conglomerate. She was appointed the first female corporate officer at Avco in 1968. In her capacity as vice president of research, she was responsible for guiding the company's various high-tech divisions. At that time, she was one of the few women to have scaled such heights on the corporate ladder, a fact that was recognized by Worcester Polytechnic Institute when conferring an honorary doctorate upon Simon in 1971. The institute cited her position as "perhaps the most important woman executive in American industry today." Simon later received a second honorary doctorate, this one from Lehigh University. She is a fellow of the American Institute of Chemists, as well as a member of the American Chemical Society and the American Institute of Aeronautics and Astronautics.

Simon is known as an outstanding speaker, who has frequently lectured and written on the challenges of space, research management, and women in science. She served on President Jimmy Carter's Committee for the National Medal of Science, the National Research Council's National Materials Advisory Board, the Department of Defense's Defense Policy Advisory Committee, and the Department of Commerce's Statutory Committee for the National Bureau of Standards. In her free time, she enjoys traveling, cooking, and gardening. Simon was married on December 6, 1946, to Sidney L. Simon—a leading scientist in his own right who became vice president at Sperry Rand. He died in 1975. Simon currently makes her home in Pittsboro, North Carolina.

SELECTED WRITINGS BY SIMON:

Periodicals

(With F.E. Belles and R.C. Weast) "Pressure Limits of Flame Propagation of Propane-Air Mixtures," *Industrial and Engineering Chemistry,* Volume 46, 1954, p. 1010.

"Diffusion Processes as Rate-Controlling Steps in Laminar Flame Propagation," *Selected Combustion Problems: Fundamentals and Aeronautical Applications,* Butterworths Scientific Publications, 1954, pp. 59–91.

SOURCES:

Books

O'Neill, Lois Decker, editor, *The Women's Book of World Records and Achievements,* Doubleday, 1979, pp. 189, 519.

Periodicals

Kelly, Mary, "Earthling Eyes Cast on Space," *Christian Science Monitor,* August 2, 1965, p. 12.

Other

Burton, David, interview with Linda Wasmer Smith conducted February 9, 1994.
Southwest Missouri State University, material including award nominations, biographical sketches, news clippings, and press release.
University of Illinois Archives, material including award nomination and citation, biographical sketch, news clipping, and résumé.

—Sketch by Linda Wasmer Smith

Herbert A. Simon
1916-

American computer scientist

Generally considered one of the fathers of artificial intelligence—computer programs capable of complex problem-solving—Herbert A. Simon has made distinguished contributions in a number of fields, including computer science, the psychology of learning, business administration, political science, economics, and philosophy. Recipient of the 1978 Nobel Prize in economics for his work on human decision-making, he also, in 1986, became the first person to receive the National Medal of Science for work in the behavioral sciences. In addition to his varied professional interests, he also paints and plays the piano and enjoys mountain-climbing, traveling, and learning foreign languages.

Simon was born in Milwaukee, Wisconsin, on June 15, 1916. His father, Arthur Simon, was a German-born electrical engineer and his mother, Edna (Merkel) Simon, was an accomplished pianist. After being skipped ahead three semesters in the Milwaukee public school system, Simon was just seventeen when he enrolled in the University of Chicago, where he would earn his B.A. in political science in 1936. As an undergraduate, Simon conducted a study of the administration of the Milwaukee Recreation Department. This study sparked Simon's interest in how administrators make decisions—a topic that would be a focal point of his career. In 1937, Simon married Dorothea Isobel Pye, also a graduate student in political science at the University of Chicago; they would have three children, Katherine, Peter, and Barbara.

After graduating, Simon was hired by the International City Managers' Association (ICMA) in Chicago as an assistant to Clarence Ridley, who had been his instructor in a course on evaluating municipal governments. Ridley and Simon became widely recognized experts on mathematical means of measuring the effectiveness of public services. While at the ICMA, Simon had his first experience with computers. As an assistant editor of the *Municipal Yearbook,* Simon started using IBM keypunch, sorting, and tabulating machines to prepare statistical tables. His consequent fascination with these machines would play a major part in his research and his career.

In 1939, Simon moved to the University of California at Berkeley to head a three-year study of local government funded by a grant from the Rockefeller Foundation. While at Berkeley, Simon completed the requirements for his Ph.D. from the University of Chicago. His dissertation, on decision-making in organizations, later evolved into his first book, *Administrative Behavior.* In 1942, Simon joined the faculty of the political science department at the Illinois Institute of Technology, where he remained for seven years, becoming department chair in 1946. Then, in 1949, he was tapped by the Carnegie Institute of Technology (later known as Carnegie-Mellon University) in Pittsburgh, Pennsylvania, to teach in its new graduate school in business administration. Simon would play a major role in shaping the curriculum, which was designed to provide students with the basic tools necessary for independent learning and problem-solving.

Defining the Field of Artificial Intelligence

In his autobiography, *Models of My Life,* Simon describes 1955 and 1956 as the most important years of his scientific career. It was at this time that Simon, along with **Allen Newell** and Clifford Shaw of the RAND Corporation, began using computers to study problem-solving behavior. To do this, they observed individuals as they worked through well-structured problems of logic. Subjects verbalized their reasoning as they worked through the problems. Simon and his colleagues were then able to code this reasoning in the form of a computer program. The program was not subject-matter specific; rather, it focused on the problem-solving process. Together, Simon, Allen, and Shaw developed Logic Theorist and General Problem Solver, the first computer programs to simulate human reasoning in solving problems. This work was at the forefront of the newly developing field of artificial intelligence. Simon and J. R. Hayes later developed the "Understand" program, which was designed to allow computers to solve even poorly structured problems. The program first worked to define the problem, and then focused on the problem's solution. Simon's work in artificial intelligence would lead to his being named Richard King Mellon University Professor of Computer Science and Psychology at Carnegie-Mellon University in 1966.

In 1957, Simon released a second edition of *Administrative Behavior*. In the new edition, Simon built on his original contention that because of the complexity of the economy, business decision-makers are unable to obtain all of the information they need in order to maximize profits. As a result, he had argued, most companies try to set goals that are acceptable but less than ideal—a behavior he termed "satisficing." In the second edition, Simon pointed out that his findings undermined a basic assumption of classical economic theory that the decision maker in an organization has access to all of the information needed to make decisions and will always make rational decisions that maximize profits. Simon's conclusions met with resistance from many economists, although those specializing in business operations were more accepting.

Research In Decision-Making Earns the Nobel Prize

Simon's distinguished career received significant recognition in the 1960s and 1970s. He was elected to the National Academy of Sciences and became chairman of the Division of Behavioral Sciences for the National Research Council in 1967; the following year, he was appointed to the President's Science Advisory Committee. In 1969, Simon received the American Psychological Association's Distinguished Scientific Contributions Award, and in 1975, he shared the Association for Computing Machinery's A. M. Turing Award with his long-time collaborator Allen Newell. This string of awards and honors culminated in 1978 when he was awarded the Nobel Prize in economic science for his research into the decision-making process within organizations.

In the 1980s, Simon continued to be an active researcher, with his work including a study of short-term memory with colleagues from China. He continued his activity with the National Academy of Sciences and published a second volume of *Models of Thought* in 1989. In 1991, he published his autobiography, *Models of My Life*. In the introduction to this book, Simon commented on the varied academic paths he has chosen: "I have been a scientist, but in many sciences. I have explored mazes, but they do not connect into a single maze. My aspirations do not extend to achieving a single consistency in my life. It will be enough if I can play each of my roles creditably, borrowing sometimes from one for another, but striving to represent fairly each character when he has his turn on stage."

SELECTED WRITINGS BY SIMON:

Books

Administrative Behavior: A Study of Decision-making Processes in Administrative Organization, Macmillan, 1947, third edition, 1976.
Models of Man, Wiley, 1958.
(With James G. March) *Organizations,* Wiley, 1958.
The New Science of Management Decision, Harper, 1960, revised edition, Prentice-Hall, 1977.
The Sciences of the Artificial, MIT Press, 1969, second edition, 1981.
(With Allen Newell) *Human Problem Solving,* Prentice-Hall, 1972.
Models of Discovery, and Other Topics in the Methods of Science, Reidel, 1978.
Models of Thought, Yale University Press, 1979.
Models of My Life, Basic Books, 1991.

SOURCES:

Books

Baars, Bernard J., *The Cognitive Revolution in Psychology,* Guilford, 1986.
Lindzey, Gardner, editor, *A History of Psychology in Autobiography,* Volume 7, Freeman, 1980.
McCorduck, Pamela, *Machines Who Think,* W. H. Freeman, 1979.

Periodicals

Business Week, December 5, 1970.
Chicago Tribune, October 27, 1986.
Newsweek, October 30, 1978.
New York Times, November 26, 1978.
New York Times Book Review, March 17, 1991, pp. 1, 28–29.
People, January 15, 1979.
Psychology Today, October, 1986.

Saturday Evening Post, May 4, 1968.
Time, October 30, 1978.
Times Literary Supplement, August 22, 1980.

—*Sketch by Daniel Rooney*

George Gaylord Simpson

George Gaylord Simpson
1902-1984
American paleontologist

George Gaylord Simpson was a pioneer in the use of statistical methods in paleontology, the scientific study of prehistoric life as revealed in the fossil record. By analyzing fossil remains, particularly those of mammals, Simpson was able to deduce much about the animals' migration patterns, distribution changes, and evolutionary histories. In addition, he was a major architect of synthetic theory, which applies the principles of modern genetics to the study of evolution. His 1944 book, *Tempo and Mode in Evolution,* is considered a seminal work in the field.

Simpson was born in Chicago, Illinois, on June 16, 1902, the youngest of three children. His parents were Joseph Alexander Simpson, a lawyer, and Helen Julia (Kinney) Simpson. While he was still a baby, the family moved to Denver, Colorado, where his father was first a claims adjuster for the railroad, and later a speculator in irrigation, land, and mining. As Simpson related in *Concession to the Improbable: An Unconventional Autobiography,* "When I was a bit older [my father and I] frequently went for weekends or longer holidays in the Colorado mountains; each with cans of food rolled in a blanket tied at the ends and slung over a shoulder, we would walk all day at a leisurely pace and sleep on the ground whenever night overtook us. . . . I acquired a deep love for nature . . . that was a factor in entering a profession that included camping out during many active years."

Rises to Curatorship at the American Museum

A gifted student, Simpson managed to pass eight grades of grammar school in only six years, despite missing an entire year for illness. He graduated from East Denver High School in 1918, shortly before his sixteenth birthday. The following autumn, he entered the University of Colorado. Financial problems the next year, however, forced him to drop out briefly and take jobs in Chicago, Texas, and the Colorado mountains. By 1920, he was back at college, thanks to a combination of scholarship money and menial jobs. Simpson transferred to Yale for his senior year at the urging of a professor of historical geology, who had himself recently made the same transition. Simpson received a bachelor's degree from Yale in 1923 and a Ph.D. in 1926.

Simpson began a prolific publishing career while still in graduate school. In his autobiography, he recalled, "I went to college thinking vaguely that I might become a writer, but I was soon bothered by the fact that unapplied writing, like unapplied mathematics, isn't *about* anything." Fortunately, he soon discovered his subject matter, as well as a knack for presenting technical information in clear, readable prose. His first papers appeared a year before he completed his doctorate, and by 1926, he already had 25 articles, abstracts, and reviews in print. At the time of his death, he had over 700 publications to his credit, including nearly 50 books.

Early in his graduate studies, Simpson began to concentrate on vertebrate paleontology. In the summer of 1924, he worked as a field assistant for an expedition that collected vertebrate fossils in Texas and New Mexico. Upon his return to Yale, Simpson made good use of the Peabody Museum's rare collection of mammal fossils dating from the Mesozoic Era—the period during which the first mammals appeared. These fossils eventually became the subject of his dissertation. The year following his graduation, Simpson was awarded a fellowship to study European Mesozoic mammals at the British Museum (Natural History) in London.

Later in 1927, Simpson returned to the United States to assume a post as assistant curator at the American Museum of Natural History in New York. It was the start of a very fruitful association lasting until 1959, during which time Simpson rose to the position of curator of fossil mammals and birds. He also became chairman of the museum's department of geology and paleontology. In addition, from 1945 to 1959, he held a joint teaching appointment at Columbia University. His position at the museum afforded Simpson many opportunities for field work. His early expeditions included trips to such places as the San Juan Basin in New Mexico, the Pleistocene deposits in Florida, and the badlands of Patagonia, a region in southern Argentina and Chile. The latter produced several technical papers, a large monograph, and a popular book, *Attending Marvels: A Patagonian Journal.* Simpson visited South America once again from 1938 to 1939, this time at the invitation of the Venezuelan government. Fossil-hunting there took Simpson to the remote territory of the Kamarakoto tribe, whose customs he recorded in another monograph.

Incorporates Genetics into Evolutionary Theory

On February 2, 1923, while Simpson was still a graduate student, he married Lydia Pedroja. That union produced four daughters—Helen, Gaylord (known as Gay), Joan, and Elizabeth—before ending in divorce in April 1938. On May 27, 1938, Simpson married Anne Roe, a psychologist who had been a childhood friend. The next year, Simpson and his second wife published a textbook, *Quantitative Zoology,* that was itself a wedding of his training in zoology and her knowledge of statistics. This book helped spur changes in zoological methodology.

Next Simpson expanded his use of statistical tools, this time applying them to the difficult task of explaining evolution. The result was *Tempo and Mode in Evolution,* a landmark book in several respects. First, Simpson demonstrated that fossil findings could be not only described, but also quantified. Second, he showed that the fossil record could indeed be reconciled with the emerging synthesis of population genetics and natural history. Synthetic theory gave scientists the means for the first time to demonstrate how natural selection could work. In brief, it stated that genetic variability among individuals in a population of sexually reproducing organisms is produced by mutation and genetic recombination. Such genetic variability is subject to natural selection. Simpson established that the fossil record was consistent with what this theory would predict.

Another major accomplishment dating from this period was the publication of a lengthy monograph titled "The Principles of Classification and a Classification of Mammals." Shortly after joining the American Museum staff, Simpson had begun compiling a catalog to help organize that institution's extensive mammal collection. In 1942, Simpson completed a greatly expanded version of this catalog, in which he classified all the mammals then known, living or extinct. To this, he appended a now-famous essay on taxonomy, the branch of biology dealing with classification. It was the first attempt to set forth the principles of evolutionary taxonomy.

Just at this point, however, World War II intervened in Simpson's career. From 1942 to 1944, he served in the U.S. Army, first as a captain and later promoted to major. His assignments—most in military intelligence—took him to Algeria, Tunisia, Sicily, and mainland Italy. Simpson continued to sport his trademark Vandyke beard, a fact that did not escape the attention of General George S. Patton. This led to an amusing incident relayed back to the States by a reporter. As Simpson told the story in his autobiography, "He sent an aide, a chicken colonel, to tell me that if I did not shave my beard he (Patton) would pluck it out hair by hair. With perfect military courtesy I explained to the colonel that according to army regulations a commissioned officer could wear a neat beard if he had permission from his commanding officer, and that General Patton was not my commanding officer. General Eisenhower was.... I received no apology, but I did keep my beard."

Resumes the Search for Vertebrate Fossils

Upon returning from the service, Simpson promptly resumed his field work. Starting in 1946, he made frequent trips to New Mexico and Colorado to search for mammal fossils from the Eocene and Paleocene, epochs beginning 54 and 65 million years ago, respectively. His most celebrated finds were the skulls of eight 15-inch-high creatures called Dawn Horses. In 1947, Simpson and his wife built a second home, dubbed Los Pinavetes, in the mountains above Cuba, New Mexico. Over the next two decades, they spent at least part of every summer and all of one winter there.

In 1949, Simpson published *The Meaning of Evolution,* in which he set about presenting the complex subject of evolution to the general public. It became his best-known work, reissued several times over the years and translated into many languages, including French, Italian, Persian, Danish, Dutch, Spanish, Japanese, Portuguese, and Finnish. Because it was widely adopted as a text for introductory physical anthropology courses, it also influenced a whole new generation of anthropologists.

In 1954, Simpson traveled to Brazil to lecture and consult as a guest of the Brazilian National Research Council. In 1956, he returned to that country to lead an expedition up the Juruá River, a tributary of the Amazon. Unfortunately, this trip ended in a serious mishap for Simpson. While clearing a campsite, an assistant felled a tree that struck Simpson, leaving the 54-year-old man with a concussion, bruised back, dislocated left shoulder and ankle, and shattered right leg. A series of twelve operations ensued, and it was two years before he could walk again with a cane. "That event changed my life quite radically," Simpson reported in his autobiography. "The then director of the American Museum removed me from the chairmanship of the department. . . . When at last I could get to my office without a wheelchair he explained to me that I would no longer be allowed to travel on any museum business and would only have to report for work in New York."

Concentrates on New Travels and Writings

Simpson resigned in 1959 rather than accept what he considered a humiliating situation. Shortly thereafter, he took a position as Alexander Agassiz Professor at Harvard's Museum of Comparative Zoology. During this period, he published his own favorite among his many books, *This View of Life: The World of an Evolutionist,* half the chapters of which were adapted from earlier lectures. He also continued to travel widely. The high point may have been a 1961 expedition to Africa. Simpson was with anthropologist **Louis Leakey** in Kenya when the latter discovered a skull fragment from a 14-million-year-old apelike creature named Ramapithecus, believed by many to have been an early human ancestor. In the early 1970s, Simpson also made three journeys to Antarctica, where he delighted in observing the many penguin colonies. Four decades earlier, he had collected a large number of penguin fossils in Patagonia, and his attention now turned to these once again. The result, characteristically, was a book: a 1976 volume titled *Penguins: Past and Present, Here and There.*

The failing health of both Simpson and his wife led to yet another move in 1967, this time to Tucson, where Simpson assumed a post as a professor of geosciences at the University of Arizona. The couple also established the Simroe Foundation, a nonprofit foundation dedicated to making their private technical libraries and research facilities more accessible to others. It was housed in a separate building especially constructed for that purpose behind the Simpsons' home. Another of Simpson's lasting preoccupations was the study of languages. In addition to English, he claimed to speak French and Spanish fluently, and German and Italian moderately well. He could also read Portuguese, and he had learned to decipher ancient Egyptian hieroglyphs. Years before, his encounter with the Kamarakoto Indians of South America had prompted him to make the first written record of their language, a phonetic rendering of hundreds of words.

Simpson's preeminence in his discipline was reflected by the many honors bestowed upon him. Honorary degrees were conferred on him by such universities as Yale, Princeton, Oxford, the University of Glasgow, and the University of Paris. In 1976, the Smithsonian Institution presented him with the International Award for distinguished contributions to natural history. Among the numerous other awards he received were the 1942 Lewis Prize of the American Philosophical Society, the 1943 Thompson Medal and the 1944 and 1961 Elliott Medals of the National Academy of Sciences, the 1952 Penrose Medal of the Geological Society of America, the 1962 Darwin Medal of the Royal Society of London, and the 1965 National Medal of Science.

Simpson was active in the founding of two professional associations: the Society of Vertebrate Paleontology and the Society for the Study of Evolution. He became the first president of both groups, and he served a term as president of the American Society of Zoologists and the Society of Systematic Zoology as well. In addition, he was a fellow or member of such select organizations as the American Academy of Arts and Sciences, the National Academy of Sciences, the American Philosophical Society, the Royal Society of London, the two Italian national academies of science, and the national academies of Venezuela, Brazil, and Argentina.

Although Simpson retired from the University of Arizona in 1982, he continued to devote himself tirelessly to his writing. A press release issued by the American Museum the following year noted that he currently had six books in progress. At the time of his death from pneumonia at the age of 82, his reputation as an world-renowned authority on vertebrate paleontology had long been secure, yet he continued to work to the end. He died in a hospital in Tucson on October 6, 1984.

SELECTED WRITINGS BY SIMPSON:

Books

Attending Marvels: A Patagonian Journal, Macmillan, 1934, reprinted, University of Chicago Press, 1982.

(With wife, Anne Roe) *Quantitative Zoology: Numerical Concepts and Methods in the Study of Recent and Fossil Animals,* McGraw-Hill, 1939, revised edition (with Roe and Richard Lewontin), Harcourt, 1960.

Tempo and Mode in Evolution, Columbia University Press, 1944, reprinted, 1984.

The Meaning of Evolution: A Study of the History of Life and Its Significance for Man, Yale University Press, 1949, revised and abridged edition, New American Library, 1951, revised edition, Yale University Press, 1967.

This View of Life: The World of an Evolutionist,
   Harcourt, 1964.
Penguins: Past and Present, Here and There, Yale
   University Press, 1976.
*Concession to the Improbable: An Unconventional
   Autobiography,* Yale University Press, 1978.
*Simple Curiosity: Letters from George Gaylord
   Simpson to His Family, 1921–1970,* edited by
   Leo F. Laporte, University of California Press,
   1987.

Periodicals

"The Principles of Classification and a Classification of Mammals," *Bulletin of the American
   Museum of Natural History,* Volume 85, 1945,
   pp. 1–350.

SOURCES:

Books

Gould, Stephen Jay, "G.G. Simpson, Paleontology,
   and the Modern Synthesis," *The Evolutionary
   Synthesis: Perspectives on the Unification of
   Biology,* edited by Ernst Mayr and William B.
   Provine, Harvard University Press, 1980, pp.
   153–172.
Hecht, Max K., Bobb Schaeffer, Bryan Patterson,
   Richard Van Frank, and Florence D. Wood,
   "George Gaylord Simpson: His Life and
   Works to the Present," *Evolutionary Biology,*
   edited by Theodosius Dobzhansky, Max K.
   Hecht, and William C. Steere, Appleton-Centu-
   ry-Crofts, Volume 6, 1972, pp. 1–29.
McGraw-Hill Modern Scientists and Engineers,
   McGraw-Hill, 1980, pp. 118–120.

Periodicals

American Journal of Physical Anthropology, Volume 84, 1991, pp. 1–16.

                              —*Sketch by Linda Wasmer Smith*

I. M. Singer
1924-
American mathematician

Ône of the eminent research mathematicians of
the twentieth century, I. M. Singer has contributed to many areas of modern mathematics, but he is
most recognized for the Atiyah-Singer Index Theo-

I. M. Singer

rem. Combining geometry, topology, and partial
differential equations, he and Sir **Michael Atiyah**
were, as Singer stated in *Science,* "able to count the
number of global solutions to differential equations.
Our theorem unified many special cases that looked
different." Cited as one of the most important
mathematical works since World War II, the Atiyah-
Singer Index Theorem has numerous applications in
many fields, including elementary particle physics.

Isadore M. Singer was born on May 3, 1924, in
Detroit, Michigan. The elder son of Simon, a printer,
and Freda (Rose) Singer, he was educated in Detroit
public schools. While he was a student at Central
High School, his English and chemistry teachers urged
him to develop his intellectual abilities. As Singer
later recalled in *The Joys of Research,* "When I
learned about science and mathematics as a teenager,
I discovered that the manipulation of abstract objects,
their construction, and their rearrangement, were
things I could do very well." Singer attended the
University of Michigan, where he majored in physics
with a specialty in infrared spectroscopy. He received
a B.S. degree in 1944 at the age of nineteen and served
in the U.S. Army from 1944 until 1946. In the
military, Singer tried to master two important areas in
physics—relativity and quantum mechanics—but
found that he needed to study more advanced mathematics. He entered the University of Chicago for
graduate studies in mathematics, earning an M.S. in
1948 and a Ph.D. two years later.

In 1950 Singer began his teaching career at the Massachusetts Institute of Technology (MIT) and has remained, for the most part, affiliated with that institution; he briefly held positions at the University of California at Los Angeles, Columbia University, the Institute for Advanced Study, and the University of California at Berkeley. Singer was appointed Institute Professor at MIT in 1987. Even though he has had a distinguished career in mathematical research, Singer has been very active in teaching young mathematicians both on the graduate and undergraduate levels.

Singer's major contributions to mathematics have been in several diverse areas. In the 1950s, the primary focus of his work was functional analysis; in the 1960s and 1970s, the major emphasis of his work was on the Atiyah-Singer Index Theorem; and in the 1980s and 1990s his research has been devoted to the interface of geometry and physics. Singer told Cathleen M. Zucco in an interview that he wanted his future accomplishments to involve "important unsolved problems in modern physics where geometry should play an important role."

Collaborates with Sir Michael Atiyah

Singer was awarded a Sloan Fellowship in 1959 and decided to write his research paper on the Isle of Capri, where there would be no distractions to his work. He found, however, that isolation was not conducive to the writing of his mathematical ideas. After three months Singer left Capri and went to Oxford so that he could have the stimulation of books and colleagues to develop his ideas. It was on his first day at Oxford's Mathematics Institute that he and professor Michael Atiyah began a conversation which nine months later evolved into the Atiyah-Singer Index Theorem. This theorem combines different fields of mathematics in a novel way. The great significance of this theorem is that applications of it are still being found in both mathematics and physics.

During the 1970s and 1980s, Singer actively served on committees in Washington which had a direct impact on national science policy. He worked to make the public aware of the important applications of mathematics and to reverse the deterioration of federal funding for mathematical research. Notably, he was chairperson of the National Academy's influential Committee on Science, Engineering, and Public Policy from 1973 to 1978, and he was a member of the White House Science Council during Ronald Reagan's administration. In 1993 Singer was bestowed with the American Mathematical Society Award for Distinguished Public Service in recognition of his efforts to support mathematics in the public sector.

Throughout his career, Singer has earned numerous accolades. He was a Guggenheim fellow twice and received the Bocher Memorial Prize in mathematics in 1969. In 1985 he was awarded the National Medal of Science, a distinct honor for a mathematician. Singer was presented, in 1988, with the Eugene Wigner Medal in physics. In addition to these numerous honors, Singer acquired a wide reputation as an eloquent spokesperson for differential geometry, his area of specialty in geometry, and how it connects to other fields of mathematics and physics.

As a research mathematician, time has been essential in the development of Singer's ideas. His research work has involved highly abstract concepts that require uninterrupted concentration. Throughout the latter part of his career, he has set aside several afternoons a week for his continuing research. Given his demanding academic schedule, Singer has noted his satisfaction in obtaining one good idea a year. When asked what he likes best about his work, Singer told Zucco that it is "the excitement of new ideas and their development."

SELECTED WRITINGS BY SINGER:

Books

"Mathematics," *The Joys of Research,* edited by Walter Shropshire, Jr., Smithsonian Institution Press, 1981, pp. 38–46.

Periodicals

(With K. Hoffman) "On Some Problems of Gelfand," *Uspekhi Matematicheskikh Nasuk,* Volume XIV, number 3 (87), 1959, pp. 99–114.

(With Michael F. Atiyah) "The Index of Elliptic Operators on Compact Manifolds," *Bulletin of the American Mathematical Society,* Volume 69, 1963, pp. 422–33.

(With H. P. McKean, Jr.) "Curvature and the Eigenvalues of the Laplacian," *Journal of Differential Geometry,* March, 1967, pp. 43–69.

(With D. B. Ray) "Reidemeister Torsion and the Laplacian on Riemannian Manifolds," *Advances in Mathematics,* October, 1971, pp. 145–210.

(With Atiyah and V. K. Patodi) "Spectral Asymmetry and Riemannian Geometry," *Bulletin of the London Mathematical Society,* Volume 5, 1973, pp. 229–34.

SOURCES:

Periodicals

Kolata, Gina Bari, "Isadore Singer and Differential Geometry," *Science,* June 1, 1979, pp. 933–34.

Notices of the American Mathematical Society,
June, 1985, pp. 366–67.
Notices of the American Mathematical Society,
March, 1993, pp. 226–28.

Other

Singer, I. M., interview with Cathleen M. Zucco
conducted January 10, 1994.

—*Sketch by Cathleen M. Zucco*

Maxine Singer
1931-
American biochemist and geneticist

Maxine Singer, a leading scientist in the field of human genetics, is also a staunch advocate of responsible use of biochemical genetics research. During the height of the controversy over the use of recombinant deoxyribonucleic acid (DNA) techniques to alter genetic characteristics, she advocated a cautious approach. She helped develop guidelines to balance calls for unfettered genetics research as a means of making medically valuable discoveries with demands for restrictions on research to protect the public from possible harm. After the DNA controversy waned, Singer continued to contribute to the field of genetics, researching cures for cancer, hemophilia, and other diseases related to genetics.

Singer was born on February 15, 1931, in New York City, to Hyman Frank, an attorney, and Henrietta (Perlowitz) Frank, a hospital admissions officer, children's camp director, and model. Singer received her B.A. from Swarthmore College in Pennsylvania in 1952, and earned her Ph.D. in biochemistry from Yale in 1957. From 1956 to 1958 she worked as a U.S. Public Health Service postdoctoral fellow at National Institute for Arthritis, Metabolism and Digestive Diseases (NIAMD), National Institutes of Health (NIH), in Bethesda, Maryland. She then became a research chemist on the staff of the section on enzymes and cellular biochemistry from 1958 to 1974. There she conducted DNA research on tumor-causing virusesas well as on ribonucleic acid (RNA). In the early 1970s, Singer also served as a visiting scientist with the Department of Genetics of the Weizman Institute of Science in Rehovot, Israel.

While Singer was working at NIH, scientists learned how to take DNA fragments from one organism and insert them into the living cells of another. This "recombinant DNA" could direct the production of proteins in the foreign organism as if the DNA was still in its original home. This technique had the potential of creating completely new types of organisms. On one hand, the new research brought unprecedented opportunities to discover cures for serious diseases, to develop new crops, and otherwise to benefit humanity. Yet the prospect of creating as-yet-unknown life forms, some possibly hazardous, was frightening to many.

In 1972, one of Singer's colleagues and personal friends **Paul Berg** of Stanford University was the first to create recombinant DNA molecules. He later voluntarily stopped conducting related experiments involving DNA manipulation in the genes of tumor-causing viruses because of some scientists' fears that a virus of unknown properties might escape from the laboratory and spread into the general population.

Warns Public of Gene-Splicing Risks

Although Berg's self-restraint was significant, the catalyst for the debate over gene-splicing was the 1973 Gordon Conference, an annual high-level research meeting. Singer, who was co-chair of the event, was approached by several nucleic acid scientists with the suggestion that the conference include consideration of safety issues. Singer agreed. She opened the discussion with an acknowledgment that DNA manipulation could assist in combatting health problems, yet such experimentation brought to bear a number of moral and ethical concerns.

The scientists present decided, by ballot, to send a public letter about the safety risks of recombinant DNA research to the president of the National Academy of Sciences, and asked *Science* magazine to publish it. Singer and her co-chair, Dieter Söll of Yale University, wrote the letter warning that organisms of an unpredictable nature could result from the new technique, and suggested that the National Academy of Sciences study the problem and recommend guidelines. Concern generated by this letter led to another meeting at the Asilomer Conference Center in Pacific Grove, California, where a debate ensued. Such proceedings—to consider the ethical issues arising from the new DNA research—were unprecedented in the scientific community. Immediately after the Asilomer Conference concluded, a NIH committee began formulating guidelines for recombinant DNA research.

In helping develop the guidelines, Singer advocated a careful analytic approach. In 1976, she presented four principles to the committee to be used in drafting the guidelines. She advised that certain experiments posed such serious hazards that they should be banned altogether; that experiments with lesser or no potential hazards should be permitted if their benefits are unobtainable through conventional methods and if they are properly safeguarded; that the more risk in an experiment, the stricter the safeguards should be; and that the guidelines should be reviewed annually.

Singer provided a calm voice of reason throughout the public debate over gene-splicing that followed. Committees of lay people, such as the Coalition for Responsible Genetic Research, held demonstrations calling for a complete ban on recombinant DNA research. Some members of the media made analogies to the nightmarish vision contained in Aldous Huxley's book *Brave New World,* which described a genetically altered society. When sent to address a public forum on the issue in 1977, for example, Singer responded to accusations that scientists ignore public concerns. As Clifford Grobstein recounted in his book, *A Double Image of the Double Helix: The Recombinant-DNA Debate,* Singer maintained that "scientists recognize their responsibility to the public . . . (but) dispute over the best way to exercise responsibility must not be confused with the negation of it." According to Grobstein, Singer explained that "while freedom of inquiry is a democratic right, it is clearly unacceptable to cause harm in the name of research. But [Singer] warned that levels of anxiety are not necessarily directly related to levels of real risk."

During her career, Singer has also served on the editorial Board of *Science* magazine and has contributed numerous articles. In her writing for that publication about recombinant DNA research, she stressed the benefits to humanity that recombinant DNA techniques could bring, especially in increasing the understanding of serious and incurable disease. After the NIH guidelines were implemented, she told *Science* readers that "under the Guidelines work has proceeded safely and research accomplishments have been spectacular." By 1980, when public near-hysteria had waned, Singer called for a "celebration" of the progress in molecular genetics. In *Science* she wrote: "The manufacture of important biological agents like insulin and interferon by recombinant DNA procedures," as well as the failure of any "novel hazards" to emerge, was evidence of the value of the cautious continuation of DNA research.

Appointed Head of Cancer Research Lab

In 1974, Singer accepted a new position at NIH as chief of the Section of Nucleic Acid Enzymology, Division of Cancer Biology and Diagnosis (DCBD) at the National Cancer Institute in Bethesda, Maryland. In 1980 she became chief of the DCBD's Laboratory of Biochemistry. She held this post until 1988, when she became president of the Carnegie Institution, a highly regarded research organization in Washington, D.C. Singer remains affiliated with the National Cancer Institute, however, as scientist emeritus, where she continues her research in human genetics.

In addition to her laboratory research, Singer has devoted considerable time and energy to other scientific and professional pursuits. In 1981, she taught in the biochemistry department at the University of California at Berkeley. A skilled and prolific writer, she has issued more than one hundred books, articles, and papers. Most are highly technical, including numerous articles published in scientific journals. Singer also compiled a graduate-level textbook with Paul Berg on molecular genetics called *Genes and Genomes: A Changing Perspective.* Reviewers gave the work high praise for its clear presentation of difficult concepts. Marcelo Bento Soares 'in *Bioscience* also commented that the book was "superbly written" and "magnificently captures the sense of discovery, understanding, and anticipation that has followed the so-called recombinant DNA breakthrough."

Singer has also written extensively on less technical aspects of science. She and Berg authored a book for laypeople on genetic engineering, and she continued to promote the benefits of recombinant DNA techniques and battle public suspicion and fear long after the controversy peaked in the 1970s. In the early 1990s, for example, Singer issued an article encouraging the public to try the first genetically engineered food to reach American supermarket shelves. In describing the harmlessness of the "Flavr Savr" tomato, she decried public objections that eating it was dangerous, unnatural, or immoral to readers of the *Asbury Park Press.* Pointing out that "almost all the foods we eat are the product of previous genetic engineering by cross-breeding," Singer said that the small amount of extra DNA in the tomato would be destroyed in the digestive tract, and that people already consume the DNA present in the other foods in their diets. Moreover, she said the decision to eat a genetically altered tomato did not reduce her admiration for nature's creations.

In addition to her writing and lecturing, Singer has served on numerous advisory boards in the United States and abroad, including science institutes in Naples, Italy, Bangkok, Thailand, and Rehovot, Israel. She also has served on an advisory board to the Pope and as a consultant to the Committee on Human Values of the National Conference of Catholic Bishops. She worked on a Yale committee that investigated the university's South African investments, and serves on Johnson and Johnson's Board of Directors. Concerned about the quality of science education in the United States, she started First Light, a science program for inner-city children.

Singer travels extensively and maintains long work weeks to accommodate all her activities. She married Daniel Singer in 1952; the couple have four children: Amy Elizabeth, Ellen Ruth, David Byrd, and Stephanie Frank. Singer is the recipient of more than forty honors and awards, including some ten honorary doctor of science degrees and numerous commendations from NIH.

SELECTED WRITINGS BY SINGER:

Books

(With P. Berg) *Genes and Genomes: A Changing Perspective,* University Science Books, 1990.
(With Berg) *Dealing with Genes: The Language of Heredity,* University Science Books, 1992.

Periodicals

"In Vitro Synthesis of DNA: A Perspective on Research," *Science,* December 22, 1967, pp. 1550–51.
"Guidelines for DNA Molecules," *Science,* September 21, 1973, p. 1114.
"The Recombinant DNA Debate," *Science,* April 8, 1977, p. 127.
"Spectacular Science and Ponderous Process," *Science,* January 5, 1979, p. 9.
"Recombinant DNA Revisited," *Science,* September 19, 1980, p. 1317.
"Seeing a Red Menace in the New Hot Tomato," *Asbury Park Press,* August 15, 1993.

SOURCES:

Books

Grobstein, Clifford, *A Double Image of the Double Helix: The Recombinant-DNA Debate,* W. H. Freeman and Company, 1979, pp. 18–19, 72–73.
Krimsky, Sheldon, *Genetic Alchemy: The Social History of the Recombinant DNA Controversy,* MIT Press, 1982, pp. 181–183.
Lappé, Marc, *Broken Code: The Exploitation of DNA,* Sierra Club Books, 1984, pp. 19–25.
Lear, John, *Recombinant DNA: The Untold Story,* Crown, 1978, pp. 68–75.
Wade, Nicholas, *The Ultimate Experiment: Man-Made Evolution,* Walker, 1977, pp. 34–36.

Periodicals

Hoffee, Patricia A., "The New Genetics," *Science,* December 13, 1991.
"The Scientific Method," *U.S. News and World Report,* August 26-September 2, 1991, p. 94.
Soares, Marcelo Bento, "Precise Genetic Concepts," *Bioscience,* March, 1992, p. 211.

Other

Singer, Maxine F., interview with Donna Olshansky, conducted August 19, 1993.
Singer, Maxine F., Curriculum Vitae, current as of August, 1993.

—Sketch by Donna Olshansky

Richard H. Sioui
1937-
American chemical engineer

Richard H. Sioui is a chemical engineer of American Indian descent who has worked on both liquid fuels and composite materials. He is most noted, however, for his extensive work in the field of abrasives and has over 30 patents in this area. Because of his achievements, the American Indian Science and Engineering Society has asked to use him as a role model to encourage children of American Indian descent to enter the engineering field.

Richard Henry Sioui, a member of the Huron tribe, was born in Brooklyn, New York, on September 25, 1937, to Joseph Fernand Sioui, a waiter, and Ellen Anita (Johnson) Sioui. His career began in the United States Air Force, in which he served from 1955 to 1959. When his tour of duty was complete, he entered a co-operative work program at Northeastern University where he studied chemical engineering. Through the co-op program, he had a chance to work on a variety of different projects at companies such as DuPont and Monsanto. In addition to studying and working, he also married Mary Ann Kapinos in July of 1962, and started a family with the addition of their first daughter in 1963.

After obtaining his B.S. degree in 1964, he spent the summer at Millers Falls Company in Greenfield, Massachusetts, where he evaluated polymer applications. He then moved to the University of Massachusetts to continue his education, studying under a National Science Foundation Traineeship. He received his M.S. in 1967, and went on to complete his Ph.D. in 1968. His graduate research looked at the combustion of small droplets of liquid fuels; research important in the design of various types of engines and rocket motors.

Following completion of his studies, Sioui joined the Norton Company's Superabrasives Division in Worcester, Massachusetts, as a Senior Research Engineer. He remained in this position until promoted to

Research Supervisor in 1971. While Research Supervisor, he was awarded patents on some of his improvements in the production of abrasive grinding tools. His first patent covered a new way to prepare abrasive surfaces used for the grinding of metals and other materials. Through the addition of silver, copper, and graphite to the resins in which industrial diamond or cubic boron nitride (CBN) abrasive were embedded, he greatly improved the performance of these grinding surfaces. Furthermore, this enhanced the economics and applicability of using CBN in place of diamond abrasives. His invention of metal/polymer composite materials has also earned praise, as well as been awarded a patent. In addition, Sioui has received patents covering the production of resin grinding wheel cores, methods of bonding the abrasive surfaces to the cores, and a new type of magnetic core.

Sioui continued to advance both his education and career. After receiving a diploma from the School of Industrial Management at Worcester Polytechnic Institute in 1976, he was promoted to Technical Manager in 1979, Research Manager in 1982, then to Research Director in 1984. Following completion of his diploma from the Tuck Executive Program at Dartmouth College in 1986, he was promoted to Director of Technology at Norton in 1987.

In his role as Director of Technology, Sioui is responsible not only for all of the ongoing research at Norton, but also for control and development of the manufacturing processes. Norton Company is one of the world's largest users of diamond and CBN abrasive, and Sioui is responsible for the quality control of materials which the company purchases. He is also accountable for the quality of the grinding products produced, which are supplied to companies all over the world.

Outside of work, his time has been taken up by his family, which grew with the addition of five more children (two boys and three girls). He has also been involved extensively with the Boy Scouts of America. Sioui has achieved the rank of Eagle Scout himself, and is a member of the National Eagle Scout Association. He has also spent five years as committee chairman of troop 178 in Holden, Massachusetts, from 1981 to 1986.

SELECTED WRITINGS BY SIOUI:

Books

"The Evolution of Tests for Diamond Wheel Performance in Dry Tool and Cutter Sharpening," *Proceedings: Diamonds in the 80's,* Industrial Diamond Association of America, 1980, pp. 131–8.

Periodicals

"The Prediction of the Burning Constants of Suspended Hydrocarbon Fuel Droplets," *Combustion and Flame,* Volume 13, 1969, p. 447.
"The Use of Silver in Diamond and CBN Wheels for Dry Grinding Hard Materials," *Cutting Tool Engineering,* July/August, 1980, pp. 6–8.

—Sketch by Jerome P. Ferrance

Folke Karl Skoog
1908-
Swedish-born American botanist

Botanist Folke Karl Skoog is renowned for his pioneering research on auxins and cytokinins (hormones responsible for plant growth) and his development of a plant growth medium. His discovery of cytokinins in 1954 and subsequent studies of them have provided new insight into plant growth and paved the way toward research in biotechnology, or applied biological science, for decades. Cytokinins also prevent the yellowing of plants and are used commercially to keep vegetables green on store shelves.

Skoog was born in Halland, Sweden in 1908, the son of Karl and Sigrid (Person) Skoog. His father worked as an agronomist (a branch of agriculture dealing with field-crop production and soil management), while his mother stayed home to raise her three sons. The young Swede left his homeland to study chemistry at California Institute of Technology, where he earned his bachelor's degree in 1932. Back then, he was better known as a runner and in 1932 represented Sweden in the Olympics.

Skoog continued his graduate studies at Cal Tech, which was then the premier institute for plant hormone research. His professors included **Frits Went**, who discovered a class of plant growth hormones called auxins. Skoog earned his Ph.D. in biology from Cal Tech in 1936, then continued his studies as a post-doctorate fellow at the University of California at Berkeley. Skoog had decided to remain in the United States and in 1935 became a citizen. Skoog accepted a teaching and research position at Harvard University in 1937, where he worked until 1941, when he moved to Johns Hopkins University to serve as an assistant professor until 1944.

Skoog took a hiatus from his plant research for two years during World War II to work as a chemist for the Defense Department in Washington, D.C. In 1946, he resumed his teaching and research career at Washington University in St. Louis, but left after only three months. He was hired in 1947 as an associate professor at the University of Wisconsin in Madison, where over the next thirty-two years he would earn his reputation as one of the world's foremost botanists. The year Skoog arrived in Madison, he married Birgit Anna Lisa Bergner. Birgit had been trained as an engineer, but gave up her career ambitions to raise their only child, Karin (Skoog) Shepard. Skoog thrived at the Wisconsin university and in 1949 was appointed as a full professor.

Discovered New Class of Growth Hormones

In the early 1950s, the only known plant growth hormones were auxins. Skoog, who had in the 1930s performed pioneering research in the field of auxins, was experimenting with tobacco tumor tissue when he realized that he could promote growth even in the absence of auxins. "He had an intuitive feel for what the growing plants were telling him," former colleague Professor Eldon Newcomb of Oregon State University told Cynthia Washam in an interview. "He could sense when the data were telling him something important." Research on the tobacco tumor tissues led to Skoog's discovery in 1954 of a new class of growth hormones, called cytokinins. These hormones are produced in plant roots and travel up the stem to leaves and fruit. Skoog's discovery was initially met with skepticism. Many botanists thought that auxins were the only hormones responsible for plant growth.

Skoog, however, proved that cytokinins did exist, and he also showed that by manipulating the levels of auxins and cytokinins, he could promote the growth of only roots, only shoots, or both. His finding revolutionized horticulture by enabling scientists to control plant propagation. Cytokinins are also used to prevent green vegetables from yellowing.

Skoog was welcomed as a member of the American Academy of Arts & Sciences in 1954, and the National Academy of Sciences in 1956. In 1954, Skoog also earned the prestigious Stephen Hales Prize from the American Society of Plant Physiologists and his first honorary Ph.D., from Lund University in Sweden.

While building his reputation worldwide as a top researcher, Skoog was building his reputation back home as everyone's favorite professor. "He was warm and patient with his students," Newcomb said. "He formed a close relationship with all of them." Although Skoog taught only graduate students, he took a strong interest in the education of undergraduates. He formed a committee in the mid–1960s to develop what became one of the strongest undergraduate biology programs in the country. Another of Skoog's major scientific contributions came in 1962, when he

developed a medium that promoted plant growth faster and more effectively than older media.

Throughout his busy career, the athletic botanist always managed to find time for recreation. Colleagues remember him taking afternoon swims in a campus lake and playing touch football with fellow professors and students. On weekends, he often retreated to the family cottage in rural Door County, Wisconsin, where he enjoyed boating, swimming, fishing and deer hunting.

Skoog retired in 1979 as a professor emeritus, giving occasional lectures and reviewing scientific papers for several years afterward. In addition to earning many honorary doctorate degrees throughout the years, Skoog was awarded the National Medal of Science, his most prestigious honor, in 1991. In addition, the Cell Culture Association honored him with its Life Membership Award in 1991, and in 1992, the Tissue Culture World Congress gave him the Distinguished Life Achievement Award.

SELECTED WRITINGS BY SKOOG:

Books

(Editor) *Plant Growth Substances,* University of Wisconsin Press, 1951.

Periodicals

"Cytokinins," *Science,* Volume 148, 1965, pp. 532–533.

SOURCES:

Newcomb, Eldon, interview with Cynthia Washam conducted March 29, 1994.
Shepard, Karin, interview with Cynthia Washam conducted March 29, 1994.

—Sketch by Cynthia Washam

John Clarke Slater
1900-1976
American theoretical physicist

John Clarke Slater was one of the foremost theoretical physicists in the United States, whose work contributed significantly to the development of atomic, molecular, and solid-state physics. He was one of very few American theoretical physicists to embrace and advance quantum mechanics, which studies the interactions between matter and radiation. Perhaps foremost among his achievements was his idea that light consists of probability waves. Slater is also remembered for his outstanding ability as a teacher and administrator, and for his prodigious output as a writer of physics textbooks and academic papers.

Slater was born on December 22, 1900, in Rochester, New York. His father was head of the English department at the University of Rochester. Slater expressed a precocious interest in all things mechanical and electrical that blossomed into a love of physics. He enrolled in the University of Rochester in 1917 as an undergraduate student in physics, chemistry, and mathematics. In his sophomore year, he worked in the physics lab. His first brush with quantum theory—which was then still in its infancy and had not yet made it into Rochester's curriculum—came from his reading of **Niels Bohr**'s 1913 paper on the specific-orbits model of atomic structure.

In 1921 Slater moved to Harvard graduate school on an assistantship. There he worked with **P. W. Bridgman** and attended Bridgman's course in fundamental physics. He was more interested, though, in a course in quantum physics offered by E. C. Kemble. Within three years, Slater had completed work on his Ph.D. thesis, an experimental study devoted to an examination of the compressibility of the alkali halides. A Harvard Sheldon fellowship enabled him to continue his studies abroad. Slater first visited Cambridge University, whose Cavendish Laboratory was producing some of the most exciting results in quantum physics, before heading for Copenhagen. His destination was Niels Bohr's center for physical research, a mecca for theoretical physicists.

Publishes Controversial Theory with Bohr

Slater explained to Bohr his theory that classical radiation fields guide light quanta, in other words, photons. Although Bohr did not accept the idea of a photon, the general principles of the idea intrigued him and his colleague H. A. Kramers. They agreed to collaborate with Slater on a paper. It appeared in a 1924 issue of *Philosophical Magazine* as "The Quantum Theory of Radiation," under all of their names. This highly controversial paper rejected the prevailing notion of light quanta—that light consists of packages of energy—and instead suggested that light consists of probability waves, that is, mathematical entities that enabled physicists to predict the probability that certain events would or would not occur. Although the mathematics used in the paper were eventually proven wrong, the basic idea Slater and his colleagues advanced was correct. Later, based on a different

mathematical model, probability waves became a central tenet of quantum mechanics.

His association with such a luminary as Bohr catapulted Slater to instant celebrity and paved the way for his invitation to join the staff of Harvard's physics department on his return to the United States. In 1925 he published two important papers. The first was on the correlation of the width of a spectral line with the reciprocal lifetime of a stationary state. The second dealt with the interpretation of the spectra of hydrogen and ionized helium. Despite being geographically isolated from the hotbed of the new quantum mechanics in Europe, Slater kept abreast of developments. In 1926 he married Helen Frankenfeld. The match produced three children—Louise Chapin, John Frederick, and Clarke Rothwell—all of whom pursued academic careers.

In 1927 Slater produced his first paper on quantum mechanics proper, entitled "Radiation and Absorption on Schrödinger's Theory." Here, Slater employed the Austrian physicist **Erwin Schrödinger**'s idea of atoms as standing waves.

Heads Department of Physics at MIT

In 1930 on his return from a brief visit to Europe on a Guggenheim fellowship, Slater was appointed chairman of the Massachusetts Institute of Technology's physics department. His ambition as a teacher and administrator was to bring American physics education up to par with that in Europe, so that young American physicists would no longer have to make the pilgrimage abroad to finish their education. He directed a member of his department, N. H. Frank, to rework the undergraduate curriculum, and personally rewrote the senior course in theoretical physics. Slater did not neglect graduate training. He reorganized the available programs and the examination system to allow students more time for research.

The upshot of all of this activity was that Slater became, at the age of thirty-one, one of the National Academy's youngest members. He justified that honor with an interminable output of papers and books. Of the latter, he published fourteen during his lifetime, on subjects ranging from microwaves and chemical physics to quantum theory. His papers examined an assortment of phenomena, including directed valence and the quantum theory of the equation of state (1931); energy bands in metals (1934); ferromagnetism in nickel (1936); the structure of alloys and the superconductive state (1937); and the structure of insulating crystals (1938).

When World War II broke out, Slater joined the staff of the Radiation Laboratory, which had been set up at MIT to develop microwave radar. His resultant book, *Microwave Transmission,* quickly became the authority in the field. Later in the war he worked at the Bell Telephone Laboratories in Manhattan. There he undertook theoretical and experimental work on magnetrons, that is, diode vacuum tubes in which the flow of electrons is controlled by an external magnetic field to generate power at microwave frequencies.

After the war Slater redirected his attention to reshaping MIT's physics department, particularly, reorienting wartime pursuits to peaceful ends. He was determined to maintain the department's unique diversity despite the trend toward specialization. He converted the Radiation Laboratory into a research laboratory of electronics, established a laboratory of nuclear science and engineering, and established an acoustics laboratory. Peacetime also enabled him to redevote himself to his own interests, especially in solid-state and molecular physics. In 1950 he set up a research group called the Solid-State and Molecular Theory Group (SSMTG), a precursor to the Interdepartmental Center for Materials Science and Engineering, which was established ten years later.

The following year, acting on his desire to free himself of his administrative burdens, Slater accepted an invitation to become an institute professor at Brookhaven National Laboratory on Long Island. There, with some members of the SSMTG, he continued his research into the quantum theory of atoms, molecules, and solids using primitive computers. Sixty people were involved with the group during its fifteen year history. Slater had a hand in almost all of its work. He also produced five books related to the group's work. Slater remarried in 1954, having divorced his first wife. His second wife, Rose Mooney, was also a physicist.

In 1964 Slater had the special pleasure of standing head to head with his father when both were awarded honorary degrees by the University of Rochester. The following year, having reached the retirement age at MIT, Slater accepted the position of research professor at the University of Florida, where the retirement age was seventy. There, he joined the Quantum Theory Project, which had been set up by one of his colleagues from the SSMTG, Per-Olov Löwdin. With its emphasis on solid-state and statistical physics, Florida represented a welcome change from MIT, which at his leaving had "been literally captured by the nuclear theorists," Slater wrote in his autobiography. He persevered in his research into quantum mechanics, aided by more powerful computers, and studied compressibility and magnetic properties of solids, binding energies and magnetic properties of polyatomic molecules, and X-ray absorption. Until his death on July 25, 1976, he led an active professional and personal life.

SELECTED WRITINGS BY SLATER:

Books

(With N. H. Frank) *Introduction to Chemical Physics,* McGraw-Hill, 1933.

Microwave Transmission, McGraw-Hill, 1942.
(With Frank) *Electromagnetism,* McGraw-Hill, 1947.
(With Frank) *Mechanics,* McGraw-Hill, 1947.
Microwave Electronics, Van Nostrand, 1950.
Quantum Theory of Matter, McGraw-Hill, 1951.
Modern Physics, McGraw-Hill, 1955.
Quantum Theory of Atomic Structure, Volumes 1 and 2, McGraw-Hill, 1960.
Solid-State and Molecular Theory: A Scientific Biography, Wiley-Interscience, 1975.

Periodicals

(With N. Bohr and H. A. Kramers) "The Quantum Theory of Radiation," *Philosophical Magazine,* Volume 47, 1924, pp. 785–802.
"Radiation and Absorption on Schrödinger's Theory," *Proceedings of the National Academy of Sciences,* Volume 13, 1927, pp. 7–12.
"Light Quanta and Wave Mechanics," *Physics Review,* Volume 31, 1928, pp. 895–899.
"The Self-Consistent Field and the Structure of Atoms," *Physics Review,* Volume 32, 1928, pp. 339–348.
"Directed Valence in Polyatomic Molecules," *Physics Review,* Volume 37, 1931, pp. 481–489.
"The Electron Theory of Solids," *American Journal of Physics,* Volume 19, 1951, pp. 368–374.
"Interaction of Waves in Crystals," *Review of Modern Physics,* Volume 30, 1958, pp. 197–222.
"Energy-Band Theory of Magnetism," *Journal of Applied Physics,* Volume 39, 1968, 761–767.
"Statistical Exchange-Correlation in the Self-Consistent Field," *Advanced Quantum Chemistry,* Volume 6, 1972, pp. 1–91.

SOURCES:

Periodicals

Biographical Memoirs of the National Academy of Sciences, Volume 53, National Academy Press, 1982.

—*Sketch by Avril McDonald*

Vesto M. Slipher
1875-1969
American astronomer

Vesto M. Slipher discovered that most spiral galaxies are racing outward into space, providing key evidence (for **Edwin Hubble** and other researchers) that the universe is expanding. For over 50 years the director of the Lowell Observatory in Flagstaff, Arizona, Slipher directed the search leading to astronomer **Clyde Tombaugh**'s 1930 discovery of Pluto and was one of the first to provide evidence that gas and dust exists between stars. Slipher also discovered that spiral galaxies are rotating, and he was the first to measure the velocities of star clusters. Slipher is generally recognized as the one of the greatest spectroscopists in astronomy in the first half of the twentieth century, for both his innovations and specific discoveries.

Vesto Melvin Slipher was born on a farm in Mulberry, Indiana, on November 11, 1875. His parents, David Clarke Slipher and Hannah (App) Slipher, were both farmers. Nicknamed "V.M.", Slipher attended high school in Frankfort, Indiana, and taught at a small rural school until 1897, when he entered Indiana University at age 21. Under the tutelage of Wilbur Cogshall, who had worked at the Lowell Observatory in 1896–97, Slipher received a B.A. in celestial mechanics and astronomy in 1901. Cogshall persuaded Percival Lowell, an influential astronomer, to hire Slipher as a temporary assistant. Lowell asked Slipher to come to his observatory on Mars Hill in western Flagstaff, and Slipher arrived on August 10, 1901. The position proved more than temporary, as Slipher remained there for the rest of his working life.

He worked as an assistant from 1901 until 1915, making the bulk of his discoveries with a 24-inch refracting telescope made by Alvan Clark. Slipher worked with this instrument only because a more powerful 40-inch telescope at the Lowell Observatory was being used to look at Mars and search for a ninth planet. Besides carrying out astronomical observations, Slipher's duties also included taking care of Lowell's cow, Venus, and its calves, as well as tending to the observatory vegetable garden when Lowell was away.

Slipher's first task as Lowell's assistant was to install and test a spectrograph—an instrument capable of breaking starlight into its component colors for analysis—which Lowell intended to use for the study of planetary rotation. Built for the observatory by John A. Brashear of the Allegheny Observatory near Pittsburgh, Pennsylvania, the device may have been the best of its kind in the world; it was especially resistant to changes in temperature and vibrations. Slipher got the spectrograph in running order by the spring of 1902, the year before he received his M.A. from Indiana University, using it first to search for the presence of water vapor and oxygen on Mars and to make a measurement of the rotation period of Venus. In 1904, Slipher married Emma Rosalie Munger at Frankfort, Indiana. They set up house at the observatory, raising two children there, Marcia Frances and David Clark. Lowell was especially intrigued by the possibility that biological life existed on Mars, and Slipher made an unsuccessful search for the spectrum of chlorophyll on Mars in 1905–1907 (and again in 1924). By 1909, Slipher had already built a reputation as a skilled astronomer, and Indiana University, waiving its residence requirement as well as any need for separate graduate study, granted him a Ph.D. on the basis of a single published paper.

Discovers Recession of Galaxies

The same year, Lowell asked him to begin a spectral study of spiral nebulae. At the time, some astronomers believed that these nebulae rested within the Milky Way, while some speculated that they were actually "island universes" or "galaxies" at vast distances from the Milky Way. Lowell thought that spiral nebulae might be solar systems in formation, and assigned Slipher the task of comparing nebular spectra with those found within the solar system. Other work came first, however. In 1912, working with Lowell, Slipher carried out a study of planetary rotation. He found that Uranus' spectrum exhibited a pattern suggesting that it rotated on its axis once every 10.8 hours. Using similar spectral analysis, he was able to determine the rotation rates of Venus, Mars, Jupiter, and Saturn.

Concentrating at last on spiral nebulae, Slipher had obtained by 1913 four images of the Andromeda nebula's spectrum. Slipher noticed a peculiarity in the images; the entire wave band of this great spiral object was shifted toward the blue end of the spectrum. Interpreting this phenomenon as a Doppler shift, Slipher deduced that the object was racing toward the earth at a high rate of speed. A *Doppler shift* is a change in the apparent frequency of a wave emitted by a moving body. This change is proportionate to the relative motion of the wave source and the wave's observer. For example, the horn of a passing car sounds higher as the car approaches an observer and lower when the car is moving away from the observer. In the same way, the spectrum of an approaching luminous object has a higher frequency (shifted toward the blue end of the spectrum), while a receding object's light has a lower frequency (shifted toward the red end of the spectrum). In February 1913, Slipher determined from the magnitude of shift that the Andromeda nebula's speed was roughly 300 km/s. This was, at the time, the highest velocity ever recorded for any object in space.

In the 18 months following this measurement, Slipher obtained the speeds of 14 other spirals. (To obtain the spectrum of a faint nebula, Slipher sometimes had to leave the spectrograph shutter open for 60 hours or more.) A number of astronomers initially questioned Slipher's results, as the nebular speeds he obtained seemed impossibly high; even Slipher remained skeptical for a time. But before long it became clear that the speed data supported the notion that spiral nebulae were not within our own Milky Way galaxy, but were in fact separate galaxies at extreme distances from our own. At an August 1914 meeting of the American Astronomical Society in Evanston, Illinois, Slipher formally announced that most of the 15 spirals for which he had obtained spectra were receding, some in excess of 1,000 km/s. For over ten years after, Slipher was the only observer obtaining such spectra. By 1917, 21 of the 25 nebular spectra recorded by Slipher showed red shifts indicating recession.

Slipher determined that spiral nebulae were rotating as well as receding. Using a spectroscopic technique, he detected the rotation of galaxy NGC 4594 in the constellation Virgo in 1914. Measurements made by Slipher in the following years indicated that spiral galaxies rotated in a fashion similar to the winding of a spring, which contradicted a widely-held view that spirals were actually spinning as if unwinding. During this period, Slipher was promoted to assistant director of the Lowell Observatory, and when Lowell died in 1916, Slipher became acting director. In the following years, Slipher led solar eclipse expeditions to Syracuse, Kansas and Ensenada, Mexico, made spectroscopic studies of the chemical components of the night sky (including a study of the aurora phenomenon), and received several important honors: the Lalande prize and the gold medal of the Paris Academy of Sciences in 1918, and an honorary Sc.D. from the University of Arizona in 1923. Slipher also continued his studies of the chemical composition of planets, helping to identify the existence of iron and copper in the spectrum of Jupiter. His observations led to the 1934 discovery (by Ruppert Wildt) of methane and ammonia in planetary atmospheres.

Slipher made additional measurements of the spectra of spiral nebulae through the mid–1920s, at which time the work was taken up by astronomers **Milton Humason** and Edwin Hubble. Hubble, a supporter of the "island universe" theory who attended Slipher's 1914 address as a graduate student, seized upon Slipher's data, working out a method to determine the distances to spiral nebulae. With Humason's help, Hubble eventually demonstrated beyond a doubt that spiral nebulae are indeed im-

mensely distant galaxies. Moreover, the work of Slipher and Hubble, integrated with the theories of astronomers **Willem de Sitter** and **Georges Lemaître**, provided the foundation for the "big bang" theory, an explanation of the origin and large-scale behavior of the universe which is widely accepted today.

Discovers Interstellar Gas and Dust

During the period in which he studied nebulae, Slipher also made significant contributions to the search for interstellar gas and dust. Analyzing the fuzzy haze of light surrounding the Pleiades star cluster in the 1910s, he detected a spectrum resembling that of the stars within it; he concluded that the diffuse light was a cloud of dust grains reflecting starlight, and detected similar clouds in other regions of space. Following up on the work of astronomer Johannes Hartmann, Slipher also detected interstellar sodium around the star Beta Scorpii as well as a number of other stars, but it took nearly 20 years before his study of interstellar gas was validated by Hertzsprung, Eddington, and others.

Slipher was named permanent director of the Lowell Observatory in 1926. After this date, he primarily busied himself with administrative duties. He paved the way for Tombaugh's discovery of Pluto by procuring a 13-inch telescope, and preparing the lab equipment needed to analyze its photographs. During this phase of his career, Slipher's pioneering work was recognized with several awards; Slipher won both the Henry Draper gold medal of the National Academy of Sciences and the gold medal of the Royal Astronomical Society in 1933, as well as the Catherine Wolf Bruce gold medal of the Astronomical Society of the Pacific in 1935. Slipher retired from the Lowell Observatory in 1954 at the age of 79.

Active in the International Astronomical Union and the American Academy of Arts and Sciences, Slipher was "deliberate, fastidious, patient, and showed a high order of technical knowledge," according to the Lowell Observatory's John S. Hall in the February 1970 issue of *Sky & Telescope*. Slipher mostly kept to himself and rarely attended scientific meetings; when thrust into the limelight by the presentation of an award, Slipher humbly downplayed his accomplishments, emphasizing instead his simple joy in exploration. Though he spent less time performing research in his later years, Slipher remained very active. Even at age 60 he could climb, with ease, the 12,661-foot San Francisco Peaks north of Flagstaff, said colleague Henry Giclas in the National Academy of Science's *Biographical Memoirs*. When asked advice on a career in astronomy, Slipher would often emphasize the need for robust health.

Beyond his astronomical studies, Slipher involved himself in a wide range of activities. He bought ranch property around Flagstaff, operated a retail furniture store, and managed rental properties. He also helped found a community hotel for which he was board chairman for many years. Slipher helped found the Northern Arizona Society for Science and Art, and the Museum of Northern Arizona. He became a member and chairman of the Flagstaff school board and helped establish Flagstaff's first high school.

Slipher died of natural causes on November 8, 1969 in Flagstaff, just three days shy of his 94th birthday. In his will, he funded an annual grant and scholarship for science students and programs on behalf of the National Academy of Sciences and the Northern Arizona University Foundation in Flagstaff.

SELECTED WRITINGS BY SLIPHER:

Periodicals

"A Spectrographic Investigation on the Rotational Velocity of Venus," *Lowell Observatory Bulletin,* no. 3 (1903), pp. 9–18.

"On the Efficiency of the Spectrograph for Investigating Planetary Rotations and on the Accuracy of the Inclination Method of Measurement: Tests on the Rotation of the Planet Mars," *Lowell Observatory Bulletin,* no. 4 (1903), pp. 19–33.

"The Radial Velocity of the Andromeda Nebula," *Lowell Observatory Bulletin,* no. 58 (1913), pp. 56–7.

SOURCES:

Books

The American Philosophical Society Year Book 1970, The American Philosophical Society, 1971, pp. 161–66.

Dictionary of Scientific Biography, Charles Scribner's Sons, 1975, pp. 454–56.

National Academy of Sciences Biographical Memoirs, Volume 52, National Academy Press, 1980, pp. 411–441.

Periodicals

New York Times, November 10, 1969, p. 47.

Parker, Barry, "Discovery of the Expanding Universe," *Sky & Telescope,* September, 1986, pp. 227–30.

—*Sketch by Sebastian Thaler*

Maud Slye
1879-1954
American pathologist

Maud Slye devoted her life to cancer research by investigating the inheritability of the disease in mice. Performing extensive breeding studies on the hereditary transmission of cancer, she kept meticulous pedigree records and autopsied thousands of mice during her lifetime. Her work was controversial, however; advocating the archiving of complete medical records for individuals, she believed that human beings could eradicate cancer by choosing mates with the appropriate genotype. Sometimes referred to as "America's Curie," Slye received wide publicity for her work and was honored by many organizations.

Slye was born in Minneapolis, Minnesota, on February 8, 1879, the daughter of James Alvin and Florence Alden Wheeler Slye. Her family, though poor, traced their ancestry back to John Alden of the Plymouth colony. At age seventeen, Slye entered the University of Chicago with savings of forty dollars and the desire to become a scientist. Attending the university for three years, she supported herself by working as a secretary for university president William Harper. After a nervous breakdown, Slye convalesced in Woods Hole, Massachusetts, then completed her B.A. degree at Brown University in 1899. Hired as a teacher at the Rhode Island State Normal School, she stayed at the institution until 1905.

In 1908 Slye received a grant to do postgraduate work at the University of Chicago. Interested in the hereditary basis of disease, she began her work with six Japanese "waltzing" mice which were afflicted with a hereditary neurological disorder. Slye became intrigued by the inheritability of cancer when she heard of several heads of cattle at the Chicago stock yards—all with cancer of the eye—that had come from the same ranch. Inspired by this and other data, Slye went forward with her studies, breeding cancerous mice with one another as well as healthy mice with other healthy mice.

In 1911, Slye became a member of the university's newly created Sprague Memorial Institute, and in 1913 she presented her first paper on cancer before the American Society for Cancer Research. Becoming director of the Cancer Laboratory at the University of Chicago in 1919, she was promoted to assistant professor in 1922, then to associate professor in 1926. In 1936, Slye left her mice in the care of an assistant and took her first vacation in twenty-six years (earlier, when she had visited her ailing mother in California, she rented a boxcar and took her mice with her).

Although Slye discredited a prevailing theory that stated cancer was contagious, it became clear as her work proceeded that the appearance of cancer in an individual was not as simple as the presence of one gene. In later years, Slye posited that two conditions were necessary to produce cancer: inherited susceptibility, and prolonged irritation of the cancer-susceptible tissues. Nonetheless, further studies by other scientists have confirmed that while heredity can be a factor in certain types of cancer, it is much more complex than Slye had perceived.

Slye's work was recognized with several awards and honors, including the gold medal of the American Medical Association in 1914, and the Ricketts Prize in 1915. She also received the gold medal of the American Radiological Society in 1922. A member of the Association for Cancer Research, the American Medical Association, and the American Association for the Advancement of Science, Slye was the author of forty-two brochures on cancer and two volumes of poetry, *Songs and Solaces* and *I in the Wind*. At the time of her retirement in 1945 Slye was made professor emeritus of pathology, and she spent her retirement years analyzing data accumulated during her years of research. Slye never married. She died September 17, 1954, and was buried in Chicago's Oak Woods Cemetery.

SOURCES:

Books

Current Biography, H. W. Wilson, 1940, pp. 743–745.
Kass-Simon, G., and Patricia Farnes, editors, *Women of Science: Righting the Record,* Indiana University Press, 1990, pp. 278–279.
O'Neill, Lois Decker, editor, *The Women's Book of World Records and Achievements,* Doubleday, 1979, p. 217.

Periodicals

Reader's Digest, March 1936, pp. 77–80.
Newsweek, April 10, 1937, pp. 26–28.
New York Times, September 18, 1954, p. 15.

—*Sketch by Jill Carpenter*

Stephen Smale
1930-
American mathematician

Stephen Smale has worked in a number of mathematical fields, including topology and dynamical systems. In the 1970s he became especially interested in the application of mathematical theory to economics. More recently, his research has focused on computer science and its relevance to fundamental principles of mathematics. In recognition of his work in these fields, Smale has been honored with the Veblen Prize, the Fields Medal, and the Chauvenet Prize.

Smale was born in Flint, Michigan, on July 15, 1930. His parents were Lawrence and Helen Smale. Smale has described his father as an "armchair revolutionary" who was once expelled from Albion College in Michigan for publishing a newsletter whose political and social views were offensive to college administrators. The elder Smale never returned to college and eventually became an assistant in the ceramics laboratory at the AC Sparkplug factory in Flint.

Becomes Politically Active at an Early Age

In 1935 when Smale was five years old, his family moved to a small farm outside of Flint and he began school in a one-room schoolhouse. In high school Smale's primary interest was chemistry, and for a while he planned on a career in that field. He also became politically active during his high-school years, organizing a protest against the omission of evolution from his biology class curriculum. The protest was not very successful, as he told Donald J. Albers and Constance Reid in *More Mathematical People,* "I am not sure I succeeded in getting even one other person to sign the petition."

In 1948 Smale enrolled at the University of Michigan planning to major in physics rather than chemistry. He did poorly in physics, however, and gradually drifted into mathematics because it was a subject in which he had always excelled. Still, until his second year in graduate school he did not make a firm decision to pursue a career in mathematics. In 1953 he added an M.S. to the B.S. he had received the year before and, three years later, he received his Ph.D., also from the University of Michigan.

During his college career Smale was involved in number of activities beyond his academic studies. As he told Albers and Reid, he "play[ed] a lot of chess and . . . a lot of Go [a Japanese game similar to chess or checkers]." Smale was also a member of the

Stephen Smale

Communist party and was very active in opposition to the Korean War. His primary motivation for staying in college, he later admitted, was to avoid being drafted into fighting a war to which he was strongly opposed.

Begins Work in Topology

The mathematical topic that first attracted Smale's attention was topology, the mathematical study of the properties of figures that are not affected by changes in shape or size. For a period of about seven years beginning in graduate school, Smale worked on topological questions, a field that he later described as "very fashionable" at the time. He chose to pursue research in topology, he told Albers and Reid, because it was "just there." Despite this attitude, his work proved valuable, and he was awarded the prestigious Fields Medal of the International Mathematical Union in 1966 for his research in the field.

Smale accepted an appointment as professor of mathematics at Columbia University in 1961, the same year he made a surprising decision: He chose to abandon his work in topology and begin research in a new field, that of dynamical systems. Dynamical systems refers to mathematical methods for dealing with changes that take place in some real or abstract system over time. For the next five years Smale vacillated among a number of mathematical fields, including the calculus of variations and infinite dimensional manifolds. He also decided to leave

Columbia University and accepted a position as professor of mathematics at the University of California in Berkeley in 1964 where he began to concentrate once again on dynamical systems. In 1970 Smale experienced yet another career transformation that was prompted by a series of conversations he had with Gerard Debreu, a Nobel laureate in economics. From these conversations, Smale began to work on the applications of mathematical theory to economic systems.

Smale remained politically active during his years at Columbia and Berkeley. He was outspoken in his opposition to the war in Vietnam and helped organize, along with Jerry Rubin and others, the "days of protest" held against the war. However, his political attitudes have undergone an evolution over the past two decades. After a series of trips to Russia in the 1960s, Smale became disillusioned with communism and eventually found himself in agreement with at least some principles of conservative political philosophy. He recently described himself to Albers and Reid as being "consistently ... against the military" and having beliefs that are "more radical than those of most liberals," but "conservative part of the time."

In recent years, Smale has become interested in computer sciences. He has expressed an interest in bringing the mathematics used in this field into closer relationship with mainstream mathematics. Although his objective is not yet defined, Smale feels that establishing such a relationship may result in some revolutionary changes in the nature of mathematics itself.

Smale married Clara Davis, a classmate at the University of Michigan, in 1955. The couple has two children, Laura, a biological psychologist, and Nat, a mathematician. Smale has a number of leisure interests including a large mineral collection and a forty-three-foot, ocean-going ketch. In addition to his Fields Medal, Smale has been given the 1966 Veblen Prize of the American Mathematical Society and the 1988 Chauvenet Prize of the Mathematical Association of America.

SELECTED WRITINGS BY SMALE:

Books

(With M. W. Hirsch) *Differential Equations, Dynamical Systems and Linear Algebra,* Academic Press, 1974.

The Mathematics of Time: Essays on Dynamical Systems, Economic Processes, and Related Topics, Springer-Verlag, 1980.

SOURCES:

Books

Albers, Donald J., Gerald L. Alexanderson, and Constance Reid, editors, *More Mathematical People,* Harcourt, 1991, pp. 305–323.

—*Sketch by David E. Newton*

Hamilton O. Smith
1931-
American molecular biologist

Hamilton O. Smith shared the 1978 Nobel Prize in physiology or medicine with fellow biologists **Werner Arber** and **Daniel Nathans** for the set of linked discoveries that started off the boom in biotechnology. Because of these discoveries, researchers can more easily elucidate the structure and coding of deoxyribonucleic acid (DNA) molecules (the basic genetic map of an organism), and they hope to correct many genetic illnesses in the future. It is also possible to design new organisms, a controversial but potentially beneficial technology. Smith purified and explained the activity of the first restriction enzyme, which became the principal tool used by genetic engineers to selectively cut up DNA. (Arber had linked restriction and modification to DNA, and predicted the existence of restriction enzymes. Nathans, under Smith's encouragement at Johns Hopkins, developed techniques that enabled their practical use.)

Hamilton Othanel Smith was born on August 23, 1931, in New York City, to Bunnie (Othanel) Smith and Tommie Harkey Smith. His father, an assistant professor of education at the University of Florida, finished his Ph.D. at Columbia University in 1937 and took a new teaching job at the University of Illinois. The family then moved to Urbana, where Smith and his brother attended public school. It was here that Smith's interest in science began. He and his brother even equipped a laboratory in their basement with money from their paper routes. Smith graduated from University High School in three years, enrolling at a local university in 1948.

Smith came to the study of genetics by way of medicine. Initially a mathematics major at the University of Illinois, he transferred to the University of California at Berkeley in 1950 to study biology and graduated with a bachelor's degree in 1952. He obtained a medical degree from the Johns Hopkins

School of Medicine in 1956. The following year, Smith married Elizabeth Anne Bolton, a nurse. They eventually had four sons and a daughter. During the years 1956 to 1962, he held various posts, including an internship at Washington University in St. Louis, Missouri, a two-year Navy stint in San Diego, California, and a residency at Henry Ford Hospital in Detroit, Michigan. He gradually taught himself genetics and molecular biology in his spare time. In 1962 he began a research career at the University of Michigan on a postdoctoral fellowship from the National Institutes of Health, before finally returning to Johns Hopkins in 1965 as a research associate in the microbiology department. He was named a full professor of microbiology in 1973, and professor of molecular biology and genetics in 1981. In 1975, Smith was awarded a Guggenheim Fellowship for a year of study at the University of Zurich in Switzerland.

Restriction Enzyme Discovery Leads to Nobel Prize

DNA, the genetic material in all cells, is a long, chain-like molecule encoded along its structure for individual genes and thereby individual proteins. Each link in the chain is one of four possible nucleotides (adenine, guanine, cytosine, and thymine) arranged in varying sequences. An individual gene's function is coded by the order of the links, as a word's meaning is coded by the order of the letters. Much of the fundamental research in biotechnology was accomplished by studying DNA from both bacteria and the viruses—also called bacteriophages—that can infect bacteria. If a bacterium can break up invading viral DNA without harming its own DNA, it destroys the virus and thus resists infection. Bacteria that resist infection chemically modify parts of their DNA, usually with a methylating enzyme called a methylase, so it cannot be cut. Then they damage the viral DNA with a specific restriction enzyme (also called a restriction endonuclease). The bacterial DNA remains undamaged because of its chemical alteration, while the viral DNA is cut apart by the endonuclease.

Restriction enzymes are classified as Class I or Class II. Class I enzymes recognize specific DNA sequences, but they do not cut DNA only at those locations. Each Class II endonuclease, however, cuts only between two specific sequences of nucleotides, and no others. The mechanism of this type of bacterial resistance is called restriction-modification and involves the matched set of Class II endonuclease—methylase enzymes. "Restriction" means cutting DNA at a specific location, and "modification" means the enzyme-driven chemical change in the DNA which prevents such cutting. (Of course, viruses eventually can evolve modifications of their own which prevent their destruction by restriction enzymes; an appropriately modified virus can thus infect a formerly resistant strain of bacteria.)

Smith had been interested in bacterial genetics for many years, and spent 1966 working in Geneva, Switzerland, with Werner Arber. After his return to the U.S., Smith purified the first Type II restriction endonuclease, which he obtained from the bacterium *Hemophilus influenzae,* and identified the nucleotide sequence which the enzyme would cut. He gave a supply of the enzyme to Daniel Nathans, who used it in his own work. The three men eventually won the 1978 Nobel Prize. The presenter of the prize noted that Smith proved Arbor's hypothesis about restriction enzymes, pointing the way for future research.

The exacting specificity of Class II restriction enzymes makes them useful because biotechnologists can now cut DNA apart selectively. Then they can add and subtract specific nucleotides, and reproducibly weld (recombine) the links back together in a new order. This new piece of DNA now codes for a different protein. The current and potential uses of these procedures are enormous. Biotechnologists can genetically engineer bacteria that produce a particular chemical; human insulin for the treatment of diabetes is now made by such "recombinant" bacteria. Other bacteria have been designed to chew up oil slicks. One of the tasks that biotechnologists would like to accomplish is the eradication of genetic illness by correcting the mistaken DNA codes that cause it. Sickle-cell anemia, for example, is a life-threatening and incurable disease resulting from a mistake in two of the genes that code for the blood protein hemoglobin. Gene therapies are still highly experimental and controversial, but tests are beginning on them.

SELECTED WRITINGS BY SMITH:

Periodicals

"A Restriction Enzyme from Hemophilus Influenzae: I. Purification and General Properties," *Journal of Molecular Biology,* Volume 51, 1970, p. 379.
"A Restriction Enzyme from Hemophilus Influenzae: II. Base Sequence of the Recognition Site," *Journal of Molecular Biology,* Volume 51, 1970, p. 393.
"Restriction Endonucleases in the Analysis and Restructuring of DNA Molecules," *Annual Review of Biochemistry,* Volume 44, 1975, pp. 273–293.

SOURCES:

Books

Nobel Prize Winners: An H.W. Wilson Biographical Dictionary, Wilson, 1987, pp. 983–985.

Periodicals

Science, December 8, 1978, pp. 1068, 1069.

—*Sketch by Gail B.C. Marsella*

Michael Smith
1932-
English-born Canadian biochemist

Michael Smith began his professional research career in salmon physiology and endocrinology, but returned to the chemical synthesis that had been his first interest, including the chemical synthesis of deoxyribonucleic acid (DNA). Smith experimented with isolating genes and invented site-directed mutagenesis, a technique for deliberately altering gene sequences. Smith's work was hailed as having tremendous implications for genetic studies and the understanding of how individual genes function, and already has been applied in the study of disease-producing viruses. In 1993 Smith shared the Nobel Prize in Chemistry independently with **Kary Mullis**. The Royal Swedish Academy of Sciences credited Smith and Mullis with having revolutionized basic research and saluted the possibilities offered by their research toward the cure of hereditary diseases.

Smith was born in Blackpool, England, on April 26, 1932. His parents were Rowland Smith, a market gardener, and Mary Agnes Armstead Smith, a bookkeeper who also helped with the market gardening. Smith was admitted to Arnold School, the local private secondary school, with a scholarship he earned based on his examination results (this examination was taken, at the time, by all English children when they finished their primary education). Without this scholarship, Smith would have had little opportunity for advanced education, as his parents did not have the money to pay for it. While at Arnold School, Smith became involved in scouting, which eventually led to a life-long interest in camping and other outdoor activities.

After graduating from Arnold School in 1950, Smith enrolled at the University of Manchester in order to study chemistry, realizing a natural inclination toward the "hard" sciences. He moved rapidly through school, receiving a B.Sc. in 1953, and a Ph.D. in chemistry in 1956, both sponsored by scholarship. Smith's desire following completion of his Ph.D. was to earn a fellowship on the West Coast of the United States. This did not work out, but he was accepted into biochemist **Har Gobind Khorana**'s laboratory in

Michael Smith

Vancouver, Canada. Smith's original plan in migrating to Canada was to work for a year, then return to England and work for a chemical company. However, his experience working with Khorana, who would win the Nobel Prize in 1968 for his contributions to genetics, changed his plans. Smith decided university research was the path he wanted to take and that British Columbia, with its natural beauty, would be his home. Smith is now a Canadian citizen.

Smith stayed with the Khorana group and moved with it in 1960 to the Institute for Enzyme Research at the University of Wisconsin. (Smith had recently married Helen Christie. The couple later separated, but they had three children, Tom, Ian, and Wendy.) Until then, Smith's work in Canada had been in several different areas of chemical synthesis. In 1961 he decided it was time for a change and decided to relocate to the West Coast. Smith accepted a position as head of the chemistry section of the Vancouver Laboratory of the Fisheries Research Board of Canada. His work there was mainly in salmon physiology and endocrinology, but he also continued to work in chemical synthesis.

Move to Academia Culminates in Nobel Prize

In 1966 Smith entered the academic field, taking an appointment as associate professor of biochemistry and molecular biology at the University of British Columbia (UBC), and bringing with him an interest in chemically synthesized DNA (the molecule of heredity). Also beginning in 1966 Smith held a concurrent position as medical research associate of the Medical Research Council of Canada. He was made full professor in 1970, and has continued his teaching duties ever since. In 1986 he was asked to establish a biotechnology laboratory on the campus of UBC, which he has headed since that time.

Smith has taken three sabbaticals from his duties at the University of British Columbia, spending three months in 1971 at Rockefeller University in New York, one year during 1975 and 1976 at the Medical Research Council laboratory in Cambridge, and eight months in 1982 at Yale University. The middle excursion was spent in English biochemist **Frederick Sanger**'s laboratory learning about DNA sequence determination, essential to Smith's later research.

Smith was first able to isolate genes using chemical synthesis in 1974. Slowly he developed what became known as site-directed mutagenesis, a technique that allows gene sequences to be altered deliberately. More specifically, it involves separating one strand of a piece of DNA and producing a mirror image of it. This mirror image can then be used as a probe into a gene. It can also be used with chemical enzymes—proteins that act as catalysts in biochemical reactions—that are able to cut and splice DNA in living cells. Jeffrey Fox, editor of *Bioscience,* called this process the "intellectual bombshell that triggered protein engineering," as quoted in the Toronto *Globe and Mail.* Smith's findings were published in 1978 in *Journal of Biological Chemistry.* This paper lays the foundation of the research Smith has done since. The paper concludes, "This new method of mutagenesis has considerable potential in genetic studies. Thus, it will be possible to change and define the role of regions of DNA sequence whose function is as yet incompletely understood."

Smith, in demonstrating that biological systems are chemical, has allowed scientists to tinker systematically with genes, altering properties one at a time to see what effect each alteration may have on the gene's functioning. Genes are the building blocks for countless proteins that make up skin, muscles, bone, and hormones. Changes in the expression of these proteins reveal to the scientist how his or her tinkering has altered the gene function. This process has been used specifically to study disease-producing viruses, such as those that cause cancer. The eventual goal is to uncover the functioning of the genes, so drugs to combat the viruses can be developed.

After being several times a nominee, Smith was awarded the Nobel Prize in Chemistry in 1993 jointly with Kary Mullis from California. Their work was not collaborative, though both dealt with biotechnology. Announcing the award, the Royal Swedish Academy of Sciences credited Smith for having "revolutionized basic research and entirely changed researchers' way of performing their experiments," as quoted in the Toronto *Globe and Mail.* The academy further said Smith's work holds great promise for the future with the "possibilities of gene therapy, curing hereditary diseases by specifically correcting mutated code words in the genetic material."

The award money from the Nobel Prize amounted to close to $500,000 Cdn for Smith. With it he established an endowment fund, half of which will be earmarked to aid research on molecular genetics of the central nervous system, specifically in relation to schizophrenia research. The other half is to be divided between general science awareness projects and the Society for Canadian Women in Science and Technology in an effort to induce more women to pursue careers in science. He also convinced both the provincial and federal governments to contribute to his funds.

In addition to his receipt of the Nobel Prize, Smith has garnered numerous other honors in the course of his career, including the Gairdner Foundation International Award in 1986, and the Genetics Society of Canada's Award of Excellence in 1988. He has assumed several administrative responsibilities, including becoming acting director of the Biomedical Research Center, a privately funded research institute, in 1991, and is a member of the Canadian Biochemical Society, the Genetics Society of America, and the American Association for the Advancement of Science. He is a fellow of the Chemical Society of London, the Royal Society of Canada, and the Royal Society of London, and has served on several medical committees, such as the advisory committee on research for the National Cancer Institute of Canada. He is a popular speaker, and has delivered over 150 addresses throughout the world during the course of his career. His scientific research articles number more than two hundred.

SELECTED WRITINGS BY SMITH:

Books

(With S. Gillam) "Constructed Mutants Using Synthetic Oligodeoxyribonucleotides as Site-Specific Mutagens," *Genetic Engineering: Principles and Methods,* edited by J. K. Setlow and A. Hollaender, Volume 3, Plenum, 1981, pp. 1–52.

Periodicals

(With G. I. Drummond and H. G. Khorana) "The Synthesis and Properties of Ribonucleoside-3',5' Cyclic Phosphates," *Journal of the American Chemical Society,* Volume 83, 1961, pp. 698–706.

(With Clyde A. Hutchison, III, Sandra Phillips, Marshall H. Edgell, and others) "Mutagenesis at a Specific Position in a DNA Sequence," *Journal of Biological Chemistry,* September 25, 1978, pp. 6551–6560.

"In Vitro Mutagenesis," *Annual Review of Genetics,* Volume 19, 1985, pp. 423–462.

SOURCES:

Periodicals

Boei, William, "Nobelist to Give Prize Money Away," *Vancouver Sun,* November 27, 1993, p. A3.

Matas, Robert, "B.C. Scientist Awarded Nobel," *Globe and Mail* (Toronto), October 14, 1993, pp. A1, A4.

Surtees, Lawrence, "Genetics Society Prize Won by UBC Scientist," *Globe and Mail* (Toronto), August 24, 1988, p. A8.

Other

Smith, Michael, interview with Kimberlyn McGrail conducted January 4, 1994.

—*Sketch by Kimberlyn McGrail*

George Davis Snell
1903-
American immunogeneticist

Geneticist George David Snell's pioneering research on the immune system in the 1930s and 1940s enabled medical science to develop the process of organ transplantation. Through skin grafts performed on mice at the Jackson Hole Laboratory, he discovered the factor (known as histocompatibility) that enables doctors to determine whether organs and tissues can be successfully transplanted from one body to another. Snell's research earned him the 1980 Nobel Prize for medicine or physiology.

One of three children, Snell was born on December 19, 1903, in Bradford, Massachusetts, to Cullen Snell and the former Kathleen Davis. Snell's father developed and manufactured many inventions, including a mechanism for starting motorboat engines. In Snell's fifth year the family moved to Brookline. Snell's interests while growing up were varied, and included science, math, sports, and music.

After enrolling at New Hampshire's Dartmouth College in 1922, Snell was influenced to major in biology after taking a genetics course taught by Professor John Gerould. He obtained a B.S. degree in that subject in 1926 and enrolled at Harvard that same year so he could study genetics under the renowned biologist William Castle, who was among the first American scientists to delve into the biological laws of inheritance regarding mammals. Snell received a Ph.D. in 1930 after completing his dissertation on linkage, the means by which two or more genes on a chromosome are interrelated. That same year he became an instructor of zoology at Rhode Island's Brown University, only to leave in 1931 to work at the University of Texas at Austin following receipt of a National Research Council Fellowship.

Snell's decision to accept the fellowship turned out to be a momentous one, as he began work for the famed geneticist **Hermann Joseph Muller**, whose research with fruit flies led to the discovery that X rays could produce mutations in genes. At the university, Snell experimented with mice, showing that X rays could produce mutations in rodents as well. Although Snell left the University of Texas in 1933 to serve as assistant professor at the University of Washington, he ventured to the Jackson Laboratory in Bar Harbor, Maine, in 1935 to return to research work. The laboratory, specializing in mammalian genetics, was well-known for its work in spite of its small size.

After continuing his work with X rays and mice, Snell decided to embark on a new study. Snell's project was concerned with the notion of transplants. Earlier scientific research had indicated that certain genes are responsible for whether a body would accept or reject a transplant. The precise genes responsible had not then been identified, however.

Snell began his experiments by performing transplants between mice with certain physical characteristics. He quickly discovered those mice with certain identical characteristics—in particular a twisted tail—tended to accept each other's skin grafts. In 1948 Peter Gorer came to Jackson Laboratory from London, England. Gorer, who had also conducted experiments on mice, developed an antiserum. He had discovered the existence of a certain antigen (foreign protein) in the blood of mice which induced an immune reaction when injected into other mice. Gorer had called this type of substance "Antigen II."

Partnership Leads to Key Discovery

In collaboration, Snell and Gorer proved that Antigen II was present in mice with twisted tails, indicating that the genetics code for Gorer's antigen and the code found by Snell to be vital for tissue acceptance were identical. They called their discovery of this factor "H–2," for "Histocompatibility Two" (a term invented by Snell to describe whether a transplant would be accepted or rejected).

Later research revealed that instead of only a single gene being responsible for this factor, a number of closely related genes controlled histocompatibility. As a result, this was subsequently designated as the Major Histocompatibility Complex (MHC). The discovery of the MHC, and subsequent research by other scientists in the 1950s which proved it also existed in humans, made widespread organ transplantation possible. Donors and recipients could be matched (as had been done with blood types) to see if they were compatible.

Eventually Snell was able to produce what he called "congenic mice"—animals that are genetically identical except for one particular genetic characteristic. Unfortunately, the first strains of these mice were destroyed in a 1947 forest fire which burned down the laboratory. However, Snell's tenacity and dedication enabled him to rebound from this setback. Within three years he had created three strains of mice which differed genetically only in their ability to accept tissue grafts. The development of congenic strains of mice opened up a new field for experimental research, with Jackson Laboratory eventually being able to supply annually tens of thousands of these mice to other laboratories.

In 1952 Snell became staff scientific director and, in 1957, staff scientist at Jackson Laboratories. In those capacities he continued his research, particularly on the role that MHC plays in relation to cancer. Experiments he conducted with congenic mice found that on some occasions the mice rejected tumors which had been transplanted from their genetic twins. This "hybrid resistance" indicated that some tumors provoke an immune response, causing the body to produce antibodies to fight the tumor. This discovery could eventually be of great importance in developing weapons to fight cancer.

Although he retired in 1968, Snell continued to visit the lab, discuss scientific and medical matters with colleagues, and write articles and books. Elected to the American Academy of Arts and Sciences in 1952 and to the National Academy of Science in 1970, he is also a member of international scientific societies, including the French Academy of Science and the British Transplantation Society. Snell won numerous awards during the 1960s and 1970s, such as the Hectoen Silver Medal from the American Medical Association, the Gregor Mendal Award for genetic research, and a career award from the National Cancer Institute. This culminated in his winning the 1980 Nobel Prize in medicine or physiology for his work on histocompatibility. He shared this with two other immunogeneticists, **Jean Dausset** and **Baruj Benacerraf**. After being told of the Nobel committee's decision, Snell said there should have been a fourth recipient—his colleague Peter Gorer who died in 1962 and was thus ineligible to receive the prize.

Married in 1937 to the former Rhoda Carson, Snell and his wife live in Bar Harbor. They have three sons—Peter, Roy, and Thomas.

SELECTED WRITINGS BY SNELL:

Books

The Biology of the Laboratory Mouse, Blakiston, 1941.
Cell Surface Antigens: Studies in Mammals Other Than Man, MSS Information Corporation, 1973.
Genetic and Biological Aspects of Histocompatibility Antigens, Munksgaard, 1973.
(With Jean Dausset and Stanley Nathanson) *Histocompatibility,* Academic Press, 1976.

SOURCES:

Books

Dowie, Mark, *"We Have A Donor": The Brave New World of Medical Transplants,* St. Martin's, 1988.
Kittridge, Mary, *Organ Transplants,* Chelsea House, 1989.

Periodicals

Borders, William, "Three Cell Researchers Win Medicine Nobel," *New York Times,* October 11, 1980, p. 1.
Clark, Matt, "A Nobel Piece of Research," *Newsweek,* October 20, 1980, p. 66.
Marx, Jean, "1980 Noble Prize in Physiology or Medicine," *Science,* November 7, 1980, pp. 621–623.

—*Sketch by Francis Rogers*

Frederick Soddy
1877-1956
English chemist

Frederick Soddy's major contribution to science was his discovery of the existence of isotopes in 1913, an accomplishment for which he was awarded the 1921 Nobel Prize in chemistry. That discovery

Frederick Soddy

came as the result of extensive research on the radioactive elements carried out first with British physicist **Ernest Rutherford** at McGill University and later with British chemist **Sir William Ramsay** at London University. Among Soddy's contributions during this period was his recognition of the relationship between helium gas and alpha particle emanations—the latter being the ejection of a type of nuclear particle during a radioactive transformation—as well as his enunciation of the disintegration law of radioactive elements (which states that when a substance decays, it emits a particle and is transformed into a totally new substance). Soddy's most important work was carried out while he was lecturer in physical chemistry at the University of Glasgow between 1904 and 1919. Later in life Soddy's interests shifted to politics and economics, although he was able to make relatively little lasting impact in these fields.

Soddy was born on September 2, 1877, in Eastbourne, England. He was the seventh and last child of Benjamin Soddy and Hannah (Green) Soddy. His mother died eighteen months after his birth and his father was a successful and prosperous corn merchant in London who was already fifty-five years of age when Frederick came into the world. Soddy's interest in science, evident from an early age, was further developed at Eastbourne College by its science master, R. E. Hughes. Hughes and Soddy coauthored a paper on the reaction between dry ammonia and dry carbon dioxide in 1894, when Soddy was only seventeen years old. Hughes encouraged Soddy to continue his education in chemistry at Oxford. Teacher and student agreed, however, that an additional year of preparation would be desirable before going on to the university, so Soddy spent a year at University College, Aberystwyth, in 1895. In that year, he won the Open Science Postmastership Scholarship, offered by Merton College, Oxford, and in 1896, he enrolled at that institution.

During his years at Merton College, Soddy published his first independent paper, on the life and work of German chemist Victor Meyer, which was received as an accomplished paper for a young undergraduate. He stood for his chemistry examination in 1898 and was awarded a First Class in the Honors School of Natural Science. One of his examiners was Sir William Ramsay, with whom he was later to collaborate in London.

Works with Rutherford at McGill and Ramsay at London

Soddy stayed on at Oxford for two years following his graduation. The chemical research he pursued during this period led to no substantial results. By 1900, however, he felt he was ready to move on and applied for a position that opened in the chemistry department at the University of Toronto. Deciding to pursue the post aggressively, Soddy traveled to Canada to make his case in person. When he failed to receive the Toronto appointment, he traveled on to Montreal, where he accepted a position as a junior demonstrator at McGill University. The McGill appointment may have been attractive both because of the superb physical facilities provided by the young institution and because of the presence of a rising young star at the university, Ernest Rutherford. In any case, Soddy's family fortune made it possible for him to accept the modest £100 annual salary without hardship.

By the fall of 1900, Soddy and Rutherford had begun to collaborate on studies of the disintegration of radioactive elements. These studies led to a revolutionary theory of nuclear disintegration. Prior to the Soddy-Rutherford research, scientists were unclear as to what happens during nuclear decay. The most common notion was that radioactive materials give off some form of energy, such as X rays, without undergoing any fundamental change themselves. Rutherford and Soddy were able to demonstrate that the process is more substantial than previously believed and that, in the process of decaying, the composition of a radioactive substance is altered.

In 1903, Soddy returned to London. He wanted to work with Ramsay on a study of the gaseous products of radioactive decay. In his brief stay at London, the two were able to demonstrate that helium is always produced during the disintegration of radium. Five years later, Rutherford was to confirm that connection when he showed that alpha particles are doubly-charged helium nuclei.

Discovery of Isotopes Brings the Nobel Prize

In the spring of 1904, Soddy accepted an appointment as lecturer in physical chemistry at Glasgow University. Before moving to Scotland, however, he also accepted another commission, that from the extension service of London University. In this assignment, Soddy gave a series of lectures on physical chemistry and radioactivity at venues in Western Australia. At the conclusion of the tour in the fall of 1904, Soddy returned to Great Britain by way of New Zealand and the United States, to begin what was to be a ten-year tenure at Glasgow.

Soddy's work at Glasgow was primarily concerned with the chemical identification of the elements involved in the radioactive decay of uranium and radium, which was the subject of intense investigation by a number of scientists. The problem was that the disintegration of uranium and radium appeared to result in the formation of about a dozen new elements, elements that were tentatively given names such as uranium X, radium A, radium B, radium C, radium D, radium E, radium F, ionium, and mesothorium. How all these elements could be fitted into the few remaining spaces in the periodic table was entirely unclear.

By 1907, some clues to the answer to this problem had begun to appear; H. N. McCoy and W. H. Ross at the University of Chicago showed that two of the elements produced during radioactive decay, thorium and radiothorium, were chemically identical to each other. Soon, similar results were being announced for other pairs, such as ionium and radium, mesothorium and thorium K, and radium D and lead. These results were similar to those being obtained by Soddy in his own laboratory. By 1910, he began to formulate a possible explanation for the research findings. In a paper published that year, he first raised the possibility that many of the products of radioactive decay are not different from each other, but are variations of the same element. He began to develop the concept of different forms of a chemical element with identical chemical properties, but different atomic weights.

That idea came to fruition in 1913 when Soddy first proposed the term isotope for these forms of an element. Soddy's paper published in *Chemical News* summarized his views on isotopes. He wrote that "it would not be surprising if the elements ... were mixtures of several homogeneous elements of similar but not completely identical atomic weights." It was for this hypothesis that Soddy would be awarded the 1921 Nobel Prize for chemistry.

At this time Soddy was also working on an explanation of the patterns observed during radioactive decay. In 1911, he pointed out that each time an element loses an alpha particle, it changes into a new element whose atomic number is two less than that of the original element. This generalization became known as the Displacement Law. Shortly thereafter, A. S. Russell and Kasimir Fajans independently extended that law to include beta decay, in which an element's atomic number increases by one after the loss of a beta particle. In 1914 Soddy left Glasgow to take a chair in chemistry at the University of Aberdeen. His major work there involved the determination of the atomic weight of lead extracted from the radioactive ore Ceylon thorite. He showed for the first time that the atomic weight of an element (lead, in this case) can differ significantly and consistently from its normally accepted value as published in the periodic table.

During World War I, Soddy was involved in military research for the marine sub-committee of the Board of Inventions and Research. The major part of this work involved the development of methods for extracting ethylene from coal gas.

Postwar Interests Shift to Economic and Political Topics

At the conclusion of the war, Soddy was appointed to the Lees Chair in Chemistry at Oxford University. He remained in this post until 1936. Soddy's interest in scientific research had largely dissipated by the time he reached Oxford, and he published no original research in chemistry during his seventeen years there. Instead, he showed interest in social, political, and economic issues, motivated to some extent by a feeling that progress in science had not produced or had not been accompanied by a comparable development of human civilization. He became—and remained—actively involved in a number of social and political causes, including the women's suffrage movement and the controversy over the status of Ireland.

Soddy's academic career ended in 1936 when he took early retirement from Oxford. The occasion for this decision was the unexpected death of his wife Winifred Moller (Beilby) Soddy. The couple had been married in 1908 and, although childless, had been happy together. They enjoyed traveling and spent some of their most pleasant moments in mountain climbing. Winifred's death from a coronary thrombosis was so distressing that Soddy almost immediately left Oxford.

Even after his retirement, Soddy continued to think, write, and speak about current events. He was particularly concerned with his fellow scientists who, he believed, had not demonstrated sufficient social conscience about the difficult issues their own re-

search had brought about. Soddy died in Brighton, England, on September 22, 1956. According to one provision of his will, a trust was to be established to study social problems in various regions of the country.

Sir Alexander Fleck, Soddy's former student, colleague, and biographer, has described Soddy's personality in *Biographical Memoirs of Fellows of the Royal Society* as "complex." On the one hand, he was often kind and generous to friends and fellow workers, and could be "a live and inspiring leader" to those students he worked with in small groups. On the other hand, he seems to have been, more generally, a failure as a teacher. "His mental processes were different from those of the ordinary run of students so that the latter could not easily follow the words with which he clothed his thoughts," Fleck wrote. Soddy held very strong moralistic views on a number of issues and was not hesitant to make those views known and to defend them with vigor and little tact. Fleck observes that "he very frequently found himself in acrimonious discussions" during his tenure at Oxford, although his personal life appears to have been filled with personal happiness and many enjoyable social events.

SELECTED WRITINGS BY SODDY:

Books

Radioactivity: An Elementary Treatise from the Standpoint of the Disintegration Theory, [London], 1904.
The Interpretation of Radium, [London], 1909.
The Interpretation of the Atom, [London], 1932.

Periodicals

"The Radio-Elements and the Periodic Law," *Chemical News,* February, 28, 1913, pp. 97–99.
"The Evil Genius of the Modern World," *Management & Human Relation in Industry,* Volume 1, [New York], 1947.

SOURCES:

Books

Biographical Memoirs of Fellows of the Royal Society, Volume 3, Royal Society (London), 1957, pp. 203–216.
Farber, Eduard, editor, *Great Chemists,* Interscience, 1961, pp. 1463–1468.
Howorth, Muriel, *Atomic Transmutation: Memoirs of Professor Frederick Soddy,* [London], 1953.

Howorth, Muriel, *Pioneer Research on the Atom,* [London], 1958.

Trenn, T. J., *The Self-Splitting Atom,* [New York], 1977.

Periodicals

Kent, A., "Frederick Soddy," *Proceedings of the Chemical Society,* November, 1963, pp. 327–330.

Paneth, F., "A Tribute to Frederick Soddy," *Nature,* Volume 180, 1957, pp. 1085–1087.

Russell, Alexander S., "F. Soddy, Interpreter of Atomic Structure," *Science,* Volume 124, 1956.

—*Sketch by David E. Newton*

Halvor Solberg
1895-1974
Norwegian meteorologist

Halvor Solberg, one of the original members of the pioneering meteorology group formed in Bergen, Norway, during the early-twentieth century, made seminal analytical and mathematical contributions to early modern dynamic meteorology research. Solberg's research on cyclonic systems and his discovery of the polar frontal boundary greatly advanced modern meteorology and weather forecasting. For his contributions to this field, Solberg received the Fridtjof Nansen Award from the Norwegian Academy of Science and Medicine in 1937.

Halvor Skappel Solberg was born in the district of Rinsaker, south of Lillehammer, Norway, in 1895. The son of farmer Petter Julius Solberg and Johanne Skappel, Solberg graduated from high school in 1912 and then attended the University of Kristiania (now the University of Oslo). While working for his bachelor's degree, which he received in 1916, Solberg also served as an assistant to the Norwegian mathematician and geophysicist **Fredrik Størmer**. That same year, on a trip to Leipzig, Germany, Solberg became acquainted with **Jacob Bjerknes**, son of the Norwegian theoretical physicist and geophysicist **Vilhelm Bjerknes**. In 1912 the elder Bjerknes had been offered the directorship of a new geophysical institute at the University of Leipzig, to validate his theories of dynamic meteorology with surface data analysis. But when Vilhelm Bjerknes lost two young collaborators—Theodor Hesselberg, who went to the Norwegian Meteorological Institute, and Harald Ulrik

Sverdrup, who had been offered a chief scientist position with Roald Amundsen's North Pole voyage for 1918—he turned to Norwegian scientists to fill these positions. He hired Johan Holtsmark, Solberg, and later, his own son Jacob. By late 1917, however, conditions at Leipzig had become untenable due to World War I, and Bjerknes accepted the opportunity to start a geophysical institute at the new University of Bergen, taking his assistants with him. Solberg and Jacob Bjerknes had already embarked on the task of promoting the elder Bjerknes' new dynamic meteorological theories and weather forecasting applications, and they carried on this research even after the move back to Norway. Further research was started in February of 1918, and by June 26, 1918, Solberg and the Bjerkneses had inaugurated the first experimental weather service for western Norway at Bergen as part of the new geophysical institute. By July, Solberg was asked by Bjerknes to head an extension office in Kristiania (Oslo) to serve eastern Norway. A year later, in 1919, the Western Norwegian Weather Bureau at Bergen was officially recognized as a division of the Norwegian Meteorological Institute in Kristiania.

Exporting the Bergen meteorological approach to research centers abroad had been planned as essential to sustaining the support of the Norwegian government. Armed with Vilhelm Bjerknes' theory and practical application agenda, Solberg and Jacob began the important task of disseminating the research to meteorologically competitive Sweden, where the Bergen ideas were initially criticized. Nevertheless, Solberg and Jacob recruited young Swedes, for the foresighted Vilhelm Bjerknes looked to younger collaborators and their interest in independent research to provide loyal and enthusiastic support. They enlisted four young scientists to collaborate with them on the research—two of the Swedes, **Carl-Gustaf Rossby** and Tor Bergeron, along with Solberg and Jacob would become long-term members of the team that further developed Bjerknes' dynamic meteorology.

Discovers the Cyclone Life Cycle and the Polar Front

Beginning in 1919, when Jacob Bjerknes published a paper on the structure of moving cyclones or the extratropical cyclone model, the research at Bergen centered on further defining airmass dynamics. Solberg contributed an acute mathematical insight to the project, as well as a gift for close analysis. In studying weather data plotted on surface maps, he noticed that, as a cyclone's wave-like "squall line" (the convergent cloud boundary which seemed to define major precipitation patterns from north to south) dissipates to the east, it generates a new wave back westward along that boundary. The configuration usually totaled four waves in all, the last leading to an outbreak of cold air southward. Solberg realized that this sequence generation of a "cyclone family," as he called it, refined the understanding of the extratropical cyclone life cycle.

Solberg, Jacob Bjerknes, and their colleagues also further described the polar temperature homogeneity to the north of the boundary line that separates the polar easterly winds from the warmer westerlies and along which the cyclone and its weather develops. They theorized that this polar demarcation delineates the potential sources for wave-like perturbations that become unstable in amplitude as warm air (called a "warm tongue") crosses the boundary and generates the extratropical cyclone phenomenon. They christened this boundary over which periodic cold air and weather invades the mid-latitudes the "polar front" and conjectured that it generally extends across an entire hemisphere.

Solberg himself took on the task of proving that the polar frontal boundary physically exists. This entailed an exhaustively detailed analysis of surface maps, particularly those plotted for North America and the North Atlantic Ocean. Basing his work on the dense surface maps prepared by another Bergen recruit, Ernst Calwagen, Solberg had finished his basic analysis by early 1920. He defined four prominent polar frontal boundaries or "leaves," rather than the continuous boundary that Vilhelm Bjerknes had originally envisioned. These findings further modified the original extratropical cyclone model. In addition, Solberg and the elder Bjerknes set about a further expansion of the Bergen mathematical formulas used in weather forecasting, to reflect further insight into the polar front.

Though the polar front was not continuously hemispheric, the theory now provided a global basis for the cyclone model, described circulation of the atmosphere in general, and justified international cooperation in a network of stations for weather analysis and forecasting. The Bergen group began to disseminate the polar front theory, sending Rossby to Sweden and Solberg to Paris. Subsequent research was focused on developing a more subtle understanding of conditions contributing to frontal development and local unstable weather. While Solberg and Jacob Bjerknes studied shower activity and its migration independent of frontal weather. The research on rain was aimed at perfecting daily forecasting for commercial aviation, and focused on humidity content, instability, and variation in moisture and temperature rather than the larger-scale pressure distribution. These more sophisticated studies of the lower three-dimensional atmosphere led Solberg and Jacob Bjerknes to detailed local airmass dynamics theory. They studied, for example, the cooling processes of air by radiation, induction, mixing, and the expansion and rise of air into the atmosphere. These ideas were published in their joint paper "Meteorological Conditions for the Formation of Rain." The classic paper Solberg co-authored with Jacob Bjerknes on cyclone life cycles, "The Life Cycle of Cyclones and the Polar Front Theory of Atmospheric Circulation," appeared a year later.

Develops Mathematics for Unstable Atmospheric Waves

By concentrating on surface and lower-level atmospheric conditions in regard to frontal analysis, the Bergen meteorologists successfully promoted the practical viability of the polar front theory. In doing so, they ensured the survival of the Geophysical Institute and the Weather Service of Bergen with commercial, government, and international cooperation. Amid his atmospheric research, Solberg continued his studies in mathematics and hydrodynamics, first at the universities of Paris and Göttingen (Germany) between 1921 and 1927. He then returned to the University of Oslo, working as a doctoral assistant to his mentor, Vilhelm Bjerknes. Solberg finished several projects, including a study of photographic techniques to determine upper atmospheric cloud height during the night (1925), but most importantly his 1928 paper on the integration of atmospheric first-order equations with the mathematics of the extratropical cyclone and polar front theories.

The initial conditions of the base model from which Solberg, a brilliant mathematician, derived his equations of this problem consisted of two fluid layers moving zonally (horizontally) on a rotating earth but with different velocities and separated by a sloping surface of discontinuity that is analogous to the frontal surface. He found solutions of integrated velocity equations for all possible waves. Most significantly, two unstable wave solutions were for a short wave (now called the Kelvin-Helmholtz Wave) and a longer period wave (1000 kilometers from crest to crest). The longer wave was indeed the cyclone wave (actually about 1000–2000 km), which Solberg and Jacob Bjerknes had analyzed in their 1922 paper. Though the complexity of Solberg's formulas made them difficult to use for many scientists, his findings were used most importantly by Jacob Bjerknes and Jörgen Holmboe in their 1944 paper on cyclone wave development coupled with an inducive upper level wave.

The publication of Solberg's classic wave equations paper in 1928 coincided with the completion of his Ph.D. Admitted to the Norwegian Science Academy in Oslo, he accepted a professorship in theoretical meteorology at the University of Oslo in 1930. His cooperative research included association with the Rockefeller Foundation in 1931 and chairing the Norwegian Geophysical Research Committee (1937–38). In 1933 he coauthored, with the Bjerkneses and Bergeron, a book on Vilhelm Bjerknes' physical hydrodynamics with applications to dynamic meteorology. His interest in the further discovery of processes of the developing extratropical cyclone was reflected in his 1936 paper on the inertial and stable states of the atmosphere. Between 1942 and 1945, Solberg was a member of the Faculty of Mathematics and Natural Sciences at Oslo. He served as general secretary of the Norwegian Science Academy from 1946 to 1953, and then as vice president of the International Council of Science Unions from 1949 to 1955. He was also called upon to chair Norwegian national committees on mechanics and geophysics/geodetics research. Solberg remained at the University of Oslo until his retirement in 1964. Solberg had married Ingeborg Germeten in 1931 but divorced in 1943. They had two daughters. Solberg died of an undisclosed illness at Oslo on January 31, 1974.

SELECTED WRITINGS BY SOLBERG:

Books

(With Vilhelm Bjerknes, Jacob Bjerknes, and T. Bergeron) *Physikalische Hydrodynamik mit Anwendung auf die dynamische Meteorologie,* Verlag Springer (Berlin), 1933.

Periodicals

(With Jacob Bjerknes) "Meteorological Conditions for the Formation of Rain," *Geofysiske Publikasjoner,* Volume 2, no. 3, 1921.

(With Jacob Bjerknes) "The Life Cycle of Cyclones and the Polar Front Theory of Atmospheric Circulation," *Geofysiske Publikasjoner* Volume 3, no. 1, 1922.

"Integrationen der Atmosphärischen Störungsgleichungen," *Geofysiske Publikasjoner,* Volume 5, no. 9, 1928.

SOURCES:

Books

Byers, Horace R., *General Meteorology,* McGraw-Hill, 1959.

Friedman, Robert Marc, *Appropriating the Weather: Vilhelm Bjerknes and the Construction of a Modern Meteorology,* Cornell University Press, 1989.

Wurtele, Morton G., *Selected Papers of Jacob Aall Bonnevie Bjerknes,* Western Periodicals Co., 1975.

Other

Bjerknes, Hedvig Borthen, interview with William J. McPeak, conducted October 30, 1993.

—*Sketch by William J. McPeak*

Susan Solomon
1956-
American atmospheric chemist

Susan Solomon played a key role in discovering the cause of a major threat to the earth—the loss of the protective ozone layer in the upper atmosphere. Ozone protects all life on earth from large amounts of damaging ultraviolet radiation from the sun. Solomon, an atmospheric chemist, was first to propose the theory explaining how chlorofluorocarbons, gases used in refrigerators and to power aerosol spray cans, could in some places on the globe lead to ozone destruction in the presence of stratospheric clouds.

Solomon said in an interview with Lee Katterman that she recalls "exactly what got me first interested in science. It was the airing of **Jacques Cousteau** on American TV when I was nine or ten years old." Solomon said that as a child she was very interested in watching natural history programming on television. This sparked an interest in science, particularly biology. "But I learned that biology was not very quantitative," said Solomon in the interview. By the time she entered the Illinois Institute of Technology, Solomon met her need for quantitative study by choosing chemistry as her major at the Illinois Institute of Technology. A project during Solomon's senior year turned her attention toward atmospheric chemistry. The project called for measuring the reaction of ethylene and hydroxyl radical, a process that occurs in the atmosphere of Jupiter. As a result of this work, Solomon did some extra reading about planetary atmospheres, which led her to focus on atmospheric chemistry.

During the summer of 1977, just before entering graduate school at University of California at Berkeley, Solomon worked at the National Center for Atmospheric Research (NCAR) in Boulder, Colorado. She met research scientist Paul Crutzen at NCAR, who introduced her to the study of ozone in the upper atmosphere. In the fall at Berkeley, Solomon sought out **Harold Johnston**, a chemistry professor who did pioneering work on the effects of the supersonic transport (SST) on the atmosphere. Solomon credits Crutzen and Johnston for encouraging her interest in atmospheric chemistry. After completing her course work toward a Ph.D. in chemistry at Berkeley, Solomon moved to NCAR to do her thesis research with Crutzen.

She received a Ph.D. in chemistry in 1981 and then accepted a research position at the National Oceanic and Atmospheric Administration (NOAA) Aeronomy Laboratory in Boulder, Colorado. Initially, Solomon's research focused on developing computer

Susan Solomon

models of ozone in the upper atmosphere. Ozone is a highly reactive molecule composed of three atoms of oxygen. By comparison, the oxygen that is essential to the metabolism of living things is a relatively stable combination of two oxygen atoms. In the upper atmosphere between about 32,000 and 100,000 feet altitude, a layer of ozone exists that absorbs much of the sun's deadly ultraviolet radiation, thereby protecting all life on earth.

Sets New Career Course with Antarctic Trip

In 1985 scientists first reported that, during the months of spring in the Southern Hemisphere (September and October), the density of the ozone layer over Antarctica had been decreasing rapidly in recent years. The cause of this "hole" in the ozone layer was unknown and many scientists began to look for its cause. In 1986 the scientific community wanted to send some equipment to Antarctica to measure atmospheric levels of ozone and nitrogen dioxide. Much to the surprise of her scientific colleagues, Solomon volunteered to travel to Antarctica to get the needed measurements; until then, she had concentrated on theoretical studies, but the chance to understand the cause of the ozone hole prompted Solomon to take up experimental work. Solomon led an expedition to Antarctica during August, September, and October of 1986, where she and co-workers measured the amounts of several atmospheric components, including the amount of chlorine dioxide in the

upper atmosphere. The level of this atmospheric chemical was much higher than anyone expected and provided an important clue in determining why the ozone hole had appeared. Back at her NOAA lab in Boulder, Solomon wrote a research article that provided a theoretical explanation for the ozone hole. Solomon showed how the high level of chlorine dioxide was consistent with fast chemical destruction of ozone triggered by reactions occurring on stratospheric clouds. The extra chlorine dioxide was derived from chlorofluorocarbons released into the atmosphere from sources such as foams and leaking refrigeration equipment. Solomon returned to Antarctica for more measurements in August of 1987. Her explanation for the cause of the ozone hole is now generally accepted by scientists, and has led many countries of the world to curtail the production and use of chlorofluorocarbons.

Solomon's scientific studies to uncover the likely cause of the ozone hole have led to public recognition and many awards. In 1989, Solomon received the gold medal for exceptional service from the U.S. Department of Commerce (the agency that oversees the NOAA) She has testified several times before congressional committees about ozone depletion and is increasingly sought out as an expert on ozone science and policy (although the latter role is one she does not welcome, Solomon admitted in her interview, since she considers herself a scientist and not a policy expert).

Solomon was born on January 19, 1956, in Chicago, Illinois. Her father, Leonard Solomon, was an insurance agent. Susan's mother, Alice Rutman Solomon, was a fourth-grade teacher in the Chicago public schools. She has one brother, Joel. She married Barry Lane Sidwell on September 20, 1988, and has a stepson by the marriage. She continues to study the atmospheric chemistry of ozone and has added Arctic ozone levels to her research subjects.

SELECTED WRITINGS BY SOLOMON:

Books

(With Guy Brasseur) *Aeronomy of the Middle Atmosphere: Chemistry and Physics of the Stratosphere and Mesosphere,* second edition, Reidel, 1986.

Periodicals

"On Depletion of Antarctic Ozone," *Nature,* June 19, 1986, pp. 755–758.
"Progress towards a Quantitative Understanding of Antarctic Ozone Depletion," *Nature,* September 27, 1990, pp. 347–354.

SOURCES:

Periodicals

Bylinsky, Gene, "America's Hot Young Scientists," *Fortune,* October 8, 1990, p. 56.

Glanz, James, "How Susan Solomon's Research Changed Our View of Earth," *R & D,* September, 1992, p. 46.

Other

Solomon, Susan, interview with Lee Katterman conducted December 14, 1993.

—*Sketch by Lee Katterman*

Arnold Sommerfeld
1868-1951
German theoretical physicist

Arnold Sommerfeld is remembered for his immense contribution to various aspects of quantum physics; he was one of the first physicists to recognize the genius of **Albert Einstein**'s theory of relativity, which he later worked to refine along with Danish theorist **Niels Bohr**'s theory of atomic structure. Sommerfeld is also celebrated as a great teacher and a firm believer in physics as a collaborative enterprise whose practitioners should work together to further the frontiers of the field rather than work in competition with each other.

Arnold Johannes Wilhelm Sommerfeld was born in Königsberg, East Prussia, on December 5, 1868, the son of a doctor. He was educated at the University of Königsberg, from which he received his doctorate in 1891. In his thesis Sommerfeld applied the theory of functions of a complex variable to boundary-value problems, initiating a topic of study that would later yield his most valuable work.

From 1895 to 1897, he lectured at the University of Göttingen in Germany, then transferred to the Bergakademie in Clausthal. There, he drew upon his experience with boundary-value problems in studying the movement of electromagnetic waves and the diffraction of X rays. He also began work with fellow German physicist Felix Klein on their *Theorie des Kreisels* (*Theory of Crystals*), which was published in a series of volumes between 1897 and 1910. Sommerfeld remained at Clausthal until 1900, teaching and continuing his work in atomic physics; he then moved to the Technische Hochschule of Aachen, where he assumed a teaching position and began collaborative investigations with a number of his colleagues on the hydrodynamics of viscous fluids. Their goal was to explain the onset of turbulence in fluids and to develop a theory of the lubrication of machines. The result was a series of papers on the general dynamics of electrons published in 1904 and 1905 which cemented Sommerfeld's reputation as one of Germany's most important theoretical physicists.

In 1906, Sommerfeld left Aachen for the University of Munich to take up its chair of theoretical physics. He would remain there for the rest of his career. At Munich, his work took a new direction as he immersed himself in the study of X rays and gamma rays. It was also in 1906 that Sommerfeld first heard of Einstein's theory of relativity. He immediately recognized its genius and was one the first physicists to do so. In 1907, he issued a vigorous defense of the theory. He also applied Einstein's theory to his own studies of electron deceleration.

Another instance of Sommerfeld's building upon and improving other physicists' work occurred in 1914. After Bohr published a paper on the constitution of atoms and molecules in 1913, Sommerfeld worked on applying Bohr's model of the atom to the splitting of spectral lines emitted in a magnetic field known as the Zeeman effect. Sommerfeld became one of the great champions of Bohr's atomic theory after overcoming his initial skepticism, to the extent that he devoted a good deal of his energies to promoting it and refining it. He and Bohr developed a close working and personal relationship and were in frequent contact by letter, exchanging ideas and critiquing each other's work.

Reworks Bohr's Atomic Theory

In 1915, Sommerfeld turned his full attention to Bohr's atomic theory, and set about reconfiguring it into a more formal structure. Bohr, in turn, improved Sommerfeld's approach. In 1916, Sommerfeld further modified Bohr's theory by suggesting that the electrons, which Bohr believed to move about an atom's central core or nucleus in circular orbits, actually moved in elliptical orbits. He took note of the relativistic increase in the mass of the electron as it sped about the nucleus, which led him to introduce a second quantum number, the azimuthal quantum number (l), in addition to that introduced by Bohr (n). This breakthrough allowed for an explanation of atomic spectral lines which Bohr's model alone had been unable to satisfactorily explain and culminated in a quantum theory of the normal Zeeman effect. Sommerfeld's improvements upon Bohr's theory, in addition to his vigorous support for it, contributed to its rapid and widespread acceptance in the international physics community. Bohr was grateful for the support, and the two continued to refine the theory.

Their joint efforts finally led to Bohr's second atomic theory (the theory of the periodic tables of the elements), known as the Bohr-Sommerfeld atomic theory.

Takes Reins of German Physical Society

In 1918, Sommerfeld was confronted with a new challenge and one for which he had had no formal training. He was elected presiding officer of the German Physical Society—the first person outside Berlin to be granted such an honor. Although gratified, Sommerfeld quickly realized the enormity of the burden he had undertaken. The group was riven with internecine strife and Sommerfeld's task of reconciliation was complicated by special interests and divided goals. At the society's inception in 1845, membership included scientists of every concentration, but by the turn of the century its bias was toward pure science. Although the task was daunting, Sommerfeld worked hard to restore peace and common purpose to the society and to build bridges between its various members, and was an amiable and much-liked leader.

In 1918, Sommerfeld was also preoccupied with applying the Bohr-Sommerfeld atomic theory to the analysis of X-ray spectra and the splitting of hydrogen spectral lines in the presence of an electric field. In 1919, Sommerfeld published an atomic physics textbook, *Atomic Structure and Spectral Lines,* which quickly established itself as the definitive text. In its preface he betrayed his passion for his subject, writing, "Today, when we listen to the language of spectra, we hear a true atomic music of the spheres." It was Sommerfeld, an amateur pianist of no mean ability, who wryly noted of the spectra of the hydrogen atom [which emits over one hundred different frequencies] that it appeared to be more complicated than a grand piano, which emits only eighty-eight.

For all the insight into atomic structure that the Bohr-Sommerfeld theory provided, it could not explain all the phenomena that confounded physicists grappling with the new quantum physics. For example, it failed to explain the optical and much of the X-ray radiations of atoms with more than one outer electron. Such atoms, when subjected to an external magnetic field, emit complex spectra. Some atomic physicists, including the German theoretician Alfred Lande, explained this as being due to some sort of magnetic coupling of the atoms, although Sommerfeld himself explained it in terms of the theory of relativity.

During Germany's Weimar years, Sommerfeld was one of the country's leading atomic physicists. His work on quantum theory brought him renown, but no less noteworthy was his record as an educator. He had a true vocation as a teacher and attracted Germany's leading young physicists to his school. He turned out a record number of doctorates and no fewer than four Nobel Prize winners. Among his star pupils was **Werner Heisenberg**, who later identified Sommerfeld's unflagging pursuit of explanations for mysterious phenomena as one of three influences from which his quantum mechanics resulted. During the 1920s, Sommerfeld was a frequent visitor to the United States, where he taught at the University of California at Berkeley. During one such visit, he revealed the key to success as a physicist: "If you want to be a physicist, you must do three things—first, study mathematics, second, study more mathematics, and third, do the same."

With the rise to power of the National Socialists in 1933, many Jewish physicists were undermined and forced to leave their posts. Sommerfeld was an ardent defender of the Jews and spoke out against the Nazi regime; his reputation as a teacher was such that his word in academic appointments carried a great deal of weight, and he did not hesitate to recommend his Jewish colleagues for academic appointments or promotions. As a result of his influence, many Jewish physicists were able to maintain their positions, at least in the short-term. Sommerfeld appeared not to be personally threatened by the Nazis. He continued to be staunchly opposed to National Socialism and especially to the movement's leader, Adolf Hitler. By 1940, however, Sommerfeld was finally denounced by the government and forced to retire.

Sommerfeld died on April 26, 1951, after being struck by a car while strolling with his grandchildren one afternoon in Munich. Victor Guillemin, writing in *The Story of Quantum Mechanics,* summarized Sommerfeld's view of the role of the scientist: "Sommerfeld, in common with many other scientists, felt that there is an intolerable arrogance in the thought of 'prescribing' to nature. Rather, scientists in a spirit of humility should hope that through unremitting labors they might achieve some small comprehension of her wonders."

SELECTED WRITINGS BY SOMMERFELD:

Books

(With Felix Klein) *Theorie des Kreisels* (*Theory of Crystals*), 1897–1910.
Atombau und Spektrallinien (*Atomic Structure and Spectral Lines*), 1919, 3rd edition, [New York], 1923.
Lectures on Theoretical Physics, Academic Press, 1949–1956.

SOURCES:

Books

Beyerchen, Alan D., *Scientists under Hitler: Politics and the Physics Community in the Third Reich,* Yale University Press, 1977.

French, A. P., and P. J. Kennedy, editors, *Niels Bohr: A Centenary Volume,* Harvard University Press, 1985.

Guillemin, Victor, *The Story of Quantum Mechanics,* Scribner, 1968.

Heilbron, John L., *The Dilemmas of an Upright Man: Max Planck as Spokesman for German Science,* University of California Press, 1986.

Kevles, Daniel J., *The Physicists: The History of a Scientific Community in Modern America,* Harvard University Press, 1987.

Periodicals

Haldane, J. B. S., "Nationality and Research," *Forum,* May, 1926, p. 720.

Harmon, L. R., "Physics Ph.D.'s: Whence, Whither, When?," *Physics Today,* October, 1962, p. 21.

Heilbron, John L., "The Kossel-Sommerfeld Theory and the Ring Atom," *Isis,* winter, 1987, pp. 451–485.

—*Sketch by Avril McDonald*

Duncan McLaren Young Sommerville
1879-1934
Scottish mathematician

Duncan McLaren Young Sommerville made important contributions to Euclidean and non-euclidean geometry as a teacher and as a researcher. His research into tesselations, the study of how geometric shapes fit together to fill a plane, led to new understanding of crystallography. In 1934, H. W. Turnbull called him the leading geometer of Scotland.

Duncan McLaren Young Sommerville was born in Beawar, Rajasthan, India, on November 24, 1879, the son of Reverend James Sommerville. He was educated in Scotland, where he attended Perth Academy and the University of St. Andrews. There he was awarded a Ramsay Scholarship in 1899 and a Bruce Scholarship the following year. His major field of study was geometry but he was interested in other sciences as well, including anatomy and chemistry.

Sommerville's first published research paper, entitled "Networks of the Plane in Absolute Geometry," appeared in 1905 in the *Proceedings of the Royal Society of Edinburgh.* That same year he became a lecturer in the mathematics department at St. An-

drews. At the college, according to Turnbull, he won the admiration of his colleagues and pupils for his teaching and for his scholarly and unobtrusive manner. He also investigated branches of geometry other than the Euclidean system, publishing several research papers. In 1911, he published the 400-page *Bibliography of Non-Euclidean Geometry,* which included a bibliography of *n*-dimensional geometry as well. In 1911 and 1912 he served as President of the Edinburgh Mathematical Society. He married Louisa Agnes Beveridge, of Belfast, Ireland, in 1912.

In 1915, Sommerville accepted a position as professor of pure and applied mathematics at Victoria College, Wellington, New Zealand. Students saw him as an outwardly shy person, but they appreciated the time and effort he devoted to his teaching. At one point, the students at the University of Otago in New Zealand were temporarily without a mathematics professor; Sommerville helped to fill the gap through weekly correspondence with the students.

Explored Non-Euclidean Geometries

Sommerville's first book, on non-euclidean geometry, appeared at a time when few people knew about systems other than Euclid's. Euclidean geometry assumes that, given a straight line and a point not on the line, there is only one line that passes through the point and is parallel to the first line. From this basic assumption, many of the concepts in high school geometry books can be shown to follow. However, if this basic assumption (the "parallel postulate") is not made, the conclusions that follow will be quite different. If, for example, it is assumed that there is no parallel line that passes through the point, the resulting system is elliptic geometry. On the other hand, if it is assumed that there is more than one parallel line through the point, the resulting geometry is hyperbolic. Sommerville and others studied these non-euclidean geometries and their relationships to Euclidean geometry.

Tesselations and crystallography also interested Sommerville. He studied how geometric shapes fit together in a mosaic-like pattern to cover a flat surface, such as a bathroom floor covered with tiles. He found that a Euclidean plane can be covered with a regular pattern of identical tiles in the shape of squares, or equilateral triangles, or regular hexagons; other shapes, such as regular pentagons, will leave gaps. He then investigated the ways that planes could be covered in non-euclidean geometries. Although the Euclidean plane could be successfully covered by only three different mosaics of regular polygons, an elliptic plane could be covered by mosaics of five regular polygons; and for the hyperbolic plane, there was an infinite number of such patterns. He found that, for each type of plane, there were more possibilities if combinations of different kinds of regular polygons were allowed.

Sommerville asked similar questions about how three-dimensional space can be filled with cubes and other polyhedrons, as in honeycombs. He went on to draw generalizations about spaces with four, five, or more dimensions—in both Euclidean and non-euclidean systems. Decades later, other geometers such as **Roger Penrose** continued the study of tiling patterns. The work of Sommerville and his successors influenced the approach taken by scientists to the study of the formation of crystals and the development of new ceramic materials.

Most of Sommerville's more than thirty papers dealt with his study of geometry. In other research, he drew connections between his geometric concepts and group theory, analyzed preferential voting in terms of geometric concepts, and developed an original analysis of the musical scale. Two of his early papers dealt with statistical issues related to research in biometrics by **Karl Pearson**. Sommerville wrote four textbooks. The first, *Elements of Non-Euclidean Geometry,* was published in 1914. It was followed by *Analytical Conics* in 1924, *An Introduction to the Geometry of n Dimensions* in 1929, and *Analytical Geometry of Three Dimensions* in 1934.

At the meeting of the Australasian Association for the Advancement of Science in 1924 in Adelaide, Sommerville presided over the mathematics section. He became interested in astronomy and was one of the founders of the New Zealand Astronomical Society, serving as its first secretary. He was skilled in making models, and he made watercolor paintings of New Zealand outdoor scenes. Sommerville died on January 31, 1934, in Wellington, New Zealand.

SELECTED WRITINGS BY SOMMERVILLE:

Books

Bibliography of Non-Euclidean Geometry, London, 1911.
Elements of Non-Euclidean Geometry, London, 1914 and 1919.
Analytical Conics, London, 1924.
An Introduction to the Geometry of n Dimensions, London, 1929.
Analytical Geometry of Three Dimensions, Cambridge, 1934.

Periodicals

"Networks of the Plane in Absolute Geometry," *Proceedings of the Royal Society of Edinburgh,* 1905, pp. 392–394.

SOURCES:

Periodicals

Turnbull, H. W., "Professor D. M. Y. Sommerville," *Proceedings of the Edinburgh Mathematical Society,* series 2, Volume 6, part 1, March, 1934, pp. 57–60.

—*Sketch by C. D. Lord*

Charles E. Sorensen
1881-1968
Danish-born American engineer

Charles E. Sorensen was a founder of the automobile industry in the United States. During his forty years at the Ford Motor Company, he helped develop the Model T and played a central role in the development of mass production. An architect of the world's first moving, fully mechanized assembly line, Sorensen was widely considered a master of production techniques, and he was an innovator in manufacturing methods for airplanes during World War II.

Sorensen was born on September 7, 1881 to Soren and Eva Abrahamsen Sorensen in Copenhagen, Denmark. He was the oldest of four children. His father had descended from a long line of Danish farmers and he worked with wood, fashioning models of household furnishings. When Sorensen was four, he and his mother moved to the United States to join his father, who had arrived a year and a half earlier. Sorensen's formal education ended at age sixteen and at seventeen he became an apprentice in a pattern shop, making wooden molds for metal castings. By the next year, he had become the foreman of a pattern shop. The family then moved to Detroit, where he began his career in the automobile industry.

In 1902, Sorensen was introduced to **Henry Ford**, who was at that time a local race-car driver. Ford and his partner were designing two race cars, for which Sorensen's employer made patterns. They kept in contact with each other during the next few years. When Sorensen quit a job as a traveling salesman he turned in his accounts to a bookkeeper named Helen Mitchell; he married her in June of 1904. Their son Clifford was born about a year later. In 1905, Sorensen joined Ford Motor Company as a pattern maker. He was soon working closely with Ford, listening to his ideas, creating sketches, and building rough models. Ford soon put him in charge of the pattern-making department and the foundry.

Develops Mass Production for the Model T

Ford had developed a handful of automobiles, but his dream was to create an inexpensive car for the masses. This required him to find methods of keeping his production costs very low. Sorensen was one of the handful of men who helped Ford develop his dream of an affordable car. During the winter of 1906 to 1907, Ford asked him to build a private room that became the birthplace of the Model T. During the years of the Model T's secret development Sorensen helped create many automotive innovations, such as the use of the new vanadium steel and a new transmission.

By 1908, Sorensen was the assistant plant superintendent in charge of all production development. His responsibilities included coordinating the movement of parts to assembly areas for Ford's Model N cars. He considered handling the numerous parts of a car harder than assembling the car itself. He saw the inefficient methods in use at the time as barriers to increasing production and lowering costs. This pushed him to search for a simpler and faster production technique, and he first tested the idea of a fully synchronized flow of car parts in 1908. After planning the experiment for several weeks, Sorensen and a few helpers pulled a Model N chassis past car parts and subassemblies which were quickly attached to the moving chassis. Sorensen showed the experiment to Ford who, according to Sorensen, was skeptical of the idea but encouraged Sorensen to continue his experiments.

Sorensen was not able to implement his idea fully for five years, primarily because Ford's Piquette Avenue plant was too small to house a moving assembly line. The enormous success of the Model T, however, helped Sorensen develop mass production; Ford now had the capital to build a larger assembly plant to meet the demand for his affordable car, and Sorensen designed most of the layout of the new Highland Park factory, which opened in 1910. Special tools and machines were designed and built for faster and more efficient parts manufacturing, and he used overhead conveyer systems to improve the movement of car subassemblies within the factory. Sorensen hired Clarence Avery to design the precise flow of parts needed to synchronize the assembly of a car. In 1913, the moving assembly line was added to Sorensen's production facility and the world's first mass production assembly plant was in operation. The result was an orderly flow of parts to subassembly operations and then to final assembly. Sorensen's efforts shortened the time to assemble a car chassis from over twelve hours to less than two. While both Ford and Sorensen later claimed to be the father of mass production, it is clearly the most famous of Sorensen's many contributions to the automotive industry, regardless of who first thought of the concept.

Contributes to War Effort during Both World Wars

Sorensen also helped Ford contribute to the World War I effort. The British government needed to increase their production of tractors, and in 1917 Sorensen and his assistants were "loaned" to them to help. British factories were too busy manufacturing munitions to produce the tractors, and Sorensen agreed to produce 5,000 tractors at fifty dollars over cost with the first shipments in just sixty days. He rushed back to Detroit to prepare facilities to build the tractors. True to his word, the first tractors were delivered on time and the entire order was completed in less than three months.

Sorensen had great loyalty to Ford and was uniquely able to maintain good relations with him, and these factors increased his influence within the company. Ford made him chief of production, manager of his enormous production facilities. Sorensen's temper could be fierce and many considered his methods domineering, even ruthless and tyrannical. But, as the *New York Times* observed in his obituary, "his judgment was unusually sound and he got spectacular results."

Sorensen played a major role in the production of B–24 bombers for World War II. In what he considered to be the greatest challenge of his career, Sorensen designed a plant to produce a B–24 every hour, at a time when they were being produced at a rate of only one plane a day. It was the first application of mass production to aircraft construction. Sorensen had difficulty persuading the designers of the aircraft to use his ideas, but the Ford Willow Run plant opened November 15, 1941. The assembly line was a mile long and the building a quarter of a mile wide. President and Mrs. Roosevelt toured the factory soon after it opened, riding right down the center of the plant on the assembly line, stopping as Sorensen explained the bomber's assembly. One historian later questioned whether the United States could have defended itself in World War II without the mass production techniques which Sorensen helped develop.

In July of 1941, Sorensen was elected executive vice-president of Ford Motor Company, but the war and changes within the Ford family made leading the company exceptionally difficult. The aging Ford resisted giving up control of the company despite his reduced leadership abilities, and politicians discussed nationalizing the company for the war effort. Harry Bennett, who had gained great favor in Ford's eyes, sought control of the company for himself. Sorensen was extensively involved in the fight for control of the company, but he was forced to resign in 1944, after Henry Ford II became president of the firm. Sorensen turned down several offers of government assignments to serve for a short time as president of Willys-

Overland, a competing automobile company. He retired soon after to his home in Miami Beach, Florida and wrote his autobiography. His wife Helen died in 1959 and Sorensen subsequently married Edith Montgomery. On August 13, 1968, he died at his summer home in Bethesda, Maryland, after a prolonged illness.

SELECTED WRITINGS BY SORENSEN:

Books

(With Samuel T. Williamson), *My Forty Years with Ford,* Norton, 1956.

SOURCES:

Books

Crabb, Richard, *Birth of a Giant,* Chilton, 1969.
Ford, Henry, and Samuel Crowther, *My Life and Work,* Doubleday, 1925.
Herndon, Booton, *Ford: An Unconventional Biography of the Men and their Times,* Weybright and Talley, 1969.
Nevins, Allan, *Ford: The Times, the Man the Company,* Scribner, 1954.
Nevins, Allan, and Frank Ernest Hill, *Ford: Decline and Rebirth, 1933–1962,* Scribner, 1963.
Rae, John B., *American Automobile Manufacturers, The First Forty Years,* Chilton, 1959.
Sward, Keith, *The Legend of Henry Ford,* Rinehart, 1948.

Periodicals

New York Times, August 14, 1968.

—*Sketch by David N. Ford*

Søren Peter Lauritz Sørensen
1868-1939
Danish chemist

The pH scale, invented by Søren Peter Lauritz Sørensen, "has become so much a part of scientific literature and its influence so important a factor in considering biological problems that one wonders how theories of acidity and alkalinity were ever formulated without a knowledge of Sørensen's

fundamental conceptions," A. J. Curtin Cosbie commented in *Nature.* Potential of hydrogen, or pH, is a simplified measure of the acidity of any given mixture. Though of immense value to scientist and layman alike, the pH scale is only one of Søren Sørensen's many achievements in a career devoted to the application of classical physico-chemical methods to the new realms of biochemistry and specifically to fermentations problems. His research on enzymes and proteins in particular—for which the invention of the pH scale was merely a methodological improvement—were invaluable, laying the groundwork for precise and thorough studies of these nitrogenous compounds.

Sørensen was born on January 9, 1868, at Havrebjerg, Slagelse, Denmark, the son of a farmer, Hans Sørensen. Sørensen was a high-strung, nervous youth, suffering from epileptic-like attacks and a pronounced stammer. His schoolwork became something of a refuge for him and upon graduation from high school in Sorø in 1886, he entered the University of Copenhagen. Initially Sørensen intended to study medicine, but was diverted from this course after studying chemistry under S. M. Jorgensen who fired him with an interest in the structure of inorganic compounds. In 1889 Sørensen was already proving his academic worth, winning a gold medal for an essay on chemical radicals. A second gold medal award came in 1896 for his research into strontium compounds. It was during this period of study that Sørensen's interest was turning toward research in analytical chemistry, a development that would later become very important for the progress of his work, as he would be able to blend his flair for experimentation with a precise attention to detail. After receiving his Master of Science degree in 1891, he worked as an assistant at the chemistry laboratory of the Danish Polytechnic Institute, consulted for the Royal Naval Dock Yard, and also found time to assist on a geological survey of Denmark. In 1899 he received his doctorate in chemistry, writing his dissertation on cobaltic oxalates.

Research Focus Shifts at Carlsberg Laboratory

Throughout the period of study for his doctorate, Sørensen focused on inorganic chemistry and related questions. In 1901, however, this focus changed with an appointment to the directorship of the prestigious Carlsberg Laboratory in Copenhagen. Sørensen, age thirty-three, took over from Johann Kjeldahl, whose work had been primarily in biochemistry, and it was with similar investigations that Sørensen would spend the rest of his scientific career. He became interested in proteins and especially in amino acids, successfully synthesizing ornithine, proline, arginine, and several others. His interest in analytical methods led him to further research into the measurement of nitrogen concentration and improving methods of titration, the process by which the concentration of ingredients in a solution is determined by adding carefully measured amounts of a reagent until a desired chemical reaction occurs.

Develops pH Scale

Much of Sørensen's fame rests in his papers on enzyme study, the first of which was a study of enzyme action utilizing the titration method. But it was in the second paper, published in 1909, where he examined the electromotive force or EMF method for determining hydrogen ion concentration, that Sørensen addressed the topic that would lead to his pH scale. Other investigators had already suggested that hydrogen ion concentrations could be used as valid indicators of the acidity or alkalinity of a solution, and the hydrogen electrode also had become the standard for such measurements. Sørensen sought to simplify the cumbersome analytical apparatus then used to measure acidity and alkalinity, and devised the familiar scale numbered 1 to 14 in which 7 represents a neutral solution, the acids are represented by numbers lower than that, and alkalines or bases by numbers above 7. Other scientists, such as Leonor Michaelis with his book on hydrogen ion concentration, and **Arnold Beckman** with a simplified pH meter, helped to popularize the pH method, which is simple enough to be grasped by laymen, yet accurate enough for scientific use.

From methodological work and studies on enzymes, Sørensen and his laboratory turned to the investigation of proteins, applying many of the classical principles of chemistry to their description and characterization, and by 1917 the laboratory had succeeded in crystallizing egg albumen, a pioneering step in the characterization of proteins. Sørensen was able to determine the molecular weight of the albumen by osmotic measurement and determine its acid and base capacity by pH. He and his assistants—later including his wife, Magrethe Høyrup Sørensen—went on to study serum proteins, lipoproteins, and the complexes of hemoglobin and carbon monoxide.

In addition to his life-long work at the Carlsberg Laboratory, Sørensen was also involved in the role of science in industry, working with spirits, yeast, and explosives. He also contributed knowledge in the medical field, his first love at university, researching epilepsy and diabetes. Honors and awards attested to his contributions to science: he was president of the Danish Scientific Society and an honorary member of societies in both Europe and the United States. Sørensen died in Copenhagen on February 12, 1939, following a year-long illness. In a memorial address delivered to the Chemical Society, E. K. Rideal remarked, "By his death the world loses a perfect example of a man whose devotion to scientific accuracy and consistency should serve as an example

to many who, claiming to be scientific in this ever-accelerating age of speed, serve their science badly by neglecting the solid in their search for the superficial and spectacular."

SELECTED WRITINGS BY SØRENSEN:

Periodicals

"Enzymstudien. II. Über die Messung und die Bedeutung der Wasserstoffionkonzentration bei enzymatischen prozessen," *Biochemische Zeitschrift,* Volume 21, 1909, pp. 131–200.
"On the Composition and Properties of Egg-Albumin Separated in Crystalline Form by Means of Ammonium Sulphate," *Comptes rendus du Laboratoire de Carlsberg,* Volume 12, 1917, pp. 164–212.

SOURCES:

Periodicals

Cohn, Edwin J., "Søren Peter Lauritz Sørensen," *Journal of the American Chemical Society,* October 9, 1939, pp. 2573–2574.
Cosbie, A. J. Curtin, "Prof. S. P. L. Sørensen," *Nature,* April 15, 1939, p. 629.
Rideal, E. K., "Søren Peter Lauritz Sørensen," *Journal of the Chemical Society,* 1940, pp. 554–561.

—Sketch by J. Sydney Jones

Mary Spaeth
1938-
American physicist

Mary Spaeth invented the tunable dye laser, an innovation that rendered lasers far more useful for research in such fields as chemistry, nuclear physics, and medicine.

Born on December 17, 1938, in Houston, Texas, Mary Dietrich Spaeth is the oldest of two children. Her father, Fred, was an insurance salesman who was often assisted in his business by his wife, Louise (Dittman) Dietrich. Intending from an early age to become a doctor, Spaeth became interested in physics as a result of a seventh-grade science lesson. Her curiosity led her into studying science and, eventually, conducting research on eyes and on saturable dyes. She received her bachelor's degree from Valparaiso University in 1960, then earned her master's degree in physics from Wayne State University in 1962; later that year she began working as a member of the technical staff at Hughes Aircraft Company.

While Spaeth was a graduate student, **Theodore Maiman** introduced the first working laser. At the time, lasers could be built to emit different colors, but once the color was chosen it could not be changed, which limited their flexibility in research applications. Research on saturable dyes increased Spaeth's interest as to whether a laser could be made to change color. While at Hughes Aircraft, she had a two-week break in a research project because equipment she needed was not available. She turned her attention to the idea of a dye laser, and within a few days had a working prototype. At the time she built the prototype, she was not aware of the work of Peter Sorokin, who showed how dyes could affect the color of a laser; another scientist at Hughes saw the article in a journal and brought it to her attention. Spaeth at first had some difficulty convincing people that her invention was a true laser because the wavelengths varied and at the time a fixed wavelength was part of the definition of a laser. However, it passed all the experimental tests for a laser.

Spaeth's tunable laser has an array of applications. It allows scientists to separate elemental isotopes, especially of plutonium and uranium. Isotopes (or varieties of the same element) absorb light differently, and the energy alters the size, shape, and electrical charge of the isotope. If the electrical charge of one of a pair of similar isotopes is changed, they can easily be separated, making the preparation of nuclear fuel for reactors far more easy. One of the most promising applications of the tunable dye laser is as part of the guide star project which will allow ground-based stellar observatories to achieve resolution comparable to that received through the Hubble Space Telescope, an orbiting observatory that was launched in 1990.

Spaeth left Hughes for Lawrence Livermore National Laboratory in 1974 in order to work on laser development. During her time there she was named deputy associate director of the isotope separation project. Divorced in 1988, Spaeth has three daughters and lives in Livermore, California.

SELECTED WRITINGS BY SPAETH:

Periodicals

(With D. P. Bortfeld) "Simulated Emission from Polymethine Dyes," *Applied Physics Letters,* Volume 9, 1966.

(With J. I. Davis and J. Z. Holtz) "Status and Prospects for Lasers in Isotope Separation," *Laser Focus,* September, 1982, pp. 49–54.

SOURCES:

Books

"Spaeth, Mary," *World of Invention,* Gale, 1994, pp. 574–75.

Other

Spaeth, Mary, interview conducted by F. C. Nicholson, February 19, 1994.

—Sketch by F. C. Nicholson

Rebecca H. Sparling
1910-
American mechanical engineer

Rebecca H. Sparling worked extensively in the fields of high temperature metallurgy and nondestructive testing of materials. She has also been an outspoken advocate for the environment and an enthusiastic promoter of engineering as a profession for women. She has been honored by the Society of Woman Engineers with their Achievement Award in 1957, and by the Institute for the Advancement of Engineering with an Outstanding Engineering Merit Award in 1978.

Rebecca Hall Sparling was born in Memphis, Tennessee, on June 7, 1910, the tenth child of Robert Meredith and Kate (Sampson) Hall. Both of her parents were college graduates; her father completed a law degree although he chose a business career. Sparling began her undergraduate education at Hollins College in Virginia, transferring later to Vanderbilt University, from which she received a B.A. degree in chemistry in 1930 and an M.S. in physical chemistry in 1931.

That same year Sparling began her career in the metallurgical department of American Cast Iron Pipe Company but stayed only a year. For the next few years, she worked in a variety of positions including writing and translating metallurgical technical papers for the American Foundrymen's Association and writing promotional materials for International Nickel Co. In 1935 she married Edwin K. Smith, a metallurgist, and continued to publish papers and do consulting work for foundries and other companies. Through 1944 she worked out of her home so that she could take care of her son, Douglas, born in 1938. From 1942 to 1944 she wrote *American Malleable Iron,* a textbook on iron castings that became an industry standard.

Sparling returned to industry in 1944, joining Northrop Aircraft's turbodyne division as chief materials and process engineer. She remained at Northrop through her divorce in 1947 and her second marriage to Joseph Sparling in 1948. In 1951 she accepted a position as design specialist in materials at General Dynamics in Pomona, California. Most of the work Sparling did at both Northrop and General Dynamics was classified, since she worked on selecting and specifying materials for use in aerospace and missile technology. As a pioneer in these new fields, her research included finding ways of using and processing materials. More importantly, it involved development of methods for testing these materials to ensure they would perform as expected. Her advances included the application of nondestructive and high temperature testing methods. This allowed better and faster testing to evaluate the performance of materials under the conditions in which they are used. She continued her pioneering work at General Dynamics until her retirement in 1968.

During her working life and her retirement, Sparling has been a prominent speaker and writer, stressing the importance of communication among engineers, government, and the public. She has given numerous presentations in high schools and colleges, promoting engineering as a career for women. Additionally she has written and testified on a variety of energy matters, including nuclear power and energy conservation. Deeply involved in technical and civic organizations, Sparling has also been elected a fellow of the American Society for Metals, Society of Woman Engineers, and the Institute for the Advancement of Engineering and has done work in a number of other societies, including the American Association of University Women. Her civic work has included being a founder of the Desert Environment Conservation Association, and president of the Conserve Our Air and Water Committee. Her efforts to use her engineering background for both civil and technical advancements won her an Engineering Merit Award from the Orange County Engineering Council in 1978.

SELECTED WRITINGS BY SPARLING:

Books

American Malleable Iron, Malleable Founders' Society, 1944.

"How I Got into Engineering," *Proceedings, First International Conference of Women Engineers and Scientists,* 1964.

Periodicals

"High Temperature Materials for Gas Turbines," *The Iron Age,* Volume 161, 1948, p. 56.

"Nondestructive Testing of Metals," *Western Metals,* Volume 7, 1949, p. 32.

"Tools of Inspection," *Nondestructive Testing,* Volume 12, 1954, p. 19.

"Of Course Women Can Be Engineers," *Western Metalworking,* Volume 22, 1964, p. 37.

SOURCES:

Sparling, Rebecca H., correspondence with Jerome Ferrance, January, 1994.

—*Sketch by Jerome P. Ferrance*

Frank Harold Spedding
1902-1984
Canadian-born American chemist

Frank Harold Spedding played an important role in the Manhattan Project—the U.S. government's effort to develop an atomic bomb during World War II. With his colleagues, he also devised chemical techniques for isolating rare-earth elements, thus making them available for industry at affordable cost.

Spedding was born in Hamilton, Ontario, Canada, on October 22, 1902, but his photographer father, Howard Leslie Spedding, and mother, the former Mary Ann Elizabeth Marshall, were American citizens. While at the University of Michigan, he majored in metallurgy, receiving his B.S. degree in 1925. He earned his M.S. degree in analytical chemistry there in 1926, and was awarded his Ph.D. in physical chemistry from the University of California, Berkeley, in 1929. While working on his doctorate at UC, Spedding studied the mathematics underlying the chemical relationships among properties of rare-earth metals, the elements consisting of scandium and yttrium, and the fifteen elements from lanthanum to lutetium. These elements exist in nature only as oxides, and are never found in the pure mineral state.

While at UC he collaborated with noted chemist **Gilbert Newton Lewis** in developing methods for concentrating heavy water, which contains deuterium, the hydrogen isotope with a mass double that of ordinary hydrogen (i.e., 2 instead of 1). The young chemist was a National Research Council fellow at UC from 1930 to 1932 and a chemistry instructor there from 1932 to 1934.

In 1931 he married Ethel Annie MacFarlane; they would eventually have one daughter, Mary Ann Elizabeth. Spedding moved to Cambridge, England, in 1934 to study theoretical chemistry and physics on a Guggenheim Fellowship. The following year, he moved to Cornell University, where he taught from 1935 to 1937. During this time, he collaborated at Cornell with **Hans Bethe**, the noted physicist and one of the developers of the atomic bomb, on studies of the atomic structures of rare-earth elements. He continued his studies of these elements at Iowa State University, where he began to develop methods for separating individual rare-earth elements and their isotopes. He was to stay at Iowa State University for much of the remainder of his career, becoming professor of physical chemistry from 1937 to 1941, professor of chemistry from 1941 to 1973, professor of physics from 1950 to 1973, and professor of metallurgy from 1962 to 1973. He was named distinguished professor of science and humanities in 1957, and emeritus professor of chemistry, physics, and metallurgy in 1973.

During World War II, Spedding began dividing his time between the University of Chicago, where scientists were trying to evoke a self-sustaining nuclear chain reaction, and Iowa. As director of the Plutonium Project, he directed chemical and metallurgical research to support the chain reaction program from 1942 to 1943. During 1942, Spedding and his colleagues developed processes for producing high-purity uranium using a column of resinous material that attracted metallic ions, a process called ion exchange. Using this technique, the team produced a third of the pure uranium that was used for the first self-sustaining nuclear chain reaction, which occurred at Stagg Field in Chicago on December 2, 1942.

Spedding's lab turned the new uranium purification process over to industry, which scaled up the process. The lab then concentrated its attention on producing pure thorium and cerium. Iowa State University received the Chemical Engineering Achievement Award for its wartime efforts, and Spedding himself received an honorary LL.D. degree from Drake University. Because the team of experts in pure materials, high-temperature metallurgy, and rare elements that Spedding had assembled was too valuable to disband after the war, the government asked Iowa State to operate a national laboratory, called the Institute for Atomic Research (later re-named the Ames Laboratory), with Spedding as director. He also served as principal scientist of the Ames Laboratory in 1968.

Spedding continued his research on the purification of rare-earth elements and the production of rare earth alloys and compounds. In the 1950s, Spedding's team developed processes for the large-scale production of yttrium, which the Atomic Energy Commission needed for research.

During his career he was awarded the William H. Nichols Medal of the American Chemical Society's New York Section for his "outstanding contributions in the constitution, properties and chemistry of the rare earth and actinide elements." He also received the James Douglas Medal of the American Institute of Mining, Metallurgical, and Petroleum Engineers in 1961 and the Francis J. Clamer Medal of the Franklin Institute in 1969. The National Academy of Sciences elected him to membership in 1952. In addition to his other honors, Spedding was technical representative for the Atomic Energy Commission at the Geneva Conference on Peaceful Uses of Atomic Energy in 1955, and a U.S. Department of State representative at the Fifth World Power Conference in Vienna in 1956. He was a member of the American Physical Society, the American Association for the Advancement of Science, the Faraday Society, and the American Association of University Professors.

After his retirement, Spedding devoted much of his time to researching and writing papers on the properties of the rare earths. He died on December 15, 1984, in Ames, Iowa.

SELECTED WRITINGS BY SPEDDING:

Books

(Editor, with A. H. Daane) *The Rare Earths and Related Elements,* Wiley, 1961.

SOURCES:

Books

McGraw-Hill Modern Scientists and Engineers, McGraw-Hill, 1980.

Periodicals

New York Times, October 2, 1951; March 15, 1952; December 17, 1984.

—*Sketch by Marc Kusinitz*

Hans Spemann
1869-1941
German embryologist

Hans Spemann was recognized for his research into the development of embryos, and in particular for his studies into the causes behind the specialization and differentiation of embryonic cells. In the mid–1930s he discovered "organizers"—regions within developing embryos that cause undifferentiated tissue to evolve in a specific way—and for this finding he was awarded the 1935 Nobel Prize for physiology or medicine. In addition to these achievements, Spemann is credited with founding the early techniques of microsurgery, the minute manipulations of tissue or living structure.

The son of a well known book publisher, Spemann was born on June 27, 1869, in Stuttgart. He was the eldest of four children of Johann Wilhelm Spemann and the former Lisinka Hoffman. The family, which was socially and culturally active, lived in a large home that was well stocked with books, which helped shape the young Spemann's intellect. Upon entering the Eberhard Ludwig Gymnasium, Spemann first wished to study the classics. Although he later turned to embryology—the branch of biology that focuses on embryos and their development—he never relinquished his love of artistic endeavors; throughout his lifetime he organized evening gatherings of friends to discuss art, literature, and philosophy.

Before entering the University of Heidelberg in 1891 to study medicine, Spemann worked at his father's business and served a tour of duty in the Kassel hussars. His strict interest in medicine lasted only until he met German biologist and psychologist Gustav Wolff at the University of Heidelberg. Only a few years older than Spemann, Wolff had begun experiments on the embryological developments of newts and had shown how, if the lens of an embryological newt's eye is removed, it regenerates. Spemann remained interested and intrigued by both Wolff's finding and also in the newt, on which he based much of his future work. But more than the regeneration phenomenon, Spemann was interested in how the eye develops from the start. He devoted his scientific career to the study of how embryological cells become specialized and differentiated in the process of forming a complete organism.

Spemann left Heidelberg in the mid–1890s to continue his studies at the University of Munich; he then transferred to the University of Würzberg's Zoological Institute to study under the well-known embryologist Theodor Boveri. Spemann quickly became Boveri's prize student, and completed his

doctorate in botany, zoology, and physics in 1895. Shortly thereafter he married Clara Binder; the couple eventually had two sons. Spemann stayed at Würzburg until 1908, when he accepted a post as professor at the University of Rostock. During World War I, he served as director of the Kaiser Wilhelm Institute of Biology (now the Max Planck Institute) in Berlin-Dahlem, and following the war, in 1919, he took a professorship at the University of Freiburg.

Crafts Precise Experiments

By the time Spemann began research at the Zoological Institute in Würzburg, he had already developed a keen facility and reputation for conducting well-designed experiments that centered on highly focused questions. His early research followed Wolff's closely. The eye of a newt is formed when an outgrowth of the brain, called the optic cup, reaches the surface layer of embryonic tissue (the ectoderm). The cells of the ectoderm then form into an eye. In removing the tissue over where the eye would form and replacing it with tissue from an entirely different region, Spemann found that the embryo still formed a normal eye, leading him to believe that the optic cup exerted an influence on the cells of the ectoderm, inducing them to form into an eye. To complete this experiment, as well as others, Spemann had to develop a precise experimental technique for operating on objects often less than two millimeters in diameter. In doing so, he is credited with founding the techniques of modern microsurgery, which is considered one of his greatest contributions in biology. Some of his methods and instruments are still used by embryologists and neurobiologists today.

In another series of experiments—conducted in the 1920s—Spemann used a method somewhat less technically demanding to make an even more critical discovery. By tying a thin hair around the jelly-like egg of a newt early in embryogenesis (embryo development), he could split the egg entirely, or squeeze it into a dumbbell shape. When the egg halves matured, Spemann found that the split egg would produce either a whole larva and an undifferentiated mass of cells, or two whole larva (although smaller than normal size). The split egg never produced half an embryo. In the case of the egg squeezed into a dumbbell shape, the egg formed into an embryo with a single tail and two heads. Spemann's primary finding in these experiments was that if an egg is split early in embryogenesis, the two halves do not form into two halves of an embryo; they either become two whole embryos, or an embryo and a mass of cells.

This led Spemann to the conclusion that at a certain stage of development, the future roles of the different parts of the embryo have not been fixed, which supported his experiments with the newt's eye. In an experiment conducted on older eggs, however,

Spemann found that the future role of some parts of the embryo had been decided, meaning that somewhere in between, a process he called "determination" must have taken place to fix the "developmental fate" of the cells.

Receives Nobel Prize for Organizer Effect

One of Spemann's greatest contributions to embryology—and the one for which he won the 1935 Nobel Prize in physiology or medicine—was his discovery of what he called the "organizer" effect. In experimenting with transplanting tissue, Spemann found that when an area containing an organizer is transplanted into an undifferentiated host embryo, this transplanted area can induce the host embryo to develop in a certain way, or into an entirely new embryo. Spemann called these transplanted cells organizers, and they include the precursors to the central nervous system. In vertebrates, they are the first cells in a long series of differentiations of which the end product is a fully formed fetus.

Spemann remained at the University of Freiburg until his retirement in the mid–1930s. When not busy with his scientific endeavors, he cultivated his love of the liberal arts. He died at his home near Freiburg on September 12, 1941.

SELECTED WRITINGS BY SPEMANN:

Books

Experimentelle Beiträge zu einer Theorie der Entwicklung, [Berlin], 1936, translated into English as *Embryonic Development and Induction,* Yale University Press, 1938.
Forschung und Leben, Errinerungen (autobiography), [Stuttgart], 1943.

SOURCES:

Books

Gillispie, Charles Coulston, editor, *Dictionary of Scientific Biography,* Volume 12, Scribner, 1975.

—Sketch by James Klockow

Elmer Sperry
1860-1930
American inventor and engineer

Elmer Sperry was one of the twentieth century's most prolific inventors. A pioneer in the applications of electricity, he held more than four hundred patents. The devices and machines he designed were used in such diverse enterprises as transportation and navigation, the production of metal and chemical products, outdoor lighting, and mining. Among his most famous inventions are an electric car, a high-intensity arc light, and the gyroscopic compass.

The Sperry family in America can be traced back to 1634, the year the first Sperry settled on a farm outside what is now New Haven, Connecticut. Elmer Ambrose Sperry was born on October 12, 1860, in Cortland, New York, to Stephen Decatur and Mary Burst Sperry. His mother died while giving birth to him, her only child, and he was reared by his widowed aunt, Helen Sperry Willett. As a young boy, Sperry demonstrated his abilities in engineering by building a tricycle that could be pedaled on railroad tracks in a game of thrill, just ahead of a pursuing freight train. In his teenage years Sperry attended the Cortland Normal School, one of the first schools in the country to offer courses about electricity. There he developed an interest in electrical devices. After graduation, he enrolled at Cornell University, a short buggy ride from the town of Cortland; he remained at the university for only one year, from 1879 to 1880—the extent of his formal education.

Sperry's work at Cornell University concentrated on generators and arc lights, which produce light by means of an arc made when a current passes through two incandescent electrodes surrounded by gas. His success in building these lights led to his first business endeavor: in December of 1879, Sperry built an assembly of electrical lights that was used to illuminate his hometown Christmas festival. Less than a year later he brought his design to Chicago and set up the Sperry Electric Illuminating and Power Company. Soon he was providing lights for towns across the Midwest, and Sperry-designed lighting equipment was responsible for most of the illumination at the Chicago World's Fair of 1892–93. Eventually Sperry sold the patents on his generator and arc lights to the General Edison Company of Schenectady, which later merged with other enterprises to become the General Electric Company.

When Sperry had first arrived in Chicago in 1880 he brought a letter of introduction from his Cortland, New York pastor. A Chicago deacon of the Baptist church arranged for him to teach Sunday school;

Sperry's classes covered a unique combination of topics, including not only religion but lighting and electricity. Sperry was introduced to the deacon's daughter, Zula Augusta Goodman, whom he married in 1887 and with whom he had four children—Helen, Edward, Lawrence and Elmer. While on his honeymoon with Zula, he had the occasion to meet a mine operator who convinced Sperry that electricity had the potential to revolutionize the mining industry.

The technical challenge Sperry had to work out was how to prevent corrosion of electrical wires in the damp environment of the mine; he accomplished this by creating small currents that raised the temperature of the copper conducting wires, evaporating the dampness before it could corrode the wires. Within a few years he had developed electrical chain cutters for carving out coal deposits, as well as an electrical locomotive that could haul out one thousand tons of coal a day; this latter device relied on a specially designed wheel-to-motor connection to keep it from toppling off the irregularly turning tracks. Applying the same design principles, Sperry was able to build an electric trolley that would take first prize in the competitive hill-climbing test at the Chicago World's Fair.

In 1890 Sperry organized the Sperry Electric Railway Company in Cleveland, Ohio; four years later, after hundreds of electric rail cars had been manufactured, the General Electric Company bought both the business and Sperry's patents. Before the business was sold, Sperry designed an electric automobile, which was eventually sold as the Waverly Electric and which enjoyed brief popularity, especially in Europe. The automobile's battery, which was the precursor to portable lead storage batteries, was also designed by Sperry. The development of the automobile battery introduced Sperry to the field of electrochemistry, and in 1900 he set up a laboratory in Washington, D.C., for electrochemical research. Over the next decade many chemical manufacturing processes were developed in this laboratory, including the Townsend process which uses salt to produce caustic soda, hydrogen, and chlorine. Sperry also developed methods for purifying lead and for chlorine detinning.

In 1905 Sperry moved his family to Brooklyn, New York, where he was to live for the rest of his life. By 1910 he had formed the Sperry Gyroscope Company to take over work on what had become his new technical interest, gyroscopes. In the 1890s, when he had encountered problems in stabilizing the motion of his electric vehicles, Sperry began studying gyros. He determined that it was possible to use them, coupled with electric motors, as stabilizing devices. Orders for ship stabilizers were filled during the early 1900s for the U.S. Navy and for various international vessels. In 1913 Sperry used his gyro-stabilizer equipment to build an automatic pilot device for airplanes. Sperry also saw the potential of gyroscopes for navigation. The heavy steel composition of ships caused magnetic navigational compasses to shift unpredictably. In 1908 Sperry began modifying his gyroscopic stabilizer so that it could sense the earth's rotation to indicate true north, and by 1911 his invention passed its first sea trial. The gyroscopic compass eventually became part of an automatic steering control system known as Metal Mike. Sperry's gyroscopic navigational instruments were in such high demand by World War I that several new production factories had to be built, both in Europe and the United States. In 1917 Sperry adapted his navigational device for airplane use, producing the gyro turn indicator.

The U.S. Navy called upon Sperry in 1914 for help with searchlights. Sperry developed the high-intensity arc light, a searchlight with one billion candlepower (a candlepower, or candela, has a frequency of 540×10^{12} hertz), capable of matching the newly expanded range of Naval turret guns. Sperry's lights were initially used to scan the skies over London and Paris during World War I; they eventually found application as airport beacons and floodlights. His lights also made outdoor drive-in movie viewing possible, illuminating the large-format screen.

Throughout the 1920s Sperry continued to design and develop machines for navigation as well as new types of searchlights, creating sighting and signaling devices for the military. Though in 1928 his health began to fail, he continued nonetheless to work on new ideas, including an automatic car transmission, a supercharged diesel engine, a variable pitch propeller for airplanes, and a rail flaw detector for railroad tracks. Sperry died on June 16, 1930, in Brooklyn, New York.

During his career he received wide recognition and honor for his inventions. He was awarded three honorary doctoral degrees; he was a member and officer of many technical and engineering societies, and he received numerous medals and trophies for his inventions, including decoration from the czar of Russia in 1915 and the emperor of Japan in 1922 and 1929.

SELECTED WRITINGS BY SPERRY:

Periodicals

"Electricity in Bituminous Mining," *American Institute of Electrical Engineers Transactions,* Volume 9, 1892, pp. 374–400.

"Electric Automobiles," *American Institute of Electrical Engineers Transactions,* Volume 16, 1899, pp. 509–525.

"Gyroscopic Stabilizers for Ships," *Scientific American,* Volume 75, 1913, pp. 203–205.

"Sperry Gyro Turn Indicator," *International Air Congress Report,* 1923, pp. 404–405.

SOURCES:

Books

Durgin, Russell L., *Dr. Sperry as We Knew Him,* Nichi-Bei Press, 1931.
Hughes, Thomas Parker, *Elmer Ambrose Sperry: Inventor and Engineer,* Johns Hopkins Press, 1971.

Periodicals

Hughes, Thomas Parker, "Science and the Instrument-Maker: Michelson, Sperry, and the Speed of Light," *Smithsonian Studies in History and Technology,* 1976, pp. 1–18.
Hunsaker, H. C., "Biographical Memoir of Elmer Ambrose Sperry," *National Academy of Sciences,* 1954, pp. 223–260.

—*Sketch by Leslie Reinherz*

Roger W. Sperry

Roger W. Sperry
1913-

American psychobiologist

Roger W. Sperry, a major contributor to at least three scientific fields—developmental neurobiology, experimental psychobiology, and human split-brain studies—conducted pioneering research in the functions of the left and right hemispheres of the brain. He was awarded the Nobel Prize for physiology or medicine in 1981 for his work. The system of split-brain research that he created has enabled scientists to better understand the workings of the human brain.

Sperry was born on August 20, 1913, in Hartford, Connecticut, to Francis Bushnell Sperry, a banker, and Florence Kramer Sperry. When Sperry was 11 years old, his father died and his mother returned to school and got a job as an assistant to a high school principal. Sperry attended local public schools through high school and then went to Oberlin College in Ohio on a scholarship. There he competed on the track team and was captain of the basketball squad. Although he majored in English, Sperry was especially interested in his undergraduate psychology courses with R. H. Stetson, an expert on the physiology of speech. Sperry earned his B.A. in English in 1935 and

then worked as a graduate assistant to Stetson for two years. In 1937 he received an M.A. in psychology.

Thoroughly committed to research in the field of psychobiology by that time, Sperry went to the University of Chicago to conduct research on the organization of the central nervous system under the renowned biologist Paul Weiss. Before Weiss's research, scientists believed that the connections of the nervous system had to be very exact to work properly. Weiss disproved this theory by surgically crossing a subject's nerve connections. After the surgery was performed, the subject's behavior did not change. From this, Weiss concluded that the connections of the central nervous system were not predetermined, so that a nerve need not connect to any particular location to function correctly.

Challenges Mentor's Theories

Sperry tested Weiss's research by surgically crossing the nerves that controlled the hind leg muscles of a rat. Under Weiss's theory, each nerve should eventually "learn" to control the leg muscle to which it was now connected. This did not happen. When the left hind foot was stimulated, the right foot responded instead. Sperry's experiments disproved Weiss's research and became the basis of his doctoral dissertation, "Functional results of crossing nerves and transposing muscles in the fore and hind limbs of the rat." He received a Ph.D. in Zoology from the University of Chicago in 1941.

Sperry did other related experiments that confirmed his findings and further contradicted Weiss's theory that "function precedes form" (that is, the brain and nervous system learn, through experience, to function properly). In one experiment, Sperry rotated a frog's eyeball and cut its optic nerve. If Weiss's theory was correct, the frog would reeducate itself, adjust to seeing the world upside down, and change its behavior accordingly. This did not happen. In fact, the nerve fibers became tangled in the scar tissue during healing. When the nerve regenerated, it ignored the repositioning of the eyeball and reattached itself correctly, albeit upside down. From this and other experiments, Sperry deduced that genetic mechanisms determine some basic behavioral patterns. According to his theory, nerves have highly specific functions based on genetically predetermined differences in the concentration of chemicals inside the nerve cells.

In 1941, Sperry moved to the laboratory of the renowned psychologist Karl S. Lashley at Harvard to work as a National Research Council postdoctoral fellow. A year later, Lashley became director of the Yerkes Laboratories of Primate Biology in Orange Park, Florida. Sperry joined him there on a Harvard biology research fellowship. While there, he disproved some Gestalt psychology theories about brain mechanisms, as well as some theories of Lashley's.

During World War II, Sperry fulfilled his military service duty by working for three years in an Office of Scientific Research and Development (OSRD) medical research project run by the University of Chicago and the Yerkes laboratory. His work involved research on repairing nerve injuries by surgery. In 1946, Sperry returned to the University of Chicago to accept a position as assistant professor in the school's anatomy department. He became associate professor of psychology during the 1952–53 school year and also worked during that year as section chief in the Neurological Diseases and Blindness division of the National Institutes of Health.

From there he moved in 1954 to the California Institute of Technology (Caltech) to take a position as the Hixon Professor of Psychobiology. At Caltech, Sperry conducted research on split-brain functions that he had first investigated when he worked at the Yerkes Laboratory. It had long been known that the cerebrum of the brain consists of two hemispheres. In most people the left hemisphere controls the right side of the body and vice versa. The two halves are connected by a bundle of millions of nerve fibers called the corpus callosum, or the great cerebral commissure.

Neurosurgeons had discovered that this connection could be cut into with little or no noticeable change in the patient's mental abilities. After experi-

ments on animals proved the procedure to be harmless, surgeons began cutting completely through the commissure of epileptic patients in an attempt to prevent the spread of epileptic seizures from one hemisphere to the other. The procedure was generally successful, and beginning in the late 1930s, cutting through the forebrain commissure became an accepted treatment method for severe epilepsy. Observations of the split-brain patients indicated no loss of communication between the two hemispheres of the brain.

From these observations, scientists assumed that the corpus callosum had no function other than as a prop to prevent the two hemispheres from sagging. Scientists also believed that the left hemisphere was dominant and performed higher cognitive functions such as speech. This theory developed from observations of patients whose left cerebral hemisphere had been injured; these patients suffered impairment of various cognitive functions, including speech. Since these functions were not transferred over to the uninjured right hemisphere, scientists assumed that the right hemisphere was less developed.

Discovers Role of Right Brain

Sperry's work shattered these views. He and his colleagues at Caltech discovered that the corpus callosum is more than a physical prop; it provides a means of communication between the two halves of the brain and integrates the knowledge acquired by each of them. They also learned that in many ways, the right hemisphere is superior to the left. Although the left half of the brain is superior in analytic, logical thought, the right half excels in intuitive processing of information. The right hemisphere also specializes in non-verbal functions, such as understanding music, interpreting visual patterns (such as recognizing faces), and sorting sizes and shapes.

Sperry discovered these different capacities of the two cerebral hemispheres through a series of experiments performed over a period of several decades. In one such experiment, Sperry and a graduate student, Ronald Myers, cut the nerve connections between the two hemispheres of a cat's brain. They discovered that behavioral responses learned by the left side of the brain were not transferred to the right, and vice versa. In an article published in *Scientific American* in 1964, Sperry observed that "it was as though each hemisphere were a separate mental domain operating with complete disregard—indeed, with a complete lack of awareness—of what went on in the other. The split-brain animal behaved in the test situation as if it had two entirely separate brains." It was evident from this experiment that the severed nerves had been responsible for communication between the two halves of the brain.

In another experiment on a human subject, he showed a commissurotomy patient (one whose corpus callosum had been surgically severed) a picture of a pair of scissors. Only the patient's left visual field, which is governed by the nonverbal right hemisphere, could see the scissors. The patient could not verbally describe what he had seen because the left hemisphere, which controls language functions, had not received the necessary information. However, when the patient reached behind a screen, he sorted through a pile of various items and picked out the scissors. When asked how he knew the correct item, the patient insisted it was purely luck.

Sperry published technical papers on his split-brain findings beginning in the late 1960s. The importance of his research was recognized relatively quickly, and in 1979 he was awarded the prestigious Albert Lasker Basic Medical Research Award, which included a $15,000 grant. The award was given in recognition of the potential medical benefits of Sperry's research, including possible treatments for mental or psychosomatic illnesses.

Awarded Nobel Prize for Split-Brain Studies

Two years later, Sperry was honored with the 1981 Nobel Prize in physiology or medicine. He shared it with two other scientists, **Torsten N. Wiesel** and **David H. Hubel**, for their research on the central nervous system and the brain. In describing Sperry's work, the Nobel Prize selection committee praised the researcher for demonstrating the difference between the two hemispheres of the brain and for outlining some of the specialized functions of the right brain. The committee, as quoted in the *New York Times,* stated that Sperry's work illuminated the fact that the right brain "is clearly superior to the left in many respects, especially regarding the capacity for concrete thinking, spatial consciousness and comprehension of complex relationships."

In his acceptance speech, as quoted in *Science* in 1982, Sperry talked about the significance of his discovery of the previously unrecognized skills of the nonverbal right half-brain. He commented that an important gain from his work is increased attention to "the important role of the nonverbal components and forms of the intellect." Because split-brain research increased appreciation of the individuality of each brain and its functions, Sperry believed that his work helped to point out the need for educational policies that took into consideration varying types of intelligence and potential.

Sperry rejected conventional scientific thinking that viewed human consciousness solely as a function of physical and chemical activity within the brain. In his view, which he discussed in his Nobel Prize lecture, "cognitive introspective psychology and related cognitive science can no longer be ignored experi-mentally.... The whole world of inner experience (the world of the humanities) long rejected by twentieth-century scientific materialism, thus becomes recognized and included within the domain of science."

Known as a private, reserved person, Sperry was, quite characteristically, camping with his wife in a remote area when the news of his Nobel Prize award was announced. He married Gay Deupree in 1949, and they have two children, Glenn Tad and Janet Hope. In addition to camping, Sperry's avocational interests include sculpture, drawing, ceramics, folk dancing, and fossil hunting.

In addition to the Nobel prize, Sperry has received many awards and honorary doctorates. He has been a member of many scientific societies, including the Pontifical Academy of Sciences and the National Academy of Sciences. Sperry always has been held in high regard by his students. One of them, Michael Gazzaniga, described him in *Science* as "exceedingly generous" to many students at Caltech. Gazzaniga also commented that Sperry "is constitutionally only able to be interested in critical issues and he drove this herd of young scientists to consider nothing but the big questions."

SELECTED WRITINGS BY SPERRY:

Books

Science and Moral Priority, Columbia University Press, 1983.

Periodicals

"The Great Commisure," *Scientific American,* January, 1964.
"Mental Unity Following Surgical Disconnection of the Cerebral Hemispheres," *Harvey Lectures* 62, 1968, pp. 293–322.

SOURCES:

Books

Nobel Prize Winners, H. W. Wilson Company, 1987, 997–1000.
The Omni Interviews, Ticknor & Fields, pp. 187–191.

Periodicals

"Brain Mappers Win a Nobel Prize," *Newsweek,* October 19, 1981, p.110.
Gazzaniga, Michael S., "1981 Nobel Prize for Physiology or Medicine," *Science,* October 30, 1981, pp. 517–18.

"The Nobel Prizes," *Scientific American,* December, 1981, p. 80.

Schmeck, Harold M. Jr., "Three Scientists Share Nobel Prize for Studies of the Brain," *New York Times,* October 10, 1981, pp. 1, 50–51.

Sperry, Roger W., reprint of Nobel Prize lecture, *Science,* September 24, 1982.

—*Sketch by Donna Olshansky*

Lyman Spitzer, Jr.

Lyman Spitzer, Jr.
1914-
American astrophysicist

Lyman Spitzer, Jr., through his research into galactic structure, made important insights into the understanding of star formation. Through continued investigations into the nature of stars, he pioneered theoretical research into the techniques of achieving controlled nuclear fusion in a laboratory setting.

Spitzer was born in Toledo, Ohio, on June 26, 1914. He studied at Phillips Academy in Massachusetts before moving on to Yale University, where he received a B.A. in Physics in 1935. He broadened his academic development as a Henry fellow, spending a year in Cambridge, England, studying with Sir **Arthur Stanley Eddington**. After returning to the United States, Spitzer worked with **Henry Norris Russell** at Princeton where he received his Ph.D. in astrophysics in 1938. He immediately obtained a National Research Council fellowship for a year of study at Harvard after which he returned to Yale as an instructor in physics and astronomy. As was the case with many young Americans, Spitzer's fast-rising career was interrupted by World War II. From 1942 to 1946, he supervised projects at Columbia University in underwater warfare research, including the development of sonar. When the war ended, Spitzer continued at Yale for a year or so. In 1947 he moved to Princeton, where he became the chair of the astronomy department. He was later appointed Charles A. Young Professor in 1951 and elected to the National Academy of Sciences in 1952.

By 1950, with the disruptions and distractions of war behind them, astronomers were poised for a new leap forward in knowledge. Helping them was the massive new 200-inch Hale telescope on Mount Palomar, which had just come on line in 1949 and promised to deliver a treasure trove of new data for scientists to ponder. Also, theories concerning the expansion of the universe in the first half of the century and more recent work on the process of stellar evolution both served to help knit the sum of astronomical progress into an emerging, coherent "story". What was missing was an understanding of how stars formed in the first place.

It was apparent from studies of the Milky Way and nearby spiral galaxies that hot, massive stars seemed to be generated almost constantly from within the spiral arms. Calculations verified that the massive stars burned their fuel at so furious a rate that they could only live for a few tens of millions of years, a short time by cosmic standards, before burning themselves out. The fact that astronomers could observe these brilliant stars at all meant that some process was continually at work replacing the burned out stars with new ones. The arms of spiral galaxies had the most plentiful abundance of such massive stars, so it became obvious that some feature or attribute of the spiral arms was responsible for star-formation. The one major feature that characterizes the spiral arms of galaxies is their large concentration of gas and dust. Lyman Spitzer, along with others, attempted to untangle the mystery of how clouds of gas and dust could combine to form stars.

Spitzer analyzed the characteristics of ionized gas clouds which existed near massive, hot stars and compared them with the cooler regions of interstellar molecular clouds. He found that the hot gas, or plasma, regions exerted a strong thermal pressure, created by temperatures of 10,000 degrees Kelvin. The pressure was sufficient to churn the nearby molecular clouds. This explained the high gas velocities observed in such regions. With instability introduced into an otherwise quiescent gas cloud, the stage was set for the cloud's gravitational collapse and the onset of star formation.

Pioneering Work on Nuclear Fusion Begins

Spitzer analyzed the effects of interstellar magnetic fields on plasma clouds and became one of the leading contributors to the burgeoning field of plasma physics. He calculated that it would be possible to contain hydrogen gas plasma at the incredible temperature of 100 million degrees Kelvin by keeping the plasma within magnetic fields. The trapped, superheated hydrogen would then fuse into helium, releasing a tremendous amount of energy. Indeed, nuclear fusion is the energy source that powers the stars, wherein the tremendous pressure of gravity at the star's core transforms hydrogen into helium at high temperatures. Spitzer's insight was to show how a hydrogen plasma could be fused to produce energy without requiring the presence of a massive star to do it. The implications of this idea, which is nothing less than the creation of energy by controlled thermonuclear fusion, is still being studied in laboratories around the world and stems directly from the work of Spitzer.

Something of the depth of Spitzer's contributions to astronomy and physics can be glimpsed from the numerous awards he received during his long career, including the Rittenhouse Medal of the Franklin Institute in 1957, the Exceptional Science Achievement Medal from NASA in 1972, The Bruce God Medal from the Astronomical Society of the Pacific in 1973, the Henry Draper Medal from the National Academy of Sciences in 1974, the James Clerk Maxwell Prize from the American Physics Society in 1975, the Distinguished Public Service Medal from NASA in 1976, the Gold Medal of the Royal Astronomical Society in 1978, the Jules Janssen Medal from the Société Astronomique de France in 1980, and the Franklin Medal from the Franklin Institute in 1980.

Spitzer also speculated on the possibility of artificial, earth-orbiting satellites and telescopes. As head of the Princeton University Observatory, he was among the first to promote the use of rockets for scientific research. Princeton played a leading part in his endeavor with programs designed to perform studies using high-altitude balloons and rockets. The critical role that orbiting observatories play in current astronomical research is testimony to the vision of Lyman Spitzer.

SELECTED WRITINGS BY SPITZER:

Books

Physics of Fully Ionized Gases, Interscience Publishers, 1956.
Diffuse Matter in Space, Interscience Publishers, 1968.
Physical Processes in the Interstellar Medium, Wiley, 1978.
Searching between the Stars, Yale University Press, 1982.
Dynamical Evolution of Globular Clusters, Princeton University Press, 1987.

—Sketch by Jeffery Bass

Franklin W. Stahl
1929-
American molecular biologist

Franklin W. Stahl, in collaboration with **Matthew Meselson**, discovered direct evidence for the semiconservative nature of deoxyribonucleic acid (DNA) replication in bacteria. In experiments, Stahl and Meselson showed that when a double stranded DNA molecule is duplicated, the double strands are separated and a new strand is copied from each "parent" strand forming two new double stranded DNA molecules. The new double stranded DNA molecules contain one conserved "parent" strand and one new "daughter" strand. Therefore, the replication of a DNA molecule is semiconservative: it retains some of the original material while creating some new material. The understanding of the semiconservative nature of DNA in replication was a major advancement in the field of molecular biology.

Franklin William Stahl, the youngest of three children, was born on October 6, 1929, in Boston, Massachusetts, to Oscar Stahl, an equipment specialist with New England Telephone and Telegraph, and Eleanor Condon Stahl, a homemaker. He received a baccalaureate degree from Harvard University in 1951 in the area of biological sciences; he continued with graduate studies in the field of biology, earning a Ph.D. degree at the University of Rochester in New York, in 1956. From 1955 to 1958, Stahl was a research fellow at the California Institute of Technology, where he collaborated with Matthew Meselson on the semiconservative replication experiment.

In 1952, having just graduated from Harvard, Stahl attended a course at Cold Spring Harbor

Laboratories in New York given by A. H. Doermann. Doermann was well known for research on bacteriophages, microscopic agents that destroy disease-producing bacteria in a living organism. This course gave Stahl his first exposure to the genetics of bacteriophages. The subject so fascinated him that he spent his summers in the laboratory of Dr. Doermann while working on his doctorate at the University of Rochester during the school year. Bacteriophage genetics would later become the major focus of his own laboratory's scientific research. Stahl would also come to teach the same course at Cold Spring Harbor.

After receiving his doctorate in biology, Stahl moved to California to work in the laboratory of **Max Delbrück** at the California Institute of Technology as a postdoctoral fellow. While at Cal Tech, he began a collaboration with graduate student Meselson to design an experiment to describe the nature of DNA replication from parent to offspring using bacteriophages. The idea was to add the substance 5-bromouracil, which would become incorporated into the DNA of a T4 bacteriophage upon its replication during a few rounds of reproduction. Phage samples could then be isolated by a density gradient centrifugation procedure which was originally designed by Stahl, Meselson, and Jerome Vinograd. It was thought that the phage samples containing the incorporated 5-bromouracil would separate in the density gradient centrifugation to a measurable degree based on the length of the new strands of DNA acquired during replication. Several attempts to obtain measurable results were unsuccessful. Despite these first setbacks, Stahl had confidence in the theory of the experiment. After further contemplation, Stahl and Meselson decided to abandon the use of the T4 bacteriophage and the labelling substance 5-bromouracil and turned to the use of a bacteria, Escherichia coli, with the heavy nitrogen isotope 15N as the labelling substance. This time, when the same experimental steps were performed using the new substitutions, the analysis of the density gradient centrifugation samples showed three distinct types of bacterial DNA, two from the original parent strands of DNA and one from the new offspring. Analysis of the new offspring showed each strand of DNA came from a different parent. Thus the theory of semiconservative replication of DNA had been proven.

Recognized as Expert in Bacteriophage Genetics

After spending 1958 at the University of Missouri as an associate professor of zoology, Stahl took a position as associate professor of biology and research associate at the Institute of Molecular Biology, located at the University of Oregon in Eugene, Oregon. In 1963, he was awarded status of professor; he was appointed acting director of the Institute from 1973 to 1975. Stahl has held a concurrent position as resident research professor of molecular genetics at the American Cancer Society.

Stahl set up his own laboratory at the Institute, contributing further to the scientific research and understanding in the area of bacteriophage genetics, as well as the genetic recombination of bacteriophages and fungi. In the early years at Eugene, he continued to focus his research in the area of genetic recombination and replication in bacteriophages using the techniques of density gradient and equilibrium centrifugations. Through the years, he was able to map the DNA structure of the T4 bacteriophage. The experiments involved T4 bacteriophages inactivated by decay of DNA incorporated radionucleotides or by X-irradiation of the DNA that would cause breaks in the DNA sequence. By performing reactivation-crosses of these bacteriophage, Stahl studied the patterns in which markers on the DNA were "knocked out" or lost. Although the inactivated phages are unable to produce offspring themselves, they can contribute particular markers to their offspring when they are grown in the presence of rescuing phages that supply the functions necessary for phage development. By the pattern of markers seen in the offspring of these reactivation crosses, a map can be constructed. From the map constructed, the correlated knockout markers reflected a linkage relationship in the form of a circle. With this map in hand, particular DNA sequences could be shown to be important for various functions of the bacteriophage.

Much of Stahl's later work focused on the bacteriophage Lambda, which has a more complex structure than bacteriophage T4, and its replication inside of a bacterial cell. He determined particular "hot spots" in the DNA sequence that were susceptible to various mutations or recombinations during the process of replication. These "hot spots" were particular sites in the DNA sequence of the phage that tended to show crossing over between two DNA strands of the chromosome. The resulting mutations (Chi mutations), which occurred at four or five particular sites in the Lambda phage, conferred a particular large plaque forming character by accelerating the rate of crossing over at these sites. These mutations affected the overall function of the bacteriophage, sometimes causing complete inactivation. Through further studies of genetic recombination in bacteriophages, Stahl became known to the scientific world as an expert on their structure and life cycle.

From 1964–85, Stahl held several year-long positions as visiting professor or volunteer scientist in various universities throughout the world. He was the volunteer scientist in the Division of Molecular Genetics for the Medical Research Council in Cambridge, England. He took a sabbatical leave from Oregon and conducted research in the Medical Research Council Unit of Molecular Genetics at the University of Edinburgh, Scotland, as well as at the

Laboratory of International Genetics and Biophysics in Naples, Italy. He held the position of Lady Davis Visiting Professor in the Genetics Department at Hebrew University in Jerusalem, Israel. Stahl also taught courses on bacterial viruses at Cold Spring Harbor Laboratories and in Naples. He is a member of the National Academy of Sciences, the American Academy of Arts and Sciences, and the Viral Study Section of the National Institutes of Health.

Reflections on a Scientific Career

During a personal interview, when asked what was a leading factor in choosing scientific research in biology as a career, Dr. Stahl responded, "The currency of science is truth and understanding opposed to power and money, leading to contact with people that are fun and exciting." This difference between the world of scientific research and the business world has been a primary factor in influencing the path of Stahl's scientific career. His main goal as a scientist was never fame or fortune, but the opportunity to interact with exciting people and share innovative ideas. According to Dr. Stahl, his greatest contribution to the scientific world has been "the ability to act as mentor to graduate students and scientists by giving encouragement and direction to their research." He has gained great pleasure in passing on his knowledge and experiences to future generations of scientists.

Throughout his career as a scientist, Stahl has written over one hundred articles published in major scientific journals, received numerous honors including two honorary degrees, and been awarded the prestigious Guggenheim Fellowship award three times. Franklin Stahl married Mary Morgan, also a scientist, in 1955; the couple had three children, Emily, Joshua and Andy. Mary worked alongside Frank in the laboratory, frequently carrying on experiments while Frank took care of administrative responsibilities. He enjoys watching "Monday Night Football" and getting together with family members.

SELECTED WRITINGS BY STAHL:

Books

The Mechanics of Inheritance, 2nd edition, Prentice-Hall, 1969.
Genetic Recombination: Thinking about It in Phage and Fungi, W. H. Freeman, 1979.

Periodicals

"The Replication of DNA in Escherichia coli," *Proceedings of the National Academy of Sciences,* Volume 44, pp. 671–682, 1958.

"Circularity of the Genetic Map of Bacteriophage T4," *Genetics,* Volume 48, pp. 659–1672, 1963.
"Circular Genetic Maps," *Journal of Cellular Physiology,* Volume 70 (Supplement 1), pp. 1–12, 1967.

SOURCES:

Books

Daintith, John, Mitchell, Sarah, and Tootill, Elizabeth, *A Biographical Encyclopedia of Scientists,* Facts on File, 1981.

Other

Stahl, Franklin W., interview with Karen S. Kelly conducted December 2, 1993.

—*Sketch by Karen S. Kelly*

Wendell Meredith Stanley
1904-1971
American biochemist

Wendell Meredith Stanley was a biochemist who was the first to isolate, purify, and characterize the crystalline form of a virus. During World War II, he led a team of scientists in developing a vaccine for viral influenza. His efforts have paved the way for understanding the molecular basis of heredity and formed the foundation for the new scientific field of molecular biology. For his work in crystallizing the tobacco mosaic virus, Stanley shared the 1946 Nobel Prize in chemistry with **John Howard Northrop** and **James B. Sumner**.

Stanley was born in the small community of Ridgeville, Indiana, on August 16, 1904. His parents, James and Claire Plessinger Stanley, were publishers of a local newspaper. As a boy, Stanley helped the business by collecting news, setting type, and delivering papers. After graduating from high school he enrolled in Earlham College, a liberal arts school in Richmond, Indiana, where he majored in chemistry and mathematics. He played football as an undergraduate, and in his senior year he became team captain and was chosen to play end on the Indiana All-State team. In June of 1926 Stanley graduated with a bachelor of science degree. His ambition was to become a football coach, but the course of his life was

Wendell Meredith Stanley

changed forever when an Earlham chemistry professor invited him on a trip to Illinois State University. Here, he was introduced to **Roger Adams**, an organic chemist, who inspired him to seek a career in chemical research. Stanley applied and was accepted as a graduate assistant in the fall of 1926.

In graduate school, Stanley worked under Adams, and his first project involved finding the stereochemical characteristics of biphenyl, a molecule containing carbon and hydrogen atoms. His second assignment was more practical; Adams was interested in finding chemicals to treat leprosy, and Stanley set out to prepare and purify compounds that would destroy the disease-causing pathogen. Stanley received his master's degree in 1927 and two years later was awarded his Ph.D. In the summer of 1930, he was awarded a National Research Council Fellowship to do postdoctoral studies with **Heinrich Wieland** at the University of Munich in Germany. Under Wieland's tutelage, Stanley extended his knowledge of experimental biochemistry by characterizing the properties of some yeast compounds.

Stanley returned to the United States in 1931 to accept the post of research assistant at the Rockefeller Institute in New York City. Stanley was assigned to work with W. J. V. Osterhout, who was studying how living cells absorb potassium ions from seawater. Stanley was asked to find a suitable chemical model that would simulate how a marine plant called *Valonia* functions. He discovered a way of using a water-insoluble solution sandwiched between two layers of water to model the way the plant exchanged ions with its environment. The work on *Valonia* served to extend Stanley's knowledge of biophysical systems, and it introduced him to current problems in biological chemistry.

Begins Chemical Studies on Tobacco Mosaic Virus

In 1932, Stanley moved to the Rockefeller Institute's Division of Plant Pathology in Princeton, New Jersey. He was primarily interested in studying viruses. Viruses were known to cause diseases in plants and animals, but little was known about how they functioned. His assignment was to characterize viruses and determine their composition and structure.

He began work on a virus that had long been associated with the field of virology. In 1892, D. Ivanovsky , a Russian scientist, had studied tobacco mosaic disease, in which infected tobacco plants develop a characteristic mosaic pattern of dark and light spots. He found that the tobacco plant juice retained its ability to cause infection even after it was passed through a filter. Six years later M. Beijerinck, a Dutch scientist, realized the significance of Ivanovsky's discovery: the filtration technique used by Ivanovsky would have filtered out all known bacteria, and the fact that the filtered juice remained infectious must have meant that something smaller than a bacterium and invisible to the ordinary light microscope was responsible for the disease. Beijerinck concluded that tobacco mosaic disease was caused by a previously undiscovered type of infective agent, a virus.

Stanley was aware of recent techniques used to precipitate the tobacco mosaic virus (TMV) with common chemicals. These results led him to believe that the virus might be a protein susceptible to the reagents used in protein chemistry. He set out to isolate, purify, and concentrate the tobacco mosaic virus. He planted Turkish tobacco plants, and when the plants were about six inches tall, he rubbed the leaves with a swab of linen dipped in TMV solution. After a few days the heavily infected plants were chopped and frozen. Later, he ground and mashed the frozen plants to obtain a thick, dark liquid. He then subjected the TMV liquid to various enzymes and found that some would inactivate the virus and concluded that TMV must be a protein or something similar. After exposing the liquid to more than 100 different chemicals, Stanley determined that the virus was inactivated by the same chemicals that typically inactivated proteins, and this suggested to him, as well as others, that TMV was protein-like in nature.

Stanley then turned his attention to obtaining a pure sample of the virus. He decanted, filtered, precipitated, and evaporated the tobacco juice many times. With each chemical operation, the juice became more clear and the solution more infectious. The end result of two-and-one-half years of work was a clear concentrated solution of TMV which began to form into crystals when stirred. Stanley filtered and collected the tiny, white crystals and discovered that they retained their ability to produce the characteristic lesions of tobacco mosaic disease.

After successfully crystallizing TMV, Stanley's work turned toward characterizing its properties. In 1936, two English scientists at Cambridge University confirmed Stanley's work by isolating TMV crystals. They discovered that the virus consisted of ninety-four percent protein and six percent nucleic acid, and they concluded that TMV was a nucleoprotein. Stanley was skeptical at first. Later studies, however, showed that the virus became inactivated upon removal of the nucleic acid, and this work convinced him that TMV was indeed a nucleoprotein. In addition to chemical evidence, the first electron microscope pictures of TMV were produced by researchers in Germany. The pictures showed the crystals to have a distinct rod-like shape. For his work in crystallizing the tobacco mosaic virus, Stanley shared the 1946 Nobel prize in chemistry with John Howard Northrop and James Sumner.

Develops Influenza Vaccine

During World War II, Stanley was asked to participate in efforts to prevent viral diseases, and he joined the Office of Scientific Research and Development in Washington D.C. Here, he worked on the problem of finding a vaccine effective against viral influenza. Such a substance would change the virus so that the body's immune system could build up defenses without causing the disease. Using fertilized hen eggs as a source, he proceeded to grow, isolate, and purify the virus. After many attempts, he discovered that formaldehyde, the chemical used as a biological preservative, would inactivate the virus but still induce the body to produce antibodies. The first flu vaccine was tested and found to be remarkably effective against viral influenza. For his work in developing large-scale methods of preparing vaccines, he was awarded the Presidential Certificate of Merit in 1948.

In 1948, Stanley moved to the University of California in Berkeley, where he became director of a new virology laboratory and chair of the department of biochemistry. In five years Stanley assembled an impressive team of scientists and technicians who reopened the study of plant viruses and began an intensive effort to characterize large, biologically important molecules. In 1955 **Heinz Fraenkel-Conrat**, a protein chemist, and R. C. Williams, an electron microscopist, took TMV apart and reassembled the viral RNA, thus proving that RNA was the infectious component. In addition, their work indicated that the protein component of TMV served only as a protective cover. Other workers in the virus laboratory succeeded in isolating and crystallizing the virus responsible for polio, and in 1960 Stanley led a group that determined the complete amino acid sequence of TMV protein. In the early 1960s, Stanley became interested in a possible link between viruses and cancer.

Stanley was an advocate of academic freedom. In the 1950s, when his university was embroiled in the politics of McCarthyism, members of the faculty were asked to sign oaths of loyalty to the United States. Although Stanley signed the oath of loyalty, he publicly defended those who chose not to, and his actions led to court decisions which eventually invalidated the requirement.

Stanley received many awards, including the Alder Prize from Harvard University in 1938, the Nichols Medal of the American Chemical Society in 1946, and the Scientific Achievement Award of the American Medical Association in 1966. He held honorary doctorates from many colleges and universities. He was a prolific author of more than 150 publications and he co-edited a three volume compendium entitled *The Viruses.* By lecturing, writing, and appearing on television he helped bring important scientific issues before the public. He served on many boards and commissions, including the National Institute of Health, the World Health Organization, and the National Cancer Institute.

Stanley married Marian Staples Jay on June 25, 1929. They had met at the University of Illinois, where they both were graduate students in chemistry. They coauthored a scientific paper together with Adams, which was published the same year they were married. The Stanleys had three daughters and one son. On June 15, 1971, while attending a conference on biochemistry in Spain, Stanley died from a heart attack.

SELECTED WRITINGS BY STANLEY:

Books

(Coeditor, with Frank Macfarlane Burnet) *The Viruses: Biochemical, Biological, and Biophysical Properties,* Academic Press (New York), 1959.
(With Evan G. Valens), *Viruses and the Nature of Life,* Dutton (New York), 1961.

Periodicals

"Chemical Studies on the Virus of Tobacco Mosaic," *Phytopathology,* 24, 1934, pp. 1055–1085.
"Isolation of a Crystalline Protein Possessing the Properties of Tobacco-Mosaic Virus," *Science,* 81, 1935, pp. 644–645.

"Preparation and Properties of Influenza Virus Vaccines Concentrated and Purified by Differential Centrifugation," *Journal of Experimental Medicine* 81, 1945, pp. 193–218.

SOURCES:

Books

Berger, Melvin, *Famous Men of Modern Biology,* Crowell, 1968, pp. 165–176.
Dictionary of Scientific Biography, Scribner's, 1976, pp. 841–848.
Nobel Prize Winners, H. W. Wilson, 1987, pp. 1001–1003.

Periodicals

"The Nobel Prize in Chemistry, 1946," *Les prix Nobel en 1946,* Stockholm, 1948, pp. 29–32.
"Wendell Meredith Stanley," *Nature,* 233, 1971, pp. 149–150.
"The William H. Nichols Medalist for 1946," *Chemical and Engineering News,* 24, 1946, pp. 750–755.

—*Sketch by Mike McClure*

Johannes Stark
1874-1957
German physicist

Johannes Stark's life can be divided into two fairly distinct and contrasting halves. During the earlier period, he demonstrated unusual skills as an experimentalist and won acclaim as a brilliant physicist, holding posts at universities throughout Germany. Founder and editor of the prestigious *Jahrbuch der Radioaktivität und Elektronik* (*Yearbook of Radioactivity and Electronics*), he is credited with discovering the Doppler effect in canal rays, and the splitting of the spectral lines of hydrogen by means of an external electrical field, a phenomenon now known as the Stark effect. For these discoveries, Stark received the 1919 Nobel Prize in physics. After 1913, however, Stark began to withdraw from the scientific community and to ally himself with Adolf Hitler's program of National Socialism. Along with **Philipp von Lenard**, Stark called for a "purification" of German science, an adoption of a non-Jewish "Aryan science." He failed to receive the recognition he sought in the political arena and eventually found himself ostracized by fellow scientists in Germany and throughout the world.

Stark was born on April 15, 1874, in Schickenhof, Bavaria. Raised on a farm, he attended local schools in Bayreuth and Regensburg. In 1894, he entered the University of München as a science major, earning his doctorate in 1897 for a dissertation entitled "Investigations on Lampblack." He then accepted a post as assistant to Eugen Lommel at München, a position he held for the next three years. In the spring of 1900, Stark moved to the University of Göttingen as assistant to Eduard Riecke, and was appointed privatdozent in 1903.

Stark Discovers the Doppler Effect in Canal Rays

During his tenure at Göttingen, Stark made the first of his important discoveries, the Doppler effect in canal rays. The Doppler effect is the change in frequency that occurs in a wave as its source advances toward or retreats from an observer. Wavelengths shorten as they approach, producing a higher pitch or frequency, and lengthen as they recede, producing a lower pitch. The apparent change in pitch of a train whistle as it passes an observer is a familiar example of the Doppler effect. The Doppler effect had been predicted by Johann Christian Doppler in 1842, and, by 1900, had been observed by the American astronomer **Edwin Hubble** in the red shift of galaxies, though no terrestrial example had yet been described. Stark decided that an appropriate way to observe the Doppler effect in the laboratory was with canal rays, beams of positively-charged particles generated in a vacuum tube. In 1905, Stark used canal rays of hydrogen atoms to conduct the experiment and observed the predicted Doppler effect in hydrogen spectral lines—as they approached they reached higher frequencies, the violet end of the spectrum, and, like Hubble's galaxies, they shifted to the red, or lower, frequencies as they receded.

In 1906, Stark was appointed lecturer in applied physics and photography at the Technical College in Hannover. During his three-year tenure there, Stark was continuously on bad terms with his superior, Julius Brecht. Finally, in 1909, Stark accepted an appointment as professor at the Technical College at Aachen, where he remained for eight years.

Observes the Splitting of Spectral Lines

Since his days at Hannover, Stark had been thinking about a problem originally suggested by the work of the Dutch physicist **Pieter Zeeman**. In 1896, Zeeman had observed that the presence of a magnetic field can cause an element's spectral lines to split. This analogy to an electric field was too obvious for physicists to miss, and while a number of them had tried in the first decade of the twentieth century to produce this effect, none were successful. But in 1913, Stark succeeded in splitting spectral lines in an electric field. He placed a third electrode a few centimeters from the cathode in a vacuum tube and applied a potential difference of 20,000 volts between the two. When canal rays were generated in the tube, Stark was able to observe the splitting of the spectral lines of hydrogen gas, a phenomenon that is now known as the Stark effect. For his work on the Doppler and Stark effects, Stark was awarded the 1919 Nobel Prize in physics. In addition, he received the Baumgartner Prize of the Vienna Academy of Sciences in 1910, the Vahlbruch Prize of the Göttingen Academy of Sciences in 1914, and the Matteuci Gold Medal of the National Academy of Sciences of Italy.

Shifts from Scientific to Political Activities

After 1913, Stark slowly fell out of the mainstream of scientific research. Scholars have suggested a number of reasons for this change. A major factor seems to have been his inability to get along with other scientists and subsequent failure to receive an appropriate academic appointment. In 1917, he accepted a post as professor of physics at the University of Greifswald. He seems to have been happy in the conservative climate of this university, but decided to leave in 1920 to accept a similar post at the University of Würzburg. Stark was much less comfortable there, as his colleagues and superiors found a number of reasons to object to his presence, including his use of Nobel Prize money to finance the construction of a new ceramics factory. Although he devoted an increasing amount of time and attention to the factory, it eventually failed. Stark's colleagues found his attention to non-academic concerns ethically questionable. In addition, Stark's increasingly conservative political views were not well received in the liberal environment of Würzburg.

By 1922, Stark had become so uncomfortable at Würzburg that he resigned his post. He then became increasingly active politically in opposition to the post-World War I Weimar Republic, and in efforts to establish conservative, anti-governmental scientific organizations. One of these, the Fachgemeinschaft der deutschen Höchschulehrer der Physik (Professional Association of the German Higher Education Teachers of Physics, he established as an attempt to counterbalance the older, more liberal Deutsche Physikalische Gesellschaft (German Physical Society), based in Berlin.

When Stark decided to return to academic life, he found that he had made too many enemies and offended too many colleagues. He was rejected for posts at the universities of Berlin and Tübingen in 1924, Breslau and Marburg in 1926, Heidelberg in

1927, and Münich in 1928. By the early 1930s, Stark had become almost entirely an administrator of science, and then only in posts that his political influence had won for him. During the mid–1930s, he worked diligently to gain control over the direction of German science policymaking, but eventually lost out in that struggle to men who were even more closely allied to Adolf Hitler and the Nazi party.

By the beginning of World War II, Stark had become a self-made loner, having angered and annoyed both his former scientific colleagues and his former political allies. He sat out the war in his estate of Eppenstatt, in Bavaria, where he had constructed a laboratory. Stark had married Louise Uepter and had five children; beyond his professional interests Stark also enjoyed forestry and cultivating fruit trees. In 1947 he was sentenced to four years in a labor camp by a German de-Nazification court; he died in Eppenstatt on June 21, 1957.

SELECTED WRITINGS BY STARK:

Books

Die Elektrizität in Gasen (title means "Electricity in Gases"), J. A. Barth (Leipzig), 1902.
Die Prinzipien der Atomdynamik, three volumes, [Leipzig], 1910–1915. *Die gegenwärtige Krisis in der deutschen Physik* (title means "The Present Crisis in German Physics"), [Leipzig], 1922.
Die Axialität der struktur und Atombindung, [Berlin], 1928.
Adolf Hitler und die deutsche Forschung, [Berlin], 1935.
(With Wilhelm Müller) *Jüdische und deutsche Physik,* [Leipzig], 1941.

Periodicals

"Beobachtungen über der Effekt des Elektrischen Feldes auf Spektrallinien, I-VI," *Annalen der Physik,* 4th series, Volume 43, 1914, pp. 965–1047, and Volume 48, 1915, pp. 193–235.
"Der Doppler Effekt und bei den Kanalstrahlen und die Spektra der Positiven Atomionen," *Physikalische Zeitschrift,* Volume 6, 1905, pp. 892–897.

SOURCES:

Books

Beyerchen, Alan D., *Scientists under Hitler: Politics and the Physics Community in the Third*

Reich, Yale University Press, 1977, pp. 103–122.

—*Sketch by David E. Newton*

Ernest H. Starling
1866-1927
English physiologist

An experimentalist who discovered a number of significant fundamental facts about the cardiovascular system, Ernest H. Starling is known for his discovery, along with long-time collaborator **William Maddock Bayliss**, of secretin. In 1902, Starling and Bayliss found that the release of digestive juices by the pancreas is caused by a chemical they named "secretin." Starling later suggested the name "hormone" for any chemical, such as secretin, that is released in one part of the body and causes an effect in another part of the body. In the course of his career, Starling also conducted studies into the circulatory system, as well as into the secretion of lymph and other body fluids. For his work, he was awarded the Medal of the Royal Society, the Baly Medal from the Royal College of Physicians, and several honorary degrees from such institutions as Trinity College, Dublin, the University of Strasburg, and the University of Sheffield.

Ernest Henry Starling was born in London on April 17, 1866. His father was Matthew Henry Starling, a clerk for the British government who served in Bombay and returned to England only once every three years. Rearing of the Starling children was the responsibility, therefore, of Matthew's wife, the former Ellen Mathilda Watkins. In *Dictionary of Scientific Biography,* essayist Carleton B. Chapman described the family as one "of limited financial means and fundamentalist religious beliefs."

Starling began his schooling at the age of six when he was enrolled at the Islington School. He then attended King's College School from 1880 to 1882 and, in the latter year, enrolled at Guy's Hospital Medical College in London. He interrupted his schooling at Guy's briefly in the summer of 1885 when he traveled to Heidelberg to study with German physiologist Wilhelm Kühne, who was known for his research into nerves and muscles. Kühne apparently had a significant impact on Stanley's growing view of the role of basic physiology in the understanding and treatment of medical disorders.

Even before receiving his medical degree in 1889, Starling achieved distinction by being appointed demonstrator in physiology at Guy's. At the time, the hospital had simple and inadequate research facilities, a condition that changed after Starling was promoted to head of the physiology department a few years later. By the time he left Guy's in 1899, Starling had overseen the construction and equipping of a new physiology building that ultimately earned a reputation as one of the best research facilities for physiology in London.

Starling was married in 1891 to Florence Amelia Wooldridge Sieveking, daughter of an eminent London physician and widow of another physiologist, Leonard Charles Wooldridge. The Starlings had four children, three daughters and a son; Florence assisted immensely with her husband's work.

The deplorable working conditions at Guy's prompted Starling to look elsewhere for research facilities even as he was working to improve those conditions at Guy's. Thus, in 1890 he was given a part-time appointment in the physiology laboratories of Edward Albert Schäfer at University College. There he met and began working with fellow physiologist William Maddock Bayliss, an association that was to last throughout Starling's life and, incidentally, resulted in the marriage of Starling's sister to Bayliss.

Starling's first important work resulted from an 1892 visit to the Breslau laboratories of German physiologist Rudolf Heidenhain, an authority on the study of lymph. During his stay in Breslau, Starling repeated many of Heidenhain's experiments (and conducted some of his own) and came to radically different conclusions about their meaning. He was able to demonstrate that a combination of hydrostatic blood pressure and osmotic forces could account for all of the observations made by Heidenhain and himself about the way lymph is formed and transported in the body. In *The Dictionary of National Biography, 1922–1930,* contributor J. Barcroft asserted that Starling's findings "so completely superseded previous work in this field as to put Starling, in his early thirties, into the first rank of experimental physiologists."

Bayliss Collaboration Results in Discovery of Secretin

Probably the discovery for which Starling is most famous occurred shortly after his return to London and his election to the Jodrell chair of physiology at University College in 1899. He and Bayliss began a study of the secretion of digestive juices by the pancreas. They eventually found that the process takes place under the control of a substance secreted by the small intestine, a substance they named "secretin." Starling suggested that the name "hormone" be given to any chemical, such as secretin, that transmits a message from one part of the body to another part. Although hormones had actually been known before the discovery of secretin in 1902, it was Starling who first clearly defined the concept and elucidated the role that such substances have in the body.

The year Starling and Bayliss discovered secretin also marked the beginning of the former scientist's research on the heart. In order to carry out this research, Starling used a "heart-lung preparation" consisting of a heart that has been isolated in an anesthetized animal from all other organs except the lungs. Starling focused his research on various factors—such as temperature and blood pressure—that affect the beating of the heart. As a result of his studies, he discovered a number of facts about the heart, including one that has become known as Starling's Law of the heart: the energy of contraction is a function of the length of the muscle fibers in the heart.

Starling's heart research was interrupted by the outbreak of World War I. After his enlistment, he first served as a medical officer at Herbert Hospital, then became a researcher on defensive mechanisms against poison gas. His contributions to the war effort were apparently somewhat limited, however, because of his "outspoken impatience with the obuseness, where scientific matters were concerned, of his military superiors," as Chapman explained in *Dictionary of Scientific Biography.*

The intensity of Starling's research diminished after the war, but he continued to exert influence in the field of physiology. In 1922 he was appointed to the newly created post of Foulerton Research Professor at the Royal Society. He also became very much interested in the state of education in Great Britain, particularly with regard to the role of the natural sciences in a liberal education. His health began to deteriorate after the war, and he died on May 2, 1927, aboard a cruise ship outside Kingston, Jamaica, where he was buried.

SELECTED WRITINGS BY STARLING:

Books

Principles of Human Physiology, Lea & Febiger, 1912.

Periodicals

(With William Maddock Bayliss), "The Mechanism of Pancreatic Secretion," *Journal of Physiology,* September 12, 1902, pp. 325–353.
(With S. W. Patterson), "On the Mechanical Factors which Determine the Output of the Ventricles," *Journal of Physiology,* September 8, 1914, pp. 357–379.
"Science in Education," *Science Progress,* 1918–1919, Volume 13, pp. 466–475.

SOURCES:

Books

Gillispie, Charles Coulson, editor, *Dictionary of Scientific Biography,* Volume 12, Scribner's, 1975. pp. 617–619.
Williams, E. T., and Helen M. Palmer, *The Dictionary of National Biography, 1922–1930,* Oxford, 1971, pp. 807–809.

—*Sketch by David E. Newton*

Chauncey Starr
1912-
American physicist

Chauncey Starr is perhaps best known as the first president of the Electric Power Research Institute. But his many contributions to the field of nuclear power are at least as important as the final episode in his long career. An accomplished researcher on nuclear propulsion systems for space vehicles, Starr foresaw the potential of nuclear energy for space applications. He has earned numerous awards for his work on peaceful uses of atomic power, and received the 1990 National Medal of Technology from the President of the United States for contributions to engineering and the electric industry.

Starr was born on April 14, 1912 in Newark, New Jersey to Rubin, a building contractor, and Rose (Dropkin) Starr. He received an electrical engineering degree in 1932 and a Ph.D. in physics in 1935 from Rensselaer Polytechnic Institute in Troy, New York. He then became a research fellow in physics at Harvard University, working with Nobel prize winner **Percy Williams Bridgman** on the physics of metals at high pressures. From 1938 to 1941, Starr was a research associate in physical chemistry at the Massachusetts Institute of Technology. Starr married Doris Evelyn Diebel in 1938 and has two children, Ross M. and Ariel E.

Space Applications of Nuclear Power

As an engineer with the Manhattan Project in the early to mid–1940s, Starr conducted research on an electromagnetic process for uranium separation, and became technical director of the Oak Ridge, Tennessee, pilot plant where the process was developed and improved. In 1946, as vice president of North American Aviation Inc., (later known as Rockwell Interna-

Chauncey Starr

tional) and president of its Atomics International Division, he was launched into the space program by a study of the technical feasibility of using nuclear rockets for the Air Force.

The team of scientists and engineers that he formed for this study went on to make significant contributions in nuclear propulsion systems. In 1956, the Atomic Energy Commission incorporated Atomic International's design for a light weight zirconium-hydride reactor (which allowed for the controllable release of nuclear energy) into its Systems for Nuclear Auxiliary Power (SNAP) program. By 1965, the reactor system was functional and was tested in orbit from California's Vandenberg Air Force Base. It operated for forty-three days, signalling the beginning of the space age.

Call for Accountability in the Power Industry

Starr's twenty year industrial career was followed by a short stay in academe. From 1967 to 1973 he was Dean of the School of Engineering and Applied Science at the University of California at Los Angeles (UCLA). During his time at UCLA, Starr pioneered the concept of risk analysis as a basis for optimal risk management in emerging engineering developments. Risk analysis calls for quantifying societal risks as part of the development process and has been incorporated into risk assessment guidelines that are used by the nuclear power industry and by government agencies.

Passionate about the environmental implications of energy production and usage, Starr has published hundreds of papers on energy-related topics. It was one of these papers ("Energy and Power", published in the September 1971 issue of *Scientific American*) that caught the attention of Shearon Harris, who was then president of the Edison Electric Institute (EEI). The EEI was working with the Electric Research Council on the creation of a comprehensive industry-sponsored research and development program. According to *EPRI Journal,* impressed with Starr's call for "sensible choices of technological alternatives" in meeting ever expanding energy demands, Harris approached Starr with the prospect of heading up the newly formed Electric Power Research Institute (EPRI).

EPRI, as it is known today, has become one of the largest private research organizations in the world. Starr, as founding president, not only ruled over the creation of the organizational structure of EPRI, but also determined the research directions and priorities the power industry would set. Given a free hand, Starr ran EPRI for its first formative five years, giving the industry much more than it expected in the process. EPRI was originally envisioned as a technical research organization, but under Starr's leadership, it took on a conscience as well. He developed a program which included broad technical, environmental, social and economic considerations, and which drew on the expertise of scientists and non-scientists alike in making conclusions. Starr became vice chairman of EPRI in 1978 and retired in 1987. He is now president emeritus and a consultant to EPRI.

In addition to numerous professional memberships, Starr is a member and past vice president of the National Academy of Engineering, and a founder and past president of the American Nuclear Society. He is also a member and past director of the American Association for the Advancement of Science, a Foreign Member of the Royal Swedish Academy of Engineering Science, and Officer of the French Legion of Honor. He has received honorary doctorate degrees from Rensselaer Polytechnic Institute, the Swiss Federal Institute of Technology, and Tulane University. In addition to the 1990 National Medal of Technology, he received the 1974 Atomic Energy Commission Award for meritorious contributions to the national atomic energy program, the 1990 United States Energy Award for long-term contributions to energy and international understanding, and numerous others.

SELECTED WRITINGS BY STARR:

Books

(With R. W. Dickinson) *Sodium Graphite Reactors,* Addison-Wesley, 1958.

Economic Growth, Employment, and Energy, IPC Science and Technology Press, 1977.
The Growth of Limits, Pergamon, 1979.
Current Issues in Energy, Pergamon, 1979.

Periodicals

"Energy, and Power," *Scientific American,* September 1971, pp. 37–49.
(With Richard Rudman and Chris Whipple) "Philosophical Basis of Risk Analysis," *Annual Review of Energy,* Volume 1, Annual Reviews, 1976.
"The Growth of Limits," *Proceedings of the Edison Centennial Symposium on Science, Technology and the Human Prospect,* Pergamon, 1979.
(With Milton F. Searl and Sy Alpert) "Energy Sources: A Realistic Outlook," *Science,* May 15, 1992, pp. 98–105.

Other

"Risk Management Commentary," for Dr. A. Allan Bromley, Assistant to the President for Science and Technology, Washington, DC, 1990.

SOURCES:

Periodicals

"The Right Person at the Right Time," *EPRI Journal* (special twentieth anniversary issue), January/February, 1993, pp. 10–14.

—*Sketch by Olga K. Anderson*

Thomas Starzl
1926-

American surgeon

Thomas Starzl is a world-renowned transplant surgeon. He performed the first human liver transplant in 1963 and was a pioneer in kidney transplantation. He has continued his pioneering work by helping to develop better drugs to make human organ transplants safer and more successful. Starzl has also contributed to the fields of general and thoracic surgery and neurophysiology.

Thomas Earl Starzl was born on March 11, 1926, in Le Mars, Iowa, to Roman F. Starzl, the editor and publisher of the *Globe Post,* a local newspaper, and Anna Laura Fitzgerald Starzl. He was the second son and was followed by two younger sisters. He finished high school during World War II and enlisted in officers' training school at Westminster College in Fulton, Missouri, in 1944. After his discharge from military service, he entered the premedical program at Westminster College, graduating in 1947. After graduation he immediately returned home to care for his mother, who was suffering from breast cancer. She died less than two months later, on June 30.

In September 1947 he entered Northwestern University Medical School in Chicago. After completing three years of medical school, Starzl took a year off to do research with Dr. Horace W. Magoun, a professor of neuroanatomy. While in Magoun's laboratory, Starzl developed a recording technique to track deep brain responses to sensory stimuli. He and his advisor published the work, which continues to be cited, in 1951. His work in Magoun's laboratory earned him a Ph.D. degree in neurophysiology from Northwestern in 1952, the same year in which he received his M.D. Starzl also received an M.A. degree in anatomy from Northwestern.

Starzl enrolled in the prestigious surgical training program at Johns Hopkins University Hospital in Baltimore in 1952. During his time at Johns Hopkins he met and married Barbara J. Brothers of Hartville, Ohio. (The two had three children, Timothy, Rebecca and Thomas. The marriage ended in divorce in 1976, in part, Starzl admits, because of his nonstop work schedule.) Starzl stayed in the Johns Hopkins training program for four years, but left in anger when he learned he would not be offered the coveted position of chief resident. He went to Jackson Memorial Hospital in Miami for his fifth and final year as a resident. During this time he was attracted to the idea of liver transplantation. In an empty garage on the grounds of Jackson Memorial Hospital, Starzl set up a laboratory and began his research on the liver, doing experimental surgeries on dogs he obtained from the city pound. He developed a new technique for removing the liver, the first step in liver transplantation. He published his method, and it quickly became the worldwide standard.

Turns to Academic Medicine

In 1958 Starzl returned to Northwestern, where he had accepted a fellowship in thoracic surgery. He passed the thoracic surgery boards in 1959. More importantly, he received two awards to fund his experimental research. One was a five-year grant from the National Institutes of Health. The other was the prestigious Markle Scholarship, which persuaded him to remain in academic medicine. Starzl was a member of Northwestern's surgical faculty for four years. During that time, he further perfected techniques for liver transplantation.

Starzl accepted a position at the University of Colorado School of Medicine as an associate professor of surgery in 1962, believing it offered better opportunities to develop an active organ transplant program. In the late 1950s surgeons had begun to experiment with the first immune suppressive drugs to prevent the body from rejecting a transplanted organ. As a consequence, transplantations became possible for the first time. Despite his interest in liver transplantation, Starzl considered a human liver transplant to be too risky given current knowledge of immunosuppression. On March 27, 1962, Starzl performed his first kidney transplantoperation in Denver. Starzl was to achieve considerable success in kidney transplantation, but his real target was the liver, and he soon turned to that challenge.

First Attempted Liver Transplant

On March 1, 1963, five years before the surgeon **Christiaan Neethling Barnard** undertook the first human heart transplant, Starzl attempted the world's first liver transplant. His patient was a three-year-old boy named Bennie Solis born with an incomplete liver. The child did not survive the operation because of uncontrolled bleeding. Starzl was widely criticized because he failed in his attempt, but, undaunted, he tried again in May 1963. This time he gave his patient, a man with cancer of the liver, huge amounts of fibrinogen, a protein that forms blood clots. The operation appeared to be a success, but the patient died three weeks later from complications due to blood clotting.

During the next few years, Starzl worked to solve the problem of uncontrolled bleeding and tissue rejection. In 1964 he directed the first extensive trial of tissue matching ever attempted. In the early 1960s, the physician Paul Terasaki of the University of California at Los Angeles had developed a method for detection of tissue antigens, the agents responsible for organ rejection. This method began the field of human histocompatibility research, the search for compatible tissue types. These efforts made it possible to match organ donors and recipients. In addition, Starzl turned his attention to development of drugs that would block the immune system from rejecting a new organ.

In the late 1960s Starzl was ready to attempt liver transplantation once again. This time all the attempts were on infants and young children with severe liver disease, and a number of them were successful, although some of the patients who survived the operation died from unrelated illnesses not too long afterwards. By the late 1970s the survival rate for liver transplants had risen to 40 percent.

During the 1970s and early 1980s Starzl's career reputation skyrocketed. He was promoted to professor of surgery at the University of Colorado in 1964 and was made chairman of the department in 1972. During the late 1970s Starzl was wooed by the University of California at Los Angeles to move his transplantation program there. But he finally settled on the University of Pittsburgh and moved there in 1981. The same year he married Joy Conger, who had been a research technician working on a project with Starzl in Denver.

In the early 1980s the availability of cyclosporin, a new, superior drug to prevent organ rejection, was an encouraging sign to Starzl that the survivor rate for liver transplantation could be raised. However, bureaucratic roadblocks were in the way of using cyclosporin and other promising new drugs in organ transplant operations other than kidney transplantations because they were considered by the federal government to be experimental. Starzl took the problem to the then-acting U.S. Surgeon General C. Everett Koop. Koop suggested Starzl appear before a government committee at the National Institutes of Health that could approve the operation. Starzl assembled a group of children who had survived liver transplants performed in the 1970s and early 1980s. They served as witnesses to the value of the operation, and after much testimony the committee approved liver transplantation as a service to mankind.

What followed was a rush by surgeons to begin performing the operation. All came to learn from Starzl and the physicians he had trained, who were scattered across the country. At the same time it became clear that the country needed a national system of organ procurement and distribution. Starzl worked diligently to get a bill passed by Congress in 1984 that would set up such as system. Starzl designed the system at the University of Pittsburgh, which became the national standard.

Performs Baboon Liver Transplants

Starzl also enhanced his fame by directing a series of multiple-organ transplants in these years. In 1984 a young child received a heart and liver in a single operation, while a young woman received a heart, liver and kidney in 1986. Starzl's attempts to transplant baboon livers into human patients remained controversial into the late 1980s, however. He had experimented with such transplantations since the early 1960s, performing the first successful one in 1989. The patient was dying from hepatitis B, to which baboon livers do not appear to be susceptible. Although the operation was initially successful, a surgical error caused a fatal infection some three weeks later. Although some people objected to the use of animals for "spare parts," a major controversy arose over the fact that the patient had been HIV positive. Virtually all medical centers take the position that organ transplants, which require a suppression of the immune system, are inappropriate for patients who have been infected with the virus that also attacks the immune system.

In 1990 Starzl underwent coronary bypass surgery himself, and shortly afterwards retired from active surgery. He now concentrates his efforts on research. He claims that the decision was motivated in part by his emotional involvement with patients, which made the surgeries particularly difficult and stressful for him.

Over the years, Starzl has won many awards and honors and has been awarded many honorary degrees, including a merit Award from Northwestern University in 1969, a Distinguished Achievement Award in Modern Medicine in 1969, Colorado Man of Year Award in 1967, David Hume Memorial Award from the National Kidney Foundation in 1978, and Pittsburgh Man of the Year Award in 1981. Starzl has written hundreds and hundreds of scientific papers, averaging fifty papers a year during the 1980s.

SELECTED WRITINGS BY STARZL:

Books

(With Charles W. Putman), *Experience in Hepatic Transplantation,* W. B. Saunders, 1969.
The Puzzle People: Memoirs of a Transplant Surgeon, University of Pittsburgh Press, 1992.

SOURCES:

Periodicals

Altman, Lawrence, K., "A Transplant Surgeon Who Fears Surgery," *New York Times,* July 7, 1992, pp. C1, C9-C10.
Clark, Matt, and Dan Shapiro, "The Master Transplanter," *Newsweek,* January 11, 1982, p. 36.
Gorner, Peter, "Cutting Edge," *Chicago Tribune,* September, 27, 1992, pp. 5-1, 5-6.
Salvatierra, O., "Renal Transplantation—The Starzl Influence," *Renal Transplantation,* February, 1988 (supplement 1), pp. 343-349.
Werth, Barry, "The Drug that Works in Pittsburgh," *New York Times Magazine,* September 30, 1990, pp. 35, 58-59.

—*Sketch by Karyn Hede George*

Hermann Staudinger
1881-1965
German organic and polymer chemist

Hermann Staudinger's interest in organic chemistry was wide-ranging and he made many important contributions in that field. He is principally known, however, for his concept of the "macromolecule," or polymer, a long chain of repeating chemical units. Although initially this idea was greeted with incredulity and scorn in the chemistry community, Staudinger eventually overcame his critics' objections with patient explanation, careful research, and dogged insistence. Polymers are now known to be extraordinarily useful substances, ubiquitous in natural systems as well as human society. The entire plastics and materials science industry bases itself on polymers, and the science of molecular biology was immeasurably aided by the concept of macromolecules. Staudinger was awarded a Nobel Prize in 1953, three years after he had retired from active research.

Staudinger was born March 23, 1881, in Worms, Germany, to Dr. Franz and Auguste (Wenck) Staudinger. His father was a philosopher and professor at various German institutions of secondary education, and was interested in social reform. Staudinger graduated from the Gymnasium at Worms in 1899 (a German *gymnasium* is roughly the equivalent of an American prep school) and began his university studies at Halle under the guidance of the botanist Professor Klebs. While there, Staudinger began a lifelong detour from his original interest in botany. His family encouraged him to study chemistry to provide a strong background for his biological investigations, and he not only took their advice, but actually stayed in chemistry for most of the rest of his career. He studied in Darmstadt under the direction of professors Kolb and Stadel, and in Munich under the direction of Professor Piloty. In 1901 he returned to the University of Halle and in 1903 finished his doctoral work under the direction of Professor Vorlander. Although Staudinger had begun his studies in the analytical subdivision of chemistry, Vorlander's influence and ideas caused him to develop an intense interest in theoretical organic chemistry. His doctoral thesis was on the malonic esters of unsaturated compounds.

Mainstream Organic Chemistry Research

Initially, Staudinger's organic chemical investigations were relatively routine, although they resulted in the synthesis of some interesting new classes of organic molecules. In 1905, while in his first teaching position (as instructor) with Professor Thiele in

Hermann Staudinger

Strassburg, he discovered the first ketene (colorless, poisonous gasses). Ketenes as a class are extremely reactive—they even react with traces of water and the oxygen in the air—and Staudinger and other researchers investigated their properties and chemistry for several years. In 1907, he prepared a special dissertation on the ketenes and was awarded the title of assistant professor. Shortly thereafter, he accepted an associate professor position at the Technische Hoshschule in Karlsruhe. Staudinger began many basic organic synthesis projects in Karlsruhe, including a new synthesis of isoprene (a constituent part of rubber), although some of the newer projects slowed when he moved to the Swiss Federal Institute of Technology (Eidgenossische Technische Hochschule) in Zurich in 1912. The Zurich position was a prestigious one, but the teaching load was many hours per week, so he curtailed his research in some areas. He proved to be a dedicated teacher and instilled in his students an appreciation not only for chemistry, but also for the power of technology in society.

During his fourteen years in Switzerland, Staudinger continued investigations on the chemistry of the ketenes, oxalyl chloride, and several materials that are shock-sensitive, that is, they explode when bumped or dropped. He also continued work on pyrethrin insecticides, and when they could not be easily synthesized, drew on his botanical interests and suggested that new strains of chrysanthemum (from which natural pyrethrines are extracted) might yield better quantities than any laboratory. During World

War I, much of Staudinger's work was driven by wartime shortages. He investigated the aromas of pepper and coffee to see if synthetic substitutes could be produced for those foods, and attempted to synthesize some important pharmaceuticals. He was successful enough to patent some of the artificial flavors and fragrances, although generally they proved uneconomical if the natural material was available. In 1926, Staudinger accepted a position as director of the chemical laboratories at Freiburg University, where he remained until his retirement in 1951. He continued to be internationally respected in his field, winning the LeBlanc medal given by the French Chemical Society in 1931 and the Cannizzarro Prize in Rome in 1933.

The Beginnings of the Macromolecule Theory

In 1924, Staudinger wrote in *Berichte der Deutschen Chemischen Gesellschaft,* "The molecules of rubber . . . have entirely different sizes . . . and these can be changed, by temperature for example. . . . It is very important here to use the idea of the molecule . . . ; [the] particles are held together by normal chemical bonds and in the structural sense we are dealing with very long carbon chains. The polymerization of isoprene to these long chains . . . goes on until a sufficiently large, little reactive, and thus strongly saturated molecule . . . has been formed. For those . . . particles in which the molecule is identical with the primary particle and in which the individual atoms of the . . . molecule are linked by normal valences, we propose to differentiate the type by the term *macromolecules.*"

The move to Freiberg University signaled Staudinger's break with traditional organic chemistry. He had first proposed the idea of macromolecules in 1920 while still in Zurich, but at Freiberg he gave up most of his other chemical research to pursue the study of rubber and synthetic polymers. It was a decision which caused his colleagues some consternation because he was well respected in his field, and they felt he would do damage to his reputation by working on such unpromising materials from such an unorthodox point of view.

When Staudinger began work on his theory of very high molecular weight compounds, several entrenched ideas about molecular weight existed. Chemists believed, for example, that the size of a molecule was governed by its "unit cell," or smallest nonrepeating piece, and that its molecular weight was a fixed number. For low molecular weight compounds, those principles remained true. Many chemical methods had been devised for determining the structure of molecules, and nonrepeating structures with unit cells of up to 5000 atomic mass units had been elucidated. The relatively new science of X-ray crystallography also helped in structure determination. Additionally, researchers knew of compounds, soaps for example, which aggregated (clumped together) in water and other solvents, instead of dissolving in the normal way. These aggregates possessed some of the same unusual physical characteristics as rubber and other known polymers. Many chemists therefore insisted that Staudinger had mistaken aggregates of smaller molecules for single large molecules.

With carefully designed experiments, Staudinger gradually accumulated evidence that a group of extremely large molecules indeed existed. They did not comprise oddly associated clumps of smaller molecules, and were not themselves single unit cells. Instead, these molecules resembled chains of repeating units, strung together and bonded to each other—like pearls on a wire. Additionally, because any number of units might be bonded together during synthesis, these large molecules had differing molecular weights, depending on the length of the chain.

While working in this area, Staudinger developed some new analytical methods and discovered a relationship between the viscosity of a polymer solution and its molecular weight. He had developed the method in desperation when he could not get funding for more sophisticated equipment, but it was soon widely used in industry because it was inexpensive, fast, and accurate. The equation, now called Staudinger's Law, allows a fairly simple estimation of molecular weight by measuring the "drag" or "stickiness" of a liquid flowing through a small tube (viscosity).

During World War II, the Freiburg University chemistry facilities were virtually destroyed in an Allied air bombardment in November 1944, and it was several years before they were fully operational again. Staudinger's work slowed after the enormous stresses of the war, although he still found the energy to start and edit two new journals, one on macromolecular chemistry. He gave many talks and wrote prolifically on the subject of macromolecules until the end of his career.

Achievements Finally Recognized with Nobel Prize in 1953

In spite of the evidence, however, chemists had difficulty in accepting his conclusions. Spirited discussions bordering on uproar often greeted him when he gave scientific lectures; his persistence and patience in the face of such hostility became legendary. Historians have noted such resistance before on the part of the scientific community whenever a truly revolutionary idea is advanced. Some have speculated that chemists simply found the idea of huge molecules too messy; they preferred the neat, tidy unit cell with its fixed structure and weight, for which they had developed many good analytical procedures.

As time went on, however, evidence from other areas of scientific study built unequivocal support for macromolecules. X-ray crystallographers had refined their techniques to the point where they could obtain structural information on polymeric materials. Various microscope and optical techniques also lent important evidence, particularly for biological molecules. Staudinger had speculated for years that living systems must require macromolecules to function, and the new science of molecular biology began to lend vigorous support to that idea.

So controversial were Staudinger's macromolecular theories, that it was not until 1953, when he was seventy-two years of age, that he was finally rewarded with the Nobel Prize for his efforts. The presenter of the prize, Professor Fredga, noted in his speech, "In the world of high polymers, almost everything was new and untested. Long standing, established concepts had to be revised or new ones created. The development of macromolecular science does not present a picture of peaceful idylls."

After his retirement, Staudinger once again took up his original interest in botany, although his biological bent had always been apparent even in his chemical work. His wife, the former Magda Woit, was a Latvian plant physiologist who often participated in his research, collaborated in writing many of his papers, and made some important connections of her own between his macromolecular theories and the molecules of biology. Staudinger listed some of her considerable contributions in his Nobel Prize address, and dedicated his autobiography to her. They married in 1927, and she survived him upon his death on September 8, 1965.

SELECTED WRITINGS BY STAUDINGER:

Books

From Organic Chemistry to Macromolecules, translated by J. Fock and M. Fried, Interscience, 1970.

Periodicals

"On Polymerization" portions translated and reprinted in *Source Book in Chemistry, 1900–1950,* Leicester, Henry M., editor, Harvard University Press, 1968, p. 260, from original in *Berichte der Deutschen Chemischen Gesellschaft,* Volume 53, 1920, pp. 1073–1085.

"On the Constitution of Rubber (Sixth Paper)" portions translated and reprinted in *Source Book in Chemistry, 1900–1950,* Leicester, Henry M., editor, Harvard University Press, 1968, p. 264, from original in *Berichte der Deutschen Chemischen Gesellschaft,* Volume 57, 1924, pp. 1203–1208.

SOURCES:

Periodicals

Flory, P. J., "Macromolecules Vis-a-Vis the Traditions of Chemistry," *Journal of Chemical Education,* Volume 50, 1973, p. 732.

Mark, H., "The Early Days of Polymer Science," *Journal of Chemical Education,* Volume 50, 1973, p. 757. Russell, C. A., editor, *Recent Developments in the History of Chemistry,* 1985, p. 128.

Olby, R., "The Macromolecular Concept and the Origins of Molecular Biology," *Journal of Chemical Education,* Volume 47, 1970, p. 168.

—*Sketch by Gail B. C. Marsella*

Milan Ratislav Stefanik
1880-1919
Hungarian-born French Czechoslovakian astronomer

Milan Ratislav Stefanik's importance to the scientific community consisted primarily in his efforts to establish astronomical observat ories and meteorological research stations in many parts of the world. However, his scientific career came to an end when he enlisted in the French army at the outbreak of World War I. He died in a plane crash shortly after accepting the position of minister of war of the newly created state of Czechoslovakia.

Son of a Protestant pastor in Hungarian Slovakia, Stefanik studied mathematics and physics in Prague, at Charles University and at the Institute of Technology. He also studied in Zurich. Upon receiving a doctorate from the Charles University in 1904, he traveled to Paris for postdoctoral work where he became an assistant at the Meudon astrophysical observatory, then under the direction of the observatory's founder, the aged patriarch of astrophysics, Pierre Jules Cesar Janssen. An invalid, Janssen had given effective control of the observatory to his wife and daughter, whom Stefanik charmed. Under Janssen's patronage, Stefanik traveled widely to make astrophysical measurements. He visited the new international observatory atop Mt. Blanc and went to Central Asia to witness an eclipse.

Further Astronomical Travels

Janssen died in 1907, and directorship of Meudon went to Henri Alexandre Deslandres. Following this change, Stefanik's association with the observatory ceased, but he now began a career as an astronomical traveler, supported by short-term grants from French authorities. He investigated setting up an observatory in the Sahara Desert in Africa, and then he landed a mission to establish an observatory on the island of Tahiti. In 1910 he brought several large telescopes to Tahiti and installed them in an observatory building with an 8-meter cupola overlooking the administrative center in Papeete, the largest island in French Polynesia. He also set up a meteorological network for French Oceania and then returned to Paris in anticipation of being named director of a permanently funded Tahitian observatory. While awaiting his appointment, he journeyed to Brazil in order to observe the eclipse of 1912 at Passa Quatro.

In 1913 French political interests finally decided to fund the Tahiti observatory. This was accomplished through a complex web of international politics. The observatory would be fitted with a radio mast capable of communicating with France through a relay station. This relay station was to be erected on the Galapagos Islands which are an island province of Ecuador, situated in the Pacific Ocean. The Ecuadoran government was asked to erect the Galapagos relay in exchange for help in renovating the Quito astronomical observatory. The real reason for the Galapagos station, however, was to have it serve as a French-controlled coaling station for ships using the new Panama Canal. Stefanik, who had become a French citizen in 1912, spent a number of months in Ecuador making arrangements to set up the radio relay-station until the outbreak of World War I scuttled French plans for the Galapagos. Upon returning to France, Stefanik traveled to Morocco as a scientific adviser to the French army which had recently conquered that kingdom.

At the beginning of the First World War, Stefanik joined the French air corps. He was most effective, not as a meteorologist (his first posting), but as an organizer of the Czech and Slovak legions that France supported. He was wounded in Serbia and rose up the ranks to become brigadier general in 1918. As a French general, he traveled to Siberia to deal with the repatriation of the Czech-Slovak legion that had been marooned there following the Russian revolution. A spokesman for the independence of his people, Stefanik became the first minister of war of the new state of Czechoslovakia. He died in 1919 when the plane that was returning him to Czechoslovakia crashed at the Bratislava airport.

SELECTED WRITINGS BY STEFANIK:

Books

Zapisnik Dr. M. R. Stefanika z Ecuadoru z r. 1913, Banska Bystrica, Czechoslovakia, 1933.

Zapisniky M. R. Stefanika, edited by Josef Bartu-
sek and Jaroslav Bohac, [Prague], 1935.
*Stefanik, knihadruha: Vzpominky, dokumenty a
jine prtsprvky,* edited by Josef Bartušek,
[Prague], 1938.

SOURCES:

Books

Ihnat, Joseph, and others, editors, *General Milan
R. Stefanik, 1880–1980: Historical Profile,*
[New York], 1981.
Pyenson, Lewis, *Civilizing Mission: Exact Sciences
and French Overseas Expansion, 1830–1940,*
Johns Hopkins University Press, 1993, pp.
318–29.

—Sketch by Lewis Pyenson

William Howard Stein
1911-1980
American biochemist

William Howard Stein, in partnership with
Stanford Moore, was a pioneer in the field of
protein chemistry. Although other scientists had
previously established that proteins could play such
roles as that of enzymes, antibodies, hormones, and
oxygen carriers, almost nothing was known of their
chemical makeup. Stein and Moore, during some
forty years of collaboration, were not only able to
provide information about the inner workings of
protein molecules, but also invented the mechanical
means by which that information could be extracted.
Their discovery of how protein amino acids function
was accomplished through a study of ribonuclease
(RNase), a pancreatic enzyme that assists in the
digestion of food by catalyzing the breakdown of
nucleic acids. But their work could not have been
accomplished without the development of a technology to assist them in collecting and separating the
amino acids contained in ribonuclease. Their invention of the fraction collector and an automated system
for analyzing amino acids was of great importance in
furthering protein research, and these devices have
become standard laboratory equipment.

Stein and Moore began their collective work in
the late 1930s under Max Bergmann at the Rockefeller Institute (now Rockefeller University). After Berg-

mann's death in 1944, the pair developed the protein
chemistry program at the Institute and began their
research into enzyme analysis. Except for a brief
period during World War II when Moore served with
the Office of Scientific Research and Development in
Washington D.C., and the two years when Stein
taught at the University of Chicago and Harvard
University, the partnership continued uninterrupted
until Stein's death in 1980. Their joint inventions and
co-authorship of most of their scientific papers were
said to make it impossible to separate their individual
accomplishments. Their combined efforts were acknowledged in 1972 with the Nobel Prize in chemistry. According to Moore, writing about Stein in the
Journal of Biological Chemistry in 1980, they received
the award "for contributions to the knowledge of the
chemical structure and catalytic function of bovine
pancreatic ribonuclease." **Christian Anfinsen** shared
the Nobel Prize with Stein and Moore for related
research.

The son of community-minded parents, Stein
was born in New York City on June 25, 1911. He was
the second of three children. His father, Fred M.
Stein, was involved in business and retired at an early
age to lend his services to various health care
associations in the community. The scientist's mother, Beatrice Borg Stein, worked to improve recreation-
al and educational conditions for underprivileged
children. From an early age, Stein was encouraged by
his parents to develop an interest in science. He
received a progressive education from grade school
on, attending the Lincoln School of the Teacher's
College of Columbia University, transferring at sixteen years of age to Phillips Exeter Academy for his
college preparatory studies. He graduated from Harvard University in 1933, then took a year of graduate
study in organic chemistry there. Finding that his real
interest was biochemistry, he completed his graduate
studies at the College of Physicians and Surgeons of
Columbia University, receiving his Ph.D. in 1938.
His dissertation concerned the amino acid composition of elastin, a protein found in the walls of veins
and arteries. This work marks the beginning of his
long search to understand the chemical function of
proteins.

Improved Methodology Solves Amino Acid Puzzle

The successful research being done at the Rockefeller Institute under the direction of Max Bergmann
caught Stein's attention. He pursued post-graduate
studies there in 1938, spending his time improving
analytical techniques for purifying amino acids.
Moore joined Bergmann's group in 1939. There, he
and Stein began work in developing the methodology
for analyzing the amino acids glycine and leucine.
Their work was interrupted when the United States
entered World War II. Then, Bergmann's laboratory
was given over to the study of the physiological effects

of mustard gases, in the hope of finding a counteractant.

The group's efforts to find accurate tools and methods for the study of amino acid structure increased in importance when they assumed the responsibility of establishing the Institute's first program in protein chemistry. Looking for ways to improve the separation process of amino acids, they turned to partition chromatography, a filtering technique developed during the war by the English biochemists **A. J. P. Martin** and **Richard Synge**. Building on this technology, as well as that of English biochemist **Frederick Sanger**'s column chromatography and the ion-exchange technique of Werner Hirs, Stein and Moore went on to invent the automatic fraction collector and develop the automated system by which amino acids could be quickly analyzed. This automated system replaced the tedious two-week sequence that was previously required to differentiate and separate each amino acid.

From then on, the isolation and study of amino acid structure was advanced through these new analytical tools. Ribonuclease was the first enzyme for which the biochemical function was determined. The discovery that the amino acid sequence was a three-dimensional, chain-like structure that folds and bends to cause a catalytic reaction was a beginning for understanding the complex nature of enzyme catalysis. Stein and Moore were certain that this understanding would result in crucial medical advances. By 1972, the year Stein and Moore shared the Nobel Prize, other enzymes had been analyzed using their methods.

Editorial Work Complements Research

Because he was extremely eager to see that research done in laboratories all over the country be disseminated as widely and as quickly as possible, Stein devoted many years in various editorial positions to the *Journal of Biological Chemistry*. Under his leadership, the journal became a leading biochemistry publication. He had joined the editorial board in 1962 and became editor in 1968. He only held the latter post for one year, however. While attending an international meeting in Denmark, he contracted Guillain-Barré Syndrome, a rare disease often causing temporary paralysis. In grave danger of dying, he managed to recover somewhat. The illness left him a quadriplegic, confined to a wheelchair for the rest of his life. Although he remained involved with the work of his colleagues both in the laboratory and at the *Journal*, he was unable to participate actively.

In addition to the Nobel Prize, Stein shared with Moore the 1964 Award in Chromatography and Electrophoresis and the 1972 Theodore Richard Williams Medal of the American Chemical Society. He served as chairperson of the U.S. National Committee

for Biochemistry from 1968 to 1969, as trustee of Montefiore Hospital, and as board member of the Hebrew University medical school. He married Phoebe L. Hockstader on June 22, 1936. They had three sons: William Howard, Jr., David, and Robert. Stein died in Manhattan on February 2, 1980.

SELECTED WRITINGS BY STEIN (JOINT PUBLICATIONS WITH STANFORD MOORE):

Periodicals

"A Chromatographic Investigation of Pancreatic Ribonuclease," *Journal of Biological Chemistry*, Volume 200, 1953.
"The Amino Acid Composition of Ribonuclease," *Journal of Biological Chemistry*, Volume 211, 1954.
"The Structure of Proteins," *Scientific American*, Volume 204, 1961.
"Chemical Structures of Pancreatic Ribonuclease and Deoxyribonuclease," *Science*, Volume 180, 1973.

SOURCES:

Books

Fruton, Joseph S., *Molecules and Life: Historical Essays on the Interplay of Chemistry, and Biology*, Wiley, 1972.

Periodicals

Moore, Stanford, "William H. Stein," *Journal of Biological Chemistry*, Volume 255, 1980, pp. 9517–9518.
Moore, Stanford, and William H. Stein, "Chemical Structures of Pancreatic Ribonuclease and Deoxyribonuclease," *Science*, Volume 180, 1973, pp. 458–464.
New York Times, October 21, 1972.
New York Times, February 3, 1980.
Richards, Frederic M., "The 1972 Nobel Prize for Chemistry," *Science*, Volume 178, 1972, pp. 492–493.

—Sketch by Jane Stewart Cook

Jack Steinberger
1921-
German-born American physicist

Jack Steinberger is an experimentalist in high-energy physics who discovered a new type of neutrino with the physicists **Leon Max Lederman** and **Melvin Schwartz**. In a groundbreaking experiment, the three scientists were able to create the first laboratory-made beam of neutrinos. Their discovery led to the development of the so-called "standard theory" of matter. In recognition of these contributions, Steinberger and his co-investigators were awarded the 1988 Nobel Prize in physics.

Steinberger was born on May 25, 1921, in Bad Kissingen, Germany. His father was Ludwig Lazarus Steinberger, a cantor and leader of the local Jewish community, and his mother was Berta May Steinberger. Jack Steinberger and his brother left Germany in 1934 and immigrated to Chicago, Illinois. There, they lived with the family of Barnard Faroll, a grain broker. Later, Faroll was instrumental in bringing the rest of Steinberger's family to the United States.

Steinberger studied chemical engineering at the Illinois Institute of Technology, but left to enlist in the U.S. army following the attack on Pearl Harbor. The army sent him to the Radiation Laboratory at the Massachusetts Institute of Technology, where he made radar bomb sights and studied physics. After the war, he enrolled at the University of Chicago, earning a bachelor of science degree in 1942, and a doctorate in physics in 1948. During his doctoral studies at Chicago, Steinberger had studied muons (semi-stable electrical particles) and showed that, when they decay, they yield two neutrons (nuclear particles with the mass of protons but not the charge) and an electron (a negatively charged atomic particle). He proposed at the time that muons could be broken down into muon-neutrinos and electron-neutrinos. (The neutrino is an elusive electrically uncharged basic particle of matter that lacks mass). The neutrino was important because Steinberger and other nuclear physicists believed neutrinos could be harnessed to study the weak nuclear force, which is responsible for certain types of radioactivity. The weak force, like electromagnetism, is one of the fundamental interactions between elementary particles.

Creates Neutrino Beam

Steinberger's professional career began at the University of California at Berkeley, with his appointment as professor of physics in 1949. He remained there for a year, and then moved on to Columbia University, also as a professor of physics. It was during a coffee break at the Pupin Physics Building of Columbia University that Melvin Schwartz, then Steinberger's graduate student, broached the idea to Leon Max Lederman and Steinberger of making beams of high-energy neutrinos for use in research. They decided to use the Brookhaven accelerator in Upton, Long Island, New York, to make the beam. They set up the accelerator to produce masses of protons at 15 billion electron volts and shoot them at a beryllium metal target. The protons (elementary positively charged particles) smashed the beryllium atomic nuclei into their component protons and neutrons. The impact also created pions, elusive short-lived particles that decay into muons and neutrinos. Seeking to filter out the neutrinos, the researchers constructed a forty-foot barrier of steel built from the scrap of the Battleship Missouri. The massive obstacle filtered out all the particles but the neutrinos, creating the first laboratory made beam of high-intensity neutrinos.

Until then, scientists had only been aware of the existence of neutrinos produced by the type of radioactive decay that also creates an electron. But the neutrinos that came out of the steel filter were accompanied by muons. These were muon-neutrinos. This finding led to the development of the "standard model theory," which posits the existence of three generations of matter: a first generation consisting of seven electrons, electron neutrinos and the up and the down quarks (hypothetical particles from which fundamental particles are built); a second generation of matter—that revealed by the experiments carried out by Steinberger and his colleagues—consisting of muons, muon-neutrinos and varieties of quarks called charmed and strange quarks; and a third generation, which physicists are exploring now and which includes tau particles (particles produced when electrons and anti-electrons are smashed together), tau neutrinos and the top and the bottom quarks. The discovery of the muon-neutrino was a pioneering step in a road that enabled high-energy physicists to use neutrinos in scientific investigations. In astronomy, for instance, neutrino telescopes detect explosions of neutrinos associated with far-off supernovas (stars that blow up with great brilliance).

Steinberger left Columbia University in 1968, moving on to become director, administrator and researcher of the European Center for Nuclear Research in Geneva. He retired from his administrative duties in 1986, but remained as a staff physicist. He has continued to work on experiments in elementary particles and conducts research using the Large Electron-Positron Collider. In 1988 Steinberger received extensive public recognition for his discovery of the muon-neutrino and for a lifetime of contributions to physics. He was awarded not only the Nobel Prize in that year, but also received the National Medal of Science from the United States. Steinberger married Joan Beauregard in 1943. The marriage ended in divorce. In 1961 he married Cynthia Eve Alff. Steinberger is the father of three sons, Joseph, Richard and John, and a daughter, Julia Karen. Steinberger has become a United States citizen.

SELECTED WRITINGS BY STEINBERGER:

Periodicals

"Observation of High-Energy Neutrino Reactions and the Existence of Two Kinds of Neutrinos," *Physical Reviews Letters,* Volume 9, 1962, p. 36.
"Resonances in Strange-Particle Production," *Physical Reviews,* Volume 128, 1962, p. 1930.
"Lifetime of the w-Meson," *Physical Reviews Letters,* Volume 11, 1963, p. 436.

SOURCES:

Books

Nobel Prize Winners: Physics, Salem Press, 1989, Volume 3, pp. 1353–64.

Periodicals

New York Times, October 20, 1988, pp. B11–12.

— *Sketch by Margo Nash*

David B. Steinman
1886-1960
American engineer

David B. Steinman designed more than four hundred bridges worldwide, including the longest cantilever bridge in the United States, the largest bridge in South America, and the bridge with the longest fixed arch in the world. Among his technical achievements were improvements in the design of suspension bridges, a new loading system for railway bridges, and simplified techniques for design analysis; he was the first to construct a bridge specifically to withstand earthquakes. He believed that bridges should be visually appealing as well as functional, and eight of his creations were recognized as being among America's most beautiful bridges.

David Barnard Steinman, who was born in New York City on June 11, 1886, and his six brothers were the sons of Eva Scollard Steinman and Louis Kelvin Steinman, an immigrant factory worker. The family lived a sparse existence in a three-room tenement on the lower East Side in view of the Brooklyn Bridge, a landmark that became a childhood inspiration to Steinman.

A talented student, Steinman enrolled at the City College of New York at age thirteen. At that time, the Williamsburg Bridge over the East River was under construction, and Steinman was awarded a pass permitting him to inspect the structure and observe the engineers at work. He received his bachelor of science degree in 1906, then applied to Columbia University, where he was granted two scholarships; in three years, he earned a master's degree and a civil engineering degree. In 1910 he accepted a post at the University of Idaho, where he taught for four years; in the meantime he completed his doctoral work at Columbia, receiving an engineering Ph.D. in 1911. His dissertation, "The Design of the Henry Hudson Memorial Bridge as a Steel Arch," became a standard text. Twenty-five years later, he would be chosen to build that bridge, which contained the world's longest fixed arch, much as he had designed it as a student.

Steinman's dissertation caught the attention of Gustav Lindenthal, the designer in charge of the $20-million Hell Gate Arch project. At Lindenthal's invitation, Steinman returned to New York in 1914 to work on that railway bridge over the East River. The extremely strong tides at the site offered unprecedented challenges, but the project was completed in 1917. Steinman then taught civil and mechanical engineering at the City College of New York until 1920, when he became an independent consultant and design engineer.

A short time later, Manhattan Bridge builder Holton D. Robinson convinced Steinman to join him in a competition to design the Florianópolis Bridge in Brazil. The pair not only won the contest but were awarded the contract to build the bridge. The duo's creation, which was the largest bridge in South America and had the longest eyebar suspension span in the world, used a revolutionary concept that achieved four times the standard rigidity while using one-third less steel. Completed in 1926, the $1.4 million structure was remarkably inexpensive, and it was constructed without a single accident.

The partnership continued until Robinson's death in 1945. During that time, Steinman designed bridges in many countries, including Thailand, England, Italy, Korea, and Iraq. His 1927 design of the Carquinez Strait Bridge, over the entrance of the Sacramento and San Joaquin Rivers into San Francisco Bay, was at the time the longest cantilever bridge in the United States. It was also the first bridge to be constructed specifically to withstand earthquakes. Decades later, a similar structure was built as a twin span next to the original bridge. A transporter bridge (a single-cable suspension span carrying people in baskets) designed by Steinman for the 1933 Chicago World's Fair remained the world's longest until 1960. Steinman's Triborough Bridge, which linked New York City's Manhattan, Queens, and the Bronx with three and one-half miles of linked suspension, truss, and vertical lift spans, was completed in 1936. Two years later, President Franklin D. Roosevelt and Canadian Prime Minister Mackenzie King dedicated Steinman and Robinson's impressive Thousand Islands International Bridge, whose eight and one-half mile length included five inter-island spans.

In 1948, Steinman was asked to repair and modernize the Brooklyn Bridge. Three years earlier, he had published a biography, *The Builders of the Bridge,* about John A. and Washington A. Roebling, the father-and-son team who had built the bridge that had been his childhood inspiration. Under Steinman's careful hand, the sixty-five-year-old structure was transformed from a two-lane roadway into a modern six-lane highway, without altering its appearance.

Connects Michigan's Peninsulas

The Mackinac Straits Bridge in Michigan is regarded as Steinman's crowning achievement. Connecting Michigan's main body with its upper peninsula across four miles of water between Lakes Michigan and Huron, the bridge was completed in 1957. According to an article in the October, 1956, issue of *Reader's Digest,* it was the longest suspension bridge in the world, from one anchorage to the other; its 3,800-foot main span was exceeded only by that of the Golden Gate Bridge. Among its technical challenges were the terrific winds common to the strait and the massive annual ice accumulations that would threaten its piers and foundations. Using his design expertise, along with new metallurgical developments and innovative construction techniques, Steinman built an impressive structure fully up to nature's challenges.

Among Steinman's 750 publications are standard engineering textbooks, poetry (much of it relating to bridges), a book about bridges for young readers, and more than six hundred technical papers. In 1934, he helped found the National Society of Professional Engineers and served as its first president. He received eighteen honorary degrees and over 150 honorary awards, including the French Legion d'Honneur. He was particularly pleased in 1947 when Columbia University presented him with its Medal for Excellence.

Professionally, Steinman had a reputation as an individualist; privately, he enjoyed playing chess and working on mechanical inventions—at one point he developed new techniques in stereo photography. He

had married Irene Hoffman in 1915; their two sons, John Francis and David, became doctors, and their daughter, Alberta, earned a doctorate in psychology. Steinman died on August 21, 1960, at his home in New York following a three-month illness. At the time of his death, he was working on several projects, including a feasibility study for adding rapid transit to the Golden Gate Bridge.

SELECTED WRITINGS BY STEINMAN:

Books

The Builders of the Bridge: The Story of John Roebling and His Son, Harcourt, 1945.
Famous Bridges of the World, Random House, 1953.
Songs of a Bridge Builder, Ind-US, 1959.
Modes and Natural Frequencies of Suspension-bridge Oscillations, New York Academy of Sciences, 1959.

SOURCES:

Books

Ratigan, William, *Highways over Broad Waters; Life and Times of David B. Steinman, Bridge-builder,* Eerdmans, 1959.

Periodicals

Obituary, *New York Times,* August 23, 1960, p. 29.
Wolfert, Ira, "Master Bridge-Builder", *Reader's Digest,* October 1956, pp. 138–142.

—*Sketch by Sandra Katzman*

Charles P. Steinmetz
1865-1923
German-born American electrical engineer and mathematician

Charles P. Steinmetz was a mathematician and electrical engineer whose theories and research fostered the widespread use of electrical energy. A scientist of prodigious inventiveness, Steinmetz was granted some two hundred patents. His discovery of the phenomenon known as magnetic hysteresis led to the development of energy-efficient motors. He worked out mathematical theories that made practical the use of alternating current in long-distance power transmission. His work in changes in electrical circuits of very short duration was used to develop new cables and improved methods of operating transmission systems. He also built artificial lightning generators that led to the development of lightning arrestors to protect electrical apparatus and transmission lines.

Charles Proteus Steinmetz was born in Breslau, Germany (now Wroclaw, Poland), on April 9, 1865. His mother, Caroline Neubert, died when he was one year old; his father, Karl Heinrich, worked for the government-owned railroad. Steinmetz was the third of three sons and had two step-sisters and one half-sister. He changed his name from Karl August Rudolph when he immigrated to America. He was born with an inherited condition that gave him a hunchback. He never married for fear of passing the trait on to his children.

As a young boy, Steinmetz had a difficult first year at school; however, the slow start and concerns soon evaporated as he quickly ascended to the top of the class. At the University of Breslau he studied mathematics and worked toward a Ph.D. He would have graduated in 1888 were it not for his political activities. While at the university, Steinmetz became a Socialist, eventually taking over the publication of a student-run Socialist newspaper. The secret police had a warrant for his arrest when he fled Germany for Switzerland on the eve of his graduation. He immigrated to the United States in 1889.

The Law of Hysteresis

Steinmetz's first job in the United States was with the Eikemeyer and Osterheld Manufacturing Company in Yonkers, New York, where he set up a small research lab and worked on alternating current (an electric current that reverses its direction at regularly recurring intervals) motors. While working at Eikenmeyer's, he discovered how the influence of a changing magnetic field operates in a motor to consume energy. Characterizing the relationship between the fluctuating strength of a magnetic field in a motor and the amount of energy lost—a phenomenon known as magnetic hysteresis—his discovery showed engineers how they could design motors with a minimal loss of energy. Steinmetz published a 178-page paper on the law of hysteresis in 1892 that brought him instant recognition.

Steinmetz then turned his attention to mathematical theories that could make practical the use of alternating current in long-distance power transmission. Alternating current had no constant value or direction, and its large-scale behavior was at that time impossible to predict. Nevertheless, Steinmetz was able to fit the principles of alternating current into predictable mathematical models.

A Lifetime Career at General Electric

The Eikemeyer plant was bought by General Electric Company (GE) in 1892, when the company was just being organized. Steinmetz was hired by GE and eventually moved to Schenectady, New York, where he lived the rest of his life. It was at GE that he completed his work on the mathematics of alternating current, and published in the late 1890s a three-volume work so complex that most engineers had trouble understanding it at first. For four years, until his theories became well understood, Steinmetz spent much of his time explaining them to engineers throughout the country.

Another of Steinmetz's major achievements was his study of changes in electrical circuits of very short duration, for which he designed a 220,000-volt experimental transformer. His research was used to develop new cables, and new and improved methods of operating transmission systems. He even created artificial lightning by designing generators that could produce electricity at very high potential. This was used to study the effect of lightning on the power lines that were just going up around the country, and led to the development of lightning arrestors, devices that protect electrical apparatus and electric transmission lines from damage by lightning. In all, Steinmetz held about two hundred patents.

A Public Servant

Steinmetz taught electrical engineering at Union College in Schenectady from 1903 to 1913, heading the new department that was formed owing to his presence. He was known as a tough lecturer, but was popular with the students. Faithful to the philosophy of his youth, he continued to espouse socialism. When George R. Lunn was elected Schenectady's Socialist mayor in 1911, Steinmetz volunteered his services to the administration. He was appointed to the board of education and was later elected president of the board. In 1915 he was elected a member of the common council in Schenectady. As president of the council, he established classes for handicapped children. He ran for state engineer in 1922.

Steinmetz, who never married and had no children, adopted Roy Hayden, his associate at General Electric. When Hayden married, he and his family lived in Steinmetz's house on Wendall Avenue in Schenectady. Steinmetz also legally adopted Hayden's three children as his grandchildren. Steinmetz loved animals and at times kept a full range of wild animals in his backyard. His favorite pets were a pair of crows, John and Mary. He was an avid grower of orchids and cacti. Steinmetz died in Schenectady on October 26, 1923, of heart failure.

SELECTED WRITINGS BY STEINMETZ:

Books

(With E. J. Berg) *Theory and Calculation of Alternating Current Phenomena,* [New York], 1897.
Theoretical Elements of Electrical Engineering, [New York], 1901.
Theory and Calculation of Transient Electrical Phenomena and Oscillations, [New York], 1909.
Electrical Discharges, Waves, Impulses, and Other Transients, McGraw-Hill, 1914.
Relativity and Space, McGraw-Hill, 1923.

SOURCES:

Books

Caldecott, E., and P. L. Alger, editors, *Steinmetz: The Philosopher,* Gordon & Breach, 1965.
Garlin, Sender, *Three American Radicals: John Swinton, Charles P. Steinmetz, and William Dean Howells,* Westview, 1991.
Hammond, John Winthrop, *Charles Proteus Steinmetz: A Biography,* Century, 1924.
Lavine, Sigmund A., *Steinmetz: Maker of Lightning,* Dodd, Mead, 1959.
Leonard, Jonathan Norton, *Loki: The Life of Charles Proteus Steinmetz,* Doubleday, 1929.

—*Sketch by Olga K. Anderson*

Patrick Steptoe
1913-1988
English gynecologist

Patrick Steptoe

Patrick Steptoe, an English gynecologist and medical researcher, helped develop the technique of in vitro fertilization. In this process, a mature egg is removed from the female ovary and is fertilized in a test tube. After a short incubation period, the fertilized egg is implanted in the uterus, where it develops as in a typical pregnancy. This procedure gave women whose fallopian tubes were damaged or missing, and were thus unable to become pregnant, the hope that they too could conceive children. Steptoe and his colleague, English physiologist Robert G. Edwards, received international recognition—both positive and negative—when the first so-called test tube baby was born in 1978.

Patrick Christopher Steptoe was born on June 9, 1913 in Oxfordshire, England. His father was a church organist, while his mother served as a social worker. Steptoe studied medicine at the University of London's St. George Hospital Medical School and, after being licensed in 1939, became a member of the Royal College of Surgeons. His medical career, though, was interrupted by World War II. Steptoe volunteered as a naval surgeon, but he and his shipmates were captured by Italian forces in 1941 after their ship sank in the Battle of Crete. Initially granted special privileges in prison because he was a physician, Steptoe was placed in solitary confinement after officials detected his efforts to help fellow prisoners escape. Steptoe left the prison camp via a prisoner exchange in 1943. Following the war, Steptoe completed additional studies in obstetrics and gynecology. In 1948 he became a member of the Royal College of Obstetricians and Gynecologists and moved to Manchester to set up a private practice. In 1951 Steptoe began working at Oldham General and District Hospital in northeast England.

Performs Groundbreaking Work in Laparoscopy

While at Oldham General and District Hospital, Steptoe pursued his interest in fertility problems. He developed a method of procuring human eggs from the ovaries by using a laparoscope, a long thin telescope replete with fiber optics light. After inserting the device—through a small incision in the navel—into the inflated abdominal cavity, Steptoe was able to observe the reproductive tract. Eventually the laparoscope would become widely used in various types of surgery, including those associated with sterility. But, at first, Steptoe had trouble convincing others in the medical profession of the merits of laparoscopy; observers from the Royal College of Obstetricians and Gynecologists considered the technique fraught with difficulties. Five years passed before Steptoe published his first paper on laparoscopic surgery.

In 1966 Steptoe teamed with Cambridge University physiologist Robert G. Edwards to propel his work with fertility problems. Utilizing ovaries removed for medical reasons, Edwards had pioneered the fertilization of eggs outside of the body. With his laparoscope, Steptoe added the dimension of being able to secure mature eggs at the appropriate moment in the monthly cycle when fertilization would normally occur. A breakthrough for the duo came in 1968 when Edwards successfully fertilized an egg that Steptoe had extracted. Not until 1970, however, was an egg able to reach the stage of cell division—into about 100 cells—when it generally moves to the uterus. In 1972 the pair attempted the first implantation, but the embryo failed to lodge in the uterus. Indeed, none of the women with implanted embryos carried them for a full trimester.

As their work progressed and word of it leaked out, the researchers faced criticism from scientific and religious circles concerning the ethical and moral issues relating to tampering with the creation of human life. Some opponents considered the duo's work akin to the scenario in Aldous Huxley's 1932 work, *Brave New World,* in which babies were conceived in the laboratory, cloned, and manipulated for society's use. Members of Parliament demanded an investigation and sources of funds were withdrawn. A *Time* reporter quoted Steptoe as saying, "All I am interested in is how to help women who are denied a baby because their tubes are incapable of doing their small part." Undaunted, Steptoe and Edwards continued their work at Kershaw's Cottage Hospital in Oldham, with Steptoe financing the research by performing legal abortions. Disturbed with the criticism, Steptoe and Edwards became more secretive, which made the speculation and criticism more intense.

Efforts Yield Success

In 1976 Steptoe met thirty-year-old Leslie Brown, who experienced problems with her fallopian tubes. Steptoe removed a mature egg from her ovary,

and Edwards fertilized the egg using her husband Gilbert's sperm. The fertilized egg—implanted after two days—thrived, and on July 25, 1978, Joy Louise Brown, a healthy five pound twelve ounce girl was born in Oldham District and General Hospital. Even before the birth, reporters and cameramen congregated outside of the four story brick hospital, hoping for a glimpse of the expectant mother. After the birth, according to an article in *Time,* headlines in Britain heralded "OUR MIRACLE and BABY OF THE CENTURY."

Steptoe and Edwards were reluctant to discuss the procedures in press conferences and did not immediately publish their findings in a medical journal. In October of 1978, Steptoe was to receive an award from the Barren Foundation, a fertility research organization based in Chicago. The foundation suddenly cancelled the presentation because Steptoe and Edwards had not published an article on the event. As reported in a 1978 issue of *Time,* Steptoe called the foundation's action "the most utterly disgraceful exhibition of bad manners I've come across in the scientific world." In addition, rumors that the pair had sold their story to the tabloid the *National Enquirer* for a six figure amount were rampant. Steptoe declared that he rejected such offers and did not make any money on the highly publicized birth. Despite the furor, the New York Fertility Society subsequently presented Steptoe with an achievement award.

As to the claim of publishing, Steptoe answered that most scientists do not publish until several months after data is in and research complete. The procedures were fully presented at the January 26, 1979 meeting of the Royal College of Obstetricians and Gynecologists and at the conference of the American Fertility Society in San Francisco. Steptoe reported that with modified techniques, ten percent of the in vitro fertilization attempts could succeed. He further predicted that there could one day be a fifty percent success rate for the procedure.

In the aftermath of the first successful test tube baby, Steptoe received thousands of letters from couples seeking help in conception. He retired from the British National Health Service and constructed a new clinic near Cambridge. For their efforts, Steptoe and Edwards were both named Commanders of the British Empire, and in 1987 Steptoe was honored with fellowship in the Royal Society. Steptoe and his wife, a former actress, had one son and one daughter. His interests outside of medicine included piano and organ, cricket, plays, and opera. Steptoe died of cancer on March 21, 1988, in Canterbury. Yet, since the birth of baby Brown and the pioneering techniques of Steptoe, couples with various physiological problems have had children in clinics throughout the world.

SELECTED WRITINGS BY STEPTOE:

Books

(With Robert Edwards) *A Matter of Life: The Story of a Medical Breakthrough,* Morrow, 1980.

SOURCES:

Books

Doctors on the New Frontier, McGraw Hill, 1980.

Periodicals

"The First Test Tube Baby," *Time,* July 31, 1978, pp. 58–69.

—*Sketch by Evelyn B. Kelly*

Otto Stern
1888-1969

German American physicist

Otto Stern received the 1943 Nobel Prize in physics for his development of molecular beam methods and the use of these methods to determine a number of important physical constants, especially the magnetic moment of atoms and nuclei. The molecular beam—the introduction of a gas or vapor into a vacuum which results in the formation of a stream of atoms or molecules that is similar to a light beam—had been discovered by French physicist Louis Dunoyer. This molecular or atomic beam can be used to study the properties of the gas or vapor of which it is made.

Stern was born in Sohrau, Upper Silesia, Germany (later Zory, Poland), on February 17, 1888. He was the oldest of five children born to Oskar Stern and the former Eugenie Rosenthal. Both parents had come from prosperous grain merchants and flour millers and eagerly encouraged the intellectual development of their children. When Otto was four years old, his family moved to Breslau (later Wroclaw, Poland), where he attended the local Johannes Gymnasium. Most of Stern's training in science came from his home, where books, conversation and even some simple experimentation were the primary means of instruction.

Earns Doctorate and Joins Einstein

As was common at the time, Stern traveled to a number of universities for his further education after graduating from the gymnasium in 1906. Finally, he undertook a doctoral program in chemistry at Breslau under Otto Sackur. He was awarded his Ph.D. in 1912 for a thesis on the kinetic theory of osmotic pressure in concentrated solutions. Through Sackur's influence, Stern was able to take a position as research assistant to **Albert Einstein** from 1912 to 1914, first in Prague and later in Zürich, at the Federal Institute of Technology. Einstein was to have an important influence on Stern's career. It was from the great man, biographer Emilio Segrè pointed out in the *Biographical Memoirs of the National Academy of Sciences,* that Stern "learned what were the really important problems of contemporary physics: the nature of the quantum of light with its double aspect of particle and wave, the nature of atoms, and relativity."

With the outbreak of World War I in 1914, Stern was drafted into the German army where he served first as a private and later as a non-commissioned officer. He was assigned with the Meteorology Corps on the Russian front. During his four years in the military, Stern had enough spare time to continue his theoretical research, writing two important papers on the application of quantum theory to statistical thermodynamics during the war years.

Begins Molecular Beam Studies at Frankfurt

As the war drew to a close, Stern was finally able to accept an appointment as Privat dozen at the University of Frankfurt-on-the-Main that he had been offered in 1915, but which the war had prevented his accepting. At Frankfurt, Stern became assistant to **Max Born**, who had just moved there from the University of Berlin. The research topic in which Stern became interested was the use of molecular beams to study atomic and molecular properties. Stern had first learned about molecular beams during the war. The techniques for using such beams had been developed in 1911 by the French physicist Louis Dunoyer. By introducing a gas or vapor into a vacuum, a beam of atoms or molecules is formed. This beam allows the researcher to study atomic structure and properties.

Stern spent the greatest part of his professional career developing the molecular beam technology and using it to determine a number of atomic and molecular properties. The first application he studied was the determination of molecular velocities in gases. In the 1850s, James Clerk Maxwell had calculated the theoretical distribution of molecular velocities in a gas. Although there was not much doubt about the accuracy of Maxwell's findings, no empirical data supporting his results had ever been obtained. In 1920, Stern completed an experiment using the molecular beam technique to find the actual distribution of molecular velocities in a gas. His results unequivocally substantiated Maxwell's predictions.

The following year, Stern went on to a more significant application of the molecular beam technique. According to quantum theory, the atom is an electrically charged particle rotating in space. As such, it was thought to have associated with it a magnetic field whose magnetic field could be expressed as its "magnetic moment." Furthermore, the atom's magnetic moment could have only a finite, discrete number of values. This notion was described as the atom's "spatial quantization." (In fact, the same argument applies to the components of an atom, its electrons, nucleus, protons, and neutrons, all of which have their own unique magnetic moments.)

In 1922, Stern used molecular beams to test the theory of spatial quantization. He passed a beam of silver atoms through a nonuniform magnetic field and found that it split into two distinct parts. The now famous experiment was given the name the Stern-Gerlach experiment for Stern and his associate in the work, Walther Gerlach. The experiment not only confirmed the concept of space quantization, but also allowed Stern to calculate the magnetic moment of the silver atom. His result was in agreement with the theoretical values calculated by means of quantum theory. For this experiment, and others like it carried out later, Stern was awarded the 1943 Nobel Prize in physics.

Stern's tenure at Frankfurt had ended in 1921 in the midst of planning for his famous experiment with Gerlach. The experiment was carried out at the University of Rostock, where he had been appointed associate professor of theoretical physics in 1921. Two years later, Stern moved on to the University of Hamburg as professor of physical chemistry and director of the Institute for Physical Chemistry. At Hamburg, Stern continued to explore the use of molecular and atomic beams. He found experimental proof for **Louis de Broglie**'s theory of the wave nature of particles and determined the magnetic moment of the proton and deuteron, subatomic particles. The value he found for the proton was at least twice that predicted by theory, a discrepancy that has yet to be totally explained.

Adolf Hitler's rise to power in Germany convinced Stern that he had to leave his homeland. Although he was probably not in any personal danger, he decided to resign his post at Hamburg in protest of the new government's anti-Semitic policies. He accepted an appointment as research professor in physics at the Carnegie Institute in Pittsburgh and became a naturalized U.S. citizen on March 8, 1939. During World War II Stern served as a consultant to the War Department and then, in 1946, resigned his post at Carnegie to move to Berkeley where he could

be near his two sisters. He lived largely in isolation for the rest of his life. He died in a Berkeley movie theater on August 17, 1969. Stern never married and was said by biographer Segrè to have "liked good cuisine, excellent cigars, and in general all the refinements of life."

SELECTED WRITINGS BY STERN:

Periodicals

"Ein Weg zür Experimentellen Prüfung der Richtungsquantelung im Magnetfeld," *Zeitschrift für Physik,* Number 7, 1921, pp. 249–253.
(With W. Gerlach) "Das Magnetische Moment des Silberatoms," *Zeitscrift für Physik,* Number 9, 1922, pp. 353–355.

SOURCES:

Books

Gillispie, Charles Coulson, editor, *Dictionary of Scientific Biography,* Volume 13, Scribner's, 1975, pp. 40–43.
Heathcote, Niels H. de V., *Nobel Prize Winners in Physics, 1901–1950,* Henry Schuman, 1953, pp. 389–397.
Segrè, Emilio, "Otto Stern," *Biographical Memoirs,* Volume 43, National Academy of Sciences, 1973.
Weber, Robert L., *Pioneers of Science: Nobel Prize Winners in Physics,* American Institute of Physics, 1980, pp. 119–121.

—*Sketch by David E. Newton*

Nettie Maria Stevens
1861-1912
American biologist and cytogeneticist

Nettie Maria Stevens was a biologist and cytogeneticist and one of the first American women to be recognized for her contributions to scientific research. "She ... produced new data and new theories," wrote Marilyn Bailey Ogilvie in *Women in Science,* "yet beyond these accomplishments passed along her expertise to a new generation. ... illustrat[ing] the importance of the women's colleges in the education of women scientists." Although Stevens started her research career when she was in her thirties, she successfully expanded the fields of embryology and cytogenetics (the branch of biology which focuses on the study of heredity), particularly in the study of histology (a branch of anatomy dealing with plant and animal tissues) and of regenerative processes in invertebrates such as hydras and flatworms. She is best known for her role in genetics—her research contributed greatly to the understanding of chromosomes and heredity. She theorized that the sex of an organism was determined by the inheritance of a specific chromosome—X or Y—and performed experiments to confirm this hypothesis.

Stevens, the third of four children and the first daughter, was born in Cavendish, Vermont, on July 7, 1861, to Ephraim Stevens, a carpenter of English descent, and Julia Adams Stevens. Historians know little about her family or her early life, except that she was educated in the public schools in Westford, Massachusetts, and displayed exceptional scholastic abilities. Upon graduation, Stevens taught Latin, English, mathematics, physiology and zoology at the high school in Lebanon, New Hampshire. As a teacher she had a great zeal for learning that she tried to impart both to her students and her colleagues. Between 1881 and 1883, Stevens attended the Normal School at Westfield, Massachusetts, consistently achieving the highest scores in her class from the time she started until she graduated. She worked as a school teacher, and then as a librarian for a number of years after she graduated; however, there are gaps in her history that are unaccounted for between this time and when she enrolled at Stanford University in 1896.

Furthers Education at Stanford and Bryn Mawr

In 1896, Stevens was attracted by the reputation of Stanford University for providing innovative opportunities for individuals aspiring to pursue their own scholastic interests. At the age of thirty-five she enrolled, studying physiology under professor Oliver Peebles Jenkins. She spent summers studying at the Hopkins Seaside Laboratory, Pacific Grove, California, and pursuing her love of learning and of biology. During this time, Stevens decided to switch careers to focus on research, instead of teaching. While at Hopkins she performed research on the life cycle of *Boveria,* a protozoan parasite of sea cucumbers. Her findings were published in 1901 in the *Proceedings of the California Academy of Sciences.* After obtaining her masters degree—a highly unusual accomplishment for a woman in that era—Stevens returned to the East to study at Bryn Mawr College, Pennsylvania, as a graduate biology student in 1900. She was such an exceptional student that she was awarded a fellowship enabling her to study at the Zoological Station in Naples, Italy, and then at the Zoological Institute of the University of Würzburg, Germany. Back at Bryn Mawr, she obtained her doctorate in

1903. At this time, she was made a research fellow in biology at Bryn Mawr and then was promoted to a reader in experimental morphology in 1904. From 1903 until 1905, her research was funded by a grant from the Carnegie Institution. In 1905, she was promoted again to associate in experimental morphology, a position she held until her death in 1912.

Contributes to the Understanding of Chromosomal Determination of Sex

While Stevens' early research focused on morphology and taxonomy and then later expanded to cytology, her most important research was with chromosomes and their relation to heredity. Because of the pioneering studies performed by the renowned monk Gregor Mendel (showing how pea plant genetic traits are inherited), scientists of the time knew a lot about how chromosomes acted during cell division and maturation of germ cells. However, no inherited trait had been traced from the parents' chromosomes to those of the offspring. In addition, no scientific studies had yet linked one chromosome with a specific characteristic. Stevens, and the well-known biologist **Edmund Beecher Wilson**, who worked independently on this type of research, were the first to demonstrate that the sex of an organism was determined by a particular chromosome; moreover, they proved that gender is inherited in accordance with Mendel's laws of genetics. Together, their research confirmed, and therefore established, a chromosomal basis for heredity. Working with the meal worm, *Tenebrio molitor,* Stevens determined that the male produced two kinds of sperm—one with a large X chromosome, and the other with a small Y chromosome. Unfertilized eggs, however, were all alike and had only X chromosomes. Stevens theorized that sex, in some organisms, may result from chromosomal inheritance. She suggested that eggs fertilized by sperm carrying X chromosomes produced females, and those by sperm carrying the Y chromosome resulted in males. She performed further research to prove this phenomenon, expanding her studies to other species. Although this theory was not accepted by all scientists at the time, it was profoundly important in the evolution of the field of genetics and to an understanding of determination of gender.

Stevens was a prolific author, publishing some thirty-eight papers in eleven years. For her paper, "A Study of the Germ Cells of *Aphis rosae* and *Aphis oenotherae,*" Stevens was awarded the Ellen Richards Research Prize in 1905, given to promote scientific research by women. Stevens died of breast cancer on May 4, 1912, before she could occupy the research professorship created for her by the Bryn Mawr trustees. Much later, **Thomas Hunt Morgan**, a 1933 Nobel Prize recipient for his work in genetics, recognized the importance of Stevens' ground-breaking experiments, as quoted by Ogilvie in the *Proceedings* *of the American Philosophical Society,* "Stevens had a share in a discovery of importance and her name will be remembered for this, when the minutiae of detailed investigations that she carried out have become incorporated in the general body of the subject."

SELECTED WRITINGS BY STEVENS:

Periodicals

"Studies in Spermatogenesis with Especial Reference to the 'Accessory Chromosome,'" *Carnegie Institution Publications,* 1905.

"A study of the Germ Cells of *Aphis rosae* and *Aphis Oenotherae,* " *Journal of Experimental Zoology,* 1905, pp. 313–333.

"Further Studies on Heterochromosomes in Mosquitoes," *Biological Bulletin of the Marine Biological Laboratory,* 1911, pp. 109–120.

SOURCES:

Books

Ogilvie, Marilyn Bailey *Women in Science: Antiquity through the Nineteenth Century,* Massachusetts Institute of Technology, 1986.

Periodicals

Isis, June, 1978, pp. 163–72.

Proceedings of the American Philosophical Society, Held at Philadelphia for Promoting Useful Knowledge, Volume 125, American Philosophical Society, 1981, pp. 292–311.

—*Sketch by Barbara J. Prouian*

H. Guyford Stever
1916-

American aeronautical engineer

One of the most significant science policy makers of the last thirty years, H. Guyford Stever has played an important and generally respected role in the shaping of the nation's scientific and technical policies. He rose to prominence in the scientific and engineering community because of his aeronautical research in the development of guided missiles and spacecraft as well as in flight aerodynamics. He gained

a reputation as an able administrator and a thoughtful advocate for applying technical expertise to the problems of the nation. As a result Stever served in several key advisory positions in the 1960s and 1970s, especially as head of the National Science Foundation and science advisor to presidents Richard M. Nixon and Gerald R. Ford.

Early Professional Experiences

Horton Guyford Stever was born on October 24, 1916, in the glass manufacturing city of Corning, New York. The son of Ralph Raymond, a merchant, and Alma Matt Stever, he was educated in the local public schools. He attended Colgate University and completed his B.A. degree in physics in 1938. From there he journeyed cross-country to work on a Ph.D. in physics at the California Institute of Technology, graduating in 1941. As World War II began, Stever, like so many of his generation and training, went to work in the defense effort as a researcher at the Massachusetts Institute of Technology's (MIT) Radiation Laboratory. There he met director Lee A. DuBridge, who later was Nixon's first science advisor in the late 1960s. Within a short time Stever joined the Office of Scientific Research and Development (OSRD), headed by **Vannevar Bush**, where he saw up close the linkage of science and government on a variety of wartime projects. This experience was critical to Stever's development as a scientific and technical advisor in the postwar era.

In 1942, with World War II underway and going badly for the Allies, Stever was sent to Great Britain as a science liaison officer at the London Mission of the OSRD. Serving there until the end of the war in 1945, he analyzed developments in German and British radar systems as a means of strengthening the defenses against German V–1 and V–2 rocket attacks. After the cross-channel invasion in June, 1944, Stever moved with forward elements of the OSRD to the continent to continue studying enemy technology.

After the war Stever returned to the United States and returned to purely civilian pursuits. He took a position with MIT as an assistant professor in the Department of Aeronautical Engineering, headed by **Jerome C. Hunsaker**. Altogether, he was at MIT almost twenty years, progressing through the academic ranks to full professor in 1956. Between 1961 and 1965 he headed the mechanical engineering and naval architecture and marine engineering departments.

While at MIT Stever was heavily involved in research projects to define and solve a number of problems associated with aerospace flight. Although trained as a physicist, Stever was adept at aeronautical engineering, and he contributed greatly to solving problems of control on guided missiles and of transonic (speeds of five hundred-fifty to nine hundred miles per hour) flight. In early experiments, conducted about 1949, Stever used the MIT wind tunnels to test models of missiles and transonic aircraft for their aerodynamic properties, and he published several important papers on the subject. Of special importance were methods Stever developed of stabilizing aircraft and missiles at transonic speeds, where normal aerodynamic rules did not apply.

At the same time, Stever was always interested in furthering the linkage between science and technology, and government, and he served on several government and military advisory committees. With his help, technology was mobilized to help the United States in its rivalry with the Soviet Union. In 1947 he became a member of the U.S. Air Force Scientific Advisory Board, and in 1955 Stever took a leave of absence from MIT to serve as chief scientist with the Air Force. He also served on advisory committees with the National Advisory Committee for Aeronautics (NACA), its successor (NASA), the National Science Foundation, and Congress in the 1950s and 1960s. In addition, Stever was a technical advisor to several private corporations such as Goodyear Tire and United Aircraft, helping them mostly with military issues.

Stever left MIT in 1965 to take over the presidency of the Carnegie Institute of Technology in Pittsburgh. He served as president until 1972, and is best known for arranging the merger of Carnegie with the Mellon Institute in 1967. Both organizations had been struggling separately, but the new Carnegie-Mellon University became a strong technical institution of higher learning. Under Stever's direction it developed a curriculum that emphasized the integration of science with other disciplines.

Becomes Governmental Advisor

Beginning in 1970 Stever served on two key advisory committees for President Nixon, the Ad Hoc Science Panel and the Task Force on Science Policy. At the same time Nixon, who was impressed with Stever's capabilities, appointed him to the National Science Board, the policy-making arm of the National Science Foundation (NSF). These positions gave him greater visibility inside the Nixon administration, and opened the way for his appointment as director of the NSF in February, 1972.

Stever suffered intense pressure in 1973 when Nixon abolished the office of science advisor to the president as being without real value and sent the responsibilities to Stever at the National Science Foundation. To many, Stever's dual role as head of NSF and science advisor to the president represented a conflict of interest. Moreover, Stever was perceived as lacking access to Nixon—a serious liability for one charged with advocating the nation's scientific and technical programs—and as being less than effective when he did get the president's ear. Well aware of the

controversy, Stever nevertheless maintained he could do both jobs and had all the access to the administration he needed.

When Nixon resigned in the aftermath of the Watergate scandal in August, 1974, Stever remained at the National Science Foundation and continued to help the Ford administration with science policy. As a result, when Ford reestablished the position of science advisor to the president in August, 1976, he asked Stever to take the position; Stever served in that capacity until the change in administrations in January, 1977. Although he again weathered criticism for his role in the Nixon administration, Stever found the situation with Ford more conducive to his position and suggested that his role was "to try to be the translator—take ideas welling up in the scientific community and see that the government takes action on them."

When he left government service, Stever continued to be very active as an advisor on several commissions, panels, and other task forces. He began consulting for several corporations, and also became a director of TRW, of Schering Plough, and of Goodyear.

SOURCES:

Books

Golden, William, editor, *Science Advice to the President,* Pergamon, 1980.

Herken, Gregg, *Cardinal Choices: Presidential Science Advising from the Atomic Bomb to SDI,* Oxford University Press, 1992.

Katz, James, *Presidential Politics and Science Advice,* Praeger, 1978.

Periodicals

Shapley, Deborah, "NSF Appointment: Science Elite, White House Reward Favorite Son," *Science,* March 31, 1972, pp. 1441, 1443.

—*Sketch by Roger D. Launius*

Frederick Campion Steward
1904-1993
English American plant physiologist

Frederick Campion Steward was a leading plant physiologist who conducted research in a broad spectrum of botanical fields; he was noted in particular for his 1958 discovery that it was possible to produce an entire plant from one cell, since all the data needed to regenerate a plant is found in a single cell. Steward also made significant contributions to the understanding of how plants absorb mineral salts, carry on respiration, and utilize nitrogen. Throughout his career, Steward wrote more than one hundred papers for scientific journals in which he described his research on these subjects. The importance of his contributions was recognized by his fellow scientists, who honored him with the Merit Award of the Botanical Society of America in 1961 and the Stephen Hales Award of the American Society of Plant Physiologists in 1964. He was also elected a Fellow of the American Academy of Arts and Sciences in 1956, and a year later became a member of the Royal Society of London, where he delivered its Crosnian Lecture in 1969.

Steward was born on June 16, 1904, in London, the son of Frederick Walter and Mary (Daglish) Steward. He received his B.Sc. in chemistry with first-class honors in 1924 from the University of Leeds, and his Ph.D. in botany in 1926. He came to the United States in 1927 to serve as a Rockefeller Foundation fellow, and two years later, on September 7, 1929, he married Anne Temple Gordon, a colleague of his in the botany department at Cornell. The couple had one son, Frederick Gordon. Upon Steward's return to England, he served as an assistant lecturer in botany at Leeds beginning in 1929, and as a reader in botany at Birkbeck College, University of London, where he also received his D.Sc. During World War II, he served as director of aircraft equipment in the British Ministry of Aircraft Production. After the war, he returned to the United States to become a visiting professor of botany—and later chair of the department—at the University of Rochester. In 1950, he became a professor of botany at Cornell University and director of the Laboratory of Cell Physiology, Growth, and Development, a post he held for nearly twenty years.

Delves into Research on Plant Metabolism

Early in his career, Steward applied his background in chemistry to problems in botany. He studied the active transport of ions such as potassium and chlorine in sections of beets and potatoes grown aseptically, and determined that variables such as oxygen supply and temperature regulated the metabolic activity. In active transport, cells utilize energy obtained from aerobic respiration to absorb increasing amounts of ions through the cell membrane against the concentration gradient. This results in a greater concentration of these ions within the cells than in the external environment. By comparison, during passive transport, when ions diffuse into a cell without the input of energy, the process does not result in a greater concentration of the ions within the cell.

After World War II, with the collaboration of a number of other scientists, Steward devoted his research to several objectives. One of his goals was to investigate how plants obtain their nitrogen for protein synthesis. Through the application of paper chromatography Steward opened doors leading to new ideas on nitrogen metabolism. In his various research projects, he studied the nutrition, growth, and metabolism of a number of plant varieties, such as carrot, potato, beet, banana, mint, and artichoke.

It was in the late 1950s, however, that Steward performed the work for which he was best known: Along with collaborators, he was able to develop complete carrot plants from isolated adult cells in nutrient culture solution, a process which required the application of aseptic techniques. This was necessary if the cultures were to be free from bacterial or fungal contamination. Steward first included the plant hormone auxin, then added coconut milk to achieve the complete development of new, entire carrot plants. Coconut milk normally nourishes the coconut embryo and has been found to contain plant hormones called cytokinins. This success illustrated the concept of totipotency, in which a mature cell can achieve the potential of its genes and can give rise to a complete plant. With the correct mixture of mineral nutrients, hormones, sucrose, and vitamins in the tissue culture medium, the genes of a mature cell can be switched on and off to differentiate into the variety of tissues needed to build an entire plant.

Assumes Additional Educational Posts

Steward remained at Cornell until 1973, then transferred to the University of Madras, India, where he served as the institution's C. V. Raman Visiting Professor. In the mid–1970s he received an honorary doctorate from the University of Delhi and also was appointed the Cecil H. and Ida Green Professor at the University of British Columbia. He later was awarded honorary positions at the State University of New York at Stony Brook and at the University of Virginia at Charlottesville, both of which involved active duties. He had been suffering from poor health, though, and died in mid-September, 1993, in Tuscaloosa, Alabama. In Steward's obituary in the *New York Times,* writer Ronald Sullivan, in addition to noting the botanist's significant scientific contributions, also pointed out the scientist's reputation as a skilled educator: Steward "was ... responsible for creating and inspiring a generation of biological scientists from his Cornell lecture halls, classrooms and laboratories," asserted Sullivan. "Former students said his lectures in advanced plant physiology were the high point of their educations. He was a spellbinding lecturer, and his classroom ultimately became a kind of international salon for visiting scientists from all over the world." Many of these students collaborated with him in research described in various scientific journals, such as *Annals of Botany, Journal of Experimental Biology,* and *Plant Physiology.*

SELECTED WRITINGS BY STEWARD:

Books

(Editor) *Plant Physiology: A Treatise,* six volumes, Academic Press, 1959–72.

(With A. D. Krikorian) *Plants at Work: A Summary of Plant Physiology,* Addison-Wesley, 1964.

About Plants: Topics in Plant Biology, Addison-Wesley, 1966.

Growth and Organization of Plants, Addison-Wesley, 1968.

(With Krikorian) *Plants, Chemicals, and Growth,* Academic Press, 1971.

Periodicals

"The Control of Growth in Plant Cells," *Scientific American,* October, 1963.

(With others) "Growth and Development of Cultured Plant Cells," *Science,* Volume 143, 1964, pp. 20–27.

SOURCES:

Books

Keeton, W. T., *Biological Science,* Norton, 1972, pp. 272–73.

Periodicals

Sullivan, Ronald, "Frederick C. Steward, 89, Leading Botanist, Dies," *New York Times,* September 18, 1993, p. 9.

—*Sketch by Maurice Bleifeld*

Thomas Dale Stewart
1901-

American anthropologist

Thomas Dale Stewart is a renowned physical anthropologist whose affiliation with the National Museum of Natural History at the Smithsonian Institution has stretched over seven decades. Stewart is an international authority in comparative human osteology (the sciences of bones), human identification, and forensic anthropology. Among his many achievements are numerous studies of pre-Columbian and early post-Columbian man in the Americas including the skeletal remains of Tepexpan man in Mexico and Midland man in Texas, among the oldest human remains found in North America. Stewart's reconstruction of Neanderthal skeletons from Shanidar in Iraq and his interpretations of Neanderthal anatomy from these fossils are considered to be major contributions. Stewart's expertise as a forensic anthropologist led him to do work for the Federal Bureau of Investigation (FBI) and the U.S. Army. He examined human skeletal remains in numerous homicide cases for the FBI and worked with the army in the identification of soldiers killed during the Korean War.

Stewart was born in Delta, Pennsylvania, on June 10, 1901, the son of Thomas Dale Stewart and Susan Price Stewart. He grew up in Delta, graduating from the local high school in 1920. Stewart moved to Washington, D.C. for his education and life's work in anthropology. While a student at George Washington University in 1924, he began his long association with the National Museum of Natural History by working as an aide under the famous Czechoslovakian-born American anthropologist **Aleš Hrdlička**. Stewart earned an A.B. degree from George Washington University and then went on to study medicine at Johns Hopkins University in Baltimore, Maryland, where he completed work on his M.D. in 1931. Stewart then returned to Washington and the Museum of Natural History where he became an assistant curator of physical anthropology in 1931, an associate curator in 1939, curator in 1942 and head curator of the department of anthropology in 1961. The following year he was appointed director of the museum and held that position until 1965. In 1966, the Smithsonian Institution honored Stewart with the rare title of senior scientist. He was given the status of emeritus physical anthropologist in 1971.

Research Carries Him in Many Directions

Stewart also has found time to teach, serving as a visiting professor of anatomy at Washington University School of Medicine in St. Louis, Missouri, during World War II and later as a visitor professor of anthropology at the Escuela Nacional de Anthropología in Mexico. Stewart's long career carried him on a number of different, yet sometimes overlapping, research tracks. He is the author of about two hundred scientific papers and books. The breadth of his research was apparent from the very start of his career. His first dozen published papers covered such topics as monkey musculature, dental caries in Peruvians, and age-change sequence differences among Eskimos and Native Americans.

Stewart inevitably became involved in the still unresolved question of when humans first crossed the Bering Sea land-bridge from Asia to the New World. His reexamination of a Florida artifact called the Melbourne Skull in the 1940s led him to contradict Hrdlička's earlier claim that it was similar to recent resident Indians. Stewart went on to study human remains in Mexico and Texas, observing the so-called Tepexpan man and Midland man, and made cases for them being the oldest known humans in North America in papers published in 1949 and 1955. Stewart delved further back on humanity's family tree when he was invited to Iraq in 1957 to help restore two Neanderthal skeletons discovered by Ralph Solecki, a Columbia University anthropologist. He returned in 1960 and 1962 to recover, restore, and study four more skeletons found by Solecki in caves at Shanidar. Stewart's careful reconstructions of the Shanidar fossils provided new anatomical data about the skull, pelvis, and shoulder blades of Neanderthals. As a curator at the National Museum of Natural History, Stewart often worked as a forensic anthropologist for the FBI. The museum and FBI are close to each other and FBI agents started bringing occasional skeletal remains of suspected homicides for analysis in the 1920s. The remains ranged from single bones or a tooth to one or more entire skeletons of unknown age. Stewart handled these cases, as well as ones from state medical examiners. These calls for expert help were infrequent at first, but by the time Stewart retired he was regularly handling a half dozen cases a month. Forensic anthropology was poorly developed when the FBI first requested help, and Stewart found that the standards for estimating such basic data as the age, sex, and stature from human remains, let alone possible ranges for these traits, were primitive. He promoted scientific study to cure these shortcomings.

Learns How Bones Mature

Stewart made significant contributions in the field of osteology, working with the U.S. Army to help identify American casualties in the Korean War. As part of this work, Stewart made detailed observations of growth change on 450 skeletons. Working with fully identified remains, Stewart looked at how bones in the human body matured. He discovered that there were far bigger variations in maturation rates than previously thought. He also developed a method of estimating skeletal age by studying pubic bones. Later on, while working with Eskimo skeletons, Stewart determined that pits and depressions in the cartilage joint between the pubic bones were tell-tale signs of childbirth and that the remains were of a female.

For this and other work Stewart was elected to the National Academy of Sciences in 1962. He was awarded the Viking Medal in Physical Anthropology in 1953 and the Smithsonian's Joseph Henry Medal in 1976. He married Julia Wright in 1932, and they had one daughter, Cornella. After his first wife died, Stewart remarried in 1952 to Rita Frame Dewey, a former newspaper reporter and editor.

SELECTED WRITINGS BY STEWART:

Books

The People of America, Scribner, 1973.

SOURCES:

Books

Modern Men of Science, McGraw-Hill, 1968.
Modern Scientists and Engineers, McGraw-Hill, 1980.

Periodicals

Angel, Lawrence J., "T. Dale Stewart," *Physical Anthropology,* November, 1976, pp. 521–530.

—*Sketch by Joel Schwarz*

George R. Stibitz
1904-
American mathematician and computer scientist

George R. Stibitz joined the Bell Telephone Laboratories as a mathematical engineer in 1930. His work at Bell Labs convinced him of the need to develop techniques for handling a large number of complex mathematical operations much more quickly than was currently possible with traditional manual systems. His research eventually led to the development of one of the first binary computers ever built. Stibitz was also the first to transmit computer data long-distance. Later in his life the mathematician became especially interested in the application of mathematics and the computer sciences to biomedical problems.

George Robert Stibitz was born on April 20, 1904, in York, Pennsylvania. His mother was the former Mildred Amelia Murphy, a math teacher before her marriage, and his father was George Stibitz, a professor of theology. Stibitz's childhood was spent in Dayton, Ohio, where his father taught at a local college. Because of the interest in and aptitude for science and engineering that he had exhibited, Stibitz was enrolled at an experimental high school in Dayton established by **Charles Kettering**, inventor of the first automobile ignition system.

For his undergraduate studies, Stibitz enrolled at Denison University in Granville, Ohio. After earning his bachelor of philosophy degree there in 1926, he went on to Union College in Schenectady, New York, where he was awarded his M.S. degree in 1927. After graduating from Union, he worked as a technician at General Electric in Schenectady for one year before returning to Cornell University to begin his doctoral program. Stibitz received his Ph.D. in mathematical physics from Cornell in 1930.

Stibitz's first job after graduation was as a research mathematician at the Bell Telephone Laboratories in New York City. His job there was to work on one of the fundamental problems with which modern telecommunication companies have to deal: How to carry out the endless number of mathematical calculations required to design and operate an increasingly complex system of telephones. At the time, virtually the only tool available to perform these calculations was the desktop mechanical calculator. It was obvious that this device would not long be adequate for the growing demands of the nation's expanding telephone network.

In the fall of 1937 Stibitz made the discovery for which he is now best known, the use of relays for automated computing. A relay is a metallic device that can assume one of two positions—open or closed—when an electrical current passes through it. The relay acts as a kind of gate, therefore, that will control the flow of electrical current, and was a common device used to regulate telephone circuits.

Stibitz Designs the "K-Model" Computing Machine

In November 1937 Stibitz decided to see if relays could be used to perform simple mathematical functions. He borrowed a few of the metal devices from the Bell stockroom, took them home, and assembled a simple computing system on his kitchen table. The system consisted of the relays, a dry cell, flashlight bulbs, and metal strips cut from a tobacco can. He soon had a device in which a lighted bulb represented the binary digit "1" and an unlighted bulb, the binary digit "0." The device was also able to use binary mathematics to add and subtract decimal numbers. Stibitz's colleagues later gave the name "K-Model" to this primitive computer because it was built on his kitchen table.

When Stibitz first demonstrated his K-model computer for company executives, they were not very impressed. "There were no fireworks, no cham-

pagne," he was quoted as saying in *The Computer Pioneers*. Less than a year later, however, Bell executives had changed their minds about the Stibitz invention. An important factor in that decision was the increasing pressure on Bell to find a way of solving its increasingly complex mathematical problems. The company agreed to finance construction of a large experimental model of Stibitz's invention. Construction on that machine began in April 1939, and the final product was first put into operation on January 8, 1940. Called the Complex Number Calculator (CNC), the machine had the capacity to add, subtract, multiply, and divide complex numbers—just the kinds of problems that were particularly troublesome for engineers at Bell.

Nine months later, Stibitz recorded another milestone in the history of computer science. At a meeting of the American Mathematical Society at Dartmouth College, he hooked up the new Complex Number Calculator in New York City with a telegraph system. He then sent problems from Dartmouth to the CNC in New York, which solved the problems and sent the answers back to Dartmouth by means of the telegraph. This type of data transmission has now become commonplace in a modern day society of modems and fax machines.

During World War II, Bell Labs permitted Stibitz to join the National Defense Research Council. There the demands of modern military artillery convinced Stibitz even more of the need for improved computer hardware, and he spent most of the war working on improved versions of the CNC, also known as the Model 1. The Model 2 computer, for instance, used punched tapes to store programs that would give the computer instructions; in this manner the computer could perform the same complex calculations many times on different sets of numbers. This proved useful in calculating weapons trajectories.

At the end of World War II, Stibitz decided not to return to Bell Labs. Instead he moved with his family to Vermont where he became a consultant in applied mathematics. After two decades in this line of work Stibitz was offered a job at Dartmouth's Medical School, where he was asked to show how computers can be used to deal with biomedical problems. He accepted that offer and was appointed professor of physiology at Dartmouth; in that capacity he investigated the motion of oxygen in the lungs and the rate at which drugs and nutrients are spread throughout the body. In 1972 he retired from his position and was made professor emeritus; nevertheless, he continued to contribute his knowledge to the department.

Stibitz was married on September 1, 1930, to Dorothea Lamson, with whom he had two daughters, Mary and Martha. Among the awards he has received are the Harry Goode Award of the American Federation for Information Processing (1965), the Piore

Award of the Institute of Electrical and Electronic Engineers (1977), and the Babbage Society Medal (1982). He was also the recipient of honorary degrees from Keene State College and Dartmouth College. The holder of 35 patents, Stibitz was named to the Inventors Hall of Fame in 1983.

SELECTED WRITINGS BY STIBITZ:

Books

(With J. A. Larivee) *Mathematics and Computers,* McGraw-Hill, 1957.
Mathematics in Medicine and the Life Sciences, Year Book Medical Publishers, 1966.

SOURCES:

Books

Ceruzzi, Paul E., *Reckoners: The Prehistory of the Digital Computer, from Relays to the Stored Program Concept, 1935–1945,* Greenwood Press, 1983, pp. 78–79.
Cortada, James W., *Historical Dictionary of Data Processing: Biographies,* Greenwood Press, 1987, pp. 240–242.
Ritchie, David, *The Computer Pioneers: The Making of the Modern Computer,* Simon & Schuster, 1986, pp. 33–52.

Periodicals

Loveday, Evelyn, "George Stibitz and the Bell Labs Relay Computer," *Datamation,* September, 1977, pp. 80–83.

—*Sketch by David E. Newton*

Alfred Stock
1876-1946
German chemist

Alfred Stock was an experimentalist who made significant contributions to chemistry and designed several important chemical instruments. He worked on the creation of new boron and silicon compounds and the development of the chemical high-vacuum apparatus, which allowed him to work with volatile materials. The latter part of his life was particularly devoted to the study of mercury and mercury poisoning and, in particular, developing precautionary guidelines for other scientists to follow in order to avoid suffering from it. Stock contracted mercury poisoning while working with the substance in laboratories since his time in school; he was afflicted with the disease the rest of his life.

Stock was born in Danzig, West Prussia (now Gdansk, Poland) on July 16, 1876. His father was a banking executive. As a schoolboy, Stock developed an early interest in science, and he earned scholarships that allowed him to pursue a degree in chemistry at the University of Berlin in 1894. He chose to work at the chemical institute at the university, directed by **Emil Fischer**, but had to wait a year for space in the lab, which was overcrowded. He finally began his doctoral research in 1895 under the auspices of organic chemist Oscar Piloty. During his summer breaks from school, Stock worked in the private laboratory of the Dutch physical chemist Jacobus van't Hoff. It was there that Stock performed his first significant research in the areas of magnesium and oceanic salt deposits. After graduating magna cum laude in 1899, he spent a year in Paris assisting the chemist **Henri Moissan** at the Ecole superieure de Pharmacie, with support of the Prussian Ministry of Culture. At Moissan's lab he first investigated compounds of silicon and boron, which were to occupy him throughout his career.

Stock began his professional career in 1900 by working for nine years as a lab assistant with Fischer at the University of Berlin. There he investigated the preparation and characterization of such elements as phosphorus, arsenic, and antimony (a brittle, white metallic element). One result of Stock's investigation was that he could clearly explain their reactions with hydrogen, sulfur and nitrogen. He also identified an unstable yellow form of antimony, and two new compounds of phosphorus: a polymeric hydride, which is a compound including hydrogen and another element or group, and a nitride, which is a compound including nitrogen and one other element. Stock's research clarified misconceptions in scientific literature and established the existence of three of today's four well-established phosphorus sulfides, which are organic compounds of phosphorous and sulfur.

Unfortunately, it was also during these early years in Berlin that symptoms associated with Stock's mercury poisoning would begin surfacing. Headaches, dizziness and upper respiratory infections started plaguing Stock while he was pioneering his work with a device known as the vapor-tension thermometer. His success with the apparatus became well known throughout Germany and he later developed it into his tension-thermometer. Many years later, the work with the tension-thermometer was traced as the first of many sources of mercury poisoning to which Stock was exposed during the course of his life.

Develops Pump for Working with Volatile Substances

In July 1909, Stock was named full professor and director of the new Inorganic Chemistry Institute at Breslau. It was here that he surpassed previous chemists' successes with his imaginative work with hydrocarbons, inorganic carbon compounds and the development of a high-vacuum apparatus that allowed Stock to work with volatile and gaseous materials. The apparatus was later referred to as the Stock high-vacuum pump. He also envisioned at this time the possibility of developing the equivalent of organic chemistry's carbon-based system around boron, an element whose unanticipated potential he was just beginning to discover. His work with borohydrides, however, was interrupted with the outbreak of World War I. Stock was then charged with studying carbon subsulfide, an irritant, to determine its effectiveness as a war gas. The gas was never used, however, due to problems with polymerization, which is a chemical reaction in which molecules combine to form larger molecules that contain repeating structural units.

Stock left Breslau in April 1916 to continue his research and take charge of **Richard Willstätter**'s laboratory at the Kaiser Wilhelm Institute near Berlin. It was not long, however, before the military moved in and took over the institute. Since his still undiagnosed physical problems (including, by that time, an acute loss of hearing) kept him from serving in the military, he and his staff moved their equipment to the University of Berlin so that they could continue their work. When the war ended, he returned to the Kaiser Wilhelm Institute and continued to study silicon and boron hydrides. His work yielded a number of halogen and alkyl derivatives which, in turn, led to the discovery of new compounds such as silyl amines and silicones. In the process, Stock developed a chemistry based on silicon; this was similar to his work with boron at Breslau. At the suggestion of Hans Goldschmidt, Stock also collaborated on the production of metallic beryllium. This substance had become a worthwhile element to pursue because it is a metal which had possible applications in industry, so a beryllium study group was formed. By 1940, their new technique for making the material yielded enough beryllium to significantly reduce the market value per kilogram, thus increasing the element's cost-effectiveness in scientific experiments.

Investigates Mercury Poisoning

Stock's unexplained medical problems kept growing worse. Besides headaches, vertigo, respiratory infections, and deafness, he now also suffered frequent numbness. None of these symptoms was alleviated by medical treatment. In 1923, he suffered virtually total hearing and memory loss, and he almost didn't make it through the winter of 1924. At that time, many scientists in addition to Stock were unknowingly being exposed to mercury poisoning. It wasn't until after he saw similar symptoms in a colleague that Stock finally realized the volatility of this odorless substance. He began researching mercury poisoning, often experimenting on himself. As a result of his investigations, Stock published several articles outlining the dangers of mercury and offered up numerous precautionary guidelines for working with the substance.

It was a difficult decision, but the opportunity to establish a new mercury-free laboratory convinced Stock to leave the Kaiser Wilhelm Institute in 1926 to become the director of the Chemical Institute at Karlsruhe. The next ten years of his life were devoted exclusively to the study of mercury poisoning and borohydrides. His concepts and working models of laboratory rooms equipped with extensive safety precautions were sought after by scientists from around the world. Further experiments proved that inhaled mercury vapor was much more dangerous than ingested mercury because the vapor, entering through the nose, moved more quickly into the pituitary gland, where it wreaked havoc on the body. Stock also pioneered a teaching method during his tenure at Karlsruhe which used reflected light to project chemical objects on a large screen. Stock worked with his lecture assistant, Hans Ramser, and with Carl Zeiss-Jena to create this apparatus, which was called an epidiascope.

Stock married Clara Venzky in August of 1906 and later had two daughters. He was the president of the Verein Deutscher Chemiker (Association of German Chemists) in Paris in 1927 and later the Deutsche Chemische Gesellschaft (German Chemical Society) from 1936 to 1938. He was a guest professor at Cornell University for several months in 1932 under the George Fisher Baker Nonresident Lectureship in Chemistry. The last ten years of Stock's life were nearly unbearable, both physically and professionally. His mercury poisoning became debilitating and interfered with his work. His political differences with the Nazi government were increasing. In 1936, at the age of 60, he asked for his retirement. He returned with his family to Berlin where he continued to trace and validate the chemical path of mercury poisoning. By 1940, movement became difficult as he developed hardening of the muscles. Stock relinquished his laboratories in 1943 because they were needed for the war effort, and he and his wife moved to Bad Warmbrunn in Silesia to live with his brother-in-law. As the Russians were approaching in 1945, Stock and his wife again moved and sought shelter with an old friend, Ernst Kuss, in Dessau. The Stocks finally found refuge in a barracks in Aken, a small city on the

Elbe. Stock died in the early morning of August 12, 1946.

SELECTED WRITINGS BY STOCK:

Books

Hydrides of Boron and Silicon, Cornell University Press, 1957.
The Structure of Atoms, Dutton, 1923.

SOURCES:

Books

Farber, Eduard, *Great Chemists,* Interscience Publishers, 1961.

—*Sketch by Amy M. Punke*

Alice M. Stoll
1917-
American biophysicist

A scientist who worked in the field of medical biophysics, Alice M. Stoll conducted research into the effects of heat and acceleration on the human body, and the rate that heat is given off by burning materials. Her investigations, which permitted evaluation of the thermal protection offered by fire resistant and fire retardant fabrics, led to the development of new fabrics for use in fire hazard protection. Among the honors accorded to Stoll in recognition for her scientific work was the 1969 Society of Women Engineers' Achievement Award.

Stoll, a native of New York City, was born on August 25, 1917. She obtained her undergraduate education at Hunter College, earning a B.A. degree in 1938. Joining the New York Hospital and Medical College at Cornell University, she worked as an assistant in the areas of metabolism, allergies, and spectroscopy. In 1943 Stoll joined the U.S. Navy, remaining in active duty until 1946, then returned to Cornell University where she began research into temperature regulation. She completed a dual M.S. degree in physiology and biophysics in 1948. Remaining at the Medical College until 1953, Stoll worked as a research associate in the area of environmental thermal radiation and as an instructor in the school of nursing. To conduct her research, Stoll had to develop the instrumentation necessary for her work. The instruments she developed—and for which she received patents—measure the heat transferred to the surroundings from flames and other thermal radiation sources. At this time, Stoll also worked as a consultant for various laboratories, including the Arctic Aerospace Medicine Lab at Ladd Air Force Base in Alaska during 1952 and 1953. Part of her time was also spent on her duties with the Naval Reserve, which she had joined upon completion of her active duty.

Leaving Cornell in 1953, Stoll joined the Naval Air Development Center (NADC) in Warminster, Pennsylvania, as a physiologist in the medical research department. Advancing to special technical assistant in 1956, she became head of the Thermal Laboratory in 1960, and then chief of the Biophysics & Bioastronautics Division in 1964. Stoll retired from the Naval Reserve in 1966 with the rank of commander, but remained at NADC where she was promoted to head of the Biophysics Laboratory in 1970, a position she held until her retirement in 1980.

Stoll conducted research at NADC into the effects of acceleration on the cardiovascular system. Most of her work, however, centered on the transfer of heat from flames and other thermal radiation sources and how this heat transfer affected the human body. Stoll's studies on tissue damage and pain sensation established a relationship between the amount of heat absorbed and the damage which resulted; she established that the source of the heat was not important, as all heat sources could cause the same damage. Models that Stoll designed based on this research were valuable in determining the amount of thermal protection needed to protect the body from different heat sources.

Stoll also investigated the heat transfer properties of various fabrics which could be used to provide thermal protection. Clothing, however, acts not only to protect the skin from heat but can also be a source of heat if it catches on fire; an accidental burning of a test participant during simulated space capsule clothing fires at NADC prompted Stoll to study the burning properties of fabrics under high oxygen concentrations—conditions which could be found in the aerospace environment. This research resulted in the development of methods for measuring the burn protection provided by clothing and fabrics, as well as the invention of "Nomex" (produced by DuPont), a fire-resistant fabric which is now widely used in apparel for fire fighters and race car drivers.

In addition to being recognized by the Society of Women Engineers, Stoll was honored in 1965 with the Federal Civil Service Award and the Paul Bert Award from the Aerospace Medical Association in 1972. A charter member of the Biophysical Society, she has been elected a fellow of the American Association for the Advancement of Science. Stoll has remained active in the American Society of Mechanical Engineers, particularly in the heat transfer and biotechnology sections.

SELECTED WRITINGS BY STOLL:

Periodicals

(With Leon C. Greene) "Relationship Between Pain and Tissue Damage due to Thermal Radiation," *Journal of Applied Physiology,* Volume 14, 1959, pp. 373–382.

(With Maria A. Chianta and L. R. Munroe) "Flame Contact Studies," *Journal of Heat Transfer,* Volume 86, 1964, pp. 449–456.

(With John A. Weaver) "Mathematical Model of Skin Exposed to Thermal Radiation," *Aerospace Medicine,* Volume 40, 1969, pp. 24–30.

(With Chianta) "Method and Rating System for Evaluation of Thermal Protection," *Aerospace Medicine,* Volume 40, 1969, pp. 1232–1237.

(With Chianta) "Thermal Analysis of Combustion of Fabric in Oxygen-Enriched Atmospheres," *Journal of Fire & Flammability,* Volume 4, 1973, pp. 309–324.

(With Munroe and others) "Facility and a Method for Evaluation of Thermal Protection," *Aviation, Space, and Environmental Medicine,* November 1976, pp. 1177–1181.

SOURCES:

Books

American Men & Women of Science, 14th Edition, R. R. Bowker, 1979, p. 4928.
Engineers of Distinction, 2nd Edition, Engineers Joint Council 1973, p. 297.
O'Neill, Lois Decker, editor, *The Woman's Book of World Records and Achievements,* Anchor Press/Doubleday, 1979, pp. 187–188.

Other

Stoll, Alice M., correspondence with Jerome Ferrance, January, 1994.

—*Sketch by Jerome P. Ferrance*

Henry Stommel
1920-
American oceanographer

Oceanographer Henry Stommel considered careers variously in ministry, law, chemistry, and astronomy, before settling on the field of oceanography. He is a pioneer in the theory of ocean currents, a field largely untouched when he began his career in 1944. His foremost achievement is the development of his Gulf Stream theory in 1947. Stommel was awarded the National Medal of Science for his contributions to oceanography in 1989.

Born September 27, 1920, in Wilmington, Delaware, Stommel first studied mathematics at Yale University, from which he received his B.S. degree in 1942. He remained at Yale as an instructor for two years, but in 1944 Stommel met Columbus Iselin, the director of the Woods Hole Oceanographic Institution, who offered him a position as research associate at Woods Hole. Stommel accepted the offer and stayed with the institution until 1959.

Develops Landmark Gulf Stream Theory

Stommel built his niche in oceanography after observing the near-complete absence of theory in the study of ocean currents. He applied relatively simple mathematical models to the study of the ocean, and devised the landmark theory of the Gulf Stream. The Gulf Stream is an ocean current that runs north along the eastern coast of the United States and Canada and then crosses the Atlantic to northern Europe. Before Stommel did his ground-breaking research, this current was considered a river of warm water that gave northern Europe its temperate climate. Stommel was able to determine that the Gulf Stream in fact forms the boundary between the cold northern waters and the warm, currentless Sargasso Sea at the center of the North Atlantic. An increase in the volume of the Gulf Stream would probably result in a drop in temperature in northern Europe.

The techniques Stommel pioneered in creating this model also proved to be applicable to other ocean currents. It had always been assumed that ocean currents are surface phenomena, but Stommel discovered that there are patterns of motion all the way down to the ocean floors. Comparing deep currents to patterns of air circulation in the atmosphere, he found that the rotation of the earth creates similar systems of currents in the earth's oceans. The Gulf Stream itself is fed by waters flowing west along the equator, propelled by the motion of the earth. The effects of the earth's rotation are known as Coriolis forces. Stommel's joint research with scientist Friedrich

Schott also established a correlation between density and velocity in ocean currents. A comprehensive account of Stommel's work on the Gulf Stream and on ocean currents in general appeared in 1965 in the book *The Gulf Stream.*

Participates in Ocean Study Programs

Stommel recognized that the Gulf Stream wanders about, and this fact led him to instigate numerous programs to gather data on the variability of ocean currents. One of these programs was the Bermuda Biweekly Hydrographic Station PANULIRUS, which he began in 1954. In 1959 Stommel left Woods Hole to take a position at the Massachusetts Institute of Technology as a professor of oceanography. The following year he moved to Harvard University and also cofounded the ARIES deep-float experiment with oceanographers John C. Swallow and James Crease. The ARIES experiment was the first systematic attempt to measure deep currents with a float newly designed by Swallow.

After three years at Harvard, Stommel returned to MIT, where he remained until 1978. In those years, he headed the MEDOC study in the Mediterranean, to gather information about deep-water formation with the scientists Henri Lacombe and Paul Tchernia. With the oceanographer Allan Robinson, Stommel began the Mid-Ocean Dynamics Experiment, which ran from 1970 to 1978, and the Seychelles Study of Equatorial Currents in the Indian Ocean, carried out with Ants Leetmaain 1975 and 1976. In 1978 Stommel returned to Woods Hole and continued his research there.

In 1987, Stommel published a book for lay readers, *A View of the Sea,* which discusses his own research into ocean circulation, focusing specifically on the upper ocean. The complex theory of ocean circulation is made simple in the book, which is set up as a dialogue between the chief engineer and an oceanographer on a research vessel. Stommel speaks to the lay reader through anecdotes, told by the fictional oceanographer, discussing Coriolis forces, density field measurements, wind-driven models, gravity and the earth's rotation. A review in *Science* describes *A View of the Sea* as "a highly successful attempt to explain important aspects of the ocean circulation to a wide audience."

Stommel has not limited himself to ocean currents, although they undoubtedly form the central focus of his life's work. Additional work carried out by Stommel includes research on cumulus clouds; a study of the diurnal thermocline (a stratum of water separating warm upper layers heated by the sun and lower, colder layers, where temperature does not vary); and a study of the distribution of phytoplankton in the oceans. Following a lifetime of innovative research in the field of oceanography, and specifically,

the theory of ocean water circulation, Henry Stommel was elected to the National Academy of Sciences in 1962 and to the former Soviet Union's Academy of Sciences in 1977. He expressed gratitude for his career in oceanography and the opportunities it gave him to explore the seas and the boundaries of his own thinking. Stommel was again honored in 1989, when he received the National Medal of Science.

SELECTED WRITINGS BY STOMMEL:

Books

The Gulf Stream, California University Press, 1965.
A View of the Sea, Princeton University Press, 1987.

SOURCES:

Books

Behrman, Daniel, *The New World of the Oceans: Men and Oceanography,* Little, Brown, 1969.

Periodicals

Hide, Raymond, review of *A View of the Sea, Science,* October, 1987.

—*Sketch by Karen Withem*

Fredrik Størmer
1874-1957
Norwegian mathematician and geophysicist

Fredrik Størmer contributed both important photographic observations and mathematical data to the understanding of the polar aurora, of stratospheric and mesospheric clouds, and of the structure of the ionosphere. Besides his many honorary academic memberships in Europe, he was elected a foreign member of the Royal Society of London in 1951.

Fredrik Carl Mülertz Størmer was born at Skien, Norway, on September 3, 1874, to Georg Størmer and Elisabeth Mülertz. The Størmer family moved to Christiania (now Oslo) while he was still a boy. Størmer's ability to excel in mathematics was already apparent in high school, and further encouragement came from a family friend, a professor of mathematics at the University of Christiania in Oslo. In 1892 Størmer published his first mathematical paper while still in secondary school; later that year he enrolled at the university, receiving his master's degree in 1898 and his doctorate in 1903. As soon as he finished his studies, he was appointed professor of pure mathematics at the university and made the acquaintance of the Norwegian physicist Olaf Kristian Birkeland, whose research centered on the earth's magnetic field.

Although Størmer had already begun to publish mature and important mathematical papers (on number and function theory, and on the nontrivial determination of trigonometric function solutions), he became thoroughly intrigued with Birkeland's momentous first laboratory demonstration of the aurora phenomenon. An aurora is the light emitted by energetic protons and electrons at the top of the Earth's atmosphere when they come in contact with solar wind particles; this phenomenon occurs regularly at both the North and South poles. In 1896 Birkeland had succeeded in simulating auroral light by bombarding a magnetized sphere with cathode ray electrons in a vacuum; French theoretical physicist Paul Villard—whose research centered on cathode ray electrons, X rays, and radioactivity—also performed this simulation in 1906. Størmer recalled in his book *The Polar Aurora* that Villard "made some very fine experiments" and "succeeded in producing threadlike currents of cathode rays, which made it possible to follow the trajectories in detail." Those trajectories were immediately significant, for the electrons collided with the sphere only at the top and bottom—analogous to the polar zones of the earth—and observation had long shown that the aurora was a high-latitude phenomenon.

Creates an Upper Atmospheric Photographic Archive

The approximate physical extent of the aurora phenomenon had already been studied for almost two hundred years beginning in 1726, when it was realized to occur at much greater altitudes than had been thought before. Størmer sought to determine the exact altitude of the aurora, as well as to derive the mathematical formulas governing the phenomenon through close observation. With the advent of photography, the possibility of more accurate altitude determination was recognized. Though the earliest photographs, made by Danish meteorologist Sophus Tromholt in 1885, did not in fact demonstrate greater accuracy, Størmer considered the photographic method essential and invaluable to the recording of auroral observations and the evaluation of his theoretical conclusions.

Possessed of an independent experimental disposition, Størmer constructed, among other instruments, a photographic apparatus by which he could take photos of actual auroral displays. Beginning in 1909, he used two cameras at different locations to take simultaneous photographs of the aurora, with the shutters of each camera synchronized by a telephone link; by comparing the parallax, or shift, of the images in the two photographs, Størmer could estimate the aurora's distance from the cameras.

Over forty years, Størmer collected a prodigious file of photographs and compiled them into a library of observational analysis, yielding data on altitudes, extent, shape, and periodicity of the polar aurora. This library was enriched by the first collection of photographs of rare noctilucent clouds (more formally known as polar stratospheric clouds, or PSCs) and the higher mesospheric nacreous, or mother-of-pearl, clouds (polar mesospheric clouds, or PMCs). These photographic observations were so significant that Størmer set up a network of observational stations to collect auroral and higher atmospheric cloud data.

Develops the Mathematics of the Auroras

Alongside his photographic efforts, Størmer developed a mathematical theory of the directional dynamics of the auroral phenomenon as it was observed in simulation experiments. He started with French mathematician **Jules Henri Poincaré**'s equations of motion for electrically charged particles influenced by a single magnetic pole, and then proceeded to the magnetic dipole—the actual case for the Earth.

Størmer's work on the mathematical theory continued from 1904 to 1950 and resulted in a configuration of the trajectories of charged particles in a magnetic dipole, rather than a cloud of particles. In order to process this information, the series of differential equations that he had derived had to be numerically integrated. With no high-speed computers to aid him, Størmer called upon a volunteer staff of his students to take on the arduous task of calculation. With their help, Størmer concluded that the electrical particles traced out only certain trajectories, which were distributed in a cone shape (known as Størmer's Cone); all other trajectories were labeled "forbidden directions." Størmer demonstrated that the particular directions traced out by particles allowed them to be bent around the earth and into the earth's dark side, which explains the nighttime occurrence of the aurora.

His further research into electron behavior in the upper atmosphere prompted the hypotheses that there is a circular electric current in the equatorial plane of the earth and that electrons might become trapped in oscillatory trajectories in the Earth's magnetic field. In the 1930s, the latitudinal variation in cosmic radiation was discovered and was found to conform to Størmer's calculations of it; furthermore, the discovery of the Van Allen Radiation Belts by **James**

Van Allen confirmed with surprising accuracy Størmer's theoretical analysis of solar charged particle trajectories in the Earth's magnetic field.

Størmer taught for forty-one years, and both his research and his teaching cast a long shadow in the foundations of the geophysics of aeronomy and of the magnetic field of the Earth. Størmer also had a great gift for communicating the abstractions of his science to the public in general articles, and most of his written work appeared in the Norwegian academic services publication *Norske Videnskabsakademiets Skrifter.* He died of heart failure in Oslo on August 13, 1957.

SELECTED WRITINGS BY STØRMER:

Books

Fra verdensrummets dybder til atomenes indre, [Oslo], 1923.
The Polar Aurora, Oxford University Press, 1955.

SOURCES:

Books

Petrie, William, *Keoeeit—The Story of the Aurora Borealis,* Pergamon Press, 1963, pp. 48–50, 122–123.

—*Sketch by William J. McPeak*

Fritz Strassmann
1902-1980

German chemist

Fritz Strassmann's experiments with the bombardment of neutrons on uranium atoms resulted in the discovery of nuclear fission, which has been employed in making the world's first atomic bomb and nuclear energy. He also developed a widely-used geological dating method employing radiation techniques, and served as a well-respected teacher of nuclear chemistry.

Friedrich Wilhelm Strassmann, the youngest of nine children, was born on February 22, 1902, in Boppard, Germany, to Richard Strassmann, a court clerk, and Julie Bernsmann. Strassmann attended primary schools in Cologne and Düsseldorf and secondary school at the Düsseldorf Oberrealschule. During this time, he became interested in chemistry. However, the death of his father in 1920 and the desperate economic conditions of post-World War I Germany made it impossible to enroll at a university. Instead, he entered the Technical Institute at Hanover, where he supported himself as a private tutor.

In 1924 Strassmann was awarded his diplomate (comparable to a master's degree) in chemistry at Hanover. He then stayed on to pursue a doctoral program in physical chemistry under Hermann Braune. Strassmann completed that program in 1929 and was awarded his Ph.D. for a thesis on the solubility of iodine in carbon dioxide. In the *Dictionary of Scientific Biography* it is noted that Strassmann's choice of physical chemistry as a major was largely due to the increased likelihood of finding employment in that field during a tight labor market.

Strassmann Begins Collaboration with Otto Hahn

Shortly after receiving his Ph.D., Strassmann was offered a scholarship to the Kaiser Wilhelm Institute for Chemistry in Berlin by its director, **Otto Hahn**. That scholarship was renewed twice and then, in 1932, Strassmann was invited to continue his work at the institute with Hahn, first at no salary and later at a minimal wage.

The 1930s were a difficult time for Strassmann, partly because of his restrictive financial situation and partly because of his views regarding the policies of Adolf Hitler's new regime. Although he was not in any immediate personal or professional danger, Strassmann decided to refuse all offers of employment that would have required his joining the Nazi party. He continued his work, therefore, with Hahn and later, **Lise Meitner** at the Kaiser Wilhelm Institute.

The subject on which Strassmann, Hahn, and Meitner were working during the mid–1930s was the bombardment of uranium by neutrons. The great Italian physicist **Enrico Fermi** had found that the bombardment of an element by neutrons often results in the formation of a new element one place higher in the periodic table. Fermi had successfully applied this technique to a number of elements during the early 1930s.

The one example that most intrigued Fermi—and other scientists familiar with his work—was the bombardment of uranium. Should earlier patterns hold, they realized, such a reaction would result in the formation of an element one place higher than uranium (number 92) in the periodic table, that is, element 93. Since no such element was known to exist naturally, a successful experiment of this design would result in the first artificially produced element.

Strassmann, Hahn, and Meitner Discover Nuclear Fission

Unfortunately, the uranium bombardment yielded results that were not easily interpreted. Original indications seemed to be that the products of the reaction were largely elements close to uranium in the periodic table, thorium, radium, and actinium, for example. Such results would not have been surprising since all nuclear reactions known up to that time involved changes in atomic number between reactants and products of no more than one or two places.

More detailed studies by Strassmann yielded troubling results, however. His chemical analysis consistently showed the presence of barium, whose atomic number is 36 less than that of uranium. The formation of barium seemed so unlikely to Strassmann and Hahn that their reports of their work were hedged with doubts and qualifications. In fact, it was not until Lise Meitner, then a refugee in Sweden, received word of the Hahn-Strassmann experiment that the puzzle was solved. With a fearlessness that Strassmann and Hahn had lacked, Meitner stated forthrightly that barium *had* been formed and that this change had occurred as a result of the splitting apart of the uranium nucleus.

The significance of this discovery can hardly be overestimated. Within a decade, it had been put to use in the development of the world's first atomic bombs and, shortly thereafter, was being touted as one of humankind's great new sources of power for peacetime applications. For his part in this historic event, Strassmann was awarded the 1966 Enrico Fermi Prize of the U.S. Atomic Energy Commission.

A second line of research in which Strassmann's analytical skills resulted in an important discovery was that of geological dating. Beginning in 1934, he and Ernst Walling studied the radioactive decay of rubidium, a process that results in the formation of strontium. Strassmann's careful analysis of the characteristics of this process eventually led to its use in the dating of geological strata, a process that has become a standard tool in geology.

Strassmann remained at the Kaiser Wilhelm Institute during the war, first in Berlin and later in Tailfingen, where the institute was moved to avoid destruction by bombing. After the war, he was appointed professor of inorganic and nuclear chemistry at the University of Mainz. At Mainz he became involved in complex negotiations over the construction of two new institutes. One was a new physical facility for the Max Planck Institute of Chemistry, successor to the former Kaiser Wilhelm Institute in Berlin. The second was a new Institute for Nuclear Chemistry, designed as part of the newly reestablished University of Mainz. Although beset by all manner of political, technical, and economic problems, Strassmann made major contributions to the establishment of both institutions. In addition, he saw through to completion the construction of the TRIGA Mark II nuclear reactor in Mainz.

Strassmann died in Mainz on April 22, 1980. He was remembered not only for his discoveries in nuclear fission and geological dating and for his skills as an administrator of scientific research, but also for his qualities as a teacher. His achievements were recognized in 1969 when the Society of German Chemists established the Fritz Strassmann award, to be given to an outstanding young nuclear chemist each year. Strassmann was married twice, the first time on July 20, 1937, to Maria Heckter, a former pupil. The couple had one son, Martin. Three years after Maria's death in 1956, Strassmann was married a second time, to Irmgard Hartmann, a good friend of his first wife.

SELECTED WRITINGS BY STRASSMANN:

Periodicals

(With E. Walling) "Die Abscheidung des Reinen Strontium-Isotops 87 aus einem Alten Rubidium Haltigen Lepidolith und die Halbwertszeit des Rubidiums," *Berichte der Deutschen Chemischen Gesselschaft,* Volume 71B, 1938, pp. 1–9.
(With O. Hahn) "Über den Nachweis und das Verhalten der bei der Bestrahlung des Urans Mittels Neutronen Entstehenden Erdalkalimetallie," *Die Naturwissenschaften,* Volume 27, 1939, pp. 89–95.

SOURCES:

Books

Dictionary of Scientific Biography, Volume 18, Scribners, 1976, pp. 880–887.
McGraw-Hill Modern Men of Science, Volume 2, McGraw-Hill, 1984, p. 527.

Periodicals

Graetzer, Hans G., "Discovery of Nuclear Fission," *American Journal of Physics,* January, 1964, pp. 9–15.
Sparberg, Esther B., "A Study of the Discovery of Fission," *American Journal of Physics,* January, 1964, pp. 2–8.

—Sketch by David E. Newton

William Levi Straus, Jr.
1900-1981

American anatomist and physical anthropologist

William Levi Straus, Jr. was a major figure in the science of physical anthropology through most of the middle decades of the twentieth century. He began his academic career as an instructor of anatomy and became increasingly interested in the comparative anatomy of the primates. At first he concentrated entirely on living members of that order, but he eventually expanded his research to include fossil primates. For many years Straus was an outspoken advocate of the theory that humans are derived not from humanoid apes, but from some earlier ancestor common to both humans and apes.

Straus was born on October 29, 1900, in Baltimore, Maryland. His parents were William Levi Straus and the former Pauline Gutman. Straus attended public schools in Baltimore and entered Harvard University in 1917. He remained at Harvard for only one year, however, before returning to Baltimore and enrolling at Johns Hopkins University. He earned his bachelor of arts degree in 1920 and his Ph.D. in 1926, both from Johns Hopkins in the field of zoology.

Begins a Long Association with Johns Hopkins

A National Research Council fellowship enabled Straus to spend a postdoctoral year at Western Reserve University (now Case Western Reserve) in Cleveland. There he studied comparative anatomy of the pelvis with T. Wingate Todd before returning to Johns Hopkins to become an instructor of anatomy at the university's medical school. After being promoted to associate professor, Straus left the medical school in 1952 to become professor of physical anthropology in the university. Five years later he returned to the medical school and was given a joint appointment as professor of anatomy and physical anthropology. Upon his retirement in 1966, Straus was made professor emeritus.

Straus was "not much of a traveler," according to his biographer T. D. Stewart in the *American Journal of Physical Anthropology.* He spent a year working with H. H. Woollard and D. H. Barron in London in 1937–38 on a Guggenheim fellowship and a brief period in 1950 as visiting professor of anatomy at Wayne University in Detroit, Michigan. But otherwise he stayed close to the Johns Hopkins campus in Baltimore.

Proposes Theory of Human Origins

Straus is noted for his extensive research on the comparative anatomy of the primates. His studies covered nearly every aspect of the primate body, including the skeleton, muscular system, internal organs, skin, fingers and toes, teeth, and skull. By 1949 Straus had come to the conclusion that humans are less complex and less advanced than are many of their primate cousins.

This notion conflicted with the accepted theory of the day that stated that humans had evolved from and were more advanced than members of the ape family. Straus argued, conversely, that humans, apes, and other primates had all evolved from some earlier common ancestor. As the science of paleoanthropology (the study of the fossilized remains of hominids) developed, increasing evidence for Straus's theory accumulated. By the mid–1950s, he had become convinced that the fossil evidence confirmed his view that Homo sapiens had never passed through a brachiating ("swinging through the trees") phase as did their cousins, the apes.

In addition to his own research career, Straus was active in a variety of professional organizations. He was a founding member of the American Association of Physical Anthropologists, of which he was president from 1953 to 1955. He also served on the editorial board of five journals, the *American Journal of Anatomy* (1946–58), *Human Biology* (1953–81), *Science* and *Scientific Monthly* (1953–64), and *Folia Primatologia* (1961–81).

Straus was married twice, the first time on September 19, 1926, to Henrietta S. Hecht. The couple had one daughter, Pauline. After his first wife's death in 1954, Straus married Bertha L. Nusbaum, on June 15, 1955. Straus was awarded the Viking Fund Medal and Award in physical anthropology of the Wenner-Gren Foundation in 1952. He was elected to the National Academy of Sciences in 1962. Straus died at his home in Baltimore on January 28, 1981.

SELECTED WRITINGS BY STRAUS:

Books

(Editor with C. G. Hartman) *Anatomy of the Rhesus Monkey,* Williams and Wilkins, 1933.

(Contributor) A. L. Kroeber, editor, *Anthropology Today: An Encyclopedic Inventory,* University of Chicago Press, 1952, pp. 77–92.

(Contributor) S. L. Washburn, editor, *Forerunners of Darwin, 1754–1859,* Johns Hopkins Press, 1959.

"The Classification of *Oreopithecus,* " S. L. Washburn, editor, *Classification and Human Evolution,* Viking Fund Publications in Anthropology, 1963, pp. 146–177.

Periodicals

"The Riddle of Man's Ancestry," *Quarterly Review of Biology,* Volume 24, 1949, pp. 200–223.

SOURCES:

Periodicals

Stewart, T. D., "William Levi Straus, Jr., 1900–1981," *American Journal of Physical Anthropology,* December, 1982, pp. 359–360.

—*Sketch by David E. Newton*

John William Strutt
1842-1919
English physicist

In 1873 John William Strutt's father, the second Baron Rayleigh, died and Strutt succeeded to that title. He is, therefore, almost universally referred to in the scientific literature as Lord Rayleigh. While the majority of his work dealt with sound and optics, Rayleigh may be most familiar to the layperson as the discover of the rare gas argon. For this accomplishment he was awarded the 1904 Nobel Prize in physics. Rayleigh served for a period of five years as director of the Cavendish Laboratory at Cambridge University. With that exception, he spent nearly all of his adult life at his home in Terling Place where he constructed a well-equipped scientific laboratory. There he carried out experiments on a remarkable variety of subjects that led to the publication of some 450 papers.

John William Strutt was born at Langford Grove, near Maldon, in Essex, on November 12, 1842. He was the eldest son of John James Strutt, second Baron Rayleigh, and the former Clara Elizabeth Vicars. Strutt's health as a child was not very good, and he was unable to remain at school for very long. He attended Eton and Harrow for about one term each and spent three years at a private school in Wimbledon. Finally, in 1857, his education was entrusted to a private tutor, the Reverend George Townsend Warner, with whom he stayed for four years.

In 1861 Strutt entered Trinity College, Cambridge, where he studied mathematics under the famous teacher E. J. Routh. During his four years at Trinity, Strutt went from being a student of only adequate skills to one who captured major prizes at graduation. One examiner is reported to have said that Strutt's answers were better than those found in books.

Following graduation, Strutt was elected a fellow of Trinity College, a position he held until 1871. In 1868 he took off on the extended "Grand Tour" vacation traditional among upper class Englishmen, except that he chose to visit the post-Civil War United States rather than the continent of Europe. In 1871, at the conclusion of his tenure at Trinity, Strutt was married to Evelyn Balfour, sister of Arthur James Balfour, later to be prime minister of Great Britain in 1902. The Strutts had three sons, Robert John, Arthur Charles, and Julian.

Within a few months of his marriage, Strutt became seriously ill with a bout of rheumatic fever. As his health returned, he decided to make a recuperative visit to Egypt and Greece with his young bride. It was on a trip down the Nile during this vacation that he began the scientific work that was to occupy his attention for most of the rest of his life, a massive work on *The Theory of Sound.*

Succeeds His Father as Lord Rayleigh

Shortly after the Strutts returned to England in the spring of 1873, his father died and Strutt succeeded to the hereditary title of Baron Rayleigh. He also took up residence in the family mansion at Terling Place, Witham, where he was to live for most of the rest of his life. He soon constructed a modest, but well-equipped, laboratory in which he was to carry out experiments for the next forty years. At first he divided his time between the laboratory and the many chores associated with the maintenance of the Rayleigh estate. Gradually he spent less time on the latter, and after 1876 he left the management of his properties to his younger brother Edward.

Rayleigh always seemed to be a man of unlimited interests. The two fields to which he devoted the greatest amount of time, however, were sound and optics. In 1871, for example, he derived a formula expressing the relationship between the wavelength of light and the scattering of that light produced by small particles, a relationship now known as Rayleigh scattering. One of his first projects in his new Terling laboratory was a study of diffraction gratings and their use in spectroscopes (instruments with which scientists may study the electromagnetic spectrum). Rayleigh appeared to be totally satisfied with his life and work at Terling Place. Then, in 1879, James Clerk Maxwell, the first Cavendish Professor of Experimental Physics at Cambridge, died. The post was offered first to Sir William Thomson, who declined, and then to Lord Rayleigh. With considerable reluctance, he accepted the appointment with the understanding that he would remain for only a limited period of time. During his tenure at Cambridge, Rayleigh made a number of changes that placed the young Cavendish Laboratory on a firm footing and prepared it for the period of unmatched excellence that was to follow in succeeding decades. The most important experimental work carried out under his auspices was a reevaluation of three electrical standards, the volt, ampere, and ohm. This work was so carefully done that its results remained valid until relatively recently.

In 1884 Rayleigh resigned his post at Cambridge and returned to his work at Terling Place. Over the next decade he took on an even more diverse set of topics, including studies of electromagnetism, mechanics, capillarity, and thermodynamics. One of his major accomplishments during this period was the development of a law describing radiation from a black body, a law later known as the Rayleigh-Jeans law.

Research Leads to the Discovery of Argon

At the end of the 1880s, Rayleigh began work on the problem for which he is perhaps best known, his discovery of the inert gas argon. That work originated as a by-product of Rayleigh's interest in Prout's hypothesis. In 1815 the English chemist William Prout had argued that all elements are made of some combination of hydrogen atoms. An obvious test of this hypothesis is to find out if the atomic weights of the elements are exact multiples of the atomic weight of hydrogen.

By 1890 most scientists were convinced that Prout's hypothesis was not valid. Still, Rayleigh was interested in examining the problem one more time. In so doing, he made an unexpected discovery, namely that the atomic weight of nitrogen varied significantly depending on the source from which it was obtained. The clue that Rayleigh needed to solve this puzzle was a report that had been written by the English chemist Henry Cavendish in 1795. Cavendish had found that whenever he removed oxygen and nitrogen from a sample of air, there always remained a small bubble of some unknown gas.

To Rayleigh, Cavendish's results suggested a reason for his own discovery that the atomic weight of nitrogen depends on the source from which it comes. Nitrogen taken from air, he said, may include a small amount of the unknown gas that Cavendish had described, while nitrogen obtained from ammonia would not include that gas. Still, Rayleigh was not entirely sure how to resolve this issue. As a result, he wrote a short note to *Nature* in 1892 asking for ideas about how to solve the nitrogen puzzle.

The answer to that note came from **William Ramsay**, who was working on the same problem at about the same time. Eventually, the two scientists, working independently, obtained an answer to the problem of the mysterious gas. They discovered that Cavendish's "tiny bubble" was actually a previously unknown element, an inert gas to which they gave the name argon, from the Greek *argos,* for "inert." On January 31, 1895, Rayleigh and Ramsay published a joint paper in the *Philosophical Transactions of the Royal Society* announcing their discovery of argon. A decade later, in 1904, Rayleigh was given the Nobel Prize in physics and Ramsay the Nobel Prize in chemistry for this discovery.

Even after returning to Terling Place in 1884, Rayleigh remained active in a number of professional positions. He was appointed professor of natural philosophy at the Royal Institute in 1887 and gave more than a hundred popular lectures there over the next fifteen years. In 1885 he became secretary of the Royal Society, a post he held until his election as president of the organization in 1905. When he left that post in 1908, he became chancellor of Cambridge University, a position he held until his death at Terling Place on June 30, 1919.

In addition to the 1904 Nobel Prize, Rayleigh received the Royal Medal of the Royal Society in 1882, Italy's Bressa Prize in 1891, the Smithsonian Institution's Hodgkins Prize in 1895, Italy's Matteuci Medal in 1895, the Faraday Medal of the Chemical Society in 1895, the Copley Medal of the Royal Society in 1899, the Rumford Medal of the Royal Society in 1914, and the Elliott Cresson Medal of the Franklin Institute in 1914.

SELECTED WRITINGS BY STRUTT:

Books

The Theory of Sound, 2 volumes, Macmillan, 1877–78.
Scientific Papers, 6 volumes, Cambridge University Press, 1899–1920.

Periodicals

"On the Light from the Sky, Its Polarization and Colour," *Philosophical Magazine,* Volume 41, 1871, pp. 107–120, 274–279.
"On the Manufacture and Theory of Diffraction Gratings," *Philosophical Magazine,* Volume 47, 1874, pp. 81–93, 193–205.
"Density of Nitrogen," *Nature,* Volume 46, 1892, pp. 512–513.
"Argon," *Proceedings of the Royal Institution,* Volume 14, 1895, pp. 524–538.

SOURCES:

Books

Davis, H. W. C., and J. R. H. Weaver, *Dictionary of National Biography: 1912–1921,* Oxford University Press, 1923, pp. 514–517.
Dictionary of Scientific Biography, Volume 13, Scribner, 1975, pp. 100–107.
Lindsay, Robert Bruce, *Lord Rayleigh: The Man and His Work,* Pergamon, 1966.
Strutt, Robert John, *Life of William Strutt, Third Baron Rayleigh, O.M., F.R.S.,* second edition, University of Wisconsin Press, 1968.
Wasson, Tyler, editor, *Nobel Prize Winners,* H. W. Wilson, 1987, pp. 1021–1023.
Weber, Robert L., *Pioneers of Science: Nobel Prize Winners in Physics,* American Institute of Physics, 1980, pp. 23–25.

—Sketch by David E. Newton

Robert Strutt
1875-1947
English physicist

Best known for his work on radioactivity and atmospheric chemistry, Robert John Strutt was born at Terling Place, Witham, Essex, England, on August 28, 1875. His father was the famous physicist and Nobel Prize winner in physics, **John William Strutt**, Third Baron Rayleigh. Robert John's mother, Evelyn Georgiana Mary Balfour, was sister of the first and second earls of Balfour. Strutt attended Eton from 1889 to 1894 and then enrolled at Trinity College. He graduated with first class honors in the natural sciences in 1898, sharing with Henry Dale (later Sir Henry) the Coutts Trotter Award. Strutt then became affiliated with the Cavendish laboratories at Cambridge, working under the direction of **J. J. Thomson**. His first scientific paper was published in 1899 during his first year at the Cavendish.

Follows in Father's Footsteps and Evolves into Prolific Scientist

In 1900, Strutt was appointed fellow at Trinity College, a position he held until 1906. Two years later, he was appointed professor of physics at the Imperial College of Science and Technology in London, where he remained until his father's death in 1919. He then succeeded his father as Fourth Baron

Rayleigh and became emeritus professor at the Imperial College in 1920.

A. C. Edgerton, Strutt's biographer in the *Dictionary of National Biography,* described him as one who "worked independently out of pure curiosity, inquiring zealously into the ways of nature." Most of Strutt's research was done in a private laboratory at his home in Terling Place. He worked primarily alone, working with only one assistant for nearly forty years. Strutt's more than three hundred scientific papers testify to his prolific nature. During his lifetime, he pursued a number of fields of study, including research into radioactivity, the nature of "active" nitrogen, and the characteristics of the atmosphere. Some of his earliest works dealt with the nature of alpha radiation—a natural decaying process where the atomic nucleus disintegrates into a lighter nucleus and an alpha particle. He contributed to **Ernest Rutherford's** later discovery that alpha particles are the same as helium nuclei in that both are made of two neutrons and two protons. Strutt also found that the concentration of helium in rocks could be used to estimate the age of those rocks. In 1904, he published one of the first books on radioactivity, *The Becquerel Rays and the Properties of Radium.* He also published two important biographies, one on his father and the other on his mentor, Thomson.

Documents Existence of Ozone

Strutt's most important work involved his studies of the atmosphere. In 1916, Strutt and a colleague, Alfred Fowler, were able to confirm the existence of ozone in the atmosphere and to estimate the upper limit of the stratosphere's ozone layer. Strutt was also very interested in nightglow and airglow —patterns of light surrounding planets which appear when solar radiation triggers atmospheric chemical reactions. In honor of Strutt's work in this field, the unit for measuring the brightness of the sky was named "raleigh" after his aristocratic title.

After taking on his hereditary title in 1919, Strutt became more active in the administrative aspects of science. He was elected foreign secretary of the Royal Society in 1929, a post he held until 1934. Strutt also served as president of the Royal Institution from 1945 and as chair of the governing board of the Imperial College from 1936, both until his death in 1947. Other posts he held include chair of the executive committee of the National Physical Laboratory from 1932 to 1939, president of the Physical Society of London from 1934 to 1936, and president of the British Association for the Advancement of Science in 1938.

Strutt was also active in a number of nonscientific roles. He was a justice of the peace in Essex for many years, served as trustee for the Beit Memorial Fellowships from 1928 to 1946, was a fellow of Eton

College from 1935 to 1945, and was chosen as president of the Central Council of Milk Recording Societies in 1939. In recognition of his scientific accomplishments, Strutt was awarded honorary doctorates by the universities of Dublin in 1913, Durham in 1929, and Edinburgh in 1933.

Strutt was married twice, first to Lady Mary Hilda Clements in 1905 and, following her death in 1919, to Kathleen Alice Culbert in 1920. His first marriage brought three sons and two daughters, while the second brought one son. Strutt died in his home in Terling on December 13, 1947.

SELECTED WRITINGS BY STRUTT:

Books

The Life of John William Strutt, Third Baron Rayleigh, Arnold, 1924.

SOURCES:

Books

Gillispie, Charles Coulson, editor, *Dictionary of Scientific Biography,* Volume 13, Scribner's, 1975, pp. 107–108.
Obituary Notices of Fellows of the Royal Society, Volume 18, Royal Society (London), 1949, pp. 503–538.

—*Sketch by David E. Newton*

JoAnne Stubbe
1946-
American chemist

JoAnne Stubbe's research has helped scientists understand the ways in which enzymes catalyze, or cause, chemical reactions. Her major research efforts have focused on the mechanism of nucleotide reductases, the enzymes involved in the biosynthesis of deoxyribonucleic acid (DNA), the molecule of heredity. Her work has led to the design and synthesis of nucleotide analogs—structural derivatives of nucleotides—that have potential antitumor, antivirus, and antiparasite activity. In 1986 the American Chemical Society honored Stubbe with the Pfizer Award which is given annually to scientists under

forty for outstanding achievement in enzyme chemistry.

Stubbe was born June 11, 1946. She earned a B.S. in chemistry with high honors from the University of Pennsylvania in 1968 and her Ph.D. in chemistry at University of California at Berkeley under the direction of George Kenyon in 1971. Stubbe's first two publications in scientific journals outlined the mechanism of reactions involving the enzymes enolase, which metabolizes carbohydrates, and pyruvate kinase.

Following completion of her doctorate, Stubbe spent a year at the University of California at Los Angeles doing postdoctoral research in the department of chemistry with Julius Rebek. In 1972 she accepted a post as assistant professor of chemistry at Williams College in Massachusetts where she stayed until 1977. In late 1975 she accepted a second postdoctoral fellowship, took a leave of absence from her teaching duties, and spent a year and a half at Brandeis University on a grant from the National Institutes of Health (NIH).

From 1977 to 1980 Stubbe was assistant professor in the department of pharmacology at the Yale University School of Medicine. She then began a seven-year association with the University of Wisconsin at Madison, beginning as assistant professor and rising to full professor of biochemistry in 1985. In 1987 the Massachusetts Institute of Technology (MIT) beckoned, and Stubbe accepted a position as professor in the department of chemistry. In 1992 she was named John C. Sheehan Professor of Chemistry and Biology.

Stubbe's research focused on the mechanism of enzymes called ribonucleotide reductases, which catalyze the rate-determining step in DNA biosynthesis. This mechanism involves radical (that is, with at least one unpaired electron) intermediates and requires protein-based radicals for catalysis. Ribonucleotide reductases are major targets for the design of antitumor and antiviral agents, because inhibiting these enzymes interferes with the biosynthesis of DNA and cell growth. In collaboration with colleague John Kozarich, Stubbe has also explained the mechanism by which the antitumor antibiotic bleomycin degrades DNA. Bleomycin is used to kill cancer cells, a function that is thought to be related to its ability to bind to and degrade DNA. Other research interests of Stubbe's include the design of so-called suicide inhibitors and mechanisms of DNA repair enzymes.

Stubbe has published over eighty scientific papers and has been recognized frequently for her research achievements. She was the recipient of a NIH career development award, the Pfizer Award in enzyme chemistry in 1986, and the ICI-Stuart Pharmaceutical Award for excellence in chemistry in 1989. She received a teaching award from MIT in 1990 and the Arthur C. Cope Scholar Award in 1993. Stubbe was elected to the American Academy of Arts and Sciences in 1991 and to the National Academy of Sciences in 1992. Stubbe is a member of the American Chemical Society, the American Society for Biological Chemists, and the Protein Society. She has been active on several committees, including review boards for the NIH grants committee and the editorial boards for various scientific journals.

SELECTED WRITINGS BY STUBBE:

Periodicals

"Ribonucleotide Reductases," *Advances in Enzymology,* Volume 63, 1989, p. 349.
(With J. M. Bollinger, D. E. Edmondson, B. H. Huynh, and others) "Mechanism of Assembly of the Tyrosyl Radical-Dinuclear Iron Cluster Cofactor of Ribonucleotide Reductase," *Science,* Volume 253, 1991, p. 292.
(With E. J. Mueller, E. Meyer, J. Rudolph, and others) "N^5-Carboxyaminoimidazole Ribonucleotide: Evidence for a New Intermediate and Two New Enzymatic Activities in the *de novo* Purine Biosynthetic Pathway of *Escherichia Coli,* " *Biochemistry,* Volume 33, 1994, pp. 2269–2278.

SOURCES:

Periodicals

"ACS Division of Biological Chemistry Awards," *Chemical and Engineering News,* April 28, 1986, pp. 75–76.

—*Sketch by Kimberlyn McGrail*

A. H. Sturtevant
1891-1970
American geneticist

A. H. Sturtevant, an influential geneticist and winner of the National Medal of Science in 1968, is best known for his demonstrations of the principles of gene mapping. This discovery had a profound effect on the field of genetics and led to projects to map both animal and human chromosomes. He is the unacknowledged father of the Human Genome Project, which is attempting to map all of man's 100,000 chromosomes by the year 2000. Sturtevant's later work in the field of genetics led to discovery of the first reparable gene defect as well as the position effect, which showed that the effect of a gene is dependent on its position relative to other genes. He was a member of Columbia University's "Drosophila Group," whose studies of the genetics of fruit flies advanced new theories of genetics and evolution.

Alfred Henry Sturtevant, the youngest of six children, was born in Jacksonville, Illinois, on November 21, 1891, to Alfred and Harriet (Morse) Sturtevant. Five of his early ancestors had come to America aboard the Mayflower. Julian M. Sturtevant, his grandfather, a Yale Divinity School graduate, was the founder and former president of Illinois College. Sturtevant's father taught at Illinois College briefly but later chose farming as a profession. When Alfred Sturtevant was seven, his family moved to a farm in southern Alabama. He attended high school in Mobile, which was 14 miles from his home and accessible only by train.

Sturtevant enrolled in Columbia University in New York City in 1908, boarding with his older brother, Edgar, who taught linguistics at Columbia's Barnard College. Edgar and his wife played a significant role in young Sturtevant's life. They sent him Columbia's entrance examination, pulled strings to get him a scholarship, and welcomed him into their home in Edgewater, New Jersey, for four years. Edgar was also responsible for steering his brother toward a career in the sciences. The young Sturtevant had discovered genetic theory at an early age and often drew pedigrees of his family and of his father's horses. Edgar encouraged him to write a paper on the subject of color heredity in horses and to submit the draft to Columbia University's **Thomas Hunt Morgan**, the future Nobel Laureate geneticist. The paper used the recently rediscovered theories of Gregor Mendel, the 19th-century Austrian monk and founder of genetics, to explain certain coat-color inheritance patterns in horses. Sturtevant somehow mastered this subject in spite of his color-blindness.

Student Work Leads to Major Genetic Breakthrough

As a result of his paper on horses, which was published in 1910, Sturtevant was given a desk in Morgan's famous "fly room," a small laboratory dedicated to genetic research using *Drosophila* (fruit flies) as subjects. Fruit flies are ideal subjects for genetic research. They mature in ten days, are less than one-eighth inch long, can live by the hundreds in small vials, require nothing more substantial than yeast for food, and have only four pairs of chromosomes.

Morgan's early work focused on the phenomenon of "crossing-over" in the fruit fly. By 1910, he had already described the sex-limited inheritance of white eye. From this observation, he postulated the idea that genes were linked because they were carried by the same chromosome and that genes in close proximity to one another would be linked more frequently than those that were farther apart. Sometimes, dominant linked traits, such as eye color and wing size, became "unlinked" in offspring. Sturtevant studied the process of crossing-over of sex-linked traits, which are carried on the X chromosome. Female fruit flies have two X chromosomes. In addition to one X chromosome, males have a Y chromosome, which carries very few genes. Sturtevant correctly hypothesized that the exchange between X chromosomes probably occurred early on in the process of egg formation, when the paired chromosomes lie parallel to each other.

Morgan believed that the relative distance between genes could be measured if the crossing-over frequencies could be determined. From this lead, Sturtevant developed a practical method for determining this frequency rate. He began by studying six sex-linked traits and measured the occurrence of this related trait. The more frequently the traits occurred, Sturtevant reasoned, the closer the genes must be. He then calculated the percentages of crossing-over between the various traits. From these percentages, he determined the relative distance between the genes on the chromosome, the first instance of gene mapping. This major discovery, which Sturtevant published in 1913 at the age of 22, eventually enabled scientists to map human and animal genes. It is often considered to be the starting point of modern genetics.

In 1914, Sturtevant received his Ph.D. from Columbia and stayed on in Morgan's lab as an investigator for the Carnegie Institution of Washington, D.C. Along with C. B. Bridges, **Hermann Joseph Muller**, and Morgan, he formed part of an influential research team that made significant contributions to the fields of genetics and entomology. He later described the lab as highly democratic and occasionally argumentative, with ideas being heatedly debated. The 16 x 24-foot lab had no desks, no separate offices, one general telephone, and very few graduate assistants. Sturtevant thrived in this environment. He worked seven days a week, reserving his mornings for *Drosophila* research and his afternoons for reading the scientific literature and consulting with colleagues. He possessed a near photographic memory and wide-ranging interests. His only shortcoming as a researcher was his incessant pipe-smoking, which often left flakes of tobacco ash mixed in with the samples of fruit flies. In spite of this minor flaw, the fly-room group raised research standards and elevated research writing to an art form. They also perfected the practice of chromosome mapping, using Sturtevant's methods to develop a chromosome map of *Drosophila,* detailing the relative positions of fifty genes.

Sturtevant published a paper in 1914 that documented cases of double crossing-over, in which chromosomes that had already crossed-over broke with one another and recrossed again. His next major paper, published in 1915, concerned the sexual behavior of fruit flies and concentrated on six specific mutant genes that altered eye or body color, two factors that played important roles in sexual selection. He then showed that specific genes were responsible for selective intersexuality. In later years, he discovered a gene that caused an almost complete sex change in fruit flies, miraculously transforming females into near males. In subsequent years, researchers identified other sex genes in many animals, as well as in humans. These discoveries led to the development of the uniquely twentieth-century view of sex as a gene-controlled trait which is subject to variability.

During the 1920s, Sturtevant and Morgan examined the unstable bar-eye trait in *Drosophila*. Most geneticists at that time believed that bar eye did not follow the rules of Mendelian heredity. In 1925, Sturtevant showed that bar eye involved a recombination of genes rather than a mutation and that the position of the gene on the chromosome had an effect on its action. This discovery, known as the position effect, contributed greatly to the understanding of the action of the gene.

In 1928, Morgan received an offer from the California Institute of Technology to develop a new Division of Biological Sciences. Sturtevant followed his mentor to California, where he became Caltech's first professor of genetics. The new genetics group set up shop in Caltech's Kerckhoff Laboratory. Sturtevant continued working with fruit flies and conducted genetic investigations of other animals and plants, including snails, rabbits, moths, rats, and the evening primrose, *Oenothera.*

In 1929, Sturtevant discovered a "sex ratio" gene that caused male flies to produce X sperm almost exclusively, instead of X and Y sperm. As a result, these flies' offspring were almost always females. In the early 1930s, giant chromosomes were discovered in the salivary glands of fruit flies. Under magnification, these chromosomes revealed cross patterns which were correlated to specific genes. The so-called "physical" map derived from these giant chromosomes did not exactly match Sturtevant's "relative" location maps. In the physical map, some of the genes tended to cluster toward one end of the chromosome and the distances between genes was not uniform. But the linear order of the genes on the chromosome matched Sturtevant's relative maps gene for gene. This discovery confirmed that Sturtevant had been correct in his assumptions about chromosomal linearity.

In 1932, Sturtevant took a sabbatical leave and spent the year in England and Germany as a visiting professor of the Carnegie Endowment for International Peace. When he returned to America, he collaborated with his Caltech colleague **Theodosius Dobzhansky**, a Russian-born geneticist, on a study of inversions in the third chromosome of *Drosophila pseudoobscura*. In the 1940s, Sturtevant studied all of the known gene mutations in *Drosophila* and their various effects on the development of the species. From 1947 to 1962, he served as the Thomas Hunt Morgan Professor of Biology at Caltech. His most significant scientific contribution during that time occurred in 1951, when he unveiled his chromosome map of the indescribably small fourth chromosome of the fruit fly, a genetic problem that had puzzled scientists for decades.

During the 1950s and 1960s, Sturtevant turned his attention to the iris and authored numerous papers on the subject of evolution. He became concerned with the potential dangers of genetics research and wrote several papers on the social significance of human genetics. In a 1954 speech to the Pacific Division of the American Association for the Advancement of Science, he described the possible genetic consequences of nuclear war and argued that the public should be made aware of these possible cataclysmic hazards before any further bomb testing was performed. One of his last published journal articles, written in 1956, described a mutation in fruit flies that, by itself, was harmless but which proved lethal in combination with another specific mutant gene.

Sturtevant was named professor emeritus at Caltech in 1962. He spent the better part of the early 1960s writing his major work, *A History of Genetics*, which was published in 1965. In 1968, he received the prestigious National Medal of Science for his achievements in genetics. He died on April 5, 1970, at the age of 78. Sturtevant married Phoebe Curtis Reed in 1923, and the couple honeymooned in Europe, touring England, Norway, Sweden, and Holland. He arranged excursions to every laboratory and museum he could find. The Sturtevants had three children.

SELECTED WRITINGS BY STURTEVANT:

Books

The Mechanism of Mendelian Heredity, Holt, 1915.
An Analysis of the Effects of Selection, Carnegie Institution of Washington, 1918.
A History of Genetics, Harper & Row, 1965.

Periodicals

"The Linear Arrangement of Six Sex-Linked Factors in *Drosophila*," *Journal of Experimental Zoology,* Volume 14, 1913, pp. 43–59.

"The Himalayan Rabbit Case, with Some Considerations on Multiple Allelomorphs," *American Naturalist,* Volume 47, 1913, pp. 234–238.
"Genetic Studies on *Drosophila* simulanus," *Genetics,* Volume 5, 1920, pp. 488–500.
"Autosomal Lethals in Wild Populations of *Drosophila pseudoobscura,*" *Biological Bulletin,* Volume 73, 1937, pp. 742–751.

SOURCES:

Books

Carlson, E. A., *The Gene: A Critical History,* Sanders, 1971.

Periodicals

Beadle, G. W., "A. H. Sturtevant," *Yearbook, American Philosophical Society,* 1970, pp. 166–171.
Emerson, S., "Alfred Henry Sturtevant," *Annual Review of Genetics,* Volume 5, 1970, pp. 1–4.

—Sketch by Tom Crawford

James B. Sumner
1887-1955
American biochemist

Biochemist James B. Sumner's natural perseverance was strengthened by his efforts to overcome a handicap suffered in an accident as a youth. He set out to isolate an enzyme in 1917—a task believed to be impossible at the time. By 1926, he had crystallized an enzyme and proven it was a protein, but spent many years defending the veracity of discovery. Sumner's achievement was finally recognized in 1946, when he shared the Nobel Prize in chemistry for proving that enzymes can be crystallized.

James Batcheller Sumner was born just south of Boston in Canton, Massachusetts, on November 19, 1887, the son of Charles and Elizabeth Kelly Sumner. They were an old New England family, whose ancestors had arrived in 1636 from Bicester, England, and Sumner's relatives included industrialists as well as artists. His own family was wealthy, and his father owned a large country estate. As a boy Sumner was interested in firearms and enjoyed hunting, a hobby that led to tragedy when he lost his left forearm and elbow to an accidental shooting. The handicap was doubly traumatic since Sumner had been left-handed, but he trained himself to use his right arm instead. He continued to participate in sports, including tennis, canoeing, and clay pigeon shooting, and he would learn to perform intricate laboratory procedures with only one arm.

Sumner received his early education at the Eliot Grammar School, and he graduated from the Roxbury Latin School in 1906. He enrolled at Harvard to study electrical engineering, but discovered he was more interested in chemistry and graduated with a degree in that discipline in 1910. He then joined the Sumner Knitted Padding Company, which was managed by an uncle, but stayed only a few months before he was offered the chance to teach chemistry for one term at a college in New Brunswick. This appointment was followed by a position at the Worcester Polytechnic Institute in Worcester, Massachusetts. He remained there for just one term as well before enrolling in the doctoral program at Harvard in 1912.

Sumner conducted his doctoral work under the supervision of Otto Folin, who had originally told him that a one-armed man could not possibly succeed in chemistry. Sumner completed his master's degree in 1913 and his doctorate in 1914. Part of his doctoral thesis was published in 1914 as "The Importance of the Liver in Urea Formation from Amino Acids" in the *Journal of Biological Chemistry*. While on a trip to Europe after completing his graduate studies, Sumner was offered an appointment as assistant professor of biochemistry at the Ithaca Division of the Cornell University Medical College. Initially detained by the beginning of World War I, he finally made it to Ithaca and discovered that he would also be teaching in the College of Arts and Sciences.

Sumner would spend his entire academic career at Cornell. He began as an assistant professor, a position he held for fifteen years, and then spent nine years as professor in the department of physiology and biochemistry at the Medical College. In 1938, Sumner was appointed professor of biochemistry in the department of zoology of the College of Arts and Sciences. In 1947 he became the founding director of the Laboratory of Enzyme Chemistry within the department of biochemistry.

Embarks on Effort to Isolate Enzyme

Sumner's teaching load at Cornell was always very heavy. He enjoyed teaching and was regarded as an excellent professor, but his schedule did not leave much time for research. His research was also limited by the minimal equipment and laboratory help available at Cornell. In his Nobel lecture Sumner recounted why had chosen to work on enzymes. "At that time I had little time for research, not much apparatus, research money or assistance," he recalled. "I desired to accomplish something of real importance. In other words, I decided to take a 'long shot.' A number of persons advised me that my attempt to isolate an enzyme was foolish, but this advice made me feel all the more certain that if successful the quest would be worthwhile."

He chose to isolate urease, an enzyme that catalyzed the breakdown of urea into ammonia and carbon dioxide. He found that relatively large amounts of urease were present in the jack bean (*Canavalia ensiformis*). Sumner disagreed with the belief, then commonly held, that enzymes were low-molecular-weight substances which were easily adsorbed on proteins but were not in fact proteins themselves. He concentrated on fractionating the proteins of the jack bean, and this effort took him nine years. In 1926, he published a paper in the *Journal of Biological Chemistry* announcing that he had isolated a new crystalline globulin, which he believed to be urease, from the jack bean. Urease was the first enzyme prepared in crystalline form and the first that was proven to be a protein.

His results, and his interpretation of them, were not immediately accepted. On the contrary, he spent years engaged in a controversy with those who believed that enzymes contained no protein. One of his strongest opponents was **Richard Willstätter**, a German chemist who had won the Nobel Prize in 1915 for his work on chlorophyll. Willstätter had tried to produce pure enzymes and failed, and he argued that what Sumner had isolated was merely the carrier of the enzyme and not the enzyme itself. Although Sumner continued to publish additional evidence over the next few years, it was not until 1930 that he received support for his discovery, when **John Howard Northrop** of the Rockefeller Institute announced he had crystallized pepsin. Sumner was jointly awarded the 1946 Nobel Prize in chemistry; his co-recipients were Northrop and **Wendell Meredith Stanley**, also at the Rockefeller Institute, honored for their preparation of enzymes and virus proteins in pure form.

After the crystallization of urease and the debates with Willstätter and others, Sumner continued his research on enzymes, among them peroxidases and lipoxidase, doing most of his own laboratory work. In 1937, he and his student Alexander L. Dounce crystallized the enzyme catalase and helped prove it was a protein. Sumner was the first to crystallize haemagglutinin concanavalin A, and he noted that this protein required the presence of a divalent metal to act. He also continued his original research work on new and improved laboratory methods. He was a prolific author, writing or contributing to about 125 research papers and a number of books.

In 1929 Sumner, who spoke Swedish, French, and German, went to the University of Stockholm to work on urease with **Hans von Euler-Chelpin** and

Theodor Svedberg . He returned to Sweden in 1937 to work at the University of Uppsala on a Guggenheim fellowship, and while there he was awarded the Scheele Medal from the Swedish Chemical Society for his work on enzymes. Other professional honors include his election to both the Polish Institute of Arts and Sciences and the American Academy of Arts and Sciences. Sumner was also a member of many associations including the National Academy of Sciences, the American Association for the Advancement of Sciences, the Society for Experimental Biology and Medicine, and the American Society of Biological Chemists.

Sumner was married three times and divorced twice. He married his first wife, Bertha Louise Ricketts on July 20, 1915, the year after he completed his Ph.D. They had five children, and were divorced in 1930. Sumner married Agnes Paulina Lundquist of Sweden in 1931; they had no children. After his second divorce, Sumner married Mary Morrison Beyer in 1943; they had two sons, one of whom died as a child.

In 1955, while preparing for his retirement from Cornell, Sumner was diagnosed with cancer. He had intended to work at the Medical School of the University of Minas Gerais, in Belo Horizonte, Brazil, organizing an enzyme research program and laboratory. However, the day after attending a symposium held partly in his honor, he was hospitalized, and died on August 12, 1955, at the Roswell Park Memorial Institute in Buffalo, New York.

SELECTED WRITINGS BY SUMNER:

Books

Textbook of Biological Chemistry, Macmillan, 1927.
(With G. Fred Somers) *Chemistry and Methods of Enzymes,* Academic Press, 1943.
(With Somers) *Laboratory Experiments in Biological Chemistry,* Academic Press, 1944.

Periodicals

(With C. H. Fiske) "The Importance of the Liver in Urea Formation from Amino Acids," in *Journal of Biological Chemistry,* Volume 18, 1914, pp. 285–295.
"The Isolation and Crystallization of the Enzyme Urease (Preliminary Paper)," in *Journal of Biological Chemistry,* Volume 69, 1926, pp. 435–441.
(With Alexander L. Dounce) "Crystalline Catalase," in *Journal of Biological Chemistry,* Volume 121, 1937, pp. 417–424.

SOURCES:

Periodicals

Dounce, Alexander L., "Prof. James B. Sumner," *Nature,* Volume 176, 1955, p. 859.
Maynard, Leonard A., "James Batcheller Sumner," *Biographical Memoirs,* National Academy of Sciences, Volume 31, 1958, pp. 376–396.

—Sketch by Marianne P. Fedunkiw

Verner E. Suomi
1915-
American meteorologist

Verner E. Suomi helped pioneer the use of space satellites to study weather on earth and other planets. A meteorologist with a knack for building gadgets, Suomi invented the spin-scan camera which takes pictures of earth from a spinning satellite. He also developed a global data system called McIDAS (Man-computer Interactive Data Access System) that gave scientists worldwide access to the satellite data. The images and information gathered in space through his developments have improved forecasting and contributed to a greater understanding of weather systems.

Verner Edward Suomi was born in the small mining town of Eveleth, Minnesota, on December 6, 1915. His father, John E. Suomi, was a carpenter for a mining company. His mother, Anna Emelia Sundquist Suomi, had seven children altogether, five girls and two boys. At the age of 22, Suomi began teaching science and mathematics at a Minnesota high school. The following year, he earned a bachelor's degree at Winona Teachers' College. Suomi married Paula Meyer in 1941, and the couple eventually had three children: Lois, Stephen, and Eric.

As an aviation student, Suomi's interest in meteorology was sparked by student handbook charts that described how the atmosphere and the amount of water in the atmosphere differed according to altitude. But it was World War II that changed the course of Suomi's career. Prompted by a radio message from noted meteorologist **Carl-Gustaf Rossby** for meteorologists to help in the war effort, Suomi returned to school. At the University of Chicago he studied under Rossby himself, an arrangement that Suomi called "a happy accident," in *Omni* magazine in 1989.

Suomi's dissertation, "The Heat Budget of a Cornfield," was a study that gave him a background that would be useful in a more ambitious project in the future: measuring the heat budget of the entire planet. Although Suomi earned his Ph.D. in 1953, he had belonged to the faculty at the University of Wisconsin at Madison since 1948. He co-founded the Space Science and Engineering Center at the University of Wisconsin in 1966 and acted as its director from its inception until his retirement in 1988.

Suomi's activities at the University of Wisconsin extended well beyond the classroom. Before any U.S. weather satellite had been launched into space, Suomi developed an instrument called a radiometer that measured the amount of heat going into and coming out of the earth's atmosphere. The radiometer was made of four metallic balls with the temperature sensors at the tips of long antennas. From a satellite orbiting the planet, it would measure the heat coming to the earth from the sun, as well as the heat reflected back into space by clouds, snow, and water. Suomi watched as the Vanguard Rocket carrying his invention was launched in 1959. Unfortunately, the rocket crashed. "When ... my gadget fell into the ocean, it was almost like a death in the family," Suomi told *Omni* magazine. Undeterred, he built another radiometer, but it too exploded along with the Juno rocket that it was aboard.

When the first successful U.S. meteorological satellite was finally launched on the Explorer VII in 1959, another of Suomi's radiometers was on board. Suomi set up a radio station in his bedroom to collect data as the satellite orbited the earth. The information he gathered showed that the energy changes in the atmosphere varied much more than scientists previously believed. Although clouds and other materials such as snow reflect sunlight, they also absorb energy. Thus, from the satellite the earth appeared dark, because it was reflecting much less solar energy back into space than people had come to believe.

One of Suomi's most noted contributions was the spin-scan camera that took pictures of the planet from a rapidly spinning satellite 22,000 miles above the earth. The images displayed dynamic weather patterns and brought about a revolution in forecasting. The satellite, designed to travel at the same speed as the earth, hovered over a given region. With each spin, the satellite viewed a narrow swath of the earth. As the satellite tilted gradually, the camera could take pictures of the entire earth in 2400 revolutions. Previous satellites had been able to take pictures, but the spin-scan camera, introduced in 1963, took sequential photos that showed how the weather was changing. Those first sets of images from the spin-scan camera caught many meteorologists by surprise. They had expected the atmosphere to appear turbulent and chaotic. Instead, the images showed organized weather patterns—"clouds that looked like someone was pulling taffy across the sky," Suomi told *Omni* magazine in 1989. The camera provided images that enabled meteorologists to study patterns of air motion, cloud growth, and atmospheric pollution which resulted in improved forecasting of storms.

In 1959 Suomi and three others founded the Global Atmospheric Research Program which attempted to form a central location for the atmospheric data which was collected by more than sixty nations. To make the best use of the immense amounts of data gathered by weather satellites, Suomi developed the Man-computer Interactive Data Access System (McIDAS) in 1972 to manage the data for research and weather forecasting. The system also made data readily accessible to other nations. In 1978 the Global Atmospheric Research Program sponsored an experiment with the spin-scan camera that doubled the amount of time for which meteorologists could forecast accurately.

In 1971 Suomi proposed an ambitious experiment to study the atmosphere's temperature and water vapor using infrared technology, but the experiment was not launched until nine years later. The results showed how storms developed over a region of several hundred thousand square miles, and the infrared technique became useful for warnings of storms and hurricanes. Looking beyond our own planet, Suomi also used satellite technology to study the atmospheres of Venus, Jupiter, and Saturn. With colleagues at the Space Science and Engineering Center, he designed and built an instrument that entered the atmosphere of Venus and discovered an intense vortex over each pole.

In addition to the directorship of the Space Science and Engineering Center at the University of Wisconsin, Suomi's other positions included a term as president of the American Meteorological Association in 1968 and a year as chief scientist of the United States Weather Bureau in 1964. Though honored for his inventions that revolutionized the way meteorologists forecast the weather, colleagues and students thought of Suomi foremost as an educator. His contributions went beyond developing technology to include fostering an interest in meteorology among several generations of students.

Suomi received the Carl-Gustaf Rossby Award in 1968, the highest honor bestowed on an atmospheric scientist by the American Meteorological Society. He was also presented with the National Medal of Science by President Carter in 1977.

SOURCES:

Periodicals

Bagne, Paul, "Verner Suomi," *Omni*, July, 1989.

Broad, William J., "A 30-Year Feud Divides Experts on Meteorology," *New York Times,* October 24, 1989, p. C1.

—*Sketch by Miyoko Chu*

Earl Sutherland
1915-1974
American biochemist

Earl Sutherland was a biochemist who expounded upon the manner in which hormones regulate body functions. His early work showed how the hormone adrenaline regulates the breakdown of sugar in the liver to release a surge of energy when the body is under stress. Later, Sutherland discovered a chemical within cells called cyclic adenosine 3'5'-monophosphate, or cyclic AMP. This chemical provided a universal link between hormones and the regulation of metabolism within cells. For this work, Sutherland was awarded the Nobel Prize in physiology and medicine in 1971.

Earl Wilbur Sutherland, Jr., the fifth of six children in his family, was born on November 19, 1915, in Burlingame, Kansas, a small farming community. His father, Earl Wilbur Sutherland, a Wisconsin native, had attended Grinnell College for two years and farmed in New Mexico and Oklahoma before settling in Burlingame to run a dry-goods business, where Earl Wilbur, Jr., and his siblings worked. Sutherland's mother, Edith M. Hartshorn, came from Missouri. She had been educated at a "ladies college," and had received some nursing training. She taught Sutherland to swim at the age of five and then allowed him to go fishing by himself, a pastime that became a lifelong passion. While in high school, Sutherland also excelled in sports such as football, basketball, and tennis. In 1933 he entered Washburn College in Topeka, Kansas. Supporting his studies by working as an orderly in a hospital, Sutherland graduated with a B.S. in 1937. He married Mildred Rice the same year. Sutherland then entered Washington University Medical School in St. Louis, Missouri. There he enrolled in a pharmacology class taught by **Carl Ferdinand Cori**, who would share the 1947 Nobel Prize in medicine and physiology with his wife Gerty Cori. Impressed by Sutherland's abilities, Cori offered him a job as a student assistant. This was Sutherland's first experience with research. The research on the sugar glucose that Sutherland undertook in Cori's laboratory started him on a line of inquiry that led to his later groundbreaking studies.

Sutherland received his M.D. in 1942. He then worked for one year as an intern at Barnes Hospital while continuing to do research in Cori's laboratory. Sutherland was called into service during World War II as a battalion surgeon under General George S. Patton. Later in the war he served in Germany as a staff physician in a military hospital.

In 1945, Sutherland returned to Washington University in St. Louis. He was unsure whether to continue practicing medicine or to commit himself to a career in research. Sutherland later attributed his decision to stay in the laboratory to the example of his mentor Carl F. Cori. By 1953, Sutherland had advanced to the rank of associate professor at Washington University. During these years he came into contact with many leading figures in biochemistry, including **Arthur Kornberg**, **Edwin G. Krebs**, T. Z. Posternak, and others now recognized as among the founders of modern molecular biology. But Sutherland preferred, for the most part, to do his research independently. While at Washington University, Sutherland began a project to understand how an enzyme known as phosphorylase breaks down glycogen, a form of the sugar stored in the liver. He also studied the roles of the hormone adrenaline, also known as epinephrine, and glucagon, secreted by the pancreas, in stimulating the release of energy-producing glucose from glycogen.

Discovers A Molecule Basic to Life

Sutherland was offered the chairmanship of the Department of Pharmacology at Western Reserve (now Case Western) University in Cleveland in 1953. It was during the ten years he spent in Cleveland that Sutherland clarified an important mechanism by which hormones produce their effects. Scientists had previously thought that hormones acted on whole organs. Sutherland, however, showed that hormones stimulate individual cells in a process that takes place in two steps. First, a hormone attaches to specific receptors on the outside of the cell membrane. Sutherland called the hormone a "first messenger." The binding of the hormone to the membrane triggers release of a molecule known as cyclic AMP within the cell. Cyclic AMP then goes on to play many roles in the cell's metabolism, and Sutherland referred to the molecule as the "second messenger" in the mechanism of hormone action. In particular, Sutherland studied the effects of the hormone adrenaline, also called epinephrine, on liver cells. When adrenaline binds to liver cells, cyclic AMP is released and directs the conversion of sugar from a stored form into a form the cell can use.

Sutherland made two more important discoveries while at Western Reserve. He found that other hormones also spur the release of cyclic AMP when they bind to cells, in particular, the adrenocorticotropic hormone and the thyroid-stimulating hormone. This implied that cyclic AMP was a sort of universal intermediary in this process, and it explained why different hormones might induce similar effects. In addition, cyclic AMP was found to play an important role in the metabolism of one-celled organisms, such as the amoeba and the bacterium *Escherichia coli,* which do not have hormones. That cyclic AMP is found in both simple and complex organisms implies that it is a very basic and important biological molecule and that it arose early in evolution and has been conserved throughout millennia.

In 1963 Sutherland became professor of physiology at Vanderbilt University in Nashville, Tennessee, a move which relieved him of his teaching duties and enabled him to devote more of his time to research. The previous year he and his first wife had divorced, and in 1963 Sutherland married Dr. Claudia Sebeste Smith, who shared with him, among other interests, a love of fishing. The couple later had two girls and two boys.

At Vanderbilt Sutherland continued his work on cyclic AMP, supported by a Career Investigatorship awarded by the American Heart Association. Sutherland studied the role of cyclic AMP in the contraction of heart muscle. He and other researchers continued to discover physiological processes in different tissues and various animal species that are influenced by cyclic AMP, for example in brain cells and cancer cells. Sutherland also did research on a similar molecule known as cyclic GMP (guanosine 3',5'-cyclic monophosphate). In the meantime, his pioneering studies had opened up a new field of research. By 1971, as many as two thousand scientists were studying cyclic AMP.

For most of his career Sutherland was well-known mainly to his scientific colleagues. In the early 1970s, however, a rush of awards gained him more widespread public recognition. In 1970 he received the prestigious Albert Lasker Basic Medical Research Award. In 1971 he was awarded the Nobel Prize for "his long study of hormones, the chemical substances that regulate virtually every body function," as well as the American Heart Association Research Achievement Award. In 1973 he was bestowed with the National Medal of Science of the United States. During his career Sutherland was also elected to membership in the National Academy of Sciences, and he belonged to the American Society of Biological Chemists, the American Chemical Society, the American Society for Pharmacology and Experimental Therapeutics, and the American Association for the Advancement of Science. He received honorary degrees from Yale University and Washington University. In 1973 Sutherland moved to the University of Miami. Shortly thereafter, he suffered a massive esophageal hemorrhage, and he died on March 9,

1974, after surgery for internal bleeding, at the age of 58.

SELECTED WRITINGS BY SUTHERLAND, JR:

Books

(With G. A. Robison and R. W. Butcher) *Cyclic AMP,* Academic Press, 1971.

Periodicals

"The Role of Cyclic 3'5'-AMP in Responses to Catechlolamines and Other Hormones," *Pharmacological Reviews,* Volume 18, 1966, pp. 145–161.

SOURCES:

Books

Cori, Carl F., "Earl Wilbur Sutherland," *Biographical Memoirs of the National Academy of Sciences,* Volume 49, National Academy of Sciences, 1978.

Periodicals

Time, October 25, 1971, p. 63.

—*Sketch by Betsy Hanson*

Ivan Sutherland
1938-
American computer scientist

Ivan Sutherland is a pioneer in the field of computer graphics. His 1960 "Sketchpad" system contributed to the development of computer graphics, computer simulation, and video games as we know them today.

Ivan Edward Sutherland was born in Hastings, Nebraska, on May 16, 1938. His first experience with computing was in high school, where as a young student he build various relay-driven machines. In the early 1950s, computers were exciting and exotic devices, and many bright students set their sights on that field.

Sutherland received his B.S. from Carnegie-Mellon University in 1959, his M.S. from the California

Institute of Technology in 1960, and his Ph.D. in electrical engineering from the Massachusetts Institute of Technology (M.I.T.) in 1963. Throughout college Sutherland was always interested in logic and computing; he held a summer job with International Business Machines (IBM) after he got his bachelor's degree, and he switched from Cal Tech to M.I.T. for his doctoral studies because of the latter's superior computer department. His doctoral thesis committee comprised some of the biggest names in computing at the time, including **Claude Shannon**, **Marvin Minsky**, and Steven Coons. At M.I.T., Sutherland worked at the Lincoln Laboratory. There he had the use of a large, modern computer called the TX–2, which played a significant role in the research for his doctoral dissertation, entitled "Sketchpad."

"Sketchpad" was arguably Sutherland's greatest work and the basis for much of what he subsequently accomplished. The principle behind "Sketchpad" is that of a pencil moving on paper, but instead it uses a light-sensitive pen moving on the surface of a computer screen. By measuring the vertical and horizontal movements of the pen by means of a grid system, the computer could recreate the lines on the computer screen. Once on the screen, lines could be manipulated (lengthened, shortened, moved to any angle) and connected to represent solid objects, which could then be rotated to display them at any angle, exactly as if they were true three-dimensional artifacts. (Previously existing graphics systems were strictly two-dimensional.) Sutherland documented his dissertation research with a film called "Sketchpad: A Man-Machine Graphical Communication System," and the film became very well known in the computer research community of the time. The concept of "Sketchpad" was revolutionary, and its direct repercussions extend down to this day.

From M.I.T., Sutherland went into the army, due to a Reserve Officers Training Corps commitment left over from Carnegie-Mellon. After brief assignments with the National Security Agency and a radar and infrared tracking project called Project Michigan, he was made director of the Information Processing Techniques Office (IPTO) of the Defense Advanced Research Projects Agency (DARPA), where he stayed for two years. This was a heady assignment for the 26-year-old lieutenant, and it had a profound influence on his later career; virtually every business partner he subsequently had was someone he had met at DARPA.

From DARPA he went to Harvard as an associate professor of engineering and applied physics. He remained at Harvard for almost three years, during which time he developed computer graphics tools that became invaluable to his later work on computer simulation. In 1967, he was recruited by David Evans, a contractor he had worked with at DARPA, to join the computer science program at the Universi-

ty of Utah. Evans, who had recently moved to Utah from Berkeley, also had in mind developing a company that would exploit some of the exciting developments in computer graphics.

At the University of Utah, Sutherland worked with a group of brilliant graduate students, and the computer department became an experimental center for computer graphics. Sutherland and his students refined the animation of their simulated figures; they developed "smooth curves" and lighting and highlight effects that began to replace the original "wireframe" models. One of Sutherland's students, Nolan Bushnell, eventually went on to develop the original video arcade and home video game Pong.

Cofounds Company to Expand Computer Simulation

In 1968, Evans and Sutherland formed the firm Evans & Sutherland in Salt Lake City. Computers at that time were being used for well-understood routine tasks, such as billing, filing, and information processing. Evans and Sutherland, however, recognized that computers had exciting possibilities as design and training tools, a potential that was not being exploited anywhere. As Evans noted in an Evans & Sutherland newsletter, computers are essentially simulators that can "replace real objects on occasions when a simulation can be built more cheaply than the physical model can be."

Evans & Sutherland's first products were computer-aided design tools, which they sold in small quantities. The company did not begin making a profit until its fifth year of operation, but by the mid–1970s it was beginning to develop a broad range of products for several market niches, principally in flight training and computer-aided design. Evans & Sutherland remains in business today. Although Sutherland left the company's day-to-day operation in 1974, he remains on the board of directors.

From 1976 to 1980, Sutherland headed the department of computer science at the California Institute of Technology. In 1980, he joined forces with Robert Sproull, the son of one of Sutherland's superiors at DARPA, to form Sutherland, Sproull & Associates in Pittsburgh, Pennsylvania, later moving to Palo Alto, California. Sutherland's last written work in computer graphics was a joint paper with Sproull titled, "A Characterization of Ten Hidden Surface Algorithms." Sutherland would say in a 1989 interview that this "seemed to tidy up a loose end," and he counts it as the time at which he stopped being involved with computer graphics for good.

Sutherland remains associated with Sutherland, Sproull & Associates, doing research in computer architecture and logic circuits. Married, with two children, he is a plain-spoken man who avoids publicity and rarely grants interviews. He has, however, been frequently honored by his peers in the computer industry. He has received many honorary degrees and has won many prestigious honors and awards, including the first Zworykin Award from the National Academy of Engineering and the first Steven Anson Coons Award.

SOURCES:

Books

Aspray, William, *An Interview with Ivan Sutherland,* Charles Babbage Institute, Center for the History of Information Processing, University of Minnesota, 1989.

Kettelkamp, Larry, *Computer Graphics: How It Works, What It Does,* Morrow, 1989.

Periodicals

Evans & Sutherland News, special issue, 1974.

—*Sketch by Joel Simon*

Walter Stanborough Sutton

Walter Stanborough Sutton
1877-1916
American geneticist, cytologist, and biologist

Walter Stanborough Sutton was a surgeon and a biologist who advanced the findings and confirmed the genetic theories of Gregor Mendel . A physician in private practice for the last half of his life, Sutton discovered the role of chromosomes in meiosis (sex cell division) and their relationship to Mendel's laws of heredity. From his research with grasshoppers collected at his parent's farm in the summer of 1899, he went on to make a major contribution to the understanding of the workings of chromosomes in sexual reproduction.

The fifth of six sons, Sutton was born in Utica, New York, on April 5, 1877, to William Bell Sutton and Agnes Black Sutton. At age ten, Sutton moved with his family to Russell County, Kansas, where he attended public schools. He studied engineering at the University of Kansas, Lawrence, beginning in 1896. Following his younger brother's death from typhoid in 1897, however, he made a pivotal change in the course of his education that would eventually lead him to the study of medicine and to his discoveries in genetics.

Sutton earned a bachelor's degree from the University of Kansas School of Arts in 1900. He was elected to Phi Beta Kappa and Sigma Xi, the scientific fraternity. While an undergraduate, he met Clarence Erwin McClung, a zoology instructor. Their four-year association would greatly influence Sutton's later work. McClung persuaded Sutton to study histology, which led the young student to other areas of inquiry, including cytological examinations of the lubber (grass)hopper (*Brachystola magna*).

Publishes Significant Papers in Graduate School

Sutton's careful camera lucida drawings of the stages of spermatogenesis in the lubber hopper were described in his first paper, "The Spermatogonial Divisions in Brachystola Magna," which appeared in the *Kansas University Quarterly* in 1900 and served as his master's thesis the following year. Following this work, McClung and other faculty members encouraged Sutton to pursue his doctoral studies under biologist **Edmund Beecher Wilson** at Columbia University. In 1901, Sutton began work there. He continued his cytological studies on chromosomal division in germ cells, and in 1902 detailed his research in "On the Morphology of the Chromosome Group in Brachystola Magna." Earlier that year, based on his readings of work done by British biologist **William Bateson** on the relationship between meiosis in germ cells and body characteristics, Sutton made the connection between cytology and heredity, and thus opened the field of cytogenetics. Sutton's hypotheses and generalizations were later published in what has become a landmark work, "The Chromosomes in Heredity" in the *Biological Bulletin,* 1903.

In these papers, Sutton explained that through his observation of meiosis he found that all chromosomes exist in pairs very similar to each other; that each gamete, or sex cell, contributes one chromosome of each pair, or reduces to one-half its genetic material, in the creation of a new offspring cell during meiosis; that each fertilized egg contains the sum of chromosomes of both parent cells; that these pairs control heredity; and that each particular chromosome's pair is based on independent assortment, that is, the maternal and paternal chromosomes separate independently of each other. The result, Sutton found, was that an individual in a species may posses any number of random combinations of different pairs of maternal and paternal chromosomes. Sutton also hypothesized that each chromosome carries in it groups of genes, each of which represents a biological characteristic—a thought that contradicted the then prevalent theory that ascribed one inherited trait to each chromosome.

At the time Sutton's paper was published, Austrian scientist **Theodor Boveri** claimed he had reached the same conclusions. As a result, the biological generalizations of the association of paternal and maternal chromosomes in pairs and their subsequent separation, which makes up the physical basis of the Mendelian law of heredity, is called the Sutton-Boveri Hypothesis. This 1903 discovery, however, was to be Sutton's last in cytology; due to unknown reasons, he never completed his course of study at Columbia.

Returning to Kansas after his laboratory research, Sutton worked as a foreman in the Chautauqua County oil fields until 1905. While there he used his abilities to solve technical problems. He developed the first technique for starting large gas engines with high pressure gas. In 1907 he patented a device to raise an oil pump mechanism from a well when worn valve components required replacement. Sutton also began a design to use electric motors to run drilling devices, but did not complete it.

Pursues Further Study in the Life Sciences

Still fascinated with the intricacies of the life sciences, and at the request of his father, Sutton returned to the Columbia University College of Physicians and Surgeons. He earned his medical degree in 1907 and for the next two years served as surgical house officer at Roosevelt Hospital in New York City. During that time, Sutton designed and built a device to deliver rectal anesthesia to patients unable to inhale ether. In 1909 he moved back to Kansas to practice privately in Kansas City, and to

teach in the department of surgery at the University of Kansas. Six years later, he took a leave of absence from the University to work at the American Ambulance Hospital in Juilly, France, during World War I. His experiences of working on injured soldiers led to a book chapter on wound surgery. In addition, Sutton developed a method of finding and removing foreign bodies in soft tissue involving the use of fluoroscopy and a simple device made from a hooked piece of wire. After the war, Sutton returned to his private practice and his teaching duties in Kansas. He continued his work there until his death from a ruptured appendix on November 10, 1916. He never married. Sutton's manual dexterity—evident in his surgical skills and handling of cells under a microscope—was nurtured by his love and talent for drawing and the mechanical abilities he practiced while working on farm machinery and oil wells. His mechanical repairs and inventions, home-built camera, and laboratory and surgical practice all bore obvious examples of his creativity, skill, and inventiveness.

SELECTED WRITINGS BY SUTTON:

Books

Binnie, J. F., "War Surgery," in *Manual of Operative Surgery,* Blakeston, 1916, pp. 1285–1316.

Periodicals

"The Spermatogonial Divisions of *Brachystola Magna,*" *Kansas University Quarterly,* Volume 9, 1900, p. 135.
"Morphology of the Chromosome Group *Brachystola Magna,*" *Biological Bulletin,* Volume 4, 1902, p. 24.
"The Chromosomes in Heredity," *Biological Bulletin,* Volume 4, 1903, pp. 231–251.
"Anesthesia by Colonic Absorption of Ether," *Annals of Surgery,* Volume 51, 1910, p. 457.
"A New Incision for Epithelioma of the Upper and Lower Lips of the Same Side," *Journal of the American Medical Association,* Volume 55, 1910, p. 647.
"The Proposed Fistuo-enterostomy of Von Stubenrauch," *Annals of Surgery,* Volume 52, 1910, p. 380.

SOURCES:

Periodicals

Whitehead, Fred, "Answer to Quiz," *Family Matters,* March, 1992.

Other

Nelson, Stanley, M.D., professor of anatomy, University of Kansas Medical Center, interview with Denise Arnold conducted October 13, 1993.

—Sketch by Denise Adams Arnold

Theodor Svedberg
1884-1971
Swedish chemist

Theodor Svedberg, helped to turn the arcane field of colloid chemistry into a vigorous and productive field of study. In so doing, he developed the ultracentrifuge, one of the most basic and useful tools in the modern biomedical laboratory, and an achievement for which he won the 1926 Nobel Prize in chemistry. Svedberg's work was not only innovative but cross-disciplinary, having valuable applications in a variety of fields, beginning with colloid chemistry. Colloids, of which milk fat and smoke are examples, are substances dispersed (as opposed to being dissolved) in a medium; colloids cannot be observed directly under the microscope, nor do they settle out under the force of gravity. Svedberg's development of the ultracentrifuge to study solutions was of enormous importance to biologists, who believed that gaining an understanding of colloids would help them to create models of biological systems.

Theodor Svedberg—called "The Svedberg" by his colleagues—was born on August 30, 1884, in Fleräng, Sweden, a small town near Gävle on the eastern coast. The only child of Elias Svedberg, a civil engineer employed at the local ironworks, and Augusta Alstermark Svedberg, the young Theodor often accompanied his father on long trips through the countryside, and performed simple experiments in a small laboratory at the ironworks under Elias's guidance.

Theodor attended the Karolinksa School in Örebro and showed a special aptitude for the natural sciences. Botany in particular peaked his interest, but he chose chemistry because of his interest in biological processes. His education progressed rapidly; he entered the University of Uppsala in January 1904, and received his B.S. in September of 1905 and his doctorate in 1907. He wrote his dissertation on colloids.

Until Svedberg's thesis describing his new method for producing colloidal solutions of metals, chemists made these mixtures by passing an electric arc between metal electrodes submerged in a liquid. Svedberg used an alternating current with an induction coil whose spark gap was submerged in a liquid to produce relatively pure colloidal mixtures of metals. The level of purity of these colloids, and the fact that the results were reproducible, permitted researchers to perform quantitative analyses during physicochemical studies. Svedberg's work propelled him quickly in the educational hierarchy at Uppsala, beginning with a lectureship in physical chemistry from 1907 to 1912. In 1912 he was awarded Sweden's first academic chair of physical chemistry, created by the University of Uppsala specifically for Svedberg and retained by him for thirty-six years.

Svedberg continued his work with colloids, using an ultramicroscope (a microscope that uses refracted light for visualizing specimens too small to be seen with direct light) to study the Brownian movement of particles. Brownian motion, the continuous random movement of minute particles suspended in liquid medium caused by collision of the particles with molecules of the medium, was named for the British botanist Robert Brown, who observed the phenomenon among pollen grains in water. Brownian movement was of great interest to a number of other researchers, including two future Nobel Prize winners, **Albert Einstein** and **Jean Perrin**. Perrin's work had provided verification of the theoretical work of Einstein and Marian Smoluchowski, and established definitively the existence of molecules. Perrin determined the size of large colloidal particles by measuring their rate of settling, a time-consuming process.

Using the ultramicroscope, Svedberg showed that the behavior of colloidal solutions obeys classical laws of physics and chemistry. But his method failed to distinguish the smallest particle sizes or determine the distribution of colloidal particles—the constant collisions of particles with water molecules kept the particles from settling out. In 1923 Svedberg and his colleague Herman Rinde began determining particle size distribution by measuring sediment accumulation in colloidal systems suspended on a balance. Although the technique itself was not new, Svedberg and Rinde increased its resolution by controlling air currents and other factors that disturbed the balance scale. While further refining this technique, Svedberg was also contemplating other approaches, especially electrophoresis (separation of particles in an electric field based on size and charge), and centrifugation.

Centrifugation—spinning solutions around a fixed circumference at high speed—mimics the force of gravity. Centrifuges were already being used to separate milk from cream and red blood cells from plasma. But fat globules and red cells are relatively large and heavy, and thus relatively easy to force out of solution. In order to force the much tinier and lighter colloidal particles out of solution, Svedberg needed a stronger centrifuge than was currently available.

In 1923 Svedberg accepted the offer of an eight-month guest professorship at the University of Wisconsin, where he taught and continued his research into centrifugation, electrophoresis, and diffusion of colloidal solutions. Working with J. Burton Nichols, Svedberg constructed the first ultracentrifuge, which could spin at up to thirty thousand revolutions per minute, generating gravitational forces thousands of times greater than earth's. This early ultracentrifuge was elaborate, equipped with both a camera and illumination for photographing samples during centrifugation. Using this device, Svedberg and Nichols determined particle size distributions and radii for gold, clay, barium sulfate, and arsenious sulfide.

Following his sabbatical in Wisconsin, Svedberg and his students continually increased the speed of successively higher-speed ultracentrifuges, pushing the limit from 100,000 g (gravitational force equivalent to that of earth's) at forty-five thousand revolutions per minute during the 1920s to 750,000 g by 1935. He used the machine to study proteins, which although huge molecules, retain their colloidal properties when in solution. Among the proteins whose weight and structure he studied using the ultracentrifuge were hemoglobin, pepsin, insulin, catalase, and albumin. The technique caught on, and Svedberg's invention became an invaluable tool used by most protein chemists. He extended his ultracentrifuge studies of large carbohydrate molecules, combining his interest in biomolecules with his interest in botany by undertaking a pioneering study of the complex sugars of the Lillifloreae family, which includes lilies and irises. His work contributed to the understanding of carbohydrate structure and provided a useful tool for later studies of evolution by biologists.

In 1926 Sweden, like much of Europe, was still recovering from the devastating effects of World War I, and research seemed destined to languish in an era of reduced government support and hopelessly outmoded facilities. Svedberg's Nobel Prize, however, gave Swedish science a boost, and led directly to the establishment in 1930 of Svedberg's proposed Institute of Physical Chemistry at Uppsala. Announced the same year that Perrin received the Nobel Prize for physics for his work with colloids, Svedberg's award greatly enhanced the recognition by science and society of the importance of the field of colloid chemistry to biological and physical processes. Svedberg became director of the new Institute for Physical Chemistry in 1931, allowing him to continue his research for the remainder of his career. During World War II, however, he was forced to switch his laboratory's research efforts to the development of polychloroprene (synthetic rubber), as well as other

synthetic polymers. Despite this distraction from his main work, he was still able to devise ways to incorporate the use of the electron microscope and X-ray diffraction to study the properties of cellulose biomolecules. And he developed the so-called osmotic balance, which weighed colloid particles by separating particles through a permeable membrane.

On reaching mandatory retirement age in 1949, the Swedish government honored Svedberg with a promotion to emeritus professor and made a special exception to the retirement rule by appointing him lifelong director of the Gustav Werner Institute for Nuclear Chemistry; there he studied radiochemotherapy and the effects of radiation on macromolecules. Physical chemists also honored Svedberg by naming the so-called centrifugation coefficient unit after him: the svedberg unit, *s*, is equal to 1×10^{-13} seconds and represents the speed at which a particle settles out of solution divided by the force generated by the centrifuge. The coefficient depends on the density and shape of the particles, with specific values of *s* corresponding to specific masses measured in daltons, a unit that expresses relative atomic masses.

Svedberg was married four times, first to Andrea Andreen (1909), then to Jan Frodi Dahlquist (1916), Ingrid Blomquist Tauson (1938), and Margit Hallen Norback (1948); he had six daughters and six sons. He held memberships in the Royal Society, the American National Academy of Sciences, the Academy of Sciences of the USSR, among many other organizations. Svedberg received honorary doctorates from the universities of Delaware, Groningen, Oxford, Paris, Uppsala, Wisconsin, and Harvard. In addition, he was active in the Swedish Research Council for Technology and the Swedish Atomic Research Council. He died in Örebro, Sweden, on February 25, 1971.

SELECTED WRITINGS BY SVEDBERG:

Books

(With Kai O. Pederson) *The Ultracentrifuge,* Clarendon, 1940.

Periodicals

(With J. Burton Nichols) "Determination of Size and Distribution of Size of Particles by Centrifugal Methods," *Journal of the American Chemical Society,* Volume 45, 1923.

(With Robin Fahraeus) "A New Method for the Determination of the Molecular Weight of the Proteins," *Journal of the American Chemical Society,* Volume 48, 1926.

"Sedimentation of Molecules in Centrifugal Fields," *Chemical Reviews,* Volume 14, 1934.

SOURCES:

Books

Abbott, David, editor, *Biographical Dictionary of Scientists: Chemists,* Peter Bedrick Books, 1984, pp. 133–134.

Magill, Frank N., editor, *The Nobel Prize Winners: Chemistry,* Salem Press, 1990, pp. 279–287.

Nobel Prize Winners, H. W. Wilson, 1987, pp. 1030–1033.

Periodicals

Tiselius, Arne, and Stig Claesson, "The Svedberg and Fifty Years of Physical Chemistry in Sweden," *Annual Review of Physical Chemistry,* Volume 18, 1967, pp. 1–8.

—*Sketch by Marc Kusinitz*

M. S. Swaminathan
1925-
Indian geneticist and agricultural scientist

As a university student in India, M. S. Swaminathan read of the terrible Bengal famine of 1942 to 1943, in which millions of his countrymen starved to death, and determined that India would make such famines a thing of the past. A genetic researcher, an agricultural administrator, and the first recipient of the World Food Prize—the equivalent of a Nobel for agriculture—Swaminathan has devoted nearly five decades of his life to making this goal a reality. At the award ceremony in Washington, Secretary General of the United Nations Javier Perez de Cuellar asserted that Swaminathan's "contributions to agricultural science have made an indelible mark on food production in India and elsewhere in the developing world."

Monkombu Sambasivan Swaminathan, born on August 7, 1925, in Kumbakonam, India, knew from a young age that much was expected of him. His father, M. K. Sambasivan, was a surgeon who worked closely with Mahatma Gandhi on the freedom movement and who established within his son a deep commitment to individual freedom as well as to national self-reliance. His mother, Shrimati Thangammal, came from an old and influential family. After his father's early death, Swaminathan, his two brothers, and one sister were brought up by other members of an extended family, academics, and government administrators. He attended Travancore and Madras Universities and appeared to have a brilliant future ahead of him in the civil service, but decided to follow a career in plant genetics instead. In 1949 he joined the department of genetics at Netherlands Agricultural University in Wageningen as a UNESCO Fellow. He completed his studies at Cambridge University in London, earning a Ph.D. at its School of Agriculture in 1952. His early research involved the origin of the cultivated potato as well as the development of new commercial varieties. This research was continued at the University of Wisconsin, where Swaminathan held a research fellowship from 1952 to 1953. Turning down a job offer from the university, Swaminathan returned to India in 1954.

Leads India's Green Revolution

Back in India, Swaminathan accepted a position as research cytogeneticist at the Central Rice Research Institute, and the following year joined the staff of the Indian Agricultural Research Institute in New Delhi, where he would remain for the next eighteen years, working mainly in the field of wheat improvement. It was during these years that Swaminathan carried out some of his most vital research in raising the yield of wheat production by the introduction of various hybrid strains of wheat—including the dwarf Mexican—into the Indian agricultural system. Swaminathan and his students also carried out genetic research into rice varieties, transferring the gene for dwarfing into the popular basmati variety of Indian rice. He also adapted strains of rice for both drought and deep water conditions and instituted a gene bank for rice plants now comprising some 75,000 varieties, many of which would otherwise be in danger of extinction. It is via this gene bank that much of the hybridization research at the institute is carried out. Additionally, Swaminathan ensured that India's Green Revolution would be in harmony with the land and that it would stress environmental issues as well as economic ones. Pesticides and inorganic fertilizers were used sparingly, and the latest technologies were passed on to illiterate farmers through his "technicracy" program, which taught advanced agricultural skills through direct work experience.

By the 1970s, the new policies had paid off: India had progressed from having the largest food deficit in the world to producing enough grain to feed all of its people. With further work in disaster preparation, Swaminathan also ensured a safe nutritional future for his country even in times of natural catastrophe. His concern for the welfare of women was also evidenced by his studies of the effects of technological changes on women in rice-based agricultural systems. Such studies have led to greater opportunities for women in the lesser developed countries to earn money and participate more fully in the economy. In 1979, Swaminathan became principal secretary of the

Ministry of Agriculture and Irrigation, a position that gave him more freedom to institute agricultural policies, particularly those relating to sustainable rice production.

Swaminathan became internationally known in 1982 when he was named director general of the International Rice Research Institute in the Philippines, a post he filled until 1989, when he founded the Center for Research on Sustainable Agricultural and Rural Development in Madras. His environmental endeavors were acknowledged by an honorary vice-presidential position with the World Wildlife Fund from 1985 to 1987. He was also the president of the International Union for Conservation of Nature and Natural Resources from 1984 to 1990. In 1991 Swaminathan was awarded the Tyler Prize for Environmental Achievement for his accomplishments in preserving biological diversity and ecologically sustainable agricultural policies. That same year he also won the prestigious Honda Award. Swaminathan holds thirty-two honorary degrees and is a member of numerous scientific societies worldwide. A tireless researcher and administrator, he is also an educator, having guided fifty-five Ph.D. students in their thesis work.

Public service is a tradition in the Swaminathan family. Married in 1955, Swaminathan is the father of three daughters. His wife, Mina, also a Cambridge graduate, gave up a government job to teach the children of unskilled laborers. One of his daughters is a pediatrician, another is an economist working with landless families, and the youngest is a rural sociologist. "Helping fellow human beings is our mission in life," Swaminathan said in the *Bangkok Post,* "because it brings the greatest satisfaction, mentally and spiritually. It would be short-sighted to think that we can be happy while millions of people are impoverished."

SELECTED WRITINGS BY SWAMINATHAN:

Books

Building a National Food Security System, Indian Environmental Society, 1981.
Science and Integrated Rural Development, Concept Publishing Company, 1982, reprinted 1991.
Science and the Conquest of Hunger, Concept Publishing Company, 1983.
(With I. P. Getubig and Volume L. Chopra) *Biotechnology for Asian Culture: Public Policy Implications,* Asian and Pacific Development Center, 1991.

Periodicals

"Wild Relatives in Potato Breeding," *Farming,* Volume 4, 1950, pp. 370–373.

"Polyploidy and Plant Breeding," *New Biology,* Volume 13, 1952, pp. 31–49.
"Disomic and Tetrosomic Inheritance in a *Solanum* Hybrid," *Nature,* Volume 178, 1956, pp. 599–600.
"Advances in Plant Genetics and Breeding in India," *Indian Journal of Agricultural Science,* Volume 31, 1961, pp. 1–7.
(With others) "Mutation Incidence in *Drosophila Melanogaster* Reared on Irradiated Medium," *Science,* Volume 41, 1963, pp. 637–638.
"New Varieties Destroy Barriers to High Rice Yields," *Indian Farming,* Volume 17, number 3, 1967, pp. 4–7.
"Dwarf Varieties Open New Yield and Income Possibilities in Wheat," *Indian Farming,* Volume 17, no. 5, 1967, pp. 4–7.
"Synergistic Effects of Coordinated Use of Fertilizer and Other Inputs," *Fertilizer News,* Volume 16, 1971, pp. 45–47.
"Indian Agriculture at the Crossroads," *Current Science,* Volume 51, 1981, pp. 13–24. "Biodiversity and Sustainable Agriculture," *Outlook on Agriculture,* Volume 20, 1991, pp. 3–4.
"Ecotechnology and Global Food Security," *Environmental Conservation,* Volume 20, 1993, pp. 6–7.

SOURCES:

Books

Science and Agriculture: M. S. Swaminathan and the Movement for Self-Reliance, Arid Zone Research Association of India, 1980.

Periodicals

Havener, Robert D., "Scientists: Their Rewards and Humanity," *Science,* September 11, 1987, p. 1281.
Thongtham, Normita, "Tribute to a Hero of the Green Revolution," *Bangkok Post,* April 28, 1985, p. 31.

Other

Swaminathan, M. S., interview with J. Sydney Jones conducted February 28, 1994.

—*Sketch by J. Sydney Jones*

Richard Synge
1914-
English biochemist and physical chemist

Richard Synge made important contributions in the fields of physical chemistry and biochemistry. He is best known for the development of partition chromatography, a collaborative effort undertaken with **A. J. P. Martin** in the late 1930s and early 1940s. As a result of their work, Synge and Martin received the 1952 Nobel Prize in chemistry.

Richard Laurence Millington Synge was born on October 28, 1914, in Liverpool, England, to Laurence Millington Synge, a stockbroker, and Katherine Charlotte (Swan) Synge. He was the oldest of three children and the only son. After growing up in the Cheshire area of England, he attended Winchester College, a private preparatory school, where he won a classics scholarship to attend Trinity College at Cambridge University. After listening to a speech given by the noted biochemist **Frederick Gowland Hopkins**, however, he decided to forego his education in the classics and instead pursue a degree in biochemistry at Trinity.

Synge undertook graduate studies at the Cambridge Biochemical Laboratory in 1936, receiving his Ph.D. in 1941. His doctoral research concerned the separation of acetyl amino acids. It was at this time that Synge first met Archer Martin, who was engaged in building a mechanism for extracting vitamin E. They began to work together on a separation process, which was delayed when Martin left for a position at the Wool Industries Research Laboratories in Leeds, England. Synge was able to join Martin there in 1939, when he received a scholarship from the International Wool Secretariat for his work on amino acids in wool.

The Development of Partition Chromatography

Synge and Martin's work built on the adsorption chromatography techniques first developed by **Mikhail Tswett**, a Russian botanist, who evolved the procedure in his work on plant colors. Like Tswett, Synge and Martin's goal was to separate the various molecules that make up a complex substance so that the constituent molecules could be further studied. In order to achieve this goal, Tswett had filled a glass tube with powder, then placed a sample of the complex material to be studied at the top of the tube. When a solvent was trickled into the tube, it carried the complex material down into the powder. As the solution moved through the tube, the molecules of the different substances would separate and move at different speeds depending on their chemical attraction to the powder. While Tswett's technique was useful, it did not have universal application; there were a limited number of materials that could be used for the powder filling, and therefore only a limited number of substances could be identified in this manner.

In addition to Tswett's adsorption chromatography, there also existed the process of countercurrent solvent extraction. This technique involves a solution of two liquids that do not mix, such as alcohol and water. When a complex substance is applied to this solution, the molecules separate depending on whether they are more attracted to the water or the alcohol. Synge and Martin's breakthrough involved the combination of adsorption chromatographyand countercurrent solvent extraction. This was achieved by using a solid substance adsorbent such as fine cellulose paper in place of Tswett's powder. In one application of the procedure, a complex mixture of molecules is spotted on one end of the paper, then that end is placed in a solution that might contain alcohol and water or chloroform and water. As the liquids flow through the paper, transporting the complex substance, the molecules in the substance separate depending both on their rate of adsorption by the paper and also by their affinity for either of the two liquids. When the process is completed, a series of spots is visible on the strip of paper. Each spot depicts one type of molecule present in the complex substance.

Synge and Martin had made early progress on partition chromatography during their time at Cambridge, but the need by industry and medicine for a more reliable technique spurred further research. At Leeds, they built a forty-unit extraction machine and experimented with various solvents and filtering materials. Their collaboration continued after Synge left to become a biochemist at the Lister Institute of Preventive Medicine in London in 1943, and by 1944 the improved cellulose filter method resulted. Later, they developed a two-dimensional chromatography process wherein two solvents flow at right angles to one another. This technique yielded an even sharper degree of molecular separation.

Partition chromatography was readily adopted by researchers for a variety of biochemical separations, especially those involving amino acidsand proteins. Using the process in his doctoral research, Synge was able to separate and analyze the twenty amino acids found in protein. The technique was used in studies of enzyme action as well as in analyses of carbohydrates, lipids, and nucleic acids. Partition chromatography also became a useful tool for the food, drug, and chemical industries. Further experimentation with the process allowed proteins to be identified through the use of radioactive markers. The result of this marking was the ability to produce a photograph of the biochemical separation. The marking technique was used extensively by other biochemists, notably **Melvin Calvin** for his work in plant photosynthesis, and **Walter Gilbert** and **Frederick Sanger** for their research into DNA sequencing. All three would later receive the Nobel Prize for discoveries made using partition chromatography.

Later Research Builds on Chromatography Knowledge

Continuing his research of amino acids and peptides, Synge traveled to the Institute of Biochemistry at the University of Uppsala, Sweden in 1946. There, he and **Arne Tiselius**, the Swedish biochemist, studied other separation methods, especially electrophoresis and adsorption. Back home, Synge applied this knowledge toward the isolation of amino acids in rye grass in order to study their structure, a subject he collaborated on with J. C. Wood. He also used the new techniques to study the molecular makeup of plant juices, examining the juices' role as a stimulator in bacteria growth. Partition chromatography was an important factor in other research carried on by Synge at that time: With D. L. Mould, he separated sugars through electrokinetic ultrafiltration in order to study the metabolic process. With Mary Youngson, he studied rye grass proteins. He and E. P. White were able to isolate a toxin called sporidesmin, which produces eczema in sheep and other cud-chewing animals. Synge's findings in all of these areas benefited efforts by agriculture, industry, and medicine to improve human health and well-being.

In 1948 Synge accepted a position as director of the Department of Protein Chemistry at Rowett Research Institute in Scotland. From 1967 until his retirement in 1976, he was a biochemist with the Food Research Institute in Norwich. He closed out his academic career as an honorary professor in the School of Biological Sciences at the University of East Anglia from 1968 until 1984. In addition to the Nobel Prize, Synge received the John Price Wetherill Medal of the Franklin Institute in 1959. He has held memberships in the Royal Society, the Royal Irish Academy, the American Society of Biological Chemists, and the Phytochemical Society of Europe. He married Ann Stephen, a physician and the niece of writer Virginia Woolf, in 1943. They have seven children.

SELECTED WRITINGS BY SYNGE:

Periodicals

(With Archer Martin) "A New Form of Chromatography Employing Two Liquid Phases," *Biochemical Journal,* Volume 35, 1941, pp. 1358–68.
"Partition Chromatography," *The Analyst,* Volume 71, 1946.

"Methods for Isolating Amino-Acids: Aminobutyric Acid from Rye Grass," *Biochemical Journal,* Volume 48, 1951.
"Applications of Partition Chromatography," Nobel lecture, in *Les Prix Nobel,* 1952.
"Note on the Occurrence of Diaminopimelic Acid in Some Intestinal Micro-organisms from Farm Animals," *Journal of General Microbiology,* Volume 9, 1953.
"Experiments on Electrical Migration of Peptides and Proteins Inside Porous Membranes: Influences of Adsorption, Diffusion and Pore Dimensions," *Biochemical Journal,* Volume 65, 1957.
"A Retrospect on Liquid Chromatography," *Biochemical Society Symposium,* Number 30, 1969.

SOURCES:

Books

The Nobel Prize Winners, Chemistry, Volume 2: *1938–1968,* edited by Frank N. Magill, Salem Press, 1990, pp. 598–607.
Wasson, Tyler, editor, *Nobel Prize Winners,* H. W. Wilson, 1987, pp. 1033–1034.

—Sketch by Jane Stewart Cook

Albert Szent-Györgyi
1893-1986
Hungarian American biochemist, molecular biologist, and physiologist

Albert Szent-Györgyi was a controversial, charismatic, and intuitive scientist whose career took many paths in the course of his life: physiologist, pharmacologist, bacteriologist, biochemist, molecular biologist. In 1937 he was awarded the Nobel Prize in physiology or medicine for his work in isolating vitamin C and his advances in the study of intercellular respiration; in 1954 he received the Albert and Mary Lasker Award from the American Heart Association for his contribution to the understanding of heart disease through his research in muscle physiology. In later years, Szent-Györgyi moved into the electron sphere, where he studied matter smaller than molecules, seeking the substances that would define the basic building blocks of life. In his late seventies,

Albert Szent-Györgyi

he founded the National Foundation for Cancer Research.

Albert Szent-Györgyi von Nagyrapolt was born in Budapest, Hungary, on September 16, 1893, to Miklos and Josephine Szent-Györgyi von Nagyrapolt. He was the second of three sons. His father, whose family claimed a title and was said to have traced their ancestry back to the seventeenth century, was a prosperous businessman who owned a two-thousand-acre farm located outside Budapest. His mother came from a long line of notable Hungarian scientists.

As a student, Szent-Györgyi did not begin to develop his potential until his last two years in high school, when he decided to become a medical researcher. In 1911 he entered Budapest Medical School. His education was interrupted by World War I, when he was drafted into the Hungarian Army. He was decorated for bravery; but in 1916, disillusioned with the country's leadership and the progress of the war, he deliberately wounded himself in his upper arm. He was released from the army and sent back home, where he resumed his medical studies. He received his medical degree in 1917 and that same year married Cornelia (Nelly) Demeny. Their daughter, Cornelia (Little Nelly), was born in 1918.

Hungary's Political Upheaval Forces Emigration

The political situation in Hungary after the Austrian defeat caused many families to lose all they had. Szent-Györgyi's family was no exception. With Budapest under Communist rule, Szent-Györgyi decided to leave and accepted a research position at Pozony, Hungary, one hundred miles away. It was there, at the Pharmacological Institute of the Hungarian Elizabeth University, that Szent-Györgyi gained experience as a pharmacologist. In 1919 war broke out between Hungary and the Republic of Czechoslovakia. The Czechs seized Pozony, renaming it Bratislava. In order to continue his scientific training, Szent-Györgyi joined the millions of intellectuals who left Hungary during this time.

In 1921 he accepted a position at the Pharmaco-Therapeutical Institute of the University of Leiden in The Netherlands. This began a period of intense productivity for Szent-Györgyi: by the time he was twenty-nine years old, he had written nineteen research papers, and his research spanned the disciplines of physiology, pharmacology, bacteriology, and biochemistry. Szent-Györgyi is quoted by Ralph W. Moss, author of his biography, *Free Radical: Albert Szent-Györgyi and the Battle over Vitamin C,* as saying: "My problem was: was the hypothetical Creator an anatomist, physiologist, chemist or mathematician? My conclusion was that he had to be all of these, and so if I wanted to follow his trail, I had to have a grasp on all sides of nature." The scientist added that he "had a rather individual method. I did not try to acquire a theoretical knowledge before starting to work. I went straight to the laboratory, cooked up some senseless theory, and started to disprove it."

It was while in The Netherlands, as assistant to the professor of physiology at Groningen, that he presented the first of a series of papers on cellular respiration (the process by which organic molecules in the cell are converted to carbon dioxide and water, releasing energy), a question whose answer was considered central to biochemistry. Competing theories put forth on this question (one citing the priority of oxygen's role in the process; the other championing hydrogen as having the primary role) had caused biochemists to take one side or the other. Szent-Györgyi's contribution was that both theories were correct: active oxygen oxidized active hydrogen. Szent-Györgyi's research into cellular respiration laid the groundwork for the entire concept of the respiratory cycle. The paper discussing his theory is considered to be a milestone in biochemistry. Here, also, was the beginning of the work for which he was eventually given the Nobel Prize.

Cambridge and Frederick Gowland Hopkins

While still at Groningen, Szent-Györgyi began studying the role of the adrenal glands (responsible for secreting adrenaline and other important hormones), hoping to isolate a reducing agent (electron donor) and explain its role in the onset of Addison's disease. This work was to occupy him for almost a decade, produce unexpected results, and bring him worldwide attention as a scientist. He was sure he had made a breakthrough when silver nitrate added to a preparation of minced adrenal glands turned black. That indicated a reducing agent was present, and he set out to explain its function in oxidative metabolism. He thought the reducing agent might be a hormone equivalent to adrenalin. Frustrated because scientists in Groningen seemed unconvinced of the importance of his discovery, he wrote to **Henry Hallett Dale**, a prominent British physiologist. As a result of their correspondence, Szent-Györgyi was invited to England for three months to continue his work.

Unfortunately, his testing proved a failure—the color change of the silver nitrate turned out to be a reaction of adrenaline with the iron in the mincer in which he ground the adrenal glands. Szent-Györgyi returned to The Netherlands, where he continued his work on cellular respiration in plants, writing a paper on respiration in the potato. But increasing friction with the head of the laboratory caused him to resign his position. Unable to support his wife and daughter, he sent them home to Budapest. In August 1926 he attended a congress of the International Physiological Society in Stockholm, Sweden. It was there that his luck turned. The chairman of the event was Sir **Frederick Gowland Hopkins**, considered to be the greatest living biochemist of his day. Much to Szent-Györgyi's surprise, Hopkins referred to Szent-Györgyi's paper on potato respiration in his address to the congress. After the address, Szent-Györgyi introduced himself to Hopkins, who invited him to Cambridge, where he was to remain until he returned to Hungary in 1932, eventually becoming president of the University of Szeged.

With the assurance of a fellowship from the Rockefeller Foundation (the foundation was to be a source of much financial support throughout his career), Szent-Györgyi sent for his family, rented a house, and set to work. Hopkins became his mentor—and the man Szent-Györgyi regarded as having the most influence on him as a scientist. While at Cambridge, he was awarded a Ph.D. for the isolation of hexuronic acid, the name given to the substance he had isolated from adrenal glands. One of the puzzling things about this substance was its similarity to one also found in citrus fruits and cabbage. Szent-Györgyi set out to analyze the substance, but the main obstacle to doing this was obtaining a sufficient supply of fresh adrenal glands. He finally was able to isolate a small quantity of a similar substance from orange juice and cabbage, learning that it was a carbohydrate and a sugar acid.

In 1929 Szent-Györgyi made his first visit to the United States. It was at this time that he visited the scientific community at Woods Hole, Massachusetts.

He then went on to the Mayo Clinic in Rochester, Minnesota, where he had been invited to use the research facilities to continue his work isolating the adrenal substance. He managed to purify an ounce of the substance, and sent ten grams of it back to England for analysis. Nothing came of this, however, as the amount sent was too small. After almost ten years, the research appeared to be at a dead end. Szent-Györgyi took what remained of the purified crystals and returned to Cambridge.

Vitamin C and the Nobel Prize

In 1928 Szent-Györgyi had been offered a top academic post at the University of Szeged in Hungary. He accepted, but did not take up his duties there until 1931 because of delays in completing the Szeged laboratory. At Szeged, in addition to his duties as teacher, Szent-Györgyi continued his research, still trying to solve the puzzle of the adrenal substance, hexuronic acid.

It had been known since the sixteenth century that certain foods, especially citrus fruits, prevented scurvy, a disease characterized by swollen gums and loosened teeth. Although scurvy could be prevented by including citrus fruit in the diet, isolation of the antiscurvy element from citrus eluded researchers. It was not until after World War I that drug companies began a concentrated search for the antiscorbutic element (now called vitamin C). Scientists in Europe and the United States began competing to be the first to isolate this element. Vitamin C was not unfamiliar to Szent-Györgyi, and he had written of its possible connection with hexuronic acid. Now he was able to positively identify hexuronic acid as vitamin C and not an adrenal hormone, as he had previously thought. He suggested the compound be called ascorbic acid, and continued his study of its function in the body, using vitamin C-rich Hungarian paprika as the source material.

Although Charles Glen King had also isolated Vitamin C and made the connection between it and hexuronic acid—and announced his findings just two weeks before Szent-Györgyi made his report, in 1937 Szent-Györgyi was given the Nobel Prize. His acceptance speech, "Oxidation, Energy Transfer, and Vitamins," gave details of the extraordinary circumstances under which his discoveries were made.

Work during Nazi Occupation

In 1941 Szent-Györgyi and his wife were divorced. He married Marta Borbiro Miskolczy that same year. Bitterly opposed to Nazi rule in Hungary, he became an active member of the Hungarian underground. It was during the war years that he made some of his most important discoveries. His work during this time still concentrated on cellular respiration. His research in this area proved to be the basis for one of the fundamental breakthroughs in biology: the citric acid cycle. This cycle explains how almost all cells extract energy from food. It was during the war years that he also studied the chemical mechanisms of muscle contraction. His discoveries about how muscles move and function were fundamental to twentieth-century physiology, and made him a pioneer in molecular biology.

By 1944 Szent-Györgyi's outspoken opposition to Hitler's regime had put his life in danger. He and his wife went into hiding for the remainder of the war, surfacing in Budapest when the Russians liberated Hungary from the Nazis in 1945. Disillusioned with Soviet rule, he emigrated to the United States in 1947, and became an American citizen in 1954.

Woods Hole, Cancer Research, and the Vietnam War

Szent-Györgyi and his wife settled in Woods Hole, Massachusetts. Research facilities were provided for him at the Marine Biological Laboratories. He struggled to find backing to continue his work. With the help of five wealthy businessmen, he set up the Szent-Györgyi Foundation (later called the Institute for Muscle Research), whose purpose was to raise money for muscle research and bring a group of Hungarian scientists to America to assist him. This endeavor met with partial success, but its full potential was not realized because of concerns about the legitimacy of the financial backing (and suspicion about the political loyalties of the Hungarians). As a result, Szent-Györgyi had a research team, but was unable to support them. To remedy this, he took a position in 1948 with the National Institutes of Health (NIH). He left there in 1950 for a short assignment at Princeton University's Institute for Advanced Studies. Then grants began to come in for his muscle research. Major funding came from Armour and Company (the Chicago meatpacking company), the American Heart Association, the Association for the Aid of Crippled Children, the Muscular Dystrophy Association, and NIH.

During these years, Szent-Györgyi and his team of researchers continued to make strides in the analysis of muscle protein. He also published three books: *Chemistry of Muscular Contraction, The Nature of Life,* and *Chemical Physiology of Contraction in Body and Heart,* and 120 scientific papers. These writings brought him to the attention of the American scientific community and had great influence on scientists worldwide.

Szent-Györgyi's wife Marta died of cancer in 1963. He married twice after her death. During the sixties and seventies, his opposition to the Vietnam War made him a hero to those connected to the peace movement. He wrote two books during this period

that characterized his personal philosophy: *Science, Ethics, and Politics* and *The Crazy Ape* (which included his poem series, "Psalmus Humanus and Six Prayers"). He spoke out against the war on numerous occasions, both in public lectures and through letters to newspapers and periodicals.

Szent-Györgyi was almost eighty years old when he founded the National Foundation for Cancer Research. Funding from the NFCR supported his research until the end of his life. For more than forty years, his research had been concerned with the development of a basic theory about the nature of life. Szent-Györgyi called this new field of endeavor "submolecular biology." It was not just a cure for cancer that he was looking for, but a new way of looking at biology. He was convinced that his study of the structure of life at the level of electrons would not only make possible a cure for cancer but would also provide the knowledge to ensure the human body's optimum health.

Ralph Moss, the author of *Free Radical,* asked Szent-Györgyi for his philosophy of life shortly before the scientist's death of kidney failure on October 22, 1986. He scrawled on a piece of paper: "Think boldly. Don't be afraid of making mistakes. Don't miss small details, keep your eyes open and be modest in everything except your aims."

SELECTED WRITINGS BY SZENT-GYÖRGYI:

Books

On Oxidation, Fermentation, Vitamins, Health, and Disease, The Abraham Flexner Lectures, Williams & Wilkens, 1937.
Chemistry of Muscular Contraction, Academic Press, 1947.
The Nature of Life, Academic Press, 1948.
Chemical Physiology of Contraction in Body and Heart, Academic Press, 1953.
Introduction to a Submolecular Biology, Academic Press, 1960.
Science, Ethics, and Politics, Vantage Press, 1963.
The Crazy Ape: Written by a Biologist for the Young, Philosophical Library, 1970.
Electronic Biology and Cancer: A New Theory of Cancer, Dekker, 1976.

SOURCES:

Books

Moss, Ralph W., *Free Radical: Albert Szent-Györgyi and the Battle over Vitamin C,* Paragon House, 1988.

—*Sketch by Jane Stewart Cook*

Leo Szilard
1898-1964
Hungarian American physicist and biophysicist

Leo Szilard

A native of Hungary, Leo Szilard was one of the leading contributors to the development of nuclear energy and the first atomic weapons. He was also among the earliest and most active campaigners for nuclear arms control. In 1942, with **Enrico Fermi**, he set up the first nuclear chain reaction. He later became increasingly interested in the fields of molecular energy and biophysics, and helped develop the electron microscope.

Leo Szilard was born in Budapest, Hungary, on February 11, 1898, to Louis Szilard, an architect and engineer, and his wife, the former Thekla Vidor. The eldest of three children, Leo was a sickly child, and for a number of years his mother taught him at home.

Educated in Budapest and Berlin

In the fall of 1916, Szilard entered the Budapest Institute of Technology, intending to major in electrical engineering. At the end of his first year at the institute, he was called to service in the Austro-Hungarian army and assigned to officer training school. He became very ill with influenza, however, and had not fully recovered by the time World War I ended in 1918. He returned to the Budapest Institute of Technology for just over a year before transferring first to the Technische Hochschule at Berlin-Charlottenburg.

At Berlin, Szilard's career outlook underwent a significant change. He came into contact with some of the finest physicists in the world, including **Albert Einstein**, **Max Planck** and **Max von Laue**, the last of whom was to become Szilard's own doctoral advisor. Szilard decided that his real interests lay in the field of physics rather than engineering, and in 1922 he was awarded his Ph.D. in that field. His doctoral thesis, written under the supervision of von Laue, dealt with the statistical implications of the second law of thermodynamics. Szilard's work on this topic continued for a number of years, culminating in a paper published in 1929, "On the Decrease of Entropy in a Thermodynamic System by the Intervention of Intelligent Beings," in which he investigated the application of thermodynamical laws to information theory. That paper is regarded as an important precursor to modern cybernetic theories.

After receiving his degree, Szilard was appointed first a research assistant and then, in 1925, *Privatdozent* at the Institute of Theoretical Physics at the University of Berlin. Director of the institute at the time was von Laue, his former advisor. In addition to his continuing work on thermodynamics during this period, Szilard also originated a series of studies on X-ray crystallography, a field in which von Laue was a world leader. Szilard also worked closely with Albert Einstein on the development of a pump for liquid metals, for which he eventually obtained a patent. In addition, he became interested in the problem of particle accelerators and invented a number of devices that were later to be incorporated into early cyclotrons.

Emigrates from Germany to England and the United States

In 1933, the rise of Adolf Hitler convinced Szilard, who was Jewish, that he should leave Germany. Fearing for both his career and his life, he fled first to Vienna and then, six weeks later, to England. There he joined the physics department at St. Bartholomew's Hospital in London. In 1935 he moved to the Clarendon Laboratory at Oxford.

It was during this period that Szilard received news of **Frédéric** and **Irène Joliot-Curie**'s discovery of artificial radioactivity. He began to think about the possibility of a nuclear chain reaction in which the nuclear decay of one atom, brought about by some type of particle, would result in the production of a new atom with the release of more particles of the kind needed to start the reaction. In such a case, the reaction, once initiated, would be self-sustaining over many, many episodes of decay. The value of such a reaction, Szilard knew, was that energy would be released in each step of the process. After countless repetitions of the reaction, huge amounts of energy—sufficient, for instance, to make a powerful bomb—would be released.

Szilard first explored the possibility of using beryllium in such a chain reaction. He and a colleague, T. A. Chalmers, found that gamma rays directed at a beryllium target would cause the emission of a neutron from the beryllium nucleus. The two hoped that this reaction could act as the first step in a chain reaction in which beryllium atoms would break apart to form helium atoms and more neutrons. The neutrons thus formed would, they hoped, then cause more beryllium atoms to break apart into helium atoms with the release of more neutrons, and so on. More detailed studies showed, however, that such a reaction could not be sustained.

In addition to his research, Szilard continued his efforts to find new jobs for scientists fleeing the Nazi purges on the continent. These efforts were characteristic of Szilard's life-long commitment to helping others. He once said that this humanitarian impulse was largely the result of reading, at the age of ten, Hungarian author Imre Madách's *The Tragedy of Man.*

Toward the end of 1938, Szilard decided to move to the United States. He had no more settled in at his new workplace, Columbia University, than he received startling news from Europe. **Otto Hahn** and **Fritz Strassman** had produced the first fission of an atomic nucleus, an event that was fully understood and explained by **Lise Meitner** in January 1939. Szilard immediately recognized the significance of this discovery. It held the potential for making possible the very kind of nuclear chain reaction on which he had been working in London.

With a colleague, Walter Zinn, Szilard set up a replica of the Hahn-Strassman experiment at Columbia. Their goal was to find out whether the fission of a uranium nucleus would result in the formation of at least one neutron, a condition necessary for the maintenance of a chain reaction. On March 3, the experiment was ready. A few flashes of light on an oscilloscope gave Szilard and Zinn the answer they sought: neutrons were being released during the fission of uranium. A nuclear chain reaction was possible. Szilard would later say he knew immediately that this discovery would cause the world great sorrow.

Leads Effort to Establish Nuclear Bomb Project

News of the discovery of nuclear fission swept through the physics community like wildfire. Few failed to grasp the military potential of the discovery.

A group of physicists in the United States who were particularly concerned about this potential became convinced that the U.S. government must take fast and aggressive action to see whether nuclear fission could really be used in the development of weapons. Szilard composed a letter, which Albert Einstein signed, presenting their arguments to President Franklin D. Roosevelt. Roosevelt responded by appointing an Advisory Committee on Uranium to investigate the issue. After some initial hesitation, the committee produced a favorable recommendation, and the Manhattan Engineering District Project was created to pursue the development of the world's first atomic bombs. The first contract let under the Manhattan Project was to a group of scientists at Columbia that included Szilard.

In 1942, Szilard left Columbia to become part of the Manhattan Project's Metallurgical Laboratory at the University of Chicago. Working there with **Enrico Fermi**, he witnessed the first controlled nuclear reaction on December 2, 1942, when the world's first atomic pile (nuclear reactor) was put into operation. The hopes and dreams—as well as the fears—that Szilard had long held for nuclear chain reactions had become a reality.

Shortly thereafter, Szilard began to argue for a cessation of research on nuclear weapons. A number of factors influenced his position. First, he was convinced that the tide of war had turned in favor of the Allies, and he thought the war could soon be ended with conventional weapons. Second, he feared that the successful development of nuclear weapons would lead to an all-out arms race with the Soviet Union after the war. Finally, he recognized the horrible human tragedies that would result from the use of an atomic bomb. His suggestions for a demonstration test of nuclear weapons in an uninhabited area to which the Japanese government would be invited fell on deaf ears, however. Instead, on August 6 and 9, 1945, the first atomic bombs were dropped on Hiroshima and Nagasaki in Japan. The war ended a week later.

Turns to Biological Studies

In the post-war years, Szilard spent a major portion of his time working for the control of the demon he had helped release, atomic energy. He joined a large number of his fellow nuclear scientists in forming the Federation of Atomic Scientists, which worked to keep control of atomic energy out of the hands of the military and within a civilian department. He also made efforts to encourage mutual disarmament and the reduction of tensions between the United States and the Soviet Union. To this end, he was active in the formation and planning of the Pugwash Conferences on Science and World Affairs, a series of conferences on nuclear safety that met in the late 1950s and early 1960s. In 1962, he helped found the Council for a Livable World, a Washington, D.C.-based lobby for nuclear arms control.

In the late 1940s, Szilard once again turned to scientific research, but this time in the field of biology. In 1946, he accepted an appointment as professor of biophysics at the University of Chicago. One of his first accomplishments was the development of the chemostat, an instrument that aids in the study of bacteria and viruses by making it possible to regulate various growth factors. Later he became interested in the biology of aging. Another topic in which Szilard became interested, memory and recall, was the subject of his final scientific paper, published after his death.

Szilard became a U.S. citizen in 1943. In 1951 he married Gertrud Weiss, whom he had first met in 1933 in Vienna, where Weiss was a medical student. The couple had no children. Szilard was awarded the Einstein Gold Medal in 1958 and the Atoms for Peace Award in 1959. He died of a heart attack on May 30, 1964, in La Jolla, California, where he had been a resident fellow at the Salk Institute.

SELECTED WRITINGS BY SZILARD:

Books

The Voice of the Dolphin and Other Stories (science fiction), Simon & Schuster, 1961.

Collected Words of Leo Szilard, edited by Bernard T. Feld and Gertrud W. Szilard, Massachusetts Institute of Technology, 1972.
Leo Szilard: His Version of the Facts: Selected Recollections and Correspondence, edited by Spencer R. Weart and Gertrud Weiss Szilard, Massachusetts Institute of Technology, 1978.

SOURCES:

Books

McGraw-Hill Modern Scientists and Engineers, Volume 10, McGraw-Hill, 1980, pp. 181–182.
Wigner, Eugene, "Leo Szilard, 1898–1964," *Biographical Memoirs,* Volume 40, National Academy of Sciences, 1969, pp. 337–341.

Periodicals

Coffin, Tristram, "Leo Szilard: The Conscience of a Scientist," *Holiday,* February 1964.
New York Times, May 31, 1964.

—*Sketch by David E. Newton*

Igor Tamm
1895-1971
Russian physicist

Igor Tamm's work on nuclear physics and elementary particles covered a wide variety of topics, including relativity, quantum theory, cosmic rays, nuclear forces, plasma physics, and the properties of mesons. His discovery of "Tamm surface levels" in crystalline solids has had application in the development of solid-state devices. In the 1950s and 1960s Tamm became deeply interested in issues of science education and the peaceful use of nuclear energy. He is best known, however, for his theoretical explanation of the origin of Cherenkov radiation, discovered by colleague **Pavel Cherenkov** in about 1935. This theory, developed with **Il'ya Frank** during the period from 1937 to 1939, was recognized by the awarding of the 1958 Nobel Prize in physics to the three Russian physicists.

Igor Evgenievich (some sources cite middle name as Yevgenyevich) Tamm was born on July 8, 1895, in Vladivostok, Russia. His parents were Evgeny Tamm, a civil engineer, and the former Olga Davydova. When Tamm was six years old, his family moved to Elizavetgrad (later renamed Kirovograd), in the Ukraine. Tamm graduated from the Elizavetgrad Gymnasium in 1913, then spent a year at the University of Edinburgh. The end of his first year in Scotland coincided with the beginning of World War I, and Tamm returned to Russia. There he enrolled in the faculty of physics and mathematics at Moscow State University. His schooling was interrupted when the battlefront moved eastward, and in 1917 he became a member of the Elizavetgrad City Soviet of Workers and Soldier Deputies. When the war came to an end, he returned to his studies and was awarded his bachelor's degree in physics in 1918.

Begins Association with Mandel'shtam

Tamm's first teaching appointments were at the Crimean University from 1919 to 1921, and the Odessa Polytechnic Institute in Simferopol. At the latter institution, he made the acquaintance of **Leonid Mandel'shtam**, later to be called the father of Russian physics. Mandel'shtam was to have a critical and long-lasting influence on Tamm's professional career.

One of Tamm's earliest research interests, for example, was crystal optics, a field in which Mandel'shtam had made important discoveries. Tamm also worked on the scattering of light (the Mandel'shtam-Brillouin effect or Rayleigh scattering), particularly on the scattering of light by crystals (the so-called Raman effect, discovered by Mandel'shtam and G. S. Landsberg in 1930).

In 1922 Tamm was offered a teaching post at the J. M. Sverdlov Communist University in Moscow, where he remained until 1925. During the same period he held appointments at the Second Moscow University (from 1923 to 1929) and Moscow State University (from 1924 to 1937). At Moscow State University he was promoted to professor of theoretical physics and made head of the department in 1930. He was granted his doctoral degree in 1933.

During the late 1920s and early 1930s, Tamm investigated a number of applications of quantum theory, which holds that energy exists in discrete units. Perhaps his best-known discovery concerned the properties of electrons on the surface of a crystalline solid. He found that these electrons are bonded in a unique way that gives a surface special properties. The discovery of these "Tamm surface levels" has had important applications in the development of solid-state devices, especially those containing semiconductors—solids whose electrical conductivity falls between that of an insulator and that of a conductor.

Another topic of interest to Tamm during the 1930s was the atomic nucleus. For example, in 1934 he predicted that the neutron, although uncharged, would have a magnetic moment with a negative sign. Although the idea did not meet with widespread approval at first, Tamm's prediction has since been shown to be correct. At about the same time, Tamm began a study of nuclear forces. He developed a theory that attributed beta decay (the spontaneous breakup of neutrons in the nucleus) to forces carried between nucleons (protons and neutrons) by means of electrons and neutrinos. He was incorrect in his choice of force carriers, but understood the general mechanism of intranuclear force transmission. In fact, **Hideki Yukawa** was to outline the correct theory for this phenomenon within a year of Tamm's own electron-neutrino hypothesis.

Explains Cherenkov Radiation

In the period from 1934 to 1936, Tamm's colleague, Pavel Cherenkov, discovered the phenomenon that now carries his name: Cherenkov radiation. The term "Cherenkov radiation" refers to the pale blue light emitted when gamma radiation passes through a (usually) liquid medium. Although Cherenkov determined a number of properties of this radiation, he was unable to develop a satisfactory theory explaining its origin.

That explanation came through the efforts of Tamm and Il'ya Frank in about 1936. Tamm and Frank found that although objects cannot travel faster than the speed of light in a vacuum, they can do so in other media. In the case of Cherenkov radiation, the passage of gamma rays through a medium results in the emission of electrons that do just that. Electrons emitted in this way form a wave that spreads out in a cone-shaped pattern in advance of the gamma ray in much the way that a sonic boom is produced by a supersonic aircraft. The blue glow is produced, then, when the wave velocity exceeds some given value. For this research, Tamm, Frank, and Cherenkov were jointly awarded the 1958 Nobel Prize in physics.

The last four decades of Tamm's life were spent at the P. N. Lebedev Physical Institute in Moscow, where he was named director of the theoretical section in 1934. After his work on Cherenkov radiation, Tamm returned to problems of nuclear physics and elementary particles. During the 1950s, he also carried out research on plasma physics, a topic critical to the development of controlled thermonuclear fusion reactions. Tamm was long interested in problems of science education and the peaceful applications of nuclear energy. In connection with the latter, he was active in the Pugwash movement for science and world affairs of the 1950s and 1960s.

In addition to the Nobel Prize in physics, Tamm was awarded two Orders of Lenin and the Order of the Red Badge of Labor. He was married to Natalie Shuiskaya on September 16, 1917. They had one daughter, Irene, and one son, Eugen. Among Tamm's writings are *Osnovy teorii elektrichestva* (title means "Principles of the Theory of Electricity"), *On the Magnetic Moment of the Neutrino,* and *Relativistic Interaction of Elementary Particles.* Tamm died in Moscow on April 12, 1971.

SELECTED WRITINGS BY TAMM:

Books

Osnovy teorii elektrichestva (title means "Principles of the Theory of Electricity"), Nauka, 1966.

Periodicals

"Exchange Forces Between Neutrons and Protons and Fermi's Theory," *Nature,* Volume 133, 1934, p. 981.

"Nuclear Magnetic Moments and the Properties of the Neutron," *Nature,* Volume 134, 1934, p. 380.

"Kogerentnoe izluchenie bystrogo elektrona v srede" (title means "Coherent Radiation of Fast Electrons Passing through Matter"), *Doklady Akademii Nauk SSSR,* Volume 14, Number 3, 1937, pp. 107–112.

SOURCES:

Books

Biographical Encyclopedia of Scientists, Volume 2, Facts on File, 1981, p. 771.
Gillispie, Charles Coulson, editor, *Dictionary of Scientific Biography,* Volume 13, Scribner's, 1975, pp. 239–242.
McGraw-Hill Modern Scientists and Engineers, Volume 3, McGraw-Hill, 1980, pp. 186–187.

—*Sketch by David E. Newton*

Tan Jiazhen
1909-
Chinese biologist and geneticist

Tan Jiazhen's work in the field of genetics resulted in a distinguished scientific career in the United States and China. His broad-ranging intellect and abilities have served the scientific community of both countries through his work at many institutes of higher learning. For example, since 1984, he has been a senior research fellow at the Eleanor Roosevelt Institute for Cancer Research in Denver, Colorado. That same year, he also became director of the Genetics Institute at Fudan University in Shanghai, People's Republic of China, where he had held the post of vice-president beginning in 1961. He has served in an advisory capacity as a member of the board of directors of the International Council for Development of Underutilized Plants, and he has held editorial and advisory positions at *The Scientist, Journal of Genetics,* and *Global Science Journal.* His work as president of the Genetics Society of China and as a member of various international science academies is well known. He capped off his affiliation with these prestigious scientific organizations by becoming, in 1991, a founding member of the World Institute of Sciences.

Tan was born on September 15, 1909, in Ningbo City, Zhejiang Province, the son of C. Y. and M. Y. Tan. He was educated at Suzhou University and obtained a biology degree in 1930. He continued his education at the California Institute of Technology, receiving a Ph.D. in genetics in 1936. A year later, he returned to China, serving as professor at Zhejiang University until 1952. During this period, he also taught for one year as visiting professor at Colorado University. He began work at Fudan University as a professor of genetics and vice president in 1961.

In the 1960s Tan experienced some difficulties given his position in China during the Cultural Revolution. Held in disgrace beginning in 1966, he went underground for a period of ten years, first surfacing in February 1978. He then began the road back to political and scientific legitimacy. First, he was elected deputy for Shanghai Municipality to the fifth National People's Congress, and in March of 1978, was elected as a member of the Standing Committee of the fifth Chinese People's Political Consultative Conference. In June of 1978, his affiliation with Fudan University was once again recognized by the government. As political repression lessened even more, Tan gradually resumed a place of importance in his country's scientific community.

Tan has been the recipient of many honors from science peers throughout the world. He was granted the Distinguished Alumni Award from the California Institute of Technology in 1983. He was given honorary doctor of science degrees from York University in 1984 and from the University of Maryland in 1985. In 1986, he was made honorary president of Ningbo University, and in 1988 Shanghai Agricultural College presented him with that same distinction. He received the Medal of Merit from Konstanz Universität, Federal Republic of Germany, in 1989, and was made an honorary citizen of the State of California in 1990.

In 1932 Tan married M. Y. Fu, who is now deceased. His second marriage was to Dr. Y. F. Qiu in 1973. He has three sons and one daughter.

—*Sketch by Jane Stewart Cook*

Richard A. Tapia
1939-
American mathematician

Richard A. Tapia is a nationally recognized educator who was named in 1990 one of the twenty most influential leaders in minority mathematics education. His four-day workshops on compu-

tational science have also received national attention by bringing secondary and middle school teachers from schools with high minority enrollments to Rice University to learn about opportunities in the computational sciences. As associate director for minority affairs in the Office of Graduate Studies at Rice, Tapia has been extremely successful in producing minority Ph.D.s.

Richard Alfred Tapia was born on March 25, 1939, in Santa Monica, California. The son of Mexican immigrant parents, Amado Tapia and Magda Tapia, he entered the University of California at Los Angeles after spending two preparatory years in junior college. He remained in that university, receiving his B.A. in 1961, his M.A. in 1966, and his Ph.D. in 1967. After graduate school, he taught at the University of Wisconsin as an assistant professor in its Mathematics Research Center from 1968 to 1970. That year he joined Rice University in Houston, Texas, as an assistant professor of mathematical science and has been there ever since. In 1972 he became an associate professor and then a full professor in 1976. Between 1978 and 1983, he was mathematical science department chair and was visiting professor at Baylor College and Stanford University. In 1989 he assumed his present position as associate director for minority affairs in Rice's Office of Graduate Studies.

Tapia has been concerned with the future role of mathematicians and mathematics in a world increasingly dominated by computers. As a member of the American Mathematics Society, he sits on its Strategic Planning Committee and has been able to lead the debate on this important issue. It is imperative, he believes, that mathematics shows itself to be relevant to the everyday world and be able to contribute to solving problems in engineering, medicine, and other applied disciplines.

Tapia's work resulted in his being named one of the twenty most influential leaders in minority mathematics education by the National Research Council of the National Science Foundation in 1990. That same year, he received the college level Education Award, one of the Society for Hispanic Professional Engineers' (SHPE) National Achievement Awards. Besides his membership in the American Mathematics Society, Tapia is a member of the Society for Industrial and Applied Mathematics, the Mathematical Association of America, the Mathematical Programming Society, and the Society for the Advancement of Chicanos and Native Americans in Science (SAC-NAS). He was also elected to the National Academy of Engineering. He is the author of over sixty technical papers as well as a textbook. He has been married to Jean Rodriguez since 1959, and they have two children, Richard and Rebecca.

SELECTED WRITINGS BY TAPIA:

Books

Nonparametric Probability Density Estimation, Johns Hopkins University Press, 1978.
Nonparametric Function Estimation, Modeling, and Simulation, Society for Industrial and Applied Mathematics, 1990.

SOURCES:

Periodicals

Mellado, Carmela C., "Math Education in the Computer Age," *Hispanic Engineer,* Spring 1991, pp. 26–27.
"1990 Award Winners," *Hispanic Engineer,* Conference Issue, 1990, pp. 66–67.

—*Sketch by Leonard C. Bruno*

Alfred Tarski
1901-1983
Polish American mathematician and logician

Alfred Tarski made considerable contributions to several areas of mathematics, including set theory and algebra, and his work as a logician led to important breakthroughs in semantics—the study of symbols and meaning in written and verbal communication. Tarski's research in this area yielded a mathematical definition of truth in language, and also made him a pioneer in studying models of linguistic communication, a subject that became known as model theory. Tarski's research also proved useful in the development of computer science, and he became an influential mentor to later mathematicians as a professor at the University of California at Berkeley.

Born Alfred Tajtelbaum in Warsaw, Poland (then part of Russian Poland), on January 14, 1901, Tarski was the elder of two sons born to Ignacy Tajtelbaum, a shopkeeper of modest means, and Rose (Iuussak) Tajtelbaum, who was known to have an exceptional memory. During his teens Tarski helped supplement the family income by tutoring. He attended an excellent secondary school, and although he was an outstanding student, he, surprisingly, did not get his best marks in logic. Biology was his favorite subject in high school, and he intended to major in this discipline when he first attended the University of War-

saw. However, as Steven R. Givant pointed out in *Mathematical Intelligence,* "what derailed him was success." In an early mathematics course at the university, Tarski was able to solve a challenging problem in set theory posed by the professor. The solution led to his first published paper, and Tarski, at the professor's urging, decided to switch his emphasis to mathematics.

Tarski received a Ph.D. from the University of Warsaw in 1924, the same year he met his future wife, Maria Witkowski. They got married on June 23, 1929, and later had two children, Jan and Ina. It is believed that the young mathematician was in his early-twenties when he changed his name from Tajtelbaum to Tarski. His son, Jan, told interviewer Jeanne Spriter James that this step was taken because Tarski believed that his new Polish-sounding name would be held in higher regard at the university than his original Jewish moniker. When Tarski was married, he was baptized a Catholic, his wife's religion.

Early Struggles in Academia

Tarski served in the Polish army for short periods of time in 1918 and 1920. While working on his Ph.D. he was employed as an instructor in logic at the Polish Pedagogical Institute in Warsaw beginning in 1922. After graduating he became a docent and then adjunct professor of mathematics and logic at the University of Warsaw beginning in 1925. That same year he also took a full-time teaching position at Zeromski's Lycee, a high school in Warsaw, since his income from the university was inadequate to support his family. Tarski remained at both jobs until 1939, despite repeated attempts to secure a permanent university professorship. Some have attributed Tarski's employment difficulties to anti-semitism, but whatever the reason, his lack of academic prominence created problems for the young mathematician. Burdened by his teaching load at the high school and college, Tarski was unable to devote as much time to his research as he would have liked. He later said that his creative output was greatly reduced during these years because of his employment situation. The papers he did publish in this period, however, quickly marked Tarski as one of the premiere logicians of the century. His early work was often concentrated in the area of set theory. He also worked in conjunction with Polish mathematician **Stefan Banach** to produce the Banach-Tarski paradox, which illustrated the limitations of mathematical theories that break a space down into a number of pieces. Other research in the 1920s and 1930s addressed the axiom of choice, large cardinal numbers, the decidability of Euclidean geometry, and Boolean algebra.

Tarski's initial research on semantics took place in the early–1930s. He was concerned here with problems of language and meaning, and his work resulted in a mathematical definition of truth as it is expressed in symbolic languages. He also provided a proof that demonstrated that any such definition of truth in a language results in contradictions. A London *Times* obituary on Tarski noted the ground-breaking nature of his work in this area, proclaiming that the mathematician's findings "set the direction for all modern philosophical discussions of truth." Tarski expanded this early work in semantics over the ensuing years, eventually developing a new field of study—model theory—which would become a major research subject for logicians. This area of study examines the mathematic properties of grammatical sentences and compares them with various models of linguistic communication.

Additionally, Tarski pursued research in many other areas of math and logic during his career, including closure algebras, binary relations and the algebra of relations, cylindrical algebra, and undecidable theories. He also made a lasting contribution to the field of computer science. As early as 1930 he produced an algorithm that was capable of deciding whether any sentence in basic Euclidian geometry is either true or false. This pointed the way toward later machine calculations, and has also had relevance in determining more recent computer applications.

Outbreak of World War II leads to New Opportunities

In 1939 Tarski left Poland for a conference and speaking tour in the United States, intending to be gone for only a short time. Shortly after his departure, however, the German Army invaded and conquered Poland, beginning World War II. Unable to return to his homeland, Tarski found himself stranded in the United States without money, without a job, and without his wife and children who had remained in Warsaw. The family would not be reunited until after the war, and in the meantime, Tarski set about finding work in America. He first served as a research associate in mathematics at Harvard University from 1939 to 1941. In 1940 he also taught as a visiting professor at the City College of New York. He had a temporary position at the Institute for Advanced Study at Princeton beginning in 1941, and in 1942 he obtained his first permanent position in the United States when he was hired as a lecturer at the University of California at Berkeley. The university would remain his professional home for the rest of his career.

Tarski became an associate professor at the university in 1945, was appointed to the position of full professor the following year, and was named professor emeritus in 1968. Tarski's contributions to mathematics and science were enhanced by his role as an educator. He established the renown Group in Logic and the Methodology of Science at Berkeley, and over his long tenure he taught some of the most-influential mathematicians and logicians to emerge after World War II, including **Julia Robinson** and Robert Montague. His stature was further enhanced through his service as a visiting professor and lecturer at numerous U.S. and international universities. In 1973 Tarski ended his formal teaching duties at Berkeley, but he continued to supervise doctoral students and conduct research during the final decade of his life. He died in 1983 from a lung condition caused by smoking.

Tarski received many awards and honors throughout his career. He was elected to the National Academy of Sciences and the Royal Netherlands Academy of Sciences and Letters, and was also made a corresponding fellow in the British Academy. In 1966 he received the Alfred Jurzykowski Foundation Award, and in 1981 he was presented with the Berkeley Citation, the university's highest faculty honor. He also was awarded numerous fellowships and honorary degrees, and was a member in many professional organizations, including the Polish Logic Society, the American Mathematical Society, and the International Union for the History and Philosophy of Science.

SELECTED WRITINGS BY TARSKI:

Books

Introduction to Logic and to the Methodology of Deductive Sciences, Oxford University Press, 1941.

Logic, Semantics, Metamathematics: Papers from 1923 to 1938, Clarendon Press, 1956, revised edition, edited by J. Corcoran, Hackett Publishing, 1983.

Alfred Tarski: Collected Papers, 4 volumes, edited by Steven R. Givant and Ralph N. McKenzie, Stuttgart, 1986.

(With Steven R. Givant) *A Formalization of Set Theory without Variables,* Colloquium Publications, 1987.

Periodicals

"The Semantic Conception of Truth and the Foundations of Semantics," *Philosophy and Phenomenological Research,* Volume 4, 1944, pp. 341–375.

SOURCES:

Books

Dictionary of Scientific Biography, Volume 18, supplement II, Scribner, 1990, pp. 893–896.

Proceedings of the Tarski Symposium, An International Symposium to Honor Alfred Tarski on the Occasion of His Seventieth Birthday, Volume 25, American Mathematical Society, 1974.

Ulam, Stanislaw M., *Adventures of a Mathematician,* Scribner, 1976, pp. 29, 40, 114, 119, 122.

Periodicals

Addison, John W., *California Monthly,* December, 1983.

Chicago Tribune, October 30, 1983.

Givant, Steven R., "A Portrait of Alfred Tarski," *Mathematical Intelligence,* Volume 13, no. 3, 1991, pp. 16–32.

Journal of Symbolic Logic, Volume 51, 1986; Volume 53, 1988.

Times (London), December 6, 1983, p. 16-G.

Washington Post, October 29, 1983.

Other

Tarski, Jan, interviews with Jeanne Spriter James conducted November 1, 2, 3, 4, and 21, 1993.

—*Sketch by Jeanne Spriter James*

Edward Lawrie Tatum

Edward Lawrie Tatum
1909-1975
American biochemist

Edward Lawrie Tatum's experiments with simple organisms demonstrated that cell processes can be studied as chemical reactions and that such reactions are governed by genes. With **George Beadle**, he offered conclusive proof in 1941 that each biochemical reaction in the cell is controlled via a catalyzing enzyme by a specific gene. The "one gene-one enzyme" theory changed the face of biology and gave it a new chemical expression. For the first time, the nature of life seemed within the grasp of science's quantitative methods. Tatum, collaborating with **Joshua Lederberg**, demonstrated in 1947 that bacteria reproduce sexually, thus introducing a new experimental organism into the study of molecular genetics. Spurred by Tatum's discoveries, other scientists worked to understand the precise chemical nature of the unit of heredity called the gene. This study culminated in 1953 with the description by **James Watson** and **Francis Crick** of the structure of DNA. Tatum's use of microorganisms and laboratory muta-

tions for the study of biochemical genetics led directly to the biotechnology revolution of the 1980s. Tatum and Beadle shared the 1958 Nobel Prize in physiology or medicine with Joshua Lederberg for ushering in the new era of modern biology.

Tatum was born on December 14, 1909, in Boulder, Colorado, to Arthur Lawrie Tatum and Mabel Webb Tatum. He was the first of three children; a younger brother and sister would follow. Both of Edward's parents excelled academically. His father held two degrees, an M.D. and a Ph.D. in pharmacology. Edward's mother was one of the first women to graduate from the University of Colorado. Presumably an interest in science and medicine ran in the Tatum family: Edward would become a research scientist, his brother a physician, and his sister a nurse. As a boy, Edward played the French horn and trumpet; his interest in music lasted his whole life. He also enjoyed swimming and ice-skating.

In 1925, when Tatum was fifteen years old, his father accepted a position as a pharmacology professor at the University of Wisconsin. Tatum studied at the University of Chicago Experimental School and for two years at the University of Chicago before transferring and completing his undergraduate work at the University of Wisconsin. He almost became a geologist before deciding in his senior year to major in chemistry.

Tatum earned his A.B. degree in chemistry from the University of Wisconsin in 1931. In 1932 he earned his master's degree in microbiology. Two years later, in 1934, he received a Ph.D. in biochemistry for a dissertation on the cellular biochemistry and nutritional needs of a bacterium. Understanding the biochemistry of microorganisms such as bacteria, yeast, and molds would persist at the heart of Tatum's career.

After receiving his doctorate, Tatum remained at the University of Wisconsin for one year as a research assistant in biochemistry. He married the same year he completed his Ph.D. In Livingston, Wisconsin, Tatum wed June Alton, the daughter of a lumber dealer, on July 28, 1934. They eventually had two daughters, Margaret Carol and Barbara Ann.

From 1936 to 1937, Tatum studied bacteriological chemistry at the University of Utrecht in the Netherlands while on a General Education Board fellowship for postgraduate study. In Utrecht he worked in the laboratory of F. Kogl, who had identified the vitamin biotin. In Kogl's lab Tatum investigated the nutritional needs of bacteria and fungi. While Tatum was in Holland, he was contacted by geneticist George Beadle. Beadle, seven years older than Tatum, had done genetic studies with the fruit fly *Drosophila melanogaster* while in the laboratory of **Thomas Hunt Morgan** at the California Institute of Technology. Beadle, newly arrived at Stanford University, was now looking for a biochemist who could collaborate with him as he continued his work in genetics. He hoped to identify the enzymes responsible for the inherited eye pigments of *Drosophila*.

Upon his return to the United States in the fall of 1937, Tatum was appointed a research associate at Stanford University in the department of biological sciences. There he embarked on the *Drosophila* project with Beadle for four years. The two men successfully determined that kynurenine was the enzyme responsible for the fly's eye color and that it was controlled by one of the eye-pigment genes. This and other observations led them to postulate several theories about the relationship between genes and biochemical reactions. Yet they realized that *Drosophila* was not an ideal experimental organism on which to continue their work.

Chooses Bread Mold Medium for Gene Experiments

Tatum and Beadle began searching for a suitable organism. After some discussion and a review of the literature, they settled on a pink mold that commonly grows on bread known as *neurospora crassa*. The advantages to working with *neurospora* were many: it reproduced very quickly, its nutritional needs and biochemical pathways were already well known, and it had the useful capability of being able to reproduce both sexually and asexually. This last characteristic made it possible to grow cultures that were genetically

identical and also to grow cultures that were the result of a cross between two different parent strains. With neurospora, Tatum and Beadle were ready to demonstrate the effect of genes on cellular biochemistry.

The two scientists began their *neurospora* experiments in March 1941. At that time, scientists spoke of "genes" as the units of heredity without fully understanding what a gene might look like or how it might act. Although they realized that genes were located on the chromosomes, they didn't know what the chemical nature of such a substance might be. An understanding of DNA (deoxyribonucleic acid, the molecule of heredity) was still twelve years in the future. Nevertheless, geneticists in the 1940s had accepted Gregor Mendel's work with inheritance patterns in pea plants. Mendel's theory, rediscovered by three independent investigators in 1900, states that an inherited characteristic is determined by the combination of two hereditary units (genes), one each contributed by the parental cells. A dominant gene is expressed even when it is carried by only one of a pair of chromosomes, while a recessive gene must be carried by both chromosomes to be expressed. With *Drosophila*, Tatum and Beadle had taken genetic mutants—flies that inherited a variant form of eye color—and tried to work out the biochemical steps that led to the abnormal eye color. Their goal was to identify the variant enzyme, presumably governed by a single gene, that controlled the variant eye color. This proved technically very difficult, and as luck would have it, another lab announced the discovery of kynurenine's role before theirs did. With the neurospora experiments, they set out to prove their one gene-one enzyme theory another way.

The two investigators began with biochemical processes they understood well: the nutritional needs of *neurospora*. By exposing cultures of *neurospora* to X rays, they would cause genetic damage to some bread mold genes. If their theory was right, and genes did indeed control biochemical reactions, the genetically damaged strains of mold would show changes in their ability to produce nutrients. If supplied with some basic salts and sugars, normal *neurospora* can make all the amino acids and vitamins it needs to live except for one (biotin).

This is exactly what happened. In the course of their research, the men created, with X-ray bombardment, a number of mutated strains that each lacked the ability to produce a particular amino acid or vitamin. The first strain they identified, after 299 attempts to determine its mutation, lacked the ability to make vitamin B_6. By crossing this strain with a normal strain, the offspring inherited the defect as a recessive gene according to the inheritance patterns described by Mendel. This proved that the mutation was a genetic defect, capable of being passed to successive generations and causing the same nutritional mutation in those offspring. The X-ray bombardment had altered the gene governing the enzyme needed to promote the production of vitamin B$_6$.

This simple experiment heralded the dawn of a new age in biology, one in which molecular genetics would soon dominate. Nearly forty years later, on Tatum's death, Joshua Lederberg told the *New York Times* that this experiment "gave impetus and morale" to scientists who strived to understand how genes directed the processes of life. For the first time, biologists believed that it might be possible to understand and quantify the living cell's processes.

Tatum and Beadle were not the first, as it turned out, to postulate the one gene-one enzyme theory. By 1942 the work of English physician **Archibald Garrod**, long ignored, had been rediscovered. In his study of people suffering from a particular inherited enzyme deficiency, Garrod had noticed the disease seemed to be inherited as a Mendelian recessive. This suggested a link between one gene and one enzyme. Yet Tatum and Beadle were the first to offer extensive experimental evidence for the theory. Their use of laboratory methods, like X rays, to create genetic mutations also introduced a powerful tool for future experiments in biochemical genetics.

Research Leads to Mass-Production of Penicillin

During World War II, the methods Tatum and Beadle had developed in their work with pink bread mold were used to produce large amounts of penicillin, another mold. Their basic research, unwittingly, thus had a very important practical effect as well. In 1944 Tatum served as a civilian staff member of the U.S. Office of Scientific Research and Development at Stanford. Industry, too, used the methods the men developed to measure vitamins and amino acids in foods and tissues.

In 1945, at the end of the war, Tatum accepted an appointment at Yale University as an associate professor of botany with the promise of establishing a program of biochemical microbiology within that department. Apparently the move was due to Stanford's lack of encouragement of Tatum, who failed to fit into the tidy category of biochemist or biologist or geneticist but instead mastered all three fields. In 1946 Tatum did indeed create a new program at Yale and became a professor of microbiology. In work begun at Stanford and continued at Yale, he demonstrated that the one gene-one enzyme theory applied to yeast and bacteria as well as molds.

Discovers Sexual Reproduction of Bacteria

In a second extremely fruitful collaboration, Tatum began working with Joshua Lederberg in March 1946. Lederberg, a Columbia University medical student fifteen years younger than Tatum, was at Yale during a break in the medical school curriculum.

Tatum and Lederberg began studying the bacterium *Escherichia coli*. At that time, it was believed that *E. coli* reproduced asexually. The two scientists proved otherwise. When cultures of two different mutant bacteria were mixed, a third strain, one showing characteristics taken from each parent, resulted. This discovery of biparental inheritance in bacteria, which Tatum called genetic recombination, provided geneticists with a new experimental organism. Again, Tatum's methods had altered the practices of experimental biology. Lederberg never returned to medical school, earning instead a Ph.D. from Yale.

In 1948 Tatum returned to Stanford as professor of biology. A new administration at Stanford and its department of biology had invited him to return in a position suited to his expertise and ability. While in this second residence at Stanford, Tatum helped establish the department of biochemistry. In 1956 he became a professor of biochemistry and head of the department. Increasingly, Tatum's talents were devoted to promoting science at an administrative level. He was instrumental in relocating the Stanford Medical School from San Francisco to the university campus in Palo Alto. In that year Tatum also was divorced from his wife June. On December 16, 1956, he married Viola Kantor in New York City. Kantor was the daughter of a dentist in Brooklyn. Owing in part to these complications in his personal affairs, Tatum left the West Coast and took a position at the Rockefeller Institute for Medical Research (now Rockefeller University) in January 1957. There he continued to work through institutional channels to support young scientists, and served on various national committees. Unlike some other administrators, he emphasized nurturing individual investigators rather than specific kinds of projects. His own research continued in efforts to understand the genetics of neurospora and the nucleic acid metabolism of mammalian cells in culture.

Contributions to Biology Recognized with Nobel Prize

In 1958, together with Beadle and Lederberg, Tatum received the Nobel Prize in physiology or medicine. The Nobel Committee awarded the prize to the three investigators for their work demonstrating that genes regulate the chemical processes of the cell. Tatum and Beadle shared one-half the prize and Lederberg received the other half for work done separately from Tatum. Lederberg later paid tribute to Tatum for his role in Lederberg's decision to study the effects of X-ray-induced mutation. In his Nobel lecture, Tatum predicted that "with real understanding of the roles of heredity and environment, together with the consequent improvement in man's physical capacities and greater freedom from physical disease, will come an improvement in his approach to, and understanding of, sociological and economic problems."

Tatum had a marked interest in social issues, including population control. In 1965 and 1966 Tatum organized other Nobel laureates in science to make public endorsements of family planning and birth control. These included statements to Pope Paul VI, whose encyclical against birth control for Catholics was issued at this time.

Tatum's second wife, Viola, died on April 21, 1974. Tatum married Elsie Bergland later in 1974 and she survived his death the following year, on November 5, 1975. Tatum died at his home on East Sixty-third Street in New York City after an extended illness. In a memoir written for the *Annual Review of Genetics,* Lederberg recalled that Tatum's last years were "marred by ill health, substantially self-inflicted by a notorious smoking habit." Lederberg noted, too, that Tatum's "mental outlook" was scarred by the painful death of his second wife.

In addition to the Nobel Prize, Tatum received the Remsen Award of the American Chemical Society in 1953 for his work in biparental inheritance and sexual reproduction in bacteria. In 1952 he was elected to the National Academy of Sciences. He was a founding member of the *Annual Review of Genetics* and joined the editorial board of *Science* in 1957. Tatum's collected papers occupy twenty-five feet of space in the Rockefeller University Archives and span the years from 1930 to 1975.

SELECTED WRITINGS BY TATUM:

Books

(With A. H. Sturtevant) *An Introduction to Genetics,* Saunders, 1939.

Periodicals

(With George W. Beadle) "Genetic Control of Biochemical Reactions in Neurospora," *Proceedings of the National Academy of Sciences,* Volume 27, 1941, pp. 499–506.

(With Joshua Lederberg) "Gene Recombination in the Bacterium Escherichia coli," *Journal of Bacteriology,* 1947.

"A Case History in Biological Search" (Nobel Lecture), *Nobel Lectures in Molecular Biology 1933–1974,* Elsevier, 1977.

SOURCES:

Periodicals

Beadle, George W., "Recollections," *Annual Review of Biochemistry,* Volume 43, 1973, pp. 1–13.

Chemical and Engineering News, May 18, 1953, p. 2099.

Kopp, Carolyn, "The J. H. B. Archive Report: The Edward Lawrie Tatum Papers at the Rockefeller University Archives," *Journal of the History of Biology,* Volume 15, 1982, pp. 153–154, 1982.

Lederberg, Joshua, "Edward Lawrie Tatum," *Annual Review of Genetics,* Volume 13, 1979, pp. 1–5.

New York Times, November 7, 1975, p. 40.

—Sketch by Liz Marshall

Henry Taube
1915-
Canadian-born American chemist

A Canadian-born American chemist and professor at Stanford, Henry Taube has dedicated over fifty years to research and teaching. In addition to conducting important research in the mechanics of electron transfer reactions in complex metals, Taube has contributed greatly to increase our understanding major concepts in inorganic chemistry with applications in the chemical industry. For his work in this field, Taube received the Nobel Prize in chemistry in 1983.

Taube, the youngest of four boys, was born on November 30, 1915, in Neudorf, Saskatchewan, Canada, to Samuel Taube and Albertina Tiledetzski. His parents were Ukrainian peasants, who moved from their home near Kiev to Saskatchewan in 1911 to escape the tyranny of the tsar. Although his parents were uneducated and poor, they were very astute and worked hard to develop a farm. Taube himself considered farm work and its lessons of perseverance a valuable part of his education. At the age of thirteen, Taube was sent to a Lutheran boarding school, from where he moved to the University of Saskatchewan. The depression brought difficult times to the Taube family, and as a result of some failed investments, Taube's father was no longer able to support the young boy at school. However, a chemistry teacher took an interest in Taube and arranged for him to help in the laboratory in order to continue his education. Although Taube received his best grades in chemistry, he loved English literature and wanted to become a writer.

Launches a Career in Chemistry

Taube received the Bachelor of Science degree in 1935 and the Master of Science degree in photochemistry in 1937. Regardless, it was not until he received an opportunity to attend the University of California, Berkeley, that Taube became deeply interested in chemistry. While at Berkeley, he won the Rosenberg prize and was considered one of the most promising students. He received the Ph.D. in 1940, following which the university employed him as an instructor. Wanting to return to Canada, Taube applied for jobs at the major universities, but the opportunities never came. Instead he received a job offer from Cornell University, which he accepted in 1941.

At Cornell Taube did not find much interest in the kind of research he wanted to pursue, and by 1946 he was ready for a change. When an opportunity arose to work at the University of Chicago, a hub of scientific activity and innovative research at the time, Taube accepted. He considered his experience at Chicago a highly productive part of his career. Chosen to develop a course in advanced inorganic chemistry, Taube found little in published textbooks. He researched widely and became interested in complex metal or coordination chemistry. In the course of these investigations, he realized that work he had done on substitution of carbon in organic reactions could be related to inorganic complexes. In 1952 he wrote a seminal paper published in *Chemical Reviews* on the rates of chemical substitution, relating them to electronic structure. Although his research is outdated in parts, Taube's work was tremendously useful to chemists in planning experiments that depend on the differential in substitution rates.

Awarded Nobel Prize for Electron Transfer Research

Taube chaired the department of chemistry at the University of Chicago form 1956 to 1959. However, he did not enjoy administrative work, and in 1961 he took a position at Stanford University that would allow him to concentrate on research. Seeking to extend his work on substitution rates, he launched into research on ruthenium and osmium, elements with an electronic structure that fascinated him. Ruthenium is a rare metallic chemical element of the platinum group first found in ores from the Ural Mountains in Russia. It has remarkable back-bonding properties with chemicals such as carbon monoxide. The element osmium has an even greater back-bonding capacity than ruthenium. As Taube investigated the way electrons were transferred between molecules in chemical reactions, he noted unexpected changes in the electrical charge and shape of the molecules. Taube's important discovery was that before the transfer of electrons occurs, molecules build a "chemical bridge." Previously, scientists had thought molecules simply exchanged electrons. Taube's work, identifying the intermediate step in electron exchanges, explained why some reactions among similar kinds of metals and ions occur at different rates.

Although inorganic reactions are important in developing principles of chemistry, interest in inorganic reactions had lagged behind the development of organic (carbon-based) chemistry. Taube's insights formed an important impulse for the further development of inorganic chemistry. For his work on the mechanisms of electron transfer, Taube won the 1983 Nobel Prize in chemistry, reversing the long-standing tradition of awarding achievements in organic chemistry.

In later work, Taube and several of his associates extended the scope of coordination chemistry with the study of ruthenium ammines and osmium, illuminating, for instance, the role of metals in catalysis. He was also able to show how the structure of the chemical bridge affects the electron transfer process in metals. In an interview with Richard Stevenson published in *Chemistry in Britain,* Taube described his work with chemistry as a love affair. "I'm a chemist and I wanted to know what happens when you mix things."

Taube is a member of fifteen societies, has received thirty-nine honors and awards, and became professor emeritus at Stanford in 1986. He has written over 330 scientific papers and articles. Taube married Mary Alice Wesche in 1952. They have two daughters and two sons. Until the mid–1960s he and his family continued to return to Saskatchewan during holidays to help with the family farm. Taube is semi-retired and spends only part of his time at Stanford tutoring small groups. He also works part-time as a consultant to various firms, including Catalytica, Inc. and Hercules, a chemical manufacturer. In his leisure time, Taube is a collector of classical vocal records from vintage 1897 to the most recent recordings, and he loves gardening.

SELECTED WRITINGS BY TAUBE:

Periodicals

"Electron Transfer between Metal Complexes: Retrospective," *Science,* 226, November 30, 1984, p. 1028.
"Use of Dihydrogen Osmium Complex," *Science,* April 10, 1992.

SOURCES:

Periodicals

Bullen, Val, "Work Can Be Fun," *Western People,* March 11, 1993, pp. 2–3.

Stevenson, Richard, "Henry Taube: The Boy From the Prairie Who Made Good," *Chemistry in Britain,* November, 1986.

—*Sketch by Evelyn B. Kelly*

Helen Brooke Taussig
1898-1986
American pediatrician and cardiologist

Helen Brooke Taussig

Physician and cardiologist Helen Brooke Taussig spent her career as the head of the Children's Heart Clinic at Johns Hopkins University. In the course of her work with young children, she discovered that cyanotic infants—known as "blue-babies"—died of insufficient circulation to the lungs, not of cardiac arrest, as had been thought. She and colleague Dr. Alfred Blalock developed a surgical procedure, the Blalock-Taussig shunt, to correct the problem. First used in 1944, the Blalock-Taussig shunt has saved the lives of thousands of children. In 1961, after investigating reports of numerous birth defects in Germany, Taussig determined that the cause was use of the drug Thalidomide, and it was her intervention that prevented Thalidomide from being sold in the United States. She was the recipient of numerous honorary degrees and awards, including the Medal of Freedom in 1964 and the 1977 National Medal of Science.

Taussig was born on May 24, 1898, in Cambridge, Massachusetts, the youngest of four children of well-known Harvard economist Frank William Taussig. Her mother, Edith Guild Taussig, who had attended Radcliffe College and was interested in the natural sciences, died of tuberculosis when Helen was eleven years old. Like her mother, Taussig attended Radcliffe, where she played championship tennis. However, wishing to be further removed from the shadow of her well-known father, she transferred to the University of California at Berkeley, where she earned her B.A. in 1921.

Having decided on a career in medicine, Taussig's educational choices were limited by sex discrimination. Although she began her studies at Harvard University, the medical school did not admit women to its regular curriculum, and would not begin to do so until 1945. Taussig enrolled in Harvard's School of Public Health, where, like other women, she was permitted to take courses but not allowed to work toward obtaining a degree. She also was permitted to study histology as a special student in the medical school. After her studies at Harvard, Taussig took anatomy at nearby Boston University. There, her anatomy professor, Alexander Begg, suggested that she apply herself to the study of the heart, which she did. Also following Begg's advice, Taussig submitted her application to attend the medical school at Johns Hopkins University, where she was accepted.

During her four years of study at Johns Hopkins Medical School, Taussig worked at the Hopkins Heart Station. After receiving her M.D. in 1927, she spent another year there as a fellow, followed by an additional year and a half there as a pediatric intern. During this time, Taussig served as an attending physician at the recently established Pediatric Cardiac Clinic. The new chair of pediatrics, Edwards A. Park, recognized Taussig's abilities and became her mentor. Upon the completion of her pediatric internship in 1930, she was appointed physician-in-charge of the Pediatric Cardiac Clinic in the Harriet Lane Home, the children's division at Johns Hopkins. Taussig would spend her entire career at Johns Hopkins until her retirement in 1963. In 1946 she was appointed associate professor of pediatrics, and was promoted to full professor in 1959, the first woman in the history of the Medical School to hold that title.

Groundbreaking Research on the Child's Heart

Taussig began her studies of congenital heart disease at the Pediatric Cardiac Clinic in 1930. Over the years she examined and treated hundreds of children whose hearts were damaged by rheumatic fever, as well as those with congenital heart disease. She developed new observational methods that led to a new understanding of pediatric heart problems. First Taussig became accomplished in the use of the fluoroscope, a new instrument which passed x-ray beams through the body and projected an image of the heart, lungs, and major arteries onto a florescent screen. Second, she used the electrocardiograph which makes a graphic record of the heart's movements. Third, she became expert at diagnosis through physical examination—made more complex in her case due to the fact that Taussig was somewhat deaf as a result of childhood whooping cough and unable to use a stethoscope, thereby necessitating her reliance on visual examination.

Taussig gradually realized that the blueness of cyanotic children was the result of insufficient oxygen in the blood. In the normal heart, bluish blood from the periphery of the body enters the right atrium (upper receiving chamber) of the heart and then goes to the right ventricle (the lower pumping chamber) to be pumped through a major artery to the lungs. In the lungs, the blood receives a new supply of oxygen that changes its color to bright red. Then it returns to the heart, entering the left atrium and descending to the left ventricle which pumps it to the rest of the body. The two sides of the heart are kept separate by a wall called the septum. Taussig discovered that the insufficient oxygen level of the blood of "blue-babies" was usually the result of either a leaking septum or an overly narrow artery leading from the left ventricle to the lungs. Although at that time surgeons were unable enter the heart to repair the septum surgically, Taussig believed that it might be possible either to repair the artery, or to attach a new vessel that would perform the same function.

She persuaded Dr. Alfred Blalock, the chairman of the Hopkins Department of Surgery, to work on the problem. Blalock was a vascular surgeon who had done experimental research on an artificial artery with the assistance of long-time associate Vivian Thomas. Accepting Taussig's challenge, Blalock set Thomas to work on the technical problems. During the next year and a half, Thomas developed the technical procedures, using about two hundred dogs as experimental animals. In 1944, although earlier than Thomas had planned, the technique was tried on a human infant, a desperately ill patient of Taussig's named Eileen Saxon. With Taussig as an observer and Thomas standing by to give advice concerning the correct suturing of the artery, Blalock performed the surgery successfully. A branch of the aorta that normally went to the infant's arm was connected to the lungs. In the years that followed, the procedure, known as the Blalock-Taussig shunt, saved the lives of thousands of cyanotic children.

The fame of the Pediatric Cardiac Clinic grew rapidly. As they became flooded with patients, Blalock and Taussig developed team methods for dealing with the different phases of treatment. Their management methods became the model for many cardiac centers, as well as other kinds of medical care. Taussig's growing reputation also brought her numerous students. She trained a whole generation of pediatric cardiologists and wrote the standard textbook of the field, *Congenital Malformations of the Heart,* first published in 1947. In addition to her work in congenital heart disease, she carried out research on rheumatic fever, the leading cause of heart problems in children. Taussig is considered the founder of the specialty of pediatric cardiology. Neither her scientific and clinical acumen, nor her enormously demanding schedule, ever prevented Taussig from being a warm, compassionate physician to her many patients and their families. She followed her patients for years, even after her own retirement. She never found it necessary to distance herself from the critically-ill children that she treated, or from their parents. Her warmth and ability to see and treat people as individuals has been recalled by many who knew her.

Influences U.S. Policy on a Dangerous Drug

In the 1950s Taussig served on numerous national and international committees. In 1962, a German graduate of her training program told her of the striking increase in his country of phocomelia, a rare congenital defect in which infants were born with severely deformed limbs. The defect was thought, but not yet proven, to be associated with a popular sedative called Contergan that was sold throughout Germany and other European countries and often taken by women to counteract nausea during early pregnancy. Taussig decided to investigate for herself and spent six weeks in Germany visiting clinics, examining babies with the abnormalities, and interviewing their doctors and mothers. She noted the absence of such birth defect in the infants of American soldiers living at U.S. military installations in Germany where the drug was banned. But there was one exception: a baby whose mother had gone off the post to obtain Contergan was born severely deformed. Taussig's testimony was instrumental in the U.S. Food and Drug Administration's rejection of the application from the William S. Merrell Company to market the drug they renamed Thalidomide in the United States.

Although Taussig formally retired in 1963, she remained deeply involved as a scientist, a clinician, and an activist in causes that affected the health of children. She fought for the right of scientists to use animals in experimental studies and advocated that women in the United States be able to choose to terminate their pregnancies through abortion. She was the author of a hundred major scientific publications, forty-one of which were written after her retirement. She occupied a home in Baltimore, often visited by guests and friends, and owned the cottage in Cape Cod where she had spent many happy childhood summers. Taussig enjoyed fishing, swimming, and gardening, as well as caring for her many pets. In the late 1970s she moved to a retirement community near Philadelphia. She became interested in the embryological causes of congenital heart defects and had begun a study of the hearts of birds when, on May 21, 1986, while driving some of her fellow retirees to vote in a primary election, she was killed in an automobile accident at the age of 87.

SELECTED WRITINGS BY TAUSSIG:

Books

Congenital Malformations of the Heart, Commonwealth Fund, 1947, second edition (two volumes), Commonwealth Fund/Harvard University Press, 1960.

Periodicals

(With Alfred Blalock) "The Surgical Treatment of Malformations of the Heart in which there is Pulmonary Stenosis or Pulmonary Atresia," *Journal of the American Medical Association,* Volume 128, May 19, 1945, pp. 189–202.

"The Thalidomide Syndrome," *Scientific American,* Volume 207, August, 1962, pp. 29–35.

SOURCES:

Books

Baldwin, Joyce, *To Heal the Heart of A Child: Helen Taussig, M.D.* (juvenile), Walker, 1992.

Nuland, Sherwin B., *Doctors: The Biography of Medicine,* Knopf, 1988, pp. 422–456.

Periodicals

Harvey, W. Proctor, "A Conversation with Helen Taussig," *Medical Times,* Volume 106, November, 1978, pp. 28–44.

—*Sketch by Pamela O. Long*

Frederick Winslow Taylor
1856-1915
American efficiency engineer

Frederick Winslow Taylor pioneered the field of time studies and functional management in an effort to increase worker productivity in manufacturing and to promote harmony between management and labor. Through empirical studies, Taylor also advanced the techniques of steel manufacturing while at Midvale Steel Company and later as an engineering consultant to various firms, including Bethlehem Steel Company. Along with J. Maunsel White, Taylor developed a process heat treating steel used for tooling, which doubled the speed of metal-cutting machinery. Taylor is most noted for his work in scientific management, an effort to quantify human labor and eliminate wasted motion. He was a dominant force within the American Society of Mechanical Engineers, serving as vice president from 1904 until he was elected president in 1906. After retiring from active engineering at age forty-five, Taylor espoused scientific management from his estate near Philadelphia, Pennsylvania.

Taylor was born on March 20, 1856, in Germantown, Philadelphia, Pennsylvania, the second of three children. His father, Franklin, was a lawyer and a poet who had inherited great wealth based on the ownership of farms and other properties in Philadelphia and Bucks County. His mother, Emily Winslow Taylor, was a staunch abolitionist who worked with American reformer Lucretia Mott. Taylor's mother played a key role in instilling discipline and a work ethic in Taylor. Even as a child, Taylor was concerned with ordering and controlling his environment; a childhood friend recalled his obsessive desire to measure a rounders court to the last inch before a backyard game. Taylor also had frequent nightmares that he associated with sleeping on his back, so, when he was twelve, he developed a harness to wake him if he rolled onto his back.

Taylor's early schooling was at the Germantown Academy. At age thirteen, he went with his family to Europe and was tutored in France and Germany. After returning to the United States in 1872, Taylor enrolled at Phillips Exeter Academy, a college preparatory school in New Hampshire. Foreshadowing his later interest in scientific management, he was intrigued by a mathematics instructor's calculation of the number of problems an average student could complete for an assignment of a specified duration. Taylor's parents wanted him to attend Harvard University and pursue a legal career. Although he passed Harvard's entrance examination, Taylor left Exeter at the beginning of his senior year because of deteriorating eyesight and never attended the university. Both he and his parents were concerned that the extensive reading required in university studies might lead to blindness, though his decision to work as a machinist—a visually demanding profession—suggests that he actually stayed out of college in order to remain loyal to his strong work ethic. In 1874, Taylor began work as an apprentice machinist at the Enterprise Hydraulics Works, also known as Ferrell and Jones, which was partly owned by a family friend.

Rises from Laborer to Chief Engineer

Once he completed his apprenticeship, Taylor went to work for the Midvale Steel Company in Philadelphia. He rose from the position of laborer to machinist, then to superintendent of machine shops, assistant foreman and foreman of the machine shops, and then to the position of chief draftsman in charge of new machinery and buildings. In June, 1883, as the result of a self-study program, Taylor received a degree in mechanical engineering from the Stevens Institute of Technology in Hoboken, New Jersey. In 1884, he was appointed chief engineer, serving in this position until 1890. As superintendent of the machine shops, Taylor had begun his campaign against "soldiering"—a term that described how workers would limit their production because they were being paid by the hour. After studying the capacity of both machines and machinists, Taylor developed his differential piece-rate policy, which paid ordinary wages (a lower rate per piece) to those workers who met a minimum output and very high wages to those who achieved maximum output. As chief engineer, Taylor supervised the forging of steel cannons for U.S. Navy warships. He developed a 25-ton steam hammer (the largest that had yet been built in the United States) that was used in the forging process. Taylor received a patent for the hammer in 1890, based on the ability of his design to maintain its alignment during use.

When the ownership of Midvale Steel changed in 1890, Taylor left to become the general manager of the Manufacturing Investment Company in Philadelphia, supervising paper mills in Maine and Wisconsin. In 1893, he embarked on a career as an industrial consultant specializing, according to his business card, in "systematizing shop management and manufacturing costs." Taylor and his associates provided services for various firms, including the Simonds Rolling Machine Company, where he introduced piece work to the manufacture of ball bearings. In 1898, Taylor was hired by the Bethlehem Steel Company to reduce the cost of armor plate manufactured for the Navy. Taylor—with the aid of Russell Davenport, Bethlehem's superintendent of manufacturing—went beyond his original mandate to reorganize the machine shop and tried to implement his "functional plan of organization" throughout the entire works. Starting with the machine shop, Taylor

established what he called "functional foremanships": gang bosses, speed bosses, inspectors, and repair bosses. Taylor's functional plan had these foremen and their workers subordinated to five "planners": the superintendent in overall control; the "order-of-work-route man"; the "instruction-card man," who prepared detailed instructions for workers on how to perform their tasks; the "time-and-cost clerk"; and the "disciplinarian." The implementation of piece-rate pay brought about reduced production costs: the cost of moving shoveled material was reduced from 7.2 cents per ton on the day rate to 3.3 cents per ton on piece rate. The large size of the Bethlehem Iron Company and management's opposition to Taylor, however, made it difficult for Taylor to implement his plan throughout the works.

In 1898, Taylor and Bethlehem metallurgist J. Maunsel White began to develop stronger steel cutting tools for use in machining steel, specifically the hard steel used by the Navy for the casings of armor-piercing shells. They claimed that heating steel close to its melting point produced superior steel for use in cutting tools. The Taylor-White process for the heat treatment of steel increased metal-cutting speed by at least 200 percent and was awarded a gold medal at the Paris Exposition in 1900. Taylor and White filed two patents for the process, both of which were granted in 1901, and they sold them to Bethlehem for $50,000 (the patents were voided in 1909; after five years of litigation, a judge ruled that they failed to define a unique process). A few months after Taylor and White received their first heat-treatment patent in February, 1901, Bethlehem executives opposed to Taylor's reorganization of the company terminated his contract. His official biographer, Frank B. Copley, wrote that Taylor retired from active work in 1901 to "serve the cause of science in management." According to recently uncovered court testimony, however, Taylor admitted that a nervous breakdown had prevented him from remaining active in business.

Becomes Foremost Spokesperson for Scientific Management

Taylor used his patent money from Bethlehem to construct Boxly, an eleven-acre estate in Chestnut Hill in northern Philadelphia. To present a more efficient environment for his visiting business clients, Taylor spent $17,000 to overhaul the gardens and removed a hill on the property to make way for a three-story colonial mansion. Boxly served as a center for Taylor's educational presentations on scientific management that were often updated by his associate, Morris L. Cooke.

Taylor wrote two books on scientific management, both published in 1911: *The Principles of Scientific Management* and *Shop Management*. The core of Taylor's managerial innovations for industry was a planning department; he believed this department should coordinate production by assigning production goals based on time-motion studies, measurements of machine capabilities, the standardization of worker tasks, routing of raw and processed materials, inventory control, centralized records, and cost accounting. In 1830, Antoine-Henri Jomini had attributed French emperor Napoleon Bonaparte's military success to an underlying science of warfare; in a similar manner, Taylor believed that business management could be reduced to an exact science. Just as Jomini's reductionism sought to simplify the chaotic dynamics of war, Taylor believed scientific management could engender harmonious relationships between management and labor. He sought to control the dynamics of the modern industrial sphere. The keys to his system were breaking the work process into the smallest components, specifying the duties of each component, employing the differential piece-rate to spur optimum production, and removing skill and creativity from the job, reserving them for management.

The belief that Taylor's scientific management offered the basis for efficiency and progress was reflected in its adoption throughout the Progressive Era, from public administration to economic theory. Progressive theorists viewed efficiency and expertise as positive components of the democratic experience and believed that scientific management, born in industry, had much to offer the nation. With the waning of Progressivism, scientific management returned to industry. The Society to Promote the Science of Management, later renamed the Taylor Society, pursued a policy of separation between management and administration within industrial firms. The view Taylorites had of the worker changed during the 1920s. Whereas Taylor himself had assumed that management and workers had a common interest in increasing prosperity, scientific managers of the 1920s saw labor not as individuals but as a group that required managerial expertise. Many economic and social planners of U.S. President Franklin Roosevelt's New Deal had been members of the Taylor Society during the 1920s.

Taylor married Louise M. Spooner in 1884. In 1901, they adopted the three youngest of four children who had survived the murder-suicide of their parents, William and Anna Aiken, distant relatives of Taylor's wife. In 1881, Taylor and his brother-in-law, Clarence M. Clark, were the first doubles champions of the U.S. Lawn Tennis Association. Taylor was also a golfer, ice skater, and cricket player, and among his forty-five patents were ones for a scoop-handled tennis racket and a two-handed putter. In 1910, Taylor's wife first manifested cyclic depression, which had a strong, adverse effect on him. During a lecture tour in Ohio in early 1915, Taylor caught a cold that developed into pneumonia; he died on March 21,

1915, after being hospitalized for nine days. He left an estate valued at approximately $1,000,000, none of which he had inherited. He was buried in Philadelphia and the epitaph on his tombstone reads "Father of Scientific Management."

SELECTED WRITINGS BY TAYLOR:

Books

The Principles of Scientific Management, Harper and Brothers, 1911.
Shop Management, Harper and Brothers, 1911.
Scientific Management: Comprising Shop Management, The Principles of Scientific Management, and Testimony Before the Special House Committee, Greenwood Press, 1972.

Periodicals

"A Piece-Rate System, Being a Step Toward Partial Solution of the Labor Problem," *Transactions of the American Society of Mechanical Engineers,* 1895, pp. 856–903.
"On the Art of Cutting Metals," *Transactions of the American Society of Mechanical Engineers,* 1907, pp. 31–280.

SOURCES:

Books

Aitken, Hugh G. J., *Taylorism at the Watertown Arsenal,* Harvard University Press, 1960.
Copley, Frank B., *Frederick W. Taylor: Father of Scientific Management,* two volumes, Harper and Brothers, 1923.
Drury, Horace B., *Scientific Management: A History and Criticism,* Columbia University Press, 1918.
Haber, Samuel, *Efficiency and Uplift: Scientific Management in the Progressive Era, 1890–1920,* University of Chicago Press, 1964.
Kakar, Sudhir,
Frederick Taylor: A Study in Personality and Innovation, MIT Press, 1970.
Nelson, Daniel, *Frederick W. Taylor and the Rise of Scientific Management,* University of Wisconsin Press, 1980.
Schachter, Hindy L., *Frederick Taylor and the Public Administration Community,* State University of New York Press, 1989.
Wrege, Charles D., and Ronald G. Greenwood, *Frederick W. Taylor, The Father of Scientific Management: Myth and Reality,* Business One Irwin, 1991.

Periodicals

"Tributes to Frederick W. Taylor," *Transactions of the American Society of Mechanical Engineers,* 1915, pp. 1459–1496.

—Sketch by William M. McBride

Joseph H. Taylor, Jr.

Joseph H. Taylor, Jr.
1941-
American astrophysicist

Joseph H. Taylor, Jr. is an astrophysicist who discovered the first binary pulsar—two extremely dense, collapsed stars in orbit around each other. He made this discovery in 1974 with **Russell A. Hulse**, who was then his graduate student at the University of Massachusetts. The two men used this binary pulsar to verify aspects of **Albert Einstein**'s general theory of relativity which scientists had not yet had an opportunity to test. Binary pulsars became what Taylor and Hulse describe in *Astrophysical Journal Letters* as "a nearly ideal relativity laboratory," and they have made particularly important contributions to the understanding of gravity. For their discovery of the binary pulsar and the application of their findings to the theory of relativity, Taylor and Hulse were awarded the 1993 Nobel Prize in physics.

Taylor was born in Philadelphia on March 29, 1941, the son of Joseph and Sylvia Evans Taylor. In 1959, Taylor entered Haverford College where he majored in physics. He graduated in 1963 with a B.A. degree and entered the doctoral program in astronomy at Harvard University. He was awarded his Ph.D. in 1968 and spent the next year as a research fellow and lecturer in astronomy at Harvard. In 1969 he joined the faculty at the University of Massachusetts in Amherst as an assistant professor of astronomy. In 1973, he was named an associate professor and four years later elevated to full professor. In the fall of 1980, Taylor left Massachusetts to become professor of physics at Princeton University; in 1986 he was named James S. McDonnell Distinguished University Professor of Physics.

Begins Search for Pulsars

While at the University of Massachusetts in 1970, Taylor was approached by one of his graduate students, Russell Hulse, in search of a thesis project. The pair agreed on an undertaking involving the use of the 300-meter diameter Arecibo telescope in Puer-

to Rico, the world's largest single-element radio telescope, to search the skies for the weak radio signals emitted by pulsars. Pulsars were first discovered in 1967 by **Susan Jocelyn Bell Burnell** and **Antony Hewish**. They are neutron stars whose diameter, in contrast with other stars, is very small, sometimes as small as ten kilometers. Their mass, on the other hand, is as great or greater than that of the sun, and the gravitational field that surrounds them is extremely high. As a result of their strong gravitational pull, radio waves are released from pulsars only at the poles; the beams reach Earth in pulses as the star spins in space, and on a radio telescope the waves from a pulsar can resemble the beam from a lighthouse. In analyzing the results of a pulsar detected on July 2, 1974, Taylor and Hulse noticed an unexpected variation in the pulsar's period. The bursts were not perfectly regular like those of known pulsars, and the irregularity revealed that there were actually two pulsars, orbiting each other.

As a press release from the Royal Swedish Academy observes, "Hulse's and Taylor's discovery in 1974 of the first binary pulsar, called PSR 1913 + 16 ... brought about a revolution in the field." Binary pulsars orbit at great speeds and at close range—approximately that of the distance from the Earth to the Moon—and the discovery of these stars gave scientists an opportunity to study the effects of gravity outside the gravitational field of our solar system. Over a period of almost twenty years, Taylor and Hulse made detailed observations of the behavior of these stars in orbit. They discovered that the path the pulsars followed is changing: their orbit is contracting and the two stars are rotating at greater speeds as they grow closer to each other.

Their examination of the timing of the pulses provided the first evidence for the existence of what *Sky & Telescope* calls the "'magnetic' aspect of gravity." In 1916, Einstein predicted that two masses in orbit around each other would have certain properties similar to electromagnetism. He predicted that bodies would emit what he called gravitational waves and thus lose energy. The small changes Taylor and Hulse have detected are consistent with this prediction; even the rate of change very nearly matches the rate Einstein predicted it would follow.

For Taylor, this indirect confirmation of the gravitational waves is only part of the support binary pulsars can offer to the general theory of relativity. As Taylor told the *New York Times,* "Continued study of binary pulsars as they spin off energy over years is essential. We've measured three of the relativity effects on this pulsar to a high accuracy, and two other consequences to somewhat lower accuracy. But there are potentially about a dozen other relativity effects we hope to measure in the future." In 1985, Taylor and a graduate student discovered another binary pulsar. His work has raised the possibility of creating a new branch of astronomy, called gravitational wave astronomy, which would enable astronomers to gather evidence about a number of events in the universe that they currently cannot observe.

In addition to the Nobel Prize, Taylor received the Dannie Heineman Prize from the American Astronomical Society and American Institute of Physics in 1980, a MacArthur Fellowship in 1981, the National Academy of Sciences' Henry Draper Medal and Tomalla Foundation Prize in gravitation and cosmology in 1985, and the Wolf Prize in Physics in 1992. He is a member of the National Academy of Sciences, the American Philosophical Society, and a fellow of the American Academy of Arts and Sciences. Taylor married Marietta Bisson on January 3, 1976. They have three children.

SELECTED WRITINGS BY TAYLOR:

Periodicals

(With Russell A. Hulse) "A Deep Sample of New Pulsars and Their Spatial Extent in the Galaxy," *Astrophysical Journal Letters,* July 15, 1974.
(With Hulse) "Discovery of a Pulsar in a Binary System," *Astrophysical Journal Letters,* October 15, 1975.

(With J. M. Wiesberg and L. A. Fowler) "Gravitational Waves from an Orbiting Pulsar," *Scientific American,* Volume 245, October, 1981, p. 66.

SOURCES:

Periodicals

"Binary Pulsar Reveals Magnetic Gravity," *Sky & Telescope,* July, 1990. pp. 10–11.
Hewish, A., "Pulsars," *Scientific American,* Volume 219, October, 1968, p. 25.
Kleppner, D., "The Gem of General Relativity," *Physics Today,* Volume 46, April, 1993, p. 9.
New York Times, October 12, 1993, p. B9.

—*Sketch by Benedict A. Leerburger*

Moddie Taylor
1912-1976
American chemist

Moddie Taylor gained distinction early in his career as an associate chemist on the U.S. Manhattan Project, which led to the development of the atomic bomb during World War II. A chemistry professor at Lincoln and later Howard universities, Taylor published a chemistry textbook in 1960 and served as head of the chemistry department at Howard from 1969 to 1976.

Moddie Daniel Taylor was born in Nymph, Alabama, on March 3, 1912, the son of Herbert L. Taylor and Celeste (Oliver) Taylor. His father worked as a postal clerk in St. Louis, Missouri, and it was there that Taylor went to school, graduating from the Charles H. Sumner High School in 1931. He then attended Lincoln University in Jefferson City, Missouri, and graduated with a B.S. in chemistry in 1935 as valedictorian and as a summa cum laude student. He began his teaching career in 1935, working as an instructor until 1939 and then as an assistant professor from 1939 to 1941 at Lincoln University, while also enrolled in the University of Chicago's graduate program in chemistry. He received his M.S. in 1939 and his Ph.D. in 1943. Taylor married Vivian Ellis on September 8, 1937, and they had one son, Herbert Moddie Taylor.

Joins Manhattan Project Team

It was during 1945 that Taylor began his two years as an associate chemist for the top-secret Manhattan Project based at the University of Chicago. Taylor's research interest was in rare earth metals (elements which are the products of oxidized metals and which have special properties and several important industrial uses); his chemical contributions to the nation's atomic energy research earned him a Certificate of Merit from the Secretary of War. After the war, he returned to Lincoln University until 1948 when he joined Howard University as an associate professor of chemistry, becoming a full professor in 1959 and head of the chemistry department in 1969.

In 1960, Taylor's *First Principles of Chemistry* was published; also in that year he was selected by the Manufacturing Chemists Association as one of the nation's six top college chemistry teachers. In 1972, Taylor was also awarded an Honor Scroll from the Washington Institute of Chemists for his contributions to research and teaching. Taylor was a member of the American Chemical Society, the American Association for the Advancement of Science, the National Institute of Science, the American Society for Testing Materials, the New York Academy of Sciences, Sigma Xi, and Beta Kappa Chi, and was a fellow of the American Institute of Chemists and the Washington Academy for the Advancement of Science. Taylor retired as a professor emeritus of chemistry from Howard University on April 1, 1976, and died of cancer in Washington, D.C., on September 15, 1976.

SELECTED WRITINGS BY TAYLOR:

Books

First Principles of Chemistry, Van Nostrand, 1960, revised edition, 1976.

SOURCES:

Books

Sammons, Vivian O., *Blacks in Science and Medicine,* Hemisphere, 1990, p. 227.

Periodicals

Jet, May 26, 1960, p. 19.
Washington Post (obituary), September 18, 1976, p. D6.

—*Sketch by Leonard C. Bruno*

Richard E. Taylor
1929-
Canadian-born American physicist

Richard E. Taylor's study of elementary particles with the use of Stanford University's Linear Accelerator Center (SLAC) led to the Nobel Prize-winning confirmation of the existence of quarks, which are thought to be the smallest and most fundamental particles in existence, and are the base substance of all matter.

Richard Edward Taylor was born in Medicine Hat, Alberta, Canada, on November 2, 1929. His father was Clarence Richard Taylor, the son of Scottish-Irish immigrants to Canada, and his mother was the former Delia Alena Brunsdale, the daughter of Norwegian immigrants. Taylor reports that his interest in science was inspired by the presence of military installations in the Medicine Hat area during World War II and by the explosion of the first atomic bombs in August 1945.

Taylor's undergraduate education took place at the University of Alberta, in Edmonton, where he earned a B.S. degree in mathematics and physics in 1950 and then a M.S. degree two years later. While working on the latter degree, Taylor married Rita Jean Bonneau, with whom he has one son, Norman Edward. After receiving his master's degree, Taylor moved to Stanford University. In 1954 Taylor accepted a job at Stanford's High Energy Physics Laboratory, where he began his long involvement in the study of elementary particles.

Taylor Begins Work with Friedman and Kendall at SLAC

Taylor's tenure at Stanford was interrupted for three years, from 1958 to 1961, a period during which he traveled to France to work on a new linear accelerator then being constructed at Orsay. Upon his return to the United States, Taylor completed his requirements for a Ph.D. degree, which was granted to him in 1962. He then began work, under the supervision of physicist **Wolfgang Kurt Panofsky**, on the design of Stanford's new two-mile-long linear accelerator (linac). Along with two colleagues, **Jerome I. Friedman** and **Henry W. Kendall**, Taylor initiated some of the first experiments to be carried out at the Stanford linac.

Those experiments were designed to be a continuation of work begun by physicist **Robert Hofstadter** at Stanford in the 1950s. Hofstadter had directed high energy beams of electrons at a variety of elements and discovered that protons and neutrons have detailed structure that had previously been unanticipated. For this discovery, Hofstadter won the 1961 Nobel Prize in physics.

Taylor, Friedman, and Kendall Discover Quarks

In the early stages of their research, Taylor, Friedman, and Kendall did not anticipate making any revolutionary discoveries. They assumed that their work would refine and extend Hofstadter's discoveries, but not break any new ground. Two factors changed that expectation. First, the newly-built particle accelerator had far more energy—twenty-billion electron volts—than the accelerator that Hofstadter had used. Secondly, the team's colleague and theoretical physicist B. J. Bjorken made the important suggestion that they focus on inelastic, rather than elastic, collisions in their experiments. In elastic collisions (the kind Hofstadter had examined), electrons are diffracted by any atomic nucleus they pass close to. The angles at which electrons are diffracted and the energies they possess provide clues as to the structure and properties of nucleons (protons and neutrons) that cause the diffraction.

Instead of continuing that line of research, Bjorken advised that Taylor, Friedman, and Kendall should look for cases in which electrons have enough energy to actually collide with and blow apart an atomic nucleus, an inelastic collision. In such cases, the researchers might be able to collect some new and entirely different kinds of information about the structure of nuclei and nucleons.

When Taylor, Friedman, and Kendall redesigned their experiment along the lines recommended by Bjorken, they made a remarkable discovery: the detailed, but fuzzy appearance of the nucleus and nucleons observed by Hofstadter was now seen clearly to consist of discrete granule-like particles. These particles were soon recognized to be the *quarks* that had been hypothesized by **Murray Gell-Mann** and, independently, by George Zweig, in the 1960s. The experiments provided confirmation of the view that protons and neutrons are not themselves discrete, fundamental particles, but are composed of even smaller units, quarks. For this discovery, Taylor, Friedman, and Kendall were jointly awarded the 1990 Nobel Prize in physics.

Long before he had received the Nobel Prize, Taylor had been promoted to associate professor (1968) and then full professor (1970) at Stanford. In 1982 he was made associate director of SLAC, a post he held until 1986. In addition to the Nobel Prize, Taylor has been awarded the Alexander von Humboldt Award in 1982 and an honorary degree from the Université de Paris-Sud in 1980. In 1989, he shared the American Physical Society's W. K. H. Panofsky Prize with Friedman and Kendall.

SELECTED WRITINGS BY TAYLOR:

Periodicals

With J. I. Friedman and H. W. Kendall, "High-Energy Inelastic Electron-Proton Scattering at Six Degrees and Ten Degrees," *Physical Review Letters,* Volume 23, 1969, p. 930.

With J. I. Friedman and H. W. Kendall, "Observed Behavior of Highly Inelastic Electron-Proton Scattering," *Physical Review Letters,* Volume 23, 1969, p. 935.

SOURCES:

Books

Nobel Prize Winners Supplement 1987–1991, H. W. Wilson, 1992, pp. 132–134.

Periodicals

Sutton, Christine, "Nobel Trophy for the Hunters of the Quark," *New Scientist,* October 27, 1990, p. 14.

Waldrop, M. Mitchell, "Physics Nobel Honors the Discovery of Quarks," *Science,* October 26, 1990, pp. 508–509.

—*Sketch by David E. Newton*

Stuart Taylor
1937-
American biologist and cell physiologist

Stuart Taylor combined his background in physiology and biophysics to delve into the mechanism by which living muscle cells contract. Working at the Mayo Foundation, he built a high-speed supercomputer imaging system called CAMERA to study rapidly, and in three-dimensions, the microscopic activity of muscle fibrils (or slender fibers). One of the findings of the CAMERA system has changed previous notions about the way in which the elements of muscle contract.

Stuart Robert Taylor was born on July 15, 1937, in Brooklyn, New York, to Rupert Robert Taylor, a physician, and Enid (Hansen) Taylor. He passed the entrance examination for the science-oriented Stuyvesant High School in Manhattan, and traveled there by subway for four years. At Cornell University, he

Stuart Taylor

majored in zoology and received his B.A. in 1958, returning to New York City to pursue a master's degree in zoology at Columbia University. Before receiving his degree in 1961, he served as a laboratory assistant, and then as a lecturer in the department of zoology. Taylor earned his Ph.D. in biology from New York University in 1966, with a dissertation entitled, "Electro-mechanical coupling in skeletal muscle," and served as a research assistant at the Institute for Muscle Disease.

In 1964, Taylor attended a lecture given by the British physiologist and Nobel Prize winner, **Andrew Huxley**, at Columbia University. Huxley's remarks covered a range of topics dealing with muscle contraction, including the microscopic image of striated muscle (muscle tissue marked by alternating light and dark bands, including cardiac muscle and skeletal muscle), changes in striation pattern, and electrical activity during contraction. The lecture, Taylor later reported, strongly influenced his career "agenda," and in 1967 he was awarded a postdoctoral research fellowship in Huxley's laboratory at University College, London. Upon his return to the United States two years later, he was appointed an instructor, and then assistant professor of pharmacology, at the Downstate Medical Center in Brooklyn. Shortly thereafter, he left for the Mayo Foundation and, in 1971, he became a staff member in pharmacology, physiology and biophysics, and assistant professor of physiology at the University of Minnesota Graduate School. In 1980, he became a professor at Mayo Medical

School and Graduate School of Medicine, where he stayed for over a decade until being appointed Distinguished Professor at Hunter College of the City University of New York.

His research at Mayo resulted in the development of the advanced cell-imaging computer called CAMERA (Computer-Assisted Measurements of Excitation-Response Activities). With this system, he was able to record the act of muscle contraction, obtaining views of up to 5,000 images per second. Previous attempts to use video cameras in imaging systems had yielded results limited to only thirty frames per second. Taylor felt that this was too slow to accurately show the effect, for example, of calcium stimulation on the individual sections of fibrils. Now, he reported in *MOSAIC,* he could see individual heart muscle cells on a "beat-to-beat basis." It has long been held that sarcomeres, the individual, contractile units of a muscle cell fibril, contract, relax, and then stretch back in unison to keep the muscle cell from tearing apart. While Taylor's research indicated similarities in certain cell response mechanisms, it also showed that adjacent sarcomeres differed in their reactions. Taylor and his colleagues concluded, as stated in *MOSAIC,* that there is some independence "between adjacent regions in a heart muscle cell, and that the links between regions are 'weak and very elastic.'" In other words, a muscle cell's twitch results from the average response of many sarcomeres, but it does not reflect the actions of individual sarcomeres. Taylor's continued use of CAMERA to further understand muscle contraction and the role of calcium in its activities has determined not only the role of calcium ions in initiating contraction, but also that there is a feedback mechanism between calcium and contraction. His CAMERA measurements also include other features of muscle cell contraction, such as changes of voltage across cell membranes, molecular rearrangements, and changes in resistance to stretching or compression.

Taylor was married in 1963, but later divorced. He has three children, Scott Carey, Nicole, and Mark Christopher. As his career developed, he gradually became an acknowledged authority on muscle cell contraction and, in 1987, was elected as a fellow of the American Association for the Advancement of Science for his research in the subject. As an African American scientist, he has become active in encouraging minority students to pursue science careers through special programs of the National Science Foundation, the Biophysical Society and the National Institutes of Health. He has also served on the editorial board of science journals, and holds memberships in many scientific societies. Since 1967, he has received some twenty grants from the U.S. Department of Health, Education and Welfare, the National Institutes of Health, the National Science Foundation, National Aeronautics and Space Administration (NASA) and other agencies, to continue his investigations in muscle physiology.

SELECTED WRITINGS BY TAYLOR:

Books

(With K. P. Roos) "High-speed Digital Imaging Microscopy of Isolated Muscle Cells," *Muscular Contraction: Andrew Huxley Festschrift,* edited by R. M. Simmons, Cambridge University Press, 1992. pp. 127–46.

Periodicals

(With I. R. Neering, L. A. Quesenberry, and V. A. Morris) "Non-uniform Volume Changes During Muscle Contraction," *Biophysics Journal,* Volume 59, 1991, pp. 926–33.
(With K. P. Roos) "High-speed Video Imaging and Digital Analysis of Microscopic Features in Contracting Muscle Cells," *Optical Engineering,* Volume 32, 1993, pp. 306–13.

SOURCES:

Periodicals

MOSAIC, fall, 1989, pp. 14–23.

—*Sketch by Maurice Bleifeld*

Maria Telkes
1900-
Hungarian-born American physical chemist

Maria Telkes devoted most of her life to solar energy research, investigating and designing solar ovens, solar stills, and solar electric generators. She is responsible for the heating system installed in the first solar-heated home, located in Dover, Massachusetts. The importance of Telkes's work has been recognized by numerous awards and honors, including the Society of Women Engineers Achievement Award in 1952 (Telkes was the first recipient) and the Charles Greely Abbot Award from the American Section of the International Solar Energy Society.

Maria de Telkes, the daughter of Aladar and Maria Laban de Telkes, was born in Budapest, Hungary, December 12, 1900. She grew up in Buda-

pest and remained there to complete her high school and college education. Studying physical chemistry at Budapest University, she obtained a B.A. degree in 1920, then a Ph.D. in 1924. The following year, on a visit to her uncle in the United States, Telkes was hired as a biophysicist at the Cleveland Clinic Foundation investigating the energy associated with living things. Her studies looked at the sources of this energy, what occurs when a cell dies, and the energy changes which occur when a normal cell is transformed into a cancer cell. In 1937, the year she became an American citizen, Telkes concluded her research at the clinic and joined Westinghouse Electric as a research engineer. She remained at Westinghouse for two years, performing research and receiving patents on new types of thermoelectric devices which converted heat energy into electrical energy.

In 1939, Telkes began working on solar energy, one of her greatest interests since her high school days. Joining the Massachusetts Institute of Technology Solar Energy Conversion Project, she continued her research into thermoelectric devices, with the heat energy now being supplied by the sun. She also researched and designed a new type of solar heating system which was installed in a prototype house built in Dover, Massachusetts, in 1948. Earlier solar heating systems stored the solar energy by heating water or rocks. This system differed in that the solar energy was stored as chemical energy through the crystallization of a sodium sulphate solution.

Telkes's expertise was also recruited by the United States government to study the production of drinking water from sea water. To remove salt from sea water, the water is vaporized to steam, then the steam is condensed to give pure water. Utilizing solar energy for vaporization of the water, she designed a solar still which could be installed on life rafts to provide water. This design was enlarged for use in the Virgin Islands, where the supply of fresh water was often a problem.

In 1953, Telkes moved to New York University and organized a solar energy laboratory in the college of engineering where she continued her work on solar stills, heating systems, and solar ovens. Transferring to the Curtiss-Wright company in 1958, she looked into the development of solar dryers and water heaters as well as the application of solar thermoelectric generators in space. Her position there, as director of research for the solar energy lab, also required her to design a heating and energy storage system for a laboratory building built by Curtiss-Wright in Princeton, New Jersey.

Working at Cryo-Therm from 1961 to 1963, Telkes developed materials for use in the protection of temperature sensitive instruments. Shipping and storage containers made of these materials were used for space and undersea applications in the Apollo and

Polaris projects. In 1963, she returned to her efforts of applying solar energy to provide fresh water, moving to the MELPAR company as head of the solar energy application lab.

Telkes joined the Institute of Energy Conversion at the University of Delaware in 1969, where her work involved the development of materials for storing solar energy and the design of heat exchangers for efficient transfer of the energy. Her advancements resulted in a number of patents—both domestic and foreign—for the storage of solar heat. Her results were put into practical use in Solar One, an experimental solar heated building at the University of Delaware.

In 1977, the National Academy of Science Building Research Advisory Board honored Telkes for her contributions to solar heated building technology; previous honorees included Frank Lloyd Wright and Buckminster Fuller. In 1978, she was named professor emeritus at the University of Delaware, and retired from active research.

SELECTED WRITINGS BY TELKES:

Books

"Thermodynamic Basis for Selecting Heat Storage Materials," *Solar Materials Science,* edited by L. E. Murr, Academic Press, 1980, pp. 405–438.

Periodicals

(With Eleanor Raymond) "Storing Solar Heat in Chemicals—a Report on the Dover House," *Heating and Ventilation,* November, 1949, pp. 80–86.

"A Review of Solar House Heating," *Heating and Ventilation,* September, 1949, pp. 68–74.

"Fresh Water from Sea Water by Solar Distillation," *Industrial & Engineering Chemistry,* Volume 45, 1953, pp. 1108–15.

"Solar Thermoelectric Generators," *Journal of Applied Physics,* Volume 25, 1954, pp. 765–777.

SOURCES:

Books

"Maria Telkes," *Current Biography,* 1950, pp. 563–564.

O'Neill, Lois Decker, editor, *The Woman's Book of World Records and Achievements,* Anchor Press/Doubleday, 1979, p. 189.

Other

University of Delaware Archives, correspondence with Jerome P. Ferrance, January 4, 1994.

—*Sketch by Jerome P. Ferrance*

Edward Teller
1908-
Hungarian-born American physicist

Trained as a theoretical physicist, Edward Teller became a leading authority on nuclear physics during the 1930s and was involved with the Manhattan Project during World War II. He was an early advocate of thermonuclear weapons, which are many times more powerful than the atomic bomb, and he is best known for the leading role he played in the development of the hydrogen bomb between 1949 and 1951. Beginning in the 1940s Teller figured prominently in policy discussions about America's nuclear arsenal, advising government officials at the highest levels and even testifying against **J. Robert Oppenheimer** at a Congressional hearing during the McCarthy era. By the 1980s a lifetime of advising politicians had given him a network of political contacts which included a friendship with President Ronald Reagan. Teller was instrumental in convincing Reagan that a system could be developed to shoot down incoming ballistic missiles. Many consider him responsible for the president's decision to support the Strategic Defense Initiate (SDI), popularly known as "Star Wars."

Teller was born in Budapest on January 15, 1908. His parents were Jewish but not orthodox, celebrating the sabbath and the high holidays. His father, Max Teller, was a lawyer from Hungarian Moravia. His mother, the former Ilona Deutch, was the daughter of a banker and a cotton-mill owner from a small town in the eastern part of the Austrian-Hungarian Empire. Teller did not speak until he was almost four years old, but once he began he spoke a great deal, and it became clear that he was quite precocious. He delighted in performing mathematical calculations in his head; when he was twelve, his father introduced him to Leopold Klug, a professor of mathematics at the University of Budapest, and Teller started seriously thinking of mathematics as a career. By the age of fourteen he was reading about **Albert Einstein** and his work on the special and general theories of relativity.

Edward Teller

In 1925, when he was eighteen, Teller won first place in a prestigious mathematics contest for all Hungarian high school students. Still, his father worried that mathematics was not a dependable occupation, so Teller agreed to study engineering as well as mathematics in college. He studied first for a short time at the University of Budapest and then at the Institute of Technology in Karlsruhe, Germany. By 1928 he was enrolled in the University of Munich as a physics student.

The year he came to Munich, Teller fell while jumping off a streetcar and lost most of one foot when he slipped beneath its wheels. The amputation was so sudden that he did not even realize what had happened until he saw his boot, with his foot still in it, lying in front of him. What was left of Teller's foot was reconstructed so he could walk without a prosthesis, which he was able to do after the accident, although he usually chose to use an artificial foot as well. Despite this injury, Teller never allowed the loss of his foot to stand in the way of his career or his life. Late that year he moved again to the University of Leipzig to study with **Werner Heisenberg**. Two years later, in 1930, he was awarded his doctorate; he had written his dissertation on experiments in which he used quantum mechanics to calculate energy levels in an excited hydrogen molecule.

Teller spent several years as an assistant at the University of Göttingen and then in 1934 he was awarded a Rockefeller Foundation fellowship. He used it to join **Niels Bohr** at the Copenhagen Institute for Theoretical Physics, where many of the great twentieth century physicists studied. On February 26, 1934, a few weeks after starting his Copenhagen fellowship, Edward married Augusta Maria Harkanyi, who he had known for over a decade. The couple spent a year in England, where Teller was a lecturer at the University of London, and then they moved to the United States, where he took a full professorship in the physics department at George Washington University.

Teller was twenty-six by this time and he had already published almost thirty papers, usually with coauthors. While at George Washinton University, he worked closely with **George Gamow**, a Russian exile; together they calculated the rules for one of the major forms of radioactivity, which became known as the Gamow-Teller selection rules for beta decay. During this early part of Teller's career he worked on many different problems, including molecular vibrations, magnetic cooling processes, and the absorption of gases on solids. One of his specialties was the behavior of matter under unusual conditions, including the interior of stars.

Advocates the Development of the Hydrogen Bomb

At the end of 1938 two German chemists, **Otto Hahn** and **Fritz Strassmann**, succeeded in splitting the atom. Within months **Leo Szilard** and Walter H. Zinn had created a chain reaction at Columbia University and it had become clear that atomic weapons were possible. Teller was one of the physicists who lobbied President Franklin D. Roosevelt and his administration to attempt to build such a weapon, and he was involved in the Manhattan Project from the beginning. From 1940 to the end of the war, Teller worked on the atomic bomb, moving between Washington, New York, Chicago, and Los Alamos, New Mexico. In 1941, Teller and his wife became naturalized U.S. citizens; their son was born in 1943 and their daughter in 1946.

One of the tasks Teller was assigned on the Manhattan Project was calculating the possibility of a thermonuclear or hydrogen bomb, also then known among nuclear physicists as the "super." He initially concluded it was impossible, but he redid his figures with Emil Konopinski and realized he had been wrong. Once he understood that a hydrogen weapon was possible, convincing the government to research and build one became a major focus of his energies, although he did continue to offer advice on the atomic bomb. Teller continued to campaign for building the hydrogen bomb even after an atomic bomb was dropped on Hiroshima (an act which Teller opposed) and World War II ended.

There was initially little interest in the hydrogen bomb project, and in 1946 Teller left Los Alamos to teach at the University of Chicago. He focused on issues in theoretical physics, such as the relation of gravitational and electromagnetic forces over time and the origins of the elements and cosmic rays. But another arms race began in earnest when the Soviets exploded their atomic bomb in 1949; the development of the H-bomb became a priority for the United States and Teller returned to Los Alamos. It was at this juncture that Teller began to exert a strong influence on nuclear policy. He convinced Paul Nitze, who was then a key State Department official (and would later be President Reagan's top arms control advisor), that the H-bomb could be built. By 1951, Teller, Stanislaw M. Ulam, and Frederic de Hoffman had made a number of crucial breakthroughs, and the path to building a thermonuclear weapon was clear.

J. Robert Oppenheimer, one of the most influential nuclear physicists in the 1930s and the director of the laboratories at Los Alamos, publicly opposed the development of thermonuclear weapons. Over his objections, Teller used his growing influence in government and lobbied for a second nuclear weapons laboratory. It was established in July, 1952 at Livermore, California, and later named after the famous experimental physicist **Ernest Orlando Lawrence**, who had proposed the site. Teller was associate director of the Lawrence Livermore Laboratory from 1954 to 1958 and director from 1958 to 1960. In 1953, he was also appointed professor at the University of California; he was named University Professor in 1960, a position he would hold until he retired in 1975. At the University of California's Davis campus, he played a major role in establishing the Department of Applied Sciences.

The political battles over the development of the H-bomb and the founding of a second nuclear weapons laboratory in Livermore, California, brought the tensions between Teller and Oppenheimer to a head. There was also a considerable amount of resentment in government circles against Oppenheimer for opposing thermonuclear weapons, and in 1953 the Atomic Energy Commission filed official charges against him, based primarily on his association with communists, including family members. He was denied his security clearance and requested a Congressional hearing. Though many scientists spoke in his favor, Teller appeared to testify against him. According to Daniel J. Kevles in *The Physicists: The History of a Scientific Community in Modern America,* Teller "considered Oppenheimer a Communist and an advocate of Soviet appeasement." At the hearing Teller testified, as quoted by Kevles, that "his actions frankly appeared to me confused and complicated . . . I would like to see to see the vital interests of this country in hands which I understand better and therefore trust more . . . I would feel personally more secure if public matters would rest in other hands." Though the committee did not find Oppen-

heimer disloyal, they decided not to restore his security clearance.

Teller's testimony alienated most of the nuclear physicists in the country and cost him many of his friendships among other scientists, but it strengthened his ties to military and political leaders. His influence on American strategic policy only increased during the 1950s. In 1956, Teller assured the Navy that Livermore could build a warhead small enough to be fired from a submarine, and four years later the first Polaris submarine was armed with the warheads Teller had enivisoned. He was less successful in fulfilling his promise that Livermore could build a "clean" nuclear weapon that would not produce dangerous radioactivity. It has never been made and many physicists believe it is impossible. During this period, Teller was also active in several other areas of nuclear policy, opposing nuclear test bans and advocating peaceful atomic projects such as power reactors and "plowshare" explosions for mining and canal digging. He was the first chairman of the Atomic Energy Commission's Advisory Committee on Reactor Safeguards, which oversaw the production of the first manual on technical aspects of reactor safety. He was especially fascinated by the prospect of nuclear fusion, where power is produced by merging atoms together, as opposed to the fission, or splitting, of atoms, and Livermore became a center for fusion research.

Argues for a Nuclear Defense System

All through the sixties and seventies Teller was an outspoken advocate of nuclear power and as early as 1962 he began advocating an "active defense system" to shoot down attacking enemy missiles. Teller became increasingly convinced that a nuclear shield could remove the threat of a retaliatory nuclear strike. Work at Lawrence Livermore National Laboratories suggested that giant X-ray lasers powered by nuclear blasts might possibly be an effective antimissile weapon; this was only a theory, however, and it was based on a number of assumptions which had not been proven and a number of scientific and technical breakthroughs which had not yet taken place.

When Teller retired from the University of California in 1975, he became a senior research fellow at Stanford University's Hoover Institute on War, Revolution, and Peace. He also continued to maintain his political contacts with policymakers both inside and outside of government. When his friend Reagan was elected president in 1980, Teller found himself with the most political influence he had ever had in his career, and he succeeded at last in his campaign to acquire government funding for an active nuclear defense system. Reagan supported the Strategic Defense Initiative (SDI) or "Star Wars," in large part because Teller convinced him it was possible.

Teller's conviction that such a defense system was possible turned out to be premature, if not entirely incorrect. His original plan for nuclear powered lasers was quickly rejected as infeasible; extensive research was done on burning small holes in the outer sheeting of enemy missiles, thereby causing them to break up in outer space. The necessary antimissile satellites for such a project were expected to be cheap but eventually turned out to be extremely costly; their effectiveness also depended upon complex computer technology.

Whatever the feasibility of the Strategic Defense Initiative, the proposal was at least partly designed to push the Soviets into an arms race they could not afford to pursue. Defense spending was already an enormous share of the Soviet Gross Domestic Product; an expensive antimissile system involving high technology items like lasars and computer tracking systems was simply beyond their means. Later commentators in both the West and Russia credit SDI with forcing the societal reforms which ended in the collapse of communism in Eastern Europe and the Soviet Union.

In *Physics Today*, Robert March writes that Teller is "best known to the public, and even to the generation of physicists educated after World War II, as the tireless and single-minded champion of the technological arms race." Teller's political influence has overshadowed many of his scientific contributions, but since World War II he has done important work in theoretical physics with **Enrico Fermi** and others. In 1962, he was given the Fermi Award, one of the highest honors in physics. In 1983, he was awarded the National Medal of Science for his research on stellar energy, fusion reaction, molecular physics, and nuclear safety. Among other awards Teller has received are the Priestley Memorial Award (1957), the Einstein Award (1959), the General Donovan Memorial Award (1959), the Robins Award (1963), the Leslie R. Groves Gold Medal (1974), the Harvey Prize (1975), the Sylvanus Thayer Award (1986), the Presidential Citizen Medal (1989), and the Order of Banner with Rubies of the Republic of Hungary. Teller is a member of the National Academy of Science and a fellow of the American Nuclear Society, the American Physical Society, the American Academy of Arts and Science, and the American Association for the Advancement of Science.

In the 1990s, Teller remained active in both physics and public policy. "I am amusing myself with a number of problems from astrophysics and superconductivity," Teller told contributor Chris Hables Gray. He went on to describe his work organizing a conference among physicists on human health and radiation levels. On his political influence, he remarked: "I tried to contribute to the defeat of the Soviets. If I contributed one percent, it is one percent of something enormous." He added that it was a great pleasure, now that Eastern Europe is free, to be able to visit his native Hungary for the first time in fifty-six years.

SELECTED WRITINGS BY TELLER:

Books

(With Francis Owen Rice) *The Structure of Matter,* J. Wiley, 1949.
(With Albert L. Latter) *Our Nuclear Future: Facts, Dangers, and Opportunities,* Criterion Books, 1958.
(With Hans Mark and John S. Foster, Jr.) *Power and Security,* Lexington Books, 1976.
(Editor) *Fusion,* Academic Press, 1981.
Better a Shield Than a Sword, Free Press, 1987.
(With Wendy Teller and Wilson Talley) *Conversations on the Dark Secrets of Physics,* Plenum Press, 1991.

SOURCES:

Books

Blumberg, Stanley A., and Louis G. Panos, *Edward Teller: Giant of the Golden Age of Physics,* Scribner, 1990.
Broad, William J., *Teller's War: The Top-Secret Story behind the Star Wars Deception,* Simon & Schuster, 1992.
Mark, Hans, and Sidney Fernbach, editors, *Properties of Matter under Unusual Conditions: In Honor of Edward Teller's 60th Birthday,* Interscience Publishers, 1969.
Hans, Mark, and Lowell Wood, editors, *Energy in Physics, War and Peace: A Festschrift Celebrating Edward Teller's 80th Birthday,* Kluwer Academic Publishers, 1988.
Kevles, Daniel J., *The Physicists: The History of a Scientific Community in Modern America,* Knopf, 1978.

Periodicals

Corn, David, "Kudos for a Con Man," *Nation,* Volume 255, September 28, 1992, p. 316.
Davis, Burton H., "B, E, & T: The Scientists behind the Surface Science," *Chemtech,* Volume 21, January, 1991, p. 18.
March, Robert, review of "Conversations on the Dark Secrets of Physics," *Physics Today,* Volume 45, January, 1992, p. 74.

Other

Teller, Edward, interview with Chris Hables Gray conducted January 29, 1994.

—Sketch by Chris Hables Gray

Howard Temin
1934-1994
American virologist

Howard Temin

Howard Temin is an American virologist who revolutionized molecular biology in 1965 when he found that genetic information in the form of ribonucleic acid (RNA) can be copied into deoxyribonucleic acid (DNA). This process, called reverse transcriptase, contradicted accepted beliefs of molecular biology at that time, which stipulated that DNA always passed on genetic information through RNA. Temin's research also contributed to a better understanding of the role viruses play in the onset of cancer. For this, he was featured on the cover of *Newsweek* in 1971, which hailed his discovery as the most important advancement in cancer research in sixty years. In addition, Temin shared the 1975 Nobel Prize in physiology or medicine for his work on the Rous sarcoma virus. His discovery of the reverse transcriptase process contributed greatly to the eventual identification of the human immunodeficiency virus (HIV). Temin's later research focused on genetic engineering techniques. A vehement antismoker, he took every opportunity to warn against the dangers of tobacco, even in his acceptance speech for the Nobel Prize.

Howard Martin Temin was born in Philadelphia on December 10, 1934, to Henry Temin, a lawyer, and Annette (Lehman) Temin. The second of three sons, Temin showed an early aptitude for science and first set foot in a laboratory when he was only fourteen years old. As a student at Central High School in Philadelphia, he was drawn to biological research and attended special student summer sessions at the Jackson Laboratory in Bar Harbor, Maine. After graduation from high school, Temin enrolled at Swathmore College in Pennsylvania where he majored and minored in biology in the school's honors program. He published his first scientific paper at the age of eighteen and was described in his college yearbook as "one of the future giants in experimental biology."

After graduating from Swathmore in 1955, Temin spent the summer at the Jackson Laboratory and enrolled for the fall term at the California Institute of Technology in Pasadena. For the first year and a half, he majored in experimental embryology but then changed his major to animal virology. He studied under **Renato Dulbecco**, a renowned biologist in his own right, who worked on perfecting techniques for studying virus growth in tissue and developed the first plaque assay (a chemical test to determine the composition of a substance) for an animal virus. Temin received his Ph.D. in biology in 1959 and worked for another year in Dulbecco's laboratory. In 1960 he

joined the McArdle Laboratory for Cancer Research at the University of Wisconsin—Madison, where he spent the remainder of his career as the Harold P. Rusch Professor of Cancer Research and the Steenbock Professor of Biological Sciences.

Studies in Viral Research Stir Controversy

Temin began studying the Rous sarcoma virus (RSV) while still a graduate student in California. First identified in the early twentieth century by **Peyton Rous**, RSV is found in some species of hens and was one of the first viruses known to cause tumors. In 1958 Temin and Harry Rubin, a postdoctoral fellow, developed the first reproducible assay *in vitro* (outside of an organism) for the quantitative measuring of virus growth. Accepting an appointment as assistant professor of oncology at Wisconsin in 1960, Temin continued his research with RSV. Using the assay method he and Rubin developed, Temin focused on delineating the differences between normal and tumor cells. In 1965 he announced his theory that some viruses cause cancer through a startling method of information transfer.

Scientists at the time thought that genetic information could only be passed from DNA to RNA. DNA is a long molecule comprised of two chains of nucleic units containing the sugar deoxyribose. RNA is a molecule composed of a chain of nucleic units containing the sugar ribose. For years, many of Temin's colleagues rejected his theory that some viruses actually reverse this mode of transmitting genetic information, and they cited a lack of direct evidence to support it. Temin, however, was convinced that RNA sometimes played the role of DNA and passed on the genetic codes that made a normal cell a tumor cell.

It took Temin several years, however, to prove his theory. Despite making further inroads in gathering evidence implicating DNA synthesis in RSV infection, many of his colleagues remained skeptical. Finally, in 1970, Temin, working with Satoshi Mitzutani, discovered a viral enzyme able to copy RNA into DNA. Dubbed "a reverse transcriptase virus," this enzyme passed on hereditary information by seizing control of the cell and making a reverse transcript of the host DNA; in other words, the enzyme synthesized a DNA virus that contained all the genetic information of the RNA virus. This discovery was made simultaneously by biologist **David Baltimore** at his laboratory at the Salk Institute in La Jolla, California.

The work of Temin and Baltimore led to a number of impressive developments in molecular biology and recombinant DNA experimentation over the next twenty years, including characterizing retroviruses, a family of viruses that cause tumors in vertebrates by adding a specific gene for cancer cells. In 1975 Temin shared the Nobel Prize in physiology or medicine with his former mentor, Renato Dulbecco, and David Baltimore. These three scientists' research illustrated how separate avenues of scientific research could converge to produce significant advances in biology and medicine. Eventually, interdisciplinary research was to become a mainstay of modern science.

In 1987 Temin reflected on his discovery of viruses' roles in causing cancer. "I measure [my discovery's importance] by comparing what I taught in the experimental oncology course 25 years ago," said Temin in a University of Wisconsin press release, pointing out that the topic of viral carcinogenesis (the viral link to cancer) was rarely the focus of any lectures at that time. "Now, in the course we're teaching, between a third and half of the lectures are related directly or indirectly to viral carcinogenesis."

Research Leads to Understanding of AIDS

Temin's continuing work into the role viruses play in carcinogenesis had an important impact on acquired immunodeficiency syndrome (AIDS) research. Temin's discovery of reverse transcriptase provided scientists with the means to find and identify the AIDS virus. His interest in genetic engineering and the causes of cancer eventually led him to another exciting discovery. He found a way to measure the mutation rate in retroviruses (viruses that engage in reverse transcriptase), which led to

insights on the variation of cancer genes and viruses, such as AIDS. Determining the speed at which genes and viruses change provided vital information for devising attempts to vaccinate or treat viral diseases. His discovery of reverse transcriptase also led to the development of standard tools used by biologists to prepare radioactive DNA probes to study the genetic makeup of viral and malignant cells. Another genetic engineering technique that arose from this research was the ability to make DNA copies of messenger RNA, which could be isolated and purified for later study.

Temin was also interested in such areas as gene therapy, which uses gene splicing techniques to "genetically improve" the host organism. As he began to apply genetic engineering techniques to his research, he recognized legitimate concerns about producing pathogens (microorganisms that carry disease) that could escape into the environment. He also served on a committee that drew up federal guidelines in human gene therapy trials.

Temin's research convinced him that science was making progress in the fight against cancer. Temin said in a 1984 United Press International release: "We know the names of some of the genes which are apparently involved in cancer. If past history is a guide, this understanding will lead to improvement in diagnosis, therapy, and perhaps prevention."

Throughout his career, Temin continued to teach general virology courses for graduates and undergraduates. He also worked with students in his laboratory. "I get satisfaction from a number of things—from discovering new phenomena, from understanding old phenomena, from designing clever experiments—and from seeing students and postdoctoral fellows develop into independent and outstanding scientists," he stated in a University of Wisconsin press release.

A scientist and family man who shunned the spotlight after winning the Nobel Prize (which he kept in the bottom drawer of a file cabinet), Temin was committed to quietly searching for clues into the mysteries of cancer-causing viruses. Temin married Rayla Greenberg, also a geneticist, in 1962, and the couple had two daughters, Miriam and Sarah. A familiar site on the Wisconsin-Madison campus, Temin bicycled to work every day on his mountain bike. Although he preferred not to attract attention so he could better concentrate on his work, Temin did not hesitate to speak out about his beliefs. For example, Temin said in an *On Wisconsin* article, "I enjoy teaching and believe I have gained a lot from doing it. As a researcher, I'm able to present to students the newest work in certain areas. I see that as a benefit." Because of this dedication to academics, he became upset when researchers started to leave the University of Wisconsin-Madison in 1984 because of a state employee wage-freeze, even though his own salary was ensured through private and foundation support. Temin wrote the governor letters criticizing his lack of support for education and faculty researchers. Eventually, he reluctantly agreed to help the governor in developing salary proposals.

Temin also spoke out against cigarette smoking. During the award ceremonies for the Nobel Prize, he told the audience that he was "outraged" that people continued to smoke even though cigarettes were proven to contain carcinogens. He instructed that eighty percent of all cancers were preventable because they resulted from environmental factors, such as smoking. "It was the most important general statement I could make about human cancer," he said later in a *People* magazine interview. "And I realized the Nobel Prize would give me an opportunity to speak out that a person does not ordinarily have." Temin went on to testify before the Wisconsin legislature and congress in support of antismoking bills. His research efforts in AIDS led him to urge the federal government to increase funding for further research into the AIDS epidemic. Despite living a lifestyle designed to minimize the risk of cancer, Temin, who never smoked, developed lung cancer in 1992. His illness was a rare form of cancer called adenocarcinoma of the lung, which is not usually associated with cigarette smoking. He died of this disease on February 9, 1994. In addition to the Nobel Prize, Temin received many other awards for his research, including the prestigious Albert Lasker Award in Basic Medical Research in 1974 and the National Medal of Science in 1992.

SELECTED WRITINGS BY TEMIN:

Periodicals

"RNA-Directed DNA Synthesis," *Scientific American,* January, 1972.

SOURCES:

Periodicals

Dorn, Patrick, "Pursuit of Knowledge Constant Motivation for Temin," *On Wisconsin,* July, 1989.
"In Hospitals and Labs, 9 Researchers Wage War on the Elusive Enemy, Cancer," *People,* August 15, 1977.
"The 1975 Nobel Prize in Physiology or Medicine," *Science,* Volume 190, 1975, pp. 650–713.

Other

"UW-Madison's Nobel Laureate Still Stalking Clues to Cancer," press release, University of Wisconsin-Madison, January 29, 1987.

"Madison Nobel Winner Continues with Simple Life," United Press International, October 8, 1984.

—*Sketch by David Petechuk*

Valentina Tereshkova
1937-
Russian cosmonaut

Valentina Tereshkova was the first woman in space. Tereshkova took off from the Tyuratam Space Station in the Vostok VI in 1963, and orbited the Earth for almost three days, showing women had the same resistance to space as men. She then toured the world promoting Soviet science and feminism, and served on the Soviet Women's Committee and the Supreme Soviet Presidium. Valentina Vladimirovna "Valya" Tereshkova was born on March 6, 1937, in the Volga River village of Maslennikovo. Her father, Vladimir Tereshkov, was a tractor driver; a Red Army soldier during World War II, he was killed when Valentina was two. Her mother Elena Fyodorovna Tereshkova, a worker at the Krasny Perekop cotton mill, singlehandedly raised Valentina, her brother Vladimir and her sister Ludmilla in economically trying conditions; assisting her mother, Valentina was not able to begin school until she was ten.

Tereshkova later moved to her grandmother's home in nearby Yaroslavl, where she worked as an apprentice at the tire factory in 1954. In 1955, she joined her mother and sister as a loom operator at the mill; meanwhile, she graduated by correspondence courses from the Light Industry Technical School. An ardent Communist, she joined the mill's Komsomol (Young Communist League), and soon advanced to the Communist Party.

In 1959, Tereshkova joined the Yaroslavl Air Sports Club and became a skilled amateur parachutist. Inspired by the flight of **Yuri Gagarin**, the first man in space, she volunteered for the Soviet space program. Although she had no experience as a pilot, her 126-jump record gained her a position as a cosmonaut in 1961. Four candidates were chosen for a one-time woman-in-space flight; Tereshkova received an Air Force commission and trained for 18 months before becoming chief pilot of the Vostok VI. Admiring fellow cosmonaut Yuri Gagarin was quoted as saying, "It was hard for her to master rocket techniques, study spaceship designs and equipment, but she tackled the job stubbornly and devoted much of her own time to study, pouring over books and notes in the evening."

At 12:30 PM on June 16, 1963, Junior Lieutenant Tereshkova became the first woman to be launched into space. Using her radio callsign Chaika (Seagull), she reported, "I see the horizon. A light blue, a beautiful band. This is the Earth. How beautiful it is! All goes well." She was later seen smiling on Soviet and European TV, pencil and logbook floating weightlessly before her face. Vostok VI made 48 orbits (1,200,000 miles) in 70 hours, 50 minutes, coming within 3.1 miles of the previously launched Vostok V, piloted by cosmonaut Valery Bykovsky. Tereshkova's flight confirmed Soviet test results that women had the same resistance as men to the physical and psychological stresses of space.

Upon her return, she and Bykovsky were hailed in Moscow's Red Square. On June 22 at the Kremlin she was named a Hero of the Soviet Union and was decorated by Presidium Chairman Leonid Brezhnev with the Order of Lenin and the Gold Star Medal. A symbol of emancipated Soviet feminism, she toured the world as a goodwill ambassador promoting the equality of the sexes in the Soviet Union, receiving a standing ovation at the United Nations. With Gagarin, she travelled to Cuba in October as a guest of the Cuban Women's Federation, and then went to the International Aeronautical Federation Conference in Mexico.

On November 3, 1963, Tereshkova married Soviet cosmonaut Colonel Andrian Nikolayev, who had orbited the earth 64 times in 1962 in the Vostok III. Their daughter Yelena Adrianovna Nikolayeva was born on June 8, 1964, and was carefully studied by doctors fearful of her parents' space exposure, but no ill effects were found. After her flight, Tereshkova continued as an aerospace engineer in the space program; she also worked in Soviet politics, feminism and culture. She was a Deputy to the Supreme Soviet between 1966 and 1989, and a People's Deputy from 1989 to 1991. Meanwhile, she was a member of the Supreme Soviet Presidium from 1974 to 1989. During the years from 1968 to 1987, she also served on the Soviet Women's Committee, becoming its head in 1977. Tereshkova headed the USSR's International Cultural and Friendship Union from 1987 to 1991, and subsequently chaired the Russian Association of International Cooperation.

Tereshkova summarized her views on women and science in her 1970 "Women in Space" article in the American journal *Impact of Science on Society:* "I believe a woman should always remain a woman and nothing feminine should be alien to her. At the same time I strongly feel that no work done by a woman in the field of science or culture or whatever, however vigourous or demanding, can enter into conflict with her ancient 'wonderful mission'—-to love, to be loved—-and with her craving for the bliss of motherhood. On the contrary, these two aspects of her life can complement each other perfectly."

SELECTED WRITINGS BY TERESHKOVA:

Periodicals

"Women in Space," *Impact of Science on Society,* Volume 20, number 1, January-March, 1970, pp. 5–12.

SOURCES:

Books

Drexel, John, editor, *Facts on File Encyclopedia of the 20th Century,* Facts on File, 1991, pp. 884–885.
O'Neill, Lois Decker, "Farthest Out of All: The First Woman in Space," in *Women's Book of World Records and Achievements,* Anchor Books, 1979, pp. 739–740.
Sharpe, Mitchell, *"It is I, Sea Gull": Valentina Tereshkova, First Woman in Space,* Crowell, 1975.
Uglow, Jennifer S., editor, *The International Dictionary of Women's Biography,* Continuum, 1982, p. 461.

Periodicals

"Soviets Orbit Woman Cosmonaut," *New York Times,* June 17, 1963, pp. 1, 8.
"2 Russians Land in Central Asia after Space Trip," *New York Times,* June 20, 1963, pp. 1, 3.

—*Sketch by Julian A. Smith*

Frederick Terman
1900-1982
American electrical engineer and educator

During his fifty-year tenure at Stanford University, Frederick Terman was instrumental in transforming the school from what he described as an "underprivileged institution" to the cornerstone of the legendary Silicon Valley. An electrical engineer, he directed the nation's secret radar laboratory at

Harvard University during World War II. The reference and text books he wrote are regarded as "bibles" of radio engineering.

Frederick Emmons Terman, an only child, was born on June 7, 1900, in English, Indiana, to Lewis and Anna Belle Minton Terman. In 1910 the elder Terman, a psychologist, joined the faculty at Stanford University, where he developed the Stanford-Binet intelligence quotient. The young Terman remained unenrolled in school until he was nine and a half because of his father's belief in natural education; he entered school at the third grade level and began a successful academic career. While in high school, he developed an interest in "ham" radio, and by age 16 he was operating his own transmitter.

Terman graduated at the top of his class when he received his bachelor's degree in chemical engineering at Stanford in 1920. Two years later, he earned an engineer's degree in electrical engineering at Stanford under Professor Harris J. Ryan, America's first professor of electrical engineering. Terman pursued his master's and doctoral degrees at the Massachusetts Institute of Technology, where he studied under Professor **Vannevar Bush**. He received his doctor of science degree in 1924 and was offered a teaching position at MIT.

Prior to beginning his new job, Terman left to visit his family in California, where he was stricken with millary tuberculosis. He was bedridden for a year at his family's Stanford campus home; he also suffered a ruptured appendix and developed eye trouble that would continue for years. Although he could not accept the faculty position at MIT, he was able to fulfill a half-time appointment in electrical engineering at Stanford in 1925. During that first year of teaching, Terman was out of bed only two hours a day. Throughout the rest of his life, he would take great care of his health, a strategy that enabled him to work 14-hour days seven days a week.

After a year, Terman was able to teach full time, and he became an assistant professor in 1927. The following year, he married Sibyl Walcutt, a graduate student in psychology. They had three sons, Frederick, Terence, and Lewis. Terman, who developed and taught Stanford's first course in electronics (then called radio engineering), headed the university's electronics laboratory and used his technical and administrative skills to encourage local industry. He suggested an idea for a marketable instrument to one of his students, **William Hewlett**, who turned the idea into an audio oscillator. Terman then helped Hewlett lure former student **David Packard** back from a General Electric job in New York. The business they started in a Palo Alto garage would grow into the huge Hewlett-Packard Company of computer manufacturing. In 1937, the year Terman became head of the electrical engineering department, the klystron tube (a

vacuum tube that generates and amplifies microwave signals) was developed at Stanford by Russell Varian and William Hansen; the invention became the foundation for World War II radar devices, the Stanford Linear Accelerator, and clinical linear accelerators used in cancer treatment. Terman already enjoyed a national reputation, and in 1942 he became the first person working west of New York state to serve as president of the Institute of Radio Engineers (later known as the Institute of Electrical and Electronic Engineering).

That same year, Vannevar Bush, who was responsible for organizing American academic scientists and engineers for the wartime defense effort, asked Terman to head the covert Radio Research Laboratory at Harvard University. Terman assembled more than 800 people to develop countermeasures against enemy radar. One of their innovations, narrow strips of aluminum foil called chaff, reflected radar when strewn by airplanes; the country sacrificed its Christmas tree tinsel and chewing gum wrappers to help provide the 20 million pounds of chaff that Allied forces used during the war in Europe. The laboratory also made tunable receivers for detecting and analyzing enemy radar signals. By the end of the war, Terman's lab had developed 150 anti-radar tools that reduced the effectiveness of German anti-aircraft efforts by 75 percent.

In 1945, Terman's achievements were recognized with an honorary doctorate from Harvard. The following year, he was elected to the National Academy of Sciences; he and his father thus enjoyed rare status as simultaneous members of that prestigious organization. He was awarded the King of England's special medal for service in the cause of freedom and, in 1948, the United States' Medal for Merit, the nation's highest civilian award.

Turns Stanford into Important Technological Research Center

Having accomplished his wartime assignment, Terman returned to Stanford in 1946 as dean of engineering. "Stanford emerged from World War II as an underprivileged institution," he was quoted as saying by Sandra Blakeslee in a Stanford News Service article. "It had not been significantly involved in any of the exciting engineering and scientific activities associated with the war." The government, whose previous support of basic research was limited to agricultural topics, showed a new interest in funding peacetime research. Terman seized the opportunity, negotiating contracts for Stanford in 1946 and 1947 that helped establish the framework for the way sponsored research would be implemented in university settings. He established a policy he called "steeples of excellence," by which Stanford would pay top salaries to attract outstanding faculty members, reasoning that these experts would attract research contracts as well as quality junior faculty and promising graduate students. Under Terman's leadership, Stanford's reputation flourished and the university was sometimes referred to as "Terman Tech" because of his shaping influence. Terman envisioned universities as more than a place for learning, seeing them also as major economic influences in the nation's industrial life. Calling the idea of creating an industrial park on plentiful Stanford land "our secret weapon," he shaped the venture into a high-technology center. Klystron tube producers Varian Associates became the first tenant in 1951. By the late 1960s, 90 businesses would employ 26,000 workers at the Stanford Industrial Park.

In 1955, Terman was named provost at Stanford; in 1959, he took on additional duties as the school's vice president. Five years later, he helped organize the National Academy of Engineering, of which he became a founding member. His career achievements were commemorated in 1977 when Stanford University dedicated the $9.2-million Frederick Emmons Terman Engineering Center.

While at Harvard, Terman had written his famous *Radio Engineer's Handbook,* the fifth of his eight books. Not counting foreign publications in at least eight languages, his books had sold over 600,000 copies by the time he retired in 1965. His texts were readable, thorough, and practical; furthermore, Terman diligently updated each new edition to reflect current developments. Results of his personal research are documented in more than 50 articles he wrote for technical journals. In 1952, he summarized his vision of modern technology, as quoted by Blakeslee: "Through its ability to control, to amplify, and to convert between light, sound, and electricity, electronics provides a nervous system for our machine-age civilization."

Terman died in his sleep of cardiac arrest at his Stanford campus home on December 19, 1982.

SELECTED WRITINGS BY TERMAN:

Books

Radio Engineer's Handbook, McGraw-Hill, 1943.
Electronic and Radio Engineering, McGraw-Hill, 1955.

SOURCES:

Periodicals

Blakeslee, Sandra, "Stanford to Honor Fred Terman at Engineering Center Oct. 6," Stanford News Service, October 5, 1977.

Palo Alto Times, December 12, 1945.
San Jose Business Journal, February 15, 1988, p. 19.

Other

Bloom, William, L. Kenneth Wilson, and Jane Morgan, *Audio Tapes of Interviews on the Occasion of the Silver Anniversary of Palo Alto,* Palo Alto, CA, 1969.

—*Sketch by Sandra Katzman*

Karl Terzaghi
1883-1963
Austrian-born American engineer

K arl Terzaghi bridged the gap between geology and civil engineering by creating the field of soil mechanics. He developed the fundamental methods and tools used to investigate the nature and behavior of soils that are still employed by soil engineers today. His theories have greatly expanded how an understanding of the behavior of soils can be used in construction projects, and designs for the foundations of most major structures now depend on his work.

Terzaghi was born in Prague, Austria-Hungary (now Czechoslovakia), on October 2, 1883, to Anton Terzaghi von Pontenuovo and Amalia Eberle Terzaghi. His father, who died while Terzaghi was a boy, was an infantry commander. Terzaghi attended military school and then the technical high school in Prague. In 1900, he entered the Technische Hochschule, a university in Graz, Austria, where he studied mechanical engineering. He also discovered an interest in geology and was once encouraged to become a professional writer by a professor who had read some of his essays. Terzaghi served a year in the army after graduating from the Technische Hochschule, during which time he translated *Outlines of Field Geology* by Scottish geologist Archibald Geikei. His interest in geology increased; he agreed to serve as a geologist on a Greenland expedition in 1906, but a mountaineering accident forced him to back out.

Terzaghi's first job was as superintendent of construction at an engineering firm in Vienna. In 1908, he moved to Croatia on the Adriatic coast, where he remained until 1910, surveying the geology of the site for a proposed hydroelectric power facility. It was here that Terzaghi became interested in applying geology to engineering problems. After the project he addressed the subject in a paper he wrote on the origin of land forms and the underground conditions of the region. During this period, he began working in Russia, helping to complete a St. Petersburg construction project that had been halted due to structural hazards. In January, 1912, he was awarded a doctorate of technical sciences from the Technische Hochschule with a thesis based on the unique design of one of his Russian construction projects.

Begins Work in Soil Mechanics

By 1912, Terzaghi had begun his search for a rational approach to foundation engineering and spent 1911 through 1913 in the United States traveling to dam sites, researching geological studies and looking for connections between them and his own construction experience. When World War I began in 1913, he returned to Austria to join the army, transferring to the newly formed Austrian air force and serving until 1916. In that year, he married Olga Byloff, with whom he would have one daughter. They were separated in 1922 and divorced in 1926.

After leaving the air force, Terzaghi accepted a position at the Imperial School of Engineers in Istanbul, Turkey, where he built his first soil mechanics laboratory. He used tools from the physics department and kitchen utensils to create a program for investigating the physical composition of clay soils. After World War I ended, Terzaghi accepted a teaching position at Roberts College, an American school in Istanbul. He developed his second soils laboratory there, remaining until 1925. Terzaghi's theories about soil mechanics advanced considerably during this period as he invented more tools and techniques for studying the behavior of soils. An example is Terzaghi's discovery that weight supported by clay soils is first carried by the liquid in the microscopic pores of the clay and then transferred over time into the clay itself. Terzaghi published a compilation of his works in 1925, which led to a visiting lectureship at the Massachusetts Institute of Technology (MIT).

During his four years at MIT, Terzaghi developed a program for teaching soil mechanics, improved his testing methods, and expanded his work to include investigations of pavement design and earth dams. Up until this time, Terzaghi had worked only in temperate climates. Curious about the effects of different climates on structures, he asked the United Fruit Company for the opportunity to study soil behavior at their Latin American locations. In 1928, he traveled to United Fruit facilities in Costa Rica, Panama, Spanish Honduras, and Guatemala, studying, among other things, the stability of sloped embankments and the flow of water through soils. After his return from Latin America, Terzaghi received a telephone inquiry about his work from Ruth Doggett, a doctoral student studying geology at Rad-cliffe College in Cambridge, Massachusetts. Their conversation led to courtship and then marriage in the summer of 1930. They would have a son and a daughter. The Terzaghis cooperated on several projects throughout their careers.

By 1930, Terzaghi had returned to Vienna to teach at the Technical University, which became, under his influence, the focal point of earthworks studies. For nine years, Terzaghi lectured and taught his laboratory techniques to engineers and students from as far away as Australia. He concentrated his research on developing new ways to measure the reactions of sand and clay to stresses such as the weight of buildings. During this period, the role of soil mechanics in engineering was becoming more widely understood by professionals; Terzaghi's role in the development of this field was recognized in 1936 when he returned to Boston, Massachusetts, for a special ceremony at Harvard University. There he was named the first president of the International Conference of Soil Mechanics and Foundation Engineering. He would remain the society's active president for twenty-one years and honorary president for several more.

Terzaghi lectured in many European cities, as well as North Africa and Central Asia. He was known for consulting on construction projects that had been interrupted by unexpected structural failures. An afternoon phone call to a place where he was staying in France once brought him to London that same evening to study a failure at an earthen dam project. This began a fruitful relationship with British engineers, and in 1939 he was invited to deliver the James Forrest Lecture to the Institution of Civil Engineers. Terzaghi was only the second non-British engineer to receive this honor since the institution was founded in 1890.

In 1938, Terzaghi accepted a visiting lectureship at Harvard University. He moved his family to the United States and settled in Winchester, Massachusetts. This developed into a very productive period of Terzaghi's career, during which he taught, consulted on a worldwide basis, and wrote two important books and almost one hundred papers. In 1946, Harvard made him Professor of the Practice of Civil Engineering. Terzaghi included adventure in his work as often as possible, such as studying the Sasumua dam site in Kenya in 1953 near the warring Mau Mau tribe. He also worked on famous projects and was chair of the Board of Consultants for the controversial High Aswan Dam in Egypt.

Terzaghi maintained a rigorous professional schedule and continued his teaching, consulting, and researching well into his seventies. His health remained excellent and he regularly out-paced much younger geologists on field investigations. Terzaghi retired from the Harvard faculty in 1956 at age seventy-three, but he still worked, and in the spring before his seventy-fifth birthday he traveled to fifteen cities throughout the United States and Europe. Over the next several years he wrote a textbook and worked with several leading engineering schools as a lecturer and research consultant. By the end of his career he had received six honorary doctoral degrees, the Norman Medal from the American Society of Civil Engineers three times, and the Frank B. Brown Medal of the Franklin Institute of Philadelphia. Terzaghi died on October 25, 1963, at his home in Winchester, Massachusetts.

SELECTED WRITINGS BY TERZAGHI:

Books

Erdbaumechanik auf bodenphysikalischer Grundlage, Deuticke (Vienna), 1925.
Principles of Soil Mechanics, McGraw-Hill, 1926.
Theoretical Soil Mechanics, Wiley, 1943.
(With Ralph Peck) *Soil Mechanics in Engineering Practice,* Wiley, 1948.
From Theory to Practice in Soil Mechanics: Selections from the Writings of Karl Terzaghi, with bibliography and contributions by L. Bjerrum, A. Casagrande, R. B. Peck, and A. W. Skempton, Wiley, 1960.

Periodicals

"Large Retaining-Wall Tests I-V," *Engineering News Record,* February 1, 1934, pp. 136–140; February 22, 1934, pp. 259–262; March 8, 1934, pp. 316–318; March 29, 1934, pp. 403–406; April 19, 1934, pp. 503–508.
"Stability of Slopes of Natural Clay," *Proceedings of the International Conference on Soil Mechanics and Foundation Engineering,* Volume 1, 1936, pp. 161–165.
"Undisturbed Clay Samples and Undisturbed Clays," *Boston Society of Civil Engineers,* Volume 28, 1941, pp. 211–231.
"Permafrost," *Journal of the Boston Society of Civil Engineers,* Volume 39, 1953, pp. 1–50.
"Egypt's Aswan High Dam," *Proceedings of the Canadian Soil Mechanics Conference,* Volume 46, 1956, pp. 47–51.
"Soil Mechanics in Action," *Civil Engineering,* Volume 29, 1959, pp. 69–70.

—Sketch by David N. Ford

Nikola Tesla
1856-1943
Serbian American inventor and electrical engineer

The first person to prove and perfect the efficient use of alternating-current electricity, Nikola Tesla saw his polyphase system become the standard for power transmission throughout the world. He also pioneered research in such areas as artificial lightning, high-frequency and high-tension currents, and radio telegraphy. Before his death in 1943, Tesla had acquired more than one hundred patents for high-frequency generators, adjustable condensers, thermomagnetic motors, transformers, his famous Tesla coil, and other inventions that were to become integral elements in modern technology. Tesla was born on July 10, 1856, the son of Serbian parents in the Croatian village of Smiljan. The settlement was located near the town of Gospić in what was then a part of the Austro-Hungarian empire, an area that later became Yugoslavia. Tesla's father and mother, Milutin Tesla and Djuka Mandić, had expected their son to follow in his father's footsteps as a Greek Orthodox clergyman. But during his early school years in Smiljan and then in nearby Gospić, where his parents moved when he was six or seven years old, he excelled in math and science. Gradually it became clear that the young and independent-minded Tesla was no candidate for the seminary.

Early Achievements in Europe

In 1871, when Tesla was fifteen, he attended the higher secondary school at Karlovac, Croatia. After four years, Tesla moved to Graz, Austria, to attend the higher technical school or polytechnic institute in 1875. As before, he excelled in math and science, seemed to have a prodigious memory (he was reputed to have memorized Johann Wolfgang von Goethe's epic drama *Faust*), and showed particular interest in electrical engineering. While attending the technical school in Graz, Tesla commented on the unnecessary (and potentially dangerous) sparks that were emitted by a Gramme dynamo, a direct-current induction motor that was being demonstrated in the classroom. The sparks emerged from where the brushes came into contact with the commutator, and Tesla commented that these sparks could be eliminated by creating a motor without a commutator. The professor was skeptical of the young scientist's theory, and at that time nothing came of the idea. Over the coming years, however, Tesla would continue to work to overcome the problems of direct-current motors.

Nikola Tesla

The details of this period of Tesla's life are unclear, but according to one of his biographers, Margaret Cheney in *Tesla: Man Out of Time,* Tesla's education was interrupted during these years by bouts of malaria and cholera. In any event, Tesla may have attempted to continue his university education at the University of Prague in 1880 (although Cheney indicates that there is no record of this). He was said to have gambled frequently in Prague, wagering for pleasure and in the often vain hope of augmenting his meager income. Tesla appears never to have completed his formal education at Prague, however, possibly because the death of his father forced him to become financially independent. As it was, Tesla may have merely audited classes and used the library without actually enrolling in the university.

Tesla's post-Prague years come into sharper focus. In January 1881 he moved to Budapest where he worked in the Hungarian government's new central telegraph office. During his brief tenure here, Tesla invented a telephone amplifier or loudspeaker, yet for reasons unknown he never patented the device. Tesla also continued to ruminate about the sparks created by the Gramme dynamo in the classroom in Graz, and about rotating magnetic fields, which would later become the basis for all polyphase induction motors. The following year, 1882, Tesla took a position with the Continental Edison Company in Paris.

Tesla's job here was to correct problems in the Edison plants in Germany and France. One of his trips took him to Strasbourg, where he earned local gratitude (but not a promised bonus) for having repaired the railroad station's lighting plant. While in Strasbourg, ever mindful of the sparking problem of direct-current motors, Tesla tried to interest the city's mayor and certain of his wealthy colleagues in his design for an alternating-current motor that would eliminate the need for a commutator. In response, the mayor and his friends rewarded Tesla with a few bottles of 1801 St. Estèphe wine but gave no financial support.

Seeks Opportunity with Edison in America

Tesla decided to try his luck in the United States where there were interesting developments in electrical engineering and presumably greater opportunities for funding. With a reference from the manager of the Edison company in Paris, Tesla secured a position in **Thomas Alva Edison**'s research laboratory in New York. Tesla embarked for the New World in 1884.

Thomas Edison had already made a reputation for himself as an electronics wizard, but he was committed to the use of direct-current electricity. When Tesla explained to Edison his plans for a motor based on alternating current, all he did was create the foundation for a difficult relationship with his unyielding new boss. Edison insisted that Tesla's designs for his new motor were impractical and dangerous. Edison hired Tesla, however, and for a year the new immigrant designed direct-current dynamos and motors for the Edison Machine Works in New York. The experience was limiting and unsatisfying for Tesla, who found that he was unable to overcome the personal and professional differences that separated him from Edison. These factors and a disagreement over compensation that Tesla felt was due to him caused the young Serb to strike out on his own.

In the ensuing year, some entrepreneurs persuaded Tesla to establish an electric company. He established the company's headquarters in Rahway, New Jersey, in 1885. In establishing his own company Tesla saw an opportunity for working out in a practical way his ideas for alternating current. His financial supporters, however, seemed mainly interested in providing arc lighting for streets and factories. Again, Tesla faced disappointment and was forced to work for at least part of 1886 as a common laborer. In his spare time, however, Tesla continued to work on his innovations. During this period he managed to acquire seven patents for his work with arc lighting. Growing interest in electrical innovations gradually worked to Tesla's advantage, and by 1887 he was able to establish the Tesla Electric Company.

Working within his own organization, Tesla was able to create the first efficient polyphase motor. This was achieved by designing a motor that incorporated several wire-taped blocks that surrounded the rotor.

When alternating current is supplied to the wires, with the current to each block being slightly out of phase with the others, a rotating magnetic field is created. The movement of the rotor is achieved as it follows this revolving field. The practical effect of Tesla's invention was that it allowed strong electrical currents to be transmitted over long distances. Edison's direct current, on the other hand, was limited to local use and required many electrical relay stations to distribute the current throughout a given area such as a city. Tesla's invention undermined Edison's assertion that alternating current was impractical, and by 1891 Tesla had acquired forty patents having to do with this technology. His inventions attracted attention, and Tesla began giving lectures in the late 1880s. Perhaps the most notable of these lectures was the one he delivered to the American Institute of Electrical Engineers in May 1888, after which his reputation as a preeminent electrical engineer was firmly established.

George Westinghouse, inventor and manufacturer, bought one of Tesla's patents for the polyphase motor and hired the man to work in his Pittsburgh plant. In 1889 Tesla became an American citizen. He was now famous and his future seemed assured. During the ensuing years, Tesla continued to research and lecture to prestigious organizations across the United States and in Europe. In Britain he addressed the Institution of Electrical Engineers and the Royal Society, and in France, the Society of Electrical Engineers and the French Society of Physics. In these lectures Tesla discussed his work in the transmission of electrical power through radio waves. At the Columbian Exposition in Chicago in 1893, the first world's fair to have electricity, Westinghouse provided it using Tesla's system of polyphase alternating current. At the Exposition Tesla also gave lectures and demonstrations of his research.

Designs First Hydroelectric Generating Plant

It was also Tesla's partnership with Westinghouse that allowed Tesla the opportunity to design what may have been the scientist's greatest achievement, the world's first hydroelectric generating plant. The plant, located at Niagara Falls, distributed electrical current to the city of Niagara Falls and to Buffalo, New York, some twenty-three miles away. The Niagara power plant, completed late in 1895, destroyed forever Edison's objections to Tesla's polyphase system of alternating current and established the kind of power system that would eventually be used throughout the United States and the world.

Meanwhile, Tesla had turned his interests to the proposition that radio waves could carry electrical energy and in 1897 demonstrated wireless communication over some twenty-five miles. Tesla also demonstrated the idea of transmitting electrical energy in

1898 with several radio-controlled model boats that he had constructed. The Spanish-American War was underway at this time, however, distracting the public from this new revelation, and it's also possible that this type of remote-control system was too advanced for its usefulness to be fully appreciated. Many of Tesla's other inventions would later prove beneficial in a number of applications. His work with high-frequency currents yielded several generating machines that were forerunners of those used in radio communication, and his Tesla coil, a resonant air-core transformer, proved capable of producing currents at a great number of frequencies and magnitudes. In 1898, Tesla moved to the clear, dry air of Colorado Springs, Colorado, where he continued his experiments on electricity, but this time on a grander scale than model boats. As before, his interests focused on transmission of high energy, sending and receiving wireless messages, and related issues pertaining to high voltage electricity. The two hundred kilowatt transmitting tower that Tesla built in Colorado Springs could produce lightning bolts that were millions of volts in strength, so powerful they could overload the city's electrical generator. Indeed, during one experiment in creating artificial lightning, Tesla did just that, causing the municipal generator to catch fire and plunging the town into darkness.

Tesla's year of experimentation in Colorado Springs produced no immediate practical results. Tesla's work did provide the basis, however, for research by later scientists. Physicist Robert Golka, for example, modeled his research in plasma physics on material he gleaned from Tesla's often cryptic Colorado Springs notes that were housed at the Tesla Museum in Belgrade after World War II. Similarly, Soviet physicist **Pyotr Kapitsa**, who shared the 1978 Nobel Prize for his research on magnetism, acknowledged Tesla's work as a model for his own research. Richard Dickinson, a researcher at Cal Tech's Jet Propulsion Laboratory, who was involved in research on the transmission of wireless energy, also invoked Tesla's concepts as a guide to further research.

Tesla in Eclipse

Although Tesla's work had enduring qualities that inspired the research scientists of later generations, Tesla's influence in the scientific community of his contemporaries began to wane after his year in Colorado Springs. Although he had received royalties from his many patents, that income gradually diminished, due in part to a royalty agreement he had renegotiated with Westinghouse before alternating-current electricity attained prominence. As a result, Tesla realized only a fraction of the fortune that alternating current generated, and he was left with scant resources for his later research. In addition, it appeared at least to some minds that Tesla was beginning to lose his grasp on rigorous scientific inquiry. For example, Tesla had received radio signals while at Colorado Springs that he suggested were from intelligent life on Mars or Venus. Although radio signals from space are now a staple of astronomical research, they were not so in the early years of the twentieth century. And to suggest intelligent life as the source of these signals, without the benefit of corroborating evidence, undermined confidence in Tesla's credibility.

During the last four decades of his life Tesla became reclusive and lived alone in a hotel room in New York City. He continued to perform such experiments as he could with his limited resources, but he never recaptured the glory of his earlier years. Those past accomplishments continued to garner attention, however. Late in 1915 the press rumored that the Nobel Prize committee had listed Tesla and Edison as candidates to share the Nobel Prize in physics. Tesla became indignant because he would have to share the prize with his arch-rival, but for reasons never made clear, the Nobel Prize committee gave the award in physics to two other candidates. In 1917, a colleague recommended Tesla for the prestigious Edison Medal of the American Institute of Electrical Engineers. Again, because of the award's association with Edison, Tesla at first refused the honor. After he was finally induced to receive the medal and attend the banquet in his honor, he soon drifted from the crowd and was found outside feeding the pigeons.

As Tesla grew older his reclusive and eccentric behavior grew more intense. He was reportedly troubled by phobias—an aversion to pearl earrings and billiard balls, for example—and his ideas seemed ever more bizarre. On his seventy-eighth birthday he told an interviewer that he had plans for an invincible death beam with a potential for 50 million volts that could instantly destroy 10,000 airplanes or one million soldiers. He publicly offered to create such a death beam for the U.S. government, which he said he could create in three months for less than $2 million dollars.

Early in morning of January 8, 1943, the maid at the Hotel New Yorker discovered Tesla's body in his room. He had been ill for the previous two years and had evidently died in his sleep on the evening of January 7 of a coronary thrombosis. He was 86 years old. In death he received much of the adulation that he did not receive during his lifetime. Scores of notable people—Franklin and Eleanor Roosevelt, New York mayor Fiorello H. LaGuardia, political figures from Yugoslavia, Nobel Prize winners, leaders in science—lauded Tesla as a visionary who provided the foundations for modern technology. Indeed, within a year of Tesla's death, the United States Supreme Court ruled that Nikola Tesla, and not Guglielmo Marconi, had invented the radio. Yugoslavia made him a national hero and established the Tesla Muse-

um in Belgrade after World War II. In addition to honorary degrees from American and foreign universities (including Columbia and Yale in 1894), and the Edison Medal, Tesla was also recipient during his lifetime of the John Scott Medal. In 1975 Tesla became an inductee into the National Inventors Hall of Fame.

SELECTED WRITINGS BY TESLA:

Books

The Inventions, Researches and Writings of Nikola Tesla, originally published in *The Electrical Engineer,* 1894, reprinted by Barnes & Noble, 1992.
Lectures, Patents, Articles, originally published by the Nikola Tesla Museum, 1956, reprinted by Health Research, 1973.

Periodicals

"Some Personal Recollections," *Scientific American,* June 1915.
"My Inventions," *Electrical Experimenter,* May, June, July, and October, 1919.

SOURCES:

Books

Cheney, Margaret, *Tesla: Man Out of Time,* Dorset Press, 1981.
Neidle, Cecyle S., *Great Immigrants,* New York, 1973.
Nikola Tesla, Édition de la Société pour la Foundation de l'Institut Nikola Tesla, 1936.
O'Neill, John J., *Prodigal Genius,* David McKay Co., 1944.
Ratzlaff, John T., and Leland I. Anderson, *Dr. Nikola Tesla Bibliography,* Ragusan Press, 1979.
Swezey, Kenneth M., "Tesla, Nikola," *Dictionary of Scientific Biography,* Volume 13, Scribner's, 1976, pp. 286–287.

Periodicals

Hall, Stephen S., "Tesla: A Scientific Saint, Wizard or Carnival Sideman?," *Smithsonian,* June 19, 1986, pp. 121–134.
Lawren, Bill, "Rediscovering Tesla," *Omni,* March, 1988, pp. 65–66, 68, 116–117.
"Nikola Tesla Dies: Prolific Inventor," *New York Times,* Jan. 8, 1943, p. 19.

Swezey, Kenneth M., "Nikola Tesla," *Science,*
   May 16, 1958, pp. 1147–1159.

—*Sketch by Karl Preuss*

Giuliana Cavaglieri Tesoro
1921-
Italian-born American chemist

Giuliana Cavaglieri Tesoro has built an international reputation as an expert on polymers, compounds consisting of large molecules formed by repeating units of smaller molecules. In a productive career during which she has been granted about 120 patents, Tesoro has made several important contributions to the field of textile chemistry. Among her accomplishments have been the development of the first antistatic chemical for synthetic fibers, the improvement of the permanent press property of textiles, and the development of flame-resistant fabrics. In honor of this research, Tesoro received the Society of Women Engineers' Achievement Award in 1978.

Tesoro was born in Venice, Italy, on June 1, 1921, one of three children born to Gino and Margherita Maroni Cavaglieri. Although her father had trained as a civil engineer, he worked as the manager of a large insurance company. He died when Tesoro was only twelve. By the time she was ready to begin her higher education in 1938, the rise of fascism in her native land meant that she could not enroll in a university there because of her Jewish ancestry. To escape such oppression, Tesoro went to Switzerland, where she briefly pursued training in X-ray technology. She immigrated to the United States in 1939, just before Italy officially entered World War II.

Tesoro, still in her teens and new to America, nevertheless set her sights high: She wanted to enter the graduate program at Yale, despite having little more than the equivalent of a high school education. As she recalled in an interview with Linda Wasmer Smith: "I went to talk to the head of the chemistry department, and he said that I could enroll in the program if I could pass certain examinations. I studied, essentially on my own, for a number of months. Then the department head and a couple of chemistry professors gave me an oral exam, on the basis of which they decided that if I took some senior courses, I could enter the graduate school." This program was accelerated due to the war. In 1943, at the age of twenty-one, Tesoro completed her Ph.D.

Patents Organic Compounds and Textile Processes

Tesoro wasted no time establishing a solid track record in the chemical and textile industries. She worked first as a research chemist at American Cyanamid in Boundbrook, New Jersey. In 1944 she moved on to Onyx Chemical Company in Jersey City, New Jersey, where she served as chemical research director until 1955. From there, she moved again to a similar position at J. P. Stevens in Garfield, New Jersey, a job in which she remained from 1958 through 1968. After that came a year spent as a senior scientist at the Textile Research Institute. In 1969 Tesoro was named director of chemical research at Burlington Industries in Greensboro, North Carolina, a position she held for the next three years. During this period Tesoro became known as a prolific inventor of products and processes, and she was granted more than two dozen U.S. patents in 1970 alone. Her papers on applied topics ranging from antistatic finishes to flame retardants appeared in dozens of journals. In 1963 she was awarded the Olney Medal of the American Association of Textile Chemists and Colorists.

In 1973 Tesoro took a post as visiting professor at the Massachusetts Institute of Technology, and so embarked on a new phase of her career. She has since maintained ties with MIT, serving at various times in the roles of adjunct professor, senior research scientist, and senior lecturer. In 1982 she accepted a new appointment as research professor at Polytechnic University in Brooklyn, New York. As an academician, she has been able to pursue less pragmatic fields of study, and she revels in the change. "I enjoy basic science-not data gathering, but rather concepts and things that remain important over a period of time. That's an attitude I've tried to impart to my students at the university as well," Tesoro explained in an interview with Linda Wasmer Smith.

Tesoro was a member of three National Research Council committees-on fire safety of polymeric materials, chemical protective clothing systems, and toxicity hazards of materials used in railway vehicles-between 1979 and 1985. She also served a term as president of the Fiber Society, and she has been a columnist for *Polymer News.* Tesoro enjoys travel; she has delivered invited papers and lectures around the United States, as well as in Western Europe, Israel, and China. She is a member of such organizations as the American Association for the Advancement of Science and the American Chemical Society, as well as a fellow of the Textile Institute in Great Britain. She was married to Victor Tesoro on April 17, 1943, in New York City. The couple have two children, Claudia and Andrew. They make their home in Dobbs Ferry, New York.

SELECTED WRITINGS BY TESORO:

Books

(With S. Backer, T. Y. Toong, and N. A. Moussa) *Textile Flammability,* MIT Press, 1976.
(Coauthor) *Fire Safety Aspects of Polymeric Materials,* National Advisory Board Publication no. 318, ten volumes, Technomic Publishing, 1977–80.

Periodicals

"An Effective New Anti-Static Finish," *Modern Textiles Magazine,* January, 1957, pp. 47–48.

SOURCES:

Books

Manly, Robert H., *Durable Press Treatments of Fabrics,* Noyes Data Corporation, 1976.
Moussa, Farag, *Women Inventors,* Coopi, 1991.
O'Neill, Lois Decker, *The Women's Book of World Records and Achievements,* Doubleday, 1979.

Periodicals

Seymour, Raymond B., "Polymer Science Pioneers: Giuliana Cavaglieri Tesoro," *Polymer News,* July, 1989, pp. 207–208.

Other

Tesoro, Giuliana Cavaglieri, interview with Linda Wasmer Smith conducted February 9, 1994.
Tesoro, Giuliana Cavaglieri, letter to Linda Wasmer Smith dated February 21, 1994.
Tesoro, Giuliana Cavaglieri, letter to Emily McMurray dated January 22, 1994.

—*Sketch by Linda Wasmer Smith*

Marie Tharp

Marie Tharp
1920-

American oceanographic cartographer and geologist

Marie Tharp is a mapmaker who charted the bottom of the ocean at a time when little was known about undersea geology. Her detailed maps showed features that helped other scientists under-stand the structure and evolution of the sea floor. In particular, Tharp's discovery of the valley that divides the Mid-Atlantic Ridge convinced other geologists that sea floor was being created at these ridges and spreading outward. The confirmation of "seafloor spreading" led to the eventual acceptance of the theory of continental drift, now called plate tectonics.

Tharp was born in Ypsilanti, Michigan, on July 30, 1920. Her father, William Edgar Tharp, was a soil surveyor for the United States Department of Agriculture's Bureau of Chemistry and Soils; he told his daughter to choose a job simply because she liked doing it. Marie's mother, Bertha Louise (Newton) Tharp, taught German and Latin. The family moved frequently because of William Tharp's mapping assignments across the country. Marie Tharp attended twenty-four different public schools in Iowa, Michigan, Indiana, Alabama (where she almost flunked out of the 5th grade in Selma), Washington, D.C., New York, and Ohio. In 1943 she received her bachelor's degree from Ohio University.

Since most young men were fighting in World War II at the time Tharp graduated, the University of Michigan opened the doors of its geology department to women for the first time. Tharp entered the masters program, which trained students in basic geology and then guaranteed them a job in the petroleum industry. Graduating in 1944, Tharp was hired as a junior geologist with Stanolind Oil & Gas in Tulsa, Oklahoma. Women were not permitted to search for oil in the field, so Tharp found herself organizing the maps and data for the all-male crews. While working for Stanolind, Tharp earned a B.S. in mathematics from the University of Tulsa in 1948.

The year of her second bachelor's degree, Tharp moved to Columbia University, where a group of scientists were about to revolutionize the study of oceanography. Hired as a research assistant by geologist Maurice Ewing, Tharp actually ended up helping graduate students with their data; she never told anyone that she had a graduate degree in geology. One student, Bruce Heezen, asked for help with his ocean profiles so often that after a while Tharp worked with him exclusively. Heezen and Tharp were to work closely together until his death in 1977. In 1950 the geophysical laboratory moved from Columbia University to the Lamont Geological Observatory in Palisades, New York.

Before the early 1950s, scientists knew very little about the structure of the ocean floor. It was much easier and cheaper to study geology on land. But without knowledge of the structure and evolution of the seafloor, scientists could not form a complete idea of how the entire earth worked. In the 1940s, most people believed that the earth was a shrinking globe, cooling and contracting from its initial hot birth. The work of Heezen, Tharp, and other geologists in the next decade—who gathered data on the sea floor using echo sounding equipment—helped replace that idea with the model of plate tectonics, where thin crustal "plates" shift around on the earth's mantle, colliding and grinding into each other to push up mountains and cause earthquakes.

The Mid-Atlantic Ridge, a mountainous bump that runs roughly parallel to and between the coastlines of the Americas and Africa, was one of the first topographical features on the sea floor to be identified. Initial studies were undertaken by those aboard the British ship *H.M.S. Challenger,* who discovered in the 1870s that the rise in the center of the Atlantic acted as a barrier between different water temperatures; and by those aboard the German ship *Meteor* who between 1925 and 1927 revealed the Mid-Atlantic Ridge as rugged and mountainous. The *Meteor* staff also found several "holes" in the center of the Ridge, but did not connect these holes into the continuous rift valley that they were later discovered to be. In the 1930s, the British geologists Seymour Sewell and John Wiseman suspected that a rift valley split the Ridge, but World War II prevented an expedition to confirm this.

By 1950, when Tharp and Heezen moved to Lamont, the time was right for a series of discoveries. In 1952, the pair decided to make a map of the North Atlantic floor that would show how it would look if all the water were drained away. This type of "physiographic" diagram looked very different from the usual method of drawing contour lines for ocean floor of equal depth. Heezen and Tharp chose the physiographic method because it was a more realistic, three-dimensional picture of the ocean floor, and also because contours were classified by the U.S. Navy from 1952 to 1962.

Tharp assembled her first drawing of the North Atlantic ocean floor in 1952, after rearranging Heezen's data into six seafloor profiles that spanned the Atlantic. This initial map showed a deep valley dividing the crest of the Mid-Atlantic Ridge. Tharp pointed out the valley to Heezen. "He groaned and said, 'It cannot be. It looks too much like continental drift,'" Tharp wrote later in *Natural History.* The valley represented the place where newly-formed rocks came up from inside the earth, splitting apart the mid-ocean ridge. At the time, Heezen, like most scientists, thought that continental drift was impossible.

While Tharp was working on detailing and clarifying the first map, Heezen kept another assistant busy plotting the location of the epicenters of North Atlantic earthquakes. **Beno Gutenberg** and **Charles F. Richter** had already pointed out that earthquake epicenters followed the Mid-Atlantic Ridge quite closely. But Heezen's group found that the epicenters actually fell within the suspected rift valley. The association of topography with seismicity convinced Tharp that the valley was indeed real.

It took Heezen eight months to agree. By studying rift valleys in eastern Africa, Heezen convinced himself that the land in Africa was simply a terrestrial analogy to what was going on in the middle of the Atlantic: the earth's crust was splitting apart in a huge tensional crack. Heezen then began to wonder whether the earthquake epicenters that had been recorded in the centers of other oceans might also lie in rift valleys. Perhaps, he thought, all the mid-ocean ridges could be connected into a huge 40,000 mile system.

Heezen told Maurice Ewing, director of Lamont, of the valley's discovery. For several years, only Lamont scientists knew of its existence. Heezen presented it to the scientific community in several talks during 1956. In 1959, most of the remaining skeptics were convinced by an underwater movie of the valley, made by French oceanographer **Jacques Cousteau** towing a camera across it. Today scientists understand how the rift valley represents the pulling apart of the seafloor as the new rock spreads outward from the ridge.

Heezen and Tharp printed their first edition of the North Atlantic map for a second time in 1959. By this time they knew that the Mid-Atlantic Ridge was cut by east-west breaks, now called transform faults. Heezen and Tharp had confirmed only one of these breaks, but they didn't know its exact length or direction. So in its place on the map they put a large legend to cover the space. In the following years,

Tharp and Heezen improved their North Atlantic map and expanded their work to cover the globe, including the South Atlantic, Indian, Arctic, Antarctic, and Pacific oceans. In 1977, three weeks before Heezen's death, they published the World Ocean Floor Panorama, based on all available geological and geophysical data, as well as more than five million miles of ocean-floor soundings. In 1978 Tharp and Heezen received the Hubbard Medal of the National Geographic Society.

After about fifteen years of work behind the scenes, Tharp finally went on research cruises herself, including trips to Africa, the Caribbean, Hawaii, Japan, New Zealand, and Australia. She retired from Lamont in 1983. Since then she has run a map distributing business in South Nyack, New York, and occasionally consults for various oceanographers. She also keeps Heezen's scientific papers and has written several articles on his life and work. Tharp enjoys gardening in her spare time.

SELECTED WRITINGS BY THARP:

Books

"Mapping the Ocean Floor 1947–1977," *The Ocean Floor,* edited by R. A. Scrutton and M. Talwani, Wiley, 1982.

Periodicals

"Mappers of the Deep," *Natural History,* October, 1986, pp. 49–62.

Other

(With Bruce C. Heezen) "World Ocean Floor" (map), painted by H. C. Berann, Office of Naval Research, 1977.

SOURCES:

Periodicals

Oceanus, winter, 1973–74, pp. 44–48.

—*Sketch by Alexandra Witze*

Max Theiler
1899-1972
South African-born American virologist

Max Theiler (pronounced Tyler) was one of the leading figures in the development of the yellow-fever vaccine. His early research proved that yellow-fever virus could be transmitted to mice. He later extended this research to show that mice which were given serum from humans or animals that had been previously infected with yellow fever developed an immunity to this disease. From this research, he developed two different vaccines in the 1930s, which were used to control this incurable tropical disease. For his work on the yellow-fever vaccine, Theiler was awarded the Nobel Prize in medicine or physiology in 1951.

Theiler was born on a farm near Pretoria, South Africa, on January 30, 1899, the youngest of four children of Emma (Jegge) and Sir Arnold Theiler, both of whom had emigrated from Switzerland. His father, director of South Africa's veterinary services, pushed him toward a career in medicine. In part to satisfy his father, he enrolled in a two-year premedical program at the University of Cape Town in 1916. In 1919, soon after the conclusion of World War I, he sailed for England, where he pursued further medical training at St. Thomas's Hospital Medical School and the London School of Hygiene and Tropical Medicine, two branches of the University of London. Despite this rigorous training, Theiler never received the M.D. degree because the University of London refused to recognize his two years of training at the University of Cape Town.

Theiler was not enthralled with medicine and had no intention of becoming a general practitioner. He was frustrated by the ineffectiveness of most medical procedures and the lack of cures for serious illnesses. After finishing his medical training in 1922, the 23-year-old Theiler obtained a position as an assistant in the Department of Tropical Medicine at Harvard Medical School. His early research, highly influenced by the example and writings of American bacteriologist **Hans Zinsser,** focused on amoebic dysentery and rat-bite fever. From there, he developed an interest in the yellow-fever virus.

Yellow-Fever Work Generates Two Life-Saving Vaccines

Yellow fever is a tropical viral disease that causes severe fever, slow pulse, bleeding in the stomach, jaundice, and the notorious symptom, black vomit. The disease is fatal in 10% to 15% of cases, the cause of death being complete shutdown of the liver or

Max Theiler

kidneys. Most people recover completely, after a painful, extended illness, with complete immunity to reinfection. The first known outbreak of yellow fever devastated Mexico in 1648. The last major breakout in the continental U.S. claimed 435 lives in New Orleans in 1905. Despite the medical advances of the 20th century, this tropical disease remains incurable. As early as the 18th century, mosquitoes were thought to have some relation to yellow fever. Cuban physician Carlos Finlay speculated that mosquitoes were the carriers of this disease in 1881, but his writings were largely ignored by the medical community. Roughly 20 years later, members of America's Yellow Fever Commission, led by **Walter Reed,** the famous U.S. Army surgeon, concluded that mosquitoes were the medium that spread the disease. In 1901, Reed's group, using humans as research subjects, discovered that yellow fever was caused by a blood-borne virus. Encouraged by these findings, the Rockefeller Foundation launched a world-wide program in 1916 designed to control and eventually eradicate yellow fever.

By the 1920s, yellow-fever research shifted away from an all-out war on mosquitoes to attempts to find a vaccine to prevent the spread of the disease. In 1928, researchers discovered that the Rhesus monkey, unlike most other monkeys, could contract yellow fever and could be used for experimentation. Theiler's first big breakthrough was his discovery that mice could be used experimentally in place of the monkey and that they had several practical research advan-

tages. When yellow-fever virus was injected into their brains, the mice didn't develop human symptoms. Instead, "when you give a mouse yellow fever, he gets not jaundice but encephalitis, not a fatal bellyache but a fatal headache," Theiler stated, according to Greer Williams author of *Virus Hunters.*

One unintended research discovery kept Theiler out of his lab and in bed for nearly a week. In the course of his experiments, he accidentally contracted yellow fever from one of his mice, which caused a slight fever and weakness. Theiler was much luckier than some other yellow-fever researchers. Many had succumbed to the disease in the course of their investigations. However, this small bout of yellow fever simply gave Theiler an immunity to the disease. In effect, he was the first recipient of a yellow-fever vaccine.

In 1930, Theiler reported his findings on the effectiveness of using mice for yellow fever research in the respected journal *Science.* The initial response was overwhelmingly negative; the Harvard faculty, including Theiler's immediate supervisor, seemed particularly unimpressed. Undaunted, Theiler continued his work, moving from Harvard University, where he was considered an upstart, to the Rockefeller Foundation in New York City. Eventually, yellow-fever researchers began to see the logic behind Theiler's use of the mouse and followed his lead. His continued experiments made the mouse the research animal of choice. By passing the yellow-fever virus from mouse to mouse, he was able to shorten the incubation time and increase the virulence of the disease, which enabled research data to be generated more quickly and cheaply. He was now certain that an attenuated live vaccine, one weak enough to cause no harm yet strong enough to generate immunity, could be developed.

In 1931, Theiler developed the mouse-protection test, which involved mixing yellow-fever virus with human blood and injecting the mixture into a mouse. If the mouse survived, then the blood had obviously neutralized the virus, proving that the blood donor was immune to yellow fever (and had most likely developed an immunity by previously contracting the disease). This test was used to conduct the first worldwide survey of the distribution of yellow fever.

A colleague at the Rockefeller Foundation, Dr. Wilbur A. Sawyer, used Theiler's mouse strain, a combination of yellow fever virus and immune serum, to develop a human vaccine. Sawyer is often wrongly credited with inventing the first human yellow-fever vaccine. He simply transferred Theiler's work from the mouse to humans. Ten workers in the Rockefeller labs were inoculated with the mouse strain, with no apparent side effects. The mouse-virus strain was subsequently used by the French government to immunize French colonials in West Africa, a hot spot for yellow fever. This so-called "scratch" vaccine was a combination of infected mouse brain tissue and cowpox virus and could be quickly administered by scratching the vaccine into the skin. It was used throughout Africa for nearly 25 years and led to the near total eradication of yellow fever in the major African cities.

Virus Work Leads to Nobel Prize

While he was somewhat pleased with the new vaccine, Theiler considered the mouse strain inappropriate for human use. In some cases, the vaccine led to encephalitis in a few recipients and caused less severe side effects, such as headache or nausea, in many others. Theiler believed that a "killed" vaccine, which used a dead virus, wouldn't produce an immune effect, so he and his colleagues set out to find a milder live strain. He began working with the Asibi yellow-fever strain, a form of the virus so powerful that it killed monkeys instantly when injected under the skin. The Asibi strain thrived in a number of media, including chicken embryos. Theiler kept this virus alive for years in tissue cultures, passing it from embryo to embryo, and only occasionally testing the potency of the virus in a living animal. He continued making subcultures of the virus until he reached strain number 176. Then, he tested the strain on two monkeys. Both animals survived and seemed to have acquired a sufficient immunity to yellow fever. In March 1937, after testing this new vaccine on himself and others, Theiler announced that he had developed a new, safer, attenuated vaccine, which he called 17D strain. This new strain was much easier to produce, cheaper, and caused very mild side effects.

From 1940 to 1947, with the financial assistance of the Rockefeller Foundation, more than 28 million 17D-strain vaccines were produced, at a cost of approximately two cents per unit, and given away to people in tropical countries and the U.S. The vaccine was so effective that the Rockefeller Foundation ended its yellow-fever program in 1949, safe in the knowledge that the disease had been effectively eradicated worldwide and that any subsequent outbreaks could be controlled with the new vaccine. Unfortunately, almost all yellow-fever research ended around this time and few people studied how to cure the disease. For people in tropical climates who live outside of the major urban centers, yellow fever is still a problem. A major outbreak in Ethiopia in 1960–62 caused 30,000 deaths. The World Health Organization still uses Theiler's 17D vaccine and is attempting to inoculate people in remote areas.

The success of the vaccine brought Theiler recognition both in the U.S. and abroad and even from his former employer, Harvard University. Over the next ten years, he received the Chalmer's Medal of the Royal Society of Tropical Medicine and Hygiene (1939), the Lasker Award of the American Public Health Association, and the Flattery Medal of Harvard University (1945).

In 1951, Theiler received the Nobel Prize in medicine or physiology "for his discoveries concerning yellow fever and how to combat it." According to Williams (in *Virus Hunters*), when Theiler was asked what he would do with the $32,000 Nobel award, he remarked, "Buy a case of scotch and watch the ole Dodgers."

After developing the yellow-fever vaccine, Theiler turned his attention to other viruses, including some unusual and rare diseases, such as Bwamba fever and Rift Valley fever. His other, less exotic research focused on polio and led to his discovery of a polio-like infection in mice known as encephalomyelitis or Theiler's disease. In 1964, he retired from the Rockefeller Foundation, having achieved the rank of associate director for medical and natural sciences and director of the Virus Laboratories. In that same year, he accepted a position as professor of epidemiology and microbiology at Yale University in New Haven, Connecticut. He retired from Yale in 1967.

Theiler married Lillian Graham in 1938. They had one daughter. His nonscientific interests included reading (mostly history and philosophy but absolutely no fiction) and watching baseball games, especially those involving his beloved Brooklyn Dodgers. Although he immigrated to the U.S. in 1923 and remained in America for the rest of his life, he never applied for U.S. citizenship. Theiler died on August 11, 1972, at the age of 73.

SELECTED WRITINGS BY THEILER:

Books

The Arthropod-Borne Viruses of Vertebrates: An Account of the Rockefeller Foundation Virus Program, 1951–1970, Yale University Press, 1973.

SOURCES:

Books

Hill, R. N., *The Doctors Who Conquered Yellow Fever,* Random House, 1957.
Strode, G. K., editor, *Yellow Fever,* McGraw-Hill, 1951.
Williams, Greer, *Virus Hunters,* Alfred A. Knopf, 1959.

Periodicals

Bendinger, Elmer, "Max Theiler: Yellow Jack and the Jackpot," *Hospital Practice,* June, 1988, pp. 211–244.

—*Sketch by Tom Crawford*

Axel Hugo Teodor Theorell
1903-1982
Swedish biochemist

Axel Hugo Teodor Theorell (also known as Hugo Theorell) spent the majority of his career studying the action of oxidation enzymes, proteins essential for the metabolic process in plants and animals. His isolation of the yellow enzyme in the mid–1930s was a breakthrough toward a clearer understanding of the transformation in the cell of food into energy, called cellular respiration. Theorell's discoveries provided basic knowledge for the eventual creation of artificial life in the laboratory, and were essential to the study of such diseases as cancer and tuberculosis. In a related area of study, his work on the alcohol-burning enzymes led to a new method for testing the alcohol content in blood. He was the first to isolate myoglobin, a substance that gives certain muscles their red color. He also studied cytochrome c, a catalytic enzyme responsible for causing energy reactions in mitochondria, the cell's "powerhouse." Theorell was awarded the 1955 Nobel Prize in physiology or medicine for "his discoveries concerning the nature and mode of action of oxidation enzymes."

Theorell was born in Linköping, Sweden, on July 6, 1903, to Thure and Armida Bell Theorell. His father was a medical officer in the local militia and enjoyed singing; his mother was a gifted pianist. Young Axel absorbed their love of music, and developed an interest in his father's profession that led him to decide on a career in medicine. He received his bachelor of medicine degree (1924) and his doctor of medicine (1930) from the Karolinska Institute in Stockholm. He also studied at the Pasteur Institute in Paris. When a crippling attack of poliomyelitis made a career as a physician impractical, he decided instead to pursue research and teaching. His academic work while at Stockholm was an inquiry into the chemistry of plasma lipids (fatty acids) and their effect on red blood cells. A technique he developed at this time to separate the plasma proteins albumin and globulin was later to prove useful in his work on isolating enzymes (globular proteins) and coenzymes, which help to activate specific enzymes.

As professor of chemistry at Uppsala University from 1930 to 1936, Theorell expanded his research on plasma lipids to concentrate on myoglobin, a muscle protein whose oxygen-carrying capacities he compared to that of hemoglobin in the blood. By isolating (purifying) myoglobin, he was able to show its absorption and storage capacities, and to measure, using centrifugal force, its molecular weight. This determination of its physical properties showed that myoglobin was a separate protein from hemoglobin.

In 1933 Theorell received a grant from the Rockefeller Foundation that enabled him to further his study of enzymes with **Otto Warburg** at the Kaiser Wilhelm Institute (now the Max Planck Institute) in Berlin. Warburg had attempted without success to isolate the yellow enzyme. Using his own methods, Theorell accomplished the isolation. He further separated the yellow enzyme into two parts: the catalytic coenzyme and the pure protein apoenzyme. He also found that the main ingredient of the yellow enzyme is the plasma protein albumin. An important corollary to the research was Theorell's discovery of the chemical chain reaction necessary for cellular oxidation or respiration. These contributions brought a test-tube creation of life closer to reality, and advanced the study of the chemical differences between normal and cancerous cells.

Returning to Stockholm, Theorell became head of the biochemistry department at the Karolinska Institute, part of a Nobel Institute established for the purpose of providing Theorell with further research opportunities. Under his direction, the department acquired a reputation for excellence that attracted biochemists from all over the world. It was here that Theorell continued his research on cytochrome c, succeeding in his attempts to purify it by 1939. He furthered this study that same year in the United States with his colleague, **Linus Pauling**, who discovered the alpha spiral (protein molecules arranged in a twisted-atom chain).

After World War II, a collaboration with **Britton Chance** of the University of Pennsylvania elucidated steps in the oxidation (breakdown) of alcohol and gave the process a name—the Theorell-Chance mechanism. Theorell's study of the enzymes that catalyze the oxidation, alcohol dehydrogenases, provided a new method for determining the level of alcohol in the bloodstream—a technique that came to be used by Sweden and West Germany to test the sobriety of their citizens. From a different perspective, Theorell's alcohol enzyme research pinpointed several bacterial strains, knowledge of which was thought to be useful in the treatment of tuberculosis.

Theorell published accounts of his findings in many scientific journals throughout Europe and the United States. His professional affiliations included membership in the Swedish Chemical Association, the Swedish Society of Physicians and Surgeons, the Royal Swedish Academy of Sciences, the International Union of Biochemistry, and the American Academy of Arts and Sciences. In addition to the 1955 Nobel Prize, he was awarded the Paul Karrer Medal in Chemistry of the University of Zurich, the Ciba Medal of the Biochemical Society in London, the Legion of Honor (France), and the Karolinska Institute 150th Jubilee Medal. Honorary degrees were bestowed upon him from Belgium, Brazil, the United States, and France.

His love for music continued throughout his life and played an important part in his social and community life. He played the violin and was active in Stockholm musical societies. In 1931 he married Elin Margit Alenius, a professional musician. They became parents of three sons. Theorell retired from the Nobel Institute in 1970. Afflicted with a stroke in 1974, his health deteriorated over the following years. He died on August 15, 1982, while vacationing on an island off the coast of Sweden.

SELECTED WRITINGS BY THEORELL:

Books

"Catalases and Peroxidases," *The Enzymes,* Academic Press, 1951, pp. 397–427.
"Introduction to Mechanisms of Enzyme Actions," *Metabolic Regulation and Enzyme Action,* Academic Press, 1970, pp. 179–180.
"My Life with Proteins and Prosthetic Groups," *Proteolysis and Physiological Regulation,* Academic Press, 1975, pp. 1–27.

Periodicals

"Function and Structure of Liver Alcohol Dehydrogenase," *Harvey Lectures,* Volume 61, 1967, pp. 17–41.

SOURCES:

Books

Magill, Frank N., editor, *The Great Scientists,* Grolier, 1989, pp. 156–160.
McGraw-Hill Modern Men of Science, McGraw-Hill, 1966, pp. 474–475.
Wasson, Tyler, editor, *Nobel Prize Winners,* Wilson, 1989, pp. 1050–1053.

—*Sketch by Jane Stewart Cook*

René Frédéric Thom
1923-
French mathematician

René Frédéric Thom is a French topologist and mathematical philosopher best known as the founder of catastrophe theory, which has received myriad applications in the exact and social sciences. Catastrophe theory provides models for the description of continuous processes that cause abrupt change.

Thom was born on September 2, 1923, at Montbéliard, France, to Gustav Thom, a pharmacist, and Louise Ramel. Thom's formal education took place at the Collège Cuvier at Montbéliard and in Paris at the Lycée Saint-Louis and the Ecole Normale Supérieure. After earning a master's degree in mathematics and a doctorate in science, Thom was Maître de Conférences at Grenoble from 1953 to 1954 and Strasbourg from 1954 to 1957. In 1957, he became a permanent professor (or Chair) in the Science Department at Strasbourg, and since 1964 he has been a professor at the Institut des Hautes Études Scientifiques at Bures-sur-Yvette.

Develops Catastrophe Theory

Most of Thom's early work focused on the mathematics of sudden change, which eventually led to the formulation of catastrophe theory. Since its full presentation in 1972 in Thom's book *Stabilité structurelle et morphogénèse* (translated as *Structural Stability and Morphogenesis*), catastrophe theory has been used to study abrupt systems changes in such diverse fields as hydrodynamics, geology, particle physics, industrial relations, embryology, economics, linguistics, civil engineering, and medicine.

Thom's catastrophe theory is generally classified as a branch of geometry because variables and results are shown as curves or surfaces. It attempts to explain predictable discontinuities in output in systems characterized by continuous inputs. Contrary to the implications of the theory's name, the "catastrophes" studied are not necessarily negative in nature. Thom uses the word simply to describe dramatic change. The inflation of an everyday balloon, for instance, may provide a simple example of the behavior studied by catastrophe theory. As a balloon is steadily filled with air, it expands and changes shape. The change in shape occurs in a relatively uniform manner until the pressure on the balloon's interior reaches a critical value. Then the balloon undergoes a more abrupt, but predictable, change: it pops. More complex phenomena, such as the refraction of light through moving water, the amount of stress that can be placed on a bridge, and the synergistic effects of the ingredients in drugs can also be effectively studied using the catastrophe theory. The theory provides a universal method for the study of all jump transitions, discontinuities, and sudden qualitative changes.

Since its introduction, some scientists have hailed Thom's catastrophe theory as a tool more valuable to mankind than Newtonian theory, which considers only smooth, continuous processes. Catastrophe theory became something of a fad in the 1970s and 1980s and was used in applications that the theory does not support. As a result of such indiscriminate application, the theory has at times been criticized, unjustly, as a cultural phenomenon or a metaphysical view rather than a legitimate branch of mathematics. Although some popularizers have presented it in a metaphysical vein as proof of the deterministic nature of the universe, catastrophe theory does not purport to abolish the indeterminacy that is central to nuclear physics.

Work Recognized with Médaille Fields

In 1958, Thom was awarded the Médaille Fields (Fields Medal), the equivalent of a Nobel Prize in mathematics, and in 1974 he was awarded the Grand prix scientifique de la Ville de Paris. Thom became a member of the prestigious French Academy of Sciences in 1976, and has also been named a Chevalier de la Légion d'honneur (a Knight of the Legion of Honor).

He married Suzanne Heimlinger on April 9, 1949, and they have three children, Françoise, Elizabeth, and Christian.

SELECTED WRITINGS BY THOM:

Books

Stabilité structurelle et morphogénèse, (Structural Stability and Morphogenesis), W. A. Benjamin, 1972, translated edition, 1976.

Periodicals

"Topological Models in Biology," *Topology 8,* 1969, pp. 313–335.

SOURCES:

Books

Arnol'd, V. I., *Catastrophe Theory,* 3rd edition, Springer-Verlag, 1992.

Periodicals

Zeeman, Christopher, "Introduction to Catastrophe Theory," *Scientific American,* April, 1976.

—*Sketch by Maureen L. Tan*

E. Donnall Thomas
1920-
American physician

E. Donnall Thomas has pioneered techniques for transplanting bone marrow, an operation that has been utilized to treat patients with cancers of the blood, such as leukemia. For proving that such transplants could save the lives of dying patients, Thomas was awarded the Nobel Prize in physiology or medicine in 1990, a commendation he shared with **Joseph E. Murray**, another American physician who has done important work in the area of transplants. Thomas has spent most of his career at the Fred Hutchinson Cancer Research Center in Seattle, Washington, which he built into the world's leading center for bone marrow transplants. The Hutchinson Center has also become an important training site for doctors learning to perform such operations, and transplant centers around the world are staffed by physicians who studied with Thomas in Seattle.

Thomas was born on March 15, 1920, in the small town of Mart, Texas, to Edward E. Thomas, a doctor, and Angie Hill Donnall Thomas, a school teacher. After graduating from a high school class of approximately fifteen students, Thomas entered the University of Texas at Austin in 1937. He received a B.A. in 1941 and continued on for a master's degree, which was awarded in 1943. In 1942 he married another University of Texas student, Dorothy Martin, who would later help him manage his research and write medical papers.

Medical Education Prepares Thomas for Early Research

After completing his master's degree, Thomas started medical school at the University of Texas Medical Branch in Galveston. After six months, however, he transferred to Harvard Medical School, where he received his M.D. in 1946. He became an intern and then a resident at Peter Bent Brigham Hospital in Boston and began to specialize in blood diseases. Thomas interrupted his formal medical training to serve as a physician in the United States Army from 1948 to 1950. He then returned to the Boston area and did research on leukemia treatments for a year as a postdoctoral fellow at the Massachusetts Institute of Technology. In 1953 he worked as an instructor at Harvard Medical School.

Thomas moved to New York in 1955 to take the position of physician-in-chief at the Mary Imogene Bassett Hospital in Cooperstown. The next year he became, in addition, an associate clinical professor of medicine at the College of Physicians and Surgeons at

Columbia University. During the next eight years Thomas had the opportunity to develop and research his ideas about bone marrow transplants, and he applied these concepts to treating cancers of the blood.

Leukemia is a type of cancer in which certain blood cells, known generally as white blood cells, are produced in abnormally large numbers by the bone marrow. In other kinds of cancer, the diseased cells pile up into a tumor, which can often be treated by simply cutting out the lump. Leukemic blood cells, however, circulate throughout the body, making them much more difficult to eliminate. Furthermore, the white blood cells that become abnormal in leukemia are an important part of the body's immune system. Even if they could be destroyed by a means such as radiation, without them the patient would be vulnerable to infections.

In the 1950s, researchers showed that inbred laboratory mice could be irradiated, thus destroying the production of white blood cells by their bone marrow, and then saved from infection by a transplant of bone marrow taken from healthy mice. Inspired by these experiments, Thomas began similar studies on dogs, but he faced two important obstacles. First, the recipient animal's immune system had to be prevented from attacking and destroying the transplanted bone marrow—such immune rejection has long been a problem for bone marrow as well as organ transplant surgery. And second, if the bone marrow transplant was successful and the donated marrow began to produce white blood cells, these cells were likely to attack the recipient's other tissues, perceiving them as foreign. Both of these problems had been avoided in the earlier studies with inbred mice because the mice were genetically identical, and hence, have identical immune systems. People are not so similar genetically, with the exception of identical twins. All attempts to graft bone marrow between a donor and recipient who were not identical twins failed. In 1956, Thomas performed the first bone marrow transplant to a leukemia patient from an identical twin. Although the patient's immune system did not reject the transplant, the cancer recurred.

Bone Marrow Transplants Succeed

Many researchers gave up working on organ transplants because the problems of immune rejection seemed insurmountable, but Thomas persisted. In 1963 he moved to Seattle to become a professor at the University of Washington Medical School. There he put together a team of expert researchers and began experimenting with new drugs that could suppress the recipient's immune system and thus prevent rejection of the new tissue. In the meantime, new methods were being developed by other researchers to identify people whose immune systems were similar, in order to match organ donors and recipients. The new methods of tissue typing were based on molecules known as histocompatibility antigens. Thomas's team performed the first bone marrow transplant to a leukemia patient from a matched donor in March 1969. During the 1970s they developed and perfected a comprehensive procedure for treating leukemia patients: first the patients receive radiation, both to kill cancer cells and to weaken the immune system so that it does not reject the transplant; then their bone marrow is replaced with marrow from a compatible donor. The patients also are given drugs that continue to suppress their immune systems. Many patients had been cured of leukemia using this technique by the late 1970s. Since then Thomas and his colleagues have improved their success rate from about 12 percent to about 50 percent. In addition to leukemia and other cancers of the blood, bone marrow transplants are used to treat certain inherited blood disorders and to aid people whose bone marrow has been destroyed by accidental exposure to radiation.

Thomas has received wide recognition for his work, including the American Cancer Society's National Award for Basic Science in 1980, and the National Medal of Science of the United States in 1990. The Nobel Prize that he received in 1990, however, came as a surprise. Thomas told reporters that the award is more often given to scientists who do basic research than to those that develop clinical treatments. Thomas shared the prize with Joseph Murray, who performed the first kidney transplant and whose research paved the way for the transplantation of other organs. As reported in *Time* magazine, both men were cited by the Nobel committee for discoveries "crucial for those tens of thousands of severely ill patients who either can be cured or given a decent life when other treatment methods are without success."

SELECTED WRITINGS BY THOMAS:

Periodicals

"Supralethal Whole Body Irradiation and Isologous Marrow Transplantation in Man," *Journal of Clinical Investigation* 38, October, 1959, pp. 1709–1716.

"Irradiation and Marrow Infusion in Leukemia: Observations in Five Patients with Acute Leukemia Treated by Whole Body Exposures of 1400 to 2000 Roentgens and Infusions of Marrow," *Archives of Internal Medicine* 107, June, 1961, pp. 829–845.

"Transplantation of Marrow and Whole Organs," *Canadian Medical Association Journal* 86, March 10, 1962, pp. 435–444.

SOURCES:

Periodicals

Kolata, Gina, "Two American Transplant Pioneers Win Nobel Prize in Medicine," *New York Times,* October 9, 1990, p. C3.

Lemonick, Michael D., "A Pair of Lifesavers," *Time,* October 22, 1990, p. 62.

Palca, Joe, "Overcoming Rejection to Win a Nobel Prize," *Science* 250, 1990, p. 378.

—*Sketch by Betsy Hanson*

Martha Jane Bergin Thomas
1926-
American chemist and engineer

Martha Jane Bergin Thomas made significant contributions to the development of phosphors, solid materials that emit visible light when activated by an outside energy source. In a productive career, she achieved many firsts, becoming the first female director at GTE Electrical Products and the first woman to receive the New England Award for engineering excellence from the Engineering Societies of New England. She is the holder of twenty-three patents, ranging from innovations in electric light technology to improvements in lamp manufacturing methods.

Thomas was born on March 13, 1926, in Boston. Her parents, both teachers, were John A. and Augusta Harris Bergin. "Even as a girl, I had an intense interest in science," Thomas recalled in an interview with Linda Wasmer Smith. After high school, she pursued that interest at Radcliffe, where she graduated with honors in 1945 at the age of nineteen. Her bachelor's degree in chemistry was supposed to be the initial step toward a medical degree. But then she was offered a job at Sylvania—later GTE Electrical Products—in Danvers, Massachusetts. It was the first nonteaching position to come her way, and Thomas accepted. So began her forty-five-year association with the company, during which she rose from junior technician to director of the technical services labs.

Thomas did not abandon her educational goals, however. She attended graduate school at Boston University, where she received an A.M. degree in 1950 and a Ph.D. two years later. In 1980 she became a part-time student once again; motivated by her new responsibilities as a manager, she obtained a master's degree in business administration from Northeastern University. Thomas has since been honored as a distinguished graduate of every institution from which she earned a degree: Boston Girl's Latin School, Radcliffe, Boston University, and Northeastern.

Develops Phosphors for Fluorescent Lighting

Thomas's first patent was for a method of etching fine tungsten coils that was designed to improve telephone switchboard lights. She went on to establish two pilot plants for the preparation of phosphors—the powdery substances used to coat the inside of fluorescent lighting tubes. Among her accomplishments was the development of a natural white phosphor that allowed fluorescent lamps to impart daylight hues. She also developed a phosphor that raised mercury lamp brightness by 10 percent. These contributions were noted by the Society of Women Engineers in 1965, when it named Thomas Woman Engineer of the Year. Thomas also was named New England Inventor of the Year at a 1991 event sponsored by Boston's Museum of Science, the Inventors Association of New England, and the Boston Patent Law Association.

In addition to her applied research, Thomas taught evening chemistry classes at Boston University from 1952 through 1970. She also served as an adjunct professor at the University of Rhode Island. She is a member of the American Chemical Society and the Electrochemical Society, a fellow of the American Institute of Chemists, and the author of numerous technical papers. In her free time, Thomas enjoys traveling, spending time with her family, and dabbling in arts and crafts.

While still in graduate school, Thomas met her future husband, a fellow chemist. She married George R. Thomas in Millbury, Massachusetts, in 1955. The couple have four daughters: Augusta, Abigail, Anne, and Susan. Thomas accorded family the highest priority in life. Yet despite the cultural norms at the time she raised her children, Thomas was never tempted to give up her scientific career for the role of full-time homemaker. As she explained to Linda Wasmer Smith in an interview, "My career was very intense; it had to be. If you were a woman in science then, you had to stay with it unequivocally. And that's what I did." Commented her husband, "If her career as a scientist was intense, then her career as a wife and mother was absolutely ferocious."

SELECTED WRITINGS BY THOMAS:

Periodicals

(With Keith H. Butler) "Measurement of Particle Size Distribution of Phosphors," *Journal of the*

Electrochemical Society, March, 1954, Volume 101, pp. 149–154.

SOURCES:

Periodicals

Fowler, Elizabeth M., "Radcliffe Girl's Success Formula," *New York Times,* August 4, 1965, pp. 43, 47.

"Inventor of the Year," *Boston Globe,* February 11, 1991, p. 45.

King, Mary Sarah, "Women in Business—Martha Thomas, Amy Spear. Two Engineers, Two Different Approaches," *Boston Evening Globe,* July 19, 1972, p. 61.

"Martha Thomas: A Lifetime of Achievement," *Electrical Products News* (GTE), March/April 1990, p. 5.

Other

Thomas, George R., letter to Linda Wasmer Smith dated February 20, 1994.

Thomas, Martha Jane Bergin, interview with Linda Wasmer Smith conducted February 7, 1994.

—*Sketch by Linda Wasmer Smith*

D'Arcy Wentworth Thompson
1860-1948

Scottish zoologist

Sir D'Arcy Wentworth Thompson combined extensive knowledge of natural history with insight into mathematics to develop a new approach to evolution and the growth of living things. His 1917 work, *On Growth and Form,* represented a significant departure from the zoology of his day and has since contributed to embryology, taxonomy, paleontology, and ecology, as well as influencing artists, engineers, architects, and poets. Thompson was also trained in the classics from a young age, and he applied his knowledge of ancient Greek culture, thought, and natural history to his *A Glossary of Greek Birds* and *A Glossary of Greek Fishes.*

Thompson was born in Edinburgh, Scotland, on May 2, 1860. His father, also named D'Arcy Wentworth Thompson, was a classical master at the Edinburgh Academy, and then a professor of Greek at Queens College, Galway. The elder Thompson wrote books expressing liberal ideas, and delivered the Lowell Institute Lectures in Boston in the late 1860s, in which he espoused the cause of women's rights. Thompson's mother, Fanny Gamgee, who died when he was born, came from a family that was active in medicine and science. Young D'Arcy thus received a scientific background from his maternal grandfather as he was growing up, and a classical education from his father. As a result, he could read, speak, and write Greek and Latin fluently.

Thompson attended Edinburgh Academy, and studied medicine at the University of Edinburgh. He showed a bent for natural history, and at the age of 19, published papers in science journals on hydroid taxonomy—or classification of invertebrate animals including corals, sea anemones, and jellyfishes—and on a Pleistocene fossil seal. He left Edinburgh for Trinity College, Cambridge, where he supplemented his finances by tutoring in Greek. While there, he translated Hermann Müller's German work, *Die Befruchtung der Blumen durch Insekten,* as *The Fertilisation of Flowers;* it was published with a preface by the naturalist Charles Darwin, about which Thompson later said, as quoted in *Science* magazine, "[It] is of peculiar interest as one of the very last of his writings."

Embarks on a Career as a Zoologist

In 1884, at the age of 24, Thompson was appointed professor of biology at University College in Dundee, where he established a teaching museum of zoology. When the college was united with the University of St. Andrews in 1897, he became the chair of natural history. He would hold that position until his death at the age of eighty-eight. Beginning in 1885, Thompson wrote scientific papers on a wide variety of zoological subjects, including the morphology of vertebrate limbs, classification of the chameleon, the nervous system and blood cells of cyclostomes (jawless fishes including hagfishes and lampreys), the newly discovered ear of the sunfish, and a fossil mammal thought to be related to whales, which he showed to be more similar to seals. He also continued to work on such varied subjects as the bones of the parrot's skull, a rare cuttlefish, the arrangement of feathers on the giant hummingbird, and a systematic survey of the sea spiders.

In 1896, when a dispute arose between Great Britain and the United States over the fur-seal fisheries in the Bering Sea, Thompson was sent to Alaska to investigate the situation. After expeditions to the Pribilof Islands, he represented Britain at the International Conference in Washington the following year. In recognition of the success of his undertaking, he was awarded the title of Companion of the Order of the Bath in 1898. In that year, he was appointed scientific adviser to the Fishery Board for Scotland, a position he held until the Board was dissolved in 1939. Thompson issued a number of scientific reports in which he made biological, statistical, and hydrographical contributions. Starting in 1902, he began to serve as the British representative to the newly founded International Council for the Study of the Sea and regularly attended meetings in Copenhagen and elsewhere in Europe until 1947. During this time, he was chair of the Statistical Committee and editor of the *Bulletin Statistique,* writing many papers on oceanography and fishery statistics.

In 1895 Thompson drew upon his predilection for the classics and published his *A Glossary of Greek Birds.* Here, he revealed a learned understanding of ancient Greek literature, as well as medieval and modern ornithology. For many years afterward, he worked on a companion book, *A Glossary of Greek Fishes,* which was finally published in 1947, and which referred not only to fish mentioned in classic Greek literature, but also to other species listed under the heading of fish by the ancients, such as crabs, cuttlefish, and oysters. In both of these books, Thompson identified the bird or fish not only from a scientific point of view, but also classically, in terms of its interest to the poets and its relation to religion, folklore, and art. In 1910, he had issued an annotated translation of Aristotle's *Historia Animalium;* he delivered the Herbert Spencer Lecture, "On Aristotle as a Biologist," three years later. He continued to express his dual interest in these subjects in his presidential address to the Classical Association, entitled *Science and the Classics,* which was published in *Nature.* In this lecture he drew connections between the two disciplines: "Science and the classics— both alike continually enlarge our curiosity, and multiply our inlets to happiness."

Blazes a New Trail in Biology

In 1908, Thompson published a paper in *Nature,* "On the Shapes of Eggs and the Causes Which Determine Them," which indicated a new direction in his explanation of morphology using mathematical interpretations. He continued with this concept in 1911 in his presidential address to section D of the British Association, entitled "Magnalia Naturae; or the Greater Problems of Biology." He had now departed from standard zoology, and its occupation with comparative morphology and evolution, and was blazing a new trail in which mathematics and physics were the tools for interpreting biological phenomena. Thompson's influential book *On Growth and Form* appeared in 1917, presenting his unorthodox new principles and explaining them with numerous illustrative examples from ancient and modern texts. The book deals with the development of form and structure in living things and how physical forces influence them in their lifetime. He demonstrated some of his

ideas by showing that various natural phenomena, such as the repeated six-sided shape of cells in a bee honeycomb, the spirals in the arrangement of seeds in a sunflower, the curve in snailshells, and even the flight of a moth attracted to light, follow mathematical principles. Thompson postulated that these and other geometrical patterns evolved as ideal adaptations in the development of the organisms. By means of graphs of grid coordinates based on logarithmic projections, he compared the changes in growth and shape of various organisms during their development. In one instance, with respect to the structure of bone, he showed that the trabeculae, or lattice-work, of calcium deposition, is aligned in the most efficient placement to cope with the stresses placed on the bone. He proved this point by comparing the metal cross structures of a hoisting crane with the internal structure of a femur.

Thompson married Maureen Drury in 1901, and they had three daughters. As his career progressed, he was received many honors. He was elected to the Royal Society in 1916, was its vice-president from 1931 to 1933, and received the Darwin Medal in 1946. In 1928 he became president of the Classical Association of England and Wales, and from 1934 to 1939, he was president of the Royal Society of Edinburgh. Thompson was knighted in 1937, and a year later, the Linnean Society presented him with the Linnean gold medal. He delivered the Lowell Lectures in Boston in 1936, seventy-nine years after his father had had this honor. In 1946, he flew to India as a member of the Royal Society delegation to the Indian Science Congress at Delhi, but contracted pneumonia soon afterward and never recovered. Thompson died on June 21, 1948. He was remembered by his colleague, Robert Chambers, in *Science* magazine, as a "towering figure with massive sculptured head and [long] flowing beard," who had a ready sense of humor and a penchant for eloquent oratory.

SELECTED WRITINGS BY THOMPSON:

Books

(Translator) Hermann Müller, *Die Befruchtung der Blumen durch Insekten,* 1873, as *The Fertilisation of Flowers,* Macmillan, 1883.

A Glossary of Greek Birds, Clarendon Press, 1895, new edition, 1936.

On Growth and Form, Cambridge University Press, 1917, new edition, 1942.

A Glossary of Greek Fishes, Oxford University Press, 1947.

Periodicals

"On the Shapes of Eggs and the Causes Which Determine Them," *Nature* 78, 1908, pp. 111–113.

"Magnalia Naturae; or the Greater Problems of Biology," *Nature* 87, 1911, pp. 325–328; reprinted in *Smithsonian Institution Annual Report,* 1911.

"Science and the Classics," *Nature,* May 25, 1929.

SOURCES:

Books

Clark, W. E. LeGros and P. B. Medawar, editors, *Essays on Growth and Form,* Clarendon Press, 1945.

Periodicals

Chambers, Robert, "Sir D'Arcy Wentworth Thompson, C.B., F.R.S. (1860–1948)," *Science* 109, 1949, pp. 138–139, 151.

Dobell, C., "D'Arcy Wentworth Thompson," *Obituary Notices of Fellows of the Royal Society* 6, 1949, pp. 599–617.

Hutchinson, G. E. "In Memoriam, D'Arcy Wentworth Thompson," *American Scientist* 36, 1948.

—Sketch by Maurice Bleifeld

Kenneth Thompson
1943-

American computer scientist

Kenneth Thompson was one of the pioneers of UNIX, perhaps the most widely used computer system in the world. Thompson conceived of the system in the late 1960s, and together with **Dennis Ritchie**, a colleague working with him at Bell Laboratories, they developed UNIX as an alternative to the old batch programming systems that dominated the industry at the time. Although Thompson created UNIX while working at Bell Labs, the system was developed independently by the two programmers and very unusual because it was not commercially marketed like other systems. Instead UNIX gained in popularity through a network of researchers long before it was released commercially, and it has had one of the longest gestation periods of any computer program. UNIX is now believed to be one of the most widely used systems in the world, supporting over twenty million dollars of equipment.

Kenneth Lane Thompson was born on February 4, 1943 in New Orleans, Louisiana, the son of Lewis Elwood Thompson, a fighter pilot in the U.S. Navy, and Anna Hazel Lane Thompson. He majored in electrical engineering at the University of California, Berkeley, also working at the computer center as well as participating in a work-study program at the General Dynamics Corporation. Thompson received his B.S. in electrical engineering in 1965 and his M.S. in electrical engineering in 1966, both from Berkeley.

Though Thompson's formal education was in electronic hardware and he built a lot of computers, he was very accomplished in developing computer software, and this is what he pursued professionally. Therefore, after receiving his master's degree, Thompson went to work for the Computing Science Research Center at Bell Laboratories in New Jersey. He married his wife Bonnie on July 2, 1967, and they had one son, Corey. Bell Labs was famous for its research productivity, and for the unconventional looks, dress, and work habits of some of its scientists. Thompson fitted in well—bearded, bespectacled, and long-haired, he wore a tee-shirt in one published picture. His work habits were also unusual, and he would sometimes put in thirty hours in a row without sleep while working on a project.

Inventing the Operating System UNIX

One of Thompson's greatest achievements at Bell Labs was inventing and then developing UNIX with Ritchie. A computer operating system manages the housekeeping functions within a computer. By enabling the user to create, open, edit, and close data files, as well as move data from a disk to the screen or printer, and to store data on disks in addition to activating and using other programs, an operating system makes computers easy and fast to run. While at Bell Labs in the late 1960s, Thompson had been assigned to work on developing such a multi-tasking and multi-user system. Together with engineers from General Electric and the Massachusetts Institute of Technology (MIT), Thompson and other Bell Lab programmers began working on what was called Multics.

This multi-tasking and multi-user system would contrast in important ways with existing batch-operation computers. Batch computers required a user to create a stack of pre-punched data cards which were then run through the computer at one time. During this process, the computer could only apply its programming abilities to the one user's stack of cards, requiring all other users to wait for their jobs to get done. After waiting an hour or longer a user would get a print-out of results on paper. If users wanted to make any changes after seeing the results on the print-outs, they would have to punch out another stack of cards and wait to resubmit them to the computer for processing. Getting the results from simple changes in a data request could take a long time.

On the other hand, multi-tasking, multi-user computer systems would be structured in such a way that the flow of data inside the computer would allow it to process many jobs at once for numerous users. The benefits were obvious: users could get their results back quickly and get much more work done. Also, if a computer screen terminal was used as an input and output device, users could key their requests into the terminal, and the computer could display its response to the requests on the screen. Changes and revisions could be made immediately, while the computer could still run other programs. Multi-tasking, multi-user computer systems like UNIX have replaced batch processing almost completely, and when Thompson invented the program at Bell Labs in 1969, he started the ball rolling to create that change. In late 1988, American Telephone & Telegraph (AT&T) licensed its millionth UNIX system.

The Cold War Adventures of a Chess-Playing Computer

In 1978 Thompson stopped working on UNIX and began other projects. Some of his later projects included another operating system called Plan 9, and computer chess. Chess had been one Thompson's boyhood hobbies, and he carried it into his adult years by making computers and computer programs that could play chess. One of these programs was so good that it became three-time American champion. Thompson also built a chess-playing computer, which he named "Belle." Besides programming, Thompson was also involved in teaching computing. During a 1975 sabbatical he taught upper division and graduate courses in computer science, including a seminar on the UNIX operating system, at the University of California at Berkeley. On another break in 1988, he taught computer science at the University of Sydney in Australia.

In 1993, after working for years on computer chess and another operating systems, Thompson began to work on digital audio encoding. He has received a number of awards for his contributions to computer programming, including the famous Turing award in 1983 from the Association for Computing Machinery, which he shared with Ritchie. The citation for the Turing award read as follows: "The success of the UNIX system stems from its tasteful selection of a few key ideas and their elegant implementation. The model of the UNIX system has led a generation of software designers to new ways of thinking about programming. The genius of the UNIX system is its framework, which enables programmers to stand on the work of others."

SELECTED WRITINGS BY THOMPSON:

Periodicals

(With Dennis Ritchie) "The UNIX time-sharing system," *Communications of the ACM,* Volume 17.7, July, 1974, pp. 365–375.
"UNIX time-sharing system: UNIX implementation," *Bell System Technical Journal,* Volume 57.6, 1978, pp. 1931–1946.

SOURCES:

Books

Slater, Robert, *Portraits in Silicon,* MIT Press, 1987.

Periodicals

Kolata, Gina, "Chess-Playing Computer Seized by Customs," *Science,* Volume 216, June 25, 1982, p. 1392.
"Dennis Ritchie and Ken L. Thompson: 1983 ACM A. M. Turing Award Recipients," *Communications of the ACM,* Volume 27.8, August, 1984, p. 757.
Rosenblatt, Alfred, "1982 Award for Achievement: Dennis M. Ritchie and Ken Thompson," *Electronics,* October 20, 1982, pp. 108–111.
"The Outlook for UNIX," *Electronic Business,* June 26, 1989, p. 30.

Other

Thompson, Kenneth, telephone interview with Patrick Moore conducted February 14, 1994.

—*Sketch by Patrick Moore*

George Paget Thomson
1892-1975
English experimental physicist

George Paget Thomson is known for providing direct experimental proof of French physicist **Louis Victor de Broglie**'s theory of matter waves, which states that matter has wave-like properties in addition to characteristics associated with particles. For this discovery, Thomson was awarded the 1937 Nobel Prize in physics jointly with the American physicist **Clinton Davisson**, who had independently

George Paget Thomson

and coincidentally reached the same findings using different methods. Thomson is also recognized for his contribution to the study of neutrons and their use in nuclear chain reactions.

Thomson was born in Cambridge, England, on May 3, 1892, the only son of **J. J. Thomson**, a Nobel Prize-winning physicist, and Rose Paget, the daughter of Sir George Paget, a distinguished professor of medicine. Thomson's mother had met her husband while she was one of his students in the Cavendish Physical Laboratory. Not surprisingly, given the family tradition of learning, particularly in the physical sciences, Thomson showed an interest in science at a young age. His first recorded scientific inquiry is said to have concerned the twisting motion of a swing that hung in his nursery. Between the ages of nine and thirteen, Thomson was sent to the King's College Choir School, an experience that did not inculcate him with any deep-seated feeling for music. Instead, Thomson was interested in literature, ships (especially war ships), and model ship building.

At Perse School, where he was sent in 1895, he demonstrated a talent for rugby, but, although he was physically agile, he never particularly enjoyed team sports. When the time came for Thomson's graduation, his headmaster advised him to study classics, but Thomson decided on a career in physics. In 1910, he entered Trinity College, Cambridge, as a Scholar, taking mathematics and physics. There, he distinguished himself by becoming a Major Scholar and attaining first class honors in mathematics at the end

of his second year and the same in physics at the end of his third.

Works at Cavendish under His Father

Upon graduating, Thomson went to work at the Cavendish Physical Laboratory with his father. He researched radicals, the single replaceable atoms of an element's reactive atomic form, and also grew interested in aerodynamics. He became a fellow and mathematical lecturer of Corpus Christi College, Cambridge, in 1914. Though he held these positions through 1922, Thomson left Cambridge for the duration of World War I.

The war gave Thomson an opportunity to develop his interest in aerodynamics. He served in France as second lieutenant and was then transferred to the Royal Aircraft Factory in Farnborough, England. There, he did more aerodynamics work, which, along with his earlier work at Cavendish, earned him the 1916 Smith Prize. He also learned to fly while in Farnborough. For a brief period, he was transferred to the British War Mission in the United States.

When the war ended, Thomson worked for the Aircraft Manufacturing Co. He wrote his first book, *Applied Aerodynamics,* before returning to Cambridge in 1919. There, he worked with positive and anode rays and discovered the existence of the two isotopes of lithium. Thomson left Cambridge in 1922 to accept an appointment as professor of natural philosophy at the University of Aberdeen. He found the college stimulating, both professionally and socially. The University's principal, Sir George Adam Smith, had a daughter, Kathleen, whom Thomson admired. They married and had four children: John, David, Clare, and Rose. Kathleen died prematurely in 1941.

At Aberdeen, Thomson continued his work with positive rays and also pursued a new direction of study. His presence at a 1926 meeting of the British Association for the Advancement of Science led him to consider the radical new matter waves theory being propounded by de Broglie. (Davisson, the physicist with whom Thomson would later share the Nobel Prize, was also at the gathering though the pair did not meet.) The meeting inspired Thomson to try to establish experimental proof of de Broglie's hypothesis.

Experimentally Proves Theory of Matter Waves

Thomson believed that he could use the same methods that had been used just three years previously to prove the wave character of X rays in order to demonstrate the same characteristic of matter. De Broglie had postulated that electrons have a wavelength proportional to their mass and velocity. In order to verify this, Thomson thought he could send a beam of electrons through a diffracting medium that would cause the electrons to bend or scatter, producing an interference pattern, if they did possess wave characteristics. However, because the wavelength that de Broglie predicted for electrons was extremely short, the diffraction apparatus required for the experiment would have to be minute. Thomson thought of using a film of metallic crystals: because crystals are composed of layers of atoms in parallel rows, they would act as a grate through which the electron beam could be shot. As he sent the electron beam through the crystal grate to a photographic plate beyond, Thomson was able to record a pattern extremely similar to that obtained from short-wave light under similar conditions. Calculating the electron's wavelength from this pattern, Thomson confirmed that it was precisely as de Broglie had predicted.

Thomson's reputation was sealed in 1930 when he was elected to London's Royal Society as a fellow. That same year, he was offered the post of professor of physics at London's Imperial College of Science and Technology. Thomson took an interest in the work of his department's various subdivisions, particularly its Technical Optics section, which sparked his interest in the recently invented electron microscope. He also worked hard to solidify the department's reputation for excellence by gathering about him some of the best minds in physics. Many of these individuals devoted themselves to continuing and extending Thomson's research into electron diffraction, using, for example, techniques of high voltage diffraction. Thomson summarized these developments in his textbook *Theory and Practice of Electron Diffraction,* which he wrote with William Cochrane. In addition to guiding the work of the department, Thomson turned his attention to nuclear physics, which had been revolutionized by the recent discovery of neutrons, positrons, and artificial radioactivity.

With his colleague J. A. Saxton, Thomson bombarded positrons (positively charged particles possessing the same mass and magnitude of charge as an electron), hoping to produce radioactivity. He invented the apparatus that they used to separate positrons from negative beta-rays. Thomson also closely supervised a series of experiments conducted by P. B. Moon and J. R. Tillman to measure the velocity of neutrons. Before these experiments could be completed, war broke out and Thomson considered the possibility of a uranium chain reaction. As P. B. Moon quoted in *Biographical Memoirs of Fellows of the Royal Society,* Thomson noted: "The military possibilities were sufficiently obvious to make me ask . . . [the] Rector of Imperial College and . . . Chairman of the Committee for the Scientific Study of Air Defence, if we ought not to do something about it." Thomson obtained a ton of uranium oxide to undertake a series of experiments at Imperial College. With the uranium oxide, Thomson carried out experiments with slowed down neutrons. His conclusion that a nuclear chain reaction could not be achieved easily or rapidly was contained in a report submitted to the Air Ministry in 1940.

Heads Government's Maud Committee during War

In April of 1940, Thomson formed and headed the Maud Committee, which fostered relationships among nuclear scientists and was the first atomic energy committee in England. By the end of July, the Committee had investigated the feasibility of making an atomic bomb and the potential of uranium as a source of power; they reported their findings to the Ministry of Aircraft. Thomson was given the title Scientific Liaison Officer and sent to Canada to investigate the possibility of transferring the British atomic project to Ottawa. He recommended that the move should go ahead. The project was realized at Chalk River in Ottawa under the leadership of English atomic physicist **John D. Cockcroft**.

Back in England, Thomson was appointed deputy chair of the Radio Board and scientific advisor to the Air Ministry, a post that involved Thomson in work on a possible hydrogen bomb. He embarked on a series of experiments at his laboratory at Imperial College. The difficulty was determining a way to control the nuclear fusion reaction. Thomson took out a provisional patent covering his idea, which employed a ring discharge. Work began on developing the paper, but Thomson soon realized the difficulty of laboring in secret with a large group. In 1951, the project was transferred to the Aldermaston Court research laboratory of Associated Electrical Industries Ltd. for security reasons. Thomson continued working on the project and, according to Professor T. E. Allibone, the director of the laboratory, "his support was a tremendous help in boosting morale," quoted Moon. During this period, Thomson was also active in scientific societies. He was vice president of the Royal Society from 1949 to 1951 and chair of both the Sectional Committee for Physics and the Warren Research Fund.

Appointed Master of Corpus Christi College, Cambridge

In 1952, Thomson returned to Cambridge as Master of his old alma mater, Corpus Christi College. He threw himself wholeheartedly into the job, overseeing major restorations of the campus, and took a keen interest in the college's finances. He was a genial and enthusiastic host who particularly enjoyed entertaining undergraduates. Moon quoted Michael McCrum, one of Thomson's colleagues and friends, on Thomson during this period: "[H]is well-stored practical memory, his wide-ranging, inquisitive mind combined with an insatiable zest for argument to make his table talk fascinating."

During his years as Master, Thomson was also active on the lecture circuit, speaking to both specialist and general audiences on topics that included the relationship of physics to technology, the education of scientists, and nuclear power. He became more involved exploring the implications of the latter as a member of a committee of the Pugwash Group, a collection of scientists who met regularly to discuss various topics such as the easing of international tensions, the establishment of systems of mutual security, nuclear proliferation and disarmament, and the role of scientists in influencing debate.

In 1958, Thomson, who had been knighted in 1943, was elected president of the Institute of Physics, a position he held until 1960, when he was elected president of the British Association for the Advancement of Science at Cardiff. Thomson was also a member of the Royal Society (he received the Hughes Medal in 1939 and the Royal Medal in 1949), a Foreign Member of the American Academy of Arts and Sciences and of the Lisbon Academy, and a Corresponding Member of the Austrian Academy of Sciences. He was an honorary graduate of the University of Aberdeen; University College, Dublin; the University of Lisbon; the University of Sheffield; the University of Wales; the University of Reading; Cambridge University; and Westminster College. Thomson also was an Honorary Fellow at Trinity and Corpus Christi Colleges, Cambridge, and at Imperial College. He served as Master of Corpus Christi until his retirement in 1962. He remained on at Cambridge and kept active both scientifically and socially. He died at the age of eighty-three on September 10, 1975.

SELECTED WRITINGS BY THOMSON:

Books

Applied Aerodynamics, Hodder and Stoughton, 1920.

(With father, J. J. Thomson) *Conduction of Electricity through Gases,* Volumes I and II, Cambridge University Press, 1928, second edition, 1933.

The Atom, Holt, 1930, sixth edition, Oxford University Press, 1962.

The Wave Mechanics of the Free Electron, McGraw, 1930.

(With William Cochrane) *Theory and Practice of Electron Diffraction,* Macmillan, 1939.

The Foreseeable Future, Cambridge University Press, 1955, revised edition, Viking, 1960.

The Inspiration of Science, Oxford University Press, 1961.

J. J. Thomson and the Cavendish Laboratory in His Day, Nelson, 1964, Doubleday, 1965, published as *J. J. Thomson, Discoverer of the Electron,* Doubleday-Anchor, 1966.

The Electron, U.S. Atomic Energy Commission, Office of Information Services, 1972.

SOURCES:

Books

Biographical Memoirs of Fellows of the Royal Society, Volume 23, Royal Society (London), 1977, pp. 529–556.

Cline, Barbara Lovett, *Men Who Made a New Physics: Physicists and the Quantum Theory,* University of Chicago Press, 1987, p. 184.

Modern Men of Science, Volume I, McGraw, 1968, pp. 479–481.

Weber, Robert L., *Pioneers of Science: Nobel Prize Winners in Physics,* Institute of Physics, 1980.

—Sketch by Avril McDonald

J. J. Thomson
1856-1940
English physicist

A scientist of diverse interests, J. J. Thomson was awarded the Nobel Prize in physics in 1906 for his theoretical and experimental research on the behavior of electricity in gases. As one consequence of that research, Thomson discovered the electron in 1897. He also was interested in a number of other topics, including optics, magnetism, radioactivity, photoelectricity, and thermionics (a branch of physics relating to the emission of charged particles from an incandescent source).

Joseph John Thomson was born at Cheetham Hill, a suburb of Manchester, England, on December 18, 1856. His father was a bookseller and publisher who specialized in antique volumes. J. J., as he was widely known, originally planned to become an engineer, and arrangements were made for him to apprentice with a friend of his father's. When the senior Thomson died in 1870, however, the family could no longer afford to pay the expense of J. J.'s apprenticeship, and he enrolled at Owen's College, now the University of Manchester. Thomson studied mathematics, physics, and chemistry under a distinguished science faculty, and with the encouragement of Thomas Baker, a professor of mathematics, Thomson applied for and won a scholarship to Baker's alma mater, Trinity College, Cambridge.

J. J. Thomson

Fellowship Brings Thomson to Cambridge for a Four-Decade Stay

Thomson entered Trinity College in 1876 and majored in mathematics, beginning an affiliation with Cambridge University that would last the rest of his life. Although some of the most exciting and important physical and chemical research was going on within a few steps of Thomson's college, he made no attempt to find out about them. However, his single-minded attention to mathematics was rewarded when, in 1880, he earned a second place in the college examination on that subject.

Thomson's first published work dealt with the research of a fellow scholar at Cambridge whom he had never met, James Clerk Maxwell. Maxwell had only recently devised his mathematical theory of electromagnetism, and Thomson became intrigued by some of its special implications. For instance, when Thomson analyzed the properties that might be expected of a charged sphere that is placed in motion, he discovered that the apparent mass of the sphere would increase as a result of its gaining electrical charge. Although Thomson did not pursue this line of research, the finding was clearly a preview of the concept of mass-energy equivalence that would be proposed by **Albert Einstein** a decade later.

In 1881 Thomson was awarded a fellowship that allowed him to stay on at Trinity College. The thesis he wrote in competition for that fellowship involved an analysis of some physical and chemical deductions that could be drawn from some very general mathematical laws, an approach Thomson used frequently in his research. He argued that it is sometimes useful simply to derive the physical implications of mathematical expressions without worrying about the physical reality that might be involved. One advantage of this approach, he said, was that new and unanticipated lines of research might be revealed.

Thomson did not disregard the role of physical reality in his research, however; he also argued that the best way to attack a problem may sometimes be to devise analogies or to construct models of the phenomenon under investigation. An example of this approach was an essay he wrote in 1882 for the Adams Prize competition. The subject of that competition was vortex rings, spinning cloud-like assemblies somewhat similar to smoke rings. Vortex rings were of great interest to scientists toward the end of the nineteenth century because many thought that atoms might consist of such arrangements. Thomson's essay won the prize but, probably more important, it eventually led him into a line of research—electrical discharges in gases—from which he was to produce his greatest accomplishments.

In 1884, Lord Rayleigh retired as Cavendish Professor of Physics—one of the most prestigious chairs of science in the English-speaking world—and he recommended that Thomson be appointed to replace him. Word of the recommendation caused an uproar within the Cambridge scientific community; numerous well-qualified and famous scholars wanted the position for themselves and were outraged that a young man of twenty-eight was being considered for the post. Critics of Thomson's candidacy perceived his background in experimental science as weak since most of his earlier studies and research had been in mathematics or theoretical science. Still, the selection committee, consisting of Lord Kelvin, George Gabriel Stokes, and George Howard Darwin, chose Thomson as Rayleigh's replacement and director of the world-famous Cavendish Laboratory at Cambridge.

Research on Electrical Discharge in Gases Reveals the Electron

The research field to which Thomson now turned was one related to the topic of his Adams Prize essay—electrical discharge in gases—which had become extremely popular among physicists during the preceding decade, largely as the result of the work of Julius Plücker, Johann Wilhelm Hittorf, William Crookes, Eugen Goldstein, and others. Most experiments followed a common model: an electrical discharge is caused to pass through a gas under very low pressure in a glass tube. Under these circumstances, a glowing beam is observed to follow the electrical discharge from one end of the tube to the other. The beam, called a cathode ray, can be deflected by an electrical or magnetic field superimposed on the tube.

The primary question that remained in the mid–1890s concerned the nature of cathode rays. Were they streams of charged particles, as Crookes and others believed, or were they of the luminiferous ether as most German physicists thought? Thomson turned his attention to the resolution of this question. A key development in his approach to the problem was the development of better equipment; he was able to show, with better vacuums, a decrease in the ambiguous and contradictory results obtained by other researchers. Using improved equipment, Thomson accomplished the deflection of cathode rays by an electrical field, which was strong evidence that the rays did consist of particles.

Thomson then went one step further: he developed an experiment in which cathode rays were deflected by both magnetic and electrical fields. By measuring the angle at which the rays were deflected by such fields of any given magnitudes, he was able to calculate the ratio of the electrical charge to the mass (e/m) for the particles that made up the rays. He found that the value of e/m was the same for any gas used in the experiment (that is, whatever particle it was that made up the cathode rays occurred in all gases and was, therefore, a component of all of the different atoms of which those gases were made).

Thomson also extended his research to other phenomena caused by electrical discharges, such as the discharge from a negatively charged heated wire. He found an occurrence similar to that observed in the original glass tube experiments, in which particles with the same e/m ratio could be detected. He concluded that some fundamental particle with a constant e/m ratio was present in all of these experiments and, hence, was a component of all atoms. The term used by Thomson for these particles, *corpuscle,* was soon replaced by a name suggested earlier by G. J. Stoney, *electron.* Thomson's reports on his discoveries to the British Association in 1889 were so well documented that the existence of a new subatomic particle was almost immediately accepted by scientists worldwide.

Thomson's discovery raised a number of fundamental questions about atomic structure. For nearly a century, scientists had thought of the atom as some kind of indivisible, uniform particle or mass of material, but Thomson had shown that this view was untenable, and that the atom must consist of at least two parts, one of which was the newly discovered electron. To account for his discovery, Thomson proposed a new model of the atom, sometimes referred to as the "plum pudding" atom. In this model, the atom was thought to consist of a cloud of positive charge in which are embedded discrete electrons, much as individual plums are embedded in

the traditional English plum pudding. However, this model was never very successful, and, in the work of Thomson's successor, **Ernest Rutherford**, a better atomic picture would soon evolve.

In recognition of his research on electrical discharges in gases, Thomson was awarded the 1906 Nobel Prize in physics. Two years later, he was knighted for his accomplishments in science. By this time, however, Thomson had gone on to a new field of research, the study of the positively charged "canal" rays that are also produced during electrical discharge in gases. Thomson used a method similar to that with which he discovered the electron, the deflection of canal rays with magnetic and electrical fields. The instrument he developed to accomplish the procedure was the forerunner of today's mass spectrometer, in which particles of differing e/m ratios can be separated from each other.

Thomson's instrumentation eventually became so sophisticated that he was able to separate two isotopes of neon, neon–20 and neon–22, from each other. He was not able to completely interpret the results of this experiment, however, and he eventually turned the work over to one of his graduate students, **Francis Aston**. Aston's continuation of this work resulted not only in a more refined form of the spectrometer, but also in a confirmation that he and Thomson had indeed discovered the first isotopes of a stable element.

Career Concludes with Accomplishments in Teaching and Administration

The work on canal rays marked the end of Thomson's most creative years. His efforts after 1912 focused more on teaching and administration, although he did remain active in research to some extent. He was elected president of the Royal Society in 1915 and was appointed Master of Trinity College in 1918. He resigned as Cavendish professor in the following year, but was then appointed to an honorary chair which allowed him to maintain university privileges. Thomson was succeeded in the Cavendish chair by one of his greatest students, Ernest Rutherford.

Thomson's impact on science was just as notable for his skills as a teacher and administrator. He was responsible for the expansion of the Cavendish Laboratories (on two occasions) as well as for its efficient operation for thirty-five years. A tribute to his talent for finding, educating, and nurturing young researchers is the fact that no less than seven of his students eventually received Nobel Prizes in the sciences. A few years before Thomson's death, he was honored by a dinner given in his honor at Cambridge. The list of guests contained most of the leading figures in physical research of the day. At the dinner, Thomson was given a testimonial signed by more than two hundred friends, students, and colleagues. Thomson died in Cambridge on August 30, 1940, and was laid to rest in Westminster Abbey close to Isaac Newton and Charles Darwin.

SELECTED WRITINGS BY THOMSON:

Books

Treatise on the Motion of Vortex Rings, [London], 1883.
Applications of Dynamics to Physics and Chemistry, [London], 1888.
Notes on Recent Research in Electricity and Magnetism, [Oxford], 1893.
Conduction of Electricity through Gases, [Cambridge], 1903.
The Corpuscular Theory of Matter, [London], 1907.
Rays of Positive Electricity and their Application to Chemical Analysis, [London], 1913.
The Electron in Chemistry, [Philadelphia], 1923.
Recollections and Reflections, [London], 1936.

SOURCES:

Books

Jaffe, Bernard, *Crucibles: The Story of Chemistry,* Simon & Schuster, 1957, chapter 12.
Rayleigh, Lord John, *The Life of J. J. Thomson,* [Cambridge], 1943.
Thomson, G. P., *J. J. Thomson and the Cavendish Laboratory in His Day,* [New York], 1965.
Weber, Robert L., *Pioneers of Science: Nobel Prize Winners in Physics,* American Institute of Physics, 1980, pp. 29–30.

Periodicals

McCommack, R., "J. J. Thomson and the Structure of Light," *British Journal of the History of Science,* (1967), pp. 362–387.

—*Sketch by David E. Newton*

William Thurston
1946-

American mathematician

William Thurston has combined curiosity with a special ability to imagine higher-dimensional shapes to advance the field of topology. He has made a hypothesis, called Thurston's conjecture, concerning three-dimensional topological shapes and is a leader in what is known as experimental mathematics. His leadership in the new experimental approach to mathematics has opened up new avenues in topology and his efforts to understand higher-dimensional shapes have contributed to theories about the shape and movement of the universe. In 1982, he won the Fields Medal, the highest award in mathematics.

William Paul Thurston was born on October 30, 1946, in Washington, D.C., to Paul and Margaret Martt Thurston. As early as age five, he was fascinated with mathematics, especially by the abacus. As a teenager he loved geometrical puzzles, and at thirteen he discovered an unusual mathematical similarity among the solutions to a "connect-the-dot" game. He imagined that he would use this discovery as a Ph.D. dissertation topic until he learned that it was already a well-known theorem. Also as a teenager, he learned of a hypothesis that three billiard balls moving on an infinitely large, open table would collide not more than three times. Thurston, by visually imagining the table and the movement of the balls, discovered paths in which the balls collided four times and disproved the hypothesis.

Thurston attended New College in Sarasota, Florida, graduating with a degree in mathematics in 1967. He went on to earn his Ph.D. in mathematics from the University of California, Berkeley, in 1972. He spent a year at Princeton University's Institute for Advanced Study and was an assistant professor on a Sloan Fellowship at the Massachusetts Institute of Technology from 1973 to 1974. He then returned to Princeton to become a professor in the department of mathematics. He remained there until 1991, when he accepted a position at the University of California, Berkeley.

Topology is the branch of geometry that studies how the shapes of objects change by bending, twisting, and stretching. Objects are considered to be topologically equivalent when they remain mathematically alike even if their shapes are otherwise very different. Thurston specializes in imagining objects in four dimensions—that is, across time—instead of the three dimensions of length, width, and depth. Objects in this fourth dimension are called hypersurfaces. Topology and hypersurfaces are particularly relevant to physics and efforts to explain the shape and movement of the universe. American physicist **Albert Einstein** theorized that the future movement of the universe depends on its current shape and suggested that the universe is four-dimensional. If time is part of the shape of the universe, questions then arise about what kind of an object the universe might be. These are some of the questions topology is helping physics answer, and Thurston has made important contributions to speculations about four-dimensional objects.

Thurston made a conjecture—an unproven theory—that suggests a method for describing all three-dimensional topological shapes with the rigid structures of geometry. In 1980, Thurston presented surprising new evidence concerning the fundamental shapes of four-dimensional objects. Prior to his presentation, most mathematicians believed that four-dimensional hypersurfaces could not be described with the same shapes used for three-dimensional objects, but Thurston's work demonstrated that hypersurfaces can be described with the three fundamental shapes (elliptical, hyperbolic, and flat) and five hybrids of these shapes. Thurston is also a leader in a new approach called experimental mathematics. Instead of using the classic approach of deducing mathematical proofs with step-by-step logic, experimental mathematics uses computers to run experiments. Thurston told *New Scientist* that computers are now powerful enough to be of use to mathematicians, and he believes computers allow them to address more complicated phenomena. He wants to see these mathematical experiments receive more scientific recognition, but many in the mathematics community continue to question the usefulness of this work.

In 1976, the American Mathematical Society presented Thurston with the Oswald Veblen Prize in Geometry. In 1979, he received the Alan T. Waterman Award by the National Science Foundation. In 1980 and 1981, he was Ulam Visiting Professor of Mathematics at the University of Colorado, Boulder. His contributions to mathematics were recognized in 1982 when he was awarded the Fields Medal (considered the equivalent of the Nobel Prize) by the International Mathematics Union. In 1992, he began directing the Mathematical Sciences Research Institute in Berkeley. He also acts as mathematics editor-in-chief for *Quantum Magazine*. Thurston married Rachel A. Findley on August 27, 1967. They have three children but were divorced in June of 1993.

SELECTED WRITINGS BY THURSTON:

Periodicals

"A Generalization of the Reeb Stability Theorem," *Topology,* Volume 13, 1974, pp. 347–352.

(With F. Almgren) "Examples of Unknotted Curves which Bound Only Surfaces of High Genus within their Convex Hulls," *Annals of Mathematics,* Volume 105, 1977, pp. 527–538.

(With M. Handel) "New Proofs of Some Results of Nielsen," *Advances in Mathematics,* Volume 56, 1985 pp. 203–247.

"A Norm of the Homology of Three-Manifolds," *Memoirs of the American Mathematical Society,* Volume 339, 1986, pp. 99–130.

SOURCES:

Periodicals

Bown, William, "New-Wave Mathematics," *New Scientist,* August 3, 1991, pp. 33–37.

Guillen, Michael, "The Shape of Things to Come," *Esquire,* December, 1984, pp. 100–103.

—Sketch by David N. Ford

Ping King Tien
1919-
Chinese-born American electronic engineer

Ping King Tien has made a number of significant contributions to the fields of microwave technology and integrated optics. In recognition of his work in the latter area, he was awarded the Morris N. Liebmann Award by the Institute of Electrical and Electronic Engineers in 1979. Yet Tien's research during a long career at AT&T Bell Laboratories has touched on almost every branch of modern electronics, and other of his fundamental findings have dealt with acoustic wave phenomena, superconductivity, lasers, microfabrication, and high-speed integrated circuits.

Tien was born on August 2, 1919, in Shan-Yu, China, then a small village in the province of Chekiang. He was the youngest of three sons born to Neu-Shing Tien, a banker, and his wife, Chao-Sing Yun Tien. At the age of eight, Tien moved with his family to Shanghai. Of his later childhood, Tien recalled in a letter to Linda Wasmer Smith, "My father decided that one of the boys should be an engineer and sent me to l'Institut Technique Franco-Chinois in Shanghai for my middle school. I was not very good at the elementary school. Somehow, I did remarkably well at the Institut. I was ranked the first in the class for the entire middle school."

From there, Tien went to the National Central University at Chunking, where he began work on an electrical engineering degree. Of his college years, Tien wrote in his letter, "I would say I was inspired by science or mathematics, for the first time, in the class of the calculus of integration and differentiation. I was intrigued by the ways the differentials and the integrals are defined. They are so abstract and yet so accurate." Tien received his bachelor's degree in 1942.

In 1947 Tien immigrated to the United States to attend Stanford University; he later became a naturalized citizen. For his thesis, he invented a new mechanism for the amplification of microwave signals. He obtained an M.S. in electrical engineering in 1948 and a Ph.D. in 1951. As one version of Tien's later résumé proudly asserted, "At Stanford University, he met Miss Nancy N. Y. Chen and married her in 1952. They now have two daughters, Emily and Julia Tien. Their two daughters and sons-in-law studied at Stanford University. It is a Stanford University family."

Advances Microwave Technology and Integrated Optics

The year after his graduation, Tien joined the research division of the communication principles department at AT&T Bell Labs. His early work there focused primarily on microwaves, which are a relatively short kind of electromagnetic wave. One application of microwaves is the carrying of information for telephone systems. Tien made some critical calculations related to traveling-wave tubes, which are used to generate microwave signals. The practical theories that resulted from his esoteric calculations were basic to the development of improved microwave tubes.

In the ensuing years, it became apparent that light waves held even greater potential than microwaves as a telecommunications carrier. Tien's interests shifted accordingly. In the late 1960s and early 1970s, he became a pioneer in the emerging discipline of integrated optics. Until this time, research on lasers and their applications had been conducted on optical benches, where beams were sent through the air from component to component, and lenses and mirrors were used to change a beam's size or direction. This classical approach was not without its problems; results could be affected by such extraneous variables as temperature change and mechanical vibration. So the development of a miniature form of laser-beam circuitry represented an important advance. Tien was a co-organizer of the first topical meeting on integrated optics, held in 1974.

Waveguides are devices designed to confine and direct electromagnetic waves, including light waves. During the 1970s, Tien was one of the first scientists to recognize the potential of thin-film waveguides, devices built from a transparent material measuring only about one micrometer-less than a ten-thousandth of an inch-thick. He also invented a prism coupler, a device that can be used to make the light from a laser beam travel within a thin-film waveguide. In all, Tien holds thirty-five patents and has published more than fifty papers in the course of a remarkably productive career.

Tien was awarded the Achievement Award of the Chinese Institute of Engineers in 1966. He has been elected a member of the National Academy of Sciences and the National Academy of Engineering, and he is a fellow of the Institute of Electrical and Electronic Engineers and the Optical Society of America. In 1983, he was honored with a chaired professorship at Shanghai Jiao Tong University in China, and he has traveled and lectured extensively in his native country. He currently maintains an office as an emeritus fellow at AT&T Bell Labs in Holmdel, New Jersey.

SELECTED WRITINGS BY TIEN:

Periodicals

(With Joseph A. Giordmaine) "Integrated Optics: Wave of the Future," *Bell Laboratories Record,* December, 1980, pp. 371–378.
(With Giordmaine) "Integrated Optics: The Components," *Bell Laboratories Record,* January, 1981, pp. 8–13.
(With Giordmaine) "Integrated Optics: Putting It All Together," *Bell Laboratories Record,* February, 1981, pp. 38–45.

SOURCES:

Books

Millman, S., editor, *A History of Engineering and Science in the Bell System: Communications Sciences (1925–1980),* AT&T Bell Laboratories, 1984.

Other

AT&T Archives, résumé.
Tien, Ping King, letter to Linda Wasmer Smith dated March 1, 1994.

—*Sketch by Linda Wasmer Smith*

J. Tyson Tildon
1931-
American biochemist

Discoverer of Coenzyme A Tranferase Deficiency, a disease of infants, J. Tyson Tildon has also made major contributions to the establishment of the Sudden Infant Death Syndrome (SIDS) Institute at the University of Maryland School of Medicine. His research interests include developmental neurochemistry and the processes that control metabolism.

James Tyson Tildon was born April 7, 1931, in Baltimore, Maryland. He received his B.S. degree in chemistry from Morgan State College in 1954 and then worked for five years as a research assistant at Sinai Hospital, where he developed and used biochemical techniques to study vitamin deficiencies in humans and animal models. Subsequently, he spent a year as a Fulbright Scholar at the Institut de Biologie Physico-Chimique in Paris and, upon his return, matriculated to the doctoral program in biochemistry at Johns Hopkins University. After receiving his Ph.D. in 1965, Tildon accepted a two-year postdoctoral fellowship at Brandeis University, where his studies included an examination of how cells assume specialized functions during development. Tildon returned to Baltimore in 1967 to assume the post of assistant professor in the department of chemistry at Goucher College. The following year, he became research assistant professor in the department of pediatrics at the University of Maryland School of Medicine, and, in 1969, assistant professor in the department of biological chemistry. He has been a full professor of pediatrics since 1974 and a professor of biological chemistry since 1982. Tildon has also served as director of the Carter Clinical Laboratories for six years and director of pediatric research in the medical school's Department of Pediatrics for nine. In addition, he was a visiting scientist in the Laboratory of Developmental Biochemistry at the University of Groningen in the Netherlands, where he did research in the developmental neurobiology.

Among Tildon's contributions is the discovery of Coenzyme A (or CoA) Transferase Deficiency in infants. In his research, he demonstrated that the brains of infants use organic molecules called ketone bodies as an energy source during their first several weeks of life, disproving the previously held theory that glucose was the major energy source of the human brain at all ages of life. Tildon was also instrumental in establishing the SIDS Institute at the University of Maryland, one of the largest research programs dedicated to the study of SIDS, a disorder that causes an infant to abruptly stop breathing. Included in the discoveries made at the Institute are those of researcher Robert G. Meny, who found that babies suffered bradycardia, or abnormally slow heartbeat, before they stopped breathing. This finding has stimulated new research into the role of the heart in SIDS.

Tildon's interests extend beyond medicine and biochemistry and into other realms of research. In his book *The Anglo-Saxon Agony,* he points out that members of western civilization rely predominately on sight and hearing to gather information while ignoring the more personal senses of taste, smell, and touch. Rather than integrating all of the brain's responses to stimuli, Tildon suggests, the Anglo-Saxon approach is to separate thinking and feeling in an effort to be dispassionate. Yet, by excluding the emotional component, he writes, westerners fail to understand fully the human condition.

Among the many societies Tildon belongs to are Sigma Xi, the American Chemical Society, the Association for the Advancement of Science, the American Society for Biochemistry and Molecular Biology, and the Society for Experimental Biology and Medicine. He received the Maryland State Senate Citation for his work with SIDS in 1983, the City of Baltimore Citizen Citation in 1986, the Baltimore Chapter of the National Technical Association's Joseph S. Tyler, Jr. Award for Achievement in Science in 1986, the National Association of Negro Business and Professional Women's Club's Community Service Award in 1987, and the Humanitarian Award from the Associated Black Charities in 1991. In addition, he has served on several boards of directors, including those of the Mental Health Association of Metropolitan Baltimore, the Maryland Academy of Sciences, and the Associated Black Charities.

SELECTED WRITINGS BY TILDON:

Books

The Anglo-Saxon Agony, Whitmore Publishing Co., 1972.
Sudden Infant Death Syndrome, Academic Press, 1983.

Periodicals

(With D. A. Sevdalian) "CoA Transferase in the Brain and Other Mammalian Tissues," *Archives of Biochemistry and Biophysics,* Volume 148, 1972, p. 382.
(With M. Cornblath) "Succinyl-CoA: 3-Ketoacid CoA-Transferase Deficiency—A Cause for Ketoacidosis in Infancy," *Journal of Clinical Investigation,* Volume 51, 1972, p. 493.

SOURCES:

Tildon, J. Tyson, interview with Marc Kusinitz conducted on April 5, 1994.

—*Sketch by Marc Kusinitz*

Stephen P. Timoshenko
1878-1972
Russian-born American mechanical engineer

Stephen P. Timoshenko was a specialist in theoretical and applied mechanics whose research in the theory of elasticity, vibration, structures, and strength of materials is documented in a dozen textbooks. His works have been published around the world in thirty-eight languages. An effective teacher who coupled a thorough theoretical foundation with practical understanding of applications, he personally instructed over ten thousand students during his fifty-year career. After immigrating to America, he worked to improve American engineering education by introducing new topics into the stagnant curriculum. He was a member of the Academy of Sciences of the United States, Russia, the Ukraine, Poland, and France.

Stephen Prokofievitch Timoshenko was born in a small Ukrainian town near Kiev on December 23, 1878. His father, Prokop Timoshenko, had been a surveyor but became a farmer so he could stay home with his family. His mother, Josefina Jacovleva Sarnevskaja Timoshenko, was of Polish extraction and had completed a gymnasium education, which was unusual for a woman. Inspired by yearly trips to Kiev, his childhood dream was to build railroads. Timoshenko was educated at home by private tutors until the age of ten, when he entered the realschule in Romny, a town twenty miles from his home. During the school year, Timoshenko lived with his grandmother, but he spent his summers on the farm. Although he learned easily and helped explain material to his classmates, he was uncomfortable in class, fearing that he would fail to answer correctly if called upon. He loved to read; one weekend he read Jules Verne's *The Mysterious Island,* feigning illness on Monday to finish it. When Timoshenko graduated in 1896, he applied for admission to the Institute of Engineers of Ways of Communication in St. Petersburg. Despite apprehension about the entrance exams, he scored among the top forty of the seven hundred applicants and easily won admission. When Timoshenko was fourteen, his father had bought one of the farms he had been leasing, and the boy helped plan and construct a new house for the family. The experience, which even included making the bricks, proved to be very useful during his summer work for a railroad in 1899 and 1900. In 1900, Timoshenko took the first of many trips abroad when the institute allowed some students to serve at its exhibit at the International Exposition in Paris. During a six-week period, he traveled through Germany, France, Switzerland, and Austria, and spent three weeks working at a construction site he had learned about at the exposition.

After graduating in 1901, Timoshenko spent the following year in required military service, part of which included a period of study in mathematics back at the institute. Since he had volunteered for military service upon graduation, he was extended privileges over draftees and was free of much of the assigned work. In order to occupy himself, he invented a bridge made of 3.5-inch poles and telegraph wire that was light enough to be carried by two men but could support the load of a twenty-five-member platoon. Upon completing his military service in 1902, Timoshenko married Alexandra Archangelskaja, a medical student. Money was short, and they shared a three-room apartment with his two brothers. He then took a job in the institute's mechanics laboratory, testing cement and the hardness and strength of railroad rails.

Timoshenko was hired in 1903 to organize a new mechanics laboratory at the St. Petersburg Polytechnic Institute and serve as a lab instructor. The following summer, he took the first of several trips to study in Germany, visiting the Munich Polytechnic Institute where he learned to do original scientific research rather than merely using laboratory equipment to repeat established experiments. In 1905, Timoshenko took several classes at the University of Göttingen, Germany, including a seminar conducted by mathematician Felix Klein. He was assigned to investigate the lateral stability of an I-beam and succeeded in writing an equation for the beam's torsion (twisting). He went on to examine the beam's stability; two years later he used the results in his dissertation.

After another year of study in St. Petersburg, Timoshenko returned to Göttingen in the summer of 1906 and studied under Ernst Zermelo and German physicist Woldemar Voigt. That fall, Timoshenko was selected for a faculty position in strength of materials at the Kiev Polytechnic Institute, where he delivered the first lecture of his career in January, 1907, to over four hundred students. One of his responsibilities was to supervise a laboratory for testing the mechanical properties of building materials; he also developed a new program to ensure that students would learn to verify experimentally the theoretical results discussed in class. In 1909, he spent another summer at Göttingen, studying elasticity theory, hydrodynamics, and aerodynamics. Returning to Kiev, he was named dean of the division of structural engineering.

That fall, Timoshenko began a year-long effort to create an entry for the Jourawski Medal competition, which was held every ten years to recognize the best work in structural mechanics. By late summer of 1911, when notified that his paper on elastic stability had won the prize, he was particularly grateful for the cash award. He had recently been fired from the institute for refusing to expel a number of Jewish students because their quota at the school had been exceeded. Moving back to St. Petersburg, Timoshenko was able to work unofficially at several schools for an hourly wage.

The following year, Timoshenko was hired as a consultant in the military shipyards; his earlier work on the stability of compressed plates was now being applied to the design of ships for the Russian navy. In 1913, his academic censure ended, and he joined the faculties at the Ways of Communication Institute and the Electrical Engineering Institute. His notable research results included the first mathematical description of the center of shear of a structural beam, and analysis of asymmetric buckling of a centrally-compressed cylindrical shell.

In 1914, in the midst of World War I, Timoshenko was asked to work on the problem of strengthening the country's railroad tracks to carry wartime loads. Existing theory treated a rail as a beam supported by a series of elastic supports, which yielded an unsolvable differential equation; he simplified the theory by considering a beam on a continuous elastic foundation. This yielded a readily solvable equation showing how variation of a rail's weight affects the stresses in the rail and the rigidity of the track. He earned the Salov Prize for his solution. By 1917, wartime conditions were difficult in St. Petersburg, and Timoshenko's parents took his wife, his son Gregor, and his daughters Anna and Marine to Kiev. At Christmas, Timoshenko visited them and was unable to leave when the Bolsheviks occupied the city. The following year, he was rehired as a professor at the Polytechnic Institute and served on a commission to organize a Ukrainian Academy of Sciences, in which he became a charter member. During the revolution, Timoshenko left the barely functioning institute to join the engineering division of the anti-communist White Army. As conditions worsened, he fled to Yugoslavia in 1920; seven months later, when the Poles occupied the Ukraine, he returned long enough to get his wife and children. Then he joined the faculty at the new Zagreb Polytechnic Institute.

In 1922, Timoshenko came to the United States to work for the Vibration Specialty Company in Philadelphia, Pennsylvania. The firm was financially insecure, and within a year, he found a better job at the Westinghouse Electric & Manufacturing Company in Pittsburgh, Pennsylvania. In addition to supervising a laboratory, he taught strength of machine structures to the newly-hired engineers. In 1927, the year Timoshenko became an American citizen, he left Westinghouse to occupy the University of Michigan's new chair of research in mechanics. He found the engineering education in America quite inferior to that in his homeland, and he strove to reorganize it.

Under his leadership, mechanics education changed from the empirical to the scientific.

Timoshenko gave a month-long series of lectures at the University of California at Berkeley in early 1935. While there, he was invited to speak at Stanford University; the following fall, he accepted a professorship at Stanford. Again, he revised the curriculum, and he organized summer sessions to teach faculty from other schools. He retired in 1944, but continued as professor emeritus at Stanford until 1953.

In 1947, Great Britain's Institution of Mechanical Engineers awarded Timoshenko the James Watt International Medal, which was presented every five years to the most outstanding engineer. In 1957, he was honored as the first recipient of the Timoshenko Medal of the American Society of Mechanical Engineers. During his lifetime, he received honorary degrees from eight institutions in six countries.

Timoshenko was of the Greek Orthodox faith. He enjoyed hiking in the mountains and was interested in music, theater, art, travel, politics, economics, and world literature. In his later years, he lived with his daughter in Wuppertal, Germany, where he died on May 29, 1972, after a brief illness following kidney problems.

SELECTED WRITINGS BY TIMOSHENKO:

Books

Theory of Elasticity, McGraw, 1934.
Theory of Plates and Shells, McGraw, 1940.
Theory of Structures, McGraw, 1945.
History of Strength of Materials, Dover, 1953.
Engineering Education in Russian, McGraw, 1959.
As I Remember (autobiography), Van Nostrand, 1968.

SOURCES:

Books

Biographical Memoirs of Fellows of the Royal Society, Volume 19, Royal Society (London), 1973.
National Cyclopedia of American Biography, Volume 57, White & Company, 1977, pp. 365–366.

—Sketch by Sandra Katzman

Nikolaas Tinbergen
1907-1988
Dutch-born English zoologist and ethologist

Nikolaas Tinbergen, a zoologist, animal psychologist, and pioneer in the field of ethology (the study of the behavior of animals in relation to their habitat), is most well known for his studies of stimulus-response processes in wasps, fishes, and gulls. He shared the 1973 Nobel Prize in physiology or medicine with Austrian zoologists **Karl von Frisch** and **Konrad Lorenz** for his work on the organization and causes of social and individual patterns of behavior in animals.

The third of five children, Tinbergen was born April 15, 1907, in The Hague, Netherlands, to Dirk Cornelius Tinbergen, a school teacher, and Jeanette van Eek. His older brother Jan studied physics but later turned to economics, winning the first Nobel Prize awarded in that subject in 1969. The Tinbergens lived near the seashore, where Tinbergen often went to collect shells, camp, and watch animals, many of which he would later formally research.

After high school, Tinbergen worked at the Vogelwarte Rossitten bird observatory and later began studying biology at the State University of Leiden, Netherlands. For his dissertation, Tinbergen studied bee-killer wasps and was able to experimentally demonstrate that the wasps use landmarks to orientate themselves. Tinbergen first established the traditional routes of the wasps near their burrows, then altered the landscape to see how the wasps' behavior would be affected. Tinbergen was awarded his Ph.D. in 1932.

Tinbergen married Elisabeth Rutten in 1932 (they had five children together). Soon afterward, the Tinbergens embarked on an expedition to Greenland, where Tinbergen studied the role of evolution in the behavior of snow buntings, phalaropes, and Eskimo sled dogs. When he returned to the Netherlands in 1933, he became an instructor at the State University, where he organized an undergraduate course on animal behavior. Tinbergen's work had been recognized in the field of biology but it was not until after he met Lorenz—the acknowledged father of ethology—that his work began to form a directed body of research. Tinbergen took his family to Lorenz's home in Austria for a summer so the two men could work together. Although they published only one paper together, their collaboration lasted a number of years.

Begins Ethology Work

During 1936, Tinbergen and Lorenz began constructing a theoretical framework for the study of

Nikolaas Tinbergen

ethology, which was then a fledgling field. They hypothesized that instinct, as opposed to simply being a response to environmental factors, arises from an animal's impulses. This idea is expressed by the concept of a fixed-action pattern, a repeated, distinct set of movements or behaviors, which Tinbergen and Lorenz believed all animals have. A fixed-action pattern is triggered by something in the animal's environment. In some species of gull, for instance, hungry chicks will peck at a decoy with a red spot on its bill, a characteristic of the gull. Tinbergen showed that in some animals learned behavior is critical for survival. The oystercatcher, for instance, has to learn which objects to peck at for food by watching its mother. Tinbergen and Lorenz also demonstrated that animal behavior can be the result of contradictory impulses and that a conflict between drives may produce a reaction that is strangely unsuited to the stimuli. For example, an animal defending its territory against a formidable attacker, caught between the impulse to fight or flee, may begin grooming or eating.

Regarding his collaboration with Lorenz, Tinbergen is quoted in *Nobel Prize Winners* as saying: "We 'clicked' at once. . . . [Lorenz's] extraordinary vision and enthusiasm were supplemented and fertilized by my critical sense, my inclination to think his ideas through, and my irrepressible urge to check out 'hunches' by experimentation." Tinbergen and Lorenz's work was disrupted by World War II.

Receives Nobel Prize

Tinbergen spent much of the war in a hostage camp because he had protested the State University of Leiden's decision to remove three Jewish faculty members from the staff. After the war ended, he became a professor of experimental biology at the University. In 1949, Tinbergen traveled to Oxford University in England to lecture. He stayed at Oxford, establishing the journal *Behavior* with W. H. Thorpe and working in the University's animal behavior division. His 1951 book *The Study of Instinct* is credited with bringing the study of ethology to many English readers. The book summarized some of the newest insights into the ways signaling behavior is created over the course of evolution. In 1955, Tinbergen became an English citizen, and in 1966 he was appointed a professor and fellow of Oxford's Wolfson College. When the work of Tinbergen, Lorenz, and von Frisch, who had demonstrated that honeybees communicate by dancing, received the Nobel Prize in 1973, it was the first time the Nobel Committee recognized work in sociobiology or ethology.

It was Tinbergen's own hope that the ethologists' body of work would help in understanding of human behavior. "With von Frisch and Lorenz, Tinbergen has expressed the view that ethological demonstrations of the extraordinarily intricate interdependence of the structure and behavior of organisms are relevant to understanding the psychology of our own species," wrote P. Marler and D. R. Griffin in *Science.* "Indeed, [the Nobel Prize] might be taken ... as an appreciation of the need to review the picture that we often seem to have of human behavior as something quite outside nature, hardly subject to the principles that mold the biology, adaptability, and survival of other organisms."

The ability of an organism to adapt to its environment is another element of Tinbergen's work. After he retired from Oxford in 1974, he and his wife attempted to explain autistic behavior in children to adaptability. The Tinbergens' assertion that autism may be caused by the behavior of a child's parents caused some consternation in the medical community. Tinbergen believed that much of the opposition to his work was caused by the unflattering view of human behavior it presented. "Our critics feel we degrade ourselves by the way we look at behavior," he is quoted as saying in *Contemporary Authors.* "Because this is one of the implications of ethology, that our free will is not as free as we think. We are determinists, and this is what they hate.... They feel that our ideas gnaw at the dignity of man."

Tinbergen was wrote a number of books and made many nature films during his lifetime. Among his publications were several children's books, including *Kleew* and *The Tale of John Stickle.* Among the numerous awards he received are the 1969 Italia prize

and the 1971 New York Film Festival's blue ribbon, both for writing, with Hugh Falkus, the documentary *Signals for Survival,* which was broadcast on English television. Tinbergen died December 21, 1988, after suffering a stroke at his home in Oxford, England.

SELECTED WRITINGS BY TINBERGEN:

Books

Eskimoland, D. Van Sijn and Zonen (Rotterdam), 1934.
The Study of Instinct, Clarendon Press, 1951.
The Herring Gull's World: A Study of the Social Behavior of Birds, Collins, 1953, revised edition, Harper, 1971.
Social Behavior in Animals, With Special Reference to Vertebrates, Wiley, 1953, second edition, 1965.
Bird Life, Oxford University Press, 1954.

SOURCES:

Books

Contemporary Authors, Volume 108, Gale, 1983, pp. 489–90.
Nobel Prize Winners, H. W. Wilson, 1987, pp. 1059–61.

Periodicals

"Learning from the Animals," *Newsweek,* October 22, 1973, p. 102.
Marler, P., and D. R. Griffin, "The 1973 Nobel Prize for Physiology or Medicine," *Science,* November 2, 1973, pp. 464–467.

—*Sketch by James Klockow*

Samuel C. C. Ting
1936-
American physicist

Samuel C. C. Ting is an American physicist who received the 1976 Nobel Prize for his discovery of the J/psi particle, which led to the detection of many new subatomic particles. Ting shared the prize with **Burton Richter,** who had made the same discovery almost simultaneously, using a different experimental

Samuel C. C. Ting

technique. Ting is known as a confident, daring theorist, as well as a precise experimenter. He is a consummate practitioner of physics in the era of "big science," when research is conducted by large international teams using costly, complex experimental apparatus.

Ting was born in Ann Arbor, Michigan, on January 27, 1936, while his father, Kuan Hai Ting, was studying engineering at the University of Michigan. He completed his studies when Ting was two months old, and the family returned to mainland China, where his father became an engineering professor. His mother, Tsun-Ying Wang, was a psychology professor. As a child, Ting was cared for mostly by his maternal grandmother while both his parents worked. Although his grandmother emphasized the strong value of education, Ting was not able to begin school until he was twelve years old, because World War II intervened. After the war, the family moved to Taiwan, where Ting's father taught at the National Taiwan University.

In 1956, Ting enrolled at the University of Michigan, studying both mathematics and physics, and in 1959 he earned bachelor's degrees in both subjects. He married Kay Louise Kune, an architect, in 1960, with whom he would have two daughters. Ting received his Ph.D. in physics in 1962, and the next year he went to the European Center for Nuclear Research (CERN) in Geneva as a Ford Foundation fellow. He worked with Giuseppe Cocconi on the

proton synchrotron, a device that accelerates protons (the nucleus of an atom) for analysis and measurement. In 1965 Ting joined the faculty of Columbia University, where he worked with **Tsung-dao Lee** and **Chien-Shiung Wu**.

Ting became interested in the production of electron (negatively charged particles of an atom) and positron (positively charged particles of an atom) pairs by photon radiation after experiments conducted at Harvard raised questions regarding some of the predictions of quantum electrodynamic theory (the theory that deals with the interaction of matter with electromagnetic radiation). He took a leave of absence from Columbia and went to Hamburg, Germany, in 1966 to repeat the Harvard experiments at the German synchrotron facility. There his team built a double-arm spectrometer (an instrument used to analyze and measure particle emissions), which enabled them to measure the momentum of two particles simultaneously. It also recorded the angles of their deflection from the radiation beam. The researchers were able to calculate the masses of the particles and their combined energy, making identification of the particles easier and clarifying their interrelationships. Results of these experiments confirmed the accuracy of the quantum electrodynamic description of pair production.

Ting's work at Hamburg led him to ponder the nature of heavy photons (particles of radiation). After his return from Germany, he moved to the Massachusetts Institute of Technology (MIT), where he became full professor in 1969. In 1971, while still at MIT, Ting began a project to determine the properties of heavy photons at Brookhaven National Laboratory in Long Island, New York. Rather than the usual method of bombarding a beryllium target with photon beams, he used a proton beam of ten trillion protons per second in hopes of creating a heavy particle that would decay into pairs of electrons and positrons.

Because the search for heavy particles requires such high energy levels, Ting's MIT team redesigned the double-arm spectrometer to detect electron-positron pairs between 1.5 and 5.5 giga-electron volts (a giga equals one billion). The spectrometer also had to be capable of adding precise but small amounts of energy incrementally, as well as detecting their effects on the particle pairs. After several months of searching, the Ting team was rewarded in August, 1974 by the appearance of a sharp spike of high-energy electron-positron pairs at 3.1 billion electron volts. This was unexpected. Ting checked his measurements carefully and decided he was looking at evidence of a new particle that had not been predicted, the J/psi particle. It was heavier than known similar particles; it also occupied a very narrow range of energy states, and it lasted a relatively long time.

Ting reported his results to the Frascati Laboratory in Italy, where physicists were able to confirm his observations in only two days. Ting's paper and the results of the Frascati experiment were accepted for publication in *Physical Review Letters*. Just a few days after Ting discussed the paper with the review's editor, he attended a routine scheduling meeting at the Stanford Linear Accelerator Center; here he shared his results with Stanford's Burton Richter. Amazingly, Richter had made the same discovery at virtually the same time by creating collisions between positrons and electrons in an accelerator.

Ting and Richter shared the 1976 Nobel Prize for physics. The two-year period between discovery and award was probably the shortest interval on record and caused considerable comment at the time, because some scientists feared the discovery would not stand the test of time. However, it has since been the basis for a virtual explosion in the detection of many other fundamental particles.

The J/psi particle's lifespan was a thousand times longer than expected for such a heavy particle (three times heavier than a proton). It was believed that most subatomic particles were made up of combinations of even more fundamental particles called quarks, of which only three types were thought to exist before the discovery of the J/psi particle. The peculiarities of the J/psi particle (especially its long life) suggested the existence of a fourth type of quark, called charm. The J/psi particle was interpreted to be composed of a charmed quark and an antiquark, creating a property called "charmonium." Charm had been predicted in 1970 and its addition to the family of quarks was thought to unify the electromagnetic and weak forces, further encouraging physicists to believe in the possibility of a grand unifying theory in which the fundamental forces of nature would be shown to be equivalent at very high energies.

There are several stories of how the Ting-Richter particle received its name of J/psi, which is a combination of Ting's name for it (J) and Richter's (psi). Classical particles were traditionally assigned Greek letters for names, while newly discovered particles are labeled with capital letters. One story says Ting called his particle J because he had been working with electromagnetic currents carrying a J label. Another story says the J derives from the physical symbol for angular momentum. A third claims Ting chose the Chinese symbol for his name. In any case, the particle has retained the double label. A similar particle, called the psi-prime, was found by Richter's team within ten days of the first discovery.

Ting is a fellow of the American, European, and Italian physical societies as well as several academies of science, including the Academia Sinica. In addition to the Nobel Prize, Ting received the 1976 E. O. Lawrence Award.

SELECTED WRITINGS BY TING:

Books

(With G. Bellini) *The Search for Charm, Beauty, and Truth at High Energies,* Plenum Press, 1984.

Periodicals

(With Stanley J. Brodsky) "Timelike Momenta in Quantum Electrodynamics," *Physical Review,* Volume 145, 1966.

SOURCES:

Books

Close, Frank, et al., *The Particle Explosion,* Oxford University Press, 1987.

Periodicals

"Choosing Detectors for the SSC," *Science,* December 21, 1990, pp. 1648–50.
Flam, Faye, "Community Asks: Has Sam Ting Found a New Particle?" *Science,* November 27, 1992, p. 1441.
Crease, Robert, "SSC Detectors: Yes, No, Maybe," *Science,* January 4, 1991, p. 24.
"1976 Nobel Prizes: Clean Sweep for U.S.," *Science News,* October 23, 1976, p. 260.

　　　　　　　　　　—Sketch by Valerie Brown

Arne Tiselius
1902-1971
Swedish chemist

Arne Tiselius was awarded the 1948 Nobel Prize in chemistry for his research in electrophoresis (the movement of molecules based on their electric charge and their size) and for his investigations into adsorption, the inclination of certain molecules to cling to particular substances. Although the phenomenon of electrophoresis had been identified decades earlier, it did not become a useful technique for analyzing chemical compounds until Tiselius developed methods which delivered accurate results.

Arne Wilhelm Kaurin Tiselius was born in Stockholm, Sweden, on August 10, 1902, to Hans

Abraham J. Tiselius, who was employed by an insurance company, and Rosa Kaurin Tiselius, the daughter of a Norwegian clergyman. Upon the death of Tiselius's father in 1906, Rosa relocated the family to Göteborg, Sweden, where Hans's family lived. Entering the gymnasium at Göteborg, Tiselius came under the tutelage of a chemistry and biology teacher who actively supported his student's interest in science. In 1921 Tiselius matriculated to the University of Uppsala—where his father had earned his degree in mathematics—and studied under the renowned physical chemist **Theodor Svedberg**. Earning his master's degree in chemistry, physics, and mathematics in 1924, Tiselius continued to work as Svedberg's research assistant in physical chemistry. Although Svedberg was interested in the electrophoretic properties of proteins, he turned the study of this over to his new assistant, and three years later Tiselius published his first paper jointly with Svedberg on the subject.

Tiselius would remain at Uppsala until his retirement in 1968, rising from researcher to full professor. His 1930 doctoral dissertation, which earned him a post as docent in the chemistry department, long stood as a standard in the field of electrophoresis. Sweden's first professorship in biochemistry was established for Tiselius at Uppsala in 1938. Besides his work in biochemistry, Tiselius had a strong interest in botany and ornithology and made frequent excursions into the Swedish countryside on photographic expeditions. On November 26, 1930, the year of his doctoral thesis, he married Ingrid Margareta Dalén, with whom he would have one son, Per, and a daughter, Eva.

Explores the Possibilities of Chromatography

Following his dissertation, Tiselius concentrated his attention in areas outside of chemistry. He expanded his research to include biochemical studies—not a typical element of the chemistry curriculum in those days—and became aware of the potential for exploiting the extremely specific electrical "signature" of proteins, as well as other substances. He became concerned, however, with the impurities in the substances under study, even those that had been carefully centrifuged, and turned to chromatography as a possible answer. In chromatographic analysis, light of a specific frequency is passed through a substance, and by using tables assembled over the course of many experiments, the "chromatic signature" of the particular sample can be detected. Tiselius applied this technique by looking into the properties of light diffusion through zeolite, a translucent mineral. While studying under Hugh S. Taylor from 1934 to 1935 at Princeton University's Frick Chemical Laboratory, Tiselius conceived of an accurate method to quantify the diffusion of water molecules through crystals of zeolite.

While at Princeton, Tiselius came to realize that a wealth of potential discoveries in the biochemical sciences awaited only the development of a method accurate enough to help separate and identify compounds. Returning to his original line of research, he completed a prototype of a new electrophoretic apparatus.

When Tiselius returned to Uppsala, he continued making improvements on his electrophoretic instrumentation. In one innovation, he filled a U-shaped tube with chemical solvents, added a solution containing the sample to be analyzed, then applied a charge to one end. As the elements migrated, they reached the solvents at different lengths along the tube. Tiselius constructed the tube so that test samples could be taken at various points along the path of migration and be analyzed to determine which of the original species had made it to that point. It was by using this technique that Tiselius was able to demonstrate that blood plasma contained a complex mix of different elements.

Tracking the movement of boundaries optically by a technique invented by August Toepler—the *Schlieren* method—Tiselius resolved the plasma into four distinct elements that showed up as separate bands in the tube. He was the first to isolate three of the blood proteins known as globulins, which he named *alpha, beta,* and *gamma.* These are important in many of the body's functions; the immunoglobulins, for example, are a critical factor in infection control. In the fourth band, located between those of *beta* and *gamma,* Tiselius discovered antibodies.

The method was a radical improvement but still dissatisfied Tiselius. At the time he was more interested in the breakdown products of polypeptides than in blood compounds. Peptides represent some of the most important proteins in the body and for a clear understanding of their function, it is essential to know their types. However, when the long chain of a polypeptide is broken down, the individual peptides are so similar in nature that even Tiselius's improved electrophoretic technique could not distinguish between them. Faced with this problem, he turned to adsorption methods of analysis, using the then-common column method. In this procedure, a mixture which contains a substance with a specific affinity for absorbing one peptide or another is flushed through a column (a tube or cylinder). The peptides which had been in the original mix can then be determined by analyzing the eluate (the wash which passed through the column).

In 1943 Tiselius introduced a critical improvement in the process. Research to that point had been carried out using a "frontal analysis method," which revealed the concentration of the components in a mixture but was unable to separate them for further study. Elution could accomplish separation, but had a major setback, "tailing," which is the corruption of one part of a solution by molecules from the other. Tiselius demonstrated that a simple modification to the old technique could reduce tailing, and this new method became known as "displacement analysis."

Advises Government on Scientific Matters

Other important work came out of Tiselius's laboratory throughout the 1940s, such as research on paper electrophoresis and zone electrophoresis. However, increasing demands from other sources took over his time and, in the summer of 1944, Tiselius became an advisor to the Swedish government. His responsibilities included sitting on a committee established to help improve conditions for advancing scientific research, with a focus on basic research. This was the beginning of a long and distinguished relationship with the Swedish Parliament, an association that ended only when Tiselius suffered a heart attack following an important meeting in Stockholm. He died the next morning on October 29, 1971.

Up to his last day, Tiselius followed an active schedule. Having accepted the four-year chairmanship of the Swedish Natural Science Research Council in 1946, he was instrumental in the creation of the Science Advisory Council to the Swedish government. Tiselius was elected vice president of the Nobel Foundation with membership on the Nobel Committee for Chemistry in 1947, one year before he was awarded his own Nobel Prize. That same year, at the International Congress of Chemistry held in London, he was elected vice president in charge of the section for biological chemistry of the International Union of Pure and Applied Chemistry—a body which he led as president four years later.

Among other honors Tiselius received were the Bergstedt Prize of the Royal Swedish Scientific Society in 1926, the Franklin Medal of the Franklin Institute in 1956, and the Paul Karrer Medal in Chemistry from the University of Zurich in 1961. He was also presented with numerous honorary degrees from universities, including those of Stockholm, Paris, Glasgow, Madrid, California at Berkeley, Prague, Cambridge, and Oxford. Tiselius was always interested in fields beyond his own and was concerned with the environmental, social, and ethical implications of science and technology. As president of the Nobel Foundation in 1960, he established the Nobel Symposium, perceiving the foundation as the perfect vehicle for raising awareness of the need to promote science as a solution to mankind's problems. This organization gathered a mix of Nobel laureates to discuss the implications of their work during symposia in each of the five prize fields.

SELECTED WRITINGS BY TISELIUS:

Periodicals

(With T. Svedberg) "A New Method for Determination of the Mobility of Proteins," *Journal of the American Chemical Society,* Volume 48, September, 1926, pp. 2272–2278.

"Adsorption and Diffusion in Zeolite Crystals," *Journal of Physical Chemistry,* Volume 40, February, 1936, pp. 223–232.

"A New Apparatus for Electrophoretic Analysis of Colloidal Mixtures," *Transactions of the Faraday Society,* Volume 33, 1937, pp. 524–31.

"Electrophoresis of Serumglobulin II: Electrophoretic Analysis of Normal and Immune Sera," *Biochemical Journal,* Volume 31, July, 1937, pp. 1464–77.

(With J. Parath and P. A. Albertsson) "Separation and Fractionation of Macromolecules and Particles," *Science,* Volume 141, July, 1963, pp. 13–20.

SOURCES:

Periodicals

Hjerten, S., "Arne Tiselius, 1902–1971," *Journal of Chromatography,* Volume 65, 1972, pp. 345–348.

—*Sketch by Nicholas Williamson*

Henry Tizard
1885-1959
English physical chemist

Henry Tizard played a pivotal role in British military policy during World War II. He advised the government on a wide variety of military applications of scientific and technological innovations, including radar and the jet propulsion engine. His scientific education and military experience allowed him to communicate effectively with people in both areas.

Sir Henry Thomas Tizard was born on August 23, 1885, in Gillingham, Kent, to Captain Thomas Henry and Mary Elizabeth (Churchward) Tizard. The family was financially solid but not wealthy. As a navy hydrographer, his father had participated in extensive naval survey work around the world. He encouraged his son's early interest in science. The young Tizard looked forward to a naval career, but just before he was to enter naval school at 13, his left eye was damaged when a fly flew into it. His sight was impaired enough to bar him from naval service. He then enrolled at Westminster preparatory school, and later at Magdalene College, Oxford, where he studied physical chemistry. The day of his final examinations he was seriously ill with the influenza that would recur throughout his life, but he still managed to take first honors.

Early Experiences Influence Career

The center of physical chemistry research at the time was with **Walther Nernst** at the University of Berlin. Tizard enrolled there in 1908 to work toward a Ph.D. Although he stayed in Berlin only a year, Tizard had two experiences there that were to prove significant for Britain: he noted the powerful changes chemistry was bringing to Germany's technological (and therefore military) status, and he met Frederick Lindemann. Lindemann, a fellow chemistry student, was the son of an Alsatian who had become a naturalized Briton. In Berlin, Tizard and Lindemann studied together, practiced boxing at a gymnasium, and ice skated. This early friendship was to sour in the midst of the anxiety and political intrigue of World War II.

In 1911 Tizard became a fellow of Oriel College, Oxford, where he taught physical chemistry. In 1914 he embarked on a British Association tour of Australia, during which he met Cambridge's **Ernest Rutherford** (a noted physicist) and other eminent scientists. The onset of World War I cut the trip short, and Tizard returned to England to enlist in the Royal Garrison Artillery. He was soon transferred to the Royal Flying Corps, where he began a lifelong commitment to aviation technology. His training as a pilot during this period enabled Tizard to understand the practical problems of flying in a way that was rare among scientific advisers and much appreciated by the other aviators. It was also during this time (1915) that he married Kathleen Eleanor Wilson. They eventually had three sons, John, Richard, and David.

At the end of the war, Tizard became assistant deputy of the newly-formed Royal Air Force and encountered Winston Churchill, then Minister of Munitions, for the first time. He never got along well with Churchill, who like Lindemann, enjoyed the intricacies of political gamesmanship which Tizard disliked intensely. In 1919, partly at Tizard's urging, the professorship of experimental philosophy at Oxford went to Lindemann. The two men continued to see each other from time to time, but hostility was already flaring up between them. One colleague remembered them getting into a shouting match over the relatively trivial question of whether oranges

should best be packed in symmetrical rows or in off-center layers.

Between the wars, Tizard consulted with the British petroleum industry. With Randall Pye, he studied adiabatic (heat neither lost nor gained) compression of gases, identifying the chemicals that were to prove most effective as fuel in internal combustion engines. Tizard also expanded his role as government adviser, working in the Department of Scientific and Industrial Research, where he hoped to encourage the application of scientific and technological discoveries. He found government and military leaders slow to assimilate new scientific knowledge, and this was to become a long-term frustration.

Politics and Science Combine for Tizard in World War II

By the early 1930s Hitler's aggression posed a threat to Europe, and the British began to worry about air attacks. They had no way to detect incoming planes which, in any effective defense strategy, would have to be intercepted at the coastlines. Various "death ray" ideas were discussed, but no technology presented itself clearly. Tizard became chair of a committee (the Tizard Committee) to investigate the possibilities, one of which was the reflection of radio waves off the atmosphere. Lindemann soon joined the committee, urging study of aerial mines and balloon intercepts, which Tizard believed were unlikely to be of much use. Lindemann also wanted to find a protection against night attacks, whereas Tizard believed the daylight threat was greater. Tension between the two men increased, as Lindemann was close to Churchill and Tizard's power was advisory rather than executive. As it turned out, Lindemann was right about the danger of night attacks. Tizard's mistake in this regard tended to obscure his foresight in pushing radar research. He was largely responsible for establishing the country's chain of radar stations that enabled Britain to survive the Battle of Britain in 1940. Credit for his role was slow in coming.

In 1939 Tizard was asked to evaluate the feasibility of an atomic bomb. He tried unsuccessfully to obtain the option for all the uranium available from the Belgian Congo, but he did manage to obtain some uranium to send to the United States, where it became the first nuclear fuel. Working as an unofficial adviser to Lord Beaverbrook (William Maxwell Aitken),Tizard served as a conduit for classified information passing between Britain and the United States. In 1940 he headed a mission to America for this purpose, taking along the cavity magnetron (called the "heart of radar"), which the British had developed but the Americans were to make practicable.

Political rivalry with Lindemann and frustration with the government's inability to set clear priorities and lines of authority led Tizard to curtail his active government service in the last years of the war. He opposed the government's policy of random bombing of German cities because he believed it would be less effective than bombing U-boats. He became president of Magdalene College, Oxford, in 1942 and retired from the Air Ministry in 1943. After the war, Tizard continued to support increased rigor in Britain's technological development, advising the government on science and military policy through the early 1950s. He received many honors, including the Order of the Bath, several honorary degrees, and membership in the Royal Society. Tizard died in Fareham, Hampshire, on October 9, 1959.

SELECTED WRITINGS BY TIZARD:

Books

(Translator) Walther Nernst, *Theoretical Chemistry,* 3rd edition, Macmillan, 1911.

Periodicals

"Methods of measuring aircraft performance," *The Aeronautical Journal,* Volume 21, 1917, pp. 108, 122.
"Experiments on the ignition of gases for sudden compression," *Philosophical Magazine,* Volume 44, 1992, p. 79.

SOURCES:

Books

Clark, Ronald W., *Tizard,* MIT Press, 1965.

—*Sketch by Valerie Brown*

Alexander Todd

Alexander Todd
1907-
English chemist

Alexander Todd was awarded the 1957 Nobel Prize in chemistry for his work on the chemistry of nucleotides. He was also influential in synthesizing vitamins for commercial application. In addition, he invesitgated active ingredients in cannabis and hashish and helped develop efficient means of producing chemical weapons.

Alexander Robertus Todd was born in Glasgow, Scotland, on October 2, 1907, to Alexander and Jane Lowrie Todd. The family, consisting of Todd, his parents, his older sister and younger brother, was not well-to-do. Todd's autobiography, *A Time to Remember,* recalls how through hard work his parents rose to the lower middle class despite having no more than an elementary education, and how determined they were that their children should have an education at any cost.

Education and Early Career

In 1918 Todd gained admission to the Allan Glen's School in Glasgow, a science high school; his interest in chemistry, which first arose when he was given a chemistry set at the age of eight or nine, developed rapidly. On graduation, six years later, he at once entered the University of Glasgow instead of taking a recommended additional year at Allan Glen's. His father refused to sign an application for scholastic aid, saying it would be accepting charity; because of superior academic performance during the first year, though, Todd received a scholarship for the rest of course. In his final year at university, Todd did a thesis on the reaction of phosphorus pentachloride with ethyl tartrate and its diacetyl derivative under the direction of T. E. Patterson, resulting in his first publication.

After receiving his B.Sc. degree in chemistry with first-class honors in 1928, Todd was awarded a

Carnegie research scholarship and stayed on for another year working for Patterson on optical rotatory dispersion. Deciding that this line of research was neither to his taste nor likely to be fruitful, he went to Germany to do graduate work at the University of Frankfurt am Main under Walther Borsche, studying natural products. Todd says that he preferred Jöns Berzelius's definition of organic chemistry as the chemistry of substances found in living organisms to Gmelin's definition of it as the chemistry of carbon compounds.

At Frankfurt he studied the chemistry of apocholic acid, one of the bile acids (compounds produced in the liver and having a structure related to that of cholesterol and the steroids). In 1931 he returned to England with his doctorate. He applied for and received an 1851 Exhibition Senior Studentship which allowed him to enter Oxford University to work under **Robert Robinson**, who would receive the Nobel Prize in chemistry in 1947. In order to ease some administrative difficulties, Todd enrolled in the doctoral program, which had only a research requirement; he received his D.Phil. from Oxford in 1934. His research at Oxford dealt first with the synthesis of several anthocyanins, the coloring matter of flowers, and then with a study of the red pigments from some molds.

After leaving Oxford, Todd went to the University of Edinburgh on a Medical Research Council grant to study the structure of vitamin B_1 (thiamine, or the anti-beriberi vitamin). The appointment came about when George Barger, professor of medical chemistry at Edinburgh, sought Robinson's advice about working with B_1. At that time, only a few milligrams of the substance were available, and Robinson suggested Todd because of his interest in natural products and his knowledge of microchemical techniques acquired in Germany. Although Todd and his team were beaten in the race to synthesize B_1 by competing German and American groups, their synthesis was more elegant and better suited for industrial application. It was at Edinburgh that Todd met and became engaged to Alison Dale—daughter of Nobel Prize laureate **Henry Hallett Dale**—who was doing postgraduate research in the pharmacology department; they were married in January of 1937, shortly after Todd had moved to the Lister Institute where he was reader (or lecturer) in biochemistry. For the first time in his career, Todd was salaried and not dependent on grants or scholarships. In 1939 the Todds' son, Alexander, was born. Their first daughter, Helen, was born in 1941, and the second, Hilary, in 1945.

The Maturing of a Scientist

Toward the end of his stay at Edinburgh, Todd had begun to investigate the chemistry of vitamin E (a group of related compounds called tocopherols), which is an antioxidant—that is, it inhibits loss of electrons. He continued this line of research at the Lister Institute and also started an investigation of the active ingredients of the *Cannabis sativa* plant (marijuana) that showed that cannabinol, the major product isolated from the plant resin, was pharmacologically inactive.

In March of 1938, Todd and his wife made a long visit to the United States to investigate the offer of a position at California Institute of Technology. On returning to England with the idea that he would move to California, Todd was offered a professorship at Manchester which he accepted, becoming Sir Samuel Hall Professor of Chemistry and director of the chemical laboratories of the University of Manchester. At Manchester, Todd was able to continue his research with little interruption. During his first year there, he finished the work on vitamin E with the total synthesis of α-tocopherol and its analogs. Attempts to isolate and identify the active ingredients in cannabis resin failed because the separation procedures available at the time were inadequate; however, Todd's synthesis of cannabinol involved an intermediate, tetrahydrocannabinol (THC), that had an effect much like that of hashish on rabbits and suggested to him that the effects of hashish were due to one of the isomeric tetrahydrocannabinols. This view was later proven correct, but by others, because the outbreak of World War II forced Todd to abandon this line of research for work more directly related to the war.

As a member, and then chair, of the Chemical Committee, which was responsible for developing and producing chemical warfare agents, Todd developed an efficient method of producing diphenylamine chloroarsine (a sneeze gas), and designed a pilot plant for producing nitrogen mustards (blistering agents). He also had a group working on penicillin research and another trying to isolate and identify the "hatching factor" of the potato eelworm, a parasite that attacks potatoes.

Late in 1943 Todd was offered the chair in biochemistry at Cambridge University, which he refused. Shortly thereafter he was offered the chair in organic chemistry, which he accepted, choosing to affiliate with Christ's College. From 1963 to 1978, he served as master of the college. As professor of organic chemistry at Cambridge, Todd reorganized and revitalized the department and oversaw the modernization of the laboratories (they were still lighted by gas in 1944) and, eventually, the construction of a new laboratory building.

Wins Nobel Prize for Work on Nucleotides

Before the war, his interest in vitamins and their mode of action had led Todd to start work on nucleosides and nucleotides. Nucleosides are compounds made up of a sugar (ribose or deoxyribose) linked to one of four heterocyclic (that is, containing rings with more than one kind of atom) nitrogen compounds derived either from purine (adenine and guanine) or pyrimidine (uracil and cytosine). When a phosphate group is attached to the sugar portion of the molecule, a nucleoside becomes a nucleotide. The nucleic acids (DNA and RNA), found in cell nuclei as constituents of the chromosomes, are chains of nucleotides. While still at Manchester, Todd had worked out techniques for synthesizing nucleosides and then attaching the phosphate group to them (a process called phosphorylating) to form nucleotides; later, at Cambridge, he worked out the structures of the nucleotides obtained by the degradation of nucleic acid and synthesized them. This information was a necessary prerequisite to **James Watson** and **Francis Crick**'s formulation of the double-helix structure of DNA two years later.

Todd had found the nucleoside adenosine in some coenzymes, relatively small molecules that combine with a protein to form an enzyme, which can act as a catalyst for a particular biochemical process. He knew from his work with the B vitamins that B_1(thiamine), B_2 (riboflavin) and B_3 (niacin) were essential components of coenzymes involved in respiration and oxygen utilization. By 1949 he had succeeded in synthesizing adenosine—a triumph in itself—and had gone on to synthesize adenosine di- and triphosphate (ADP and ATP). These compounds are nucleotides responsible for energy production and energy storage in muscles and in plants. In 1952, he established the structure of flavin adenine dinucleotide (FAD), a coenzyme involved in breaking down carbohydrates so that they can be oxidized, releasing energy for an organism to use. For his pioneering work on nucleotides and nucleotide enzymes, Todd was awarded the 1957 Nobel Prize in chemistry.

Todd collaborated with **Dorothy Crowfoot Hodgkin** in determining the structure of vitamin B_{12}, the antipernicious anemia factor, which is necessary for the formation of red blood cells. Todd's chemical studies of the degradation products of B_{12} were crucial to Hodgkin's X-ray determination of the structure in 1955.

Another major field of research at Cambridge was the chemistry of the pigments in aphids. While at Oxford and working on the coloring matter from some fungi, Todd observed that although the pigments from fungi and from higher plants were all anthraquinone derivatives, the pattern of substitution around the anthraquinone ring differed in the two cases. Pigment from two different insects seemed to be of the fungal pattern and Todd wondered if these were derived from the insect or from symbiotic fungi they contained. At Cambridge he isolated several pigments from different kinds of aphids and found that they were complex quinones unrelated to anthra-

quinone. It was found, however, that they are probably the products of symbiotic fungi in the aphid.

A Senior Scientist and Government Advisor

In 1952 Todd became chairman of the advisory council on scientific policy to the British government, a post he held until 1964. He was knighted in 1954 by Queen Elizabeth for distinguished service to the government. Named Baron Todd of Trumpington in 1962, he was made a member of the Order of Merit in 1977. In 1955 he became a foreign associate of the United States' National Academy of Sciences. He has traveled extensively and been a visiting professor at the University of Sydney (Australia), the California Institute of Technology, the Massachusetts Institute of Technology, the University of Chicago, and Notre Dame University.

A Fellow of the Royal Society since 1942, Todd served as its president from 1975 to 1980. He increased the role of the society in advising the government on the scientific aspects of policy and strengthened its international relations. Extracts from his five anniversary addresses to the society dealing with these concerns are given as appendices to his autobiography. In the forward to his autobiography, Todd reports that in preparing biographical sketches of a number of members of the Royal Society he was struck by the lack of information available about their lives and careers and that this, in part, led him to write *A Time to Remember*.

SELECTED WRITINGS BY TODD:

Books

A Time to Remember: The Autobiography of a Chemist, Cambridge University Press, 1983.

Periodicals

"Chemistry of Nucleotides," *Proceedings of the Royal Society,* Volume A227, 1954, pp. 70–82.
"Chemical Structure of Nucleic Acids," *Proceedings of the National Academy of Sciences,* Volume 40, 1954, pp. 748–755.
(With Dorothy Crowfoot Hodgkin and A. W. Johnson) "The Structure of Vitamin B_{12}," *Chemical Society Special Publication,* Number 3, 1955, pp. 109–123.

SOURCES:

Books

Current Biography, H. W. Wilson, 1958, pp. 437–439.

Nobel Lectures Including Presentation Speeches and Laureate's Biographies—Chemistry: 1942–1962, Elsevier, 1964, pp. 519–538.

—Sketch by R. F. Trimble

Clyde W. Tombaugh
1906-

American astronomer

Clyde W. Tombaugh, an astronomer and master telescope maker, spent much of his career performing a painstaking photographic survey of the heavens from Lowell Observatory in Flagstaff, Arizona. This led to the discovery of Pluto (1930), the ninth planet in the solar system. Although Tombaugh is best known for this early triumph, he went on to make other contributions, including his work on the geography of Mars and studies of the distribution of galaxies. Tombaugh also made valuable refinements to missile-tracking technology during a nine-year stint at the U.S. Army's White Sands Proving Grounds in New Mexico.

Clyde William Tombaugh, the eldest of six children, was born on February 4, 1906, to Muron Tombaugh, a farmer, and Adella Chritton Tombaugh. He spent most of his childhood on a farm near Streator, Illinois. In 1922 the family relocated to a farm in western Kansas. Tombaugh glimpsed his first telescopic view of the heavens through his uncle Leon's three-inch refractor, a kind of telescope that uses a lens to gather faint light from stars and planets. In 1925, inspired by an article in *Popular Astronomy,* Tombaugh bought materials to grind an eight-inch light-collecting mirror for a reflecting telescope. He ground that first mirror by hand, using a fence post on the farm as a grinding stand.

The finished instrument, a seven-foot-long, rectangular wooden box, was equipped with wooden setting circles for aligning it to objects of interest in the sky. Tombaugh had not ground the mirror very accurately, and thus the telescope was unsuitable for the planetary observing he had in mind. However, it launched a lifetime of building, improving, and maintaining telescopes, tasks at which Tombaugh excelled. Tombaugh biographer and amateur astronomer David H. Levy estimated that Tombaugh ground some thirty-six telescope mirrors and lenses in his career. He continued to use a few of his early telescopes for decades after he first constructed them

(for example, his nine-inch reflector, whose mechanical mounting included parts from a 1910 Buick).

Hired to Search for Ninth Planet

Tombaugh's nine-inch reflector, which he completed in 1928, led to a career as a professional observer as well as to sharper views of the planets and stars. After a 1928 hailstorm wiped out the Tombaughs' wheat crop and foiled Clyde's plans for college, the young observer turned his new telescope to Jupiter and Mars. Subsequently, he sent his best drawings of these planets to Lowell Observatory, which had been founded in the late nineteenth century by famed Mars watcher Percival Lowell.

Hoping only for constructive criticism of his drawings, Tombaugh instead received a job offer from the astronomers at Lowell. He accepted, and in January 1929 began his work on the search for the predicted ninth planet beyond the orbit of Neptune. Working full time as a professional observer (although lacking any formal education in astronomy), Tombaugh used Lowell's thirteen-inch telescope to systematically photograph the sky. He then used a special instrument, called a blink comparator, to examine the plates for telltale signs of moving bodies beyond the orbit of Earth. A blink comparator, or blink microscope, rapidly alternates—up to ten times per second—two photographic images, taken at different times, of the same field or area of the sky. Seen through a magnifying lens, moving bodies will appear to jump back and forth or "blink" as the images are switched.

Using his knowledge of orbital mechanics and his sharp observer's eye, Tombaugh was able to discern asteroids and comets from possible planets; a third "check" plate was then taken to confirm or rule out the existence of these suspected planets. On February 18, 1930, after ten months of concentrated, painstaking work, Tombaugh zeroed in on Pluto, fulfilling a search begun by Percival Lowell in 1905. The discovery of Pluto secured the twenty-four-year-old Tombaugh's reputation and his place in the history of astronomy, and he remained with the survey until 1943.

After his discovery, Tombaugh took some time off to obtain his formal education in astronomy. He left for the University of Kansas in the fall of 1932, returning to Lowell each summer to resume his observing duties. At college, he met Patricia Irene Edson, a philosophy major. They married in 1934, and subsequently had two children, Alden and Annette. Tombaugh paused only once more for formal education in science, taking his master's degree in 1938–39 at the University of Kansas. For his thesis work, he restored the university's twenty-seven-inch reflecting telescope to full health and studied its observing capabilities.

In 1943 Tombaugh taught physics at Arizona State Teachers College in Flagstaff; that same year, the U.S. Navy asked him to teach navigation, also at Arizona State. In what little spare time remained, Tombaugh struggled to continue the planet survey. The following year, he taught astronomy and the history of astronomy at the University of California in Los Angeles. Tombaugh's stint on the planet survey ceased abruptly in 1946. Citing financial constraints, observatory director **Vesto M. Slipher** asked Tombaugh to seek other employment.

Tombaugh's contribution to the "planetary patrol" at Lowell proved enormous. From 1929 to 1945, he cataloged many thousands of celestial objects, including 29,548 galaxies, 3,969 asteroids (775 of them previously unreported), two previously undiscovered comets, one nova, and, of course, the planet Pluto. However, as Tombaugh pointed out to biographer David Levy, tiny Pluto cast a long and sometimes burdensome shadow over the rest of his career, obscuring subsequent astronomical work. For instance, in 1937 Tombaugh discovered a dense cluster of 1,800 galaxies, which he called the "Great Perseus-Andromeda Stratum of Extra-Galactic Nebula." This suggested to Tombaugh that the distribution of galaxies in the universe was more patchy and irregular than some astronomers believed at the time.

Tombaugh was also an accomplished observer of Mars. He predicted in 1950 that the red planet, being so close to the asteroid belt, would have impact craters like those on the moon. These craters are not easily visible from Earth because Mars always shows its face to astronomers fully or nearly fully lighted, masking the craters' fine lines. Images of the Martian surface captured in the 1960s by the Mariner IV space probe proved Tombaugh's prediction to be correct.

In 1946 Tombaugh began a relatively brief career as a civilian employee of the U.S. Army, working as an optical physicist and astronomer at White Sands Proving Grounds near Las Cruces, New Mexico, where the army was developing launching facilities for captured German V–2 missiles. Tombaugh witnessed fifty launchings of the forty-six-foot rockets and documented their performance in flight using a variety of tracking telescopes. Armed with his observing skills and intimate knowledge of telescope optics, Tombaugh greatly increased the quality of missile tracking at White Sands, host to a number of important postwar missile-development programs.

Tombaugh resumed serious planetary observing in 1955, when he accepted a teaching and research position at New Mexico State University in Las Cruces. There he taught astronomy, led planetary observation programs, and participated in the care and construction of new telescopes. From 1953 to 1958, Tombaugh directed a major search for small, as-yet-undetected objects near the Earth—either asteroids or tiny natural satellites—that might pose a threat to future spacecraft. He and colleagues developed sensitive telescopic tracking equipment and used it to scan the skies from a high-altitude site in Quito, Ecuador. The survey turned up no evidence of hazardous objects near the Earth, and Tombaugh issued a closing report on the program the year after the Soviet Union launched Sputnik (1957), the first artificial satellite.

Upon his retirement in 1973, Tombaugh maintained his links to New Mexico State University, often attending lunches and colloquia in the astronomy department that he helped to found. He also remained active in the local astronomical society and continued to observe with his cherished homemade telescopes. Indeed, asked by the Smithsonian Institution in Washington, D.C., to relinquish his nine-inch reflector to its historical collections, Tombaugh refused, explaining to *Smithsonian* magazine, "I'm not through using it yet!"

SELECTED WRITINGS BY TOMBAUGH:

Books

(With Patrick Moore) *Out of Darkness: The Planet Pluto,* Stackpole Books, 1980.

Periodicals

"Plates, Pluto, and Planet X," *Sky & Telescope,* April, 1991, pp. 360–361.

SOURCES:

Books

Levy, David H., *Clyde Tombaugh: Discoverer of Planet Pluto,* University of Arizona Press, 1991.

Periodicals

Levy, David H., "Clyde Tombaugh: Planetary Observer and Telescope Maker," *Sky & Telescope,* January, 1987, pp. 88–89.

Trefil, James, "Phenomena, Comment and Notes," *Smithsonian,* May, 1991, pp. 32–36.

—Sketch by Daniel Pendick

Sin-Itiro Tomonaga
1906-1979
Japanese physicist

S in-Itiro Tomonaga was a pioneer in the field of quantum electrodynamics, a broad theory that uses principles from quantum mechanics and special relativity to explain a wide variety of physical phenomena. He developed a theory about subatomic particles that was consistent with the theory of relativity about the same time that **Richard P. Feynman** and **Julian Schwinger** independently reached similar solutions. The three were jointly awarded the 1965 Nobel Prize in physics for their efforts in quantum theory.

Sin-Itiro (also transliterated as Sin-Ichiro) Tomonaga was born in Tokyo on March 31, 1906, to Sanjuro and Hide Tomonaga. When Sin-Itiro was a child, his family moved to Kyoto, where his father had been appointed professor of philosophy at the Kyoto Imperial University. Sin-Itiro enrolled at Kyoto's prestigious Third High School where he was a classmate of **Hideki Yukawa**, later to become Japan's first Nobel Prize winner (in the field of physics) in 1949. After graduation, Tomonaga and Yukawa both went on to Kyoto Imperial University, where both majored in physics and earned their bachelor's degrees in 1929. The two then stayed on as research assistants to Kajuro Tamaki.

In 1932, Tomonaga and Yukawa finally went their separate ways, with Tomonaga accepting a position as research assistant to Yoshio Nishina at the Institute of Physical and Chemical Research in Tokyo. After five years in this post, Tomonaga traveled to the University of Leipzig where he studied under physicist Werner Heisenberg. While at Leipzig, Tomonaga wrote a paper on the atomic nucleus that earned him a Ph.D. from Kyoto Imperial upon his return to Japan in 1939. In 1941 Tomonaga became professor of physics at Tokyo's Bunrika University (now Tokyo University of Education), a post he held until 1956, when he became president of the university. After leaving Tokyo University in 1962, Tomonaga served as president of the Science Council of Japan and director of the Institute for Optical Research.

Attacks Problems of Quantum Electrodynamics

The topic that dominated Tomonaga's research throughout most of his life was quantum electrodynamics (QED). QED arose during the 1920s when the successes of quantum theory and relativity made it apparent that classical laws of physics were inadequate to explain the behavior of elementary particles. A number of theorists attempted to develop new

Sin-Itiro Tomonaga

equations that would take into consideration both quantum mechanics and relativity theory to explain the behavior of particles and their interaction with energy.

By the late 1920s, impressive progress had been made in dealing with this problem, especially as a result of the work of the English physicist **Paul Dirac**. Dirac's theory successfully predicted the qualitative properties of atomic particles and the way they interacted with energy. Over time, however, it became apparent that Dirac's theory was quantitatively inadequate. Among the most serious problems of the Dirac theory was the prediction that, under certain circumstances, particles would have infinite mass and infinite charge. The physical absurdity of these predictions, commonly known as "divergence difficulties," deeply troubled physicists, many of whom decided that a totally knew approach to QED would be needed.

Success with Quantum Electrodynamics Brings Nobel Prize

Tomonaga, however, took another view. He was convinced that techniques could be found that would allow the retention of Dirac's fundamental approach while resolving the "divergence difficulties" inherent within it. The mathematical technique he used, called renormalization, worked. Tomonaga was eventually able to demonstrate that infinite mass and charge are indeed a fundamental part of the Dirac theory, but that they apply to situations that would never be encountered in the real world.

Tomonaga's fundamental paper on QED was published in Japan in 1943. Because of the war, however, news and translation of the paper did not reach the rest of the world until 1947. At about the same time, similar papers dealing with QED written by Schwinger at Harvard and Feynman at the California Institute of Technology were also being published. When the 1965 Nobel Prize for physics was announced, therefore, it was divided among the three physicists for the independent solutions of the "divergence difficulties" problem.

Tomonaga's prize-winning research had been carried out at Tokyo's Bunrika University of Science and Literature, where he had been appointed professor of physics in 1941. He remained in this post, after the university had been incorporated into the Tokyo University of Education, until 1949. He then accepted an invitation to become a visiting scholar the Institute for Advanced Studies at Princeton, New Jersey. He returned to Tokyo in 1951 to become head of the Institute for Scientific Research. Four years later, he was instrumental in the founding of the Institute for Nuclear Studies at the University of Tokyo and then, in 1956, became president of the university. Upon his retirement in 1962, Tomonaga accepted an offer to become president of the Science Council of Japan and director of the Institute for Optical Research, posts he held until 1969.

Tomonaga was married in 1940 to Ryoko Sekiguchi, daughter of the director of the Tokyo Metropolitan Observatory. They had two sons, Atsushi and Makoto, and a daughter, Shigeko. In addition to the Nobel Prize, Tomonaga was awarded the Japan Academy Prize in 1948, the Order of Culture of Japan in 1952, and the Lomonosov Medal of the Soviet Academy of Sciences in 1964. Tomonaga died in Tokyo on July 8, 1979.

SELECTED WRITINGS BY TOMONAGA:

Books

Quantum Mechanics, 2 volumes, Misuzu Publishing Company, 1949.
Scientific Papers of Tomonaga, 2 volumes, Misuzu Shobo Publishing Company, 1971–76.

SOURCES:

Books

McGraw-Hill Modern Scientists and Engineers, Volume 3, McGraw-Hill, 1980, pp. 224–225.

Wasson, Tyler, editor, *Nobel Prize Winners,* H. W. Wilson, 1987, pp. 1068–1071.
Williams, Trevor, editor, *A Biographical Dictionary of Scientists,* Wiley, 1974, pp. 610–611.

Periodicals

Dyson, Freeman J., "Tomonaga, Schwinger, and Feynman Awarded Nobel Prize for Physics," *Science,* October 29, 1965, pp. 588–589.

—*Sketch by David E. Newton*

Susumu Tonegawa
1939-
Japanese molecular biologist

In 1987, Susumu Tonegawa became the first Japanese recipient of the Nobel Prize in physiology and medicine for his study of the immune system and his subsequent discovery of the causes of antibody diversity—the ability of an antibody to resist infection from millions of different viruses and bacteria. Tonegawa provided direct evidence that a gene's ability to encode antibody proteins is produced from separate, chain-like segments of DNA (deoxyribonucleic acid) molecules which mutate to code for different antibodies. Since 1981, Tonegawa has worked at the Massachusetts Institute of Technology (MIT), and was honored as Howard Hughes Medical Institute Investigator in 1988.

Tonegawa was born in Nagoya, Japan, on September 5, 1939, the second of four children born to Tsutomu Tonegawa and the former Miyoko Masuko. Tonegawa's father was an engineer whose work required him to move frequently from town to town across the country. As a result, Tonegawa and his older brother were sent to Tokyo to live with an uncle. In Tokyo, the boys attended the prestigious Hibiya High School, where Tonegawa eventually developed an interest in chemistry. After graduation, he entered the University of Kyoto in 1959 to pursue a degree in chemistry. He earned his degree in 1963 and began graduate studies in a then-emerging branch of biology—molecular biology—which is the study of molecules that perform biological operations.

While he was still a student at Kyoto, Tonegawa learned about the field of molecular biology and decided that it was an area in which he wanted to specialize. In 1953, **James Watson** and **Francis Crick** had discovered the mechanism by which genetic information is stored in molecules. That discovery

Susumu Tonegawa

provided an exciting new way to understand biological phenomena in terms of atomic and molecular structure. Research in this promising new field developed very rapidly. In 1963, Tonegawa applied to the University of California at San Diego and began his graduate study in the Department of Biology under Masaki Hayashi. Tonegawa's research in genetic transcription in bacteriophages resulted in three scientific papers, published between 1966 and 1970 with Hayashi, and a Ph.D. in biology by 1968.

For his postdoctoral work, Tonegawa chose to stay in San Diego, working first with Hayashi from September, 1968, to April, 1969, and then moving to the Salk Institute in nearby La Jolla from May, 1969, to December, 1970. At the Salk Institute, Tonegawa studied genetic transcription in simian virus 40 (SV40), an important virus in genetic engineering, with **Renato Dulbecco**, who would go on to win a Nobel Prize in 1975.

Joins Institute of Immunology

In the fall of 1970, Tonegawa was confronted with a dilemma. His United States immigration visa was due to expire at the end of the year, and he had to decide where he was going to continue his studies. At that time, Tonegawa received a letter from Dulbecco notifying him of an opening for a molecular biologist at the Institute of Immunology in Basel, Switzerland. Tonegawa had no formal training in immunology, but applied for the position, and was accepted. By

February, 1971, Tonegawa found himself "surrounded by immunologists," as he was to point out in his Nobel Prize lecture many years later as cited in *Bioscience Reports*. It was a challenging position, and he soon became deeply involved in the research for which he was to win the Nobel Prize.

Biologists had long known that an individual vertebrate has the ability to generate millions of different antibodies before it ever encounters an antigen that stimulates a specific defense antibody. Biologists speculated on the mechanism by which the organism's immune system adapts with two theories. According to the first, named the "germ line" theory, all the genes needed to make an antibody are part of the genetic code. The problem was that it seemed impossible for a single gene to carry that much information. A second theory, "somatic mutation," suggested that the antibody genes mutate readily, rearranging themselves in a variety of ways to code for different antibodies. According to this hypothesis, a relatively small number of genes would be able to generate a very large number of variants.

Solves the Antibody Diversity Puzzle

After half a decade of research, Tonegawa was able to report the first firm evidence on the antibody diversity debate. With Nobumichi Hozumi, a colleague, Tonegawa was able to prove that the somatic mutation theory was correct. The biologists demonstrated that the parts of a DNA molecule can rearrange themselves in many different ways—just as the fifty-two cards in a deck can be shuffled and rearranged—in response to an attack by a hostile organism. The antibody which is thus selectively produced then attacks the invader. As explained in a comment in *Nobel Prize Winners Supplement,* "DNA recombination and mutation could generate perhaps 10 billion different kinds of antibodies, more than enough to solve the diversity problem."

Among Tonegawa's contributions to molecular biology is the discovery, with Hozumi, that the DNA segments which undergo rearrangement are separated by seemingly inactive (noncoding) strands of DNA, now known as introns. Additionally, Tonegawa's research into the immune system resulted in the breakthrough discovery of a gene control element "enhancer" in the intron. Jean L. Marx, writing in *Science,* observed that Tonegawa's work has far-reaching significance: "One unexpected consequence of the antibody gene research was new information about the possible causes of cancer, especially the blood cancers known as lymphomas and leukemias."

Tonegawa stayed at Basel until 1981 when he was offered a position as professor of biology in the Center for Cancer Research and Department of Biology at MIT. In 1988, he was made Howard Hughes Medical Institute Investigator. In addition to the Nobel Prize in 1987, Tonegawa has received numerous honors and awards, including the Genetics Grand Prize of the Japanese Genetics Promotions Foundation in 1981, the V. D. Mattia Award of the Roche Institute of Molecular Biology in 1983, the Robert Koch Prize in 1986, the Albert and Mary Lasker Award for Basic Research in 1987, the Rabbi Shai Shacknai Memorial Prize in Immunology and Cancer Research in 1989, and Brazil's Order of the Southern Cross in 1991. In 1992, Tonegawa and his colleagues at MIT identified, for the first time, a specific gene which has an effect on the ability to learn. The *New York Times* reported that this research is "the first step toward discovering the entire repertoire of genes that affect brain function." Tonegawa was married to the former Mayumi Yoshinari on September 28, 1985. The couple has three children.

SELECTED WRITINGS BY TONEGAWA:

Periodicals

(With C. Steinberg, S. Dube, and A. Bernardini) "Evidence for Somatic Generation of Antibody Diversity," *Proceedings of the National Academy of Sciences, USA,* 1974, pp. 4027–31.

(With Steinberg) "Too Many Chains—Too Few Genes," *The Generation of Antibody Diversity: A New Look,* edited by A. Cunningham, Academic Press, 1976, pp. 175–82.

(With Richard Maki, John Kearney, and Christopher Paige) "Immunoglobulin Gene Rearrangement in Immature B Cells," *Science,* Volume 209, 1980, pp. 1366–69.

"The Molecules of the Immune System," *Scientific American,* October, 1985, pp. 122–31.

"Somatic Generation of Immune Diversity," *Bioscience Reports,* Volume 8, November 1, 1988, pp. 3–26.

SOURCES:

Books

McGuire, Paula, editor, *Nobel Prize Winners Supplement 1987–1991,* Wilson, 1992, pp. 136–139.

Periodicals

Marx, Jean L., "Antibody Research Garners Nobel Prize," *Science,* October 23, 1987, pp. 484–85.

New York Times, July 14, 1992, p. C3.

—*Sketch by David E. Newton*

Charles H. Townes
1915-
American physicist

Charles H. Townes was awarded a share of the 1964 Nobel Prize in physics for his discovery in 1951 of the maser, a device that can amplify microwaves for practical applications. About six years later, Townes speculated on the possibility of building a maser-like instrument using solid crystals instead of gases. A device of this kind—the laser—was actually constructed two years afterwards by **Theodore Maiman**.

Charles Hard Townes was born in Greenville, South Carolina, on July 28, 1915. His father was Henry Keith Townes, an attorney, and his mother was the former Ellen Sumter Hard. Townes grew up in an intellectually stimulating environment in which both parents had an avid interest in natural history. He later told Shirley Thomas in a sketch for the book *Men of Space* that "there was always an inclination toward science" in his family. He was convinced that had the opportunity been available, his father "would have become a very excellent scientist."

Townes's genius was obvious early on. His parents allowed him to skip seventh grade, and by age 16 he was ready to enter Furman University in his hometown of Greenville. Although he planned to major in science, he also took a full schedule of language classes. As a result, he was able to graduate in 1935 with a B.S. in physics and a B.A. in modern languages. He continued his mastery of French, German, Italian, Russian, and Spanish throughout his life. In addition to his demanding class work at Furman, Townes was also curator of the college museum and a member of the band, glee club, swimming team, and newspaper staff.

Townes entered Duke University in the fall of 1935 to work on his master's degree. In addition to his thesis research on van der Graaf generators, he continued his study of French, Italian, and Russian. Having completed his work at Duke (various biographers credit him with either an M.A. or an M.S., awarded in either 1936 or 1937), Townes headed for the California Institute of Technology (Cal Tech) in Pasadena, California. There he completed his doctoral research on the spin of the carbon-13 nucleus in 1939 and was awarded his Ph.D.

War Research Leads to Interest in Microwaves

An offer from Bell Laboratories to pay Townes a salary of $3,016 a year "astonished" him, according to Mary Ann Harrell in *Those Inventive Americans.*

He could scarcely believe that a career in physics would be "so highly paid," and he accepted the Bell offer quickly. Townes found an apartment in New York City and began to take full advantage of the city's cultural opportunities. He took evening classes at the Julliard School of Music and, according to Harrell, "changed apartments every three months to explore the city thoroughly."

For most of his time at Bell, Townes worked on projects related to national defense. In particular, he was involved in the development of radar systems. At one point he warned the army against using a three-centimeter band radar wave detection system because he knew that water molecules absorb in this range and that the system would, therefore, be ineffective. Having ignored this advice, the Army built three-centimeter radar devices anyway, only to find that they would not work.

As the pressures of war research receded, Townes turned his attention to a problem many scientists and engineers were thinking about: finding a way to amplify microwaves so that they could be used in practical applications, as were radio and radar waves. **Albert Einstein** had outlined a theoretical method for accomplishing this goal in 1917. He suggested using individual atoms as resonators rather than using macroscopic-sized objects. The problem was that, by 1950, no one had found a way to build a working device based on Einstein's principle.

Townes's breakthrough in this area came while he was sitting on a park bench in Washington D.C.'s Franklin Square in 1951, waiting for a restaurant to open so that he could have breakfast. As Harrell tells the story, "six years of work suddenly blossomed into insight: a way to make ammonia molecules amplify . . . microwaves by the process Einstein had outlined." In classic storybook fashion, Townes outlined his ideas on the back of an old envelope he found in his pocket.

Producing a device that actually worked according to his theory, however, was no simple matter. Townes worked with two colleagues, James P. Gordon and H. J. Zeiger, for more than two years before they had success. Finally, in late 1953, the three produced a successful model of Townes's Franklin Square idea, a device that amplified an incoming microwave beam while maintaining the signal wave's phase. They gave to their invention the name *maser* (for microwave amplification by stimulated emission of radiation). For his discovery of the maser, Townes was awarded a share of the 1964 Nobel Prize in physics. He shared that prize with two Russian scientists, **N. G. Basov** and **Aleksandr Prokhorov**, who had independently and somewhat earlier come up with a similar method for using the Einstein principle to build a maser-like device, which they called a "molecular generator."

Outlines Laser Theory

By the time Townes announced the first working maser in 1954, he had already been at Columbia University for six years, having been appointed full professor there in 1954. He continued to teach and do research at Columbia until 1961, when he resigned to become professor of physics and provost at the Massachusetts Institute of Technology (MIT). While still at Columbia, he developed a theory with his brother-in-law **Arthur L. Schawlow** that described a method by which a maser-like device could be built that would operate with visible light instead of microwaves. Theodore Maiman's laser provided proof of Townes and Schawlow's theory some two years later.

In 1966 Townes left MIT to become University Professor of Physics at the University of California at Berkeley, where he remained until his retirement in 1986. Townes was married on May 4, 1941, to the former Francis H. Brown, and they raised four children. Townes has received many honors and awards in addition to his 1964 Nobel Prize in physics. These include the Liebmann Memorial Prize of the Institute of Radio Engineers, the Sarnoff Award of the Institute of Electrical Engineers, the Comstock Medal of the National Academy of Sciences, the Ballantine Medal of the Franklin Institute, the Distinguished Public Service Medal of the National Aeronautics and Space Administration, and the National Medal of Science from the National Science Foundation.

SELECTED WRITINGS BY TOWNES:

Books

(With A. L. Schawlow) *Microwave Spectroscopy,* McGraw-Hill, 1955.
(Editor) *Quantum Electronic: A Symposium,* Columbia University Press, 1960.

Periodicals

(With J. P. Gordon and H. J. Zeiger) "Molecular Microwave Oscillator and New Hyperfine Structure in the Microwave Spectrum of NH_3XN," *Physical Review,* July 1, 1954, pp. 282–84.

SOURCES:

Books

Current Biography 1963, H. W. Wilson, 1963, pp. 423–425.

Harrell, Mary Ann, in *Those Inventive Americans,*
National Geographic Society, 1971, pp.
218–227.
McGraw-Hill Modern Scientists and Engineers,
Volume 10, McGraw-Hill, 1980, pp. 227–228.
Thomas, Shirley, *Men of Space,* Volume 5, Chilton Books, 1962, pp. 221–251.
Weber, Robert L., *Pioneers of Science: Nobel Prize Winners in Physics,* American Institute of
Physics, 1980, pp. 195–196.

Periodicals

Gordon, J. P., "Research on Maser-Laser Principle Wins Nobel Prize in Physics," *Science,*
November 13, 1964, pp. 897–899.

—*Sketch by David E. Newton*

Mildred Trotter
1899-1991
American anatomist

Mildred Trotter was an anatomist and physical anthropologist whose pioneering bone studies contributed to a wide range of disciplines, including medicine, forensics, engineering, and aeronautics. "She has been responsible for the largest single increase in our knowledge of bone, both as a tissue and as the primary locus of the mineral mass of the human body," observed Dr. Stanley M. Garn, professor of nutrition at the University of Michigan. Her method for using the length of certain bones to estimate the height of their owners in life has been a primary tool of forensic experts and physical anthropologists since its formulation in 1952. Also, her studies of human hair have disproved many popular myths and contributed to the understanding of hypertrichosis, or excessive hair growth.

Trotter was born on February 3, 1899, to farmers of German and Irish extraction. James R. and Jennie (nee Zimmerley) Trotter also produced two other daughters, Sarah Isabella and Jeannette Rebecca, and a son, Robert James. Trotter's parents were active Presbyterians and Democrats, and, in addition to farming, her father served for a time as community school director. Trotter attended grammar school in a one-room facility, graduating in 1913. She completed high school in nearby Beaver, Pennsylvania, where, as her hometown paper would report in a career retrospective, the principal objected to her choice of geometry over home economics as a subject for study.

Trotter enrolled at Mt. Holyoke College where she majored in zoology. While there she found role models in female professors and the zoology department head. In an interview late in life, Trotter recalled that she "never even thought, let alone worried, about being a woman in science" as a result of their influence. Upon graduating, Trotter rejected a better paying job as a high school biology teacher to work as a research assistant to Dr. C. H. Danforth, an associate professor of anatomy at Washington University in St. Louis, Missouri. Danforth had received funding to study hypertrichosis from an anonymous donor whose wife and daughters suffered from excessive facial hair. Trotter's work on the subject earned her credit toward a masters degree in anatomy, which she received in 1921. After the donor pledged more funds, she continued her study of hair, using it as the basis of her doctoral thesis in 1924. As a result of her analysis, Trotter determined that hair follicles keep to fixed patterns of growth, resting, and shedding; she also discovered that women have as much facial hair as men. In addition she disproved such common myths as the belief that sun exposure cures baldness or that shaving thickens hair. Trotter's collected papers on hair were published serially, then in book form by the American Medical Association in 1925 under Danforth's name.

Farmer's Daughter Turns "Bone Detective"

Upon completing her studies, Trotter was made an instructor at Washington University. Not long afterwards, she accepted a National Research Council Fellowship to study physical anthropology at Oxford for the year 1926. Although she had planned to continue her research on hair, she was asked instead to study bones, specifically museum specimens from ancient Egypt and Roman era Britain. During the course of her stay at Oxford, Trotter discovered that she "liked studying skeletons better than studying hair." When she received yet another fellowship, the head of Washington's anatomy department offered her a promotion to assistant professor, which she accepted over the grant. Her career stalled, however, despite a steadily increasing workload, and she did not receive another promotion until sixteen years later when she straightforwardly asked the department chair to explain why she had been passed over. He responded by convening a review committee, and in 1946 Trotter became the first woman to attain full professorship at Washington University's Medical School. In all, Trotter spent over fifty-five years on the university's staff, during which time she published numerous papers on the human skeleton, including studies of growth cycles, sexual and racial differences, and changes in mineral mass and density occurring with age.

In 1948 Trotter, growing restless in her position at the university, took an unpaid sabbatical to volunteer as director of the Central Identification Laboratory at Schofield Barracks, Oahu, Hawaii. For the next fourteen months she and her team identified the skeletal remains of war dead found in the Pacific theater. During this time she also secured permission from the U.S. Army to conduct allometric studies using the long limb bones of identified dead, one of the first times that war casualties were used for scientific research. From these studies Trotter then devised a formula for estimating the stature of a person based upon the relative length of the long bones. Published in 1952, her update of nineteenth-century French stature estimation tables was described in a 1989 *Journal of Forensic Sciences* article as "a landmark study in physical anthropology."

Trotter returned to Washington University in 1949. Soon after, the new department chair eliminated the adjective "gross" from her title Professor of Anatomy—an important distinction to Trotter who had fought to be accepted as an equal in a field dominated by microscopic research. During the 1950s and 1960s Trotter began attracting national and international attention for her work. In 1955 she was asked to serve as president of the American Association of Physical Anthropologists, an organization she helped found in 1930. A year later she became the first female recipient of the Wenner-Gren Foundation's Viking Fund Medal. She was asked by the editors of *Encyclopedia Britannica* to contribute entries on the skin and exoskeleton for their 1953 and 1956 editions. In addition she gathered material for reference books in her field, such as a lab guide, an anatomical atlas, and a dictionary of Latin nomenclature. Trotter also served as a consultant to the Rockefeller Foundation, lecturing in London and Washington, D.C., and as a visiting professor to Uganda's Makerere University College.

Along with her academic responsibilities, Trotter also sat on the St. Louis Anatomical Board and Missouri State Anatomical Board, serving as president of the latter from 1955 to 1957. St. Louis detectives regularly consulted with Trotter on missing persons and "John Doe" cases as well as on partial, sometimes nearly obliterated, physical evidence. For example, when police recovered a handful of blackened bones from a furnace, Trotter identified them as being from a human infant, not a small animal as originally suspected. She was also instrumental in passing legislation that enabled Missourians to donate their bodies to universities for medical research. When asked in 1980 about her practical approach to such morbid subjects, Trotter observed, "the attitude of our culture toward death is silly. We all know we have to die."

Coaches Nobel Laureates

Trotter's work as an instructor proved as important as her research. During her forty-one year career as a full-time professor at Washington University, Trotter's students totaled into the thousands. Hundreds went on to careers as medical school faculty, prepared by her rigorous coursework. As Dr. John C. Herweg recalled in 1975, "we learned because we admired and respected her and because, to an extent, we feared her. After we had passed Gross Anatomy, we grew to love her as a friend." Her belief that students should learn not from books but from observing nature guided Trotter's instruction. "Learning to observe is one of the chief benefits of studying anatomy," she asserted during an interview in 1975. Two of Trotter's students, **Earl Sutherland** and **Daniel Nathans**, went on to win Nobel Prizes in medicine.

Upon her retirement in 1967, Trotter was named professor emeritus and lecturer in anatomy and neurobiology. She continued to publish scientific papers, and eight years later she became the first female faculty member to be honored by the medical school with a lectureship in her name. Trotter, who never married, spent leisure time in later years knitting, gardening, or auditing classes at the university until she suffered a disabling stroke. Upon her death on August 23, 1991, her body was donated to the Washington University School of Medicine.

SELECTED WRITINGS BY TROTTER:

Books

(With R. R. Peterson), *Laboratory Guide for Gross Anatomy,* 2nd ed., Bardgett Printing and Publishing Co., 1957.

"Estimation of Stature from Intact Long Limb Bones," in *Personal Identification in Mass Disasters,* edited by T. D. Steward, Smithsonian Institution, 1970, pp. 71–83.

(With D. N. Menton), "Hair," in *Encyclopedia of Microscopy and Microtechnique,* pp. 233–234, edited by Peter Gray, Van Nostrand Reinhold Co., 1973.

Periodicals

(With G. C. Gleser), "Estimation of Stature from Long Limb Bones of American Whites and Negroes." *American Journal of Physical Anthropology,* no. 10, 1952.

(With G. C. Gleser), "Corrigenda to 'Estimation of Stature from Long Limb Bones of American Whites and Negroes,' American Journal of Physical Anthropology, 1952," *American Journal of Physical Anthropology,* no. 47, 1977.

SOURCES:

Periodicals

Kerley, Ellis R., "Forensic Anthropology: Increasing Utility In Civil and Criminal Cases," *Trial,* January, 1983, pp. 66–111.

Wood, W. Raymond and Lori Ann Stanley, "Recovery and Identification of World War II Dead: American Graves Registration Activities in Europe," *Journal of Forensic Sciences,* Volume 34, 1989, pp. 1365–1373.

Other

Trotter Papers, Resource & Research Center for Beaver County & Local History, Inc., Carnegie Free Library, Beaver Falls, PA.

Trotter Papers, Washington University School of Medicine Library Archives, St. Louis, MO.

—Sketch by Jennifer Kramer

John G. Trump
1907-1985
American electrical engineer

John G. Trump is best remembered for introducing key advances in radiation therapy for cancer. At the Massachusetts Institute of Technology (MIT), he worked closely with **Robert Van de Graaff** and adapted the latter's high-voltage electrostatic system for use as a generator of energetic x-ray beams. These beams offered the basis for Trump's cancer treatments. Initial clinical tests in the late 1930s showed promise, and Trump and Van de Graaff went on to found High Voltage Engineering Corporation, which built and sold such x-ray systems commercially.

John George Trump was born in New York City on August 21, 1907, the son of Frederick and Elizabeth (Christ) Trump. He received a B.S. in electrical engineering from Brooklyn Polytechnic Institute in 1929, followed by an M.A. in physics from Columbia University in 1931. He continued onward to MIT, where the dean of engineering, **Vannevar Bush**, suggested that he talk to Van de Graaff about a topic for a Ph.D. dissertation. Van de Graaff had invented an electrostatic accelerator, a machine capable of sustaining very high voltages using static electricity. In turn, these voltages could accelerate beams of electrons and other particles, for research in

nuclear physics. Trump worked with him and won a D.Sc. in 1933, in electrical engineering.

Launches New Initiatives against Cancer

As a disease, cancer dates to antiquity; its name comes from Hippocrates. In the 1930s, the only effective treatment lay in surgery. X-ray systems of the era could generate beams with as much as 200,000 volts of energy, but such beams could not be focused on a tumor, particularly if it lay deep within a patient's body. Instead the rays would scatter throughout adjacent tissues, damaging these tissues while doing little harm to the cancer.

Trump appreciated that the Van de Graaff system offered a route toward x-ray beams of much higher energy. Its high voltage could produce a particularly energetic electron beam, which would produce x-rays when this beam struck a target of heavy metal. In turn, energetic x-rays could penetrate the body with ease, delivering their energy to the tumor while producing much less damage to nearby tissues. Working with colleagues from Harvard Medical School, Trump built a million-volt x-ray source at Boston's Huntington Memorial Hospital. The first cancer patient was treated with the equipment in March 1937. Trump meanwhile was pursuing research that showed how to raise the voltage of such a system while reducing its size. This led to development of a far more compact x-ray source of 1.25 million volts. It entered clinical use at Massachusetts General Hospital in the spring of 1940.

World War II then intervened, with Trump taking an active role in the development and use of radar. He served as chairman of the radar division of the National Defense Research Committee. In 1944 he became director of the British branch of MIT's Radiation Laboratory, the nation's principal center for radar development. He also served as a member of a specialist group advising General Carl Spaatz, who led the Eighth Air Force, the nation's main force of heavy bombers in the war against Germany. Returning to MIT after the war, he took over the directorship of that university's High Voltage Research Laboratory, a post he held until 1980. Also in 1946, he cofounded the firm of High Voltage Engineering. Its purpose lay in taking the Van de Graaff generator out of the esoteric world of physics research, selling these systems commercially for use in treating cancer. Trump's firm faced competition from General Electric (GE) and from Allis-Chalmers, which also were entering this field. But Trump proposed to offer a 2-million-volt unit for $75,000, about $50,000 less than a similar system from GE. This allowed him to win start-up funding from a Boston venture capital firm, American Research and Development. Trump also introduced the technique of rotating the patient. This permitted the x-ray beam to strike the tumor from all directions, while delivering minimal doses to surrounding tissues. In 1949 the first patients received this treatment at Boston's Lahey Clinic.

Radiation therapy combined with rotation did not offer a magic bullet against cancer—indeed, no such bullet exists to this day—but it offered a valuable new treatment that could stand alongside the standard approach of surgery. Radiation could combat many inoperable or hard-to-reach tumors, as in the pituitary gland, which lies below the brain. At times radiation could also open the way to successful surgery, by stopping the spread of a malignancy and reducing the size of the primary tumor. Hugh Hare, head of the Department of Radiology at the Lahey Clinic, told *Collier's* magazine in 1953 that "this is the most promising method evolved so far of treating deep tumors susceptible to radiation, including many cases previously considered inaccessible."

Honored Repeatedly for Achievements

For his work in both war and peace, Trump received a number of high distinctions during his career. In 1946 the King of England, George VI, presented him with His Majesty's Medal for contributions to the Allied victory. Two years later, President Harry Truman awarded Trump a Presidential Citation. His work with cancer won him the Gold Medal of the American College of Radiology. This 1982 award was particularly noteworthy because it is generally bestowed on physicians, whereas Trump was an electrical engineer.

In 1935 Trump married Elora Gordon Sauerbrun. They had three children: John Gordon, Christine Elora, and Karen Elizabeth. He was also the uncle of Donald Trump, the real-estate magnate. Trump died in Winchester, Massachusetts, on February 21, 1985, following a long illness. A month later the White House cited him anew, presenting him posthumously with the National Medal of Science.

SELECTED WRITINGS BY TRUMP:

Periodicals

"Roentgen Rays against Cancer," *Technology Review*, December, 1947, reprinted in *Annual Report of the Board of Regents of the Smithsonian Institution*, 1948, pp. 209–16.

SOURCES:

Periodicals

Cantwell, J. L., H. R. Stewart, and J. G. Trump, "John G. Trump: 1960 Lamme Medalist," *Electrical Engineering*, August, 1961, pp. 596–600.

Ratcliff, J. D., "The X-Ray Cannon and the Rotating Chair," *Collier's*, January 3, 1953, pp. 36–38.

Robinson, Denis M., "John George Trump," *Physics Today*, September, 1985, pp. 90, 92.

"Supervoltage Machines," *Fortune*, April, 1950, pp. 113–124.

—*Sketch by T. A. Heppenheimer*

George T. Tsao
1931-
Chinese-born American chemical engineer

As director of the Laboratory of Renewable Resources Engineering at Purdue University, George T. Tsao has been in the forefront of research in biomass conversion—the process of extracting new energy sources from organic waste material. His studies in the development of alcohol fuels such as gasahol from cellulose materials, including urban organic garbage and agricultural waste, have won him international respect as well as helped to create viable alternatives to the burning of petroleum products in order to meet rising world energy demands.

Tsao was born on December 4, 1931, in Nanking, China, and received his early education in Taiwan. He earned his B.S. from National Taiwan University in 1953, and then travelled to the United States for graduate studies, completing his M.S. in 1956 at the University of Florida, and his Ph.D. in chemical engineering in 1960 at the University of Michigan. After graduation, Tsao held a one-year assistant professorship in physics at Olivet College, and then worked as a chemical engineer for Merck & Company for another year, before becoming research chemist for the Tennessee Valley Authority. Tsao's career continued to alternate between industry and academia for the next years: From 1962 to 1965, he worked for Miles Labs in the research department, specializing in hydrolysis and fermentation; in 1966 he accepted a position at Iowa State University, first as an associate professor of chemical engineering, and then as a full professor; and in 1977 he moved to Purdue University as a professor of chemical engineering and agricultural engineering, eventually becoming the director of Purdue's Laboratory of Renewable Resources Engineering (LORRE).

Focuses on Biomass Conversion

At Purdue, Tsao set himself a formidable task: to convert cellulose—the primary carbohydrate substance in plants—into glucose, a type of sugar. By converting cellulose waste materials such as garbage and grain stalks into glucose, Tsao could then ferment the sugar into ethanol, a burnable fuel alcohol. Others before Tsao had tackled this problem with little success. Not only does cellulose have a strong crystalline structure, it is also protected by a layer of lignin, a substance that binds the cellulose fiber together. As Tsao said in *Pioneers of Alcohol Fuels,* "The structure of a piece of cellulosic material resembles that of a reinforced concrete pillar with cellulose fibers being the metal rods, and lignin the natural cement." The problem, then, was not only to break down the crystalline structure of cellulose, but also to somehow tear apart the lignin shield.

Tsao's solution was to use sulfuric acid in a multi-step process by which crop waste is converted into three usable by–products: glucose, lignin, and hemicellulose, a carbohydrate containing several sugars that occurs in plants and that is more easily hydrolyzed or decomposed than cellulose. The glucose, which is the primary by–product, is fermented into ethanol; the lignin is dried and then processed into a coal-like substance for fuel; and the hemicellulose is processed to extract sugars that can be made into plastic. In effect, Tsao came up with a biomass conversion process that would not only produce ethanol at approximately eighty cents per gallon, but also would—as a result of the secondary products—pay for the energy it used in the conversion process. Yet Tsao's work was far from done. He spent much time during the next several years testifying before Congress and campaigning for sufficient funds to support the project.

In addition to his work in biomass conversion, Tsao has also studied industrial carbohydrates, enzyme engineering, and the utilization of agricultural and natural products as well as waste disposal. He is a member of the American Chemical Society, the American Institute of Chemical Engineers, and the American Society of Engineering Educators.

SELECTED WRITINGS BY TSAO:

Books

(With others) *Research in the General Field of the Mechanism of Cellulose Synthesis and Degradation,* University of Florida, 1955.
Treatment of Aqueous Agricultural Wastes for Clean Water and for Microbial Protein Production, Iowa State University, 1971.
(With others) *Investigations on Mixing, Flow, and Fluidization in Systems of Cereal Starches and Flours,* Iowa State University, 1975.
Conversion of Biomass from Agriculture into Useful Products, U.S. Department of Energy, 1978.

Periodicals

"Ethanol and Chemicals from Cellulosics," *ASPAC Technical Bulletin,* December, 1984, pp. 1–9.
(With others) "Methane Generation from Chemically Pretreated Cellulose by Anaerobic Fluidized-Bed Reactors," *Biological Wastes,* Volume 29, 1989, pp. 201–210.
(With others) "Some Considerations for Optimization of Desorption Chromatography," *Biotechnology and Bioengineering,* January 5, 1991, pp. 65-70.
(With others) "Hydrolysis of Maltose and Cornstarch by Glucoamylase Immobilized in Porous Glass Fibres and Beads," *Process Biochemistry,* May, 1992, pp. 177–181.
(With P. B. Beronio) "An Energetic Model for Oxygen-Limited Metabolism," *Biotechnology and Bioengineering,* December, 1993, pp. 1270–1276.

SOURCES:

Books

Burns, Paul, and others, *Pioneers of Alcohol Fuels,* Volume 1, Citizens' Energy Project, 1981, pp. 29–32.

—*Sketch by J. Sydney Jones*

Konstantin Tsiolkovsky
1857-1935
Russian aerospace engineer

Konstantin Tsiolkovsky was almost entirely self-educated, yet became one of the greatest Russian scientists of the early twentieth century. He studied and wrote about a wide range of scientific topics, but is best known for his pioneering work in astronautics. As early as the 1890s he had begun preliminary calculations on the mathematics and physics of space flight, which he saw as the first step in the colonization of space by humans. When the Soviet Union was prepared to launch the world's first artificial satellite, *Sputnik 1,* it attempted to do so on the one-hundredth anniversary of Tsiolkovsky's birth. It failed to meet that precise deadline, but the flight was still dedicated as a memorial to Tsiolkovsky's life and work. Throughout his life, Tsiolkovsky saw himself as far more than a scientist working on

Konstantin Tsiolkovsky

abstract problems; his goal was to work for the betterment of life for all humans.

Konstantin Eduardovich Tsiolkovsky was born on September 17, 1857, in the Russian village of Izhevskoye in the province of Ryazan. His mother was the former Maria Yumasheva and his father, Eduard Tsiolkovsky, a forester, teacher, and minor government official. The Tsiolkovsky family moved frequently while Konstantin was young, and their financial situation was often very difficult.

Until the age of ten, Tsiolkovsky led a childhood that was typical for the time. His biographer V. N. Sokolsky says that "he liked games, went skating in winter, sent up kites, climbed fences, and dreamt of becoming strong and agile." Then disaster struck. Tsiolkovsky was taken seriously ill with scarlet fever in 1867, which caused him to lose his hearing.

For a period of time, Tsiolkovsky was despondent about his misfortune. He later wrote in his autobiography that the three years that followed his illness "was the saddest time of my life." Gradually, however, he worked his way through this difficult period. He began to develop an intense interest in science, teaching himself at every step along the way. Once again in his autobiography, Tsiolkovsky explained that "there were very few books, and I had no teachers at all. . . . There were no hints, no aid from anywhere; there was a great deal that I couldn't understand in those books and I had to figure out everything by myself."

In 1873 Tsiolkovsky's father found enough money to send his son to Moscow. There Tsiolkovsky continued his self-education, albeit in an intellectually richer surrounding. He built himself an ear trumpet that allowed him to attend lectures, but could not afford to enroll in any formal college or university program. At the end of three years in Moscow, Tsiolkovsky returned to his home town where he continued to teach himself science, build models of all kinds of machines, and carry out original experiments.

Early Studies

In 1879 Tsiolkovsky passed the examination for a school teaching license and took a job as instructor of arithmetic and geometry at the Borovsk Uyzed School in Kaluga. Simultaneously he continued his own research and in 1880 wrote his first scientific paper, "The Graphical Depiction of Sensations." The paper was an attempt to express human sensations in strict mathematical formulas.

A year later, in 1881, Tsiolkovsky wrote his second paper, "The Theory of Gases." The paper is extraordinary in that it outlines a theory very similar to one developed two decades earlier by James Clerk Maxwell. Tsiolkovsky, however, had not heard of Maxwell's work nor was he familiar with any of the studies that Maxwell had used as the basis of his theory, including those of Rudolf Clausius, Ludwig Boltzmann, and **Johannes van der Waals**. The Russian Physico-Chemical Society, to which Tsiolkovsky sent his paper, greatly admired his work and offered its support for his future research, but decided that the paper did not qualify for publication.

Tsiolkovsky's next paper, written in 1882–83, was "On the Theoretical Mechanics of a Living Organism." In that paper Tsiolkovsky analyzed the ways in which natural forces, such as gravity, affect the structure and movement of human beings. This paper was not published either, although it impressed the Physico-Chemical Society sufficiently to elect Tsiolkovsky as one of its members.

Tsiolkovsky's interest in flight can be traced at least to the age of fifteen, when he posed for himself the problem "what size a balloon should be to carry people aloft if made of a metal shell of a definite thickness." More than a decade later he wrote his first paper on this subject, "The Theory and Experiment of a Horizontally Elongated Balloon." In 1887 he was invited to lecture to a meeting of the Society of Lovers of Natural Science on his ideas. He continued to work on lighter-than-air machines for more than a decade, but failed to obtain funding with which to build working models of his ideas. Those who controlled the purse strings for scientific research could see no practical utility for the metal dirigible that Tsiolkovsky envisioned.

By the mid-1880s, Tsiolkovsky had also begun to think about heavier-than-air craft. One of his first papers on the subject, written in 1890, was entitled "On the Problem of Flying by Means of Wings." In it, Tsiolkovsky completed one of the earliest mathematical studies of the forces operating on the wings and body of an aircraft. The 1890 paper was followed by other studies on the shape of aircraft fuselages, the cantilevering of wings, the use of internal combustion engines in aircraft, the shape of wings, and other important features of heavier-than-air machines. His research was essentially unaffected by his acceptance of a high-school teaching job in Kaluga in 1892.

Constructs the First Wind Tunnel

Tsiolkovsky was well aware of the fact that most of his ideas were theoretical speculations that needed to be tested in actual experiments. To that end, he designed the first wind tunnel to be built in Russia. The wind tunnel, first put to use in Kaluga in 1897, produced a stream of air that could be forced over aircraft bodies and wings of various size, shape, and design. Tsiolkovsky described the preliminary results of his wind tunnel experiments in an 1897 paper on "Air Pressure on Surfaces Introduced into an Artificial Air Flow." Encouraged by his success, Tsiolkovsky appealed to the Russian Academy of Sciences for a grant that would allow him to continue and to extend his wind tunnel experiments. He was successful in getting an award of 470 rubles (worth about $235 at the time) to build a larger wind tunnel. The grant was apparently the only financial assistance that Tsiolkovsky ever received while Russia was ruled by czarist governments. In May 1900, construction on the larger wind tunnel began, and experiments in it were started before the end of the same year.

For all his many achievements, Tsiolkovsky will probably best be remembered for his accomplishments in the field of astronautics or space travel. He first began to wonder about this subject during his three-year stay in Moscow from 1873 to 1876. In a 1904 article, he wrote that his first thoughts on space travel dazzled him. "I was excited, even staggered," he wrote, "to such an extent that I could not sleep all night; I wandered about Moscow and kept thinking of the great consequences of my discovery."

By the late 1870s, Tsiolkovsky's ideas about spacecraft and space travel were pouring forth at an astonishing rate. They dealt with virtually every aspect of the subject. In about 1879, for example, he designed an instrument for measuring the effects of gravitational acceleration on the human body. Four years later he outlined the mechanism by which a jet rocket could carry an object into space. In the early 1890s he was writing about space travel to the moon, other planets, and beyond. His 1895 article "Dreams of the Earth and Sky and the Effects of Universal Gravitation" first set forth the concept of an artificial Earth satellite, which he describes as "something like the moon, but arbitrarily close to our planet, just outside its atmosphere." By 1896, Tsiolkovsky was also deriving the mathematical formulas needed to describe the movement of a spacecraft. A year later he worked out the fundamental relationship among the velocity and mass of a rocket and the exhaust velocity of the propellant used to send it into space. That formula is now known as the basic rocket equation.

One of the consequences of Tsiolkovsky's research was his realization that the most efficient way of placing rockets into space is to arrange them in packets, or "cosmic rocket trains" as he called them in a 1929 article. These trains made use of the concept of "staging," as it is known today, in which a series of rocket engines are fired successively to put an object into space.

Argues for the Colonization of Space

In his work on astronautics, Tsiolkovsky investigated virtually every technical question that bears on the subject. He worked intensively, for example, on the kinds of fuels that would work best as rocket propellants eventually settling on a mixture of liquid hydrogen and liquid oxygen as the best choice. In 1903, he completed a historic paper, "Investigations of Outer Space by Reaction Devices," that summarized his work in a variety of fields. That paper did not actually appear in print until it was published in the journal *Vestnik vozdukhoplavaniya* (*Herald of Aeronautics*) in 1911–12. This paper also provided an outline of Tsiolkovsky's views on the colonization of space. He argued that space travel should not be viewed as some abstract scientific experiment, but as a way of creating new human communities outside the Earth. "In all likelihood," he wrote in the paper, "the better part of humanity will never perish but will move from sun to sun as each one dies out in succession." In 1920, Tsiolkovsky wrote a popular exposition of his ideas about space travel in a book called *Beyond the Earth*. The book was an attempt to describe to nonscientists what space travel and living in space would be like.

The first sixty years of Tsiolkovsky's life were extremely difficult, not only because of the suffocating poverty in which he lived, but also because of the indifference of his colleagues to his work. He once wrote that "it is hard to work by oneself many years and under unfavorable conditions and not experience any gratification or support at all."

The October Revolution of 1917 brought about a remarkable change in Tsiolkovsky's life, however. He was elected a member of the Socialist Academy and was given a pension by the Council of the Peoples' Commissariats of the Russian Federation. For the first time in his life, Tsiolkovsky could concentrate on his scientific research with some degree of comfort. An indication of the impact this pension made on Tsiolkovsky's productivity is the fact that about one-quarter of his five-hundred-plus papers were written in the six decades between 1857 and 1917, and the remaining three-quarters in the last two decades of his life.

During the late 1920s, Tsiolkovsky began to spend more time on problems of aeronautics. Typical of the papers written during this period were "A New Airplane" and "Reactive Airplane," as well as studies of issues further removed from air and space travel, including "A Common Alphabet for the Human Race," "The Future of Earth and Man," "Auto-Trailer on Tracks," "Solar Energy and Its Applications," and "The Elasticity of Solids."

On September 13, 1935, in an effort to gain a pension for his family, Tsiolkovsky bequeathed all of his books and papers to the Communist Party and the Soviet government. He died of cancer at his home in Kaluga six days later. His home was later made into a museum that was badly damaged during World War II. After the launching of *Sputnik 1* in 1957, the home-museum became a popular sightseeing stop for visitors.

SELECTED WRITINGS BY TSIOLKOVSKY:

Books

Kosmicheskaia raketa: opytnaia podgotovka, Gosti-pografiia, 1927.
Atlas dirizhablia iz volnistoi stali, Mosoblpoligraf, 1931.
Reaktivnye letatel'nye apparaty, Nauka, 1964.
The Will of the Universe. Intellect Unknown. Mind and Passiona, Pamiat', 1992.

Periodicals

"Free Space," unpublished manuscript, 1883.
"The Aeroplane or Bird-Like (Aviation) Flying Machine," *Nauka i zhizn,*Volume 46, 1894.
"Investigation of World Spaces by Reactive Vehicles," *Vestnik vozdukhoplavaniya,* Volume 9, 1912.

SOURCES:

Books

Dictionary of Scientific Biography, Volume 13, Scribner's, 1975, pp. 482–484.
Sharpe, Mitchell R., "Tsiolkovsky," in *The McGraw-Hill Encyclopedia of World Biography,* Volume 11, McGraw-Hill, 1973, pp. 8–10.

Sokolsky, Volume N., compiler, *K. E. Tsiolkovsky: Selected Works,* translated by G. Yankovsky, Mir, 1968.

—Sketch by David E. Newton

Daniel Chee Tsui
1938-
Chinese-born American physicist

Daniel Chee Tsui's research in solid state physics has laid important groundwork for the development of superconductors, which are substances that can conduct an electric current with no resistance (or loss of energy) and which can also create powerful magnetic fields. Tsui was the first scientist to measure energy levels in the surface space charge layer of a semiconductor at the quantum, or sub-atomic level.

Tsui was born February 28, 1938, in Henan, China. Receiving his bachelor of arts degree from Augustana College in 1961, he went on to the University of Chicago, where he earned both his master's degree and Ph.D. in 1967. After graduation, Tsui remained at the university as a research fellow from 1967 to 1968. He then joined the technical staff at Bell Labs in Murray Hill, New Jersey, where he and his colleagues began studying the two-dimensional electron gas that is present at semiconductor interfaces. Examining the far infrared wavelengths of this gas through spectroscopy—a method by which the electromagnetic spectra can be observed—they were able to note the localization of the gas as well as the lack of a mobility edge in such a two-dimensional system. In 1981, Tsui and his colleagues discovered the fractional quantum Hall effect, which addresses the movement of electrons in a conductor at the quantum level.

In 1982, Tsui joined the faculty of Princeton University's electrical engineering department as the Arthur LeGrand Doty Professor. He is also a member of the associated faculty in physics at Princeton. Tsui's research there has concentrated on the electronic properties of metals (including cadmium and nickel), the surface properties of superconductors, and low-temperature superconductors. He is particularly interested in conduction in ultra-small structures and quantum physics of electronic materials in strong magnetic fields and low temperatures. Tsui has published more than two hundred forty scientific papers.

A member of the National Academy of Sciences since 1987, Tsui has been married since 1964 and has two children. In recognition of his work in solid state physics, particularly for the discovery of the fractional quantized Hall effect, Tsui received the American Physical Society's Oliver E. Buckley Prize in 1984. Sharing the prize with him that year were H. L. Stormer and A. C. Gossard of Bell Laboratories. Since discovering the effect, Tsui has continued to research it.

SELECTED WRITINGS BY TSUI:

Periodicals

"The Fractional Quantum Hall Effect," *IEEE Journal of Quantum Electronics,* Volume 22, 1986.

SOURCES:

Periodicals

"Awards of Prizes by the American Physical Society," *Bulletin of the American Physical Society,* Volume 29, March, 1984.

—*Sketch by F. C. Nicholson*

Mikhail Tswett
1872-1919
Russian chemist and botanist

Although recognized only belatedly, Mikhail Tswett (sometimes spelled Tsvet) was the first to lay out in detail the methods of the separation technique called chromatography. Tswett himself regarded chromatography only as a tool in his chemical and biological studies; his purpose was to separate and identify the many different pigments in leaves and other plant parts, and he considered it merely an improvement on existing techniques such acid-extraction, base-extraction, and fractional crystallization. Since he first described this process, many kinds of chromatography have been developed, and no laboratory is considered complete without a number of chromatographic instruments.

Mikhail Semyonovich Tswett was born May 14, 1872, in Asti, in the northwest part of Italy about seventy miles from the Swiss border. His parents were Semyon Nikolaevich and Maria de Dorozza Tswett. His father was a Russian civil servant and his mother,

who was very young, died soon after his birth. His father returned to Russia after her death, and left his son with a nurse in Lausanne. Tswett was educated in Lausanne and Geneva, becoming multilingual in the process. He received his secondary education at the Collège Gaillard in Lausanne and the Collège de St. Antoine in Geneva; he entered the University of Geneva in 1891, studying chemistry, botany, and physics. His baccalaureate in both physical and natural sciences was awarded in 1892. He began plant research during his undergraduate years, earning the Davy Prize while a doctoral student with a paper on plant physiology that was subsequently published. In 1896 he defended his thesis, "Études de physiologie cellulaire," and received his doctoral degree.

Thereafter he moved to Russia, and in 1897 he began working at the laboratory of plant anatomy and physiology at the Academy of Sciences and the St. Petersburg Biological Laboratory. His academic horizon was limited by the fact that foreign degrees were not recognized in tsarist Russia, and he set to work earning another master's degree in botany at Kazan University. He finished in 1901, with a thesis in Russian whose title is translated "The Physicochemical Structure of the Chlorophyll Grain." In 1902 Tswett became an assistant in the laboratory of plant anatomy and physiology at the University of Warsaw, which was under Russian control at that time, where he became a full professor in 1903. In 1907 he took on the additional task of teaching botany and microbiology at the Warsaw Veterinary Institute; a year later he was also teaching at the Warsaw Technical University. He resigned his teaching post at the University of Warsaw but took a second doctorate there in 1910 with a dissertation on plant and animal chromophils. This apparently led to his only book, published in the same year, whose title is translated as "The Chromophils in the Animal and Vegetable Kingdoms." The book itself has never been translated. By 1914 Tswett's brief, brilliant research career was essentially at an end. The German invasion of Poland in 1915 forced the Technical University to move to Moscow, and then to Nizhni Novgorod in 1916. Tswett's time was largely consumed with organizing the work of the botanical laboratories after each of these moves. In 1917 he accepted a position at the University at Yuryev in Estonia, but that too was overrun by the German army a year later. The university moved to Voronezh in 1918, but Tswett's health, never robust, failed quickly, and he died of a heart ailment at age forty-seven, on June 26, 1919.

Tswett's strength as a scientist lay in how well he understood both chemistry and botany. He had always been interested in the internal molecular structures of plants, often inquiring what their purpose might be, and the work he did on chlorophyll was one of his most important research efforts. He had long doubted the contention, which was widely accepted at the time, that chlorophyll was a compound that actually existed in plants. He decided this belief was the result of a misunderstanding; he hypothesized that chemists had been confused either because chlorophyll was combined nearly inseparably with other molecules within the leaf or because a compound recovered by a particular separation technique might in fact be an artifact of the technique. He was able to demonstrate all of these misunderstandings in the work of others, both by his deployment of the chemical separation methods of the time (fractional solution and precipitation, diffusion, differential solution) and by the adsorption methods he developed, culminating in chromatography.

Develops Chromatography Process

"Adsorbent" means holding molecules on the surface of the material, not in the body, and chromatography is a process which employs substances which have this property. It is a separation technique in which a very finely powdered adsorbent material is held in a vertical tube or "column." The mixture to be separated is placed on the top of the column, dissolved in as small an amount of solvent as possible, so that it forms a narrow band of adsorbed mixture; then more solvent is allowed to flow through the column, top to bottom. The molecules in the mixture are more or less strongly held by the adsorbent; those weakly held are washed down the column most rapidly, and those strongly held move less rapidly. After a suitable development time, the components of the mixture separate into a series of bands spaced along the column. The plug of wet adsorbent is blown out of the column onto a plate, where the bands can be cut apart and the components recovered separately. As the mixtures separated in these early experiments were colored, and the bands absorbed light in the visible spectrum, Tswett named the process *chromatography* ("color-writing"), and the developed separation he called a *chromatogram*. Even though most mixtures are not colored, this terminology is retained; the components must be detected by some means other than the eye. Many sophisticated varieties of chromatography are in use today: paper, thin-layer, gas-liquid, and ion exchange, to name but a few. Still, Tswett's column method has not been totally displaced.

Tswett used this technique to demonstrate that chlorophyll indeed does not exist in the plant as a free molecule but is complexed with albumin. He named this complex "chloroglobin," by analogy with the heme complex of the blood, hemoglobin. There was, however, widespread skepticism of his research methods, and this finding was sharply criticized. Tswett next analyzed the plant pigments themselves, which were understood at the time to be only two: green chlorophyll and yellow xanthophyll. Using not chromatography but the standard chemical methods of the

time, he demonstrated that there are two chlorophylls: xanthophyll and carotene. This finding was hotly disputed, partly because chlorophyll passed the test of a single pure compound: it could be crystallized. Tswett was able to show that the "crystallizable chlorophyll" formed by lengthy extraction with hot ethanol was in fact another compound; it is known today as an ethyl ester formed by transesterification of one of chlorophyll's ester groups.

During the course of his pigment work Tswett had found that when he ground the plant leaves with powdered calcium carbonate to neutralize acids, all but carotene were adsorbed on the solid carbonate. He used this as a method to separate carotene. It is not clear that this led to his devising column chromatography, but once he had developed this technique he found that in addition to two chlorophylls there were four xanthophylls and, of course, carotene. These findings came to be accepted later, but mainly through the work of the German chemist **Richard Willstätter**.

The technique of column chromatography was not widely used in Tswett's lifetime, being regarded by his most vocal opponent, L. Marchlewski, as no more than a "filtration experiment." It was only later in the century that his work was reevaluated and his status as one of the originators, though probably not the sole inventor, of chromatography, was confirmed. This is his legacy today, although some would consider the plant pigment work to be at least as important.

SELECTED WRITINGS BY TSWETT:

Books

Michael Tswett's First Paper on Chromatography (translated by Gerhard Hesse and Herbert Weil from 1903 Russian paper), M. Woelm, 1954.

Periodicals

"Adsorption Analysis and Chromatographic Methods; Application to the Chemistry of the Chlorophylls" (translated by Harold H. Strain and Joseph Sherma from 1906 German paper), *Journal of Chemical Education*, Volume 44, 1967, pp. 238–242.

SOURCES:

Books

Heftmann, E., editor, *Chromatography*, Elsevier, 1983.

Periodicals

Dhere, C., "Michel Tswett," *Candollea,* Volume 10, 1943, pp. 23–63.

Robinson, Trevor, "Michael Tswett," *Journal of Chemical Education,* Volume 36, 1959, pp. 144–147.

Robinson, Trevor, "Michael Tswett," *Chymia,* Volume 6, 1960, pp. 146–161.

Strain, Harold H., and Joseph Sherma, "Michael Tswett's Contributions to Sixty Years of Chromatography," *Journal of Chemical Education,* Volume 44, 1967, pp. 235–237.

—*Sketch by Robert M. Hawthorne Jr.*

Alan Turing

Alan Turing
1912-1954
English mathematician

Mathematician Alan Turing is recognized as a pioneer in computer theory. His classic 1936 paper, "On Computable Numbers, with an Application to the Entscheidungs Problem," detailed a machine that served as a model for the first working computers. During World War II, Turing took part in the top-secret ULTRA project and helped decipher German military codes. During this same time, Turing conducted groundbreaking work that led to the first operational digital electronic computers. Another notable paper was published in 1950 and offered what became known as the "Turing Test" to determine if a machine possessed intelligence.

Alan Mathison Turing was born on June 23, 1912, in Paddington, England, to Julius Mathison Turing and Ethel Sara Stoney. Turing's father served in the British civil service in India, and his wife generally accompanied him. Thus, for the majority of their childhoods, Alan and his older brother, John, saw very little of their parents. While in elementary school, the young Turing boys were raised by a retired military couple, the Wards. At the age of 13, Turing entered Sherbourne school, a boys' boarding school in Dorset. His record at Sherbourne was not generally outstanding; he was later remembered as untidy and disinterested in scholastic learning. He did, however, distinguish himself in mathematics and science, showing a particular facility for calculus. Turing also developed an interest in competitive running while at Sherbourne.

Produces Prophetic Paper

Turing twice failed to gain entry to Trinity College in Cambridge, but was accepted on scholarship at King's College (also in Cambridge). He graduated in 1934 with a master's degree in mathematics. In 1936 Turing produced his first, and perhaps greatest, work. His paper "On Computable Numbers, with an Application to the Entscheidungs Problem," answered a logical problem staged by German mathematician **David Hilbert.** The question involved the completeness of logic—whether all mathematical problems could, in principle, be solved. Turing's paper, presented in 1937 to the London Mathematical Society, proved that some could not be solved. Turing's paper also contained a footnote describing a theoretical automatic machine, which came to be known as the Turing Machine, that could solve any mathematical problem—provided it was give the proper algorithms, or problem-solving equations or instructions. Although it may not have been Turing's intent at the time, his Turing Machine defined the modern computer.

After graduating from Cambridge, Turing was invited to spend a year in the United States studying at Princeton University. He returned to Princeton for a second year—on a Proctor Fellowship—to finish his doctorate. While there, he worked on the subject of computability with **Alonso Church** and other mathematicians. Turing and his associates worked with binary numbers (1 and 0) and Boolean Algebra, developed by George Boole, to develop a system of equations called logic gates. These logic gates were useful for producing problem-solving algorithms such as would be needed by an automatic computing machine. From the initial paper exercise, it was a simple matter to develop logic gates into electrical hardware, using relays and switches, which could—theoretically, and in huge quantities—actually perform the work of a computing machine. As a sideline, Turing put together the first three or four stages of an electric multiplier, using relays he constructed himself. After receiving his doctorate, Turing had an opportunity to remain at Princeton, but decided to accept a Cambridge fellowship instead. He returned to England in 1938.

Helps Crack German War Codes

Cryptology, the making and breaking of coded messages, was greatly advanced in England after World War I. The German high command, however, had modified a device called the Enigma machine that mechanically enciphered messages. The English found little success in defeating this method. The original Enigma machine was not new, or even secret; a basic Enigma machine had been in operation for several years, mostly used to produce commercial codes. The Germans' alterations, though, greatly increased the number of possible letter combinations in a message. The Allies were able to duplicate the modifications, but it was a continual cat-and-mouse game; each time Allied analysts figured out a message, the Germans' changes made all of their work useless.

In the fall of 1939, Turing found himself in a top-secret installation in Bletchley, where he played a critical role in the development of a machine that deciphered the Enigma's messages by testing key codes until it found the correct combinations. This substitution method was uncomplicated, but impractical to apply because possible combinations could range into the tens of millions. Here Turing was able to put his experience at Princeton to good use; no one else had bridged the gap between abstract logic theory and electric hardware as he had with his electric multiplier. Turing helped construct relay-driven decoders (which were called Bombes, after the ticking noise of the relays) that shortened the code-breaking time from weeks to hours. The Bombes helped uncover German movements, particularly the U-boat war in the Atlantic, for almost two years. Eventually, however, the Germans changed their codes and the new level of complexity was too high to be solved practically by electrical decoders. British scientists agreed that although a Bombe of sufficient size could be made for further deciphering work, the machine would be slow and impractical.

Yet other advances would prove advantageous for the decoding machine. Vacuum tubes used as switches (the British called them thermiotic valves) used no moving parts and were a thousand times faster than electrical relays. A decoder made with tubes could do in minutes what it took a Bombe several hours to accomplish. Thus work began on a device which was later named Collosus. Based on the same theoretical principles as earlier Bombes, Collosus was the first operational digital electronic computer. It used 1800 vacuum tubes, proving the practicality of this approach. Much information concerning Collosus remained classified by the British government in the early 1990s. Some claimed that Turing supervised the construction of the first Collosus.

Many stories were circulated about Turing during the war; mostly surrounding his eccentricity. Andrew Hodges noted in his book *Alan Turing, The Enigma,* "With holes in his sports jacket, shiny grey flannel trousers held up with an ancient tie, and hair sticking out at the back, he became the cartoonist's 'boffin'—an impression accentuated by his manner of practical work, in which he would grunt and swear as solder failed to stick, scratch his head and make a strange squelching noise as he thought to himself." Unconvinced of England's chances to win the war, Turing converted all of his funds to two silver bars, buried them, and was later unable to locate them. He was horrified at the sight of blood, was an outspoken atheist, and was a homosexual. Still, for his unquestionably vital role in the British war effort, he was later awarded the Order of the British Empire, a high honor for someone not in the combat military.

In the waning months of the war, Turing turned his thoughts back to computing machines. He conceived of a device, built with vacuum tubes, that would be able to perform any function described in mathematical terms and would carry instructions in electronic symbols in its memory. This universal machine, clearly an embodiment of the Turing machine described in his 1936 paper, would not require separate hardware for different functions, only a change of instructions. Turing was not alone in his ambition to construct a computing machine. A group at the University of Pennsylvania had built a computer called ENIAC (Electronic Numerical Integrator and Computer) that was similar to, but more complex, than Collosus. In the process, they had concluded that a better machine was possible. Turing's design was possibly more remarkable because he was working alone out of his home while they were a large university research group with the full backing of the American military. The American group published well before Turing did, but the British government subsequently took a greater interest in Turing's work.

Postwar Work

In June of 1945 Turing joined the newly formed Mathematics Division of the National Physical Laboratory (NPL). Here he finalized plans for his Automatic Computing Engine (ACE). The rather archaic term "engine" was chosen by NPL management as a tribute to Charles Babbage's Analytical Engine (and also because it made a pleasing acronym). Turing, however, was unprepared for the inertia and politics of a bureaucratic government foundation. All of his previous engineering projects had been conducted during wartime, when time was of the essence and no budget constraints existed. More than a year after the ACE project was approved, though, no engineering work had been completed and there was little cooperation between participants. A scaled-down version of the ACE was finally completed in 1950. But Turing had already left NPL in 1948, frustrated at the slow pace of the computer's development.

In 1950 Turing produced a widely read paper titled "Computing Machinery and Intelligence". This classic paper expanded on one of Turing's interests—if computers could possess intelligence. He proposed a test called the "Imitation Game", still used today under the name "Turing Test." In the test, an interrogator was connected by teletype (later, by computer keyboard) to either a human or a computer at a remote location. The interrogator is allowed to pose any questions and, based on the replies, the interrogator must decide whether a human or a computer is at the other end of the line. If the interrogator cannot distinguish between the two in a statistically significant number of cases, then artificial intelligence has been achieved. Turing predicted that within fifty years, computers could be programmed to play the game so effectively that after a five-minute question period the interrogator would have no more than a seventy-percent chance of making the proper identification.

Personal Troubles Mount

Turing's personal life deteriorated in the early 1950s. After leaving NPL he took a position with Manchester College as deputy director of the newly formed Royal Society Computing Laboratory. But he was not involved in designing or building the computer on which they were working. By this time, Turing was no longer a world-class mathematician, having for too long been sidetracked by electronic engineering, nor was he engineer: The scientific world seemed to be passing him by.

While at Manchester, Turing had an affair with a young street person named Arnold Murray, which led to a burglary at his house by one of Murray's associates. The investigating police learned of the relationship between Turing and Murray; in fact Turing did nothing to hide it. Homosexuality was a felony in England at the time, and Turing was tried and convicted of "gross indecency" in 1952. Because of his social class and relative prominence, he was sentenced to a year's probation and given treatments of the female hormone estrogen in lieu of serving a year in jail.

Turing committed suicide by eating a cyanide-laced apple on June 7, 1954. His death puzzled his associates; he had been free of the hormone treatments for a year, and, although a stigma remained, he had weathered the incident with his career intact. He left no note, nor had he given any hint that he had contemplated this act. His mother tried for years to have his death declared accidental, but the official cause of death was never seriously questioned.

SELECTED WRITINGS BY TURING:

Periodicals

"On Computable Numbers, with an Application to the Entscheidungs Problem," *Proceedings of the London Mathematical Society,* Volume 42, 1937, pp. 230–265.
"Computing Machinery and Intelligence" *Mind,* Volume 59, 1950, pp. 433–460.

SOURCES:

Books

Carpenter, B. S., and R. W. Doran, editors, *A. M. Turing's ACE Report of 1946 and Other Papers,* MIT Press, 1986.
Hodges, Andrew, *Alan Turing, The Enigma,* Simon and Schuster, 1983.
Shurkin, Joel, *Engines of the Mind,* W.W. Norton, 1984.
Slater, Robert, *Portraits in Silicon,* MIT Press, 1987.
Turing, Sara, *Alan M. Turing,* Heffers, 1959.

—*Sketch by Joel Simon*

Charles Henry Turner
1861(?)-1923
American entomologist

Charles Henry Turner, an African American scientist, made major contributions to the field of entomology during the early years of the twentieth century. Through meticulous analytical research and untiring observation, he proved conclusively that insects can hear and distinguish pitch and that roaches learn by trial and error. In 1910 he discovered that the common honey bee can distinguish color and is drawn to flowers not just by odor but by sight as well. He was the first person to note that ants are guided back to their colony by light rays, not odors. He showed that wasps use visual landmarks to find their way back to their nests, disproving the long-held assumption that their homing skills resulted from an instinctual sixth sense. He also demonstrated that invertebrates often display certain "turning" behaviors when stimulated by light (in ants, the behavior is now known as Turner's circling). His research led to many journal publications, all of which advanced existing knowledge about ants, bees, wasps, and other insects.

Turner was born in Cincinnati, Ohio, on February 3, 1861 (one source says 1867), to Thomas and Addie Campbell Turner. His father was a church custodian and his mother worked as a practical nurse. The education-minded Turners owned a library containing several hundred volumes and instilled a love of reading in their son. At an early age, he decided to pursue a career in science. He received both his bachelor of science (1891) and master of science (1892) degrees from the University of Cincinnati.

From 1892 to 1893, Turner held an assistant professorship in biology at the University of Cincinnati. With the help of Booker T. Washington, he received an appointment as professor of biology at Clark College in Atlanta. From 1894 to 1897, he pursued a doctoral degree at the University of Chicago. He received his Ph.D. (magna cum laude) in 1907; his dissertation was entitled "The Homing of Ants: An Experimental Study of Ant Behavior." That same year, he began his long affiliation with Sumner High School in St. Louis, where he taught biology and psychology. He died in Chicago on February 14, 1923.

Constrained throughout his professional life by a lack of facilities and equipment, Turner made clever use of tools and techniques. He used his window shades to prove that wasps use landmarks (and not instinct) in finding their way. Colored disks and colored boxes filled with honey were used in experiments that showed that sight as well as odor leads bees to flowers. He observed death feinting in ant lions, and a "turning" activity of some invertebrates in response to sensory excitation—the scuttling away of roaches when the lights go on, for instance. A particular kind of movement in ants came to be known as Turner's circling. Turner published numerous papers on his work between 1911 and 1923, and he also wrote a book on nature for children and a collection of poems.

Turner was, undoubtedly, the nation's leading authority on insect behavior. While racism kept him far removed from the established academic mainstream, the importance of his research could not be ignored. Despite having to work with inadequate equipment and specimens, many of which were purchased at his own expense, the ingenuity of his experiments and his analytical genius led to discoveries and observations that forever changed scientific thinking about insects.

SOURCES:

Periodicals

Ferguson, Charles, "Charles Henry Turner and His Contributions," *Journal of Negro Education,* Volume 10, October, 1940.

Books

Hudson, G. H., "Charles Henry Turner," in *American Black Scientists and Inventors,* National Science Teachers Association, 1975.

—*Sketch by Tom Crawford*

Merle A. Tuve
1901-1982
American physicist

Merle A. Tuve left his mark on a number of fields of scientific research, beginning as a graduate student with his confirmation of the existence of the ionosphere, which led directly to the development of radar. He later explored the structure of the atomic nucleus, discovering the existence of the strong force and developing the particle accelerator as a tool in conducting nucleus research. During World War II, he was largely responsible for the development of a new and more efficient system of detonating bombs, the proximity fuse. After the war, he used surplus weapons to study the structure and composition of the Earth's interior. Beginning in the 1950s, Tuve turned his attention to astronomy, developing systems for greatly improving the sensitivity of observational devices.

Merle Antony Tuve was born in Canton, South Dakota, on June 27, 1901. His parents were Anthony E. and Ida Marie Larsen Tuve. Coincidentally, another man destined to earn international fame as a scientist, **Ernest O. Lawrence**, was also born in the small town of Canton, just two months after Tuve.

Tuve and Lawrence played together as children and on one occasion constructed a telegraph between their homes. When Lawrence moved away, the two boys continued to communicate—by ham radio.

After completing his secondary education at the Augustana Academy in Canton, Tuve enrolled in the University of Minnesota, where he planned to major in chemistry. Those plans changed, however, and he received his bachelor's degree in electrical engineering in 1922. During his undergraduate years, Tuve came into contact with John T. Tate, a theoretical physicist, and became convinced that it was physics, not engineering, that interested him most. Accordingly, he entered the master's program in physics at Minnesota and began a study of the microwave radiation produced in vacuum tubes. For this research, he received his master's degree in 1923.

Doctoral Research Reveals Ionosphere

After graduation, Tuve was offered a teaching position at Princeton University but transferred after a single year to Johns Hopkins University, where he entered the doctoral program in physics in 1924. It was at Johns Hopkins that Tuve made his first important discovery. Scientists had known for many years that radio signals can be transmitted over long distances. The explanation for this phenomenon at the time was that radio waves generated at one location on the Earth's surface pass into the upper atmosphere, where they are reflected off a layer of charged particles. Those waves then return to the Earth's surface, where they can be detected at some distant location. For his doctoral research, Tuve and colleague **Gregory Breit** developed a method for generating very short radio-wave pulses that could be directed into the atmosphere. By measuring the time it took for these pulses to be received at a detection station, Tuve and Breit were able to calculate the height of the atmospheric reflecting layer, a region later named the ionosphere. This process of measuring reflected pulses was later utilized in the development of radar. Upon completion of this research, Tuve was awarded his Ph.D. in 1926.

In the same year, Tuve accepted a position as staff researcher at the Carnegie Institute in Washington, D.C. He was to remain at Carnegie for the next four decades, becoming director in 1946 and distinguished service member in 1966, the year of his retirement. Tuve was joined at Carnegie in 1926 by Breit, and the two physicists then began a research project designed to study the forces that exist within the atomic nucleus. By the 1920s, it had become apparent that the only charged particles present in the nucleus are positively charged protons. The question that arose, therefore, was how the nucleus was able to remain stable when it seemed that electrostatic forces of repulsion would tend to drive it apart.

To study this question, Tuve, working initially with Breit and later with Lawrence R. Hafstad and Odd Dahl, developed devices for the acceleration of particles to very high speeds. At first, they adapted Tesla coils for thier particle accelerator but then found Van de Graaff generators more effective. Their goal was to cause a stream of rapidly moving protons to collide with a stationary mass of protons (hydrogen gas) and observe the results of these collisions. After a decade of study with increasingly more powerful machines, Tuve and his colleagues eventually made an important discovery. They found that there exists within the nucleus a force far stronger than the electrostatic force, indeed, the most powerful force yet discovered. That force was eventually given the apt name "the strong force."

Just prior to World War II, Tuve learned of the discovery of atomic fission by **Otto Hahn** and **Fritz Strassmann** and immediately confirmed their findings in his own laboratory at Carnegie's Department of Terrestrial Magnetism. He served briefly on the Uranium Committee appointed to study the application of atomic fission to the construction of nuclear weapons. He soon decided, however, to devote his wartime efforts to the problems of more conventional weapons. In particular, he worked on the development of a new device for explosive detonation.

At the time, detonation of explosives was accomplished by one of two methods: a bomb could be set off either by means of a timing device or by impact with another object. Neither mechanism was adequately effective against rapidly moving objects, such as the high-speed "buzz bombs" being used by the Germans. Tuve's solution to this problem was the proximity fuse, an instrument that transmitted radio waves as an explosive device traveled through the air. The reflection of the waves emanating from an intended target could be used to measure the distance between bomb and target and, at a certain point, facilitate detonation.

Turns Attention to Earth's Interior

Tuve did not return to nuclear physics after World War II but instead became interested in the structural characteristics of the Earth's crust. He was able to obtain war surplus land mines and depth charges that could be used to generate shock waves. By timing and tracking the passage of these shock waves through the crust, Tuve was able to determine properties of the crust to a depth of about 125 miles. In one application of this work, Tuve supervised the establishment of a network of seismic stations in the Andes plateau as part of the 1957 International Geophysical Year.

From the 1950s on, Tuve become involved in astronomical research. He and his colleagues developed devices to improve the collection and analysis of telescopic data. He also become interested in the study of radio-wave emission by hydrogen clouds located between galaxies.

Tuve married Winifred Gray Whitman, a medical doctor, in 1927. The Tuves had two children, Trygve Whitman, who was to become a health care administrator, and Lucy Winifred, who became a cell biologist. Tuve died of heart disease in Bethesda, Maryland, on May 20, 1982.

SELECTED WRITINGS BY TUVE:

Books

Velocity Structures in Hydrogen Profiles: A Sky of Neutral Hydrogen Emission, Carnegie Institution of Washington, 1973.

SOURCES:

Books

Steinhart, John S., editor, *The Earth Beneath the Continents: A Volume of Geophysical Studies in Honor of Merle A. Tuve,* American Geophysical Union, 1966.

Periodicals

Cornell, Thomas D., "Merle Antony Tuve: Pioneer Nuclear Physicist," *Physics Today,* January, 1988, pp. 57–64.

—*Sketch by David E. Newton*

George Uhlenbeck
1900-1988
Dutch American physicist

George Uhlenbeck made the discovery for which he became famous, electron spin, while still a graduate student at the University of Leiden studying under the eminent physicist **Paul Ehrenfest**. His collaborator in that work was another graduate student, **Samuel Goudsmit**. Many scholars believe that the failure of the Nobel Prize committee to award Uhlenbeck and Goudsmit a physics prize for this discovery has been one of its greatest errors of omission.

George Eugene Uhlenbeck was born on December 6, 1900, in Batavia, Java (now Djakarta, Indonesia), part of what was then the Dutch East Indies. He came from a prominent Dutch family with roots in Germany. A paternal ancestor, Johannes Wilhelmus Uhlenbeck, had served in the army of Frederick the Great of Prussia, fled the country after a duel, and joined the Dutch East India Company in Ceylon (now Sri Lanka). That episode marked the beginning of the Dutch line of Uhlenbecks. George's father, Eugenius Marius Uhlenbeck, was born on the island of Sumatra and later joined the Dutch East Indian Army. George's mother was the former Annie Beegers, daughter of a major general in the Dutch East Indian Army.

Uhlenbeck's education began in the town of Padangpandjang on Sumatra, but was interrupted by his family's return to Holland in 1907. He then completed his elementary and secondary schooling in the Hague. His interest in physics was first aroused by a three-year course at the higher burgher school he attended.

Encounters Paul Ehrenfest

Upon graduation from high school in 1918, Uhlenbeck entered the Technische Hogeschool at Delft. He would have preferred to attend the University of Leiden, but national regulations required a university student to be proficient in Latin and Greek, which Uhlenbeck was not. Only a few months into his first semester at Delft, however, those regulations were changed, and Uhlenbeck found it possible to transfer to Leiden.

As a graduate student at Leiden Uhlenbeck came into contact with the man who was to become the most influential force in his life, Paul Ehrenfest. Abraham Pais writes in *Physics Today* that "in all the years I knew Uhlenbeck, in Utrecht, in Ann Arbor, and in New York, a single picture always stood on his desk: a small photograph of a warmly smiling Ehrenfest." Uhlenbeck obtained his first teaching job, in fact, as a result of Ehrenfest's influence. That job was as a private tutor to a son of the Dutch ambassador to Italy, stationed in Rome.

Begins Work with Goudsmit

During his three years in Rome, from September 1922 to June 1925, Uhlenbeck returned to Holland during the summers to continue his studies at Leiden. By September 1923, he had completed the requirements for the degree of doctorandus, the equivalent of a master's degree. Two years later, he resigned from his job in Rome and returned to Leiden to work on his Ph.D. The summer and fall of 1925 were a momentous period for Uhlenbeck. In June, Ehrenfest had introduced Uhlenbeck to Samuel A. Goudsmit, another of his graduate students, and suggested that the two work on the problem of line spectra. The topic on which they were to concentrate in particular was doublet lines, the splitting of lines in a spectrum when subjected to an external magnetic field.

This phenomenon had been known for some time, but no satisfactory explanation as to its cause had been developed. From June to October, Uhlenbeck and Goudsmit worked on the problem, finally arriving at a solution. Suppose, they said, that one imagines the electron as a tiny spinning sphere. As such, it would generate its own magnetic field that, depending on its alignment, could either oppose or reinforce the external magnetic field. These two positions would have similar, but not identical, energies that could account for the formation of doublet lines.

The Uhlenbeck-Goudsmit discovery came only months after **Wolfgang Pauli** had concluded that a fourth quantum number was needed to explain existing data on atomic structure. Pauli had no idea as to how the new quantum number could be interpreted physically, but knew that it could have only one of two values. Uhlenbeck and Goudsmit showed that the numerical value associated with electron spin could be either $+\frac{1}{2}$ or $-\frac{1}{2}$, values that satisfied Pauli's theoretical constraints for the fourth quantum number.

Uhlenbeck was awarded his Ph.D. in physics from Leiden in 1927, two years after the discovery of electron spin. In the same year, he immigrated to the United States, where he took a position teaching physics at the University of Michigan in Ann Arbor. He became professor of theoretical physics in 1939, and Henry Carhart Professor of Physics in 1954. During World War II, Uhlenbeck was head of the theoretical division at the Radiation Laboratory of the Massachusetts Institute of Technology. He married Else Ophorst in 1947, and together they had one son, Olke. In 1961, he was offered an opportunity to establish a new department of theoretical physics at the Rockefeller Medical Research Center of the State University of New York, later Rockefeller University. He remained at Rockefeller until his retirement in 1974. Among the honors he received during his lifetime were the Research Corporation Award in 1953, the Oersted Medal of the American Association of Physics Teachers in 1955, the Max Planck Medal in 1964, the Lorentz Medal of the Royal Netherlands Academy of Science in 1970, and the National Medal of Science in 1977. Uhlenbeck died in Boulder, Colorado, on October 31, 1988.

SOURCES:

Periodicals

Pais, Abraham, "George Uhlenbeck and the Discovery of Electron Spin," *Physics Today,* December, 1989, pp. 34–40.

—*Sketch by David E. Newton*

Karen Uhlenbeck
1942-
American mathematician

Karen Uhlenbeck is engaged in mathematical research that has applications in theoretical physics and has contributed to the study of instantons, models for the behavior of surfaces in four dimensions. In recognition of her work in geometry and partial differential equations, she was awarded a prestigious MacArthur Fellowship in 1983.

Karen Keskulla Uhlenbeck was born in Cleveland, Ohio, on August 24, 1942, to Arnold Edward Keskulla, an engineer, and Carolyn Windeler Keskulla, an artist. When Uhlenbeck was in third grade, the family moved to New Jersey. Everything interested her as a child, but she felt that girls were discouraged from exploring many activities. In high school, she read American physicist **George Gamow**'s books on physics and English astronomer **Fred Hoyle**'s books on cosmology, which her father brought home from the public library. When Uhlenbeck entered the University of Michigan, she found mathematics a broad and intellectually stimulating subject. After earning her B.S. degree in 1964, she became a National Science Foundation Graduate Fellow, pursuing graduate study in mathematics at Brandeis University. In 1965, she married Olke Cornelis Uhlenbeck, a biophysicist; they later divorced.

Uhlenbeck received her Ph.D. in mathematics from Brandeis in 1968 with a thesis on the calculus of variations. Her first teaching position was at the Massachusetts Institute of Technology in 1968. The following year she moved to Berkeley, California, where she was a lecturer in mathematics at the University of California. There she studied general relativity and the geometry of space-time, and worked on elliptic regularity in systems of partial differential equations.

In 1971, Uhlenbeck became an assistant professor at the University of Illinois at Urbana-Champaign. In 1974, she was awarded a fellowship from the Sloan Foundation that lasted until 1976, and she then went to Northwestern University as a visiting associate professor. She taught at the University of Illinois in Chicago from 1977 to 1983, first as associate professor and then professor, and in 1979 she was the Chancellor's Distinguished Visiting Professor at the University of California, Berkeley. An Albert Einstein Fellowship enabled her to pursue her research as a member of the Institute for Advanced Studies at Princeton University from 1979 to 1980. She published more than a dozen articles in mathematics journals during the 1970s and was named to the editorial board of the *Journal of Differential Geometry* in 1979 and the *Illinois Journal of Mathematics* in 1980.

In 1983, Uhlenbeck was selected by the John D. and Catherine T. MacArthur Foundation of Chicago to receive one of its five-year fellowship grants. Given annually, the MacArthur fellowships enable scientists, scholars, and artists to pursue research or creative activity. For Uhlenbeck, winning the fellowship inspired her to begin serious studies in physics. She believes that the mathematician's task is to abstract ideas from fields such as physics and streamline them so they can be used in other fields. For instance, physicists studying quantum mechanics had predicted the existence of particle-like elements called instantons. Uhlenbeck and other researchers viewed instantons as somewhat analogous to soap films. Seeking a better understanding of these particles, they studied soap films to learn about the properties of surfaces. As soap films provide a model for the behavior of surfaces in three-dimensions, instantons provide analogous models for the behavior of surfaces in four-dimensional space-time. Uhlenbeck cowrote a book on this subject, *Instantons and 4-Manifold Topology,* which was published in 1984.

After a year spent as a visiting professor at Harvard, Uhlenbeck became a professor at the University of Chicago in 1983. Her mathematical interests at this time included nonlinear partial differential equations, differential geometry, gauge theory, topological quantum field theory, and integrable systems. She gave guest lectures at several universities and served as the vice president of the American Mathematical Society. The Alumni Association of the University of Michigan named her Alumna of the Year in 1984. She was elected to the American Academy of Arts and Sciences in 1985 and to the National Academy of Sciences in 1986. In 1988, she received the Alumni Achievement award from Brandeis University, an honorary doctor of science degree from Knox College, and was named one of America's 100 most important women by *Ladies' Home Journal.*

In 1987, Uhlenbeck went to the University of Texas at Austin, where she broadened her understanding of physics in studies with American physicist **Steven Weinberg**. In 1988, she accepted the Sid W. Richardson Foundation Regents' Chair in mathematics at the University of Texas. She also gave the plenary address at the International Congress of Mathematics in Japan in 1990.

Concerned that potential scientists were being discouraged unnecessarily because of their sex or race, Uhlenbeck joined a National Research Council planning group to investigate the representation of women in science and engineering. She believes that mathematics is always challenging and never boring, and she has expressed the hope that one of her accomplishments as a teacher has been communicating this to her students. "I sometimes feel the need to apologize for being a mathematician, but no apology is needed," she told *The Alcalde Magazine.* "Whenever I get a free week and start doing mathematics, I can't believe how much fun it is. I'm like a 12-year-old boy with a new train set."

SELECTED WRITINGS BY UHLENBECK:

Books

(With D. Freed) *Instantons and 4-Manifold Topology,* Springer Verlag, 1984.

SOURCES:

Periodicals

Benningfield, Damond, "Prominent Players," *The Alcalde Magazine,* September/October, 1988, pp. 26–30.

Other

Uhlenbeck, Karen, "Some Personal Remarks on My Partly Finished Life," unpublished manuscript.

—Sketch by C. D. Lord

Harold Urey
1893-1981
American chemist and physicist

In 1934 Harold Urey was awarded the Nobel Prize in chemistry for his discovery of deuterium, an isotope, or species, of hydrogen in which the atoms weigh twice as much as those in ordinary hydrogen. Also known as heavy hydrogen, deuterium became profoundly important to future studies in many scientific fields, including chemistry, physics, and medicine. Urey continued his research on isotopes over the next three decades, and during World War II his experience with deuterium proved invaluable in efforts to separate isotopes of uranium from each other in the development of the first atomic bombs. Later, Urey's research on isotopes also led to a method for determining the earth's atmospheric temperature at various periods in past history. This experimentation has become especially relevant because of concerns about the possibility of global climate change.

Harold Clayton Urey was born in Walkerton, Indiana, on April 29, 1893. His father, Samuel Clayton Urey, was a schoolteacher and lay minister in the Church of the Brethren. His mother was Cora Reinoehl Urey. Urey's father died when Harold was only six years old, and his mother later married another Brethren minister. Urey had a sister, Martha, a brother, Clarence, and two half-sisters, Florence and Ina.

After graduating from high school, Urey hoped to attend college but lacked the financial resources to do so. Instead, he accepted teaching jobs in country schools, first in Indiana (1911–1912) and then in Montana (1912–1914) before finally entering Mon-

Harold Urey

tana State University in September of 1914 at the age of 21. Urey was initially interested in a career in biology, and the first original research he ever conducted involved a study of microorganisms in the Missoula River. In 1917 he was awarded his bachelor of science degree in zoology by Montana State.

Early Job Experience Leads to Career in Chemistry

The year Urey graduated also marked the entry of the United States into World War I. Although he had strong pacifist beliefs as a result of his early religious training, Urey acknowledged his obligation to participate in the nation's war effort. As a result, he accepted a job at the Barrett Chemical Company in Philadelphia and worked to develop high explosives. In his Nobel Prize acceptance speech, Urey said that this experience was instrumental in his move from industrial chemistry to academic life.

At the end of the war, Urey returned to Montana State University where he began teaching chemistry. In 1921 he decided to resume his college education and enrolled in the doctoral program in physical chemistry at the University of California at Berkeley. His faculty advisor at Berkeley was the great physical chemist **Gilbert Newton Lewis**. Urey received his doctorate in 1923 for research on the calculation of heat capacities and entropies (the degree of randomness in a system) of gases, based on information obtained through the use of a spectroscope. He then

left for a year of postdoctoral study at the Institute for Theoretical Physics at the University of Copenhagen where **Niels Bohr**, a Danish physicist, was researching the structure of the atom. Urey's interest in Bohr's research had been cultivated while studying with Lewis, who had proposed many early theories on the nature of chemical bonding.

Upon his return to the United States in 1925, Urey accepted an appointment as an associate in chemistry at the Johns Hopkins University in Baltimore, a post he held until 1929. He interrupted his work at Johns Hopkins briefly to marry Frieda Daum in Lawrence, Kansas, on June 12, 1926. Daum was a bacteriologist and daughter of a prominent Lawrence educator. The Ureys later had four children, Gertrude Elizabeth, Frieda Rebecca, Mary Alice, and John Clayton.

Discovery of Deuterium Leads to Nobel Prize

In 1929, Urey left Johns Hopkins to become associate professor of chemistry at Columbia University, and in 1930 he published his first book, *Atoms, Molecules, and Quanta,* written with A. E. Ruark. Writing in the *Dictionary of Scientific Biography,* Joseph N. Tatarewicz called this work "the first comprehensive English language textbook on atomic structure and a major bridge between the new quantum physics and the field of chemistry." At this time he also began his search for an isotope of hydrogen. Since **Frederick Soddy**, an English chemist, discovered isotopes in 1913, scientists had been looking for isotopes of a number of elements. Urey believed that if an isotope of heavy hydrogen existed, one way to separate it from the ordinary hydrogen isotope would be through the vaporization of liquid hydrogen. Since heavy hydrogen would be more dense than ordinary hydrogen, Urey theorized that the lighter hydrogen atoms would vaporize first, leaving behind a mixture rich in heavy hydrogen. Urey believed that if he could obtain enough of the heavy mixture through a process of slow evaporation, spectroscopic readings would show spectral lines that differed from that of ordinary hydrogen.

With the help of two colleagues, Ferdinand Brickwedde and George M. Murphy, Urey carried out his experiment in 1931. The three researchers began with four liters of liquid hydrogen which they allowed to evaporate very slowly. Eventually, only a single milliliter of liquid hydrogen remained. This sample was then subjected to spectroscopic analysis which showed the presence of lines in exactly the positions predicted for a heavier isotope of hydrogen. This was deuterium.

The discovery of deuterium made Urey famous in the scientific world, and only three years later he was awarded the Nobel Prize in chemistry for his discovery. Since his wife was pregnant at the time, he declined to travel to Stockholm and was allowed to participate in the award ceremonies the following year. Urey's accomplishments were also recognized by Columbia University, and in 1933 he was appointed the Ernest Kempton Adams Fellow. A year later he was promoted to full professor of chemistry. Urey retained his appointment at Columbia until the end of World War II. During this time he also became the first editor of the new *Journal of Chemical Physics,* which became one of the principal periodicals in the field.

During the latter part of the 1930s, Urey extended his work on isotopes to other elements besides hydrogen. Eventually his research team was able to separate isotopes of carbon, nitrogen, oxygen, and sulfur. One of the intriguing discoveries made during this period was that isotopes may differ from each other chemically in very small ways. Initially, it was assumed that since all isotopes of an element have the same electronic configuration, they would also have identical chemical properties. Urey found, however, that the mass differences in isotopes can result in modest differences in the *rate* at which they react.

Work on Isotopes Proves of Value during World War II

The practical consequences of this discovery became apparent all too soon. In 1939, word reached the United States about the discovery of nuclear fission by the German scientists **Otto Hahn** and **Fritz Strassmann.** The military consequences of the Hahn-Strassmann discovery were apparent to many scientists, including Urey. He was one of the first, therefore, to become involved in the U.S. effort to build a nuclear weapon, recognizing the threat posed by such a weapon in the hands of Nazi Germany. However, Urey was deeply concerned about the potential destructiveness of a fission weapon. Actively involved in political topics during the 1930s, Urey was a member of the Committee to Defend America by Aiding the Allies and worked vigorously against the fascist regimes in Germany, Italy, and Spain. He explained the importance of his political activism by saying that "no dictator knows enough to tell scientists what to do. Only in democratic nations can science flourish."

As World War II drew closer, Urey became involved in the Manhattan Project to build the nation's first atomic bomb. In 1940, he became a member of the Uranium Committee of the project, and two years later he was appointed director of the Substitute Alloys Materials Laboratory (SAML) at Columbia. SAML was one of three locations in the United States where research was being conducted on methods to separate two isotopes of uranium. As a leading expert on the separation of isotopes, Urey made critical contributions to the solution of the Manhattan Project's single most difficult problem, the isolation of uranium–235 from its heavier twin.

At the conclusion of World War II, Urey left Columbia to join the Enrico Fermi Institute of Nuclear Studies at the University of Chicago. In 1952 he was named Martin A. Ryerson Distinguished Service Professor there. The postwar period saw the beginning of a flood of awards and honorary degrees that was to continue for more than three decades. He received honorary degrees from more than two dozen universities, including doctorates from Columbia (1946), Oxford (1946), Washington and Lee (1948), the University of Athens (1951), McMaster University (1951), Yale (1951), and Indiana (1953).

The end of the war did not end Urey's concern about nuclear weapons. He now shifted his attention to work for the control of the terrible power he had helped to make a reality. Deeply conscious of a sense of scientific responsibility, Urey was opposed to the dropping of an atomic bomb on Japan. He was also aggressively involved in defeating a bill that would have placed control of nuclear power in the United States in the hands of the Department of Defense. Instead, he helped pass a bill creating a civilian board to control future nuclear development. In later years Urey explored peaceful uses of nuclear energy, and in 1975 he petitioned the White House to reduce production in nuclear power plants. He was also a member of the Union of Concerned Scientists.

More Applications of Isotope Research Uncovered

Urey continued to work on new applications of his isotope research. In the late 1940s and early 1950s, he explored the relationship between the isotopes of oxygen and past planetary climates. Since isotopes differ in the rate of chemical reactions, Urey said that the amount of each oxygen isotope in an organism is a result of atmospheric temperatures. During periods when the earth was warmer than normal, organisms would take in more of a lighter isotope of oxygen and less of a heavier isotope. During cool periods, the differences among isotopic concentrations would not be as great. Over a period of time, Urey was able to develop a scale, or an "oxygen thermometer," that related the relative concentrations of oxygen isotopes in the shells of sea animals with atmospheric temperatures. Some of those studies continue to be highly relevant in current research on the possibilities of global climate change.

In the early 1950s, Urey became interested in yet another subject: the chemistry of the universe and of the formation of the planets, including the earth. One of his first papers on this topic attempted to provide an estimate of the relative abundance of the elements in the universe. Although these estimates have now been improved, they were remarkably close to the values modern chemists now accept.

Urey also became involved in a study of the origin of the solar system. For well over 200 years, scientists had been debating the mechanism by which the planets and their satellites were formed. From his own studies, Urey concluded that the creation of the solar system took place at temperatures considerably less than those suggested by most experts at the time. He also proposed a new theory about the origin of the Earth's moon, claiming that it was formed not as a result of being torn from the Earth, but through an independent process of a gradual accumulation of materials.

Urey's last great period of research brought together his interests and experiences in a number of fields of research to which he had devoted his life. The subject of that research was the origin of life on Earth. Urey hypothesized that the Earth's primordial atmosphere consisted of reducing gases such as hydrogen, ammonia, and methane. The energy provided by electrical discharges in the atmosphere, he suggested, was sufficient to initiate chemical reactions among these gases, converting them to the simplest compounds of which living organisms are made, amino acids. In 1951, Urey's graduate student **Stanley Lloyd Miller** carried out a series of experiments to test this hypothesis. In these experiments, an electrical discharge passed through a glass tube containing only reducing gases resulted in the formation of amino acids.

In 1958 Urey left the University of Chicago to become Professor at Large at the University of California in San Diego at La Jolla. At La Jolla, his interests shifted from original scientific research to national scientific policy. He became extremely involved in the U.S. space program, serving as the first chairman of the Committee on Chemistry of Space and Exploration of the Moon and Planets of the National Academy of Science's Space Sciences Board. Even late in life, Urey continued to receive honors and awards from a grateful nation and admiring colleagues. He was awarded the Johann Kepler Medal of the American Association for the Advancement of Science (1971), the Priestley Medal of the American Chemical Society (1973), National Aeronautics and Space Administration (NASA) Exceptional Scientific Achievement Award (1973), and the 200th Anniversary Plaque of the American Chemical Society (1976). Urey died of a heart attack in La Jolla on January 5, 1981, at the age of 87.

SELECTED WRITINGS BY UREY:

Books

(With A. E. Ruark) *Atoms, Molecules, and Quanta,* McGraw-Hill, 1930.
The Planets: Their Origins and Development, Yale University Press, 1952.

"The Origin of the Earth," in *Nuclear Geology,* edited by Henry Faul, Wiley, 1954, pp. 355–71.
"Earth's Daughter, Sister, or Uncle?" in *America's Race for the Moon,* edited by W. Sullivan, Random House, 1962.

Periodicals

"On the Relative Abundances of Isotopes," *Physical Review,* Volume 38, 1931, pp. 718–24.
"Some Thermodynamic Properties of Hydrogen Deuterium," *Angewandte Chemie,* Volume 48, 1935, pp. 315–20.
"A Hypothesis Regarding the Origin of the Movement of the Earth's Crust," *Science,* October 28, 1949, pp. 445–46.
"Meteorites and the Origin of the Solar System," *Yearbook of the Physical Society,* New York, 1957.
"As I See It," *Forbes,* July 15, 1969, pp. 44–48.

SOURCES:

Books

Holmes, Frederic L. editor, *Dictionary of Scientific Biography*, Volume 18, Supplement II, Scribner, 1990.
Schoenebaum, Eleanora W., *Political Profiles: The Truman Years,* Facts on File, 1978, pp. 571–72.

Periodicals

Brickwedde, Ferdinand G., "Harold Urey and the Discovery of Deuterium," *Physics Today,* September 1982, pp. 34–39.
Brush, Stephen G., "Nickel for Your Thoughts: Urey and the Origin of the Moon," *Science,* Volume 217, 1982, pp. 891–98.
Garfield, Eugene, "A Tribute to Harold Urey," *Current Comments,* December 3, 1979, pp. 5–9.
Sagan, Carl, "Obituary, Harold Clayton Urey, 1893–1981," *Icarus,* Volume 48 1981, pp. 348–52.

—Sketch by David E. Newton

Seiya Uyeda
1929-
Japanese geophysicist

Geophysicist Seiya Uyeda became an expert on tectonics—the study of the Earth's crust and its motions—through his studies of the Japanese island arc. Using this knowledge, he demonstrated the relationship between terrestrial heat flow around Japan and earthquake and volcanic activity. He also developed, with D. Forsyth, a theory explaining the motion of the Earth's tectonic plates. Uyeda was born in Tokyo on November 28, 1929, to Seiichi, a government official, and Hatsuo (Okino) Uyeda. He attended the University of Tokyo, majoring in geophysics. He was awarded his bachelor of science in 1952 and his D.Sc. in 1958. In 1952 Uyeda married Mutsuko Kosaka; they have three children, Taro, Makiko and Naoko.

For his doctoral research, Uyeda studied the phenomenon of the self-reversal of magnetism in some rock minerals. This means that the direction of the magnetism of some rocks was exactly opposite of that of the Earth's geomagnetic field. The reversal of magnetism in some minerals indicated that in the geological past, the Earth's magnetic field had experienced reversals. This area of study was very important at the start of Uyeda's career, as it corresponded with the continental drift theory. Originally proposed in 1912 by **Alfred Wegener**, the theory was experiencing a revival in the scientific community. It proposed that the Earth's continents were not fixed in place, which contradicted the earlier theory that the surface of the Earth was rigid and unchanging.

Wegener's continental drift theory claimed that all of the current continents were once one large land mass. Although now discounted, that theory was connected to the related theories of sea-floor spreading and plate tectonics. According to plate tectonics, the ocean floor was created at the mid-oceanic trenches, then spread horizontally and finally ended in the deep trenches. Plate tectonics posit that the Earth's surface was made of fifteen rigid blocks or plates. The collisions and other interactions of these plates explain the appearance of the Earth's crust.

Researches Plate Tectonics and Heat Flow

Plate tectonics can explain the current appearance of island arcs, the area of study that Uyeda pioneered in association with other scientists. Island arcs are the series of island chains along the northern and western edges of the Pacific. Named for their typical arc shape, they have trenches which are more than six thousand meters (twenty thousand feet) deep, usually lying on the ocean side of each arc. From 1957 to 1964, Uyeda was a research associate at the Earthquake Research Institute at the University of Tokyo, where he studied the distribution of terrestrial heat flow over the Japanese island arc and its surrounding seas. He found that the flow was low on the ocean side of the arc and high on the continental side; the heat flow in the Sea of Japan was always higher than that of the Japan Trench and the Pacific on the east of Japan. Uyeda's research demonstrated that the distribution of heat flow was related to the distribution of volcanoes and earthquakes. These findings were used as the basis of a theory of typical heat flow for island arcs.

Uyeda's research on island arcs led to his discovery, with colleagues, of magnetic lineations in the Pacific Ocean. From this finding, he posited that the Pacific floor had undergone a major northward move sometime in the geological past. Uyeda also co-originated, with Forsyth in 1975, a theory based on a pulling at the trenches of plates that explained the origin of plate motions.

Uyeda became an associate professor at the Geophysical Institute in 1964, where he remained until he returned to the Earthquake Research Institute as a professor from 1969 to 1990. Since 1990, he has served as both a professor in the department of marine science and technology at Tokai University in Simizu, Japan, and a professor at the Texas A & M University College Station. Throughout his career Uyeda also has spent many years as a visiting scientist at prestigious institutions. He has taught at Cambridge and Oxford Universities, the Scripps Institution of Oceanography, Stanford University, the Massachusetts Institute of Technology, the Lamont-Doherty Geological Observatory, and the California Institute of Technology.

Uyeda has received numerous prizes and honors, including the Tanakadte Prize of the Society of Terrestrial Magnetism and Electricity in 1955, the Agassiz Medal of the U.S. National Academy of Sciences in 1972, the Academy Prize of the Japanese Academy in 1987, and the G. P. Woollard Award of the Geological Society of America in 1989. Uyeda is a foreign associate of the National Academy of Science, and an associate member of the Societé Géologique de France.

SELECTED WRITINGS BY UYEDA:

Books

(With A. Sugimura) *Island Arcs: Japan and its Environs,* Elsevier, 1973.
The New View of the Earth: Moving Continents and Moving Oceans, W. H. Freeman, 1978.

SOURCES:

Books

McGraw-Hill Modern Scientists and Engineers, Volume 3, McGraw-Hill, 1980, pp. 241–242.

—*Sketch by Terrie M. Romano*

Henri-Victor Vallois
1889-1981
French anatomist and paleontologist

Henri-Victor Vallois was one of the major proponents of the presapiens theory of human evolution, one of a number of theories which attempted to determine the evolutionary position of the fossilized remains of an early form of human known as the Neanderthal.

Born in Nancy, France, in 1889, Vallois received degrees in medicine and natural science and joined the faculty of medicine in Toulouse in 1922. In 1933 he became director of the laboratory of the École Pratique des Hautes Études. A prolific writer, Vallois published more than four hundred works between 1908 and 1980. He served as professor at the Musée d'Histoire Naturelle, held the post of director of the Institut de Paléontologie Humaine in Paris from 1942, and was Marcellin Boule's successor as director of the Musée de l'Homme from 1950 to 1959.

As was common in the early part of the twentieth century, Vallois's research concerned the origin of the racial differences recognized in modern humans, and he established a system of classification of humans by racial type. He identified twenty-seven races, distinguished by such features as size, skin color, and head shape, which he grouped into four major categories: the australoid, the leucoderme, the melanoderm, and the xanthoderm. This classification was substantially criticized by other scientists; however, it produced two influential books, *Les races de l'empire français* (1943) and *Les races humaines* (1944).

His most significant work, however, concerned the development of the modern human, *Homo sapiens,* from earlier forms now known as *Homo erectus.* Vallois was the first to critique the three most prevalent theories of human origin, each of which is identified by the position attributed to the Neanderthal in the sequence of human evolution. The Neanderthal-phase hypothesis holds that humans developed in a relatively linear manner, from the earliest forms through *Homo erectus,* the Neanderthals, and *Homo sapiens,* that is, placing modern humans in a direct line from the Neanderthals. The presapiens theory maintains that the Neanderthal was too primitive a form of human living too late in the sequence to have been a direct ancestor of modern humans; rather, a more advanced type of human had already developed, and with their superior tools and more advanced culture, these humans eventually displaced the more primitive Neanderthals. The pre-Neanderthal hypothesis offers a compromise, accepting the premise that the European Neanderthals (the "classic" Neanderthals) were too primitive to have been direct ancestors of modern humans, but suggesting that another branch of Neanderthal had been the intermediate stage between *Homo erectus* and modern *Homo sapiens.*

Vallois first organized these theories in his 1958 monograph on the fossil remains found at Fontéchevade in France. He rejected the Neanderthal-phase theory, associated with the ideas of **Franz Weidenreich** and **Aleš Hrdlička**, believing, on the basis of certain anatomical indexes derived from analysis of Neanderthal remains, that the species was too specialized to fall within the evolutionary sequence. Vallois also believed that two nearly contemporaneous human forms, the Neanderthal and the more modern-appearing Cro-Magnon, or Aurignacian, were too different morphologically to have been part of the same line of descent; he maintained that modern humans were descended from the Aurignacian, who, he theorized, had originated in Western Asia independent of the Neanderthals and migrated into Europe between glacial periods.

Vallois criticized the pre-Neanderthal theory, concluding that the fossils grouped together as pre-Neanderthals were too different from each other to form a coherent type, and he believed that the Neanderthals as a group exhibited relatively little interindividual variation. In his view, some of the so-called pre-Neanderthal fossils were morphologically too close to modern humans—especially in their lack of a prominent brow ridge—to be ancestral to the Neanderthals.

Vallois's main evidence in support of the presapiens theory, which was upheld by such paleoanthropologists as **Arthur Keith** and **Louis Leakey**, came from European sites, notably Fontéchevade, with corroborating evidence taken from skull fragments found in Swanscombe, England. Although these fossils lacked the portion of the skull on which the brow ridge would have appeared or were of immature individuals who would not yet have developed such a ridge, Vallois's reconstruction of the skulls led him to conclude that these provided evidence of a modern human species predating the Neanderthals and the pre-Neanderthals as well, and provided the link between ancient and modern humans. The theory held that anatomically modern humans could be very ancient, in fact developing earlier than some more primitive types. Additional evidence from the fossil remains found at Piltdown, England, was quickly discarded when it was found to be fraudulent, but the presapiens theory was already losing support. Even by the time of publication of his monograph in 1958, few scholars supported Vallois's view. Further research into the Fontéchevade and Swanscombe remains led an increasing number of scholars to the conclusion that these were actually ancestral to the Neanderthals, and the pre-Neanderthal theory gained prominence. Vallois retired in 1961 and died in 1981.

SELECTED WRITINGS BY VALLOIS:

Books

La paléontologie et l'origine de l'homme, Paris, 1950.
(With Marcellin Boule) *Fossil Men,* Dryden, 1957.
"The Social Life of Early Man: The Evidence of Skeletons," in *Social Life of Early Man,* edited by Sherwood L. Washburn, Aldine, 1961.

Periodicals

"Les preuves anatomatiques de l'origine mono-phyletique de l'homme," *L'anthropologie,* Volume 39, 1929, pp. 77–101.
"The Fontéchevade Fossil Man," *American Journal of Physical Anthropology,* Volume 7, 1949, pp. 339–362.
"Neanderthals and Presapiens," *Journal of the Royal Anthropological Institute,* Volume 84, 1954, pp. 111–130.

SOURCES:

Books

Smith, Fred H., and Frank Spencer, *The Origins of Modern Humans: A World Survey of the Fossil Evidence,* Liss, 1984.
Trinkaus, Erik, and Pat Shipman, *The Neanderthals: Changing the Image of Mankind,* Knopf, 1993.

Periodicals

Delmas, André, tribute in *L'anthropologie,* December, 1981.

—*Sketch by Michael Sims*

James Van Allen
1914-
American physicist

James Van Allen is best known for his discovery of bands of high-level radiation surrounding the earth. Popularly known as the Van Allen radiation belts, these belts are part of the earth's magnetosphere. Although Van Allen's discovery of the belts has been the highlight of his career, he has also been associated with other significant scientific research. During World War II Van Allen made his first significant scientific contribution by creating the radio proximity fuse, a small tracking device that triggered weapons when they were close to the target. The knowledge and skills Van Allen developed in weapons research and miniaturization later proved useful in his studies of the atmosphere using rockets and satellites.

James Alfred Van Allen was born in Mount Pleasant, Iowa, on September 7, 1914. He was the second of four sons of Alfred M. Van Allen, an attorney, and Alma E. (Olney) Van Allen. His interest in science developed early, and when he was twelve, he and a brother built their own electrostatic generator. The boys used their machine to produce bolts of artificial lightning. By the time Van Allen reached high school, physics had become a passion for him. According to biographer D. S. Halacy, Jr., in *They Gave Their Names to Science,* "Teachers sometimes had to forcibly eject him from laboratories after the day was over!"

After graduating from high school, Van Allen entered Wesleyan College in his hometown. At Wesleyan he was strongly influenced by Thomas Poulter, later to become director of the Stanford Research Institute at Stanford University. In 1935 Van Allen received his bachelor of science degree from Wesleyan and entered the State University of Iowa at Iowa City for graduate study. He earned his master of science degree in 1936 and his Ph.D. in 1939.

Van Allen's work at the State University of Iowa caught the attention of the Carnegie Institute in Washington, D.C., and he was offered a position as research fellow there in the Department of Terrestrial Magnetism. After three years at Carnegie, he moved on to the Applied Physics Laboratory at Johns Hopkins University in 1942.

War Brings New Opportunities

By 1942, however, World War II had become the dominant factor in Van Allen's life. He left Johns Hopkins to accept a commission in the U.S. Navy, where he served until 1946. Van Allen's first important scientific accomplishment—the radio proximity fuse—came as a result of his war research. The fuse was a device consisting of a radio transmitter and receiver that was attached to weapons. Signals sent out and received by the fuse indicated when the weapon was close to the target, allowing it to explode before actual impact. This greatly increased the effeciency of the missiles, as it eliminated the need for a direct hit.

Van Allen's work on the fuse was to shape his future scientific career in unexpected ways. At the end of World War II, American scientists inherited about one hundred V–2 rockets built by German scientists. Far more advanced than anything produced by Americans at the time, these rockets promised to be valuable for scientists studying the earth's atmosphere. As a result of his research on the fuse, Van Allen had become a leading authority on the miniaturization of instruments, a skill crucial in rocket research. The U.S. Army therefore appointed him to administer and coordinate rocket-based research, and in 1946 Van Allen took charge of the V–2 research program based at the White Sands Proving Ground in New Mexico. His primary responsibilities were to design payloads to be sent into the atmosphere and to select projects to be used in the rocket research. From 1947 to 1958 he also served as chairman of the committee overseeing this research, originally called the V–2 Rocket Panel and, later, the Rocket and Satellite Research Panel.

This change of name reflected a change in actual rocket research itself. With a limited number of V–2 rockets available, scientists soon began to explore alternative instruments. Although American scientists could not produce an equivalent of the V–2, under Van Allen's direction they eventually constructed an acceptable substitute, the Aerobee. The Aerobee carried smaller payloads than the V–2, and although it reached altitudes of only 60 miles, compared to the German rocket's 100 miles, it became a research workhorse for American scientists over the next decade.

The Return to Iowa

In 1951 Van Allen returned to his native state of Iowa as professor of physics and head of the department of physics and astronomy at the State University of Iowa, positions he held until 1985. Shortly after this move, Van Allen developed a new approach for the study of the atmosphere. For over a century, balloons had been the most effective way to accumulate information about the atmosphere. Instruments were carried aloft in balloons to heights of up to fifteen miles and then parachuted back to earth with their data.

Van Allen combined ballooning techniques with modern rocket technology to make a "rockoon," which consisted of a balloon carrying a rocket. When the balloon reached its maximum altitude, the rocket was fired off by remote control. It traveled straight upward, through the balloon itself, another 50–70 miles into the atmosphere. Readings obtained from such rockoon launchings provided better information about the outer atmosphere than ever before.

Information from two rockoons sent up in 1953 produced data that puzzled Van Allen. He discovered that levels of radiation at an altitude of 30 miles were much higher than had been expected. These results made Van Allen curious about what he might find at even higher altitudes. At this time scientists were discussing the next stage in rocket development: an artificial Earth satellite that would remain in long-term orbit around the planet. As part of the International Geophysical Year planned for 1957–58, the U.S. government had made a commitment to finance such a satellite. The first satellite in that program, *Explorer I,* was launched on January 31, 1958. Results obtained from the satellite were intriguing; the levels of cosmic radiation in the upper atmosphere were much higher than had been anticipated. Instruments on *Explorer II* and *Explorer III* gave similar results.

By May of 1958, Van Allen was ready with an explanation for these results. He hypothesized the existence of two belts of radiation, one at an altitude of 600–3000 miles, the other at an altitude of 9,000–15,000 miles. Later research confirmed this hypothesis and proved that the belts consist of high-velocity protons and electrons spiraling around the earth's magnetic lines of force. These are the Van Allen radiation belts. In scientific terms, these belts form part of Earth's magnetosphere, an area of space around the planet dominated by charged particles that are held there by Earth's magnetic field. For his discovery of the belts and other contributions to science, Van Allen has received many scientific awards and honors, including the Space Flight Award of the American Astronautical Society, the John A. Fleming Award of the American Geophysical Union, and the Elliott Cresson Medal of the Franklin Institute.

Van Allen married Abigail Fithian Halsey on October 13, 1945. They have five children, Cynthia (Schaffner), Margot (Cairns), Sarah (Trimble), Thomas, and Peter.

SELECTED WRITINGS BY VAN ALLEN:

Books

Editor, *Scientific Uses of Earth Satellites,* University of Michigan Press, 1956.

(With Richard O. Fimmel and Eric Burgess) *Pioneer: First to Jupiter, Saturn, and Beyond,* National Aeronautics and Space Administration, 1980.

Origins of Magnetospheric Physics, Smithsonian Institution Press, 1983.

SOURCES:

Books

Halacy, D. S., Jr., *They Gave Their Names to Science,* Putnam's, 1967.

—*Sketch by David E. Newton*

Robert J. Van de Graaff

Robert J. Van de Graaff
1901-1967
American physicist

Robert J. Van de Graaff invented a particle accelerator named for him that tremendously advanced research in nuclear physics. He devoted his life to the improvement and commercial construction of his Van de Graaff accelerator, which has found widespread application in nuclear research, medicine, and industry around the world. At the time of his death, he was immersed in an effort to further extend the capabilities of his accelerator. Robert Jemison Van de Graaff was born and raised in Tuscaloosa, Alabama. His mother was Minnie Cherokee Hargrove, and his father was Adrian Sebastian Van de Graaff, a jurist. He was educated in Tuscaloosa's public schools, and then attended the University of Alabama, from which he received his B.S. degree in 1922 and his M.S. degree in 1923, both in mechanical engineering. After graduation, Van de Graaff worked for the Alabama Power Company for a year as a research assistant, continuing his studies of the conversion of heat into mechanical energy.

The young engineer's desire to understand the physical forces that drive natural phenomena—rather than work only with practical methods to harness and use those forces—led him to the study of physics. He began with studies at the Sorbonne in Paris from 1924 to 1925 and while there attended **Marie Curie**'s lectures on radiation. In 1925 he went to Oxford University in England as a Rhodes Scholar, where he received another B.S. degree, this time in physics in 1926, followed by his Ph.D. in physics in 1928 for work on ion mobility. He stayed at Oxford for one more year on a fellowship. While at Oxford, Van de Graaff absorbed **Ernest Rutherford**'s 1927 address to the Royal Society expressing that pioneer nuclear experimenter's hope that particles could someday be accelerated to speeds sufficient to disintegrate nuclei. Study of a nucleus as it disintegrated and scattered would reveal much about the nature of individual atoms. Only very high-speed particles would have enough force to smash apart an atomic nucleus, and nature does not supply enough of these: hence the need for an acceleration machine.

Develops New Atom Smasher

Van de Graaff realized the importance of research on atomic nuclei, and, impressed by Rutherford's address, worked out the principle of a device to accelerate elementary particles to high energies, drawing on his mechanical engineering background. He based his design on the oldest kind of electricity known: static electricity, the kind that causes small effects like static cling and large effects like lightning. Van de Graaff decided to generate high voltages using a direct-current electrostatic method. A moving belt would carry an electric charge inside an insulating tube into an insulated metal sphere, which would store the accumulated electricity on its surface. High-voltage discharges of this electricity into an acceleration tube would provide the required particle acceleration. From his engineering background, Van de

Graaff knew that a polished and rounded surface for the electric terminal would greatly reduce the possibility of electric stress and breakdown.

In 1929 Van de Graaff returned to the United States, joining Princeton University's Palmer Physics Laboratory as a National Research Fellow. That fall, he verified his particle acceleration principles by constructing the first working model of his device, which developed 80,000 volts. It was not sophisticated, consisting as it did of a silk ribbon, a tin can, and a small motor. E. Alfred Burrill in *Physics Today* wrote that in order to construct this elementary model, Van de Graaff searched through Princeton's local millinery shops for pure silk, going so far as to set at least one sample on fire—in the shop—to be sure of its purity. More working models followed, and Van de Graaff introduced his invention to fellow physicists in September 1931 at a meeting of the American Physical Society. He followed with a demonstration in November 1931 at the inaugural dinner of the American Institute of Physics, producing over a million volts.

Particle Accelerator Makes Dramatic Debut

Fellow physicist Karl T. Compton encouraged Van de Graaff in his work at Princeton. When Compton became president of the Massachusetts Institute of Technology (MIT) in 1931, Van de Graaff accepted Compton's invitation to come to MIT as a research associate and further developed his accelerator. In 1932 and 1933, Van de Graaff constructed his first large generator, in an aircraft hangar at Round Hill, on the shore of Buzzard's Bay in South Dartmouth, Massachusetts. The machine was truly enormous. It consisted of two polished aluminum spheres each fifteen feet in diameter mounted on cylindrical insulating columns twenty-five feet high and six feet in diameter. The columns were mobile, mounted on trucks operating on a railway track which boosted the spheres to forty-three feet above ground level. This machine had its debut performance on November 28, 1933, with spectacular effects choreographed for half an hour by Van de Graaff as he directed the switches controlling the generator's current. The spheres, acting as voltage terminals, sent out seven-million-volt bolts of blue lightning between each other and between themselves and the hangar's walls and floor. Observers could feel their hair rise from the static force. The *New York Times,* reporting on the demonstration on November 29, 1933, headlined its story "Man Hurls Bolt of 7,000,000 Volts," and went on to describe the "brilliance and the savage fury of [the generator's] unleashed power," the "magic wands which spat out flaming streaks of blue, liquid fire," and the "snakelike tongues of violet, pink and lavender flames [that] lashed out" as the participating scientists calmly monitored their switches. Operating the generator in the hangar caused problems, so the

machine was moved to a pressurized enclosure at MIT in 1937. A vacuum tube to contain the current was added. By 1940, a modified version was producing voltages of 2.75 MV, and after its productive years as a tool of nuclear and radiography research ended, it became a permanent "atom smasher" exhibit at the Boston Museum of Science.

The Van de Graaff accelerator was an immediate success, as its advantages over existing machines were immediately apparent. **John D. Cockcroft** and **Ernest Walton** of the Cavendish Laboratory in England had built a successful particle accelerator in 1932, which used voltage-multiplier circuits to produce the required high voltages. This machine was bulky and complicated, however, and maximum voltages were limited. The Van de Graaff device, in contrast, was extremely simple and (ultimately) compact, based as it was on electrostatic generation, employing a simple belt rather than multiple transformers. Because its voltage was relatively easy to stabilize, it permitted precisely controllable particle acceleration, which the Cockcroft-Walton accelerator did not, and it achieved significantly higher energies. The simplicity of Van de Graaff's principle is made apparent by the fact that it is possible to produce a small, homemade Van de Graaff generator—and many science students and laboratory assistants do so with, for example, loaf pans (for the base and dome), a plastic fruit-juice mixer (for the insulating tube), a rubber belt, and a toy motor.

Guided by Compton and by **Vannevar Bush**, MIT's vice president, Van de Graaff toiled through the writing of his patent application and was rewarded with a patent for his invention in 1935. Through the 1930s and 1940s Van de Graaff worked with **John G. Trump**, a professor of electrical engineering at MIT, and William W. Buechner, a professor in MIT's physics department, to modify and improve his particle accelerator, aiming for higher voltages, vertically mounted and more compact designs, and steadier, more homogeneous particle beams. With Trump, Van de Graaff adapted his design into a machine that could treat cancerous tumors with precisely penetrating X rays. The medical Van de Graaff machine was first used clinically in 1937 at Harvard Medical School's Huntington Memorial Hospital.

Launches Commercial Production of the Accelerator

During World War II, Van de Graaff remained at MIT as director of the High Voltage Radiographic Project, sponsored by the Office of Scientific Research and Development. Working with Buechner, he directed the adaptation of the electrostatic generator to precision radiographic examination of U.S. Navy ordnance. This opened up the possibility of industrial applications for the Van de Graaff accelerator. After the war, a 1945 Rockefeller Foundation grant funded the development of an improved accelerator at MIT, which involved Van de Graaff in continued nuclear research and experimentation. On December 19, 1946, Trump and Van de Graaff formed the High Voltage Engineering Corporation (HVEC) in Burlington, Massachusetts, for the commercial production of particle accelerators. Denis M. Robinson, a professor of electrical engineering from England, became president. Trump was technical director. Van de Graaff was chief physicist and a board member; he acted in the capacity of consultant while retaining his post as associate professor of physics at MIT.

Under the direction of these three men, HVEC produced a series of ever more technologically advanced Van de Graaff particle accelerators. Soon the company was the leading supplier of electrostatic generators, which were used in cancer therapy, in industry for radiography, and in studies of nuclear structure in both chemistry and physics. In 1951 **Luis W. Alvarez** at the University of California in Berkeley rediscovered the tandem principle of particle acceleration first invented by Willard Bennett in 1937. Van de Graaff became very involved in efforts at HVEC to develop a tandem Van de Graaff accelerator, which uses the same high voltage twice to accelerate the particles twice, resulting in particle energies double the machine's voltage. The first of these machines was purchased for use in 1956 by the Chalk River Laboratories of Atomic Energy of Canada and put into use in 1959. HVEC's tandem Van de Graaff accelerators became very successful.

Pursues Further Innovations

Van de Graaff solved other difficult and limiting problems inherent with the electrostatic generator. His uniform-field electrode configuration and inclined field tubes overcame problems in the insulating tubes that could inhibit acceleration. His insulating-core transformer of the late 1950s generated high-voltage direct current via magnetic flux rather than by the electrostatic charging belt, thereby permitting higher dc voltages than previously attainable with electrostatic machines. This invention had important applications in high-voltage electric power utilities and industrial processes, and the inspiration for it came from a magnetic circuit Van de Graaff had observed in an Alabama Power company hydroelectric generator decades earlier. Van de Graaff also devised many methods of controlling particle beams after their acceleration so they could be adapted to precise and individual research requirements. Using Van de Graaff accelerators, experimenters accumulated a vast amount of information on nuclear disintegrations and reactions, which led directly to very sophisticated theories of nuclear structure.

Toward the end of his life, Van de Graaff was absorbed with adapting his insulating-core concept to produce triple tandem accelerators powerful enough to accelerate heavy ions, which in turn could smash the nuclei of even the heaviest atoms—in particular, uranium. He envisioned the possibility of creating new elements if a uranium nucleus bombarded by a high-speed proton captured the proton rather than disintegrating. He also was excited by the powerful nuclear reaction that would result if two uranium nuclei could be induced to fuse. His goal for particle acceleration was to be able to produce and use precisely controlled charged-particle beams of any element, including heavy ones. In the fall of 1966, shortly before his death, Van de Graaff launched an intensive research program at HVEC bombarding uranium nuclei with uranium ions, thereby producing highly charged uranium atoms and yielding valuable data on heavy particle motion.

In 1936, Van de Graaff married Catherine Boyden; they had two sons, John and William. He was an associate professor of physics at MIT from 1934 until 1960, when he resigned to devote himself to his ever-increasing involvement with HVEC. In 1966, he was awarded the Tom W. Bonner Prize by the American Physical Society "for his contribution to and continued development of the electrostatic accelerator, a device that has immeasurably advanced nuclear physics." (The prize was named for a scientist who had used Van de Graaff particle accelerators to achieve the results of his fundamental research.) Van de Graaff also advanced physics in his role as a teacher and mentor, producing many proteges who themselves advanced particle accelerator technology and basic nuclear knowledge. Van de Graaff was courteous and unassuming, but nevertheless was inspirational and effective as a teacher and research leader because he was able to communicate his ideas clearly, visually, and with excitement. He published many articles in scientific journals, often coauthored with colleagues, and was granted many patents, including those for the electrostatic generator and the insulating-core transformer. He received honorary doctorates from several universities and many honors and awards, including the 1947 Duddell Medal of the Physical Society of Great Britain. Van de Graaff died of a heart attack on the morning of January 16, 1967, in Boston at the age of sixty-five. At the time of his death, over five hundred Van de Graaff particle accelerators were in use in more than thirty countries.

SELECTED WRITINGS BY VAN DE GRAAFF:

Periodicals

"A 1,500,000 Volt Electrostatic Generator," *Physical Review,* Volume 38, 1931, pp. 1919–1920.
(With W. W. Buechner and J. G. Trump) "Electrostatic Generators for the Acceleration of Charged Particles," *Progress in Physics,* Volume 11, 1948, pp. 1–18.

(With Trump) "Irradiation of Biological Materials by High-Energy Roentgen Rays and Cathode Rays," *Journal of Applied Physics,* Volume 19, 1948, pp. 599–604.

"Tandem Electrostatic Accelerators," *Nuclear Instruments and Methods,* Volume 8, 1960, pp. 195–202.

"Electrostatic Acceleration of Very Heavy Ions, with Resulting Possibilities for Nuclear Research," *Bulletin, American Physical Society,* August 29, 1966.

SOURCES:

Books

Livingston, M. Stanley, *Particle Accelerators: A Brief History,* Harvard University Press, 1969.

Rosenblatt, J., *Particle Acceleration,* Methuen, 1968.

Wilson, Robert R., and Raphael Littauer, *Accelerators: Machines of Nuclear Physics,* Doubleday, 1960.

Periodicals

Burrill, E. Alfred, "Van de Graaff, the Man and His Accelerators," *Physics Today,* February, 1967, pp. 49–52.

Huxley, L. G. H., "Dr. R. J. Van de Graaff," *Nature,* April 8, 1967.

"Man Hurls Bolt of 7,000,000 Volts," *New York Times,* November 29, 1933, p. 14.

Rose, P. H., "In Memoriam: Robert Jemison Van de Graaff, 20 December 1901—16 January 1967," *Nuclear Instruments and Methods,* Volume 60, 1968.

—*Sketch by Kathy Sammis*

Simon van der Meer
1925-
Dutch physicist

Simon van der Meer is one of the world's authorities on particle accelerator engineering. Beginning in 1968, he worked out a technique for accumulating nonoverlapping bunches of particles in an accelerator with a system he invented known as stochastic cooling. He utilized this technique in a series of experiments carried out in the early 1980s that led to the discovery of the W and Z bosons, force-carrying particles by which the electroweak force is transmitted. For his contributions to this discovery, van der Meer shared with **Carlo Rubbia** the 1984 Nobel Prize in physics.

Van der Meer was born on November 24, 1925, in the Hague, the Netherlands, the only son of Pieter van der Meer, a teacher, and Jetske Groeneveld. Van der Meer graduated from the local gymnasium in 1943 and hoped to enter college, but the colleges had been closed by the German army, which occupied Holland. As a result, he remained at the gymnasium for an additional two years; in 1945, he was finally able to enroll at the technical college at Delft to study physics. He graduated in 1952 with an engineering degree.

Van der Meer took a job that same year with the Phillips Research Laboratory in Eindhoven. Over the next four years, his work dealt primarily with the development of electron microscopy and high voltage equipment. He left Phillips in 1956 for a job at the European Center for Nuclear Research (CERN) in Geneva, where he has remained ever since. CERN had been established two years earlier as a thirteen-nation, intergovernmental research institute for the study of elementary particles and has become one of the leading particle research laboratories in the world.

At CERN, van der Meer worked on the design of the new proton synchrotron (PS). The technical challenge of this work was daunting. The plan was to produce masses of charged particles and then accelerate them to speeds near that of light in a smaller accelerator before injecting them into the larger accelerator, the PS, where they would be given even more energy. The primary engineering challenge involved in the PS was to design the electrical and magnetic fields so they would be imposed on the revolving particles in such a way as to keep them in a very precise path; these fields had to prevent the particles from drifting away from the center of the accelerator tube and getting lost in collisions with each other and with the tube itself.

Develops Stochastic Cooling

By the 1970s, a major focus of research at CERN had become the search for W and Z bosons. Electromagnetism and the so-called weak force are two of the forces in nature recognized by quantum theory. In the 1960s, hypotheses that would explain both these theories were developed by American physicist **Sheldon L. Glashow**, Pakistani physicist **Abdus Salam**, and American physicist **Steven Weinberg**. Essential to their theory was the existence of the force-carrying W and Z bosons. In 1976, van der Meer joined a project led by Rubbia, a scientist at CERN and professor of physics at Harvard University, who had made it his goal to discover the hypothesized bosons.

To accomplish this task, Rubbia proposed to redesign CERN's PS accelerator. He suggested rebuilding the machine so that two beams of particles, one consisting of protons and one of antiprotons, would be accelerated in opposite directions. Then, at various positions in the accelerator ring, the two beams would be allowed to collide. These collisions would release enough energy, Rubbia predicted, to allow the formation of W and Z bosons. The proton-antiproton colliding beam was extremely difficult to design and build, however; antiprotons—a form of antimatter—have a tendency to interact with ordinary forms of matter and change into energy. A critical problem involved the injection of antiprotons into the accelerator as well as maintaining a sufficient supply of them within the accelerator tubes.

It was van der Meer's solution to this problem that made the discovery of the W and Z bosons possible. For more than a decade, he had been developing stochastic cooling, which involves an elegant statistical technique for compressing many bunches of particles into a relatively small region, thus cooling them. In most instances, bunches of particles introduced into an accelerator have a tendency to overtake each other, causing the loss of the preceding bunch. Van der Meer was able to design an electrical system that prevented the "bunching up" of antiprotons, even when their density became quite high within the accelerator tubes. Using van der Meer's design, the CERN PS was converted to a Super Proton Synchrotron (SPS). The SPS began operation in early 1983 and, within a short period of time, the first W bosons were observed. Less than a year later, Z bosons were also detected.

For his share in this work, van der Meer was awarded the 1984 Nobel Prize in physics with Rubbia. Van der Meer has also been given honorary doctorates by the universities of Amsterdam, Geneva, and Genoa. He is a member of the Royal Netherlands Academy of Arts and Sciences and the American Academy of Arts and Sciences. Van der Meer married Catharina M. Koopman on April 26, 1966. They have a daughter and a son.

SELECTED WRITINGS BY VAN DER MEER:

Periodicals

"Stochastic Cooling Theory and Devices," *Lawrence Berkeley Laboratory Report LBL–7574,* 1978, pp. 93–97.
"Antiproton Production and Collection for the CERN Antiproton Accumulator," *IEEE Transactions in Nuclear Science,* Part I, 1983, pp. 2778–80.

SOURCES:

Books

Nobel Prize Winners, H. W. Wilson, 1987, pp. 689–691.

Periodicals

Lederman, Leon M., and Roy F. Schwitters, "The 1984 Nobel Prize in Physics," *Science,* January 11, 1985, pp. 131–134.

—*Sketch by David E. Newton*

Johannes Diderik van der Waals
1837-1923
Dutch physicist

Johannes Diderik van der Waals received his doctorate in physics from the University of Leiden at the relatively late age of thirty-six. His doctoral dissertation, "On the Continuity of Gaseous and Liquid States," quickly became known among his colleagues and made his reputation almost immediately. The Nobel Prize in physics, awarded him in 1910, recognized the line of work begun in his dissertation, eventually resulting in a famous equation of state relating the pressure, volume, and temperature of a gas. He also demonstrated why a gas cannot be liquified above its critical temperature. Van der Waals also investigated the weak nonchemical bond forces between molecules that now carry the name *van der Waals forces.*

Van der Waals was born in Leiden in the Netherlands on November 23, 1837. His parents were Jacobus van der Waals, a carpenter, and the former Elisabeth van den Burg. Van der Waals attended local primary and secondary schools and then took a job teaching elementary school in his hometown. In 1862 he began taking courses at the University of Leiden and, two years later, received the credentials necessary to teach high school physics and mathematics. He then accepted a job teaching physics in the town of Deventer and, a year later in 1866, became headmaster of a secondary school in The Hague.

During his year at Deventer, van der Waals married Anna Magdalena Smit, who bore him three daughters, Anne Madeleine, Jacqueline Elisabeth, and Johanna Diderica, and one son, Johannes Diderik.

Biographers note that Anna Magdalena died while the children were still very young; Van der Waals never remarried.

While in The Hague, van der Waals continued to attend the University of Leiden on an informal basis. Since he had never studied Greek and Latin in high school, he was not allowed by federal law to enroll in a doctoral program. When that regulation was abolished in the late 1860s, van der Waals was admitted as a regular graduate student at Leiden. For his dissertation he chose to study the nature and behavior of the particles that make up gases and liquids.

Studies Relationship of Gases and Liquids

Van der Waals's choice of topics, he later said, was strongly influenced by a paper written by the German physicist Rudolf Clausius in 1857. In that paper Clausius had argued that the molecules of a gas can be considered tiny points of matter in constant motion. From this initial premise, Clausius was able to derive theoretically a law relating gas pressure and volume originally stated empirically by Robert Boyle in 1662. It occurred to van der Waals that the molecules of both gases and liquids might be considered in the same way, as tiny points of matter. In such a case, according to van der Waals, there might be no fundamental difference between gases and liquids, the latter being only compressed gas at a low temperature.

It was this concept that van der Waals explored in detail in his doctoral thesis, presented to the faculty at Leiden in 1873. He pointed out that two fundamental assumptions of earlier gas laws were not valid. In the first place, such laws had assumed that the particles of which a material is made had no effective size. Van der Waals argued that they did have measurable volume and that such volume affected the behavior of a gas. A second assumption of gas laws was that gas particles do not interact with each other. Van der Waals argued instead that particles do indeed exert forces on each other.

Given these modifications in starting assumptions, van der Waals was able to develop an equation that more closely matches the actual behavior of gases. Laws such as those of Robert Boyle and J. A. C. Charles had been regarded as correct for "ideal" gases, but always failed to some extent when applied to any real gas. Under van der Waals's formulation, the revised gas law applied with remarkable precision to any real gas. Van der Waals's work earned him almost instantaneous fame among his colleagues. His thesis was translated into German, English, and French, and gained him notice in the science world. Van der Waals was elected to the Royal Dutch Academy of Sciences in 1877, and two years later he was appointed professor of physics at the newly created University of Amsterdam. He remained in

that post for three decades, retiring in 1907, to be succeeded by his son.

Develops Concepts of Binary Solutions and Pseudoassociation

Van der Waals continued to work on the relationship between gases and liquids for the rest of his career. In 1890 he suggested the notion of binary solutions—states in which a substance exists as both a gas and a liquid at the same time. The calculations that van der Waals made on binary solutions later proved crucial in the fledgling field of cryogenics, specifying the conditions under which a gas can be converted to a liquid. One of the pioneers of this field, **Heike Kamerlingh Onnes**, acknowledged his debt to van der Waals in an article in Eduard Farber's book *Great Chemists,* in which he said, "How much I was under the influence of its great importance as much as forty years ago may be best judged by my taking it then as a guide for my own researches."

For many students of science, van der Waals may be best known for the weak intermolecular forces that now carry his name. Originally called by him "pseudoassociation," these forces were hypothesized by van der Waals to explain the aggregation of particles in liquid solutions that occurred, for example, during the formation of binary solutions. Today, van der Waals forces are invoked to describe a host of situations in which rapidly shifting electron distributions in a molecule result in the formation of weak, but nonzero, transient attractions between molecules.

During the last ten years of his life, van der Waals gradually grew frail; he died in Amsterdam on March 8, 1923. Van der Waals had been elected to membership in the French Academy of Sciences, the British Chemical Society, the U.S. National Academy of Sciences, the Royal Academy of Sciences of Berlin, and the Russian Imperial Society of Naturalists.

SELECTED WRITINGS BY VAN DER WAALS:

Books

Over de Continuiteit van den Gasen-Vloeistoftoestand, A. W. Sijthoff, 1873.
De Relativiteitstheorie, F. Bohn, 1923.
Lehrbuch der Thermostatik, das Heisst, des Thermischen Gleich Gewichtes Materieller Systeme, J. A. Barth, 1927.

SOURCES:

Books

Gillispie, Charles Coulson, editor, *Dictionary of Scientific Biography,*Volume 14, Scribner's, 1975, pp. 109–111.

Kamerlingh Onnes, Heike, "Johannes Diderik van der Waals," *Great Chemists,* edited by Eduard Farber, Interscience, 1961, pp. 751–755.

Periodicals

Oesper, R. E., "Johannes Diderik van der Waals," *Journal of Chemical Education,* Volume 31, 1954, p. 599.

—*Sketch by David E. Newton*

Laurel van der Wal
1924-

American aeronautical engineer and space biologist

Laurel van der Wal spent a large part of her career in the fields of aeronautical and aerospace engineering, including the design of missiles, rocket systems, and manned spacecraft. But she is also known for her research into the physical effects of spaceflight on mice. This pioneering work in space biology, known as Project MIA (Mouse-In-Able), later led to the scientist's work on life support systems in space craft for human passengers.

Van der Wal was born in Spokane, Washington, on September 22, 1924, to the former Lillian Gerischer and Richard van der Wal. As a teenager during World War II, van der Wal was drawn to the field of aviation. This interest carried over into her career; in 1944 she began working at the Hamilton Air Force Base in California as an aircraft engine mechanic. She began training to become a woman air services pilot, or WASP, and left California for Nevada to acquire the required number of flying hours. After she had completed her hours, however, the war ended and the program was terminated. Van der Wal decided to pursue engineering because she realized that the opportunities for female pilots were limited at that time.

She enrolled at the University of California at Berkeley where she studied mechanical engineering and carried out research on wind tunnel operation. In 1949 van der Wal graduated with a bachelor of science degree and an option in aeronautics. From 1950–51 she was a laboratory research analyst for the guided missiles division of the Douglas Aircraft Company in Santa Monica, California. In 1953 the scientist moved briefly to the east coast to take up a position as associate engineer for Reaction Motors,

Inc. in New Jersey. There she investigated the starting time of turbopump-rocket systems. She returned to California the same year, accepting a position as a design engineer at the Rheem Manufacturing Company, where she was responsible for the design and test of fuse components for fast burning rockets. During her three years at Rheem, she also worked in the Aircraft Engineering Department, analyzing the aerodynamics of the design, performance, and operation of various aircraft and missiles. Van der Wal moved in 1956 to the Ramo-Wooldridge Corporation, where she worked on the design of missile and space-probe systems in the Guided Missiles Research Division.

In 1958, van der Wal took a position with Space Technology Laboratories, Inc., where she carried out the research for which she is most noted. She was first hired to work on missile programs, but after discussions with some of the bioengineering scientists there she became curious about the problems associated with manned spaceflight. She developed the idea of putting mice into the missile nose-cones that were being tested. By simply adding the animal tests onto already existing experiments to determine the viability of the missiles on re-entry into the atmosphere, the mice experiments were done at almost zero cost. Van der Wal eventually became the head of the company's Bioastronautics Group. In this position she focused on designing space systems to accommodate the life support requirements of human (or other living) beings. Her research group was responsible for experiments providing information about the environmental, mechanical, physical, and biomedical requirements of manned space systems.

While at Space Technology Laboratories, van der Wal had been appointed an airport commissioner for the city of Los Angeles and had become interested in transport. After taking a break from engineering in the period when her two sons were born, she worked for Rand Corporation on domestic transportation systems from 1967 to 1974. She briefly moved to Nigeria with her children to work on domestic transport systems, but was forced to return, to the United States when a coup d'etat in the African nation made it impossible for her to take up the position. On her return she worked for the Community Redevelopment Agency in Los Angeles on a proposed people mover. Van der Wal's final professional post was with the Southern California Association of Governments.

During her career, van der Wal received many honors, including a National Research Council Fellowship in aeronautics. In 1961 she was doubly honored; van der Wal was chosen by the Society of Women Engineers for their annual Achievement Award and by the Los Angeles Times as one of its women of the year.

SELECTED WRITINGS BY VAN DER WAL:

Periodicals

With W. D. Young, "Project MIA (Mouse-In-Able), Experiments on Physiological Response to Spaceflight," *American Rocket Society Journal,* October, 1959.

SOURCES:

Books

Significant Achievements in Space Bioscience, 1958–1964, United States National Aeronautics and Space Administration Scientific and Technical Information, 1966.

Other

van der Wal, Laurel, interview with Terrie M. Romano conducted March 29, 1994.

—*Sketch by Terrie M. Romano*

John R. Vane
1927-
English pharmacologist

John R. Vane's research on prostaglandins, hormone-like substances produced by the body, has had enormous consequences for the research and treatment of such illnesses as heart disease, strokes, ulcers and asthma. Through his studies, first at the Royal College of Surgeons and then at the Wellcome pharmaceutical company, Vane was able to discover how these previously little-known secretions function. For these contributions to medicine and to how the body works, he shared the 1982 Nobel Prize in medicine or physiology.

John Robert Vane was born March 29, 1927, in Tardebigge, Worcester, the son of Maurice Vane and the former Frances Fisher. Vane's father, the son of Russian immigrants, owned a small manufacturing company; his mother came from a family of farmers. Their Christmas gift of a chemistry set sparked Vane's interest in science when he was twelve, and his home became the site of numerous experiments. However, upon entering the University of Birmingham in 1944, he found that the work given him was not as challenging as he anticipated. At the advice of a professor, he decided to go to Oxford University to study pharmacology under Harold Burn after receiving his B.S. in chemistry from Birmingham in 1946. Vane became a fellow on Oxford's Therapeutic Research Council for the next two years. He obtained a B.S. in pharmacology from Oxford in 1949, a year after marrying Elizabeth Daphne Page, and earned his doctorate in 1953. Vane and his wife eventually had two daughters, Nicola and Miranda. After leaving Oxford, Vane came to America to teach at Yale University as an instructor and assistant professor of pharmacology. He returned to England in 1955 as a senior lecturer in pharmacology at the Royal College of Surgeons, at its Institute of Basic Medical Sciences.

Vane became interested in prostaglandins in the late 1950s. Discovered in the 1930s, they were originally thought to be secreted by the prostate gland, which is how they got their name. Prostaglandins are natural compounds, developed from fatty acids, which control many bodily functions. Different prostaglandins regulate blood pressure and coagulation, allergic reactions to substances, the rate of metabolism, glandular secretions, and contractions in the uterus.

For many years after the discovery of prostaglandins, scientists were unaware of how they were produced and how they functioned. In the early 1960s Vane expanded upon the procedure known as biological assay (bioassay), by which the strength of a substance is measured by comparing its effects on an organism with those of a standard preparation. Vane developed the dynamic bioassay, which allows scientists to measure more than one substance in blood or body fluids. This method enabled Vane and his colleagues at the Royal College to prove that prostaglandins are produced by many tissues and organs in the body. Further research led the scientists to discover that, unlike hormones, certain prostaglandins are effective only in the areas where they were formed.

In 1966 Vane advanced to professor of experimental pharmacology at the Institute for Basic Medical Sciences and continued his studies. An experiment he conducted in 1969 resulted in the discovery of the methods by which aspirin alleviates pain and reduces inflammation. Using the lung tissue of guinea pigs, Vane found that aspirin inhibited the production of a certain prostaglandin that causes inflammation. He published the results in a June, 1971, issue of *Nature New Biology,* a science magazine.

Leaves Academia to Head Pharmaceutical Research

In 1973 Vane resigned his post at the Institute to enter the business world as director of research and development at the Wellcome Foundation, a pharmaceutical company. Following up on research by the Swedish chemist **Bengt Samuelsson** (who found that a type of prostaglandin was responsible for allowing blood to clot), Vane discovered the existence of a prostaglandin with the opposite quality, which inhibits clot formation. With the assistance of the Upjohn Chemical Corporation, Vane isolated the secretion, which he named prostacyclin. This discovery proved to be of great assistance in dissolving clots blocking the blood supply in stroke and heart attack victims and is also useful for keeping blood from clotting during surgery. Scientists have discovered even more uses for prostaglandins, including the treatment of ulcers, alleviating pain from menstruation and gallstones, and stimulating contractions for childbirth.

Vane, along with Samuelsson and Swedish chemist **Sune Bergström**, was given the Albert Lasker Basic Medical Research Award in 1977 for his work on prostaglandins. Five years later the Nobel Committee gave the trio the Nobel Prize for medicine or physiology. After receiving the award, Vane predicted that future research on prostaglandins would create major breakthroughs in the areas of medicine. "In the next 20 years we should see a substantial attack on the disease process," *Time* quoted him as saying. "We will be able to find new drugs that have effects on cardiovascular disease, on asthma, on heart attack," and even health problems associated with old age, the magazine reported.

During the 1980s Vane embarked on a crusade for greater research on new drugs to fight both new diseases (such as acquired immunodeficiency syndrome, known as AIDS) and drug-resistant strains of old diseases, such as malaria. In articles for scientific and medical journals, he stressed the need for greater international cooperation in the search for a cure or vaccine for AIDS and advocated the creation of an Institute for Tropical Diseases to research new drugs to battle disease in the tropics.

Vane's professional activities also include memberships in the British Pharmacological Society and the American Academy of Arts and Sciences. A popular lecturer, he has received more than a dozen awards for his accomplishments. In addition to the many hours he devotes to his work, Vane finds time for his hobbies of photography, travel, snorkeling, and water-skiing.

SELECTED WRITINGS BY VANE:

Books

(With Maeve O'Connor and G. E. W. Wolstenholme) *Adrenergic Mechanisms,* Little, Brown, 1960.
(With Harry Robinson) *Prostaglandin Synthetase Inhibitors—Their Effects on Physiological Functions and Pathological States,* Raven Press, 1974.

Anti-Inflammatory Drugs, Springer Verlag, 1979.
(With Sune Bergström) *Prostacyclin,* Raven Press, 1979.
Prostacyclin in Health and Disease, Royal College of Physicians, 1982.

Periodicals

"Inhibition of Prostaglandin Synthesis as a Mechanism of Action for Aspirin-like Drugs," *Nature New Biology,* June 23, 1971.
(With Win Guttridge) "TDR and the Drug Industry," *World Health,* May, 1985.

SOURCES:

Books

Butt, Wilfred, *Hormone Chemistry,* Van Nostrand, 1967.
Connor, Julius, *Exploring the Heart—Heart Diseases and High Blood Pressure,* Norton, 1983.
Current Biography, H. W. Wilson, 1986, pp. 575–78.
Nobel Prize Winners Biographical Dictionary, H. W. Wilson, 1987, pp. 1082–84.

Periodicals

Miller, J. A., "Nobel Prize in Medicine for Prostaglandin Discoveries," *Science News,* October 16, 1982, p. 245.
"Sharing the Nobel Prize," *Time,* October 25, 1982, p. 84.

—Sketch by Francis Rogers

Florence W. van Straten
1913-
American physicist and meteorologist

Florence W. van Straten worked for many years with the U.S. Navy researching the causes of weather patterns and investigating the possibility of human weather modification. She served as the head of naval tests in cloud seeding to create and dissipate clouds, as well as an educator and writer.

Florence Wilhelmina van Straten was born on November 12, 1913, in Darien, Connecticut, the daughter of Jacques and Rosette (Roozeboom) van Straten, Dutch immigrants. Her father was an executive for Metro-Goldwyn-Mayer, and she thus grew up in various cities in North America and Europe. From an early age, van Straten wanted to be a writer. Influenced by her practical father, she agreed to take chemistry classes in addition to English at New York University, and it was the chemistry that won out. She earned her B.S. in 1933, the M.A. in 1937, and a Ph.D. in chemistry in 1939. From her senior year in college, she had been an instructor of freshman chemistry courses. After graduation, she accepted a teaching fellowship at New York University. With the advent of World War II she joined the Waves, becoming a specialist in meteorology and doing postgraduate work at the Massachusetts Institute of Technology.

Researches Weather Modification

After the war, van Straten continued working for the Navy in a civilian capacity, becoming director of its Technical Requirements Branch of the U.S. Naval Weather Service. During the war she had already begun researching a problem meteorologists had been looking at for generations: how to control and modify the weather so as to stop a hurricane or end rain in flooded areas. In her view, rain was often caused by atmospheric events in tropical areas, for which the standard model involving sub-freezing temperatures in the tops of clouds would not hold. Finally, van Straten developed the theory that rain is dependent upon evaporation rates within a cloud. She concluded that she could create or dissipate clouds by 'seeding' them with some material that could change temperatures by absorbing light. In 1958 van Straten had a chance to test these theories, seeding carbon particles into clouds and successfully dissipating seven clouds, marking the conclusion of fifteen years of theorizing.

In 1962 van Straten left the Naval Weather Service and made her home near Washington, DC, but remained a consultant in atmospheric physics as well as a lieutenant commander in the reserves. She was awarded for her researches in weather modification with the Meritorious Service Award of the U.S. Department of the Navy in 1958 and the Woman of the Year award from the Aerospace Medical Association in 1959. Retirement brought van Straten the time she had always lacked to devote to her first love—writing. She authored a popular study of weather, short stories, and pamphlets on radar and radioactive fallout.

SELECTED WRITINGS BY VAN STRATEN:

Books

Radar as a Meteorological Tool, U.S. Government Printing Office, 1957.
Weather or Not, Dodd, 1966.

SOURCES:

Periodicals

"Does Something about It: Florence Wilhelmina van Straten," *New York Times,* September 24, 1958, p. 52.

—Sketch by J. Sydney Jones

John Van Vleck
1899-1980
American physicist

John Van Vleck was one of the United States' first theoretical physicists, specializing in problems of chemical physics, magnetism, quantum theory, and spectroscopy. Some of his work has had important practical applications in such devices as the atomic clock, lasers and transistors. He shared the 1977 Nobel Prize in physics for his "fundamental theoretical investigations of the electronic structure of magnetic and disordered systems."

John Hasbrouck Van Vleck was born in Middletown, Connecticut, on March 13, 1899, into a prosperous family with a history of notable intellectual accomplishments. His paternal grandfather had been a professor of astronomy at Connecticut's Wesleyan College, and his father, Edward Burr Van Vleck, was professor of mathematics at Wesleyan at the time of his son's birth. Van Vleck's mother was the former Hester Lawrence (also given as Laurence) Raymond. It has been noted that his parents' overbearing manner may have been responsible for their only child's shyness as a youngster. When Van Vleck was seven years old his father accepted an appointment at the University of Wisconsin. John attended public schools in Madison and then entered the University of Wisconsin, graduating in 1920 with a bachelor's degree in physics. For his graduate work, Van Vleck chose to attend Harvard University, where his father was serving as visiting professor of mathematics.

Chooses a Career in Theoretical Physics

At Harvard, Van Vleck decided to concentrate on theoretical physics, a field with little tradition in American science at the time. In fact, when he received his doctorate in 1922, his thesis was one of the first, if not actually *the* first, in America based on a purely theoretical subject—the ionization energy of a particular model of the helium atom. Upon completing his degree, Van Vleck was invited to stay on at Harvard as an instructor in physics.

In 1923, based largely on his doctoral work, the University of Minnesota offered Van Vleck a job in its physics department; he accepted and remained at Minnesota until 1928. During his tenure there, Van Vleck worked on problems involving the application of quantum mechanical theory to a variety of physical phenomena. His magnum opus during this period was his first book, *Quantum Principles and Line Spectra,* published in 1926. Though the book came out just as major modifications in quantum theory were being made, much of what he had written remained valid and the book was an unexpected commercial success.

Begins Work on Magnetism

Van Vleck's years at Minnesota were also marked by his first venture into the field for which he is best known, the quantum explanation of magnetic effects. He tried to find a way in which modern developments in quantum theory could be used to explain the various forms of magnetism—efforts which resulted in the publication of *The Theory of Electric and Magnetic Susceptibilities* in 1932. The work on magnetism was by no means the only topic Van Vleck researched at Minnesota, but it would prove to be the most important, earning him both a share of the 1977 Nobel Prize in physics and the title "father of modern magnetism."

Van Vleck was married to Abigail June Pearson on June 10, 1927. The following year he moved to the University of Wisconsin, where he accepted a post as professor of physics. He was attracted to Wisconsin, in part, by the university's visiting scholars program. Each semester, an outstanding authority in some field was invited to be in residence on the Madison campus. Van Vleck knew that the program would be an excellent way for him to stay in touch with developments in modern physics, a field in which American scientists were woefully deficient. In 1934, Van Vleck was offered an opportunity to return to Harvard, one that he accepted. He remained at Harvard until his retirement in 1969, serving the last eighteen years of his tenure there as Hollis Professor of Mathematical and Natural Philosophy, the oldest endowed science chair in North America.

One of Van Vleck's areas of interest at Harvard was crystal field theory. He again used quantum theory to evaluate the relationship between electron and ion energy levels in bound systems such as crystals. Understanding these relationships is critical in solid-state theories and in their applications in devices such as lasers and semiconducting devices.

At the beginning of World War II, Van Vleck was asked to serve on a committee evaluating the feasibility of building an atomic bomb. That committee's favorable decision eventually led to the creation of the Manhattan Project, under which the world's first nuclear weapons were designed and built. For the majority of the war years, however, Van Vleck worked on the development of radar at the Radio Research Laboratory in Cambridge, Massachusetts.

Van Vleck worked on a host of other problems on his return to Harvard after the war, including nuclear magnetic resonance, molecular spectra, and the cohesive energy of metals. In addition to the Nobel Prize, he was awarded the title of Chevalier in the French Legion of Honor, and was the recipient of the Irving Langmuir Award of the General Electric Foundation in 1965, the National Medal of Science in 1966, and the Lorentz Medal of the Royal Netherlands Academy of Science in 1974, among others. Van Vleck died in Cambridge on October 27, 1980.

SELECTED WRITINGS BY VAN VLECK:

Books

Quantum Principles and Line Spectra, National Research Council, 1926.
The Theory of Electric and Magnetic Susceptibilities, Oxford University Press, 1932.

Periodicals

"Quantum Theory of the Specific Heat of Hydrogen. I. Relation to the New Mechanics, Band Spectra, and Chemical Constants," *Physical Review,* Volume 28, 1926, pp. 980–1021.
"Magnetic Susceptibilities and Dielectric Constants in the New Quantum Mechanics," *Nature,* Volume 118, 1927, pp. 226–27.
"The New Quantum Mechanics," *Chemical Reviews,* Volume 5, 1928, pp. 467–507.

SOURCES:

Books

Dictionary of Scientific Biography, Volume 18, Scribner, 1982, pp. 949–57.
McGraw-Hill Modern Scientists and Engineers, Volume 3, McGraw, 1980, pp. 251–52.
Nobel Prize Winners, H. W. Wilson, 1987, pp. 1086–88.
Weber, Robert L., *Pioneers of Science: Nobel Prize Winners in Physics,* American Institute of Physics, 1980, pp. 249–50.
World of Scientific Discovery, Gale, 1994.

—Sketch by David E. Newton

Harold E. Varmus
1939-
American microbiologist and virologist

When Harold E. Varmus was appointed director of the National Institutes of Health (NIH) in November, 1993, he was already famous throughout the world for his investigations into cancer-causing genes and other fundamental areas of biology, including the complex mechanisms of viruses. Varmus, who helped prove that there is a genetic component to cancer, was the co-recipient of a 1989 Nobel Prize for his research into oncogenes (genes with the capacity to turn normal cells into cancerous ones). Varmus's title of director of the NIH carries with it immense responsibilities, including the managing of a ten billion-dollar-plus NIH budget and the determination of grant awards for many types of medical research.

Harold Eliot Varmus was born in Oceanside, New York, on December 18, 1939, to Frank and Beatrice (Barasch) Varmus. He attended Amherst College, graduating with a B.A. degree in 1961 (twenty-three years later, Amherst would award him with an honorary doctorate). Varmus went on to perform graduate work at Harvard University, receiving an M.A. degree in 1962, then he studied medicine at Columbia University, receiving an M.D. in 1966.

Varmus practiced medicine as an intern and resident at the Presbyterian Hospital of New York City between 1966 and 1968. He then worked as a clinical associate at the National Institutes of Health in Bethesda, Maryland, from 1968 to 1970. Moving to California, Varmus served as a lecturer in the department of microbiology at the University of California in San Francisco, becoming an associate professor in 1974—the same year that he was named associate editor of *Cell and Virology*—then, in 1979, he was promoted to full professor of microbiology, biochemistry and biophysics. During the 1980s, Varmus began to accumulate a number of prestigious honors for his research, including the 1982 California Academic Scientist of the Year award and the 1983 Passano Foundation award; he was also the co-recipient of the Lasker Foundation award. In 1984, Varmus received both the Armand Hammer Cancer prize and the General Motors Alfred Sloan award, and the American Cancer Society made him an honorary professor of molecular virology. These honors were followed by the Shubitz Cancer prize and, in 1989, the Nobel Prize in physiology or medicine.

Cancer Gene Research Wins Nobel Prize for Medicine

Varmus and **J. Michael Bishop**, his colleague from the University of California at San Francisco,

were awarded the Nobel Prize in honor of their 1976 discovery which showed that normal cells contain genes that can cause cancer. Varmus and Bishop, working with Dominique Stehelin and Peter Vogt, helped to prove the theory that cancer has a genetic component, demonstrating that oncogenes are actually normal genes that are altered in some way, perhaps due to carcinogen-induced mutations. Their research focused on Rous sarcoma, a virus which can produce tumors in chickens by attaching to a normal chicken gene as it duplicates within a cell. Since then, research has identified a number of additional "proto-oncogenes" which, when circumstances dictate, abandon their normal role of overseeing cell division and growth and turn potentially cancerous. Varmus's and Bishop's oncogene studies had a tremendous impact on the efforts to understand the genetic basis of cancer. The results of their work quickly found practical applications, especially in cancer diagnosis and prognosis.

Director of the National Institutes of Health

Varmus was nominated by U.S. President Bill Clinton to the directorship of the National Institutes of Health and was confirmed in November, 1993. The director of the NIH plays a vital part in setting the course for biomedical research in the United States. Varmus's nomination was strongly supported by biomedical scientists, but there was some opposition from AIDS activists. They—as well as others who were concerned with the health of women and members of minority groups—were concerned that Varmus would be more interested in basic biomedical research than in applied studies and feared that the medical research related to their specific concerns might be neglected. Varmus has argued that basic research in science, especially investigations of the fundamental properties of cells, genes, and tissues, could eventually lead to cures for many diseases, such as AIDS and cancer. As director, Varmus is also interested in revitalizing the intramural research program at NIH. He believes that science education in the United States needs to be improved and that students should be exposed to a science curriculum sooner, in smaller classes, by better-informed teachers.

A licensed physician in the state of California, Varmas is a member of numerous professional and academic associations, including the National Academy of Sciences, the American Society of Microbiologists, the American Society of Virologists, and the American Academy of Arts and Sciences. He married Constance Louise Casey on October 25, 1969, and they have two sons, Jacob Carey and Christopher Isaac.

SELECTED WRITINGS BY VARMUS:

Books

(With Robert A. Weinberg) *Cells, Development, and the Biology of Cancer,* Freeman, 1992.

(With Weinberg) *Genes and the Biology of Cancer,* Scientific American Library, 1993.

Periodicals

"The Molecular Genetics of Cellular Oncogenes," *Annual Review of Genetics,* Volume 18, 1984, pp. 513–612.

"Reverse Transcription," *Scientific American,* Volume 257, September, 1987, pp. 56–59.

"Oncogenes and Transcriptional Control," *Science,* Volume 238, December 4, 1987, pp. 1337–1339.

(With J. Michael Bishop and Marc Kirschner) "Retroviruses," *Science,* Volume 240, June 10, 1988, pp. 1427–35.

(With Bishop and Kirschner) "Science and the New Administration" *Science,* Volume 259, January 22, 1993, pp. 444–446.

SOURCES:

Periodicals

Angier, Natalie, "Out of the Lab and Into the Bureaucracy," *New York Times,* November 23, 1993, p. C1.

Campbell, Neil A., "A conversation with . . . Michael Bishop and Harold Varmus," *American Biology Teacher,* Volume 54, November/December, 1992, pp. 476–481.

—*Sketch by Jessica Jahiel*

Arlette Vassy
1913-

French atmospheric physicist

Arlette Vassy is a leading authority on ozone in the atmosphere. As one of France's premier atmospheric physicists, she undertook a series of positions that made use of both her laboratory and field study skills. In this work she examined the role of ozone gas, a triatomic form of oxygen formed by photochemical reactions that, while extant in lower areas, makes up a layer in the high atmosphere that protects the earth from harmful ultraviolet lights. In connection with her atmospheric studies, Vassy also participated in France's early space exploration, acting as a scientific advisor on numerous rocket launches.

Vassy was born in St-Nexans (Dordogne) to Pierre Tournaire and the former Jeanne Vitrac. Her father was a physics teacher and had passed the rigorous state pedagogical licensing procedure known as the *agrégation.* Entering higher education herself, Vassy matriculated into her father's career. In 1934 she took a *licence* in physics at the University of Paris, known since medieval times as the Sorbonne. She then received a *diplôme d'études supérieures* in physics in 1935. (These diplomas correspond in a formal sense to B.S. and M.S. degrees, although they represent a more sophisticated mastery of material than was then typical in North America.) The following year, 1936, Vassy married fellow physicist Etienne Vassy, with whom she would collaborate on much of her work.

Begins Work in Atmospheric Physics

Vassy and her husband dedicated themselves to upper-atmospheric physics, a field in which the French were leaders. In 1937 the couple spent five months studying the absorption of light in the atmosphere at a newly-opened geophysical station in Ifrane, located in the mountains of Morocco. This and related work led to Sorbonne doctoral dissertations— Etienne in 1937 and Arlette in 1941.

Vassy's career was carried out within the Centre National de la Recherche Scientifique (CNRS). This national research organization, created in 1939, was the result of nearly twenty years of experimentation with the administration of scientific research. At its debut, the CNRS acted as a central authority for funding laboratories and employing scientists. In a notable innovation (already anticipated in the national German laboratories of the Kaiser-Wilhelm Gesellschaft and those of diverse foundations like the Solvay, Nobel, and Carnegie), researchers had no teaching responsibilities. Vassy received predoctoral funding from the CNRS and then obtained an appointment as a scientist there. She rose to senior scientist (*maître de recherche*) in 1954 and, in 1968, became director of a CNRS laboratory devoted to atmospheric ozone.

Atmospheric ozone and its related problems required both laboratory analysis and observations in the field. Vassy's research ideally suited her for playing an active role in the inception of France's space program. Beginning in 1954 she participated in nearly forty rocket launches; from 1963 to 1967 she directed the scientific side of France's high-altitude ballistic rocket research. In 1959 Vassy became an officer in the Order of Academic Palms—France's national society of merit; in 1988 she received the gold medal of the Society for the Encouragement of Progress.

SELECTED WRITINGS BY VASSY:

Books

Fondements théoriques de la photographie, Editions de la Revue d'optique, 1953.

(Editor with M. Morand) *Colloque sur la sensibilité des cristaux et des émulsions photographiques,* Editions de la Revue d'optique, 1953.

"Atmospheric Ozone," in *Advances in Geophysics,* Volume 2, Academic Press, 1965, pp. 115–73.

La Luminescence nocturne, Springer, 1976.

—*Sketch by Lewis Pyenson*

V. I. Veksler
1907-1966
Russian physicist

Physicist V. I. Veksler's early research covered a variety of topics, including X rays, cosmic radiation, nuclear physics and particle detection devices. He is best known for his development of the principle of phase stability of particles in accelerators. This principle, discovered independently and concurrently in the United States by **Edwin M. McMillan**, became the basis for a whole new class of particle accelerators that included the synchrocyclotron in the United States and the synchrophasotron in the Soviet Union.

Vladimir Iosifovich Veksler was born in Zhitomir, Russia, on March 4, 1907, according to the Julian calendar in use in Russia at the time. His father, Iosif Lvovich Veksler, was an engineer. Veksler took his first job as an assembler in a factory before entering the Moscow Energetics Institute, where he received his diploma in electrical engineering in 1931. A year earlier he had taken a job with the All-Union Electrotechnical Institute, where he worked primarily on X rays. He continued his studies at the Institute of Energetics over the next decade, eventually earning both his candidate of physico-mathematical sciences degree (similar to a master's degree) in 1934 and his doctorate in 1940.

Moves to the Lebedev Institute

In 1936, Veksler moved from the All-Union Institute to a new post at the P. N. Lebedev Institute of Physics in Moscow. During his twenty years in this position he carried out extensive studies of cosmic radiation, conducting much of that work in the Pamir Mountain range of Central Asia. As a means of providing science with a more comprehensive understanding of the the atomic nucleus, Veksler began devising methods for increasing the effectiveness of existing particle accelerators. **Ernest Orlando Lawrence**'s invention of the cyclotron in the early 1930s had made available to physicists a powerful new tool for the investigation of the atomic nucleus. In a cyclotron, subatomic particles, such as protons and electrons, are accelerated by a changing electrical field at opposite sides of the cyclotron. The particles are then forced into a spiral path by a fixed magnetic field perpendicular to the plane of the particles' path. An instrument of this design can accelerate particles to velocities close to the speed of light.

At such velocities, however, technical problems begin to accumulate. Raising the energy of particles can no longer be accomplished by increasing their speed since, according to **Albert Einstein**'s theory of relativity, they can never go faster than the speed of light; further increases in speed can only result in an increase in the particles' mass. This so-called relativistic mass increase creates serious problems in cyclotron design, since the heavier particles take longer than expected to reach the point at which they are supposed to receive their next "push" from the electrical field.

Solves the Problem of Relativistic Mass Increase

In 1944, Veksler proposed a method by which this problem could be resolved. He showed how particles can be treated in "bunches" and accelerated in orbits that remain stable even during relativistic mass increases. An almost identical proposal to Veksler's was developed shortly thereafter by Edwin M. McMillan at the University of California at Berkeley. Phase stability was incorporated almost immediately into the design of a whole new generation of particle accelerators that had energy capacities significantly greater than any that had previously been possible. Those machines included the synchrocyclotrons used in the United States, and the corresponding synchrophasotrons built in the Soviet Union. For their independent development of the concept of phase stability in particle accelerators, Veksler and McMillan were jointly awarded the sixth Atoms for Peace Award in 1963.

Veksler was elected an associate member of the U.S.S.R.'s Academy of Science in 1946, becoming a full member in 1958. In 1956, Veksler moved on to a new assignment as director of the high-energy laboratory at the Joint Institute of Nuclear Research at Dubna, where he directed the construction of the ten billion-electron-volt synchrotron that was, at that time, the most powerful particle accelerator in the world.

Veksler died of a heart attack in Moscow on September 22, 1966. In his obituary in *Physics Today,* McMillan described him as "a quiet, modest man with a gentle sense of humor [who] was known as a strong proponent of international amity among scientists." In addition to the Atoms for Peace Award, Veksler also received both the Lenin and State Prizes of the U.S.S.R.

SELECTED WRITINGS BY VEKSLER:

Books

Eksperimentalnye Metody Yadernoy Fiziki, [Moscow-Leningrad], 1940.
Ionizatsionnye Metody Issledovania Izlucheny, [Moscow], 1950.

Periodicals

"Novy Metod Uskorenia Relyativistskikh Chastis," *Doklady Akademii Nauk SSR,* Volume 43, number 8, 1944, p. 346.
"Kogerentny Metod Uskoremia Zaryazhennykh Chastis," *Atomnaya Energiya,* Volume 11, number 5, 1957, p. 427.

SOURCES:

Books

Daintith, John, editor, *A Biographical Encyclopedia of Scientists,* Facts on File, 1981, p. 808.
Gillispie, Charles Coulson, editor, *Dictionary of Scientific Biography,* Volume 13, Scribner, 1975, pp. 600–01.
Turkevich, John, *Soviet Men of Science,* Van Nostrand, 1963, p. 409–10.

Periodicals

"Atoms for Peace Award," *Physics Today,* September, 1963, p. 94.
McMillan, Edwin M., "Vladimir Iosifovich Veksler," *Physics Today,* November, 1966, pp. 103–04.
Walkinshaw, W., "Academician Volume I. Veksler," *Nature,* November 12, 1966, p. 674.

—Sketch by David E. Newton

Vladímir Ivanovich Vernadsky
1863-1945
Russian mineralogist, geochemist, and biogeochemist

In a life that spanned two centuries, eight decades, and dozens of Russian and Soviet regimes, Russian geologist Vladímir Ivanovich Vernadsky successfully combined mineralogy with chemistry and biology, using this new approach to investigate evolution. Vernadsky's biosphere theory—the concept that living matter and the atmosphere's essential gases exist in a mutual relationship—lay the groundwork for modern environmentalism.

Vernadsky's ability to meld the scientific and the political can be traced back to his childhood and early adolescence. He was born on March 12, 1863, in St. Petersburg, Russia. His father, Ivan, was a professor of political economy and edited a liberal journal that barely escaped the Tsarist regime's censorship. Vladímir's mother, Anna Petrovna Konstantinovich, was a teacher of singing who was neither as intellectual nor as politically inclined as her husband. When Vernadsky was five, the family moved to the more provincial town of Kharkov, where he received an introduction to nature and astronomy from his uncle. At the age of 13, Vernadsky moved with his family back to St. Petersburg, where he attended a classical gymnasium. Because a classical Russian education in this era did not include the sciences, Vernadsky and his friends were forced to form a study group of their own.

In 1881 Vernadsky entered the physics and math departments at St. Petersburg University. Although it was the custom for men of his class to study abroad, Vernadsky remained close to home to help care for his father, who had suffered a stroke the previous spring. At St. Petersburg, Vernadsky studied with Dmitri Ivanovich Mendeleev, who derived the periodic table of the elements, chemist Aleksandr Butlerov, and mineralogist V. V. Dokuchaev. He published two scientific articles during his undergraduate years, one on mineral analysis and the other on the prairie rodent. Vernadsky's undergraduate thesis on isomorphism so impressed his professors that they urged him to pursue an academic career. That same year he joined an underground committee on literacy, which wrote and distributed reading materials for the common people. Through the committee, Vernadsky met Natalia Egorovna Staritskaya, who was three years his senior. Though their age difference concerned Natalia, the two began courting. When Vernadsky was appointed curator of the university's mineralogical collection in 1886, he persuaded her to accept his offer of marriage.

But Vernadsky was not to enjoy the peaceful existence of the newlywed for long. Russia in the late 1880s was in turmoil and few places were more tumultuous than the university campuses. After a group of students there were found guilty of a plot to kill Alexander III, the Tsarist government considered St. Petersburg University a hotbed of radicalism. Administrators at the state-run university targeted students and faculty suspected of rebellious feelings towards the autocracy. The 25-year-old Vernadsky was among the suspects, not because of any radical activities but because of his decision not to study abroad, a decision which, according to administrators, branded him an avowed rabble-rouser. Vernadsky's father-in-law, a well-respected government official, appealed his ouster and the government decided to allow Vernadsky to continue his association with the university as long as he now sought that international education. As soon as his first child, George (later a Russian historian) was born, Vernadsky began studying at the University of Naples.

Undertakes Research on Polymorphism

Soon after his arrival in Italy, Vernadsky realized that the Naples department no longer led the field, so he transferred to Munich to study with the German crystallographer Paul Groth. Although in letters to his wife Vernadsky poked fun at the German professors' pedantic lecturing style, he also admitted that he learned how to observe and experiment in practical mineralogy in Germany. In 1889 Vernadsky transferred to Paris's Mining Academy, where, under the guidance of Henri Le Châtelier, he chose polymorphism—the ability of some chemical compounds to assume different forms—as the topic for his master's thesis. Whereas it was previously believed that the aluminosilicate minerals which make up most of the earth's crust were silicic acid salts, Vernadsky showed them to have a different structure, with aluminum that is chemically analogous to silicon. He proposed the theory of the kaolin nucleus, a structure which is made up of two aluminum, two silicon, and seven oxygen atoms, and which forms the basis of many minerals. The theory has since been confirmed, and is considered essential to an understanding of minerals.

Vernadsky started lecturing at Moscow University in 1891, the year he received his master's degree. Like many intellectuals of his time and place, he found himself balancing academic interests with political ones. In 1897, Vernadsky earned a doctoral degree with his dissertation on crystalline matter, qualifying him for a full professorship. The following year his daughter Nina (later a psychiatrist) was born.

The first decade of the twentieth century proved a productive one for Vernadsky. His new approach of combining geologic interests with other scientific fields, such as chemistry and biology, attracted supporters. By 1901, when he created the Mineralogical Circle at Moscow University, he had a devoted cadre of students and colleagues who formed a scientific school that was heavily influenced by the latest theories in chemistry and evolutionary biology. He also maintained an interest in politics, helping to found the Union of Liberation, a group that sought to end the Russian autocracy peacefully. In 1902 he published a summary of his political views, disguised as science, in *On a Scientific World View*. The next year, he published his first scientific book, *Fundamentals of Crystallography*. When the universities again erupted in turmoil in 1905, Vernadsky operated a lab until the university closed. Caught up in the fervor of the times, he helped organize the Constitutional Democratic party, the largest opposition party to pose candidates for the nation's newly created Duma. His political work did not deter him from amassing scientific honors, however. In 1906 Vernadsky was elected as an adjunct member of the Academy of Sciences and appointed director of St. Petersburg's Mineralogical Museum; two years later he melded his interests with his appointment to the Agrarian Commission of the State Council.

After the university riots of 1905, the campus situation calmed down somewhat, allowing the faculty to return to teaching and research. For Vernadsky, that meant expanding the field of mineralogy to include evolutionary concerns. As he explained in volume 2 of *Izbrannye sochinenia,* his version of mineralogy held that "mineralogy, like chemistry, must study not only the products of chemical reactions but also the very processes of reaction." He was particularly interested in paragenesis, or the way in which essential minerals formed. By studying the many layers of the earth's crust in this manner, Vernadsky hoped to be able to piece together some of the planet's evolutionary history. In 1911 strikes interrupted his work once more. In retaliation for the liberal faculty's support of miscreant students, the government fired three professors. Twenty-eight percent of the faculty—including Vernadsky—resigned in protest. Soon after resigning, Vernadsky was expelled from the state council.

Introduces Theory of the Biosphere

Loss of both these positions translated into free time for Vernadsky to pursue his scientific interests. He moved to St. Petersburg, where he took a job as a scientific administrator and continued research on the distribution of rare elements such as cesium, rubidium, scandium, and indium. He made one expedition per year to remote areas in the Russian empire to catalog the nation's resources. During World War I, Vernadsky spearheaded a movement to conserve Russian natural resources, culminating in the formation of the Commission for the Study of the Natural Productive Forces of Russia in 1915. When the Tsarist regime collapsed in 1917, Vernadsky became involved in politics again, joining a campaign to persuade Russians to take pride in and preserve their culture. Vernadsky served briefly as the government's assistant minister in charge of universities and institutions, until the October revolution, which ushered in a government whose politics did not mesh with Vernadsky's. In 1919, he moved to Kiev to found and become president of the Ukrainian Academy of Sciences. When the Red Terror of 1919 drove him into hiding, Vernadsky spent his time in isolation, developing the blueprints for a new field he called biogeochemistry. As he saw it, this new discipline studied the nexus between geology, chemistry, and biology, determining how prevalent life was, the rates at which different forms of life multiply, and the processes and speed of adaptation.

Vernadsky left Russia in 1921 for France, where he worked with the grande dame of radiation physics, **Marie Curie**. During this period, he coalesced his thoughts on the interconnection of all living and nonliving beings on earth into a book entitled *The Biosphere*. After four years in the West, Vernadsky's wife lobbied to move there permanently, rather than returning to Soviet Russia. But the government was eager to attract prominent scholars such as Vernadsky and offered him a chair in the Academy with the promise of time and funding for his own work, an offer that no Western institution matched. In 1926 he founded and headed the Commission on the History of Knowledge of the Academy of Sciences of the U.S.S.R. and lay the basis for the organization that later became the Vernadsky Institute of Geochemistry and Analytical Chemistry .

During the Stalin years, Vernadsky continued working, relatively uninterrupted. His earlier years of protest against the Tsar, combined with his image as an elder statesman of science, protected him from the government persecution that many of his colleagues experienced. In 1935 he began writing philosophical essays on the nature of the world. In 1940 his years of interest in radioactivity culminated in the creation of the Uranium Institute. During World War II, he argued for Russia to develop its atomic energy program. His wife of 56 years died in 1943 while the couple was evacuated from their home. Vernadsky passed away two years later on January 6, 1945, a few months after suffering a cerebral hemorrhage.

SELECTED WRITINGS BY VERNADSKY:

Books

Izbrannye sochinenia (title means "Selected Works"), six volumes, [Moscow], 1954-1960.

Biosfera (title means "The Biosphere"), [Leningrad], 1926, [Moscow], 1967.

SOURCES:

Books

Bailes, Kendall, *Science and Russian Culture in an Age of Revolutions: V. I. Vernadsky and His Scientific School, 1863–1945,* Indiana University Press, 1990.

Balandin, R. K., *Outstanding Soviet Scientists: Vladimir Vernadsky,* translated by Alexander Repyev, Mir Publishers (Moscow), 1982.

—*Sketch by Shari Rudavsky*

Artturi Ilmari Virtanen
1895-1973
Finnish biochemist

Artturi Ilmari Virtanen was a Finnish biochemist who discovered many of the nutritionally important components of plants, including vitamins and amino acids. His most important discovery, a method of preserving green fodder and silage, led to an improved understanding of the mechanism of plant decay. For his biochemical investigations in agriculture and nutrition he received the 1945 Nobel Prize in chemistry.

Virtanen was born January 15, 1895, in Helsinki, Finland, to Serafina (Isotalo) and Kaarlo Virtanen. He began his education at the Classical Lyceum in Viipuri (now Vyborg, Russia). Upon graduation, he entered the University of Helsinki to study biology, chemistry, and physics. Virtanen received his master of science degree in 1916 and worked briefly as an assistant chemist in the Central Industrial Laboratory of Helsinki. That same year he returned to the University to continue his studies and in 1919 he received his doctorate. Interested in a broad range of scientific subjects, Virtanen traveled extensively to pursue his studies. In 1920 he left for Zurich, Switzerland, to undertake postgraduate work in physical chemistry. The next year he had moved to Stockholm, Sweden, to study bacteriology, and in 1923 he worked on enzymology with **Hans von Euler-**

Chelpin . At this time Virtanen discovered the subject that would become his life work, biochemistry.

Career and Discoveries in Agricultural Chemistry

In 1921 Virtanen was appointed Laboratory Director of the Finnish Cooperative Dairies Association in Valio, where he was responsible for controlling the manufacture of dairy products such as cheese and butter. A decade later, in 1931, he was appointed the Director of the Biochemical Research Institute in Helsinki. In that same year, he began teaching as professor of biochemistry at the Finland Institute of Technology. Late in 1939 he became professor of biochemistry at the University of Helsinki.

Virtanen was interested in both the theoretical and practical aspects of biochemistry. His first important study was an investigation of the fermentation reactions of some biologically important acids. His research showed how enzymes were necessary for bacterial fermentation. Enzymes, the complex organic catalysts of living cells, were thought to speed up chemical reactions without being chemically changed. Virtanen, who believed that enzymes were composed of proteins, began an exhaustive study of the protein content and enzyme activity of plants.

Proteins are rich in nitrogen, an essential element in both human and animal nutrition. Virtanen realized that nitrogen was plentiful in the atmosphere but almost completely unavailable to most plants and animals. He began to study legumes (peas, clover, and soybeans), which are able to convert atmospheric nitrogen into nitrogen compounds suitable for plant growth. Virtanen became interested in what happened to plants after they were cut and stored for cattle fodder. It was found that fodder stored as silage could lose one quarter to one half of its nutrients to bacterial decay. Animals consuming this silage produced poor quality butter, milk, and cheese. After study and experimentation, Virtanen discovered that the addition of a simple mixture of dilute hydrochloric and sulfuric acids to stored silage could slow down bacterial decay and prevent the destruction of nutritionally important vitamins and proteins.

Virtanen fed his acid-treated silage to dairy cows and tested the milk to determine the safety and effectiveness of his method. He discovered that milk remained rich in protein, carotene, and vitamin C, and that the milk cows remained healthy and strong. The method Virtanen devised for treating silage—called the Artturi Ilmari Virtanen (AIV) method—was first used in Finland in 1929.

Although most of Virtanen's scientific investigations had practical agricultural applications, his later work was more theoretical. He studied how bacteria in the root nodules of legumes synthesize nitrogen compounds, and how plant cells assimilate simple molecules into large complex vitamins. He discovered a red pigment in plant cells similar in structure and function to hemoglobin, the molecule that transports life-giving oxygen in human blood. He also studied the composition of plants, discovering many important amino acids—the building blocks of proteins. For his work on the AIV method of silage preservation and for his research in agricultural chemistry Virtanen received the 1945 Nobel Prize in chemistry.

After winning the Nobel Prize, Virtanen remained actively engaged in research. He published a book on animal and human nutrition and served on the editorial boards of several leading biochemical journals. He represented Finland on a United Nations Commission on Nutrition, and in 1948 he was elected president of Finland's State Academy of Science and Arts. Virtanen, remembered as one of Finland's leading scientists, died November 11, 1973, in the city of his birth, Helsinki.

SELECTED WRITINGS BY VIRTANEN:

Books

Cattle Fodder and Human Nutrition with Special Reference to Biological Nitrogen Fixation, Cambridge, 1938.

SOURCES:

Books

Dictionary of Scientific Biography, Volume XIV, Scribner, 1976.
Nobel Prize Winners, H. W. Wilson, 1987.

—*Sketch by Mike McClure*

Richard Vollenweider
1922-
Swiss Canadian limnologist

Richard Vollenweider is best known for his innovative research in eutrophication (nutrient enrichment and its effects) which advanced the fields of modern limnology, the study of the properties of fresh waters, and lake management. Eutrophication is generally seen as a problem of the middle and late stages of the twentieth century, a consequence of society's urban, industrial and agricultural use of plant nutrients and their disposal. The term eutrophication describes the biological effects of an increase in concentration of plant nutrients, usually nitrogen and phosphorous, but can also include silicon, potassium, calcium, iron or manganese, on aquatic systems. Vollenweider was the first to recognize phosphorus as the primary element in lake production, a discovery which laid the foundation for the restoration of the Great Lakes and for eutrophication control models employed internationally.

Richard Albert Vollenweider was born in Zurich, Switzerland, on June 27, 1922. He grew up in Lucerne where he finished high school and obtained a teacher's diploma in 1942. He attended the University of Zurich where he earned a diploma in biology in 1946, and completed a Ph.D. in biology in 1951, with a thesis on "Experimental Studies on Phytoplankton Ecology." He was awarded an honorary doctorate of science from McGill University in Montreal in 1986.

Vollenweider devoted much of his career to education. He taught in undergraduate schools in Lucerne, Switzerland from 1949 to 1954, followed by two fellowships studying limnology. The first fellowship took him to the Italian Hydrobiological Institute in Palanza, Italy, from 1954 to 1955, and the second to the Swedish Research Council in Uppsala, Switzerland, from 1955 to 1956.

From 1957 to 1959 he worked as a field expert in limnology and fisheries for the United Nations Educational, Scientific and Cultural Organization (UNESCO) Department of Agriculture in Egypt. He then returned to the Italian Hydrobiological Institute to work as a research associate from 1959 to 1966, followed by a position as a water pollution consultant for the Organization for Economic Cooperative development in Paris from 1966 to 1968. He served as chief limnologist and head of the Fisheries Research Board for the Canadian Centre for Inland Waters (CCIW), Burlington, Ontario, from 1968 to 1970, followed by a position as chief of the National Water Research Institute Lakes Research Division from 1970 to 1973. Vollenweider's final professional position was as a senior scientist with the Canadian Centre of Inland Waters from 1973 to 1988, which he held concurrently with a position as professor of biology at McMaster University in Hamilton, Ontario, from 1978 to 1988.

While head of the Fisheries Research Board laboratories at CCIW, Vollenweider administered a research staff of 140 scientists and technicians. In this capacity he was responsible for organizing and developing the early research activities on the Laurentian Great Lakes and other limnological studies in Canada. CCIW created the position of senior scientist for Vollenweider to allow him to continue his own research as well as to serve as chair of the Centre's Scientific Committee for Research Coordination.

Water Purification Research Earns International Recognition

Vollenweider's primary contribution to the study of limnology began at the theoretical stage when he designed a mathematical model for measuring the levels of phosphorus in the Great Lakes. This model determined the appropriate level of reduction of phosphorus necessary to stabilize the aquatic environments. His prior research, as well as that of others, concluded that the dumping of massive quantities of phosphorous had resulted in the destructive overgrowth of algae in these lakes. Vollenweider's theory of maximum tolerable levels of phosphorus in the lakes became the accepted standard among scientists and extended to the political arena when it formed the basis of the 1972 Great Lakes Water Quality Agreement between Canada and the United States. This recognition of the work of a single scientist within international law is an unusual distinction. Vollenweider's experiment to reduce phosphorous in the Great Lakes, begun in 1972, has proved successful and has stimulated similar projects around the world.

Vollenweider studied the primary production of Swiss, Italian, Swedish and Egyptian lakes using oxygen techniques and radioactive carbon, and developed mathematical models for calculating integral photosynthesis. He also explored the relationship between primary production and absorption characteristics and the spectral correlation of underwater light over a broad range of lakes. This early line of research became the frame for later efforts to resolve the question about eutrophication. Further, he discovered the acidification process of lakes due to industrial ammonia pollution.

In addition to his research work in Canada, Vollenweider served as a consultant to many United Nations organizations and the governments of Italy, Argentina, Venezuela, Japan and Ecuador. He has been instrumental in helping these countries develop programs to deal with major water management issues and in supporting purification projects. Vollenweider also served as a consultant to the Pan American Health Organization for Venezuela from 1977 to 1980; Italy in 1977; Argentina in 1980; Ecuador in 1982; and Brazil and Mexico in 1983. He worked for the International Lake Environment Commission and the World Health Organization in 1985.

Vollenweider has published more than 90 scientific papers in current scientific and technical journals, two books, and authored and/or co-authored numerous other scientific and technical reports in the fields of aquatic primary production, algal nutrition, optical conditions in lakes, water chemistry, freshwater and marine eutrophication, and modelling. In addition to several papers on these topics, the primary outcome from Vollenweider's studies was the International Biological Programme (IBP) handbook on

"Methods for Measuring Primary Production in the Aquatic Environment," of which he was the primary contributor.

Vollenweider's honors and awards include the International Award, Premio Cervia/Ambiente in 1978; the International Tyler Prize for Global Environmental Achievement in 1986; and the Societas Internationalis Limnologiae Naumann-Thienemann Medal in 1987. He has been a member of the Italian Association of Ecology, the Italian Association of Theoretical and Applied Limnology, and the Royal Society of Canada.

In recognition of his scientific leadership and public involvements for the environmental safeguard of the Adriatic Sea from eutrophication and pollution, Vollenweider has been conferred honorary citizenship of the City of Cesenatico, Italy. He has been a frequent guest on Italian television regarding Adriatic pollution, and his activities have been reported in many Italian daily newspapers. He currently divides his time between Canada and Italy.

The annual R. A. Vollenweider Lectureship in Aquatic Sciences was established in his honor by the National Water Research Institute upon his retirement in 1988 to commemorate his global contribution to the advancement of the aquatic sciences. At the time of his retirement, Vollenweider was the National Water Research Institute's senior scientist.

Vollenweider was married in 1965 and has no children.

SELECTED WRITINGS BY VOLLENWEIDER:

Books

Water Management Research; Scientific Fundamentals of the Eutrophication of Lakes and Flowing Waters, with Particular Reference to Nitrogen and Phosphorus as Factors in Eutrophication, Organization for Economic Cooperation and Development (OECD), Paris, 1968.
(With J. F. Talling and D. F. Westlake) *A Manual on Methods for Measuring Primary Production in Aquatic Environments,* 2nd edition, Blackwell Scientific Publishers, 1974.

Periodicals

(With M. Munawar and P. Stadelmann) "A Comparative View of Phytoplankton and Primary Production in the Laurentian Great Lakes," *Journal of the Fisheries Research Board of Canada,* Volume 31, 1974.
Input-Output Models with Special Reference to the Phosphorous Loading Concept in Limnology, Schweizische Zeitschrift fuer Hydrologie, Volume 37, 1975.

SOURCES:

Vollenweider, Richard A., interview with Kelly Otter Cooper conducted December 3, 1993.

—Sketch by Kelly Otter Cooper

Vito Volterra
1860-1940
Italian mathematician and physicist

Vito Volterra has been called a modern Renaissance man for the extraordinary variety of his interests, his great scientific curiosity, and his love of art, literature, and music. In a scientific career that spanned fifty-nine years, Volterra made his most important contributions in the areas of higher analysis, mathematical physics, celestial mechanics, the mathematical theory of elasticity, and mathematical biometrics. His name is most often associated with the creation of the theory of functionals and with the theory of integral and integro-differential equations.

Volterra was born in Ancona, Italy, on May 3, 1860, the only child of Abramo Volterra, a cloth merchant, and Angelica Almagià. After the death of his father in 1862, Volterra and his mother went to stay with her brother, Alfonso Almagià, who raised Volterra as his own son. Volterra spent most of his childhood in Florence and considered himself a native of that city. From a very early age, Volterra demonstrated an aggressive curiosity and an uncanny talent in mathematics and science. At the age of thirteen, inspired by Jules Verne's novel *From the Earth to the Moon,* Volterra tried to determine the trajectory of a projectile in the combined gravitational fields of the earth and moon. To solve this restricted version of the so-called three-body problem, he divided passing time into sufficiently small intervals to allow the forces operating on the projectile to be treated as constant in each interval. Volterra used this technique again and again over the years as he attacked such problems as differential linear equations, the theory of functionals, and linear substitutions.

Volterra attended the Scuola Tecnica Dante Alighieri and the Instituto Tecnico Galileo Galilei in Florence, Italy, graduating in 1878. Over the opposition of his mother and uncle, he enrolled at the University of Florence, where he was offered the position of assistant in the Physical Laboratory. He studied mineralogy and geology as well as mathematics and physics. In 1878, he transferred to the

University of Pisa, and in 1880 won a competition to become a resident student at the Scuola Normale Superiore, where he remained for three years. While there, he wrote his first original paper on the theory of aggregates and the functions of a real variable. In 1882, Volterra was awarded a doctorate in physics for a thesis in the area of hydrodynamics.

In 1883, at the age of twenty-three, Volterra won the competition for a professorship of mechanics at the University of Pisa and went on to become the chair of mathematical physics. In 1892, he was appointed professor of mechanics at the University of Turin. Eight years later, in 1900, he became the chair of mathematical physics at the University of Rome. He was a gifted teacher and lectured in many different European countries in the course of his life.

From his first paper in 1881 to a 1940 paper in *Acta* of the Pontifical Academy of Sciences, Volterra demonstrated a keen intelligence and a curiosity about many areas. Beyond his seminal work on the theory of functionals and on the theory of integro-differential equations, Volterra made important scientific contributions in many areas of applied science, including elasticity, physics, astronomy, mathematical biology, and hereditary phenomena. One of his most important achievements in applied science was his work on the mathematics of population growth, which took this field of inquiry beyond the Malthusian approach that any given environment can only sustain a strictly limited population. Volterra argued that cooperation among human beings would allow for increases in the food supply and thus accommodate a greater increase in population. He developed a mathematical model of population growth that takes these considerations into account.

Career Interrupted by World War II

In March 1905, at the comparatively young age of forty-five and in recognition of his scientific achievements, Volterra was made a Senator of the Kingdom of Italy. The Italian government also appointed him Chairman of the Polytechnic School at Turin. Although Volterra would have preferred to pursue a career of pure science, politics and war disrupted his plans. Throughout his life, Volterra was touched by these forces. When Volterra was three months old, he was nearly killed by a bomb that destroyed his cradle during a siege by the Italian Army. In 1914, at the outbreak of World War I, Volterra was among those who urged his government to join the Allies. When Italy entered the war on the Allied side in 1915, Volterra enlisted in the army (at the age of fifty-five) and joined the air force. For more than two years he worked to perfect a new type of airship and developed a system for firing a gun from it. He was the first to propose the use of helium as a substitute for hydrogen, which is highly explosive,

and he organized the manufacture of the slightly heavier gas. He also experimented with early aircraft designs and published mathematical works relating to aerial warfare. In 1917, he established the Office for War Inventions and, as its chairman, worked successfully to promote scientific and technical collaboration among the Allies. He was decorated with the War Cross and mentioned in dispatches for his work.

Forced from Homeland by Fascism

At war's end, Volterra returned to his research and teaching. But in 1922, at a time when he was generally recognized as the most eminent man of science in Italy, his academic life was again disrupted by politics. From the beginning, Volterra opposed fascism, especially objecting to changes in the educational system that deprived the Italian Middle Schools of their liberty. At great personal risk, Volterra and a small group of his fellow senators opposed the "laws of national security." In 1931, one year after the Italian parliamentary system had been abolished, Volterra refused to take the Oath of Allegiance imposed by the fascist government and was forced to leave the University of Rome, where he had taught and studied for more than thirty years. In 1932, he was compelled to resign from all Italian scientific academies and, from that time on, lived mostly abroad.

Despite the political disruptions, Volterra's life was generally happy and productive. He was much honored and well recognized for the excellence of his scientific work. He was a member of almost every major scientific and mathematical society, including the Royal Society, which he joined in 1910. In 1936, he was elected to the Pontifical Academy of Sciences after being nominated by Pope Pius XI. He was a Grand Officer of the French Legion of Honor. In 1921, he received an honorary knighthood from George V of England. He was also awarded honorary doctorates by many universities, including Cambridge, Oxford, and Edinburgh. In 1900, Volterra married Virginia Almagià, a distant cousin. They had six children. In 1938, Volterra developed phlebitis but continued his academic pursuits until his death on October 11, 1940, in Rome.

SELECTED WRITINGS BY VOLTERRA:

Books

Opere Matematiche. Memorie e Note (collected works), five volumes, [Rome], 1954–1962.

SOURCES:

Books

American Philosophical Society Yearbook, 1940, Lancaster Press, 1941, pp. 448–451.

Manheim, J., *The Genesis of Point Set Topology*, Macmillan, 1964.

Obituary Notices of Fellows of the Royal Society, Volume 3, Morrison & Gibb, 1939–41, pp. 691–729.

—*Sketch by Maureen L. Tan*

Wernher von Braun
1912-1977

German-born American rocket engineer

Wernher von Braun was the most famous rocket engineer of his time as well as a scientist and noted promoter of spaceflight. Teams under his direction designed the V–2, Redstone, Jupiter, and Pershing missiles, as well as the Jupiter C, Juno, and Saturn launch vehicles that carried most of the early U.S. satellites and spacecraft beyond the earth's atmosphere and ultimately to the moon. He became both a celebrity and a national hero in the United States, winning numerous awards, including the first Robert H. Goddard Memorial Trophy in 1958, the Distinguished Federal Civilian Service Award (presented by President Dwight D. Eisenhower) in 1959, and the National Medal of Science in 1977. As President Jimmy Carter stated at the time of his death: "To millions of Americans, [his] name was inextricably linked to our exploration of space and to the creative application of technology. He was not only a skillful engineer but also a man of bold vision; his inspirational leadership helped mobilize and maintain the effort we needed to reach the Moon and beyond."

The second of three children (all male), Wernher Magnus Maximilian von Braun was born on March 23, 1912, in the east German town of Wirsitz (later, Wyrzysk, Poland). He was the son of Baron Magnus Alexander Maximilian von Braun—then the principal magistrate (*Landrat*) of the governmental district and later (1932-early 1933) the minister of nutrition and agriculture in the last two governments of the Weimar Republic before Hitler rose to power in Germany—and of Emmy (von Quistorp) von Braun, a well-educated woman from the Swedish-German aristocracy with a strong interest in biology and astronomy. She inspired her son's interest in spaceflight by supplying him with the science fiction works of Jules Verne and H. G. Wells and by giving him a telescope as a gift upon his confirmation into the Lutheran church in his early teens instead of the customary watch or camera. Despite these influences, the young

von Braun was initially a weak student and was held back one year in secondary school because of his inability in math and physics. Due to his interest in astronomy and rockets, he obtained a copy of space pioneer **Hermann Oberth**'s book *Die Rakete zu den Planeträumen* ("Rockets to Planetary Space") in 1925. Appalled that he could not understand its complicated mathematical formulas, he determined to master his two weakest subjects. Upon completion of secondary school, von Braun entered the Berlin-Charlottenburg Institute of Technology, where he earned a bachelor of science in mechanical engineering and aircraft construction in 1932.

Begins Career in Rocketry

In the spring of 1930 von Braun found time to work as part of the German Society for Space Travel, a group founded in part by Hermann Oberth which experimented with small, liquid-fueled rockets. Although Oberth returned to a teaching position in his native Romania, von Braun continued working with the society. When the group ran short of funds during the Depression, von Braun, then twenty, reluctantly accepted the sponsorship of the German military. In 1932 he went to work for the German army's ordnance department at Kummersdorf near Berlin, continuing to develop liquid-fueled rockets. Entering the University of Berlin about this same time, he used his work at Kummersdorf as the basis for his doctoral dissertation and received his Ph.D. in physics in 1934.

Von Braun's staff at Kummersdorf eventually grew to some eighty people, and in early 1937 the group moved to Peenemünde, a town on the Baltic coast where the German army together with the air force had constructed new facilities. Before the move, engineers at Kummersdorf had begun developing ever larger rockets, and in 1936 they completed the preliminary design for the A–4, better known as the V–2. This was an exceptionally ambitious undertaking, since the missile was to be 45 feet long, deliver a 1-ton warhead to a target some 160 miles distant, and employ a rocket motor that could deliver a 25-ton thrust for 60 seconds, compared to the 1.5 tons of thrust supplied by the largest liquid-fueled rocket motors then available. Von Braun's team encountered numerous difficulties—perfecting the injection system for the propellants, mastering the aerodynamic properties of the missile, and especially in developing its guidance and control system. Thus, even with the assistance of private industry and universities, the first successful launch of the A–4 did not occur at Peenemünde until October 3, 1942. Despite this success, failed launches continued to plague the project, and as a result the first fully operational V–2s were not fired until September 1944. Between then and the end of the war, approximately 6,000 rockets were manufactured at an underground production site named *Mittelwerk,* using the slave labor of concentration camp inmates and prisoners of war. Although several thousand V–2s struck London, Antwerp, and other allied targets, they were not strategically significant in the German war effort. Their importance lies in the technological advances they brought to the development of rocketry.

This fact and von Braun's later importance in the American spaceflight effort often overshadows the issue of his ethical responsibility for the suffering and loss of life associated with the V–2. Although the youthful, blond, blue-eyed von Braun always gave credit to his whole team for the technical success of this and other programs, he clearly played a key role in the development of the missile. Thoroughly familiar with its technical details, he also had a remarkable ability to express ideas clearly, to resolve problems, and to promote a sense of belonging to and functioning as a team. He and his Army superior, General Walter Dornberger, were also notably successful in obtaining funding and other support for the V–2. While he had no direct responsibility for production at *Mittelwerk,* von Braun was aware of conditions in the concentration camp that provided the factory's labor. Moreover, he had joined the Nazi party on May 1, 1937, and had even become an officer in the elite, quasi-military SS on May 1, 1940. While more research is needed on this subject, available American records support his claim that he had joined both organizations only because failure to do so would have forced him to abandon his work on rocketry. He further stated that his motivation in building army missiles was their ultimate use in space travel and scientific endeavors and that his own arrest by Nazis in 1944 resulted from this concern for the future and lack of interest in the immediate uses of the V–2. All of this makes von Braun's ethical responsibility a difficult issue to resolve, but any blame would appear to be indirect rather than direct—a failure to take the possibly dangerous step of protesting against Nazi policies, rather than any overt support for the abuse of concentration camp labor. Regardless of how this ethical question is answered, it is clear that von Braun was a remarkable individual with a wide range of accomplishments beyond his role as a space pioneer. A musician who played the piano and cello, he loved the music of Mozart, Chopin, and Puccini. At the same time, he was an ardent outdoorsman who enjoyed scuba diving, fishing, hunting, sailing, piloting an airplane, and sail planing.

Moves to America

As the war drew to a close in Europe in the early months of 1945, von Braun organized the move of hundreds of people from Peenemünde to Bavaria so they could surrender to the Americans rather than the Soviets. Subsequently, about 120 of them went to Fort Bliss near El Paso, Texas, as part of a military operation called Project Paperclip. They worked on rocket development and employed captured V–2s for high altitude research at the nearby White Sands Proving Ground in New Mexico. In the midst of these efforts, von Braun returned to Germany to marry his second cousin, Maria Louise von Quistorp, on March 1, 1947, returning with her to Texas after the wedding. In 1950, the von Braun team transferred to the Redstone Arsenal near Huntsville, Alabama, where between April 1950 and February 1956 it developed the Redstone medium-range ballistic missile under his technical direction. Deployed in 1958, the Redstone was basically an offshoot of the V–2 but featured several modifications including an improved inertial guidance system. The Redstone also served as a launch vehicle, placing Alan B. Shephard and Virgil I. "Gus" Grissom in suborbital flight in May and July 1961, respectively. Meanwhile, in February 1956 von Braun became the director of the development operations division of the newly established Army Ballistic Missile Agency (ABMA) in Huntsville. While located there, he and his wife raised three children—Iris Careen (born in 1948), Margrit Cecile (1952), and Peter Constantine (1960)—and von Braun himself became a U.S. citizen on April 14, 1955.

The next missile designed by von Braun and his team was the Jupiter intermediate range ballistic missile. Unlike the Redstone and the V–2, which used liquid oxygen and an alcohol-water mixture as propellants, the Jupiter employed liquid oxygen and kerosene. Following development, it was assigned to the Air Force for deployment after 1958. In the meantime, von Braun's engineers had developed the Jupiter C, which consisted of three parts or "stages." Its first stage was a modified Redstone missile, while the second and third stages were derived from the Sergeant missile, initially developed by the Jet Propulsion Laboratory. In its third launch on August 8, 1957, the Jupiter C carried a nose cone that became the first man-made object to be recovered from outer space. It also proved the feasibility of a new technique to carry off the excessive heat produced by friction upon the nose cone of a missile or spacecraft during re-entry into the atmosphere. In addition, the von Braun team developed the Pershing—a two-stage, solid-fuel ballistic missile that had its first test launch in February 1960. Another group of rockets developed under von Braun was the Juno series. Juno I, a four-stage version of Jupiter C, launched America's first satellite, Explorer I, on January 31, 1958. Juno II, using the Jupiter missile as its first stage and Jupiter C upper stages, launched a number of satellites in the Pioneer and Explorer series, including Pioneer IV that went past the moon and entered solar orbit following launch on March 3, 1959.

Transfers to NASA

Undoubtedly the greatest claim to fame of von Braun and his team was the powerful Saturn family of rockets, which propelled Americans into lunar orbit and landed 12 of them on the moon between July 1969 and January 1971. Development of these launch vehicles began under ABMA and was completed during the decade after July 1, 1960, when von Braun and over 4,000 ABMA personnel transferred to the National Aeronautics and Space Administration (NASA), forming the George C. Marshall Space Flight Center, which von Braun directed until February 1970. The Saturn I and Ib were developmental rockets leading to the massive Saturn V that actually launched the astronauts of the Apollo program. Propelled by liquid oxygen and kerosene in its first stage, liquid oxygen and liquid hydrogen for the two upper stages, the Saturn V stood 363 feet high, six stories above the level of the Statue of Liberty. Its first stage constituted the largest aluminum cylinder ever produced; its valves were as large as barrels, its fuel pumps larger than refrigerators.

As von Braun repeatedly insisted, he and his team were not alone responsible for the success of the Saturn and Apollo programs. In fact, the engineers at Marshall often urged more conservative solutions to problems occurring in both programs than NASA ultimately adopted. To von Braun's credit, he invariably accepted and supported the more radical approaches once he was convinced they were right. One example involved the debate over all-up versus step-by-step testing of Saturn V. Having experienced numerous rocket system failures going back to the V–2 and beyond, the German engineers favored testing each stage of the complicated rocket. At NASA headquarters, however, administrator George Mueller preferred the Air Force approach, which relied much more heavily on ground testing. He therefore insisted upon testing Saturn V all at once in order to meet President John F. Kennedy's ambitious goal of landing an American on the moon before the end of the decade. Ever cautious, von Braun hesitated but finally concurred in the ultimately successful procedure.

Beyond his role as an engineer, scientist, and project manager, von Braun was also an important advocate for spaceflight, publishing numerous books and magazine articles, serving as a consultant for television programs and films as well as testifying before Congress. Perhaps most important in this regard were his contributions, with others, to a series of *Collier's* articles from 1952 to 1953 and to a Walt Disney television series produced by Ward Kimball from 1955 to 1957. Both series were enormously influential and, along with the fears aroused by the Soviet space program, galvanized American efforts to conquer space. As von Braun said to Kimball in late 1968 after the Apollo 8 orbit of the moon: "Well, Ward, it looks like they're following our script."

In March 1970, NASA transferred von Braun to its headquarters in Washington, D.C., where he became Deputy Associate Administrator. He had hoped to renew interest in the space program, but a much smaller NASA budget, as he said, "reduced my function in Washington eventually to one of describing programs which I knew could not be funded for the next 10 years anyway." Consequently, he resigned from the agency effective July 1, 1972, to become vice president for engineering and development with Fairchild Industries of Germantown, Maryland. Besides his work for that aerospace firm, he continued his efforts to promote human spaceflight, helping to found the National Space Institute in 1975 and serving as its first president. On June 16, 1977, he died of cancer at a hospital in Alexandria, Virginia.

SELECTED WRITINGS BY VON BRAUN:

Books

Across the Space Frontier, with J. Kaplan and others, Viking Press, 1952.

Man on the Moon, Sidgwick and Jackson, 1953.

The Mars Project, University of Illinois Press, 1953.

Exploration of Mars, with Willy Ley, Viking Press, 1956.

"The Redstone, Jupiter, and Juno," in *The History of Rocket Technology,* Eugene M. Emme, editor, Wayne State University Press, 1964, pp. 107–121.

History of Rocketry and Space Travel, with F. I. Ordway III, Crowell, 1966.

Periodicals

"Man on the Moon—The Journey," *Colliers,* October 18, 1952, pp. 52–60.

"Baby Space Station," with Cornelius Ryan, *Colliers,* June 27, 1953, pp. 33–40.

"Can We Get to Mars?" with Cornelius Ryan, *Colliers,* April 30, 1954, pp. 22-28.

SOURCES:

Books

Bergaust, Erik, *Wernher von Braun,* National Space Institute, 1976.

Bilstein, Roger E., *Stages to Saturn: A Technological History of the Apollo/Saturn Launch Vehicles,* NASA SP-4206, 1980.

Hunt, Linda, *Secret Agenda: The United States Government, Nazi Scientists, and Project Paperclip, 1945 to 1990,* St. Martin's Press, 1991.

Huzel, Dieter K., *Peenemünde to Canaveral,* Prentice-Hall, Inc., 1962.

Kennedy, Gregory P., *Vengeance Weapon 2: The V–2 Guided Missile,* Smithsonian Institution Press, 1983.

Neufeld, Michael J., "The Guided Missile and the Third Reich: Peenemünde and the Forging of a Technological Revolution," in *Science, Technology and National Socialism,* Monika Renneberg and Mark Walker, editors, Cambridge University Press, 1993.

Stuhlinger, Ernst and Frederick I. Ordway III, *Wernher von Braun: Crusader for Space,* Volume I, *A Biographical Memoir,* Krieger, 1994.

Periodicals

Biddle, Wayne, "Science, Morality and the V–2," *New York Times,* October 2, 1992, p. A31.

Hutchins, Timothy, "Space Hero Von Braun Dead at 65," *Washington Star,* June 17, 1977, pp. 9–10.

Wilford, John Noble, "Wernher von Braun, Space Pioneer, Dies," *New York Times,* June 18, 1977, pp. 16–18.

Other

Agent Report on Von Braun, Wernher Magnus Maximilian, prepared by Milton F. Gidge, 10 April 1953, available in "Wernher von Braun," biographical files, NASA Historical Reference Collection, Washington, D.C.

Letter, Thomas J. Ford, Colonel, GSC, Director, to Commanding General, United States Forces, European Theater, Attention: G–2, subject: Request for Information on German Scientist [Wernher von Braun], 3 March 1947, available in biographical files, NASA Historical Reference Collection, Washington, D.C.

National Aeronautics and Space Administration Biographical Data, Dr. Wernher von Braun, February 1971.

—*Sketch by J. D. Hunley*

Theodore von Kármán
1881-1963
Hungarian aerodynamicist

Often referred to as "the father of aerodynamics," Theodore von Kármán's studies of aerodynamics resulted in a number of important and fundamental discoveries, including the existence of Kármán vortex streets, a characteristic flow of air that has passed over a cylindrical surface. These discoveries had significant applications in the design of aircraft frames, bridges, and other structures subject to winds and other types of air flow. Von Kármán, who lived both in Europe and the United States, was very active in developing the practical applications of his scientific discoveries. Equally interested in dealing with the political implications of these discoveries, he served as consultant and advisor to a number of private corporations and governmental agencies. Von Kármán died in Germany in 1963.

Theodore von Kármán was born in Budapest, Hungary, on May 11, 1881. His father was Moritz von Kármán, founder of the modern Hungarian system of secondary education and professor of education at the University of Budapest. His mother was the former Helen Konn, a member of a distinguished Bohemian-Jewish family that included many teachers and rabbis. For his secondary education, von Kármán attended the Minta Gymnázium in Budapest, a demonstration school established by his father. He showed an interest in mathematics and science at an early age and decided to major in mechanical engineering at the Technical University of Budapest, where he was awarded an engineering degree with high honors in 1902. After serving a year of compulsory military service, von Kármán returned to the university as an assistant professor of hydraulics. He also began his long consulting career while working with the manufacturing firm of Granz and Company.

Becomes Interested in Aerodynamics

In 1906, von Kármán was awarded a two-year fellowship by the Hungarian Academy of Sciences. He chose to use the fellowship at the University of Göttingen, then home to a number of first-rate scholars in science. Among these was the German physicist **Ludwig Prandtl**, who would later carry out many of the earliest fundamental experiments in the field of aerodynamics. Von Kármán's own research at Göttingen, however, was directed toward other topics. His doctoral thesis dealt with the stability of structures under various conditions of stress. He also worked with his friend, a German physicist named **Max Born**, on problems concerning the theory of specific heats.

Eventually, von Kármán increasingly concentrated on aerodynamics and, in 1911, he made the discovery for which he is most famous. It had been known that air, or fluid, moving over a cylindrical surface creates a particular pattern of vortices in its wake. In considering that flow, von Kármán was the first to use a mathematical approach to understanding the distribution of vortices in an alternating double row, now recognized as a Kármán vortex street. Under certain conditions, a Kármán vortex street can have disastrous consequences for the object with which it is associated. The collapse of the Tacoma Narrows bridge in 1940, for example, was later found to have resulted from the formation of Kármán vortices, when winds reached a velocity of forty-two miles per hour over the bridge.

In 1912 von Kármán left Göttingen to become professor of the theory of machines at the College of Mining Engineering in Selmecbánya, Hungary. However, that same year he was offered an opportunity to organize the new Aeronautical Institute at the Technical University of Aachen. He accepted the offer and became professor of aerodynamics and mechanics as well as director of the new institute. Von Kármán retained his affiliation with Aachen until 1930, interrupted briefly by a leave of absence during the first world war.

Turns to Issues of Aircraft Design

During World War I, von Kármán was assigned work on the design of aircraft parts for the newly created Austro-Hungarian air force. That experience apparently solidified his interest in airfoil design that had been aroused some years earlier. His military tasks included finding a solution for the problem of synchronizing machine gun fire with rapid propeller rotation and designing improvements in helicopter design. After the war, von Kármán returned to Aachen and the task of building up the aeronautical institute there. He also became active as a consultant to various aircraft manufacturers, including the Junkers Aeroplane Works and Luftschiffbau Zepplin in Germany, Handley-Paige Limited in England, and Kawanishi Aircraft Company in Japan.

Von Kármán's first visit to the United Sates came in 1926, when he was asked to consult on the design of the recently endowed Guggenheim Aeronautical Laboratory and its accompanying wind tunnel at the California Institute of Technology (Caltech). He made a strong impression on **Robert A. Millikan**, then president of Caltech, and was eventually persuaded to leave Aachen for a permanent position as director of the Guggenheim Laboratory. He retained an affiliation with Caltech until 1949, although that connection became increasingly tenuous in the latter years.

Von Kármán exerted a powerful influence on the science of aerodynamics at the Guggenheim Laboratory because of the many specialists he helped to train. His establishment of the Jet Propulsion Laboratory at Caltech, which he directed from 1938 to 1945, would also prove critical in the development of future U.S. space programs. However, as von Kármán became increasingly involved with the military applications of aerodynamic research, he gradually withdrew from Caltech. In 1938 he became consultant to the U.S. Army Ballistic Research Laboratory, and in the following year he was appointed as a consultant to the U.S. Army Air Corps. After the war, he became

even more involved in a number of governmental activities with the objective of garnering scientific cooperation on an international level. He conceived of an aeronautical collaboration between European scientists through the North Atlantic Treaty Organization (NATO) Advisory Group for Aeronautical Research and Development, for which he served as chair from its conception in 1952 until his death a decade later.

Von Kármán also expanded his activities into the private sector. Disappointed by the lack of willingness among established industries to explore the potential applications of rockets, von Kármán was instrumental in the formation of the Aerojet Engineering Corporation in 1942. Aerojet was later reorganized as Aerojet-General Corporation, a subsidiary of General Tire and Rubber Company. In *Biographical Memoirs of Fellows of the Royal Society,* S. Goldstein points out that by 1951, von Kármán's many government-related activities had caused him to establish his "main headquarters" in Washington, DC, although he maintained a residence in Pasadena until his death. Von Kármán never married, but lived most of his life with his mother and his sister, Josephine. Among the many awards and honorary doctorates he received were the U.S. Medal for Merit in 1946, the Franklin Gold Medal of the Franklin Institute in 1948, and the National Medal of Science in 1963. Von Kármán died on May 7, 1963, in Aachen, while on a projected four-month visit to Europe in connection with the NATO advisory group.

SELECTED WRITINGS BY VON KÁRMÁN:

Books

(With M. A. Biot), *Mathematical Methods in Engineering,* McGraw-Hill, 1940.

Aerodynamics: Selected Topics in the Light of Their Historical Development, Cornell University Press, 1954.

Collected Works of Dr. Theodore von Kármán, Butterworths, 1956.

From Low-Speed Aerodynamics to Astronautics, Pergamon Press, 1961.

SOURCES:

Books

Biographical Memoirs, Volume 38, National Academy of Sciences, 1965.

Biographical Memoirs of Fellows of the Royal Society, Volume 12, Royal Society (London), 1966.

—*Sketch by David E. Newton*

Klaus von Klitzing
1943-
German physicist

Klaus von Klitzing was awarded the 1985 Nobel Prize in physics for his discovery of the quantized Hall effect, a variation on an electrical phenomenon first observed by the American physicist Edwin Hall in about 1880. Von Klitzing's discovery has had a number of profound effects in both theoretical and practical fields of physics, exhibiting one of the first instances in which quantum effects had been observed on a macroscopic scale. In addition, it made possible the establishment of an entirely new international standard for the ohm, the unit of measure of electrical resistance.

Von Klitzing was born on June 28, 1943, in Schroda, Germany, close to the Polish border, to Bogislav von Klitzing, a forester, and Anny Ulbrich. As World War II turned against Germany, the von Klitzing family decided to stay ahead of the advancing Soviet army and moved westward to the town of Lutten. Three years later, in 1948, they moved again to Oldenburg and finally, in 1951, to the northern town of Essen. Von Klitzing eventually completed his secondary education at the Artland Gymnasium in Quakenbrück.

Begins His Studies of Semiconductors

In 1962, von Klitzing entered the Technical University of Braunschweig, intending to major in physics. He was awarded his baccalaureate degree in 1969 for a dissertation on the electrical properties of indium antimonide, a compound of two semiconducting elements, indium and antimony. Von Klitzing then moved to the University of Würzburg for his doctoral studies, planning to continue his work on semiconductors there. He also accepted a job at the University teaching physics to premedical students. At Würzburg, von Klitzing became particularly interested in the effects of strong magnetic fields on the conducting properties of semiconductors. In 1971, he published his first scientific paper on this topic, "Resonance Structure in the High Field Magnetoresistance of Tellurium," with G. Landwehr, one of his instructors, and was awarded his Ph.D. the following year for this line of research.

A key feature of von Klitzing's ongoing research was the need for stronger and stronger magnetic fields. He spent the 1975 academic year at Oxford University because of the powerful superconducting magnets being manufactured there and, in 1979, continued his research at the High-Field Magnet Laboratory of the Institute Max von Laue-Paul Lan-

gevin in Grenoble, France. It was at Grenoble that von Klitzing made the discovery that earned him the Nobel Prize.

Observes Quantization of the Hall Effect

The Hall effect is a three-dimensional phenomenon in which an electrical current is passed in one direction through a conducting material while a magnetic field is applied at right angles to the current. The accumulation of electrons along one edge of the conductor results in a potential difference along the face of the material that is called the Hall voltage. The Hall resistance, then, is the Hall voltage divided by the current in the conductor. Under these conditions, von Klitzing observed a totally unexpected effect. As the magnetic field on the sample was strengthened, the Hall resistance also increased as a linear function over a certain range, and then levelled off. Further increases in the magnetic field had no effect on the Hall resistance over another range, but then the Hall resistance began to increase again. After another period, the Hall resistance again levelled off. The final results of the experiment appear graphically as a series of steps. Under conventional experimental conditions, however, the Hall resistance is a continuous, linear function of the imposed magnetic field.

To analyze his contradictory findings, von Klitzing devised an experiment with a number of conditions. Most important was his use of a very thin sheet of silicon that constrained the movement of electrons to two dimensions rather than the three normally allowed. In addition, the experiment was carried out in a powerful magnetic field at temperatures close to absolute zero. In this manner, von Klitzing demonstrated that the Hall effect is quantized; changes in the external magnetic field only induce electrical changes in the silicon in certain steps and not continuously. Von Klitzing found that all the possible quantum steps had a value of a fundamental constant divided by an integer number. That constant, 25,813 ohms, is significant because it is the ratio of two fundamental constants of nature, the square of an electron's electrical charge and Planck's constant. In fact, an effect of this type had been foreseen in 1975 by three Japanese theoretical physicists, T. Ando, Y. Matsumoto, and Y. Uemura. The theory did not predict, however, the high degree of precision that von Klitzing had found.

Von Klitzing's discovery is a significant one for physics. It is one of the few instances in which quantum effects have been observed directly in the laboratory; such effects are normally important only at the level of individual particles such as the electron or atom. In addition, the high precision of von Klitzing's results means that a new and more exact standard for the ohm, the unit of electrical resistance, may be possible.

In 1971, von Klitzing married Renate Falkenberg, with whom he had two sons and a daughter. In addition to the Nobel Prize, von Klitzing was awarded the Walter-Schottley Prize of the German Physical Society in 1981 and the Hewlett Packard Prize of the European Physical Society in 1982.

SELECTED WRITINGS BY VON KLITZING:

Periodicals

(With G. Landwehr), "Resonance Structure in the High Field Magnetoresistance of Tellurium," *Solid State Communications,* Volume 9, 1971, pp. 1251–54.

(With G. Dorda and M. Pepper), "New Method for High-Accuracy Determination of the Fine-Structure Constant Based on Quantized Hall Effect," *Physical Review Letters,* Volume 45, 1990, p. 494.

SOURCES:

Books

Nobel Prize Winners, H. W. Wilson, 1987, pp. 558–60.

Periodicals

Halperin, Bertrand I., "The 1985 Nobel Prize for Physics," *Science,* February 21, 1986, pp. 820–22.

"1985 Nobel Prize Winners: Physics," *Scientific American,* December 1985, pp. 75–76.

Schwarzschild, Bertram, "Von Klitzing Wins Nobel Physics Prize for Quantized Hall Effect," *Physics Today,* December, 1985, pp. 17–20.

—*Sketch by David E. Newton*

Richard von Mises
1883-1953

Austrian-born American mathematician and aerodynamicist

Richard von Mises was an aerodynamicist and applied mathematician who made significant contributions to the theory of probability and statistics. A student of logical positivism, he believed in solving problems through rational reasoning. Although his mathematical theories have been widely explored, they have not been universally accepted.

Richard Martin Edler von Mises was born on April 19, 1883, in Lemberg, Austria (now Lvov, Ukraine). His father, Arthur Edler von Mises, was an engineer with the Austrian railway system, who held a doctorate of technical sciences. His mother, Adele Landau von Mises, hailed from a family of literary scholars. He had a younger brother who died in infancy, and an older brother, Ludwig, who became an economist. Although his family was Jewish, von Mises converted to Catholicism as a young man.

Except for occasional temporary relocations for his father's work assignments (including an 1883 stay in Lemberg), von Mises lived in Vienna. During his teenage years, he studied the classics and the humanities at Vienna's Akademische Gymnasium, graduating with distinction in Latin and mathematics in 1901. Shortly thereafter, von Mises entered the Vienna Technical University, where he studied mechanical engineering and published his first mathematical paper. Following graduation, von Mises enrolled in the German Technical University in Brünn at the beginning of 1906, working part time in a factory while completing his doctoral dissertation. He received his doctorate from the University of Vienna in 1907 and lectured the following year at Brünn. In 1909 von Mises took the post of Professor of Applied Mathematics at the University of Strassburg in Germany (now Strasbourg, France).

Shaped the Development of Flight Mechanics

Von Mises began his career investigating fluid mechanics. Dramatic advances in heavier-than-air flying machines drew his attention to aerodynamics and aeronautics. After learning to fly, he taught a summer class in 1913 that apparently was the first university course in the mechanics of powered flight. His own contributions to the field included improvements in boundary layer flow theory and refinements in airfoil design, and he also worked on problems of elasticity, plasticity, and turbulence.

When World War I began in 1914, von Mises returned to his homeland to volunteer for military service, becoming an officer in the new Flying Corps of the Austro-Hungarian Army. He was first given a field assignment, but later assigned to teach at the Fliegerarsenal in Aspern. While there he led a team that devised, built, and tested a 600-horsepower military airplane featuring a new wing profile of his own design. His booklet on flight, published in Vienna in 1916, formed the basis of his work *Theory of Flight,* which von Mises published with English colleagues in 1945. At his own request, he returned to field duty in 1918.

After World War I ended, von Mises returned to Strassburg. The war had cost him his university position as well as much of his personal property. He moved to Germany and worked as a lecturer in mathematics at the University of Frankfurt. In 1919 von Mises took the position of full professor of mechanics at the Technical University in Dresden.

In 1920 von Mises became a professor of applied mathematics and Director of the Institute for Applied Mathematics at the University of Berlin. He published nearly 150 technical works throughout his career and was particularly proud of having founded the journal *Zeitschrift für angewandte Mathematik und Mechanik* in 1921, serving as its editor for the first 12 years. While in Berlin, von Mises met **Hilda Geiringer**, a student from Vienna. She became his assistant, then his collaborator, and eventually his wife. After his death, she edited and completed several of his unfinished manuscripts.

Formalized the Frequency Theory of Probability

Von Mises explored topics ranging from the philosophy of science to practical computational techniques, viewing applied mathematics as the crucial link between theory and scientific observation. He saw the field of statistics as fundamentally important: repetitions of an experiment yield a set of different measurements, which must be analyzed to obtain a single result for comparison with theoretical predictions. Statistics, in turn, are intimately related to probability, especially as von Mises developed the concept.

Recognizing that the existing theory of probability was vague and non-rigorous, von Mises developed a formal, axiomatic treatment of the subject. Pierre-Simon Laplace's original definition of the probability of an event, formulated in 1820, held that the ratio of the number of favorable outcomes to the number of possible outcomes, assuming each outcome to be equally likely. This worked adequately for artificial applications such as games of chance, but failed when applied to natural-occurring events (such as expressing the probability of rain on a given day). Half a century later, John Venn and others proposed defining the probability of an event as the relative frequency with which the event would actually occur "in the long run" (i.e., after an unlimited number of trials). This approach seemed promising, but it was not developed with sufficient precision to validate it.

In 1919 von Mises proposed two axioms which probability must satisfy. His axiom of convergence states that as a sequence of trials is extended, the proportion of favorable outcomes tends toward a definite mathematical limit; such a limit must exist in order to define the probability of an event as the long-term relative frequency of its occurrence. The axiom of randomness was von Mises' most important new

concept. It states that the limiting value of the relative frequency must be the same for all possible infinite subsequences of trials chosen solely by a rule of place selection within the sequence (i.e., the outcomes must be randomly distributed among the trials).

With probability clearly defined as a relative frequency, statistics comprises the system of strategies and tools for designing and evaluating experiments to determine the probability of a specific event. Von Mises' 1928 book, *Probability, Statistics and Truth,* offers an interesting explanation of the subject for the lay reader.

Various mathematicians have identified inconsistencies in von Mises' treatment of probability, which implies that the observation of any finite number of trials is insufficient to determine the probability of an event. Nonetheless, von Mises' contributions have significantly affected the development of modern theories of probability and its relationship to statistics.

When Adolph Hitler became chancellor of Germany in 1933, von Mises moved to Turkey and taught at the University of Istanbul. In 1939 he left for the United States and joined the faculty at Harvard University in Boston.

Throughout his life, von Mises was a scholar with wide-ranging interests. He studied German literature and published eight articles and books on Rainer Rilke's life and poetry; he amassed the largest privately owned collection of Rilke's works, which is now housed at Harvard University. Von Mises even developed a hobby of bookbinding during his years in Berlin. Besides German, he was also fluent in several other languages, including Turkish and English. During a 1951–52 leave of absence from Harvard to lecture on statistics in Rome, he looked forward to teaching in Italian and was reportedly disappointed at being asked to use French instead. In 1944 von Mises was named Gordon McKay Professor of Aerodynamics and Applied Mathematics at Harvard, a position he filled until his death from cancer on July 14, 1953.

SELECTED WRITINGS BY VON MISES:

Books

Selected Papers of Richard von Mises, two volumes, American Mathematical Society, 1963.
Positivism: A Study in Human Understanding, Dover, 1968.
Probability, Statistics, and Truth, Dover, 1981.

SOURCES:

Books

Abbott, David, editor, *The Biographical Dictionary of Scientists: Mathematicians,* Blond Educational, 1985, pp. 130–131.

Gillispie, Charles Coulston, editor, *Dictionary of Scientific Biography,* Volume IX, Charles Scribner's Sons, 1974, pp. 419–420.

Magill, Frank N., editor, *Great Events from History II,* Volume 2, 1991, pp. 664–668.

—*Sketch by Loretta Hall*

John von Neumann

John von Neumann
1903-1957
Hungarian American mathematician

John von Neumann, considered one of the most creative mathematicians of the twentieth century, made important contributions to quantum physics, game theory, economics, meteorology, the development of the atomic bomb, and computer design. He was known for his problem-solving ability, his encyclopedic memory, and his ability to reduce complex problems to a mathematically tractable form. Von Neumann served as a consultant to the United States government on scientific and military matters, and was a member of the Atomic Energy Commission. According to mathematician Peter D. Lax, von Neumann combined extreme quickness, very broad interests, and a fearsome technical prowess; the popular saying was, "Most mathematicians prove what they can; von Neumann proves what he wants." The Nobel Laureate physicist **Hans Albrecht Bethe** said, "I have sometimes wondered whether a brain like von Neumann's does not indicate a species superior to that of man."

Max and Margaret von Neumann's son Janos was born in Budapest, Hungary, on December 28, 1903. As a child he was called Jancsi, which later became Johnny in the United States. His father was a prosperous banker. Von Neumann was tutored at home until age ten, when he was enrolled in the Lutheran Gymnasium for boys. His early interests included literature, music, science and psychology. His teachers recognized his talent in mathematics and arranged for him to be tutored by a young mathematician at the University of Budapest, Michael Fekete. Von Neumann and Fekete wrote a mathematical paper which was published in 1921.

Von Neumann entered the University of Budapest in 1921 to study mathematics; he also studied chemical engineering at the Eidgenössische Technische Hochschule in Zurich, receiving a diploma in 1925. In those same years, he spent much of his time in Berlin, where he was influenced by eminent scientists and mathematicians. In 1926 he received a Ph.D. in mathematics from the University of Budapest, with a doctoral thesis in set theory. He was named *Privatdozent* at the University of Berlin (a position comparable to that of assistant professor in an American university), reportedly the youngest person to hold the position in the history of the university. In 1926 he also received a Rockefeller grant for postdoctoral work under mathematician **David Hilbert** at the University of Göttingen. In 1929 he transferred to the University of Hamburg. By this time, he had become known to mathematicians through his publications in set theory, algebra, and quantum theory, and was regarded as a young genius.

Extends Theory in Pure Mathematics and Quantum Physics

In his early career, von Neumann focused on two research areas: first, set theory and the logical foundations of mathematics; and second, Hilbert space theory, operator theory, and the mathematical foundations of quantum mechanics. During the 1920s, von Neumann published seven papers on mathematical logic. He formulated a rigorous definition of ordinal numbers and presented a new system of axioms for set theory. With Hilbert, he worked on a formalist approach to the foundations of mathematics, attempting to prove the consistency of arithmetic. In about 300 B.C., Euclid's *Elements of Geometry* had proved mathematical theorems using a limited number of axioms. Between 1910 and 1913, **Bertrand Russell** and **Alfred North Whitehead** had published *Principia Mathematica,* which showed that much of the newer math could similarly be derived from a few axioms. With Hilbert, von Neumann worked to carry this approach further, although in 1931 **Kurt Gödel** proved that no formal system could be both complete and consistent.

Hilbert was interested in the axiomatic foundations of modern physics, and he gave a seminar on the subject at Göttingen. The two approaches to quantum mechanics—the wave theory of **Erwin Schrödinger** and the particle theory of **Werner Karl Heisenberg**—had not been successfully reconciled. Working with Hilbert, von Neumann developed a finite set of axioms that satisfied both the Heisenberg and Schrödinger approaches. Von Neumann's axiomatization represented an abstract unification of the wave and particle theories.

During this period, some physicists believed that the probabilistic character of measurements in quantum theory was due to parameters that were not yet clearly understood and that further investigation could result in a deterministic quantum theory. However, von Neumann successfully argued that the indeterminism was inherent and arose from the interaction between the observer and the observed.

In 1929 von Neumann was invited to teach at Princeton University in New Jersey. He accepted the offer and taught mathematics classes from 1930 until 1933, when he joined the elite research group at the newly established Princeton Institute for Advanced Study. The atmosphere at Princeton was informal yet intense. According to mathematician Stanislaw Ulam, writing in the *Bulletin of the American Mathematical Society,* the group "quite possibly constituted one of the greatest concentrations of brains in mathematics and physics at any time and place." During the 1930s von Neumann developed algebraic theories derived from his research into quantum mechanics. These theories were later known as von Neumann algebras. He also conducted research into Hilbert space, ergodic theory, Haar measure, and noncommutative algebras. In 1932 he published a book on quantum physics, *The Mathematical Foundations of Quantum Mechanics,* which remains a standard text on the subject. After becoming a naturalized citizen of the United States, von Neumann became a consultant to the Ballistics Research Laboratory of the Army Ordnance Department in 1937. After the attack on Pearl Harbor in 1941, he became more involved in defense research, serving as a consultant to the National Defense Research Council on the theory of detonation of explosives, and with the Navy Bureau of Ordnance on mine warfare and countermeasures to it. In 1943 he became a consultant on the development of the atomic bomb at the Los Alamos Scientific Laboratory in New Mexico.

Develops Design for Stored-Program Computer

At Los Alamos, von Neumann persuaded **J. Robert Oppenheimer** to pursue the possibility of using an implosion technique to detonate the atomic bomb. This technique was later used to detonate the bomb dropped on Nagasaki. Simulation of the technique at the Los Alamos lab required extensive numerical calculations which were performed by a staff of twenty people using desk calculators. Hoping to speed up the work, von Neumann investigated using computers for the calculations and studied the design and programming of IBM punch-card machines. In 1943 the Army sponsored work at the Moore School of Engineering at the University of Pennsylvania, under the direction of **John William Mauchly** and **J. Presper Eckert**, on a giant calculator for computing firing tables for guns. The machine, called ENIAC (Electronic Numerical Integrator and Computer), was brought to von Neumann's attention in 1944. He joined Mauchly and Eckert in planning an improved machine, EDVAC (Electronic Discrete Variable Automatic Computer). Von Neumann's 1945 report on the EDVAC presented the first written description of the stored-program concept, which makes it possible to load a computer program into computer memory from disk so that the computer can run the program without requiring manual reprogramming. All modern computers are based on this design.

Von Neumann's design for a computer for scientific research, built at the Princeton Institute for Advanced Study between 1946 and 1951, served as the model for virtually all subsequent computer applications. Those built at Los Alamos, the RAND Corporation, the University of Illinois and the IBM Corporation all incorporated, besides the stored program, the separate components of arithmetic function, central control (now commonly referred to as the central processing unit or CPU), random-access memory (or RAM) as represented by the hard drive, and the input and output devices operating in serial or parallel mode. These elements, present in virtually all personal and mainframe computers, were all pioneered under von Neumann's auspices.

In addition, von Neumann investigated the field of neurology, looking for ways for computers to imitate the operations of the human brain. In 1946 he became interested in the challenges of weather forecasting by computer; his Meteorology Project at Princeton succeeded in predicting the development of new storms. Because of his role in early computer design and programming techniques, von Neumann is considered one of the founders of the computer age.

Formulates Game Theory and Its Application to Economics

While in Germany, von Neumann had analyzed strategies in the game of poker and wrote a paper presenting a mathematical model for games of strategy. He continued his work in this area while he was at Princeton, particularly considering applications of game theory to economics. When the Austrian economist Oskar Morgenstern came to Princeton, he and von Neumann started collaborating on applications of game theory to economic problems, such as the exchange of goods between parties, monopolies and oligopolies, and free trade. Their ambitious 641-page book, *Theory of Games and Economic Behavior,* was published in 1944. Von Neumann's work opened new channels of communication between mathematics and the social sciences.

Von Neumann and Morgenstern argued that the mathematics as developed for the physical sciences was inadequate for economics, since economics seeks to describe systems based not on immutable natural laws but on human action involving choice. Von Neumann proposed a different mathematical model to analyze strategies, taking into account the interdependent choices of "players." Game theory is based on an analogy between games and any complex decision-making process, and assumes that all participants act rationally to maximize the outcome of the "game" for themselves. It also assumes that participants are able to rank-order possible outcomes without error. Von Neumann's analysis enables players to calculate the consequences or probable outcomes of any given choice. It then becomes possible to opt for those strategies that have the highest probability of leading to a positive outcome. Game theory can be applied not only to economics and other social sciences but to politics, business organization and military strategy, to mention only a few areas of its usefulness.

Serves as Advisor to Government and Military

After the war, von Neumann served as a scientific consultant for government policy committees and agencies such as the CIA and National Security Agency. He advised the RAND Corporation on its research on game theory and its military applications, and provided technical advice to companies such as IBM and Standard Oil. Following the detonation of an atomic bomb by the Soviets in 1949, von Neumann contributed to the development of the hydrogen bomb. He believed that a strong military capacity was more effective than a disarmament agreement. As chairman of the nuclear weapons panel of the Air Force scientific advisory board (known as the von Neumann committee), his recommendations led to the development of intercontinental missiles and submarine-launched missiles. Herbert York, the director of the Livermore Laboratory, said, "He was very powerful and productive in pure science and mathematics and at the same time had a remarkably strong streak of practicality [which] gave him a

credibility with military officers, engineers, industrialists and scientists that nobody else could match."

In 1954 President Eisenhower appointed von Neumann to the Atomic Energy Commission. Von Neumann was hopeful that nuclear fusion technologies would provide cheap and plentiful energy. According to the chairman of the Commission, Admiral Lewis Strauss, "He had the invaluable faculty of being able to take the most difficult problem, separate it into its components, whereupon everything looked brilliantly simple, and all of us wondered why we had not been able to see through to the answer as clearly as it was possible for him to do." He received the Enrico Fermi Science Award in 1956, and in that same year the Medal of Freedom from President Eisenhower.

Von Neumann has been described as a genius, a practical joker, and a raconteur. Laura Fermi, wife of the associate director of the Los Alamos Laboratory, wrote that he was "one of the very few men about whom I have not heard a single critical remark. It is astonishing that so much equanimity and so much intelligence could be concentrated in a man of not extraordinary appearance."

Von Neumann married Mariette Kovesi, daughter of a Budapest physician, in 1929. Their daughter, Marina, was born in 1935. Mariette obtained a divorce in 1937. The following year, von Neumann married Klara Dan, from an affluent Budapest family. In 1955, von Neumann was diagnosed with bone cancer. Confined to a wheelchair, he continued to attend Atomic Energy Commission meetings and to work on his many projects. He died in 1957 at the age of fifty-three.

SELECTED WRITINGS BY VON NEUMANN:

Books

Mathematische Grundlagen der Quanton-mechanik (title means "Mathematical Foundations of Quantum Mechanics.") [Berlin], 1932.
(With Oskar Morgenstern) *The Theory of Games and Economic Behavior,* Princeton University Press, 1944.
The Collected Works of John von Neumann, edited by A. H. Traub, Macmillan, 1963.

SOURCES:

Books

Aspray, William, *John von Neumann and the Origins of Modern Computing,* MIT Press, 1990.

Glimm, James, John Impagliazzo, and Isadore Singer, editors, *The Legacy of John von Neumann: Proceedings of Symposia in Pure Mathematics,* Volume 50, American Mathematical Society, 1990.

Heims, Steve J., *John von Neumann and Norbert Wiener: From Mathematics to the Technologies of Life and Death,* MIT Press, 1980.

Macrae, Norman, *John von Neumann,* Pantheon, 1992.

Poundstone, William, *Prisoner's Dilemma,* Doubleday, 1992.

Periodicals

Ulam, Stanislaw, "John von Neumann," *Bulletin of the American Mathematical Society,* May, 1958, pp. 1–49.

—*Sketch by C. D. Lord*

Joan George Erardus Gijsbert Voûte
1879-1963
Indonesian Dutch astronomer

In spite of an unorthodox career, Joan George Erardus Gijsbert Voûte became a significant figure in mid-twentieth-century astronomy as a result of his observations at Bosscha Observatory on Java, Indonesia. Over a period of almost thirty years, Voûte identified and described 11,000 binary star systems.

Voûte was born at Madioen (Java, Indonesia) in 1879, the eldest child of Dutch colonists Christoffel Voûte, who was descended from Huguenot exiles, and Maria Antoinnetta de Dieu Stierling. Joan Voûte and his brothers were educated in the Netherlands. Voûte attended a *gymnasium* (a classical secondary school with a curriculum centered on Greek and Latin) in Amsterdam, where he lived with his Welsh grandmother. Upon graduation, he enrolled in the Delft Institute of Technology, one of the finest engineering schools in Europe. He received a civil-engineering diploma from the school in 1908, at the rather late age of twenty-eight. By this time both his parents had died, leaving him a modest inheritance.

Fascinated by astronomy, Voûte worked at the Leiden Observatory for two years without salary, from 1908 to 1910, when he was named to the post of "third observer." It was normal for professional astronomers to work their way up from the bottom, and this lowest post in the observatory hierarchy could indeed lead into something more prestigious: the third observership had been created in 1896 for the talented astronomer and socialist Antonie Pannekoek, who eventually received an associate professorship at the University of Amsterdam; previously, in 1878, Jacobus Cornelius Kapteyn jumped from the post of "second observer" to a full professorship at the University of Groningen. Voûte remained third observer for five years. Financially independent, he was in no hurry to begin publishing or even take a doctorate at the university.

Voûte married Anna Lorch around 1908. With money from his in-laws, he purchased some astronomical equipment and set off for South Africa. There he carried out observations at the Royal Observatory of the Cape of Good Hope, a British institution that had long cooperated with Dutch astronomers—notably Kapteyn and **Willem de Sitter**. While in South Africa, Voûte's personal life underwent major changes. He divorced, remarried, and divorced a second time. By 1918 he began a campaign to find a permanent astronomical position, either in Leiden or at the new Afrikaans-language University of Stellenbosch. In 1919, at the age of forty and with few accomplishments in the world of science, Voûte returned to his native land, accepting the position of temporary scientist at the Royal Magnetical and Meteorological Observatory in Batavia (now Jakarta)—the finest geophysical institution in Asia.

Directs Bosscha Observatory

He arrived at the moment when Indonesia's principal scientific philanthropist, Karel Albert Rudolf Bosscha, had endowed a magnificent institute of technology at Bandung on central Java. Bosscha and his first cousin Rudolf Albert Kerkhoven had long been interested in astronomy, and they then decided to erect the finest observatory in the southern hemisphere, creating a private association to finance the project. Voûte, with his heritage and family ties in the Dutch colony, became Bosscha's choice as the observatory's first director; his lack of a doctorate was no drawback for Bosscha, who himself had been forced to withdraw from the Delft Institute of Technology without taking a diploma.

By the middle 1920s, the new Bosscha observatory at Lembang, near Bandung on Java, had become the finest one in Dutch hands. The observatory's jewel was a 60-centimeter double photographical refractor, constructed by Zeiss in Jena, Germany, complemented by a 37-centimeter Schmidt telescope, constructed in Mittweida. Voûte, as director of the new observatory at Lembang, energetically resisted the attempts of physicists in the Netherlands to control his operation.

Voûte remarried in 1923 (to Frieda Johanna Gertrud Elsbeth Adloff), and he and his wife lived in a villa on the observatory grounds. They hosted a string of temporary observers, including Dutch astronomers P. G. Meesters, Pannekoek, and Egbertus A. Kreiken, German astronomer Paul Bruggencate, Russian astronomer Gleb Victor Simonow, and Swedish astronomer Åke Anders Edvard Wallenquist. Voûte's own observing program focused on binary star systems, which are systems of two stars that orbit around a common center of gravity. The binary stars play an important role in astronomy because their orbits reveal the nature of the gravitational field of each star. Knowledge of a star's gravitational field in turn makes it possible to deduce its mass. Eventually astronomers were able to construct a theory of stellar evolution in part on the basis of stellar mass. Voûte found partners in his endeavors to identify double stars in the Jesuit astronomers at Riverview Observatory, located in a suburb of Sydney, Australia, and provided them with a telescope.

Voûte retired as director in 1939. In his place came Aernout de Sitter (son of astronomer **Willem de Sitter**). With a war footing, however, research at the observatory slowed. De Sitter, his assistant Willem Christiaan Martin, and the observatory's mechanic A. J. Witlox became prisoners of the Japanese in 1942; all three died in a labor camp. Voûte was permitted to return to the observatory under the Japanese administrator Misasi Miyadi. After Indonesian independence, Voûte retired to Amsterdam, where he died in 1963.

SELECTED WRITINGS BY VOÛTE:

Periodicals

"Description of the Observatory," *Annalen,* Volume 1, part 1, 1933.

"Measures of Double Stars, War Series, Made at the Bosscha Observatory Lembang (Java)," *Journal des observateurs,* Volume 78, number 6, 1955, pp. 109–163.

SOURCES:

Books

Pannekoek, Antonie, *Herinneringen,* edited by B. A. Sijes, [Amsterdam], 1982, pp. 229–274.

Pyenson, Lewis, *Empire of Reason: Exact Sciences in Indonesia, 1840–1940,* E. J. Brill, 1989, pp. 45–82.

Periodicals

O'Connell, D. J. K., "Joan George Erardus Gijsbertus Voûte," *Quarterly Journal of the Royal Astronomical Society,* Volume 5, 1964, pp. 296–297.

van der Bilt, J., "Het eerste decennium der Bosscha-Sterrenwacht," *Hemel en Dampkring,* Volume 29, 1931, pp. 1–8.

van der Hucht, Karel, and C. L. M. Kerkhoven, "De Bosscha-Sterrenwacht: Van thee tot sterrenkunde," *Zenit,* Volume 9, 1982, pp. 292–300.

Wallenquist, A. A. E., "Over het leven en werken op de Bosscha Sterrewacht bij Lembang: Een halve eeuw geleden," *Moesson,* December 15, 1982, pp. 6–9.

—*Sketch by Lewis Pyenson*

Hugo de Vries
1848-1935
Dutch botanist and geneticist

Hugo de Vries was a Dutch plant physiologist who developed a great interest in the infant disciplines of evolution and genetics around the turn of the twentieth century. He is best known for his rediscovery of the work of Gregor Mendel in plant genetics and for his own work on the theory of mutation, the changes in the genetic makeup of plants and animals that provide a mechanism for evolution. His research also laid the foundation to the discovery that the genes on chromosomes form the "blueprint" of a cell.

Hugo de Vries was born in Haarlem, the Netherlands, on February 16, 1848. His father, Gerrit de Vries, a lawyer and legislator, was also an expert on water management, and later the minister of justice in the cabinet of William III. De Vries' paternal grandfather was a minister and the librarian for the city of Haarlem as well as an expert on the history of printing. Hugo de Vries' mother, Maria Everardina Reuvens, also came from a scholarly family. Her father was the first professor of archaeology at the University of Leiden.

At a young age, de Vries began collecting varieties of plants to add to his herbarium. After the family moved to The Hague in 1862, de Vries went to Leiden on weekends for religion classes. There he met Willem Suringar, a professor of botany, who asked de Vries to classify plants for the Netherlands Botanical Society. By the time he entered the University of Leiden in 1866, de Vries was already quite an expert on the flora of the Netherlands.

Hugo de Vries

Conducts Independent Research in Plant Physiology

During his university days, two new disciplines in the forefront of science held great interest for de Vries: plant physiology and evolution, the latter stemming from his reading of Charles Darwin's *Origin of Species.* Because of these interests, de Vries grew increasingly dissatisfied with his education at the university. Plant physiology was not taught at Leiden and his work on his dissertation was conducted in his own attic laboratory. His former mentor from Leiden, Suringar, was not open to the idea of evolution, and this caused a permanent rift between the two.

In 1870 De Vries left the Netherlands for Heidelberg and then Wurzburg in Germany, where he studied plant physiology under Julius von Sachs, a noted botanist and author. His work was primarily on the growth patterns in plants, including zones of growth in climbing plants, geotropism (the movement of plant roots toward the earth) and heliotropism (stem growth toward the sun). When de Vries returned to Amsterdam the next year to teach natural history, he continued to spend summers at Sachs's laboratory in Wurzburg. Upon a recommendation from Sachs, de Vries began work for the Prussian Ministry of Agriculture in 1875, writing monographs on important crops such as potatoes and sugar beets. During this time, he also became interested in osmosis in plant cells, which concerns the flow of fluid through the cell wall in order to balance the pressure inside and outside of the cell. By investigating this, he sought to find out how much of the growth of a cell was due to stretching of its cell wall. This involved calculating the amount of pressure caused by the fluid within the cell, or turgor pressure.

De Vries did further work on the stretching of cells in 1877 after which he received an appointment at the University of Hall. His teaching there was short-lived and after returning to Amsterdam in 1877, de Vries became the first instructor in plant physiology in the Netherlands. That summer he and another great mind of science, Charles Darwin, met when de Vries visited England.

For the next decade, de Vries taught while conducting experiments on plant plasmolysis, or the shrinking of the cytoplasm—the substance between the cell wall and the nuclear membrane—away from the cell wall due to the outward flow of water by osmosis. He did this by analyzing the pressure due to osmosis caused by different cell components and their concentrations. He came up with coefficients to determine the proportional contribution to the total pressure for each component in the fluid of a cell's protoplasm (the organic and inorganic substances within a cell and its nucleus), and also conjectured about the compounds that contribute to cell turgor and theorized about the function of minerals.

Reaches Breakthrough in Genetic Study with Mutation Theory

In the latter part of the 1880s de Vries abandoned his work on plant physiology and began devoting his study to heredity, a work that he would carry on until his death. He studied the experiments and writings of Darwin and others and came up with his own theory that "pangenes" were the structures that carried inherited traits. Later, Johannsen would derive the term "gene" from de Vries' term "pangene."

De Vries studied the distribution of variations of traits in about twenty species, showing how traits segregate, or become inherited by separate independent units that can be studied. His theoretical model of a pangene was made of molecules which divided when the cells divided into daughter cells, separating before blending in the next generation. After checking the literature for any earlier research along these lines, in 1900 de Vries happened upon a reprint of Gregor Mendel's paper in which Mendel had proposed these same ideas after conducting his experiments with pea plants. Although in 1866 Mendel's ideas had made little impact, now at the turn of the twentieth century, de Vries gave credit to Mendel's work. Because de Vries did make note of Mendel's work, two other scientists also working on heredity, Karl Erich Correns and Eric Tschermak von Seysenegg, were obligated to follow suit. Thus at the turn of the century, Mendel's work was "rediscovered" by all three men.

De Vries's ideas, however, went beyond Mendel's theory of the segregation of traits. He proposed that most characters are inherited unchanged from one generation to the next, but that sometimes pangenes start to multiply in extraordinary ways and change somehow during cell division. This change creates a new characteristic, known as a mutant. Such new varieties provide changes that can be acted upon by natural selection and thus hasten the evolution of a species.

While crossing flowers with a genus of plants, *Oenotheras,* the evening primrose, de Vries' work would prove most fascinating. De Vries came up with many mutants which he considered to be new species. Some other scientists of the time disputed de Vries' idea, hypothesizing that these plants were merely varieties of the same species. But de Vries had the notion that mutations were changes in the pangenes that provided the mechanisms by which variations were introduced into a population and thus caused evolution. Along the way he also made the discovery that some mutants are lethal. His major work on mutations, *Die Mutationstheorie,* gained him fame in Europe and in the United States. De Vries was invited to lecture at the University of California at Berkeley in 1904 and 1906. Several years later in 1912, de Vries again came to the United States and lectured at the Rice Institute in Houston, Texas.

Despite the imperfections, de Vries' theory of mutations provided much of the groundbreaking work in genetics, having great impact on geneticists working on both continents. At Columbia University, **Thomas Hunt Morgan** and his students **A. H. Sturtevant**, **Hermann Joseph Muller** and Calvin Bridges were experimenting on *Drosophila* (fruit flies) and attempting to describe mutations of that species. They never discovered the great number of mutants that de Vries had with the evening primrose, but found enough mutants to provide data for the first map of chromosomes.

Later studies conducted by followers of de Vries showed that inheritance in the evening primrose was indeed very complicated. Some of the varieties were not different species, but rather plants in which the chromosomes were tetraploid, that is, they had double the normal number of chromosomes. Although mutations were not as abundant as de Vries predicted, his work still was seminal to the discovery that the cell's genetic makeup was found on the genes located in the chromosomes and to the theory of evolution, which depends on research into mutant species.

For his work, De Vries was bestowed with eleven honorary doctorates and awarded seven gold medals and memberships into major academic societies. After retiring to a country house in Lunteren, Holland, de Vries continued experimenting, using plants from his own garden. Many of his friends and pupils visited his remote laboratory, breaking up his rather solitary life of experimenting which continued to yield scientific papers. He died there on May 21, 1935.

SELECTED WRITINGS BY DE VRIES:

Books

De invloed der temperatuur op de levensverschijnselen der planten, The Hague, 1870.
Original works are collected in *Opera e periodicis collata,* seven volumes, Utrecht, 1918–1927.

Periodicals

"Sur la perméabilité du protoplasme des betteraves rouges," *Archives néerlandaises des sciences exactes et naturelles,* Volume 6, 1871, pp. 117–126.
"Sur la mort des cellules végétales par l'effet d'une température éleveé," *Archives néerlandaises des sciences exactes et naturelles,* Volume 6, 1871, pp. 245–295.
Die Mutationstheorie, Versuche und Beobachtungen über die Entstehung von Arten im Pflanzenreich, two volumes, [Leipzig], 1901–1903, edited version translated as *The Mutation Theory, Experiments and Observations on the Origin of Species in the Vegetable Kingdom,* two volumes, [Chicago], 1909–1910.

SOURCES:

Books

Gillispie, Charles Coulston, editor, *Dictionary of Scientific Biography,* Volume 14, Scribner, 1976, pp. 95–104.

Periodicals

Allen, G. E. "Hugo de Vries and the Reception of the Mutation Theory," *Journal of the History of Biology,* number 2, 1969, pp. 55–87.

—Sketch by Barbara A. Branca

Salome Waelsch
1907-
German American geneticist

Salome Waelsch was born and educated in Germany, but came to the United States in 1933 after the rise of Nazi dictator Adolf Hitler. She trained as a geneticist under 1935 Nobel Prize winner **Hans Spemann** in Germany and Leslie Dunn at Columbia University. For more than half a century Waelsch has studied the role of genes in the early stages of development and cellular differentiation, research that has important implications for the treatment of congenital diseases. In addition, she taught the first course on medical genetics in the United States.

Salome Gluecksohn Waelsch was born in Danzig, Germany, on October 6, 1907, to Ilyia and Nadia Gluecksohn. Waelsch's early life was made difficult by a number of factors. First, her father died during the flu epidemic of 1918, when she was only eleven years old. Next, her mother lost all the family's money in the inflation following World War I. Finally, as a young girl Waelsch had to deal with both anti-female and anti-Jewish taunts of her schoolmates and neighbors.

Waelsch persevered in her goal of obtaining a college education. She attended the universities of Königsberg, Berlin, and Freiburg, intending at first to major in classical languages. Her interest in biology arose as the result of a friend's offhand suggestion that she take a course in that subject. "That was the beginning," she later told Jamie Talan, an interviewer for *Newsday*. "I found my love." Eventually Waelsch entered a doctoral program in genetics at Freiburg. Her advisor there was the eminent geneticist Hans Spemann; Waelsch completed the work required of her and was awarded her Ph.D. from Freiburg in 1932.

Waelsch's job prospects did not seem particularly bright at the time. In an interview with Harriet Zuckerman and Jonathan R. Cole for *The Outer Circle: Women in the Scientific Community,* she reported that in 1932 one prospective employer said to her: "You—a woman and a Jew—forget it." Despite such prejudice, she obtained an appointment as a research assistant in cell biology at the University of Berlin after leaving Freiburg. Perhaps the most important event that occurred during her one year at Berlin was her marriage to Rudolf Schoenheimer, a young biochemist at the university.

Immigrates to the United States

Given the rabid anti-Semitic policies and pronouncements of Hitler's government, it rapidly became clear to Salome and Rudolf that they had no future in Germany. Thus they moved to the United States, where Schoenheimer was offered a position at Columbia University's College of Physicians and Surgeons. His equally qualified wife received no similar offer, however, although she was allowed three years later to work in the laboratories of the famous geneticist Leslie Dunn, without pay. Waelsch became a naturalized citizen of the United States in 1938.

Initiates Studies on Differentiation

It was in Dunn's laboratories that Waelsch began the studies that were to occupy her for the next fifty years. The studies were designed to find out how specific genes in an organism affect the development and differentiation of various body parts within the embryo. Waelsch's studies have been particularly helpful in understanding how errors occur during embryonic development and may ultimately lead to the discovery of methods for curing genetic disorders that begin before birth.

Rudolf Schoenheimer died in 1941, and a little more than a year later, on January 8, 1943, Salome was married a second time, again to a biochemist, Heinrich B. Waelsch. The couple had two children, Naomi Barbara and Peter Benedict. Waelsch was widowed a second time in 1966. In 1953, after seventeen years in Dunn's laboratories, Waelsch was appointed a research associate in the department of obstetrics at the College of Physicians and Surgeons.

Two years later, Waelsch's major professional break came with the founding of the Albert Einstein College of Medicine in New York City. She was offered the post of associate professor of anatomy, a position she held until 1958, when she was promoted to full professor. During this period Waelsch offered what are believed to be the first courses in medical genetics taught at any U.S. university. In 1963 her title was changed to professor of genetics and she was made chair of the department of genetics at Einstein. Although she retired officially in 1978 and was named professor emerita, she has continued her research.

During her career Waelsch has authored or co-authored more than one hundred papers on developmental genetics. She was elected to the National Academy of Sciences in 1979 and awarded the National Medal of Science by President Bill Clinton in 1993. In 1982 she was awarded a gold doctoral diploma by her alma mater, the University of Freiburg, in recognition of her life's work. She declined the award, however, because of her terrible memories of the Holocaust and her forced departure from her homeland.

SOURCES:

Books

Zuckerman, Harriet, Jonathan R. Cole, and John T. Bruer, editors, *The Outer Circle: Women in the Scientific Community,* Norton, 1991, pp. 71–93.

Periodicals

Talan, Jamie, "The Mouse Lady: 60 Years of Genes," *Newsday,* September 30, 1993.

—*Sketch by David E. Newton*

Julius Wagner-Jauregg
1857-1940
Austrian physician

Julius Wagner-Jauregg was an Austrian psychiatrist whose experimental work in the first part of the twentieth century led to a new appreciation of the beneficial effects of bodily stress in the treatment of mental illness. In 1927 he became the first psychiatrist to win the Nobel Prize for his discovery that syphilis, a chronic, usually venereal disease caused by spirochete bacteria, could be cured by clinically induced malaria, which is characterized by symptoms of fever and chills.

Wagner-Jauregg was born Julius Wagner on March 7, 1857, in the village of Wels, Austria. He was the oldest son of Ludovika Ranzoni and Adolf Johann Wagner, a government official. The family name became "Wagner von Jauregg" when Adolf Johann was raised to the nobility, but following the collapse of the Austro-Hungarian empire in 1918, the "von" was dropped. After the early death of his mother, Julius Wagner-Jauregg was raised at home. In his youth he successfully fought off typhoid and tuberculosis to graduate from Vienna's prestigious Schotten-gymnasium.

While attending medical school at the University of Vienna, Wagner-Jauregg received thorough training in experimental biology and met the father of psychoanalysis, Sigmund Freud, who was studying at the Institute of General and Experimental Pathology. Despite Wagner-Jauregg's lack of interest in psychoanalysis, the two remained lifelong friends. In 1880 Wagner-Jauregg was awarded a medical degree for his thesis on the heart under conditions of acceleration.

Originally, Wagner-Jauregg hoped to practice general medicine, but when Vienna's two teaching hospitals turned him down, he reluctantly accepted a position as an assistant in the university's psychiatric clinic. Although he had little training in mental illness, he quickly became a qualified instructor in psychiatry and neurology. Wagner-Jauregg was a clinician, skilled in detailed observation and careful case analysis. Using the latest techniques of animal experimentation, he spent his life working to advance the biological understanding of mental illness. His first research entailed the investigation of how certain chemicals stimulate breathing after strangulation.

In 1889 Wagner-Jauregg was appointed professor of psychiatry at the University of Graz and for the next four years studied the effect of the thyroid gland on behavior. An ardent vivisectionist, he discovered that when the thyroid was removed from a cat, the animal's behavior became convulsive and violent. Cretinism in humans, Wagner-Jauregg put forth in an early paper, was due to a malfunction of the thyroid. During his years in Graz, he travelled frequently in central and southeastern Austria studying peasants with goiter and found that small amounts of iodine reduced their hugely swollen necks. He urged the sale of iodized salt in alpine regions, a measure the Austrian government undertook belatedly in 1923.

In 1893 Wagner-Jauregg was made a full professor at the University of Vienna and appointed director of the Hospital for Nervous and Mental Diseases and the State Mental Asylum. As a member of the Austrian Board of Health, he helped draft important legislation protecting the rights of the mentally ill and regulating the certification of the insane. At his urging, psychiatry became a compulsory subject in the undergraduate curriculum.

Discovers That Fever Can Cure the Mentally Ill

While still only a medical assistant, Wagner-Jauregg had studied the beneficial effect of high fever on psychotic patients. For a monograph that he published in 1888, he surveyed instances where epidemics of typhoid, malaria, small pox, and scarlet fever had swept through mental asylums. In 30 cases reaching back to antiquity, he described how bouts of high fever had brought dramatic relief in cases of melancholy, mania, and paresis. At the end of his monograph, Wagner-Jauregg suggested that malaria might be used experimentally to induce a "fever cure" in psychotic patients, although at the time he lacked the authority to undertake so radical a treatment.

The monograph received little notice when it was published. In it, Wagner-Jauregg had formulated two bold hypotheses: first, that some psychoses were organic in nature, and second, that one disease might be employed to eradicate another disease. In Graz, he had produced fever with injections of tuberculin, a protein used to treat tuberculosis, until it was learned that tuberculin was unsafe. In Vienna, he injected paralytic patents with typhus vaccine and staphylococci but was disappointed by the results. Most of the cures proved to be temporary, and patients soon relapsed.

It was not until World War I that conditions were ripe for a radical trial. By then a series of important discoveries had confirmed the link between paresis and syphilis. In 1905 researchers had identified the syphilis bacillus, *Spirochaete pallida*. A year later, the Wasserman test for syphilis revealed that paresis was a progressive disease of the brain caused by untreated syphilis. In Wagner-Jauregg's time, paresis accounted for fifteen percent of the patients confined to mental hospitals. The disease was thought to be incurable and invariably ended in insanity, paralysis, and death within three to four years.

In the final years of World War I, Wagner-Jauregg was treating victims of shell shock when he encountered a soldier suffering from malaria. On June 14, 1917, Wagner-Jauregg used blood drawn from the malarial soldier to infect nine patients suffering from paresis. Quinine, the medicine used to treat malaria, was withheld until each patient had endured seven to eleven attacks of fever. The results were astonishing. Six patients experienced a dramatic remission of symptoms, and three were able to return to normal life. In 1919 Wagner-Jauregg began full-scale clinical trials.

At first, Wagner-Jauregg's reports were greeted with considerable skepticism by the medical community. Some physicians considered it unethical to deliberately induce a disease as serious as malaria. Others feared the outbreak of malaria epidemics in major metropolitan centers. But trials elsewhere produced similar results. Employing only a mild strain of malaria easily cured by quinine, mortality remained low while complete recovery was experienced by thirty to forty percent of all patients. Patients who had only recently contracted syphilis could be cured completely when the "malaria cure" was used in conjunction with injections of Salvarsan and Neosalvarsan, two drugs used to treat early syphilis. In 1927

Wagner-Jauregg became the first psychiatrist to be awarded the Nobel Prize in physiology or medicine.

Safer methods of inducing fever were tried—preparations of colloidal sulfur, hot-water baths, and "fever cabinets"—but none had the high rates of success typical of malaria. Until the discovery of penicillin during World War II, malaria remained the preferred treatment for advanced syphilis. Medical opinion differed on just how the fever cure worked since it seemed unlikely that the fever killed all of the spirochete bacteria, which cause syphilis. Instead, it was believed that the stress produced by the malaria attack in some way strengthened the body's defenses against the syphilitic infection. Stress treatments such as electroshock continue to play a role in the treatment of psychiatric disorders.

In 1928, one year after receiving the Nobel Prize, Wagner-Jauregg retired at the age of seventy-one. In his youth he had been an avid mountaineer, and he was an accomplished chess player. During his long career he published some eighty papers and received several distinguished honors. In 1935 the University of Edinburgh awarded Wagner-Jauregg the Cameron Prize, and in 1937 he received the Gold Medal of the American Committee for Research on Syphilis. Julius Wagner-Jauregg died on September 27, 1940, in Vienna at age eighty-four, shortly before the discovery of penicillin made his fever cure obsolete. He was survived by his wife, Anna Koch, a daughter, Julia, and a son, Theodor, who became a distinguished professor of chemistry at the University of Vienna.

SELECTED WRITINGS BY WAGNER-JAUREGG:

Books

Fieber und Infektionstherapie. Ausgewählten Beitrage 1887–1935, Verglag für Medizin, Weidmann, 1936.

Lebenserinnerungen, edited by L. Schönbauer and M. Jantsch, Springer, 1950.

Periodicals

"Über die Einwirkung Fieberhafter Erkrankungen auf Psychosen," *Jahrbuch für Psychiatrie und Neurologie,* Volume 7, 1887, pp. 94–131.

"Über den Einwirkung der Malaria auf die progressive Paralyse," *Psychiatrisch-neurologische Wochenschrift,* Volume 20, 1918–1919, pp. 132–134.

SOURCES:

Books

De Kruif, Paul, *Men Against Death,* Harcourt, 1932, pp. 249–279.

Fox, Daniel M. et al, editors, *Nobel Laureates in Medicine or Psychology: A Biographical Dictionary,* Garland Publishing, 1990, pp. 545–548.

Magill, Frank N., editor, *The Nobel Prize Winners: Physiology or Medicine,* Volume 1, 1901–1944, Salem Press, 1991, pp. 277–284.

Valenstin, E. S., *Great and Desperate Cures: The Rise and Decline of Psychosurgery and Other Radical Treatments for Mental Illness,* Baru Book, 1986, pp. 29–31.

Periodicals

Breutsch, W. L., "Julius Wagner von Jauregg— Eminent Psychiatrist and Originator of the Malaria Treatment of Dementia Paralytica (1857–1940)," *Archives of Neurology and Psychiatry,* Volume 44, 1940, pp. 1319–1322.

Riebl, L., and P. Sharp, "Julius Wagner von Jauregg: A Reappraisal," *Australian and New Zealand Journal of Psychiatry,* June 1, 1992, pp. 302–306.

—Sketch by Philip Metcalfe

Selman Waksman

Selman Waksman
1888-1973
Russian-born American microbiologist

Selman Waksman revolutionized medicine, thanks to his discoveries of life-saving antibacterial compounds. His investigations have also spawned further studies for other disease-curing drugs. Waksman isolated streptomycin, the first chemical agent that was effective against tuberculosis. Prior to his discovery, tuberculosis was a lifelong debiliting disease, and was fatal in some forms. Streptomycin effected a cure, and for this discovery, Waksman received the 1952 Nobel Prize in physiology or medicine. In pioneering the field of antibiotic research, Waksman had an inestimable impact on human health and well-being, creating both a new field of medicine and a new industry.

The only son of a Jewish furniture textile weaver, Selman Abraham Waksman was born in the tiny Russian village of Novaya Priluka on July 22, 1888. Life was hard in late-nineteenth-century Russia. Waksman's only sister died from diphtheria when he was nine. There were particular tribulations for members of a persecuted ethnic minority. As a teen during the Russian revolution, Waksman helped organize an armed Jewish youth defense group to counteract oppression. He also set up a school for underprivileged children and formed a group to care for the sick. These activities prefaced his later role as a standard-bearer for social responsibility.

Several factors led to Waksman's immigration to the United States. He had received his diploma from the *Gymnasium* in Odessa and was poised to attend university, but he doubtless recognized the very limited options he held as a Jew in Russia. At the same time, in 1910, his mother died, and cousins who had immigrated to New Jersey urged him to follow their lead. Waksman did so, and his move to a farm there, where he learned the basics of scientific farming from his cousin, likely had a pivotal influence on Waksman's later choice of field of study.

Begins Research on Soil Microbes

In 1911 Waksman enrolled in nearby Rutgers College (later University) of Agriculture, following the advice of fellow Russian immigrant Jacob Lipman, who led the college's bacteriology department. He worked with Lipman, developing a fascination with the bacteria of soil, and graduated with a B.Sc. in 1915. The next year he earned his M.S. degree. Around this time he also became a naturalized United States citizen and changed the spelling of his first name from Zolman to Selman. Waksman married Bertha Deborah Mitnik, a childhood sweetheart and the sister of one of his childhood friends, in 1916. Deborah Mitnik had come to the United States in

1913, and in 1919 she bore their only child, Byron Halsted Waksman, who eventually went on to a distinguished career at Yale University as a pathology professor.

Waksman's intellect and industry enabled him to earn his Ph.D. in less than two years at the University of California, Berkeley. His 1918 dissertation focused on proteolytic enzymes (special proteins that break down proteins) in fungi. Throughout his schooling, Waksman supported himself through various scholarships and jobs. Among the latter were ranch work, caretaker and night watchman, and tutor of English and science.

Waksman's former advisor invited him to join Rutgers as a lecturer in soil bacteriology in 1918. He was to stay at Rutgers for his entire professional career. When Waksman took up the post, however, he found his pay too low to support his family. Thus, in his early years at Rutgers he also worked at the nearby Takamine Laboratory, where he produced enzymes and ran toxicity tests.

In the 1920s Waksman began to gain recognition in scientific circles. Others sought out his keen mind, and his prolific output earned him a well-deserved reputation. He wrote two major books during this decade. *Enzymes: Properties, Distribution, Methods, and Applications,* coauthored with Wilburt C. Davison, was published in 1926, and in 1927 his thousand-page *Principles of Soil Microbiology* appeared. This latter volume became a classic among soil bacteriologists. His laboratory produced more than just books. One of Waksman's students during this period was **René Dubos**, who would later discover the antibiotic gramicidin, the first chemotherapeutic agent effective against gram-positive bacteria (bacteria that hold dye in a stain test named for Danish bacteriologist Hans Gram). Waksman became an associate professor at Rutgers in the mid–1920s and advanced to the rank of full professor in 1930.

During the 1930s Waksman systematically investigated the complex web of microbial life in soil, humus, and peat. He was recognized as a leader in the field of soil microbiology, and his work stimulated an ever-growing group of graduate students and postdoctoral assistants. He continued to publish widely, and he also established many professional relationships with industrial firms that utilized products of microbes. These companies that produced enzymes, pharmaceuticals, vitamins, and other products were later to prove valuable in Waksman's researches, mass producing and distributing the products he developed. Among his other accomplishments during this period was the founding of the division of Marine Bacteriology at Woods Hole Oceanographic Institution in 1931. For the next decade he spent summers there and eventually became a trustee, a post he filled until his death.

Research Finds Practical Applications in Wartime

In 1939 Waksman was appointed chair of the U.S. War Committee on Bacteriology. He derived practical applications from his earlier studies on soil microorganisms, developing antifungal agents to protect soldiers and their equipment. He also worked with the Navy on the problem of bacteria that attacked ship hulls. Early that same year Dubos announced his finding of two antibacterial substances, tyrocidine and gramicidin, derived from a soil bacterium (*Bacillus brevis*). The latter compound, effective against gram-positive bacteria, proved too toxic for human use but did find widespread employment against various bacterial infections in veterinary medicine. The discovery of gramicidin also evidently inspired Waksman to dedicate himself to focus on the medicinal uses of antibacterial soil microbes. It was in this period that he began rigorously investigating the antibiotic properties of a wide range of soil fungi.

Waksman set up a team of about fifty graduate students and assistants to undertake a systematic study of thousands of different soil fungi and other microorganisms. The rediscovery at this time of the power of penicillin against gram-positive bacteria likely provided further incentive to Waksman to find an antibiotic effective against gram-negative bacteria, which include the kind that causes tuberculosis.

In 1940 Waksman became head of Rutgers' department of microbiology. In that year too, with the help of Boyd Woodruff, he isolated the antibiotic actinomycin. Named for the actinomycetes (rod- or filament-shaped bacteria) from which it was isolated, this compound also proved too toxic for human use, but its discovery led to the subsequent finding of variant forms (actinomycin A, B, C, and D), several of which were found to have potent anti-cancer effects. Over the next decade Waksman isolated ten distinct antibiotics. It is Waksman who first applied the term antibiotic, which literally means against life, to such drugs.

Breakthrough with Isolation of Streptomycin

Among these discoveries, Waksman's finding of streptomycin had the largest and most immediate impact. Not only did streptomycin appear nontoxic to humans, but it was highly effective against gram-negative bacteria. (Prior to this time the antibiotics available for human use had been active only against the gram-positive strains.) The importance of streptomycin was soon realized. Clinical trials showed it to be effective against a wide range of diseases, most notably tuberculosis.

At the time of streptomycin's discovery, tuberculosis was the most resistant and irreversible of all the major infectious diseases. It could only be treated with a regime of rest and nutritious diet. The tuberculosis bacillus consigned its victims to a lifetime of invalidism and, when it invaded organs other than the lungs, often killed. Sanatoriums around the country were filled with persons suffering the ravages of tuberculosis, and little could be done for them.

Streptomycin changed all of that. From the time of its first clinical trials in 1944, it proved to be remarkably effective against tuberculosis, literally snatching sufferers back from the jaws of death. By 1950 streptomycin was used against seventy different germs that were not treatable with penicillin. Among the diseases treated by streptomycin were bacterial meningitis (an inflammation of membranes enveloping the brain and spinal cord), endocarditis (an inflammation of the lining of the heart and its valves), pulmonary and urinary tract infections, leprosy, typhoid fever, bacillary dysentery, cholera, and bubonic plague.

Waksman arranged to have streptomycin produced by a number of pharmaceutical companies, since demand for it soon skyrocketed beyond the capacity of any single company. Manufacture of the drug became a $50-million-per-year industry. Thanks to Waksman and streptomycin, Rutgers received millions of dollars of income from the royalties. Waksman donated much of his own share to the establishment of an Institute of Microbiology there. He summarized his early researches on the drug in *Streptomycin: Nature and Practical Applications* (1949). Streptomycin ultimately proved to have some human toxicity and was supplanted by other antibiotics, but its discovery changed the course of modern medicine. Not only did it directly save countless lives, but its development stimulated scientists around the globe to search the microbial world for other antibiotics and medicines.

Research Yields Other Antibiotics

In 1949 Waksman isolated neomycin, which proved effective against bacteria that had become resistant to streptomycin. Neomycin also found a broad niche as a topical antibiotic. Other antibiotics soon came forth from his Institute of Microbiology. These included streptocin, framicidin, erlichin, candidin, and others. Waksman himself discovered eighteen antibiotics during the course of his career.

Waksman served as director of the Institute for Microbiology until his retirement in 1958. Even after that time, he continued to supervise research there. He also lectured widely and continued to write at the frenetic pace established early in his career. He eventually published more than twenty-five books, among them the autobiography *My Life with the Microbes,* and hundreds of articles. He was author of popular pamphlets on the use of thermophilic (heat-loving) microorganisms in composting and on the enzymes involved in jelly-making. He wrote biographies of several noted microbiologists, including his own mentor, Jacob Lipman. These works are in addition to his numerous publications in the research literature.

On August 16, 1973, Waksman died suddenly in Hyannis, Massachusetts, of a cerebral hemorrhage. He was buried near the institute to which he had contributed so much over the years. Waksman's honors over his professional career were many and varied. A complete listing of his awards would fill many pages. Besides receiving the Nobel Prize in 1952, he was recognized by the French Legion of Honor, won the Lasker award for basic medical science, was elected a fellow of the American Association for the Advancement of Science, and received commendations from academies and scholarly societies in Brazil, Britain, Denmark, Italy, Japan, the Netherlands, Spain, and other countries. It can safely be said that Selman Waksman changed the face of modern medicine around the world.

SELECTED WRITINGS BY WAKSMAN:

Books

(With Wilburt C. Davison) *Enzymes: Properties, Distribution, Methods, and Applications,* Williams & Wilkins, 1926.
Principles of Soil Microbiology, Williams & Wilkins, 1927, revised edition, 1932.
(Editor) *Streptomycin: Nature and Practical Applications,* Williams & Wilkins, 1949.
My Life with the Microbes, Simon & Schuster, 1954.

SOURCES:

Books

Magill, F. N., editor, *The Nobel Prize Winners: Physiology or Medicine, Volume 2, 1944–1969,* Salem Press, 1991, pp. 647–657.

Periodicals

Nature, December 7, 1973, p. 367.
New York Times, August 17, 1973, pp. 1, 34.
Sakula, Alex, "Selman Waksman (1888–1973), Discoverer of Streptomycin: A Centenary Review," *British Journal of Diseases of the Chest,* Volume 82, number 1, 1988, pp. 23–31.

—*Sketch by Ethan E. Allen*

George Wald
1906-
American biochemist

George Wald first won a place in the spotlight as the recipient of a Nobel Prize for his discovery of the way in which hidden biochemical processes in the retinal pigments of the eye turn light energy into sight. Among Wald's important experiments were the effects of vitamin A on sight and the roles played by rod and cone cells in black and white and color vision. Outside the laboratory, his splendid lectures at Harvard to packed audiences of students generated great intellectual excitement. It was as a political activist during the turbulent 1960s, however, that Wald garnered further public recognition. Wald's personal belief in the unity of nature and the kinship among all living things is evidenced by the substantial roles he played in the scientific world as well as the political and cultural arena of the 1960s.

Wald's father, Isaac Wald, a tailor and later a foreman in a clothing factory, immigrated from Austrian Poland, while his mother, Ernestine Rosenmann Wald, immigrated from Bavaria. Most of Wald's youth was spent in Brooklyn, New York, where his parents moved after his birth on the Lower East Side of Manhattan on November 18, 1906. He attended high school at Brooklyn Tech, where he intended to study to become an electrical engineer. College changed his mind, however, as he explained for the *New York Times Magazine* in 1969, "I learned I could talk, and I thought I'd become a lawyer. But the law was man-made; I soon discovered I wanted something more real."

Wald's bachelor of science degree in zoology, which he received from New York University in 1927, was his ticket into the reality of biological research. He began his research career at Columbia University, where he was awarded a master's degree in 1928, working under Selig Hecht, one of the founders of the field of biophysics and an authority on the physiology of vision. Hecht exerted an enormous influence on Wald, both as an educator and a humanist. The elder scientist's belief in the social obligation of science, coupled with the conviction that science should be explained so the general public could understand it, made a great impression on the young Wald. Following Hecht's sudden death in 1947 at the age of 55, Wald wrote a memorial as a tribute to his colleague.

In 1932 Wald earned his doctorate at Columbia, after which he was awarded a National Research Council Fellowship in Biology. The two-year fellowship helped to support his research career, which first took him to the laboratory of **Otto Warburg** in Berlin. It was there, in 1932, that he discovered vitamin A is one of the major constituents of retinal pigments, the light sensitive chemicals that set off the cascade of biological events that turns light into sight.

Warburg sent the young Wald to Switzerland, where he studied vitamins with chemist **Paul Karrer** at the University of Zurich. From there Wald went to **Otto Meyerhof**'s laboratory of cell metabolism at the Kaiser Wilhelm Institute in Heidelberg, Germany, finishing his fellowship in the department of physiology at the University of Chicago in 1934. His fellowship completed, Wald went to Harvard University, first as a tutor in biochemistry and subsequently as an instructor, faculty instructor, and associate professor, finally becoming a full professor in 1948. In 1968 he became Higgins Professor of Biology, a post he retained until he became an emeritus professor in 1977.

Wald did most of his work in eye physiology at Harvard, where he discovered in the late 1930s that the light-sensitive chemical in the rods—those cells in the retina responsible for night vision—is a single pigment called rhodopsin (visual purple), a substance derived from opsin, a protein, and retinene, a chemically modified form of vitamin A. In the ensuing years, Wald discovered that the vitamin A in rhodopsin is "bent" relative to its natural state, and light causes it to "straighten out," dislodging it from opsin. This simple reaction initiates all the subsequent activity that eventually generates the sense of vision.

Wald's research moved from rods to cones, the retinal cells responsible for color vision, discovering with his co-worker Paul K. Brown, that the pigments sensitive to red and yellow-green are two different forms of vitamin A that co-exist in the same cone, while the blue-sensitive pigments are located in separate cones. They also showed that color blindness is caused by the absence of one of these pigments.

For much of his early professional life, Wald concentrated his energy on work, both research and teaching. His assistant, Brown, stayed with him for over 20 years and became a full-fledged collaborator. A former student, Ruth Hubbard, became his second wife in 1958, and they had two children, Elijah and Deborah. (His previous marriage to Frances Kingsley in 1931 ended in divorce; he has two sons by that marriage, Michael and David.) Wald, his wife, and Brown together became an extremely productive research team.

Research Efforts Receive Recognition with Nobel Prize

By the late 1950s Wald began to be showered with honors, and during his career he received numerous honorary degrees and awards. After Wald was awarded (with **Haldan K. Hartline** of the United States and **Ragnar Granit** of Sweden) the Nobel Prize in physiology or medicine in 1967 for his work with vision, John E. Dowling wrote in *Science* that Wald and his team formed "the nucleus of a laboratory that has been extraordinarily fruitful as the world's foremost center of visual-pigment biochemistry."

As Wald's reputation flourished, his fame as an inspiring professor grew as well. He lectured to packed classrooms, inspiring an intense curiosity in his students. The energetic professor was portrayed in a 1966 *Time* article that summarized the enthusiasm he brought to teaching his natural science course: "With crystal clarity and obvious joy at a neat explanation, Wald carries his students from protons in the fall to living organisms in the spring, [and] ends most lectures with some philosophical peroration on the wonder of it all." That same year, the *New York Post* said of his lectures, "His beginnings are slow, sometimes witty. . . . The talk gathers momentum and suddenly an idea *pings* into the atmosphere—fresh, crisp, thought-provoking."

Six days after he received the Nobel Prize, Wald wielded the status of his new prestige in support of a widely popular resolution before the city council of Cambridge, Massachusetts—placing a referendum on the Vietnam War on the city's ballot of November 7, 1967. Echoing the sentiments of his mentor Hecht, he asserted that scientists should be involved in public issues.

The Cambridge appearance introduced him to the sometimes stormy arena of public politics, a forum from which he has never retired. The escalating war in Vietnam aroused Wald to speak out against America's military policy. In 1965, during the escalation of that war, Wald's impromptu denunciation of the Vietnam war stunned an audience at New York University, where he was receiving an honorary degree. Shortly afterward, he threw his support and prestige behind the presidential campaign of Eugene McCarthy. His offer to speak publicly on behalf of McCarthy was ignored, however, and he became a disillusioned supporter, remaining on the fringe of political activism.

Political Activism Punctuated with "The Speech"

Then on March 4, 1969, he gave an address at the Massachusetts Institute of Technology (M.I.T.) that, "upended his life and pitched him abruptly into the political world," according to the *New York Times Magazine*. Wald gave "The Speech," as the talk came to be known in his family, before an audience of radical students at M.I.T. The students had helped to organize a scientists' day-long "strike" to protest the influence of the military on their work, a topic of much heated debate at the time.

Although much of the M.I.T. audience was already bored and restless by the time Wald began, even many of those students who were about to leave the room stopped to listen as the Nobel laureate began to deliver his oration, entitled, "A Generation in Search of a Future." "I think this whole generation of students is beset with a profound sense of uneasiness, and I don't think they have quite defined its source," Wald asserted as quoted in the *New York Times Magazine*. "I think I understand the reasons for their uneasiness even better than they do. What is more, I *share* their uneasiness."

Wald's discourse evoked applause from the audience as he offered his opinion that student unease arose from a variety of troublesome matters. He pointed to the Vietnam War, the military establishment, and finally, the threat of nuclear warfare. "We must get rid of those atomic weapons," he declared. "We cannot live with them." Speaking to the students as fellow scientists, he sympathized with the their unease at the influence of the military establishment on the work of scientists, intoning, "Our business is with life, not death. . . ."

The speech was reprinted and distributed around the country by the media. Through these reprints, Wald told readers that some of their elected leaders were "insane," and he referred to the American "war crimes" enacted in Vietnam. In the furor that followed, Wald was castigated by critics, many of whom were fellow academics, and celebrated by sympathizers. A letter writer from Piney Flats, Tennessee was quoted in the *New York Times Magazine* as saying, "So good to know there are still some intellects around who can talk downright horsesense." Wald summed up his role as scientist-political activist in that same article by saying, "I'm a scientist, and my concerns are eternal. But even eternal things are acted out in the present." He described his role as gadfly as putting certain controversial positions into words in order to make it "easier for others to inch toward it."

His role as a Vietnam war gadfly expanded into activism in other arenas of foreign affairs. He served for a time as president of international tribunals on El Salvador, the Philippines, Afghanistan, Zaire, and Guatemala. In 1984 he joined four other Nobel Prize laureates who went with the "peace ship" sent by the Norwegian government to Nicaragua during that country's turmoil.

In addition to his interests in science and politics, Wald's passion includes collecting Rembrandt etchings and primitive art, especially pre-Columbian pottery. This complex mixture of science, art, and political philosophy was reflected in his musings about religion and nature in the *New York Times Magazine:* "There's nothing supernatural in my mind. Nature is my religion, and it's enough for me. I stack it up against any man's. For its awesomeness, and for the sense of the sanctity of man that it provides."

In addition to the Nobel Prize, Wald has received numerous awards and honors, including the Albert Lasker Award of the American Public Health Association in 1953, the Proctor Award in 1955 from the Association for Research in Ophthalmology, the Rumford Premium of the American Academy of Arts and Sciences in 1959, the 1969 Max Berg Award, and the Joseph Priestley Award the following year. In addition, he was elected to the National Academy of Science in 1950 and the American Philosophical Society in 1958. He is also a member of the Optical Society of America, which awarded him the Ives Medal in 1966. In the mid–1960s Wald spent a year as a Guggenheim fellow at England's Cambridge University, where he was elected an Overseas fellow of Churchill College for 1963–64. Wald also holds honorary degrees from the University of Berne, Yale University, Wesleyan University, New York University, and McGill University.

SELECTED WRITINGS BY WALD:

Books

General Education in a Free Society, Harvard University Press, 1945.
Visual Pigments and Photoreceptors: Review and Outlook, Academic Press, 1974.

Periodicals

"The Molecular Basis of Visual Excitation," *American Scientist,* January, 1954.

SOURCES:

Periodicals

Dowling, John E., "News And Comment; Nobel Prize: Three Named for Medicine, Physiology Award," *Science,* October 27, 1967.
Dudar, Helen, profile in *New York Post,* May 1, 1966, p. 32.
"George Wald: The Man, the Speech," *New York Times Magazine,* August 17, 1969, pp. 28–29.
Time, May 6, 1966.

—*Sketch by Marc Kusinitz*

Otto Wallach
1847-1931
German chemist

Otto Wallach was a highly regarded professor of chemistry whose curiosity about essential oils led to research that benefited both organic chemistry and an important industry. For his meticulous procedures and initiative in the study of terpenes, a class of compounds he identified and named as essential oils, Wallach received the Nobel Prize in chemistry in 1910. Essential oils, called ethereal oils in Wallach's time, are fragrant extracts from plant materials that are used in perfumes, flavorings, and medicines. Terpenes are responsible for much of the pleasant odor associated with essential oils. Wallach's work provided a scientific foundation for the fragrance industry.

Otto Wallach was born on March 27, 1847, in Königsberg, in East Prussia (Königsberg is now called Kaliningrad and is part of the reorganized former Soviet Union). Wallach's mother was Otillia Thoma Wallach; his father, Gerhard Wallach, was an official in the Prussian government whose post necessitated moves from Königsberg to Stettin (now in Poland and called Szczecin) and then to Potsdam, near Berlin, Germany. Wallach graduated from the Potsdam *Gymnasium* (high school). In school he became fascinated with chemistry and the history of art, and pursued both interests throughout his life. Early in 1867 he entered the University of Göttingen and received his doctorate in chemistry in 1869. Wallach never married.

Doctoral Dissertation and Chance Lead to Important Discoveries

Wallach's doctoral dissertation was on isomers of toluene. Isomers (*iso* means same; *mer* means parts) are substances with identical composition, but different arrangements of the parts, giving the substances different physical and chemical properties. Toluene is one of the products of distillation of coal, and among its many uses is as a solvent in the preparation of fragrances. Wallach's doctoral studies were to provide the background for his most important research.

After graduation Wallach worked briefly in Berlin, then went to the University of Bonn to assist August Kekulé (1829–1896), a renowned German professor of chemistry whose most noted contribution was the discovery of the structural formula of benzene, another important coal product and a substance similar to toluene. Kekulé was interested in turning much of his laboratory work over to a young assistant. Wallach remained at the University of Bonn until

1889, except for a period of two years, from 1871 to 1873, when he tried research at Aktiengesellschaft für Anilinfabrikation (Agfa).

In 1879, as a professor at the University of Bonn, Wallach was assigned to teach pharmacy. He had little background in the chemistry of essential (ethereal) oils, used in medicines. In Kekulé's laboratory he found abandoned samples of essential oils that Kekulé thought were too complex even to attempt to analyze. A very patient researcher, Wallach distilled and redistilled each oil sample until he could identify a pure substance. By 1881 he had repeated his procedure with different oils and identified eight pure, very similar, fragrant substances that he named terpenes, from the Greek *terebinthos*—turpentine.

Work Rewarded with Nobel Prize

Wallach did not work alone. While some colleagues worked on synthesizing new and similar compounds, he devoted most of his effort to studying how the terpenes he separated from essential oils were related. By 1887 Wallach discovered that all the terpenes he identified in essential oils are derived from a multiple of a particular arrangement of five carbon atoms, now called isoprene units. Some examples of terpenes found naturally are bayberry, rose oil, peppermint, menthol, camphor, and turpentine.

In 1889 Wallach was appointed director of the Chemical Institute at the University of Göttingen, where he continued his work on terpenes. In 1910 he received the Nobel Prize in chemistry "for his initiative work in the field of alicyclic substances," the terpenes, discovered to have carbon atoms arranged in rings, or cycles. Kekulé was the first person to identify a compound (benzene) as shaped like a ring.

One of the most important outcomes of Wallach's work was the research it spawned, which, combined with his own work, forever changed the fragrance industry. Before Wallach, there was little scientific background for production of fragrances. Processes used were much like the ones brought to Europe by the Crusaders. Wallach described the change his work inspired in his Nobel address. "The fragrant components of plants were merely distilled and the distillate brought to market. In this process, the products obtained were not always handled rationally, in the absence of all knowledge of their chemical nature, and the doors were wide open for every kind of falsification. When this was carried out with only some skill, the consumer was helpless against it.

"This has now been changed thoroughly. Thanks to the possibility of distinctly characterizing single components of the ethereal oils, we now possess a significant analytical system to detect falsifications and to guard against them." Wallach's work, com-

bined with the work of others he inspired, was credited with putting science into the production of perfumes, flavorings, and medicines that use terpenes.

Many universities and scientific societies honored Wallach. In 1912 he received the Davy Medal, awarded to outstanding scientists in memory of the British chemist, Sir Humphrey Davy (1778–1829), who identified a number of chemical elements through his pioneering work with electrochemistry. Wallach retired from Göttingen in 1915, but continued with research until he was eighty years old. In his lifetime Wallach published 126 papers on his research of essential oils. He died in Göttingen, Germany, on February 26, 1931, a month short of his eighty-fourth birthday.

SELECTED WRITINGS BY WALLACH:

Books

Die Terpene und Campher ("Terpenes and Camphor"), Leipzig, 1909.
Eduard Farber, *Nobel Prize Winners in Chemistry* (contains translation of portions of his Nobel Prize address), Henry Schuman, 1953, pp. 43–44.

SOURCES:

Books

Dictionary of Scientific Biography, Scribner, 1980, Volume 14, pp. 141–142.

Periodicals

Partridge, William S., and Ernest R. Schierz, "Otto Wallach: The First Organizer of the Terpenes," *Journal of Chemical Education,* Volume 24, 1947, pp. 106–108.

—*Sketch by M. C. Nagel*

Ernest Walton
1903-
Irish experimental physicist

Ernest Walton is an Irish experimental physicist who gained renown for achieving, with physicist **John D. Cockcroft**, the first artificial disintegration of an atomic nucleus, without the use of radioactive

Ernest Walton

elements. Their breakthrough was accomplished by artificially accelerating a beam of protons (basic particles of the nuclei of atoms which carry a positive charge of electricity) and aiming it at a target of lithium, one of the lightest known metals. The resultant emission of alpha particles, that is, positively charged particles given off by certain radioactive substances, indicated not only that some protons had succeeded in penetrating the nuclei of the lithium atoms but also that they had somehow combined with the lithium atoms and had been transformed into something new. Although the process was not an efficient energy producer, the work of Walton and Cockcroft stimulated many theoretical and practical developments and influenced the whole course of nuclear physics. For their pioneering work, Walton and Cockcroft shared the 1951 Nobel Prize in physics.

Ernest Thomas Sinton Walton was born October 6, 1903, in Dungarven, County Waterford, in the Irish Republic. His father, John Arthur Walton, was a Methodist minister, while his mother, Anna Elizabeth (Sinton) Walton, was from a very old Ulster family, who had lived in the same house in Armagh for over two-hundred years. The young Walton was sent to school at Belfast's Methodist College, where he demonstrated an aptitude for science and math. It was no surprise, then, when in 1922 he decided to enroll in math and experimental science at Dublin's Trinity College. He graduated in 1926 with a B.A. degree, in 1928 with a M.Sc., and in 1934 with a M.A.

Joins the Cavendish During its Heyday

The following year he headed to Cambridge University, England, on a Clerk Maxwell research scholarship. There, he joined the world-famous Cavendish Laboratory, headed by the great New Zealand-born physicist, **Ernest Rutherford**. Walton was assigned cramped laboratory space in a basement room. While his quarters were less than luxurious, he was at least blessed by having roommates with whom he struck up an immediate friendship, physicists T. E. Allibone and John D. Cockcroft. Walton would go on to make scientific history, in collaboration with the latter, for a project that would pave the way for the development of the atom bomb. Walton had first to learn to crawl before he could take such giant steps. At the suggestion of Rutherford, he began attempting to increase the velocity of electrons (the negatively charged particles of the atom) by spinning them in the electric field produced by a changing circular magnetic field as a method of nuclear disintegration. Although the method was not successful, he was able to figure out the stability of the orbits of the revolving electrons, and the design and engineering problems of creating an accelerating machine with minimal tools and materials. This early work of Walton's later led to the development of the betatron, that is, a particle accelerator in which electrons are propelled by the inductive action of a rapidly varying magnetic field.

Next, Walton tried to build a high frequency linear accelerator. His goal was to produce a stream of alpha particles traveling at high speed which could be used to shed light on various aspects of the atomic nucleus. Rutherford had long been keen to get his hands on such as source of alpha particles but despaired of any short-term breakthrough. As it transpired, Rutherford's wish was granted sooner than he expected.

What was needed was a fundamentally different way of viewing the problem. Walton and his colleagues at the Cavendish were trying to accelerate electrons to a speed sufficient to enable them to penetrate an atomic nucleus. Such high velocities were necessary, they believed, in order to counteract the repulsive charge of the nuclei. The speeding electrons, they figured, would literally bully their way through. However, achieving such high speeds was easier said than done. It required the application of enormous amounts of electricity, about four million volts, which at that time was impossible to generate in a discharge tube (a tube that contains a gas or metal vapor which conducts an electric discharge in the form of light). A crucial breakthrough came in 1929, when the Russian physicist **George Gamow**, visited the Cavendish laboratory. With physicist **Niels Bohr** in Copenhagen, he had worked out a wave-mechanical theory of the penetration of particles, in which they believed particles tunneled through rather than over potential barriers. This meant that particles propelled by about 500,000 volts, as opposed to millions, could possibly permeate the barrier and enter the nucleus, if present in sufficiently large numbers. That is, one would need a beam of many thousands of millions of moving particles to produce atomic disintegrations that would be capable of being observed.

Rutherford gave Walton and Cockcroft the go-ahead to test the supposition. It was a measure of his confidence in them—the high voltage apparatus they constructed to enable them to accelerate atomic particles cost almost £1,000 (British pounds) to build. It was an enormous sum in those days, and represented almost the entire annual budget for the laboratory.

The machine, the first of its kind ever built, and today on view at the London Science Museum in South Kensington, was built out of an ordinary transformer, enhanced by two stacks of large condensers (or what would today be called capacitors), which could be turned on and off by means of an electronic switch. This arrangement generated up to half a million volts, which were directed at an electrical discharge tube. At the top of the tube protons were produced. The velocity of the protons was increased into a beam which could be used to hit any mark at the bottom of the tubes. Although it would be considered primitive by today's standards, their apparatus was, in fact, an ingenious construction, cobbled together from glass cylinders taken from old fashioned petrol pumps, flat metal sheets, plasticene, and vacuum pumps. The current generated by the discharge tube was almost one hundred-thousandth of an ampere, which meant that about 50 million million protons per second were being produced. The availability of such a large and tightly controlled source of particles—compared with that produced by, say, a radioactive source—greatly increased the odds of a nucleus being penetrated by the speeding atomic particles.

Halfway through 1931, while their experiment was still in its early stages, Walton and Cockcroft were forced to vacate their subterranean basement when it was taken over by physical chemists. They were obliged to deconstruct their installation and build it again. As it happened, it turned out to be a lucky break. Their new laboratory was an old lecture theater, whose high ceiling was much more suitable for their purposes. When Walton and Cockcroft went to reassemble their massive apparatus, they used the opportunity to introduce a few modifications. This time around, they incorporated a new voltage multiplying circuit, which Cockcroft had just developed, into their apparatus. It took them until the end of 1931 just to produce a steady stream of five or six hundred volts.

When the accelerator was finally completed, they restarted the laborious process of trying to penetrate

an atomic nucleus using a stream of speeded up protons. They positioned a thin lithium target obliquely across from the beam of protons, in order to observe the alpha particles on either side of it. In order to detect the alpha particles that they hoped would be produced, they set up a tiny screen made of zinc sulfide, which they observed with a low-power microscope; a technique borrowed from Rutherford.

Walton's Scintillating Discovery

The first few months of 1932 were spent in rendering the installation more reliable and measuring the range and speed of the accelerated protons. It was not until April 13, 1932, that they achieved a breakthrough. On that fateful date, Walton first realized that their experiment had been successful. On the tiny screen, he detected flashes, called scintillations. These indicated that not only had the steam of protons succeeded in boring through the atomic nuclei but also that, in the process, a transformation had occurred. The speeding protons had combined with the lithium target to produce a new substance, the alpha particles, which appeared on the screen as scintillations.

Walton and Cockcroft confirmed Walton's observations using a paper recorder with two pens, each operated by a key. Walton worked one key, Cockcroft the other. When either noticed a flash, he pressed his key. As both keys were consistently pressed at the same time, it was clear that the alphas were being emitted in pairs. The implication was that the lithium nucleus, with a mass of seven and a charge of three had, on contact with an accelerated proton, split into two alpha particles, each of mass four and charge two. In the transformation, a small amount of energy was lost, equivalent to about a quarter of a percent of the mass of lithium.

Walton and Cockcroft's achievement was groundbreaking and historic in many ways. It represented the first time that anyone had produced a change in an atomic nucleus by means totally under human control. They had also discovered a new energy source. Furthermore, they had confirmed Gamow's theory that particles could tunnel or burrow their way into a nucleus, despite the repulsion of the electrical charges. And finally, they furnished a valuable confirmation of physicist **Albert Einstein's** theory that energy and mass are interchangeable. The extra energy of the alpha particles, when allowance was made for the energy of the proton, exactly corresponded to the loss of mass.

Walton and Cockcroft's achievement was announced in a letter in *Nature* and later at a meeting of the Royal Society of London, on June 15, 1932. By that time, they had succeeded in splitting the nuclei of fifteen elements, including beryllium, the lightest, to uranium, the heaviest. All produced alpha particles, although the most spectacular results were obtained from fluorine, lithium, and boron. The news caused a sensation throughout the world. As a result of their discovery, Walton and Cockcroft were the star attractions at the Solvay Conference, an important gathering of international physicists, held in 1933, and at the International Physics Conference, held in London in 1934.

Walton and Cockcroft's particle accelerator spawned many more sophisticated models, including one built by their colleague physicist Marcus Oliphant at the Cavendish. It was capable of producing a more abundant supply of particles; not only protons, but also deuterons (nuclei of heavy hydrogen). With this, many groundbreaking nuclear transformations were carried out. Their invention also inspired the American nuclear physicist, **Ernest Orlando Lawrence**, to build a cyclotron, a cyclical accelerator, capable of reaching tremendous speeds. Although scientists in the close of the twentieth century may regard the equipment Walton and Cockcroft used as primitive, the basic idea behind the particle accelerator has stayed the same.

In 1932, Walton received his Ph.D. from Cambridge and two years later, returned to Dublin as a fellow of Trinity College, his reputation preceding him. He remained there for the rest of his career. The year 1934 was memorable not only for Walton's shifting bases but also because it was the year he married Freda Wilson, a former pupil of the Methodist College, Belfast. They had two sons and two daughters, Alan, Marian, Philip, and Jean.

The next few years passed rather uneventfully for Walton. While his erstwhile partner, John D. Cockcroft went from one high profile position to another, Walton preferred to remain slightly aloof from the mainstream of physics. He concentrated instead on establishing his department's reputation for excellence. His efforts were rewarded in 1946 when he was appointed Erasmus Smith Professor of Natural and Experimental Philosophy.

Shares 1951 Nobel Prize with Cockcroft

In 1951, almost twenty years after achieving the breakthrough that changed the face of nuclear physics, Walton and Cockcroft finally achieved the recognition that many believed was long overdue them. The Nobel Prize for physics was awarded to them jointly for their pioneering work on the transmutation of atomic nuclei by artificially accelerated atomic particles. The following year, Walton became chairman of the School of Cosmic Physics of the Dublin Institute for Advanced Studies. He was elected a senior fellow of Trinity College in 1960.

Outside of his scientific work, Ernest Walton has been active in committees concerned with the government, the church, research and standards, scientific academies, and the Royal City of Dublin Hospital. He has been described as "quiet, undemonstrative, and little given to talk," according to Robert L. Weber in *Pioneers or Science: Nobel Prize Winners in Physics.* Walton celebrated his ninetieth birthday in 1993.

SELECTED WRITINGS BY WALTON:

Other

The First Penetration of Nuclei by Accelerated Particles (sound recording), Educational Materials and Equipment Co., Spring Green Multimedia, 1974.

SOURCES:

Books

Andrade, E. N. da C, *Rutherford and the Nature of the Atom,* Doubleday Anchor, 1964.
Biographical Dictionary of Scientists, Volume 2, Facts-on-File, 1981, pp. 823.
Crowther, J. G., *The Cavendish Laboratory, 1874–1974,* Science History Publications, 1974.
Modern Men of Science, McGraw-Hill, 1966, pp. 509.
Oliphant, Mark, *Rutherford: Recollections of the Cambridge Days,* Elsevier Publishing Co., 1972.
Weber, Robert L., *Pioneers of Science: Nobel Prize Winners in Physics,* Bristol and London, The Institute of Physics, 1980, pp. 141.
Wilson, David, *Rutherford: Simple Genius,* MIT Press, 1983.

—Sketch by Avril McDonald

An Wang
1920-1990
Chinese-born American computer scientist

An Wang, a computer scientist and commercial computing executive, is best remembered for founding Wang Laboratories, a prominent manufacturer of office wordprocessing and dataprocessing computers in the 1970s and 1980s. His early work as a computer scientist focused on the development of

An Wang

magnetic core memories for computers in the late 1940s and early 1950s.

Wang, whose name means "Peaceful King" in Chinese, was born in Shanghai, China, on February 7, 1920. Because of its strategic location at the mouth of the Yangtze River, Shanghai was often a war zone during Wang's youth. Other areas of China were also at war: Japan captured the Chinese province of Manchuria in 1931. Wang's father, Yin Lu Wang, taught English in a private school and practiced traditional Chinese herbal medicine. Wang's mother was Zen Wan Chien. In elementary school, Wang excelled in math and science, but his grades in other subjects were so bad that he almost did not graduate. In high school some of his textbooks were written in English, which was to help him later when he moved to the United States.

Wang entered the prestigious Chiao-Tung University after high school and was elected class president. He studied electrical engineering, but spent more time competing at table tennis than studying. During this time, the Japanese began to conquer more and more of China. Wang managed to stay safe because the fighting was usually far away from him. He received his Bachelor of Science degree from Chiao-Tung University in 1940, remaining at the university as a teaching assistant from 1940 to 1941. As his part in the Chinese war effort against Japan, he designed and built radio transmitters at the Central Radio Works in China from 1941 to 1945.

In April of 1945, Wang left China for America with some fellow engineers on a two-year apprenticeship. They were to learn about Western technology so they could rebuild China after the war. Wang, however, did more to build Western technology than to rebuild China. After arriving in the United States, Wang decided to apply to Harvard, where some of his teachers at Chiao-Tung University had studied. Many American men were still at war (Japan would not surrender until August, 1945), and Harvard needed students, so they admitted Wang. He performed well in Harvard's electrical engineering courses because he already had years of experience designing radios for the Chinese government. He received his Master of Science in electrical engineering in 1946.

Wang intended to return to China after he got his degree, but he had no money for the transportation. Through a school friend, he obtained a job with the Chinese Government Supply Agency in Ottawa, Ontario, Canada, where he worked from 1946 to 1947. The job was clerical, and he found it very boring. He decided to return to Harvard for a Ph.D., and he was accepted into the Applied Physics Department. He completed his program quickly and wrote his doctoral dissertation on nonlinear mechanics. Late in 1948, he finished his doctorate in applied physics.

Developing Magnetic Core Computer Memories at Harvard

Wang got his start in applied computer electronics when he went to work as a research fellow for **Howard Aiken** at the Harvard Computation Laboratory in May of 1948. Aiken, a computer pioneer, had developed the Mark I, the first automatic binary computer, in 1944. Wang did his most important work at Harvard in computer memories. Computer memories are essential to the development of computers as we know them today. Without computer memories, stored programs cannot exist, nor can programming languages or computer applications. When Wang went to work in the Harvard Computation Lab, there were already several kinds of memories: magnetic drums, punched cards, vacuum tubes, electromechanical relays, mercury delay lines, and cathode ray tubes. Each kind of memory had its disadvantages. Magnetic drums and punched cards were too slow, vacuum tubes burned out too often, and electromechanical relays were too noisy. Mercury delay lines made it hard for users to retrieve specific bits of data in a larger data set, and cathode ray tubes required a constant source of power or the data were lost.

Howard Aiken wanted Wang to invent a memory that would let a computer read and record data magnetically without the mechanical movement involved in a relay or rotating drum. Wang was perplexed for a while, because he found that when magnetic data were read, the process of reading the data destroyed them. But Wang soon discovered that he could use the data to rewrite the information in magnetic cores immediately after he destroyed it in the process of reading. Wang's ideas were used extensively in computers until magnetic core memories were replaced in the late 1960s by silicon chips. In 1955 Wang patented his ideas about reading and rewriting the information in magnetic memory cores.

In 1948, Wang met Lorraine Chiu, who was also from Shanghai, though her parents had been born in Hawaii. She was in the United States studying English at Wellesley College. They married in 1949. In September, 1950, their first child, Frederick, was born. A second son, Courtney, and a daughter, Juliette, were to follow. In April of 1955, both Wang and his wife became naturalized American citizens.

Building Wang Laboratories

Harvard preferred to sponsor basic research and decreased its work in computers when they started to be developed commercially. Aware of this, Wang began thinking about starting his own company. On June 22, 1951, he founded Wang Laboratories in Cambridge, Massachusetts, to manufacture magnetic core memories. He had $600, and, as he said in his autobiography, "I had no orders, no contracts, and no office furniture." He subsisted for a while on contracts for manufacturing memories, on teaching, and on consulting. In November, 1953, Wang began a consulting contract with IBM for a thousand dollars a month that was to bring him some financial stability. In March of 1956 Wang sold his patent on magnetic core memories to IBM for $500,000.

In the early 1960s, Wang Laboratories developed a popular typesetting system that would justify and hyphenate text on a page. By 1964 the company had sales of more than $1,000,000 for the first time. Then Wang began to develop desktop calculators. One of these, the Model 300, was very successful because it was user friendly, small, and relatively cheap at $1,695. By 1967, Wang's sales were up to $6.9 million per year. To raise money and eliminate some of its debt, Wang Labs publicly offered its stock for sale in August of 1967. The stock was so popular that the value of the company soared. Before the sale of stock, on August 22, Wang Labs was worth about one million dollars. One day later, after its stock went on sale, it had a market capitalization of $70,000,000.

Wang began to realize that the future of the company was not in desktop calculators but in computers. He feared that desktop calculators would become lower-valued commodities because of increasing competition. In 1971 the first pocket calculator was manufactured by Bowmar Instruments, and in the following decades, the appliances became even smaller and less expensive. Wang Laboratories began producing its first word processors, the Wang 1200s, in 1972. The Wang 1200 was very primitive by today's standards. It stored data on a tape cassette and had no means of displaying text. Wang decided on some major improvements, and Wang Labs caused a sensation when it demonstrated its first CRT (cathode ray tube)-based word processor in June of 1976. In two years it was the largest distributor of such systems in the world. By 1982, Wang Laboratories had over a billion dollars in sales a year. By 1989, sales were $3 billion a year.

Wang received over a dozen honorary doctorates for his accomplishments, and, among other honors, was a fellow of the American Academy of Arts and Sciences. He underwent surgery to remove a cancerous tumor of the esophagus in 1989. He was readmitted to Massachusetts General Hospital in March of 1990 and died of cancer at the age of 70 on March 24, 1990.

SELECTED WRITINGS BY WANG:

Books

(With Eugene Linden), *Lessons: An Autobiography,* Addison-Wesley, 1986.

SOURCES:

Books

Cortada, James W., *Historical Dictionary of Data Processing: Biographies,* Greenwood Press, 1987.

Periodicals

Bulkeley, William M. and John R. Wilke, "Steep Slide: Filing in Chapter 11, Wang Sends Warning to High-Tech Circles," *Wall Street Journal,* August 1992, pp. A1, A6.
Wilke, John R. "Wang Labs Reorganization Is Cleared, Allowing Emergence from Chapter 11," *Wall Street Journal,* September 21, 1993, p. B6.

—*Sketch by Patrick Moore*

James C. Wang
1936-
Chinese-born American biochemist

James C. Wang is a biochemist who trained as a chemical engineer before turning to biophysical chemistry and molecular biology. Wang discovered deoxyribonucleic acid (DNA) topoisomerases (or local enzymes) and proposed a mechanism for their operation in the 1970s. He also studied the configuration (or topology) of DNA, an approach that proved fruitful in helping to explain how the structure of the double helix coils and relaxes.

Wang was born in mainland China on November 18, 1936. Less than a year later the Sino-Japanese War began. Wang lost his mother during the conflict, and shortly after it ended, his older sister also died. His father remarried, moving the family to Taiwan in 1949. Because of the war, Wang received only about two years of elementary education before starting junior high school in Taiwan. As a child, he wanted to study medicine, but his father encouraged him to become an engineer. A high school teacher inspired him to follow his interest in chemistry. Chemical engineering became Wang's course of study, and he earned a B.S. in 1959 from National Taiwan University. Continuing his studies in the field of chemistry, he earned a masters from the University of South Dakota in 1961, and a doctorate from the University of Missouri in 1964.

In the same year that Wang received his doctorate, he became a research fellow at the California Institute of Technology, remaining there until 1966. He then taught at the University of California in Berkeley from 1966 until 1977, when he joined the faculty at Harvard University. He was named the Mallinckrodt Professor of Biochemistry and Molecular Biology at Harvard in 1988.

Study of DNA Topology Leads to Revelations

Wang once noted that his interest in DNA topology came about by chance. His training in engineering and chemistry had led him to study the physical basis of chemical processes. He began to think about the questions raised by the double helix structure of DNA soon after its discovery by molecular biologists **James Watson** and **Francis Crick**. His own study of DNA confirmed the unique structure. But it was not clear how the two tightly intertwined strands could unravel at the speed at which the biochemical processes were thought to occur. Topologically, it did not seem possible for the strands to unravel at all. Wang studied supercoiling in *E. coli* bacteria and found that the rotation speed of an unraveling DNA strand is 10,000 revolutions per minute. He also found that the same enzyme, a DNA topoisomerase, is responsible for both breaking and rejoining the DNA strands.

Wang believed that the topological characteristics of the double helix affected all its chemical transformations, including transcription, replication, and recombination. In a 1991 interview in *Cell Science*, Wang remarked that he relied on intuition to further his scientific understanding, particularly when trying to make sense of "bits and pieces of information" that didn't obviously fit together. "There are times," he told the interviewer, "when results that seem to make no sense are key to new advances."

Wang has served on the editorial boards of several scholarly journals, including *Journal of Molecular Biology, Annual Review of Biochemistry,* and *Quarterly Review of Biophysics.* He was a Guggenheim fellow in 1986, and was elected to the U.S. National Academy of Sciences in 1984. In 1961 Wang married a former classmate; they have two daughters.

SELECTED WRITINGS BY WANG:

Periodicals

"DNA Topoisomerases," *Scientific American,* Volume 247, 1982, pp. 94–109.
"DNA Gyrations in Reverse," *Nature,* Volume 309, 1984, pp. 682–87.
"DNA Topoisomerases: Why So Many?," *Journal of Biological Chemistry,* Volume 266, 1991, pp. 6659–62.

—*Sketch by Valerie Brown*

Felix Wankel
1902-1988
German inventor

The distinction for designing the first practical rotary engine belongs to Felix Wankel, who experimented for years to properly integrate the necessary systems. Although concepts for an engine with pistons that spin rather than move back and forth had existed for centuries, Wankel was the first to develop the technologies required for its use in internal combustion engines. He became the leading developer of engine improvements based upon rotation and engine sealing systems, and Wankel engines are still used in thousands of automobiles manufac-

Felix Wankel

Wankel continued to perform experiments and develop new projects until his death in Lindau, Germany, on October 9, 1988.

Felix Heinrich Wankel was born to Rudolf Wankel and Gerty Heidlauff Wankel on August 13, 1902, in the town of Lahr, located in the Black Forest region of Germany. Wankel's father, a forest commissioner, was killed at the beginning of World War I when Wankel was twelve years old. As a result, Wankel worked to support himself and his mother after he finished high school. This prevented him from pursuing an apprentice position in foreign industry, the route often followed by men of his day who were talented in mechanics. Instead, Wankel moved to Heidelberg and worked in the print shop of a university book store until illness forced him to move from the print shop to the stock room. While there, however, he devised an improved method of stacking books for storage.

After work, Wankel attended night school and took correspondence courses. At the age of twenty-two he opened a machine shop in Heidelberg, quickly learning the important aspects of machining, production, and precision shaping and finishing of parts. Wankel began to experiment with improvements to automobile engines, specifically with reciprocating internal combustion engines, which use pistons and valves that move in a back-and-forth motion.

Wankel was aware of the shortcomings of reciprocating engines. Many parts were required to achieve the back-and-forth motion, which in turn caused a high degree of vibration and noise. In addition, as the speed of the engine increased, power losses occurred more frequently. Wankel believed that a rotary engine, one based on pistons which move in a circular motion, could perform much better than engines based upon reciprocating motion, and he began sketching designs of internal combustion engines with rotary pistons as early as 1924. He knew that ideas for rotary engines had been proposed since the sixteenth century, but a model that could withstand the heat, pressure, and wear created by internal combustion engines had not yet been developed. Wankel's own evaluations of his earliest designs led him to the conclusion that they did not justify further pursuit.

Designs Innovative Leak-Proof Valves

Wankel initially experimented with adapting rotary valves for motorcycle engines. His work in 1926 included improvements to the valve seals to prevent leakage of gas from the cylinders that house the pistons. He recognized that the lack of such seals in previous rotary valve designs was a primary cause of their failure. He began experimenting with a disc valve, rotating valves which turned on top of the engine cylinders, and by 1933 Wankel had successfully operated a disk valve engine on a motorcycle. His innovations in sealing became one of the most important steps in Wankel's development of a rotary engine.

In 1928 Wankel met Wilhelm Keppler, who later became the business consultant to Adolf Hitler. At their meeting Wankel expressed his desire to help Germany maintain her position as a great nation by building his technologically superior rotary engine. Keppler played a central role in Wankel's work on the engine during World War II and for several years after the war.

In 1933 Wankel contracted with Daimler-Benz A.G., an auto manufacturer, to research sealing, rotary valves, and engines. After a year he began conducting similar research for another automobile maker, Bayerische Motoren Werke (BMW). As a result of this work, Wankel obtained a patent for "packing bodies" in 1936. Packing bodies were specially-designed materials that were attached to primary components to achieve the seal. This customized approach provided much tighter seals than previous sealing attempts by precisely finishing primary components and pressing them tightly together in direct contact. Wankel also used the pressure of the gases in the engine to help tighten the seals. Wankel received many patents for his work on sealing systems, and by 1936 all possible rotary valve applications to internal combustion engines and compressors were covered by his patents. Wankel developed his first rotary piston internal combustion engine, one with rotating instead of reciprocating pistons, during this period. This first engine was impractical, but Wankel's unique solution to sealing the cylinders proved critical to future development.

War Research Provides Avenue for Improved Rotary Technology

As Germany became involved in the Second World War, Wankel's work toward the development of a practical rotary engine slowed. He was branded a traitor and imprisoned by then-State Chancellor Hitler for his assistance in uncovering an embezzlement operation run by members of Hitler's party. Hans Nibel, the chief engineer at Daimler-Benz, learned of Wankel's circumstances and convinced Wilhelm Keppler to have Wankel released. Keppler acted as Wankel's protector throughout World War II.

Upon his release from prison in 1935, Wankel moved his workshop closer to his home in Lahr. The following year Hermann Goering, the head of Germany's air force, heard of Wankel's work and invited him to conduct his research in Berlin. Wankel declined to move to Berlin, but convinced Goering to establish a separate research facility for him on Lake Constance near his home. Goering's air ministry invested millions of dollars in Wankel's facility and the development of a rotary valve airplane engine. By 1939 Wankel's rotary disk valve was part of the new Daimler-Benz DB601 aircraft engine. The outbreak of World War II prevented a scheduled speed flight that was expected to break records, but by 1942 the DB601 engine was in production for use in many German fighter planes and light bombers.

During the war, another company, Junkers, began using Wankel's rotary valves in the designs for their torpedo engines. The valves were critical to the development of Junkers's product because they greatly reduced the amount of space required by the engine. Junkers designed and tested several engines using Wankel's valves. The final design was for an engine that fit inside a twenty-one inch diameter torpedo.

Wankel was in Berlin performing research for Goering's air ministry from 1940 through 1944. He was able to use the successful DB601 engine as a springboard for further development of rotary valves. In 1944 Wankel built a rotary compressor, and by 1945 he had contracts with several government agencies and automobile and railroad corporations to develop rotary parts.

At the conclusion of World War II, the politics of war again interrupted Wankel's work. French occupation forces jailed the inventor from 1945 to 1946 as a war criminal for his work on German airplane engines. His research facility on Lake Constance was dismantled, and he was forbidden to conduct research or experiments. Wankel used this time to review his work, write papers, and work on designs for engines that included his rotary valves and pistons and sealing system.

Develops Practical Rotary Engine in Partnership with NSU

In 1951 Wilhelm Keppler helped Wankel open a new research and development facility on Lake Constance, not far from the site of his wartime laboratories. Keppler had influence in German industry and guided Wankel into a working relationship with NSU Werke, the motorcycle manufacturer. Some of Wankel's early work at NSU included the development of sealing systems for air compressors and conventional pistons. Wankel carefully developed his relationship with NSU, never becoming a company employee. Instead he contracted with NSU for the company's use of his motorcycle engines and future research. In addition, Wankel negotiated his contracts so that he was free to work with other clients and run his own shop.

NSU funded the development of Wankel's compressor into a supercharger for their racing motorcycles. The supercharger, completed in 1954, pushed the mixture of gas and air into the cylinder of a small NSU moped engine, increasing the power by more than 800 percent. For three and a half years Wankel and NSU experimented with ways to develop a rotary engine from the supercharger's fundamental design. The shape of the chamber in which a rotary piston spins is particularly critical to a practical rotary engine. Wankel identified the shapes for his early engines empirically. Only later would Professor Othmar Baier of the Technical College in Stuttgart employ geometric principles. Professor Baier's work greatly facilitated the analysis of Wankel's engine and simplified manufacturing by allowing the application of analytic mathematics to the shape of the Wankel engine.

During this time Wankel was assisted by a team of NSU engineers led by Dr. Walter Froede. On February 1, 1957, the group successfully tested their first rotary engine. A second, larger test engine was built and tested that same year. It produced no mechanical vibration, proving the ability of the Wankel engine to overcome a primary disadvantage of reciprocating engines. However, the engine required additional modifications before it could be used for such practical applications as the power plant in an automobile. In this early design, while the triangular shaped piston spun inside the chamber, the chamber itself rotated as well. A stationary housing would be required to protect the engine for use in practical applications, but instead of adding the cost and weight of an additional housing to the engine, Dr. Froede redesigned it so that the chamber remained stationary instead of turning. This allowed the chamber to act as the engine's protective housing. Froede's design resulted in the KKM engine, which made the Wankel engine truly practical. Wankel initially opposed the KKM on technical grounds, but after testing the improved engine design, his research and experimentation with NSU progressed.

Wankel was forced to divert some of his attention away from the development of his engine during its long technological progression. Financial difficulties at NSU forced him to find additional funding in order to continue his research. Wankel joined forces with Ernst Hutzenlaub, an architect turned inventor who provided $250,000 to market licenses for Wankel's engine. In order to use the Wankel engine in their airplanes, in 1958 Curtiss-Wright became one of the first companies to purchase a license. NSU continued to have a volatile financial status, but Wankel was able to conduct further research.

Wankel and the NSU engineers improved and modified the design of the KKM engine over the course of several years until a production model of the Wankel engine was ready. The KKM became the basis for numerous applications, including a water cooled version for boats. Wankel and NSU were very interested in using the engine for automobiles. In 1963 Toyo Kogyo (Mazda) produced the Cosmo Sports, the first prototype car using a Wankel engine. Several other corporations with licenses for Wankel engines, including Mercedes-Benz and General Motors, developed improvements to Wankel's basic design. In 1970 the first publicly available automobile powered by a Wankel engine arrived in the United States from Japan. Wankel's dream of a rotary piston engine for automobiles had finally become reality. After the development of a practical version of the engine, Wankel continued to experiment with new seals and geometric applications. He also performed extensive research into adapting the engine for diesel power and large rotary compressors.

Wankel showed unusual innovation and persistence in the pursuit of his dream of a practical rotary engine, and in 1969 the Technical Institute of Munich awarded him an honorary doctorate. Based upon an idea that is centuries old, Wankel's efforts have resulted in the development of valuable innovations in power systems.

SELECTED WRITINGS BY WANKEL:

Books

Rotary Piston Machines, Illiffe Books Ltd., 1965.

Periodicals

"Rotary Piston Engine Performance Criteria," *Automotive Engineer,* September, 1964.

SOURCES:

Books

Corbett, Scott, *What About the Wankel Engine?,* Four Winds Press, 1974.
Dark, Harris Edward, *The Wankel Rotary Engine, Introduction and Guide,* Indiana University Press, 1974.
Faith, Nicholas, *Wankel, the Curious Story Behind the Revolutionary Rotary Engine,* Stein and Day, 1975.
Norbye, Jan P., *The Wankel Engine,* Chilton Book Co., 1971.
Yamamoto, Kenichi, *Rotary Engine,* Sankaido Co. Ltd., 1981.

Periodicals

"Is the Wankel the Auto Engine of the Future?" *Changing Times,* July, 1972.
"Wangle Yourself a Wankel," *Forbes,* December 15, 1972.

—*Sketch by David N. Ford*

Otto Warburg
1883-1970
German biochemist

Otto Warburg is considered one of the world's foremost biochemists. His achievements include discovering the mechanism of cell oxidation and identifying the iron-enzyme complex, which catalyzes this process. He also made great strides in developing new experimental techniques, such as a method for studying the respiration of intact cells using a device he invented. His work was recognized with a Nobel Prize for medicine and physiology in 1931.

Otto Heinrich Warburg was born on October 8, 1883, in Freiburg, Germany, to Emil Gabriel Warburg and Elizabeth Gaertner. Warburg was one of four children and the only boy. His father was a physicist of note and held the prestigious Chair in Physics at University of Berlin. The Warburg household often hosted prominent guests from the German

Otto Warburg

scientific community, such as physicists **Albert Einstein**, **Max Planck**, **Emil Fischer**—the leading organic chemist of the late-nineteenth century, and **Walther Nernst**—the period's leading physical chemist.

Warburg studied chemistry at the University of Freiburg beginning in 1901. After two years, he left for the University of Berlin to study under Emil Fischer, and in 1906 received a doctorate in chemistry. His interest turned to medicine, particularly to cancer, so he continued his studies at the University of Heidelberg where he earned an M.D. degree in 1911. He remained at Heidelberg, conducting research for several more years and also making several research trips to the Naples Zoological Station.

Warburg's career goal was to make great scientific discoveries, particularly in the field of cancer research, according to the biography written by **Hans Adolf Krebs**, one of Warburg's students and winner of the 1953 Nobel Prize in medicine and physiology. Although he did not take up problems specifically related to cancer until the 1920s, his early projects provided a foundation for future cancer studies. For example, his first major research project, published in 1908, examined oxygen consumption during growth. In a study using sea urchin eggs, Warburg showed that after fertilization, oxygen consumption in the specimens increased 600 percent. This finding helped clarify earlier work that had been inconclusive on associating growth with increased consumption of oxygen and energy. A number of years later, Warburg did some similar tests of oxygen consumption by cancer cells.

World War I Interrupts Research

Warburg was elected in 1913 to the Kaiser Wilhelm Gesellschaft, a prestigious scientific institute whose members had the freedom to pursue whatever studies they wished. He had just begun his work at the institute when World War I started. He volunteered for the army and joined the Prussian Horse Guards, a cavalry unit that fought on the Russian front. Warburg survived the war and returned to the Kaiser Wilhelm Institute for Biology in Berlin in 1918. Now 35 years old, he would devote the rest of his life to biological research, concentrating on studies of energy transfer in cells (cancerous or otherwise) and photosynthesis.

One of Warburg's significant contributions to biology was the development of a manometer for monitoring cell respiration. He adapted a device originally designed to measure gases dissolved in blood so it would make measurements of the rate of oxygen production in living cells. In related work, Warburg devised a technique for preparing thin slices of intact, living tissue and keeping the samples alive in a nutrient medium. As the tissue slices consumed oxygen for respiration, Warburg's manometer monitored the changes.

During Warburg's youth, he had become familiar with Einstein's work on photochemical reactions as well as the experimental work done by his own father, Emil Warburg, to verify parts of Einstein's theory. With this background, Warburg was especially interested in the method by which plants converted light energy to chemical energy. Warburg used his manometric techniques for the studies of photosynthesis he conducted on algae. His measurements showed that photosynthetic plants used light energy at a highly efficient sixty-five percent. Some of Warburg's other theories about photosynthesis were not upheld by later research, but he was nevertheless considered a pioneer for the many experimental methods he developed in this field. In the late 1920s, Warburg began to develop techniques that used light to measure reaction rates and detect the presence of chemical compounds in cells. His "spectrophotometric" techniques formed the basis for some of the first commercial spectrophotometers built in the 1940s.

Discovers Details of Cell Respiration

His work on cell respiration was another example of his interest in how living things generated and used energy. Prior to World War I, Warburg discovered that small amounts of cyanide can inhibit cell oxidation. Since cyanide forms stable complexes with heavy metals such as iron, he inferred from his experiment that one or more catalysts important to oxidation must contain a heavy metal. He conducted other experiments with carbon monoxide, showing that this compound inhibits respiration in a fashion similar to cyanide. Next he found that light of specific frequencies could counteract the inhibitory effects of carbon monoxide, at the same time demonstrating that the "oxygen transferring enzyme," as Warburg called it, was different from other enzymes containing iron. He went on to discover the mechanism by which iron was involved in the cell's use of oxygen. It was Warburg's work in characterizing the cellular catalysts and their role in respiration that earned him a Nobel Prize in 1931.

Nobel Foundation records indicate that Warburg was considered for Nobel Prizes on two additional occasions: in 1927 for his work on metabolism of cancer cells, then in 1944 for his identification of the role of flavins and nicotinamide in biological oxidation. Warburg did not receive the 1944 award, however, because a decree from Hitler forbade German citizens from accepting Nobel Prizes. Two of Warburg's students also won Nobel Prizes in medicine and physiology: Hans Krebs (1953) and **Axel Theorell** (1955).

In 1931 Warburg established the Kaiser Wilhelm Institute for Cell Physiology with funding from the Rockefeller Foundation in the United States. During the 1930s, Warburg spent much of his time studying dehydrogenases, enzymes that remove hydrogen from substrates. He also identified some of the cofactors, such as nicotinamide derived from vitamin B3 (niacin), that play a role in a number of cell biochemical reactions.

Warburg conducted research at the Kaiser Wilhelm Institute for Cell Physiology until 1943 when the Second World War interrupted his investigations. Air attacks targeted at Berlin forced him to move his laboratory about 30 miles away to an estate in the countryside. For the next two years, he and his staff continued their work outside the city and out of the reach of the war. Then in 1945, Russian soldiers advancing to Berlin occupied the estate and confiscated Warburg's equipment. Although the Russian commander admitted that the soldiers acted in error, Warburg never recovered his equipment. Without a laboratory, he spent the next several years writing, publishing two books that provided an overview of much of his research. He also traveled to the United States during 1948 and 1949 to visit fellow scientists.

Survives Nazi Germany

Even though Warburg was of Jewish ancestry, he was able to remain in Germany and pursue his studies unhampered by the Nazis. One explanation is that Warburg's mother was not Jewish and high German officials "reviewed" Warburg's ancestry, declaring

him only one-quarter Jewish. As such he was forbidden from holding a university post, but allowed to continue his research. There is speculation that the Nazis believed Warburg might find a cure for cancer and so did not disturb his laboratory. Scientists in other countries were unhappy that Warburg was willing to remain in Nazi Germany. His biographer Hans Krebs noted, however, that Warburg was not afraid to criticize the Nazis. At one point during the war when Warburg was planning to travel to Zurich for a scientific meeting, the Nazis told him to cancel the trip and to not say why. "With some measure of courage," wrote Krebs, "he sent a telegram [to a conference participant from England]: 'Instructed to cancel participation without giving reasons.'" Although the message was not made public officially, the text was leaked and spread through the scientific community. Krebs believed Warburg did not leave Germany because he did not want to have to rebuild the research team he had assembled. The scientist feared that starting over would destroy his research potential, Krebs speculated.

In 1950 Warburg moved into a remodeled building in Berlin which had been occupied by U.S. armed forces following World War II. This new site was given the name of Warburg's previous scientific home—the Kaiser Wilhelm Institute for Cell Physiology—and three years later renamed the Max Planck Institute for Cell Physiology. Warburg continued to conduct research and write there, publishing 178 scientific papers from 1950 until his death in 1970.

For all of his interest in cancer, Warburg's studies did not reveal any deep insights into the disease. When he wrote about the "primary" causes of cancer later in his life, Warburg's proposals failed to address the mechanisms by which cancer cells undergo unchecked growth. Instead, he focused on metabolism, suggesting that in cancer cells "fermentation" replaces normal oxygen respiration. Warburg's cancer studies led him to fear that exposure to food additives increased one's chances of contracting the disease. In 1966 he delivered a lecture in which he stated that cancer prevention and treatment should focus on the administration of respiratory enzymes and cofactors, such as iron and the B vitamins. The recommendation elicited much controversy in Germany and elsewhere in the Western world.

Warburg's devotion to science led him to forego marriage, since he thought it was incompatible with his work. According to Karlfried Gawehn, Warburg's colleague from 1950 to 1964, "For him [Warburg] there were no reasonable grounds, apart from death, for not working." Warburg's productivity and stature as a researcher earned him an exemption from the Institute's mandatory retirement rules, allowing him to continue working until very near to the end of his life. He died at the Berlin home he shared with Jakob Heiss on August 1, 1970.

SELECTED WRITINGS BY WARBURG:

Books

The Metabolism of Tumors, Constable and Co., 1930.
Heavy Metal Prosthetic Groups and Enzyme Action, translated by Alexander Lawson, Clarendon Press, 1949.
New Methods of Cell Physiology, Interscience Publishers, 1962.

Periodicals

"On the Origin of Cancer Cells," *Science,* Volume 123, 1956, p. 312.

SOURCES:

Books

Krebs, Hans, *Otto Warburg: Cell Physiologist, Biochemist and Eccentric,* Clarendon Press, 1981.

—*Sketch by Lee Katterman*

Warren M. Washington
1936-
American meteorologist

Warren M. Washington is an atmospheric scientist whose research focuses on the development of computer models that describe and predict the earth's climate. He is the director of the Climate and Global Dynamics Division of the National Center for Atmospheric Research (NCAR), in Boulder, Colorado. He has advised the U.S. Congress and several U.S. presidents on climate-system modeling, serving on the President's National Advisory Committee on Oceans and Atmosphere from 1978 to 1984.

Washington was born on August 28, 1936, in Portland, Oregon. His father, Edwin Washington, Jr., had hoped to be a school teacher, but in the 1920s Portland wouldn't hire a black man to teach in the public schools. Instead, the elder Washington supported Warren and his four brothers by waiting tables in Pullman cars. His wife, Dorothy Grace (Morton) Washington, became a practical nurse, after the Washington children were grown.

Washington's interest in scientific research developed early and was nurtured by high school teachers who encouraged him to experiment. Refusing once to directly answer his question about why egg yolks were yellow, a chemistry teacher inspired Washington to study chicken diets and eventually to learn about the chemistry of sulfur compounds. Despite the boy's aptitude for science, Washington's high school counselor advised him to attend a business school rather than college, but Washington's dream was to be a scientist. He earned his bachelor's degree in physics in 1958, from Oregon State University. As an undergraduate, Washington become interested in meteorology while working on a project at a weather station near the campus. As part of the project, the station used radar equipment to track storms as they came in off the coast. In 1960 he earned his master's degree in meteorology from Oregon State. When he completed his graduate work in 1964 at Pennsylvania State University, he became one of only four African Americans to receive a doctorate in meteorology.

Washington began working for the NCAR in 1963 and has remained affiliated with that institution throughout his career. His research there has attempted to quantify patterns of oceanic and atmospheric circulation. He has helped to create complex mathematical models that take into account the effects of surface and air temperature, soil and atmospheric moisture, sea ice volume, various geographical features, and other parameters on past and current climates. His research has contributed to our modern-day understanding of the greenhouse effect, in which excess carbon dioxide in the Earth's atmosphere causes the retention of heat, giving rise to what is known as global warming. Washington's research also provided understanding for other mechanisms of global climate change.

Washington was appointed the director of the Climate and Global Dynamics Division at NCAR in 1987. In 1994 he was elected President of the American Meteorological Society. He is a fellow of the American Association for the Advancement of Science and a member of its board of directors, a fellow of the African Scientific Institute, a Distinguished Alumnus of Pennsylvania State University, a fellow of Oregon State University, and Founder and President of the Black Environmental Science Trust, a nonprofit foundation that encourages African American participation in environmental research and policymaking.

Washington has published over 100 professional articles about atmospheric science. He coauthored, with Claire Parkinson, *An Introduction to Three-Dimensional Climate Modeling* in 1986, and the book has since become a standard reference text for climate modeling. Washington, a widower, has six children and ten grandchildren.

SELECTED WRITINGS BY WASHINGTON:

Books

(With Claire Parkinson), *An Introduction to Three-Dimensional Climate Modeling,* Oxford University Press, 1986.

Periodicals

"Where's the Heat?" *Natural History,* March, 1990, pp. 66–70.

SOURCES:

Periodicals

Clemmitt, Marcia, "Minority Scientists Broaden Efforts to Fight Environmental Woes of Poor," *Scientist,* April 29, 1991, p.1.

Hill, Richard, "Acclaimed Scientist Rejected Advice to Go to Business School," *Oregonian,* November 18, 1993, p. A–21.

Jackson, Robert, "Coloradan to Head Meteorologists," *Rocky Mountain News* (Colorado), February 9, 1993.

Roberts, Chris, "Mr. Washington Goes to Washington," *Daily Camera,* February 11, 1993, pp. 1–2C.

Saunders, Ellen, "Global Warming Expert Hopes to Encourage Others," *Oregon Stater,* December, 1990, p. 21.

—Sketch by Leslie Reinherz

Levi Watkins, Jr.
1945-

American cardiac surgeon

Levi Watkins, Jr., the first black graduate of Vanderbilt University School of Medicine, has conducted research on congestive heart failure and also performed the first implantation of the automatic defibrillator in February 1980 at Johns Hopkins Hospital in Baltimore. The Automatic Implantation Defibrillator (AID) is designed to restore the heart's normal rhythm during an attack of ventricular fibrillation or arrhythmia, an irregularity of the heartbeat caused by coronary scar tissue or hardening of the coronary artery. When arrhythmia occurs, the heart is unable to pump blood and, unless corrected by devices such as the AID, the sufferer can die.

Watkins was born on June 13, 1945, in Parsons, Kansas, to Levi Watkins, Sr., an educator who became the president of Alabama State University, and Lillian Bernice Varnado. He graduated from Tennessee State University with honors in 1966. Watkins received his medical degree from the Vanderbilt University School of Medicine in Nashville in 1970 and completed his residency at the Johns Hopkins University Hospital, where he was the first black chief resident of cardiac surgery.

After his residency, Watkins was appointed assistant professor and then professor of surgery at Johns Hopkins. Watkins also spent two years conducting research at Harvard Medical School's Department of Physiology, investigating the relationship between congestive heart failure and the renin angiotensin system. Within the renin angiotensin system, a kidney enzyme is associated with the production of a hormone that causes dilation of blood vessels and contraction of muscles. Watkins's research led to the use of angiotensin blockers to treat congestive heart failure.

In 1982, discussing the ground-breaking AID device in *Ebony,* Watkins observed that "Now we can give patients the ultimate protection from this sudden death." At that time, it was estimated that 500,000 people died from arrhythmia annually, making the disorder one of the leading causes of death in the United States. Invented by Michel Mirowski, the director of the coronary care unit at Sinai Hospital in Baltimore, the AID is a small, battery-operated generator that is implanted in the patient's abdomen. One electrode leading from the AID is inserted into the right chamber of the heart; a second electrode is affixed to the tip of the heart. When the AID senses an abnormal heart rhythm, it administers mild shocks to restore the normal rhythm. The success of the device means a positive prognosis for patients who do not respond to medication for the disorder (about twenty-five percent). Watkins's initial AID surgical procedure was soon followed by dozens of successful implantations, and representatives of medical centers throughout the country applied to be trained for the procedure.

In addition to his work with cardiac arrhythmia at Johns Hopkins, Watkins has been a pioneer in the application of lasers to heart surgery, and has directed research on heart disease, particularly as it affects minorities, through Maryland's Minority Health Commission and Panel for Coronary Artery Bypass Surgery. An aggressive recruiter of black students for Johns Hopkins Medical School, he was appointed in 1979 to the university's admissions committee. In 1983, Watkins joined the national board of the Robert Wood Johnson Minority Faculty Development Program. His other professional affiliations include the American Board of Surgery and the American Board of Thoracic Surgery.

SELECTED WRITINGS BY WATKINS:

Periodicals

(With others) "Termination of Malignant Ventricular Arrhythmias with an Implanted Automatic Defibrillator in Human Beings," *The New England Journal of Medicine,* August 7, 1980, pp. 322–324.

(With others) "Implantation of the Automatic Implantable Cardioverter Defibrillator," *Journal of Cardiac Surgery,* March 3, 1988, pp. 1–7.

"Treatment of Impending Sudden Cardiac Death," *Annals of Thoracic Surgery,* March, 1989, pp. 484–485.

SOURCES:

Periodicals

"Device Averts Heart Attacks," *Science Digest,* March, 1981, p. 103.

"Finding New Breakthroughs in Heart Care," *Black Enterprise,* October, 1988, p. 58.

"Young Surgeon Brings New Hope to Heart Patients," *Ebony,* January, 1982, pp. 96–98; 100.

—*Sketch by Jane Stewart Cook*

James D. Watson

James D. Watson
1928-
American molecular biologist

James D. Watson won the 1962 Nobel Prize in physiology and medicine along with **Francis Crick** and **Maurice Wilkins** for discovering the structure of DNA, or deoxyribonucleic acid, which is the carrier of genetic information at the molecular level. Watson and Crick had worked as a team since meeting in the early 1950s, and their research ranks as a fundamental advance in molecular biology. More than thirty years later, Watson became the director of the Human Genome Project, an enterprise devoted to a difficult goal: the description of every human gene, the total of which may number up to one hundred thousand. This

is a project that would not be possible without Watson's groundbreaking work on DNA.

James Dewey Watson was born in Chicago, Illinois, on April 6, 1928, to James Dewey and Jean (Mitchell) Watson. He was educated in the Chicago public schools, and during his adolescence became one of the original Quiz Kids on the radio show of the same name. Shortly after this experience in 1943, Watson entered the University of Chicago at the age of fifteen.

Watson graduated in 1946, but stayed on at Chicago for a bachelor's degree in zoology, which he attained in 1947. During his undergraduate years Watson studied neither genetics nor biochemistry—his primary interest was in the field of ornithology; in 1946 he spent a summer working on advanced ornithology at the University of Michigan's summer research station at Douglas Lake. During his undergraduate career at Chicago, Watson had been instructed by the well-known population geneticist **Sewall Wright**, but he did not become interested in the field of genetics until he read **Erwin Schrödinger**'s influential book *What is Life?;* it was then, Horace Judson reports in *The Eighth Day of Creation: Makers of the Revolution in Biology,* that Watson became interested in "finding out the secret of the gene."

Work with the "Phage Group"

Watson enrolled at Indiana University to perform graduate work in 1947. Indiana had several remarkable geneticists who could have been important to Watson's intellectual development, but he was drawn to the university by the presence of the Nobel laureate **Hermann Joseph Muller**, who had demonstrated twenty years earlier that X rays cause mutation. Nonetheless, Watson chose to work under the direction of the Italian biologist **Salvador Edward Luria**, and it was under Luria that he began his doctoral research in 1948.

Watson's thesis was on the effect of X rays on the rate of phage lysis (a phage, or bacteriophage, is a bacterial virus). The biologist **Max Delbrück** and Luria—as well as a number of others who formed what was to be known as "the phage group"—had demonstrated that phages could exist in a number of mutant forms. A year earlier Luria and Delbruck had published one of the landmark papers in phage genetics, in which they established that one of the characteristics of phages is that they can exist in different genetic states so that the lysis (or bursting) of bacterial host cells can take place at different rates. Watson's Ph.D. degree was received in 1950, shortly after his twenty-second birthday.

Watson was next awarded a National Research Council fellowship grant to investigate the molecular structure of proteins in Copenhagen, Denmark. While Watson was studying enzyme structure in Europe, where techniques crucial to the study of macromolecules were being developed, he was also attending conferences and meeting colleagues.

From 1951 to 1953, Watson held a research fellowship under the support of the National Foundation for Infantile Paralysis at the Cavendish Laboratory in Cambridge, England. Those two years are described in detail in Watson's 1965 book, *The Double Helix: A Personal Account of the Discovery of the Structure of DNA.* (An autobiographical work, *The Double Helix* describes the events—both personal and professional—that led to the discovery of DNA.) Watson was to work at the Cavendish under the direction of **Max Perutz**, who was engaged in the X-ray crystallography of proteins. However, he soon found himself engaged in discussions with Crick on the structure of DNA. Crick was twelve years older than Watson and, at the time, a graduate student studying protein structure.

Intermittently over the next two years, Watson and Crick theorized about DNA and worked on their model of DNA structure, eventually arriving at the correct structure by recognizing the importance of X-ray diffraction photographs produced by **Rosalind Franklin** at King's College, London. Both were certain that the answer lay in model-building, and Watson was particularly impressed by Nobel laureate **Linus Pauling**'s use of model-building in determining the alpha-helix structure of protein. Using data published by Austrian-born American biochemist **Erwin Char-**

gaff on the symmetry between the four constituent nucleotides (or "bases") of DNA molecules, they concluded that the building blocks had to be arranged in pairs. After a great deal of experimentation with their models, they found that the double helix structure corresponded to the empirical data produced by Wilkins, Franklin, and their colleagues. Watson and Crick published their theoretical paper in the journal *Nature* in 1953 (with Watson's name appearing first due to a coin toss), and their conclusions were supported by the experimental evidence simultaneously published by Wilkins, Franklin, and Raymond Goss. Wilkins shared the Nobel Prize with Watson and Crick in 1962.

Career Since the Discovery of DNA

After the completion of his research fellowship at Cambridge, Watson spent the summer of 1953 at Cold Spring Harbor, New York, where Delbruck had gathered an active group of investigators working in the new area of molecular biology. Watson then became a research fellow in biology at the California Institute of Technology, working with Delbruck and his colleagues on problems in phage genetics. In 1955, he joined the biology department at Harvard and remained on the faculty until 1976. While at Harvard, Watson wrote *The Molecular Biology of the Gene* (1965), the first widely used university textbook on molecular biology. This text has gone through seven editions, and now exists in two large volumes as a comprehensive treatise of the field. In 1968, Watson became director of Cold Spring Harbor, carrying out his duties there while maintaining his position at Harvard. He gave up his faculty appointment at the university in 1976, however, and assumed full-time leadership of Cold Spring Harbor. With John Tooze and David Kurtz, Watson wrote *The Molecular Biology of the Cell,* originally published in 1983 and now in its third edition.

In 1989, Watson was appointed the director of the Human Genome Project of the National Institutes of Health, but after less than two years he resigned in protest over policy differences in the operation of this massive project. He continues to speak out on various issues concerning scientific research and is a strong presence concerning federal policies in supporting research. In addition to sharing the Nobel Prize, Watson has received numerous honorary degrees from institutions, including one from the University of Chicago, which was awarded in 1961, when Watson was still in his early thirties. He was also awarded the Presidential Medal of Freedom in 1977 by President Jimmy Carter. In 1968, Watson married Elizabeth Lewis. They have two children, Rufus Robert and Duncan James.

Watson, as his book *The Double Helix* confirms, has never avoided controversy. His candor about his colleagues and his combativeness in public forums have been noted by critics. On the other hand, his scientific brilliance is attested to by Crick, Delbruck, Luria, and others. The importance of his role in the DNA discovery has been well supported by Gunther Stent—a member of the Delbruck phage group—in an essay that discounts many of Watson's critics through well-reasoned arguments.

Most of Watson's professional life has been spent as a professor, research administrator, and public policy spokesman for research. More than any other location in Watson's professional life, Cold Spring Harbor (where he is still director) has been the most congenial in developing his abilities as a scientific catalyst for others. His work there has primarily been to facilitate and encourage the research of other scientists.

SELECTED WRITINGS BY WATSON:

Books

The Molecular Biology of the Gene, Benjamin, 1965.
The Double Helix: A Personal Account of the Discovery of the Structure of DNA, Norton, 1968.
(With John Tooze) *The DNA Story,* 1981.
(With Tooze and David Kurtz) *The Molecular Biology of the Cell,* Benjamin, 1983.

Periodicals

(With Francis Crick) "A Structure for Deoxyribose Nucleic Acid," *Nature,* April 25, 1953, pp. 738–740.
(With Francis Crick) "Genetical Implications of the Structure of DNA," *Nature,* May 30, 1953, pp. 964–967.

SOURCES:

Books

Crick, Francis, *What Mad Pursuit: A Personal View of Scientific Discovery,* Basic Books, 1988.
Judson, Horace Freeland, *The Eighth Day of Creation: Makers of the Revolution in Biology,* Simon and Schuster, 1979.
Olby, Robert, *The Path to the Double Helix,* Macmillan, 1974.
Stent, Gunther, *Paradoxes of Progress,* Chicago, 1985.

—Sketch by Russell Aiuto

Robert Watson-Watt
1892-1973
Scottish physicist

Robert Watson-Watt's major contribution to science was the development of radar, the process of using radio waves to detect objects. First used successfully as a defense mechanism during World War II, many authorities have described it as one of the two most significant scientific achievements (along with nuclear weapons) resulting from research conducted during the war. The discovery stemmed from Watson-Watt's research on tracking thunderstorms by means of radio waves during World War I, when he served as a member of the British Meteorological Office. Following the war, Watson-Watt ended his long affiliation with the British government and established his own business, Sir Robert Watson-Watt and Partners.

Robert Alexander Watson-Watt was born on April 13, 1892, in Brechin, Scotland. His father, Patrick Watson Watt, a master carpenter, took his last name from his father (Watt) and his mother (Watson) and passed them both along to his son. Watson-Watt's mother was the former Mary Small Matthew. The hyphenation of Watson-Watt's name occurred in 1942, when he was knighted.

Develops Early Interest in Radio Sciences

Watson-Watt attended the Damacre Road School and then the local high school in Brechin. After graduation, he won a scholarship to University College, Dundee, where he pursued a degree in electrical engineering and was introduced to the field of wireless telegraphy. His fascination with the subject would eventually guide and motivate nearly all of the research he was to conduct throughout his life. In 1912, Watson-Watt was granted a bachelor of science degree in electrical engineering and offered a post as assistant professor of physics at his alma mater, a position he would hold only briefly. At the outbreak of World War I in 1914, his application for a job with the British War Office was denied, but he succeeded in obtaining a position with the government's Meteorological Office, where he proposed a method for tracking severe weather patterns by triangulation with radio waves. Progress in the development of this technique was slow, however, because the technology required to perform related experiments had not yet been perfected.

At the conclusion of the war, Watson-Watt in 1919 received a bachelor of science in physics from the University of London and was transferred to a field observing station at Ditton Park, Slough. In

1927, that station was combined with a nearby facility of the National Physical Laboratory to form a single unit called the Radio Research Station under the authority of the Department of Scientific and Industrial Research. Watson-Watt was appointed director of the new station. Over the next decade, Watson-Watt directed research on the radio location of thunderstorms, the detection of naval signals, and studies of the atmosphere. In connection with the latter work, he proposed the name "ionosphere" for the reflecting layer of the atmosphere discovered in 1924 by Sir **Edward Appleton**.

Invents Radar

Watson-Watt's most notable accomplishment, the invention of radar, came about as the result of an inquiry made by an official of the Air Ministry in 1935. He asked if it would be possible to concentrate radio waves in such a way that they could be used to destroy enemy aircraft. Though Watson-Watt's assistant, A. F. Wilkins, pointed out the impossibility of creating such a device, they explained how radio waves could at least be used for detecting aircraft. This can be accomplished by sending out a beam of radio waves in the direction of a given object. The time required for the beam to reflect off of the object and return to its source provides a means of accurately calculating the object's distance.

Watson-Watt outlined this method in a memo to the Air Ministry dated February 12, 1935. In his autobiography, Watson-Watt identifies that date clearly as being "the birth of radar and as being in fact the invention of radar." The term radar, coined in the United States, is an acronym for "radio detection and ranging." The British government quickly initiated a program for the development of Watson-Watt's idea. Radar stations in Britain were fully operational by the opening months of World War II and, most military authorities agree, served as the deciding factor in repulsing Germany's air invasions during the Battle of Britain in 1940.

Throughout his life, Watson-Watt displayed an interest in important social issues outside the field of science. From 1929 to 1936, for example, he was an active member of the Institute of Professional Civil Servants, serving as vice-chairman of the organization in 1932, and as chairman in 1934. He was also a fellow and treasurer of the Institute of Physics, a fellow of the Royal Society, and the recipient of numerous honorary degrees and other recognitions. In 1946, Watson-Watt formed the private consulting company, Sir Robert Watson-Watt and Partners, and consulted with a number of agencies within the British government.

Watson-Watt was married three times between 1916 and 1966. His last wife, Air Chief Commandant Dame Katherine Jane Trefusis-Forbes, formerly head of the Women's Royal Air Force, died in 1971. Details surrounding the last two decades of his life are somewhat clouded. In his obituary of Watson-Watt in the *Biographical Memoirs of the Fellows of the Royal Society,* J. A. Ratcliffe writes: "From about 1952 onwards, Watson-Watt lived chiefly in Canada and the U.S.A., and it is difficult to find anyone who can give much account of his activities. From what evidence there is it seems that he acted from time to time as a freelance scientific advisor, occasionally with a small staff of one or two people." Watson-Watt died in Inverness, Scotland, on December 5, 1973.

SELECTED WRITINGS BY WATSON-WATT:

Books

(With J. F. Herd and L. H. Bainbridge-Bell) *Applications of Cathode-Ray Oscillograph in Radio Research,* H. M. Stationery Office, 1933.
Three Steps to Victory: A Personal Account by Radar's Greatest Pioneer (autobiography), Odhams, 1957, abbreviated version published in the U.S. as *The Pulse of Radar,* Dial, 1959.
Man's Means to His End, Heinemann, 1962.

Periodicals

"Radar in War and Peace," *Nature,* Volume 156, 1945, p. 319.
"The Evolution of Radiolocation," *Journal of the Institute of Electrical Engineering,* Volume 93, III A, 1946, p. 11.

SOURCES:

Books

Biographical Memoirs of Fellows of the Royal Society, Volume 21, Royal Society (London), 1975, pp. 549–568.
Contemporary Authors, Permanent Series, Volume 1, Gale, 1975.
Holmes, Frederic L., *Dictionary of Scientific Biography,* Volume 18, Scribner, 1982, pp. 977–978.

—*Sketch by David E. Newton*

Anne Antoinette Weber-van Bosse
1852-1943
Dutch botanist

Anne Antoinette Weber-van Bosse, one of the world's leading experts on algae and marine botany, was born in Amsterdam to Jacob van Bosse, a successful merchant, and Jaquéline Jeanne Beynvaan. She had three brothers and a sister, ten years her senior, who ran the Van Bosse household after their mother died. She received her education at home from a Swiss governess, and from an early age she was fascinated by botany and by exotic animals at the Amsterdam zoo. In 1870 Van Bosse married the painter Wilhelm Ferdinand Willink van Collen; when van Collen died in 1877, van Bosse returned to live with her father.

In 1880 she enrolled at the University of Amsterdam, where she was one of three women botanical students. There she was captivated by the courses in plant physiology taught by **Hugo De Vries**. After three years of study she specialized in algae, the subject which would become her life's work. In 1883 she married Max Weber, a university lecturer in anatomy, who in 1884 became professor of zoology and director of the zoological museum at Amsterdam.

Begins Research on Algae

Weber-van Bosse's first research on algae concerned those varieties that lived on the body of the South American sloth. She later accompanied her husband on research trips to Norway and, in 1889, to Indonesia. While in the tropics she studied the symbiosis between algae and sponges, as well as the algae that lives on the leaves of the plant *Pilea*. In 1898 her husband undertook an ambitious deep-sea oceanographical expedition on board the ship *Siboga;* the analysis of the material collected during this expedition occupied the Webers for the rest of their lives.

Weber-van Bosse often assisted her husband in his research, but she also published independent papers and monographs. On her own account she analyzed algae collected on the *Siboga,* and she published a popular account of the expedition. In 1934 she gave her algae herbarium of 50,000 specimens to the Royal Herbarium at Leiden. Among her other interests, she was active in the Montessori educational movement. Her scientific work resulted in an honorary doctorate, awarded by the University of Utrecht in 1910; in 1935 she was made a knight of the Order of Orange-Nassau, one of the highest honors in the Netherlands.

SELECTED WRITINGS BY WEBER-VAN BOSSE:

Books

Monographie des Caulerpes, E. J. Brill, 1898.
Een jaar an boord H. M. Siboga, E. J. Brill, 1904.
Liste des algues du Siboga, E. J. Brill, 1928.

SOURCES:

Books

Koster, Joséphine Th. and Tera S. S. van Benthem Jutting, *Blumea: Tijdschrift voor de systamatiek en de geografie der planten,* supplement II, [Leiden], 1942.
Querner, Hans, "Max Wilhelm Carl Weber (1852–1937)," in *Dictionary of Scientific Biography,* Scribner, 1976, p. 203.

—Sketch by Lewis Pyenson

Julia Weertman
1926-
American physicist

Julia Weertman is a physicist who significantly furthered knowledge of high temperature metal failure and the nanocrystalline structures of metals. Her study of small angle neutron scattering also aided in understanding the basic characteristics of different materials.

Weertman was born Julia Randall on February 10, 1926, in Muskegon, Michigan. Her parents, Louise Neumeister Randall and Winslow Randall, had one other daughter, Louise. Weertman grew up in Pittsburgh, graduating from Mount Lebanon High School in 1943. As a youngster, Weertman loved airplanes and flying. She announced to her parents that she wanted to fly. Weertman's parents replied that she would have to become an aeronautical engineer before they would consent to letting her learn to fly. Pursuing this goal, Weertman studied science vigorously, eventually deciding that she liked physics best.

After high school, Weertman received her bachelor of science degree in physics in 1946, her master's in 1947, followed by a doctorate in 1951, all from the Carnegie Institute of Technology. While at graduate school, Weertman met Johannes Weertman, and they married on her birthday, February 10, 1950.

Under the auspices of a Rotary International Fellowship, Weertman followed graduate school with post-doctorate work at the Ecole Normale Superieure in Paris during 1951 and 1952. In 1952, Weertman returned to Washington, D.C. to work at the Naval Research Laboratory. Most of her work centered around ferro-magnetic spin resonance and study of the basic concepts of magnetism. Weertman's work at the Naval Research Laboratory lasted until 1958, when her husband accepted a position in London, working for the Office of Naval Research. By this time, Weertman had a daughter, Julia. She put her career on hold to raise her daughter.

In early 1960, Johannes Weertman accepted a position at Northwestern University in Evanston, Illinois. A year later, son Bruce was born. During this interval, Weertman occupied herself with raising her children, community work, and being a Girl Scout troop leader. During this time, she also collaborated with her husband to write a textbook entitled *Elementary Dislocation Theory,* published in 1964.

Much of the work Weertman did early in her career centered not only on dislocation, a condition which allows metals to be manipulated more easily, but on studying the effects of very high temperatures on pure metals and alloys with respect to their fatigue and failure. Weertman studied the mechanical effects of high heat as it related to such properties as tensile strength and brittleness. Weertman also studied small angle neutron scattering. Her work helped characterize materials so that boundary interactions and mechanical properties were more easily understood.

In 1972, Weertman became a visiting assistant professor at Northwestern University. After her third year at Northwestern, Weertman was teaching fulltime, eventually receiving tenure. By 1982, she was a full professor, working in the Material Science and Engineering Department. In 1986, she briefly taught at a technical college in Switzerland. She returned to Northwestern University and assumed leadership of the Material Science and Engineering Department in 1987, serving until 1992.

Weertman has been active in a number of professional organizations, receiving awards from many of them. She was a member of the American Institute of Physics, the American Crystalline Association, the Mining, Metals and Materials Society, and was also an ASM International fellow. Weertman served on one of the National Academy of Sciences' standing committees as chairman of the Solid States Science Committee. She was also an advisor to the National Science Foundation, the United States Department of Energy, the National Bureau of Standard and Technology, and Argonne and Oak Ridge National Laboratories.

From the National Science Foundation, Weertman twice received the Creativity Award, in 1981 and 1986. The City of Evanston presented her with its Environmental Award in 1979. In 1988, Weertman received the National Academy of Engineering Award. The Society of Women Engineers awarded Weertman its highest honor in 1991.

SELECTED WRITINGS BY WEERTMAN:

Books

Weertman, Johannes and Julia R., *Elementary Dislocation Theory,* Macmillan, 1964.

Periodicals

(With J. G. Barker) "Growth Rates of Grain Boundary Cavities During High Temperature Fatigue of Copper," *Scripta Metallurgica et Materialia,* February 1, 1990, p. 227.

(With L. L. Lisieck) "Orientation Effects on the Elevated Temperature Fatigue of Copper Single Crystals," *Acta Metallurgica et Materiallia,* March 1, 1990, p. 509.

(With Y. C. Chen and M. E. Fine) "Microstructural Evolution and Mechanical Properties of Rapidly Solidified Al-Zr-V Alloys at High Temperatures," *Acta Metallurgica et Materialia,* May 1, 1990, p. 771.

(With P. R. Jemian and G. G. Long) "High-Resolution, Small-Angle X-Ray Scattering Camera for Anomalous Scattering," *Journal of Applied Crystallography,* February 1, 1991, p. 30.

(With G. W. Nieman and R. W. Siegel) "Mechanical Behavior of Nanocrystalline Cu and Pd," *Journal of Materials Research,* May 1, 1991, p. 1012.

"Hall-Petch Strengthening in Nanocrystalline Metals," *Material Science and Engineering,* July 15, 1993, p. 161.

(With Fine and R. Mitra) "Chemical Reaction Strengthening of Al/TiC Metal Matrix Composites by Isothermal Heat Treatment at 913K," *Journal of Materials Research,* September 1, 1993, p. 2370.

SOURCES:

Weertman, Julia R., interview with Susan Kolmer conducted February 18, 1994.

—Sketch by Susan E. Kolmer

Alfred Wegener
1880-1930
German meteorologist and geophysicist

Alfred Wegener was primarily a meteorologist who became much more famous for proposing the idea of continental drift. Decades after his death, the theory of continental drift that he had proposed in 1912 became the well-established foundation for the plate tectonics revolution in the earth sciences. Wegener heard mostly ridicule of his continental drift idea during his lifetime, but in the 1960s oceanic data convinced scientists that continents do indeed move. Wegener was an eminent meteorologist in his time, but he was appointed professor late in his professional career and died during one of his scientific trips to Greenland.

Wegener was born in Berlin on November 1, 1880, to Richard, a minister and director of an orphanage, and Anna Wegener. From an early age he hoped to explore Greenland, and he walked, hiked, and skated in order to build up his endurance for such a trip. He studied at the universities in Heidelberg, Innsbruck, and Berlin, receiving a doctorate in astronomy from the latter in 1905. Wegener's thesis involved conversion of a thirteenth-century set of astronomical tables into decimal notation; thereafter he abandoned astronomy in favor of meteorology. He carried out experiments with kites and balloons, fascinated with the new science of weather. In 1906, he and his brother Kurt set a world record in an international balloon contest by flying for 52 hours straight.

That year Wegener also fulfilled his dream of going to Greenland. Wegener was chosen as official meteorologist for a Danish expedition to northeastern Greenland from 1906 to 1908. It was the first of four trips to Greenland he would take. In 1912 he returned to Greenland with an expedition to study glaciology and climatology; this trip was the longest crossing of the ice cap ever made on foot.

In 1908, Wegener accepted a job teaching meteorology at the University of Marburg. His lectures were very popular with students for their clarity and frankness. He admitted disliking mathematical details, yet in 1911 he published a textbook on the thermodynamics of the atmosphere, which included in embryonic form the modern theory on the origins of precipitation. The following year Wegener married Else Köppen, the daughter of the "Grand Old Man of Meteorology" in Germany, Wladimir Köppen. During World War I Wegener served as a junior military officer and was wounded twice. After the war he succeeded his father-in-law as director of the meteoro-

Alfred Wegener

logical research department of the Marine Observatory near Hamburg. There he conducted experiments to reproduce lunar craters by hurling projectiles at various ground substances, demonstrating that the craters were probably of impact, rather than volcanic, origin. He also continued to analyze the data from Greenland, observe meteorological phenomena, and develop his earlier ideas on the origin of the continents and the oceans.

Continental Drift Is Born

Wegener had first thought of the idea of continental drift in late 1910 while looking at a world map in an atlas. He noticed that the east coast of South America matched like a puzzle piece with the west coast of Africa, but dismissed the idea of drifting continents as improbable. The next year, however, he came across a list of sources arguing that a land bridge must have connected the two continents at one time, since similar fossils from the same time period appeared in both Africa and Brazil. Wegener immediately began to search out fossil evidence to support the idea of drifting continents. Within a few months he presented his hypothesis in two public forums.

Wegener spoke on "The Geophysical Basis of the Evolution of the Large-Scale Features of the Earth's Crust (Continents and Oceans)" at a meeting of geologists in Frankfurt on January 6, 1912. Four days later he addressed a scientific society in Marburg on the same topic. For the first time, he proposed that the continents had actually moved thousands of miles away from each other instead of being connected by a stationary land bridge. Wegener wrote up his theory in two brief papers that year before leaving for his second expedition to Greenland.

Wegener published an extended account of his idea as *Die Entstehung der Kontinente und Ozeane* (*The Origin of Continents and Oceans*) in 1915. The first edition was only 94 pages long with no index. The second edition, much expanded and revised, attracted attention in Europe. The third edition was translated into English, French, Spanish, Swedish, and Russian in 1924 and was then widely read for the first time. The first English translation correctly referred to the idea of "continental displacement," as Wegener had termed it. The name "continental drift" was coined later.

Wegener was not the first to come up with the idea of continental drift. In 1620, English philosopher and author Francis Bacon noted the physical similarities between the American and African coasts. In 1858 Antonio Snider-Pellegrini published a book that described the breaking up of a giant continent, accompanied by deluges and other biblical catastrophes; his work sunk into relative oblivion. In 1910 German physicist Frank Bursey Taylor published a carefully worked-out hypothesis that anticipated Wegener's theory by two years. But Taylor's paper did not address the mechanism of continental movement and thus had little impact on the geological community.

Wegener's was the first coherent and logical argument for continental drift that was also supported by concrete evidence. He proposed that a huge supercontinent had once existed, which he named Pangaea, meaning "all land." He suggested that Pangaea was surrounded by a supersea, Panthalassa, and that two hundred million years ago, in the Mesozoic period, Pangaea began to rift into separate continents that moved away from each other. The Americas drifted westward from Europe and Africa, forming the Atlantic Ocean. India moved east from Africa, and Australia severed its ties with Antarctica and moved towards the equator.

Wegener's hypothesis departed radically from the accepted view of the earth in his day. Other geologists believed that the earth was still cooling and contracting from a molten mass, and that lighter rocks such as granite (termed "sial"), moved towards the surface, underlain by denser rocks such as basalt ("sima"). Mountain ranges, they believed, were produced by the cooling contraction, like wrinkles appearing on a drying fruit. To these scientists, the continents and the ocean basins were initial and set features. It seemed impossible for continents to move through the ocean rocks.

Wegener instead proposed that the lighter sial that made up continents could move horizontally through the oceanic sima; if the continents can rise up vertically, he argued, they must be able to move horizontally as well, as long as sufficient force is provided. Thus the Rocky Mountains and the Andes, on the western edges of the Americas, were formed by the resistance of the sima layer to the continents plowing through them. Island arcs like Japan and the West Indies were fragments left behind in the wake of these giant drifting continents.

Wegener's strongest argument was the similarities of rocks, animals, and plants on both sides of the Atlantic. He pointed to the fossils of several reptiles and flora that were known only in Africa and South America, and to the fact that the distribution of some living animals was hard to explain unless the continents had once been connected. Scientists had previously explained these in terms of a land bridge that had once connected the continents and then sunk into the ocean. Wegener argued that this was impossible; if a bridge was made of sial, it could not simply sink and disappear.

However, Wegener couldn't find an adequate mechanism to explain continental drift. He suggested two mechanisms, which were later disproved. One was *Pohlflucht*, or "flight from the poles," to explain why continents seemed to drift towards the equator. *Pohlflucht*, also known as the Eötvös force, came from the fact that the earth is an oblate spheroid, slightly flattened at the poles and bulging at the equator. Second, Wegener had to explain the westward movement of the Americas; he suggested that some kind of tidal force must be doing the work.

Reactions to Wegener's Hypothesis: Then and Now

Wegener's hypothesis was received with ridicule. For decades, other geologists scoffed at the idea of drifting continents. Some scientists supported him, but there was not enough geological evidence to prove beyond a doubt that he was essentially right. Wegener's first critic was his father-in-law, Köppen, who apparently wanted Wegener to stay in meteorology and not wander into unknown areas like geophysics. At the first lecture in Frankfurt in 1912, some geologists were apparently indignant at the very notion of continental drift. The initial reaction was mixed at best and hostile at worst. In 1922, when *The Origin of Continents and Oceans* first appeared in English, it was blasted in a critical review and at a scientific meeting. Subsequently continental drift provoked a huge international debate, with scientists ranging themselves on both sides.

Detractors had plenty of ammunition. It was soon shown that *Pohlflucht* and tidal forces were about one millionth as powerful as they needed to be to move continents. The paleontological evidence was thought to be inconclusive. In 1928, at a meeting of fourteen eminent geologists, seven opposed it, five supported it without reservation, and two supported it with reservations. From then until after World War II, the subject was put on the back burner of scientific debate. In the only major variant on the theory, South African geologist Alex du Toit, a vigorous defender of continental drift, proposed in 1937 that instead of Pangaea there were two supercontinents, Laurasia in the northern hemisphere and Gondwanaland in the south.

Many eminent geologists, such as **Sir Harold Jeffreys** in England and, later, American paleontologist George Gaylord Simpson, were vehement critics of Wegener and his continental drift theory. Science historians consider it likely that the prestige of the critics often carried too much weight in the argument over the theory itself. Wegener himself often complained about the narrow-mindedness of geophysicists who could not accept new ideas. In 1926 Wegener was finally given a professorship in meteorology and geophysics at the University of Graz. Four years later he sailed from Copenhagen to Greenland as leader of a major expedition. On November 1 of that year, he and others in the party celebrated his fiftieth birthday at a camp in the center of the Greenland ice cap. Wegener headed for the west coast that day, and apparently died of heart failure. His body was later found about halfway between the two camps.

After World War II, and several decades after Wegener's disappearance, other geologists began to uncover clues that eventually led to the plate tectonics revolution. The development of paleomagnetism in the early 1950s demonstrated that rocks in different continents appeared to have different directions of magnetization, as if continents had drifted apart from each other. In addition, oceanographers began to map the ocean floor to learn about its origin. They learned that the ocean floor was not a fixed glob of sima at all. In 1960, American geologist **Harry Hammond Hess** proposed the theory of seafloor spreading: that the ocean floor is constantly being created at underwater ridges in the middle of the oceans, spreading outward, and being consumed in trenches underneath the continents. By the mid 1960s, new data on magnetic anomalies in the Pacific Ocean revealed that seafloor spreading did indeed occur. Here was the mechanism by which Wegener's continents could drift: The ocean floor was constantly regenerating itself. By the end of the 1960s, continental drift had begun to be accepted by the entire earth science community. It had taken half a century, but Wegener's hypothesis became the foundation for a revolution among geologists and a cornerstone for modern views of the earth's history.

SELECTED WRITINGS BY WEGENER:

Books

Thermodynamik der Atmosphäre, Leipzig, 1911.

Die Entstehung der Kontinente und Ozeane, Brunswick, 1915, fourth revised edition translated by John Biram as *The Origin of Continents and Oceans,* Dover Publications, 1966.

SOURCES:

Books

Hallam, *A Revolution in the Earth Sciences: From Continental Drift to Plate Tectonics,* Clarendon Press, 1973.
Hallam, Anthony, *Great Geological Controversies,* Oxford University Press, 1983.
LeGrand, H. E., *Drifting Continents and Shifting Theories,* Cambridge University Press, 1988.
Marvin, Ursula B., *Continental Drift: The Evolution of a Concept,* Smithsonian Institution Press, 1973.

—*Sketch by Alexandra Witze*

Franz Weidenreich
1873-1948
German anatomist and physical anthropologist

Most closely associated with the study of Peking man (the name given to early human remains found in Asia), Franz Weidenreich earned a reputation as an exceptionally thorough and meticulous cataloger of human fossils, as well as one of the most prolific writers on the subject. He studied the source of human evolution from what he believed to be a single common ancestor through various racial developments, influenced by environment and other factors, to modern human beings. Weidenreich's work helped establish current knowledge of human evolution.

Born on June 7, 1873, in Edenkoben, Palatinate, Germany, Weidenreich was the youngest of the four children of Carl Weidenreich and Frederike Esesheimer. He received his early education at the Landau Humanist Gymnasium and later attended the universities of Munich, Kiel, and Berlin. He received his M.D. from the University of Strassburg in 1899, where he taught anatomy from 1899 until 1918; he became a professor there in 1904. At Strassburg he studied under Gustav Schwalbe, a prominent specialist in the study of Neanderthal humans. He also served as president of the democratic party of Alsace-

Lorraine during World War I but was expelled from France in 1918 because he was a German national.

In the field of anatomy, Weidenreich specialized in the study of blood cells, the hemopoietic and lymphatic systems, and the central nervous system. It was his studies of skeletal anatomy, however, that led him to anthropology through his investigation of locomotion, posture, and bone structure as they related to human evolution. He became professor of anthropology at the University of Heidelberg from 1921 until 1924 and held the same post at the University of Frankfurt from 1928 until 1933, at which time he was removed from his position by the Nazis because he was Jewish. Leaving Germany, he had a brief tenure at the University of Chicago; this was followed by a position at the Peking Union Medical College, replacing **Davidson Black**, who had died suddenly. There he began his studies of the early human remains found in China, concentrating on the dentition, jawbones, and skull. During this period he also published a study of three *Homo sapiens* skulls from sites at Choukoutien, China.

Examines Link between Early Human Forms and Modern Humans

Weidenreich believed that the development of modern human types resulted from the evolution of a number of major lineages from a single ancestral group. He proposed that isolated populations evolved from groups that had already become differentiated into "racial" types. Although he acknowledged the effects of genetic mixing resulting from migration, he felt that remnants of the original genetic material could be found in modern populations.

In addition to its concern with the origin of racial types in modern humans, much of the research on human evolution during this period was devoted to the discovery of the links between the earliest human forms and modern man. Part of the theoretical investigation of the link between the earliest remains then known and modern humans was concerned with the position of the Neanderthals. Although most paleontologists now see the Neanderthals as an evolutionary dead end, some scientists early in the twentieth century—including Weidenreich's teacher, Schwalbe—held to the so-called Neanderthal-phase theory, which posited that Neanderthals were a distinct species that was transitional between *Homo erectus* forms and modern *Homo sapiens*. This belief formed the basis for Weidenreich's own view. Such a linear view of human evolution came under increasing attack during the 1930s as more fossil evidence became available and seemed to indicate otherwise. Others adopted the view that the Neanderthals were not ancestral to modern humans but rather had been displaced by a more advanced population with more sophisticated tools. This scheme, known as the presa-

piens theory, dominated paleontology in the years between the world wars; it postulated an earlier development of modern humans than the Neanderthal-phase theory and was based in part on the belief that there had not been enough evolutionary time for the Neanderthals to develop into modern humans.

Weidenreich's initial study of human fossil remains, in 1926, focused on the Neanderthal skull found at Ehringsdorf in 1925. Weidenreich's theory, first presented in 1928, held that early Neanderthal types migrated out of Africa after they had already developed "racial" distinctions. The groups in various parts of the world continued to undergo development, producing the various racial varieties existing today. He based his theory in part on the perception that there were morphological similarities between specific fossil remains and certain modern populations—what he called local regional continuity.

Partakes in Study of Peking Man

When Weidenreich began his investigation into human evolution, remains found in Java, designated *Pithecanthropus erectus* and popularly known as Java man, comprised the bulk of human fossil remains discovered up to that time. In the late 1920s Davidson Black had discovered a fossilized human tooth in Zhoukoudien (then called Choukoutien), southwest of Beijing, that was from approximately the same era as the *Pithecanthropus* remains and assigned it the designation *Sinanthropus pekinensis* (Peking man). (Both *Pithecanthropus* and *Sinanthropus* are now considered examples of *Homo erectus*.) Further finds in 1928 and many more between 1929 and 1932, including a complete skull, along with signs that the remains were indeed human (stone tools and evidence of fire), contributed to the creation of a new prehistoric figure in the scientific and popular communities: Peking man. These *Sinanthropus* remains became the focus of Weidenreich's detailed study, an endeavor that produced an extensive series of monographs, including *The Mandibles of Sinanthropus pekinensis* (1936), *The Dentition of Sinanthropus pekinensis* (1937), *The Extremity Bonds of Sinanthropus pekinensis* (1941), and *The Skull of Sinanthropus pekinensis* (1943). Publication of these works was fortunate, as the specimens themselves, packed for shipment to the United States, were apparently destroyed during the Japanese invasion of China in the 1940s.

Discovery of the *Sinanthropus* specimens in China rekindled interest in the *Pithecanthropus* remains found in Java, and additional discoveries by Ralph von Koenigswald during the 1930s of *Pithecanthropus* led Weidenreich to comparative studies of the two. He theorized that they were not separate species but rather variants of a form ancestral to the Neanderthals and therefore to modern humans. He held that there was at no time more than one species of human living concurrently. Significantly, he stated that these variants represented racial distinctions maintained throughout the subsequent stages of evolution. In Weidenreich's model, there was a single path of hominid descent consisting of parallel lines representing racial variants; these developed from the early hominids to modern humans independently, each going through the same evolutionary phases, all with increasing cranial capacity and increasingly erect posture, and maintaining their racial distinctions to the present day. He defined three phases of human development: the Archanthropine of approximately one million years ago, representing the period of *Pithecanthropus erectus* and *Sinanthropus pekinensis;* the Paleoanthropine (the period of the Neanderthals); and the Neoanthropine, which includes subsequent evolutions up to modern man. He divided modern humans into four major groups: Australian, Mongolian, African, and Eurasian, and theorized that modern Europeans were descended from a western subgroup of the Asian Neanderthals.

In Weidenreich's best-known book, *Apes, Giants, and Man* (1946), he theorized that before the separation of humans into various "racial" types, the common ancestor of modern humans was a massive creature—especially in regard to its skull and jaw. This conclusion was corroborated by evidence derived from the so-called Solo skulls, the subject of Weidenreich's last phase of research.

From 1941 until his death on July 11, 1948, Weidenreich was associated with the American Museum of Natural History in New York. In 1947 he was awarded the Viking Fund Medal for his work in physical anthropology. At the time of his death, he was married, with three daughters, to the former Matilda Neuberger.

SELECTED WRITINGS BY WEIDENREICH:

Books

Apes, Giants, and Man, University of Chicago Press, 1946.

Periodicals

"Facts and Speculations Concerning the Origin of Homo Sapiens," *American Anthropologist,* Volume 49, 1947, pp. 187–203.
"The Trend of Human Evolution," *Evolution,* Volume 1, 1947, pp. 221–36.

SOURCES:

Books

Bowler, Peter J, *Theories of Human Evolution: A Century of Debate 1844–1944,* Johns Hopkins University Press, 1986.

Gregory, W. K., "Franz Weidenreich, 1873–1948," *Anthropological Papers of Franz Weidenreich 1939–1948,* edited by S. L. Washburn and Davida Wolffson, Viking Fund, 1949, pp. 251–56.
Smith, Fred H., and Frank Spencer, *The Origins of Modern Humans: A World Survey of the Fossil Evidence,* Alan R. Liss, 1984.

Periodicals

Howells, W. W., "Franz Weidenreich, 1873–1948," *American Journal of Physical Anthropology,* Volume 56, 1981, pp. 407–10.

—*Sketch by Michael Sims*

André Weil
1906-
French mathematician

André Weil is responsible for important advances in algebraic geometry, group theory, and number theory and belonged to the group of French mathematicians who published many important works under the collective pseudonym of Nicolas Bourbaki. Many of his peers in the 1950s considered him the finest living mathematician in the world. In 1980, he was presented with the Barnard Medal by Columbia University; prior recipients of the medal, which is awarded every five years, include **Albert Einstein**, **Ernest Rutherford**, and **Neils Bohr**. The prize recognizes outstanding accomplishment in physical or astronomical science or a scientific application of great benefit to humanity.

Weil was born May 6, 1906, in Paris, France, to free-thinking Jewish parents. His father, Bernard, was a physician, and his mother, Selma Reinherz Weil, came from a cultured Russian family. His sister was the famous writer, social critic, and World War II French Resistance activist, Simone Weil. When he was eight years old, Weil happened upon a geometry book and began to read it for recreation. By the time he was nine, he was absorbed in mathematics and was solving difficult problems. In her biography of Weil's sister, Simone Pétrement quotes Weil's mother as saying that at nine years of age André "is so happy that he has given up all play and spends hours immersed in his calculations." Weil's father was drafted into the military in 1914, and the family accompanied him to various medical assignments around France during World War I. At age sixteen,

Weil was accepted at the elite Ecole Normale Supérieure in Paris, where he received his doctorate in 1928. He also studied at the Sorbonne, the University of Göttingen, and the University of Rome. From 1930 to 1932, he taught at the Aligarh Muslim University in India. From 1933 to 1940, he was a professor of mathematics at the University of Strasbourg in France. In 1937, he married.

Weil was in Finland with his wife when France entered World War II. He believed that he could do France more good as a mathematician and refused to return to his home country and join the army. He was walking near an anti-aircraft gun emplacement when the Russians invaded Finland, and the Finns arrested him, thinking that he was a spy. The letters to Russian mathematicians in his room did not help his case, and for a while it appeared that he would be executed. The Finns, however, released Weil to the Swedes, who sent him to England, from where he returned to France to be imprisoned and tried for not reporting for military service. He was tried on May 3, 1940 and convicted, and he asked to be sent to the front. The court obliged, and he was to be sent to an infantry unit along the English Channel at Cherbourg. Weil's boat, however, wound up in a British port, and he made his way back to France later in 1940. He soon rejoined his wife, Eveline, and they escaped the war to the United States. Their daughter, Sylvie, was born on September 12, 1942. Weil taught at Haverford and Swarthmore colleges in the United States in 1941 and 1942, and at the University of São Paulo in Brazil from 1945 to 1947.

In 1947, Weil was recruited to the mathematics department at the University of Chicago, where he taught until 1958. One of his colleagues at Chicago was Irving Kaplansky, who gives a sense of Weil's personality in *More Mathematical People:* "There we were at Chicago, lucky enough to have André Weil, one of the greatest mathematicians in the world. There were several times in my life that I've, one way or another, got that feeling, my gosh, here is a tremendous mathematician.... He was very impatient with what he regarded as incompetence." Kaplansky added, "Then there is his extraordinary quickness.... You can take an area of mathematics that he presumably never heard of before and just like that he'll have something to say about it." From 1958 until his retirement, Weil taught at the Institute for Advanced Study at Princeton.

Reveals Discovery of "Uniform Space"

Weil's mathematical innovations are highly technical and involve complex formulas. One of his discoveries was the concept of "uniform space," a kind of mathematical space that cannot be readily visualized like the three-dimensional space that we occupy in our daily lives. The *Science News Letter* pronounced Weil's discovery of uniform space one of the most important mathematical discoveries of 1939. In 1947, Weil developed some formulas in the field of algebraic geometry, which are known as the "Weil conjectures." Weil's conjectures, as Ian Stewart explains in *Scientific American,* "give formulas for the number of solutions to an algebraic equation in a finite field. In particular they allow one to deduce that a given equation does or does not have solutions; this information can be transferred to analogous equations involving integers or algebraic numbers.... [T]hey are of fundamental importance in algebraic geometry."

Weil's algebraic and geometrical innovations of the first half of the twentieth century were especially important for the technological innovations of the second half of the twentieth century. Complex computer software that models black holes for astronomers, scientific graphics for research physicists, and special effects visualizations for Hollywood filmmakers all rely in part on mathematical innovations in algebra and geometry. As the *Science News Letter* said in 1939, in the decades to come, mathematical innovations like Weil's may lead to "some concept that will illumine the universe as glimpsed by the 200-inch telescope or the atom as created or smashed by the powerful cyclotron."

Becomes Involved with Influential Group

In the mid–1930s, Weil and other important young French mathematicians—among them Jean Dieudonné, Claude Chevallier, and Henri Cartan—began to write a series of mathematical works under the pseudonym of Nicolas Bourbaki. As Paul Halmos said in *Scientific American,* one writer called Bourbaki a "polycephalic mathematician." The group has varied in number from ten to twenty and has been composed, predominantly, of those of French nationality. Their purpose was quite serious: to write a series of books about such fundamental mathematical areas as set theory, algebra, and topology. The resulting series of books, which to date number over thirty, was called the *Elements of Mathematics.* As Halmos said, "The main features of the Bourbaki approach are a radical attitude about the right order for doing things, a dogmatic insistence on a privately invented terminology, a clean and economical organization of ideas, and a style of presentation which is so bent on saying everything that it leaves nothing to the imagination." Their work has been very thorough (for example, it took them two hundred pages to define the number "1") and influential. Among other things, they inspired the "new math" that was introduced into American schools in the 1960s.

While their purpose is serious, the Bourbakians cultivate an atmosphere of mystery about their identities: they attempt to keep their names secret, they like to make up stories about themselves, and they love pranks. One story about their origin, which could well be a hoax, is that they got the idea for their name from the annual visit of a character named Nicolas Bourbaki to the Ecole Normale Supérieure, where many of them were educated. This character was an actor who gave a mock-serious lecture on mathematics in double-talk. Some of their own double-talk consists of saying that the home institution of Nicolas Bourbaki is the "University of Nancago," a fusion of the Universities of Nancy and Chicago, where several members of the group teach. Another story reported is that the name was inspired by General Charles Denis Sauter Bourbaki, a colorful figure in the Franco-Prussian war. One of the group's pranks was to apply for a membership to the American Mathematical Society under the name of N. Bourbaki. They played another prank on Ralph P. Boas, the executive editor of *Mathematical Reviews.* Boas had said in one of the *Encyclopedia Britannica*'s annual *Book of the Year* volumes that Nicolas Bourbaki did not exist. The Bourbakians sent a letter to the editors of the *Britannica* complaining about Boas's charge. Later, as Paul Halmos said in *Scientific American,* the Bourbakians "circulated a rumor that Boas did not exist. Boas, said Bourbaki, is the collective pseudonym of a group of young American mathematicians who act jointly as the editors of *Mathematical Reviews.*"

SELECTED WRITINGS BY WEIL:

Books

Foundations of Algebraic Geometry, American Mathematical Society, 1946.
Basic Number Theory, 3rd edition, Springer-Verlag, 1974.
Number Theory, Birkhäuser, 1984.

SOURCES:

Books

Albers, Donald J., Gerald Alexanderson, and Constance Reid, *More Mathematical People,* Harcourt, 1990.
Pétrement, Simone, *Simone Weil: A Life,* translated by Raymond Rosenthal, Pantheon, 1976.

Periodicals

Halmos, Paul R., "Nicolas Bourbaki," *Scientific American,* May, 1957, pp. 88–99.
"New Kind of Space, Year's Discovery in Mathematics," *Science News Letter,* January 21, 1939, pp. 45–46.

Stewart, Ian, "Gauss," *Scientific American,* July, 1977, pp. 122–131.

—*Sketch by Patrick Moore*

Robert A. Weinberg
1942-
American molecular biologist and biochemist

Robert A. Weinberg has made important discoveries in the field of cancer research. Along with colleagues, he produced tumors in healthy mice by transferring individual, cancer-causing genes, called oncogenes, to normal cells. These oncogenes were almost indistinguishable from normal genes—in some cases, the difference between a normal gene and an oncogene was a single amino acid along the chain. Weinberg used new forms of genetic engineering to isolate genes in the cells of human tumors. He demonstrated that these oncogenes, when introduced into normal mouse cells grown in a laboratory environment, modified the normal cells and made them cancerous. This work was of great importance to cancer research, as it shifted the focus of biomedical research to investigations at the molecular level. Medical researchers had previously thought cancer was caused in several different ways: by chemical carcinogens, tumor viruses, and radiation. Weinberg's work with oncogenes made it apparent that normal cells have genes with malignant potential, and that those previously mentioned causes of cancer must be viewed in terms of their effect in activating genes that exist in a dormant state in normal cells.

Robert Allan Weinberg was born in Pittsburgh, Pennsylvania, on November 11, 1942. He was the son of dentist Fritz E. Weinberg and Lore (Reichhardt) Weinberg, who both had escaped Nazi Germany and emigrated to the United States in 1938. Weinberg studied at the Massachusetts Institute of Technology, receiving a B.S. in 1964, an M.A. in 1965, and a Ph.D. in 1969, all in biology. He also worked as an instructor in biology at Stillman College in Tuscaloosa, Alabama, from 1965 to 1966. Upon graduation, Weinberg went to Israel where he spent two years as a research fellow at the Weizmann Institute in Rehovoth, working with Dr. Ernest Winocour. He received a fellowship from the Helen Hay Whitney Foundation in 1970, and worked with Dr. **Renato Dulbecco** as a fellow of the Salk Institute in LaJolla, California, from 1970 to 1972. Returning to MIT as a research associate in 1972, he began work with Dr. **David Baltimore**.

Before the 1970s, scientists had spent much time searching for viruses as the cause of cancer. But in spite of all efforts, researchers could not establish a connection between viruses and the great majority of human cancers. Then cancer research began to take another direction—this was the beginning of the scientific search for oncogenes.

From 1972 to 1973, Weinberg also worked as an assistant professor in the Department of Biology and at the Center for Cancer Research at MIT. He received the resident scholar award from the American Cancer Society from 1974 to 1977. In 1976, he was promoted to associate professor at MIT; he was also designated as Rita Allen Foundation scholar from 1976 to 1980.

DNA Transfer Yields Results

Weinberg tackled the problem of oncogenes in his own way. By the late 1970s, although about a dozen oncogenes had been identified, no one had managed to prove that these oncogenes could cause cancer without the presence of a virus to activate them. Weinberg finally demonstrated this in 1980. Taking DNA from active cancer cells in humans, he transferred it into normal mouse cells. The altered cells became cancerous.

Weinberg's next step was to attempt to identify particular genes as the oncogenes associated with specific cancers in humans. In 1981 he and his colleagues were able to identify genes for human leukemia, as well as colon and bladder cancers. Once the molecular basis of carcinogenesis had been established, and once it was possible to isolate and characterize specific oncogenes, it still remained to analyze those genes in exact structural detail, to find out precisely what changes in the DNA had induced the normal cell to behave differently.

Weinberg, through cloning bladder and lung cancer oncogenes in 1981, proved that the transforming genes are actually present in normal cells, but are either dormant or active at much lower levels, until they are activated or stimulated by some change. This activation might come about as a response to a seemingly insignificant change—in theory, a carcinogen might affect the gene, causing a slightly different amino acid protein to be manufactured along the chain, and somehow disrupting the cell's normal regulatory mechanism. This implied that there might be a two-step system for developing cancer: first, the creation of an oncogene, and second, an exposure to a carcinogen of some sort, perhaps even years later. And this two-step system, if accurate, might offer some explanation for the fact that the incidence of cancer increases with advancing age.

In 1982, Weinberg was promoted to professor of biology at MIT. During that same year, he was made

Millard Schult lecturer at Massachusetts General Hospital, became a member of the Whitehead Institute for Biomedical Research, and was named 1982 Scientist of the Year by *Discover* Magazine. In 1983, while teaching at MIT, he was awarded the Warren Triennial Prize and the Robert Koch Foundation Medal (Bonn, Germany). In 1984, Weinberg was the recipient of the National Academy of Science's Armand Hammer Cancer Foundation Award and U.S. Steel Foundation Award, as well as the Howard Taylor Ricketts Award from the University of Chicago Medical Center, the Brown-Hazen Award from the New York State Department of Health, and the Antonio Feltrinelli Prize from Academia Lincei in Rome. He also received the Bristol-Meyer Award for Distinguished Achievement in Cancer Research, and was awarded an honorary doctorate by Northwestern University.

In 1985 Weinberg was made honorary professor of biology by the American Cancer Society. He received the Katherine Berkann Judd Award from the Memorial Sloan-Kettering Cancer Center in 1986, the Sloan Prize from General Motors Cancer Research Foundation in 1987, and was made a member of the MIT Medical Consumers Advisory Committee in 1988, at which time he was also the recipient of an honorary doctorate from State University of New York at Stonybrook.

The next year, 1989, brought Weinberg yet another honorary doctorate, this time from City University, New York. He became a member of the Committee on Biological Warfare, Federation of American Scientists, and received the Lucy Wortham James Award from the Society of Surgical Oncologists. In 1990, Weinberg was given the Research Recognition Award by the Samuel Roberts Noble Foundation, the distinguished basic scientist award by the Milken Family Medical Foundation, and the Lila Gruber cancer research award by the American Academy of Dermatology.

Weinberg married Amy Shulman, a teacher, in 1976, and they had two children: Aron and Leah Rosa. Weinberg has many other interests in addition to science. He built his own vacation house in New Hampshire, literally from the ground up. He cleared the land himself, then framed the house and created a garden. He is also interested in genealogy.

SELECTED WRITINGS BY WEINBERG:

Books

Selected Abstracts on DNA Viral Transforming Proteins, [Bethesda, MD], 1983.
Selected Abstracts on Protein Kinases Associated with Growth, Differentiation, and Transformation, [Bethesda, MD], 1983.

Periodicals

"The Dark Side of the Genome," *Technology Review,* April, 1991, pp. 44–48.
"Tumor Supressor Genes," *Science,* November 22, 1991, pp. 1138–1139.

SOURCES:

Periodicals

NY Times Magazine, October 24, 1982, p. 39.
Science News, November 13, 1982, p. 316.

—*Sketch by Jessica Jahiel*

Steven Weinberg
1933-
American physicist

Steven Weinberg shared the 1979 Nobel Prize in physics with **Sheldon Glashow** and **Abdus Salam** for his contributions to the development of a theory unifying the electromagnetic and weak forces, two of the four forces governing nature. He predicted that one of the three particles inherent in the weak force could be found in "neutral currents." Its subsequent discovery in 1983 may have brought scientists one step closer to a unified theory of the universe.

Weinberg was born in New York City on May 3, 1933, to Frederick Weinberg, a court stenographer, and the former Eva Israel. Weinberg's early interests in science were nurtured both at home and at the world-famous Bronx High School of Science, from which he graduated in 1950. Like Glashow, his classmate at the Bronx High School, Weinberg decided to major in physics at Cornell University, graduating with a B.A. in 1954. He then spent a year at the Niels Bohr Institute (formerly the Institute for Theoretical Physics) in Copenhagen, studying under the noted theoretical physicist Gunner Källén. In 1955, Weinberg returned to the United States and Princeton University, where he began his doctoral research under Samuel Treiman; he was awarded a Ph.D. for his thesis on weak interactions in 1957.

Weinberg took teaching positions at Columbia University from 1957 to 1959, the Lawrence Berkeley Laboratories of the University of California from 1959 to 1969, the Massachusetts Institute of Technology (MIT) from 1969 to 1973, and Harvard Universi-

ty in 1973, where he replaced **Julian Schwinger** as Eugene Higgins Professor of Physics. He took a concurrent position beginning in 1973 at the Smithsonian Astrophysical Observatory, where he served as senior scientist. During much of this period, Weinberg was engaged in a relatively wide variety of research, including studies on muon physics, scattering theory, broken symmetries, and Feynman graphs.

Weinberg Focuses on Problems of the Electroweak Force

For nearly half a century, physicists had recognized the existence of four fundamental forces: gravity, the strong nuclear force, the weak nuclear force, and electromagnetism. At no time, however, were physicists entirely convinced that these forces acted as separate entities. In fact, there had been a continuing effort to find a theory allying the four forces into a single fundamental force. A model of that nature had already been conceived during the mid-nineteenth century by James Clerk Maxwell, who showed that two apparently different kinds of forces, the electrical and magnetic forces, were actually two manifestations of a single, more basic electromagnetic force.

By the early 1960s, efforts toward unification were directed specifically at finding ways of relating the electromagnetic and weak forces. Electromagnetism causes such phenomena as sunlight and radio waves, and the weak force operates over very short distances within the nucleus and is responsible for some forms of radioactive decay. The theories put forth all assumed that while the electromagnetic and weak forces are clearly distinct at energy levels we encounter in everyday life, they are indistinguishable at much greater energies, such as those encountered in cosmic rays and the most powerful particle accelerators.

Between 1960 and 1968 a theory unifying the electromagnetic and weak forces was developed independently by Weinberg, Pakistani physicist Salam, and, to an extent, by Glashow. There were a number of ways in which the premises and conclusions of these theories could be tested, including the detection of "neutral currents." Weinberg in 1971 had indicated that in the collisions of neutrinos and matter, a neutral current was produced which contained one of the three weak force carrying particles. In 1973, experiments at the European Center for Nuclear Research (CERN) confirmed the existence of these currents, and a decade later, the three types of particles were detected in further experiments carried out at CERN by a group headed by the Italian and Dutch physicists **Carlo Rubbia** and **Simon van der Meer.** For their contributions to the development of the electroweak theory, Weinberg, Glashow, and Salam were jointly awarded the 1979 Nobel Prize in physics.

Weinberg has continued to work on a wide variety of topics in physics and cosmology. In 1974, with Howard Georgi and Helen Quinn, he made the first estimate of the energy at which the strong, weak, and electromagnetic forces would all be unified. In 1982, Weinberg joined the physics and astronomy departments of the University of Texas at Austin as Josey Regental Professor of Science.

Weinberg was married on July 6, 1954, to Louise Goldwasser, a professor of law. The couple has one daughter, Elizabeth. Weinberg's numerous honors include the 1977 Dannie Heineman Prize of the American Physical Society, the 1979 Elliott Cresson Medal of the Franklin Institute, election to the Royal Society of London in 1981, the 1992 National Medal of Science, and many honorary doctoral degrees. Weinberg, who left Harvard in 1983 to become Josey Professor of Science at the University of Texas at Austin, lists his primary leisure time interest as reading history and walking in the Austin Hills.

SELECTED WRITINGS BY WEINBERG:

Books

Gravitation and Cosmology: Principles and Applications of the General Theory of Relativity, Wiley, 1972.
The First Three Minutes: A Modern View of the Origin of the Universe, Basic Books, 1977.
The Discovery of Subatomic Particles, W. H. Freeman, 1983.
Dreams of a Final Theory, Pantheon, 1993.

Periodicals

"A Model of Leptons," *Physical Review Letters,* Volume 19, 1967, p. 1264.
"Recent Progress in Gauge Theories of the Weak, Electromagnetic and Strong Interactions," *Reviews of Modern Physics,* Volume 46, 1974, pp. 255–77.

SOURCES:

Books

McGraw-Hill Modern Scientists and Engineers, Volume 10, McGraw-Hill, 1980, pp. 286–287.
Pioneers of Science: Nobel Prize Winners in Physics, American Institute of Physics, 1980, pp. 261–262.

Periodicals

Coleman, Sidney, "The 1979 Nobel Prize in Physics," *Science,* December 14, 1979, pp. 1290–1291.

"Nobel Prizes: To Glashow, Salam and Weinberg for Physics . . . ," *Physics Today,* December, 1979, pp. 17–19.
"Nobels for Getting It Together in Physics," *New Scientist,* October 18, 1979, pp. 163–164.

—*Sketch by David E. Newton*

Wilhelm Weinberg
1862-1937
German geneticist

Wilhelm Weinberg was an obstetrician in private practice who used his experience delivering babies for gathering data and wrote a number of pioneering papers on genetics and medical statistics. At the beginning of the twentieth century, he was one of the first to apply Gregor Mendel's laws of heredity to observable human characteristics. Working independently for most of his life, Weinberg collected data on multiple births, genetic diseases, and mortality, and he used these statistics to derive generalized mathematical laws and statistical relationships. The most notable of these, the Hardy-Weinberg law, is now widely used to predict gene frequencies within a population, and it has become one of the fundamental laws of genetics.

Weinberg was born December 25, 1862 in Stuttgart, Germany. His father, Julius Weinberg, was a cloth merchant and a member of Stuttgart's Jewish middle class; Wilhelm Weinberg and his mother, the former Maria Magdelena Humbert, were Protestant. Weinberg attended secondary school at the Stuttgart Realgymnasium, then enrolled as a medical student at the University of Tübingen. He finished his academic career at the University of Munich, where he received his medical degree in 1886, and he began his clinical work as a medical assistant in Berlin, Frankfurt, and Vienna. In 1889, Weinberg returned home to Stuttgart, where he established a practice in general medicine and obstetrics.

Medical Practice Stimulates Interest in Genetics

Over the course of his career, Weinberg supervised a large number of twin births. This experience not only established him as an authority on obstetrics but also stimulated his interest in heredity, especially concerning families which had experienced multiple births. He was initially interested in the differences between twins who were identical and twins who were fraternal, as well as the question of whether a woman could inherit a tendency to give birth to twins. In 1901, Weinberg wrote his first important paper on heredity, in which he developed the "difference method"—a mathematical rule that geneticists could use to determine the proportion of identical versus fraternal twin births within a population, simply by knowing the number of same-sex twin pairs. Weinberg did not invent the difference method and he acknowledged that it had been used previously, but he was the first to use the method without unnecessary alteration of data. Weinberg also discovered a number of differences between fraternal and identical twins, and he concluded that women could inherit a tendency to bear fraternal twins but not identical twins.

In the early twentieth century, new attention paid to the work of Gregor Mendel was transforming the field of genetics. In 1866, Mendel had determined that observable biological traits are passed down from generation to generation according to certain proportional laws. Weinberg became interested in Mendelism through Valentin Haecker, a Stuttgart zoologist and associate of renowned geneticist August Weismann, and he began looking for ways to apply it to his work. Since his medical practice brought him into contact with hundreds of families, and he witnessed the creation of new generations on a daily basis, Weinberg decided to explore the ways in which Mendelian laws influenced the genetic relationships between family members, thus testing Mendel's equations on observable human characteristics.

Weinberg would publish over 220 papers in his career, but between 1908 and 1910 he wrote four of the most important. These publications represented his attempts to apply the mathematical laws of Mendelian genetics to his statistical observations. Mendel had determined that genetic characteristics, whether rare or common, appear in the population according to predictable laws and occur in particular proportions. Weinberg expanded this notion to demonstrate that over several generations of a randomly mating population, one may consistently predict the frequency of an inherited trait according to a mathematical law, called the law of equilibrium. In 1904, British geneticist **Karl Pearson** had published an equilibrium law for special cases of Mendelian genetics, but in January 1908 Weinberg generalized Pearson's rule for all populations, and in doing so laid the foundation for modern genetics. A few months later, **Godfrey Harold Hardy**, an English mathematics professor at Cambridge University, independently published a similar finding, and the equilibrium law eventually became known as the Hardy-Weinberg formula.

Weinberg also applied his new knowledge of Mendelian genetics to older studies he had done on multiple births. In several of his earlier experiments on multiple births, Weinberg had pointed to his data as proof of "blending inheritance," which is incompatible with Mendelism. Now he was able to demonstrate that the tendency to bear twins, for example, could be inherited as a recessive trait (a weaker genetic characteristic, often masked). He was also one of the first geneticists to apply equilibrium laws and Mendelian proportions to common human traits, rather than unusual ones such as albinism or rare birth defects. In addition, he was the first to distinguish between genetic and environmental factors in the variance of observed characteristics between close relatives—work which anticipated the research of well-known population biologists **Ronald A. Fisher** and **Sewall Wright** by several years. For his work in medicine and genetics, Weinberg was awarded the title of Sanitätsrat by the King of Württemberg in 1911.

Weinberg changed the face of genetics over the span of only three years, and he continued to produce original ideas even after his most prolific period. In 1912, he made a significant contribution not only to the analysis of statistical data but also to the methodology which determined how that data should be collected. Weinberg published useful new techniques for ascertainment, the process of ensuring that statistical data truly represent a random selection of individuals. For Weinberg's research on the frequency of twin births, for example, he realized that if he only counted births within families of women who had already given birth to twins, he must subtract that original twin birth from his statistics to have a truly random sample. In other words, to determine the correct proportion of a certain observable trait, a researcher must use the ratio of affected to nonaffected persons only among the siblings of someone who is already affected—otherwise the researcher is guilty of unintentional selection of data. This simple trick was called the sibling method, and was adapted by Munich psychiatrist Ernst Rüdin to become a fundamental procedure in German psychiatry.

In addition to his landmark discoveries in population genetics, Weinberg was also instrumental in the gradual refinement of the methods of medical statistics. He was an expert at analysis as well as collection of data, and he was responsible for correcting several long-standing but mistaken assumptions in the interpretation of data. He also supervised many thorough, specialized studies of mortality statistics, as well as studies of the genetics of specific diseases such as cancer, tuberculosis, and mental illness. Many of Weinberg's contemporaries used his numerous methods of correction, ascertainment, and statistical analysis to refine their own data.

Weinberg was not unaware of the broader, societal implications of his work, particularly in the area of eugenics. Eugenics is the science of improving genetic fitness by imposing artificial selection. Weinberg agreed with Karl Pearson that certain restrictions on fertility should be imposed by the government to improve the human gene pool, including legal sterilization and marriage prohibition in families with heritable genetic diseases. Weinberg did not, however, approve of eugenic abortions.

Recognition of Weinberg's Work Delayed

Weinberg's professional life was an unusual one: He continued to practice medicine even as he performed his most important research in genetics. In a medical career of forty-two years, he worked on a private basis for fees but also served the poor. He had relatively little interest in making money and occasionally forgot to collect the fees owed him. He never had a single student or collaborator, and it was this independence, along with a relatively inaccessible writing style, which isolated Weinberg from his contemporaries, both in the scope of his ideas and the recognition of his work.

Even though Weinberg had developed his equilibrium principle several months before Hardy's work was published, the formula was known as Hardy's Law for decades, even in Germany. His resentment regarding this oversight was evident as early as 1909, when he argued for his own priority in a review of Hardy's paper. Weinberg insisted that his work had been more inclusive and yet more simple than that of his British counterpart, and in 1927 he publicly defended his priority once again at the Berlin International Congress of Genetics. Weinberg was neglected, at least in part, because he was not member of the academic establishment, but his 1908 paper had been published in a relatively obscure German journal, while Hardy's article had appeared in *Science*. It was only in 1943, after diligent lobbying by his friend Curt Stern, that Hardy's Law became known as the Hardy-Weinberg Law. Also, whether an effect or an additional cause of his isolation, Weinberg was known for his unpleasantness in professional correspondence. He did not hesitate to turn professional debates into personal ones, and he frequently engaged in public feuds with Pearson and Lenz, among others, arguments which often concerned their ignorance or oversight of his work.

In an obituary in *Genetics*, Curt Stern compared Weinberg's career to Mendel's, claiming that "both men made their discoveries at a time when their contemporaries were unable to appreciate them." Weinberg's work on ascertainment was given proper credit and his statistical methodology borrowed by geneticists worldwide. However, his most important work in population genetics, perhaps because he was not a professional population geneticist, was overlooked for decades, just as Mendel's had been, and it was left to be rediscovered by others in a later generation.

Weinberg retired from his medical practice in 1931 and moved to Tübingen, Germany, with his wife, the former Bertha Wachenbrönner, whom he had married in 1896. Weinberg and his wife had one daughter and four sons, the oldest of whom died in World War I. In Tübingen, he lived in poverty and poor health for six years until his death on November 27, 1937. Despite his professional reputation as caustic, he was remembered by friends as an essentially gentle man whose impatience was the result of his bitterness over his scientific career. As quoted in *Genetic Counseling*, H. Luxenburger wrote of Weinberg: "It was to his own harm that he carefully hid his goodness, his kindness, and his sense of justice. Therefore, it is largely his own fault that his achievement was not noticed in the way it should have deserved."

SELECTED WRITINGS BY WEINBERG:

Periodicals

"Uber den Nachweis der Vererbung beim Menschen," *Jahreshefte des Vereins für Vaterländische Naturkunde in Württemburg,* Volume 64, 1908, pp. 368–382.

SOURCES:

Books

Dunn, L. C., *A Short History of Genetics,* McGraw-Hill, 1965, pp. 121–123.
Gillispie, C. C., editor, *Dictionary of Scientific Biography,* Scribners, Volume 14, 1976, pp. 230–231
Provine, William B. *The Origins of Theoretical Population Genetics,* University of Chicago Press, 1971, pp. 134–136.
Tiley, N. A., *Discovering DNA,* Van Nostrand, 1983, p. 29.

Periodicals

Kallman, F. J., "Wilhelm Weinberg, M.D.," *Journal of Nervous and Mental Diseases,* Volume 87, 1938, pp. 263–264.
Luxenburger, H., "Wilhelm Weinberg," *Allgemeine Zeitschrift für Psychiatrie,* Volume 107, 1938, pp. 378–381.
Stern, Curt, "Wilhelm Weinberg," *Genetics,* Volume 47, 1962, pp. 1–5.
Süss, Jochen and Dorothee Früh, "Wilhelm Weinberg, M.D. (1862–1937): The Man Behind the 'Hardy-Weinberg-Equilibrium,'" *Genetic Counseling,* Volume 1, pp. 279–285.

—Sketch by G. Scott Crawford

Carl F. Von Weizsäcker
1912-
German physicist

Carl F. Von Weizsäcker's achievements encompass both the scientific and philosophical examination of the creation of the universe. In a career that spanned several decades, Von Weizsäcker taught at several institutions, published over thirty books, and founded the renowned Max Planck Institute for Social Sciences in Starnberg, Germany. His best-known scientific theory is known as the "Carbon Cycle," which he, along with fellow German physicist **Hans Bethe**, proposed as a nuclear reactive process by which energy is generated in stars.

Carl Friedrich Freiherr von Weizsäcker was born on June 28, 1912, in Kiel, Germany. The term *Freiherr*, which means "free man," is more loosely translated as *baron*, a name by which von Weizsäcker is often addressed. His parents were Ernest Freiherr von Weizsäcker and the former Marianne von Graevenitz. Von Weizsäcker's lineage included distinguished scholars and civil servants, including a famous Protestant theologian (von Weizsäcker's great-grandfather), the last prime minister of the Kingdom of Württemburg (his grandfather), and one of the founders of psychosomatic medicine (an uncle). His own father was a high official in Adolf Hitler's Nazi government in Germany. As a child, von Weizsäcker was fascinated by both science and religion. Even very early in his life, he did not view them as two distinct subjects, but as two facets of a single topic. In this respect, von Weizsäcker was following a tradition from the early days of modern science when boundaries between science and religion were often difficult to distinguish. By the twentieth century, however, this tradition had become a minor theme for most scientists who, with a few exceptions, saw clear distinctions between their own work and religious or philosophical speculations.

Von Weizsäcker completed undergraduate and graduate work at the Universities of Berlin, Göttingen, and Copenhagen, receiving his Ph.D. in physics from the University of Leipzig in 1933. He then began working as a researcher at Leipzig's Institute of Theoretical Physics, going on to become a lecturer in theoretical physics at the University of Berlin. His work during this period focused largely on nuclear physics, and his most notable accomplishment was the derivation of a method for calculating the total energy of an atomic nucleus.

Works on Problems of Astrophysics

In the early years of World War II, von Weizsäcker was appointed to the post of associate professor of theoretical physics at the University of Strasbourg, located in a German-occupied region of France. He was also assigned to work on the development of Germany's atomic bomb. However, the project received little attention from Hitler's government and never made significant progress. It was during these years that von Weizsäcker also worked on the two scientific problems for which he is best known, the origin of stellar energy and the creation of the planets.

Scientists had long been puzzled about the mechanism by which stars produce energy. Well-known and obvious processes, such as combustion, could not explain the conversion since stars would rapidly exhaust the raw materials needed for such a procedure. In the late 1930s, at approximately the same time, von Weizsäcker and a German physicist, Hans Bethe, proposed that a series of nuclear reactions generated energy in stars. The net result of these reactions, said the scientists, was the conversion of four protons (hydrogen nuclei) to one helium atom. Since carbon was a catalyst in this process, the series of reactions became known as the carbon cycle.

During the 1940s, von Weizsäcker turned his attention to the study of planetary formation. In particular, he applied his knowledge of nuclear physics to a theory originally proposed by the French mathematician and philosopher, René Descartes in the seventeenth century. The theory had subsequently developed by German philosopher, Immanuel Kant in the eighteenth century and, especially, by the French mathematician and physicist, Pierre-Simon Laplace around the late 1700s. According to the Descartes-Kant-Laplace theory, the planets were originally formed when large clumps of matter condensed from a disk of gases rotating around the sun. Although von Weizsäcker's own elucidation of this problem did not resolve all the questions about planetary formation, his update of this "nebular" theory was a significant step forward in the evolution towards understanding planetary formation.

Shifts Attention to Problems of Philosophy, Religion and Social Activism

After World War II, von Weizsäcker took the post of professor of theoretical physics at the University of Göttingen and also became department head at the university's Max Planck Institute for Physics. While working here, he continued his research on nuclear and astrophysics. Then, in 1957, he accepted an appointment as professor of philosophy at the University of Hamburg, a move that startled many of his colleagues. This decision was indicative of his intention to spend more time in thinking, writing, and talking about the need for integrating the sciences with each other and with other aspects of human life, especially religion and philosophy. Von Weizsäcker, who has more than thirty books to his credit, outlined some of these ideas in his work titled *The Relevance of Science: Creation and Cosmogony.* Explaining the historical process by which the various sciences became compartmentalized, von Weizsäcker went on to expound on the harmful effects of this change on science and on society, showing how and why this process should be reversed in modern society. During the 1960s, von Weizsäcker became very active in the peace movement and became a strong spokesman for nuclear disarmament.

In 1970 von Weizsäcker founded the Max Planck Institute on the Preconditions of Human Life in the Modern World (later renamed the Max Planck Institute for Social Sciences) in Starnberg, Germany. He served as director of the institute until his retirement in 1980. Also in 1970, he became honorary professor of philosophy at the University of Munich. Von Weizsäcker was married to Gundalena Wille on March 30, 1937. Their children are Carl Christian, Ernest Ulrich, Elizabeth, and Heinrich. Among his awards are the Max Planck Medal in 1957 and 1966, the Goethe Prize from the city of Frankfurt in 1958, the Order of Merit for Sciences and Arts in 1961, the Arnold Reymond Prize for Physics in 1965, the Wilhelm Boelsche Gold Medal in 1965, and the Erasmus Prize in 1969.

SELECTED WRITINGS BY VON WEIZSÄCKER:

Books

The History of Nature, translated by F. D. Wieck, University of Chicago Press, 1949.
(With J. Juilfs) *The Rise of Modern Physics,* translated by A. J. Pomerans, Braziller, 1957.
The Relevance of Science: Creation and Cosmogony, Harper, 1964.
The Biological Basis of Religion and Genius, NC Press, 1971.
The Politics of Peril: Economics, Society and the Prevention of War, translated by M. Shaw, Seabury Press, 1978.

SOURCES:

Books

Tango, Gerardo G., "Von Weizsäcker Finalizes His Quantitative Theory of Planetary Formation," *Great Events from History II,* edited by Frank N. Magill, Science and Technology Series, Volume 3, 1931–1952, pp. 1208–11.

—*Sketch by David E. Newton*

Thomas Weller
1915-
American pediatrician, parasitologist, and virologist

Thomas Weller was corecipient, with **John F. Enders** and **Frederick Robbins**, of the Nobel Prize in physiology or medicine in 1954. This award was given for the trio's successful growth of the poliomyelitis (polio) virus in a non-neural tissue culture. This development was significant in the fight against the crippling disease polio, and eventually led to the development, by **Jonas Salk** in 1953, of a successful vaccination against the virus. It also revolutionized viral work in the laboratory and aided the recognition of many new types of viruses. Weller also distinguished himself with his studies of human parasites and the viruses that cause rubella and chicken pox.

Thomas Huckle Weller was born June 15, 1915, in Ann Arbor, Michigan. His parents were Elsie A. (Huckle) and Dr. Carl V. Weller. He received his B.S. in 1936 and M.S. in 1937, both from the University of Michigan, where his father was chair of the pathology department. He continued his studies at Harvard Medical School, where he met and roomed with his future Nobel corecipient Robbins. In 1938 Weller received a fellowship from the international health division of the Rockefeller Foundation, which allowed him to study public health in Tennessee and malaria in Florida, topics which first interested him during his undergraduate years.

Weller graduated from Harvard with magna cum laude honors in parasitology, receiving his M.D. in 1940. He also received a fellowship in tropical medicine and a teaching fellowship in bacteriology. He completed an internship in pathology and bacteriology (1941) at Children's Hospital in Boston. He then began a residency at Children's, with the intention of specializing in pediatrics, before enlisting in the U.S. Army during World War II.

Weller served in the Army Medical Corps from 1942 to 1945. He was initially given teaching assignments in tropical medicine, but he was soon made officer in charge of bacteriology and virology work in San Juan, Puerto Rico. His major research there related to pneumonia and the parasitic disease schistosomiasis, an infection that is centered in the intestine and damages tissue and the circulatory system. Before his military service ended, he moved to the Army Medical School in Washington D.C. Upon his discharge in 1945, Weller was married to Kathleen Fahey, with whom he had two sons and two daughters. Returning to Boston's Children's Hospital, he finished his residency and began a post-doctoral year working with Enders.

Helps Solve the Polio Puzzle

During 1948, Weller was working with the mumps virus, which Enders had been researching since the war. After one experiment, Weller had a few tubes of human embryonic tissue left over, so he and Enders decided to see what the virus poliomyelitis might do in them. A small amount of success prompted the duo, who had been joined in their research by Robbins, to try growing the virus in other biological mediums, including human foreskin and the intestinal cells of a mouse. The mouse intestine did not produce anything, but the trio finally had significant viral growth with human intestinal cells. This was the first time poliomyelitis had been grown in human or simian tissue other than nerve or brain. Using antibiotics to ward off unwanted bacterial invasion, the scientists were able to isolate the virus for study.

Once poliomyelitis was grown and isolated in tissue cultures it was possible to closely study the nature of the virus, which in turn made it possible for Salk to create a vaccine in 1953. Besides leading to an inhibitor against a debilitating disease, a major result of the trio's development was a decrease in the need for laboratory animals. As Weller was quoted saying in the *Journal of Infectious Diseases,* "In the instance of poliomyelitis, one culture tube of human or monkey cells became the equivalent of one monkey." In times prior, viruses had to be injected into living animals to monitor their potency. Now, with tissue culture growth, cell changes were apparent under the microscope, showing the action of the virus and eliminating the need for the animals. The techniques for growing cells in tissue cultures developed by Weller and his associates were not only applicable to the poliomyelitis virus, however. They were soon copied by many other labs and scientists and quickly led to the identification, control, and study of several previously unrecognized virus types. For their work, and the improvements in scientific research it made possible, Weller, Enders, and Robbins shared the 1954 Nobel Prize in physiology or medicine.

Concurrent with his work with Enders and Robbins, Weller was named assistant director of the research division of infectious diseases at Children's Hospital in 1949. He held this position until 1954. At the same time, he began teaching at Harvard in tropical medicine and tropical public health, moving from instructor to associate professor. In 1953, Weller and Robbins shared the Mead Johnson Prize for their contributions to pediatric research. Then, in 1954, Weller was named Richard Pearson Strong Professor of Tropical Public Health and chair of the public health department at Harvard. As a consequence, he moved his research facilities to the Harvard Medical School. Later, he was appointed director of the Center for Prevention of Infectious Diseases at the Harvard School of Public Health.

Advances Knowledge of Parasites and Viruses

From the end of World War II until 1982 Weller also continued his research on two types of helminths, *trichinella spiralis* and *schistosoma mansoni.* Helminths are intestinal parasites, and these two cause, respectively, trichinosis, which can also severely affect the human musculature, and schistosomiasis. Weller was concerned with the parasites' basic biology and performed various diagnostic studies on them. His contributions to current understanding of these parasites are significant, advancing an understanding of the ailments they cause.

Weller spent a portion of the same period (1957 to 1973) establishing the basic available knowledge concerning cytomegalovirus (commonly known as CMV), which causes cell enlargement in various organs. Weller's most important finding in this area regarded congenital transmission of both CMV and rubella, a virus also known as German measles. A pregnant woman infected with either of these viruses may pass the infection on to her fetus. Weller showed that infected newborns excreted viral strains in their feces, providing another source for the spread of the diseases. His findings became significant when it was also learned that children born to infected mothers often risked birth defects.

In 1962 Weller, along with Franklin Neva, was able to grow and study German Measles in tissue cultures. These two also went on to grow and isolate the chicken pox virus. Subsequently, Weller was the first to show the common origin of the varicella virus, which causes chicken pox, and the herpes zoster virus, which causes shingles. In 1971, Weller was the first to prove the airborne transmission of *pneumocystis carinii,* a form of pneumonia that later appeared as a frequent side effect of the human immunodeficiency virus commonly known as HIV.

Weller was elected to the National Academy of Sciences in 1964. In addition, he served on advisory committees of the World Health Organization, the Pan American Health Organization, the Agency for Internation Development, and the National Institute of Allergy and Infectious Disease. He continued his position at Harvard until 1985, when he became professor emeritus. While at Harvard, he helped establish the Public Health Department's international reputation. In 1988, Weller gave the first John F. Enders Memorial Lecture to the Infectious Disease Society of America. In addition to his Nobel Prize, Weller was the recipient of many awards and honorary degrees during his career.

SELECTED WRITINGS BY WELLER:

Periodicals

(With J. F. Enders and F. C. Robbins) "Cultivation of the Lansing Strain of Poliomyelitis Virus in Cultures of Various Human Embryonic Tissues," *Science,* January 28, 1949, pp. 85–87.

(With D. L. Augustine and R. Thomas) "The Importance of Tropical Public Health to World Peace," *Post Graduate Medicine,* Volume 13, 1953, pp. 339–43.

"As It Was and As It Is: A Half-Century of Progress," *Journal of Infectious Diseases,* March 1989, pp. 378–83.

SOURCES:

Books

Chernin, Eli, *Tropical Medicine at Harvard: The Weller Years, 1954–1981. A Personal Memoir,* Harvard University Press, 1985.

Current Biography Yearbook 1955, H. W. Wilson, 1955, pp. 183–84.

Nobel Laureates in Medicine or Physiology, Garland, 1990, pp. 563–66.

McGraw-Hill Modern Scientists and Engineers, Volume 3, Mcgraw-Hill, 1980, pp. 292–94.

Periodicals

Time, November 1, 1954, p. 49.

—*Sketch by Kimberlyn McGrail*

Frits Went
1903-1990
Dutch-born American botanist

Lush, weed-free lawns owe their beauty in large part to American botanist Frits Went's discovery of the role of the plant growth hormone auxin. Went's 1927 discovery paved the way for the development of modern fertilizers and weed killers and the genetic engineering of plants. Went also developed a greenhouse that has enhanced botanical research by enabling scientists to control the plants' climate. Later in his career, the versatile scientist turned his atten-

Frits Went

tion toward environmental problems, including smog and the degradation of the Amazon rain forest.

A career in botany seemed virtually destined for Went, who was born in a garden and raised in a botany lab. He was born May 18, 1903, in Utrecht, Netherlands, the son of Catharina Jacomina (Tonckens) and Friedrich August Ferdinand Christian Went. The Wents lived in a 300-year-old house in the botany garden of the State University of Utrecht, where the senior Went worked as a professor and director of the garden and botany lab. Just across from the house was the newly rebuilt laboratory, which was considered one of the finest in the world.

The young Went was fascinated by the Venus fly traps, cacti, palms, and other exotic plants in the garden's greenhouse. Many hours of his boyhood years were spent there and in the laboratory. Went considered himself lucky to have been surrounded by such a variety of plants and some of the best minds in the field of botany. He credited his career choice to his boyhood at the university, although his father carefully avoided pushing him into science. Went earned his bachelor's, master's and doctoral degrees at the State University of Utrecht between 1920 and 1927.

Discovers Role of Plant Hormone

For the subject of his doctoral thesis, Went chose the plant growth hormone auxin. He was intrigued by phototropism, the tendency of plants to bend toward light. He knew they bent by growing faster on the dark side of the stem and slower on the side facing the light. He suspected the growth hormone auxin was responsible, but he was not sure how. Went conducted his research on oat seedlings. His most important finding was that auxin, which is produced at the tip of the stem, is unevenly distributed under unidirectional light. More auxin flows down the dark side, making it grow faster. His theory also explained why the phototropic curve in plants moves farther down the stem over time. Went made his discovery in 1927, at the same time as Russian botanist N. Cholodny. Since then, their theory of phototropism has been called the Cholodny-Went theory.

Knowledge of growth hormones in plants later gave rise to the field of agricultural chemistry. Many herbicides, fungicides, and fertilizers use auxins. These hormones are also used in genetic engineering to develop better plant species. Back in the 1920s and 1930s, however, Went's theory was rejected by many of his peers. The controversy disturbed the gentle, amiable scientist. Yet dispute seemed to follow him throughout his career. After earning his Ph.D. in 1927, Went accepted his first job as a botanist at the botanical garden in Bogor, Java. That same year he married Catharina Helena van de Koppel. They would have two children, Hans Went and Anneke (Went) Simmons.

Two years after arriving in Bogor, Went was appointed director of the Foreigners Laboratory there. He left in 1933 to become an assistant professor of plant physiology at California Institute of Technology in Pasadena. He was named a full professor in 1935, a position he held until he left the institute in 1958. While there, Went continued his research on auxins, which culminated in the 1937 publication of the book *Phytohormones,* which he wrote with K. V. Thimann.

The book's publication ended Went's research into the internal control of plant growth. By that time he had grown discouraged by the naysayers. "If a field becomes too controversial or too theoretical, I prefer to leave it, as I did the growth factor field in the early 1940s," he wrote in an introductory chapter for the *Annual Review of Plant Physiology.* "After Thimann and I had written *Phytohormones,* I felt that I degenerated to a policeman, overseeing the auxin field, checking doubtful statements or questionable results." Went shifted his studies from the internal factors affecting plant development to the external ones.

The laboratory for his new field was the first air-conditioned research greenhouse, which California Institute of Technology opened in 1939. By varying the temperature, Went learned that plants grew best when the daytime temperature was several degrees higher than at night. Since his discovery, commercial greenhouses have routinely varied the day and night temperatures for optimal growth. Went also learned that greenhouse plants cultivated under temperatures similar to those occurring in the wild would grow just like those in nature. The best way to research the effects of climate on plant growth, he reasoned, was to duplicate the natural climate. So he persuaded his friend H. Earhart from Michigan to finance a phytotron—a greenhouse that could duplicate the full range of naturally occurring temperature, lighting, wind, and humidity conditions—at the Institute. In June of 1949, the Institute opened the Earhart Plant Research Laboratory as the first phytotron. Soon, phytotrons became a fixture of the best botany departments at universities throughout the world.

In 1947, Went was elected to the prestigious National Academy of Sciences. He would be elected to the French Academy of Sciences in 1956, the Dutch Academy of Sciences in 1958, and the German Academy for Natural Sciences in 1977.

Theorizes Smog Comes From Plants

In the 1950s, Went again shifted his focus, this time toward the effects of plants on the environment. He began by analyzing the smog that hovers over Los Angeles. Until that time, it had been assumed that the smoky haze was sulfur dioxide. But Went rejected that assumption based on the reaction of plants to the smog. He organized a joint venture of the California Institute of Technology, the University of California, and the Los Angeles County Air Pollution Control District to identify the components of the haze. Went theorized that most of the smog in the atmosphere comes not from cars and factories, but from plants. During the process of photosynthesis, he claimed, the hydrocarbons in plants—known as terpene—decompose to produce a blue haze. This natural haze inspired the names of the Blue Ridge and the Smoky Mountains in Virginia and North Carolina. Went lacked the scientific data to prove his theory and had no desire to obtain it. He had grown away from the detailed analysis used in his early research on auxins. Yet his reluctance to research his hypothesis once again subjected his theory to widespread rejection.

"He was so far in front that mainstream scientists could shoot his theories full of holes," said Thomas Sharkey, Went's former colleague and chair of the department of botany at the University of Wisconsin in Madison, in an interview for *NTCS.* "The idea that most of hydrocarbon comes from plants turns out to be correct. Now the atmospheric scientists agree with him." Not all of Went's far-flung theories turned out to be correct. He theorized that the greenhouse effect leading to global warming was caused by the smoky vapors coming from vegetation, rather than carbon dioxide. In that case, Went was proven wrong. Carbon dioxide from fossil fuels contributes greatly to the greenhouse effect.

While spending his days with textbooks and microscopes, Went never lost his appreciation of the beauty of gardens. He was elected president of the California Arboretum Foundation and was the sponsor of the Los Angeles State and County Arboretum. In his *Annual Review* article, Went wrote that those positions "gave me the advantage of coming close to the living plant, to acquaint myself not only with its appearance and occurrence, but also with its workings. And it has prevented me from becoming a narrow specialist, spending my life on the response of a single plant or organ."

Went's second book, *The Experimental Control of Plant Growth,* was published in 1957. The following year, he left California to become a professor at Washington University in St. Louis and the director of the Missouri Botanical Gardens. Also in 1958, Went received the Stephen Hales Award from the American Society of Plant Physiologists for his outstanding career contributions. In 1959, he was awarded an honorary Ph.D. from McGill University.

Went used his knowledge of the phytotron in 1960 to build a large display greenhouse at the Botanical Gardens, where different climates could be replicated in different areas of the greenhouse. He ran the Botanical Gardens until 1963 and taught at the university until 1965. In 1964, his third book, *The Plants,* was published. Went returned to research in 1965 as a distinguished professor of botany at the University of Nevada's Desert Research Institute in Reno. That same year, the American Society of Plant Physiologists gave him the Charles Reid Barnes Life Membership Award.

Finds Key to Sustaining Amazon Rain Forest

In the late 1960s, Went made one of his most important discoveries on the floor of the Amazonian rain forest. He was travelling aboard the research vessel *Alpha Helix* and planned to conduct research on the Amazon basin. When Brazilian customs agents impounded his laboratory equipment, Went turned his attention toward the ground. There he found a garden of fungi among the dead leaves, branches, and other debris, making up a litter layer. Running throughout this layer was a network of tree roots. Went concluded that the fungi digest the litter and pass the extracted nutrients to the tree roots in a continuous nutrient cycle.

Converting this rich land to temperate-zone agriculture irreparably harms the rain forest, Went warned. He urged rain forest developers to avoid annual crops and instead plant Brazil nuts, oil palms, or cacao trees, which would perpetuate the rich forest. Although clear-cutting of the rain forest continues, by

the late 1980s, Went's warning had become gospel for the growing movement to save the Amazonian rain forest.

In 1967, Went received the Hodgkins Award from the Smithsonian Institute for his contribution to the understanding of the environment. He retired from the Desert Research Institute as a research professor emeritus in 1975, but his devotion to studying the living world never ceased. Went spent his last years researching the effects of smog on weather. He concluded that most of the soot collects on the surface of cumulus clouds, then returns to the earth as dirty rain or snow. In 1989, months before his death, he received the Henry Shaw Medal from the Missouri Botanical Gardens.

The 86-year-old scientist died of a heart attack on May 2, 1990, during a visit from his retirement home in Portland, Oregon, to the Desert Institute in Reno. A manuscript he had written for a book about hydrocarbons and their relationship to thunderstorms was found in his suitcase. His children published the book posthumously to distribute to Went's friends and peers. It is titled *Black Carbon, Blue Sky.* Had he lived longer, Went most likely would have continued his research. In his 1974 article for the *Annual Review of Plant Physiology,* he wrote of his dream to delve into such uncharted fields as the sociology and physiology of ants and galls, or tumors, that insects develop on leaves. Went's son Hans, a retired zoology professor, told *NTCS* in an interview that even in his leisure time, his father's sole interest was science. "He was always out looking at plants, analyzing, comparing," Hans said of his father. "Science was his life."

SELECTED WRITINGS BY WENT:

Books

(With K. Volume Thimann) *Phytohormones,* Macmillan, 1937.
The Experimental Control of Plant Growth, With Special Reference to the Earhart Plant Research Laboratory at the California Institute of Technology, Chronica Botanica Co., 1957.
(With the editors of *Life* magazine) *The Plants,* Time, Inc., 1964.
"Reflections and Speculations," *Annual Review of Plant Physiology,* Annual Reviews, 1974, pp. 1–26.

Periodicals

"Blue Hazes in the Atmosphere," *Nature,* Volume 187, 1960, pp. 641–643.

SOURCES:

Other

Sharkey, Thomas, interview with Cynthia Washam conducted August 11, 1993.

Went, Hans, interview with Cynthia Washam conducted August 15, 1993.

—*Sketch by Cynthia Washam*

Alfred Werner
1866-1919
Swiss chemist

Alfred Werner was a chemist and educator whose accomplishments included the development of the coordination theory of chemistry. This theory, in which Werner proposed revolutionary ideas about how atoms and molecules are linked together, was formulated in a span of only three years, from 1890 to 1893. The remainder of his career was spent gathering the experimental support required to validate his new ideas. For his work on the linkage of atoms and his coordination theory, Werner became the first Swiss chemist to win the Nobel Prize.

Werner was born December 12, 1866, in Mulhouse, a small community in the French province of Alsace. He was the last of four children born to Jean-Adam Werner, a factory foreman and farmer, and Salome Jeanette Tesche, daughter of a wealthy German family. Alsace was French when Werner was born but was annexed into Germany during the Franco-Prussian war. Although the Werner family maintained strong patriotic ties with France and continued to speak French in their home, young Werner began his education in German schools.

At age six he was enrolled at the Ecole Libre des Freres, partly because of his mother's recent conversion to Catholicism. In 1878 he entered the Ecole Professionelle, a technical school, and began studying chemistry. The family had moved from the city to take up residence on a nearby farm, where Werner's father was engaged in dairying. The farm provided an ideal place for young Werner to begin his experiments. During this time, an unpleasant explosion in his home lab almost ended his career in chemistry and forced him to move his vials and chemicals into the barn. Werner's earliest known work was a paper on urea that he submitted in 1885 to the director of the Mulhouse Chemie Schule. He was 18. Although the paper was scientifically unsound and showed youthful inexperience, it did reveal a talent for classification and systematization that would prove invaluable in later years.

In late 1885 Werner began serving a one year term of compulsory military duty. Stationed in the town of Karlsruhe, Werner enrolled in two organic chemistry courses taught at the Technical University there. After his tour of duty, he relocated to Zurich, Switzerland, to continue his education in chemistry at the Federal Institute of Technology. Werner excelled in chemistry but performed poorly in mathematical courses, especially descriptive geometry. After six semesters of work and completion of a paper describing the successful preparation of five compounds, he received a diploma in technical chemistry. A year later, in 1890, he was awarded a Ph.D.

Werner's doctoral thesis in 1890 was his first publication and his most important work in organic chemistry. Along with his graduate advisor, Werner showed that the shape of nitrogen compounds are similar to carbon compounds. His second paper, "Contribution to the Theory of Affinity and Valence," concerned the forces of attraction that hold carbon atoms together. Werner attacked the traditional theory that pictured atoms of carbon held together in rigid formations. He suggested that attractive forces emanate in all directions from the center of a central atom. Using this novel idea, Werner was able to derive kekulé formulas—notations for chemical structures in which valence bonds are illustrated with short lines—for organic carbon compounds.

Dream Inspires Coordination Theory

His most important paper, "Contribution to the Construction of Inorganic Compounds," was written in 1893. Werner awoke at 2 a.m. one morning with the solution to the riddle of molecular structure. He began writing furiously and by 5 p.m. his monumental paper on coordination theory was finished. In his paper Werner proposed that single atoms or molecules could be grouped around a central atom according to simple geometrical principles. These coordination bonds were immensely successful in explaining the properties of observed compounds and in predicting the existence of unknown compounds.

During this time, Werner had been developing other dimensions of his career as well. In 1891 he went to Paris as a post-doctoral student and worked with the French chemist Pierre Berthelot on thermochemical problems. Werner began his teaching career during the summer semester of 1892, as a lecturer in atomic theory at the Federal Institute of Technology. In the fall of 1893, as a result of his almost overnight success with the publication of his theory, he was appointed professor of organic chemistry at the University of Zurich. In his first course, the chemistry of aromatic compounds, Werner proved to be a demanding professor whose exuberance and contagious enthusiasm for atoms and molecules inspired and enthralled students. Although Werner's theoretical and experimental work was primarily in the field of inorganic chemistry, it was not until 1902 that he was allowed to teach inorganic chemistry.

After writing his ground-breaking papers, Werner had set about immediately to prove his theory. In a span of some 25 years he painstakingly prepared over 8000 compounds and published his findings in more than 150 publications. In 1907 he succeeded in preparing a beautiful ammonia-violeo salt, a compound predicted by his theory. With this preparation his opponents finally conceded defeat. Werner's greatest experimental success came in 1911 with the successful resolution of optically active coordination compounds—substances able to deflect polarized light. A few years later he resolved carbon-free coordination compounds and ended forever carbon's dominance in stereochemistry. For his theoretical and experimental work on coordination theory, Werner was awarded the Nobel Prize in chemistry in 1913.

Werner married Emma Wilhelmine Giesker in 1894, the same year he became a Swiss citizen. They had two children, a boy and a girl. Werner was a robust man with a jovial sense of humor. He was a connoisseur of good foods and wine and enjoyed billiards and chess with friends and family. Werner's hobbies included photography, stamp collecting, mountain climbing, and ice skating.

Werner published prolifically in both organic and inorganic chemistry. He wrote two textbooks on inorganic and stereochemical topics. In addition to the Nobel Prize, he was the recipient of many awards and honorary degrees, including the prestigious Leblanc Medal of the French Chemical Society. Werner died on November 15, 1919, at a Zurich psychiatric institution, from arteriosclerosis of the brain. At his funeral he was remembered for his numerous contributions to science and teaching.

SELECTED WRITINGS BY WERNER:

Books

Lehrbuch der Stereochemie, Verlab von Gustav Fischer, Jena, 1904.

SOURCES:

Books

Kauffman, George B., *Alfred Werner, Founder of Coordination Chemistry,* Springer-Verlag, 1966.

Nobel Prize Winners, H. W. Wilson, 1987, pp. 1110–12.

—*Sketch by Mike McClure*

Harold Dadford West
1904-1974
American biochemist

For forty-seven years Harold Dadford West was involved in biochemical research and education at Meharry Medical College. For thirteen of those years, he was president of the institution. He was selected to be the first honorary member of the National Medical Association, and the Science Center at Meharry was named for him.

Born in Flemington, New Jersey, on July 16, 1904, West was the son of George H. West and the former Mary Ann Toney. He attended the University of Illinois, where he received a bachelor of arts degree in 1925. He was an associate professor and head of the science department at Morris Brown College in Atlanta from 1925 to 1927. On December 27, 1927, West married Jessie Juanita Penn. They eventually had one daughter and one son.

In 1927 West joined the faculty of Meharry Medical College in Nashville, Tennessee, as an associate professor of physiological chemistry. Meharry Medical College had become an independent institution in 1915. Prior to that it was part of Central Tennessee College, established by the Freedmen's Aid Society of the Methodist Episcopal Church after the American Civil War in 1866. During his early years on the faculty of Meharry Medical College, West completed a master of arts degree and a doctorate. He was a recipient of a fellowship from the Julius Rosenwald Fund at the University of Illinois while he earned a master of arts degree in 1930. Following that he was a Rockefeller Foundation Fellow, receiving a doctorate degree from the same university in 1937. The title of his dissertation was "The Chemistry and Nutritive Value of Essential Amino Acids." In 1938 West became professor of biochemistry and chairperson of the department.

West's work in biochemical research was vast, including studies of tuberculosis and other bacilli, the antibiotic biocerin, and aromatic hydrocarbons. He worked with amino acids, becoming the first to synthesize threonine. As noted in the *Journal of the National Medical Association,* among his other investigations were "the role of sulfur in biological detoxi-

Harold Dadford West

fication mechanisms; blood serum calcium levels in the Negro in relation to possible significance in tuberculosis; relation of B-vitamins, especially pantothenic acid, to detoxification of sulfa-drugs and susceptibility to bacillary disease."

West's studies were supported by the John and Mary R. Markle Foundation, the Nutrition Foundation, the National Institutes of Health, and the American Medical Association. His research papers were published in a number of professional journals, including the *American Journal of Physiology, Southern Medical Journal,* and *Journal of Biological Chemistry.*

In 1952 West was named the fifth president of Meharry Medical College, its first African American president. In 1963 he was the first black American to serve on the State Board of Education. West retired as president in 1965, returning to the position of professor of biochemistry. When he retired from Meharry in 1973 he became a trustee of the college. In his final years he worked on a complete history of the college. West died on March 5, 1974.

During his career, West was awarded two honorary degrees. In 1955 he received a doctor of laws from Morris Brown College, and in 1970 a doctor of science from Meharry Medical College. He was a member of many honorary and professional societies, including the American Chemical Society, the Society of Experimental Biology and Medicine, and the American Society of Biological Chemists. He was also elected to Sigma Xi, the scientific research society, which describes itself "as an honor society for scientists and engineers. . . . Its goals are to foster interaction among science, technology and society."

SOURCES:

Books

Sammons, Vivian Ovelton, *Blacks in Science and Medicine,* Hemisphere, 1990, p. 246.

Periodicals

Journal of the National Medical Association, September 1974, pp. 448–449.

—*Sketch by M. C. Nagel*

George West Wetherill
1925-
American geophysicist

George West Wetherill is a geophysicist and planetary scientist who is involved in many fields of research. He has done work on geochronology—the study of the earth from its origin to the present—and lunar history, but he is probably best known for his work on the origins of our solar system. He has concentrated much of his research on the asteroid belt, and he has been extensively involved in debates about what the belt, and the asteroids that fall to Earth as meteorites, can tell us about how the planets were formed. He has designed computer simulations to model how bodies orbit in a solar system and what happens when they collide.

Wetherill was born to George and Leah Victoria Wetherill on August 12, 1925 in Philadelphia, Pennsylvania. He attended the University of Chicago, where he received a succession of degrees, including an M.S. in 1951 and a Ph.D. in physics in 1953. At the conclusion of his schooling, Wetherill joined the Department of Terrestrial Magnetism of the Carnegie Institution of Washington; he remained there until 1960, when he moved the University of California at Los Angeles. While at UCLA, he served as a professor of geophysics and geology and then as chair of the department of planetary and space science from 1968 to 1972. Wetherill returned to the Carnegie Institution in 1975, where he assumed the title of Director of the Department of Terrestrial Magnetism. He remained as director until 1991, when he moved to a consultative position with the institution.

In astronomy, it is generally accepted that the solar system formed from an initial cloud of dust and gas with the Sun at the center. In this cloud there were innumerable tiny bodies, also referred to as planetesimals, which were in revolution around the Sun. The conventional scientific wisdom is that these bodies eventually combined to form planetary "embryos," about the size of our moon. Over time, the embryos pulled in more and more matter until they reached their present form. This theory, however, fails to explain the existence of the asteroid belt. Located between Mars and Jupiter, the belt measures 400 million kilometers in width and is in orbit around the Sun. There are over 4000 asteroids within the belt, and one of the problems facing astronomers is explaining why they would not have combined to form a planet of their own.

In 1991, Wetherill completed work on a project dealing with this problem and other aspects of the origin of the solar system. His project made use of complex three-dimensional computer models. By randomly selecting distributions of matter, energy, and angular momentum, Wetherill was able to create solar systems by chance. Surprisingly, the simulations yielded systems similar to our present solar system nearly every time. Through these experiments Wetherill observed the evolution of asteroid regions, and they underwent a process of "self clearing." During the evolution of the solar system, the collision of planet embryos have a different result in the areas where asteroid belts are formed, such as the area between Mars and Jupiter. The collision of these embryos causes varying degrees of fragmentation, but instead of being drawn into a planet like Jupiter, they are flung away from it. The gravitational field of the planet acts like a slingshot, which propels the fragments out of orbit.

Wetherill ran twenty-seven simulations with his computer models and found, on average, that 4.2 planets formed in the area occupied in our solar system by Mercury, Venus, Mars, and Earth. He also discovered that a large body like Jupiter did not always form, but a planet similar to Earth in size always formed at approximately the same distance from the Sun. Wetherill believes that the asteroid fragments which fall to earth may also provide some answers. He considers meteorite collections to be fossil evidence of the origin of the solar system.

Wetherill is often consulted for his opinion on the controversies of the day. There is an ongoing debate between meteoriticists and the revisionist astronomers over the origin of asteroids. The meteoriticists hold that the asteroids have remained unchanged in the 4.5 billion years since their origin. The revisionists contest this theory, claiming that aster-

oids underwent severe heating to the point of melting, thus experiencing radical alterations. An expert in the orbital and collisional behavior of solar systems bodies, Wetherill sides with neither group. He does, however, reject the revisionists' theory that smaller bodies exist in the belt which are of a radically different constitution than other asteroids in the belt. Wetherill made use of the revisionists' own belief in fragmentation of asteroids through collisions, and he pointed to the lack of larger bodies of a radical nature in the belt from which the smaller bodies would have to have been chipped.

Wetherill is a regular contributor to many periodicals and professional journals. He is an editor with the *Annual Review of Earth and Planetary Science*. He is also affiliated with both *Icarus* and *Meteoritics* as an associate editor. He has been retained as a consultant by the National Science Foundation, the National Academy of Science, and NASA. He is a member of the American Astronomical Society and the National Academy of Science and a fellow of the American Academy of Arts and Sciences and the American Geophysical Society. Wetherill served as vice president of the Meteoritical Society from 1972 to 1974, and again from 1980 to 1982. He was elected president in 1982 and served in this capacity until 1984. He served as vice president and president of the Geochemical Union from 1973 to 1975. Wetherill's work has brought him recognition from many quarters. He received the Leonard Medal from the Meteoritical Society in 1981, and the G. K. Gilbert Award from the Geological Society of America in 1984. He was awarded the G. P. Kuiper prize from the American Astronomical Society in 1986, and the American Geophysical Society made him the recipient of their 1991 H. H. Hess Medal.

Wetherill married Phyllis May Steiss on June 17, 1950. They have three children. Wetherill is currently a member of the staff at the Department of Terrestrial Magnetism and is active in the International Society for the Study of the Origin of Life.

SELECTED WRITINGS BY WETHERILL:

Books

"Origin of the Asteroid Belt," in *Asteroids II,* edited by Richard P. Binzel, Tom Gehrels, and Mildred S. Matthews, University of Arizona Press, 1989.

Periodicals

"Occurrence of Giant Impacts During the Growth of Terrestrial Planets," *Science,* May 17, 1985, pp. 877–879.

"Occurrence of Earth-like Bodies in Planetary Systems," *Science,* August 2, 1991, pp. 535–538.

SOURCES:

Periodicals

Kerr, Richard, "The Great Asteroid Roast: Was It Rare or Well-done?", *Science,* February 2, 1990, pp. 527–528.
Suplee, Curt, "Astronomy: Solar System Pattern May Be Typical," *The Washington Post,* August 5, 1991.

—*Sketch by Chris McGrail*

Nancy Wexler
1945-
American neuropsychologist

Nancy Wexler's research on Huntington's disease has led to the development of a presymptomatic test for the condition as well as the identification of the genes responsible for the disease. The symptoms of this fatal, genetically based disorder (for which Wexler herself is at risk) usually appear around middle age, and the disease leads to the degeneration of mental, psychological, and physical functioning. For her pivotal role in these achievements, Wexler was granted the Albert Lasker Public Service Award in 1993.

Nancy Sabin Wexler was born on July 19, 1945, to Milton Wexler, a Los Angeles psychoanalyst, and Leonore Sabin Wexler. She studied social relations and English at Radcliffe and graduated in 1967. Wexler subsequently traveled to Jamaica on a Fulbright scholarship and studied at the Hampstead Clinic Child Psychoanalytic Training Center in London.

In 1968 Wexler learned that her mother had developed the symptoms of Huntington's disease, a condition to which Wexler's maternal grandfather and three uncles had already succumbed. Efforts to fight the disease became a primary mission for Wexler and her family: Her father founded the Hereditary Disease Foundation in 1968, and Wexler herself, who was then entering the doctoral program in clinical psychology at the University of Michigan, eventually wrote her doctoral thesis on the "Perceptual-motor, Cognitive, and Emotional Characteristics of Persons-at-Risk for Huntington's Disease," and received her Ph.D. in 1974.

After graduating from University of Michigan, Wexler taught psychology at the New School for Social Research in New York City and worked as a researcher on Huntington's disease for the National Institutes of Health (NIH). In 1976 she was appointed by congress to head the NIH's Commission for the Control of Huntington's Disease and its Consequences. In 1985 she joined the College of Physicians and Surgeons at Columbia University.

In 1979 Wexler's research led her to Lake Maracaibo in Venezuela, where she studied a community which had a high incidence of Huntington's disease. Wexler kept medical records, took blood and skin samples, and charted the transmission of the disease within families. Wexler sent the samples she collected to geneticist James Gusella at Massachusetts General Hospital, who used the blood samples to conduct a study to locate the gene—the first such genetic mapping of a disease. Gusella eventually discovered a deoxyribonucleic acid (DNA) marker close to the Huntington's gene. Based on this study, Gusella introduced a test that was ninety-six percent accurate in detecting whether an individual bears the Huntington's gene. Because there was still no cure for the Huntington's disease, the test proved to be controversial, raising many issues involving patient rights, childbearing decisions, and discrimination by employers and insurance companies. In her interviews and writings Wexler has stressed the importance of keeping such genetic information confidential.

In 1993 the Huntington's gene was identified through research based on the Venezuelan blood samples and the work of the Huntington's Disease Collaborative Research Group. In October, 1993, Wexler received an Albert Lasker Public Service Award for her role in this effort. In addition, she has served as an advisor on social and medical ethics issues to the Human Genome Project—a massive international effort to map and identify the approximately 100,000 genes in the human body. Wexler also has assumed directorship of the Hereditary Disease Foundation founded by her father, to which she donated the honorarium that accompanied the Lasker Award.

SELECTED WRITINGS BY WEXLER:

Books

Advances in Neurology, Volume 23: Huntington's Disease, Raven, 1979.
Mama Can't Remember Anymore: Care Management of Elders and Their Families, Wein & Wein, 1991.

SOURCES:

Books

Newsmakers, Gale, 1992, pp. 530–33.

Periodicals

"An Array of New Tools Against Inherited Diseases," *U.S. News & World Report,* April 22, 1985, pp. 75–76.

Bluestone, Mimi, "Science and Ethics: The Double Life of Nancy Wexler," *Ms.,* November/December 1991, pp. 90–91.

Grady, Denise, "The Ticking of a Time Bomb in the Genes," *Discover,* June 1987.

Jaroff, Leon, "Making the Best of a Bad Gene," *Time,* February 10, 1992, pp. 78–79.

Konner, Melvin, "New Keys to the Mind," *New York Times Magazine,* July 17, 1988, pp. 49–50.

New York Times, October 1, 1993, p. A24.

—*Sketch by David Sprinkle*

Hermann Weyl

Hermann Weyl
1885-1955
German-born American mathematician

Hermann Weyl was one of the most wide-ranging mathematicians of his generation, following in the footsteps of his teacher **David Hilbert**. Weyl's interests in mathematics ran the gamut from foundations to physics, two areas in which he made profound contributions. He combined great technical virtuosity with imagination, and devoted attention to the explanation of mathematics to the general public. He managed to take a segment of mathematics developed in an abstract setting and apply it to certain branches of physics, such as relativity theory—a theory that holds that the velocity of light is the same for all observers, no matter how they are moving, that the laws of physics are the same in all inertial frames, and that all such frames are equivalent—and quantum mechanics—a theory that allows mathematical interpretation of elementary particles through wave properties. His distinctive ability was integrating nature and theory.

Claus Hugo Hermann Weyl was born on November 9, 1885, at Elmshorn, near Hamburg, Germany. The financial standing of his parents (his father, Ludwig, was a clerk in a bank and his mother, Anna Dieck, came from a wealthy family) enabled him to receive a quality education. From 1895 to 1904 he attended the Gymnasium at Altona, where his performance attracted the attention of his headmaster, a relative of an eminent mathematician of that time, David Hilbert. Weyl soon found himself at the University of Göttingen where Hilbert was an instructor. He remained there for the rest of his student days, with the exception of a semester at the University of Munich. He received his degree under Hilbert in 1908 and advanced to the ranks of privatdocent (unpaid but licensed instructor) in 1910.

Weyl married Helene Joseph (known as Hella to the family) in 1913 and in the same year took a position as professor at the National Technical University (ETH) in Zurich, Switzerland. He declined the offer to be Felix Klein's successor at Göttingen, despite the university's central role in the mathematical world. It has been suggested that he wanted to free himself, somewhat, of the influence of Hilbert, especially in light of the fact that he had accepted an invitation to take a chair at Göttingen when Hilbert retired. In any case, he brought a great deal of mathematical distinction to the ETH in Zurich, where his sons Fritz Joachim and Michael grew up.

It is not surprising that Weyl's early work dealt with topics that which Hilbert held an interest. His *Habilitationsschrift* was devoted to boundary conditions of second-order linear differential equations. (The way the German educational system worked, it was necessary to do a substantial piece of original research beyond the doctoral dissertation in order to qualify to teach in the university. This "entitling document" was frequently the launching point of the mathematical career of its author.) In other words, he was looking into the way functions behaved on a given region when the behavior at the boundary was specified. His results were sufficient for the purpose of enabling him to earn a living, but he rapidly moved on to areas where his contributions were more innovative and have had a more lasting effect.

One of the principal areas of Weyl's research was the topic of Hilbert spaces. The problem was to understand something about the functions that operated on the points of Hilbert space in a way useful for analyzing the result of applying the functions. In particular, Weyl wanted to know where the functions behaved more simply than on the space as a whole, since the behavior of the function on the rest of the space could be represented in terms of its behavior on the simpler regions. Different kinds of functions behaved in radically different ways on a Hilbert space, so Weyl had to restrict his attention to a subclass of functions small enough to be tractable (for example, the functions could not "blow up") but large enough to be useful. His choice of self-adjoint, compact operators was justified by their subsequent importance in the field of functional analysis.

Among the areas he brought together were geometry and analysis from the nineteenth century and topology, which was largely a creation of the twentieth century. Topology sought to understand the behavior of space in ways that require a less-detailed understanding of how the elements of a structure fit together than geometry demanded. One of the basic ideas of topology is that of a "manifold," first introduced by G. F. B. Riemann in his *Habilitationsschrift* as a student of Gauss. Riemann had little material with which to work, while Weyl was able to take advantage of the work of Hilbert and the Dutch mathematician **Luitzen Egbertus Jan Brouwer**. This effort culminated in his 1913 book on Riemann surfaces, an excellent exposition on how complex analysis and topology could be used together to analyze the behavior of complex functions.

Weyl served briefly in the German army at the outbreak of World War I, but before this military interlude, he did research that led to one of his most important papers. He looked at the way irrational numbers (those that cannot be expressed as a ratio of two whole numbers) were distributed. What he noticed was that the *fractional* parts of an irrational number and its integral multiples seemed to be evenly distributed in the interval between O and 1. He succeeded in proving this result, and it is known as the Kronecker-Weyl theorem, owing half of its name to an influential number theorist who had had an effect on Hilbert. Although the result may seem rather narrow, Weyl was able to generalize it to sequences of much broader application.

During his time in Zurich, Weyl spent a year in collaboration with **Albert Einstein** and picked up a dose of enthusiasm for the relativity theory. Among the other results of this collaboration was Weyl's popular account of relativity theory, *Space, Time, Matter* (the original German edition appeared in 1918). In those early days of general relativity, which describes gravity in terms of how mass distorts space-time, the correct mathematical formulation of some of Einstein's ideas was not clear. He had been able to use ideas developed by differential geometers at the end of the nineteenth century that involved the notion of a tensor. A tensor can be thought of as a function on a number of vectors that takes a number as its value. Weyl used the tensor calculus that had been developed by the geometers to come up with neater formulations of general relativity than the original version proposed by Einstein. In later years, he took the evolution of tensors one step further while maintaining a strict mathematical level of rigor.

Constructs New Foundations

One of the most visible areas in which Weyl worked after World War I was in the foundations of mathematics. He had used some of the topological results of the Dutch mathematician Brouwer in working on Riemann surfaces. In addition, he had looked at some of Brouwer's ideas about the philosophy of mathematics and was convinced that they had to be taken seriously. Although it was not always easy to understand what Brouwer was trying to say, it was clear that he was criticizing "classical" mathematics, that is, the mathematics that had prevailed at least since Euclid. One of the standard methods of proof in classical mathematics was the reductio ad absurdum, or proof by contradiction. If one wished to prove that P was true, one could assume that not-P was true and see if that led to a contradiction. If it did, then not-P must not be true, and P must be true instead. This method of proof depended on the principle that either P was true or not-P was true, which had seemed convincing to generations of mathematicians.

Brouwer, however, found this style of argument unacceptable. For reasons having to do with his understanding of mathematics as the creation of the human mind, he wanted to introduce a third category besides truth and falsity, a category we could call "unproven." In other words, there was more to truth than just the negation of falsity—to claim P or not-P, something had to be proven. This argument of Brouwer was especially directed against so-called nonconstructive existence proofs. These were proofs in which something was shown to exist, not by being constructed, but by arguing that if it didn't exist, a contradiction arose. For ordinary, finite mathematics it was usually easy to come up with a constructive proof, but for claims about infinite sets nonconstructive arguments were popular. If Brouwer's objections were to be sustained, a good part of mathematics even at the level of elementary calculus would have to be rewritten and some perhaps have to be abandoned.

This attitude aroused the ire of David Hilbert. He valued the progress that had been made in mathematics too highly to sacrifice it lightly for philosophical reasons. Although Hilbert had earlier expressed admiration for Brouwer's work, he felt obliged to negate Brouwer's philosophy of mathematics known as intuitionism. What especially disturbed Hilbert was Weyl's support of Brouwer's concepts, since Hilbert knew the mathematical strength of his former student. In the 1920s, while the argument was being considered, Hilbert was discouraged about the future of mathematics in the hands of the intuitionists.

Although Weyl never entirely abandoned his allegiance to Brouwer, he also recognized that Hilbert's program in the philosophy of mathematics was bound to appeal to the practicing mathematician, more than Brouwer's speculations. In 1927, responding to one of Hilbert's lectures concerned with the foundations of mathematics, Weyl commented on the extent to which Hilbert had been led to a reinterpretation of mathematics by the need to fight off Brouwer's criticisms. The tone of Weyl's remarks suggested that he would not have been unhappy if Hilbert's point of view was to prevail. This flexibility with regard to the foundations of mathematics indicates that Weyl was sensitive to the changes in attitude that others ignored, but also may explain why Weyl never founded a philosophical school: he was too ready to recognize the justice of others' points of view.

In general, Weyl took questions of literature and style seriously, which goes far to explain the success of his expository writings. His son recalls that when Weyl would read poetry aloud to the family, the intensity and volume of his voice would make the walls shake. He kept in touch with modern literature as well as the classics of his childhood. While he continued to enjoy the poetry of Friedrich Hölderlin and Johann Wolfgang von Goethe, he also read Friedrich Nietzsche's *Also Sprach Zarathustra* and Thomas Mann's *The Magic Mountain.* He could cite quotations from German poetry whenever he needed them. For those of a psychologizing bent, it has even been argued that his fondness for poetry may be in line with his preference for intuitionism as a philosophy of mathematics. The kind of poetry he preferred spoke to the heart, and he used quotations to add a human dimension to otherwise cold mathematical writing.

Leaves Germany for the United States

After he accepted a chair at Göttingen in 1930, Weyl did not have long to enjoy his return to familiar surroundings. In 1933 he decided that he could no longer remain in Nazi Germany, and he took up a permanent position at the Institute for Advanced Study, newly founded in Princeton, New Jersey.

Although Weyl himself was of irreproachably Aryan ancestry, his wife was partly Jewish, and that would have been enough to attract the attention of the authorities. There may have been the additional attraction of the wealth of intellectual company available at the institute, between its visitors from all over the globe and permanent residents such as Einstein. Weyl took his official duties as a faculty member seriously, although his reputation could be terrifying to younger mathematicians unaware of the poet within.

Weyl's work continued to bridge the gap between physics and mathematics. As long ago as 1929, he developed a mathematical theory for the subatomic particle the neutrino. The theory was internally consistent but failed to preserve left-right symmetry and so was abandoned. Subsequent experimentation revealed that symmetry need not be conserved, with the result that Weyl's theory reentered the mathematical physics mainstream all the more forcefully. Another area for the interaction of mathematics and physics was the study of spinors, a kind of tensor that has proven to be of immense use in quantum mechanics. Although spinors had been known before Weyl, he was the first to give a full treatment of them. Perhaps it was this work that led **Roger Penrose**, one of the most insightful mathematical physicists of the second half of the twentieth century, to label Weyl "the greatest mathematician of this century."

One of the challenges of physical theories is to find quantities that do not change (are conserved) during other changes. Felix Klein in the nineteenth century had stressed the importance of group theory, then a new branch of mathematics, in describing what changed and what remained the same during processes. Weyl adapted Klein's ideas to the physics of the twentieth century by characterizing invariant quantities for relativity theory and for quantum mechanics. In a 1923 paper Weyl had come up with a suitable definition for congruence in relativistic space-time. Even more influential was his 1928 book on group theory and quantum mechanics, which imposed a model that would have been welcome to Klein due to the previously rather disjointed results assembled by quantum physicists. Weyl was an artist in the use of group theory and could accomplish wonders with modest mathematical structure.

After the end of World War II, Weyl divided his time between Zurich and Princeton. His first wife died in 1948, and two years later he married Ellen Bär. He took a serious view of the history of mathematics and arranged with Princeton to give a course on the subject. One of his magisterial works was a survey of the previous half-century of mathematics that appeared in the *American Mathematical Monthly* in 1951. Although he never became as fluent in English as he had in German, he retained a strong commitment to the public's right to be informed about scientific developments.

John Archibald Wheeler, an American physicist, called attention to Weyl's anticipation of the anthropic principle in cosmology. In a 1919 paper Weyl had speculated on the coincidence of the agreement of two enormous numbers of very different origin. In the 1930s this speculation had been given with the title "Weyl's hypothesis," although later authors referred more to its presence elsewhere. What cannot be denied is that the recent discussion of the anthropic principle concerning features necessary for human existence in the universe has, as Wheeler noted, taken up Weyl's point once again.

Weyl was unaware of the rules governing the length of time that a naturalized citizen could spend abroad at one time without losing citizenship. By inadvertence he exceeded the time limit and lost his American citizenship in the mid 1950s. To remedy the situation required an act of Congress, but there was no lack of help in securing it. In the meantime, Weyl celebrated his seventieth birthday in Zurich amid a flurry of congratulations. On December 8, 1955, as he was mailing some letters of thanks to well-wishers, he died of a heart attack. With his death passed one of the links with the great era of Göttingen as a mathematical center and one of the founders of contemporary mathematical physics, but even more, a mathematician who could convey the poetry in his discipline.

SELECTED WRITINGS BY WEYL:

Books

Die Idee der Riemannschen Fläche, Teubner, 1913.
Raum, Zeit, Materie, Springer, 1918.
Philosophie der Mathematik und Naturwissenschaft, R. Oldenbourg, 1926.
Grüppentheorie und Quantenmechanik, Hirzel, 1928.
Symmetry, Princeton University Press, 1952.
Selecta Hermann Weyl, Birkhäuser, 1956.
Gesammelte Abhandlungen, four volumes, Springer, 1968.

SOURCES:

Books

Chandrasekharan, K., editor, *Hermann Weyl: Centenary Lectures,* Springer, 1986.
Deppert, Wolfgang, and others, editors, *Exact Sciences and Their Philosophical Foundations,* Peter Lang, 1988.

Dictionary of Scientific Biography, Volume 14, Scribner's, pp. 281–285.

—Sketch by Thomas Drucker

John Archibald Wheeler
1911-
American physicist

John Archibald Wheeler's work with **Niels Bohr** and Edward Teller helped advance the processes of nuclear fission and fusion. Wheeler conducted a variety of military research in association with the Manhattan Project, the effort which developed the atomic bomb during World War II, and also was instrumental in the creation of the hydrogen bomb. A professor of physics and director of the Center for Theoretical Physics at the University of Texas at Austin, Wheeler added the term "black hole" to astronomy dictionaries. Throughout his career, Wheeler has made fundamental contributions to the studies of nuclear structure, nuclear fission, scattering theory, relativity, geometrodynamics, and other subjects. A long-time professor at Princeton University, his students include the Nobel-honored physicist **Richard P. Feynman**. Wheeler was born in Jacksonville, Florida, on July 9, 1911. His parents, Dr. Joseph Lewis Wheeler and Mabel Archibald Wheeler, were both librarians. Dr. Wheeler was later head of the Enoch Pratt Free Library in Baltimore, Maryland, when his son entered Johns Hopkins University as an undergraduate. Wheeler's plans to major in electrical engineering changed after his first year, according to Dennis Overbye's essay on Wheeler in *A Passion To Know,* because of "a frustrating summer spent rewinding electrical motors in a silver mine in New Mexico." Wheeler then changed his major to theoretical physics, a field in which he earned his Ph.D. in 1933.

Studies at Copenhagen Lead to Nuclear Model

A postdoctoral fellowship from the National Research Council in 1933 allowed Wheeler to continue his studies first at New York University with **Gregory Breit** and then at the Institute for Theoretical Physics in Copenhagen. There, he worked closely with Bohr; Wheeler would later tell Overbye that "you can talk about people like Buddha, Jesus, Moses, Confucius, but the thing that really convinced me that such people existed were the conversations with Bohr."

While studying with Bohr, Wheeler began to think about one of the questions that was to occupy his attention for many years: the structure of the atomic nucleus. At the time, two models of the nucleus were popular, one which emphasized the properties of the nucleus as a whole and one that emphasized the properties of the nucleons (protons and neutrons) that make up the nucleus. More than a decade later, in 1953, Wheeler and a colleague, D. L. Hill, made one of the first and most successful attempts to combine these two models into a single theory, the "collective model" of the atomic nucleus. Wheeler, in collaboration with Bohr, also devised a theory explaining the process of nuclear fission, predicting the fissility of plutonium produced from the uranium isotope ^{238}U. The Wheeler-Bohr discovery was later to become critical in the development of the first atomic weapons.

Works on Theoretical Problems and Military Research

Throughout his career, Wheeler has pursued some of the most difficult and most fundamental questions in all of physics. Some of his earlier research dealt with the search for a unified field theory, which would show how the fundamental forces of nature (the strong, weak, electromagnetic, and gravitational forces) are related to each other. His 1962 book, *Geometrodynamics,* is a collection of his papers on this subject. He also worked during the 1940s with Feynman on the problem of action at a distance, a line of research for which Feynman shared the 1965 Nobel Prize in physics.

During World War II, Wheeler took a leave of absence from Princeton to consult on various aspects of the Manhattan Project, working at the University of Chicago's Metallurgical Laboratory, where the first atomic pile was constructed; at Washington States' Hanford Engineering Works, where plutonium was manufactured; and at the Los Alamos Scientific Laboratory, where the first atomic bombs were assembled and tested. Wheeler maintained scientific affiliations with the government, serving as a member of the U.S. General Advisory Committee on Arms Control and Disarmament from 1969 to 1976, science advisor to the U.S. Senate Delegation to the 1957 NATO Conference of Parliamentarians, project chairman of the Department of Defense Advance Research Project Agency in 1958, and consultant to the U.S. Atomic Energy Commission in 1958. Wheeler received the Albert Einstein Award of the Strauss Foundation in 1965 for his contributions in the field of nuclear energy.

One of Wheeler's best known and most controversial activities was his participation in the design and construction of the first thermonuclear fusion (hydrogen) bomb. Invited by Teller in 1949 to assist in this project, Wheeler was at first hesitant to become involved, but eventually became convinced that such a weapon was necessary to preserve world-wide peace. Wheeler's part in the project took place primarily between 1951 and 1953 at his Princeton offices under the code name Project Matterhorn.

Expands on Black Holes and Collapsing Universes

In 1939, **J. Robert Oppenheimer** described the theoretical effects of the curvature of space, when thermonuclear reactions cease to function in stars and gravitational forces cause their collapse. Wheeler carried out his own investigations into this phenomenon and, in 1967, coined the term "black hole." Expanding upon this concept even further, he rationalized that the whole universe might be subject to what he called the Big Crunch. As the universe contracts upon itself to super-dense dimensions, it would cause an explosion similar to that of the big bang, creating a totally new universe. As part of this research, Wheeler has developed the concept of "superspace," a highly complex mathematical construct that may be all that remains of the universe after the Big Crunch. His ideas on the Big Crunch and superspace have continued to evolve over time, resulting in the better understanding of black holes and imaginative theoretical constructs such as "wormholes," which deal with holes in space containing electrical forces.

Wheeler was married to Janette Latourette Zabriskie Hegner in 1935, "three days after [his] return from Copenhagen," according to Overbye. The couple has three children, one son and two daughters. Upon his return, Wheeler accepted a job as assistant professor of physics at the University of North Carolina. He remained there three years before taking a similar post at Princeton University, an affiliation that lasted until 1976. Wheeler took early retirement in order to accept an appointment at the University of Texas at Austin, as professor of physics and director of the Center for Theoretical Physics and then, in 1979, as Ashbell Smith Professor of Physics. He has also retained his Princeton rank of Joseph Henry Professor Emeritus.

Wheeler has received a host of honors and awards, including the Cressey-Morrison Prize of the New York Academy of Sciences, 1946, the Enrico Fermi Award of the U.S. Energy Research and Development Agency, 1968, the Franklin Medal of the Franklin Institute, 1969, the National Medal of Science, 1971, the Niels Bohr International Gold Medal, 1982, the Oersted Medal, 1983, and the J. Robert Oppenheimer Memorial Prize, 1984.

SELECTED WRITINGS BY WHEELER:

Books

Geometrodynamics, Academic Press, 1962.

(With B. K. Harrison, K. S. Thorne, and Masami Wakano), *Gravitation Theory and Gravitational Collapse,* University of Chicago Press, 1965.

(With Edwin F. Taylor), *Spacetime Physics,* W. H. Freeman, 1966.

(With M. Rees and R. Ruffini), *Black Holes, Gravitational Waves and Cosmology,* Gordon & Breach, 1974.

SOURCES:

Books

Contemporary Authors, Volumes 57–60, Gale, 1976.

McGraw-Hill Modern Scientists and Engineers, Volume 3, McGraw-Hill, 1980, pp. 299–302.

Overbye, Dennis, "John Wheeler: Messenger at the Gates of Time," in *A Passion To Know,* edited by Allen L. Hammond, Scribner, 1984.

—*Sketch by David E. Newton*

John R. Whinnery
1916-

American electrical engineer

John R. Whinnery has made significant contributions to the field of electrical engineering, both as a researcher and as an educator. His research includes work on microwave electron devices, wave guiding systems, optical guiding systems, and laser communications. As an educator at the University of California, Berkeley, Whinnery progressed from lecturer in 1946 to Dean of the College of Engineering in 1959. He has received numerous honors and awards, including the National Medal of Science in 1992, the 1976 Institute of Electrical and Electronics Engineers (IEEE) Microwave Career Award, and the 1974 Lamme Medal of the American Society for Engineering Education. In 1993 he was named to the Hall of Fame of the American Society for Engineering Education.

John Roy Whinnery was born in Read, Colorado, on July 26, 1916, to Ralph V. and Edith Mable (Bent) Whinnery. His father was a farmer whose hobbies included mechanics and electricity, and Whinnery became interested in electrical engineering at an early age. After attending high school and junior college in Modesto, California, Whinnery enrolled at the University of California, Berkeley, and graduated with a B.S. in electrical engineering in 1937. Following graduation he joined the research staff of the General Electric Company in Schenectady, New York. He spent one year as an assistant engineer before becoming supervisor of the High Frequency Section. There he was one of the leading members of a team working on the disk seal triode, a device significant in the field of high-frequency (microwave) electronics. This device, and others which he helped develop at GE, remain important elements of electronic technology in the fields of communication and radar. While at GE, Whinnery also worked on problems in waveguide discontinuities. Waveguides, like transmission lines, are devices which transmit electromagnetic energy. Discontinuities dissipate the transmitted energy, preventing it from reaching the intended destination.

Whinnery did not spend all his time conducting research, however. With Simon Ramo, a colleague at GE, he coauthored the textbook *Fields and Waves in Modern Radio.* This publication, and later editions under a slightly different name, became the definitive text on electromagnetic theory, both in the U.S. and abroad. Additionally, Whinnery was active during the Second World War, teaching training classes and lecturing at Union College in Schenectady. On September 17, 1944, Whinnery married his childhood sweetheart, Patricia Barry.

A Return to Berkeley: From Lecturer to Dean

Returning to the University of California in 1946 as an electrical engineering lecturer, Whinnery began work toward his doctorate. He was awarded a Ph.D. in 1948 and was promoted to associate professor. From 1951 to 1952 he was on leave from the university as head of Microwave Tube Research at the Hughes Aircraft Company. He then returned to Berkeley, attained full professorship, and became director of the Electronics Research Laboratory. Whinnery held this position until 1956, when he was named chairperson of the engineering department.

Throughout this time, Whinnery taught courses in electromagnetic theory and microwave networks and continued his research in microwave electronics with the aid of his graduate students. This research centered on problems with antennae, electron tube noise, and crossed-field amplifiers, and led to significant developments, including the backward wave amplifier. In 1959, after being honored with a Guggenheim Fellowship, Whinnery was made dean of the College of Engineering at Berkeley. He remained in that position until 1963, when he took another leave of absence, this time going to Bell Laboratories in Murray Hill, New Jersey. At Bell, he began research in quantum electronics, specifically lasers and optical communication problems. A year later, Whinnery again returned to Berkeley, where he continued the research begun at Bell.

A Leader in Education

After 1964 Whinnery remained primarily at Berkeley, where he continued to act as a lecturer and a researcher in optics, lasers, and optical communications. Additionally, he has served both the engineering community at large, and the nation, by assuming a leadership role in educating students and in formulating engineering education programs. This leadership has included chairing the Commission on Engineering Education from 1966 to 1968, serving as a visiting professor at Stanford University and the University of California, Santa Cruz, and serving on advisory committees for engineering departments at Massachusetts Institute of Technology, California Institute of Technology, Harvard, Yale, and Worcester Polytechnic Institute. Whinnery also achieved international acclaim as a visiting professor at the National Defense Academy in Yokosuka, Japan, and when he was made an Honorary Professor at Chengdu Institute of Radio Engineering in the People's Republic of China.

In addition to his efforts regarding engineering education, Whinnery has also served on various government committees, including the Science and Technical Advisory Committee for Manned Space Flight at NASA from 1963 to 1969, the President's Committee for the National Medal of Science from 1970 to 1972 and 1979 to 1981, and the Atomic Energy Commission's standing committee on controlled thermonuclear research from 1970 to 1973. He has won numerous engineering awards, including the 1992 National Medal of Science, the 1985 Institute of Electrical and Electronics Engineers Medal of Honor, and the 1967 IEEE Education Medal, and was named Outstanding Educator of America in 1974. He was also elected to both the National Academy of Engineering and the National Academy of Sciences. Whinnery has also served on the board of directors of the IEEE and on a number of IEEE award committees. In addition to his many honors, in a letter to G. A. Ferrance, Whinnery wrote that he is "most proud of the outstanding students I have had the privilege to work with."

SELECTED WRITINGS BY WHINNERY:

Books

(With S. Ramo) *Fields and Waves in Modern Radio*, John Wiley & Sons, 1944.
(With D. O. Pederson and J. J. Studer) *Introduction to Electronic Systems, Circuits and Devices*, McGraw-Hill, 1964.
(Editor) *The World of Engineering*, McGraw-Hill, 1965.

Periodicals

"Power Amplifiers with Disk-Seal Tubes," with H. W. Jamieson, *Proceedings of the Institute of Radio Engineers,* 34, July, 1946.
"The Effect of Input Configuration Antenna Impedance," *Journal of Applied Physics,* 21, October, 1950.
"Thermal Lens Effect in Laser Beams," *IEEE Student Journal,* Volume 6, No. 2, March, 1968, pp. 7–10.
"Laser Measurement of Optical Absorption in Liquids," *Accounts of Chemical Research,* 7, June, 1974, pp. 225–31.
"The Teaching of Electromagnetics," *IEEE Transactions on Education,* Volume 33, No. 1, February, 1990, pp. 3–7.

SOURCES:

Books

McGraw-Hill Modern Scientists and Engineers, McGraw-Hill, 1980, pp. 302–303.

Other

Whinnery, John R., personal correspondence with G. A. Ferrance, January 19, 1994.

—*Sketch by George A. Ferrance*

Fred Lawrence Whipple
1906-
American astronomer

The discoverer of six comets, Fred Lawrence Whipple is best known for his work on advancing the understanding of the nature of comets and meteors. His other interests include planetary nebulae (gases and dust), spectrophotometry (the measurement of intensities of light in different parts of a spectrum), the evolution of stars and the solar system, and the earth's upper atmosphere. Whipple also was at the forefront of tracking artificial satellites following the 1957 launch of *Sputnik*.

Fred Lawrence Whipple was born on November 5, 1906, in Red Oak, Iowa, the son of Henry Lawrence and Celestia (MacFarland) Whipple. The Whipples were farmers, and the youngster spent his first fifteen years on the farm. When Fred Whipple

Fred Lawrence Whipple

was a teenager, his family moved to California. After completing high school, Whipple enrolled at Occidental College, which he attended from 1923 to 1924, then entered the University of California at Los Angeles (UCLA), where he majored in mathematics. Following his graduation from UCLA in 1927, he married his first wife, Dorothy Woods. The couple had one son, Earle Raymond, before they divorced in 1935. Eleven years later, on August 20, 1946, Whipple married his second wife, Babette Frances Samuelson, and the couple had two daughters: Dorothy Sandra and Laura. In the meantime Whipple had attended the University of California at Berkeley and received his Ph.D. in astronomy in 1931. He had also accepted an invitation to join the staff of the Harvard College Observatory. His main areas of interest were comets, meteors, and interplanetary dust.

Although astronomers had long observed comets, scientists had virtually no clue as to the origin of the phenomena. Some observers of the 1600s believed comets had been flung out into space by rapidly rotating planets. Various astronomers of the nineteenth century theorized that comets were caused by the eruption of volcanoes on Jupiter and Saturn, or on their moons; the explosive eruptions had ejected the comets into highly elliptical orbits. Other scientific theories suggested that comets were densely packed hailstorms that orbited around the sun. In 1932 Estonian astronomer Ernst Julius Öpik proposed that an invisible cloud, lying far out in deep space, surrounded the solar system, and this was where comets and meteors originated.

Enters the Fray

Whipple began his investigation into meteors by developing a "two-station" photographic method of observing. Using cameras with rotating shutters, he was able to measure a meteor's trajectory, atmospheric drag, velocity, and orbit around the sun. His observing program, which lasted approximately fifteen years, led him to theorize that all visual meteors were related to comets—meteors were made up of the debris that followed comet-type orbits around the sun. Analyses of the spectra of meteors, as they burned in the atmosphere, indicated they contained silicon, iron, and other materials. It seemed reasonable to conclude that comets were comprised of much the same material.

The fact that comets did not precisely obey the laws of English physicist and mathematician Isaac Newton caused considerable consternation; Newton's First Law of Motion essentially states that the velocity of an object does not change unless a force acts on it. Some comets, like Halley's Comet, gain energy, causing their orbits (and consequently the amount of time it takes to complete their orbits) to increase. Meanwhile, other comets, like Comet Encke, lose energy, causing their orbits to decrease. Among the questions confronting scientists was: What is the force that changes the orbits of comets? Whipple devised a theory that not only explained the mysterious force, but also resolved the question of the composition of comets and revealed how they could survive close encounters with the sun.

The Demystification of Comets

To account for the mysterious force, Whipple suggested in 1949 that comets contain a solid nucleus several kilometers in diameter, composed chiefly of frozen water, ammonia, methane, and dust (silicates and primitive hydrocarbons)—in essence, Whipple proposed that comets were massive, dirty snowballs. When far from the influence of the sun, and in the cold darkness of space, the comet was a solid, frozen ice-ball. As the comet drew closer to the sun it would begin to heat up. The nucleus of the comet would undoubtedly be rotating, Whipple presumed, and as the ice layer began to melt, a thin layer of "dirt" would be left behind. This layer would absorb energy from the sun and prevent it from penetrating deeper into the nucleus. However, the heat would eventually radiate through the dirt layer, penetrate the nucleus, reach the highly volatile gases within the nucleus, and cause a "jet" of gas to erupt. This would have the same effect as a rocket engine on a spacecraft: If the jet was aimed behind the comet, it would cause the velocity to increase; if the jet was aimed in front of the comet, it would cause the velocity to decrease. (If the jet occurred on either side of the comet, an appropriate deviation would be introduced to the orbit.)

By studying the orbits of approximately sixty comets, Whipple and his colleague S. Hamid found that their results were consistent with the "dirty snowball" model. While comets lose material with each passage around the sun, an extremely large nucleus would permit repeated visits; hence, a short period comet, such as Comet Encke, could last a very long time. On the other hand, a comet with a small nucleus might last only a few orbits before disintegrating, and this would explain why some periodic comets fail to return when predicted. The dirty snowball model also explained how a comet could survive a passage through the sun's outer atmosphere. Undoubtedly, there would be a considerable loss of cometary material by such an event, but the solid nucleus would resist disintegration by holding the comet together. Whipple also considered the fact that great amounts of gas are emitted by comets with each visit; in previous studies of comets, scientists had wondered if the gases constituted an atmosphere surrounding the comet, and, if so, how the gases were replenished. Scientists had supposed that if comets had solid surfaces, they wouldn't be able to absorb enough gas to replenish themselves, and, in addition, there simply isn't enough gas in space to replenish their reserves. With Whipple's model, however, there is no need for replenishment: frozen gas is distributed throughout the nucleus, and it is released as the snowball evaporates.

The Emergence of Additional Theories

At about the same time that Whipple published his dirty snowball theory (in 1950), Dutch astronomer **Jan Hendrik Oort** revised Öpik's theory–that comets and meteors originated in an invisible cloud that surrounded the solar system—and suggested a manner in which comets could be "replenished." He conceived of passing stars whose gravitational attraction disturbed the distant Öpik cloud, continually sending cometary debris hurtling into the inner solar system. According to Oort, the comets would all arrive at different times and establish individual orbits as they plummeted toward the sun. Some of the orbits would become periodic, and these comets would return regularly; others would skim the solar system, and still others would fall into the sun and never again be seen.

The Whipple dirty snowball and the Oort cloud theories are presently the accepted models of comets and their origin, although they are not the only ones. In 1978 Thomas Van Flandern suggested that approximately five million years ago a gigantic planet orbiting the sun between Mars and Jupiter broke apart. The debris of that planet is the source of the comets.

Halley's Comet Provides Whipple with His Proof

In 1986, Halley's Comet returned, an event that had been long awaited and which became one of the most vigorously observed astronomical phenomena in history. In addition to a battery of telescopes and cameras of professionals and amateurs on the earth, as well as in high-flying aircraft, there were six spacecraft on a flyby trajectory to observe Halley. The United States sent the International Comet Explorer, and other countries, including Japan and the former Soviet Union, also sent space probes. The measurements and photographs attained from these launches confirmed Whipple's predictions: the "jets" he had forecasted were observed directly on Comet Halley's surface. It was learned that most of the comet's dust was composed of carbon and hydrocarbon compounds, rather than silicates, but Whipple's theory was more than substantiated, for Comet Halley had provided direct proof. In 1986 Mauritania, a West African republic, issued a postage stamp to commemorate the return of Halley, and an engraving of Whipple was included on it to honor his contribution to the understanding of the previously misunderstood celestial spectacles.

Prior to the excitement surrounding the return of Comet Halley, Whipple had been occupied with other endeavors. In 1942 he published his book *Earth, Moon, and Planets,* which is regarded as an authoritative volume on its subject; the work has been revised several times and went into a third edition in 1968. In the years 1943 to 1945, Whipple conducted war-related work at the Harvard Radio Research Laboratories, where he was in charge of researching, developing, and producing "confusion reflectors." These were small pieces of aluminum foil that were dropped from Allied planes. Tuned to interact with German radar, the foil simulated a multitude of aircraft on German radar scopes. In 1948 Whipple received the Presidential Certificate of Merit for his work, and two years later he assumed the position of professor of astronomy at Harvard, a post he retained for more than twenty-five years. In 1955 he became the director of the Smithsonian Institution's Astrophysical Observatory in Cambridge, and remained in that capacity until 1973, when he became Senior Scientist. He also served as a participant in the International Geophysical Year of 1957–58, during which time he organized multitudes of professional and amateur observers to keep track of artificial satellites, following the surprising launch of the Soviet Union's *Sputnik* in October of 1957. He also worked to formulate reliable ways of tracking the increasing number of satellites, for which he received the American Astronautical Society's Space Flight Award in 1960.

Throughout his career, Whipple has received several other honors: He was awarded the Donahue Medal six times (for independently discovering six new comets), and he received the J. Lawrence Smith

Medal of the National Academy of Sciences in 1949. In 1960 he was the recipient of a medal from the University of Liège for his astronomical research, and in 1971 the American Association for the Advancement of Science presented him with their Kepler Medal. In addition to his ongoing interest in astronomy, Whipple is a science fiction enthusiast and cultivates roses for relaxation.

SELECTED WRITINGS BY WHIPPLE:

Books

Earth, Moon, and Planets, Blakiston Co., 1942, revised 3rd edition, Harvard University Press, 1968.

History of the Solar System, Astrophysical Observatory, Smithsonian Institution, 1964.

(With Richard B. Southworth and Carl S. Nilsson) *Studies in Interplanetary Particles,* Astrophysical Observatory, Smithsonian Institution, 1967.

(Editor with Charles Lundquist) *Smithsonian Astrophysical Observatory Star Atlas of Reference Stars and Nonstellar Objects,* MIT Press, 1969.

Orbiting the Sun: Planets and Satellites of the Solar System, Harvard University Press, 1981.

The Mystery of Comets, Smithsonian Institution Press, 1985.

SOURCES:

Books

Abell, George, David Morrison, and Sidney Wolff, *Exploration of the Universe,* 6th edition, Holt, 1991.

Berry, Arthur, *A Short History of Astronomy,* Dover, 1961.

Calder, Nigel, *The Comet Is Coming!,* Viking, 1981.

Sagan, Carl, *Cosmos,* Random House, 1980.

—*Sketch by Raymond E. Bullock*

George Hoyt Whipple

George Hoyt Whipple
1878-1976
American pathologist

George Hoyt Whipple knew he would be a physician from the time he was in elementary school at the turn of the century. The son and grandson of doctors, Whipple followed the family tradition by choosing a career in medicine, researching the creation and breakdown of oxygen-carrying hemoglobin in the blood; this research resulted in not only a treatment for pernicious anemia, but also in a share of the 1934 Nobel Prize. An industrious, hardworking Yankee from New Hampshire, Whipple authored more than 200 publications on anemia, pigment metabolism, liver injury and repair, and other related subjects. Yet in his last days, it was as an educator that he hoped to be remembered.

Whipple was born on August 28, 1878, in Ashland, New Hampshire, the son of Frances Anna Hoyt Whipple and Ashley Cooper Whipple, a general practitioner held in high esteem by his patients and colleagues. Whipple's father died of typhoid fever just two years after the birth of his son, and Whipple and his sister Ashley were brought up by their mother and grandmothers. His was an outdoor life in rural New Hampshire, and he took a love of hunting, fishing, and camping with him into adulthood. At the age of fourteen Whipple entered Phillips Academy in Andover, Massachusetts, enrolling at Yale College (now Yale University) as a premedical student four years later. At Yale, he was a star baseball player and was on the gymnastics and rowing teams, as well as an outstanding student. Though versed in the humanities in these years of public and private schools, he had always been attracted by science and mathematics. After graduating with high standing in 1900, Whipple spent a year teaching and coaching at Holbrook Military Academy in New York to earn money for medical studies, and in 1901 he entered Johns Hopkins University's School of Medicine.

Sets His Course for Research

During his years as a student at Johns Hopkins, Whipple earned his way with a paying instructorship. Initially Whipple had considered going into pediatrics, but upon receiving his M.D. in 1905 instead joined the Johns Hopkins staff as an assistant in pathology, working under the renowned pathologist William Henry Welch. It was as a 29-year-old assistant performing an autopsy on a missionary doctor that Whipple made his first notable medical contribution, describing a rare condition in the intestinal tissues, which has since come to be called Whipple's disease. A year spent at a hospital in the Panama Canal Zone led to further notable advances in malaria and tuberculosis research.

When he returned to Johns Hopkins in 1908, Whipple turned his attention to studies in liver damage and the way in which liver cells repair themselves. Studies with dogs led Whipple to realize the importance of bile, a substance manufactured in the liver by the breakdown of hemoglobin, a complex pigment in red corpuscles. In normal concentrations, bile helps to break down fats during digestion, but can produce jaundice when present in excessive amounts. Beginning his assistant professorship at Johns Hopkins in 1911, Whipple came to focus on the interrelationship of bile, hemoglobin, and the liver. In 1913, along with a talented medical student, Charles W. Hooper, Whipple was able to show that bile pigments could be produced outside of the liver, solely from the breakdown of hemoglobin in the blood. Using this experiment as a starting point, Whipple set a new course for his studies. Since bile pigments are formed from hemoglobin, Whipple reasoned that he should tackle the question of hemoglobin itself, beginning with how it is manufactured. It was a fateful decision.

In 1914 Whipple accepted a position as director of the Hooper Foundation for Medical Research at the University of California in San Francisco. In that same year he also married his long-time sweetheart, Katharine Ball Waring, and the couple moved to California. Though burdened with administrative duties, Whipple continued his researches into hemoglobin production. His assistant, Hooper, came with him to California and together with a new assistant, Frieda Robscheit-Robbins, they began experiments which would lead to a major breakthrough. By systematically bleeding laboratory dogs, Whipple and his team were able to induce a controlled anemic condition. They then tested various foods and their effects upon hemoglobin regeneration, finding that a diet of liver produced a pronounced increase in hemoglobin regeneration. While such short term

effects were encouraging, they were still far from conclusive.

Research Proved Conclusive at Rochester

Though in 1920 Whipple was named dean of the University of California Medical School, he remained in California for just a year before accepting (somewhat reluctantly) a similar position at a new medical complex at the University of Rochester in New York—a facility heavily endowed by Kodak founder George Eastman and the Rockefeller Foundation. Courted enthusiastically by Eastman and university president Rush Rhees, Whipple moved home and laboratory to New York, bringing Robscheit-Robbins and the group of anemic dogs with him.

The next decade proved busy for Whipple: he directed the building and staffing of the University of Rochester School of Medicine and Dentistry, all the while directing further hemoglobin research. Perfecting their technique of bleeding the dogs, Whipple and Robscheit-Robbins induced long-term anemia and were able to prove conclusively that a liver diet was successful in counteracting its effects by increasing the production of hemoglobin. His results were published in 1925, and the pharmaceutical firm of Eli Lilly, with Whipple's cooperation, began producing a commercially available liver extract within a year. Whipple refused to patent his findings, and directed all royalties from the sales of the extract to fund additional research. Whipple's experiments paved the way for further studies by two Boston researchers, **George Richards Minot** and **William P. Murphy**, who used liver therapy to successfully treat pernicious anemia in 1926.

Whipple's work soon won international repute and in 1934 he received word that he, along with Minot and Murphy, was going to receive the Nobel Prize for Physiology or Medicine for their separate work in liver therapy. Whipple did not let fame slow him down. He continued his hemoglobin experiments, turning now to the study of iron in the body and utilizing the new technology of radioisotope elements to follow the distribution of iron in the body. He also made important contributions to the study of an anemic disorder peculiar to people of Mediterranean extraction, a disorder for which Whipple suggested the name *thalassemia*. Other studies involved the use of plasma or tissue proteins to rebuild hemoglobin in cases of anemia. A spin-off of this latter research was the development of intravenous feeding.

Despite the administrative and research duties that pressed upon him, Whipple did not forget his students, and took real pleasure in teaching. When in later years he was offered the position of Director of the Rockefeller Institute, he politely but adamantly declined, preferring his classes and his research.

Whipple finally relinquished his chair as dean in 1953 at the age of 75, after a long and distinguished career that had seen the once-small university grow to more than 12,000 graduates in medicine and other related fields. He remained on the faculty of the University of Rochester teaching pathology until 1955. In 1963 he established a medical and dental library for the university valued at $750,000. In addition to the Nobel Prize, Whipple was also a trustee of the Rockefeller Foundation from 1927-43, a Kober Medal winner in 1939, and a recipient of the Kovalenko Medal of the National Academy of Sciences in 1962, among others.

Whipple's life was long and productive. He was an active outdoorsman well into his ninth decade. With his wife Katharine, he had two children: a son, Hoyt, who followed in the Whipple tradition of medicine, and a daughter, Barbara. He died in Rochester on February 1, 1976, in the hospital he had helped to build.

SELECTED WRITINGS BY WHIPPLE:

Books

Hemoglobin, Plasma and Cell Protein, Charles C. Thomas, 1948.
The Dynamic Equilibrium of Body Proteins, Charles C. Thomas, 1956.

Periodicals

"A Hitherto Undescribed Disease Characterized Anatomically by Deposits of Fat and Fatty Acids in the Intestines and Mesenteric Lymphatic Tissues," *Johns Hopkins Hospital Bulletin,* Volume 18, 1907, pp. 382ff.
"The Metabolism of Bile Acids," with Marjorie G. Foster and C. W. Hooper, *Journal of Biological Chemistry,* Volume 38, 1919, pp. 367–433.
"Blood Regeneration in Severe Anemia, parts 1–3," with Frieda Robscheit-Robbins, *American Journal of Physiology,* Volume 72, 1925, pp. 395–430.
"Hemoglobin Generation as Influenced by Diet and Other Factors, Nobel Prize Lecture," *Journal of the American Medical Association,* Volume 104, 1935, p. 791ff.
"Mediterranean Disease—Thalassemia (Erythroblastic Anemia of Cooley). Associated Pigment Abnormalities Simulating Hemochromatosis," *Journal of Pediatrics,* Volume 9, 1936, pp. 279ff.
"Autobiographical Sketch," *Perspectives in Biology and Medicine,* Volume 2, 1959, pp. 253–87.

SOURCES:

Books

Corner, George W., *George Hoyt Whipple and His Friends,* Lippincott, 1963. *Nobel Laureates in Medicine or Physiology,* Garland Publishing, 1990.
Nobel Prize Winners, H. W. Wilson, 1987.

Periodicals

Diggs, Lemuel W., "Dr. George Hoyt Whipple," *The Johns Hopkins Medical Journal,* November, 1976, pp. 196–200.
New York Times, February 2, 1976, p. 26.
Young, Lawrence E., "George Hoyt Whipple 1878–1976," *Transactions of the Association of American Physicians,* Volume 89, 1976, pp. 34–37.

—Sketch by J. Sydney Jones

Augustus White
1936-
American orthopedic surgeon

A surgeon and biomedical engineer, Augustus White is an expert on back pain whose mechanical studies of the human spine have helped to develop technologies with direct clinical value. His surgical and engineering systems have aided patients in recovering more rapidly from spinal injuries. Throughout a career as a professor at both Yale and Harvard Medical Schools, and as a surgeon at Beth Israel Hospital in Boston, White has educated the public on preventative measures to head off chronic back pain.

Augustus Aaron White III, son of Augustus, Jr., and Vivian Dandridge White, was born on June 4, 1936, in Memphis, Tennessee. Attending Brown University, White initially intended to go into psychiatry. This career goal was altered, however, when he played football for Brown and became interested in sports injuries and their treatment. As a result, White decided on a career as an orthopedic surgeon, and after graduating cum laude from Brown in 1957, he went on to Stanford University where he earned his M.D. in 1961.

After serving an internship at University Hospital in Ann Arbor, Michigan, White worked as a resident orthopedic surgeon in both San Francisco and New Haven, Connecticut. He then served in

Vietnam from 1966 to 1968, rising to the rank of captain in the medical corps and being awarded the Bronze Star. In 1969 White joined the faculty of Yale Medical School as assistant professor and remained at the university for the next decade, becoming a full professor and then director of its biomechanical research department for orthopedics.

In 1969 White was awarded a doctorate from the Karolinska Institute in Sweden for his research in the biomechanics of the spine, work which focused on all aspects of spine mechanics and on fracture healing. He then went on to coauthor a basic and first-of-its kind text on the subject, *Clinical Biomechanics of the Spine*. Leaving Yale in 1978 to accept a position as professor of orthopedic surgery at Harvard Medical School, he also assumed a concurrent position as orthopedic surgeon-in-chief at Beth Israel Hospital in Boston. Not limiting his studies to orthopedics, White graduated in 1984 from the advanced management program at the Harvard Business School.

Married to Anita Ottemo, White is the father of three children, Alissa Alexandra, Atina Andrea, and Annica Akila. His work has been recognized by numerous awards and honors, including the Martin Luther King, Jr., Medical Achievement Award in 1972, the National Award for Outstanding Orthopedic Research from Kappa Delta in 1975, the *Ebony* Magazine Black Achievement Award in 1980, and the William Rogers Award from the Associated Alumni of Brown University in 1984.

White's work has helped to draw attention to back pain, a malady that effects eighty per cent of Americans between the ages of thirty and fifty. Almost anyone who has to sit for long periods at either a desk or behind the wheel of a vehicle is susceptible to back pain, according to White. The results of his research on the mechanics of the human spine have had practical applications; White advises that one should use the proper chair to provide lower back support, should know the correct way to lift heavy weights, and should practice sufficient exercise in between long periods of sitting. Involving the patient in the cure for back pain through education—spelling out the do's and don'ts of lifting and sitting, for example—was highly encouraged by White.

SELECTED WRITINGS BY WHITE:

Books

(With Manohar Panjabi) *Clinical Biomechanics of the Spine*, Lippincott, 1978.
(Editor with Stephen L. Gordon) *Symposium on Idiopathic Low Back Pain*, Mosby, 1982.
Your Aching Back: A Doctor's Guide to Relief, Bantam, 1983.

Periodicals

(With C. Hirsch) "An Experimental Study of the Immediate Load Bearing Capacity of Some Commonly Used Iliac Bone Grafts," *Acta Orthopaedica Scandanavica*, Volume 42, 1971, pp. 482–490.
"Kinematics of the Normal Spine As Related to Scoliosis," *Journal of Biomechanics*, October, 1971, pp. 405–411.
(With W. O. Southwick and R. J. De Pont) "Cervical Spine Fusions—Psychological and Social Considerations," *Archives of Surgery*, February, 1973, pp. 150–152.
(With D. Johnson and D. M. Griswold) "Chronic Ankle Pain Associated with the Peroneus Accessorius," *Clinical Orthopaedics and Related Research*, Volume 103, 1974, pp. 53–55.
(With S. M. Southwick) "The Use of Psychological Tests in the Evaluation of Low-Back Pain," *Journal of Bone and Joint Surgery*, April, 1983, pp. 560–565.
(With M. Shea, W. T. Edwards, and W. C. Hayes) "Variations of Stiffness and Strength Along the Human Cervical Spine," *Journal of Biomechanics*, Volume 24, 1991, pp. 95–107.

SOURCES:

Books

Hawkins, Walter L., *African American Biographies*, McFarland, 1992, pp. 440–442.

Periodicals

Ebony, June, 1964, p. 215; February, 1980, p. 84.
Howell, Ronald, "My Aching Back," *Ebony*, June, 1979, pp. 44–52.

—*Sketch by J. Sydney Jones*

Gilbert Fowler White
1911-
American geographer

Gilbert Fowler White is admired for his many contributions to the fields of geography and natural resource management. His research has covered a number of subjects that affect people on a personal, regional, and global basis, including water-systems in developing countries; global environmental change; nuclear winter; geography education; and strategies for coping with natural hazards. Many scientists particularly hold in high esteem White's ideas about a broad range of alternatives needed to cope with the risks of floods, calling him "the father of flood-plain management." For his work on the environment, White has won a number of awards, including the United Nations Sasakawa International Environment Prize in 1985 and the Tyler Prize for Environmental Achievement in 1987.

White was born on November 26, 1911, in Chicago, Illinois, where his father, Arthur Edward White, worked for the Burlington Railroad. The White family lived near the University of Chicago because Arthur wanted his children to have a good education and his wife, Mary Louise (Guthrie) White, was impressed by the president of the new university. Their son Gilbert attended the University of Chicago High School and eventually received an S.B., S.M., and Ph.D. from the university. Later in life he would join the University of Chicago faculty, teaching there from 1956 to 1969.

White's family influenced his education and career in other ways. In addition to his job with the railroad, White's father was a partner in a ranch in Tongue River Valley, Wyoming. Young White worked at the ranch during the summer months and saw first-hand the impact of decisions about water and land use, an interest he never lost. While an undergraduate, White discovered a group in the University of Chicago geography department that studied water, land, and natural resources. He had found his intellectual niche.

As a graduate student in 1934, White obtained a six-month appointment in Washington, D.C., as a geographer. In this capacity he conducted community-oriented research, a characteristic of much of his work since. The job was stretched to eight years, beginning with work on the Mississippi Valley Committee and ending with the President's Bureau of the Budget. Studying the Mississippi River Basin for the federal government in the 1930s, White opposed prevailing views about flood management, which called for the construction of levees and dams. He instead advocated the prevention of disastrous consequence from floods by keeping people out of the path of floodwaters. The wisdom of White's assessment reported in his 1942 landmark doctoral dissertation, *Human Adjustment to Floods,* was evident a half century later, when severe flooding of the Mississippi River devastated people and commerce in the American midwest for several weeks during the summer of 1993.

White has often expressed the opinion that solutions to complex problems are likely to be found in local activities. He told a *New York Herald Tribune* Forum audience in October 1952, "The tide of poverty will be turned only by the concurrent development of a vast number of small-scale projects centering on the patient, simple action of workers in rural communities of Asia, the Middle East, and Latin America."

White's belief in the importance of local activities is evident in the work he considers his most important. With his wife, the economist Anne Elizabeth (Underwood) White, and David Bradley of the London School of Tropical Hygiene and Medicine, he studied 30 sites in East Africa where women drew and carried all the water consumed for domestic use. The resulting 1972 report, *Drawers of Water,* put forth for the first time information about the collection and transport by women of domestic water, activities critical to 60 percent of the world's population. From their data, the scientists calculated the participants' costs in time and energy and the impact of those expenditures on resources, discovering in the process that the amounts of water used and the behaviors associated with the task varied enormously. The research results of White and his collaborators changed the attitudes of many governments toward the quality and quantity of water provisions. In a 1992 interview for *Summit,* White noted that this project "certainly was the most influential research work I've done in terms of affecting the lives of people."

Warns of Environmental Dangers in International Forums

Throughout his career, White has taken this concern for people on an individual and community level and applied it to efforts with a more global perspective. In 1953, White served in the Arid Zone Program of the United Nations Education and Cultural Organization (UNESCO). The arid lands research conducted by the organization paved the way for the concerns discussed at the 1972 Stockholm conference on the world's environment, which in turn led to the massive 1992 United Nations Conference on Environment and Development held in Rio de Janeiro.

In 1979 White spoke to the world community about the environment when he issued a declaration with Mostafa Tolba, head of the United Nations Environment Programme, suggesting that human activities might lead to climate change. His concerns with human activity and the earth have extended to issues of nuclear danger as well. As president of the Scientific Committee on Problems of the Environment (SCOPE), White launched a study of the environmental effects of nuclear war and helped draft *The Environmental Effects of Nuclear War,* a 1984 document providing a unified statement on nuclear disaster from a community of 300 scientists in 30 countries.

The leadership and organizational abilities demonstrated by White's ability to bring such a wide range of people together in the SCOPE project has been seen in White's other efforts as a scholar and administrator. At the age of 35, he became the president of Haverford College, a small liberal arts college near Philadelphia, Pennsylvania, founded by Quakers. He remained president there for ten years. His years at the University of Colorado have been equally productive. There he founded the school's Natural Hazards Research and Applications Information Center and served as director of the university's Institute for Behavioral Science. He is currently Gustavson Distinguished Professor Emeritus at the university.

White has been honored for his work on numerous occasions. In 1973, he was elected to the National Academy of Sciences. His many other recognitions and awards have included the Association of American Geographers' Distinguished Service Award in 1955 and 1974; the National Council for Geographic Education's Master Teacher award in 1985; the United Nations Sasakawa International Environment Prize in 1985; the Tyler Prize for Environmental Achievement in 1987; and the Vautrin Lud International Prize in Geography in 1992.

White's Quaker heritage underlies his activist approach to the problems he has studied. The great-grandson of Quakers, White was drawn to the religion's beliefs while in college. His adaption of the Quakers' philosophy of non-violence compelled him to serve as a conscientious objector during World War II, during which time he worked for the American Friends Service Committee (AFSC) as an administrator of Quaker relief efforts. White's active participation with AFSC has continued throughout his life, an influence which is evident in his strong views on the sanctity of life and on the responsibility humans have to care for the natural world. White's late wife Anne, whom he married in 1944 and with whom he had two sons and a daughter, was quoted in *Summit* as once attributing his ability to get things done to these very beliefs. She observed that White was driven by his "Quaker faith in the ability of humans to marshal their inner resources to deal competently and lovingly with the outer world and with their fellow human beings. . . . And not least there is his innate and humble desire to leave the world a bit better place than he found it."

SELECTED WRITINGS BY WHITE:

Books

Human Adjustment to Floods, University of Chicago Department of Geography, 1942.

Strategies of American Water Management, University of Michigan Press, 1969.
(With David J. Bradley and Anne White) *Drawers of Water: Domestic Water Use in East Africa,* University of Chicago Press, 1972.
Natural Hazards: Local, National, and Global, Oxford University Press, 1974.
(With Julius London) *The Environmental Effects of Nuclear War,* Westview Press (Boulder, CO), 1984.
Geography, Resources, and Environment, Volume I: *The Selected Writings of Gilbert White,* edited by Robert W. Kates and Ian Burton, University of Chicago Press, 1986.

Periodicals

"The Future of the Great Plains Revisited," *Great Plains Quarterly,* Volume 6, 1986, pp. 84–93.
"SCOPE: The First Sixteen Years," *Environment,* Volume 14, number 1, 1987, pp. 7–13.

SOURCES:

Books

Reuss, Martin, *Water Resources People Issues: An Interview with Gilbert F. White,* Office of History, U.S. Army Corps of Engineers (Fort Belvoir, VA), 1993.

Periodicals

Caughey, Peter, "A Quiet Leader," *Summit* (University of Colorado-Boulder publication), winter, 1992–93, pp. 16–19.
New York Herald-Tribune, October 26, 1952, p. 8.

—*Sketch by Margaret DiCanio*

Alfred North Whitehead
1861-1947
English American mathematician

Albert North Whitehead began his career as a mathematician, but eventually became at least as famous as a philosopher. His first three books, *A Treatise on Universal Algebra, The Axioms of Projective Geometry,* and *The Axioms of Descriptive Geometry,* all dealt with traditional mathematical topics. In 1900, Whitehead first heard about the new system for

Alfred North Whitehead

expressing logical concepts in discrete symbols developed by the Italian mathematician **Giuseppe Peano**. Along with **Bertrand Russell**, his colleague and former student, Whitehead saw in Peano's symbolism a method for developing a rigorous, nonnumerical approach to logic. The work of these two men culminated in the publication of the three-volume *Principia Mathematica,* widely regarded as one of the most important books in mathematics ever written. In 1924 Whitehead became professor of philosophy at Harvard University, where he devoted his time to the development of a comprehensive and complex system of philosophy.

Whitehead was born on February 15, 1861, at Ramsgate in the Isle of Thanet, Kent, England. Both his grandfather, Thomas Whitehead, and his father, Alfred Whitehead, had been headmasters of a private school in Ramsgate. Alfred Whitehead had later joined the clergy and become vicar of St. Peter's Parish, about two miles from Ramsgate. In his autobiography, Whitehead said of his father that he "was not intellectual, but he possessed personality." Whitehead's mother was the former Maria Sarah Buckmaster, daughter of a successful London businessman. As a young man, Whitehead often traveled to London to visit his maternal grandmother.

Educated at Sherborne and Trinity College

For the first fourteen years of his life, Whitehead was educated at home primarily by his father. Then,

in 1875, he was sent to the public school at Sherborne in Dorsetshire. Whitehead described his education as traditional, with a strong emphasis on Latin and Greek. But, he continued, "we were not overworked," so that he had plenty of time for sports such as cricket and football, private reading, and a study of history. At Sherborne he also had his introduction to science and mathematics, at which he excelled. In fact, he was apparently excused from some Latin requirements in order to have more time for his mathematical studies.

In 1880 Whitehead received a scholarship to continue his studies at Trinity College, Cambridge. While at Trinity, all of Whitehead's formal education was in the field of mathematics, the British system not having yet accepted the concept of a broad liberal education for all students. Still, he later wrote, his mathematics courses "were only one side of the education" he experienced at Trinity. Another side consisted of regular evening meetings with other undergraduates at which virtually all subjects were discussed. Whitehead later referred to these meetings as "a daily Platonic dialogue." Through these dialogues, Whitehead rapidly expanded his knowledge of history, literature, philosophy, and politics.

Whitehead was awarded his bachelor of arts degree in 1884 for a thesis on James Clerk Maxwell's theory of electromagnetism. A few months later he was elected a fellow of Trinity College and appointed assistant lecturer in mathematics. Whitehead was awarded his M.A. in 1887, and in 1903, was named senior lecturer. Two years later he was granted his doctor of science degree.

Meets and Marries Evelyn Wade

While still at Trinity, Whitehead met Evelyn Willoughby Wade, described in the *Dictionary of American Biography* as the "daughter of impoverished Irish landed gentry" who was "witty, with passionate likes and dislikes, a great sense of drama, and . . . a keen aesthetic sense." Whitehead himself credits his wife with teaching him "that beauty, moral and aesthetic, is the aim of existence; and that kindness, and love, and artistic satisfaction are among its modes of attainment." The two were married on December 16, 1890. They later had four children, Thomas North in 1891, Jesse Marie in 1893, Eric Alfred in 1898, and an unnamed boy who died at birth in 1892. Eric later became a pilot with the Royal Flying Corps and was killed in March, 1918, during World War I.

Whitehead's first book, *A Treatise on Universal Algebra,* was begun in January, 1891, and published seven years later. The book was an attempt to expand on the works of three predecessors, Hermann Grassmann, William Rowan Hamilton, and George Boole, the founder of symbolic logic. Whitehead later wrote that Grassmann, in particular, had been "an original genius, never sufficiently recognized." All of Whitehead's future work on mathematical logic, he said, was derived from the contributions of these three men. Whitehead's book was a tour de force that earned him election to the Royal Society five years after its publication. In the book, Whitehead argues that algebraic concepts have an existence of their own, independent of any connection with real objects.

Begins a Long Working Relationship with Russell

The year of Whitehead's marriage, 1890, also marked the beginning of another long and fruitful relationship, with Russell. The two had met when Russell was still a freshman at Cambridge; Whitehead was one of his teachers. In later years their student-and-teacher relationship blossomed into a full-blown working relationship as professional colleagues. They were eventually to collaborate on a number of important mathematical works.

An important event in their association occurred in July, 1900, when they attended together the First International Congress of Philosophy in Paris. It was there that Whitehead and Russell were introduced to the techniques of symbolic logic developed by the Italian mathematician Giuseppe Peano. They immediately saw that Peano's symbolism could be used to clarify fundamental concepts of mathematics. When Russell returned to England, he began to incorporate Peano's approach into the book on which he was then working, *Principles of Mathematics.*

Before long, however, it occurred to Russell that he and his former teacher were both working on very similar topics, he on his *Principles of Mathematics* and Whitehead on a second volume of his *Universal Algebra.* The two agreed to start working together, with the result that the second volume of neither work ever appeared. Instead, they developed the three-volume masterpiece, *Principia Mathematica.* The fundamental concept behind the book was that the basic principles of mathematics can be derived in a strict way through the precise rules of symbolic logic. The *Principia Mathematica* has since been described by one of Whitehead's biographers, Victor Lowe, in the *Dictionary of American Biography* as "one of the great intellectual monuments of all time."

Moves from Cambridge to London

In 1910, the year in which the first volume of *Principia Mathematica* appeared, Whitehead ended a twenty-five-year teaching career at Trinity College and moved to London. He remained without an academic appointment for one year, during which time he wrote his *Introduction to Mathematics,* which James R. Newman has called "a classic of popularization" of mathematics. Whitehead then accepted an appointment as lecturer in applied mathematics and mechanics at University College, London, and two years later, was made reader in geometry there. In 1914 he was named professor of applied mathematics at the Imperial College of Science and Technology in Kensington.

The London period was for Whitehead a particularly busy time in the political and administrative arenas. He served on a number of faculty and governmental committees and was outspoken in his concern about educational reform. Perhaps his best-known remarks on this subject came in a 1916 address to the Mathematical Association, "The Aims of Education: A Plan for Reform." In this address, Whitehead pointed out that the narrow view of education in which the classics are taught to a select number of upper-class men had become outmoded in a world of a "seething mass of artisans seeking intellectual enlightenment, of young people from every social grade craving for adequate knowledge."

During the latter years of his London period, Whitehead's interests shifted from mathematics to the philosophy of science. The fourth volume of *Principia Mathematica,* dealing with the foundations of geometry, was never completed. Instead, Whitehead began to write on the philosophical foundations of science in books such as *An Enquiry Concerning the Principles of Natural Knowledge* in 1919, *The Concept of Nature* in 1920, and *The Principle of Relativity, with Applications to Physical Science* in 1922.

The main theme of these books was that there exists a reality in the physical world that is distinct from the descriptions that scientists have invented for that reality. Scientific explanations certainly have their functions, according to Whitehead, but they should not be construed as being the reality of nature itself.

Joins Harvard's Philosophy Department

As early as 1920, Harvard University had been interested in offering Whitehead a position in its philosophy department. For financial reasons, a firm offer was not made until 1924, when Whitehead was sixty-three years old. He accepted the offer partly because he was nearing mandatory retirement age at Imperial College and partly because he looked forward to the opportunity of expanding his intellectual horizons. On September 1, 1924, Whitehead's appointment at Harvard became official.

Until the Harvard post became available, Whitehead had remained rather strictly within the areas of mathematics and natural science. After 1924, however, he extended the range of his writings to include far broader topics. His first work published in the United States, *Science and the Modern World,* discussed the significance of the scientific enterprise for other aspects of human culture. The book was an instant professional and commercial success and earned Whitehead an immediate reputation as a profound thinker and a writer of great clarity and persuasiveness.

His next book, *Religion in the Making,* was the first of a number that carried Whitehead far beyond the fields of mathematics and science. Its publication in 1926 was followed by *Symbolism, Its Meaning and Effect* in 1927, *The Aims of Education and Other Essays* in 1929, *The Function of Reason,* also in 1929, and a half dozen more books over the next two decades. In recognition of his work, Whitehead was elected a fellow of the British Academy in 1931, and he was awarded the Order of Merit, the highest honor that Great Britain can bestow on a man of letters, in 1945. Whitehead retired from active teaching at Harvard in 1937, at which time he was named emeritus professor of philosophy. He died at his home in Cambridge, Massachusetts, on December 30, 1947.

SELECTED WRITINGS BY WHITEHEAD:

Books

A Treatise on Universal Algebra, Cambridge University Press, 1898.
The Axioms of Projective Geometry, Cambridge University Press, 1906.
The Axioms of Descriptive Geometry, Cambridge University Press, 1907.
(With Bertrand Arthur William Russell) *Principia Mathematica,* three volumes, Cambridge University Press, 1910–13.
An Introduction to Mathematics, Williams & Norgate, 1911.
An Enquiry Concerning the Principles of Natural Knowledge, Cambridge University Press, 1919.
The Concept of Nature, Cambridge University Press, 1920.
The Principle of Relativity, with Applications to Physical Science, Cambridge University Press, 1922.
Science and the Modern World, Macmillan, 1925.
Religion in the Making, Macmillan, 1926.
Symbolism, Its Meaning and Effect, Macmillan, 1927.
The Aims of Education and Other Essays, Macmillan, 1929.
The Function of Reason, Princeton University Press, 1929.
Process and Reality: An Essay in Cosmology, Macmillan, 1929.
Adventures of Ideas, Macmillan, 1933.
Nature and Life, University of Chicago Press, 1934.
Modes of Thought, Macmillan, 1938.
Essays in Science and Philosophy, Philosophical Library, 1947.

Dialogues of Alfred North Whitehead, edited by L. Price, Little, Brown, 1954.
The Interpretation of Science: Selected Essays, edited by A. H. Johnson, Bobbs Merrill, 1961.

SOURCES:

Books

Johnson, R. C., "Alfred North Whitehead," in *Dictionary of Literary Biography,* Volume 100, edited by Robert Baum, 1990, pp. 306–315.
Newman, James R., *The World of Mathematics,* Volume 1, Simon & Schuster, pp. 395–401.
Price, Lucien, *Dialogues of Alfred North Whitehead,* Little, Brown, 1954, pp. 3–20.
Schilpp, Paul Arthur, *The Philosophy of Alfred North Whitehead,* Tudor, 1941.

—Sketch by David E. Newton

Robert Harding Whittaker
1920-1980
American ecologist

Robert Harding Whittaker was a central figure in twentieth-century ecology, developing a variety of innovative research methods and advancing novel theories on plant community ecology. He was an influential teacher, directing the research of a number of graduate students. He also conducted numerous field studies of his own, both in the United States and abroad. According to R. K. Peet, who edited a collection of essays in Whittaker's honor, his meticulous field research helped to advance his sometimes unorthodox and controversial hypotheses.

Born December 27, 1920 in Wichita, Kansas, Whittaker was raised in the small farming community of Eureka. His parents, Clive and Adeline Whittaker, were teachers at Fairmount College (now the University of Wichita). Though Clive Whittaker left his zoology teaching post when Robert was born and took up oil-drilling, he passed on to his son a love of natural history and an interest in academic studies. As a child, Whittaker collected butterflies and enjoyed summer holidays climbing mountains in Colorado, where his family often vacationed.

Challenges Orthodoxies as a Young Researcher

Like many of his generation, Whittaker saw his university education interrupted by World War II. He attended Washburn Municipal University in Topeka, was awarded a B.A. in Biology in 1942, and promptly joined the Air Force, where he served as a weather observer in England. After the war, he returned to the United States and entered the graduate school of the University of Illinois. Though his original application to the botany program was rejected, he later applied and was accepted to the university's zoology program.

During the 1930s and 1940s, the field of natural history was highly charged with divergent theories on how species interacted in communities. Whittaker began his graduate career with ties to two alternative opinions of species distribution. His official advisor, Charles Kendeigh, held to the traditional Clementsian theory of plant association; this theory argued for a holistic view of plant community, focusing on interdependence and cooperation. Whittaker, however, was drawn to the alternative theory put forth by Henry Gleason, who argued for individualism rather than cooperation as a basis for species interaction.

Whittaker's graduate research ultimately provided vital evidence to support Gleason's view. In order to complete his doctorate, Whittaker undertook field research in the Great Smoky Mountains. Originally intended to focus on insects, the project eventually became an examination of vegetation patterns and densities. Whittaker found ample evidence to demonstrate that plant species exist independently along different gradients—in other words, at different elevations and topographies, the distribution of vegetation species tends to vary rather than form discrete communities. Later, Whittaker would describe the distribution pattern as a continuum.

Whittaker's research on species distribution became the basis for his dissertation, which he defended in 1948. Although the research impressed leading ecologists and was generally considered to represent revolutionary methodology, according to Peet, it was not published until 1956, when it appeared in *Ecological Monographs* as "Vegetation of the Great Smoky Mountains."

After receiving his Ph.D., Whittaker taught for several years at Washington State College, continuing field work in and around southern Oregon. However, his teaching contract was not renewed, and in 1951 he left academia for a brief stint in industry. He joined the Aquatic Biology Unit of General Electric in Richland, Washington, where he studied the movement of microcosmic aquatic nutrients. At General Electric he met Clara Buehl, whom he married on January 1, 1953. They raised three sons.

In 1954, Whittaker landed a position in the Biology Department of Brooklyn College, City University of New York. During his years at Brooklyn, he spent summers in the Great Smoky Mountains conducting field research on plant productivity. In subsequent years, working first at Brookhaven National

Laboratory (from 1964 to 1966) and then at the University of California at Irvine (from 1967 to 1968), he developed a reputation as a skilled field-based ecologist and ecological theorist.

Whittaker continued to produce studies on gradient analysis and plant productivity, developing important data that challenged traditional theories of plant communities. One field-research project, undertaken with William Niering of Connecticut College, eventually resulted in Whittaker and Niering sharing the 1966 Mercer Award of the Ecological Society of America.

With his growing reputation came recognition and an appointment as Professor of Biology at Cornell University in 1968, where he would remain for the rest of his life. There he advised graduate students and became involved in a number of important research projects. One, concerning the use of ordination techniques to compare and analyze vegetation in Mendocino County, led Whittaker into potential conflict with European ecologists, who were wedded to an approach that favored traditional classification of species. In a successful attempt to negotiate a middle ground, Whittaker delivered a paper entitled "Convergences of Ordination and Classification" at the Rinteln symposium in Germany.

International Recognition Grows

Whittaker's Rinteln paper marked his growing importance as an international figure in the field of ecology. In 1973 he became the editor of the influential journal *Vegetatio*. To this international journal he brought a new perspective, soliciting articles by American ecologists advancing the ordination and gradient analysis approach, which he published alongside articles by Europeans representing the more traditional classification approach.

During his career, Whittaker translated his research into scores of articles and textbooks. He was the senior author for many of these articles, and he authored, edited, co-authored, or co-edited numerous books and texts. His works were often cited in the works of other ecologists. Among his most influential books are *Communities and Ecosystems*, 1970; *Handbook of Vegetation Science, Part V: Ordination and Classification of Vegetation*, 1973; *Niche: Theory and Application*, 1975; *Classification of Plant Communities*, 1978.

Whittaker received numerous honors during his years at Cornell, including election to the Academy of Sciences, election to the American Academy of Arts and Sciences, and honorary membership in the British Ecological Society and the Swedish Phytogeographical Society. He served as Vice-President of the Ecological Society of America in 1971, and at the time of his death was serving as the President of the

American Society of Naturalists. Shortly before his death Whittaker was awarded the Ecological Society of America's highest honor, Eminent Ecologist.

After the death of his wife in 1977, Whittaker continued field research both in the United States and abroad. In 1979 he married one of his doctoral students, Linda Olsvig; the two traveled to Israel and South Africa, where Whittaker continued a study comparing the diversity of species in similar climates—a project he was still working on when he died of cancer in 1980.

SELECTED WRITINGS BY WHITTAKER:

Books

Communities and Ecosystems, Macmillan, 1970.
Handbook of Vegetation Science, Part V: Ordination and Classification of Vegetation, W. Junk, 1973.
(Editor, with Helmut Lieth) *Primary Productivity of the Biosphere,* Springer-Verlag, 1975.
(Editor, with Simon Levin) *Niche: Theory and Application,* Dowden, Hutchinson & Ross, 1975.
(Editor) *Classification of Plant Communities,* W. Junk, 1978.

SOURCES:

Books

Peet, R. K., editor, *Plant Community Ecology: Papers in Honor of Robert H. Whittaker,* Kluwer Academic Publishers, 1985.

—*Sketch by Katherine Williams*

Frank Whittle
1907-
English aviation engineer

Frank Whittle, along with German engineer Hans von Ohain, invented the jet engine. Neither Whittle nor von Ohain was aware of the other's work, however, until after World War II. Whittle first began working on the concept of a jet engine in the 1920s, but he was repeatedly rebuffed by those who insisted that the idea was unworkable or impractical. With persistence during the 1930s and into World War II, Whittle developed his concept into the first flyable jet airplane outside of Germany. His creation, the Gloster-Whittle E28/39, first flew on May 15, 1941.

Whittle was born to working-class parents in Coventry, England, on June 1, 1907. His father had talents as a machinist and inventor, and in 1916 he bought a small business that he called the Leamington Valve and Piston Ring Company. The young Whittle acquired some experience here in manufacturing, helping with odd jobs such as drilling valve stems or working on the lathe. Whittle later wrote in his autobiography that he inherited his inventiveness and love for things mechanical from his father.

When Whittle turned eleven he received a small scholarship to attend secondary school. His school work was spotty. Most of the subjects he liked best, such as astronomy, engineering, and natural science, were not taught at the school. He read whatever he could find on popular science and became interested in chemistry. Still, he hated homework, and excelling at school seems to have been undermined by what Whittle himself called, in *Jet: The Story of a Pioneer,* "a natural laziness."

It was in secondary school that Whittle developed an interest in aeronautics and flying, an interest that would carry him through a brilliant and sometimes frustrating career as an aviation engineer. After graduating from secondary school, Whittle joined the Royal Air Force as an aircraft apprentice, although he had difficulty getting accepted because he stood only five feet tall. After he spent three years rigging aircraft, the RAF College at Cranwell accepted Whittle as a cadet. While at Cranwell he joined the Model Aircraft Society, which, Whittle later wrote, played a critical role in his early education as an engineer.

After graduating from the cadet college, Whittle was assigned to 111 Fighter Squadron, where he reported in August 1928. Here, along with his regular duties, Whittle continued pilot training, this time at Central Flying School at Wittering. Lectures at Wittering added to his fund of knowledge and helped nurture to maturity Whittle's ideas about jet propulsion. The problem under much discussion then was that propellers and piston engines limited an airplane's altitude and speed. The air was too thin at higher altitudes to properly engage a propeller, and the content of oxygen in the air was too lean to keep a piston-driven engine from stalling. Whittle thought that the problem could be solved by using a turbine instead of a piston engine. This way a lean mixture of oxygen could be compressed, combined with fuel, and ignited. The expanding gases caused by igniting the mixture of compressed oxygen and fuel would result in a jet blast that would propel the aircraft forward.

Overcomes Resistance

Convincing officials in the Air Ministry, however, was perhaps as great a challenge as developing the engine itself. One of the main objections was that materials did not yet exist that could withstand the heat and stress present in a jet engine. Whittle persisted. Eventually he found supporters who were willing to give him financial backing for his project. In return for their support, Whittle promised his backers each a quarter share of the commercial rights. The result of their agreement was the formation in March 1936 of a small corporation called Power Jets.

Development and testing of prototype jet engines continued into the war years after the German invasion of Poland in September 1939. The British surmised that Germany was also working on a jet engine, but could only speculate on the nature of that work. As for Whittle, he eventually prevailed over what at times seemed like insurmountable odds posed by technical difficulties and bureaucratic infighting.

By April 1941 Whittle and the Power Jet corporation began testing their W.1 jet engine in the Gloster-Whittle E28/39 airplane (after Gloster Aircraft Company, which constructed the airplane) by making taxi runs to see how the engine handled on the ground. With this testing and confidence-building measure, the engineers were able to make further adjustments, so that by the evening of May 15, 1941, a test pilot could take the aircraft aloft. The flight lasted seventeen minutes during which the aircraft reached a speed of 370 miles per hour at an elevation of twenty-five thousand feet. This easily exceeded the speed of the next fastest airplane in the Royal Air Force, the redoubtable Spitfire, which in many minds had defeated Germany's best aircraft in the Battle of Britain.

Despite the successful flight of the E28/39 with its W.1 engine (other models of this engine were also undergoing tests), more refinement was needed before they could be mass produced. With this in mind, engineers and other decision makers decided to start production of aircraft and engines in June 1942. As it was, production models of Britain's first jet did not appear in the skies until mid–1944. The production model, dubbed the Meteor I, was used against the German V–1 rockets that pummeled London late in the war.

In 1944 Great Britain nationalized the Power Jets company, which had been taken over by Rolls-Royce in 1943. The company was now called Power Jets R & D, and was limited to research and development. Whittle became chief technical advisor to the board, but because of poor health he played an increasingly marginal role, the more so since by the end of 1944 it had become clear that further development of a jet fighter would contribute little to what then seemed like the inevitable defeat of Germany. Morale sank and Whittle left the company in January, 1946.

Awarded Knighthood

By this time, Whittle's fame had become well established, and he was in demand as a lecturer in the United Kingdom. During the latter part of 1946 Whittle undertook a lecture tour in the United States, but again fell ill and required two months' hospitalization. In the United Kingdom, Whittle had received the Clayton Prize (£1,000) from the Institution of Mechanical Engineers for his work on jet engines. The Royal Commission on Awards to Inventors honored Whittle in 1945 with an interim award of £10,000, which it increased in 1948 to £100,000. That same year, King George VI granted him knighthood. Whittle's personal life was subsumed by his career, and *Jet,* his book about his work on jet propulsion, gives scant attention to life at home. Nonetheless, Whittle married Dorothy Mary Lee, whom he had known in Coventry, in 1930. Their first son, Francis David, was born in May of the following year.

After the war, Whittle worked for a while as a mechanical engineering specialist for the Dutch oil company, Bataafsche Petroleum Maatschappij, where he designed an oil-drilling motor called the Whittle turbo-drill. Thereafter he became a technical consultant to a number of aerospace firms and finally emigrated to the United States in 1976 after having accepted a lectureship with the U.S. Naval Academy. Whittle also worked on jet propulsion at Wright-Paterson Air Force Base in Dayton, Ohio, and became chief scientist at Wright-Paterson's Aero Propulsion Laboratory. Thereafter, Whittle worked as a senior research engineer at the University of Dayton Research Institute.

Whittle's research in jet propulsion revolutionized air travel and provided the technical groundwork for America's first jet airplane, the Bell XP–59A, which had its maiden flight in 1942. In recognition of Whittle's achievements, in 1991 the National Academy of Engineering in Washington, D.C., awarded him and Hans von Ohain its prestigious Charles Draper Prize, which included a grant of $375,000 to be divided between the two engineers.

SELECTED WRITINGS BY WHITTLE:

Books

Jet: The Story of a Pioneer, Frederick Muller, 1953.
Gas Turbine Aero-Thermodynamics, Pergamon, 1981.
(With John Golley and Bill Guston) *Whittle: The True Story,* Smithsonian Institution Press, 1987.

SOURCES:

Periodicals

Fink, Donald E., "Jet Engine Milestone," *Aviation Week & Space Technology*, April 13, 1987, p. 15.

Joyce, Christopher, "Jet Pioneers Win Engineering's 'Nobel Prize,'" *New Scientist*, October 5, 1991, p. 31.

Stix, Gary, "Smaller World: The Draper Prize Recognizes the Fathers of the Jet Age," *Scientific American*, December, 1991, p. 15.

"Turbojet's Inventors Earn Draper Prize," *Science News*, October 19, 1991, p. 252.

Vietmeyer, Noel, "They Created the Jet Age," *Reader's Digest*, May, 1987, pp. 162–166.

—*Sketch by Karl Preuss*

William E. Wickenden
1882-1947
American engineer

William E. Wickenden was a noted engineer and educator who, as president of Cleveland's Case School of Applied Science—as the institution was then known—brought the worlds of science and industry together. During his tenure from 1930 to 1947, Wickenden became a national spokesman for the engineering profession, enhancing not only the reputation and teaching standards of Case, but also attracting young scholars to the sciences. As a president of the American Institute of Electrical Engineering, Wickenden also promoted engineering as an educational option, while at the same time stressing the importance of a well-rounded education as the starting point for "turning a life experience into an education." A humanistic scientist, Wickenden served as the model for an entire generation of new scientists who blended the ideas of culture and technology.

William Elgin Wickenden was born on December 24, 1882, one of eight children of Thomas Rogers and Ida Consaul Wickenden. The elder Wickenden was a self-trained civil engineer who had immigrated to Toledo, Ohio, from England. He worked as an engineer for the city of Toledo, married the daughter of a local farmer, and raised his large family with a respect not only for God, but also for the humanizing effects of education. Seven of the eight Wickenden children graduated from college, a high ratio indeed

for the late nineteenth century. William Wickenden graduated valedictorian of his high school class, working year-round delivering papers and in the summer for a construction firm, and saving enough money to enter Denison University in Granville, Ohio, in 1900.

A small liberal arts college, Denison was also supported by the Baptist Church. While at college, Wickenden worked setting type for the *Granville Times,* and in 1904 earned his B.S., was Phi Beta Kappa, and valedictorian of his class. After a brief stint as an instructor at Mechanics Institute in Rochester, New York, Wickenden won a physics scholarship to the University of Wisconsin and became an instructor of electrical engineering at that university from 1905 to 1909. On September 2, 1908, he married Marion Susan Lamb of Toledo, Ohio, a fellow graduate of Denison University.

In 1910, Wickenden's first book, *Illumination and Photometry,* was published. Thereafter, he accepted a post as assistant professor of electrical engineering at the Massachusetts Institute of Technology (MIT), and was made associate professor in 1914. He was a popular teacher and a most approachable scholar. The years he spent at MIT were fruitful ones, and indicative of the direction that the mature Wickenden would take: teaching and encouraging interest in engineering.

From 1918 to 1923, Wickenden left academia, first to become a personnel manager for Western Electric Company in New York, and then from 1921 to 1923 as the assistant vice-president for American Telephone and Telegraph. But the pull of engineering scholarship soon brought him back to education. As director of investigations for the Society for the Promotion of Engineering Education, Wickenden worked from 1923 to 1929 studying engineering schools worldwide, using a Carnegie endowment to help fund his researches. He researched schools in the U.S. and Canada and spent a full 18 months in Europe and Great Britain. His final report, known popularly as the "Wickenden report," was published in 1929 and greatly influenced universities and technical schools. As the pre-eminent specialist in engineering education, Wickenden found himself a man in demand.

Tenure at Case an Inspiration

In 1929, just finishing up on his study of engineering schools, Wickenden was offered and accepted the position of president of the Case School of Applied Science in Cleveland, Ohio. Case, established in 1881, had been intended as a strong magnet school for science in the American heartland. By 1929 several attempts had failed at establishing real national prominence for the school, though it did enjoy a strong regional reputation. Sister college to Western

Reserve University, with which it shared a vast building site, Case had a long and contentious rivalry with the older institution. To Wickenden it made sense that the two schools cooperate instead of compete—a dream only fully realized in the 1960s when the two institutions merged into Case Western Reserve University. To that end, he proposed the sharing of teaching responsibilities between the two: Case being responsible for undergraduate science courses, and Western Reserve's Adelbert College tackling the humanities for both schools. It was only a cooperative effort, but it met with much opposition from those who feared Reserve would swallow up the smaller institution. In any event, Case's reputation grew because of the association, and Wickenden's model of the all-round scientist—both researcher and humanist—became more of a reality because of the shared teaching.

Other obstacles stood in the way of Wickenden's high hopes for creating a national institution out of Case: the Great Depression dried up funds not only from benefactors, but also from new students. By 1934 the student body had dwindled by a third, necessitating a corresponding reduction in faculty. It was this last action which hurt the most, for Wickenden had made a concerted effort since coming to Case to recruit well qualified faculty, making Ph.D. status a requirement. Thereafter, however, the situation improved, and with the coming of the World War II, Case became a training center for much needed civil engineers as well as for U.S. Navy officers. Wickenden—a critic of Roosevelt's conduct of defense preparation and production—instituted year-round schooling to enable students to graduate in three years. During the war years another barrier was broken: undergraduate women were admitted for the first time in 1943. The postwar years were again ones of growth for Case: the advent of the G.I. Bill enabled thousands of young men to pursue academic careers who might otherwise have not been able to afford such an investment. The years of the Cold War also made technology increasingly valued, and engineers were more in demand than ever before in the country's history.

Wickenden was a tireless proselytizer for engineering. In the early 1940s he served as president of the American Institute of Electrical Engineers and travelled more than 40,000 miles through North America and Mexico speaking on over 100 occasions annually at regional meetings of the association. Known for his eloquence as well as his great erudition, Wickenden was a personal example of the well-rounded scientist for which he campaigned. He was widely honored for his work both in education and civic activities: the recipient of 11 honorary degrees, he was awarded the Lamme Medal from the Society for the Promotion of Engineering Education in 1933, and served on the boards of both academic institu-

tions and private industries. In 1947, citing declining energy and a wish to spend more time with his wife and two children, Elizabeth and William C., Wickenden decided to retire from Case. He presided over the 68th commencement exercises, but suffered a massive heart attack on August 23 at his summer home in New Hampshire. He died on September 1, 1947, in Peterboro, New Hampshire, one day after his retirement had become effective. As reported in *Case Western Reserve: A History of the University 1826–1976,* Wickenden's friend and pastor, Dr. Frank Ferris, summed up the man in a funeral tribute: "He was one of the most completely civilized men it has been my good fortune to know."

SELECTED WRITINGS BY WICKENDEN:

Books

Illumination and Photometry, McGraw-Hill, 1910.
A Comparative Study of Engineering Education in the United States and Europe, Lancaster Press, 1929.
A Professional Guide for Junior Engineers, Engineers' Council for Professional Development, 1949.

SOURCES:

Books

Cramer, C. H., *Case Western Reserve: a History of the University,* Little, Brown, 1976, pp. 245–260.

Periodicals

"Dr. W. E. Wickenden of Case Institute," *New York Times,* September 2, 1947, p. 21.

Other

"William Elgin Wickenden, 1882–1947," *curriculum vitae* courtesy of Case Western Reserve University Archives.

—*Sketch by J. Sydney Jones*

Sheila E. Widnall
1938-
American aeronautical engineer

Sheila E. Widnall is an accomplished researcher, educator, and writer in the field of aerospace engineering. A specialist in fluid dynamics at the Massachusettes Institute of Technology (MIT) for nearly three decades, she has also served in numerous administrative and advisory posts in industry, government, and academia. In August, 1993, Widnall was appointed Secretary of the United States Air Force, the first woman to head one of the country's military branches.

Sheila Evans Widnall was born to Rolland John and Genievieve Alice Evans in Tacoma, Washington, on July 13, 1938. Her father worked as a rodeo cowboy before becoming a production planner for Boeing Aircraft Company and, later, a teacher. Her mother was a juvenile probation officer. Interested in airplanes and aircraft design from her childhood, Widnall decided to pursue a career in science after she won the first prize at her high school science fair. She entered MIT in September, 1956, one of twenty-one women in a class of nine hundred, and received her Bachelor of Science degree in aeronautics and astronautics in 1960. She continued on at MIT to earn a Master of Science degree in 1961 and the Doctor of Science degree in 1964, both in aeronautics and astronautics. Upon graduation, MIT awarded Widnall a faculty post as assistant professor in mathematics and aeronautics. She was the first alumna to serve on the faculty in the school of engineering. In 1970 MIT promoted her to associate professor, and in 1974 to full professor. During her tenure at MIT, Widnall served as head of the Division of Fluid Mechanics from 1975 to 1979, and as director of the Fluid Dynamics Laboratory from 1979 to 1990.

Establishes the Anechoic Wind Tunnel

Widnall specialized in the theories and applications of fluid dynamics, particularly in problems associated with air turbulence created by rotating helicopter blades. Her research focused on the vortices or eddies of air created at the ends and at the trailing edge of helicopter blades as they swirl through the air. These vortices are the source of noise, instability, and vibrations that affect the integrity of the blades and the stability of the aircraft. Widnall pursued similar interests in relation to aircraft that make vertical, short take-offs and landings (that is, V/STOL aircraft) and the noise associated with them. To this end, her studies led her to establish the anechoic wind tunnel at MIT, where researchers study

Sheila E. Widnall

the phenomenon of noise and V/STOL aircraft. During her tenure at MIT, Widnall established a reputation as an expert in her field and lectured widely on her research in vortices and their relation to aerodynamics. Widnall is the author of seventy papers on fluid dynamics as well as other areas of science and engineering; she has also served as associate editor for the scientific publications *Journal of Aircraft, Physics of Fluids,* and the *Journal of Applied Mechanics.*

In addition to writing about aerodynamics, Widnall has also published articles and delivered talks about the changing attitudes and trends in education for prospective engineers and scientists. In 1988, as newly elected president of the American Association for the Advancement of Science (AAAS), Widnall addressed the association on her longstanding interest in seeing more women become scientists and engineers and the problems they face in attaining higher degrees and achieving professional goals. In recognition of Widnall's efforts on behalf of women in science and engineering, in 1986 MIT awarded her the Abby Rockefeller Mauze chair, an endowed professorship awarded to those who promote the advancement of women in industry and in the arts and professions.

Begins a Distinguished Public Career

Along with her technical and scientific interests, Widnall has been active in administration, public policy, and industry consulting. In 1974 she became the first director of university research of the U.S. Department of Transportation. In 1979 MIT nominated Widnall to be the first woman to chair its 936-member faculty; she chaired MIT's Committee on Academic Responsibility for a year beginning in 1991; and she was named associate provost at the university in 1992. In addition to her term as president of the AAAS, Widnall has served on the board of directors for the American Institute of Aeronautics and Astronautics, as a member of the Carnegie Commission on Science, Technology, and Government, and as a consultant to businesses and colleges, including American Can Corporation, Kimberly-Clark, McDonnell Douglas Aircraft, and Princeton University. Her career has been recognized with numerous awards, including the Lawrence Sperry Award from the American Institute of Aeronautics and Astronautics in 1972, the Outstanding Achievement Award from the Society of Women Engineers in 1975, and the Washburn Award from the Boston Museum of Science in 1987. She was elected to the National Academy of Engineering in 1985.

Widnall's association with the Air Force developed through her appointment by President Carter to two three-year terms on the Air Force Academy's board of visitors, which she chaired from 1980–1982. She also served on advisory committees to the Military Airlift Command and to Wright-Patterson Air Force Base in Dayton, Ohio. As Secretary of the Air Force, Widnall is responsible for all administrative, training, recruiting, logistical support, and personnel matters, as well as research and development operations.

She married William Soule Widnall, also an aeronautical engineer, in June, 1960. The couple has two grown children, William and Ann Marie. In her spare time, Widnall enjoys bicycling, wind surfing, and hiking in the Cascade Mountains with her husband in her native Washington.

SELECTED WRITINGS BY WIDNALL:

Periodicals

"Science and the Atari Generation," *Science,* August 12, 1983, p. 607.
"AAAS Presidential Lecture: Voices from the Pipeline," *Science,* September 30, 1988, pp. 1740–1745.

SOURCES:

Periodicals

Ewing, Lee, "Panelists Laud Widnall, Approve Her Nomination," *Air Force Times,* August 2, 1993, p. 4.

Jehl, Douglas, "M.I.T. Professor Is First Woman Chosen as Secretary of Air Force," *New York Times,* July 4, 1993, sec. 1, p. 20.
Sears, William R., "Sheila E. Widnall: President-Elect of AAAS," *Association Affairs,* June 6, 1986, pp. 1119–1200.
Stone, Steve, "Air Force Secretary Salutes Female Aviators," *Norfolk Virginian-Pilot,* October 10, 1993, p. B3.
"USAF Head Approved," *Aviation Week & Space Technology,* August 9, 1993, p. 26.
"Widnall of MIT Is New President-elect Of AAAS," *Physics Today,* February 1986, p. 69.

Other

Biography, "Dr. Sheila E. Widnall," Office of the Secretary of the Air Force/Public Affairs, November 1993.

—Sketch by Karl Preuss

Emil Wiechert
1861-1928
German geophysicist

Emil Wiechert's contributions to the fields of geophysics and seismology laid the foundations of the modern understanding of the internal movement and constitution of the earth. He also invented the most accurate seismographs of his day. Wiechert's other research topics included atmospheric structure and electricity. He was the founder of the University of Göttingen Institute of Geophysics and one of the founders of the International Association of Seismology.

Wiechert was born on December 26, 1861, in Tilsit, Germany, to Johann Christian Wiechert, a merchant who died when his son was a child. Wiechert's mother encouraged her son in his studies and accompanied him to Königsberg when he enrolled as a physics student at the university there. After receiving his bachelor's degree in 1889, Wiechert became a lecturer and began his graduate studies with a research project on atomic structure in relation to basic properties of matter and electrical particle theory.

In 1890 Wiechert began the first of several scientific collaborations with graduate and post-graduate students which involved geophysical problems that resulted in his designs for instruments to be used in applied physics. The Physics and Economics

Society at the University of Königsberg awarded a prize for the interpretation of the data on the earth's temperature collected at the school's meteorological observatory. Wiechert and **Arnold Sommerfeld**, a theoretical physicist whose specialty was boundary value mathematics, constructed a harmonic analyzer to facilitate interpretation of the data. The analyzer reduced the data, plotted as a temperature curve, to a series of trigonometric figures. The harmonic analyzer's results allowed for an interpretation of the earth's temperature variations as a function of thermodynamic heat conduction.

In 1897 Wiechert moved to the University of Göttingen, and his career as a geophysicist began in earnest. Shortly after his arrival he founded the Göttingen Institute of Geophysics, where he studied seismology, the study of earthquakes and other vibrations of the earth. The seismograph, an instrument that records earth oscillations, dates back to the second century A.D., but it was not until 1892 that a seismograph was developed that was capable of worldwide monitoring rather than local recording. Wiechert's entrance into the field of seismology occurred shortly after this data became available for study. However, his experience with a variety of seismographs convinced him that he could invent a more accurate instrument than those in use at that time. He turned to the idea of an inverted pendulum design to obtain the accuracy he desired.

Develops an Improved Seismograph

Wiechert applied his acumen for instrumental design when he invented the inverted pendulum seismograph in 1900. The design used a heavy inertial mass equilibrium positioned to overcome friction and balanced on a knife-edge pen indicator. Support for oscillation was afforded by sets of small springs anchored at the top of the seismograph frame, a design much different than other seismographs of the day. Wiechert's first model only recorded the two horizontal component directions of earth movement. Further modifications enabled recording in the vertical component as well, so that all three required directions of seismic oscillation were eventually covered.

Wiechert's seismographs were the largest of the time, some with masses of more than two tons. Whereas earlier seismographs had used an optical method (light reflected through the oscillating horizontal pendulum arm onto light-sensitive paper) to register seismic activity, Wiechert used a mechanical method employing a sheet of smoked paper wrapped on a rotating drum, which shifted with each rotation to avoid superimposition of the recording. This was a simpler recording method, and the resulting chart, or seismogram, was more detailed and closer to a true reflection of earth activity. By 1920 there were eighty Wiechert seismographs in operation, more than any other type in use worldwide. Prior to World War I, Wiechert himself was able to establish several geophysical observatories in the German colonies, which provided an important link to the early world network of seismic stations.

Using his seismograph, Wiechert and a group of dedicated students and collaborators, most notably Karl Zöppritz and **Beno Gutenberg**, provided a landmark perspective on the earth's internal structure from their data, which helped establish the fundamentals of modern seismological theory. One of their most important results was determining seismic wave travel time through the layered structure of the earth, which Zöppritz compiled into comprehensive tables. Another addition to the theory came from Gutenberg, who later emigrated to the United States and became director of the seismology lab at the California Institute of Technology. Wiechert and his colleagues formed a basic theoretical model of the earth, concluding that there were three basic layers in the earth: a dense core, a liquid mantle, and a solid crust. Using the seismic wave data and the mathematical theory of the wave time-depth relation, Gutenberg calculated the depth of the earth's core to be 2,900 kilometers or 1,780 miles.

Contributions to the Inter-Geophysical Community

Wiechert remained active in his research endeavors even though a progressive deafness overtook him in later years. He finalized the work on the mathematics of seismic waves with Gustav Herglotz, which culminated in their equations determining deep-earth seismic wave velocities derived from the travel-time tables (Wiechert-Herglotz method). He eventually returned to seismograph design to create smaller-sized, portable instruments for use with controlled explosions to study shock wave propagation in the earth's crust. Wiechert's artificial detonation method was used in exploratory geophysics and solid earth structural research and prospecting.

Relatively late in his career Wiechert returned to elementary electrical theory but applied it to the study of the atmosphere. His research contributed to the development of planetary electrodynamics as a discipline. Wiechert also supervised the development of galvanometric instruments—those used to measure small electric currents in the atmosphere—and experiments to determine potential gradients of atmospheric layers and their electrical conductivity. Further research involved applying his knowledge of seismic waves to studies regarding the atmosphere. By transmitting sound waves through the atmosphere, he was able to better understand how it was stratified.

Wiechert helped found the International Association of Seismology in 1905. Wiechert married the daughter of a Göttingen lawyer in 1908. The couple, who had no children, lived with Wiechert's mother until her death in 1927. Wiechert died on March 19, 1928, in Göttingen.

SELECTED WRITINGS BY WIECHERT:

Periodicals

"Theorie der automatischen Seismographen," *Abhandlungen der K. Gesellschaft der Wissenschaften zu Göttingen,* number 1, 1903.

"Our Present Knowledge of the Earth," *Report of the Board of Regents of the Smithsonian Institution,* 1908, pp. 431–449.

(With L. Geiger) "Bestimmung des Weges der Erdbebenwellen im Erdinneren," *Physikalische Zeitschrift,* Volume 11, 1910, pp. 294–311.

—*Sketch by William J. McPeak*

Heinrich Wieland
1877-1957
German chemist

Heinrich Wieland was one of the greatest organic chemists of the century, admired for the breadth of his knowledge and his devotion to arduous, painstaking research. Wieland is known for his studies on the structures of important complex natural products, from toad poisons to butterfly pigments. He also made major contributions to biochemistry, especially in the study of the mechanism of biological oxidation. His most famous work, for which he was awarded the Nobel Prize in chemistry in 1927, was the determination of the molecular structure of the bile acids. This research combined superb experimental skill with precise deductive reasoning and remains a model of organic chemical investigation.

Heinrich Otto Wieland was born on June 4, 1877, in Pforzheim, Germany, to Theodor and Elise Blom Wieland. Theodor Wieland was a pharmaceutical chemist, and Heinrich studied the subject in school in Pforzheim. At that time, instead of studying at a single university to obtain a degree, a student enrolled at several universities, listening to the lectures of the best professors. Wieland spent 1896 at the University of Munich, 1897 at the University of Berlin, and 1898 at the Technische Hochschule at Stuttgart. In 1899 he returned to Munich to work toward his Ph.D. under the direction of Johannes Thiele, in the laboratory of Adolf von Baeyer. After he

received his Ph.D. in 1901, Wieland remained at Munich to do research, eventually becoming a lecturer in 1904 and a senior lecturer in 1913. In 1917 he was appointed professor at the Technische Hochschule in Munich, but was granted leave to work for **Fritz Haber**'s chemical warfare research organization at the Kaiser Wilhelm Institute in Berlin. At the end of World War I he returned to Munich, but left in 1921 to accept a professorship at the University of Freiburg. In 1925, Wieland returned to the University of Munich as professor and director of the Baeyer Laboratory, succeeding **Richard Willstätter**, who personally recommended Wieland for the position. By this time, Wieland was recognized as a world leader in organic chemistry, and he remained at Munich until his retirement in 1950.

Wieland's early research was concerned with the chemistry of organic nitrogen compounds. He explored the addition of dinitrogen trioxide and nitrogen dioxide to carbon-carbon double bonds. A large series of papers described the reactions of aromatic amines (a type of organic compound derived from ammonia), especially their oxidations. One line of experiments led to the discovery of nitrogen free radicals, unusually reactive short-lived species in which nitrogen is bonded to two atoms, instead of the usual three atoms. Wieland published almost one hundred papers on organic nitrogen chemistry, which in itself was a notable achievement.

Another series of experiments led to Wieland's 1912 theory of biological oxidation, a process by which biologic substances are changed by combining with oxygen or losing electrons. For years, the accepted theory involved some kind of change to molecular oxygen inside the cell in which the oxygen becomes "activated" and reacts with the oxidizable substance. Wieland proposed that the oxidizable substance itself becomes "activated" and loses hydrogen atoms in the oxidation process. Wieland published more than fifty papers from 1912 to 1943 on biological oxidation and was able to demonstrate that many reactions proceed through dehydrogenation and could proceed in the absence of oxygen. He was challenged, however, by the German physiologist **Otto Warburg**, who showed that respiratory enzymes which contain iron (sometimes copper) do activate oxygen, and both types of oxidation mechanism are found in nature. Warburg received the Nobel Prize in 1931 for his contribution to understanding oxidation, but Wieland's work has been recognized as equally significant by biochemists.

Determining Structure of Bile Acids Leads to Nobel Prize

In 1912, the year Wieland proposed his theory of biological oxidation, he published his first paper on the structure of the bile acids. This topic would occupy his interest for twenty years and earn him the

Nobel Prize. Bile is a golden yellow liquid which is produced in the liver, stored in the gall bladder, and secreted in small amounts into the intestines. The sodium salts of bile acids, the principal constituent of bile, are essential to the digestion of fats. Although bile acids had been isolated early in the nineteenth century, their structural formulas were unknown when Wieland began his work. As the work progressed, it was shown by **Adolf Windaus**, a chemist at the University of Göttingen, that cholesterol and the bile acids share a common basic structure, allowing Windaus's research results on the structure of cholesterol (for which he won the Nobel Prize in 1928) to be used by Wieland, and vice versa. Later it was shown that the common basic structure, the steroid nucleus, is found in many naturally occurring sources, such as the sex hormones, adrenal hormones (cortisone), digitalis (a plant cardiac poison, used medicinally as a stimulant), and toad poison. Steroid chemistry became essential to the development of many powerful medicines, as well as oral contraceptives. The pioneering work of Wieland and his students on the bile acids became a foundation of modern pharmaceutical chemical research.

The work on bile acids was an enormous challenge for organic chemistry in the first quarter of the century. First, a procedure for isolation and purification of the various acids, obtained from ox bile, was required. Then, each acid had to be characterized and chemically related to the others. The acids each contain 24 carbon atoms and differ in the number of hydroxyl (alcohol) groups. Wieland used the method of selective degradation to break the acids into simpler compounds, thus allowing him to identify the smaller molecules. Although his work was somewhat simplified because he could use the results of Windaus, Wieland admitted in his Nobel Lecture that "the task would appear to be a long and unspeakably wearisome trek through an arid desert of structure." In this lecture he outlined the course of his research, showing the failures as well as successes. Although the structures of the bile acids and cholesterol appeared to be solved when Wieland and Windaus received their Nobel prizes, in fact a conclusion which they had made based on analogous reactions was not correct, and the final, unequivocal structures were proposed by Wieland and others in 1932.

In addition to the bile acids, Wieland also investigated other natural products. He contributed to the determination of the structures of morphine, lobeline, and strychnine alkaloids, as well as butterfly wing pigments and mushroom and toad poisons. He had a wide range of interests, encompassing all areas of organic chemistry, and for twenty years he was editor of the major chemical journal *Justus Liebigs Annalen der Chemie*. His work was recognized throughout his career, and he was honored by scientific societies and universities in many countries. In 1955 he was named the first recipient of the German Chemical Society's Otto Hahn Prize for Physics and Chemistry.

Wieland remained at the University of Munich during World War II. He had little regard for the Nazi government in Germany and made no secret of it. He protected Jews in his laboratory and in 1944 testified on behalf of students who had been accused of treason.

Wieland married Josephine Bartmann in 1908. All three of their sons became scientists: Wolfgang, a pharmaceutical chemist; Theodor, a professor of chemistry; and Otto, a professor of medicine. Their daughter, Eva, married **Feodor Lynen**, a professor of biochemistry who won the Nobel Prize in physiology or medicine in 1964. In addition to his love of family and his work, Wieland also enjoyed painting and music. He died in Starnberg, Germany, on August 5, 1957, two months after his eightieth birthday.

SELECTED WRITINGS BY WIELAND:

Books

On the Mechanism of Oxidation, Yale, 1932.
"The Chemistry of the Bile Acids," in *Nobel Lectures: Chemistry, 1922–1941,* Elsevier, 1966, pp. 94–104.

SOURCES:

Books

Farber, Eduard, "Heinrich Wieland," in *Great Chemists,* edited by E. Farber, Interscience, 1961, pp. 1442–51.

Fieser, Louis F. and Mary Fieser, "Structure of the Bile Acids and of Cholesterol," in *Steroids,* Reinhold, 1959, pp. 53–89.

Follweiler, Joanne M., "Heinrich Wieland" in *Nobel Laureates in Chemistry, 1901–1992,* edited by L. K. James, American Chemical Society, 1993, pp. 164–68.

Shuman, R. Baird, "Heinrich Otto Wieland," in *The Nobel Prize Winners: Chemistry,* Volume 2, edited by F. N. Magill, Salem, 1990, pp. 291–98.

—Sketch by Martin R. Feldman

Wilhelm Wien
1864-1928
German physicist

Wilhelm Wien is best known for his studies of radiation. Of the two laws he developed dealing with this topic, one was later confirmed, and is now known as Wien's displacement law. The second law was later shown to be inadequate and was replaced by **Max Planck**'s brilliant theoretical analysis of the quantum nature of energy emission. Although Wien never made discoveries later in life of the quality of those from his early career, he eventually became a highly respected leader of German science in the early part of the twentieth century.

Wilhelm Carl Werner Otto Fritz Franz Wien was born on January 13, 1864, on his family's farm at Gaffken, near Fischhausen, in East Prussia. He was the only child of Carl Wien and the former Caroline Gertz, both descended from land-owning Prussian aristocracy. When Wien was two years old, the family moved to a smaller farm at Drachenstein, in the district of Rastenburg. As a young child, Wien received private tutoring and learned to speak French before he could write his native German. He was quite introverted, however, and spent a great deal of time by himself riding and swimming. Wien's mother was a particularly strong influence in her son's life. She was responsible for operating the Drachenstein farm after her husband had become ill, and according to Wien's entry in the *Dictionary of Scientific Biography,* "her excellent knowledge of history and literature stimulated [Wien's] interest in those subjects." Wien was sent to the local Gymnasium at Rastenburg in 1875, but he showed little interest in his classes and was brought home five years later without graduating. For a period of time, he stayed at home learning agriculture and studying with another private tutor. He then returned to formal classes at the Königsberg Altstädtisches Gymnasium, graduating in 1882.

Undecided about Becoming a Farmer

At his mother's urging, Wien then enrolled at the University of Göttingen to study mathematics and natural science. After only one semester, he became bored and left the university, setting off for an extended vacation through the Rhineland and Thüringen. He returned home once again, convinced that as the only child in the family he should take over the farm from his parents. That commitment lasted only a few months, however, and he headed back to school again in the fall of 1883, this time to the University of Berlin.

His academic experience this time was very different. He came under the tutelage of the great German physicist, mathematician, and physiologist Hermann von Helmholtz and, according to his own reports, "really came into contact with physics for the first time." He now applied himself vigorously to his studies and in the spring of 1886 received his doctorate. His dissertation dealt with the behavior of light diffracted by the sharp edge of a piece of metal.

After receiving his doctorate, Wien returned yet another time to the Drachenstein farm. The occasion for this trip was a disastrous fire that had destroyed some of the farm buildings. For four years Wien remained in a mood of indecision, feeling that he should continue to operate the farm, but still maintaining an interest in physics and continuing to do research on his own.

Joins Helmholtz at Charlottenberg

In 1890 a decision was made for Wien. An extended period of drought forced the Wien family to sell the farm, and Wien decided to take a job as Helmholtz's assistant at the newly established Physikalisch-Technische Reichsanstalt in Charlottenberg, outside Berlin. His parents also moved to Berlin, where his father died less than a year later. In 1892 Wien was promoted to lecturer at Berlin and then, four years later, he was offered a position as professor of physics at the Technical University in Aachen. He remained at Aachen for three years before moving on to the University of Giessen in 1899 and then to the University of Würzburg in 1900.

Wien's most productive period was the decade of the 1890s, when his main area of interest was the nature of blackbody radiation. The term *blackbody* refers to a theoretical substance that absorbs all of the radiation that falls on it; the fact that it reflects none of the radiation makes it black. In the 1860s, Gustav Kirchhoff had thoroughly studied the thermal properties of blackbodies. He pointed out that they are a perfect tool for studying radiation since when heated they emit radiation of all wavelengths. This fact makes it possible to study in great detail the nature of radiation emitted at different temperatures.

In about 1893 Wien began a theoretical analysis of the characteristics of blackbody radiation beginning with the fundamental laws of thermodynamics. He eventually developed two important conclusions. The first of these, now known as Wien's displacement law, says that the wavelength of radiation emitted by a blackbody is inversely proportional to the temperature of the body. That is, at low temperatures a blackbody will radiate energy with a long wavelength (red light). As the temperature rises, the most abundant wavelength radiated becomes smaller, and the color of the emitted light changes to orange, yellow, and then white.

Wien next attempted to find a mathematical formula that would fit the empirical graphical representation of the relationship between the amount of energy radiated at each wavelength for various temperatures. He obtained a complex equation that works fairly well at short wavelengths, but not very well at long wavelengths. He published this result in June 1896. In the meantime **J. W. Strutt** (Lord Rayleigh) in England had derived a formula that worked well at long wavelengths, but not at short wavelengths. It was not until Max Planck introduced the concept of a quantum of energy in 1900 that the problem of blackbody radiation was finally solved.

By 1897 Wien had moved on to a new field of interest, cathode rays. Although he completed some excellent studies in this field, he did not produce any major breakthroughs. His two most notable accomplishments were probably his confirmation of the nature of cathode rays as rapidly moving negatively charged particles (1897–98) and of canal rays as rapidly moving positively charged particles (1905). He also carried out some of the earliest studies on the diffraction of X rays by crystals, anticipating the discoveries of **Max von Laue** in this area by at least five years.

Wien's tenure at Würzburg lasted for two decades, during which time he was awarded the 1911 Nobel Prize in physics for his work on radiation. He also traveled extensively, including trips to Norway, Spain, Italy, and England (in 1904), to Greece (in 1912), to the United States (where he visited Columbia, Yale, and Harvard in 1913), and to the Baltic states (in 1918). Wien's last academic position was at the University of Munich, where he became professor of physics in 1920. There he supervised construction of a new physics institute and served as rector from 1925 to 1926. He died in Munich on August 30, 1928.

Wien was married to Luise Mehler in 1898. They had two sons, Waltraut and Karl, and two daughters, Gerda and Hildegard. In addition to the Nobel Prize, Wien was honored with membership in the scientific societies of Berlin, Göttingen, Vienna, and Stockholm. He was also a member of the U.S. National Academy of Sciences. From 1906 until his death, he was joint editor with Planck of the prestigious *Annalen der Physik* and later, with F. Harms, of the *Handbuch der Experimental Physik.*

SELECTED WRITINGS BY WIEN:

Books

Lehrbuch der Hydrodynamik, S. Hirzel, 1900.
Kanalstrahlen, Akademische Verlagsgesellschaft, 1917.
Aus dem Leben und Wirken eines Physikers, J. A. Barth, 1930.

Periodicals

"Über die Energievertheilung im Emissionsspectrum eines schwarzen Körpers," *Annalen der Physik,* Volume 294, 1896, pp. 662–669.
"Zur Theorie der Strahlung schwarzer Körper: Kritisches," *Annalen der Physik,* Volume 308, 1900, pp. 530–539.

SOURCES:

Books

Dictionary of Scientific Biography, Volume 14, Scribner, 1975, pp. 337–342.
Magill, Frank N., editor, *The Nobel Prize Winners: Physics,* Volume 1, *1901-1937,* Salem Press, 1989, pp. 159–165.
Wasson, Tyler, editor, *Nobel Prize Winners,* Wilson, 1987, pp. 1118–1121.
Weber, Robert L., *Pioneers of Science: Nobel Prize Winners in Physics,* American Institute of Physics, 1980, pp. 42–44.

—*Sketch by David E. Newton*

Alexander Wiener
1907-1976
American physician and immunohematologist

Alexander Wiener was a physician who, along with fellow scientist **Karl Landsteiner**, discovered the Rh factor in blood. He also discovered a number of other antigens (substances in the blood that cause the development of antibodies). The Rh factor is an antigen named after the rhesus monkey, the animal in which it was first discovered. Blood that contains the factor is called Rh-positive, whereas blood that lacks it is labeled Rh-negative. The discovery of the Rh factor led to an understanding of adverse reactions to blood transfusions that occurred inexplicably in some patients even though compatibility of blood type (A, B, AB, and O) in donor and recipient had been observed. The discovery of the Rh factor also brought about an understanding of the possible adverse reactions when an Rh-negative mother carried an Rh-positive fetus. Wiener developed a life-saving method of replacing the damaged blood of new-born infants who had erythroblastosis fetalis, the infant blood disease that sometimes results from Rh incompatibility. He was also instrumental in getting the results of his research applied to legal issues such as disputed paternity, and to cases involving crimes such as homicide and assault. Author or co-author of more than five hundred scientific articles, he also wrote several books, including what for years was the standard textbook on the subject, *Blood Groups and Transfusion*. His many awards include the Lasker Award of the American Public Health Association, which he received in 1946, and the Passano Foundation Award, received in 1951.

Alexander Solomon Wiener was born March 16, 1907, in Brooklyn, New York, the son of George Wiener, an attorney who had emigrated from Russia in 1903, and Mollie (Zuckerman) Wiener. He attended Brooklyn public schools, graduating from Brooklyn Boys' High School at the age of 15. He was awarded scholarships to attend Cornell University, where he was elected to Phi Beta Kappa in his senior year. Both in high school and in college he pursued an interest in mathematics. In high school he took courses in analytic geometry and calculus and was a member of the mathematics team and president of the mathematics club. He continued his study of mathematics at Cornell University, and contributed mathematical problems to the *American Mathematical Monthly*. He majored in biology, however, receiving his A.B. in 1926. He then entered the Long Island College of Medicine (now the SUNY College of Medicine) and was awarded an M.D. in 1930.

While he was in medical school, Wiener began his first research on blood groups at the Jewish Hospital of Brooklyn, where he would also intern from 1930 to 1932 and with which he would be affiliated for his entire professional career. From 1933 to 1935 he served as the head of the Division of Genetics and Biometrics, from 1932 to 1952 as head of the blood transfusion division, and thereafter as attending immunohematologist. From 1949 he was also affiliated with Adelphi Hospital, including three years (1949–1952) as the head of the blood transfusion division. In addition, he began a private medical practice in 1932, but three years later he founded Wiener Laboratories, where he limited his practice to clinical pathology and blood grouping. In 1938 he joined the faculty of the Department of Forensic Medicine of New York University School of Medicine, moving up the academic ranks to professor by 1968. In 1938 he also began his long-time association with the Office of the Chief Medical Examiner of New York City. He married Gertrude Rodman in 1932. They had two daughters, Jane Helen and Barbara Rae. Wiener died of leukemia in New York on November 6, 1976.

Searches for Blood Antigens

The background to the discovery of the Rh factor lay in earlier discoveries concerning the nature of blood. In 1901 Karl Landsteiner had distinguished four main human blood groups: A, B, AB, and O. These classifications refer to antigens (substances that produce antibodies) on the surface of the red blood cells. Blood type A contains the A antigen, B contains the B antigen, AB contains both, and O contains neither. However, in the 1920s other blood factors or antigens were discovered—M, N, and P.

In the 1930s Wiener began collaborating with Landsteiner, who was affiliated with the Rockefeller Institute for Medical Research in New York. In 1937 Landsteiner and Wiener were studying the M factor in apes and monkeys, focussing on its action as an agglutinogen (its ability to clump red blood cells together). They showed that different anti-M sera (blood sera samples with antibodies opposing the M antigen) produced differing reactions, and concluded that there were at least five distinct M blood factors. This led to further experimentation in which they tested the sera of rabbits immunized with rhesus monkey blood cells. The antibodies produced by rabbit blood in response to rhesus monkey antigens led them to believe that unknown blood factors might be discovered in human blood by the same method. They began experiments using human blood and the anti-sera from rhesus blood, and thereby discovered a new antigen that they called the Rh factor. The importance of this discovery in transfusions was recognized in 1939 when it was understood that although the first transfusion of Rh-positive blood into an Rh-negative person may be harmless, the sensitization that resulted meant that a second transfusion could cause a dangerous hemolytic reaction involving the damage or destruction of red blood cells.

Wiener then studied the sera from Rh negative patients who had hemolytic transfusion reactions, and the sera from Rh-negative mothers of erythroblastotic babies. These babies have Rh positive blood, some of which enters the mother's blood, usually shortly before or during birth. The mother's blood forms an antibody to the Rh factor and crosses back to the fetal blood supply. The result is the damage or destruction of the fetal red blood cells containing the Rh antigen. He discovered that the expected Rh antibodies often could not be found. He hypothesized that there must be two different forms of Rh antibodies, one that caused the agglutination of cells (which he called bivalent antibodies), the other capable of coating the red blood cells without clumping them (which he called univalent or blocking antibodies). In 1944 and 1945 he developed tests for both types of antibodies.

Wiener noted the fallacy of assuming a one-to-one correspondence between antigens and antibodies. One antigen could produce multiple blood specificities. He soon discovered additional Rh factors that were related to the original one. In the human Rh system (now known as the Rh-Hr system), Wiener and others established as many as 25 different blood factors that form the basis of a large number of blood types.

Practical Implications of Wiener's Discoveries

Wiener's research had many practical implications. It led to an understanding of erythroblastosis fetalis, for which Wiener himself devised (1944–1946) a treatment by means of a complete exchange transfusion replacing the damaged Rh-positive blood of the infant with Rh-negative blood. This treatment led to a significant decline in the rate of infant mortality. Knowledge of Rh factors also made blood transfusions far safer. Other implications of Wiener's research derived from the fact that all blood factors are inherited in predictable fashion, and that they combine in a highly specific way in individuals, allowing a sophisticated method of "fingerprinting." Blood factor analysis became important in legal matters (such as establishing paternity), as well as criminal matters, such as the use of blood for identification in homicide and assault. It also facilitated advances in physical anthropology—different groups of people have different proportions of various blood factors, so that tribal movements can sometimes be traced by analysis of blood factor percentages in populations.

Wiener's research had significant legal implications. He was a member of the American Medical Association legal committee that sponsored blood test laws in all states, and he was the co-author of its 1935 report. He was instrumental in the passage of the New York State law allowing blood tests in disputed paternity cases. He and his father, attorney George Wiener, assisted in drafting a number of laws concerning blood testing that became part of the New York State domestic relations, civil, and criminal codes.

Wiener liked playing the piano, going to the movies, and playing cards. He also enjoyed tennis and gulf. In addition, he continued his life-long interest in mathematics and physics by avidly reading in these areas. A member of many professional organizations, he was also an honorary member of the Mystery Writers of America.

SELECTED WRITINGS BY WIENER:

Books

Blood Groups and Transfusion, 3rd ed., Hafner, 1943.
Rh-Hr Blood Types: Applications in Clinical and Legal Medicine and Anthropology, Grune, 1954.
(With Irving B. Wexler), *Heredity of the Blood Groups,* Grune, 1958.
Advances in Blood Grouping, Grune, 1961.

(With Wexler) *An Rh-Hr Syllabus: The Types and Their Applications,* 2nd ed., Grune, 1963.
(With Wladyslaw W. Socha) *A-B-O Blood Groups and Lewis Types: Questions and Answers; Problems and Solutions: A Teaching Manual,* Stratton Intercontinental Medical Book Corp., 1976.

SOURCES:

Books

McGraw-Hill Modern Scientists and Engineers, Volume 3, McGraw, 1980, pp. 314–315.
National Cyclopaedia of American Biography, Volume G, 1943–1946, James T. White, 1946, pp. 469–470.
New York Times, November 7, 1976.

—Sketch by Pamela Long

Norbert Wiener
1894-1964
American mathematician

Norbert Wiener was one of the most original mathematicians of his time. The field concerning the study of automatic control systems, called cybernetics, owes a great deal not only to his researches, but to his continuing efforts at publicity. He wrote for a variety of popular journals as well as for technical publications and was not reluctant to express political views even when they might be unpopular. Perhaps the most distinctive feature of Wiener's life as a student and a mathematician is how well documented it is, thanks to two volumes of autobiography published during his lifetime. They reveal some of the complexity of a man whose aspirations went well beyond the domain of mathematics.

Wiener was born in Columbia, Missouri, on November 26, 1894. His father, Leo Wiener, had been born in Bialystok, Poland (then Russia), and was an accomplished linguist. He arrived in New Orleans in 1880 with very little money but a great deal of determination, some of it visible in his relations with his son. He met his wife, Bertha Kahn, at a meeting of a Browning Club. As a result, when his son was born, he was given the name Norbert, from one of Browning's verse dramas. In light of the absence of Judaism from the Wiener home (Norbert was fifteen before he

Norbert Wiener

learned that he was Jewish), it is surprising that one of Leo Wiener's best-known works was a history of Yiddish literature.

As the title of the first volume of his autobiography *Ex-Prodigy* suggests, Wiener was a child prodigy. Whatever his natural talents, this was partly due to the efforts of his father. Leo Wiener was proud of his educational theories and pointed to the academic success of his son as evidence. Norbert was less enthusiastic and in his memoirs describes his recollections of his father's harsh disciplinary methods. He entered high school at the age of nine and graduated two years later. In 1906 he entered Tufts University, as the family had moved to the Boston area, and he graduated four years later.

Up until that point Wiener's education had clearly outrun that of most of his contemporaries, but he was now faced with the challenge of deciding what to do with his education. He enrolled at Harvard to study zoology, but the subject did not suit him. He tried studying philosophy at Cornell, but that was equally unavailing. Finally, Wiener came back to Harvard to work on philosophy and mathematics. The subject of his dissertation was a comparison of the system of logic developed by **Bertrand Russell** and **Alfred North Whitehead** in their *Principia Mathematica* with the earlier algebraic system created by Ernst Schröder. The relatively recent advances in mathematical research in the United States had partly occurred in the area of algebraic logic, so the topic was a reasonable one for a student hoping to bridge

the still-existent gap between the European and American mathematical communities.

Although Wiener earned a Harvard travelling fellowship to enable him to study in Europe after taking his degree, his father still supervised his career by writing to Bertrand Russell on Norbert's behalf. Wiener was in England from June 1913 to April 1914 and attended two courses given by Russell, including a reading course on *Principia Mathematica.* Perhaps more influential in the long run for Wiener's mathematical development was a course he took from the British analyst **G. H. Hardy**, whose lectures he greatly admired. In the same way, Wiener studied with some of the most eminent names in Göttingen, Germany, then the center of the international mathematical community.

Wiener returned to the United States in 1915, still unsure, despite his foreign travels, of the mathematical direction he wanted to pursue. He wrote articles for the *Encyclopedia Americana* and took a variety of teaching jobs until the entry of the United States into World War I. Wiener was a fervent patriot, and his enthusiasm led him to join the group of scientists and engineers at the Aberdeen Proving Ground in Maryland, where he encountered Oswald Veblen, already one of the leading mathematicians in the country. Although Wiener did not pursue Veblen's lines of research, Veblen's success in producing results useful to the military impressed Wiener more than mere academic success.

Takes the Mathematical Turn

After the war two events decisively shaped Wiener's mathematical future. He obtained a position as instructor at the Massachusetts Institute of Technology (MIT) in mathematics, where he was to remain until his retirement. At that time mathematics was not particularly strong at MIT, but his position there assured him of continued contact with engineers and physicists. As a result, he displayed an ongoing concern for the applications of mathematics to problems that could be stated in physical terms. The question of which tools he would bring to bear on those problems was answered by the death of his sister's fiancé. That promising young mathematician left his collection of books to Wiener, who began to read avidly the standard texts in a way that he had not in his earlier studies.

The first problem Wiener addressed had to do with Brownian motion, the apparently random motion of particles in substances at rest. The phenomenon had earlier excited **Albert Einstein**'s interest, and he had dealt with it in one of his 1905 papers. Wiener took the existence of Brownian motion as a sign of randomness at the heart of nature. By idealizing the physical phenomenon, Wiener was able to produce a mathematical theory of Brownian motion that had wide influence among students of probability. It is possible to see in his work on Brownian motion, steps in the direction of the study of fractals (shapes whose detail repeats itself on any scale), although Wiener did not go far along that path.

The next subject Wiener addressed was the Dirichlet problem, which had been reintroduced into the mathematical mainstream by German **David Hilbert**. Much of the earliest work on the Dirichlet problem had been discredited as not being sufficiently rigorous for the standards of the late nineteenth century. Wiener's work on the Dirichlet problem produced interesting results, some of which he delayed publishing for the sake of a couple of students finishing their theses at Harvard. Wiener felt subsequently that his forbearance was not recognized adequately. In particular, although Wiener progressed through the academic ranks at MIT from assistant professor in 1924 to associate professor in 1929 to full professor in 1932, he believed that more support from Harvard would have enabled him to advance more quickly.

Wiener had a high opinion of his own abilities, something of a change from colleagues whose public expressions of modesty were at odds with a deep-seated conviction of their own merits. Whatever his talents as a mathematician, Wiener's expository standards were at odds with those of most mathematicians of his time. While he was always exuberant, this was often at the cost of accuracy of detail. One of his main theorems depended on a series of lemmas, or auxiliary propositions, one of which was proven by assuming the truth of the main theorem. Students trying to learn from Wiener's papers and finding their efforts unrewarding discovered that this reaction was almost universal. As Hans Freudenthal remarked in the *Dictionary of Scientific Biography,* "After proving at length a fact that would be too easy if set as an exercise for an intelligent sophomore, he would assume without proof a profound theorem that was seemingly unrelated to the preceding text, then continue with a proof containing puzzling but irrelevant terms, next interrupt it with a totally unrelated historical exposition, meanwhile quote something from the 'last chapter' of the book that had actually been in the first, and so on."

In 1926 Wiener was married to Margaret Engemann, an assistant professor of modern languages at Juniata College. They had two daughters, Barbara (born 1928) and Peggy (born 1929). Wiener enjoyed his family's company and found there a relaxation from a mathematical community that did not always share his opinion of the merits of his work.

During the decade after his marriage, Wiener worked in a number of fields and wrote some of the papers with which he is most associated. In the field of harmonic analysis, he did a great deal with the decomposition of functions into series. Just as a polynomial is made up of terms like x, x^2, x^3, and so forth, so functions in general could be broken up in various ways, depending on the questions to be answered. Somewhat surprisingly, Wiener also undertook putting the operational calculus, earlier developed by Oliver Heaviside, on a rigorous basis. There is even a hint in Wiener's work of the notion of a distribution, a kind of generalized function. It is not surprising that Wiener might start to move away from the kind of functions that had been most studied in mathematics toward those that could be useful in physics and engineering.

In 1926 Wiener returned to Europe, this time on a Guggenheim fellowship. He spent little time at Göttingen, due to disagreements with **Richard Courant**, perhaps the most active student of David Hilbert in mathematical organization. Courant's disparaging comments about Wiener cannot have helped the latter's standing in the mathematical community, but Wiener's brief visit introduced him to Tauberian theory, a fashionable area of analysis. Wiener came up with an imaginative new approach to Tauberian theorems and, perhaps more fortunately, with a coauthor for his longest paper on the subject. The quality of the exposition in the paper, combined with the originality of the results, make it Wiener's best exercise in communicating technical mathematics, although he did not pursue the subject as energetically as he did some of his other works.

In 1931 and 1932 Wiener gave lectures on analysis in Cambridge as a deputy for G. H. Hardy. While there, he made the acquaintance of a young British mathematician, R. E. A. C. Paley, with whom a collaboration soon flourished. He brought Paley to MIT the next academic year and their work progressed rapidly. Paley's death at the age of twenty-six in a skiing accident early in 1933 was a blow to Wiener, who received the Bôcher prize of the American Mathematical Society the same year and was named a fellow of the National Academy of Sciences the next. Among the other areas in which Wiener worked at MIT or Harvard were quantum mechanics, differential geometry, and statistical physics. His investigations in the last of these were wide ranging, but amounted more to the creation of a research program than a body of results.

Creates Cybernetics

The arrival of World War II occupied Wiener's attention in a number of ways. He was active on the Emergency Committee in Aid of Displaced German Scholars, which began operations well before the outbreak of fighting. He made proposals concerning the development of computers, although these were largely ignored. One of the problems to which he devoted time was antiaircraft fire, and his results were of great importance for engineering applications regarding filtering. Unfortunately, they were not of much use in the field because of the amount of time required for the calculations.

Weiner devoted the last decades of his life to the study of statistics, engineering, and biology. He had already worked on the general idea of information theory, which arose out of statistical mechanics. The idea of entropy had been around since the nineteenth century and enters into the second law of thermodynamics. It could be defined as an integral, but it was less clear what sort of quantity it was. Work of Ludwig Boltzmann suggested that entropy could be understood as a measure of the disorder of a system. Wiener pursued this notion and used it to get a physical definition of information related to entropy. Although information theory has not always followed the path laid down by Wiener, his work gave the subject a mathematical legitimacy.

An interdisciplinary seminar at the Harvard Medical School provided a push for Wiener in the direction of the interplay between biology and physics. He learned about the complexity of feedback in animals and studied current ideas about neurophysiology from a mathematical point of view. (Wiener left out the names of those who had most influenced him in this area in his autobiography as a result of an argument.) One area of particular interest was prosthetic limbs, perhaps as a result of breaking his arm in a fall. Wiener soon had the picture of a computer as a prosthesis for the brain. In 1947 he agreed to write a book on communication and control and was looking for a term for the theory of messages. The Greek word for messenger, *angelos,* had too many connections with angels to be useful, so he took the word for helmsman, *kubernes,* instead and came up with *cybernetics.* It turned out that the word had been used in the previous century, but Wiener gave it a new range of meaning and currency.

Cybernetics was treated by Wiener as a branch of mathematics with its own terms, like signal, noise, and information. One of his collaborators in this area was **John von Neumann**, whose work on computers had been followed up much more enthusiastically than Wiener's. The difference in reception could be explained by the difference in mathematical styles: von Neumann was meticulous, while Wiener tended to be less so. The new field of cybernetics prospered with two such distinct talents working in it. Von Neumann's major contribution to the field was only realized after his death. Wiener devoted most of his later years to the area. Among his more popular books were *The Human Use of Human Beings* in 1950 and *God and Golem, Inc.* in 1964.

In general, Wiener was happy writing for a wide variety of journals and audiences. He contributed to the *Atlantic, Nation,* the *New Republic,* and *Collier's,* among others. His two volumes of autobiography, *Ex-Prodigy* and *I Am a Mathematician,* came out in 1953 and 1956, respectively. Reviews pointed out the extent to which Wiener's memory operated selectively, but also admitted that he did bring the mathematical community to life in a way seldom seen. Although Wiener remarked that mathematics was a young man's game, he also indicated that he felt himself lucky in having selected subjects for investigation that he could pursue later in life. He received an honorary degree from Tufts in 1946 and in 1949 was Gibbs lecturer to the American Mathematical Society.

In 1964 Wiener received the National Medal of Science. On March 18, while travelling through Stockholm, he collapsed and died. A memorial service was held at MIT on the June 2, led by Swami Sarvagatananda of the Vedanta Society of Boston, along with Christian and Jewish clergy. This mixture of faiths was expressive of Wiener's lifelong unwillingness to be fit into a stereotype. He was a mathematician who talked about the theology of the Fall. He did not discover that he was Jewish until he was in graduate school but found great support in the poems of Heinrich Heine. Nevertheless, his intellectual originality led him down paths subsequent generations have come to follow.

SELECTED WRITINGS BY WIENER:

Books

Cybernetics, MIT Press, 1948.
The Human Use of Human Beings, Houghton, 1950.
Ex-Prodigy, Simon & Schuster, 1953.
I Am a Mathematician, Doubleday, 1956.
God and Golem, Inc., MIT Press, 1964.
Selected Papers, MIT Press, 1964.

SOURCES:

Books

Dictionary of Scientific Biography, Scribner, Volume 14, 1970–1978, pp. 344–347.
Heims, Steve J., *John von Neumann and Norbert Wiener,* MIT Press, 1980.
Masani, P. R., *Norbert Wiener,* Birkhäuser, 1990.

—Sketch by Thomas Drucker

Torsten Wiesel
1924-
Swedish-born American neurophysiologist

Torsten Wiesel, in collaboration with **David H. Hubel**, has been instrumental in describing the physiology of vision. His work on charting the visual or striate cortex, the posterior section of the cerebral cortex, has not only provided new insights into the complexity of the visual process, but has also had direct clinical applications. His discovery of critical periods in childhood development for "learning" to see has led to earlier clinical intervention in visual problems in children. In 1981 Wiesel, along with Hubel and another brain researcher, **Roger W. Sperry**, shared the Nobel Prize for Physiology or Medicine.

Torsten Nils Wiesel was born on June 3, 1924, in Uppsala, Sweden, the son of Anna-Lisa Bentzer Wiesel and Fritz S. Wiesel, the chief psychiatrist at the Beckomberga Mental Hospital in Stockholm. Wiesel lived at his father's hospital as a youth, attending a private school where he was more interested in sports than academics. But this attitude changed in 1941 when Wiesel entered medical school at the Karolinska Institute in Stockholm and studied neurophysiology under **Carl Gustaf Bernhard**. He also studied psychiatry during this time, and in 1954 he received his medical degree, becoming an instructor at the institute as well as an assistant in the Department of Child Psychiatry at Karolinska Hospital. Wiesel then came to the United States in 1955 to do postdoctoral work at the Wilmer Institute of Johns Hopkins School of Medicine in Baltimore, Maryland.

Focuses on the Neurophysiology of Vision

At Johns Hopkins, Wiesel worked under Stephen Kuffler, a researcher in visual physiology who had studied the nerve activity in the retina of the cat as well as in animals of other classes. Kuffler's exhaustive work had proved that the vision of mammals is distinctly different from that of non-mammals. Research with frogs had shown that their vision occurred in the optical nerve: that they had neurons, or nerve cells, sensitive not only to light and dark, but also to shapes, movements, and the boundaries between light and dark. Cats have no such specification in their ganglia, no ability to give the detailed boundary information that is found in frogs. Yet mammalian vision is stereoscopic, whereas non-mammalian appears to be in most cases binocular but lacking three dimensions. Wiesel became interested in the direction in which such investigations must logically lead: namely that the critical level of visual perception must take place in the brain of mammals. In 1958 David Hubel, a graduate of McGill University, returned to the institute from military service, and together Wiesel and Hubel set off on researches that would result in a new theory of visual perception.

The striate or visual cortex is located at the back of the brain, an area of about 15 square centimeters in some of the monkeys Wiesel and Hubel would study. It had long been known, from accident victims, that this region of the cortex was involved with vision, and it is here that Wiesel and Hubel began their studies. They painstakingly measured electrical discharge of cells in the visual cortex with the aid of a microelectrode, a microscopic needle with an electrode built in to measure electrical impulses. Initially using anesthetized cats whose sight was trained on various patterns of light and dark, lines and circles, and probing the animal's visual cortex with their microelectrode at various angles, they discovered which cells in the cortex responded to which pattern or level of light. They also conducted experiments in which they injected the eyes of experimental animals with radioactively labeled amino acid. These amino acids would be taken up by the cell bodies of the retina and transported to cells in the visual cortex, giving a map of the pathway of vision. In some cases the laboratory animals were sacrificed and their visual cortexes dissected in order to see, by the use of autoradiographs or X-ray like photos, where the labeled amino acids actually ended up. Such experiments, begun in 1959, used both cats and macaque monkeys. That same year Kuffler was appointed a professor at the Harvard University Medical School, and Wiesel and Hubel joined him there. Wiesel was appointed assistant professor of physiology, and became a full professor in 1964.

Complexity of Visual Process Revealed

The Wiesel-Hubel team soon began publishing the results of their experimental method, and it was clear that they had uncovered new complexities to the visual process. Mapping the path of vision with radioactive amino acid, they showed that vision passed in coded signals from neuron to neuron through the optic nerve and split at the optic chiasm so that a representation of each half of the visual scene is projected deep in the brain on a nest of cells called the lateral geniculate nucleus, a way station to the cells in the cortex. From here the path of vision continues to the back of the brain to various parts of the visual cortex, depending on the specialization of each cell. But the pathway does not end there; indeed, the visual cortex was shown to be an early step in the processing of visual information. Information is sent back to parts of the brain from the cortex as well as back to the geniculate nuclei.

Within the visual cortex itself, Wiesel and Hubel made two important discoveries. First they showed that there is a hierarchy of types of cells in the cortex, ranking from simple to complex to hypercomplex, depending on the information each is able to process. They termed the process of putting the millions of building blocks of visual information back together into a picture convergence. Various cells have preferences for the bits of visual information they process: size, shape, light, and sharpness of boundary differentiation, as well as which eye is sending the information. Such a complexity of visual processing destroys the old notion of sight being simply a film played in the mind. Instead, the accretion of bits of visual information into visual representation appears more similar to language processing than to an analogy of a film. Cells in the visual cortex "read" neuron messages. Their second major discovery was a further organization of the cortical cells into roughly vertical divisions of two types: orientation columns and ocular dominance columns. The orientation columns transform what is essentially circular information from the retina and geniculate nerve cells into linear information, while the ocular combine the neural information from both eyes to provide three-dimensional vision. Within these columns are simple, complex, and hypercomplex cells working toward a progressive convergence of visualization. Until the time of Wiesel's and Hubel's work, it was assumed that all cells of the cerebral cortex were more or less uniform. Wiesel and Hubel showed that the visual cortex is constituted of a cell pattern, which appears to be designed specifically for vision. As a result of their discovery, current theory now posits that the rest of the cerebral cortex may follow this form-follows-function rule.

Later Work Yields Clinical Results

Wiesel and Hubel researched another experimental model in which they used kittens to study the effect of various visual impairments on development. They discovered that if one eye were deprived of certain or all visual stimuli during the third to fifth postnatal weeks, the central functioning of that eye would always be suppressed from cortical processing. Kittens, and by extension mammals in general, though born with a complete visual cortex, must still "learn" to see. Even if an early impairment is later corrected, the repaired eye will still remain functionally impaired as far as the visual cortex is concerned. The realization that there is a critical stage for visual development revolutionized the field of pediatric ophthalmology, calling for the earliest possible intervention in cases of strabismus, or crossed eyes, and congenital cataracts.

By 1973 Wiesel succeeded Kuffler as chair of the Department of Neurobiology at Harvard, and was named the Robert Winthrop Professor of Neurobiolo-

gy in 1974. His first marriage, to Teiri Stenhammer, ended in divorce after 14 years in 1970. Wiesel was married again in 1973, to Grace Yee. The couple had one child, Sara Elisabet. His second marriage also ended in divorce in 1981. Wiesel became a naturalized U.S. citizen in 1990. Wiesel has been the recipient of many awards over the years, including the Lewis S. Rosentiel Award in 1972, the Jonas S. Friedenwald Memorial Award in 1975, the Karl Spencer Lashley Prize in 1977, the Louisa Gross Horowitz Prize in 1978, and the George Ledlie Prize in 1980. But none were as prestigious as the Nobel Prize, which he and Hubel won in 1981, sharing it with Sperry from Caltech. The Karolinska Institute in Stockholm, which administers the prize and where Wiesel began his professional career, praised Hubel and Wiesel for their discoveries concerning information processing in the visual system. Wiesel and Hubel continued their close working relationship until Wiesel left Harvard in 1984 to head the neurobiology lab at Rockefeller University where he continued his researches on vision. In 1992 he was named president of Rockefeller University.

SELECTED WRITINGS BY WIESEL:

Periodicals

(With David H. Hubel) "Receptive Fields of Single Neurons in the Cat's Striate Cortex," *Journal of Physiology,* Volume 148, 1959, pp. 574–91.

(With Hubel) "Integrative Action in the Cat's Lateral Geniculate Body," *Journal of Physiology,* February, 1961, pp. 385–98.

(With Hubel) "Receptive Fields, Binocular Interaction and Functional Architecture in the Cat's Cortex," *Journal of Physiology,* January, 1962, pp. 106–54.

(With Hubel) "Single-cell Responses in Striate Cortex of Kittens Deprived of Vision in One Eye," *Journal of Neurophysiology,* November, 1963, pp. 1003–17.

(With Hubel) "Extent of Recovery from the Effects of Visual Deprivation in Kittens," *Journal of Neurophysiology,* November, 1965, pp. 1060–72.

(With Hubel) "Receptive Fields and Functional Architecture in Two Non Striate Visual Areas (18 and 19) of the Cat," *Journal of Neurophysiology,* November, 1965, pp. 229–89.

(With Hubel) "Receptive Fields and Functional Architecture of Monkey Striate Cortex," *Journal of Physiology,* Volume 195, 1968, pp. 215–43.

(With Hubel and M. P. Stryker) "Anatomical Demonstration of Orientation Columns in Macaque Monkey," *Journal of Comparative Neurology,* Volume 177, 1978, pp. 361–80.

(With Hubel) "Brain Mechanisms of Vision," *Scientific American,* September, 1979, pp. 150–62.

SOURCES:

Books

Hubel, David H. *Eye, Brain, and Vision,* Scientific American Library, 1988.

Periodicals

Altman, Lawrence K., "Studies Advance Work on Brain," *New York Times,* October 10, 1981, p. 50.
Barinaga, Marcia, "At Rockefeller, Wiesel Is the Calm after the Storm," *Science,* June 4, 1993, pp. 1426–8.
Lettvin, Jerome Y, "Filling out the Forms: An Appreciation of Hubel and Wiesel," *Science,* October 30, 1981, pp. 518–20.
"Nobel Prize Goes to Two Americans, Swedish Scientist," *Los Angeles Times,* October 10, 1981, p. 1.
Russell, Christine, "Three in U.S. Win Nobel Prize for Brain Research," *Washington Post,* October 10, 1981, p. 1.
Schmeck, Harold M., Jr., "Three Scientists Share Nobel Prize for Studies of the Brain," *New York Times,* October 10, 1981, p. 1.
"Torsten Nils Wiesel," *New York Times,* October 10, 1981, p. 50.

—*Sketch by J. Sydney Jones*

Vincent Wigglesworth
1899-1994
English entomologist

Vincent Wigglesworth was a British entomologist who took the study of entomology from the mere collection and classification of insects to a field of knowledge with significant scientific applications. He specialized in insect physiology, conducting studies to determine how brain hormones trigger molting, metamorphosis, and reproduction in insects. As Antony Tucker writes in an obituary in the *Guardian,* Wigglesworth's most important contribution may have been his recognition "that insects could be used—instead of mice or other laboratory animals—

for the fundamental investigation of animal physiology and function."

Vincent Brian Wigglesworth was born on April 17, 1899 in Kirkham, Lancashire, England. His father, Sidney Wigglesworth, was a medical doctor in general practice. Wigglesworth attended Repton School and then Gonville and Caius College at Cambridge. He entered the army during World War I, and he served in the field artillery in France from 1917 to 1918. Upon his return, he completed his graduate work in physiology and biochemistry at Cambridge, including two years as a researcher under **John Burdon Sanderson Haldane** and **Frederick Gowland Hopkins**. Wigglesworth demonstrated an aptitude for and a deep interest in basic research. He decided to take up the challenge, issued by Patrick Buxton, to improve the practical application of entomology by increasing the scientific knowledge of insect physiology. Most of Wigglesworth's research at the time was on the role of insects in the transmission of human diseases; diseases such as malaria and Chagas' disease made this issue of immediate importance but it was poorly understood.

In order to further his understanding of human diseases, Wigglesworth completed a medical degree at St. Thomas's Hospital in London. In 1926, he became a lecturer at the London School of Hygiene and Tropical Medicine, where he began his famous studies with *Rhodnius prolixus,* a South American blood-sucking insect known to be a carrier of Chagas' disease. The insect was thereafter known among entomologists as "Wigglesworth's bug." Wigglesworth was appointed Reader in Entomology at London University in 1936. He returned to Cambridge in 1945 and in 1952 was named Quick Professor of Biology at Cambridge. He served as director of the Agricultural Research Council's entomological unit from 1943 to 1967.

Wigglesworth's research concentrated on insect hormones and how they affected physiological processes. It was known that brain secretions initiated certain physiological processes; for example, a decapitated insect would live but it would not molt. Wigglesworth implanted different sections of the brain into the bodies of decapitated insects, and he was thus able to identify the particular areas of the brain where neurosecretory cells were located. He also proved that the brain was the only place in the body of these insects that produced the triggering hormones. This was the first time the role of neurosecretory brain cells in animal development was established experimentally.

Wigglesworth's further studies of insect hormones showed that brain secretions controlled not only molting but also how and when insect larvae would metamorphose into adult forms. He established that it was a hormone, identified as the juvenile hormone, which prevented larvae from developing adult characteristics until they were fully grown. He conducted an experiment in which larvae were continually exposed to the juvenile hormone; as a result of this exposure, larvae maintained their immature form but continued to grow in size. The study of this and other phenomena associated with insect hormones led Wigglesworth to develop a theory of metamorphosis which proposes that the genetic factors necessary for larval development are regulated by the juvenile hormone.

Wigglesworth's research did not concentrate solely on neurological issues but ranged over a wide array of physiological phenomena. He determined how insects are able to make their feet adhere to walking surfaces, how insect eggs breathe, and how symbiotic microorganisms provide vitamins to insects which live solely on blood. The comprehensive nature of his curiosity and understanding enabled him to write books integrating the complete scope of knowledge about insect physiology. His book, *Principles of Insect Physiology,* first published in 1939, became a standard international text. His work has become so basic to entomology that most of it has been incorporated into the standard body of educational material.

Tucker writes of Wigglesworth: "His manner always remained that of a very senior medical consultant; the careful form of question, the cautious, almost shy, analytical progression of thought, and the decisive separation of important and trivial evidence." Wigglesworth continued to work full time until shortly before his death. Known for his strong scientific judgment, care in formulating hypotheses, and precision in discussing scientific ideas, Wigglesworth also advocated caution in using sweeping measures to control insects. He warned against heavy use of pesticides and supported the study of species-specific pheromones to affect insect populations.

Wigglesworth was a member of scientific societies around the world, and he lectured at many universities in the United States and Europe. He was a member of the Royal Entomological Society and the U.S. National Academy of Sciences, and he received several honorary degrees. He was awarded the Gregor Mendel Gold Medal in 1967 from the Czechoslovak Academy of Science. He was knighted in 1964, and the British Royal Entomological Society awards a Wigglesworth Medal in his name.

Wigglesworth married Mabel Katherine Semple in 1928. They had three sons and a daughter. His wife died in 1986. One of their sons, William R. B. Wigglesworth, became England's Deputy Director General of Telecommunications. Wigglesworth died on February 12, 1994.

SELECTED WRITINGS BY WIGGLESWORTH:

Books

Insect Physiology, Methuen & Co., 1934, 2nd edition, 1938.
The Principles of Insect Physiology, E. P. Dutton, 1939.
Physiology of Insect Metamorphosis, Cambridge University Press, 1954.
Control of Growth and Form, Cornell University Press, 1959.
The Life of Insects, New American Library, 1964.
Insect Hormones, W. H. Freeman, 1970.
Insects and the Life of Man, Wiley, 1976.

SOURCES:

Books

McGraw-Hill Modern Scientists and Engineers, Volume 3, McGraw-Hill, 1980, pp. 316–17.

Periodicals

Tucker, Anthony, "Unearthing Insects' Mysteries" (Obituary), *Guardian,* February 14, 1994, p. 12.

—*Sketch by Valerie Brown*

Eugene Paul Wigner
1902-
Hungarian American mathematical physicist

Eugene Paul Wigner's enormous contribution to various branches of physics, notably quantum and nuclear, was confirmed by his receipt of the 1963 Nobel Prize for Physics (he shared the award with **Maria Goeppert-Mayer** and **J. Hans D. Jensen**). Recognizing the role of symmetry principles in predicting certain physical processes, Wigner formulated many of the laws governing this theory. Wigner is remembered as being one of the first physicists to call attention to the problems of nuclear energy, and also as one of the first scientists to forge links between science and industry around nuclear energy.

Wigner was born in Budapest, Hungary, on November 17, 1902, the son of a businessman. At school, Wigner discovered an interest in physics, but he realized that job opportunities as a physicist in

Eugene Paul Wigner

electron emitted from a nucleus will be indifferent as to whether it is ejected to the left or right and will shoot off in equal numbers in both directions along the spin axes of the aligned nucleus. This theory remained steadfast until 1956 when two Chinese-American physicists, **Tsung-Dao Lee** and **Chen Ning Yang**, disproved it by showing experimentally that parity is not conserved in weak interactions. Instead, their experiments revealed that far more electrons were emitted from the south end of the nucleus than from the north. For invalidating the widely held concept of the conservation of parity, they shared the 1957 Nobel Prize for Physics.

Wigner returned in 1928 to the Technische Hochschule and continued his work on group theory until 1930, when he moved to the United States to accept a position as lecturer in mathematical physics at Princeton University. For eight years he served as a part-time professor at Princeton, until he was elevated to the position of Thomas D. Jones Professor of Mathematical Physics in 1938. The year before, Wigner had become an American citizen.

Develops Short Periodicity of Binding Energies

Wigner's tenure at Princeton afforded him the time and space to do his most important work. As a young physicist, he had become interested in symmetry principles, especially with the patterns found in atomic and molecular spectra. Important discoveries in the 1930s of the binding forces within a nucleus paved the way for Wigner's research. It was found that nuclei containing even numbers of protons (the positively charged particles in the nucleus) and neutrons (the neutral particles) are bound together more strongly than those with an uneven number of protons and neutrons. This is referred to as the short periodicity of binding energies. Longer periods of binding energy are also possible, and show especially strong binding when the number of protons or neutrons or both is 2, 8, 20, 28, 40, 50, 82, or 126. The longer binding periods are thought to be caused by the existence in the nucleus of shells or orbits, similar to those that surround the nucleus and contain the electrons, the negatively charged particles. Armed with this data, Wigner forecasted an optical spectra based on the long periodicity model. His findings were published in one of the first papers on the subject. Wigner also contributed significantly to the understanding of short periodicity in his application of mathematical group theory to the energy levels of nuclei up to atomic weight 50. His book on group theory has become a classic in the physics canon.

In 1933, the year after **James Chadwick** discovered the neutron, Wigner composed a paper which postulated the existence of an energy state of the deuteron which differed from the ground state that had been observed. A deuteron is the nucleus of an

Hungary would be very limited. He therefore decided to study chemical engineering. After receiving a doctorate in chemical engineering from the Technische Hochschule in Berlin in 1925, Wigner returned to Budapest for a year to take up a post in a leather-tanning plant. He left Hungary for the last time in 1926 upon receiving an invitation to return to Berlin to work as an assistant to the well-known physical chemist R. Becker. "The whole of quantum physics was being created within my own eyesight," he said of physics in Germany during the 1920s, as quoted in *Pioneers of Science: Nobel Prize Winners in Physics*. Inspired by such inventiveness, Wigner began writing papers of his own; specifically, he was interested in exploring how the mathematical concept known as group theory could be used as a tool in the new quantum mechanics. On the strength of this work, Wigner was invited in 1927 to join the physics department of the University of Gottingen, as assistant to the mathematician David Hilbert.

At Gottingen Wigner developed his law of the conservation of parity, which states that no fundamental distinction can be made between left and right in physics. The laws of physics are the same in a right-handed system of coordinates as they are in a left-handed system. Based on Wigner's law of parity conservation, particles emitted during a physical interaction should emanate from the nucleus to the right and the left in equal numbers. In practical terms, the law meant that a nuclear process should be indistinguishable from its mirror image, that is, an atom of deuterium, the hydrogen isotope that has twice the mass of regular hydrogen, and which occurs in water. A deuteron contains one proton and one neutron. Wigner's theory provided an explanation for a hitherto unaccounted-for phenomenon: the large deflections of slow neutrons when they pass close to protons. Although Wigner discounted the idea's importance and did not deem it worthy of publication, it proved to be the foundation for numerous other papers.

In 1936, while working with **Gregory Breit**, Wigner examined the phenomenon of neutron absorption by a compound nucleus. Their Breit-Wigner formula did much to throw light on this subject. Continuing his work around atomic nuclei, Wigner postulated in 1937 that protons and neutrons were analogous to isotopes in the periodic table of the elements. The manifestation of a particle as a proton or as a neutron could be accounted for by different degrees of spin on the particle, known as isotopic spin or isospin for short.

Turning his attention to nuclear fission in 1938, Wigner developed a number of theoretical techniques of reactor calculations, some of which formed the basis of the first controlled chain reaction carried out by the Italian physicist **Enrico Fermi**. Together with his fellow Hungarians, **Leo Szilard** and **Edward Teller**, Wigner persuaded **Albert Einstein** to send a letter to President Franklin Roosevelt urging him to beat Hitler in the race to develop an atom bomb. The letter was crucial in convincing the American government to build nuclear reactors and was also directly responsible for the establishment of the Manhattan Project, on which Wigner played a key role.

In 1941 Wigner married Mary Annette Wheeler, with whom he had two children, David and Martha. Despite his many scientific commitments, Wigner tried to find time to devote to his family and to pursue his hobbies of bowling and figure skating.

The outbreak of war in Europe caused Wigner to turn his full attention to nuclear physics. At the Metallurgical Laboratory at the University of Chicago, he began work on the Manhattan Project as the chief engineer of the water-cooled Hanford plutonium reactors. Wigner's colleagues observed that, for a theorist, he had a remarkably precise knowledge of the engineering design of reactors. Also remarkable was the tremendous speed at which the latest scientific findings in the laboratory were converted into engineered chain reactors. After the war, Wigner accepted a position as director of research and development at the Clinton Laboratories at Oak Ridge from 1946 to 1947.

Career Honored with Copious Awards

Wigner's many contributions to physics have been recognized in a variety of prizes and honorary degrees. He was elected to the National Academy of Sciences in 1945. He was awarded the U.S. Atomic Energy Commission's Enrico Fermi Prize in 1958 and the Atoms for Peace Award in 1960. Most significantly, in 1936, Wigner won the Nobel physics prize for "systemically improving and extending the methods of quantum mechanics and applying them widely." Specifically, he was commended for his contribution to the theory of atomic nuclei elementary particles, especially for his discovery and application of fundamental principles of symmetry. This marked an unusual departure for the Nobel Committee, which normally awards the prize for a single discovery or invention.

Wigner, who retired from Princeton in 1971, has also been active on behalf of other scientists. He was one of thirty-three Nobel Prize winners who sent a telegram to President Podgorny of the former Soviet Union asking that **Andrei Sakharov** be permitted to receive the Nobel Peace Prize in Stockholm.

SELECTED WRITINGS BY WIGNER:

Books

(With Leonard Eisenbud) *Nuclear Structure,* Princeton University Press, 1961.
Symmetries and Reflections, Indiana University Press, 1967.
Who Speaks for Civil Defense?, Scribner, 1968.
Survival and the Bomb, Indiana University Press, 1969.
Aspects of Quantum Theory, Cambridge University Press, 1972.
(With Behram N. Kursunoglu) *Reminiscences about a Great Physicist: Paul Adrian Maurice Dirac,* Cambridge University Press, 1987.

SOURCES:

Books

Asimov, Isaac, *Atom: Journey Across the Subatomic Cosmos,* Truman Talley Books, 1991, p. 273.
Great American Scientists: America's Rise to the Forefront of World Science, Prentice Hall, 1967, pp. 21–22, 119.
Weber, Robert L., *Pioneers of Science: Nobel Prize Winners in Physics,* The Institute of Physics, 1980, p. 188.

—Sketch by Avril McDonald

Andrew J. Wiles
1953-
English-born American mathematician

A professor of mathematics at Princeton University, Andrew J. Wiles has formulated a proof which may solve a puzzle which has frustrated mathematicians for centuries. In his seven-year quest to solve the famous Fermat's Last Theorem, Wiles brought together separate schools of mathematical thought; his work has been submitted to a review process by other mathematicians and if it passes, the ancient problem will be considered solved.

Wiles was born in Cambridge, England, in April 1953. His father was a professor of theology. Wiles attended Clare College at Cambridge University, where he studied elliptical curves, earning his master's degree in 1977 and his Ph.D. in 1980. Elliptical curves would play a central role in his proof of Fermat's Last Theorem, but it was years before Wiles recognized this. He came to the United States in 1980 to accept a position as professor of mathematics at Princeton University. In 1988, Wiles received the Whitehead Prize from the London Mathematics Society, and he returned to England for two years as Research Professor in Maths and Professorial Fellow at Merton College, Oxford. He returned to Princeton in 1990.

Fermat's Last Theorem is the most famous problem in mathematics, and Wiles became intrigued with it when he was ten years old. He even worked on it as a teenager, but as he began his professional life he realized it was more complicated than he had initially thought. In 1637, French lawyer and number theorist Pierre Fermat scrawled a general math equation in the margin of his copy of Diophantus's *Arithmetic,* along with a very bold statement declaring that the equation $a^n + b^n = c^n$ can never be true when the exponent n is greater than two. Fermat provided no proof of his theorem because, he wrote, "the margin is too small to hold it." The theorem concerns an equation similar to the well-known Pythagorean theorem. Pythagorus said that the square of the longest side of a right triangle equals the sum of the squares of the other two sides ($a^2 + b^2 = c^2$). For example three squared (nine) plus four squared (sixteen) equals five squared (twenty five). Many other values also make this equation true, as long as the exponent is two. According to Fermat's theorem, however, an equation of the same form will never be true with any other whole number.

Like Wiles, many mathematicians had tested and tried to prove or disprove Fermat's Last Theorem in the 300 hundred years since it was published. Fermat himself had shown that when the exponents are four, the equation cannot be true. In 1780, Leonhard Euler proved the same for the exponent three. Others proved that exponents of five, seven, and thirteen cannot produce correct equations. Eventually computers were used to search for an equation which was true and would thereby disprove Fermat's Last Theorem. Exponents up to 4,000,000 were tested without finding an equation which showed that Fermat's Last Theorem was wrong. But an infinite number of possibilities remained to be tested. A different approach was needed to provide a definitive proof of Fermat's Last Theorem. In 1954, a Japanese mathematician named Yutaka Taniyama proposed a modular form to a set of mathematical equations called elliptical curves. His proposal was called the Taniyama conjecture. A conjecture in mathematics is a fascinating but unproved theory. The next advance came out of Germany in the 1980s from Gerhard Frey, who suggested that proving the Taniyama conjecture might indirectly prove Fermat's Last Theorem; an elliptical curve could be used to represent all the solutions to Fermat's equation. Kenneth Ribet in the United States proved Frey's idea in 1986, and this changed Wiles's perception of the theorem. He dedicated himself to solving Fermat's Last Theorem on the same day he heard of Ribet's proof.

Begins Seven-Year Journey to Prove the Theorem

Wiles believed he could prove that the elliptical curve representing the solutions to Fermat's equation could not exist and thereby prove Fermat's Last Theorem to be true. He virtually withdrew from professional life, except to teach classes at Princeton, and pursued his quest. Wiles spent seven years in seclusion in the attic of his home, without computer or telephone, working exhaustively to prove the theorem. He wanted to develop the proof completely on his own, and he was extremely secretive about his attic work, consulting only with one trusted colleague. He made steady progress in the first few years; progress eventually slowed, but in 1991 he made a discovery that reduced the problem to a calculation that had been used unsuccessfully by others. Wiles worked without interruption on this calculation, and by May of 1993 he felt he had a proof that was complete except for one single but critical special case. While reading a paper by Harvard mathematician Barry Mazur, Wiles realized that a mathematical construction described in the paper was the approach that would help him over this last hurdle.

Wiles announced his proof in an unusual manner. His withdrawal from most professional activities within the mathematics community had made his presentations at conferences rare. He asked to give three lectures at a small mathematics meeting in Cambridge, England, and rumors of an exciting announcement abounded, though the title of his lectures had no relationship to Fermat's theorem. In his first lecture, Wiles remained secretive about the final outcome of his series of talks, but twice as many people attended his second lecture. On the third day, June 23, 1993, Wiles announced that he had proven the Taniyama conjecture. Almost as an afterthought, he added that this meant that Fermat's Last Theorem was also proven to be true. Word of Wiles's proof spread throughout the mathematics world at the speed of electronic mail, and both mathematics journals and the general press hounded him for interviews. He sought refuge from the media coverage at his parents' home near the conference but was discovered there. He soon returned to Princeton, and he has continued his secretive approach to his proof of Fermat's Last Theorem even after his announcement. He withheld the document from almost everyone but the reviewers, unwilling to release it until he considers it to be absolutely correct and ready for publication.

When asked how he felt about his proof, Wiles told *People Weekly,* "There is a sense of loss, actually." But his work on Fermat's Last Theorem was not finished. Acceptance of a proof as important and complex as this is neither automatic nor immediate; there is an exhaustive review process used to verify that mathematical proofs are complete and clearly stated. Only a handful of mathematicians are fully able to understand the work Wiles has done, making the process one that may last as long as a year. Some refinement of the 200-page document was considered inevitable; Wiles resolved many of the reviewer's concerns quickly, though one particular flaw found in December of 1993 requires more work. But neither Wiles nor others believe that the integrity of his proof is threatened. In the meantime, Wiles continues to live in Princeton with his wife and two daughters.

SELECTED WRITINGS BY WILES:

Periodicals

"An Ordinary Lambda-adic Representation Associated to Modular Forms," *Annals of Mathematics,* Volume 94, 1988, pp. 529–573.
"The Iwasawa Conjecture for Totally Real Fields," *Annals of Mathematics,* Volume 131, 1990, pp. 493–540.
"On a Conjecture by Brumer," *Annals of Mathematics,* Volume 131, 1990, pp. 555–565.

SOURCES:

Periodicals

Cipra, Barry, "Fermat's Last Theorem Finally Yields," *Science,* Volume 261, July 2, 1993, pp. 32–33.

Davidson, K., "Amazement to the Nth," *San Francisco Chronicle,* June 27, 1993, p. A4
Folger, Tim. "Sure, Pierre. Sure You Knew," *Discover,* January 1994, p. 61.
Gleick, James, "Fermat's Theorem," *New York Times Magazine,* October 3, 1993, pp. 52–53.
Grossman, Ron, "He's Numero Uno," *Chicago Tribune,* July 14, 1993, p. D1.
Kolata, Gina. "At Last, Shout of 'Eureka!' In Age-Old Math Mystery," *New York Times,* June 24, 1993, p. A1.
Kolata, Gina. "Math Whiz Who Battled 350-Year-Old Problem," *New York Times,* June 29, 1993, p. C1.
Kolata, Gina. "Flaw Is Found in Math Proof, but Repairs Are Under Way," *New York Times,* December 11, 1993, p. A9.
Schwartz, John, "This Equation Figures to Answer a 17th Century Puzzle," *The Washington Post,* August 2, 1993, p. A3.
"The 25 Most Intriguing People of 1993—Andrew Wiles," *People Weekly,* December 27, 1993, p. 104.

—*Sketch by David N. Ford*

Maurice Wilkes
1913-
English computer engineer

Maurice Wilkes developed an interest in radio as a child and specialized in radar research during World War II. After the war, Wilkes became involved in pioneering research on the development of computers and is best known for his development of EDSAC, the Electronic Delay Storage Automatic Calculator, the first computing machine to make use of the concept of a stored program. Over the last five decades, Wilkes has been actively involved in the formation of a number of computer organizations and associations.

Maurice Vincent Wilkes was born on June 26, 1913, in Dudley, England. His father, Vincent J. Wilkes, was employed at the time on the South Staffordshire estate of the Earl of Dudley. His mother's name is not mentioned in the usual biographical records nor in Wilkes's own autobiography *Memoirs of a Computer Pioneer.* She is described in the latter reference, however, as "one of a pioneering band of women who went into offices in their hobble skirts and worked the new-fangled type-writing machines."

Develops an Early Interest in Science and Mathematics

Wilkes's early education in Dudley was interrupted by severe bouts of asthma, which he apparently inherited from his mother's side of the family. While he was still young, Wilkes's father moved the family to nearby Stourbridge in order to find a more congenial environment for his mother's health. Wilkes entered the King Edward VI Grammar School in Stourbridge at the age of eight and quickly developed an interest in science and mathematics. He was later to report in his *Memoirs*, "I think it was already clear to me [in the Sixth Form] that my life would be in physics or in physics-based engineering. I had seen enough to realize that there was a magic power in mathematics and I burned to be initiated fully into that mystery."

The other field that attracted Wilkes's interest at an early age was radio. The early 1920s were an era when "the wireless" was just becoming popular, with small amateur stations and crystal sets beginning to proliferate. Wilkes subscribed to *Wireless World* while he was still a teenager and a short time later was asked to build some equipment for station G6OJ, operated by the chemistry master at King Edward VI. In 1931 Wilkes applied for and received his own amateur radio operator's license.

Continues His Education at St. John's College and Cambridge University

Also in 1931 Wilkes graduated from King Edward VI and was accepted as a student at St. John's College, Cambridge. He concentrated in mathematics there and in June 1934 graduated with honors. He then applied for and received a research grant from the department of scientific and industrial research. He chose to use that grant to continue his studies at the Cavendish Laboratories at Cambridge, where he began work with the radio group in July 1934.

The first topic on which Wilkes was asked to work at the Cavendish involved a study of long radio waves. As he completed this project, the future direction of his career became more clear to him. He found that he was not particularly interested in pure or theoretical mathematics itself, but math "as application to any sort of physics was concerned. I did not have," he later wrote, "and indeed have never had, that interest in mathematical puzzles and fine points that characterize the natural theoretician. I looked forward to being able to apply the math I had learnt to physical problems."

Introduced to the Differential Analyzer

An important turning point in Wilkes's life came in March 1936 when he attended a lecture given by D. R. Hartree of Manchester University. Hartree's lecture involved the demonstration of a differential analyzer, a mechanical device for solving differential equations. Wilkes says that he found the machine "irresistible," and, more than that, exactly the tool he needed to solve some of the mathematical problems involved in his study of long waves. His future in the computing sciences appears to have been set.

Before long, Wilkes was involved in the operation of Cambridge's own differential analyzer and, in later 1937 he was asked to join the university's newly established "Mathematical Laboratory," which was, in fact, a "computing laboratory." (The facility's name was actually corrected thirty-three years later.) Wilkes's official appointment at the time was as university demonstrator. In early 1938 he was awarded his M.A. degree and in October of the same year, his Ph.D.

Begins Wartime Research on Radar

The year of Wilkes's graduation was one of profound unrest in Great Britain and across Europe. Some observers expected the outbreak of war momentarily and were encouraging preparation for that event. Others held to the hope that peace could still be salvaged. Within a year of receiving his degree, Wilkes had been drafted into the program for the development of radarlike devices for the detection of, at first, submarines, and, later, surface ships and aircraft. His first assignment was at the radar station at Dunkirk, where he reported on August 28, 1939. Within a short time he was back in Cambridge, working on antisubmarine devices before returning to Dunkirk and, later, to other stations along the coast.

By 1941 Wilkes had been assigned to the Operations Research Group (ORG) headquartered in Petersham. Most of his work with the ORG involved the development of ten-centimeter radar instruments and, in particular, of the GL Mark I, II, and III detection systems. In 1943 Wilkes moved on to a new assignment in Malvern, where he worked on the development of the Oboe system. In his autobiography, Wilkes describes Oboe as a "blind-bombing system that depended on measurement of range from two land-based stations to the bombing aircraft."

At the war's conclusion, Wilkes volunteered for an assignment in Germany interviewing captured German scientists. His account of the two months he spent in Germany is an equal mix of new information gained from his interviewees, sparkling travelogue about the German countryside, and ongoing complaints about endless bureaucratic confusion. Wilkes returned to Cambridge from his Germany assignment on August 1, 1945, to an offer of a university lectureship and the post of acting director of the mathematical laboratory. In May 1946 Wilkes was given a copy of **John von Neumann**'s "Draft Report on EDVAC." The report contained, Wilkes later wrote, "the principles on which the development of the modern digital computer was to be based." "I recognized this at once as the real thing," he went on, "and from that time on never had any doubt as to the way computer development would go." In October 1946 Wilkes was given the title of director of the laboratory.

Wilkes's interest in computers had not precluded his continued research on atmospheric physics begun before the war. Indeed, this topic was one to which he kept returning for many years, even after he had earned his reputation in computer science. One of his accomplishments in the immediate postwar period was to confirm, using the differential analyzer, a prediction by C. L. Pekeris regarding factors affecting resonance in the atmosphere.

Makes Important Contacts at a Moore School Course

In early 1946 Wilkes was invited to attend a course on Electronic Computing to be held at the Moore School of Electrical Engineering in Philadelphia on August 8–31. Travel was still difficult in the postwar year of 1946, and Wilkes actually arrived two weeks late for the class. However, he had an opportunity to see the world's first electronic computer, the ENIAC, which, although it had already become something of a dinosaur in the computer world, still provided the standard for the future of computer development.

During this visit to the United States—the first of many over the next forty years—Wilkes spoke with most of the pioneers of computer science in the United States, including **Howard Aiken** at Harvard, S. H. Caldwell at the Massachusetts Institute of Technology (MIT), and **John William Mauchly** and H. H. Goldstine at the Moore School. It was during this visit that Wilkes "first began to sketch out the design of the machine that finally became the EDSAC," he states in his autobiography. Actual work on the machine then began about two months after his return to England.

The key innovation in Wilkes's EDSAC was that the programs needed to operate the machine were actually built into the machine itself rather than having to be fed into it, as in earlier machines. The key part of the machine was a 1.5 meter-long, mercury-filled tank, called a "tube," that held sixteen words of thirty-five bits each. The final design of the EDSAC was to consist of thirty-two such tubes.

Actual construction of the EDSAC was a long and complex process, filled with the problems and frustrations to be expected of such an undertaking. At a key point, officials of J. Lyons and Company offered an infusion of cash that made completion of the computer possible and at the same time led to the

development of the first commercial versions of EDSAC, LEO 1, LEO 2, and LEO 3.

The first successful run of EDSAC took place on May 6, 1949. The machine read a program tape for computing a table of squares and correctly printed out the results. In a short period of time, researchers were making use of the powerful new computing tool. In early 1949, for example, the eminent statistician **Ronald A. Fisher** inquired about the use of EDSAC in the solution of a second-order nonlinear differential equation. A year later, Wilkes provided him with the results, results about which Wilkes later wrote, "I do not think that he had for one moment expected that we would produce." In 1950 Wilkes wrote a report describing the development and uses of EDSAC, a report that was published in 1951 by Addison-Wesley as *Preparation of Programs for an Electronic Digital Computer, with Special Reference to the EDSAC and the Use of a Library of Subroutines*. The book was reissued in 1982 as volume 1 of the Charles Babbage Institute reprint series on the history of computing. In July 1950 Wilkes left for his second visit to the United States, one that was to last for two months and was to include stops at every major computing center in the country. He visited the Institute for Advanced Studies in Princeton, New Jersey; the Eckert-Mauchly Corporation in Philadelphia; the National Bureau of Standards in Washington, D.C.; the U.S. Army proving ground in Aberdeen, Maryland; Harvard and MIT in Cambridge, Massachusetts; IBM World Headquarters in New York City; the navy proving ground in Dahlgren, Virginia; the University of Illinois; and the University of California at Berkeley.

Begins Work on EDSAC 2

Less than six months after his return from the United States, Wilkes had become deeply involved in the planning for the next stage in computing machinery, EDSAC 2. He recognized that the time had come to move from the experimental level represented by EDSAC 1 to a fully operational working machine that could begin to take on many of the research projects already envisioned by university researchers in many departments. By June 1951 funding had been obtained from the Nuffield Foundation, and construction was under way by the summer of 1953. An intermediary model, EDSAC 1.5, passed initial tests, and early in 1958 EDSAC 2 was formally put into operation. A few months later, on July 11, 1958, EDSAC 1 was formally closed down and dismantled, its parts sold for scrap.

In very little time, EDSAC 2 proved its worth to the scientific community. Its first notable success was in connection with the work of **John Kendrew**, who was working on the molecular structure of myoglobin. Kendrew had used EDSAC 1 to help analyze four hundred X-ray diffraction patterns in the early part of his research and had then turned to EDSAC 2 to examine ten thousand more photographs when that machine became available. In his 1962 Nobel lecture, Kendrew acknowledged the role of the EDSAC machines in facilitating the research for which he had received that coveted prize.

At nearly the same time, astronomer **Martin Ryle** found another use for EDSAC 2. Ryle was working on the problem of creating a radio telescope with a very large aperture capable of obtaining resolutions far better than any existing instruments. Ryle's approach was to construct the telescope of movable sections whose individual photographs could then be analyzed and combined by means of complex computer programs. The EDSAC 2 provided the technology that made that approach workable and that brought to Ryle the 1974 Nobel Prize in physics.

By the time EDSAC 2 was powered down on November 1, 1964, Wilkes had become a senior statesman in the field of computer hardware. Although he continued to be active in research, he also began to assume more responsibility in professional organizations. For example, in 1957 he was elected the first president of the British Computer Society, a post he held for three years. In 1965 he was appointed chairman of the Computer Advisory Committee of the Agricultural Research Council, a post he held for ten years. After 1950 Wilkes made many trips to the United States; when he reached mandatory retirement age at Cambridge in 1980, he moved to Maynard, Massachusetts, and took a job as staff consultant at the Digital Equipment Corporation. A year later he was also appointed adjunct professor at MIT. In 1986 Wilkes returned to Cambridge, where he became a consultant for the Olivetti Research Board.

Wilkes was married to Nina Twyman in 1947. They have three children, Margaret, Helen, and Anthony. Among his many awards have been the Harry Goode Memorial Award (1968) and the Eckert-Mauchly Award (1980) of the American Federation of Information Processing Societies, the McDowell Award of the Institute of Electrical and Electronics Engineers (1981), the Pender Award of the University of Pennsylvania (1982), the C and C Prize (Tokyo, 1988), and the Italgas Prize (Turin, 1991). He has also received honorary doctorates from eight universities.

SELECTED WRITINGS BY WILKES:

Books

Oscillations of the Earth's Atmosphere, Cambridge University Press, 1949.
Preparation of Programs for an Electronic Digital Computer, with Special Reference to the EDSAC and the Use of a Library of Subroutines, Addison-Wesley, 1951.

Automatic Digital Computers, Methuen, 1958.
A Short Introduction to Numerical Analysis, Cambridge University Press, 1966.
Time-Sharing Computer Systems, Elsevier, 1968.
The Cambridge CAP Computer and Its Operating System, North Holland, 1979.
Memoirs of a Computer Pioneer, MIT Press, 1985.

SOURCES:

Books

Cortada, James W., *Historical Dictionary of Data Processing: Technology,* Association for Computing Machinery, 1987, pp. 149–151.

—*Sketch by David E. Newton*

J. Ernest Wilkins, Jr.
1923-
American mathematician and physicist

A distinguished applied mathematician and nuclear engineer, J. Ernest Wilkins, Jr., has enjoyed a diverse career spanning governmental, industrial, and academic positions. He was involved in the Manhattan Project—the top-secret quest to construct a nuclear bomb during the 1940s—and was a pioneer in nuclear reactor design. He served as President of the American Nuclear Society, and contributed to the mathematical theory of Bessel functions, differential and integral equations, the calculus of variations, and to optical instruments for space.

Jesse Ernest Wilkins, Jr. was born in Chicago on November 27, 1923, the son of J. Ernest Wilkins, Sr., and Lucile Beatrice Robinson Wilkins. The senior Wilkins was a prominent lawyer who was president of the Cook County Bar Association in 1941–42, and an Assistant Secretary of Labor in the Eisenhower administration. Wilkins' mother was a schoolteacher with a master's degree. Both parents remained active in the Methodist church. Wilkins' two brothers became lawyers, but Wilkins preferred mathematics, entering the University of Chicago at the age of thirteen, and becoming the youngest student ever admitted to that institution. He completed his baccalaureate in 1940, his master's in 1941, and, by the age of nineteen, had earned his doctoral degree.

Wilkins went to the Institute for Advanced Study on a Rosenwald scholarship in 1942, then taught at

Tuskegee Institute in 1943–44. He returned to the University of Chicago, where he worked on the Manhattan Project at the Metallurgical Laboratory from 1944 to 1946. Wilkins spent the bulk of his career in industry, however, starting with a position as Mathematician at the American Optical Company in Buffalo, New York, in 1946. He left to become a Senior Mathematician at the Nuclear Development Corporation of America (NDA), later United Nuclear Corporation, in White Plains, New York, in 1950. There he became Manager of the Physics and Mathematics Department in 1955 and later Manager of Research and Development. While he was at NDA, Wilkins earned a B.M.E. degree in 1957, and an M.M.E. in 1960, from New York University.

Beginning in the sixties, Wilkins held various offices in the American Nuclear Society, becoming President of the organization during 1974–75. In the early sixties, Wilkins moved to the General Atomic Division of General Dynamics Corporation in San Diego, where he remained until 1970. Wilkins next took an academic position as Distinguished Professor of Applied Mathematical Physics at Howard University in Washington, DC., remaining in that position for the next seven years.

In 1977 Wilkins went to EG&G Idaho in Idaho Falls, where he was Associate General Manager and then Deputy General Manager. Leaving in 1984, Wilkins was an Argonne Fellow at Argonne National Laboratory in 1984 and 1985, and although retired beginning in 1985, he remained active as a consultant. In 1990, Wilkins joined Clark Atlanta University as Distinguished Professor of Applied Mathematics and Mathematical Physics.

Completes Gamma Ray Research

During his career Wilkins published roughly a hundred papers and reports on pure and applied mathematics, nuclear engineering, and optics. He is best-known for studies with Herbert Goldstein on gamma-ray penetration, the results of which are used for the design of nuclear reactor and radiation shielding, and of neutron absorption, which produced the Wigner-Wilkins approach to estimating the distribution of neutron energies in nuclear reactors. Wilkins also wrote papers on reactor operation and design and heat transfer. In addition, Wilkins continued to write on optical optimization problems and did interesting work on the estimation of the number of real roots of polynomials with random coefficients.

Wilkins served on advisory committees on scientific and engineering education for the National Academy of Engineering, the National Research Council, and other organizations and universities. Wilkins married Gloria Stewart in 1947. They had two children, Sharon and J. Ernest III. Wilkins remarried in 1984.

SELECTED WRITINGS BY WILKINS:

Books

(With Robert L. Hellens and Paul E. Zweifel) "Status of Experimental and Theoretical Information on Neutron Slowing-Down Distributions in Hydrogenous Media," *Proceedings of the International Conference on the Peaceful Uses of Atomic Energy,* United Nations, 1956, Volume 5, pp. 62–76.

"The Landau Constants," *Progress in Approximation Theory,* Academic Press, 1991, pp. 829–842.

"Mean Number of Real Zeroes of a Random Trigonometric Polynomial, II," *Topics in Polynomials and Their Applications,* World, 1993, pp. 581–594.

Periodicals

(With Herbert Goldstein and L. Volume Spencer) "Systematic Calculations of Gamma-Ray Penetration," *Physical Review,* Volume 89, 1953, p. 1150.

(With G.B. Melese-d'Hospital) "Steady-state Heat Conduction in Slabs, Cylindrical and Spherical Shell with Non-uniform Heat Generation," *Nuclear Engineering and Design,* Volume 24, 1973, pp. 62–77.

(With K.N. Srivastava) "Minimum Critical Mass Nuclear Reactors, Part I and Part II," *Nuclear Science and Engineering,* Volume 82, 1982, pp. 307–315, 316–324.

(With J. N. Kibe) "Apodization for Maximum Central Irradiance and Specified Large Rayleigh Limit of Resolution, II," *Journal of the Optical Society of America A, Optics and Image Science,* Volume 1, 1984, pp. 337–343.

SOURCES:

Books

Glasstone, Samuel and Alexander Sesonske, *Nuclear Engineering,* Van Nostrand, 1955.

In Black and White, A Guide to Magazine Articles, Newspaper Articles and Books Concerning more than 15,000 Black Individuals and Groups, Volume 2, third edition, Gale, 1980, p. 1040.

Periodicals

Ebony, February, 1958, pp. 60–67.

—*Sketch by Sally M. Moite*

Maurice Hugh Frederick Wilkins
1916-
New Zealand-born English biophysicist

Maurice Hugh Frederick Wilkins is best known for the assistance he provided to molecular biologists **James D. Watson** and **Francis Crick** in their quest to uncover the structure of deoxyribonucleic acid (DNA), the genetic blueprint of heredity in humans and many other organisms. Specifically, Wilkins' contribution to their discovery involved discerning the structure of DNA through the use of X ray diffraction techniques. For his efforts, Wilkins shared the 1962 Nobel Prize in physiology or medicine with Watson and Crick.

Wilkins was born in Pongaroa, New Zealand on December 15, 1916, to Irish immigrants Edgar Henry, a physician, and Eveline Constance Jane (Whittaker) Wilkins. Superior education began at an early age for Wilkins, who began attending King Edward's School in Birmingham, England, at age six. He later received his B.A. in physics from Cambridge University in 1938. After graduation, he joined the Ministry of Home Security and Aircraft Production and was assigned to conduct graduate research on radar at the University of Birmingham. Wilkins' research centered on improving the accuracy of radar screens.

Soon after earning his Ph.D. in 1940, Wilkins, still with the Ministry of Home Security, was relocated to a new team of British scientists researching the application of uranium isotopes to atomic bombs. A short time later Wilkins became part of another team sent to the United States to work on the Manhattan Project—the military effort to develop the atomic bomb—with other scientists at the University of California at Berkeley. He spent two years there researching the separation of uranium isotopes.

Switches Research Focus to Biophysics

Wilkins' interest in the intersection of physics and biology emerged soon after his arrival to the United States. He was significantly influenced by a book by **Erwin Schrödinger**, a fellow physicist, entitled *What is Life? The Physical Aspects of the Living Cell.* The book centers on the possibility that the science of quantum physics could lead to the understanding of the essence of life itself, including the process of biological growth. In addition to Schrödinger's book, the undeniable and undesirable ramifications of his work on the atomic bomb also played a role in Wilkins' declining interest in the field of nuclear physics and emerging interest in biology.

Maurice Hugh Frederick Wilkins

After the war, the opportunity arose for Wilkins to begin a career in biophysics. In 1945, Wilkins' former graduate school professor, Scottish physicist John T. Randall, invited him to become a physics lecturer at St. Andrews University, Scotland, in that school's new biophysics research unit. Later, in 1946, Wilkins and Randall moved on to a new research pursuit combining the sciences of physics, chemistry and biology to the study of living cells. Together they established the Medical Research Council Biophysics Unit at King's College in London. Wilkins was, for a time, informally the second in command. He officially became deputy director of the unit in 1955 and was promoted to director in 1970, a position he held until 1972.

Delves into Research on DNA Structure

It was at this biophysics unit, in 1946, that Wilkins soon concentrated his research on DNA, shortly after scientists at the Rockefeller Institute (now Rockefeller University) in New York announced that DNA is the constituent of genes. Realizing the enormous importance of the DNA molecule, Wilkins became excited about uncovering its precise structure. He was prepared to attack this project by a number of different methods. However, he fortuitously discovered that the particular makeup of DNA, specifically the uniformity of its fibers, made it an excellent specimen for X ray diffraction studies. X ray diffraction is an extremely useful method for photographing atom arrangements in molecules. The regularly-spaced atoms of the molecule actually diffract the X rays, creating a picture from which the sizing and spacing of the atoms within the molecule can be deduced. This was the tool used by Wilkins to help unravel the structure of DNA.

Physical chemist **Rosalind Franklin** joined Wilkins in 1951. Franklin, who had been conducting research in Paris, was very adept in X ray diffraction. Although their personal relationship was not ideal, (Franklin was more outgoing whereas Wilkins was a quiet, non-confrontational person), together they were able to retrieve some very high quality DNA patterns. One initial and important outcome of their research was that phosphate groups were located outside of the structure, which overturned **Linus Pauling**'s theory that they were on the inside. In another important finding, Wilkins thought the photographs suggested a helical structure, although Franklin hesitated to draw that conclusion. Subsequently, Wilkins, some say unbeknownst to Franklin, passed on to Watson one of the best X ray pictures Franklin had taken of DNA. These DNA images provided clues to Watson and Crick, who used the pictures to solve the last piece of the DNA structure puzzle.

X Ray Images Lead to Discovery of DNA Structure

Consequently, in 1953, Watson and Crick were able to reconstruct the famous double-helix structure of DNA. Their model shows that DNA is composed of two strands of alternating units of sugar and phosphate on the outside, with pairs of bases—including the molecular compounds adenine, thymine, guanine, and cytosine—inside, bonded by hydrogen. It is important to note that while Wilkins' contribution to the discernment DNA's structure is undeniable, controversy surrounds the fact that Franklin was not recognized for this scientific breakthrough, particularly in terms of the Nobel Prize. Some feel that Franklin, who died of cancer in 1958, did not receive due recognition, whereas others maintain that it was solely Watson's ability to discern the structure in Franklin's photograph that made possible the discovery of the DNA structure.

The knowledge of the DNA structure, which has been described as resembling a spiral staircase, has provided the impetus for advanced research in the field of genetics. For example, scientists can now determine predispositions for certain diseases based on the presence of certain genes. Also, the exciting but sometimes controversial area of genetic engineering has developed.

Studies Composition of RNA

Wilkins, Watson, and Crick were awarded the 1962 Nobel Prize for physiology or medicine for their work which uncovered the structure of hereditary material DNA. After winning the Nobel Prize, Wilkins focused next on elucidating the structure of ribonucleic acids (RNA)—a compound like DNA associated with the control of cellular chemical activities—and, later, nerve cell membranes. In 1962 he was able to show that RNA also had a helical structure somewhat similar to that of DNA. Besides his directorship appointments at the Medical Research Council's Biophysics Unit, Wilkins was also appointed director of the Council's Neurobiology Unit, a post he held from 1974 to 1980. Additionally, he was a professor at King's College, teaching molecular biology from 1963 to 1970 and then biophysics as the department head from 1970 to 1982. In 1981, he was named professor emeritus at King's College. Utilizing some of his professional expertise for social causes, Wilkins has maintained membership in the British Society for Social Responsibility in Science (of which he is president), the Russell Committee against Chemical Weapons, and Food and Disarmament International.

Wilkins is an honorary member of the American Society of Biological Chemists and the American Academy of Arts and Sciences. He was also honored with the 1960 Albert Lasker Award of the American Public Health Association (given jointly to Wilkins, Watson, and Crick), and was named Fellow of the Royal Society of King's College in 1959.

Wilkins, known to be a quiet and polite man, married Patricia Ann Chidgey in 1959. The couple has four children, two sons and two daughters.

SOURCES:

Books

Current Biography, H. W. Wilson, 1963, pp. 465–466.

McGraw-Hill Modern Scientists and Engineers, McGraw-Hill, 1980, pp. 320–321.

Wasson, Tyler, editor, *Nobel Prize Winners,* H. W. Wilson, 1987, pp. 1127–1129.

Periodicals

Judson, Horace Freeland, "The Legend of Rosalind Franklin," *Science Digest,* January, 1986, pp. 78–81.

New York Times, October 19, 1962, p. 1.

—Sketch by Carla Mecoli-Kamp

Geoffrey Wilkinson
1921-
English chemist

Geoffrey Wilkinson is best known for establishing the structure of a "sandwich molecule" he called ferrocene. In sandwich compounds a metal atom is the "filling" between two "slices" which are flat, typically carbon-based, rings. Since Wilkinson's original discovery of an iron filling between two cyclopentadienyl (five carbon atoms linked in a circle) slices, many different sandwiches have been built. Various metal fillings have been used, as have numerous other slices. Sandwich compounds have found widespread use as catalysts in industrial processes, and their previously unknown chemical bonding structure has proven to be of great theoretical interest to various branches of chemistry. Wilkinson's discovery revolutionized how chemists thought about chemical structure and opened up new avenues of chemical exploration.

Wilkinson was born on July 14, 1921, in Yorkshire, England, to Henry and Ruth Crowther Wilkinson. It was an uncle, the owner of a small chemical company in the town of Todmorden, who encouraged Wilkinson's interest in chemistry and had the most influence on his career choice. Wilkinson attended the Todmorden Secondary School and then the Imperial College of Science and Technology at the University of London. Supported by a scholarship, he obtained his B.S. degree in 1941 and his doctorate in 1946.

In 1942, while still a doctoral student, Wilkinson worked with the National Research Council on a joint atomic energy project. His work involved separating the various products of atomic fission reactions from one another so they could be studied and the fission process better understood. In the course of this work Wilkinson developed a new technique, ion-exchange chromatography, which has since proven useful in many chemical analyses. Using this technique, Wilkinson identified a number of new isotopes, atomic species which vary only in the number of neutrons within their nuclei. After the Second World War, Wilkinson continued his research on nuclear chemistry at the University of California at Berkeley. His work there focused on identifying neutron-deficient isotopes, products of atomic fission that are unstable because they have too few neutrons in their nuclei.

In 1950, Wilkinson moved to the Massachusetts Institute of Technology as a research associate. He had come to the end of what he considered to be his effectiveness in nuclear synthesis research, and began to study the chemical nature of the transition elements. These are the elements found in the center of the periodic table; they often have more than a single stable electrical charge state and unusual magnetic properties. One of Wilkinson's first major breakthroughs was to synthesize a compound in which the transition element nickel was chemically bound to phosphorus within a larger molecule.

Despite his decision to change the focus of his research, it was Wilkinson's expertise as a nuclear chemist that earned him a position as an assistant professor at Harvard University in 1951. He would only remain at Harvard for four years, but it was a very productive time in his life. It was here that he first deduced the sandwich-type molecular structure.

Discovers Structure of Ferrocene

Early in 1952, while preparing to teach an inorganic chemistry course, Wilkinson read about a newly synthesized compound, bicyclopentadienyl iron (a chemical made from an iron atom bonded to two five-carbon rings). The structure proposed seemed unlikely to Wilkinson. Based on theories developed by **Linus Pauling**, he thought that the key to the structure must lie in the distribution of the so-called pi electrons in the cyclopentadienyl ring. Pauling's work indicated that this ion would have its pi electrons very evenly distributed in rings parallel to the plane of the carbon atoms. Wilkinson realized that a stable structure would result if the iron atom bonded through the pi electrons and was thus held equidistant from all of the carbon atoms in the cyclopentadienyl ring. In bicyclopentadienyl iron this would be possible only by having the iron atom "sandwiched" between the two flat cyclopentadienyl groups.

Along with a colleague, **Robert B. Woodward**, Wilkinson experimentally proved this novel structure in a few days. Woodward coined the term ferrocene, due to the similarity of the structure to the well-known compound benzene. Wilkinson rapidly adapted the synthesis methods to create a number of other sandwich compounds. For discovering this previously unknown class of chemical structure, Wilkinson shared the 1973 Nobel Prize in chemistry with **Ernst Otto Fischer**. Fischer had also worked on these compounds, and in presenting the award the committee congratulated both men for creating a new field of chemistry.

While at Harvard in the 1950s, Wilkinson also pioneered the use of the nuclear magnetic resonance (NMR) technique in chemical analysis. In NMR spectroscopy, chemists study the movement of atoms (most often hydrogen) within a magnetic field; each atom emits a distinct spectral line according to its bond. This technique helped to explain the concept of fluctionality, a theory which states that some chemical species may fluctuate back and forth from one bonding structure to another. This technique has since also found considerable use in medicine, where it is called magnetic resonance imaging or MRI. But despite the widespread recognition of the importance of his work, Harvard University did not offer Wilkinson tenure.

In 1955 Wilkinson returned to the Imperial College of Science and Technology to assume the chair of the inorganic chemistry department. Here he continued his work on transition elements and how they form complexes with organic species through pi electrons. In particular, Wilkinson concentrated on several ways in which transition metal complexes serve as catalysts. (A catalyst speeds up a chemical reaction and is then converted back into its original form, enabling it to serve for multiple cycles of the reaction.)

Wilkinson wrote widely, publishing more than four hundred articles on the transition metals and their complexes with organic compounds. He also coauthored *Advanced Inorganic Chemistry* (1962), which has remained a classic text in the field, and *Basic Inorganic Chemistry* (1976). Wilkinson received numerous honors in addition to the Nobel Prize. The French Chemical Society honored him in 1968 with its Lavoisier Medal, the Royal Society presented him with the Transition Metal Chemistry Award in 1972, and he won the Gallileo Medal from the University of Pisa, Italy, in 1973.

Wilkinson married Lise Solver Schau in 1951, soon after arriving at Harvard. They have two daughters.

SELECTED WRITINGS BY WILKINSON:

Books

(With F. A. Cotton) *Advanced Inorganic Chemistry,* Interscience, 1962.
(With Cotton) *Basic Inorganic Chemistry,* Wiley, 1976.

Periodicals

(With W. F. Grummit) "Chemical Separation of Fission Products by Oxidation-Reaction," *Nucleonics,* Volume 9, 1951.
(With R. B. Woodward, M. C. Whiting, and M. Rosenblum) "The Structure of Bicyclopentadienyl Iron," *Journal of the American Chemical Society,* Volume 74, 1952.
"The Iron Sandwich: A Recollection of the First Four Months," *Journal of Organometallic Chemistry,* Volume 100, 1975, pp. 273–278.

—*Sketch by Ethan E. Allen*

Anna W. Williams
1863-1954
American bacteriologist

Anna W. Williams' work as one of America's pioneering bacteriologists was accomplished during her long tenure at the research laboratory of the New York City Department of Health. Her discovery of the *Corynebacterium diphtheriae* bacillus led to the development of a diphtheria antitoxin and the conquering of this dreaded childhood disease. Williams' wide-ranging research also led to the development of a rabies vaccine and an improved method for diagnosing rabies.

Anna Wessels Williams was born in Hackensack, New Jersey, on March 17, 1863, to William and Jane (Van Saun) Williams. Although her English-born father was a private school teacher, the family, which included her five siblings and several half-siblings, could not afford private school tuition. Williams was schooled at home until she was twelve; she then entered the State Street Public School, where her father was a trustee. Williams attended the New Jersey State Normal School in Trenton, New Jersey, in 1883; she subsequently taught school until 1885. Williams decided on a medical career in 1887, the year one of her sisters suffered a severe illness. She obtained her medical degree in 1891 from the Women's Medical College of the New York Infirmary, and remained there as a pathology and hygiene instructor until 1893 and as department assistant until 1895. Williams also served as consulting pathologist at the Women's Medical College from 1902 to 1905.

Discovery of Diphtheria Antitoxin and Rabies Vaccine

In 1894, Williams volunteered to serve in the bacteriology laboratory at the New York City Department of Health, the nation's first city-operated diagnostic laboratory, whose director was William H. Park. Her work at the Department of Health began with a search for a antitoxin for diphtheria—at that time a leading cause of death among children. Williams' discovery in 1894 of the *Corynebacterium diphtheria* bacillus (a disease-producing bacterium) led to the development of a diphtheria antitoxin soon in use for immunization throughout North America and Great Britain. The isolation of this bacillus strain, known as Park-Williams #8, was generally credited to Park, even though he was not involved in the initial discovery. In 1895, Williams joined the laboratory staff as assistant bacteriologist.

Williams also researched streptococcal and pneumococcal infections (caused by the bacterium responsible for "strep throat" and pneumonia, respectively), and conducted diagnostic studies related to trachoma and the chronic eye infections commonly found among the city's underprivileged children. In 1896, she traveled to the Pasteur Institute in Paris in the hopes of developing an antitoxin for scarlet fever. Although she was not successful in this effort, her experiments with a rabies virus culture she obtained at the Pasteur Institute resulted in the mass production of a rabies vaccine by 1898. In 1905, Williams was named assistant director of the laboratory at the Department of Health.

In this same year, Williams published an improved method of rabies diagnosis based on a technique of analyzing brain tissue samples. This method stemmed from her own research and the parallel studies of Adelchi Negri, an Italian physician, on the presence of distinctive cells in rabies-infected brain tissue. Until Williams' publication of her method, a diagnosis of rabies took ten days; her technique took minutes, and was not improved upon for over thirty years. In recognition of this advance, the American Public Health Association in 1907 appointed Williams as chair of its newly-formed committee on the diagnosis of rabies.

In 1915, Williams became president of the Women's Medical Association. During World War I, she served on the influenza commission, trained medical laboratory workers, and contributed to a military program to detect meningococcal carriers. In 1931, she was elected vice-chair of the laboratory section of the American Public Health Association. Williams also published extensively over the course of her career. She was co-author, with Park, of the widely-used *Pathogenic Microörganisms Including Bacteria and Protozoa: A Practical Manual for Students, Physicians and Health Officers;* their edition first came out in 1905. She published her authoritative treatise, *Streptococci in Relation to Man in Health and Disease,* in 1932. Williams' controversial forced retirement in 1934 came about because of Mayor Fiorello La Guardia's decree of mandatory retirement for all city employees over seventy years old. Despite the urging of Williams' colleagues and other scientists that she be allowed to continue her important research, La Guardia refused to make an exception. She left New York City for retirement in Woodcliff Lake, New Jersey, and subsequently moved to Westwood, New Jersey, where she lived with her sister, Amelia Wilson. Williams died from heart failure on November 20, 1954, at the age of ninety-one.

SELECTED WRITINGS BY WILLIAMS:

Books

(With William H. Park) *Pathogenic Microörganisms Including Bacteria and Protozoa: A Practical Manual for Students, Physicians and Health Officers,* Lea Brothers, 1905.

(With Park) *Who's Who among the Microbes,* Century, 1929.
Streptococci in Relation to Man in Health and Disease, Williams & Williams, 1932.

Periodicals

"Persistence of Varieties of the Bacillus Diphtheriae and of Diphtheria-like Bacilli," *Journal of Medical Research,* June, 1902.
"A Study of Trachoma and Allied Conditions in the Public School Children of New York City," *Journal of Infectious Diseases,* March, 1914.

SOURCES:

Books

Notable American Women: The Modern Period, Belknap, 1980, pp. 737–739.

Periodicals

New York Times, November 21, 1954, p. 86.

—*Sketch by Jane Stewart Cook*

Daniel Hale Williams
1858-1931
American surgeon

Arguably the most prominent black physician of his time, Daniel Hale Williams performed the first recorded successful heart surgery; founded Provident Hospital in Chicago; reorganized Freedmen's Hospital in Washington, D.C.; instituted policies and programs that made Meharry Medical College in Nashville a first-class institution for the training of black medical practitioners; and helped found the National Medical Association, the black counterpart to the segregated American Medical Association. Williams' distinguished career was recognized in 1913 when he was asked to become a charter member of the American College of Surgeons, the only black doctor so honored.

Williams was born January 18, 1858, in Hollidaysburg, Pennsylvania. He was the fifth child of Daniel Williams, a barber, and Sara (Price) Williams. After his father's death, his mother moved the family to Rockford, Illinois, and later to Janesville, Wiscon-

Daniel Hale Williams

sin, where Williams completed his secondary education. In 1878, he began an apprenticeship under Henry Palmer, a physician who had served as Wisconsin's surgeon general. His training under Palmer enabled him to enter Chicago Medical College, an affiliate of Northwestern University, where he received his medical degree in 1883. After serving an internship at Mercy Hospital in Chicago, Williams opened his practice in an integrated neighborhood on the south side of Chicago.

These early years saw Williams successful in his new practice, where he was meticulous in observing the sterilization and antiseptic procedures (newly advanced by the English surgeon Joseph Lister, based on the germ theory of French microbiologist Louis Pasteur) in the domestic locales of his surgeries. In 1884, he became a surgeon for the South Side Dispensary and an attending physician at the Protestant Orphan Asylum. He began instructing in anatomy at Chicago Medical College in 1885 and also served during this time as surgeon to the City Railway Company. In 1889, he was appointed to a four-year term on the Illinois State Board of Health, where he played a role in drafting important public health regulations.

Founding of Provident Hospital

In spite of his many medical commitments, "Doctor Dan," as he was affectionately called, was determined to establish a progressive interracial hos-

pital that would focus on offering internships to black doctors and training for black nurses. Williams realized this dream in 1891 with the opening of Provident Hospital. It was here that he performed the first recorded heart surgery by suturing a tear in a stabbing victim's pericardium (the membrane that encloses the heart); the patient completely recovered from the risky operation. Williams was subsequently to perfect a suture for spleen hemorrhage.

In 1894, President Cleveland appointed Williams as surgeon-in-chief of Freedmen's Hospital in Washington, D.C. At Freedmen's, Williams used his administrative skills to reorganize and upgrade what was essentially a collection of decrepit Army buildings that had been converted to civilian medical use. Under his guidance, Freedmen's hospital was divided into seven departments: dermatological, genito-urinary, gynecological, medical, obstetrical, surgical, and throat and chest. The number of internships was increased, the nurses training program was strengthened, and a horse-drawn ambulance was put into service. During his tenure, the hospital saw a significant decrease from its former ten percent mortality rate. Williams' administrative achievement at Freedmen's was substantial, although he did not realize all of his far-reaching plans for the institution. In 1895, Williams helped found the Medico-Chirurgical Society of Washington. Ultimately discouraged by political infighting, he resigned from Freedmen's in 1897 and returned to Chicago.

In Chicago, Williams resumed his affiliation with Provident, and also began practicing at other hospitals. In 1899, in addition, Williams accepted a professorship of clinical surgery at Meharry Medical College in Nashville, Tennessee, where he began holding annual surgery clinics. In 1900, Williams presented research to the Chicago Medical Society refuting the myth that black women were not at risk for ovarian cysts. His association with the white-clientele St. Luke's Hospital, beginning in 1913, was instrumental in building one of the largest gynecological practices in Chicago. Over this period, Williams also helped establish forty hospitals in twenty states to serve black communities.

Although Williams retained his affiliation with Provident for many years, his return to Chicago and the hospital came at a time of dissension: it was said that jealous and powerful associates, among them Dr. George C. Hall, looked unfavorably on Williams' advancements within the white medical establishment. The rivalry between Williams and George C. Hall eventually forced Williams to cut his ties to the hospital he had founded. In 1925, Williams invited Leon Tancil to assist him in his practice. Tancil remained for a few years, but then left to establish his own office. Shortly thereafter, Williams' failing health forced him to end his long and distinguished practice.

Williams married Alice Johnson, a school teacher, in 1898; their only child died during birth a year later. Williams' favorite hobby was music; he often played his bass viol for charitable affairs. In 1926, two years after the death of his wife, Williams suffered a stroke and remained in ill health. He died at his summer home in Idlewild, Michigan, on August 4, 1931, and was buried in Chicago's Graceland Cemetery.

SELECTED WRITINGS BY WILLIAMS:

Periodicals

"Stab Wound of the Heart and Pericardium, Suture of the Pericardium. Recovery. Patient Alive Three Years Afterward," *New York Medical Record*, March 27, 1897, pp. 437–439.

"The Need of Hospitals and Training Schools for the Colored People of the South," *National Hospital Record*, Detroit (Reprint of paper read before the Phillis Wheatley Club, Nashville, Tennessee, January 23, 1900).

SOURCES:

Books

The African American Encyclopedia, Marshall Cavendish, 1993, pp. 1705–1707.
Blacks in Medicine and Science, Hemisphere, 1990, pp. 251–252.
Buckler, Helen, *Daniel Hale Williams, Negro Surgeon*, Pitman, 1968.
Buckler, Helen, *Doctor Dan, Pioneer in American Surgery*, Little, Brown, 1954.
Fenderson, Lewis R., *Daniel Hale Williams: Open-Heart Doctor*, McGraw-Hill, 1971.
Patterson, Lillie, *Sure Hands, Strong Heart: The Life of Daniel Hale Williams*, Abingdon, 1981.
Scientists in the Black Perspective, The Lincoln Foundation, 1974, pp. 101–103.

—*Sketch by Jane Stewart Cook*

Frederic C. Williams
1911-1977
English electrical engineer

Sir Frederic C. Williams, an electrical engineer, is best known for his development of the Williams tube, an early data storage system for electronic digital computers. Although his invention was soon superseded by the magnetic-core system developed by **Jay Forrester**, it was a significant development at the time and allowed electronic computers to access data in memory randomly instead of serially, which made for much faster data retrieval. Williams was such a prolific inventor and developer of electronic and mechanical devices that his name ultimately appeared in over one hundred patent applications. His work extended from airplane radar and storage devices for electronic computers to early automatic transmissions for automobiles.

Frederic Calland Williams was born on June 26, 1911 in Romiley, Cheshire, England, the only son of Frederic Williams, a locomotive draftsman, and Ethel Alice Williams (whose maiden name was Smith). He entered the school of engineering at the University of Manchester on a scholarship in 1929, graduating with honors in 1932 and winning the Fairbairn prize. A year later he received his Master of Science degree. After a brief apprenticeship at the Metropolitan-Vickers Electrical Company, he entered Magdalen College of Oxford University in 1934 on a scholarship awarded by the Institution of Electrical Engineers. His research in the engineering laboratories at Oxford focused on the study of circuit and valve noise. For recreation, he was a coxswain (steersman) in the eight-man boating races on the Thames River.

After receiving his Doctor of Philosophy degree from Oxford in 1936, Williams returned to the University of Manchester and became an assistant lecturer in the school of engineering. In 1939, the University of Manchester awarded him a Doctorate in Science for his research. Williams married Gladys Ward in 1938, and they had two children, a daughter and a son. Their son eventually became a professor of civil engineering.

Major Contributions to the War Effort

During World War II, Williams worked on several important projects, including the development of radar and of automatic target acquisition equipment for aircraft. Although airplanes had played only a minor role in World War I, developments in aeronautical engineering made the war in the air vastly more important during World War II. Now far larger and having much greater ranges, aircraft could traverse great distances with many men and large stores of supplies. Aircraft had also become much more varied, comprising bombers, cargo planes, long-range reconnaissance aircraft, and fighter planes. Some kinds of planes were crewed by one person; others needed a large crew to carry out their complicated missions. All these aircraft had to be able to fly in all kinds of weather.

As part of his contribution to the war effort, Williams developed many of the instruments that enabled different aircraft to carry out their missions. In 1939, Williams went to the Bawdsey Research Station, where he worked on the equipment that enabled radar operators to distinguish between friendly and enemy aircraft. His work on aircraft identification systems also included developing intricate coding procedures that allowed aircraft to disguise themselves electronically so that they could not be detected by enemy radar. For single-seat airplanes, Williams developed a fully automatic radar system that took up little of the pilot's attention. Williams' system could automatically locate a target, filter out distracting ground echoes and echoes from other airplanes with electronic identification signals, and indicate the direction of the target and its range. This equipment enabled accurate bombing through heavy cloud cover and permitted planes to navigate by radio at night or during bad weather when the crew could not see the stars or geographical landmarks.

Developed the First Random Access Memory

After the war, Williams made his most important discovery, a way of storing data on a cathode-ray tube similar to those used in television receivers. For electronic computers to process data, they need some way to store instructions in memory and to access them in performing operations on data in a systematic way. In early electronic digital computers, the memory storage consisted of mercury delay lines. These lines, however, were highly sensitive and difficult to manufacture. Also, they could only store data serially. That is, to read a single instruction in the middle of the instruction set, the computer had to start at the beginning and read all the way through to the middle for the one instruction that it needed to use. It was like reading all of a dictionary's entries from A through M in order to access the word "Neolithic." Obviously, this serial method of accessing memory took a long time.

Working at the University of Manchester in 1946, Williams discovered a way to store instructions in spots on a cathode-ray tube that would serve as a computer memory. A key problem with storing spots on a cathode-ray tube was that the spots would fade away rapidly. One of Williams' innovations was to develop electronic circuits for refreshing the spots on the tube, so that a spot could be stored indefinitely.

An important benefit of using cathode-ray tubes for storing instructions in memory was that the instructions could be accessed randomly. That is, if the instruction that the computer needed was at the middle of the instruction set, then the computer could find that instruction immediately, without having to start from the beginning. As Andrew Hodges has said, another benefit of the Williams tube was that "one could actually see the numbers and instructions held in the machine, as bright spots on the three monitor tubes. Indeed, at this stage it was essential to see them, for there was no other output mechanism. Nor was there any form of input but that of hand switches, used to insert digits one at a time into the storage tube."

Using this innovation, Williams and other electronics experts working with him at the University of Manchester built one of the first working stored-program digital computers in the world. The Manchester Mark I or MADM computer was produced commercially by Ferranti, Ltd., and approximately twenty of the computers were installed in Britain and other countries.

Williams went on to develop a second computer before turning his attention to work with motors. Late in his career he built an automatic transmission for automobiles, which he used in his own car. Williams was named an Officer of the British Empire in 1945 and Commander of the British Empire in 1961; he was knighted in 1976. He received several honorary doctorates and many awards in Britain and the United States, including the Benjamin Franklin medal from the Royal Society of Arts in 1957 and the John Scott award from the city of Philadelphia in 1960. He was elected a Fellow of the Royal Society in 1950. Williams died in Manchester, England, on August 11, 1977.

SOURCES:

Books

Biographical Memoirs of Fellows of the Royal Society, Volume 24, Royal Society (London), 1978.

Cortada, James W., *Historical Dictionary of Data Processing: Biographies,* Greenwood Press, 1987.

Hodges, Andrew, *Alan Turning: The Enigma,* Simon & Schuster, 1983.

Shurkin, Joel, *Engines of the Mind,* Pocket Books, 1984.

—Sketch by Patrick Moore

O. S. Williams
1921-
American aeronautical engineer

The second African American to receive a degree in aeronautical engineering, O. S. Williams headed the team that originated the first experimental airborne radio beacon for tracking crashed aircraft. Williams also managed the development of the control rocket systems that successfully guided the Apollo lunar landers.

Oswald S. "Ozzie" Williams was born on September 2, 1921 in Washington, D.C., to Oswald S. Williams, a postal worker, and Marie (Madden) Williams, a housewife. He grew up in New York, graduating from Boys High School in Brooklyn in 1938. Williams became interested in engineering as a teenager. He loved to make model airplanes and decided to become an engineer after a family friend described an engineer as a person who designs things.

When Williams went to New York University, he was discouraged by a dean. As he recounted in an interview with Terrie M. Romano, the dean told him that "people of your race are not ready for engineering, and engineering is not ready for you. I warn you not to waste your ambition and training where you cannot get a job." Despite such advice, Williams completed his bachelor's degree in aeronautical engineering at New York University in 1943; he received his master's degree in aeronautical engineering from the same institution in 1947.

Aids in Design of War Planes

During World War II, Williams was a senior aerodynamicist with the Republic Aviation Corporation. He helped to design the P47 Thunderbolt, which was pivotal in the war effort. The P47 was the escort plane that protected the American high-altitude bombers. As an aerodynamicist, he was responsible for estimating and calculating from wind tunnel testing, the lift of the plane's wings, its propelling forces and its drag in order to determine how well the airplane would fly and its overall stability.

In 1947 Williams moved to the Babcock and Wilcox company, where he was a design draftsman. He then spent two years as a technical writer with the United States Navy Material Catalog Office, leaving in 1950 to take an engineering position at Greer Hydraulics, Inc. At Greer, as a group project leader, he was responsible for the development of the first experimental airborne radio beacon, which was used to locate crashed airplanes. The project was very challenging since the beacon had to operate equally well wherever it landed and whatever the weather conditions. The beacon would be fired by catapult and parachute to the ground as the airplane disintegrated, potentially landing anywhere: in water, in a tree, on level ground, or on a mountainside. Williams's team developed a beacon that could recognize where it had landed and transmit its position, but unfortunately, it was never produced commercially.

In 1956, Williams moved to the Reaction Motors Division of Thiokol Chemical Corporation, where he was responsible for pioneering work on small rocket engines. Williams was hired as a propulsion engineer by Grumman International in 1961 because of his expertise on liquid-fuel rockets. He had published several papers on the subject, one of which, "On the feasibility of liquid bipropellant rockets for spacecraft attitude control," was translated into Russian by Dr. Leonid Sedov, the president of the Soviet Space Academy.

Helps Develop Apollo Lunar Module

At Grumman, Williams managed the development of the Apollo Lunar Module reaction control subsystem. Williams was fully responsible for the $42 million effort for eight years. He managed the three engineering groups that developed the small rocket motors—which used one hundred pounds of thrust in comparison to the 10,500 pounds of thrust of the lunar module's main engine—that guided the lunar module, the part of the Apollo spacecraft that actually landed on the moon.

Williams went on to a career in marketing at Grumman, culminating in his election as a company vice president in 1974. After leaving Grumman he became a marketing professor at St. John's University in Queens, New York, where he had completed an M.B.A. in 1981. Williams was a member of the American Institute of Aeronautics and Astronautics, as well as an associate fellow and past chair of its Liquid Rockets Technical Committee. His varied career was profiled on Queens Public Television in the one-hour program, *O.S. Williams, A Man of Three Careers.*

In 1993, O. S. and Doris Reid Williams celebrated their fiftieth wedding anniversary. They had three children: Gregory (who died in 1982), Bruce, and Meredith.

SOURCES:

Biography provided by Grumman International Inc., dated August, 1985.

O. S. Williams, interviews with Terrie M. Romano, conducted March 18 and 21, 1994.

—Sketch by Terrie M. Romano

James S. Williamson
1949-
American mathematician

James S. Williamson, a Chippewa scientist, has gained recognition in many fields including mathematics, solar energy, and education. He was instrumental in developing the nation's first solar central receiver electric generating plant and later improving the receiver's design. Throughout his career, Williamson has taught and has also helped formulate new methods for educating students in mathematics. He has also been active in government; in 1978, he was appointed by President Jimmy Carter to the Domestic Policy Review Panel for Solar Energy Research.

Williamson was born November 30, 1949, the eighth of twelve children, in Williston, North Dakota. His mother, Cecelia (Falcon) was a homemaker and his father, Fritz Williamson, was a civil servant. His oldest brother, F. Dale Williamson, is also a scientist, with a doctorate in chemistry. Academically, Williamson's background is in mathematics, a discipline which he has applied to several career fields. He graduated with a bachelor of science degree from Montana State University in 1971 and then completed his master's degree at the University of California, Berkeley, in 1974. His research centered on the hyperbolic and elliptical functions of imaginary numbers, which, at that point, only had application in space travel. While at Berkeley, he taught undergraduate courses in mathematics, as well as being part of a curriculum development team deriving new teaching methods for mathematics.

His career in solar energy research began as Project Manager for the Atomic Energy Commission in 1971, first in Idaho Falls, Idaho, then in Oakland, California. For six years he provided project management for solar systems for satellite power, managed subcontractor projects for the development of a nuclear reactor system and radio-isotope thermonuclear power systems for satellites, and directed the design of the solar thermal test facility. Williamson told contributor Marianne Fedunkiw in an interview that he was originally hired as a mathematician/statistician to evaluate, using mathematical models, how to clean up fuels coming out of a spent reactor. When an opportunity arose to work on applications in space, he took it, a move which brought him into the field of solar energy. "Solar energy was used in space long before it was on the ground," he said. Williamson was the program manager for the design of the central receiver test facility in Albuquerque, New Mexico, and for the design of the nation's first solar central receiver electric generating plant at Barstow, California. The Barstow plant has more than 1,800 large mirrors, each of which reflect onto a steam boiler mounted on a tower several hundred feet in the air to make steam; this steam, in turn, drives a turbine to generate electricity for the Los Angeles area.

In 1977 Williamson moved to the Martin Marietta Corporation in Denver, Colorado, as Deputy Program Manager for Advanced Solar Technologies, followed by eight years (1978–86) as Program Director for International Solar Energy Programs at Midwest Research Institute. He spent the first four years in Golden, Colorado, and then the next four years in Kansas City, Missouri. His research concentrated on water desalination, independent utility power systems, and solar systems. Although he was active in government and the private sector, he never abandoned teaching. During his last two years at Midwest, he taught evening courses in mathematics at the University of Missouri in Kansas City.

Williamson left Midwest in 1986 to become Associate Partner and Director of the Technology Management Group, Meridian Corporation in Washington, where he had a staff of sixty who provided management support to the Department of Energy as well as conducted biomass resource surveys and developed a technology assessment guide for public utilities. He also spent seven months of 1989 as the President of Engineering and Product Services, a small engineering consulting firm. One project of this firm was the development of a recruiting strategy for Native American health centers.

The late 1980s marked another shift in Williamson's career, applying solar energy programs and activities to increase young students' interests in science and mathematics. Since 1989, he has been Assistant to the Director for Education & Special Projects at the National Renewable Energy Laboratory, originally in Washington, D.C. Later, in 1992, he returned to Golden, Colorado. He has also served as Adjunct Lecturer at Regis University in Denver, Colorado, lecturing on the business and economics of alternative energy technologies, and at the Air Force Academy, Colorado Springs, Colorado, lecturing on thermodynamic applications in solar energy. His most recent work has been in developing science, mathematics, and technology education for students from kindergarten to the university level. "This includes curriculum modules, organizing and managing student competitions," he explained to Fedunkiw, "basically things to get kids interested in science." One example was the development of a mini solar-powered car competition, complete with ramp tests, speed tests, and a design contest.

Evaluating his contributions to science to Fedunkiw, Williamson divided it into two periods: he considers his early mathematics work at Berkeley to have been significant as well as his later work in solar energy—specifically the development of advanced solar central receiver technology while at Martin Marietta. He was a codesigner, with Tom Tracy, of advanced concepts for heat transfer and solar receiver designs using a molten salt transfer fluid.

Williamson's achievements also include joint solar energy research projects between Saudi Arabia and the United States; researching air conditioning systems to generate electricity from sunlight; nuclear material safeguards systems for nuclear power plants; and the design of nuclear and solar power systems for space travel to Saturn, Mars, and Jupiter.

Williamson is a charter member of the American Indian Science and Engineering Society, as well as a member of the American Solar Energy Society and International Solar Energy Society. He also holds memberships to the Institute of Electrical and Electronic Engineers and the American Management Association. Among his awards are the 1991 Organization Committee Award, Conference for Economics of Ethanol Fuels, Montana State University and the Management Award, given by the Saudi Arabian National Center for Science and Technology in 1983 for contributions made as U.S. Program Director for the Joint U.S./Saudi Arabia Solar Research Program.

Williamson married Virginia Hansen in 1968. They have two children, James and Kerry. When he is not working, Williamson raises and breeds paint horses on a small farm. "My father used to raise horses," he told Fedunkiw. "I started about ten years ago."

SELECTED WRITINGS BY WILLIAMSON:

Periodicals

"Energy Policies of Ethanol Fuels," Ethanol Producers and Consumers Conference, November, 1990.
"Chemistry of Solar Energy Technologies," *College Chemistry,* November, 1990.
"Economics of Alternative Fuels," Women Involved in Farm Economics, Arkansas Conference, June, 1991.
"Education Programs at the National Renewable Energy Laboratory," American Solar Energy Society Annual Conference, June, 1992.

Books

Unsolicited Proposal Evaluation, Solar Energy Research Institute, 1979.
(Editor) *Solar Energy Water Desalination,* Conference Proceedings of U.S./Saudi Arabian Joint Research Program for Solar Energy, 1982.
(Editor) *Solar for Remote Applications,* Conference Proceedings of U.S./Saudi Arabian Joint Research Program for Solar Energy, 1986.

SOURCES:

Books

Directory of the National Society of the Sons of the American Revolution, 1993.

Other

American Indian Science and Engineering Society Biography Booklet, 1984–85, p. 29.
Williamson, James S., interview with Marianne Fedunkiw, conducted March, 1994.

—*Sketch by Marianne Fedunkiw*

Richard Willstätter
1872-1942
German chemist

A gifted experimentalist, Richard Willstätter's pioneering work on natural products, especially chlorophylls and anthocyanins (plant pigments), was honored with the 1915 Nobel Prize in chemistry. In 1924 Willstätter, who was Jewish, resigned from his position at the University of Munich in protest against the anti-Semitism of some of the faculty. This act of conscience seriously hampered his research activity. In 1939 the anti-Semitic policies of the Third Reich forced him to emigrate to Switzerland, where he spent the remaining few years of his life.

Education and Early Career

Richard Martin Willstätter was born in Karlsruhe, Germany on August 13, 1872, the second of two sons of Max and Sophie Ulmann Willstätter. Willstätter's father was a textile merchant and his mother's family was in the textile business. Willstätter's education began in the classical Gymnasium in Karlsruhe. When he was eleven years old, his father moved to New York in search of better economic opportunities and to escape the circumscribed life in Karlsruhe; although this separation was meant to be short, it lasted seventeen years. Willstätter's mother took him and his brother to live near her family home in Nürnberg, a change to which Willstätter had difficulty adjusting, in part because of the more overt anti-Semitism he experienced there.

One effect of the move to a new school was that, although receiving good grades in his other subjects, he did poorly in Latin, the most important subject in

Richard Willstätter

the gymnasia of the time. A family council decided he should switch to the Realgymnasium and be educated for business instead of a profession. Ironically, it was at this time, stimulated by some home experiments and good teachers, that he decided to become a chemist. In his autobiography, Willstätter observed that excellence in academic subjects caused one to be disliked, while athletic excellence resulted in popularity. He was also attracted to medicine and might have become a physician instead of a chemist, but because of the longer schooling required his mother would not permit him to change. An interest in biological processes remained with him, though, and is evident in the kinds of chemical problems he attacked. Much later, while teaching at Zurich, he still thought of studying physiology and internal medicine, but the death of his wife ended the idea.

In 1890 the eighteen-year-old Willstätter entered the University of Munich and also attended lectures at the Technische Hochschule. In 1893 he began his doctoral studies and was assigned to do his research under Alfred Einhorn on some aspects of the chemistry of cocaine. It was at this time that **Adolf von Baeyer**, the leading organic chemist in Germany, began to take Willstätter under his wing. Although Willstätter never worked directly for Baeyer, he thought of himself as Baeyer's disciple. Willstätter completed his doctoral work in a year and stayed on doing independent research, becoming a privatdocent, or unsalaried lecturer, in 1896.

In his work with Einhorn, Willstätter had come to suspect that the structure assigned to cocaine by Einhorn and others was incorrect. When he started his independent research, Einhorn forbade him to work on the cocaine problem. Willstätter, with Baeyer's approval, decided to work instead on the closely related chemical tropine, whose structure was suspected to be similar to that of cocaine; once the structure of tropine was known, the structure of cocaine could be easily derived. Willstätter showed that, indeed, the cocaine structure was not what it had been thought to be; for the remainder of his stay at Munich, Einhorn refused to speak to him. In 1902 Willstätter was appointed professor extraordinarius (roughly equivalent to associate professor), although Baeyer thought he should have accepted an industrial position. Baeyer, himself partly Jewish, also recommended that Willstätter be baptized, an act that would have removed the legal barriers he faced as a Jew. This Willstätter refused to consider. During Easter vacation in 1903 Willstätter met the Leser family from Heidelberg, and that summer he and Sophie Leser were married. Their son Ludwig was born in 1904 and their daughter, Margarete, in 1906.

Switzerland and Nobel Prize Work

In 1905 Willstätter accepted a call to the Eidgenössische Technische Hochscuhle in Zurich as professor of chemistry, beginning the most productive phase of his career. While at Munich he had begun an investigation into the chemical nature of chlorophyll, the green pigment in plants that converts light into energy through photosynthesis; at Zurich, he and his students made great strides in understanding this important material. They developed methods for isolating chlorophyll from plant materials without changing it or introducing impurities. Willstätter was then able to prove that the chlorophyll from different plants (he examined over two hundred different kinds) was substantially the same—a mixture of two slightly different compounds, blue-green chlorophyll a and yellow-green chlorophyll b, in a 3 to 1 ratio.

He also showed that magnesium, which had been found in chlorophyll by earlier workers, was not an accidental impurity but an essential component of these chlorophyll molecules, bonded in a way very similar to that in which iron is bonded in hemoglobin, the oxygen-carrying constituent of blood. The later work of others, especially **Hans Fischer**, in elucidating the detailed structures of the chlorophylls and hemoglobin would not have been possible without the pioneering work of Willstätter and his students. In 1913, Willstätter, in collaboration with his former student and good friend, Arthur Stoll, reviewed the work on chlorophyll in a book, *Untersuchungen über Chlorophyll*. In all, between 1913 and 1919, Willstätter published twenty-five papers in a series on chlorophyll. A preliminary step in the isolation of chlorophyll from plant materials yielded a yellow solution that on further study proved to contain carotenoid pigments. These had been described before, but Willstätter's work marked the beginning of our understanding of these materials that produce the color of tomatoes, carrots, and egg yolk.

In 1908, Willstätter suffered a devastating blow in the death of his wife after an operation for appendicitis had been delayed for thirty-six hours after the appendix had ruptured. He consoled himself with the care of his two children and with his work; in his autobiography he wrote that he took no vacations for the next ten years. During his stay at Zurich, Willstätter also did work on quinones and the mechanism of the oxidation of aniline to aniline black—a process of importance to the dye industry. He also completed a project begun eight years earlier, by synthesizing the chemical cyclooctatetraene and showing that it did not behave as an aromatic compound despite its structural similarities to benzene.

Berlin and the War

The Kaiser Wilhelm Institutes were founded in 1910 to afford outstanding scientists the chance to do research on problems of their own choosing, free of any teaching obligations. In 1911 Willstätter accepted the position of director of the Kaiser Wilhelm Institute of Chemistry and in 1912 moved into the new building at Berlin-Dahlem. The institute was situated next to the Institute for Physical Chemistry and Electrochemistry, headed by **Fritz Haber**, and a deep and lasting friendship developed between the two directors.

At Zurich, Willstätter had initiated a study of the pigments of various red and blue flowers, a class of compounds now known as anthocyanins. He began with dried cornflowers, or bachelor's button, because it was winter and they were commercially available. This choice, as it turned out, was not a good one; cornflowers only contained a percent or less of the pigment. In Berlin, Willstätter planted fields of double cornflowers, asters, chrysanthemums, pansies, and dahlias around the Institute and his residence. In these fresh flowers he found a much higher pigment content, up to 33 percent in blue-black pansies. Before World War I brought an end to this line of research, Willstätter published eighteen papers in an anthocyanin series between 1913 and 1916. He showed that the various shades of red and blue in these flowers as well as in cherries, cranberries, roses, plums, elderberries, and poppies all arose mainly from three closely related compounds, cyanidin, pelargonidin, and delphinidin chlorides, and were very dependent on the acidity or alkalinity of the flower. During the first year of the war, most of Willstätter's co-workers went into military service, and the flowers were taken to

military hospitals instead of to the laboratory. Willstätter was bitterly disappointed by this interruption and could not bring himself to return to the problem after the war.

In 1915 Haber, who was in charge of Germany's chemical warfare work, asked Willstätter's assistance in developing the chemical absorption unit for a gas mask that would protect against chlorine and phosgene (a severe respiratory irritant). In five weeks, Willstätter came up with a canister containing activated charcoal and hexamethylenetetramine (also called urotropin). The use of charcoal was not new, but the use of hexamethylenetetramine was. When asked after the war how he had come to try so unusual a compound, he said that the idea had just popped into his head. For this work he received an Iron Cross, Second Class. He was also involved in an industrial research project with **Friedrich Bergius** on the hydrolysis of cellulose with hydrochloric acid to give dextrose, which could then be fermented to produce alcohol. The process, which was only perfected later, is now known as the Bergius-Willstätter process.

In the spring of 1915 Willstätter's ten-year-old son, Ludwig, died suddenly, apparently from diabetes. Willstätter wrote that his memory of the months following was blurred. Ironically, in November, while engaged in the work on gas masks, Willstätter learned that he had been awarded the 1915 Nobel Prize in chemistry in recognition of his work on chlorophylls and anthocyanins. Because of wartime conditions he did not travel to Stockholm to receive the prize until 1920, when a ceremony was held for a group of those who had been honored during the war. Willstätter made the trip in the company of fellow German awardees **Max Planck**, Fritz Haber, **Max von Laue**, and **Johannes Stark**.

The Return to Munich and the Final Years

An offer of a full professorship to succeed Baeyer at Munich also came in 1915. This offer, recommended by Baeyer, was precipitated by an offer to succeed **Otto Wallach**, a pioneer in natural product chemistry, at Göttingen. Willstätter maintained that left to his own inclinations, he would have preferred Göttingen, because a medium-sized university would provide more contact with colleagues and greater interaction with different disciplines than was possible at large institutions. However, he accepted the appointment as professor and director of the state chemical laboratory in Munich and moved there in the spring of 1916.

He made two major demands before accepting the offer: that the old institute building be remodeled and a large addition to the chemical institute be built housing laboratories and a large lecture hall, and that a full professorship in physical chemistry be established. The first of these was contrary to the advice that the physical chemist **Walther Nernst** gave him before he left Berlin, "Don't ever build!" In fact, the construction, delayed by the war and post-armistice turmoil in Munich, was not completed until the spring of 1920.

At Munich, as before, Willstätter experienced the anti-Semitism that had troubled him during his earlier residence, and that finally brought about his resignation in 1924. The final straw was the refusal of the faculty to appoint the noted geochemist **Victor Goldschmidt** of Oslo, Norway, to succeed the mineralogist Paul von Groth, who had himself named Goldschmidt as the only one who could take his place. The sole reason for the refusal was that Goldschmidt was Jewish. When Willstätter's resignation became known, students and faculty joined in expressions of respect and confidence, urging him to reconsider. Nonetheless, he remained only for the time needed to see his students finish their research and to install **Heinrich Wieland** in his place. He received offers of positions at universities and in industry in Germany and abroad, but he declined all of them, finally leaving the university in September 1925 never to return.

Some of Willstätter's assistants continued work at the University, and in 1928 Wieland made room in what had been Willstätter's private laboratory for Willstätter's private assistant, Margarete Rohdewald, one of his former students. From 1929 until 1938 she collaborated with him in a series of eighteen papers on various aspects of enzyme research. It was an odd collaboration, conducted almost entirely over the telephone; Willstätter never saw her at work in the laboratory.

During the few years at Munich before his resignation, Willstätter began to concentrate his research on the study of enzymes. He had first encountered these biological catalysts in his early work on chlorophyll. Now he worked to develop methods for their separation and purification. His method for separation was to adsorb the materials on alumina or silica gel and then to wash them off using solutions of varying acidity, among other solvents. In this connection, Willstätter carried out a systematic study (comprised of nine papers) of hydrates and hydrogels during which he, with his assistants Heinrich Kraut and K. Lobinger, was able to show that aluminum hydroxide, silicic acid, ferric hydroxide, and stannic hydroxide do actually exist in solution and are not colloidal sols (dispersions of small solid particles in solution) of the corresponding oxides. Willstätter reported that this foray of an organic chemist into inorganic chemistry was not well received by inorganic chemists.

The enzyme studies were not as successful, in part because Willstätter thought that enzymes were relatively small molecules adsorbed on a protein or some other giant (polymer) molecule. The modern view, of course, is that enzymes are themselves proteins. Though Willstätter's chemical intuition failed him, there were positive results—for example, the enzymatic reduction of chloral and bromal resulted in the formation of trichloroethanol, a sedative (Voluntal), and tribromoethanol, an anesthetic (Avertin).

In 1938 the situation for Jews in Germany was becoming impossible. On a visit to Switzerland, Stoll tried to persuade Willstätter to stay, but he insisted on returning to Munich. There, after some trouble with the Gestapo, he was ordered to leave the country. After much red tape, which entailed the confiscation of much of his property, papers, and art collection, and an abortive attempt to leave unofficially, he entered Switzerland in March 1939 to stay for a while with Stoll and then to settle in the Villa Eremitaggio in Muralto. There he wrote his autobiography to pass the time. On August 3, 1942, Willstätter died of cardiac failure in his sleep. Among the honors received by Willstätter in addition to the Nobel prize were honorary membership in the American Chemical Society (1927), honorary fellowship in the Chemical Society (1927), the Willard Gibbs Medal for distinguished achievement in science from the Chicago Section of the American Chemical Society (1933), and election as foreign member of the Royal Society (1933). Willstätter's obituary by Sir **Robert Robinson** in *Obituary Notices of Fellows of the Royal Society,* has an eleven page bibliography, probably incomplete, listing over three hundred papers between 1893 and 1940.

SELECTED WRITINGS BY WILLSTÄTTER:

Books

(With Arthur Stoll) *Investigations on Chlorophyll; Methods and Results,* translated by F. M. Schertz and A. R. Merz, Science Press, 1928.
From My Life (autobiography), foreword by Stoll, translated by Lilli S. Hornig, Benjamin, 1965.

Periodicals

"A Chemist's Retrospects and Perspectives," *Science,* Volume 78, 1933, pp. 271–274.

SOURCES:

Books

Dictionary of Scientific Biography, Volume 14, Scribner, 1976, pp. 411–412.

Nobel Lectures Including Presentation Speeches and Laureates' Biographies, Volume 3, *Chemistry: 1901–1921,* Elsevier, 1966, pp. 297–314.

Obituary Notices of Fellows of the Royal Society, Volume 8, Morrison & Gibb, 1954, pp. 609–634.

Partington, J. R., *A History of Chemistry,* Macmillan, 1964, pp. 860–866.

Periodicals

Huisgen, Rolf, "Richard Willstätter," *Journal of Chemical Education,* Volume 38, number 1, 1961, pp. 10–15.

Robinson, Robert, "Willstätter Memorial Lecture," *Journal of the Chemical Society,* 1953, pp. 1012–1026.

—*Sketch by R. F. Trimble*

C. T. R. Wilson

C. T. R. Wilson
1869-1959
Scottish physicist

the exam that he was awarded a scholarship to Sidney Sussex College.

Begins Career at Cambridge

In 1888, when he was nineteen years old, Wilson entered Cambridge to study physics and chemistry. He found it a thoroughly stimulating environment. He attended physics lectures at its world-renowned Cavendish Laboratory—he was, in fact, the only student in his year taking physics as a main subject—and began to develop what would be a lifelong interest in meteorological physics. After graduating from Cambridge in 1892, Wilson found work as a demonstrator and a private coach. Although it helped him to keep body and soul together, it left him with precious little time or energy for his own research. At the time, his work was devoted to a comparison of the behavior of different substances in solution. In a bid to secure his future, Wilson somewhat reluctantly accepted the post of science teacher at Bradford Grammar School, but he quickly realized that his career was on the wrong track. In 1894 he decided, therefore, to return to Cambridge, where the University's decision to extend the teaching of physics to medical students had opened up a post as supervisor of the students' practical work.

Returning to Cambridge afforded him more time and space to continue his own work. With the encouragement of the eminent physicist, **J. J. Thomson**, who at the time headed the Cavendish, he began

A Scottish physicist, C. T. R. Wilson invented the cloud or expansion chamber, which enabled physicists to track the paths of individual atoms and electrons. It was described by the physicist W. B. Lewis as being "to the atomic physicist what the telescope is to the astronomer." Lord Ernest Rutherford described the cloud chamber as "the most original and wonderful [invention] in scientific history." For his invention, Wilson shared the 1927 Nobel Prize for physics with **Arthur Holly Compton**. Wilson is also credited with the discovery of cosmic rays, that is, speeding atomic nuclei from outer space that enter the earth's atmosphere.

Charles Thomson Rees Wilson was born on the 14th of February, 1869, in Glencorse, near Edinburgh, Scotland, to John Wilson, a sheep farmer, and his second wife, Annie Clark Harper Wilson. When Wilson senior died in 1873, the family moved to Manchester. There Wilson attended first a private school then, when he was fifteen, Ownes College, later renamed the Victoria College of Manchester. Although he had registered as a medical student, he switched to science and graduated with a First Class degree in zoology when he was only eighteen years of age. At the urging of his tutors, he decided to sit for the scholarship exams for Cambridge in practical physics and chemistry. Although he had received no instruction in either subject, he performed so well in constructing an expansion chamber which would enable him to track the paths of atoms and electrons. In 1895, the first cloud chamber was finished. Wilson intended to use the apparatus to create artificial clouds in the laboratory. His work was inspired by the meteorological phenomena he had witnessed during a visit to Ben Nevis, Britain's highest mountain, in the Scottish Highlands the year before. During a two-week stint as temporary observer to the observatory atop Ben Nevis, he had been captivated by the extraordinary sight of the sun shining on the clouds and the magical optical effects it produced. He was so awestruck that he vowed to create similar clouds to the ones he had witnessed. His theory was that if he expanded moist air in an enclosed chamber, a cloud would thereby be created.

Wilson's hunch was based on results that had been obtained in 1888 by another Scottish physicist, John Aitken. Aitken had discovered that when compressed air is permitted to suddenly expand, a cloud is formed if the air contains dust particles. The latter act as nuclei on which the water vapor can condense—in their absence, the air becomes supersaturated and no clouds are formed. At the beginning of 1895, Wilson began trying to manufacture clouds in the Cavendish laboratory. Within a short space of time, he succeeded in producing them and in recreating the optical effects he had witnessed on the mountain. In the process, he obtained some interesting results. Using his cloud chamber, Wilson discovered that, contrary to Aitken's theory, a cloud could indeed form even if the air was dust free, so long as the moist air was expanded beyond a certain precise limit. No drops were formed unless the expansion exceeded this limit, in which case a shower of drops was produced.

Encouraged by his preliminary results, Wilson embarked on a series of experiments using more sophisticated equipment. He now discovered that if the air was expanded beyond a second precise limit, equivalent to an approximately eight-fold supersaturation of the vapor, dense clouds were formed in dust-free air. In the process, extraordinary optical effects were also created. Wilson published his results in early 1895. They indicated that two different kinds of clouds could be produced in dust-free air by different degrees of expansion, corresponding to two different types of nuclei. The first kind were less common than the second, which were very numerous, but required more expansion to come into effect.

In 1895, Wilson was appointed one of Cambridge's Clerk Maxwell Students. That same year, he also began investigating electrical fields and thunderstorms inspired, once again, by the weather; during another visit to the Scottish Highlands he had witnessed a mighty thunderstorm, which started him thinking about electrical fields in the atmosphere. Over the next five years he developed his basic knowledge of atmospheric electricity and put forward the proposition that atmospheric ions, which produce electricity, might in fact be produced by sources of radiation outside the earth's atmosphere.

In 1895, X rays were discovered. Wilson quickly took advantage of the new technology and used X rays to investigate the behavior of ions as condensation nuclei. He found that X rays produced large numbers of the nuclei in gases that Wilson had been creating in much smaller amounts in his cloud chamber. He found that not only X rays, but also other ionizing agents such as uranium rays and ultraviolet rays, produce condensation nuclei in gases, which are identical with respect to the supersaturation needed to enable water to condense on them and form clouds. These ionizing agents allowed Wilson to successfully test his idea that the two kinds of nuclei he had discovered when he expanded moist air in his dust free cloud chamber were in fact positive and negative ions, of the kind that had been discovered in ionized gases. This work preoccupied him from 1896 to 1898. Between 1898 and 1899, he was engaged full-time in studying condensation on negative and positive ions. Eventually, he was able to render individual ions visible to the eye, and to distinguish between positive and negative ions.

In 1899, Wilson joined the Meteorological Council as a researcher on atmospheric electricity. The following year, he was elected fellow of Sidney Sussex College, Cambridge, and appointed a lecturer in physics. For the next eighteen years, he remained in this position, building a solid advanced physics research team around him and teaching at the Cavendish. Wilson preferred a practical method of instruction. He liked to set his students minor research problems to carry out in the laboratory themselves rather than having them rely on textbook experiments. His was a close and small coterie, however. He felt comfortable working at a measured pace with just a few, well-chosen pupils to whom he could devote his full attention. He was a dedicated mentor, who took his responsibilities as a teacher extremely seriously. Although he was known as a shy and somewhat plodding lecturer, his insights were considered second to none and inspired subsequent generations of experimental physicists.

Since Wilson had invented his first cloud chamber in 1895, much more had been learned about the phenomena of electricity in ions. But a mystery remained as to where the ions originated. Wilson himself provided the answer in 1900. Using his cloud-expansion chamber, he demonstrated that ions are constantly present in the air, incessantly regenerating. He was able to prove this because, given the right degree of expansion of moist air in the cloud chamber, he was always able to obtain nuclei. Their presence meant that the air should always be conducting. He tested his hypothesis using a gold-leaf electroscope, and discovered that positive and negative ions are constantly being produced in air in equal numbers, at the rate of about 14 per cubic meters of air per second. This discovery provided an explanation as to how an electrical discharge could pass through air, in the laboratory or in the atmosphere, in the form of lightning. Moreover, it represented the first step in the discovery of cosmic rays. These are the streams of atomic nuclei of heterogeneous, extremely penetrating character, that enter the earth's atmosphere from outer space at speeds approaching that of light; when they enter the earth's atmosphere, they bombard atmospheric atoms to produce mesons as well as secondary particles possessing some of the original energy. However, it was not until 1912 that Wilson had obtained enough information about the phenomena that he felt confident enough to postulate their existence. His cloud chamber, particularly the more sophisticated versions of it devised by the English physicist, Sir **Patrick Blackett**, was an essential tool in the study of cosmic radiation.

In 1908, at the age of thirty-nine, Wilson married Jessie Fraser Dick. The marriage produced two children. In 1910, he started work on designing a new, much improved cloud chamber. His first two prototypes had been used, respectively, to create clouds and to help in research on ions. The third model was to be used to measure an atom's electrical charge. He proposed to do this by condensing drops of nuclei on atoms and thus rendering them visible. By measuring the total charge and counting the number of drops, the charge per atom could be figured. Before Wilson could finish his research, however, another scientist discovered the charge per atom before him.

Wilson's attention turned to the possibility of rendering visible the vapor trail or tracks of positively charged alpha rays. By 1911, he had built an apparatus to carry out the experiment. Although he did not have high hopes of success, he was pleasantly surprised when the tracks were actually revealed. When the cloud chamber was subjected to a magnetic field, the nature of the curved path showed if the charge was positive or negative and what size the particle was.

In 1911, Wilson was appointed observer in meteorological physics at the Solar Physics Observatory. He was promoted reader in electrical meteorology in 1918. In 1925, he was made Jacksonian Professor of Natural Philosophy at the University of Cambridge. He retired from Cambridge in 1934. Wilson remained highly active after his retirement. He moved back to Scotland where he was able to indulge his love of mountain climbing until he was well into his eighties. Until the age of eighty-six, he took weather flights over the Outer Scottish Isles as an honorary member of the University of Edinburgh's meteorology department.

Honored with Many Awards

During his long career, Wilson received many honors. He was elected a Fellow of the Royal Society of London in 1900 and awarded its Hughes Medal in 1911. He received the Hopkins Prize of the Cambridge Philosophical Society in 1920, the Royal Society of Edinburgh's Gunning Prize in 1921, and the Franklin Institute's Howard Potts Medal in 1925. He was given the highest honor in 1927 when he was awarded the Nobel Prize for physics, "for his discovery of the vapor condensation method of rendering visible the paths of electrically charged particles." He shared the award with the American theoretical physicist, Arthur Holly Compton, whose theory of the scattering of X rays upon contact with matter was confirmed using Wilson's cloud chamber.

Wilson kept working right up to the end of his long life. In 1956, at the age of eighty-seven, he presented his paper, *A Theory of Thundercloud Electricity,* to the Royal Society. It was the last presentation given by the Society's oldest fellow. Wilson died in 1959 at Carlops, Peebleshire, Scotland.

SELECTED WRITINGS BY WILSON:

Books

Condensation Nuclei, Smithsonian Institution, 1905.
A Theory of Thundercloud Electricity, Royal Society, 1957.

SOURCES:

Books

Crowther, J. G., *The Cavendish Laboratory, 1874–1974,* Science History Publications, 1974.
Heathcote, Niels H. deV, *Nobel Prize Winners in Physics, 1901–1950,* Books for Libraries Press, 1953, p. 269.
Johnston, Marjorie, editor, *The Cosmos of Arthur Holly Compton,* Knopf, 1967.
Weber, Robert L., *Pioneers of Science: Nobel Prize Winners in Physics,* Institute of Physics (London), 1980, pp. 85–87.
Wilson, David, *Rutherford: Simple Genius,* MIT Press, 1983, p. 556.

—*Sketch by Avril McDonald*

Edmund Beecher Wilson
1856-1939
American biologist

Edmund Beecher Wilson emphasized careful experimentation and analysis in biology at a time when the field was rife with theories based on little more than speculation. Indeed, Wilson's work was instrumental in transforming biology into a rigorous, scientific discipline. Although known for his meticulous approach to the study of the structure and function of the cell, he never lost sight of biology as a unified field that included embryology, evolution, and genetics. His influence in biology was felt through his position as a professor first at Bryn Mawr College and then at Columbia University, and through his highly influential textbook, *The Cell in Development and Inheritance.* His study of chromosomes, and especially his discovery of the sex chromosomes, helped lay the foundation for the study of genetics and evolution in the early-twentieth century. Many of the problems that Wilson tackled, including the details of cell development, remain unsolved today.

Edmund Wilson was born on October 19, 1856, in Geneva, Illinois. He was the second of four surviving children of Isaac Grant Wilson, a lawyer and eventually judge, and Caroline Louisa Clark, both of whom were originally from New England. When Edmund was two years old, his father was appointed a circuit court judge in Chicago. Rather than separate him from her childless sister and brother-in-law in Geneva, Edmund's mother left him to live with them while the rest of the family moved to Chicago. In this manner, he was "adopted" by Mr. and Mrs. Charles Patten and grew up counting himself very lucky to have two homes and four parents.

Shortly before he turned 16, Wilson taught school for one year from 1872 to 1873. As his older brother, Charles, had done the previous year, Wilson taught everything, including reading and arithmetic, to twenty-five pupils aged six to eighteen in a one-room schoolhouse. The following year he attended Antioch College (Yellow Springs, Ohio), following in the footsteps of an older cousin, Samuel Clarke. At Antioch, Wilson decided to devote himself to the study of biology, which, at that time, largely meant natural history.

In the fall of 1874, Wilson did not return to Antioch because he wished to prepare for studying at the Sheffield Scientific School of Yale University, which had been highly recommended to him by his cousin. To ready himself for Yale, Wilson moved to Chicago where he lived with his parents and took courses at the old University of Chicago from 1874 to

1875. He entered Yale in 1875 and received his bachelor's degree in 1878.

Lifelong Research Interest in Cell Development

Although Wilson's particular focus of research changed many times in his long career, his work was always concerned with gaining a better understanding of how the single fertilized egg gave rise to a complete individual, whether that individual be an earthworm, jellyfish, or human. This interest in the development of the organism led Wilson to study cell structure and function, heredity, and evolution.

During his years of graduate and postgraduate work, Wilson studied the embryology and morphology of earthworms, sea spiders, the colonial jellyfish (*Renilla*), and other invertebrates. After Yale, he again followed Sam Clarke's educational path, this time to Johns Hopkins University. A close friend, William T. Sedgwick, entered Johns Hopkins along with him. From 1878 to 1881, Wilson worked closely with William Keith Brooks, obtained his Ph.D. in 1881, and remained at Johns Hopkins for an additional year of postdoctoral work. In 1882 Wilson studied in Europe with the help of a loan from his older brother, Charles. He studied in Cambridge, and, with Thomas H. Huxley's recommendation, gave a paper on *Renilla* before the Royal Society in London. From England, he went to Leipzig, Germany, and then to the Zoological Station at Naples. Wilson worked for almost a year there and formed strong friendships with director Anton Dohrn and zoologist Theodor Boveri. (For Wilson, the embryos of marine invertebrates were more easily studied than those of terrestrial animals, and for almost 50 years, Wilson spent his summers working at the Marine Biological Laboratory in Woods Hole, Massachusetts.)

To visit Naples, Wilson had worked out an arrangement with Clarke, who was then teaching at Williams College (Massachusetts). The college would pay for a laboratory bench at Naples for two years as part of a professorship at Williams. Wilson would work at Naples the first year while Clarke taught at Williams, then the two would switch places. Wilson's stint at Williams College lasted between 1883 and 1884.

From Williams, Wilson moved to the Massachusetts Institute of Technology as an instructor from 1884 to 1885. There, he collaborated with his friend, William T. Sedgwick, in the creation of a textbook titled *General Biology* (1886). Wilson's next teaching appointment, unlike his previous two, offered him the time and opportunity to continue his research. M. Carey Thomas, the first dean of Bryn Mawr College (Bryn Mawr, PA), invited Wilson to become the first professor of biology at the new women's college. he taught there between 1885 and 1891. While at Bryn Mawr, the scientist tackled the problem of cell differentiation—the way in which the fertilized egg gives rise to many kinds of specialized cells. To do this, he studied the cell-by-cell development of the earthworm and *Nereis,* a marine worm. This work, known as "cell lineage," established Wilson's reputation as a biologist of considerable skill. His 1890 and 1892 papers on *Nereis* demonstrated the value of cell lineage and inspired other scientists to pursue this fruitful avenue of research.

In 1891 Wilson accepted an appointment to become an adjunct professor of zoology in the new zoology department at Columbia University being organized by Henry Fairfield Osborn. He spent the rest of his career at Columbia, eventually becoming chair of the department, and retiring as DaCosta Professor in 1928. Before settling on campus, however, Wilson spent another fruitful year in Munich and Naples from 1891 to 1892. A series of lectures on the study of the cell that he gave during his first teaching year at Columbia formed the basis of his textbook *The Cell in Development and Inheritance,* published in 1896. Written before the fundamentals of heredity were understood, the book added a balanced, careful voice to the fierce debates over modes of inheritance and cell development that were occurring in biology at that time. The book, which illuminated Wilson's penchant for observation and experimentation, was hugely influential and further cemented his already substantial reputation. The book was dedicated to Boveri, the Italian zoologist.

On September 27, 1904, Wilson married Anne Maynard Kidder. Kidder and her family lived in Washington, D.C., but spent their summers at their cottage in Woods Hole, and it was there that the two met. Their only child, Nancy, became a professional cellist. Wilson himself was an avid amateur musician, and his trips to Europe were warmly remembered as much for the music he heard as for the science he learned. A flutist as a young man, he began taking cello lessons while he was living in Baltimore. For the rest of his life, in Bryn Mawr and then New York, he always found himself a quartet of amateur musicians with which to play.

Helps Usher in Modern Era of Genetics

In 1900 the modern era of genetics was born. Three scientists, working independently from each other, stated that inherited characteristics were determined by the combination of two hereditary units, one from each parent. (Today, those two hereditary units are known as genes.) This theory had actually been published 36 years earlier by Gregor Johann Mendel, but had lain dormant until it was "revived" at the turn of the 19th century by **Hugo De Vries,** Karl Erich Correns, and Erich Tschermak von Seysenegg.

Wilson quickly saw the connection between the rediscovery of the laws of heredity and his own work with cells and cell structures. The laws of heredity stated that the fertilized egg received half of the blueprint for its own expression from each parent. Chromosomes, he theorized, were the cell structures responsible for transmitting the units of inheritance. By following instructions from the chromosomes, the fertilized egg gave rise to a complete individual.

In 1905 Wilson and **Nettie Maria Stevens** of Bryn Mawr College independently showed that the X and Y chromosomes carried by the sperm were responsible for determining gender: in many species, including humans, females had an XX pair of chromosomes while males had an XY pair. In eight papers published from 1905 to 1912 entitled "Studies on Chromosomes," Wilson brilliantly extended his study of the chromosomal theory of sex determination, and it is for this work with chromosomes that he is best remembered. He is also recognized for setting the stage for the zoology department's future excellence in genetics, as personified by **Thomas Hunt Morgan** and **Hermann Joseph Muller.**

In the last years of his career, Wilson continued his study of cell structures. Despite failing health, he also wrote the third edition of *The Cell in Development and Inheritance,* over 1200 pages, which was published in 1925. In most respects, this was actually a completely new book that included the new discoveries in biology of the twentieth century. Wilson retired from Columbia University in 1928. He died in New York, on March 3, 1939, of bronchial pneumonia, and his ashes were buried in the churchyard of the Church of the Messiah in Woods Hole, Massachusetts.

SELECTED WRITINGS BY WILSON:

Books

(With William T. Sedgwick) *General Biology,* [New York], 1886.
The Cell in Development and Inheritance, [New York], 1896, second edition, 1900, third edition, revised and enlarged as *The Cell in Development and Heredity,* 1925.

Periodicals

"Science and Liberal Education," *Science,* Volume 42, 1915, pp. 625–30.

SOURCES:

Books

Biographical Memoirs, Volume 21, National Academy of Sciences, 1941, pp. 315–42.

Obituary Notices of the Fellows of the Royal Society, Volume 3, Royal Society (London), 1939–41, pp. 123–38.

Periodicals

Morgan, Thomas Hunt, "Edmund B. Wilson—An Appreciation," *The American Naturalist,* Volume 77, 1943, pp. 5–37 (January/February issue) and pp. 142–72 (March/April issue).

—*Sketch by Liz Marshall*

Edward O. Wilson

Edward O. Wilson
1929-
American zoologist

World-renowned entomologist Edward O. Wilson is nicknamed "Dr. Ant," but his achievements impact much of the field of biology. He is co-founder of the modern field of sociobiology, believed by some to be one of the great paradigms of science, which has touched off much controversy but also a great deal of research in animal and human social behavior. From his posts as Harvard Univeristy's Frank B. Baird, Jr. Professor of Science and Mellon Professor of Science, Wilson is the recipient of Sweden's Crafoord Prize (equal in stature to the Nobel Prize), a 1979 Pulitzer Prize for literature, and the 1977 National Medal of Science. He has influenced the field of animal taxonomy through his work in speciation theory, conducted research which led to the discovery of pheromones—chemicals which cause behavior in animals—and has been a harbinger of the threat of mass extinction resulting from man's unchecked use of the environment.

Fateful Fishing Trip Determines Career

Edward Osborne Wilson was born on June 10, 1929 in Birmingham, Alabama. A descendant of farmers and shipowners in subtropical Alabama, Wilson had already decided to become a naturalist explorer by age seven. Fate intervened, however, when on a fishing trip he vigorously pulled his catch out of the water and its fin hit and damaged his right eye. He thus developed the habit of examining animals and objects close-up with his keen left eye, and when he subsequently read a National Geographic article entitled "Stalking Ants, Savage and Civilized" at age 10, the entomologist was born. Wilson later studied biology at the University of Alabama, obtaining a B.S. degree in this discipline in 1949 and

an M.S. in 1950. In 1955, at age 26, he received his Ph.D. in biology from Harvard. He gained full professorship in 1964, and became Frank B. Baird, Jr. Professor of Science in 1976.

The field of new systematics—the attempt to classify species based on the principles of evolutionary theory—occupied Wilson during the early years of his career. With his colleague William L. Brown, Wilson critiqued the utilization of the subspecies category, prompting revised procedures among taxonomists. In 1956, Wilson also co-developed the concept of "character displacement," which occurs when two similar species begin a process of genetic differentiation to avoid competition and cross-breeding.

During the mid- to late–1950s, Wilson traveled to Australia, the South Pacific islands, and Melanesia to further study and classify ants native to those regions. As a result of his field work in the Melanesian archipelagoes, he developed the concept of the taxon cycle, which has since been found among birds and other insects. Wilson described the taxon cycle of Melanesian ants as the process through which a species disperses to a new, harsher habitat and evolves into one or more new "daughter" species, which then adapt to the new habitat.

All the while, Wilson was developing the foundation for what would he would term "sociobiology" two decades later. In 1959, influenced by the rise of molecular biology, he proved his hypothesis that social insects such as ants communicate through chemical releasers. Wilson crushed a venom gland extracted from a fire ant and created a trail of the chemical near a colony of the same species. He had anticipated that a few ants would trace the chemical path. Instead, dozens of fire ants swarmed out of the colony to follow the trail, and were baffled at its end. "That night I couldn't sleep," Wilson notes. "I envisioned accounting for the entire social repertory of ants with a small number of chemicals." Indeed, the chemicals came to be known as pheromones, and this discovery launched an "explosion of research" on the behavior of social insects—research which continues still. Wilson wrote later that pheromones were "not just a guidepost, but the entire message." These chemicals communicate complex instructions for fellow ants—everything from the location of food and how to obtain it to a call for help when in distress.

First to Identify Species Equilibrium Theory

In the early and middle 1960s, Wilson collaborated with Princeton University mathematician **Robert H. MacArthur** to develop the first quantitative theory of species equilibrium. Prior to their work in this area, it was believed that the regularity of species in a given area was maintained through incomplete colonization. Wilson and his coauthor hypothesized that the number of species on a small island would remain constant, though the variety of species would undergo constant reshuffling.

Two factors affect the number of species in an ecosystem: extinction and immigration. In Wilson and MacArthur's island model, these factors are determined by the size and proximity of the islands—larger, less crowded islands typically have lower extinction rates, for example, and islands that are close together experience greater species immigration from one island to another. The "equilibrium hypothesis of island biogeography" describes the relationship between these factors in a mathematical model. The two determinants in the number of species are the rate of extinction of species (depicted by a positive sloping curve) and the rate of immigration of new species (indicated by a negative sloping curve). The actual number of species is found at the intersection of the two curves.

MacArthur and Wilson's hypothesis was borne out by a 1968 study by Wilson and biologist Daniel Simberloff, who examined the insect life on six islands off the Florida Keys. They first counted the number of insect species, then fumigated the islands and recounted eight months later. As Wilson had predicted, the number of species remained the same, while the composition of species was significantly different and did in fact evolve over time.

For this landmark work, Wilson received the Crafoord Prize in 1990, awarded by the Royal Swedish Academy of Sciences. "This relatively simple idea transformed the study of species richness into a quantitative and experimental branch of biology," the academy noted. "Arguably, hardly a single important work in conservation biology is written today without the author making use of this theory as a launching ramp."

Founds Field of Sociobiology

But Wilson's greatest milestone probably was his 1975 book, *Sociobiology: The New Synthesis.* In it he defines sociobiology as "the systematic study of the biological basis of all social behavior." The term was in use prior to Wilson's landmark book, but he identified the interdisciplinary endeavor as one which was to change the way animal and human behavior is viewed and researched by the scientific community. Arthur Fisher, in *Society* magazine, declares, "Many biologists believe that sociobiology is indeed one of the great scientific paradigms, a powerful new tool for understanding some of the most baffling phenomena in the living world." Fisher compares the new framework to Darwin's theory of natural selection and Einstein's revolution of space/time theory. In fact, many of the tenets Wilson put forth in his book have gained widespread acceptance, and have aroused controversy over the ideological implications for human behavior.

The roots of Wilson's journey into this field lay in the beginning of his career. "In the forties and fifties," he says in *Society,* "we were in the midst of a very exciting development, called the new synthesis, which reinvigorated evolutionary biology by applying modern population genetics to what had previously been scattered and highly descriptive subjects. . . . It was a period of grand synthesis in which it seemed possible to understand some of the most intrinsically interesting phenomena."

Simultaneously, the field of molecular biology was gaining prominence, and Wilson observed that this threatened to relegate the softer study of animal behavior to a tiny corner of Harvard's biology department. Wilson began focusing on the significance of organisms as carriers of genetic information. Viewing the complex behavior of ants and other social insects in this framework prompted Wilson to describe behavior which served survival not of the individual, but of the population.

Thus Wilson was able to explain, in Darwinian terms, such characteristics as altruism, significance of kinship, communication, and specialization of labor—characteristics which had previously confounded scientists. Cooperation among individuals or between species was consistent with early evolutionary theory because it enabled individuals to survive and carry on the gene pool. But altruism (behavior in which one individual helps another at possible or certain cost to itself) and spiteful behavior (when an individual harms another and itself) were largely unexplained by biologists.

Explains Altruism in Ants

The answer lies in the broader view of population survival. In a colony of ants, sterile members will work for their family members who share similar genes and who will reproduce on their behalf. Wilson maintains that selflessness is a characteristic of most ant species. He describes their colonies as "superorganisms," in which the welfare of the colony—not the individual—is paramount. On the other end of the behavioral spectrum, a species of Malaysian ants will rupture glands of poison on their own bodies if invaded by enemies—killing themselves and their intruders, while signaling for help from members of their own colony. Other complex and intricate behavior is explained by Wilson's sociobiology. The European red amazon ant, for example, is an aggressive creature which actually invades the nests of more peaceful ant species, killing some individuals and capturing others for use as slaves in their own nests. The slave ants actually do "housework," digging chambers and feeding and nurturing the young Amazons.

Applies Sociobiology to Humans

It was the twenty-seventh chapter of *Sociobiology* which touched off a controversy that continues today. In "Man—From Sociobiology to Biology," Wilson argued for expanded research on the role of biology in human behavior. "There is a need for a discipline of anthropological genetics," he wrote. "By comparing man with other primate species, it might be possible to identify basic primate traits that lie beneath the surface and help to determine the configuration of man's higher social behavior."

Wilson noted that humans have always been characterized by "aggressive dominance systems, with males generally dominant over females." He also wrote that "a key early step in human social evolution was the use of women in barter." In a separate article, Wilson wrote: "In hunter-gatherer societies, men hunt and women stay at home. This strong bias ... appears to have a genetic origin. Even with identical education and equal access to all professions, men are likely to continue to play a disproportionate role in political life, business, and science."

The anger with which Wilson's words were received led to noisy protests at a 1978 meeting of the American Association for the Advancement of Science. Intruders on the meeting first yelled a diatribe against him and then poured a pitcher of water over him. A letter of protest signed by, among others, two of Wilson's colleagues at Harvard, asserted that

theories such as his in the past had led to the "sterilization laws and restrictive immigration laws by the United States between 1910 and 1930 and also for the eugenics policies which led to the establishment of gas chambers in Nazi Germany."

Wilson's worst detractors believed that the inevitable conclusion of his theories was "biological determinism." Harvard Professor **Stephen Jay Gould** (who had signed the letter of protest) sought a middle ground, since Wilson's theory didn't preclude the possibility that "peacefulness, equality, and kindness are just as biological as violence, sexism and general nastiness." But Gould maintained that there is no direct evidence in existence that specific human behaviors are genetically determined. In 1978, Wilson penned a follow-up to *Sociobiology,* the Pulitzer Prize–winning *On Human Nature.* In this volume he attempted to defend his hypotheses forwarded in chapter twenty-seven of *Sociobiology,* as well as to clear up certain areas that had become targets for controversy and prejudice. In particular, Fisher notes, Wilson "aimed for a fuller explanation of his views of the issues of free will, ethics, and development." Wilson's continuing research led to a collaboration with University of Toronto professor Charles Lumsden, with whom he penned 1981's *Genes, Mind and Culture* and 1983's *Promethean Fire*—the latter of which Wilson describes as his "last word on the subject" of human sociobiology.

Whatever the ramifications of Wilson's attempt to apply his entomological expertise to human behavior, his books and life's research represent great forward strides in the field of biology. His fascination with ants, begun in his childhood, culminated with the publication of 1990's *The Ants,* which he co-authored with German entomologist Bert Holldobler. Wilson, the world's leading authority on the creature with 8,800 species, believes they are essential to the world's ecosystems.

Wilson also is forthright in arguing for increased protection of the environment to minimize the mass species extinction now underway. He has warned that the current extinctions due to rainforest destruction will rival those which marked the end of the dinosaur age. Wilson has argued for surveyance of the earth's flora and fauna (the majority of which remain unclassified), the promotion of sustainable development, the wise use of the earth's plant and animal resources for food and medicine, and the restoration of terrains already damaged.

His many achievements include the Cleveland Prize (1967), the Mercer Award of the Ecological Society of America (1971), the Founders' Memorial Award from the Entomological Society of America (1972), the Leidy Medal (1978), the Carr Medal (1978), the L. O. Howard Award of the Entomological Society of America (1985), and the Tyler Prize for

Environmental Achievement (1984). Wilson served on the World Wildlife Fund Board of Directors from 1984 to 1990. He is a member of the National Academy of Sciences, a fellow of the American Academy of Arts and Sciences, a fellow of the American Philosophical Society, the former president of the Society for the Study of Evolution, and an honorary member of the British Ecological Society.

Of his lifelong exploration of the insect world, Wilson says, "God is in the details." His contributions to species classification, biogeography, insect social organization, and his founding of sociobiology, have left a legacy the depth of which is yet to be measured.

SELECTED WRITINGS BY WILSON:

Books

(With R. H. MacArthur) *The Theory of Island Biogeography,* Princeton University Press, 1967.
The Insect Societies, Belknap Press, 1971.
(With W. H. Bossert) *A Primer of Population Biology,* Sinauer Associates, 1971.
(Co-author) *Life on Earth,* Sinauer Associates, 1973.
Sociobiology: The New Synthesis, Belknap Press, 1975.
(With George F. Oster) *Caste and Ecology in Social Insects,* Princeton University Press, 1978.
On Human Nature, Harvard University Press, 1978.
(With Charles J. Lumsden) *Genes, Mind, and Culture: The Coevolutionary Process,* Harvard University Press, 1981.
(With Lumsden) *Promethean Fire: Reflections on the Origin of the Mind,* Harvard University Press, 1983.
Biophilia: The Human Bond to Other Species, Harvard University Press, 1984.
(With Bert Holldobler) *The Ants,* Harvard University Press, 1990.
The Diversity of Life, Harvard University Press, 1992.

SOURCES:

Books

McGraw-Hill Modern Scientists and Engineers, McGraw-Hill 1980, pp. 334–35.

Periodicals

Brownlee, Shannon, "A Celebration of Pests," *U.S. News & World Report,* May 7, 1990, pp. 63–66.
Fisher, Arthur, "Sociobiology: Science or Ideology?," *Society,* July/August 1992, pp. 67–79.
Murphy, Jamie, "The Quiet Apocalypse," *Time,* October 13, 1986, p. 80.
Scientific American, March, 1993, pp. 146–50.

—*Sketch by Karen Withem*

J. Tuzo Wilson
1908-1993
Canadian geophysicist

An early proponent of the continental drift theory, J. Tuzo Wilson is chiefly remembered for his proposition that transform faults were present in the ocean floor, an idea that led to conclusive evidence that the sea floor and the earth's crust are constantly moving. Wilson later hypothesized that an ancestral Atlantic Ocean basin had opened and closed during the Paleozoic era, in turn creating the huge land mass known as Pangaea. This theory helps account for the presence of the Appalachian mountains in eastern North America, the striking similarity of many rock features in Western Europe and North America, and parallel cyclical developments on the seven continents.

John Tuzo Wilson was born in Ottawa, Ontario, Canada, on October 24, 1908. His father, John Armitstead Wilson, was an engineer who held a civil service position. His mother, Henrietta Tuzo, was an avid mountain climber who met her husband at the first gathering of Canada's Alpine Club. The Wilsons later shared their love of geology and the outdoors with their children, who were brought up to respect the pursuit of knowledge and were educated under the direction of an English governess.

Chooses Career in Geophysics

In 1924 Wilson's father obtained a position for him at a forestry camp. Wilson grew so fond of outdoor work that he signed on as an assistant to the legendary mountaineer Noel Odel, who persuaded him to pursue a career in geology. Following his freshman year at the University of Toronto, Wilson switched majors from physics to geology. After earning a B.A. in 1930, Wilson received a scholarship to study at Cambridge University under Sir **Harold Jeffreys**. When Wilson returned to Canada in the early 1930s, he had difficulty finding work, so he continued his education, enrolling in Princeton University, where he earned a Ph.D. in 1936. He made the first recorded ascent of Mount Hague in Montana in 1935, and in 1938 married Isabel Jean Dickson, with whom he had two children, Patricia and Susan.

With the outbreak of World War II in 1939, Wilson joined the Canadian Army. During his seven-year stint, he authored more than 500 technical reports and later claimed that these military papers had helped him develop the lucid prose style which he utilized in a number of scientific studies. By 1946 he had reached the rank of colonel. That same year, after resigning from the army, he succeeded his professor at the University of Toronto. Geophysics had finally become a lucrative field of study in Canada, thanks in large part to the discovery of oil in Alberta, which increased demand for geophysical exploration and led to the development of more advanced instruments and measurement techniques. Wilson investigated a number of geological mysteries, including Canadian glaciers, mountain building, and mineral production. He conducted these investigations with a characteristic reverence toward nature: "Everywhere in science modern tools and ideas bring to light the elegant and orderly skeins by which nature builds the glory that we see about us, knit in regular patterns from simple stitches," he wrote in *I.G.Y.: The Year of the New Moons* (1961). "Indeed, we may think of all nature in terms of music, as infinitely ingenious and elaborate variations on a few simple themes."

Geophysical Work Legitimizes Theory of Continental Drift

From 1957 to 1960 Wilson served as president of the International Union of Geodesy and Geophysics. During his tenure he led a series of geologic expeditions to China and Mongolia, the details of which are recorded in his highly praised book, *One Chinese Moon* (1959). In the early 1960s he became a key figure in what was then the most controversial issue in geology—the continental drift theory.

The origins of the continental drift theory date back hundreds of years. Since the time of the first global maps people have reasoned that at one time the continents might have been a single huge land mass. However, the first formal hypothesis of continental drift was made by German geophysicist **Alfred Wegener** in 1912. The idea was generally overlooked for decades but reemerged prominently in 1960, when geologist **Harold Hess** theorized that the ocean floors were being continuously created and changed. Hess attributed this activity to two physical structures: mid-ocean ridges, where the ocean floor is created, and ocean trenches, where the sea floor is destroyed.

Wilson was one of the first scientists to recognize the immense implications of this idea. For the next decade, he was at the very center of this theoretical debate. Using Hess's theory, Wilson postulated the existence of a third category of physical structure on the ocean floor which he called "transform faults," horizontal shears located between ridge sites and trenches. He suggested that transform faults could not exist unless the earth's crust was moving, and that the physical confirmation of these faults might prove the scientific validity of the continental drift theory. In 1967, seismologist Lynn Sykes partially tested Wilson's theory by studying seismic patterns and oceanic focal mechanisms. Wilson brought the idea to the attention of the general public by exhibiting a continental drift model at Montreal's Expo '67. By the late 1960s the theory had gained wide acceptance and was eventually incorporated into the larger concept of plate tectonics, which maintains that the Earth's lithosphere is made up of a number of plates that move independently.

Wilson's hypothesis and the publicity it garnered earned him numerous honors, including a Fellowship in the Royal Society (1968), the Penrose Medal of the Geological Society of America (1968), the Walter H. Bucher Medal of the American Geophysical Union (1968), the John J. Carty Medal of the National Academy of Sciences (1975), the Vetlesen Prize of Columbia University (1978), and the Wollaston Medal of the Geological Society of London (1978).

Wilson retired from his professorship at the University of Toronto in 1974. He then assumed the directorship of the Ontario Science Centre and in that capacity helped transform the center from a traditional science museum into an interactive science lab for public use. Of the center's roughly 1,000 exhibits, 400 were designed to be handled by patrons, and during the late 1970s and 1980s, the exploratory museum attracted approximately 1.5 million visitors annually.

Throughout his life Wilson traveled extensively. He lectured at more than 200 colleges and universities. One of his passions was collecting books on the Arctic and Antarctic, both of which he had visited. A mountain range in Antarctica was named the Wilson range in his honor. He died in Toronto on April 15, 1993, at the age of 84. In an obituary tribute in *Nature,* colleague Fred Vine wrote, "Tuzo Wilson was a big man; in stature, in his magnanimity, on the Canadian science scene, and internationally in the Earth sciences. His seminal contributions to our new view of the Earth will be long remembered."

SELECTED WRITINGS BY WILSON:

Books

One Chinese Moon, Hill and Wang, 1959.
I.G.Y.: The Year of the New Moons, Knopf, 1961.
(Editor) *Continents Adrift: Readings from "Scientific American,"* W. H. Freeman, 1972.
Unglazed China, Saturday Review Press, 1973.

(Editor) *Continents Adrift and Continents Aground: Readings from "Scientific American,"* W. H. Freeman, 1976.

SOURCES:

Books

The Continental Crust and Its Mineral Deposits (proceedings of a symposium held in honor of Wilson), Geological Association of Canada, 1980.

Periodicals

Vine, Fred, "John Tuzo Wilson (1908–1993)," *Nature,* 363, June 3, 1993, p. 400.

—*Sketch by Tom Crawford*

Kenneth G. Wilson
1936-
American physicist

Kenneth G. Wilson was awarded the 1982 Nobel Prize in physics for his development of a theory to describe phase changes that take place close to critical points. Phase transitions are changes that take place in the physical state of a system (a simple and familiar phase transition is the melting of ice, during which water changes from the solid to the liquid state). The critical point is the temperature or pressure at which the transition takes place. The award was described by colleague P. W. Anderson in *Science* as one of the most clearly justified of all Nobel Prizes in physics "in terms of [its] total influence on the world of theoretical and experimental physics and chemistry."

After earning his Ph.D. under **Murray Gell-Mann** at the California Institute of Technology in 1961, Wilson spent terms as junior fellow at Harvard University from 1959 to 1962 and as a Ford Foundation Fellow at the European Organization for Nuclear Research (CERN) from 1962 to 1963. Working his way up the professorial ranks at Cornell University, he was appointed James A. Weeks Professor of Physical Science in 1974. In 1988, Wilson left Cornell to accept an appointment as Hazel C. Youngberg Trustees Distinguished Professor of Physics at Ohio State University. In recent years, his research has focused on computer simulations and modeling of a variety of physical phenomena.

Born in Waltham, Massachusetts, on June 8, 1936, Kenneth Geddes Wilson was the oldest of six children born to Edgar Bright Wilson, Jr., and the former Emily Fisher Buckingham. Wilson's parents were both involved in the sciences; his father was professor of chemistry at Harvard University and an authority in microwave spectroscopy, while his mother had completed a year of graduate study in physics before her marriage. Kenneth's maternal grandfather had been a professor of mechanical engineering at the Massachusetts Institute of Technology, and his paternal grandfather had been a lawyer and one-time speaker of the Tennessee House of Representatives.

Exhibits a Flair for Science

Wilson showed a talent for mathematics at an early age; according to a writer for the *New York Times,* when Wilson was a boy he spent his time waiting for the school bus by calculating the cube roots of numbers in his head. He attended grade schools in Wellesley and Woods Hole and at the Shady Hill School in Cambridge, all in Massachusetts; and his secondary education was completed at the Magdalen College School in Oxford and at the George School in Bucks County, Pennsylvania (a Quaker school). Wilson also studied a great deal on his own, teaching himself the basic principles of calculus and learning symbolic logic from his father.

At the age of sixteen, Wilson was accepted as a freshman into Harvard University, from which he received a B.A. in math and physics in 1956. He chose to do his graduate work in theoretical physics at the California Institute of Technology, where his advisor was Murray Gell-Mann. Wilson's doctoral thesis dealt with quantum field theory, an area of physics that attempts to integrate relativity theory with quantum mechanics (the object behind combining these two major theories was to develop an overall conceptual picture of the physical world). In particular, Wilson investigated an aspect of quantum electrodynamics (QED) that had been particularly troubling for theoretical physicists. The use of traditional QED theory, which describes the interaction of particles within an electromagnetic field, sometimes resulted in bizarre and nonsensical results, such as the prediction of particles with infinite electrical charges. One way around this dilemma had been the use of a mathematical procedure developed by Gell-Mann, among others, known as renormalization; this procedure could extract important physical values from a calculation running into infinity. In his own thesis, Wilson used the techniques of renormalization to study the properties of an elementary particle known as the K meson.

After completing his doctorate, Wilson spent three years at Harvard University as a junior fellow in

Harvard's Society of Fellows. He then continued his research on elementary particles as a Ford Foundation Fellow at the CERN particle accelerator facility in Geneva. At the completion of that fellowship in 1963, he was appointed assistant professor of physics at Cornell University. Over the next few years, Wilson was promoted to associate, and then full professor in 1970. In 1974, he was appointed to the James A. Weeks Chair of Physical Science at Cornell.

The Investigation of Phase Transitions

It was at Cornell that Wilson became interested in a new aspect of theoretical physics, the study of phase transitions at critical points. Physicists had been studying critical phenomena since the early 1870s; in the process, they discovered a number of examples of phase transitions, such as the sudden loss of magnetism demonstrated by iron, cobalt, and nickel at a distinctive temperature, the "Curie point." But most critical phenomena are complex events, and early theories were able to do no more than to predict that they did occur, not how or under what circumstances.

Wilson's approach was to break a phase transition down into smaller, more easily studied subunits, a technique that had been developed by others. He then applied the principles of renormalization to these subunits. In a pair of articles published in 1971 in *Physical Review B* Wilson outlined the result of his analysis, a theory that correctly predicts known critical data. It was for this work that Wilson received the 1982 Nobel Prize for physics. At the presentation ceremonies, Stig Lundqvist of the Royal Swedish Academy of Sciences stated that Wilson's theory "gave a complete theoretical description of the behavior close to the critical point and gave also methods to calculate numerically the crucial quantities."

Since the mid–1970s, Wilson has returned to the research of his graduate years, the study of elementary particles. Like many others, he has been attempting to use the methods of renormalization to understand the interaction of quarks, one group of fundamental particles of which all matter seems to consist. As a result of this research, he has also developed another interest: the development of faster and more efficient computers. As he has seen how his own research and that of others is limited by existing computer technology, he has become an outspoken advocate for the development of improved hardware to deal with problems of particle physics. In connection with this interest, Wilson accepted an appointment as director of the Center for Theory and Simulation in Science and Engineering at Cornell in 1985.

Wilson was married in 1982 to Alison Brown, a computer specialist at Cornell Computer Services, whom he had met in 1975. He enjoys hiking, folk dancing, and playing the oboe. Outdoor activities in general have long been an important part of Wilson's life. During high school, he ran the mile and cross country for his track team; as a graduate student, he spent one summer hiking the John Muir Trail from Yosemite Park to Mount Whitney. And in 1962, he climbed Mount Blanc with fellow physicists **Henry Kendall** and James Bjorken.

Elected a member of the National Academy of Sciences in 1975, Wilson has been awarded a number of prestigious honors including the Dannie Heineman Prize of the American Physical Society in 1973, Israel's Wolf Prize in 1980 (shared with Michael Fisher and Leo Kadanoff), and the Franklin Medal of the Franklin Institute in 1982. In 1988, he ended his long affiliation with Cornell to become Hazel C. Youngberg Trustees Distinguished Professor at Ohio State University. Since 1990, Wilson has also become active on two important national committees dealing with science policy, the National Academy of Science's Committee on Physical Science, Mathematics and Applications and the Committee on the Federal Role in Educational Research.

SELECTED WRITINGS BY WILSON:

Periodicals

"Renormalization Group and Critical Phenomena," *Physical Review B,* November 1, 1971, pp. 3174–3205.

SOURCES:

Books

Nobel Prize Winners, H. W. Wilson, 1987, pp. 1136–1138.
Weber, Robert L., *Pioneers of Science: Nobel Prize Winners in Physics,* American Institute of Physics, 1980, pp. 277–278.

Periodicals

New York Times, October 10, 1982, p. C6.
Science, November 19, 1982.

—Sketch by David E. Newton

Robert R. Wilson
1914-
American physicist

Robert R. Wilson is a rare combination of particle physicist, philosopher, and artist. His work on protons in the 1950s significantly advanced knowledge of these elementary particles. He also made contributions to the use of magnetic forces to guide beams of particles. In addition, Wilson had been an active sculptor during his years as a physicist, and his experience in both fields culminated in the design of the Fermi National Accelerator Laboratory at Batavia, just west of Chicago, Illinois. Fermilab, as it is known, is a high-energy particle accelerator, designed to collide electrically charged particles at high speeds. The debris from the collisions gives scientists valuable information regarding the structure and behavior of matter. Wilson was director of Fermilab from its inception in the mid–1960s until 1978.

Wilson brought a philosophical approach to the building of Fermilab, comparing the process of building the lab to the process of building the great cathedrals in Europe. Physicist Leon Lederman, in his book *The God Particle: If the Universe Is the Answer, What Is the Question?*, quotes Wilson as follows: "I even found, emphatically, a strange similarity between the cathedral and the accelerator: The one structure was intended to reach a soaring height in space; the other is intended to reach a comparable height in energy." Wilson's unusual approach to building scientific instruments had roots in his early years. He was born Robert Rathbun Wilson in Frontier, Wyoming, on March 4, 1914. His father was Platt Elvin Wilson, a local politician, and his mother was Edith (Rathbun) Wilson. When he was eight, his parents divorced. His youthful experiences on the cattle ranches of Wyoming—particularly his exposure to the blacksmith shop—familiarized him with toolmaking and repair. This experience and an attitude that nothing was impossible would prove useful in the future when Wilson designed Fermilab.

The young Wilson was as much a tinkerer as a physicist. In high school, he designed and constructed scientific devices, including a vacuum and a hand-sized particle accelerator. When it came time to go to college, he enrolled at the University of California at Berkeley, intending to study philosophy. But the year was 1932—the middle of the Great Depression—and philosophy seemed impractical during those years of hardship. He became attracted to physics when he walked by a lab one day and saw machines and generators whirring inside. He felt an immediate affinity with the scientists and students working those machines.

Contributes to Atomic Bomb

Wilson remained at the University of California as a graduate student, working with **Ernest Orlando Lawrence** who had invented the cyclotron, a type of particle accelerator. After receiving his Ph.D. in 1940, Wilson took a position as physics instructor at Princeton University. When the United States became involved in World War II, he was asked, along with thousands of other expert scientists and mathematicians, to help with the effort to develop an atomic bomb. From 1943 to 1946 he lived in Los Alamos, New Mexico, serving as leader of a group of scientists working on a cyclotron. In 1944 he became head of the division researching experimental nuclear physics, which eventually became responsible for designing instruments to measure the flash produced by the first test bomb.

Wilson had, at first, been a reluctant participant in the war efforts. He had initially opposed the war, but in the early 1940s, with the fighting in Europe escalating, he had accepted an invitation by Dr. Lawrence to attend a conference at the Massachusetts Institute of Technology to discuss the war. There, he heard testimony from witnesses regarding the devastation in Europe. He agreed that Germany must be stopped.

During his stay in Los Alamos, it became clear that the United States government was not going to let the inventors of the weapon have any input about how the bomb was going to be used. Wilson, along with many other scientists involved, became discouraged about the political uses of the weapon they had designed. The power of the bomb was extraordinary; yet only the scientists seemed aware of its awesome power and the ramifications of misuse.

After World War II, Wilson took a position at Harvard University, designing a 150 MeV cyclotron—a machine that accelerates particles to 150 million electron volts. The early machines sprayed out protons in all directions, so that measurements were difficult. Wilson realized that magnets could be used to focus the emerging protons into a concentrated beam. As Lederman wrote in *The God Particle,* Wilson was "the first to understand the subtle but crucial effect the magnetic forces had in keeping the protons from spraying out." As accelerators became more powerful they also became longer, eventually being designed in circular shapes. Magnetic fields were used to guide the particle beams around the accelerator rings.

In 1946 Wilson became a full professor at Cornell University, where he was also named director of the Laboratory of Nuclear Studies. There, he oversaw the construction of a new type of particle accelerator, a 300 MeV synchrotron. (A synchrotron enabled particles to travel in a circular path at increasing speeds.) In the following years he built ever more powerful accelerators to help explore the nature of the proton. From his experiments, the structure of the proton was established.

Builds Fermilab

In the early 1960s, however, Wilson became discouraged with his research in particle physics. He seemed not to be making headway in his field. By the mid–1960s, he was considering a total change. He thought perhaps he should pursue full-time what had been a lifelong hobby, sculpture. It was at this time, when Wilson was casting about for change, that he was offered the opportunity to construct the 200-billion-electron-volt (200 GeV, or gigaelectron volts) synchrotron—the Fermi National Accelerator Laboratory. Wilson approached his new project with zeal and creativity. Construction at Fermilab was started in 1968 and finished in 1971—far less time than had been estimated by other experts. The new accelerator was contained at the world's best experimental facility in particle physics. Protons traveled near the speed of light, with collisions reaching an energy level of 400 gigaelectron volts. A few initial problems were resolved, and it became clear that the power of Fermilab would be useful in many ways. In 1977, for example, upsilon particles were discovered by Wilson's colleague **Leon Lederman**, who went on to win the 1988 Nobel Prize in physics. Wilson was convinced that the discovery was a direct result of the power of the accelerator. One of Wilson's powerful innovations during his tenure at Fermilab was the use of superconducting magnets to optimize energy efficiency and produce a more powerful magnetic field to guide the beams of particles.

By 1974, it was clear that, in order to remain the world's best, Fermilab's power would have to be increased even more. In 1977, Wilson appealed to Congress for increased funding. During his congressional testimony, Wilson remarked that the value of accelerators "has only to do with the respect with which we regard one another, the dignity of men, our love of culture. . . . It has to do with, are we good painters, good sculptors, great poets? I mean all the things we really venerate and honor in our country and are patriotic about. It has nothing to do directly with defending our country except to make it worth defending." Wilson wanted to build a second ring of magnets to boost the energy level to 1000 gigaelectron volts, but Congress denied the funding. Early in 1978, Wilson resigned as director, convinced that he could do more to advance physics on his own than as a director of a minimally funded lab.

Although Wilson remained involved with the lab as director emeritus and architectural consultant, he has spent most of his time after his resignation teaching. From 1978 to 1980, he was the Peter B. Ritzma Professor at the University of Chicago and from 1980 to 1983, the Michael Pupin Professor at Columbia. He has been a guest lecturer at Harvard, the University of Washington and the Los Alamos Scientific Laboratory. Currently, he is professor of physics emeritus at Cornell University. He lives in Ithaca, New York, with his wife, Jane Inez Scheyer, whom he married in 1940. They have three sons. Several of Wilson's sculptures—metal constructions and stone carvings—are displayed at Fermilab.

SOURCES:

Books

Hilts, Philip, *Scientific Temperaments: Three Lives in Contemporary Science,* Simon & Schuster, 1982.

Lederman, Leon, and Dick Teresi, *The God Particle: If the Universe Is the Answer, What Is the Question?,* Houghton, 1993.

—Sketch by Dorothy Barnhouse

Robert Woodrow Wilson
1936-
American astronomer

Robert Woodrow Wilson is best known for the discovery, with coresearcher **Arno Penzias**, of the cosmic background radiation believed to be the remnant of the "big bang" that started the universe. For their work, Wilson and Penzias were honored with numerous awards, including the 1978 Nobel Prize in physics, which they shared with **Pyotr Kapitsa**.

Wilson was born in Houston, Texas, on January 10, 1936. He attended Rice University where he received a B.A. in physics in 1957. He then moved on to the California Institute of Technology (Caltech) for graduate study and received his Ph.D. in 1962. Wilson's thesis work, and post-doctoral research, involved making radio surveys (the use of radio waves bounced off of stellar bodies to create visual approximations) of the Milky Way Galaxy. When he heard of the existence of specialized radio equipment at Bell

Robert Woodrow Wilson

Laboratories, he left Caltech and accepted a job at Bell's research facility in Holmdel, New Jersey. This was the very same research facility from which **Karl Jansky**, in the 1930s, almost single-handedly invented the science of radio astronomy. Wilson and Penzias, who had preceded Wilson at Bell Labs by about a year, were about to embark on a research odyssey that would culminate in an extremely important discovery almost by accident.

Just as Jansky had done thirty years earlier, Wilson and Penzias were studying the possible causes of static interference that impaired the quality of radio communications. At least, this was what the management at Bell hoped would transpire as the two radio astronomers conducted their research. Wilson and Penzias's long range plan was to measure radiation in the galactic "halo," a theorized but not well understood cloud of matter and radiation surrounding the Milky Way and other galaxies. Then, they hoped to look for hydrogen gas in clusters of galaxies. Their research instrumentation included a small, sensitive twenty-foot microwave "horn" originally designed to receive bounced radio reflections from the Echo communications satellite.

Since galactic radio radiation is, by its nature, not very energetic, the central problem in measuring its precise intensity was to eliminate all conceivable sources of heat, or thermal noise, which could obscure an accurate reading of the weak radio signals from space. To this end, Penzias had laboriously constructed a "cold load," using frigid liquid helium, which

would cool the radio detector down to within only a few degrees above absolute zero. When the equipment was finally ready in the spring of 1964, the radio horn was turned to the sky.

Discovers Cosmic Background Radiation with Penzias

Very early in the research project, it became apparent that the antenna was measuring more radio radiation than Wilson and Penzias had anticipated. The source of the excess radiation could not be determined. A similar problem had surfaced earlier when the twenty-foot horn was used for Echo satellite communications. At that time, researchers added up all the known sources of accounted radio noise, which totaled a heat measurement of nineteen degrees Kelvin. It was therefore puzzling to them that the radio receiver was measuring twenty-two degrees. Wilson and Penzias's results were similar. They had hoped that their carefully modified apparatus would yield more accurate results, but this apparently was not the case. They were measuring a significant amount of excess microwave radiation. The intensity of the signal did not change regardless of where they pointed the receiver. Nor did the radio static appear to be coming from any discrete object in space. The Milky Way Galaxy was not the source either, since the radio signal seemed to be coming from everywhere in the universe at once, not from just a limited zone across the sky. Based on the known sources of radio radiation, the strength of this radiation was far more powerful than expected.

Wilson and Penzias checked for possible explanations for this phenomenon, concluding that atmospheric effects were not to blame. Since the hill upon which their radio horn was perched overlooked New York City, the possibility of interference from man-made sources was considered. After repeated observations, however, Wilson and Penzias were convinced that New York was not to blame. To insure that the signal was not the result of interference from their own electronic apparatus, Wilson and Penzias tracked down and eliminated every conceivable source of noise—including the effects of bird dung, which coated the inside of the radio horn, courtesy a pair of nesting pigeons. The interior of the radio horn was cleaned out.

The attempts to improve the performance of the radio horn took time. Finally, in 1965, the antenna was re-activated and careful observations were made of the radio flux from the sky. The results revealed that the telescope was performing better than ever, but the mysterious excess signal remained. The intensity of the excess radio noise was what would be expected from an object, or source, with a very low temperature—only a few degrees above absolute zero. In this case, as with the previous observation, the static was not coming from a discrete source but was emanating uniformly from every direction in the sky.

While Wilson and Penzias were trying to make sense of what seemed to them to be a failed experiment, Robert Dicke and his colleagues at Princeton University, unaware of the project at Bell Labs, were building a radio receiver of their own designed to look for the very radiation that Wilson and Penzias had unintentionally observed. Whereas Wilson and Penzias had rather modest hopes of making simple surveys of galactic radio flux, Dicke was looking for physical evidence of the creation of the universe. Dicke had been researching the theoretical effects of the big bang, the expanding fireball theorized as the birth of the universe.

The line of reasoning Dicke followed was this: as the universe expanded after the big bang, gases cooled and thinned but were still dense enough to block electromagnetic radiation. All thermal energy released by atoms, including light and heat, was reabsorbed by other atoms in the gas almost instantly. One consequence of this condition was that if someone could have viewed the universe from the "outside" at this point, they would have seen only blackness, since no light could escape the opaque, light-absorbing gas. Eventually, there must have come a time, thousands of years after the big bang, when the average density of the expanding universe was finally low enough to allow heat and light to escape from atoms unimpeded, much as the light and heat generated in the sun's interior eventually escapes through the sun's transparent photosphere. According to the theory that Dicke was exploring, the rapid release of newly freed energy in the thinning, early universe would have taken the form of an incredibly sudden blaze of heat and light, almost like an explosion.

Hearing the "Echo" of the Big Bang

How could this "primeval fireball," as it came to be called, be observed today? If the remnant of this energy flash had survived after several billion years, it would be detected as a kind of "whisper" in a radio telescope. It would have a specific color and temperature and would be present in nearly equal intensities in every direction, forming a cosmic background radiation. This radiation would flood every available volume of space. In time, the radiation would appear to cool down to a point near absolute zero, due to the further expansion of the universe, but it would still be detectable even in the present-day universe. It was precisely this radiation that Robert Dicke was preparing to look for with his own radio telescope. It was also this radiation, measuring close to absolute zero (around three degrees Kelvin) in uniformity across the sky, that Wilson and Penzias had already discovered.

Wilson and Penzias were not cosmologists, however. They could not explain their observation of the

microwave radiation at the 7.3 cm wavelength, and so they contacted Dicke, who they knew was working on this problem. When Dicke heard the details of their findings, he knew that Wilson and Penzias had discovered exactly what he was looking for; the cold, background radiation left over from the big bang. In 1965, Wilson and Penzias published their results in a paper entitled "A Measurement of Excess Antenna Temperature at 4,080 Mc/s." A companion paper written by Dicke, P. J. E. Peebles, P. G. Roll, and D. T. Wilkinson explained the profound cosmological implications of the finding.

The discovery of the cosmic background radiation was like finding the intact skeleton of a dinosaur. The radiation is a "fossil," an ancient relic from a time when the universe was barely 100,000 years old. The discovery of the radiation was to become the second great pillar upon which the big bang theory would rest, second only to the 1920s discovery of the expansion of the universe. The fact that the background radiation was predicted in advance of its discovery helped to strengthen the big bang theory, so much so that most competing theories about the birth of the universe, such as steady state, almost immediately fell away after 1965.

As scientists around the world began making their own confirming observations of the cosmic background radiation, it became apparent to those searching past research papers that clues to the existence of the radiation had existed for over twenty-five years. The most striking example came from 1938, in which optical telescopic observations revealed that interstellar cyanogen gas was being heated, unaccountably, by a 3 degree source. This source was nothing less than the cosmic background radiation. But at the time, no one imagined that the seemingly innocuous source of heat could be the remnants of the big bang fireball. It would not be until Wilson and Penzias's discovery that the cosmic radiation would be identified for what it was.

Wilson and Penzias's discovery was acclaimed by scientists around the world. Less impressed was the management of Bell labs who, according to Wilson in *Serendipitous Discoveries in Radio Astronomy*, essentially held the point of view, "You guys have been doing radio astronomy full time; the effort is supposed to be sort of half time, let's get on with something for the telephone company." In 1976, Wilson was named head of the Radio-Physics department of Bell Telephone. For his work on the cosmic background radiation he also received the Henry Draper Award, in 1977, from the National Academy of Sciences. In 1978, the importance of their achievement in the history of science was fully recognized when Wilson and Penzias shared the Nobel Prize in physics with Kapitsa.

SELECTED WRITINGS BY WILSON:

Periodicals

"Discovery of the Cosmic Microwave Background," *Serendipitous Discoveries in Radio Astronomy,* edited by K. Kellermann and B. Sheets, National Radio Astronomy Observatory, 1983, pp. 185–95.

SOURCES:

Books

Astronomers, Peter Bedrick Books, 1984, pp. 157–58.
Weinberg, Steven, *The First Three Minutes,* Basic Books, 1988.

—*Sketch by Jeffery Bass*

Adolf Windaus
1876-1959
German organic chemist

Adolf Windaus devoted his professional life to the investigation of the chemistry of natural products. He was awarded the Nobel Prize for chemistry in 1928 for his work on sterols, which led to his clarifying the chemical structure of cholesterol, and he is also noted for his discoveries of the structure of vitamin D, some of the B vitamins, and histamine. The impact of his work made it possible for many other scientists to study the structures of other natural products; for example, his work on cholesterol helped to establish the study of sex hormones. Windaus's research on digitalis was used in the treatment of heart disease, and his studies of vitamin D led to the development of irradiation, a process of exposing foods, such as milk and bread, to ultraviolet light in order to prevent nutritional deficiencies that could lead to disease.

Adolf Otto Reinhold Windaus came from a family of artisans and craftspeople on his mother's side and from weavers and clothing manufacturers on his father's side. He was born in Berlin to Adolf and Margarete (Elster) Windaus on December 25, 1876. In his youth, he attended the French Gymnasium in Berlin, where literature, not science, was the primary area of study. Young Windaus decided to become a physician after reading about the work of French

chemist and microbiologist Louis Pasteur and German physician and microbiologist **Robert Koch**. His mother, who was a widow at the time of his decision, was disappointed, since she had hoped he would continue the long tradition of the family business.

Windaus's career in science began at the University of Berlin in 1895. The chemistry lectures given by **Emil Fischer** there were to be major influences which would shape his future. The physiological applications of Fischer's approach became the foundation of Windaus's investigations. After receiving a bachelor's degree in 1897 from the University of Berlin and abandoning any ideas of pursuing a career in medicine, he continued his studies at the University of Freiburg, where he was influenced by Heinrich Kiliani. Under Kiliani's direction he researched digitalis, which later was found to be a powerful stimulant to the heart and became widely used in the treatment of heart failure. Windaus wrote his dissertation on the chemistry of this substance and received his doctorate in 1899 from Freiburg.

Embarks on the Study of Cholesterol

After a year in military service, Windaus returned to Freiburg to work with Kiliani, turning now to the study of cholesterol. A seroid alcohol present in animal cells and body fluids, cholesterol regulates membrane fluidity and is involved in the process of metabolism. Because it was so widely found in animal cells, Windaus speculated that it must be closely connected with other important compounds. By 1906, he was appointed assistant professor at Freiburg. In 1913, Windaus moved to the University of Innsbruck in Austria to become a professor of applied medical chemistry. Two years later, he was at the University of Göttingen, where he was appointed director of the Laboratory for General Chemistry, succeeding chemist **Otto Wallach**. He remained at Göttingen for twenty-nine years, retiring in 1944.

While Windaus pursued his studies of natural products, a number of other chemists were working in related areas. During his investigation of cholesterol (the best known sterol) and associated substances, **Heinrich Wieland**, a colleague in Munich, was researching the structure of bile acids. By 1919, Windaus was able to show an affinity between sterines, a group of sterols he had established earlier, and bile acids. After this, the work between Wieland and Windaus in both of their laboratories proceeded in close collaboration and led to the clarification of the chemical structure of the sterol ring in 1932.

It was known that rickets could be cured with cod liver oil, which contained vitamin D. Some scientists, such as physiologist Alfred Hess in New York, felt that cholesterol was somehow involved with vitamin activity, which led him to ask Windaus to collaborate in efforts to find the chemical nature of vitamin D.

Windaus's cooperation with scientists in New York and London resulted in the findings of other D vitamins and made Göttingen a center for vitamin research.

The results of the research taking place during the 1920s and 1930s on vitamins made it possible for Windaus to identify and characterize many other compounds formed in the process of the photochemical reactions under study. In 1927, Wieland was given the Nobel Prize in chemistry for his study of bile acids, and Windaus received the same award in 1928 for his discovery of the structure of sterols and their connection with vitamins. Windaus was granted numerous honorary degrees and other awards as well, including the Louis Pasteur Medal of the French Academy of Sciences in 1938 and the Goethe Medal of the Goethe Institute in 1941.

Collaboration Leads to the Discovery of Histamine

During his early work on cholesterol, Windaus also had collaborated with biochemist Franz Knoop. They studied the reaction of sugar with ammonia, hoping that they could convert sugar into amino acids, and possibly do the same for carbohydrates into proteins. This work led to the discovery of histamine, a compound that is significant in allergies and inflammation. Consequently, Windaus became involved with pharmaceutical companies that began to suggest problems for him to solve, and supplied him with much of the materials he needed for his work.

Windaus's work on a B vitamin, thiamine, helped to establish its correct structure and synthesis, while other work involved clarifying the structure of colchicine, a substance used in cancer therapy. Although Windaus abandoned the idea of becoming a physician early in his academic career, his contributions to organic chemistry paved the way for new medical treatments of disease.

Windaus's studies on cholesterol opened new research areas for many other investigators and led to an important branch of organic chemistry and biochemistry. He was considered a valuable collaborator because of the close work he did with chemists in Germany and other countries on natural products. He was generous with his students, giving them both freedom to pursue their research interests and full credit for contributions they made. His influence on other research was considerable. For instance, one of his students, **Adolf Friedrich Johann Butenandt**, presented the structure of sex hormones shortly after Windaus presented the structure of the sterol ring.

Windaus married Elisabeth Resau in 1915 and they had two sons, Gunter and Gustav, and a daughter, Margarete. While he was not sympathetic to the Nazi government during World War II, his reputation made it possible for him to continue his

work without interference. After his retirement in 1944, he did not publish any further research, but a journal on which he had served editorially, the *Justus Liebigs Annalen der Chemie,* dedicated several volumes to him in 1957 in celebration of his eightieth birthday. He died at the age of eighty-two on June 9, 1959, at Göttingen.

SELECTED WRITINGS BY WINDAUS:

Periodicals

"Die Konstitution des Cholesterins," *Nachrichten Gesellschaft d. Wissenschaften,* Göttingen, 1919.
"Anwendungen der Spannugstheorie," *Nachrichten Gesellschaft d. Wissenschaften,* Göttingen, 1921.
"Ultraviolet Bestrahlung von Ergasterin," *Nachrichten Gesellschaft d. Wissenschaften,* Göttingen, 1929, pp. 45–59.
"Chemistry of Irradiated Ergosterol," *Proceedings of the Royal Society* B, Volume 108, 1931, pp. 131–138.

SOURCES:

Books

Gillispie, Charles Coulson, editor, *Dictionary of Scientific Biography,* Scribner, 1970, pp. 443–446.

—*Sketch by Vita Richman*

Niklaus Wirth
1934-
Swiss computer programmer

Computer language pioneer Niklaus Wirth is well-known to anyone who has studied even the basics of computer programming and technology. His contributions to the field of computer language development—in particular, the creation of the programming language PASCAL—have played an important role in shaping the arts of computer design and programming.

Wirth was born on February 15, 1934 in Winterthur, Switzerland to Walter, a geography professor, and Hedwig (Keller) Wirth. He attended the Federal

Institute of Technology (known by the initials ETH) in Zurich, Switzerland, receiving his bachelor's degree in 1958. Moving to Canada, he continued his education with a Master of Science degree in 1960 from Laval University in Quebec. Moving once again, this time to California, he received his doctorate from the University of California at Berkeley in 1963. At the time Wirth received his Ph.D. from Berkeley, nearby Stanford University was assembling its Computer Science Department, and Wirth was offered a position as an assistant professor in the department. There, Wirth and his colleagues developed a host of computer languages, including PL360 and AL-GOL-W. Soon, Wirth had established himself as an expert in computer language development.

The Birth of PASCAL and Structured Programming

In 1967 Wirth moved back to his native Switzerland as an assistant professor of computer science at the University of Zurich. One year later, he accepted a position as a professor of computer science at ETH, his alma mater. Between 1968 and 1970 he developed the computer language PASCAL. Initially, Wirth had not intended for PASCAL to have commercial applications; because the language is so well suited for the microprocessors of today's computer systems, however, it has seen widespread use and development. Phillipe Kahn, an ETH graduate, formed his California-based computer software company around Wirth's language, selling more than a million copies of a modified PASCAL.

In 1971 Wirth introduced the concept of "structured programming," the idea that a program should be designed by dividing it into general but distinct steps, then refining each step until the final product is stripped down to its simplest elements. This concept, while creating quite a stir at the time, has become a standard methodology for most computer program development, and is taught in today's university computer science curriculums. Wirth "changed the way people think about programming," Kahn said in *Business Week*.

By design, structured programming leads to simpler programs. Similarly, Wirth's languages are defined so that programs written with them are easier to read and more bug-free than systems coded in other languages. In today's age of growing reliance upon computer systems, it is critical that those systems be both extremely reliable and user-friendly. Wirth himself traces his respect for simplicity back to his childhood hobby of building model airplanes; in an article in *Business Week*, he was quoted as saying, "If you have to pay [for a model airplane repair] out of your own pocket money, you learn not to make the fixes overly complicated." The journal of the Association of Computing Machinery said in a recent article

that Wirth "has established a foundation for future research in the areas of computer language, systems, and architecture."

Beginning in 1979, Wirth developed the language Modula-2 and later a high-performance computer workstation called "Lilith," designed to utilize Modula-2. More recently, he has finished a new language called Oberon, which he hopes will lead to computer programs that are even simpler and more powerful than those created using PASCAL.

Honors and Awards

Wirth was the chairman of ETH's computer science division from 1982 until 1984 and again from 1988 through 1990; he was also appointed to lead the Institute of Computer Systems at ETH. He holds honorary doctorates from the University of York (England) and the Institute of Technology in Lausanne, Switzerland. He received the Emanuel Priore award from the Institute of Electrical and Electronics Engineers (IEEE) in 1983 and the coveted A. M. Turing award from the Association of Computing Machinery (ACM) in 1984. In 1987 Wirth received the Outstanding Contributions to Computer Science Education award from the ACM. In 1988 he was named a Computer Pioneer by the IEEE Computer Society and he was nominated as a Distinguished Alumnus of the University of California at Berkeley in 1992. Wirth and his wife, Nani Tucker, have three children, Carolyn, Christian, and Tina.

SELECTED WRITINGS BY WIRTH:

Books

Systematic Programming, Prentice-Hall, 1973.
(With Kathleen Jensen) *PASCAL: User Manual and Report,* Springer-Verlag, 1974.
Algorithms and Data Structures: Programs, Prentice-Hall, 1975.
Programming in Modula-2, second corrected edition, Springer-Verlag, 1982.

Periodicals

"Program Development by Stepwise Refinement," *Communications of the ACM,* April, 1971.
"Toward a Discipline of Real-Time Programming," *Communications of the ACM,* August, 1974.
"What Can We Do about the Unnecessary Diversity of Notation," *Communications of the ACM,* November, 1974.
"Niklaus Wirth: 1984 ACM A. M. Turing Award Recipient," *Communications of the ACM,* February, 1985, pp. 159–164.

SOURCES:

Books

Contemporary Authors New Revision Series, Volume 21, Gale, 1986.

Periodicals

Levine, Jonathan, "An Endless Campaign to Simplify Software," *Business Week,* June 15, 1990, p. 136.

—*Sketch by Roger Jaffe*

Evelyn Maisel Witkin
1921-
American geneticist

E velyn Maisel Witkin is a specialist in bacterial mutation who has published more than forty-five papers in journals such as *Proceedings of the National Academy of Sciences, Bacteriological Reviews,* and *The Cold Spring Harbor Symposia of Quantitative Biology.* Her research focused on the genetic effects of radiation, spontaneous and induced mutation in bacteria and the enzymatic repair of DNA damage.

Witkin was born in New York City on March 9, 1921, the daughter of Joseph Maisel and the former Mary Levin. After completing high school, she attended New York University, from which she received her bachelor of arts degree magna cum laude in 1941. She then did her graduate work at Columbia University and received her master of arts degree in 1943 and her Ph.D. in 1947. Between 1947 and 1949 Witkin did postdoctoral research at the American Cancer Society. On July 9, 1943, she was married to Herman A. Witkin, with whom she had two children, Joseph, born in 1949, and Andrew, born in 1952. Witkin's husband died in July of 1979.

Begins Teaching Career

In 1950 Witkin accepted an appointment as a member of the genetics department at the Carnegie Institute in Washington, D.C., a post she held until 1955. She was then appointed to the faculty at the Downstate Medical Center of the State University of New York (SUNY) in Brooklyn. She remained at SUNY until 1971, rising to the rank of professor of medicine. In 1971 Witkin became professor of biolog-

ical sciences at Douglass College of Rutgers University. Eight years later she was named Barbara McClintock Professor of Genetics at Douglass. On her retirement in 1991, she was made Barbara McClintock Professor Emerita.

In addition to her role as a teacher, Witkin also served as editor of the journal *Microbial Genetics* from 1950 to 1964 and as a member of the editorial board of *Mutation Research* since 1960. Among the honors accorded Witkin have been the Prix Charles Leopold Mayer of the French Academy of Sciences in 1977 and the Lindback Award in 1979. She was also elected to membership in the National Academy of Sciences.

SELECTED WRITINGS BY WITKIN:

Periodicals

"UV Mutagenesis and Inducible DNA Repair in *E. Coli,*" *Bacteriological Review,* 1976.
"Overproduction of DnaE Protein (Alpha Subunit of DNA Polymerase III) Restores Viability in a Conditionally Inviable *Escherichia Coli* Strain Deficient in DNA Polymerase I," *Journal of Bacteriology,* Volume 174, 1992, pp. 4166–4168.

—*Sketch by David E. Newton*

Edward Witten
1951-
American mathematical physicist

E dward Witten's work combines physics with advanced mathematical techniques, and he has made major contributions to the field of theoretical physics. Many consider him not only the most brilliant physicist of his generation but a rival to greats such as **Albert Einstein** and Isaac Newton. He is best known for his work on a unified theory of physics called superstring theory, which theorizes that the universe is composed of extremely small particles called strings and posits the existence of ten dimensions.

Witten was born on August 26, 1951, in Baltimore, Maryland. He is the son of Louis W. Witten, a gravitational physicist who is currently at the University of Cincinnati in Ohio. Witten went to a Baltimore Hebrew school as a child and then attended Brandeis University near Boston, Massachusetts. He graduated with a degree in history in 1971, although his real interest was linguistics. After graduation he wrote articles for such publications as the *Nation* and the *New Republic.* In 1972 he worked on George McGovern's campaign for president as an aide to a legislative assistant, but he decided against a career in journalism or politics in favor of returning to school. He was still considering whether to study physics or mathematics when he entered the doctoral program at Princeton University; he earned his master's degree in physics in 1974 and his Ph.D. in 1976.

In 1977 Witten was named junior fellow of the Society of Fellows at Harvard University. Despite receiving several offers from other universities, Witten returned to Princeton in 1980, where he was named full professor in the department of physics at the age of twenty-eight. Although highly respected by his students, Witten's behavior occasionally made him seem otherworldly. Habits such as frequent long pauses for thought during his unusually soft-spoken lectures caused some students at Princeton refer to him as "The Martian."

Witten's early research remained relatively close to traditional physics. He studied electromagnetism, as well as the forces that hold the nuclei of atoms together and the forces responsible for nuclear decay. While a professor at Princeton, Witten excelled in developing new approaches to describing the universe with quantum theory. By 1982 he had become very interested in supersymmetry—a theory which describes how matter and energy particles can be interchanged. In that year he was awarded a MacArthur Fellowship, an honor he earned for his many original theoretical proposals. By the mid 1980s, Witten found himself increasingly drawn to the search for a unified theory in physics, one which would explain all the forces in the universe with a single set of rules. Traditional theories of physics lack a single model that explains all the observed forces in this way.

To search for a unified theory, Witten studied the fundamental building blocks of everything from atoms to the cosmos. He used advanced mathematics, which allowed him to describe these fundamental building blocks using more dimensions than the four used in traditional physics, and in doing so he drew on the work of a number of mathematicians and theoretical physicists who had preceded him. In 1918, a German physicist named Theodor Kaluza attempted to use a fifth dimension to explain inconsistencies between gravity and other laws of nature, particularly electromagnetism. The principal difficulty with Kaluza's theory was that it did not explain why the fifth dimension was not observable. In 1926, the Swedish mathematician Oskar Klein elaborated on Kaluza's theory by explaining a possible reason for failures to find the fifth dimension. He suggested the fifth dimension was so compact or "rolled up" that it

existed, in effect, between subatomic particles and was thus too small to be seen by any known technology. The combination of these two ideas is called the Kaluza-Klein theory, and Witten used it in his effort to develop an understanding of the characteristics shared by all the forces found in nature.

String theory had been proposed earlier in the 1970s as a possible unified theory. String theory differed from traditional theories in two basic ways: the shape of the fundamental building blocks it proposed and the number of dimensions used to describe those blocks. According to theories of physics before quantum theory, the fundamental building blocks are tiny ball-shaped pieces of matter. These particles move in a world which is described with the four traditional dimensions of length, width, depth, and time. Forces such as gravity and electricity cause the particles to move. This view of the universe was revolutionized by quantum theory, which proposed that the fundamental building blocks are really locations where matter and energy become interchangeable. The existence of matter results from fields of energy, energy which exists in varying amounts with varying patterns of resonances. The problem with quantum theory, however, is that it cannot account for gravity, and string theory began as an effort to solve this problem. String theory proposes that the fundamental building blocks are mathematical curves or strings formed into loops and that these shapes can only be described with more than four dimensions. Different vibrations of the strings create the many types of matter and energy found in the universe; an example these theorists use is the way different vibrations of the strings on a musical instrument create many different sounds.

Witten first learned about string theory in 1975, and studying it allowed him to combine his unusual mathematical abilities with advanced theoretical physics. Little attention was given to string theory for many years after its introduction, and Witten played a major role in popularizing it among physicists. One problem with the theory was that it originally proposed the existence of twenty-six dimensions, a concept many physicists found difficult to accept. In the 1970s, two researchers combined string theory and supersymmetry into superstring theory, which only required ten dimensions. However, a ten-dimensional universe still had six dimensions more than most physicists were prepared to believe existed, so string theory remained relatively unpopular. In 1984, Witten wrote an important paper with **Luis Alvarez** which identified new anomalies in certain kinds of radioactive decay. Anomalies are mathematical inconsistencies or theoretical defects that yield unacceptable results. Witten and Alvarez first established that these anomalies were topological, or related to intrinsic geometric shapes. They then showed that the topology of these anomalies could only be studied using ten dimensions but not using four dimensions. A paper written in response to theirs showed how string theory could explain the elements as well.

By 1985 Witten was completely committed to the study of string theory. He became its foremost proponent, writing nineteen papers about the theory in that year alone. Witten also won both the Einstein Medal and the New York Academy of Science's Award for Physics and Math Science in 1985. The following year the National Science Foundation awarded him its Alan T. Waterman Award for his work in elementary-particle physics and its application to cosmology. In an interview with *Scientific American* Witten remarked: "It was very clear that if I didn't spend my life concentrating on string theory, I would simply be missing my life's calling." A number of traditional physicists remain skeptical about the theory, primarily because the existence of ten dimensions is not substantiated by anything except mathematics. But Witten has observed, as quoted in the *New York Times Magazine,* that mathematical consistency has been "one of the most reliable guides to physicists in the last century."

Witten ended his teaching career in 1987 and joined the Institute for Advanced Study at Princeton, where research is the focus. To delve deeper into string theory Witten created a new technique which combined topology and quantum field theory, naming it topological quantum field theory. He applied his technique to the adjacent mathematical field of knot theory as well as to string theory. According to Witten, his discovery of new symmetries in knot theory using topological quantum field theory was his "single most satisfying piece of work." And for this work, Witten shared the Fields Medal, the most prestigious prize in mathematics, in 1990.

Witten is married to Chiara Nappi, who is also a physicist at Princeton University. They have three children. He is active in the Middle East peace movement through the Tel Aviv based International Centre for Peace in the Middle East, and he traveled to Jerusalem in order to attend their Emergency World Jewish Leadership Peace Conference. He is also a board member of Americans for Peace Now.

SELECTED WRITINGS BY WITTEN:

Books

(With M. B. Green and J. H. Schwarz) *Superstring Theory,* Cambridge University Press, 1987.

Periodicals

(With L. Alvarez-Guamé) "Gravitational Anomalies," *Nuclear Physics,* Volume B234, 1984, p. 269.

"Search for a Realistic Kaluza-Klein Theory," *Nuclear Physics,* Volume B186, 1987, p. 412.
"On the Structure of the Topological Phase of Two-Dimensional Gravity," *Nuclear Physics,* Volume B340, 1990, pp. 281–332.
"String Theory and Black Holes," *Physical Review,* Volume D44, 1991, pp. 314–324.
"Three Months Later, A Mixed Bag of Results," *Jewish Post,* April 8, 1993.

SOURCES:

Periodicals

Cole, K. C., "A Theory of Everything," *New York Times Biographical Service,* Volume 18, October, 1987, pp. 1062–1067.
Horgan, John, "The Pied Piper of Superstrings," *Scientific American,* November, 1991, pp. 42–46.
"Muller, Wilczek and Witten Are MacArthur Foundation Fellows," *Physics Today,* December, 1982, pp. 68–70.
"NSF Honors Rabi and Witten, Names Young Investigators," *Physics Today,* September, 1987, pp. 95–96.
Siegel-Itzokovich, Judy, "The Martian," *Jerusalem Post Magazine,* March 23, 1990, pp. 6–8.

—Sketch by David N. Ford

Georg Wittig
1897-1987
German chemist

Organic chemist Georg Wittig's investigations led him to discover in 1953 a chemical process for synthesizing complex compounds such as vitamin A, vitamin D derivatives, steroids, and biological pesticides. Because of this process, known as the Wittig reaction, such compounds can now routinely be synthesized. For his work in organic synthesis, and especially for the Wittig reaction, he shared the 1979 Nobel Prize in chemistry with **Herbert C. Brown**.

Georg Friedrich Karl Wittig was born on June 16, 1897, in Berlin, Germany, to Gustav Wittig, a professor of fine arts at the University of Berlin, and Martha (Dombrowski) Wittig. He went to grade school at the Wilhelms-Gymnasium in Kassel. In 1916 he enrolled at the University of Tübingen, but interrupted his college years to serve in World War I. After moving to the University of Marburg in 1920, he began postgraduate studies in chemistry under the guidance of Karl von Auwers. After receiving his doctorate in 1923, Wittig stayed on at Marburg to teach and do research for many years. In 1932, he became associate professor at the technical university in Brunswick. He went to the University of Freiburg five years later in the capacity of associate professor. In 1944 he was appointed full professor and director of the University of Tübingen's Chemical Institute. After twelve years, he transferred to the University of Heidelberg, where he became emeritus professor in 1967. After retirement, he continued to work and publish with various students at the University of Heidelberg.

Among his peers, Wittig won renown as an original thinker and gifted deviser of experiments. During Wittig's tenure at Tübingen, he and his research team started working with a family of organic compounds called ylides. These compounds formed the basis of the Wittig reaction, which easily and predictably joins two carbon atoms from different molecules to form a double bond. The Wittig reaction's reliability enabled other chemists to pursue and publish findings on thousands of applications for linking large carbon molecules.

Prior to the Nobel Prize, Wittig received many accolades, including the Adolf von Baeyer Medal in 1953, the 1967 Otto Hahn Prize of the German Chemical Society, the 1972 Paul Karrer Medal in Chemistry from the University of Zurich and the 1975 Roger Adams Award from the American Chemical Society. He had also been granted honorary degrees from the universities of Hamburg, Tübingen, and Paris. Wittig married Waltraut Ernst in 1930. Together, they had two daughters. Wittig loved the out-of-doors and was an avid mountaineer. While young, he had shown considerable musical ability. Those who knew him often remarked that he could have had a career in music had his early inclinations led him away from chemistry. Wittig died on August 26, 1987, in Heidelberg at the age of ninety.

SELECTED WRITINGS BY WITTIG:

Books

Stereochemie, Akademische verlag (Leipzig), 1930.

SOURCES:

Books

Nobel Prize Winners, H. W. Wilson, 1987.

—*Sketch by Hovey Brock*

Abel Wolman
1892-1989
American engineer

Abel Wolman was one of the world's foremost sanitary engineers. His career spanned three-quarters of a century. He is perhaps best known for establishing, in collaboration with Linn H. Enslow, the standards for application of chlorine to drinking water now used throughout the world. On the occasion of Wolman's death, John B. Mannion wrote in the *Journal of the American Water Works Association*, "No other chemical application undertaken by man has had the public health benefit of the disinfection of water by chlorine." Wolman influenced generations of students in engineering, public health, and environmental science and was an advisor on water problems to more than fifty foreign governments.

Wolman was born June 10, 1892, in Baltimore, Maryland, to Morris and Rosa Wachsman Wolman. He received a B.A. from Johns Hopkins University in 1913, and a B.S. in engineering there in 1915. In 1937 Johns Hopkins granted him an honorary doctorate in engineering when he accepted the position of professor and chair of the departments of sanitary engineering at both the School of Engineering and the School of Hygiene and Public Health. He continued at Johns Hopkins until 1962. He also taught at Harvard, Princeton, the University of Chicago, and the University of Southern California.

Engineering in the Service of Public Health

Wolman began his career in health services even before completing his engineering degree. In 1913 he conducted pollution studies of the Potomac River in Washington for the U.S. Public Health Service. In 1914 he took a position with the Maryland State Department of Health, serving as chief engineer for the department from 1922 to 1939. He oversaw the formation of the Washington Suburban Sanitary Commission and the consolidation of the Baltimore metropolitan area into a single water supply region, and developed during these years a firm belief in regional solutions to problems of sewerage and water supply.

In 1919 Wolman and former Hopkins classmate Linn H. Enslow published a paper that established standards for the application of chlorine to drinking water. The benefits of using hypochlorite salts to kill bacteria in water had been demonstrated as early as 1896 by George Fuller; however, because no method existed for determining the absorption of chlorine into different kinds of water, it could not be applied to drinking water safely or reliably. Wolman and

Abel Wolman

Enslow devised a formula for calculating the correct amount of chlorine based on particular water conditions and desired qualities. Their methods soon gained universal acceptance.

At the federal level Wolman's advice was sought by the Senate Select Committee on National Water Resources, the House Committee on Science and Astronautics, and the U.S. Geological Survey. At the state level as well, his reputation for careful analysis and his ability always to see the broader impact of policy decisions earned him consultancies to the Tennessee Valley Authority, the Potomac River Commission, and the New Jersey Master Water Plan. Cities around the nation as well as the international community (more than fifty foreign governments, including Brazil, India, and Senegal) benefited from Wolman's knowledge and experience concerning drinking water and waste water systems.

Wolman's expertise guided the National Research Council in its efforts to improve sanitary engineering and environmental health issues in the U.S. military during World War II. When the United Nations was organized after the war, Wolman was chosen to assist the surgeon general of the U.S. Public Health Service in negotiations that established the World Health Organization (WHO). Under his influence the agency broadened its initial mandate to promote health by medical intervention, vaccines, and medicines to include an emphasis on controlling and preventing water-borne disease. Wolman's associ-

ation with WHO was to last the rest of his life. His work with the National Research Council led to a position as consultant to the Department of Defense, and he later became a consultant to the U.S. Atomic Energy Commission. Wolman formulated sanitary engineering guidelines for the commission, and in the 1940s became a member of its advisory committee on reactor safety.

In the 1950s Wolman became uneasy about the environmental impact of the growing nuclear power industry and made his case eloquently to scientists such as **J. Robert Oppenheimer** and **Edward Teller**. It was Wolman who insisted that the first of the commercial nuclear power plants in West Milton, New York, include a concrete containment structure. Toward the end of his life he was increasingly concerned that overpopulation would neutralize the benefits of improvements to the world's water supply and supporting environmental systems, particularly in developing countries.

Wolman's lifelong contributions were recognized with numerous honors and awards, including the Sedgwick Memorial Medal of the American Public Health Association in 1948 and the Albert Lasker Special Award in 1960. In 1967 he received the William Proctor Prize from the Science Research Society of America. He also received the National Medal of Science in 1974 and the Tyler Ecology Award in 1976. He was a member of the American Association for the Advancement of Science, as well as Britain's Faraday Society and Royal Institute of Public Health. He was elected to the National Academy of Sciences in 1963 and to the National Academy of Engineering in 1965. In 1983 Wolman held his last organizational position as honorary president of the Pan American Health and Education Foundation.

Wolman was editor-in-chief of the *Journal of the American Water Works Association* from 1920 to 1937 and editor of the *Journal of the American Public Health Association, Manual of Water Works Practice,* and *Municipal Sanitation.* He contributed more than 135 papers to professional journals.

Wolman married Anne Gordon on June 10, 1920, and had one son, Markley Gordon. He enjoyed playing the violin, often accompanied by his wife on the piano. Wolman died on February 22, 1989, at the age of ninety-six. Steven Muller, president of Johns Hopkins University, told the *New York Times,* "I can think of no other Johns Hopkins faculty member and alumnus who has touched so many lives around the globe with his life's work."

SELECTED WRITINGS BY WOLMAN:

Books

(With Arthur E. Gorman) *The Significance of Waterborne Typhoid Fever Outbreaks: 1920–1930,* Williams & Wilkins, 1931.

(Contributor) William L. Thomas, editor, *Man's Role in Changing the Face of Earth,* University of Chicago Press, 1956, p. 807–816.

Water, Health, and Society: Selected Papers, edited by Gilbert F. White, Indiana University Press, 1959.

Present and Prospective Means for Improved Reuse of Water, U.S. Government Printing Office, 1960.

(Contributor) *Cities,* Knopf, 1965, pp. 156–174.

Periodicals

"Wanted: A National Water Policy," *State Government,* Volume 19, September, 1946, pp. 215–217, 239.

"Basic Principles of a National Water Resources Policy: Committee Report," *Journal of the American Water Works Association,* Volume 49, July, 1957, pp. 825–833.

SOURCES:

Books

Cohen, Harry, and Itzhak J. Carmin, *Jews in the World of Science,* Monde, York, 1956, p. 258.

McGraw-Hill Modern Scientists and Engineers, Volume 3, McGraw, pp. 344–345.

Periodicals

"Abel Wolman; Helped Perfect Water Purification Technique," *Los Angeles Times,* February 24, 1989, part 1, p. 22.

Sullivan, Walter, "Prof. Abel Wolman, 96, Is Dead; Led Efforts to Chlorinate Water," *New York Times,* February 24, 1989, p. B4.

Valentine, Paul W., "Pushing 96, His Creativity Flows; Wolman Still a Water Science Titan," *Washington Post,* January 9, 1988, p. M1.

—Sketch by Kelly Otter Cooper

Harland G. Wood
1907-1991
American biochemist

Harland G. Wood is best known for his work in demonstrating how carbon dioxide is used by heterotrophic as well as autotrophic organisms. An autotroph is any organism that requires only inorganic compounds (carbon dioxide and metals, for example) for nutrition (most plants are autotrophs). Heterotrophs need organic compounds in the form of amino acids, carbohydrates, or vitamins. All animals and some plants are heterotrophs. In collaboration with the scientist C. H. Werkman, Wood proved that carbon dioxide was more than merely a by-product for heterotrophs.

Wood was born in Delavan, Minnesota, on September 2, 1907, the son of William Clark and Inez Goff Wood. He attended Macalester College in St. Paul, Minnesota, from which he received a B.A. in chemistry and mathematics in 1931. He did his graduate work at Iowa State University and received his Ph.D. in 1935. Upon his graduation, Wood began his collaboration with Werkman, and the two demonstrated that carbon dioxide is used by propionic acid bacteria, which are heterotrophic. (Propionic acid is used as a mold inhibitor in bread.) By measuring oxidation levels in controlled experiments, the two scientists were able to determine that some carbon dioxide was in fact used by the organism. This finding was significant because up until then scientists had maintained that the primary distinction between autotrophs and heterotrophs was that only autotrophs could use carbon dioxide.

Wood was named a National Research Council fellow at the University of Wisconsin in 1936, where he and biochemist **Edward Lawrie Tatum** conducted research to prove vitamin B_1 is a requirement for growth of bacteria. He returned to Iowa State University, where he conducted research until 1943. He then joined the faculty of the physiology department at the University of Minnesota. In 1946 he moved on to Case Western Reserve University in Cleveland, Ohio. He remained there for the rest of his career.

Helps Validate Krebs Cycle

During these years Wood was hard at work collaborating with Werkman and several other scientists on a variety of experiments. In the early 1940s, Wood's experimentation with carbon isotopes helped prove the validity of the Krebs cycle and the critical role that carbon dioxide plays in that process. (The Krebs cycle is a series of enzymatic reactions that occur within cells whose ultimate function is to break down glucose to release energy.) Wood and his colleagues attempted to determine how carbon dioxide fit into the equation. The British scientist A. B. Hastings discovered carbon dioxide fixation (the transformation from a volatile to a stable state) while Wood and his colleagues were doing similar research. Sir **Hans Adolf Krebs** noted in his memoirs, *Reminiscences and Reflections,* that Wood "missed the discovery of carbon dioxide fixation ... by a hair's breadth." But Wood was able to show how various chemicals reacted on the basis of the by-products they created, and his research showed carbon dioxide is an essential element of the cycle.

Up to this point, all of Wood's experiments with labeled carbon had been done in a laboratory setting. He wanted to prove that the same results could be obtained through experimentation not only with lab specimens but also with living, normal animals. Using rats and then cows, he and his colleagues conducted experiments with labeled carbon, acetate, propionate, butyrate, lactate, and other chemicals. The results, when compared with similar experiments done on lab specimens, proved that laboratory culture experiments are an accurate reflection of what occurs in animal metabolism.

Wood's later career focused on enzymology. He worked to isolate enzymes to discover new sources of energy in organisms. He showed that enzymes can have more complex reactions than scientists had previously believed. He also worked to show that adenosine triphosphate (ATP), a key source of energy in the Krebs cycle, is not the only energy source used by cellular organisms.

Acts As Advisor to Several Organizations

Upon his arrival at Case Western, Wood chaired the biochemistry department. He became dean of sciences in 1967. He served as president of the American Society of Biological Chemists in 1959 and general secretary of the International Union of Biochemistry from 1970 to 1973. He also served on the advisory committee of the American Cancer Society from 1965 to 1969 and the President's Scientific Advisory Committee from 1968 to 1971. He received a Fulbright fellowship in 1955 and a Guggenheim fellowship in 1962.

His later years brought him many honors, notably the President's National Medal of Science in 1989 and the William C. Rose Award in 1990. He also received three honorary degrees, the last coming from Case Western Reserve in 1991. He remained active and vigorous, conducting lab research and meeting with other scientists until his death.

Wood married Mildred Lenora Davis in 1929; the couple had three daughters, one of whom predeceased them. Outside the lab, he was an avid sportsman. The family actually developed a forty-acre deer camp in Minnesota, where Wood hunted, fished, and canoed in his spare time. He learned to ski at the age of fifty-five. Wood died of lymphoma in Cleveland on September 12, 1991, and was buried in Mankato, Minnesota.

SELECTED WRITINGS BY WOOD:

Books

"Then and Now," in *Annual Review of Biochemistry,* Volume 54, 1985, pp. 1–41.

SOURCES:

Books

Krebs, Hans with Anne Martin, *Reminiscences and Reflections,* Clarendon Press, 1981.

Periodicals

Cleveland Plain Dealer, September 13, 1991, p. C4.

—*Sketch by George A. Milite*

Joseph Woodland
1921-
American engineer and inventor

Joseph Woodland is a mechanical engineer who spent 35 years with the IBM corporation. In the late 1940s, he conceived and patented what later became Universal Product Code (UPC) symbols. While with IBM, he was instrumental in the practical development of this system. which has become an integral part of everyday life. Norman Joseph Woodland was born in Atlantic City, New Jersey, on September 6, 1921, to Lewis Woodland and Lena Peiken. His father was a successful businessman who developed a furniture outlet into a chain of discount stores; his mother was involved in the business as well, eventually becoming the chain's buyer for women's sportswear. Lewis Woodland was an inquisitive, inventive man as well as an entrepreneur, and his son developed his own love of invention from helping his father in their workshop at home.

College and the Manhattan Project

The younger Woodland graduated from high school in 1939. He decided not to follow his father into business, but found other employment opportunities scarce in depression-struck Atlantic City. Instead, he moved to Philadelphia where he enrolled at the Drexel Institute of Technology (later called Drexel University). He joined the Army Reserve at the beginning of World War II, and was called into active duty in 1942.

The Army enrolled him in a crash course at the University of Maryland, then sent him to Oak Ridge, Tennessee, where he was involved in the top-secret Manhattan Project. Woodland spent the next three years as Technical Assistant to the Unit Chief of the

"Liquid Thermal Diffusion Project," which separated the uranium isotope U–235 to be used as fissionable material in the atomic bomb. Woodland returned to Drexel after his discharge, and graduated in 1947; after graduation, he accepted a short-term teaching position.

The Conception of Bar Codes

While Woodland was teaching at Drexel, an electrical engineer named Bob Silver came to him and repeated a conversation he had just overheard in the Dean of Engineering's office. "The president of a supermarket chain [Sam Friedland, president of Food Fair] was trying to interest the Dean in undertaking a project that would enable them to automatically capture item prices at the front end of the store," recalls Woodland. "The Dean turned it down because, as I recall, it wasn't in Drexel's charter to undertake that kind of research and development work."

Silver thought it was a great opportunity and asked Woodland how they might go about it. Woodland devised a way to use several colors of fluorescent pigment and an ultraviolet light to encode product prices on the packages. Woodland and Silver constructed the device, proved to themselves that it had some limited potential, then put it aside.

That might have been the end of the matter. Woodland, however, was attending some graduate-level courses in business administration, and one of his assignments was to analyze the investment potential of a local company. In the course of his research he learned that Atlantic City Electric Company's stock was badly undervalued, and showed promise of dramatically increasing in value in the next few months. With borrowed money he bought all the stock he could, doubling his investment in less than a year. This windfall gave Woodland the freedom to pursue the opportunity he and Silver had seen. He resigned his faculty position at the end of the term, moved to Florida, and stayed in his grandfather's apartment while he continued his research.

It was already apparent that his original idea of multicolored codes was not feasible. As a youngster he had learned Morse code, in which data is encoded in dots and dashes. He pondered the idea of stretching the dots and dashes into bars, then shining light on the printed code and using an optical scanner to "read" the information. To make the code omni-directional, he shaped the lines into concentric circles, like a bullseye.

Woodland returned to Philadelphia where he carefully documented his findings. He knew, however, that a product code, however practical, was of little value without a decoder. So before applying for a patent on his code, he enlisted Silver's aid in developing the hardware they needed for a complete system.

On October 20, 1949, they jointly applied for a patent; that patent, for a "Classifying Apparatus and Method," was awarded on October 7, 1952.

To their mutual shock, Woodland and Silver found that the very supermarket people who had originally expressed the need were not interested in their invention. The system still needed a lot of development, and none of the supermarket chains wanted to take that plunge. But Woodland knew he had a viable approach to supermarket checkout automation. What he needed was a company with the financial resources to make it happen.

Begins Work at IBM

After researching several companies, he joined IBM's facility at Endicott, New York. Though IBM was not involved with product coding and knew nothing of Woodland's work, he hoped for a chance to change that. For a time Woodland worked on an IBM military contract, developing an electromechanical airborne computer. (This was before digital electronic computers were widespread, or small enough to fit in even a large airplane.) When Tom Watson, Jr. became president of IBM, Woodland sent him a letter of congratulations which also contained detailed plans for an automated supermarket checkout system. Watson was intrigued, and put Woodland in touch with W. W. McDowell, who headed IBM's research & development activity.

McDowell was also interested, and asked that Woodland be moved out of the project to which he had been assigned. For several years little development was done on supermarket scanners; during this time, Woodland designed a bar code scanner at home, a project which took several years. Meanwhile, he took night classes at nearby Syracuse University, receiving his Master's degree in mechanical engineering in 1956.

In 1959 Woodland finally got his chance to head a full-scale development project for a supermarket scanner when IBM conducted a pilot study in conjunction with an Atlanta supermarket chain. Using a scanner built into the supermarket counter, the device scanned a bar code symbol attached to the bottom of market items. The scanner worked, but it had severe limitations. For one thing, the light source—a 500 watt incandescent bulb—produced far too much heat, and provided a very shallow field of focus. Also, the electronics needed for decoding and inventory control (which depended upon thousands of individual transistors) were far too costly for large-scale use. Woodland reluctantly concluded that the concept behind his device was too far ahead of the available technology, and he suggested that his idea be shelved until the necessary scanning light and electronics could become available. Ironically, IBM did not agree at first; they hired a California firm called Stanford Research, Inc.

to critique the work to date. They eventually endorsed Woodland's recommendation, and the project was shelved.

Scanning Technology Becomes Available

In 1962, after rejecting two IBM offers as too low, Woodland and Silver sold their patent to Philco. It expired in 1969, and the technology came into the public domain. Shortly after that, RCA put on an exhibition of bullseye-shaped bar codes at a major supermarket trade show. An IBM executive who knew of Woodland's work watched in dismay as crowds flocked to the RCA booth. The very next day, IBM management tracked Woodland down and assigned him to the revitalized project.

A number of important factors had changed in the twelve years since IBM had shelved Woodland's invention. Low-cost integrated circuit chips and readily-available helium neon lasers provided the needed technology boost. Also, in 1970 the National Association of Food Chains had formed a committee to study product codes for inventory control, and in 1971 the food industry settled on a bar code configuration based largely on Woodland's original concentric circles.

When Woodland got involved the first thing he did was cast doubt on their choice of configurations. Having more experience with bar code configurations than anyone in the world, Woodland had learned the fundamental flaws of the bullseye. When asked what was wrong with it, he replied, "It was a very good idea when I invented it back in 1949." They did not believe they were speaking to the original inventor until he produced a copy of his patent. From then on, as he recalled, "I think I really had them in my hand. I really got their attention." Woodland sold the grocery industry on a parallel-line bar code, and the UPC symbol was launched.

In his 35 years with IBM, Woodland held many senior assignments in mechanical and optical design, system development, long-range planning, and most recently artificial intelligence and expert systems—a field he grew interested in during his final years with IBM. Since his retirement in 1987 he has continued his research, and along with a collaborator is working on a development which he says he is quite excited about, and which he hopes to patent shortly. He has lectured at his alma mater, Drexel University, where in 1992 he was elected to the "Drexel 100," being one of the 100 most distinguished Drexel graduates. He has received other honors for his work as well, including IBM's Outstanding Contribution Award (1973) in appreciation for development of the UPC symbol, and the National Medal of Technology (1992) by President George Bush.

SOURCES:

Periodicals

Regardie's Magazine, December, 1990, pp. 42–58
Supermarket News, December, 28 1992, p. 81

—*Sketch by Joel Simon*

Robert B. Woodward
1917-1979
American organic chemist

Robert B. Woodward was arguably the greatest organic synthesis chemist of the twentieth century. He accomplished the total synthesis of several important natural products and pharmaceuticals. Total synthesis means that the molecule of interest— no matter how complex—is built directly from the smallest, most common compounds and is not just a derivation of a related larger molecule. In order to accomplish his work, Woodward combined physical chemistry principles, including quantum mechanics, with traditional reaction methods to design elaborate synthetic schemes. With Nobel Laureate **Roald Hoffmann**, he designed a set of rules for predicting reaction outcomes based on stereochemistry, the study of the spatial arrangements of molecules.

When Woodward won the Nobel Prize in chemistry in 1965, the committee cited his contributions to the "art" of organic synthesis. Upon Woodward's acceptance of the award, Bartlett, Westheimer, and Buchi wrote in *Science,* "Woodward's style is polished, showing an insight and sense of proportion that afford him strong convictions and a well-developed dramatic sense. In the laboratory, identifications and structural assignments must be complete, spectra exact, compounds not merely pure but beautifully crystallized, or he will not accept them. His lectures, given without notes or slides, are elegantly organized and illustrated with artistic blackboard formulas, with the key atoms shown in color. . . . Most of the polish comes naturally to a man with such intellectual vitality."

Robert Burns Woodward was born in Boston on April 10, 1917, to Arthur and Margaret (Burns) Woodward. His father died when he was very young. Woodward obtained his first chemistry set while still a child and taught himself most of the basic principles of the science by doing experiments at home. By the time he graduated at the age of sixteen from Quincy High School in Quincy, Massachusetts, in 1933, his

Robert B. Woodward

knowledge of chemistry exceeded that of many of his instructors. He entered the Massachusetts Institute of Technology (MIT) the same year but nearly flunked out a few months later, apparently impatient with the rules and required courses.

The MIT chemistry faculty, however, recognized Woodward's unusual talent and rescued him. They obtained funding and a laboratory for his work and allowed him complete freedom to design his own curriculum, which he made far more rigorous than the required one. Woodward obtained his doctorate degree from MIT only four years later, at the age of 20, and then joined the faculty of Harvard University after a year of postdoctoral work there.

Woodward spent virtually all of his career at Harvard but also did a significant amount of consulting work with various corporations and institutes around the world. As is true in most modern scientific endeavors, Woodward's working style was characterized by collaboration with many other researchers. He also insisted on utilizing the most up-to-date instrumentation, theories, and other available tools, which were sometimes looked upon with suspicion by more traditional organic chemists. He was known as an intense thinker, personally reserved and imperiously confident of his intellectual skills. His graduate students, however, still found ways to joke with him; one Halloween, noticing that he virtually always had the same color tie, office, and car, they painted his parking space "Woodward blue."

Contributions to the Theories of Synthesis

The design of a synthesis, the crux of Woodward's work, involves much more than a simple list of chemicals or procedures. Biochemical molecules exhibit not only a particular bonding pattern of atoms, but also a certain arrangement of those atoms in space. The study of the spatial arrangements of molecules is called stereochemistry, and the individual configurations of a molecule are called its stereoisomers. Sometimes the same molecule may have many different stereoisomers; only one of those, however, will be biologically relevant. Consequently, a synthesis scheme must consider the basic reaction conditions that will bond two atoms together as well as determine how to ensure that the reaction orients the atoms properly to obtain the correct stereoisomer.

Physical chemists postulate that certain areas around an atom or molecule are more likely to contain electrons than other areas. These areas of probability, called orbitals, are described mathematically but are usually visualized as having specific shapes and orientations relative to the rest of the atom or molecule. Chemists visualize bonding as an overlap of two partially full orbitals to make one completely full molecular orbital with two electrons. Woodward and Roald Hoffmann of Cornell University established the Woodward-Hoffmann rules based on quantum mechanics, which explain whether a particular overlap is likely or even possible for the orbitals of two reacting species. By carefully choosing the shape of the reactant species and reaction conditions, the chemist can make certain that the atoms are oriented to obtain exactly the correct stereochemical configuration. In 1970 Woodward and Hoffmann published their classic work on the subject, *The Conservation of Orbital Symmetry;* Woodward by that time had demonstrated repeatedly by his own startling successes at synthesis that the rules worked.

Organic Synthesis Work Leads to Nobel Prize

Woodward and his colleagues synthesized a lengthy list of difficult molecules over the years. In 1944 their research, motivated by wartime shortages of the material and funded by the Polaroid Corporation, prompted Woodward—only twenty-seven years old at the time—and William E. Doering to announce the first total synthesis of quinine, important in the treatment of malaria. Chemists had been trying unsuccessfully to synthesize quinine for more than a century.

In 1947 Woodward and C. H. Schramm, another organic chemist, reported that they had created an artificial protein by bonding amino acids into a long chain molecule, knowledge that proved useful to both researchers and workers in the plastics industry. In 1951 Woodward and his colleagues (funded partly by Merck and the Monsanto Corporation) announced the first total synthesis of cholesterol and cortisone, both biochemical steroids. Cortisone had only recently been identified as an effective drug in the treatment of rheumatoid arthritis, so its synthesis was of great importance.

Woodward's other accomplishments in synthesis include strychnine (1954), a poison isolated from *Strychnos* species and often used to kill rats; colchicine (1963), a toxic natural product found in autumn crocus; and lysergic acid (1954) and reserpine (1956), both psychoactive substances. Reserpine, a tranquilizer found naturally in the Indian snake root plant *Rauwolfia,* was widely used to treat mental illness and was one of the first genuinely effective psychiatric medicines. In 1960, after four years of work, Woodward synthesized chlorophyll, the light energy capturing pigment in green plants, and in 1962 he accomplished the total synthesis of a tetracycline antibiotic.

Total synthesis requires the design and then precise implementation of elaborate procedures composed of many steps. Each step in a synthetic procedure either adds or subtracts chemical groups from a starting molecule or rearranges the orientation or order of the atoms in the molecule. Since it is impossible, even with the utmost care, to achieve one hundred percent conversion of starting compound to product at any given step, the greater the number of steps, the less product is obtained.

Woodward and Doering produced approximately a half a gram of quinine from about five pounds of starting materials; they began with benzaldehyde, a simple, cheap chemical obtained from coal tar, and designed a seventeen-step synthetic procedure. The twenty-step synthesis that led to the first steroid nucleus required twenty-two pounds of starting material and yielded less than a twentieth of an ounce of product. The best synthesis schemes thus have the fewest number of steps, although for some very complicated molecules, "few" may mean several dozen. When Woodward successfully synthesized chlorophyll (which has an elaborate interconnected ring structure), for example, he required fifty-five steps for the synthesis.

Woodward's close friend, Nobel Laureate **Vladimir Prelog**, helped establish the CIBA-Geigy Corporation-funded Woodward Institute in Zurich, Switzerland, in the early 1960s. There Woodward could work on whatever project he chose, without the intrusion of teaching or administrative duties. Initially, the Swiss Federal Institute of Technology had tried to hire Woodward away from Harvard; when it failed, the Woodward Institute provided an alternative way of ensuring that Woodward visited and worked frequently in Switzerland. In 1965 Woodward and his Swiss collaborators synthesized Cephalosporin C, an important tantibiotic. In 1971 he succeeded in synthesizing vitamin B_{12}, a molecule bearing some chemical

similarity to chlorophyll, but with cobalt instead of magnesium as the central metal atom. Until the end of his life, Woodward worked on the synthesis of the antibiotic erythromycin.

Woodward, who received a Nobel Prize in 1965, helped start two organic chemistry journals, *Tetrahedron Letters* and *Tetrahedron,* served on the boards of several science organizations, and received awards and honorary degrees from many countries. Some of his many honors include the Davy Medal (1959) and the Copley Medal (1978), both from the Royal Society of Britain, and the United States' National Medal of Science (1964). He reached full professor status at Harvard in 1950 and in 1960 became the Donner Professor of Science. Woodward supervised more than three hundred graduate students and postdoctoral students throughout his career.

Woodward married Irji Pullman in 1938 and had two daughters, Siiri and Jean. He was married for the second time in 1946 to the former Eudoxia Muller, who had also been a consultant at the Polaroid Corporation. The couple had two children, Crystal and Eric. An inveterate smoker and coffee-drinker, his only exercise was an occasional game of softball. Woodward died at his home of a heart attack on July 8, 1979, at the age of 62.

SELECTED WRITINGS BY WOODWARD:

Books

(With Roald Hoffmann) *The Conservation of Orbital Symmetry,* VCH Publishers, 1970.

SOURCES:

Periodicals

Bartlett, P. D., F. H. Westheimer, and G. Buchi, "Robert Burns Woodward, Nobel Prize in Chemistry for 1965," *Science,* October 29, 1965, p. 585.

"Robert Woodward Is Dead at Age 62," *Chemical and Engineering News,* July 16, 1979, p. 6.

"Synthesis, General Approach Bring Nobel Prize," *Chemical and Engineering News,* November 1, 1965, p. 38.

—*Sketch by Gail B. C. Marsella*

George M. Woodwell
1928-
American ecologist

From the uproar in the 1960s over the insecticide dichlorodiphenyltrichloroethane (DDT), through the debate in the 1990s over global warming, American ecologist George M. Woodwell has been involved in nearly every environmental controversy of the late twentieth century. "I'm a citizen," Woodwell explained in a November, 1993, interview with Cynthia Washam, "and citizens have a role in steering the democracy." Woodwell has taken an active role in ecological issues throughout his career, holding such positions as founder of the Environmental Defense Fund, founding member of the Natural Resources Defense Council, president of the Ecological Society of America, founding trustee of the World Resources Institute, and chair of the World Wildlife Fund. Through his frequent articles and speeches, he has taken his plea to conserve the Earth's resources to politicians, fellow scientists, and laypeople.

While known to the general public as an activist, Woodwell also has earned the respect of his scientific colleagues. Walter Orr Roberts, director emeritus of the National Center for Atmospheric Research in Colorado, has stated that Woodwell "is characterized by solid scientific work that goes into tough issues with total objectivity," as cited by Denise Grady and Thomas Levenson in *Discover*. Woodwell has received four honorary doctoral degrees, won several scientific awards, and served on the editorial boards of three scientific journals. His research has focused on ecosystems, or communities of plants and animals and their environment, and he consistently delves into controversial issues that have significant implications for public policy, using the results of his research to support his activism.

Woodwell traces his interest in ecology to his childhood. Born October 23, 1928, in Cambridge, Massachusetts, he developed an appreciation of nature at his family's farm in Maine, where he spent his summers. There, along with his parents, Philip and Virginia (Sellers) Woodwell, both high school teachers, the young Woodwell cultivated potatoes, made maple syrup, and assisted neighbors on their farms. In 1946 Woodwell began his formal education in ecology at Dartmouth College, where he earned a bachelor's degree in botany in 1950. He joined the U.S. Navy as a lieutenant shortly after graduating and served for three years before returning to academia. While studying for his master's degree at Duke University, Woodwell met fellow graduate student Alice Katharine Rondthaler, who later dropped out of the program. In 1955 the couple married, and eventually

they had four children: Caroline, John, Marjorie, and Jane. In 1956, Woodwell completed his master's degree in botany at Duke, and received his doctorate two years later. In the late 1950s he returned to New England as an assistant professor of botany at the University of Maine in Orono, and for several years he taught introductory ecology.

DDT Research Prompts Activist Role

During this time, Woodwell became involved in a project that changed the course of his career. He had been asked by the privately funded Conservation Foundation to study the effects of DDT on Maine forests. At first, he supported the use of the popular pesticide. He changed his mind a short time later, however, when he discovered that only about one half of the DDT sprayed on crops and forests actually settled on the soil—the rest was scattered by the wind. This drifting pesticide made its way into the food chain, as eagles, pelicans, ospreys, and other birds ate contaminated fish, then laid eggs with shells that were too fragile to survive. In 1966, Woodwell, along with some of his colleagues, filed the first of a series of lawsuits calling for a ban on the use of DDT. Their efforts eventually led to the Environmental Protection Agency's ban on the insecticide in 1972. The experience made Woodwell realize the value of taking environmental issues to court. To support further litigation, he founded the Environmental Defense Fund in 1967, which has become a thriving conservation law organization with more than two hundred thousand members. He also helped a group of Yale University law students establish the Natural Resources Defense Council.

By the early 1960s, Woodwell had left his post at the University of Maine to become an assistant scientist at Brookhaven National Laboratory in Upton, New York. At Brookhaven, he conducted an experiment that is recognized as a major contribution to ecological research. He planted radioactive cesium–137 in the center of a fourteen-acre oak and pine forest, and for the next eighteen years studied the radiation's effect on the ecosystem. The forest died in systematic stages: First the pine trees died, then the oaks, and then later the shrubs and grasses. Finally, only some mosses, bacteria, and lichens (plants made up of algae and fungi) were left. His experiment proved that the most sensitive species in an ecosystem died first and that only the most resistant ones survived. It also showed that, when under stress, a community could die in a much smaller amount of time than it had taken to develop.

Founding of Ecosystems Center Leads to Research into Deforestation

The ecologist eventually decided his opportunities for ecological research were limited at the physics laboratory, and in 1975 he left to establish the Ecosystems Center at the Marine Biological Laboratory in Woods Hole, Massachusetts. Woodwell's first major project there was studying sources of carbon dioxide in the atmosphere. Carbon dioxide is a greenhouse gas; in other words, it traps the sun's heat and contributes to dangerous global warming. Woodwell learned that atmospheric carbon dioxide is produced not only by industrial and auto emissions, but also when forests are burned or plowed under: When trees are destroyed, he found, they release the carbon dioxide they normally absorb. Woodwell concluded that deforestation increases atmospheric carbon dioxide in two ways—first, by releasing carbon dioxide, and second, by destroying the forests' ability to absorb the gas. These findings prompted Woodwell to publicly condemn the destruction of the Earth's forests and call for drastic cuts in carbon dioxide emissions. "There's no chance that people will continue on an Earth that continues to warm," he told Washam. "It's important to see that the warming does not proceed. We would control it by reducing the use of fossil fuels by sixty percent and by stopping deforestation." Woodwell has taken his plea to the U.S. Congress several times, but has seen no action. The government's apparent reluctance to take strong steps to save the environment has been his greatest frustration. Still, he persists in fighting for conservation. In 1983, he served as chair of an international conference on the biological effects of nuclear war. There, he succeeded in gaining a consensus among more than one hundred scientists, who ultimately agreed that even a small-scale nuclear war would cause temperatures to drop below zero for months, a phenomenon called nuclear winter. In addition, in the early 1990s, Woodwell proposed the creation of an International Commission on the Conservation and Utilization of World Forests to stem the global destruction of forests. He had the support of several countries, including the United States. "I have no doubt the commission will exist," he told Washam. "The question is when."

Establishes Ecology Research Center

In 1985, Woodwell decided to leave the Ecosystems Center in order to develop his own ecology institute: the Woods Hole Research Center. With funding from federal grants and private foundations, the non-profit center focuses on the ecological impact of toxic waste, air pollution, deforestation, and other major environmental threats. Woodwell, as the director, uses the results of the center's studies to support his demand for an end to environmental destruction.

Woodwell's involvement with ecological issues has been recognized several times by his peers as well as by environmental organizations. In 1975, he garnered the Green World Award from the New York Botanical Garden, and in 1982 he received a Distinguished Service Award from the American Institute of Biological Sciences. He was elected to the National Academy of Sciences in 1990, won the Dartmouth College Class of 1950 Award in 1991, and received the Hutchinson Medal from Garden Clubs of America in 1993. He also has been awarded honorary doctorates from Williams College, Miami University, Carleton College, and Muhlenberg College.

While calling for action from industry and government, Woodwell takes care to monitor his own influence on the health of the planet. He walks to work every day and often travels around the village of Woods Hole on his bicycle. Several years ago, he and his son erected a twenty-eight-foot high structure containing more than twenty solar panels in order to heat the water in their home. Though Woodwell rarely takes a break from his work, he enjoys spending any free time on his boat, whose source of power is simply the wind.

SELECTED WRITINGS BY WOODWELL:

Books

(Editor) *Diversity and Stability in Ecological Systems,* Brookhaven National Laboratory, 1967.
(Editor with Erene Pecan) *Carbon and the Biosphere: Proceedings,* DOE, 1973.
(Editor) *The Earth in Transition: Patterns and Processes of Biotic Impoverishment,* Cambridge University Press, 1991.
(Editor with F. T. MacKenzie) *Biotic Feedback in the Global Climatic System: Will the Warming Feed the Wakening?,* Oxford University Press, 1993.
(Editor with Kilaparti Ramakrshna) *Forests for the Future: Their Use and Conservation,* Yale University Press, 1993.

Periodicals

"Global Deforestation: Contribution to Atmospheric Carbon Dioxide," *Science,* December 9, 1983, pp. 1081–86.
"Global Climatic Change," *Scientific American,* April, 1989, pp. 36–44.
"Do the Right Thing," *Natural History,* May, 1990, pp. 84–85.
"Forests, Scapegoats and Global Warming," *New York Times,* February 11, 1992, p. A25.

SOURCES:

Books

Ehrlich, Paul R., *Healing the Planet: Strategies for Solving the Environmental Crisis,* Addison-Wesley, 1992.

Hardin, Garrett, *Living within Limits: Ecology, Economics, and Population,* Oxford University Press, 1993.

Kennedy, Paul M., *Preparing for the Twenty-First Century,* Random House, 1993.

Periodicals

Grady, Denise, and Thomas Levenson, "George Woodwell: Crusader for the Earth," *Discover,* May, 1984, p. 44.

Raeburn, Paul, "George Woodwell: A Practical Man of Great Conviction," *Sunday Telegram,* January 5, 1986.

Other

Woodwell, George M., interview with Cynthia Washam, conducted November 24, 1993.

—Sketch by Cynthia Washam

Stephen Wozniak
1950-
American electronics engineer

Stephen Wozniak, along with **Steven Jobs**, co-founded Apple Computer, Inc., and developed one of the most popular personal computers ever marketed. His contributions to Apple were almost exclusively technical—Jobs pushed the marketing potential of the Apple, while Wozniak provided the engineering know-how.

Wozniak's father, Jerry, was a Lockheed engineer, and his mother, Margaret, was president of a local Republican women's club. Young Wozniak grew up in Sunnyvale, a suburban development located in the Santa Clara Valley, now known as Silicon Valley. He was surrounded by the technological wizardry that grew out of Sputnik and the race for space. His parents provided a stable, close-knit environment.

Wozniak was an early devotee of electronics and in the fifth grade created a voltmeter from a kit. His interest in science and engineering led to a number of homemade devices: a ham radio, a makeshift electronic tic-tac-toe game, a calculator. By the time he entered Homestead High School, Wozniak had learned so much about the theory and practice of electronics that he became a prize student in the school's electronics courses.

When Wozniak met Steven Jobs in 1968, Wozniak was an accomplished student of electronics, although largely self-taught. Having flunked out of the University of Colorado, he was back home constructing a computer with a friend who also knew Jobs. Both Wozniak and Jobs took summer jobs at Hewlett-Packard, and Wozniak later returned to Hewlett-Packard after dropping out of Berkeley.

Early Work in Computer Design Leads to the Apple II

Together with Jobs, Wozniak spent the early years of the 1970s heavily immersed in the burgeoning computer culture of Silicon Valley, particularly among the hobbyists and video game enthusiasts who were to become the first market for the personal computer. Both young men belonged to the Homebrew Computer Club, a Bay Area users' group that sprang up during the personal computer revolution of the mid-seventies.

This revolution would not have been possible without the development of the microprocessor in 1970 and the later discovery by hobbyists that this inexpensive silicon chip not only shrank the size of the computer but also shrank its price tag. The January 1975 issue of *Popular Electronics* announced the first computer kit, the Altair 8800, using an Intel 8080 microprocessor. Orders from hungry computer enthusiasts poured in—despite the fact that there seemed to be little to do with the computer once it was assembled.

In 1976, Wozniak, who was unable to afford the Altair, took the personal computer revolution a step further by constructing a computer out of a cheaper microprocessor and adding several chips for memory. The result was a naked circuit board, without case, keyboard, or screen, which was able to outperform the Altair. The Apple I formed the basis for the future Apple Computer, Inc. Steven Jobs marketed the crude computer through contacts from the Homebrew club.

The next step was the construction of a computer with a keyboard and color video display. Wozniak's engineering emphasized power and meticulous design. He was able to extract both speed and power out of relatively few chips. By fall 1976, Wozniak and Jobs were able to display their newest computer at a national computer fair. Their new machine attracted attention, although it clearly needed refinement. With Jobs's marketing efforts, Apple Computer, Inc., began to grow. In 1977, Wozniak, who had left Hewlett-Packard to work full time at Apple, completed the technical design of the Apple II.

The Apple II was the first personal computer that could be bought ready-made "off the shelf." Its success was due in part to its sleek design and its ability to accept "add-ons," such as music synthesizers, modems, and enhanced graphics. By 1978, Wozniak had incorporated a floppy disk drive into the

Apple II, replacing the cassette tapes that had previously stored information. Using a floppy drive, the user could retrieve information in seconds. With this addition, and the availability in 1979 of VisiCalc, a spreadsheet program, the Apple II became a multimillion dollar success. In 1980, when Apple Computer, Inc., went public, sales stood at $117 million; in 1983, they reached $985 million.

Reaffirms Democratic Values in Computing

Although Wozniak's association with Apple Computer left him a multimillionaire (in 1980, his stock in Apple was worth $88 million), his interest never wavered from the electronics and technical side of the business. He shared with Jobs a vision of democratic computing and believed that computers should be accessible to ordinary people. Early in his design career, he recognized the need for user-friendly software; by the late 1970s, the Apple II provided a growing market for software programs, especially in the educational field.

In 1981, Wozniak was piloting a single-engine plane near his home when it crashed on take-off. He was hospitalized and suffered amnesia. His convalescence lasted two years, during which time he became involved in New Age ventures, providing financial backing for two large music festivals near Los Angeles.

He returned to Apple in 1983, working as an engineer in the Apple II division. Despite the company's successes, its position within the personal computer market was being threatened by IBM. In the next tempestuous years at Apple, Wozniak remained aloof from corporate infighting. In January 1985, he (along with Jobs) was presented with the National Technology Award by President Reagan for his work at Apple. During that month, he resigned from the company to found a new operation called "CL–9 Inc." ("Cloud 9"), which produced remote control devices. The operation shut its doors in 1989.

Wozniak's life after Apple included several business ventures. He became involved in the Electronic Frontier Foundation, founded by Mitch Kapor (developer of Lotus), a user group dedicated to preserving First Amendment rights in the computer and communications fields. With his third wife and their six children, he built an elaborate home with mock caverns and prehistoric carvings in Los Gatos, California. After his retirement from Apple, he returned to the University of California at Berkeley and attained his bachelor's degree in computer science and electrical engineering.

SOURCES:

Books

Butcher, Lee, *The Accidental Millionaire: The Rise and Fall of Steve Jobs at Apple Computer,* Paragon House, 1988.
Garr, Douglas, *Woz,* Avon, 1984.
Rose, Frank, *West of Eden,* Viking, 1989.

Periodicals

Alexander, Michael, "Kapor Group Lines Up for Rights Fight," *Computerworld,* July 16, 1990, p. 6.
Dalglish, Brenda, "Wonder Boys Hit Middle Age," *Maclean's,* May 11, 1992, pp. 36–37.

—*Sketch by Katherine Williams*

Almroth Edward Wright
1861-1947
English bacteriologist

Almroth Edward Wright made several significant contributions to science and is perhaps best known for introducing a vaccination against typhoid fever. Developed near the turn of the twentieth century, the vaccine was used on British soldiers during World War I and was responsible for saving many lives. The disease only claimed the lives of 1,191 British soldiers, instead of a projected 125,000 without the vaccination, according to estimates outlined in Leonard Colebrook's biography, *Almroth Wright: Provocative Doctor and Thinker.* Numerous honors were bestowed upon Wright for his scientific work, including a knighthood and election as a Fellow of the Royal Society of London, both of which were awarded in 1906.

Wright was born August 10, 1861, in Middleton Tyas, Yorkshire, England. He was the second son of Reverend Charles Henry Hamilton and Ebba Johanna Dorothea (Almroth) Wright. His father was an Old Testament scholar and a militant protestant. His mother was the daughter of a chemistry professor who was also governor of the Royal Mint in Stockholm. In his early years Wright was educated by tutors and lived in Germany and France where his father worked as a minister. Eventually, the family settled in Ireland, and Wright received his university education at Trinity College in Dublin, earning a degree in modern literature in 1882 and a degree in medicine in 1883.

Winning a traveling scholarship to the University of Leipzig in Germany, Wright studied medicine there for a year.

Wright then returned to England, and was a bit unsure as to whether the future direction of his career led to literature or medicine; he soon decided to read law, and after two years took the civil service exam. Eventually Wright's interest in science took precedence over his other pursuits. After securing a fairly non-demanding position at the Admiralty in 1885, he also immediately began working evenings at the Brown Institution (University of London) as a science researcher on a volunteer basis. Wright was next offered a demonstratorship in the department of pathology at Cambridge in 1887, then soon after transferred to the department of physiology. Upon working in Germany for several months, Wright accepted a demonstratorship at the University of Sydney, in Australia, in 1889. That same year Wright married Jane Georgina Wilson, with whom he had two sons and a daughter.

In 1892 Wright was offered the chair of the pathology department at the Army Medical School in Netley, England. This was the first time Wright worked close to patients, and he claimed the atmosphere was productive since it never allowed the scientist to become too far removed from the ultimate goal of his work, which was to cure the sick. It was at this time Wright began his research on the phenomenon of blood coagulation, eventually linking clotting time to the presence of calcium in the blood. Laboratory instruments during this period were generally crude and home-made, so Wright—a pioneer in laboratory testing—made his own, developing and producing capillary tubes large enough to hold only a few drops of blood. These instruments could test blood without the necessity of drawing a great deal of it from a patient; all that would be required was a finger prick. Wright also recognized the importance of uniformity in laboratory testing, so he made sure each tube was identical.

Wright discovered that if blood was clotting too slowly, giving the patient a dose of calcium by mouth would speed up the process. Conversely, if clotting occurred too quickly, he found administering citric acid to the patient slowed it down. These same principles were also applied to a situation Wright was experiencing at home. Wright's young child seemed to experience distress when fed cow's milk; upon testing, Wright found cow's milk to have a greater concentration of calcium with harder, thicker clots than breast milk. Adding citrate of soda to the milk made the clots softer and thinner, rendering the milk easier for his child to digest, and thus decreasing digestive pains. Wright then tried feeding lemons to the family cow to see if it would change the concentration of calcium in the milk produced. The cow did not

respond, but the housekeeper by this point had had enough and turned in her resignation.

Begins Work on Typhus

Near the turn of the century typhoid fever had a death rate of ten to thirty percent. Although the disease had been partially eradicated with better sewage handling, Wright did not think this would eliminate the problem and believed these methods would break down during a war. Wright wanted to test the effects of injection with a heat-killed typhoid culture, to see if it would produce antibodies. He found it did, but there was what he termed a "negative phase"—a period of one to two days where antibodies seemed to decrease. Nonetheless, he believed his vaccine would be beneficial and set out trying to convince medical authorities of its merits. Wright convinced the War Office committee to set up an experimental situation, using military units over a three year period. Frequencies of inoculation and instances of typhoid records were measured, and in 1909 very positive results were published: Colebrook relates in *Almroth Wright* that deaths per 1,000 inoculated soldiers were 0.38, while for uninoculated were 3.93.

In 1906, prior to the publication of the typhoid inoculation results, Wright had been knighted and elected to Fellow of the Royal Society. After this success, he turned his lab over to serum production, so the vaccination would be available. Wright also wrote a long letter to the editor of the *New York Times* urging mandatory inoculation of troops. In 1914, only British troops entered World War I fully inoculated.

In the midst of his typhoid work, Wright had changed positions in 1902, from his professorship at the Army Medical School at Netley to pathologist and professor of pathology at St. Mary's Hospital in London. In 1911, Wright traveled to South Africa to help produce a pneumonia inoculation for the men who were working in the mines. The system Wright developed to inoculate the miners resembled the one he instituted earlier to fight typhus.

During World War I Wright served in France as head of a research lab which worked primarily on wound infections. Wright developed at this time a method using a hypertonic salt solution to draw lymph into open wounds (lymph is a fluid derived from blood and which contains lymphocytes, a type of white blood cell which repels infection). Wright also developed a scientific basis for early wound closure, or suturing, which was not in practice up until that time. Several citations were presented to Wright after World War I, including a special medal of the Royal Society of Medicine in 1920 which credited him with providing the best medical work during the war.

Engages in Philosophical Debate

Wright's direct influence on scientific research seemed to taper off after World War I. His indirect influence was felt for many years, however, as several of his students went on to great fame, including **Alexander Fleming**, the scientist who discovered penicillin. For Wright this era was more a time for reflection and what Colebrook describes in *Almroth Wright* as the scientist's "search for truth".

Among the reasons contributing to Wright's declining influence may be his rather unpopular views. The treatise *The Unexpurgated Case Against Woman Suffrage,* for example, attempted to demonstrate the intellectual and psychological inferiority of women. Although the playwright George Bernard Shaw disagreed with this claim, he was, nevertheless, an admirer of Wright; the lead character in Shaw's play *The Doctor's Dilemma* is modeled after Wright, and the idea for the play came from the many discussions the writer shared with Wright as well as other members of the medical profession.

Wright published over 150 papers during his career. He advanced the truly scientific component of research to a great degree due to his insistence on the use of the scientific method, which involves several steps, including the formation of a hypothesis and the testing and confirmation of that hypothesis. Commonly accepted now, the scientific method was a revolutionary idea during Wright's time.

Wright continued his work at St. Mary's Hospital until 1946 and died shortly after in Buckinghamshire, England, on April 30, 1947. Wright was working—literally to the end—on a philosophical work *Alethetropic Logic* (in Wright's words, "a system of Logic which searches for the Truth"), which was published posthumously through the efforts of his grandson.

SELECTED WRITINGS BY WRIGHT:

Books

Principles of Microscopy, Constable, 1906.
Studies in Immunization, Constable, 1909.
The Unexpurgated Case Against Woman Suffrage, Constable, 1913.
Technique of the Teat and Capillary Glass Tube, Constable, 1921.
Alethetropic Logic, Heinemann, 1953.

SOURCES:

Books

Colebrook, Leonard, *Almroth Wright: Provocative Doctor and Thinker,* Heinemann, 1954.

Colebrook, Leonard, *Bibliography of the Published Writings of Sir Almroth E. Wright,* Heinemann, 1952.
Cope, Zachary, *Almroth Wright: Founder of Modern Vaccine-Therapy,* Thomas Nelson, 1966.

Periodicals

Mummest, R. T., "Sir Almroth Wright, K.B.E., C.B., F.R.S." (obituary), *Nature,* May 31, 1947, pp. 731–732.

—Sketch by Kimberlyn McGrail

Jane Cooke Wright
1919-
American physician

Jane Cooke Wright has carried on the medical legacy of her prominent family through a career in internal medicine, cancer research, and medical education. She has served as director of the Cancer Research Foundation of Harlem Hospital in New York City, faculty member and director of cancer chemotherapy at the New York University Medical Center, and professor of surgery and associate dean at New York Medical College and its affiliate hospitals. Wright has also devoted her efforts to educating fellow practitioners about advances in chemotherapy, a service she performed in her 1983 convention lecture to the National Medical Association entitled "Cancer Chemotherapy: Past, Present, and Future".

Wright was born in New York City on November 20, 1919, to Louis Tompkins and Corinne (Cooke) Wright. Her paternal grandfather was one of the first graduates of Tennessee's Meharry Medical College, an institution founded to give former slaves professional training. Another relative, **Harold D. West**, was Meharry's first black president. Her step-grandfather, William Penn, was the first black person to earn a medical degree from Yale. Her father, **Louis Tompkins Wright**—one of the first black graduates of Harvard medical college—was the first black physician to be appointed to the staff of a New York City hospital; he was also a pioneer in cancer chemotherapy, and New York City's first black police surgeon. Jane Cooke Wright was the first of two daughters; her sister, Barbara, also became a physician.

Wright was educated in private elementary and secondary schools and won a four-year scholarship to Smith College in Massachusetts, where she set records as a varsity swimmer. Graduating in 1942, Wright entered New York Medical College, again on a four-year scholarship, and received her medical degree with honors in 1945. An internship and assistant residency followed at Bellevue Hospital in New York City. After leaving Bellevue Hospital, she completed her training with a two-year residency in internal medicine at Harlem Hospital.

Wright's first position after residency was as a school and visiting physician at Harlem Hospital in 1949. She became a clinician later that year at the hospital's Cancer Foundation, which was then headed by her father. There she studied the response of tumors and growths to drugs and the application of chemotherapy in the treatment of cancer. She explored the complex relationships and variations between test animal and patient, tissue sample and patient, and individual patient responses to various chemotherapeutic agents. Upon her father's death in 1952, she became the Cancer Foundation's director.

In 1955, Wright joined the New York University Medical Center to direct the cancer chemotherapy research department and teach research surgery. Her continuing research explored animal and human responses to chemotherapeutic agents (such as triethylene thiophosphoromide, CB 1348 and Dihydro E. 73) and isolation perfusion and regional perfusion chemotherapy techniques. In 1961, Wright became adjunct professor of research surgery at the medical center and also served as vice-president of the African Research Foundation, a position which took her on a medical mission to East Africa. In 1964, she was appointed to the President's Commission on Heart Disease, Cancer, and Stroke; the commission's work resulted in a nationwide network of treatment centers for these diseases. The Albert Einstein College of Medicine presented Wright with its Spirit of Achievement Award in 1965.

Wright became associate dean and professor of surgery at New York Medical College in 1967, where she was also responsible for administrating the medical school and developing a program for the study of cancer, heart disease, and stroke. She was awarded the Hadassah Myrtle Wreath in 1967, and the Smith College medal in 1968. In December, 1975, Wright was one of eight scientists saluted by *Cancer Research* in its observation of International Women's Year, and in 1980 was featured on an Exceptional Black Scientists poster by Ciba Geigy. Since 1987, she has been emerita professor of surgery at New York Medical College.

Wright has served on the editorial board of the *Journal of the National Medical Association* and as a trustee of Smith College and of the New York City division of the American Cancer Association. She married David D. Jones, Jr., a graduate of Harvard Law School, on July 27, 1947; the couple have two daughters, Jane and Alison. Her hobbies include sailing, painting, and reading mystery novels.

SELECTED WRITINGS BY WRIGHT:

Periodicals

"Cancer Chemotherapy: Past, Present, and Future" *Journal of the National Medical Association,* August, 1984, pp. 773–784; September, 1984, pp. 865–876.

SOURCES:

Books

Blacks in Medicine and Science, Hemisphere, 1990, p. 258.
Notable Black American Women, Gale, 1992, pp. 1283–1285.

—*Sketch by Jane Stewart Cook*

Louis Tompkins Wright
1891-1952
American surgeon and hospital administrator

Louis Tompkins Wright, one of the first black graduates of the Harvard Medical School, was a distinguished surgeon, hospital administrator, and civil rights activist. His talents and determination as a black leader improved access to quality health care for black people and the professional prospects of his fellow African American medical practitioners. During Wright's prolonged affiliation with Harlem Hospital in New York City, he became the hospital's surgical director and founded its Cancer Research Center. An active member of the New York City chapter of the National Association for the Advancement of Colored People (NAACP), Wright ultimately chaired its national board of directors, holding that position from 1934 until his death.

Wright was born on July 23, 1891, in La Grange, Georgia. He was the younger son of Ceah Ketcham and Lula Tompkins Wright. His father, a doctor who practiced for only a short period before becoming a clergyman, died in 1895; in 1899, his mother married William Fletcher Penn, also a physician. Wright enrolled in Clark University in Atlanta, where he was valedictorian of the class of 1911. After being subjected to a special examination, Wright was accepted by the Harvard Medical School, where he was to graduate *cum laude* and fourth in his class in 1915. After a two-year internship at Freedmen's Hospital in Washington, D.C., he briefly joined his stepfather's practice in Atlanta.

In 1917, in the midst of World War I, Wright entered the U.S. Army Medical Corps, and was eventually appointed director of surgical wards for an Army field hospital in France. While in France, he was exposed to phosgene gas, which caused him permanent lung damage. For his military service, Wright was awarded the Purple Heart and discharged at the rank of captain, later achieving the rank of lieutenant-colonel in the U.S. Medical Reserve Corps through examination. When Wright returned from France in the spring of 1919, he settled into private practice in New York City.

Association with Harlem Hospital

Shortly thereafter, the Medical Board of Harlem Hospital was persuaded by Civil Service Commissioner Ferdinand Q. Morton to admit Wright and some other black physicians as provisional adjunct surgeons. A few white doctors on the staff of the hospital (whose clientele was then a prosperous white community) resigned in protest, but Wright quickly established himself professionally. In 1926, he was granted a permanent appointment at the hospital. A few years later, in addition to his hospital commitments, he began his service as surgeon for the New York City Police Department, a post he held for more than twenty years. In 1943, he was named director of Harlem Hospital's Department of Surgery. In 1948, he became president of the medical staff board and director of the hospital's Cancer Research Foundation, and founded the *Harlem Hospital Bulletin.*

Wright's contributions to medicine were various. Early in his career, while an intern at Freedmen's Hospital, he was critical of the medical establishment's belief that the Schick test for diphtheria (which, for diphtheria susceptible individuals, reddens the skin where injected) was not useful on black patients; his research proved this supposition to be without basis. He originated an intradermal smallpox vaccination method that minimized undesirable side effects. Wright directed the research team that first tested the antibiotic aureomycin for the treatment of venereal disease, and also conducted research with the antibiotic terramycin; he was to publish over thirty papers on aureomycin and eight papers on terramycin. Wright invented several surgical devices, including a brace for cervical fractures and a plate used in repairing fractures of the knee. His research into skull and brain injuries led to the first authoritative publication in this area by a black doctor. His cancer research, which led to fifteen publications, focussed

on the use of teropterin, triethylene melamine, folic acid, and hormones in chemotherapy. Throughout his career, moreover, Wright opposed various forms of medical discrimination, such as efforts to establish segregated medical facilities (including a segregated Veterans Hospital) in New York. Another achievement was fostering solidarity and harmony among Harlem Hospital's ethnically diverse medical staff.

In 1934, Wright became the second black doctor to be admitted to the American College of Surgeons. He received an honorary doctorate from Clark University in 1938, and was awarded the NAACP's Spingarn Medal in 1940. In 1952, he was honored by the John A. Andrews Memorial Hospital of the Tuskegee Institute in Alabama. Wright held membership in numerous professional associations in addition to the American College of Surgeons, including the American Medical Association, the National Medical Association, and the American Board of Surgery; he was also a founding member of the American Academy of Compensation Medicine. In connection with his civil rights activism, he served as president of the Crisis Publishing Company, printers of the *Crisis,* which was to become the official organ of the NAACP.

Wright married Corinne Cooke in 1918. They had two daughters: **Jane Cooke Wright**, a physician who became director of the Cancer Research Foundation on her father's death; and Barbara Penn Wright, also a physician. Wright died of a heart attack on October 8, 1952. The Louis T. Wright Medical Library at Harlem Hospital had been established in his honor that same year; in 1969, the Louis T. Wright Surgical Building at Harlem Hospital was dedicated in his memory.

SELECTED WRITINGS BY WRIGHT:

Books

"Head Injuries," Chapter 22 of *The Treatment of Fractures* (11th edition), edited by Charles L. Scudder, W. B. Saunders, 1938.

SOURCES:

Books

Blacks in Medicine and Science, Hemisphere, 1990, p. 259.
Dictionary of American Negro Biography, W. W. Norton, 1982, pp. 670–671.
Scientists in the Black Perspective, The Lincoln Foundation, 1974, pp. 105–107.

Periodicals

New York Times, October 9, 1952, p. 31.

—*Sketch by Jane Stewart Cook*

Sewall Wright
1889-1988
American geneticist

During his long and productive life, Sewall Wright achieved international standing in the disciplines of experimental physiological genetics, which is the study of heredity, as well as quantitative evolutionary biology. He made significant contributions to the fields of genetics, zoology, biometrics (the use of statistics to analyze biological data) and animal breeding but is best known for his comprehensive theory of evolution, the so-called "shifting-balance" theory (which accounts for the spread of certain gene combinations within a population). This theory changed the way scientists think about evolution and took a more mathematical and analytical approach to population genetics. Wright's work brought serious statistical analysis to the forefront of biological science and touched off a long-running debate about the nature of animal species development.

Wright, the oldest of three children, was born on December 21, 1889, to Philip Green Wright, a college professor, and Elizabeth Quincy (Sewall) Wright. When he was seven years old, he wrote a small booklet he called "The Wonders of Nature," a hand-sewn volume printed in capital letters. The precocious Wright spent only five years in grade school as his learning was supplemented at home by his intellectual parents. In 1902, he entered Galesburg High School in Illinois, where he excelled at languages, especially Latin and German. The courses that intrigued him most, however, were algebra, geometry, and physics, all of which he would put to good use in later years. He graduated fifth in his class in 1906, having achieved a grade-point-average of 98.35. Wright then attended Lombard College in Galesburg, where his father was employed. His original intention was to continue the study of languages, but the language professors were not up to Wright's high standards. He enrolled in several classes taught by his father, including general mathematics and economics and a course on the fiscal history of the United States. In his senior year, Wright took two biology classes from Wilhemine Key, who introduced him to the relatively new discipline of theoretical biology and to **R. C.**

Punnett's groundbreaking article, "Mendelism," which had just appeared in the eleventh edition of *Encyclopaedia Britannica*. Key steered Wright toward graduate study in biology and set up an internship in zoology for him at Columbia University's Cold Spring Harbor laboratory on Long Island, New York. After graduating from Lombard College in 1911, Wright spent the summer at Cold Spring Harbor, where he studied marine invertebrates. While there, he also met a number of influential geneticists and began to take an interest in the field.

With the help of a modest state scholarship, Wright moved on to the University of Illinois and received his M.S. in zoology in 1912. The same year, he attended a lecture by the prominent Harvard zoologist, W. E. Castle, who spoke of his selection and mammalian genetics experiments in hooded rats. Castle's work centered on the notion that Mendelian factors, such as recessive and dominant traits, were sometimes variable. He later altered this view, but his experiments seemed to indicate that certain genetic combinations could yield unexpected results. Intrigued by these ideas, Wright signed on as Castle's personal assistant and graduate student.

Introduction to Guinea Pigs Sparks Evolutionary Investigations

In addition to his doctoral classwork, Wright also worked at Harvard's Bussey Institution, a biological research facility, helping Castle maintain a colony of hooded rats and working with other researchers to develop a guinea pig colony. Wright had learned about the genetics of guinea pigs while at Cold Spring Harbor, and Castle assumed that Wright would eventually use the colony for his own research. Wright thought the guinea pig was a valuable research animal, despite the fact that they are disease prone, relatively large and cumbersome, and have long reproductive cycles. At that time, no one knew exactly how many chromosomes the guinea pig had and a number of questions remained about their inheritance patterns; Wright's work with the guinea pig would continue until 1961 and answer many of these questions. His first major finding occurred in 1914, when he discovered a series of four alleles (a series of two or more genes that can occupy the same position on a chromosome) that produced various effects on coat and eye color. Over the next forty years, he would study the inheritance factors of color patterns, hair direction, digit size, and abnormalities in guinea pigs. When Wright received his Sc.D. in zoology from Harvard in 1915, his dissertation was entitled *An Intensive Study of the Inheritance of Color and of Other Coat Characters in Guinea Pigs, with Especial Reference to Graded Variations.*

In 1915, Wright accepted a position as senior animal husbandman at the U.S. Department of

Agriculture (USDA) in Washington, D.C. Inheriting an extensive inbreeding study of guinea pigs (which the USDA had begun in 1906), Wright was charged with analyzing the mountains of data generated by this on-going experiment. To make his task easier, he developed a mathematical theory of inbreeding in 1920, the methods of which were published in 1921 under the title *Correlation and Causation.* Wright's early work with Castle had led him to the notion that interaction systems between genes had important implications for evolution and that inbreeding in small populations led to variation within a given species. His mathematical theory enabled him to quantify the effects of inbreeding, and he used this theory extensively during the next ten years.

Wright spent the summer of 1920 at Cold Spring Harbor, where he met Louisa Williams, then an instructor at Smith College in Massachusetts. She had earned her master's degree from Denison University while working under Harold Fish, who had been Wright's colleague at the Bussey Institution. Despite a congenital hip problem, she, like Wright, enjoyed long walks and equally long conversations. She had come to Cold Spring Harbor to help Fish set up a rabbit colony for genetic research and, because of similar interests, became one of Wright's close friends. The two began dating that summer, Wright's first romantic relationship of any kind. The couple married on September 10, 1921, and moved to Washington. They had two sons over the next four years, Richard and Robert.

Wright left the USDA in 1925 and accepted a position in the department of zoology at the University of Chicago, where he would remain until 1954. During the late 1920s, Wright refined his ideas on evolution and developed a more comprehensive theory. He believed that the "random drift" of genes due to inbreeding and the isolation of small groups within a species were important factors in the evolution of any species. These ideas led to his often spirited, life-long scientific debate with geneticist **Ronald A. Fisher**, who proposed that natural selection worked best in large populations in which more mutant genes—genes in which the hereditary material has changed—were available. Fisher believed that each population had a complex gene structure and that many genes affected each characteristic. He postulated the idea of the population as a "gene pool" in which gene frequency was determined by natural selection.

Debate with Fisher Leads to "Shifting-Balance" Theory

When Fisher's *Genetical Theory of Natural Selection* appeared in 1930, Wright reviewed the book, pointing out several errors and stating his overall objections to the theory. The two corresponded and

agreed on some common points, but never reached a consensus. In 1931, Wright published a long paper describing in detail his own evolutionary theory, which he called the "three-phase shifting-balance" theory. The three phases were (1) random gene-frequency drift within subpopulations, (2) increase of the preferred combination of genes or what has become known as mass selection, and (3) the dispersal of the preferred gene combination throughout the population.

During the early 1930s, as Wright's reputation grew, his theory attracted worldwide attention. As a result, he was elected to membership in the American Philosophical Society (1932), the National Academy of Sciences (1934), and the Genetics Society of America (1934). He was asked to serve on a number of scientific boards and was sought out as a guest lecturer and reviewer. He received numerous requests from researchers to perform quantitative data analysis on their experimental data. His work with Russian-born geneticist **Theodosius Dobzhansky**, then at the California Institute of Technology, helped further the cause of quantitative genetics. Dobzhansky used Wright's mathematical methods and conclusions to develop an extension of Wright's own evolutionary theory. In 1937, Dobzhansky published *Genetics and the Origin of the Species,* which set the research agenda in population genetics for decades to come.

During the 1940s Wright divided his research between physiological genetics and theoretical population genetics, becoming one of the most respected scientists in the nation as more and more researchers began to grasp the importance of his theories. He was awarded nine honorary doctorates over the next thirty years and also received the National Academy of Sciences Daniel Giruad Elliot Award and Oxford University's Weldon Memorial Medal. During this period, Wright authored a series of papers which argued that genes were responsible for replicating and coding the enzymes (complex proteins which facilitate bio-chemical reactions) that determine an organism's physiology. He continued his genetic experiments with guinea pigs, but the 1947 discovery of DNA—the molecular components of heredity—moved the field more toward the realm of molecular biology; when Wright retired from the University of Chicago in 1954 and moved on to the University of Wisconsin in Madison, he left his guinea pigs behind. It took him years to analyze the cumulative data from these experiments and his final papers on inbreeding in guinea pigs did not appear until 1961.

For the next twenty-five years Wright worked on his massive *Evolution and the Genetics of Populations,* a four-volume text that explained the history of genetics in minute scientific and mathematical detail. These volumes contributed to Wright's growing status. In recognition of his remarkable achievements in genetics and quantitative evolution, he received the

National Medal of Science in 1967, the Darwin Medal of the Royal Society of London in 1980, and the Balzan Prize in 1984. His wife, Louisa, died of pneumonia in 1975. During the 1980s, he continued his habit of taking long, vigorous walks and retained his interest in the sciences. Although he began to lose his vision in 1980, he continued to read vociferously with the aid of a magnifying closed-circuit television device. Wright's last paper appeared in 1988 in *American Naturalist,* one of his favorite outlets, when he was ninety-nine years old.

Wright's work had a profound effect on evolutionary biology. In 1991, geneticists M. J. Wade and C. J. Goodnight published an account of an experiment that simulated Wright's shifting-balance theory. They separated a common base population of flour beetles into a series of small subpopulations, produced a migrant pool, and introduced migrants into various groups. The results of this experiment, which were published in *Science,* indicated that Wright's shifting-balance theory was credible and could work under certain favorable conditions. But, like most theories, the shifting-balance idea probably cannot be proven one hundred percent correct. It remains, however, one of the most intriguing evolutionary theories and a lasting testament to Wright's genius.

SELECTED WRITINGS BY WRIGHT:

Books

Evolution and the Genetics of Populations, four volumes, University of Chicago Press, 1968–1978.

Periodicals

"Duplicate Genes," *American Naturalist,* Volume 48, 1914, pp. 638–639.
"The Effects in Combination of the Major Color Factors of the Guinea Pig," *Genetics,* Volume 12, 1927, pp. 530–569.
"Evolution in Mendelian Populations," *Genetics,* Volume 16, 1931, pp. 97–156.

SOURCES:

Books

Provine, William B., *Sewall Wright and Evolutionary Biology,* University of Chicago Press, 1986.

Periodicals

Crow, James F., "Was Wright Right?" *Science,* 1991, Volume 253, p. 973.

—*Sketch by Tom Crawford*

Wilbur Wright
1867-1912
Orville Wright
1871-1948
American inventors and aviators

Wilbur and Orville Wright were inventors with little formal training who are best remembered for inventing the first heavier-than-air, engine-powered passenger flying craft. They not only invented the airplane, but some of the systems we use for flight control today. Had it not been for a bit of over-control of his craft, Wilbur Wright might have been the one who actually flew first, instead of Orville. The brothers were insatiably curious and tenacious tinkerers, two qualities which were vital in overcoming the obstacles to flight posed at the time of their endeavors. They also had a unique partnership as evidenced by this assessment of their relationship by Wilbur Wright, as cited in their *Papers:* "From the time we were little children my brother Orville and myself lived together, played together, worked together and, in fact thought together."

Born the third of five children, Wilbur was born on April 16, 1867, near Millvale, Indiana, with Orville following on August 19, 1871, in Dayton, Ohio. Their parents, Milton and Susan Catharine Koerner Wright, married in 1859 while she was a student and he an instructor at Hartsville College in Indiana. Milton was also pastor of a local church and later rose to become Bishop of the United Brethren Church. It was in 1878 that Bishop Wright brought home a novel toy for his children—a miniature toy helicopter. Wilbur and Orville were fascinated by the toy and how it flew. This sparked the love for aviation that would eventually be their life's undertaking.

From Recluse and High School Dropout to Bicycle Businessmen

Among other things, Wilbur was a keen athlete who loved to compete, excelling at gymnastics. At the age of eighteen, however, his face was smashed with a hockey stick. Wilbur suffered the loss of most of his upper teeth and several lower ones. Even though a lot of medical and dental reconstruction work was done, Wilbur's health suffered significantly. For a long time thereafter, he endured stomach trouble and claimed to suffer heart ailments as well. After his injury, Wilbur became rather reclusive, tending to his mother, who had tuberculosis, and rarely going far from home.

Nonetheless, Wilbur did finish high school, although he opted not to attend graduation ceremonies.

Orville didn't even finish his education, having become bored with school in his senior year. Afterward, Wilbur studied Greek and trigonometry and read voraciously. Orville also loved reading and tinkering with printing presses, building bigger ones whenever he felt the need. In the late 1880s, Wilbur assisted Orville in several journalistic ventures, acting as both editor and humor essayist for the *West Side News* and *The Evening News,* which Orville launched from their home using the printing presses he had built.

Then in 1892, the brothers bought two new "safety bicycles." The bicycles were considered new because of their chain-driven gearing and wheels which were the same size. The bikes were quite different from the unwieldy two-wheelers of this period. The Wrights became enamored not only of the sport aspect of bicycling, but of the business aspect, too. Within one year, they opened their own bicycle outlet and repair shop. Business was good, and by 1896, the Wrights were making their own bikes, including the eighteen dollar Wright Special. Within the first year, Orville ended his journalism career to devote full time to the bicycle shop.

Gears Shift into Aviation Research

August of 1896 brought the tragic crash in which German glider pilot Otto Lilienthal died. Lilienthal was a leading aviation pioneer at the time, having made numerous glider flights and having published tables showing lift on wings of different camber, or curvature. His death caught the Wrights' attention, and rekindled their interest in aviation. The Wright Cycle Company did a brisk business in the spring, summer and early fall, but little during winter. Nonetheless, the business brought in enough money to see the Wrights comfortably through winter, so it was during that season that they started seriously tinkering with the idea of flight.

Being methodical, the Wrights' first steps were to examine all of the current literature on flying. Most of this was done by Wilbur, to the extent that he even wrote to the Smithsonian Institution for information; the Smithsonian at that time was headed by Samuel Pierpoint Langley, another aviation pioneer. They also studied the flights of French-American aviator Octave Chanute, as well as those of Lilienthal. Several things struck Wilbur and Orville as they researched flying: there was very little actual data, and not enough emphasis on flight control. Wilbur also came to the realization that they would have to master the art of flying in an unpowered machine before they attempted anything powered.

Wilbur observed the flight of buzzards and noticed the twisting or warping of their wings as they flew; he then realized that wing warping was a necessary aspect of flight. A customer came in to buy an inner tube one day and stayed to chat. While conversing, Wilbur absent-mindedly twisted the ends of the narrow cardboard box in which the inner tube had come. When the customer left, Wilbur saw how he had twisted the box ends in opposite directions. He instantly envisioned two pairs of wings, one above the other, which would be rigid in the vertical plane but able to move to opposing angles at their tips. Orville quickly caught on to Wilbur's idea. The two fashioned a bi-wing kite with maneuverable wings. Orville was gone on a camping trip when Wilbur tested it. It was such a success that he visited Orville's camp to tell him about it. This led to the development of a glider based on the idea of attaching wings to wires so that they could be warped as needed to provide flight control. It was a significant and innovative development.

On May 13, 1900, Wilbur wrote to aviator Chanute for his advice and opinions. Thus started a long friendship between the brothers and Chanute. Wilbur also wrote to the United States Weather Bureau asking about wind and terrain conditions around the country. The reply indicated that Kitty Hawk, North Carolina, might best suit the Wrights' purposes. So on September 13, 1900, Wilbur arrived there. Being a very remote place at the time, Wilbur stayed with Postmaster William Tate until Orville came with the camping gear on September 28th. Together they finished the glider Wilbur had been assembling.

After several glider experiments, it became clear that they weren't getting the lift they expected from the wings. So on October 28, they broke camp and returned to Dayton. However, the flying bug had bitten, and the brothers realized they were closer to flying than anyone else. Thus Wilbur and Orville pursued aviation single-mindedly.

Hiring Charles Taylor to mind the bicycle store for them, the Wrights advanced their plans to return to Kitty Hawk, arriving July 10, 1901. This time they used a much larger and heavier glider with the camber nearly doubled on the wings. Wilbur was the first to try the glider, and it immediately plopped to the ground. As he had to lie prone to fly the glider, Wilbur realized that he was too far forward and inched back until the glider flew on the ninth try. Its center of gravity had shifted back one foot.

By August, the Wrights had a good feel for the glider and decided to try banking turns. Despite brisk winds, Wilbur made the attempt, and encountered many problems, not the least of which was getting into a spin. He and Orville continued experiments until August 20th, when they left for Dayton. Much careful analysis led the Wrights to the conclusion that the Lilienthal lift tables were wrong—even though they were considered gospel by the flying world of the time.

Closing in on Powered Flight

By this time, Chanute was so impressed by the brothers' achievements that he invited Wilbur to speak at a meeting for the Western Society of Engineers in Chicago. There, in a ten-thousand-word paper, Wilbur made the startling claim that Lilienthal's lift tables were wrong. Later, to assuage self-doubts about their claim, the Wrights decided to do laboratory work, testing different wing shapes at different wind angles. This eventually led them to build a primitive wind tunnel, only eighteen inches long. Although English inventor Frank Wenham had invented the wind tunnel in 1870, the Wrights were the first to realize its full potential. The result was that they found Lilienthal's tables to be seriously in error, so they researched until they had made a set of their own, using nearly 48 different wings. According to Orville: "I believe we possessed more data on cambered surfaces, a hundred times over, than all of our predecessors put together."

Armed with this new knowledge, the Wrights returned to Kitty Hawk on August 28, 1902. Their new glider had longer, narrower wings and a shallower curvature. For the first time, it also had a tail: two vertical fins for preventing spins. Their first test on September 19th was very good. However, later testing showed that falling into spins was still possible. Eventually, Orville realized that the tail was adding to the problem and that it needed to be controlled just like the wings. Then Wilbur devised the idea of linking the tail fins (today called rudders) to the wing-warping wires. This innovation was a stunning success. When the brothers broke camp that year on October 28th, they knew their next step would be a powered craft.

Of all the problems flying a powered craft presented, however, two were especially challenging. One was the need for a propeller, and the other was the need for an engine with sufficient power which was also lightweight. The brothers got their store manager, Charles Taylor, to work on the engine. Meanwhile, they researched propellers. Those used in ships of the time were hit-and-miss devices: shipwrights tried a number of different sizes and shapes until they got a propeller which worked satisfactorily. Wilbur did much library research on the subject, turning up virtually nothing.

The two brothers argued over the propeller problem for weeks. Finally, they realized that a propeller was in reality a wing rotating in the vertical plane. This revelation led to weeks more of calculations and research resulting in tables showing how to design propellers with adequate thrust. The propellers the Wrights used were rear-mounted and rotated in opposite directions. The brothers had already realized that a yaw, or swerving motion, would result if the propellers rotated the same way.

The Wrights returned to Kitty Hawk September 25, 1903. By November 5th, the new machine was assembled. They performed pre-flight tests on the engine, with terrible results. It sputtered and backfired. The propellers didn't work well either, rotating jerkily. Finally they came off, damaging their shafts.

It was December, and winter was becoming a problem when the machine was finally ready to try again. On December 14th, the brothers flipped a coin, and Wilbur won the toss. Using the new track they had built to launch their flyer, Wilbur took off. However, the take-off was too fast and Wilbur became nose-high. He was unused to how quickly it could all happen and crashed, but not seriously.

The next try was December 17th. This time, it was Orville's turn. At 10:35 a.m., Orville took off, rising ten feet, falling, climbing again and landing roughly 100 feet from where he started. In winds as high as 27 miles per hour, Orville became the first man carried by a machine-powered craft which took off under its own power and landed as high as it had started. Thus was born the airplane.

They flew several more times that day, each flight covering a longer distance and time. Then, as they and several helpers were attempting to return the machine to its hangar, the wind caught it and sent it reeling end over end. It was smashed beyond repair. Even after a terse statement issued by the brothers on January 5, 1904, the world took almost no notice of what the Wrights had done.

Uncle Sam Turns a Cold Shoulder, But Europe Is Enthusiastic

The brothers spent 1904 refining the new machine, which the Wrights called Flyer II, since the first Flyer was hopelessly damaged. They built it so they could test it in the more confined flying spaces around Dayton, on what was known as the Huffman Farm. On September 20th, Wilbur flew the first complete circle, setting a new distance record of 3/4 mile in one minute and 35.4 seconds. Flyer III debuted in June of 1905. On October 5th, it flew 24.2 miles in just over 38 minutes, landing only because it was out of fuel.

Feeling that it was their duty to let the United States Government have the first chance to buy airplanes, the Wrights approached the War Department about their invention. They were brushed off. However, on February 8, 1908, the Army Signal Corps accepted the Wrights' bid to make a plane according to Army specifications for $25,000. The 14th of May brought the first time two men ever flew together. In 1908, Wilbur undertook a tour of Europe to demonstrate the flying machine, and it was wildly successful. Europe was so crazed by the invention that a number of would-be producers launched into the aircraft-making business. Wilbur also returned home with a number of contracts in his pocket.

Meanwhile, on September 17th, Orville made the first one-hour flight at Ft. Myer, Virginia, hoping for an Army contract. But the flight ended tragically when a guy wire broke, hurting a propeller and impairing control. In the ensuing crash, Orville's passenger, Lieutenant Thomas Selfridge, was killed— the first man to die in an airplane. Orville suffered a broken leg, four broken ribs and a multi-fractured hip.

It wasn't until 1909 that the brothers were finally recognized for their achievements. Upon Wilbur's return from Europe, Dayton threw a surprise parade and bash on June 17th and 18th in their honor. Both brothers were presented with gold medals from the City of Dayton, the State of Ohio and the United States Congress. In Europe, they had been awarded gold medals from French and British aero clubs, among others. May 21, 1910, turned out to be Wilbur's last flight as the pilot. On May 30, 1912, Wilbur succumbed to typhoid fever. He was forty-five. Orville succeeded him as president of the Wright Company.

In 1914, Orville bought all of the stock in the Wright Company, except for that of Robert Collier. In October of 1915, with Collier's consent, Orville sold the company to an Eastern syndicate. He then founded the Wright Aeronautical Corporation, later becoming Director of the Wright Aeronautical Laboratory in Dayton.

Content to make their refinements gradually, the Wrights relied on their numerous patents to protect them from the innovations of would-be competitors. Both in the United States and in Europe, they became embroiled in patent suits. Particularly acrimonious was the fight between the Herring-Curtiss Company and the Wright Company. Although the courts found for the Wrights in nearly every case, they also allowed ways their competitors could work around them without violating their patents. The net effect was that Europeans made rapid advances in the development of the airplane, while in the United States, the many patent fights and attitude of flying as merely a form of high-flying entertainment stagnated American aviation.

World War I ended the patent bickering. The United States government forced the Wright Company to work with Glenn Curtiss, a partnership that turned out well for all those involved. Then the Navy Bureau of Aeronautics forced Wright Aeronautical Corporation to produce an airplane using the radial air-cooled engine that engineer Charles Lawrance had invented. Although initially reluctant due to their own research into water-cooled, in-line engines, Orville Wright did as ordered. The result, named the Whirlwind, became an international standard almost instantly, proving quite lucrative.

Split flaps were Orville's last major invention. Recognized as a scientific pioneer, Orville received several honorary degrees: from Earlham College in Indiana and Royal Technical College of Munich in 1909, from Yale in 1919 and from Harvard in 1931, as well as a doctorate of Engineering from the University of Dayton in 1943. Wilbur also received honorary degrees from Earlham College in 1909 and Oberlin College of Ohio in 1910. In addition, Orville was also awarded a medal from the French Academy of Sciences in 1909 (with Wilbur), the Langley Medal from the Smithsonian Institution in 1910, the Elliot Cresson Medal from the Franklin Institute in 1914, a Cross of an Officer of the Legion of Honor in 1924, and the Distinguished Flying Cross in February 1929. Orville also became the first recipient of the Daniel Guggenheim Medal in 1930.

Orville was also a member of various aeronautical and technical societies, both in the United States and abroad. In 1940, he was issued Honorary Pilot Certificate #1 by the new Civil Aeronautics Authority. In 1944, Orville took the pilot's controls for the last time, flying Lockheed's new, fast C–69 Constellation, nicknamed "Connie." A few years later, on January 30, 1948, Orville died of a heart attack. Never married, neither he nor Wilbur left any descendants, but together, they left a legacy that reached to the skies and beyond.

SELECTED WRITINGS BY THE WRIGHTS:

Books

The Papers of Wilbur and Orville Wright, edited by Marvin W. McFarland, McGraw-Hill, 1953.

Periodicals

Wright, Wilbur, "Aeronautical Experiments," *Smithsonian Institute Report,* 1902, p. 133.

Wright, Orville and Wilbur, "Mechanical Flight," *Science,* April 6, 1906, p. 557.

Wright, Wilbur, "Flying as a Sport," *Scientific American,* February 29, 1908, p. 139.

Wright, Orville and Wilbur, "Our Aeroplane Tests at Kitty Hawk," *Scientific American,* June 13, 1908, p. 423.

Wright, Orville and Wilbur, "Wright Brothers' Aeroplane," *Century,* September, 1908, p. 641.

Wright, Wilbur, "Earliest Wright Flights," *Scientific American,* July 16, 1910, p. 47.

Wright, Orville, "Stability of Aeroplanes," *Scientific American,* September 26, 1914, p. 206.

SOURCES:

Books

Boyne, Walter J., *The Leading Edge,* Stewart, Tabori & Chang, 1986.

Boyne, Walter J., *The Smithsonian Book of Flight,* Smithsonian Books, 1987.

Hallion, Richard P., *Legacy of Flight,* University of Washington Press, 1977.

Kelly, Fred C., *The Wright Brothers,* Harcourt, 1943.

Moolman, Valerie, *The Road to Kitty Hawk,* Time-Life Books, 1980.

Periodicals

"Mr. Wright Disparages the Glider," *Literary Digest,* January 6, 1923, p. 59.

"Portrait of Orville Wright," *Scientific American,* November 1, 1913, p. 338.

"Portrait of Wilbur Wright," *Independent,* June 6, 1912, p. 194.

"Visiting the Wright Boys," *St. Nicholas,* November, 1910, p. 76.

—*Sketch by Susan E. Kolmer*

Chien-Shiung Wu

Chien-Shiung Wu
1912(?)-
Chinese American physicist

For more than thirty years, Chien-Shiung Wu was a member of the physics department at Columbia University, where she earned a reputation as one of the world's foremost nuclear physicists. Wu is best known for a classic experiment on beta decay, completed in 1957, which confirmed a prediction made a year earlier by **Tsung-Dao Lee** and **Chen Ning Yang** regarding the conservation of parity (the basic symmetry of nature) in reactions involving the weak force. A number of observers have commented on the apparent inequity of the Nobel Prize committee's not having included Wu in the 1957 physics prize, which was awarded to Lee and Yang for this work.

Chien-Shiung Wu was born in May of 1912 (some sources say 1915; one source says 1913), in Liu Ho near Shanghai, China. Her father, Wu Zhongyi, was a former engineer who had abandoned his profession in 1911 to take part in the revolution that overthrew the Manchu dynasty. After the war, Wu returned to Liu Ho to open a school for girls. Still filled with revolutionary zeal, he saw it as his mission to make sure that girls as well as boys were able to have an education in the "new China." Chien-Shiung's mother, Fan Fuhua, helped her husband in this effort, providing education to their students' families in their own homes.

Wu attended her father's school until she was nine and then continued her education at the Soochow Girls School, about fifty miles from her home. During her high school years, Wu was active in a number of political causes; her fellow classmates chose her to represent them in some of the causes because, with her stellar scholastic record, she could not readily be dismissed from school on the basis of her involvement in political issues. In 1930 Wu graduated from Soochow as valedictorian of her class and then entered the National Central University in Nanking. By that time she had decided to pursue physics as a career, and in 1934 was awarded a bachelor's degree in that field. After teaching and doing research for two years, Wu left China in 1936, intending to obtain the graduate training in physics that was not then available in her native land. Her original plans to enroll in the University of Michigan changed abruptly when she reached San Francisco and was offered an opportunity to attend the University of California at Berkeley.

Among the factors influencing Wu's decision to remain in California was the presence of **Ernest Orlando Lawrence**, inventor of the atom-smashing cyclotron (a device that accelerates the speed of nuclear particles), on the Berkeley campus. The chance to study with Lawrence was, Wu decided, too important to pass up. Another factor in her decision was the presence of "Luke" Chia Liu Yuan—a young man she met soon after arriving in San Francisco. Wu and Yuan were married in 1942 and eventually had one son, Vincent Wei-Chen Yuan.

Teaches at Smith, Princeton, and Columbia

Wu received her Ph.D. in 1940, a time of great turmoil in her homeland and in the world at large. The Japanese army had already invaded China, and U.S. involvement in World War II was only a year away. Wu stayed on as a research assistant at Berkeley for two years after receiving her degree, but spent much of that time on war-related work. In 1942 she was offered her first teaching position, at Smith College in Northampton, Massachusetts. She remained at Smith for only one year before accepting an appointment at Princeton University, where she was assigned to teach introductory physics to naval officers. She held this position for only a few months before she was offered a post at Columbia University, where she would join the Manhattan Project—through which the world's first atomic bombs were designed and built. That job, which began in March 1944, was the beginning of a long relationship with Columbia; she eventually became a research associate in 1945, associate professor in 1952, and finally full professor in 1958. She retired from Columbia in 1981.

Tests the Lee-Yang Theory of Parity Nonconservation

The work for which Wu gained fame took place in 1957. It was based on a revolutionary theory proposed by two colleagues, Tsung-Dao Lee, also of Columbia, and Chen Ning Yang, of the Institute for Advanced Study in Princeton, New Jersey. In 1956 Lee and Yang had raised the possibility that a property known as parity may not be conserved in certain types of nuclear reactions. Conservation laws had long been at the heart of physical theories. These laws said that a number of important physical characteristics—mass, energy, momentum, and electrical charge, for instance—were always conserved during physical or chemical changes. As an example, the law of conservation of electrical charge says that the total electrical charge on all particles involved in a physical change would be the same both before and after the event.

Lee and Yang found theoretical reasons to question the conservation of parity in some instances. Parity refers to the theory that the laws of nature are not biased in any particular direction, a concept long held by physicists. When beta particles are emitted by nuclei during radioactive decay, for example, classical theory predicts that they will be emitted without preference to any particular spin orientation. Lee and Yang developed a mathematical argument showing that this might not be the case and outlined experiments through which their theory could be tested.

Lee and Yang presented their ideas to Wu, already recognized as an authority on beta decay (a radioactive nuclear transformation) and the weak force that causes it. Even before her colleagues had published a paper on their theory, Wu had begun to design experiments to test their ideas. Working with colleagues at the National Bureau of Standards's Low Temperature Physics Group, Wu labored almost without rest for six months. In January of 1957, she announced her results: clear evidence for the violation of parity conservation had been observed. Later that same year, Lee and Yang were awarded the Nobel Prize in physics—an award that many observers in the field believe might easily have been shared with Wu.

Although she did not receive a Nobel Prize, Wu has won a host of other awards, including the first Wolf Prize awarded by the state of Israel (1978), the first Research Corporation Award (1959) given to a woman, the Comstock Award of the National Academy of Sciences (1964), and the National Science Medal (1975). She was elected to the National Academy of Sciences in 1958.

SELECTED WRITINGS BY WU:

Books

(With others) *An Experimental Test of Parity Conservation in Beta Decay,* [New York], 1957.
(Editor with Luke C. L. Yuan) *Nuclear Physics,* Academic Press, 1961.

SOURCES:

Books

Kass-Simon, G., and Patricia Farnes, editors, *Women of Science: Righting the Record,* Indiana University Press, 1990, pp. 205–208.
McGraw-Hill Modern Men of Science, Volume 2, McGraw-Hill, 1984, pp. 541–542.
McGrayne, Sharon Bertsch, *Nobel Prize Women in Science,* Birchlane Press, 1993, pp. 255–279.
Yost, Edna, *Women of Modern Science,* Dodd, 1959, pp. 80–93.

—*Sketch by David E. Newton*

Y. C. L. Susan Wu
1932-
Chinese-born American aerospace engineer

Aerospace engineer Y. C. L. Susan Wu is a researcher who has excelled in both academics and industry. Her work has earned the respect of leading engineers and scientists and has advanced the potential for cleaner and more efficient methods of coal-fired power generation in the United States.

Ying-Chu Lin Wu was born in Peking, China, on June 23, 1932. Her mother, Kuo-Chun Kung, was a personnel employee for the Taiwanese government; her father, Chi-Yu Lin, was a government accountant. Wu developed an early interest in science, but at that time women were generally discouraged from such pursuits. Her mother's encouragement gave Wu the impetus to continue her studies, and in 1955 she received a bachelor's degree in mechanical engineering from the National Taiwan University.

Engineering jobs were scarce for women in China in the mid–1950s. Because employers viewed jobs as a lifetime commitment for the employee, firms were reluctant to hire women, recognizing the potential pressures of marriage and child-rearing. Wu moved to the United States in 1957 and earned a master's degree from Ohio State University in aeronautical engineering in 1959. After achieving a doctorate from the California Institute of Technology in 1963, Wu found employment at an optics engineering company in Pasadena, California, as a senior engineer. In 1965 Wu accepted a position as an assistant professor at the University of Tennessee Space Institute (UTSI). In 1967 she was promoted to associate professor, and a full professorship in aerospace engineering followed in 1973. She held that position at UTSI for fifteen years.

Focuses on Energy Research

During Wu's tenure at UTSI her research focused on magnetohydrodynamics (MHD) and its application to cleaner coal-fired power generation. Conventional power generators use steam, coal, or oil power to turn an armature on which a continuous wire is wrapped. A magnetic field surrounds the armature and as the wires cut through the magnetic field, a current is induced in the wire, thereby producing electricity. MHD uses conventional power generation theory, but the armature is replaced by plasma, a very hot gas on the order of 5,000°F. When a gas is very hot it becomes an electrical conductor. Sometimes such elements as cesium or potassium ions are introduced into the gas to increase its conductivity. As the electrically conductive plasma cuts through the mag-

netic field, an electric current is generated. This method of power generation is cleaner and more efficient than traditional coal-fired power plants.

In 1988 Wu left UTSI after twenty-three years to start her own business. She founded ERC, Inc., an aerospace engineering and MHD consulting firm based in Tullahoma, Tennessee. ERC, Inc., works with such agencies as the National Aeronautics and Space Administration (NASA), the Department of Energy, Argonne National Laboratory, Boeing, McDonnell Douglas, and UTSI.

Wu's many honors include the University of Tennessee Chancellor's Research Scholar Award in 1978, Outstanding Educators of America Award in 1973 and 1975, and the Society of Women Engineers Achievement Award in 1985. She was honored by the National Science Foundation in 1987, and she received the Amelia Earhart Fellowship in 1958, 1959, and 1962, the only three-time recipient of the award. A naturalized U.S. citizen, Wu married Jain-Ming (James) Wu in 1959, and they have three children: Ernest, a biologist; Albert, an aerospace engineering consultant; and Karen, a quality control engineer. In her spare time, Wu enjoys classical music, reading, and civic activities.

SELECTED WRITINGS BY WU:

Periodicals

(With D. P. Duclos, R. Denison, and R. W. Ziemer) "Physical Property Distribution in a Low-Pressure Crossed Field Plasma Accelerator," *AIAA Journal*, November, 1965.

"The Limiting Circles of One-Dimensional MHD Channel Flows," *AIAA Journal*, August, 1968.

(With E. S. Jett and D. L. Denzel) "Eddy Currents in an Infinitely Finely Segmented Hall Generator," *AIAA Journal*, September, 1970.

(With G. D. Roy) "Study of Pressure Distribution along Supersonic Magnetohydrodynamic Generator Channels," *AIAA Journal*, September, 1975.

(With J. N. Chapman and S. S. Strom) "MHD Steam Power—Promise, Progress, and Problems," *Mechanical Engineering*, September, 1981.

(With F. L. Galanga and others) "Experimental Results of the UTSI Coal-Fired MHD Generator," *Journal of Energy*, May-June, 1982, p. 179.

(With J. T. Lineberry and others) "Comparison of Experimental Results from the UTSI Coal-Fired MHD Generator to Theoretical Predictions," *Journal of Energy*, May-June, 1982.

(With M. Ishikawa and M. H. Scott) "Power Take-off Analysis and Comparison with Experiments in a Coal-Fired MHD Generator," *Journal of Energy,* September-October, 1983.

(With Ishikawa and Scott) "Fault Analysis of Mid Channel Power Takeoff in Diagonal Conducting Wall Magnetohydrodynamic Generators," *Journal of Propulsion and Power,* September-October, 1985.

(With R. C. Attig, Chapman, and A. C. Sheth) "Emission Control by Magnetohydrodynamics," *Chemtech,* November, 1988.

"SWE Personality Profile: Y. C. L. Susan Wu, 1985 SWE Achievement Award Winner," *U.S. Woman Engineer,* March-April, 1990, pp. 31–32.

SOURCES:

Periodicals

Congressional Record, July 15, 1985, p. S–9510.

Other

Wu, Y. C. L. Susan, interview with Roger Jaffe conducted January 20, 1994.

—*Sketch by Roger Jaffe*

Xie Xide
1921-
Chinese physicist

Xie Xide is a Chinese physicist and the president of Fudan University in Shanghai, China. During the decade of China's Cultural Revolution she was removed from her teaching post and was not allowed to conduct scientific research. Reinstated in 1972, as a university administrator she has been an outspoken advocate for science education in China.

Born in 1921, in South China, she spent her early years in Peking, where her father was a professor of physics at Yenching University, now a part of Peking University. When the Japanese occupied Peking in July of 1937, she fled with her family. Traveling halfway across China, they eventually reached Guiyang, in Guizhou Province. During the journey Xie became ill with tuberculosis, and was hospitalized in Guiyang for close to four years. After recovering, she began her university studies in physics at Amoy University, where her father had found a new teaching post. To escape the Japanese, Amoy University had been evacuated to the remote hill town of Changding in Fukien Province. In 1946 she received her B.Sc.

Shortly after the war ended Xie took a teaching position in physics at the University of Shanghai. A year later, in 1947, she set sail for the United States, part of a wave of young Chinese intellectuals who were seeking higher education abroad. Leaving behind the civil war and political chaos that preceded the emergence of the Communist government in China, she enrolled in a master's degree program at Smith College, in Amherst, Massachusetts. She received her M.A. in 1949, and then began her doctoral studies in the physics department at the Massachusetts Institute of Technology. Her thesis work there concerned the wave function of electrons in highly compressed gases. She was granted her Ph.D. in 1951.

Unable to return directly home because of U.S. government restrictions on travel to China at the time, Xie instead went to England, where she married Cao Tianqin, a biochemist. Together, in 1952, they made their way back to Shanghai on an arduous route via the Suez Canal and Singapore. Back in China, Xie took a post at Fudan University. Her husband joined the Shanghai branch of the Chinese Academy of Science. Xie soon distinguished herself as one of China's top physicists, publishing many professional articles and two texts, *Semi-conductor Physics* (1958) and *Solid Physics* (1962). In 1962 she was promoted in rank to Professor and was appointed the Deputy Director of the Institute of Technical Physics in Shanghai.

In 1966 when the Cultural Revolution began, Xie and her husband were subjected to the anti-intellectual tyranny of Mao Tse-tung's government. Despite her allegiance to the Communist Party, she was kept imprisoned in her own laboratory for a period of nine months. Her husband was incarcerated as well, at his own institute, leaving their then ten-year-old boy to look after himself alone in the family's apartment. Xie was forced to clean bathrooms at the university, and was eventually sent to the countryside to work in a silicon wafer factory. In 1972 she was allowed to return to her teaching post, where she taught physics to peasants, workers and soldiers, most of them ill-prepared for university classes. The Cultural Revolution came to a close in 1976, when the "Gang of Four" were arrested. Since then Xie has worked hard to regain her footing. She resumed research in surface physics, and in 1977 founded the educational Modern Physics Institute. One year later Xie was appointed vice-president of Fudan University, and in 1982 she became its president. That same year, she was elected to the Central Committee of the Chinese Communist Party, one of the few women and scientists among this elite body of policy-making leaders. Xie has been awarded numerous honorary degrees and is a member of the Chinese Academy of Sciences and the Praesidium. She continues to work to improve the educational opportunities for students in China.

SELECTED WRITINGS BY XIE:

Books

Semi-conductor Physics, 1958.
Solid Physics, 1962.

SOURCES:

Periodicals

Oka, Takashi, "Xie Xide—The Gentle President of China's Fudan University," *Christian Science Monitor,* March 28, 1984, p. 21.

—*Sketch by Leslie Reinherz*

Rosalyn Sussman Yalow
1921-
American medical physicist

Rosalyn Sussman Yalow was co-developer of radioimmunoassay (RIA), a technique that uses radioactive isotopes to measure small amounts of biological substances. In widespread use, the RIA helps scientists and medical professionals measure the concentrations of hormones, vitamins, viruses, enzymes, and drugs, among other substances. Yalow's work concerning RIA earned her a share of the Nobel Prize in physiology or medicine in the late 1970s. At that time, she was only the second woman to receive the Nobel in medicine. During her career, Yalow also received acclaim for being the first woman to attain a number of other scientific achievements.

Yalow was born on July 19, 1921, in The Bronx, New York, to Simon Sussman and Clara Zipper Sussman. Her father, owner of a small business, had been born on the Lower East Side of New York City to Russian immigrant parents. At the age of four, Yalow's mother had journeyed to the United States from Germany. Although neither parent had attended high school, they instilled a great enthusiasm for and respect of education in their daughter. Yalow also credits her father with helping her find the confidence to succeed in school, teaching her that girls could do just as much as boys. Yalow learned to read before she entered kindergarten, although her family did not own any books. Instead, Yalow and her older brother, Alexander, made frequent visits to the public library.

During her youth, Yalow became interested in mathematics. At Walton High School in the Bronx, her interest turned to science, especially chemistry. After graduation, Yalow attended Hunter College, a women's school in New York that eventually became part of the City University of New York. She credits two physics professors, Dr. Herbert Otis and Dr. Duane Roller, for igniting her penchant for physics. This occurred in the latter part of the 1930s, a time when many new discoveries were made in nuclear physics. It was this field that Yalow ultimately chose for her major. In 1939 she was further inspired after hearing American physicist **Enrico Fermi** lecture about the discovery of nuclear fission, which had earned him the Nobel Prize the previous year.

Rosalyn Sussman Yalow

Overcomes Sex Bias

As Yalow prepared for her graduation from Hunter College, she found that some practical considerations intruded on her passion for physics. At the time, most of American society expected young women to become secretaries or teachers. In fact, Yalow's parents urged her to pursue a career as an elementary school teacher. Yalow herself also thought it unrealistic to expect any of the top graduate schools in the country to accept her into a doctoral program or offer her the financial support that men received. "However, my physics professors encouraged me and I persisted," she explained in *Les Prix Nobel 1977*.

Yalow made plans to enter graduate school via other means. One of her earlier college physics professors, who had left Hunter to join the faculty at the Massachusetts Institute of Technology, arranged for Yalow to work as secretary to Dr. Rudolf Schoenheimer, a biochemist at Columbia University in New York. According to the plan, this position would give Yalow an opportunity to take some graduate courses in physics, and eventually provide a way for her to enter a graduate a school and pursue a degree. But

Yalow never needed her plan. The month after graduating from Hunter College in January, 1941, she was offered a teaching assistantship in the physics department of the University of Illinois at Champaign-Urbana.

Gaining acceptance to the physics graduate program in the College of Engineering at the University of Illinois was one of many hurdles that Yalow had to cross as a woman in the field of science. For example, when she entered the University in September, 1941, she was the only woman in the College of Engineering's faculty, which included four hundred professors and teaching assistants. She was the first woman in more than two decades to attend the engineering college. Yalow realized that she had been given a space at the prestigious graduate school because of the shortage of male candidates, who were being drafted into the armed services in increasing numbers as America prepared to enter World War II.

Yalow's strong work orientation aided her greatly in her first year in graduate school. In addition to her regular course load and teaching duties, she took some extra undergraduate courses to increase her knowledge. Despite a hectic schedule, Yalow earned A's in her classes, except for an A- in an optics laboratory course. While in graduate school she also met Aaron Yalow, a fellow student and the man she would eventually marry. The pair met the first day of school and wed about two years later on June 6, 1943. Yalow received her master's degree in 1942 and her doctorate in 1945. She was the second woman to obtain a Ph.D. in physics at the University.

After graduation the Yalows moved to New York City, where they worked and eventually raised two children, Benjamin and Elanna. Yalow's first job after graduate school was as an assistant electrical engineer at Federal Telecommunications Laboratory, a private research lab. Once again, she found herself the sole woman as there were no other female engineers at the lab. In 1946 she began teaching physics at Hunter College. She remained a physics lecturer from 1946 to 1950, although by 1947 she began her long association with the Veterans Administration by becoming a consultant to Bronx VA Hospital. The VA wanted to establish some research programs to explore medical uses of radioactive substances. By 1950, Yalow had equipped a radioisotope laboratory at the Bronx VA Hospital and decided to leave teaching to devote her attention to full-time research.

That same year Yalow met Solomon A. Berson, a physician who had just finished his residency in internal medicine at the hospital. The two would work together until Berson's death in 1972. According to Yalow, the collaboration was a complementary one. In Olga Opfell's *Lady Laureates* Yalow is quoted as saying, "[Berson] wanted to be a physicist, and I wanted to be a medical doctor." While her partner

had accumulated clinical expertise, Yalow maintained strengths in physics, math, and chemistry. Working together, Yalow and Berson discovered new ways to use radioactive isotopes in the measurement of blood volume, the study of iodine metabolism, and the diagnosis of thyroid diseases. Within a few years, the pair began to investigate adult-onset diabetes using radioisotopes. This project eventually led them to develop the groundbreaking radioimmunoassay technique.

Diabetes Mystery Leads to a Discovery

In the 1950s some scientists hypothesized that in adult-onset diabetes, insulin production remained normal, but a liver enzyme rapidly destroyed the peptide hormone, thereby preventing normal glucose metabolism. This contrasted with the situation in juvenile diabetes, where insulin production by the pancreas was too low to allow proper metabolism of glucose. Yalow and Berson wanted to test the hypothesis about adult-onset diabetes. They used insulin "labeled" with iodine–131. (That is, they attached, by a chemical reaction, the radioactive isotope of iodine to otherwise normal insulin molecules.) Yalow and Berson injected labeled insulin into diabetic and non-diabetic individuals and measured the rate at which the insulin disappeared.

To their surprise and in contradiction to the liver enzyme hypothesis, they found that the amount of radioactively labeled insulin in the blood of diabetics was higher than that found in the control subjects who had never received insulin injections before. As Yalow and Berson looked into this finding further, they deduced that diabetics were forming antibodies to the animal insulin used to control their disease. These antibodies were binding to radiolabeled insulin, preventing it from entering cells where it was used in sugar metabolism. Individuals who had never taken insulin before did not have these antibodies and so the radiolabeled insulin was consumed more quickly.

Yalow and Berson's proposal that animal insulin could spur antibody formation was not readily accepted by immunologists in the mid–1950s. At the time, most immunologists did not believe that antibodies would form to molecules as small as the insulin peptide. Also, the amount of insulin antibodies was too low to be detected by conventional immunological techniques. So Yalow and Berson set out to verify these minute levels of insulin antibodies using radiolabeled insulin as their marker. Their original report about insulin antibodies, however, was rejected initially by two journals. Finally, a compromise version was published that omitted "insulin antibody" from the paper's title and included some additional data indicating that an antibody was involved.

The need to detect insulin antibodies at low concentrations led to the development of the radioimmunoassay. The principle behind RIA is that a radiolabeled antigen, such as insulin, will compete with unlabeled antigen for the available binding sites on its specific antibody. As a standard, various mixtures of known amounts of labeled and unlabeled antigen are mixed with antibody. The amounts of radiation detected in each sample correspond to the amount of unlabeled antigen taking up antibody binding sites. In the unknown sample, a known amount of radiolabeled antigen is added and the amount of radioactivity is measured again. The radiation level in the unknown sample is compared to the standard samples; the amount of unlabeled antigen in the unknown sample will be the same as the amount of unlabeled antigen found in the standard sample that yields the same amount of radioactivity. RIA has turned out to be so useful because it can quickly and precisely detect very low concentrations of hormones and other substances in blood or other biological fluids. The principle can also be applied to binding interactions other than that between antigen and antibody, such as between a binding protein or tissue receptor site and an enzyme. In Yalow's Nobel lecture, recorded in *Les Prix Nobel 1977,* she listed more than one hundred biological substances—hormones, drugs, vitamins, enzymes, viruses, non-hormonal proteins, and more—that were being measured using RIA.

In 1968 she became a research professor at the Mt. Sinai School of Medicine, and in 1970, she was made chief of the Nuclear Medicine Service at the VA hospital. Yalow also began to receive a number of prestigious awards in recognition of her role in the development of RIA. In 1976, she was awarded the Albert Lasker Prize for Basic Medical Research. She was the first woman to be honored this laurel—an award that often leads to a Nobel Prize. In Yalow's case, this was true, for the very next year, she shared the Nobel Prize in physiology or medicine with **Andrew V. Schally** and **Roger Guillemin** for their work on radioimmunoassay. Schally and Guillemin were recognized for their use of RIA to make important discoveries about brain hormones.

Berson had died in 1972, and so did not share in these awards. Ecstatic to receive such prizes, Yalow was also saddened that her longtime partner had been excluded. According to an essay in *The Lady Laureates,* she remarked that the "tragedy" of winning the Nobel Prize "is that Dr. Berson did not live to share it." Earlier Yalow had paid tribute to her collaborator by asking the VA to name the laboratory, in which the two had worked, the Solomon A. Berson Research Laboratory. She made the request, as quoted in *Les Prix Nobel 1977,* "so that his name will continue to be on my papers as long as I publish and so that his contributions to our Service will be memorialized."

Yalow has received many other awards, honorary degrees, and lectureships, including the Georg Charles de Henesy Nuclear Medicine Pioneer Award in 1986 and the Scientific Achievement Award of the American Medical Society. In 1978, she hosted a five-part dramatic series on the life of French physical chemist **Marie Curie**, aired by the Public Broadcasting Service (PBS). In 1980 she became a distinguished professor at the Albert Einstein College of Medicine at Yeshiva University, leaving to become the Solomon A. Berson Distinguished Professor at Large at Mt. Sinai in 1986. She also chaired the Department of Clinical Science at Montefiore Hospital and Medical Center in the early- to mid–1980s.

By all accounts, Yalow was an industrious researcher, rarely taking time off. For example, some reports claim that she only took a few days off of work following the birth of her two children. In *The Lady Laureates,* Opfell reported that when the VA Hospital put on a party in honor of Yalow's selection for the Lasker Prize, Yalow herself "brought roast turkeys from home and stood in the middle of a meeting peeling potatoes and making potato salad while fellows reported to her."

The fact that Yalow was a trailblazer for women scientists was not lost on her, however. At a lecture before the Association of American Medical Colleges, as quoted in *Lady Laureates,* Yalow opined: "We cannot expect that in the foreseeable future women will achieve status in academic medicine in proportion to their numbers. But if we are to start working towards that goal we must believe in ourselves or no one else will believe in us; we must match our aspirations with the guts and determination to succeed; and for those of us who have had the good fortune to move upward, we must feel a personal responsibility to serve as role models and advisors to ease the path for those who come afterwards."

SELECTED WRITINGS BY YALOW:

Books

Luft, R. and R. S. Yalow, *Radioimmunoassay: Methodology and Applications in Physiology and in Clinical Studies,* Publishing Sciences Group, 1974.

Periodicals

(With Solomon A. Berson, A. Bauman, M. A. Rothschild, and K. Newerly) "Insulin-I131 Metabolism in Human Subjects: Demonstration of Insulin Binding Globulin in the Circulation of Insulin Treated Subjects," *Journal of Clinical Investigation,* Volume 35, 1956, pp. 170–190.

(With Berson) "Assay of Plasma Insulin in Human Subjects by Immunological Methods," *Nature,* Volume 184, 1959, pp. 1648–1649.

SOURCES:

Books

Les Prix Nobel 1977, Almquist & Wiskell International, Stockholm, 1978, pp. 237–264.

Opfell, Olga, *The Lady Laureates: Women Who Have Won the Nobel Prize,* Scarecrow Press, Inc., 1978.

—*Sketch by Lee Katterman*

Chen Ning Yang
1922-
Chinese American physicist

Chen Ning Yang

In 1945, Chen Ning Yang came to the United States, where he studied physics at the University of Chicago under **Enrico Fermi**. At Chicago, Yang struck up a friendship with another graduate student from China, **Tsung-Dao Lee**, with whom he would have a long and productive professional relationship. In 1956 Yang and Lee developed a hypothesis that one of the fundamental laws of physics, the conservation of parity, might not in fact be valid. As a result of experiments conducted by **Chien-Shiung Wu** along lines suggested by Yang and Lee, that hypothesis was confirmed. The discovery was momentous because it called into question the validity of all conservation laws—laws that support a major part of modern physical theory. For the discovery of the violation of parity conservation, Yang and Lee were jointly awarded the 1957 Nobel Prize for Physics.

Chen Ning Yang was born in the city of Hofei, in Anhwei province, China, on September 22, 1922, to Ke Chuan Yang, a professor of mathematics, and the former Meng Hwa Loh. The Yang family moved in 1929 from Hofei to Peking, where Professor Yang took a job with Tsinghua University. In Peking, Yang attended the Chung Te Middle School. The family moved once more eight years later to escape the invading Japanese army. At that time, Tsinghua University was moved to Kunming, where it was consolidated with National Southwest Associated University. When Yang finished high school, he entered the National Southwest Associated University, where he majored in physics and earned his B.S. degree in 1942. He then continued his studies at Tsinghua University, where his father was still professor of mathematics. Yang earned his M.S. at Tsinghua in 1944. He then taught high school for one year before deciding to begin work on a Ph.D. in physics. Because doctoral programs in physics were not then available in China, Yang decided to come to the United States, where he particularly wanted to study with physicist Enrico Fermi. According to an article by Jeremy Bernstein in the *New Yorker,* Yang traveled to New York City (by way of India, the Suez Canal, and Europe) under the impression that Fermi was still at Columbia, where he had come upon his arrival in the United States in 1938. When Yang heard that Fermi had only recently left for a new post at the University of Chicago, he followed Fermi and enrolled in the doctoral program at Chicago.

One of the many benefits of Yang's tenure at Chicago was the association he developed with fellow student Tsung-Dao Lee. Yang and Lee had attended Southwest University in China at the same time, but Yang was a year ahead of Lee, and the two were not particularly close. The situation at Chicago was very different. The two compatriots shared housing at the university's International House and soon became close friends. They began to spend time together, talking almost every day about issues in physics. When Yang received his doctorate in 1948, he remained at Chicago as an instructor for one year and then took a job at the Institute for Advanced Study in

Princeton, New Jersey. As Lee was not to complete his own degree for two more years, it appeared that their close association was to end; however, in 1951 Lee joined Yang at Princeton for a period of two years. When Lee then took a job at Columbia University in 1953, the two agreed to continue meeting once each week, alternating between New York and Princeton. By the spring of 1956 they had settled on a problem of particular interest to both of them, the decay of the K-meson (a subatomic particle) and the question of parity conservation.

Considering the Possibility of Parity Conservation Violation

Conservation laws lie at the heart of physics, and they are familiar to most students of high school physics. Such laws say that a particular property—mass, energy, momentum, or electrical charge, for instance—is conserved during any change. As an example, when two moving objects strike each other, their total momentum after the collision must be the same as their total momentum before the collision.

The law of parity conservation, first proposed in 1925, defines the basic symmetry of nature, referring to the theory that the laws of nature are not biased in any particular direction. Consequently, nature is unable to distinguish between right- and left-handedness in particles—the smallest building blocks of energy and matter. Any reaction that involves a right-handed particle would be the same for a left-handed particle. By the 1950s, however, one particular kind of nuclear reaction had raised some questions about the validity of that law. That reaction involved the decay of an elementary particle called the K-meson.

Experiments appear to have shown that K-mesons can decay in one of two ways. The explanation that had been postulated for this observation was that two kinds of K-mesons exist; Yang and Lee suggested another possibility. Perhaps only one form of the K-meson exists, they said, and it sometimes decays in such a way that parity is conserved and sometimes in such a way that parity is not conserved. In June of 1956 Yang and Lee formulated their thoughts on the K-meson puzzle in a now-classic paper titled "Question of Parity Conservation in Weak Interactions." They not only explained why they thought that parity conservation might not occur, but they also outlined experimental tests by which their hypothesis could be evaluated.

Within a matter of months, the proposed experiments were under way. They were carried out by a group of researchers under the direction of Chien-Shiung Wu, a compatriot of Yang and Lee at Columbia University. Wu assembled a team of colleagues at Columbia and at the National Bureau of Standards to study K-meson decay along the lines suggested by Yang and Lee. By January of 1957, the preliminary results were in. The evidence confirmed that Yang and Lee were correct: Parity was not conserved in the decay of K-mesons. For their work on this problem, Yang and Lee were awarded the Nobel Prize for Physics only ten months after Wu's experiments had been completed—almost record time for recognition by a Nobel Prize committee.

In 1965, Yang ended his long affiliation with the Institute for Advanced Study to accept an appointment as Albert Einstein Professor of Physics and Director of the Institute of Theoretical Physics at the State University of New York at Stony Brook. In 1950 he had married Chih Li Tu, a former high school student of his in China. They have two sons, Franklin and Gilbert, and a daughter, Eulee. In addition to the Nobel Prize, Yang has been awarded the 1957 Albert Einstein Award and the 1980 Rumford Medal of the American Academy of Arts and Sciences.

SELECTED WRITINGS BY YANG:

Books

Selected Papers, 1945–80, with Commentary, W. H. Freeman, 1983.

Periodicals

(With Tsung-Dao Lee and M. Rosenbluth) "Interaction of Mesons with Nucleons and Light Particles," *Physical Review,* Volume 75, 1949, p. 905.
(With T. D. Lee) "Mass Degeneracy of the Heavy Mesons," *Physical Review,* Volume 102, 1956, pp. 290–291.
(With T. D. Lee) "Question of Parity Conservation in Weak Interactions," *Physical Review,* Volume 104, 1956, pp. 254–258.
(With T. D. Lee) "Remarks on Possible Noninvariance under Time Reversal and Charge Conjugation," *Physical Review,* Volume 106, 1957, pp. 340–345.

SOURCES:

Books

Magill, Frank N., editor, *The Nobel Prize Winners—Physics,* Volume 2, Salem Press, 1989, pp. 707–713.
McGraw-Hill Modern Men of Science, Volume 1, McGraw-Hill, 1984, pp. 545–546.
Wasson, Tyler, editor, *Nobel Prize Winners,* H. W. Wilson, 1987, pp. 1150–1152.

Periodicals

Bernstein, Jeremy, "A Question of Parity," *New Yorker,* May 12, 1962, pp. 49–104.

—*Sketch by David E. Newton*

Shing-Tung Yau
1949-

Chinese-born American mathematician

Shing-Tung Yau has made fundamental contributions to differential geometry which have influenced a wide range of scientific disciplines, including astronomy and theoretical physics. With Richard Schoen, Yau solved a long-standing question in **Albert Einstein**'s theory of relativity by proving that the sum of the energy in the universe is positive; their proof has provided an important tool for understanding how black holes form. Yau was awarded the Fields Medal in 1982, the highest award in mathematics, and he won the 1994 Crafoord Prize from the Royal Swedish Society with **Simon Donaldson** of Oxford University, in recognition of his "development of nonlinear techniques in differential geometry leading to the solution of several outstanding problems." Yau was born April 4, 1949, in Swatow, in southern China, the fifth of the eight children of Chen Ying Chiou and Yeuk-Lam Leung Chiou. Within the year, Communists had overthrown the government and the family fled to Hong Kong, where his father, a respected economist and philosopher, obtained a position at a college which would later be part of Hong Kong University. His mother knit and created other goods by hand to help support the family, for professors were poorly paid. During high school in Hong Kong, Yau told contributor F. C. Nicholson, much emphasis was placed on mathematics, partly because the laboratories for the sciences were ill equipped. He credits his father, who died when Yau was fourteen, with encouraging him to study mathematics and he has retained a passion for it: "It's clean, clear-cut, beautiful, and has a lot of applications," he told the *Harvard Gazette.*

Yau entered the Chinese University of Hong Kong, earning his undergraduate degree in 1968. One of his professors had attended the University of California at Berkeley and suggested he study there. An IBM fellowship made it possible for Yau to attend Berkeley; he studied with Shiing-Shen Chern, the legendary geometer (Yau would later edit a collection of papers honoring his teacher). Yau completed his Ph.D. in mathematics in 1971 at the age of twenty-two. Yau spent a year after receiving his doctorate with the Institute for Advanced Study at Princeton, and then in 1972 he accepted a position as assistant professor of mathematics at the State University of New York at Stony Brook. In 1974, he became a full professor of mathematics at Stanford, where he was to remain until 1979. After leaving Stanford in 1979, Yau returned to the Institute for Advanced Study. He left there in 1984 to become professor of mathematics and chairman of the department at the University of California, San Diego.

Differential geometry, which is Yau's field, was developed during the 1800s, and it uses derivatives and integrals to describe geometric objects such as surfaces and curves. Differential geometry is particularly concerned with geometrical calculations across many dimensions. The simplest kind of geometry would be one and two dimensional, analyzing figures such as squares or circles; the geometry of a three-dimensional figure, such as a cube or a cylinder, is more complicated. Differential geometry is primarily concerned with calculations about geometrical figures in four or more dimensions. An example of a four-dimensional figure would be a three-dimensional one changing over time—the stretching and snapping of a rubber band, for instance, or a drop of water splashing on a surface.

One of the most important applications of differential geometry is Einstein's theory of relativity: Einstein used differential geometry in his original calculations and it was central to his theory of gravity. The general theory of relativity includes a conjecture—that is, an unproven postulate—which proposes that in an isolated physical system the total energy, including gravity and matter, would be positive. Called the positive mass conjecture, this was fundamental to the theory of relativity but no one had been able to prove it.

Yau's first major contribution to differential geometry was his proof of another conjecture, called the Calabi conjecture, which concerns how volume and distance can be measured not in four but in five or more dimensions. But in 1979, Yau and Richard Schoen proved Einstein's positive mass conjecture by applying methods Yau devised. The proof was based on their work with minimal surfaces. A minimal surface is one in which a small deformation creates a surface with a larger area—soap films are often used as an example of minimal surfaces. The mathematic equations that must be used to describe minimal surfaces differ from those used for most problems in differential geometry. The latter use differential equations to describe curves and surfaces, while mathematicians working with minimal surfaces use partial, nonlinear differential equations, which are far more difficult to work with. Schoen and Yau's proof analyzed how such surfaces behave in space and time and showed that Einstein had correctly defined mass. Their methods allowed for the development of a new theory of minimal surfaces in higher dimensions, and they have had an impact on topology, algebraic geometry, and general relativity.

In 1987, Yau joined the faculty of Harvard University as a professor of mathematics. During 1991 and 1992 (concurrent with his position at Harvard), he served as the Wilson T.S. Wang Distinguished Visiting Professor at the Chinese University of Hong Kong and Special Chair of National Tsing Hua University in Hsinchu, Taiwan. In addition to the Fields Medal and the Crasoord Prize, Yau has received the Veblen Prize (1981). He was named an Alfred Sloan Fellow in 1974, and in 1985 he was awarded a MacArthur Fellowship. He received an honorary degree from Harvard University in 1987 and was named an Honorable Doctor of Science by the Chinese University of Hong Kong in 1980. Among his many professional affiliations, Yau is a member of the American Physical Society, the American Academy of Arts and Sciences, the National Academy of Sciences, and the Society for Industrial and Applied Mathematics. He has published over 150 scientific papers and served as editor-in-chief of the *Journal of Differential Geometry,* as well as editor of both *Communications in Mathematical Physics* and *Letters in Mathematical Physics.* Yau married a fellow Berkeley student, Yu Yun Kuo, in 1976; they have two children.

SELECTED WRITINGS BY YAU:

Books

(Editor) *Chern: A Great Geometer of the Twentieth Century,* International Press, 1992.

Periodicals

(With R. Schoen) "On the Proof of the Positive Mass Conjecture in General Relativity," *Communications in Mathematical Physics,* Volume 65, 1979, pp. 45–76.

(With R. Schoen) "The Existence of a Black Hole Due to the Condensation of Matter," *Communications in Mathematical Physics,* Volume 90, 1983, pp. 575–579.

SOURCES:

Periodicals

"Shing-Tung Yau: Breaking Through Geometric Barriers," *Harvard Gazette,* November 5, 1987, p. 5.

Other

Yau, Shing-Tung, interview with F. C. Nicholson, February 14, 1994.

—*Sketch by F. C. Nicholson*

Grace Chisholm Young
1868-1944
English mathematician

A distinguished mathematician, Grace Chisholm Young is recognized as being the first woman to receive a Ph.D. in any field from a German university. Working closely with her husband, mathematician William Henry Young, she produced a large body of published work that made contributions to both pure and applied mathematics.

Grace Emily Chisholm Young was born on March 15, 1868, in Haslemere, Surrey, England, to Anna Louisa Bell and Henry William Chisholm. Her father was a British career civil servant who (following his own father) rose through the ranks to become the chief of Britain's weights and measures. Grace Emily Chisholm was the youngest of three surviving children. Her brother, Hugh Chisholm, enjoyed a distinguished career as editor of the eleventh edition of the *Encyclopaedia Britannica.*

As befitted a girl of her social class, Young received an education at home. Forbidden by her mother to study medicine—which the youngster wanted to do—she entered Girton College, Cambridge (one of two women's colleges there) in 1889. She was twenty-one years of age, and the institution's Sir Francis Goldschmid Scholar of mathematics. In 1892 she graduated with first-class honors, then sat informally for the final mathematics examinations at Oxford; there, she placed first. In 1893 she transferred to Göttingen University in Germany, where she attended lectures and produced a dissertation entitled "The Algebraic Groups of Spherical Trigonometry" under noted mathematician Felix Klein. In 1895 she became the first woman to receive a Göttingen doctorate in any subject. The degree bore the distinction magna cum laude.

She returned to London and married her former Girton tutor, William Henry Young, who had devoted years to coaching Cambridge students. After the birth of their first child, the Youngs moved to Göttingen. There, William Young began a distinguished research career in mathematics, which would be supported in large part by the work of his wife. Grace Chisholm Young studied anatomy at the university and raised their six children, while collaborating with her husband on mathematics in both co-authored papers and those published under his name alone. In 1905 the pair authored a widely regarded textbook on set theory. Grace Chisholm Young's most important work was achieved between 1914 and 1916, during which time she published several papers on derivates of real functions; in this work she contributed to what is known as the Denjoy-Saks-Young theorem.

The Young family lived modestly, and William Young traveled frequently to earn money by teaching. In 1908, with the birth of their sixth child, the Youngs moved from Göttingen to Geneva. William Young continually sought a well-paying professorship in England, but he failed to obtain such a position; in 1913 he obtained a lucrative professorship in Calcutta, which required his residence for only a few months per year, and after World War I he became professor at the University of Wales in Aberystwyth for several years. Switzerland, however, remained the family's permanent home.

With advancing years, Grace Chisholm Young's mathematical productivity slackened; in 1929 she began an ambitious historical novel, which was never published. Writing fiction was but one of her many varied interests, which included music, languages, and medicine. She also wrote children's books, in which she introduced notions of science. Her children followed the path she had pioneered, becoming accomplished scholars of mathematics, chemistry, and medicine. Her son Frank died as a British aviator during the First World War.

Grace Chisholm Young had lived with her husband's extended absences for her entire married life, and the spring of 1940 found them separated again: she in England, and he in Switzerland. From that time onward, neither spouse was able to see the other again—both were prevented from doing so by the downfall of France during the war. William Young died in 1942, and Grace Chisholm Young died of a heart attack in 1944.

SELECTED WRITINGS BY YOUNG:

Books

(With husband, William Henry Young) *The First Book of Geometry*, Dent, 1905, reprinted, 1969.
(With William Henry Young) *The Theory of Sets of Points*, Cambridge University Press, 1906, reprinted, 1972.

Periodicals

"On the Form of a Certain Jordan Curve," *Quarterly Journal of Pure and Applied Mathematics*, Volume 37, 1905, pp. 87–91.

(With William Henry Young) "An Additional Note on Derivates and the Theorem of the Mean," *Quarterly Journal of Pure and Applied Mathematics*, Volume 40, 1909, pp. 144–145.
"A Note on Derivatives and Differential Coefficients," *Acta Mathematica*, Volume 37, 1914, pp. 141–154.
(With William Henry Young) "On the Reduction of Sets of Intervals," *Proceedings of the London Mathematical Society*, Volume 14, 1914, pp. 111-130.
"On the Solution of a Pair of Simultaneous Diophantine Equations Connected with the Nuptial Number of Plato," *Proceedings of the London Mathematical Society*, Volume 23, 1925, pp. 27–44.

SOURCES:

Books

Grinstein, Louise S., and Paul J. Campbell, editors, *Women of Mathematics: A Biobibliographic Sourcebook*, Greenwood Press, 1987, pp. 247–254.

Periodicals

Cartwright, M. L., "Grace Chisholm Young," *Journal of the London Mathematical Society*, Volume 19, 1944, pp. 185–192.
Grattan-Guinness, Ivor, "A Mathematical Union: William Henry and Grace Chisholm Young," *Annals of Science*, Volume 29, 1972, pp. 105–186.

—*Sketch by Lewis Pyenson*

J. Z. Young
1907-
English biologist

J. Z. Young is a highly acclaimed biologist whose research on the squid and the octopus has helped greatly in making neurology an exact science. His studies of the regeneration of the nerves of the octopus qualified him, during World War II, to work with a team of scientists investigating the problems of peripheral nerve injuries and their surgical repair. Young was the first to prove that the giant fibers of the squid are nerves. For his work, which has shed light on the nature of memory, Young was named a fellow of the Royal Society, which also bestowed on him its Royal Medal in 1967. In 1973, he was awarded the Linnean Gold Medal, and two years later he received the London Medal from the Zoological Society.

John Zachary Young, the eldest of five children, was born on March 18, 1907 in Fishponds, Bristol, England, to Philip Young and Constance Maria Lloyd Young. His father's family were yeoman farmers in Gloucestershire and Somerset, becoming prosperous in the eighteenth and nineteenth centuries. His mother's ancestors were Welsh, and they became industrialists and bankers in Birmingham and the West Midlands.

Research on Octopus and Squid Flourishes in Naples

In 1928, Young graduated in zoology at Oxford University. His interest in octopus research led him to the Zoological Station of Naples, which was the first international marine biological observatory in Europe. Young's first paper, on the regeneration of the nerves of octopus, was published in Italian in 1929. It was also at this time that he began research that led to the discovery of the giant nerve fibers of the squid. His studies of squid, which were described in various papers published during the 1930s, provided the basis for the research into the study of nerve impulses in higher animals. "In a squid, the whole jet propulsion system is worked by just *two* nerve cells; but the learning part of the squid's brain has many millions, as has that of an octopus. Multiplicity is a prime clue to the nature of memory," Young wrote in his book, *Philosophy and the Brain.* In 1945, Young was appointed to the Chair of Anatomy at University College London (U.C.L.), a post he held until 1974. Upon his retirement, he chose to work in the Psychology Department at Oxford, where he continued to do experimental work on octopus and squid.

Young's appointment to the chair of anatomy at U.C.L. marked a departure for the college, which previously had sought traditional anatomists for this position. However, by the time of his appointment, Young had acquired a considerable reputation as a researcher on the physiology of lampreys, the nervous system of cephalopods, the autonomic nervous system, as well as the regeneration of mammalian nerves, which assumed much importance during the Second World War. During his tenure as chair, Young continued his research on the octopus. "He must be the first man to have made a really detailed study of the brain of an invertebrate. Perhaps he has reached a greater understanding of the brain of a single type of animal than any other biologist, and it was a stroke of genius on his part to choose such a fascinating and intelligent creature," wrote the editors of *Essays on*

the Nervous System, a book dedicated to Young on the occasion of his sixty-seventh birthday. Young's research touched many people through his books and also through the radio lectures he gave on the British Broadcasting Corporation (BBC). The first of these, the Reith Lectures, were given in 1950 and later published in book form as *Doubt and Certainty in Science.* Young, who had sent a copy of the Reith lectures to the English writer Lewis Mumford, commented in a letter to him dated November 28, 1951, "I cannot help feeling that we are at a point where we could develop a new 'science' lying between fields as wide apart as physics, physiology and history. The more I think of it, the more convinced I become that all scientific study is a study of the behaviour of observers and reactors, which, I suppose, is the same as History."

Young's Work at U.C.L. Inspires Colleagues

At the college itself, Young's octopus research, which shed a great deal of light upon the relationship between brain structure and behavior in higher animals, inspired psychiatrists, neurologists and engineers. One result was a model electronic brain, devised by an electrical engineer named W. K. Taylor. This model was able to discriminate between various shapes, and even between portraits of people. Young continued his work on the reaction of nerves to injury, gathering around him a group of eager young anatomists who went on to become important researchers in the fields of anatomy and neurology. Several years after Young was chosen to head the anatomy department, he persuaded the college to purchase an electron microscope, which had so impressed him at the American embassy in London. Its use threw much light on the study of cell membranes.

Research on Octopus Brain Illuminates Nature of Memory

The research that Young embarked upon in Naples as a young man continued to absorb him. Focusing on the brain of the octopus, Young also analyzed the structure and functions of the various lobes concerned in memory, differentiating between the short- and long-term memory systems. He demonstrated that there are two separate sets of lobes for recording information about visual and tactile events. Both sets are organized on the same principles, allowing the signals of the results of actions (pleasure and pain) to provide the information for inductive forecasting of the best course of future action. From this work, Young formulated a theory about the units that accumulate in the memory by the release of inhibitory substances, which limit the possible outputs for the classifying cells of the receptors. These researches have illuminated one of the most complex and most challenging of all biological problems—the nature of memory. During his tenure at U.C.L., Young divided his time between research and teaching; one of the first things he did as department chairman was to revise the teaching of gross anatomy. As a result, he substantially reduced the burden it imposed on medical students. In addition, Young played an important role in developing B.Sc. courses in anatomy at the college, thus offering opportunities to young biologists both within and without the medical field.

Young married Phyllis Elizabeth Heaney in 1938 and they had one son and two daughters. He subsequently married Raymonde May, with whom he had one daughter. Young wrote numerous scientific papers and books, and delivered several notable lectures. He received many awards and medals and was made an honorary fellow of numerous academies and societies both in the U.K. and abroad.

SELECTED WRITINGS BY YOUNG:

Books

Doubt and Certainty in Science, Oxford University Press, 1960.
(With Tom Margerison) *From Molecule to Man,* Crown Publishers, 1969.
Philosophy and the Brain, Oxford University Press, 1987.

SOURCES:

Books

Bellairs, R. and E. G. Gray, editors, *Essays on the Nervous System,* Clarendon Press, 1974.

Other

Letter from J. Z. Young to Lewis Mumford, dated November 28, 1951.

—*Sketch by Rayma Prince*

Hideki Yukawa
1907-1981
Japanese physicist

Hideki Yukawa was the first citizen of Japan to receive a Nobel Prize, an award given to him in 1949 for his theory of the meson, the subatomic particle that binds the nucleus' protons and neutrons.

In addition to that honor, Yukawa received the Imperial prize of the Japan Academy in 1940, the Lomonosov Gold Medal of the Soviet Academy of Sciences in 1964, the Order of Merit of the Federal Republic of Germany in 1964, and the Order of the Rising Sun (Japan) in 1977.

Hideki Yukawa was born Hideki Ogawa in Tokyo on January 23, 1907. He was the fifth of seven children born to Takuji and Koyuki Ogawa. His father was employed at the Geological Survey Bureau in Tokyo at the time of Hideki's birth and a year later was appointed professor of geology at Kyoto Imperial University. In his autobiography, *Tabibito* (*The Traveler*), Yukawa describes the experience of growing up in a large household which included, in addition to his parents and siblings, three grandparents. One of these, his maternal grandmother, had once taught at the samurai school at Tokugawa Castle and was a particularly strong influence in Yukawa's life. She taught him to read and write kanji (Chinese pictographs) before he entered elementary school.

Learns Modern Physics

Yukawa attended the Third High School in Kyoto from 1923 to 1926. There he was a classmate of future Nobel Laureate **Sin-Itiro Tomonaga** who, for his work on quantum electrodynamics, would go on to share the Nobel Prize with **Paul Dirac**. After graduation, Yukawa entered Kyoto Imperial University, where he majored in physics. Yukawa's interest in the subject had been aroused in high school when he discovered a number of books on quantum mechanics and relativity in the school library. One of the most influential of the books he found, **Max Planck**'s *Introduction to Theoretical Physics,* he was able to read only after he had taught himself German.

In 1929, Yukawa received his master's degrees from Kyoto, and then stayed on as a research assistant in the laboratory of Kajuro Tamaki. Then, in 1932, Yukawa accepted an appointment as lecturer in physics at Kyoto. Just prior to accepting his new teaching post, Hideki married Sumi Yukawa, a classical Japanese dancer. He adopted his new wife's family name and went to live with them in Osaka. The Yukawas eventually had two sons, Harumi and Takaai.

In 1933 Yukawa accepted a second position as lecturer in physics, this time at Osaka Imperial University. He continued teaching at Osaka for the next five years, working on his doctorate in physics at the same time. In 1936 he was promoted to associate professor of physics and, two years later, was awarded his Ph.D.

Proposes the Meson Theory

It was during his years at Osaka that Yukawa made the discovery for which he is best known, the meson theory. The early 1930s were a period of some confusion for physicists interested in the atomic nucleus. They had learned from **Werner Karl Heisenberg** that nuclei consist of only two particles, protons and neutrons. Of these two, only protons have electrical charge, a positive charge. It would appear, then, that nuclei should be inherently unstable: the electrostatic force of repulsion among protons should, according to classical theory, tend to blow the nucleus apart.

Yukawa became interested in this problem in about 1930. It occurred to Yukawa that there must be some force far stronger than the electromagnetic force that could hold nucleons (protons and neutrons) together. As he developed his theory, Yukawa came to the conclusion that such a force must take the form of a particle, carrying a force of attraction back and forth between pairs of nucleons.

In his calculations, Yukawa found that this force-carrying particle would have a mass about 200 times greater than the electron, but only one-ninth that of a proton or neutron. Because of the particle's intermediary mass, it was later given the name *meson,* from the Greek for "middle." (Scientists actually considered naming the particle the "yukon," in honor of its discoverer, but discarded it to avoid possible geographical confusion.)

Yukawa first announced his theory of the meson at scientific meetings in Osaka and Tokyo in October and November, 1934, and then in the *Proceedings of the Physico-Mathematical Society of Japan* in February, 1935. For about two years his ideas remained largely ignored; then, in 1937, **Carl D. Anderson** and Seth Neddermeyer discovered a particle that appeared to have many of the properties predicted by Yukawa. The scientific community's initial enthusiasm for this discovery soon died out, however, as additional studies showed that Anderson's meson—later named the mu-meson, or muon—differed in some fundamental ways from Yukawa's prediction. It was not until 1947 that Yukawa's work was fully confirmed. That year, **Cecil Frank Powell** found the Yukawa particle—now called the pi-meson—in a cosmic ray shower. Two years later, Yukawa was awarded the 1949 Nobel Prize in physics for his discovery of the meson—an honor that brought substantial pride to the war-torn Japanese scientific community.

In the mean time, Yukawa had returned to Kyoto University where he had been appointed professor of theoretical physics in 1939. The year he was awarded the Nobel Prize, Yukawa came to the United States on a one-year visiting professorship at the Institute for Advanced Studies in Princeton, New Jersey. At the end of that year he accepted an appointment at Columbia Univeristy, where he remained for four more years. In 1946 he founded the scientific journal

Progress of Theoretical Physics, for which he also served as editor.

In 1953 Columbia awarded Yukawa tenure, but he decided nonetheless to return to Japan. There he assumed his previous post at Kyoto University, as well as the newly-created position as director of the Research Institute for Fundamental Physics, an institute established specifically for him by the Japanese government. Although he retired officially from his academic positions in 1970, Yukawa continued to write, speak, and edit his journal. He was also active in organizations that promoted the peaceful use of science and technology: for example, in 1955 he, along with other scientists, signed the Russell-Einstein paper advocating the settling of political disputes through peaceful means; Yukawa was also in attendance at a number of Pugwash Conferences, in which scientists discussed options for disarmament. He died from pneumonia in Kyoto on September 8, 1981.

SELECTED WRITINGS BY YUKAWA:

Books

Yukawa Hideki Jishenshu (title means *Selected Works of Hideki Yukawa*), Asahi Shimbunsha, 1971.
Creativity and Intuition: A Physicist Looks at East and West, Kodansha, International, 1973.
Hideki Yukawa: Scientific Works, Iwanami Shoten, 1979.
Tabibito (title means *The Traveler*), translated by L. Brown and R. Yoshida, [Singapore], 1982.

Periodicals

"On the Interaction of Elementary Particles," *Proceedings of the Physico-Mathematical Society of Japan,* Volume 17, 1935, p. 48.

SOURCES:

Books

Dictionary of Scientific Biography, Scribner, 1982, pp. 999–1005.
Heathcote, Niels H. de V., *Nobel Prize Winners in Physics, 1901–1950,* Henry Schuman, 1953, pp. 446–447.
McGraw-Hill Modern Men of Science, McGraw-Hill, 1984, pp. 360–361.
Nobel Prize Winners, H. W. Wilson, 1987, pp. 1155–1157.
Weber, Robert L., *Pioneers of Science: Nobel Prize Winners in Physics,* American Institute of Physics, 1980, pp. 133–134.

—*Sketch by David E. Newton*

Lotfi Asker Zadeh
1921-
Russian-born American electrical engineer

Lotfi Asker Zadeh, who described himself in an interview with Jeanne Spriter James as an "American, mathematically oriented, electrical engineer of Iranian descent, born in Russia," is responsible for the development of fuzzy logic and fuzzy set theory. Zadeh is also known for his research in system theory, information processing, artificial intelligence, expert systems, natural language understanding, and the theory of evidence. His first two papers that set forth the fuzzy theories, "Fuzzy Sets" and "Outline of a New Approach to the Analysis of Complex Systems and Decision Processes," have been listed as "Citation Classics" by the *Citation Index,* a publication that counts and lists those papers which have been cited most often in the writings of others. Zadeh received the prestigious Honda Prize—an award that was introduced in 1977 to honor technology that advances a "humane civilization"—from the Honda Foundation in Japan in 1989. That same year Japan's Ministry of Trade and Industry, along with almost fifty corporate sponsors, opened a laboratory for International Fuzzy Engineering Research (LIFE) with a budget of approximately $40 million for a six-year period. Six months after its initiation, Zadeh became an advisor to LIFE. Although fuzzy theory has received less attention in the United States, industrial applications have begun to appear in U.S. organizations as well.

Zadeh was born February 4, 1921, in Baku, a city on the Caspian Sea in the Soviet Republic of Azerbaijan. Originally named Lotfi Aliaskerzadeh, he simplified his name to Lotfi Asker Zadeh when he arrived in the United States. His father, Rahim Aliaskerzadeh (Asker), was a correspondent for Iranian newspapers and also an importer-exporter; his mother, Fannie (Fania) Koriman Aliaskerzadeh (Asker), was a pediatrician. Zadeh and his parents settled in Teheran (Tehrän), the capital city of Iran, in 1931, when he was ten years old. Zadeh explained in an interview that the culture shock he felt as a result of this move was caused by the change from a school which promoted "atheism and the persecution of anyone religiously oriented, to a religious school run by American missionaries where he attended chapel

every morning." Zadeh was taught in Persian—a language he had to learn after his arrival in Iran—at American College, the Presbyterian missionary school. He attended this school for eight years and then took the entrance exams for the University of Teheran, scoring third in the country. As an electrical engineering major he was first in his class his freshman and sophomore years. However, the disruption of World War II was felt at the university and in the electrical engineering department, which graduated only three students, Zadeh among them, in 1942.

During the year after his graduation, Zadeh worked with his father supplying construction materials to the U.S. Army in Iran. His contacts with Americans made him decide to move to the United States in 1943. Arriving in 1944, he enrolled at the Massachusetts Institute of Technology (MIT), which awarded him an M.A. in electrical engineering in 1946. During his years at MIT, the university was abuzz with excitement over developments in cybernetics, information and communication theory, and advances in computer applications. Zadeh caught the excitement as well and enrolled in the doctoral program at Columbia University. At the same time he was appointed an instructor there. He received his Ph.D. in 1949. Rising from instructor to professor of electrical engineering, he was on staff at Columbia from 1946 to 1959, when he moved on to the University of California at Berkeley.

Develops Fuzzy Theory

In 1963 Zadeh was appointed chairman of the electrical engineering department at Berkeley. It was in the following years that he developed the first outlines of fuzzy theory. Fuzzy logic is the logic that underlies inexact or approximate reasoning, and it is most usefully seen as a branch of set theory. While traditional set theory works with sets of clearly defined objects, fuzzy theory deals with objects that belong to sets with what has been called varying degrees of membership. The set of tall trees, for instance, comprises trees that are tall, trees that are very tall, and trees that are not quite so tall. While the human mind can swiftly make qualitative—and therefore to some extent subjective—judgments of what is tall, machines, particularly computers, could traditionally be programmed only to deal with quantitative measures. Fuzzy logic as Zadeh developed it, however, prescribes the rules by which linguistic models containing qualitative judgments are translated into computer algorithms. In effect, machines can then be programmed to process "approximate" data and deal with the gray areas of life.

Although fuzzy theory was enthusiastically received and applied in Japan, China, and several European countries, it was greeted with a great deal of skepticism in the United States. Many scientists claimed that probability theory was already successfully being used to tackle the same problems that fuzzy theory solved. However, probability theory deals with uncertainty arising in a quantitative, mechanistic universe, while fuzzy theory clarifies uncertainty that follows from the subjective aspects of human cognition. Recently, fuzzy theory has gained a foothold in the United States as well. The most important application of the theory to be developed in the United States is AT&T's expert system on a chip. Hiroyuki Watanabe, the computer scientist who built the "first known expert system on a chip" with Masaki Togai, said in an interview with Jeanne Spriter James that manipulation of information is easier with fuzzy logic, which he described as a sophisticated method that allows for a minimum of engineering time to develop applications. Daniel McNeill and Paul Freiberger, in their book *Fuzzy Logic,* sum up Zadeh's contribution to the world of science as follows: "Fuzzy logic is practical in the highest sense: direct, inexpensive, bountiful. It forsakes not precision, but pointless precision. It abandons an either/or hairline that never existed and brightens technology at the cost of a tiny blur. It is neither a dream like AI [artificial intelligence] nor a dead end, a little trick for washers and cameras. It is here today, and no matter what the brand name on the label, it will be here tomorrow."

In 1968 Zadeh took a sabbatical from Berkeley. He spent half a year at IBM and another six months at MIT. When he returned from his leave, he began teaching only computer science courses at Berkeley. Since then he has spent periods as a visiting scientist at the IBM Research Laboratory in San Jose, California, in 1973 and 1978, as a visiting scholar at the Artificial Intelligence Center of SRI International at Menlo Park, California, in 1981, and as a visiting member of the Center for the Study of Language and Information at Stanford University in 1988.

Zadeh's research has earned him many honors and awards, including the Congress Award from the International Congress on Applied Systems, Research and Cybernetics (1980), the Outstanding Paper Award from the International Symposium on Multiple-valued Logic (1984), and the Berkeley Citation, from the University of California at Berkeley (1991). Zadeh is a member of many organizations, including the American Association for Artificial Intelligence, the World Council on Cybernetics, the American Mathematics Society, the National Academy of Engineers, and the Russian Academy of Natural Sciences. He has received honorary doctorates in the United States and Europe, from universities including the State University of New York in Binghamton, Paul Sabatier University in France, Dortmund University in Germany and the University of Granada in Spain. Zadeh still supervises doctoral dissertations at Berkeley and keeps a busy calendar of speaking engagements. He founded the Berkeley Initiative in Soil Computing (called the BISC group) in 1991 and serves as its director, and is a member of the editorial boards of forty journals.

Zadeh married Fay Sand, his childhood sweetheart from Iran, on March 21, 1946, and they have two children, Stella and Norman. He is an accomplished amateur photographer, specializing particularly in portraiture, and has made portraits of many famous scientists and artists.

SELECTED WRITINGS BY ZADEH:

Books

(With C. A. Desoer) *Linear System Theory,* McGraw, 1963.

(Editor with E. Polak) *System Theory,* McGraw, 1969.

Fuzzy Sets and Applications: Selected Papers, edited by R. R. Yager, S. Ovchinnikov, R. M. Tong and H. T. Nguyen, Wiley, 1987.

Periodicals

"Fuzzy Sets," *Information and Control,* June, 1965, pp. 338–353.

"Outline of a New Approach to the Analysis of Complex Systems and Decision Processes," *IEEE Transactions on Systems, Man and Cybernetics,* January, 1973, pp. 28–44.

"Fuzzy Logic, Neural Neutral Networks and Soil Computing," *Communications of the ACM (Association of Computer Machinery),* March, 1994.

SOURCES:

Books

Klir, George J., and Tina A. Folger, *Fuzzy Sets, Uncertainty and Information* Prentice-Hall, 1988.

Kosko, Bart, *Neural Networks and Fuzzy Systems,* Prentice-Hall, 1991.

McNeill, Daniel, and Paul Freiberger, *Fuzzy Logic,* Simon & Schuster, 1993.

Periodicals

Dvorak, Wes, "Fuzzy Logic Aids New Expert Chip," *Bell Labs News,* January 26, 1986.

London Times, July 17, 1992, p. 26E.
New York Times, April 2, 1989, p. 1.

Other

Watanabe, Hiroyuki, interview with Jeanne Spriter James conducted August 23, 1993.

Zadeh, Lotfi Asker, interview with Jeanne Spriter James conducted February 28, 1994.

—*Sketch by Jeanne Spriter James*

E. C. Zeeman
1925-
English mathematician

A pure mathematician E. C. Zeeman has devoted most of his career to various aspects of topology —a type of geometry that examines the properties of shapes in many dimensions. He is best known for his work in catastrophe theory and his attempts to apply this method of mathematical modelling to other scientific fields, including biology and psychology. In addition to his contributions to mathematical research, Zeeman has proven to be an effective administrator and a successful educator. He joined the University of Warwick in England in 1964, the year it was founded, and built the mathematics department there into an internationally known research center. He has also spent much time teaching mathematics to children, giving talks on both radio and television, and he was knighted in 1991 by Queen Elizabeth II for his leadership role in the advancement of mathematics education. He has been principal of Hertford College at Oxford University since 1988.

Erik Christopher Zeeman was born in Japan on February 4, 1925, to Christian and Christine Bushnell Zeeman. His mother was an English governess and his father a Danish exporter and importer who died when Zeeman was four years old. After his father's death, his mother took him and his sister back to England, where they grew up. In an interview reprinted as "Private Games," Zeeman recalled his mother showing him how to solve a problem using variables when he was seven years old. This was his first introduction to algebra: "I was absolutely flabbergasted at this technique and I've never forgotten it. And then at school maths was always very easy."

When World War II began in 1939 Zeeman was only fourteen. Four years later with the war still raging, he had joined the Royal Air Force, and he served as a Flying Officer until 1947. He entered Christ's College at Cambridge University the year he left the service; he earned his bachelor's degree and remained there until 1953, when he moved to another Cambridge college, Gonville and Caius, as a lecturer. He did his doctoral work in pure mathematics under Shaun Wylie, receiving his Ph.D. in 1954 for a thesis on knots. "I was particularly intrigued," he recalls in "Private Games," "by all the algebraic machinery you need to actually prove knots exist." Zeeman began his research career in what is known as algebraic topology, using algebra to address geometric problems, such as the question of whether knots can be tied in many dimensions. In his doctoral dissertation, he was not able to prove that a knot could be tied in more than four dimensions, but he returned to the problem seven years later. He used geometry instead of algebra and discovered he could prove it was possible to untie knots in five dimensions. This proof turned out to have many important ramifications for geometric topology, and he had many research students who subsequently earned their doctorates working on theorems suggested by this proof.

But his best known and most controversial work has been in catastrophe theory. First developed by the French mathematician **René Thom** in the 1960s, catastrophe theory creates models to predict the consequences of a chain of events that has certain discontinuous elements. In the *Times Literary Supplement,* Zeeman describes the applications of this theory: "Throughout nature we observe continuous changes giving rise to discontinuous jumps: for example a continuous rise in temperature will cause water to boil suddenly, which is a sudden jump in density." Catastrophe theory uses multi-dimensional images to model these sudden changes and Zeeman has argued that it can be used in disciplines as disparate as meteorology and behavioral psychology. He has used catastrophe theory to model anorexia nervosa as well as the concept of punctuated equilibria in evolution. In his paper, "On the Psychology of a Hijacker," Zeeman employs the theory to analyze what could be expected from various types of hijacking cases, arguing that mathematics can help make accurate predictions in hostage situations.

Always concerned about the relevance of mathematics, Zeeman became increasingly interested in the intersection between pure and applied mathematics throughout the course of his career. In a talk on British Broadcasting Corporation radio, he once offered an example of the practical applications of topology: if a ball is entirely covered with hair, it would be impossible to comb the hair down smoothly all around it, without leaving a tuft anywhere. He calls this an example of a topological theorem and observes that one consequence of this theorem is that there can never be a stable weather situation: The wind can never be blowing smoothly all around the globe.

Zeeman has also made contributions to brain modelling and he has been involved in the development of chaos theory.

Zeeman joined Warwick University when it was founded in 1964 as Foundation Professor and Director of the Mathematics Research Centre. An articulate man, with an ability to command financial support for research projects in mathematics, he was the driving force behind the development of the department there. In 1982 he was awarded the Whitehead Prize for "his personal work and his leadership," according to a citation published in the *Bulletin of the London Mathematical Society.* In building his department at the University of Warwick into an international center for mathematics, he "displayed talents as a manager and a leader exceptional among pure mathematicians," and the citation continues: "The strong British school of geometrical topologists now consists almost entirely of Zeeman's pupils, his pupil's pupils, and so on to the third or fourth generation."

Zeeman is often conscious of the difference between the way mathematicians see their subject and the way others do, and this awareness is part of what has made him an effective educator, not only of doctoral students and undergraduates but also of children and the public in general. In 1978 he delivered the Royal Institution Christmas Lectures—television broadcasts designed to introduce school children to various scientific disciplines. In the 1980s, he delivered the Mathematics Masterclasses for the Royal Institution. The original television broadcasts of these classes have since been released on videotape, and their purpose, as Zeeman writes in "Christmas Lectures and Mathematics Masterclasses," is "to provide enrichment for the more gifted, because today the gifted can be amongst the educationally most deprived."

In addition to the Whitehead Prize and his knighthood in 1991, Zeeman received the Queen's Jubilee Medal in 1977 and the Faraday Medal in 1988. He was elected to the Royal Society in 1975, and he was president of the London Mathematical Society from 1986 to 1988. He was made an honorary fellow of Christ's College, Cambridge in 1989, and he has received honorary degrees from the University of Strasbourg and the University of York.

Zeeman married for the second time in 1960, to Rosemary Gledhill; they have three sons and two daughters. He also has another daughter from a previous marriage. One of his daughters has followed in his footsteps, pursuing a career in mathematics, and he has collaborated with her on some research projects. Zeeman told contributor Jeanne Spriter James that his primary leisure activity is his family. Dressmaking is another of his hobbies and he has even written an academic paper on the subject, called "The Mathematics of Dressmaking." Of mathematics in general, Zeeman says in "Private Games" that "It's a very noble subject. It's probably one of the oldest and noblest of man's activities. And I would identify, historically, with that very long tradition."

SELECTED WRITINGS BY ZEEMAN:

Books

Catastrophe Theory: Selected Papers, 1972–1977, Addison Wesley, 1977.

Periodicals

"Unknotting Spheres in Five Dimensions," *Bulletin of the American Mathematical Society,* May, 1960, p. 198.
"Mathematics and Creative Thinking," *Psychiatric Quarterly,* Volume 40, 1966, pp. 348–354.
"The Geometry of Catastrophe," *Times Literary Supplement,* December 10, 1971, pp. 1556–1557.
"The Psychology of a Hijacker," *Analysis Conflict and Its Resolution,* edited by P. G. Bennett, Oxford University Press, 1987, pp. 71–91.
"Private Games," *A Passion for Science,* edited by L. Wolpert, Oxford University Press, 1988, pp. 52–65.
"Christmas Lectures and Mathematics Masterclasses," *The Popularization of Mathematics,* edited by A. G. Howson and J. P. Kahane, Cambridge University Press, 1990, pp. 194–206.

SOURCES:

Books

Thompson, Michael, *Rubbish Theory,* Oxford University Press, 1979.

Periodicals

"Citation for Erik Christopher Zeeman, F.R.S.," *Bulletin of the London Mathematical Society,* Volume 14, 1982, p. 569.

Other

Zeeman, Erik Christopher, interview with Jeanne Spriter James, conducted November 6, 1993.

—Sketch by Jeanne Spriter James

Pieter Zeeman
1865-1943
Dutch physicist

In 1902 Pieter Zeeman, along with theoretical physicist **Hendrik Lorentz**, received the Nobel Prize for Physics for their research on the effects of magnetism on electromagnetic radiation. That research had been suggested when James Clerk Maxwell demonstrated in the 1860s that light is composed of electrical and magnetic fields oscillating at right angles to each other. That formulation meant that light should be affected by the imposition of external magnetic and electrical fields—phenomena that had already been observed by Michael Faraday in 1845 and John Kerr in 1875. Zeeman's detection of the splitting of the spectral lines of sodium in a strong magnetic field was, however, the most impressive confirmation of Maxwell's theory up to that time.

Pieter Zeeman was born in Zonnemaire, Zeeland, the Netherlands, on May 25, 1865. He was the son of Catharinus Farandinus Zeeman, a Lutheran minister, and the former Wilhelmina Worst. Zeeman's primary education took place in Zonnemaire and his secondary education in the somewhat larger town of Zierikzee, five miles away. From 1883 to 1885 he attended the Delft gymnasium to study the Greek and Latin that were then required for attendance at any Dutch university. At Delft he met physicist **Heike Kamerlingh Onnes**, who was impressed by Zeeman's understanding of Scottish physicist James Clerk Maxwell's famous textbook, *Theory of Heat*.

Begins Research on the Kerr Effect

In 1885 Zeeman was admitted to the University of Leiden, where he was a student of both Kamerlingh Onnes and Lorentz. Five years later he obtained a post as assistant to Lorentz and began his doctoral research on the Kerr effect. First observed by the Scottish physicist John Kerr in 1875, the Kerr effect is produced when plane-polarized light is reflected off a highly polished pole of an electromagnet. During reflection, the light becomes elliptically polarized.

The Kerr effect was an example of the kind of phenomena suggested by Maxwell's theory of electromagnetism, announced in the 1860s. Maxwell demonstrated that a light ray has associated with it an electric field and a magnetic field, both oscillating at right angles to each other and to the direction in which the light ray is moving. It follows from this formulation that one or the other of these two components should be affected by the presence of an external electrical or magnetic field—an effect that would be observed by some change in a light beam forced to pass through an electrical or magnetic field.

The first of these predicted effects had actually been observed by English chemist and physicist Michael Faraday as early as 1845. Faraday had shown that a plane-polarized beam of light experiences a rotation of planes when it passes through a magnetic field. Kerr's 1875 discovery was the first post-Maxwellian confirmation of the same effect. For his doctoral studies, Zeeman repeated and refined Kerr's experiments, obtaining such impressive results that he was awarded a gold medal by the Netherlands Scientific Society of Haarlem in 1892. Zeeman received his Ph.D. from Leiden a year later.

After receiving his doctorate, Zeeman spent a semester at the Kohlrausch Institute in Strasbourg and then returned to Leiden as a privatdocent (an unpaid instructor). In January of 1897, Zeeman moved to the University of Amsterdam as a lecturer in physics. Three years later he was promoted to full professor, and in 1908 he was made director of the university's Physical Institute. In 1923 he also was appointed director of the newly established Laboratorium Physica, which was later renamed the Zeeman Laboratory in his honor. He retired from these posts in 1935.

Observes the Splitting of Spectral Lines

It was during his brief stay at Leiden from 1896 to 1897 that Zeeman made the discovery for which he was to become famous: the splitting of spectral lines. He learned that in 1862 Faraday had attempted—without success—to produce a splitting of spectral lines by placing a sodium flame within a magnetic field. Zeeman decided to repeat the Faraday experiment, but to make use of a more powerful magnetic field and a more accurate detection system. In August of 1896 he was successful. He found that each of the two yellow "D" lines in the sodium spectrum divided into two distinct parts when the sodium flame was situated within the magnetic field. This phenomenon is now universally known as the Zeeman effect.

Although he announced these results on October 31, 1896, Zeeman continued his work using other elements and improved techniques. In the spring of 1897, after he had taken up residence in Amsterdam, he observed the tripling of lines that had been predicted by Zeeman's former advisor Lorentz. Zeeman's last series of confirmatory experiments was conducted at the University of Gröningen, located in a rural part of Holland. This setting was necessary to escape from background noises, such as street traffic, that would have affected the most precise of Zeeman's experiments.

Zeeman also was able in this series of experiments to make very precise measurements of the particle responsible for the sodium radiation. He discovered that the ratio of electrical charge to mass for this particle was identical to that determined by **Joseph John Thomson** for the electron. Zeeman concluded that it was the vibration of electrons in the sodium atom that was responsible for the emission of the D lines in the element's spectrum.

In his later research, Zeeman continued to employ the high precision that had revealed to him the splitting of the sodium spectral lines. In 1915, for example, he carried out a series of experiments on the speed of light in water as a follow-up on the tests of American physicists **Albert Michelson** and **Edward Williams Morley**. Zeeman also became interested in the study of isotopes—groups of chemically identical atoms of the same element and atomic number with differing atomic mass—and he discovered a new argon isotope.

Zeeman married Johanna Elisabeth Lebret in 1895, and they had four children. In addition to the Nobel Prize, Zeeman was awarded the Rumford Medal of the Royal Society, the Wilde Prize of the French Academy of Sciences, the Baumgartner Prize of the Austrian Academy of Sciences, and the Henry Draper Medal of the U.S. National Academy of Sciences. He died in Amsterdam on October 9, 1943.

SELECTED WRITINGS BY ZEEMAN:

Books

Researches in Magneto-Optics, with Special Reference to the Magnetic Resolution of Spectrum Lines, Macmillan, 1913.
Verhandelingen van Dr. P. Zeeman over Magneto-Optische Verschijnselen, E. Ijdo, 1921.

SOURCES:

Books

Gillispie, Charles Coulson, editor, *Dictionary of Scientific Biography,* Volume 14, Scribner, 1975, pp. 597–599.
Magill, Frank N., editor, *The Nobel Prize Winners—Physics,* Volume 1, Salem Press, 1990, pp. 45–52.
Wasson, Tyler, editor, *Nobel Prize Winners,* H. W. Wilson, 1987, pp. 1157–1160.
Weber, Robert L., *Pioneers of Science: Nobel Prize Winners in Physics,* American Institute of Physics, 1980, pp. 10–11.

—*Sketch by David E. Newton*

Yakov Borisovich Zel'dovich
1914-1987
Russian physicist and cosmologist

Yakov Borisovich Zel'dovich is perhaps best known for his work in cosmology, the study of the origins and nature of the universe, a field he did not even begin to plumb until he was almost fifty years old. At that age Zel'dovich evolved his famous "pancake model," which described the formation of clusters of galaxies in the early universe. But as a brilliant young scientist who rose through the then-Soviet ranks without a formal education, Zel'dovich made earlier significant contributions as well in the theory of explosions and shock waves, the theoretical foundation of chain reactions, and such basic physics questions as the conservation of baryon and lepton numbers and the theory of electroweak interactions.

Zel'dovich was born March 8, 1914, three years before the Russian Revolution, at his grandfather's house in Minsk. His father, a lawyer, and his mother, a translator of French fiction, moved while Yakov was still an infant to Petrograd (later Leningrad and now St. Petersburg). There, at age 15, Yakov finished high school and began taking courses to become a laboratory technician. But he was nudged off that path by a fortuitous class trip to the Leningrad Physical-Technical Institute in March 1931. During his visit to this center of Soviet physics, young Zel'dovich asked such penetrating questions that he was invited to work at the Institute in his free time. He seized the opportunity and excelled at his work; so impressed was the chemical physics department with his presentation on the ortho-para transformations of hydrogen that he was promptly recruited as a department member. Senior residents at the Institute, which broke off to become the Institute of Chemical Physics, told stories for years afterwards about the youth who stumped the experts and was so well regarded that one laboratory head was said to have traded an expensive oil pump for him.

Zel'dovich's "unusual training strongly influenced the surprising imagery and solidness of his thinking—his ability to see the phenomenon behind every formula, to find physically justified approximations, to simplify the route of problem solving while preserving essential components of the theory," colleague Vitalii Goldanskii recalled in *Physics Today* in December, 1988. In fact, Zel'dovich simply learned on his own, asking questions, observing. Despite his lack of formal university training, in 1936 he earned a Candidate of Science degree with his defense of a thesis that laid the foundations for the theory of adsorption (the adhesion on a surface of a very thin layer of molecules) on heterogenous surfaces. His doctoral thesis, which was awarded in 1939 and gave him the Soviet equivalent of a full professorship in the United States, showed that the oxidation of nitrogen is an unbranched chain reaction with an equilibrium concentration of oxygen atoms serving as active centers—a finding that has major application to today's environmental pollution dilemma. The kinetic scheme of nitrogen oxidation, named after Zel'dovich himself, makes it possible to calculate the amount of pollution from internal combustion engines, chemical industries and coal power stations, and is useful in devising counter-measures.

Zel'dovich Makes Shock Waves

During the 1930s Zel'dovich applied his genius to the theory of explosions and shock waves. In collaboration with David Frank-Kamenetzky, he came up with the first physically grounded theory of flame propagation, based on treating flame as a combustible wave. The Zel'dovich-Neumann-Doring theory of detonation, developed in 1940, made key contributions to the understanding of detonation wave structure. In the early 1940s, while working on theoretical problems related to gunpowder ignition, Zel'dovich discovered a phenomenon of combustion that under certain conditions can cause burning gunpowder in solid-propellant rocket engines to be extinguished. He also made important discoveries about changes in the rate of combustion in rocket engines under the effect of circumfluent gas flow. His work in this area laid the basis for the interior ballistics of solid-propellant rockets.

Zel'dovich's work had obvious military applications, particularly after the discovery of uranium fission. His work with Yuliy B. Khariton on the theoretical bases of explosive and controlled fission reactions—the last such Soviet research to be published openly before the Cold War closed the door on scientific exchange—contributed to the development of the first nuclear reactors. World War II and the Nazi invasion of the Soviet Union brought home the importance of such studies. For his 1940s work on atomic and, later, thermonuclear weapons, Zel'dovich was awarded three Orders of Lenin, three Hero of Socialist Labor awards, the Lenin Prize and four State Prizes (then called Stalin Prizes). In the 1950s Zel'dovich worked on nuclear physics and the physics of elementary particles, proposing the existence and conservation of baryonic and leptonic charges and contributing to the confirmation of the standard model of electroweak interactions, which was not demonstrated until two decades later.

Zel'dovich, who died before the fall of Communism, navigated the treacherous political waters of the Stalinist and post-Stalinist U.S.S.R. by remaining distinctly apolitical. In a 1991 article in *Nature,* John

Peacock repeated a famous story of how the famous scientist once protected himself from police harassment by donning his medals before going out drinking. From 1948 to 1968, Zel'dovich worked closely with famous fellow physicist (and later political dissident) **Andrei Sakharov**. But unlike Sakharov, Zel'dovich chose to ignore risky and potentially disturbing political issues. "Zel'dovich strongly disapproved of my social work, which irritated and even frightened him," Sakharov recalled in an obituary published in *Nature* in February 1988. "He once said, 'People like [English astrophysicist **Stephen**] **Hawking** are devoted to science. Nothing can distract them.' I did not understand why he could not give the help which, given our relationship, I considered myself justified in asking for. I know that all this tormented Zel'dovich."

Turns His Attention to the Stars

In the 1960s Zel'dovich turned his attention to a very different field, cosmology, the study of the nature and evolution of the universe. His work on the dynamics of neutron emission during the formation of black holes led to the acceptance of black holes as observable objects. He is best known for his "pancake model," which suggests that galaxies formed on the surfaces of pancake-like shock fronts created as a result of the "Big Bang," the massive explosion theorized to have generated the universe. Married, with several children, Zel'dovich has been described as a born teacher. "His effect on his pupils was remarkable," Sakharov wrote in his obituary. "He often discovered in them a capacity for scientific creativity which without him would not have been realized or could have been realized only in part and with great difficulty." Zel'dovich died of a heart attack on December 2, 1987.

SELECTED WRITINGS BY ZEL'DOVICH:

Books

Higher Mathematics for Beginners, Nauka, 1960.
(With I. D. Novikov) *Relativistic Astrophysics,* 2 volumes, 1971, republished by University of Chicago Press, 1982, 1983.
(With A. D. Dolgov and M. Volume Sazhin) *Basics of Modern Cosmology,* 1986, translation published by Editions Frontières, 1991.
Selected Works of Yakov Borisovich Zel'dovich, Volume 1: Chemical Physics and Hydrodynamics, edited by J. P. Ostriker, Princeton University Press, 1992.

SOURCES:

Periodicals

Goldanskii, Vitalii I., "Obituaries: Ya. B. Zel'dovich," *Physics Today,* December 1988, p. 98.

Maddox, John, "Differences of Style in Science," *Nature,* October 29, 1987, p. 786.

Peacock, John, "This Strange Universe," *Nature,* May 30, 1991, p. 359.

Priester, Wolfgang, "The Universe of Yakov Zel'dovich," *Sky & Telescope,* October 1988, p. 354.

Sakharov, Andrei, "A Man of Universal Interests," *Nature,* February 1988, p. 671.

Schwarzschild, Bertram, "Redshift Surveys of Galaxies Find a Bubbly Universe," *Physics Today,* May 1986, p. 17.

—*Sketch by Joan Oleck*

E-an Zen
1928-
Chinese-born American geologist and petrologist

E-an Zen's work in the origin and constitution of rocks and minerals has made him an acknowledged expert on New England geology, as well as the geology of the southern Appalachians. His work in applying the principles of thermodynamics and physical chemistry to problems in the structure of granites, sedimentary rocks, and batholiths—masses of igneous rock that have forced themselves into surrounding strata—have earned him awards from both the Geological and Mineralogical Societies of America and the respect of colleagues around the world. Zen's work extends beyond the theoretical, and his field researches have included everything from granites to potholes.

This blending of both intellectual and pragmatic qualities could be foretold from Zen's background. Born in Beijing, China, on May 31, 1928, Zen was the child of versatile academics. His father, Hung-chun Zen, was a chemist, science administrator, and educator, and his mother, Heng-chih Chen Zen, was a historian, essayist, and social reformer. His first decade was spent in Beijing, but then with the coming of World War II, Zen and his family kept one step ahead of the invading Japanese, traveling from Lushan to Kunming to Chungking. What education he had

in those years came from his parents, and it was during that difficult time that Zen developed a love for mineralogy. "I was about ten years old," Zen said in an interview, "and my father and I went out for a stroll in the countryside. He picked up a crystal of calcite (Iceland spar) from the roadside gutter and explained to me how the crystal would break repeatedly along fixed directions because of intrinsic arrangement of atoms in the crystal. A casual remark that stuck!" During the war Zen read books on geomorphology and geology, but at this time it was still maps and geography he loved the most.

Pursues Geological Career in the United States

After the war, his mother—who, like her husband had been educated in the United States—sent Zen to America. Despite very little formal education up to that time, he graduated from high school in 1947 and then attended Cornell University, where he initially planned to study geography. Discovering that the university did not offer a major in physical geography, he opted for geology, earning his A.B. in 1951. His advanced study was done at Harvard University, where he won an M.A. in geology in 1952 and his Ph.D. in the same field in 1955. But his education was gained at great personal cost: he was never to see his father again, and it would be thirty years before he could visit his mother, trapped behind the Chinese Communist bamboo curtain.

As early as the time of his Ph.D., Zen was an acknowledged master of the geology of New England. An early stint as assistant professor at the University of North Carolina also brought him into contact with the geology of the Appalachian Mountains. By 1959, he was a geologist for the U.S. Geological Survey, a position he held until 1989. In the 1960s he conducted field mapping of the stratigraphy and structure of western Vermont, solving the long-standing problem of the tectonic origin of those rocks. Other early research and papers that won him scientific renown include those on the thermodynamics of so-called mix-layered minerals and of multisystems of rocks. His research into the petrology or origin and structure of granites and plutonic rocks also formed a major focus of his work in those years. In 1986, he was awarded the Arthur L. Day Medal from the Geological Society of America for his outstanding work in applying thermodynamics and physical chemistry to the problems of geology. Five years later, he was recognized by the Mineralogical Society of America, winning its Roebling Medal for his career-long work in the field of mineralogy.

In 1990, Zen became an adjunct professor at the University of Maryland and turned his attention from pure research to helping to train a future generation of committed geologists. He was married to Cristina

Coney Silber, a geologist and school teacher, from 1967 to 1982.

SELECTED WRITINGS BY ZEN:

Periodicals

"Metamorphism of Lower Paleozoic Rocks in the Vicinity of the Taconic Range in West-Central Vermont," *American Mineralogist,* Volume 45, 1960, pp. 129–175.

"Stratigraphy and Structure in the Vicinity of the Taconic Range in West-Central Vermont," *Geological Society of America Bulletin,* Volume 72, 1961, pp. 293–338.

"Some Topological Relationships of N+3 Phases, I. General Theory; Unary and Binary Systems," *American Journal of Science,* Volume 264, 1966, pp. 401–427.

"The Phase-Equilibrium Calorimeter, the Petrogenic Grid, and a Tyranny of Numbers," *The American Mineralogist,* Volume 62, 1977, pp. 189–204.

"Exotic Terranes in the New England Appalachians," *Geologic Society of America Memoir,* Volume 158, 1983, pp. 55–81.

"Phase Relations of Peraluminous Granitic Rocks and Their Petrogenic Implications," *Annual Review of Earth and Planetary Sciences,* Volume 16, 1988, pp. 21–51.

"Phanerozoic Denudation History of the Southern New England Appalachians Deduced from Pressure Data," *American Journal of Science,* Volume 291, 1991, pp. 401–424.

SOURCES:

Periodicals

Kieffer, Susan W., "Presentation of the Roebling Medal of the Mineralogical Society of America for 1991 to E-an Zen," *American Mineralogist,* July/August, 1992, pp. 863–864.

McPhee, John, "Travels of the Rock," *New Yorker,* February 26, 1990, pp. 108–117.

Skinner, Brian, J., "Presentation of the Arthur L. Day Medal to E-an Zen," *Geological Society of America Bulletin,* July, 1987, pp. 136–138.

Other

Zen, E-an, interview with J. Sydney Jones, conducted February 10, 1994.

—Sketch by J. Sydney Jones

Frits Zernike
1888-1966
Dutch physicist

Frits Zernike won the 1953 Nobel Prize in physics for his invention of the phase-contrast microscope, an instrument which enabled scientists to study living tissue samples under magnification for the first time. Zernike's background in statistical mathematics and thermodynamics was responsible for his groundbreaking discovery. A conventional microscope utilizes ordinary light, and under these instruments living tissues, particularly transparent ones, are not visible unless stained. Yet staining usually kills the specimen or produces artifacts that are impossible to differentiate from the specimen. The phase-contrast microscope utilizes a diaphragm and a diffraction plate. The diaphragm funnels light into a cone, which is focused on the specimen; the diffraction plate is placed between the lenses, changing the speed of the light if the specimen has diffracted the light. The phase-contrast technique can reveal variations in opacity as well as variations in the thickness of transparent objects.

Born on July 16, 1888, in Amsterdam, Zernike was the son of two mathematicians, Carl Frederick August Zernike and Antje Dieperink Zernike. He was recognized while still young for his mathematical abilities. He received both his B.S. and his Ph.D. in physics from the University of Amsterdam, and he worked at an astronomical laboratory while pursuing his graduate studies. His doctoral thesis, "Critical Opalescence, Theoretical and Experimental," quickly established him as a leader in his field. In 1915 he was appointed lecturer in theoretical physics at the University of Groningen. In 1920, he was promoted to professor, and he remained at Groningen for the rest of his career.

Glitch in Telescopes Leads to New Microscope

It was while working in the field of astronomy that Zernike first discovered the advantages of phase-contrast techniques. Irregularities on the surfaces of the curved mirrors of telescopes were a common problem at that time; these mirrors sometimes produced "ghost" images and Zernike hypothesized that they were caused by out-of-phase wavelengths. If he could somehow bring direct and diffracted images back into phase, perhaps these aberrations would disappear. He developed a glass plate with tiny grooves etched in it to be placed in the focal plane of the telescope, and he called this a "phase plate." His experiment worked: when looking through the phase plate, the out-of-phase areas became clearly visible.

Zernike published these findings in 1934, and by 1935 he was applying these same principles to microscopes, which he knew had optical problems that were similar to telescopes. He inserted a phase strip into the focal plane of a microscope and immediately it brought the direct and the diffracted beams into phase.

Although the practical applications of Zernike's findings seem obvious now, it was some years before he could find a manufacturer for a phase-contrast microscope. He first approached a German company, Carl Zeiss, in 1932. "They understood the theoretical background but did not think the practical use would be great," Zernike recalled in an interview when he won the Nobel Prize. "They said if it was practical they already would have developed it." Finally, in 1941, Carl Zeiss agreed to produce the instrument. But it was not until American troops arrived in Germany in 1945 and discovered photomicrographs taken by a phase-contrast microscope that Zernike's instrument received worldwide attention. When he won the Nobel Prize in 1953, the phase-contrast microscope was cited as being a key to insights into cancer research.

Unlike many instrument makers, Zernike worked first from theoretical principles and then moved to practical applications. "Perhaps Dr. Zernike's most outstanding characteristic," said the author of his *New York Times* obituary, "was his ability to blend theory with experiment." Though the phase-contrast microscope is considered his crowning achievement, Zernike is also known for other work. Early in his career he invented the Zernike galvanometer, an instrument used to detect and measure small electrical currents. The Zernike polynomials are a method he developed regarding the wave theory of light and are widely used by mathematicians. He also made many improvements in infrared and ultraviolet spectroscopy, as well as in the construction of the electromagnet.

Although Zernike stayed at his alma mater for his entire career, he was a visiting professor of physics at the Johns Hopkins University in Baltimore in 1948. In 1950 he was elected to the Royal Microscopical Society of London, and he was presented with the Rumford Medal of the British Royal Society in 1952.

Zernike married Dora van Bommel van Vloten in 1929. The couple had two children; his wife died in 1944. In 1954, Zernike remarried, to L. Koperberg-Baanders. He retired in 1958 and died in Groningen on March 10, 1966.

SELECTED WRITINGS BY ZERNIKE:

Periodicals

"Diffraction Theory of the Knife-Edge Test and Its Improved Form, the Phase-Contrast Method," *Monographs of the National Royal Astronomical Society,* Volume 94, 1934, p. 377.

"The Propagation of Order in Cooperative Phenomena," *Physica,* Volume 7, 1940, p. 565.

"How I Discovered Phase Contrast," *Les prix Nobel en 1953,* Stockholm, 1953, pp. 107–114.

SOURCES:

Periodicals

New York Times, March 16, 1966, p. 45.

—*Sketch by Dorothy Barnhouse*

Karl Ziegler
1898-1973
German chemist

Karl Ziegler had a long and distinguished career in diverse areas of chemistry. Although he is considered an organic chemist, he applied the methods and principles of inorganic, physical, and analytical chemistry to his research problems. He thought of himself as a chemist who carried out "pure" research, but his greatest contribution was a discovery that led to a revolution in "applied" research and was of great benefit to industry. This breakthrough related to catalysts—substances that provoke a chemical reaction—and Ziegler's work became the foundation of the modern plastics industry. The discovery and application of the "Ziegler catalysts" were rewarded with lucrative licensing fees and the 1963 Nobel Prize in chemistry, which Ziegler shared with **Giulio Natta**, an Italian chemist who significantly extended Ziegler's work.

Ziegler was born on November 26, 1898, in Helsa, Germany, to Luise (Rall) and Karl Ziegler, a Lutheran minister. As a youth he showed an early interest in chemistry, and had a laboratory at home. In 1916 he matriculated at the University of Marburg, from which his father had graduated, and was so advanced in his studies that he was able to complete his Ph.D. in 1920, when he was only twenty-one. His thesis adviser was Karl von Auwers, a noted organic chemist of his time. Ziegler remained at Marburg as a lecturer until 1925, then spent a year as a visiting lecturer at the University of Frankfurt. In 1926 Ziegler moved to the University of Heidelberg, receiving a promotion to professor the following year. He remained at Heidelberg until 1936, when he was appointed professor and director of the Chemical

Institute at the University of Halle. In 1943 Ziegler accepted the directorship of the Kaiser Wilhelm Institute (later known as the Max Planck Institute) for Coal Research in Müllheim, located in Germany's Ruhr valley. Ziegler agreed to the appointment on condition that he could work on any research project of his choice and not be limited to the chemistry of coal. It was at Müllheim that he discovered the catalyst that brought him great renown, but the discovery was a natural consequence of research which he had begun as a graduate student and developed over his long career.

From 1923 to 1943 Ziegler concentrated his research on free radicals (atoms or groups of atoms having one or more unpaired electrons), organometallic compounds and their reactions with double bonds, and the synthesis of large rings, which are cyclic compounds of molecules. He was primarily interested in the fundamental aspects of structural chemistry, such as the strength of the carbon-carbon bond. He studied the nature of free radicals while looking for compounds whose bonds could be broken easily to form a trivalent species, or one containing a carbon atom bound to three other substances. Usually free radicals exist only briefly and rapidly react to form normal tetravalent compounds—carbon most often has a bonding capacity of four—but Ziegler found many examples of complex free radicals that could survive and be manipulated like ordinary compounds, as long as reactive species such as oxygen were excluded.

In the course of his work on free radicals, Ziegler investigated the organic derivatives of reactive metals, such as sodium and potassium, and later, lithium. With a chemical composition similar to that of the organomagnesium compounds explored earlier by French chemist and Nobel Prize–winner **Victor Grignard**, lithium proved to be extremely useful in organic synthesis. Unlike Grignard's reagent, however, Ziegler found that certain organopotassium compounds could add to a carbon-carbon double bond to make a more complex organopotassium compound. Ziegler applied the reaction to butadiene, a compound that contains two double bonds, and found that the butadiene molecules could form long chains.

As this research progressed, Ziegler considered the problem of joining the ends of long chain molecules to form large rings. This problem had considerable practical importance, for example, in the synthesis of the natural perfume base, muscone. Ziegler eventually used a strong base—a material that accepts protons in solution—with a long-chain compound in very high dilution in order to prepare a large-ring ketone, a compound with fourteen to thirty-three carbons.

Discovery of Polymerization Catalysts Revolutionizes the Chemical Industry

When Ziegler moved to the Institute for Coal Research in 1943, he continued the lines of research he had earlier developed. Ziegler tried many experiments to add lithium hydride to the carbon-carbon double bond, but the reaction was slow and unsuccessful. The compound lithium aluminum hydride was reported by Schlesinger at the University of Chicago in 1947, and Ziegler tried this as a substitute for lithium hydride in 1949. This was successful, and led Ziegler to the conclusion that the aluminum was the vital component. Ziegler found that organoaluminum compounds reacted with double-bond compounds at one hundred degrees centigrade to produce long chains of carbons attached to the aluminum atom. The organoaluminum compounds could be converted into long-chain alcohols (alcohols are characterized by a hydroxyl, or oxygen-hydrogen, group attached to a hydrocarbon chain) by allowing air into the reaction, and these alcohols were useful in the formulation of detergents.

In the course of the investigation of organoaluminum reactions in 1953, one experiment delivered a product that did not contain the expected long chains. The reaction had been carried out in an autoclave—an apparatus suited to special conditions such as high or low pressure or temperature—and careful analysis showed that the autoclave had been previously used in a reaction that contained nickel, with small traces of nickel salts remaining. Ziegler and his colleagues investigated the addition of other metal salts and found that in contrast with nickel, which caused the reaction to fail, certain salts dramatically improved the reaction. When ethylene, the simplest compound containing a carbon-carbon double bond, is bubbled into a hydrocarbon solvent containing a very small amount of an organoaluminum compound and titanium tetrachloride (a volatile liquid compound used now chiefly in skywriting and smoke screens because it fumes in moist air), there is formation of polyethylene (a long, straight hydrocarbon chain). The reaction conditions are very mild, consisting of atmospheric pressure and room temperature.

Polyethylene had been previously produced by the British company Imperial Chemicals Industries, but their method required temperatures up to two hundred degrees centigrade and pressures up to two thousand atmospheres. The ICI polyethylene had shorter chains, and the chains were branched; the substance was waxy and products made from it were soft and easily deformed. On the other hand, Ziegler's polyethylene was hard and rigid, and could be drawn into fibers. Many useful products could be made from Ziegler's low-pressure polyethylene, starting from inexpensive, abundant starting materials. Ziegler refined the process and investigated other catalyst systems. Chemical companies worldwide showed immediate interest in Ziegler's discovery and paid for the right to use it. Among those who extended Ziegler's work was Natta, a chemist at the University of Milan, who showed how the geometry of the polymer could be controlled by the catalyst, and made different polypropylenes, whose physical properties were determined by their molecular geometries.

The discovery of the Ziegler catalysts had a profound effect on the course of chemical research and development. Industrial and academic chemists turned their attention to the wide area of organometallic chemistry in order to understand the fundamental chemistry and to discover useful catalysts for polymerization and other commercial reactions. In Ziegler's Nobel lecture, he showed a world map that indicated large chemical plants that were producing polyethylene and other products based on his research only ten years after his initial discovery. Ziegler became wealthy as a result of his research, and when he was seventy years old, he established the Ziegler Fund for Research with ten million dollars. Ziegler had no political connections with the Nazi government, and he was welcomed at the Institute for Coal Research because his work could continue in the postwar period without interference from the Allies. After resurrecting the German Chemical Society in 1949, Ziegler served as its first president. He retired from the institute in 1969 after bringing great prestige and funding to it.

Ziegler had a long and happy marriage to Maria Kurz, whom he married in 1922. His daughter Marianne was a physician and his son Erhart was a physicist. Ziegler was able to enjoy himself outside the laboratory; among his hobbies were collecting paintings and hiking in the mountains. Ziegler died on August 12, 1973, after a short illness.

SELECTED WRITINGS BY ZIEGLER:

Books

"A Forty Years' Stroll through the Realms of Organometallic Chemistry," *Advances in Organometallic Chemistry,* Volume 6, edited by F. G. A. Stone and R. West, Academic Press, 1968, pp. 1–17.

"Consequences and Development of an Invention," *Nobel Lectures: Chemistry, 1963–1970,* Elsevier, 1972.

SOURCES:

Books

Bonnesen, Peter V., "Karl Ziegler," *Nobel Laureates in Chemistry, 1901–1992,* edited by L. K. James, American Chemical Society, 1993, pp. 449–455.

Boor, J., Jr., *Ziegler-Natta Catalysts and Polymerization,* Academic Press, 1979.

Lagrone, Craig P., "Karl Ziegler," *The Nobel Prize Winners: Chemistry,* Volume 3, edited by F. N. Magill, Salem Press, 1990, pp. 744–754.

Periodicals

Eisch, J. J., "Karl Ziegler: Master Advocate for the Unity of Pure and Applied Research," *Journal of Chemical Education,* Volume 60, 1983, pp. 1009–1014.

—*Sketch by Martin R. Feldman*

Norton Zinder
1928-
American molecular geneticist

Norton Zinder is a molecular geneticist and John D. Rockefeller Jr. Professor of molecular genetics at Rockefeller University in New York City. He also serves as the university's dean of graduate and postgraduate studies. Zinder is known primarily for his research during the late 1940s and early 1950s, when he discovered a new mechanism of genetic transfer called bacterial transduction. This process refers to the transfer of genetic material between bacteria through bacterial viruses. The discovery has shed new light on the location and behavior of bacterial genes. Zinder is the recipient of numerous awards and honors, including the 1962 Eli Lilly Award in Microbiology and Immunology from the American Society of Microbiology.

Norton David Zinder, the older of two boys, was born on November 7, 1928, in New York City to Harry Zinder, a manufacturer, and Jean (Gottesman) Zinder, a homemaker. He attended New York City public schools, graduating from the prestigious Bronx High School of Science, and went on to attend Columbia University, where he received his B.A. in biology in 1947. The following year, at the recommendation of Francis Ryan, a professor of zoology at Columbia and in whose laboratory he had worked, Zinder commenced his graduate career at the University of Wisconsin. There, he studied under American geneticist **Joshua Lederberg**, who had already discovered genetic conjugation (or "mating") a few years earlier and who would win a Nobel Prize in 1958 for his viral and bacterial research. Zinder focused his research on microbial genetics (the study of the genetics of microorganisms), at a time when the field

Norton Zinder

was relatively new and when many basic phenomena were as yet undiscovered.

In 1946, Lederberg had researched mating in *Escherichia coli*—a bacterium that is found in the intestinal tract of animals and which can cause bacterial dysentery. Zinder wished to continue Lederberg's investigations, and he chose to study the closely related genus of *Salmonella*—bacteria that cause illnesses such as typhoid fever or food poisoning in humans and other warm-blooded animals. For his work, Zinder needed to obtain large numbers of mutant strains, which were, at the time, acquired by randomly testing the survivors among bacteria that had been treated with mutagens, or agents that increase both the chance and extent of mutation. Zinder, however, wanted to experiment with a different method of acquisition: He knew that mutant bacteria will not grow in a nutritionally deficient medium and that antibiotic penicillin will kill only growing bacteria. So, he was able to collect bacteria into an environment that was nutritionally inadequate, then kill any normal bacteria by administering penicillin.

Discovers Genetic Transduction

Zinder obtained large numbers of mutant bacteria using this method, and he began his experiments to investigate conjugation in *Salmonella;* however, instead of observing conjugation, he stumbled upon a different method of genetic transfer in bacteria:

genetic transduction. As Zinder continued his research, he determined that genetic material is transferred from one bacterial cell to another by means of a phage, or a virus that invades the bacterial cell, assumes control over the cell's genetic material, reproduces, then eventually destroys the cell. Zinder's discovery of this genetic transfer has led to further studies into the mapping and behavior of genes found in bacteria. For example, Milislav Demerec and other researchers at New York's Cold Spring Harbor Laboratory later found that the bacterial genes that regulate biosynthetic steps are grouped in what have become known as "operons," a term coined in 1960 to describe closely linked genes that function as an integrated whole.

In subsequent investigations, Zinder and his team also discovered the F2 phage, very small in size and the only virus known to contain RNA (ribonucleic acid) as its genetic substance. The researchers ascertained that the RNA generated by the virus contains codes for specific amino acids—the building blocks of protein molecules—as well as signals to control the termination and initiation of protein chains.

Zinder received his M.S. in genetics in 1949 from the University of Wisconsin and married Marilyn Estreicher in December of that same year; the couple eventually had two sons, Stephen and Michael. In 1952 Zinder completed his Ph.D. in medical microbiology, then accepted the post of assistant professor at Rockefeller University (then Rockefeller Institute for Medical Research). By 1964 he had become a full professor of genetics, and approximately ten years later he was named John D. Rockefeller Jr. Professor of Molecular Genetics; in 1993 he was appointed dean of graduate and postgraduate studies. The primary focus of Zinder's research has been in the molecular genetics of phages.

In addition to his positions at Rockefeller, Zinder also has been associated with other institutions. In the mid–1970s he began lengthy affiliations with the science departments of Harvard University, Yale University, and Princeton University, and, beginning in the same period, he also worked in the viral cancer program at the National Cancer Institute. In 1988 he assumed the position of chair of the program advisory committee for the National Institute of Health (NIH) human genome project, and remained in that capacity for three years. He has served in editorial capacities for scientific journals, such as *Virology* and *Intervirology,* and has published numerous articles in professional journals.

Throughout his career Zinder has received several honors, including the United States Steel Award in Molecular Biology from the National Academy of Sciences in 1966, the Medal of Excellence from Columbia University in 1969, and an honorary doctorate of science from the University of Wisconsin in 1990. He was named a fellow of the American Academy of Arts and Sciences, and is associated with such organizations as the National Academy of Sciences, the American Society of Microbiology, Genetics Society of America, the American Society of Virology, and HUGO (Human Genome Organization).

SELECTED WRITINGS BY ZINDER:

Books

(Editor) *RNA Phages,* Cold Spring Harbor Laboratory Press, 1975.

Periodicals

(With J. Lederberg) "Concentration of Biochemical Mutants of Bacteria with Penicillin," *Journal of American Chemical Society,* Volume 70, 1948, p. 4267.
(With Volume Enea, K. Horiuchi, and B. G. Turgeon) "Physical Map of Defective Interfering Particles of Bacteriophage F1," *Journal of Molecular Biology,* Volume 111, 1977, pp. 395–414.
"The Genome Initiative: How to Spell 'Human,'" *Scientific American,* July, 1990, p. 128.

—*Sketch by Kala Dwarakanath*

Hans Zinsser
1878-1940
American bacteriologist

Hans Zinsser was one of the leading bacteriologists and immunologists in the United States during the first half of the twentieth century. His work in advancing the understanding of typhus fever as well as a number of fundamental features of immunology remains central to this day. Zinsser was born on November 17, 1878, in New York City, and grew up in a household where German was the primary language that was spoken. Both of his parents had emigrated from Germany: His father, August Zinsser, was a wealthy manufacturing chemist originally from the Rhineland, and his mother, Marie Theresa (Schmidt), was from the Black Forest region, an area long dominated by French tradition. For this reason, the young Zinsser soon became fluent in a second language: French.

The youngest of August and Marie's four sons, Zinsser did not start formal schooling until age ten. At that time he was sent to a private school in New York City operated by Julius Sachs, and only then did Zinsser begin using English as his first language. The school emphasized the liberal arts, an area of learning especially valued by Zinsser, who had the fortune of spending some portion of every one of his first twenty years of life visiting the art galleries and concert halls of Europe. In 1895, at age seventeen, Zinsser entered nearby Columbia University, where he was intent on studying literature and pursuing a writing career. Studying under comparative literature specialist George Edward Woodberry, the already broadly educated Zinsser showed great promise in the writing of poetry. In an article in *Memoirs of the National Academy of Sciences,* Zinsser's principal biographer, Simeon Burt Wolbach, noted that the "world of things and thoughts" had occupied Zinsser until that time. Although his intellectual life was about to change, Zinsser remained an accomplished poet and essayist as well as lucid writer of scientific prose for the remainder of his more than sixty years. On his deathbed, after battling leukemia for the final two years of his life, he wrote his last sonnet. The poem, which was published posthumously in his collection *Spring, Summer and Autumn,* ends with the lines: "Then, ageless, in your heart I'll come to rest / Serene and proud as when you loved me best."

Enters the Field of Bacteriology

It was only after his tutelage under biologists **Edmund Beecher Wilson** and Bashford Dean during his junior year at Columbia that Zinsser realized that the life sciences would be his career. He went on to Columbia's College of Physicians and Surgeons in 1899, deciding to devote his career to the application of his interest in biology to real human problems. Earning both an M.A. and an M.D. in 1903, he interned at Roosevelt Hospital, then began to practice medicine. He left that vocation after a short while, however, when Columbia offered him a post as instructor in bacteriology. In the meantime, he had married Ruby Handforth Kunz in 1905.

Zinsser taught bacteriology for a short time at Columbia and teamed with Philip Hanson Hiss, Jr., with whom in 1910 he coauthored *A Textbook of Bacteriology,* which has become a standard microbiology text. Simultaneously, he served as assistant pathologist at New York's St. Luke's Hospital. The same year *A Textbook of Bacteriology* was released, Zinsser moved his wife and first child, Gretel, to Palo Alto, California, to accept a position as associate professor of bacteriology and immunology at Stanford University. There, he set up a bacteriology laboratory with the most minimal of equipment in some space borrowed from the anatomy department. In 1913,

Zinsser returned to Columbia University, where he concentrated his research in the field of immunology.

Encounters an Outbreak of Typhus

As a professor of bacteriology and immunology at Columbia, Zinsser experienced a decade that was both exciting and dismaying. In 1915, in the midst of World War I, Zinsser served first as a member of the Red Cross Typhus Commission and later as an officer in the U.S. Army Medical Corps. Arriving in Serbia in 1915, Zinsser had his first field contact with an epidemic of typhus—a disease that is caused by the family of bacteria known as rickettsia, and is characterized by stupors, delirium, high fevers, severe headaches, and dark rashes. Approximately one hundred and fifty thousand cases of typhus existed at the Belgrade front, with a fatality rate of about sixty to seventy percent. During their experiences in the Eastern Front, the scientists in the commission began to gain a rudimentary understanding of the bacteriology and pathology of the disease. For his contributions during the war, Zinsser was awarded the U.S. Distinguished Service Medal, the French Legion of Honor, and the Order of Sava, a major Serbian citation.

In 1918, Zinsser left the U.S. Army Medical Corps as a lieutenant colonel, and continued his professorial duties at Columbia, where he specialized in immunology. In particular, Zinsser focused on discovering a way to immunize patients against the chronic and contagious disease syphilis. Though he did not succeed in his quest to discover a successful method of immunization, he did contribute to the existing knowledge of spirochete, a type of bacteria that causes syphilis and relapsing fevers. In addition, Zinsser continued to study typhus, since he had became an expert on military sanitation, especially with regards to typhus, during his service in the war. He wrote articles and books on the subject in the course of his career, and during his lifetime took a number of trips to distant lands to study epidemic typhus or cholera—a diarrheal disease caused by bacteria. Among his expeditions were excursions to the Soviet Union in 1923, to Mexico in 1931, and to China in 1938, where he lectured at the Peiping, Beijing, Medical College. His Columbia years came to an end in 1923 when, at the age of forty-five, he was offered a teaching position at Harvard University Medical School. Within two years he was named the Charles Wilder Professor of Bacteriology. Zinsser remained in Boston for the remainder of his life. The Zinsser family, along with their second and last child, Hans Handforth Zinsser (who later graduated from Columbia's College of Physicians and Surgeons), lived in a house in the city and traveled often to their country farm in Dover, Massachusetts. The farm became a retreat and entertainment site for Zinsser's colleagues and his medical students.

By 1930, Zinsser had decided to concentrate his studies on typhus fever research, and began a lengthy friendship with **Charles J. H. Nicolle**, the Nobel Prize–winning French physician and bacteriologist who discovered that typhus is transmitted by body lice. During the 1930s, Zinsser was able, either alone or with a variety of co-workers, to aid in the understanding of the cause of the several forms of typhus, including Brill's disease, named for American physician Nathan Edwin Brill, who investigated the malady. Zinsser was able to prove that the disease is caused by the microorganism *Rickettsia prowazekii* as opposed to *Rickettsia mooseri,* as was commonly believed, and hypothesized that Brill's disease is a form of recrudescent (or renewing) typhus. His theory was confirmed by later studies, and the disease has since been renamed Brill-Zinsser's disease. In addition, Zinsser worked on a vaccine against typhus and assisted in conceiving of a way to prepare the vaccine commercially, thus making the treatment available to large numbers of people. These endeavors have guaranteed him a place in the history of bacteriology and medicine.

In addition to his significant contributions to bacteriology, Zinsser also made advancements in the field of immunology. He discovered that it is not possible to create a grand conceptual unification for an understanding of the phenomenon of allergic reaction. Near the beginning of the twentieth century, Austrian pediatrician Clemens von Pirquet and Hungarian pediatrician Bela Schick, then leading figures in immunology, sought to explain allergic reactions as if all were antibody-mediated. They also believed that an allergic reaction was a typical step in the recovery process. Zinsser showed that certain forms of bodily responses to infection, including those involving the body's reaction to tuberculin (a substance that was later, and to this day, used in the test for tuberculosis infection), are fundamentally different from other types of allergic responses.

In several books and papers, Zinsser detailed his scientific studies in the fields of bacteriology and immunology; among the most well known of these volumes is his 1935 work *Rats, Lice and History*. An examination of the history of typhus, the book intermixes philosophy and wit along with scientific information. The book became a best-seller and was praised by several literary critics. Zinsser delved into his private life with his 1940 autobiography, *As I Remember Him: The Biography of R. S.* Made up of some of the author's thoughts regarding living with leukemia—the disease that eventually caused his death—*As I Remember Him* was a popular book whose somewhat odd subtitle was derived from Zinsser's use of a pseudonym for his literary writings. In these writings he often referred to himself as R. S. There is disagreement as to what R. S. stood for: Some say it meant "Romantic Self"; others believe that it was derived from a German author, Rudolf Schmidt, who in 1908 had written on pain and its significance in medicine.

During his lifetime, Zinsser won numerous awards and was actively involved in many scientific societies, such as serving as president of the American Association of Immunologists in 1919 and of the Society of American Bacteriologists in 1926. His major honors include the receipt of honorary doctorates from Columbia University in 1929, Western Reserve University in 1931, Lehigh University in 1933, Yale University in 1939, and Harvard University in 1939. Among his other accolades are his elections to the Harvey Society and Sigma Xi. His published articles number more than 270.

Zinsser possessed a life-long devotion to personal fitness—enjoying activities ranging from horseback riding to hounds (at which he was expert) to shooting. "Throughout his life," Wolbach reported in *Memoirs of the National Academy of Sciences,* "he carried the aura of youth." Zinsser died of leukemia in his native New York City on September 4, 1940.

SELECTED WRITINGS BY ZINSSER:

Books

(With Philip Hanson Hiss, Jr.) *A Textbook of Bacteriology,* D. Appleton, 1910.
Infection and Resistance, Macmillan, 1914.
(With J. G. Hopkins and Reuben Ottenburg) *Laboratory Course in Serum Study,* [New York], 1916.
(With R. P. Strong, G. C. Shattuck, A. W. Sellards, and J. G. Hopkins) *Typhus Fever with Particular Reference to the Serbian Epidemic,* Harvard University Press, 1920.
Rats, Lice and History, Little, Brown, 1935.
As I Remember Him: The Biography of R. S., Little, Brown, 1940.
Spring, Summer and Autumn (poems), Knopf, 1942.

Periodicals

(With H. Yu) "The Bacteriology of Rheumatic Fever and the Allergic Hypothesis," *Archives of Internal Medicine,* Volume 42, 1928, pp. 301–309.
"Varieties of Typhus Fever and the Epidemiology of the American Form of European Typhus Fever (Brill's Disease)," *American Journal of Hygiene,* Volume 20, 1934, pp. 513–534.

SOURCES:

Periodicals

Wolbach, Simeon Burt, "Biographical Memoir of Hans Zinsser: 1878–1940," *Memoirs of the*

National Academy of Sciences, Volume 24, 1947, pp. 323–360.

—*Sketch by Donald J. McGraw*

Richard Zsigmondy
1865-1929
German colloidal chemist

Although trained as an organic chemist, Richard Zsigmondy earned fame in the field of colloidal chemistry, the study of fine dispersions of a material in a solution of another substance. Colloids had been well known and widely used for centuries, but at the dawn of the twentieth century very little was known about their physical and chemical nature. To learn more about this class of materials, Zsigmondy invented a number of tools, including the ultramicroscope, with which he was able to study colloids more closely. Such equipment allowed Zsigmondy to make a number of fundamental discoveries about the composition and properties of colloids. For this work he was awarded the 1925 Nobel Prize in chemistry, the first and one of the few times this award has been given for research on colloids.

Richard Adolf Zsigmondy was born in Vienna on April 1, 1865. His father, Adolf Zsigmondy, a dentist and an inventor of surgical instruments, and his mother, the former Irma von Szakmáry, oversaw their four sons' home experiments in chemistry and physics. After Zsigmondy graduated from high school in 1883, he enrolled at the Vienna Technische Hochschule, where he majored in chemistry. At the time, the Hochschule emphasized organic chemistry, which eventually became Zsigmondy's major field of study. However, he also became interested in the colorization of glasses, and he collaborated with a Prague chemist in some original research at a nearby glass factory. In 1887 Zsigmondy completed his studies at the Hochschule and began a graduate program in organic chemistry.

Some disagreement among scholars surrounds the conditions of Zsigmondy's doctoral work. Most authorities say that he attended the University of Munich and was granted his Ph.D. in organic chemistry in 1885. In one of the most complete biographies available, however, George Fleck in the American Chemical Society's *Nobel Laureates in Chemistry, 1901–1992,* claims that Zsigmondy did his research on chlorine derivatives at the Munich Technische Hochschule, which "was the basis for the doctor of philosophy degree awarded to Zsigmondy by the University of Erlangen in December 1889."

Interest in Glass Colorization Leads to Research on Colloids

After receiving his doctorate, Zsigmondy became an assistant to A. A. Kundt at the University of Berlin's Institute of Physics. Kundt, an authority on the colorization of glass by inorganic materials, further encouraged Zsigmondy's interest in this field. In 1893 Zsigmondy became qualified to teach and accepted a job as privatdozent at the Technische Hochschule in Graz. He joined the Schott Glass Manufacturing Company in Jena, Germany, in 1897; there he continued his work on the colorization of glass and invented a product known as *Jena milk glass* that was later to attain wide commercial popularity.

Zsigmondy's work with colored glass led to an increased interest in colloids, which are often responsible for the colorization of glassy materials. Colloids are mixtures of two substances that do not form a solution, but that do not separate even after standing for long periods of time. For example, if one were to add powdered iron to water, the iron would not dissolve, but would remain suspended for some period of time. Eventually, however, the iron would settle at the bottom of the container.

Under certain conditions, however, the iron can be made into such fine particles that, although still not dissolved, remain in suspension essentially forever. The science of colloidal chemistry is devoted to a study of the ways in which such mixtures can be made, of their properties, and of the ways the particles can be made to settle out.

A fundamental problem with colloidal research is that, although not of atomic size, colloidal particles are too small to be seen with ordinary light microscopes. Direct observation of such particles was therefore impossible before Zsigmondy's time. The one method that was (and is) commonly available for the study of colloids relies upon the so-called Tyndall effect. The Tyndall effect occurs when colloidal particles scatter light shined through a mixture. A common example of this effect is the scattering of light that occurs when a beam of light shines through a smoky room.

Invents the Ultramicroscope for the Study of Colloids

Zsigmondy concluded that an instrument could be developed that makes use of the Tyndall effect. In this instrument, called the ultramicroscope, light is reflected off particles not in the same direction as the incident light, as in a conventional microscope, but at right angles to the incident beam.

From 1900 to 1907 Zsigmondy's work was supported by his family's own fortune, and he pursued his research without any official professional affiliation. During this time he was invited, however, to make use of the superb facilities at the Zeiss Optical Company in Jena for his research on the ultramicroscope. There he collaborated with Zeiss physicist H. F. W. Siedentopf; together, the two men produced the first microscope of Zsigmondy's design, with which he soon made a number of discoveries about colloidal materials. For example, in 1898 Zsigmondy discovered that the valuable dye known as Cassius purple is actually a suspension of colloidal gold and stannic acid particles. In 1907 Zsigmondy returned to academia as assistant professor of inorganic chemistry and director of the Institute for Inorganic Chemistry at the University of Göttingen. Twelve years later he was promoted to full professor, a post he held for the rest of his life. Zsigmondy died from arteriosclerosis at his home in Göttingen on September 24, 1929.

Zsigmondy was married to Laura Luise Müller in 1903; the couple had two daughters. Zsigmondy's work was recognized by his election to the scientific academies of Göttingen, Vienna, Uppsala, Zaragoza, Valencia, and Haarlem. He was awarded honorary doctorates from the University of Königsberg and the Technische Hochschules at Vienna and Graz. Throughout his life, Zsigmondy's leisure-time passions were hiking and mountain climbing.

SELECTED WRITINGS BY ZSIGMONDY:

Books

Über Kolloid-Chemie: mit besonderer Berücksichtigung der anorganischen Kolloide, J. A. Barth, 1906.
Colloids and the Ultramicroscope: A Manual of Colloid Chemistry and Ultramicroscopy, translated by J. Alexander, John Wiley, 1909.
The Chemistry of Colloids, translated by E. B. Spear, John Wiley, 1917.
Das kolloide Gold, Akademische Verlagsgesellschaft, 1925.
"The Immersion Ultramicroscope" and "Membrane Filters and Their Uses," chapters in *Colloid Chemistry: Theoretical and Applied,* edited by J. Alexander, The Chemical Catalog Company, 1926.

SOURCES:

Books

Fleck, George, "Richard Zsigmondy," in *Nobel Laureates in Chemistry, 1901–1992,* edited by Laylin K. James, American Chemical Society and The Chemical Heritage Foundation, 1993, pp. 151–157.

Gillispie, Charles Coulson, editor, *Dictionary of Scientific Biography,* Volume 14, Scribner, 1975, pp. 632–634.

Madden, Paul, "Richard Zsigmondy," in *The Nobel Prize Winners: Chemistry,* Volume 1, 1901–1937, edited by Frank N. Magill, Salem Press, 1990, pp. 271–276.

—*Sketch by David E. Newton*

Konrad Zuse

Konrad Zuse
1910-1973
German computer scientist

Konrad Zuse was one of the most honored figures in the history of computing, with his influence on computing in Britain and America abated only because of World War II. In 1938, in Germany, Zuse built a binary calculator, the Z1. A young engineering student without knowledge of similar inventions being built simultaneously in other parts of the world, Zuse created several computers that equaled in some respects and surpassed in many ways the capabilities of American-built computers of the same generation. With the war intervening, it was not until several years later that Zuse's inventions were known outside Germany.

Born in 1910 in Berlin-Wilmersdorf, Zuse grew up in East Prussia, where his family moved shortly after his birth. He attended school in Braunsberg, experiencing an early education that revolved around a curriculum based on the classics and Latin. By his mid-teens he had developed a fascination for engineering and in 1927, at the age of seventeen, he enrolled at the Technical University (Technische Hochschule) in Berlin. He graduated eight years later with a degree in civil engineering.

Develops Computer to Facilitate Job

While at engineering school, Zuse became disillusioned by the "long and awful" calculations he had to perform, according to David Ritchie in *The Computer Pioneers.* Some equations were so tedious it would take the better part of a year to solve on a desktop calculator. Upon graduation he went to work at the Henschel Flugzeugwerke (aircraft factory) in Berlin, where he was a stress analyst, studying the amount of stress an airplane in flight could stand before it began to break apart. Because of the extreme difficulty Zuse came across working with differential equations, he

knew he would have to build a machine that could automatically do his calculations.

The biggest problem Zuse found when making the initial sketches for his machine was not in the calculations themselves, but in the steps in between—the recording and transferring of intermediate results. And, as the equations became larger, the transfer became more difficult. Getting those intermediate results from one part of a problem to another was Zuse's main task. He considered several options before arriving at the idea of creating a calculator with a mechanical keyboard. In fact, twenty years after the war, Zuse admitted in a speech which is quoted in *The Computer Pioneers,* "I did not know anything about computers, nor had I heard about the early work of Charles Babbage." Babbage was a contemporary of Zuse who also made early discoveries in the field of computing.

Zuse's ideal computer contained an arithmetic unit and storage unit, a selection mechanism to link the two, and a control unit that would be directed by punched tape and would deliver instructions to the selection mechanism and arithmetic unit. Once he had finalized his computer design, he devoted full time to its realization, using his parents' living room as his workshop.

Although he was a competent draftsman and skilled mechanic, he was relatively ignorant when it came to electrical engineering. He also knew very little about how to go about constructing a mechanical calculator. With his lack of knowledge Zuse was able to approach his project without the burden of conventional ideas. Later, after the war, he said, "Thus—unprejudiced—I could go new ways," according to Ritchie in *The Computer Pioneers.*

Since Zuse was more familiar with binary arithmetic—math based on a two digit system rather than ten—he decided to make his machine a binary device. Zuse's reasoning was that if he didn't have to represent ten numbers when two would work, why should he? A major influence on him was the writings of Gottfried Wilhelm Leibniz, who several centuries earlier imagined the entire universe reduced to binary values. In fact, one of Zuse's reports about his work was entitled, "Hommage to Leibniz."

The computer that Zuse designed and built, with the help of friends, had a mechanical memory unit that used movable pins in slots to indicate, by their position, zeroes and ones. Because of his use of the binary approach, the memory space was surprisingly compact, occupying about a cubic meter. Zuse's first computer was produced in 1938 when he connected his mechanical memory with a crude mechanical calculating unit.

With the help of friends and a supply of second-hand telephone relays, Zuse built his second computer, the Z2 computer, using electromechanical relays. Although the Z2's relays were problematic, making it less reliable than the Z1, it sparked the interest of the German Experimental Aircraft Institute, or Deutsche Versuchanstalt für Luftfahrt (DVL). The problem of trying to overcome flutter, a shivering of aircraft wings, demanded extensive calculations and the DVL was not equipped to handle the tasks. The Z2 was seen as a possible solution to the DVL's perplexing problem.

Zuse received money from the DVL for the design and manufacture of a relay computer. He began work on the Z3 while still using his parents' living room. The Z3, with two thousand relays and the capability to multiply, divide, or extract a square root in only three seconds, was completed in 1941. The Z3 was extremely compact (occupying only the volume of a closet) and had a sophisticated push-button control panel enabling the user to carry out operations with the touch of a finger. A single keystroke would convert decimal numbers into binary and, with another keystroke, switch them back again.

Zuse even created an innovative programming notation that included the now familiar symbols $\geq$ (greater than or equal to) and $\leq$ (less than or equal to). He used punched motion picture film for input. In addition to designing and building a sophisticated yet compact computer, Zuse, with the Z3, also created the first computer to achieve automatic control of a sequence of calculations. A person was no longer needed to continually punch in numbers. Zuse's

computer could automatically carry out a string of calculations.

In fact, Zuse became a software pioneer before the concepts of software and hardware were fully developed. As noted in *The Computer Pioneers,* Zuse remarked in a postwar speech to an American audience, "In the early forties nobody knew the difference between hardware and software. We concentrated ourselves on purely technological matters, both logical design and programming."

Enhanced Computer Aids in War Effort

Although the Z3 was totally destroyed in 1944 when an Allied bomb fell on the apartment building where the Zuses lived, he did produce another computer, the S1, that was a non-programmable version of the Z3 that was used to design German glider bombs, unmanned aircraft that carried high explosives and were carried aloft by bombers. Directed to their targets by radio control, the bombs were usually dropped on British ships. In fact, the British feared glider bombs more than almost any other aerial weapon because, since it was pilotless, it could not be disabled. During the last two years of the war, glider bombs were used against Allied shipping in the Mediterranean. Zuse's S1 assisted in plotting a glider bomb's actual flight path as well as its deviations. With those factors in place the control surfaces on the glider bomb's wings and tail could be adjusted to ensure a steady flight and a direct hit.

With the Allied armies moving toward Germany from the west and the Russians advancing from the east, Zuse finished the Z4 an even more advanced mechanical computer. To escape damage from Allied bombs he kept moving the Z4 around Berlin. By 1945 Zuse moved the Z4 to the university town Göttingen, a fair distance west of Berlin. The computer was left with the Experimental Aerodynamics Institute, or Aerodynamische Versuchanstalt (AVA). As the Allies continued to advance, Zuse, once again, moved the Z4, this time to Hinterstein, a small Alpine village, where he hid it in a barn.

Although Zuse felt he needed to keep his computer from harm's way, his brilliant work was also hidden from the rest of the world until years after Germany surrendered. In fact, it wasn't until French troops discovered Zuse and the Z4 in Hinterstein that word of the computer reached the British and Americans.

Observers who saw the Z4 in operation were amazed at what Zuse had accomplished. Without any knowledge of other, previous computer designs to assist him, as well as no information about contemporaneous computer projects in the United States and Britain, Zuse had designed and built his computers practically from scratch. In 1951, Zuse demonstrated the Z4 in Zurich, where one observer, quoted in *The Computer Pioneers*, wrote, "I could not believe it."

There were several contributing factors in addition to the isolation of his work at Hinterstein as to why Zuse's wartime achievements took so long to be recognized. The Z4 looked more like a typesetting machine than the huge American machines. Also, Zuse resented the Allies so he did not cooperate with their inquiries about his machines.

It was only well after the war that Zuse learned about other computer scientists such as **Howard H. Aiken** and his team at Harvard, who worked extensively on technological development during the war years. Although they had constructed computers larger than Zuse thought possible, it was Konrad Zuse who had brought computer design farther than they had.

After the war Zuse continued to design calculating machines and in 1949 established a small computer company, Zuse KG, that developed into a leading manufacturer of small scientific computers. He remained with the firm until 1966. After retirement, he remained as a consultant to the firm but devoted most of his remaining years to painting, his lifelong hobby. He died in 1973.

FOR FURTHER READING:

Books

Augarten, Stan, *Bit by Bit,* Ticknor & Fields, 1984.
Fang, Irving E., *The Computer Story,* Rada Press, 1988.
Ritchie, David, *The Computer Pioneers,* Simon & Schuster, 1986.
Slater, Robert, *Portraits in Silicon,* Massachusetts Institute of Technology Press, 1987.
Wulforst, Harry, *Breakthrough to the Computer Age,* Scribner, 1982.

Periodicals

Golden, Frederic, "Big Dimwits and Little Geniuses," *Time,* January 3, 1983, pp. 30–32.

—*Sketch by Dorothy Spencer*

Vladimir Zworykin
1889-1982
Russian-born American physicist and engineer

Vladimir Zworykin is best remembered for developing the iconoscope and the kinescope, two inventions for which he became known as "the father of television." During his lifetime he obtained more than 120 patents on a wide variety of electronic devices and applied many of the principles from his work with television to microscopy, leading to the development of the electron microscope.

Vladimir Kosma Zworykin was born to Kosma and Elaine (Zworykin) Zworykin on July 30, 1889, in Mourom, Russia. His early years were spent in Mourom, where his father owned and operated a fleet of river boats on the Oka River. He was educated locally before studying electrical engineering at the St. Petersburg Institute of Technology (also known as Petrograd Institute of Technology). In St. Petersburg, he studied with professor Boris Rosing, who maintained that cathode ray tubes, with their ability to shoot a stream of charged particles, would be useful in the development of television. This belief contrasted with efforts at the time to use mechanical systems based on a variety of synchronized moving parts. Although Rosing's ideas could only be demonstrated by transmission of crude geometric images in his laboratory in St. Petersburg, these early experiments inspired much of Zworykin's later successful work on the television.

After receiving his degree from St. Petersburg in 1912, Zworykin entered the prestigious College de France in Paris, where he studied X-ray technology under the well-known French physicist **Paul Langevin**. With the outbreak of World War I in 1914, he returned to Russia and spent the war years as a radio officer in the Russian signal corps. During the war Zworykin married Tatiana Vasilieff, a union that produced two children. At the war's end in 1918, he left Russia and traveled widely before emigrating with his family to the United States in 1919. When he arrived in the U.S., Zworykin obtained a position as a bookkeeper for the financial agent of the Russian embassy.

Television Is Born

In 1920 Zworykin was invited to join the research laboratories at Westinghouse to work on the development of radio tubes and photoelectric cells (small devices whose electrical properties are modified by the action of light). While at Westinghouse, Zworykin earned his Ph.D. in physics at the University of Pittsburgh, writing his dissertation on the

Vladimir Zworykin

improvement of photoelectric cells. It was the concept of television, however, that most excited him, and in December 1923 he filed a patent application for his iconoscope, an invention that would revolutionize the development of television (although the actual patent was not granted until 1938). Until this time most television research involved mechanical systems. These relied on a rapidly rotating, perforated disk. The perforations were arranged in a spiral which could be quickly rotated. Light was transmitted from a photoelectric device behind the disk through the holes to form a series of successive parallel lines on a viewing screen. Unfortunately, the amount of light transmitted for each picture was very small, making the pictures quite dim and lacking in detail.

Zworykin's landmark iconoscope was an attempt to reproduce the human eye electronically. In human vision, light enters the eye through the iris, passes through a lens, and focuses an image on the retina, which registers colors via photosensitive receptor cells known as cones and light intensities via cells called rods. The optic nerves of the eye transmit this information to the brain in the form of electrical impulses which register as an image for the viewer. The iconoscope, like the eye, used a lens to focus an image on a signal plate of mica, covered with tiny dots of photoelectric cells (corresponding to and simulating the rods and cones of the retina). An electron beam (corresponding to and simulating the optic nerves) scanned the signal plate from top to bottom in parallel lines detecting the electrical emissions. This

formed the picture. This system was more sensitive than any mechanical system then being explored and greatly reduced the amount of light necessary to produce a clear picture.

To reconstruct the transmitted image, Zworykin needed a special kind of cathode-ray tube which could send a steady stream of electrons to the signal plate. The kinescope was his ingenious solution, an idea whose essential elements were suggested by Scottish physicist A. A. Campbell Swinton in 1908 and amplified in an address to the Roentgen Society of London in 1911. Until Zworykin's efforts, however, a series of technical barriers had prevented a practical demonstration of Swinton's ideas. The kinescope, or picture tube, corresponded to the brain in human vision. An electron beam is applied to an electrode grid (invented in 1906 by the American Lee DeForest) with modulation occurring through the use of electromagnetic fields. With the addition of the kinescope, for which Zworykin filed a patent in 1924, television as we know it was now feasible.

In 1924, the year Zworykin gained American citizenship, he demonstrated his new system to Westinghouse executives. As he later wrote in an article in *American Magazine,* "l was terribly excited and proud. After a few days I was informed, very politely, that my demonstration had been extremely interesting, but that it might be better if I were to spend my time on something 'a little more useful'." Apparently, Zworykin was too forthcoming about the technological problems still to be surmounted even as he persisted in pleading his cause with management. Westinghouse decided not to pursue Zworykin's research, a decision they surely lived to regret many times over in subsequent years as a whole industry developed around this new communications medium.

In 1929 Zworykin, still determined to prove the worth of his ideas, found a receptive audience at Radio Corporation of America (RCA) and was hired away from Westinghouse as associate research director of the RCA electronic research laboratory in Camden, New Jersey. The story is told that when RCA's president, the famous scientist-administrator David Sarnoff, asked Zworykin how much it would cost to perfect his system, he replied, "About $100,000." Sarnoff later said, as quoted in the *New York Times,* "RCA spent $50 million before we ever got a penny back from TV." The same year that Zworykin moved to RCA, he filed his first patent for color television. It took the end of World War II, however, with the lifting of restrictions on manufacturing of receivers to fuel explosive growth in television communications. As a result of the quality of his efforts at RCA, Zworykin was elevated to director of electronic research in 1946 and to vice president of the laboratories division in 1947, a position he held in an emeritus capacity until his death.

Turns to New Ventures

A man of many interests, Zworykin began work with G. A. Morton in 1930 on the infrared (electron) image tube, which converted infrared rays into visible light. This device enabled humans to see in the dark and became the basis for the Sniperscope and Snooperscope used during World War II and all subsequent night sighting instruments.

Believing that the refinement of television could be left to fellow engineers, Zworykin then sought to apply television technology to microscopy. Under his leadership the electron microscope was developed by James Hillier and others at the RCA labs. This device enabled researchers to see objects much smaller than was possible with a conventional microscope and revolutionized scientific understanding of the fine structure of matter, especially in the fields of molecular and cell biology. The number of scientific applications for this technology continue to multiply. Zworykin's remaining patents consisted of such inventions as the electric eye used in security systems and automatic door openers, electronically-controlled missiles and automobiles, a clock which operated without moving parts, and a device which enabled the blind to read print—a very early precursor to textual recognition systems which combine light-based technologies with electronics and microprocessors.

During World War II, Zworykin served on the Scientific Advisory Board to the U.S. Air Force and on a number of committees of the National Defense Research Council which advised the U.S. government on scientific contributions to the war effort. In the early years of the Cold War, Zworykin collaborated with **John von Neumann** of the Institute for Advanced Study at Princeton University to lay the conceptual groundwork for a computer sophisticated enough to open the possibility of accurate weather forecasting—an application whose possibilities were not lost on the American military command.

Zworykin was honored with numerous awards during his lifetime. The first major award he received was the Morris Liebmann Memorial prize given him in 1934 for his television contributions by the Institute of Radio Engineers. The American Institute of Electrical Engineers bestowed its highest honor, the Edison Medal, on Zworykin in 1952 citing his "outstanding contributions to the concept and development of electronic components and systems." In 1967 he was awarded the National Medal of Science by the National Academy of Sciences for his work in television, science, and engineering and the application of science to medicine. Among other tributes, he was elected to the National Academy of Sciences in 1943, was one of the earliest inductees into the newly founded National Academy of Engineering in 1965, and was honored by the French Legion of Honor.

With his first marriage ended in divorce, Zworykin married Katherine Polevitsky in 1951. He retired from RCA in 1954 at which time he was named an honorary vice president and technical consultant for the company. He was appointed director of the Medical Electronics Center at the Rockefeller Institute for Medical Research (now Rockefeller University), where he worked for a number of years in an attempt to broaden the range of electronically-based applications in medicine.

Zworykin died July 29, 1982, one day before his 93rd birthday. He is best remembered for his pioneering work in the development of television, a technology which has evolved into a major shaper of cultures and events around the world. Ironically, as quoted in his *New York Times* obituary, when asked to comment on the content of American television in an interview in 1981, Zworykin replied, "Awful."

SELECTED WRITINGS BY ZWORYKIN:

Books

Television: The Electronics of Image Transmission, Wiley, 1940, 2nd edition, 1954.
Electron Optics and the Electron Microscope, Wiley, 1946.
Photoelectricity and Its Applications, Wiley, 1949.
Television in Science and Industry, Wiley, 1958.

SOURCES:

Books

Current Biography 1949, H. W. Wilson, 1950, pp. 654–56.
Parker, Sybil P., editor, *McGraw-Hill Modern Scientists and Engineers,* Volume 3, McGraw Hill, 1980.

Periodicals

Abramson, A., "Pioneers of Television," *Journal of the Society of Motion Picture and Television Engineers,* July, 1981, pp. 579–90.
Thomas, Robert McG., Jr., "Vladimir Zworykin, Television Pioneer, Dies at 92," *New York Times Biographical Service,* August, 1982, p. 1119.

—*Sketch by Dennis W. and Kim A. Cheek*

Selected Biographical Sources

Asimov, Isaac, *Asimov's Biographical Encyclopedia of Science and Technology: The Lives and Achievements of 1510 Great Scientists from Ancient Times to the Present Chronologically Arranged,* 2nd revised edition, New York: Doubleday, 1982.

Blacks in Science: Ancient and Modern, edited by Ivan Van Sertima, New Brunswick, NJ: Transaction Books, 1983.

Bridges, Thomas C., and Hubert H. Tiltman, *Master Minds of Modern Science,* New York: L. MacVeagh, 1931.

Darrow, Floyd L., *Masters of Science and Invention,* New York: Harcourt, 1923.

Dash, Joan, *The Triumph of Discovery: Women Scientists Who Won the Nobel Prize,* Englewood Cliffs, NJ: Julian Messner, 1991.

Defries, Amelia D., *Pioneers of Science,* London: Routledge and Sons, 1928.

Dunlap, Jr., Orrin E., *Radio's One Hundred Men of Science: Biographical Narratives of Pathfinders in Electronics and Television,* New York: Harper, 1944.

Feldman, Anthony, *Scientists and Inventors,* New York: Facts on File, 1979.

Gaillard, Jacques, *Scientists in the Third World,* Lexington: University Press of Kentucky, 1991.

Lives in Science, New York: Simon and Schuster, 1957.

Makers of Modern Science: A Twentieth Century Library Trilogy, New York: Scribner, 1953.

McGraw-Hill Modern Men of Science: 426 Leading Contemporary Scientists, New York: McGraw-Hill, 1966-68.

McGraw-Hill Modern Scientists and Engineers, New York: McGraw-Hill, 1980.

McGrayne, Sharon Bertsch, *Nobel Prize Women in Science: Their Lives, Struggles, and Momentous Discoveries,* Secaucus, NJ: Carol Publishing Group, 1993.

McSpadden, J. Walker, *How They Blazed the Way: Men Who Have Advanced Civilization,* New York: Dodd, 1960.

A Passion to Know: 20 Profiles in Science, New York: Scribner, 1984.

Pioneers of Science in America: Sketches of Their Lives and Scientific Work, revised and edited by William J. Youmans, New York: Arno Press, 1978.

Scott, Michael Maxwell, *Stories of Famous Scientists,* London: Barker, 1967.

Siedel, Frank, and James M. Siedel, *Pioneers in Science,* Boston: Houghton, 1968.

The Twentieth-Century Sciences: Studies in the Biography of Ideas, New York: Norton, 1972.

Van Wagenen, Theodore F., *Beacon Lights of Science: A Survey of Human Achievement from the Earliest Recorded Times,* New York: Thomas Y. Crowell, 1924.

Weisgerber, Robert A., *The Challenged Scientists: Disabilities and the Triumph of Excellence,* New York: Praeger, 1991.

Zuckerman, Harriet, *Scientific Elite: Nobel Laureates in the United States,* New York: Free Press, 1979.

Autobiographical Collections

The Excitement and Fascination of Science: A Collection of Autobiographical and Philosophical Essays, Palo Alto, CA: Annual Reviews, 1965-78.

Scientists Who Believe: Twenty-One Tell Their Own Stories, edited by Eric C. Barrett and David Fisher, Chicago: Moody Press, 1984.

Studying Animal Behavior: Autobiographies of the Founders, edited by Donald A. Dewsbury, Chicago: University of Chicago Press, 1989.

Historical Collections

Elliott, Clark A., *Biographical Dictionary of American Science: The Seventeenth through the Nineteenth Centuries,* Westport, CT: Greenwood Press, 1979.

Engstrand, Iris W., *Spanish Scientists in the New World: The Eighteenth-Century Expeditions,* Seattle: University of Washington Press, 1981.

Gascoigne, Robert Mortimer, *A Historical Catalogue of Scientists and Scientific Books: From the Earliest Times to the Close of the Nineteenth Century,* New York: Garland Pub., 1984.

The Golden Age of Science: Thirty Portraits of the Giants of 19th-Century Science by Their Scientific Contemporaries, edited by Bessie Zaban Jones, New York: Simon and Schuster, 1966.

Hutcgubgs, D., and E. Candlin, *Late Seventeenth Century Scientists,* 1st edition, Oxford, NY: Pergamon Press, 1969.

Kohler, Robert E., *Partners in Science: Foundation Managers and Natural Scientists, 1900-1945,* Chicago: University of Chicago Press, 1991.

Late Eighteenth Century European Scientists, 1st edition, edited by Robert C. Olby, Oxford, NY: Pergamon Press, 1966.

Lenard, Philipp Eduard Anton, *Great Men of Science: A History of Scientific Progress,* translated from the second German edition by H. Stafford Hatfield, New York: Macmillan, 1933.

Murray, Robert H., *Science and Scientists in the Nineteenth Century,* New York: Macmillan, 1925.

North, J., *Mid-Nineteenth-Century Scientists,* 1st edition, Oxford, NY: Pergamon Press, 1969.

Dictionaries and Encyclopedias

The Biographical Dictionary of Scientists, 1st edition, New York: P. Bedrick Books, 1983-85.

Biographical Encyclopedia of Scientists, 2nd edition, edited by John Daintith, Sarah Mitchell, Elizabeth Tootill, and Derek Gjertsen, Philadelphia: Institute of Physics Publishing, 1994.

Concise Dictionary of Scientific Biography, New York: Scribner, 1981.

Howard, Arthur Vyvyan, *Chambers's Dictionary of Scientists,* New York: Dutton, 1961.

Directories

American Men and Women of Science, 1995-96: A Biographical Directory of Today's Leaders in Physical, Biological, and Related Sciences, 19th edition, New York: R. R. Bowker, 1994.

Cassutt, Michael, *Who's Who in Space: The First 25 Years,* Boston: G. K. Hall, 1987.

Ireland, Norma, *Index to Scientists of the World from Ancient to Modern Times: Biographies and Portraits,* Boston: Faxon, 1962.

Pelletier, Paul A., *Prominent Scientists: An Index to Collective Biographies,* 3rd edition, New York: Neal-Schuman, 1994.

Who's Who in Computer Education and Research: U.S. Edition, edited by T. C. Hsiao, Latham, NY: Science and Technology Press, 1975.

Who's Who in Science and Engineering, 1994-1995, 2nd edition, New Providence, NJ: Marquis Who's Who, 1994.

Who's Who in Technology, 6th edition, edited by Amy L. Unterburger, Detroit, MI: Gale Research Inc., 1989.

Who's Who in Science in Europe, 8th edition, Essex, England: Longman, 1994.

Who's Who of British Scientists, 1980-81, New York: St. Martin's, 1981.

Who's Who of Nobel Prize Winners, 2nd edition, edited by Bernard S. Schlessinger and June H. Schlessinger, Phoenix, AZ: Oryx Press, 1991.

Field of Specialization Index

Acoustic Design

Harris, Cyril **2:** 866

Aerodynamics

Prandtl, Ludwig **3:** 1610

Aeronautical Engineering

Draper, Charles Stark **1:** 518
Durand, William F. **1:** 534
Flügge-Lotz, Irmgard **2:** 662
Fokker, Anthony H. G. **2:** 663
Harris, Wesley L. **2:** 868
Heinkel, Ernst **2:** 889
Hunsaker, Jerome C. **2:** 980
Johnson, Clarence L. **2:** 1027
Ochoa, Ellen **3:** 1496
Piasecki, Frank **3:** 1579
Shurney, Robert E. **4:** 1839
Sikorsky, Igor I. **4:** 1843
Stever, H. Guyford **4:** 1922
van der Wal, Laurel **4:** 2078
von Kármán, Theodore **4:** 2096
von Mises, Richard **4:** 2099
Widnall, Sheila E. **4:** 2184
Williams, O. S. **4:** 2216
Wright, Wilbur **4:** 2262

Aerospace Engineering

Alcorn, George Edward **1:** 16
Armstrong, Neil **1:** 63
Bluford, Guion S. **1:** 201
Brill, Yvonne Claeys **1:** 255
Gutierrez, Orlando A. **2:** 831
Harris, Wesley L. **2:** 868
Johnson, Barbara Crawford **2:** 1026
Korolyov, Sergei **2:** 1127
Liepmann, Hans Wolfgang **3:** 1248
MacGill, Elsie Gregory **3:** 1296
Rockwell, Mabel M. **3:** 1698
Rogers, Marguerite M. **3:** 1700
Ross, Mary G. **3:** 1710
Tereshkova, Valentina **4:** 1992
Tsiolkovsky, Konstantin **4:** 2048
von Braun, Wernher **4:** 2093
Wu, Y. C. L. Susan **4:** 2268

Agriculture

Brown, Lester R. **1:** 265

Carver, George Washington **1:** 325
Evans, Alice **1:** 604
Khush, Gurdev S. **2:** 1091
Sanchez, Pedro A. **4:** 1774
Swaminathan, M. S. **4:** 1954
Tsao, George T. **4:** 2047

Anatomy

Alcala, Jose **1:** 15
Banting, Frederick G. **1:** 102
Barr, Murray Llewellyn **1:** 115
Cobb, William Montague **1:** 371
Crosby, Elizabeth Carolyn **1:** 431
Dart, Raymond A. **1:** 456
Dubois, Eugène **1:** 526
Fell, Honor Bridget **2:** 621
Hoyle, Fred **2:** 960
Keith, Arthur **2:** 1075
Lloyd, Ruth Smith **3:** 1263
Papanicolaou, George **3:** 1529
Romer, Alfred Sherwood **3:** 1704
Sabin, Florence Rena **4:** 1754
Scharrer, Berta **4:** 1787
Straus, William Levi, Jr. **4:** 1936
Trotter, Mildred **4:** 2044
Vallois, Henri-Victor **4:** 2069
Weidenreich, Franz **4:** 2140

Anthropology

Dart, Raymond A. **1:** 456
Keith, Arthur **2:** 1075
Leakey, Louis **3:** 1187
Leakey, Mary **3:** 1191
Leakey, Richard E. **3:** 1194
Stewart, Thomas Dale **4:** 1925
Weidenreich, Franz **4:** 2140

Astronomy

Adams, Walter Sydney **1:** 5
Baade, Walter **1:** 83
Banks, Harvey Washington **1:** 101
Bell Burnell, Jocelyn Susan **1:** 141
Cannon, Annie Jump **1:** 304
Davis, Raymond, Jr. **1:** 463
de Sitter, Willem **1:** 490
Eddington, Arthur Stanley **1:** 546
Faber, Sandra M. **2:** 607
Geller, Margaret Joan **2:** 742

Gold, Thomas **2:** 778
Hertzsprung, Ejnar **2:** 904
Hogg, Helen Sawyer **2:** 943
Hubble, Edwin **2:** 969
Humason, Milton L. **2:** 979
Jeffreys, Harold **2:** 1012
Kuiper, Gerard Peter **2:** 1143
Leavitt, Henrietta **3:** 1196
Le Cadet, Georges **3:** 1200
Lemaître, Georges **3:** 1221
Lin, Chia-Chiao **3:** 1252
Lippmann, Gabriel **3:** 1256
Massevitch, Alla G. **3:** 1324
Maunder, Annie Russell **3:** 1333
Maury, Antonia **3:** 1334
Minkowski, Rudolph **3:** 1389
Moulton, Forest Ray **3:** 1434
Oort, Jan Hendrik **3:** 1510
Osterbrock, Donald E. **3:** 1519
Payne-Gaposchkin, Cecilia **3:** 1552
Ponnamperuma, Cyril **3:** 1600
Reber, Grote **3:** 1655
Roman, Nancy Grace **3:** 1703
Rubin, Vera Cooper **3:** 1725
Russell, Henry Norris **3:** 1737
Sagan, Carl **4:** 1757
Sandage, Allan R. **4:** 1775
Shapiro, Irwin **4:** 1816
Shapley, Harlow **4:** 1817
Slipher, Vesto M. **4:** 1861
Stefanik, Milan Ratislav **4:** 1910
Taylor, Joseph H., Jr. **4:** 1980
Tombaugh, Clyde W. **4:** 2037
Voûte, Joan George Erardus
  Gijsbert **4:** 2104
Whipple, Fred Lawrence **4:** 2167
Wilson, Robert Woodrow **4:** 2235

Astrophysics

Banks, Harvey Washington **1:** 101
Breit, Gregory **1:** 248
Burbidge, E. Margaret **1:** 277
Burbidge, Geoffrey **1:** 280
Carruthers, George R. **1:** 319
Chandrasekhar, Subrahmanyan **1:** 340
Dirac, Paul **1:** 503
Friedmann, Aleksandr A. **2:** 699

Sørensen, Søren Peter Lauritz **4:** 1883

Tatum, Edward Lawrie **4:** 1970

Theorell, Axel Hugo Teodor **4:** 2007

Tildon, J. Tyson **4:** 2023

Tsao, George T. **4:** 2047

Vernadsky, Vladimir Ivanovich **4:** 2086

Virtanen, Artturi Ilmari **4:** 2088

Wald, George **4:** 2115

Wang, James C. **4:** 2124

Warburg, Otto **4:** 2127

Weinberg, Robert A. **4:** 2144

West, Harold Dadford **4:** 2157

Wood, Harland G. **4:** 2246

Biology

Alvariño, Angeles **1:** 34

Arber, Werner **1:** 57

Astbury, William **1:** 69

Avery, Oswald Theodore **1:** 75

Beltrán, Enrique **1:** 143

Booker, Walter M. **1:** 214

Carson, Rachel **1:** 322

Chang, Min-Chueh **1:** 344

Cloud, Preston **1:** 368

Cobb, Jewel Plummer **1:** 369

Cohen, Stanley N. **1:** 378

Cohn, Zanvil **1:** 382

Commoner, Barry **1:** 387

Cox, Geraldine V. **1:** 419

Dallmeier, Francisco **1:** 445

Djerassi, Carl **1:** 505

Dobzhansky, Theodosius **1:** 506

Dole, Vincent P. **1:** 510

Dubos, René **1:** 528

Earle, Sylvia A. **1:** 541

Ehrlich, Paul R. **1:** 568

Fell, Honor Bridget **2:** 621

Goldstein, Avram **2:** 789

Goodall, Jane **2:** 798

Gould, Stephen Jay **2:** 803

Govindjee, **2:** 808

Horn, Michael Hastings **2:** 954

Hubel, David H. **2:** 972

Isaacs, Alick **2:** 996

Jacob, François **2:** 1002

Janzen, Dan **2:** 1007

Johannsen, Wilhelm Ludwig **2:** 1024

Just, Ernest Everett **2:** 1049

Konishi, Masakazu **2:** 1123

Lancaster, Cleo **3:** 1156

Laveran, Alphonse **3:** 1182

Leopold, Estella Bergere **3:** 1228

Levi-Montalcini, Rita **3:** 1233

Li, Ching Chun **3:** 1242

Lillie, Frank Rattray **3:** 1250

Lovelock, James E. **3:** 1279

Lwoff, André **3:** 1284

MacArthur, Robert H. **3:** 1292

Margulis, Lynn **3:** 1319

Maynard Smith, John **3:** 1336

Mayr, Ernst **3:** 1338

Medawar, Peter Brian **3:** 1353

Merrifield, R. Bruce **3:** 1361

Nabrit, Samuel Milton **3:** 1451

Nathans, Daniel **3:** 1454

Osborn, Mary J. **3:** 1518

Palade, George **3:** 1525

Pardue, Mary Lou **3:** 1530

Perutz, Max **3:** 1572

Pincus, Gregory Goodwin **3:** 1586

Ray, Dixy Lee **3:** 1653

Russell, Frederick Stratten **3:** 1735

Sager, Ruth **4:** 1760

Scharrer, Berta **4:** 1787

Sharp, Phillip A. **4:** 1820

Sheldrake, Rupert **4:** 1825

Spemann, Hans **4:** 1888

Sperry, Roger W. **4:** 1891

Stahl, Franklin W. **4:** 1895

Stevens, Nettie Maria **4:** 1920

Sturtevant, A. H. **4:** 1941

Sutton, Walter Stanborough **4:** 1950

Tan Jiazhen **4:** 1966

Taylor, Stuart **4:** 1983

Thompson, D'Arcy Wentworth **4:** 2012

Turner, Charles Henry **4:** 2056

Wilson, Edmund Beecher **4:** 2225

Young, J. Z. **4:** 2280

Biomathematics

Cardús, David **1:** 309

Biomedical Engineering

Cohen, Stanley N. **1:** 378

Estrin, Thelma **1:** 599

Greatbatch, Wilson **2:** 814

Hounsfield, Godfrey **2:** 957

Jarvik, Robert K. **2:** 1009

Jemison, Mae C. **2:** 1016

Kolff, Willem Johan **2:** 1119

Lee, Raphael C. **3:** 1208

Micheli-Tzanakou, Evangelia **3:** 1370

Weinberg, Robert A. **4:** 2144

Biophysics

Bronk, Detlev Wulf **1:** 256

Chance, Britton **1:** 338

Cohn, Mildred **1:** 381

Deisenhofer, Johann **1:** 482

Hartline, Haldan Keffer **2:** 870

Hauptman, Herbert A. **2:** 873

Hodgkin, Alan Lloyd **2:** 935

Neher, Erwin **3:** 1460

Quimby, Edith H. **3:** 1629

Sakmann, Bert **4:** 1765

Stoll, Alice M. **4:** 1930

Szilard, Leo **4:** 1961

Wilkins, Maurice Hugh Frederick **4:** 2208

Botany

Adams, Roger **1:** 4

Arber, Agnes **1:** 56

Borlaug, Norman **1:** 218

Diener, Theodor Otto **1:** 498

Earle, Sylvia A. **1:** 541

Engler, Adolph Gustav Heinrich **1:** 591

Esau, Katherine **1:** 599

Johannsen, Wilhelm Ludwig **2:** 1024

Khush, Gurdev S. **2:** 1091

Leopold, Estella Bergere **3:** 1228

Marie-Victorin, Frère **3:** 1321

Parker, Charles Stewart **3:** 1532

Skoog, Folke Karl **4:** 1857

Todd, Alexander **4:** 2034

Tswett, Mikhail **4:** 2052

Vries, Hugo de **4:** 2105

Weber-van Bosse, Anne Antoinette **4:** 2136

Went, Frits **4:** 2153

Cardiology

Healy, Bernadine **2:** 885

Cellular Biology

Claude, Albert **1:** 361

Cobb, Jewel Plummer **1:** 369

Cohn, Zanvil **1:** 382

de Duvé, Christian **1:** 473

Elion, Gertrude Belle **1:** 582

Farquhar, Marilyn G. **2:** 610

Margulis, Lynn **3:** 1319

Nirenberg, Marshall Warren **3:** 1474

Olden, Kenneth **3:** 1504

Petermann, Mary Locke **3:** 1577

Sheldrake, Rupert **4:** 1825

Chemical Engineering

Dicciani, Nance K. **1:** 495

Greenewalt, Crawford H. **2:** 815

Hawkins, W. Lincoln **2:** 879

Johnson, Marvin M. **2:** 1032

Katz, Donald L. **2:** 1072

Le Beau, Désirée **3:** 1198

Lewis, Warren K. **3:** 1240

Little, Arthur D. **3:** 1259

Patrick, Jennie R. **3:** 1534

Sioui, Richard H. **4:** 1856

Tsao, George T. **4:** 2047

Chemical Evolution

Ponnamperuma, Cyril **3:** 1600

MacDonald, Gordon **3:** 1295
Schneider, Stephen H. **4:** 1790
Solberg, Halvor **4:** 1874
Washington, Warren M. **4:** 2130
Went, Frits **4:** 2153

Computer Science
Aiken, Howard **1:** 12
Amdahl, Gene M. **1:** 35
Atanasoff, John **1:** 71
Backus, John **1:** 88
Bell, Gordon **1:** 140
Cormack, Allan M. **1:** 405
Cray, Seymour **1:** 423
Dennis, Jack B. **1:** 488
Dijkstra, Edsger W. **1:** 500
Eckert, J. Presper **1:** 544
Estrin, Thelma **1:** 599
Feigenbaum, Edward A. **2:** 618
Forrester, Jay W. **2:** 670
Gates, Bill **2:** 733
Goldberg, Adele **2:** 780
Gourneau, Dwight **2:** 807
Hannah, Marc R. **2:** 856
Hopper, Grace **2:** 951
Jobs, Steven **2:** 1022
Kay, Alan C. **2:** 1074
Kilburn, Thomas M. **2:** 1092
Knuth, Donald E. **2:** 1109
Kurtz, Thomas Eugene **2:** 1146
Mauchly, John William **3:** 1331
McCarthy, John **3:** 1342
Micheli-Tzanakou, Evangelia **3:** 1370
Minsky, Marvin **3:** 1392
Newell, Allen **3:** 1466
Reddy, Raj **3:** 1656
Rigas, Harriett B. **3:** 1686
Ritchie, Dennis **3:** 1687
Roberts, Lawrence **3:** 1691
Shannon, Claude **4:** 1814
Shaw, Mary **4:** 1823
Simon, Herbert A. **4:** 1847
Stibitz, George R. **4:** 1926
Sutherland, Ivan **4:** 1948
Thompson, Kenneth **4:** 2014
von Neumann, John **4:** 2101
Wang, An **4:** 2121
Washington, Warren M. **4:** 2130
Wilkes, Maurice **4:** 2203
Williams, Frederic C. **4:** 2214
Wirth, Niklaus **4:** 2239
Wozniak, Stephen **4:** 2254
Zuse, Konrad **4:** 2302

Conservation
Durrell, Gerald **1:** 535
Ehrlich, Paul R. **1:** 568
Janzen, Dan **2:** 1007
Leopold, Aldo **3:** 1226

Schaller, George **4:** 1781

Cosmochemistry
Anders, Edward **1:** 41

Cosmology
Bondi, Hermann **1:** 212
Penrose, Roger **3:** 1562

Crystallography
Goldschmidt, Victor **2:** 788
Karle, Isabella **2:** 1059
Lonsdale, Kathleen **3:** 1270
Perutz, Max **3:** 1572
Vernadsky, Vladimir Ivanovich **4:** 2086

Cytology
Hay, Elizabeth D. **2:** 883
Rowley, Janet D. **3:** 1722
Sutton, Walter Stanborough **4:** 1950
Wilson, Edmund Beecher **4:** 2225

Dermatology
Lawless, Theodore K. **3:** 1184

Ecology
Adamson, Joy **1:** 7
Darden, Christine **1:** 455
Dubos, René **1:** 528
Ehrlich, Paul R. **1:** 568
Eisner, Thomas **1:** 579
Elton, Charles **1:** 586
Gadgil, Madhav **2:** 715
Hutchinson, G. Evelyn **2:** 982
Janzen, Dan **2:** 1007
Maathai, Wangari **3:** 1291
MacArthur, Robert H. **3:** 1292
Mittermeier, Russell **3:** 1397
Odum, Eugene Pleasants **3:** 1501
Odum, Howard T. **3:** 1502
Pimentel, David **3:** 1583
Sanchez, Pedro A. **4:** 1774
Vernadsky, Vladimir Ivanovich **4:** 2086
Whittaker, Robert Harding **4:** 2178
Woodwell, George M. **4:** 2252

Efficiency Engineering
Gilbreth, Frank **2:** 759
Gilbreth, Lillian **2:** 761
Taylor, Frederick Winslow **4:** 1977

Electrical Engineering
Armstrong, Edwin Howard **1:** 60
Ayrton, Hertha **1:** 81
Baird, John Logie **1:** 93
Boykin, Otis **1:** 236

Bundy, Robert F. **1:** 277
Chestnut, Harold **1:** 351
Cho, Alfred Y. **1:** 356
Edgerton, Harold **1:** 552
Fleming, John Ambrose **2:** 652
Forrester, Jay W. **2:** 670
Hewlett, William **2:** 918
Kilby, Jack St. Clair **2:** 1094
Marconi, Guglielmo **3:** 1313
Nishizawa, Jun-ichi **3:** 1475
Ochoa, Ellen **3:** 1496
Packard, David **3:** 1523
Peden, Irene Carswell **3:** 1558
Rigas, Harriett B. **3:** 1686
Rockwell, Mabel M. **3:** 1698
Steinmetz, Charles P. **4:** 1915
Terman, Frederick **4:** 1993
Tesla, Nikola **4:** 1997
Tien, Ping King **4:** 2022
Trump, John G. **4:** 2046
Whinnery, John R. **4:** 2166
Williams, Frederic C. **4:** 2214
Zadeh, Lotfi Asker **4:** 2285

Embryology
Hamburger, Viktor **2:** 850
Mintz, Beatrice **3:** 1394
Spemann, Hans **4:** 1888
Wilson, Edmund Beecher **4:** 2225

Endocrinology
Guillemin, Roger **2:** 826

Engineering
Alcorn, George Edward **1:** 16
Alexander, Archie Alphonso **1:** 20
Alexanderson, Ernst F. W. **1:** 23
Ammann, Othmar Hermann **1:** 40
Armstrong, Edwin Howard **1:** 60
Armstrong, Neil **1:** 63
Ayrton, Hertha **1:** 81
Baird, John Logie **1:** 93
Bishop, Alfred A. **1:** 176
Bluford, Guion S. **1:** 201
Bosch, Karl **1:** 224
Boykin, Otis **1:** 236
Brill, Yvonne Claeys **1:** 255
Bundy, Robert F. **1:** 277
Bush, Vannevar **1:** 285
Cambra, Jessie G. **1:** 301
Carrier, Willis **1:** 318
Chestnut, Harold **1:** 351
Cho, Alfred Y. **1:** 356
Clarke, Edith **1:** 360
Conway, Lynn Ann **1:** 392
Crosthwait David Nelson, Jr. **1:** 433
Dalén, Nils **1:** 443
Daniels, Walter T. **1:** 452
de Forest, Lee **1:** 475

Dicciani, Nance K. **1:** 495
Douglas, Donald W. **1:** 516
Draper, Charles Stark **1:** 518
Drucker, Daniel Charles **1:** 525
Durand, William F. **1:** 534
Dyson, Freeman J. **1:** 539
Eckert, J. Presper **1:** 544
Edgerton, Harold **1:** 552
Estrin, Thelma **1:** 599
Evans, James C. **1:** 605
Fitzroy, Nancy D. **2:** 648
Fleming, John Ambrose **2:** 652
Flügge-Lotz, Irmgard **2:** 662
Fokker, Anthony H. G. **2:** 663
Ford, Henry **2:** 667
Forrester, Jay W. **2:** 670
Fukui, Kenichi **2:** 708
Gilbreth, Frank **2:** 759
Gilbreth, Lillian **2:** 761
Goethals, George W. **2:** 777
Goldmark, Peter Carl **2:** 782
Gourdine, Meredith Charles **2:** 805
Greatbatch, Wilson **2:** 814
Greenewalt, Crawford H. **2:** 815
Groves, Leslie Richard **2:** 823
Gutierrez, Orlando A. **2:** 831
Harmon, E'lise F. **2:** 865
Harris, Wesley L. **2:** 868
Hawkins, W. Lincoln **2:** 879
Heinkel, Ernst **2:** 889
Henderson, Cornelius Langston **2:** 895
Hewlett, William **2:** 918
Hicks, Beatrice **2:** 924
Hounsfield, Godfrey **2:** 957
Hubbard, Philip G. **2:** 966
Hunsaker, Jerome C. **2:** 980
Iverson, F. Kenneth **2:** 998
Jansky, Karl **2:** 1005
Jarvik, Robert K. **2:** 1009
Jemison, Mae C. **2:** 1016
Jewett, Frank Baldwin **2:** 1020
Jobs, Steven **2:** 1022
Johnson, Barbara Crawford **2:** 1026
Johnson, Clarence L. **2:** 1027
Johnson, Marvin M. **2:** 1032
Juran, Joseph M. **2:** 1047
Katz, Donald L. **2:** 1072
Kettering, Charles Franklin **2:** 1085
Kilby, Jack St. Clair **2:** 1094
Kolff, Willem Johan **2:** 1119
Korolyov, Sergei **2:** 1127
Kuhlmann-Wilsdorf, Doris **2:** 1141
Latimer, Lewis H. **3:** 1173
Le Beau, Désirée **3:** 1198
Lee, Raphael C. **3:** 1208
Lewis, Warren K. **3:** 1240
Liepmann, Hans Wolfgang **3:** 1248
Little, Arthur D. **3:** 1259

MacGill, Elsie Gregory **3:** 1296
Marconi, Guglielmo **3:** 1313
Matthews, Alva T. **3:** 1329
Micheli-Tzanakou, Evangelia **3:** 1370
Midgley, Thomas, Jr. **3:** 1374
Morgan, Arthur E. **3:** 1417
Nichols, Roberta J. **3:** 1471
Nishizawa, Jun-ichi **3:** 1475
Ochoa, Ellen **3:** 1496
Ochoa, Ellen **3:** 1496
Packard, David **3:** 1523
Patrick, Jennie R. **3:** 1534
Peden, Irene Carswell **3:** 1558
Piasecki, Frank **3:** 1579
Pressman, Ada I. **3:** 1616
Qöyawayma, Alfred H. **3:** 1627
Reid, Lonnie **3:** 1663
Rickover, Hyman G. **3:** 1680
Rigas, Harriett B. **3:** 1686
Rockwell, Mabel M. **3:** 1698
Rockwell, Mabel M. **3:** 1698
Rogers, Marguerite M. **3:** 1700
Ross, Mary G. **3:** 1710
Shurney, Robert E. **4:** 1839
Sikorsky, Igor I. **4:** 1843
Sioui, Richard H. **4:** 1856
Sorensen, Charles E. **4:** 1881
Sparling, Rebecca H. **4:** 1885
Sperry, Elmer **4:** 1889
Steinman, David B. **4:** 1914
Steinmetz, Charles P. **4:** 1915
Stever, H. Guyford **4:** 1922
Taylor, Frederick Winslow **4:** 1977
Tereshkova, Valentina **4:** 1992
Terman, Frederick **4:** 1993
Terzaghi, Karl **4:** 1995
Tesla, Nikola **4:** 1997
Thomas, Martha Jane Bergin **4:** 2011
Tien, Ping King **4:** 2022
Timoshenko, Stephen P. **4:** 2025
Trump, John G. **4:** 2046
Tsiolkovsky, Konstantin **4:** 2048
van der Wal, Laurel **4:** 2078
von Braun, Wernher **4:** 2093
von Kármán, Theodore **4:** 2096
von Mises, Richard **4:** 2099
Whinnery, John R. **4:** 2166
Whittle, Frank **4:** 2180
Wickenden, William E. **4:** 2182
Widnall, Sheila E. **4:** 2184
Williams, Frederic C. **4:** 2214
Williams, O. S. **4:** 2216
Wolman, Abel **4:** 2244
Woodland, Joseph **4:** 2247
Wright, Wilbur **4:** 2262
Wu, Y. C. L. Susan **4:** 2268
Zadeh, Lotfi Asker **4:** 2285
Zworykin, Vladimir **4:** 2304

Entomology
Eisner, Thomas **1:** 579
Henry, John Edward **2:** 896
Janzen, Dan **2:** 1007
Kettlewell, Bernard **2:** 1088
Pimentel, David **3:** 1583
Turner, Charles Henry **4:** 2056
Wigglesworth, Vincent **4:** 2198

Environmental Engineering
Colmenares, Margarita **1:** 385

Environmentalism
Eisner, Thomas **1:** 579

Environmental Science
Ames, Bruce N. **1:** 38
Brooks, Ronald E. **1:** 261
Brown, Lester R. **1:** 265
Colmenares, Margarita **1:** 385
Commoner, Barry **1:** 387
Cox, Geraldine V. **1:** 419
Durrell, Gerald **1:** 535
Ehrlich, Paul R. **1:** 568
Hansen, James **2:** 856
Janzen, Dan **2:** 1007
Landsberg, Helmut E. **3:** 1166
Leopold, Aldo **3:** 1226
Leopold, Luna **3:** 1229
Lovelock, James E. **3:** 1279
MacDonald, Gordon **3:** 1295
Munk, Walter **3:** 1445
Pimentel, David **3:** 1583
Pinchot, Gifford **3:** 1584
Powless, David **3:** 1609
Revelle, Roger **3:** 1665
Rowland, F. Sherwood **3:** 1719
Sanchez, Pedro A. **4:** 1774
Schaller, George **4:** 1781
Schneider, Stephen H. **4:** 1790
Tsao, George T. **4:** 2047
Vernadsky, Vladimir Ivanovich **4:** 2086
Washington, Warren M. **4:** 2130
Went, Frits **4:** 2153
White, Gilbert Fowler **4:** 2173

Epidemiology
Blumberg, Baruch Samuel **1:** 203
Gayle, Helene Doris **2:** 737
Macdonald, Eleanor Josephine **3:** 1293

Ethnobotany
Schultes, Richard Evans **4:** 1798

Ethology
Lorenz, Konrad **3:** 1277

Field of Specialization Index

Robbins, Frederick **3:** 1689
Rock, John **3:** 1696
Ross, Ronald **3:** 1712
Rous, Peyton **3:** 1717
Sabin, Albert **4:** 1750
Sakmann, Bert **4:** 1765
Salk, Jonas **4:** 1768
Schou, Mogens **4:** 1792
Shockley, Dolores Cooper **4:** 1831
Slye, Maud **4:** 1863
Starzl, Thomas **4:** 1905
Steptoe, Patrick **4:** 1917
Sutton, Walter Stanborough **4:** 1950
Szent-Györgyi, Albert **4:** 1957
Taussig, Helen Brooke **4:** 1975
Temin, Howard **4:** 1990
Theiler, Max **4:** 2004
Thomas, E. Donnall **4:** 2009
Tildon, J. Tyson **4:** 2023
Vane, John R. **4:** 2079
Varmus, Harold E. **4:** 2083
Wagner-Jauregg, Julius **4:** 2110
Watkins, Levi, Jr. **4:** 2131
Weller, Thomas **4:** 2151
Whipple, George Hoyt **4:** 2170
White, Augustus **4:** 2172
Wiener, Alexander **4:** 2190
Williams, Daniel Hale **4:** 2212
Wright, Jane Cooke **4:** 2257
Wright, Louis Tompkins **4:** 2258
Yalow, Rosalyn Sussman **4:** 2273

Metallurgical Engineering
Iverson, F. Kenneth **2:** 998
Kuhlmann-Wilsdorf, Doris **2:** 1141

Metallurgy
Chaudhari, Praveen **1:** 349
Jeffries, Zay **2:** 1014
Pellier, Laurence Delisle **3:** 1560
Weertman, Julia **4:** 2136

Meteorology
Bjerknes, Jacob **1:** 179
Bolin, Bert **1:** 210
Coulomb, Jean **1:** 408
Diaz, Henry F. **1:** 494
Fujita, Tetsuya Theodore **2:** 706
Gadgil, Sulochana **2:** 717
Johnston, Harold S. **2:** 1035
Landsberg, Helmut E. **3:** 1166
Le Cadet, Georges **3:** 1200
Lorenz, Edward N. **3:** 1274
Mohorovičić, Andrija **3:** 1399
Richardson, Lewis Fry **3:** 1672
Rossby, Carl-Gustaf **3:** 1713
Solberg, Halvor **4:** 1874
Suomi, Verner E. **4:** 1945
van Straten, Florence W. **4:** 2080

Wegener, Alfred **4:** 2138

Microbiology
Abelson, Philip Hauge **1:** 1
Alexander, Hattie **1:** 21
Avery, Oswald Theodore **1:** 75
Baltimore, David **1:** 98
Behring, Emil von **1:** 137
Bordet, Jules **1:** 214
Claude, Albert **1:** 361
Cobb, Jewel Plummer **1:** 369
Cohn, Zanvil **1:** 382
Colwell, Rita R. **1:** 386
de Duvé, Christian **1:** 473
d'Hérelle, Félix **1:** 492
Dubos, René **1:** 528
Ehrlich, Paul **1:** 564
Elion, Gertrude Belle **1:** 582
Evans, Alice **1:** 604
Farquhar, Marilyn G. **2:** 610
Fibiger, Johannes **2:** 631
Fleming, Alexander **2:** 649
Flexner, Simon **2:** 654
Friend, Charlotte **2:** 701
Gajdusek, D. Carleton **2:** 719
Griffith, Frederick **2:** 817
Gross, Carol **2:** 820
Hay, Elizabeth D. **2:** 883
Hazen, Elizabeth Lee. **2:** 883
Hershey, Alfred Day **2:** 900
Hobby, Gladys Lounsbury **2:** 934
Huang, Alice Shih-hou **2:** 965
Koch, Robert **2:** 1111
Kornberg, Arthur **2:** 1124
Lancefield, Rebecca Craighill **3:** 1157
Landsteiner, Karl **3:** 1167
Lwoff, André **3:** 1284
MacLeod, Colin Munro **3:** 1299
Margulis, Lynn **3:** 1319
Moore, Ruth **3:** 1413
Nicolle, Charles J. H. **3:** 1472
Nirenberg, Marshall Warren **3:** 1474
Noguchi, Hideyo **3:** 1482
Northrop, John Howard **3:** 1487
Olden, Kenneth **3:** 1504
Petermann, Mary Locke **3:** 1577
Poindexter, Hildrus A. **3:** 1594
Reed, Walter **3:** 1657
Robbins, Frederick **3:** 1689
Rowley, Janet D. **3:** 1722
Salk, Jonas **4:** 1768
Sheldrake, Rupert **4:** 1825
Sutton, Walter Stanborough **4:** 1950
Szent-Györgyi, Albert **4:** 1957
Varmus, Harold E. **4:** 2083
Waksman, Selman **4:** 2112
Williams, Anna W. **4:** 2211
Wright, Almroth Edward **4:** 2255

Zinsser, Hans **4:** 2298

Microscopy
Zworykin, Vladimir **4:** 2304

Mineralogy
Fersman, Aleksandr Evgenievich **2:** 627
Goldschmidt, Victor **2:** 788
Vernadsky, Vladimir Ivanovich **4:** 2086

Molecular Biology
Altman, Sidney **1:** 29
Ames, Bruce N. **1:** 38
Arber, Werner **1:** 57
Bachrach, Howard L. **1:** 86
Benzer, Seymour **1:** 147
Bishop, J. Michael **1:** 177
Blackburn, Elizabeth H. **1:** 187
Brenner, Sydney **1:** 249
Crick, Francis **1:** 426
Delbrück, Max **1:** 484
Fedoroff, Nina V. **2:** 616
Fraenkel-Conrat, Heinz **2:** 683
Franklin, Rosalind Elsie **2:** 689
Gilbert, Walter **2:** 756
Hershey, Alfred Day **2:** 900
Itakura, Keiichi **2:** 997
Klug, Aaron **2:** 1105
Luria, Salvador Edward **3:** 1281
Meselson, Matthew **3:** 1363
Monod, Jacques Lucien **3:** 1405
Nomura, Masayasu **3:** 1485
Perutz, Max **3:** 1572
Ponnamperuma, Cyril **3:** 1600
Smith, Hamilton O. **4:** 1866
Stahl, Franklin W. **4:** 1895
Stanley, Wendell Meredith **4:** 1897
Szent-Györgyi, Albert **4:** 1957
Tonegawa, Susumu **4:** 2040
Watson, James D. **4:** 2132

Mutagenesis
Auerbach, Charlotte **1:** 74

Mycology
Hazen, Elizabeth Lee. **2:** 883

Natural Science
Adamson, Joy **1:** 7
Bailey, Florence Merriam **1:** 92
Dobzhansky, Theodosius **1:** 506
Durrell, Gerald **1:** 535
Janzen, Dan **2:** 1007
Noble, G. K. **3:** 1478
Rothschild, Miriam **3:** 1716
Schaller, George **4:** 1781

Physiology

Gender Index

Female

Adamson, Joy
Alexander, Hattie
Alvariño, Angeles
Andersen, Dorothy
Anderson, Gloria L.
Arber, Agnes
Auerbach, Charlotte
Ayrton, Hertha
Bailey, Florence Merriam
Baker, Sara Josephine
Bascom, Florence
Bell Burnell, Jocelyn Susan
Berkowitz, Joan B.
Bernstein, Dorothy Lewis
Bishop, Katharine Scott
Blackburn, Elizabeth H.
Blodgett, Katharine Burr
Brill, Yvonne Claeys
Brown, Rachel Fuller
Browne, Marjorie Lee
Burbidge, E. Margaret
Caldicott, Helen
Cambra, Jessie G.
Canady, Alexa I.
Cannon, Annie Jump
Carson, Rachel
Chinn, May Edward
Clarke, Edith
Clay-Jolles, Tettje Clasina
Cobb, Jewel Plummer
Cohn, Mildred
Colmenares, Margarita
Colwell, Rita R.
Conway, Lynn Ann
Conwell, Esther Marly
Cori, Gerty T.
Cowings, Patricia S.
Cox, Geraldine V.
Cox, Gertrude Mary
Crosby, Elizabeth Caroline
Curie, Marie
Daly, Marie M.
Darden, Christine
Davis, Margaret B.
Davis, Marguerite
Dicciani, Nance K.
Dresselhaus, Mildred S.

Earle, Sylvia A.
Edinger, Tilly
Edwards, Cecile Hoover
Edwards, Helen T.
Ehrenfest-Afanaseva, Tatiana
Elion, Gertrude Belle
Emerson, Gladys Anderson
Esau, Katherine
Estrin, Thelma
Evans, Alice
Faber, Sandra M.
Farquhar, Marilyn G.
Farr, Wanda K.
Fedoroff, Nina V.
Fell, Honor Bridget
Fieser, Mary Peters
Fisher, Elizabeth F.
Fitzroy, Nancy D.
Flügge-Lotz, Irmgard
Fossey, Dian
Franklin, Rosalind Elsie
Friend, Charlotte
Gadgil, Sulochana
Gardner, Julia Anna
Gayle, Helene Doris
Geiringer, Hilda
Geller, Margaret Joan
Giblett, Eloise R.
Gilbreth, Lillian
Goeppert-Mayer, Maria
Goldberg, Adele
Goldring, Winifred
Good, Mary L.
Goodall, Jane
Granville, Evelyn Boyd
Gross, Carol
Hamilton, Alice
Hardy, Harriet
Harmon, E'lise F.
Hay, Elizabeth D.
Hazen, Elizabeth Lee
Healy, Bernadine
Herzenberg, Caroline L.
Hicks, Beatrice
Hobby, Gladys Lounsbury
Hodgkin, Dorothy Crowfoot
Hogg, Helen Sawyer
Hopper, Grace

Horstmann, Dorothy Millicent
Huang, Alice Shih-hou
Hyde, Ida H.
Jackson, Shirley Ann
Jemison, Mae C.
Johnson, Barbara Crawford
Johnson, Katherine Coleman Goble
Johnson, Virginia E.
Joliot-Curie, Irène
Jones, Mary Ellen
Karle, Isabella
Kelsey, Frances Oldham
Kittrell, Flemmie Pansy
Knopf, Eleanora Bliss
Krim, Mathilde
Kuhlmann-Wilsdorf, Doris
Ladd-Franklin, Christine
Lancaster, Cleo
Lancefield, Rebecca Craighill
Leakey, Mary
Leavitt, Henrietta
Le Beau, Désirée
Leeman, Susan E.
Lehmann, Inge
Leopold, Estella Bergere
Levi-Montalcini, Rita
Lloyd, Ruth Smith
Logan, Myra A.
Long, Irene D.
Lonsdale, Kathleen
Maathai, Wangari
Macdonald, Eleanor Josephine
MacGill, Elsie Gregory
Manton, Sidnie Milana
Margulis, Lynn
Massevitch, Alla G.
Matthews, Alva T.
Maunder, Annie Russell
Maury, Antonia
Maury, Carlotta Joaquina
McClintock, Barbara
Meitner, Lise
Mendenhall, Dorothy Reed
Micheli-Tzanakou, Evangelia
Miller, Elizabeth C.
Mintz, Beatrice
Moore, Charlotte E.
Moore, Ruth

Bishop, J. Michael
Bjerknes, Jacob
Bjerknes, Vilhelm
Black, Davidson
Black, James
Blackett, Patrick Maynard Stuart
Blackwell, David
Bloch, Felix
Bloch, Konrad
Bloembergen, Nicolaas
Bluford, Guion S.
Blumberg, Baruch Samuel
Bohr, Aage
Bohr, Niels
Bolin, Bert
Bondi, Hermann
Booker, Walter M.
Bordet, Jules
Borel, Émile
Borlaug, Norman
Born, Max
Bosch, Karl
Bose, Satyendranath
Bothe, Walther
Bott, Raoul
Bovet, Daniel
Bowie, William
Boyer, Herbert W.
Boykin, Otis
Brady, St. Elmo
Bragg, William Henry
Bragg, William Lawrence
Branson, Herman
Brattain, Walter Houser
Braun, Karl Ferdinand
Breit, Gregory
Brenner, Sydney
Bressani, Ricardo
Bridgman, Percy Williams
Bronk, Detlev Wulf
Brønsted, Johannes Nicolaus
Brooks, Ronald E.
Brouwer, Luitzen Egbertus Jan
Brown, Herbert C.
Brown, Lester R.
Brown, Michael S.
Bucher, Walter Herman
Buchner, Eduard
Bullard, Edward
Bundy, Robert F.
Burbidge, Geoffrey
Burnet, Frank Macfarlane
Burton, Glenn W.
Bush, Vannevar
Butenandt, Adolf
Cairns, John, Jr.
Calderón, Alberto P.
Callender, Clive O.
Calvin, Melvin

Cantor, Georg
Cardona, Manuel
Cardozo, W. Warrick
Cardús, David
Carlson, Chester
Carothers, Wallace Hume
Carrel, Alexis
Carrier, Willis
Carruthers, George R.
Carson, Benjamin S.
Carver, George Washington
Castro, George
Cech, Thomas R.
Chadwick, James
Chain, Ernst Boris
Chamberlain, Owen
Chamberlin, Thomas Chrowder
Chance, Britton
Chandrasekhar, Subrahmanyan
Chang, Min-Chueh
Chargaff, Erwin
Charpak, Georges
Chaudhari, Praveen
Cherenkov, Pavel A.
Chestnut, Harold
Chew, Geoffrey Foucar
Child, Charles Manning
Cho, Alfred Y.
Chu, Paul Ching-Wu
Church, Alonzo
Claude, Albert
Claude, Georges
Clay, Jacob
Cloud, Preston
Cobb, William Montague
Cockcroft, John D.
Cohen, Paul
Cohen, Stanley
Cohen, Stanley N.
Cohn, Zanvil
Commoner, Barry
Compton, Arthur Holly
Cooke, Lloyd M.
Coolidge, William D.
Cooper, Leon
Corey, Elias James
Cori, Carl Ferdinand
Cormack, Allan M.
Cornforth, John
Coulomb, Jean
Courant, Richard
Cournand, André F.
Cousteau, Jacques
Cox, Elbert Frank
Cram, Donald J.
Cray, Seymour
Crick, Francis
Cronin, James W.
Crosthwait, David Nelson, Jr.

Curie, Pierre
Dale, Henry Hallett
Dalén, Nils
Dallmeier, Francisco
Dalrymple, G. Brent
Daly, Reginald Aldworth
Dam, Henrik
Daniels, Walter T.
Dantzig, George Bernard
Dart, Raymond A.
Dausset, Jean
Davis, Raymond, Jr.
Davisson, Clinton
DeBakey, Michael Ellis
de Broglie, Louis Victor
Debye, Peter
de Duvé, Christian
de Forest, Lee
de Gennes, Pierre-Gilles
Dehmelt, Hans
Deisenhofer, Johann
Delbrück, Max
Deligné, Pierre
Dennis, Jack B.
de Sitter, Willem
d'Hérelle, Félix
Diaz, Henry F.
Diels, Otto
Diener, Theodor Otto
Dijkstra, Edsger W.
Dirac, Paul
Djerassi, Carl
Dobzhansky, Theodosius
Doisy, Edward A.
Dole, Vincent P.
Domagk, Gerhard
Donaldson, Simon
Douglas, Donald W.
Draper, Charles Stark
Drew, Charles R.
Drucker, Daniel Charles
Dubois, Eugène
Dubos, René
Dulbecco, Renato
Durand, William F.
Durrell, Gerald
du Vigneaud, Vincent
Dyson, Freeman J.
Eccles, John C.
Eckert, J. Presper
Eddington, Arthur Stanley
Edelman, Gerald M.
Edgerton, Harold
Edison, Thomas Alva
Ehrenfest, Paul
Ehrlich, Paul
Ehrlich, Paul R.
Eigen, Manfred
Eijkman, Christiaan

Einstein, Albert
Einthoven, Willem
Eisner, Thomas
Eldredge, Niles
El-Sayed, Mostafa Amr
Elton, Charles
Enders, John F.
Engler, Adolph Gustav Heinrich
Enskog, David
Erlanger, Joseph
Ernst, Richard R.
Esaki, Leo
Euler, Ulf von
Euler-Chelpin, Hans von
Evans, James C.
Farnsworth, Philo T.
Fauci, Anthony S.
Favaloro, René Geronimo
Feigenbaum, Edward A.
Feigenbaum, Mitchell
Ferguson, Lloyd N.
Fermi, Enrico
Fersman, Aleksandr Evgenievich
Feynman, Richard P.
Fibiger, Johannes
Fieser, Louis
Fischer, Edmond H.
Fischer, Emil
Fischer, Ernst Otto
Fischer, Hans
Fisher, Ronald A.
Fitch, Val Logsdon
Fleming, Alexander
Fleming, John Ambrose
Flexner, Simon
Florey, Howard Walter
Flory, Paul
Fokker, Anthony H. G.
Forbush, Scott Ellsworth
Ford, Henry
Forrester, Jay W.
Forssmann, Werner
Fowler, William A.
Fox, Sidney W.
Fraenkel, Abraham Adolf
Fraenkel-Conrat, Heinz
Franck, James
Frank, Il'ya
Fraser-Reid, Bertram Oliver
Fréchet, Maurice
Freedman, Michael H.
Frenkel, Yakov Ilyich
Friedman, Jerome
Friedmann, Aleksandr A.
Frisch, Karl von
Frisch, Otto Robert
Fujita, Tetsuya Theodore
Fukui, Kenichi
Fuller, Solomon

Gabor, Dennis
Gadgil, Madhav
Gagarin, Yuri A.
Gajdusek, D. Carleton
Gallo, Robert C.
Gamow, George
Garrod, Archibald
Gasser, Herbert Spencer
Gates, Bill
Gates, Sylvester James, Jr.
Gaviola, Enrique
Geiger, Hans
Gell-Mann, Murray
Ghiorso, Albert
Giacconi, Riccardo
Giaever, Ivar
Giauque, William F.
Gibbs, William Francis
Gilbert, Walter
Gilbreth, Frank
Glaser, Donald
Glashow, Sheldon Lee
Glenn, John H., Jr.
Goddard, Robert H.
Gödel, Kurt Friedrich
Goethals, George W.
Gold, Thomas
Goldmark, Peter Carl
Goldschmidt, Richard B.
Goldschmidt, Victor
Goldstein, Avram
Goldstein, Joseph L.
Golgi, Camillo
Goudsmit, Samuel A.
Gould, Stephen Jay
Gourdine, Meredith Charles
Gourneau, Dwight
Govindjee
Granit, Ragnar Arthur
Greatbatch, Wilson
Greenewalt, Crawford H.
Griffith, Frederick
Grignard, François Auguste Victor
Grothendieck, Alexander
Groves, Leslie Richard
Guillaume, Charles-Edouard
Guillemin, Roger
Gullstrand, Allvar
Gutenberg, Beno
Guth, Alan
Gutierrez, Orlando A.
Haagen-Smit, A. J.
Haber, Fritz
Hadamard, Jacques
Hahn, Otto
Haldane, John Burdon Sanderson
Hale, George Ellery
Hall, Lloyd Augustus
Hamburger, Viktor

Hanafusa, Hidesaburo
Hannah, Marc R.
Hansen, James
Harden, Arthur
Hardy, Alister C.
Hardy, Godfrey Harold
Harris, Cyril
Harris, Wesley L.
Hartline, Haldan Keffer
Hassel, Odd
Hauptman, Herbert A.
Hausdorff, Felix
Hawking, Stephen
Hawkins, W. Lincoln
Haworth, Walter
Heimlich, Henry Jay
Heinkel, Ernst
Heisenberg, Werner Karl
Hench, Philip Showalter
Henderson, Cornelius Langston
Henry, John Edward
Henry, Warren Elliott
Herschbach, Dudley R.
Hershey, Alfred Day
Hertz, Gustav
Hertzsprung, Ejnar
Herzberg, Gerhard
Hess, Harry Hammond
Hess, Victor
Hess, Walter Rudolf
Hevesy, Georg von
Hewish, Antony
Hewlett, William
Heymans, Corneille Jean-François
Heyrovský, Jaroslav
Hilbert, David
Hill, Archibald V.
Hill, Henry A.
Hinshelwood, Cyril N.
Hinton, William Augustus
Hitchings, George H.
Hodgkin, Alan Lloyd
Hoffmann, Roald
Hofstadter, Robert
Holley, Robert William
Holmes, Arthur
Hopkins, Frederick Gowland
Horn, Michael Hastings
Houdry, Eugene
Hounsfield, Godfrey
Houssay, Bernardo
Hoyle, Fred
Hrdlička, Aleš
Hubbard, Philip G.
Hubbert, M. King
Hubble, Edwin
Hubel, David H.
Huber, Robert
Huggins, Charles B.

Hulse, Russell A.
Humason, Milton L.
Hunsaker, Jerome C.
Hutchinson, G. Evelyn
Huxley, Andrew Fielding
Huxley, Julian
Hyman, Libbie Henrietta
Imes, Elmer Samuel
Ioffe, Abram F.
Isaacs, Alick
Itakura, Keiichi
Iverson, F. Kenneth
Jacob, François
Jansky, Karl
Janzen, Dan
Jarvik, Robert K.
Jason, Robert S.
Jeffreys, Harold
Jeffries, Zay
Jensen, J. Hans D.
Jerne, Niels K.
Jewett, Frank Baldwin
Jobs, Steven
Johannsen, Wilhelm Ludvig
Johnson, Clarence L.
Johnson, John B., Jr.
Johnson, Joseph Lealand
Johnson, Marvin M.
Johnston, Harold S.
Joliot-Curie, Frédéric
Jones, Fred
Josephson, Brian D.
Julian, Percy Lavon
Juran, Joseph M.
Just, Ernest Everett
Kamerlingh Onnes, Heike
Kan, Yuet Wai
Kapitsa, Pyotr
Karle, Jerome
Karlin, Samuel
Karrer, Paul
Kastler, Alfred
Kates, Robert W.
Kato, Tosio
Katz, Bernard
Katz, Donald L.
Kay, Alan C.
Keith, Arthur
Kemeny, John G.
Kendall, Edward C.
Kendall, Henry W.
Kendrew, John
Kettering, Charles Franklin
Kettlewell, Bernard
Khorana, Har Gobind
Khush, Gurdev S.
Kilburn, Thomas M.
Kilby, Jack St. Clair
Kimura, Motoo

Kinoshita, Toichiro
Kinsey, Alfred
Kishimoto, Tadamitsu
Kistiakowsky, George B.
Klug, Aaron
Knudsen, William Claire
Knuth, Donald E.
Koch, Robert
Kocher, Theodor
Kodaira, Kunihiko
Kohler, Georges
Kolff, Willem Johan
Kolmogorov, Andrey Nikolayevich
Kolthoff, Izaak Maurits
Konishi, Masakazu
Kornberg, Arthur
Korolyov, Sergei
Kossel, Albrecht
Kountz, Samuel L.
Krebs, Edwin G.
Krebs, Hans Adolf
Krogh, August
Kuhn, Richard
Kuiper, Gerard Peter
Kurchatov, Igor
Kurtz, Thomas Eugene
Kurzweil, Raymond
Kusch, Polycarp
Lamb, Willis E., Jr.
Land, Edwin H.
Landau, Lev Davidovich
Landsberg, Helmut E.
Landsteiner, Karl
Langevin, Paul
Langmuir, Irving
Latimer, Lewis H.
Lattes, C. M. G.
Laub, Jakob Johann
Laue, Max von
Lauterbur, Paul C.
Laveran, Alphonse
Lawless, Theodore K.
Lawrence, Ernest Orlando
Leakey, Louis
Leakey, Richard E.
Lebesgue, Henri
Le Cadet, Georges
Leder, Philip
Lederberg, Joshua
Lederman, Leon Max
Lee, Raphael C.
Lee, Tsung-Dao
Lee, Yuan T.
Leevy, Carroll
Leffall, LaSalle D., Jr.
Lehn, Jean-Marie
Leloir, Luis F.
Lemaître, Georges
Lenard, Philipp E. A. von

Leopold, Aldo
Leopold, Luna
Lester, William Alexander, Jr.
Levi-Civita, Tullio
Lewis, Gilbert Newton
Lewis, Julian Herman
Lewis, Warren K.
Li, Ching Chun
Li, Choh Hao
Libby, Willard F.
Liepmann, Hans Wolfgang
Lillie, Frank Rattray
Lim, Robert K. S.
Lin, Chia-Chiao
Lipmann, Fritz
Lippmann, Gabriel
Lipscomb, William Nunn, Jr.
Little, Arthur D.
Lizhi, Fang
Loeb, Jacques
Loewi, Otto
London, Fritz
Lorentz, Hendrik Antoon
Lorenz, Edward N.
Lorenz, Konrad
Lovelock, James E.
Luria, Salvador Edward
Lwoff, André
Lynen, Feodor
Lynk, Miles Vandahurst
MacArthur, Robert H.
MacDonald, Gordon
Mac Lane, Saunders
MacLeod, Colin Munro
Macleod, John James Rickard
Maillart, Robert
Maiman, Theodore
Maloney, Arnold Hamilton
Mandelbrot, Benoit B.
Mandel'shtam, Leonid Isaakovich
Marchbanks, Vance H., Jr.
Marconi, Guglielmo
Marcus, Rudolph A.
Margulis, Gregori Aleksandrovitch
Marie-Victorin, Frère
Markov, Andrei Andreevich
Martin, A. J. P.
Massey, Walter E.
Massie, Samuel P.
Masters, William Howell
Matuyama, Motonori
Mauchly, John William
Maynard Smith, John
Mayr, Ernst
McAfee, Walter S.
McCarthy, John
McCarty, Maclyn
McCollum, Elmer Verner
McConnell, Harden

McMillan, Edwin M.
Medawar, Peter Brian
Merrifield, R. Bruce
Meselson, Matthew
Metchnikoff, Élie
Meyerhof, Otto
Michel, Hartmut
Michelson, Albert
Midgley, Thomas, Jr.
Miller, James A.
Miller, Stanley Lloyd
Millikan, Robert A.
Milne, Edward Arthur
Milnor, John
Milstein, César
Minkowski, Hermann
Minkowski, Rudolph
Minot, George Richards
Minsky, Marvin
Mitchell, Peter D.
Mittermeier, Russell
Mohorovičić, Andrija
Moissan, Henri
Molina, Mario
Moniz, Egas
Monod, Jacques Lucien
Montagnier, Luc
Moore, Raymond Cecil
Moore, Stanford
Morgan, Arthur E.
Morgan, Garrett A.
Morgan, Thomas Hunt
Mori, Shigefumi
Morley, Edward Williams
Morrison, Philip
Moseley, Henry Gwyn Jeffreys
Mössbauer, Rudolf
Mott, Nevill Francis
Mottelson, Ben R.
Moulton, Forest Ray
Muller, Hermann Joseph
Müller, K. Alex
Müller, Paul
Mulliken, Robert S.
Mullis, Kary
Munk, Walter
Murphy, William P.
Murray, Joseph E.
Nabrit, Samuel Milton
Nagata, Takesi
Nambu, Yoichiro
Nathans, Daniel
Natta, Giulio
Neal, Homer Alfred
Néel, Louis
Neher, Erwin
Nernst, Walther
Newell, Allen
Newell, Norman Dennis

Nicolle, Charles J. H.
Nier, Alfred O. C.
Nirenberg, Marshall Warren
Nishizawa, Jun-ichi
Nishizuka, Yasutomi
Noble, G. K.
Noguchi, Hideyo
Nomura, Masayasu
Norrish, Ronald G. W.
Northrop, John Howard
Novikov, Sergei
Noyce, Robert
Oberth, Hermann
Ochoa, Severo
Odum, Eugene Pleasants
Odum, Howard T.
Olden, Kenneth
Oldham, Richard Dixon
Onsager, Lars
Oort, Jan Hendrik
Oparin, Aleksandr Ivanovich
Oppenheimer, J. Robert
Osterbrock, Donald E.
Ostwald, Friedrich Wilhelm
Packard, David
Palade, George
Panofsky, Wolfgang K. H.
Papanicolaou, George
Parker, Charles Stewart
Parsons, John T.
Patterson, Claire
Patterson, Frederick Douglass
Paul, Wolfgang
Pauli, Wolfgang
Pauling, Linus
Pavlov, Ivan Petrovich
Peano, Giuseppe
Pearson, Karl
Pedersen, Charles John
Penrose, Roger
Penzias, Arno
Perrin, Jean Baptiste
Perutz, Max
Piasecki, Frank
Piccard, Auguste
Pimentel, David
Pinchot, Gifford
Pincus, Gregory Goodwin
Planck, Max
Pogue, William Reid
Poincaré, Jules Henri
Poindexter, Hildrus A.
Polanyi, John C.
Pólya, George
Ponnamperuma, Cyril
Porter, George
Porter, Rodney
Poulsen, Valdemar
Pound, Robert

Powell, Cecil Frank
Powless, David
Prandtl, Ludwig
Pregl, Fritz
Prelog, Vladimir
Prigogine, Ilya
Prokhorov, Aleksandr
Punnett, R. C.
Purcell, Edward Mills
Qöyawayma, Alfred H.
Quarterman, Lloyd Albert
Quinland, William Samuel
Rabi, I. I.
Rainwater, James
Ramalingaswami, Vulimiri
Raman, C. V.
Ramanujan, S. I.
Ramón y Cajal, Santiago
Ramsay, William
Ramsey, Frank Plumpton
Ramsey, Norman Foster
Rao, C. N. R.
Reber, Grote
Reddy, Raj
Reed, Walter
Reichstein, Tadeus
Reid, Lonnie
Reines, Frederick
Revelle, Roger
Richards, Dickinson Woodruff, Jr.
Richards, Theodore William
Richardson, Lewis Fry
Richardson, Owen W.
Richet, Charles Robert
Richter, Burton
Richter, Charles F.
Rickover, Hyman G.
Risi, Joseph
Ritchie, Dennis
Robbins, Frederick
Roberts, Lawrence
Roberts, Richard J.
Robinson, Robert
Rock, John
Roelofs, Wendell L.
Rohrer, Heinrich
Romer, Alfred Sherwood
Romero, Juan Carlos
Röntgen, Wilhelm Conrad
Ross, Ronald
Rossby, Carl-Gustaf
Rous, Peyton
Rowland, F. Sherwood
Rubbia, Carlo
Runcorn, S. K.
Ruska, Ernst
Russell, Bertrand
Russell, Frederick Stratten
Russell, Henry Norris

Russell, Loris Shano
Rutherford, Ernest
Ružička, Leopold
Ryle, Martin
Sabatier, Paul
Sabin, Albert
Sagan, Carl
Sakharov, Andrei
Sakmann, Bert
Salam, Abdus
Salk, Jonas
Samuelsson, Bengt
Sanchez, David A.
Sanchez, Pedro A.
Sandage, Allan R.
Sanger, Frederick
Satcher, David
Schaller, George
Schally, Andrew V.
Scharff Goldhaber, Gertrude
Schawlow, Arthur L.
Schneider, Stephen H.
Schou, Mogens
Schrieffer, J. Robert
Schrödinger, Erwin
Schultes, Richard Evans
Schwartz, Melvin
Schwinger, Julian
Seaborg, Glenn T.
Segrè, Emilio
Seitz, Frederick
Semenov, Nikolai N.
Serre, Jean-Pierre
Shannon, Claude
Shapiro, Irwin
Shapley, Harlow
Sharp, Phillip A.
Sharp, Robert Phillip
Sheldrake, Rupert
Shepard, Alan B., Jr.
Sherrington, Charles Scott
Shockley, William
Shoemaker, Eugene M.
Shokalsky, Yuly Mikhaylovich
Shtokman, Vladimir Borisovich
Shurney, Robert E.
Siegbahn, Kai M.
Siegbahn, Karl M. G.
Sikorsky, Igor I.
Simon, Herbert A.
Simpson, George Gaylord
Singer, I. M.
Sioui, Richard H.
Skoog, Folke Karl
Slater, John Clarke
Slipher, Vesto M.
Smale, Stephen
Smith, Hamilton O.
Smith, Michael

Snell, George Davis
Soddy, Frederick
Solberg, Halvor
Sommerfeld, Arnold
Sommerville, Duncan McLaren
   Young
Sorensen, Charles E.
Sørensen, Søren Peter Lauritz
Spedding, Frank Harold
Spemann, Hans
Sperry, Elmer
Sperry, Roger W.
Spitzer, Lyman, Jr.
Stahl, Franklin W.
Stanley, Wendell Meredith
Stark, Johannes
Starling, Ernest H.
Starr, Chauncey
Starzl, Thomas
Staudinger, Hermann
Stefanik, Milan Ratislav
Stein, William Howard
Steinberger, Jack
Steinman, David B.
Steinmetz, Charles P.
Steptoe, Patrick
Stern, Otto
Stever, H. Guyford
Steward, Frederick Campion
Stewart, Thomas Dale
Stibitz, George R.
Stock, Alfred
Stommel, Henry
Størmer, Fredrik
Strassmann, Fritz
Straus, William Levi, Jr.
Strutt, John William
Strutt, Robert
Sturtevant, A. H.
Sumner, James B.
Suomi, Verner E.
Sutherland, Earl
Sutherland, Ivan
Sutton, Walter Stanborough
Svedberg, Theodor
Swaminathan, M. S.
Synge, Richard
Szent-Györgyi, Albert
Szilard, Leo
Tamm, Igor
Tan Jiazhen
Tapia, Richard A.
Tarski, Alfred
Tatum, Edward Lawrie
Taube, Henry
Taylor, Frederick Winslow
Taylor, Joseph H., Jr.
Taylor, Moddie
Taylor, Richard E.

Taylor, Stuart
Teller, Edward
Temin, Howard
Terman, Frederick
Terzaghi, Karl
Tesla, Nikola
Theiler, Max
Theorell, Axel Hugo Teodor
Thom, René Frédéric
Thomas, E. Donnall
Thompson, D'Arcy Wentworth
Thompson, Kenneth
Thomson, George Paget
Thomson, J. J.
Thurston, William
Tien, Ping King
Tildon, J. Tyson
Timoshenko, Stephen P.
Tinbergen, Nikolaas
Ting, Samuel C. C.
Tiselius, Arne
Tizard, Henry
Todd, Alexander
Tombaugh, Clyde W.
Tomonaga, Sin-Itiro
Tonegawa, Susumu
Townes, Charles H.
Trump, John G.
Tsao, George T.
Tsiolkovsky, Konstantin
Tsui, Daniel Chee
Tswett, Mikhail
Turing, Alan
Turner, Charles Henry
Tuve, Merle A.
Uhlenbeck, George
Urey, Harold
Uyeda, Seiya
Vallois, Henri-Victor
Van Allen, James
Van de Graaff, Robert J.
van der Meer, Simon
van der Waals, Johannes Diderik
Vane, John R.
Van Vleck, John
Varmus, Harold E.
Veksler, V. I.
Vernadsky, Vladímir Ivanovich
Virtanen, Artturi Ilmari
Vollenweider, Richard
Volterra, Vito
von Braun, Wernher
von Kármán, Theodore
von Klitzing, Klaus
von Mises, Richard
von Neumann, John
Voûte, Joan George Erardus
   Gijsbert
Vries, Hugo de

Wagner-Jauregg, Julius
Waksman, Selman
Wald, George
Wallach, Otto
Walton, Ernest
Wang, An
Wang, James C.
Wankel, Felix
Warburg, Otto
Washington, Warren M.
Watkins, Levi, Jr.
Watson, James D.
Watson-Watt, Robert
Wegener, Alfred
Weidenreich, Franz
Weil, André
Weinberg, Robert A.
Weinberg, Steven
Weinberg, Wilhelm
Weizsäcker, Carl F. Von
Weller, Thomas
Went, Frits
Werner, Alfred
West, Harold Dadford
Wetherill, George West
Weyl, Hermann
Wheeler, John Archibald
Whinnery, John R.
Whipple, Fred Lawrence
Whipple, George Hoyt
White, Augustus

White, Gilbert Fowler
Whitehead, Alfred North
Whittaker, Robert Harding
Whittle, Frank
Wickenden, William E.
Wiechert, Emil
Wieland, Heinrich
Wien, Wilhelm
Wiener, Alexander
Wiener, Norbert
Wiesel, Torsten
Wigglesworth, Vincent
Wigner, Eugene Paul
Wiles, Andrew J.
Wilkes, Maurice
Wilkins, J. Ernest, Jr.
Wilkins, Maurice Hugh Frederick
Wilkinson, Geoffrey
Williams, Daniel Hale
Williams, Frederic C.
Williams, O. S.
Williamson, James S.
Willstätter, Richard
Wilson, C. T. R.
Wilson, Edmund Beecher
Wilson, Edward O.
Wilson, J. Tuzo
Wilson, Kenneth G.
Wilson, Robert R.
Wilson, Robert Woodrow
Windaus, Adolf

Wirth, Niklaus
Witten, Edward
Wittig, Georg
Wolman, Abel
Wood, Harland G.
Woodland, Joseph
Woodward, Robert B.
Woodwell, George M.
Wozniak, Stephen
Wright, Almroth Edward
Wright, Louis Tompkins
Wright, Sewall
Wright, Orville
Wright, Wilbur
Yang, Chen Ning
Yau, Shing-Tung
Young, J. Z.
Yukawa, Hideki
Zadeh, Lotfi Asker
Zeeman, E. C.
Zeeman, Pieter
Zel'dovich, Yakov Borisovich
Zen, E-an
Zernike, Frits
Ziegler, Karl
Zinder, Norton
Zinsser, Hans
Zsigmondy, Richard
Zuse, Konrad
Zworykin, Vladimir

Nationality/Ethnicity Index

Scientists are listed by country of origin and/or citizenship as well as by ethnicity (see African American, Asian American, Hispanic American, Native American).

African

Leakey, Louis **3:** 1187
Leakey, Richard E. **3:** 1194

African American

Alcorn, George Edward **1:** 016
Alexander, Archie Alphonso **1:** 020
Allen, William E., Jr. **1:** 028
Anderson, Gloria L. **1:** 047
Banks, Harvey Washington **1:** 101
Barber, Jesse B., Jr. **1:** 106
Barnes, William Harry **1:** 114
Berry, Leonidas Harris **1:** 163
Bishop, Alfred A. **1:** 176
Blackwell, David **1:** 190
Bluford, Guion S. **1:** 201
Booker, Walter M. **1:** 214
Boykin, Otis **1:** 236
Brady, St. Elmo **1:** 237
Branson, Herman **1:** 244
Brooks, Ronald E. **1:** 261
Browne, Marjorie Lee **1:** 270
Bundy, Robert F. **1:** 277
Callender, Clive O. **1:** 297
Canady, Alexa I. **1:** 303
Cardozo, W. Warrick **1:** 309
Carruthers, George R. **1:** 319
Carson, Benjamin S. **1:** 320
Carver, George Washington **1:** 325
Chinn, May Edward **1:** 354
Cobb, Jewel Plummer **1:** 369
Cobb, William Montague **1:** 371
Cooke, Lloyd M. **1:** 394
Cowings, Patricia S. **1:** 417
Cox, Elbert Frank **1:** 418
Crosthwait David Nelson, Jr. **1:** 433
Daly, Marie M. **1:** 448
Daniels, Walter T. **1:** 452
Darden, Christine **1:** 455
Drew, Charles R. **1:** 523
Edwards, Cecile Hoover **1:** 559
Evans, James C. **1:** 605
Ferguson, Lloyd N. **2:** 622
Fuller, Solomon **2:** 710
Gates, Sylvester James, Jr. **2:** 734
Gayle, Helene Doris **2:** 737
Gourdine, Meredith Charles **2:** 805
Granville, Evelyn Boyd **2:** 811

Hall, Lloyd Augustus **2:** 848
Hannah, Marc R. **2:** 856
Harris, Wesley L. **2:** 868
Hawkins, W. Lincoln **2:** 879
Henderson, Cornelius Langston **2:** 895
Henry, Warren Elliott **2:** 897
Hill, Henry A. **2:** 929
Hinton, William Augustus **2:** 931
Hubbard, Philip G. **2:** 966
Imes, Elmer Samuel **2:** 993
Jackson, Shirley Ann **2:** 1001
Jason, Robert S. **2:** 1011
Jemison, Mae C. **2:** 1016
Johnson, John B., Jr. **2:** 1029
Johnson, Joseph Lealand **2:** 1030
Johnson, Katherine Coleman Goble **2:** 1031
Jones, Fred **2:** 1041
Julian, Percy Lavon **2:** 1045
Just, Ernest Everett **2:** 1049
Kittrell, Flemmie Pansy **2:** 1104
Kountz, Samuel L. **2:** 1130
Lancaster, Cleo **3:** 1156
Latimer, Lewis H. **3:** 1173
Lawless, Theodore K. **3:** 1184
Leffall, LaSalle D., Jr. **3:** 1215
Lester, William Alexander, Jr. **3:** 1231
Lewis, Julian Herman **3:** 1238
Lloyd, Ruth Smith **3:** 1263
Logan, Myra A. **3:** 1267
Long, Irene D. **3:** 1269
Lynk, Miles Vandahurst **3:** 1288
Maloney, Arnold Hamilton **3:** 1305
Marchbanks, Vance H., Jr. **3:** 1312
Massey, Walter E. **3:** 1325
Massie, Samuel P. **3:** 1327
McAfee, Walter S. **3:** 1341
Moore, Ruth **3:** 1413
Morgan, Garrett A. **3:** 1419
Nabrit, Samuel Milton **3:** 1451
Neal, Homer Alfred **3:** 1457
Olden, Kenneth **3:** 1504
Parker, Charles Stewart **3:** 1532
Patrick, Jennie R. **3:** 1534
Patterson, Frederick Douglass **3:** 1539
Poindexter, Hildrus A. **3:** 1594

Quarterman, Lloyd Albert **3:** 1628
Quinland, William Samuel **3:** 1631
Reid, Lonnie **3:** 1663
Satcher, David **4:** 1780
Shockley, Dolores Cooper **4:** 1831
Shurney, Robert E. **4:** 1839
Taylor, Moddie **4:** 1981
Taylor, Stuart **4:** 1983
Tildon, J. Tyson **4:** 2023
Turner, Charles Henry **4:** 2056
Washington, Warren M. **4:** 2130
Watkins, Levi, Jr. **4:** 2131
West, Harold Dadford **4:** 2157
White, Augustus **4:** 2172
Wilkins, J. Ernest, Jr. **4:** 2206
Williams, Daniel Hale **4:** 2212
Williams, O. S. **4:** 2216
Wright, Jane Cooke **4:** 2257
Wright, Louis Tompkins **4:** 2258

Algerian

Coulomb, Jean **1:** 408

American

Abelson, Philip Hauge **1:** 001
Adams, Roger **1:** 004
Adams, Walter Sydney **1:** 005
Ahlfors, Lars V. **1:** 010
Aiken, Howard **1:** 012
Aki, Keiiti **1:** 014
Alcala, Jose **1:** 015
Alcorn, George Edward **1:** 016
Alexander, Archie Alphonso **1:** 020
Alexander, Hattie **1:** 021
Alexanderson, Ernst F. W. **1:** 023
Alfvén, Hannes Olof Gösta **1:** 024
Allen, William E., Jr. **1:** 028
Altman, Sidney **1:** 029
Alvarez, Luis **1:** 031
Alvariño, Angeles **1:** 034
Amdahl, Gene M. **1:** 035
Ames, Bruce N. **1:** 038
Ammann, Othmar Hermann **1:** 040
Anders, Edward **1:** 041
Andersen, Dorothy **1:** 043
Anderson, Carl David **1:** 044
Anderson, Gloria L. **1:** 047
Anderson, Philip Warren **1:** 049

Subject Index

References to individual volumes are listed in **boldface;** numbers following a colon refer to page numbers. A **boldface** page number indicates the full entry for a scientist.

Abbot, William R. **3:** 1657
ABC
    See Atanasoff-Berry Computer (ABC)
Abderhalden, Emil **1:** 497
Abegg, Richard **1:** 154
Abel, John Jacob **3:** 1302
Abel, Niels Henrik **3:** 1199
Abelian functions **3:** 1593
Abell, George O. **3:** 1519
Abelson, Philip Hauge **1:** 1; **3:** 1352; **4:** 1804
ablation cooling **4:** 1846
ablative coatings for missile reentry **4:** 1846
abortions, spontaneous, in cows **1:** 604
abrasives **4:** 1856
absolute motion **3:** 1593
absolute zero **2:** 1054; **3:** 1165, 1650
abstract algebra **3:** 1481
abstract spaces **2:** 694
AC
    See alternating current (AC)
accelerated flow modification **1:** 339
accommodation theory of optics **2:** 828
acetanilide **1:** 78
acetate **1:** 196
acetic acid **2:** 859
acetone, production of **3:** 1488
acetyl amino acids **4:** 1956
acetyl coenzyme A **2:** 1090; **3:** 1287, 1288
acetyl phosphate **3:** 1254
acetylcholine **1:** 442, 601; **3:** 1218, 1266
acetylcholine neurotransmitter **1:** 543
acetylene **1:** 363, 443; **4:** 1750
acid phosphatase **2:** 976
acid rain **1:** 210, 211; **3:** 1167
acid-base equilibria **1:** 260
acidimeter **1:** 132
acidity **1:** 132
acids **1:** 258, 260
Ackerman, Thomas **4:** 1759
Acoustic Thermometry of Ocean Climate (ATOC) **3:** 1446
acoustical design **2:** 867
acoustics **2:** 866
acquired immunodeficiency syndrome (AIDS) **1:** 30, 382, 384; **2:** 613, 614,

692, 721–723, 737, 738, 1035, 1101, 1136, 1138; **3:** 1408; **4:** 1991, 1992
acquired immunological tolerance **3:** 1355
Acta Chimica Scandinavica **2:** 872
ACTH
    See adrenocorticotropic hormone (ACTH)
actinide concept **4:** 1804
actinium radioactive decay series **3:** 1567
actinomycetes **1:** 269
actinomycin **4:** 2113
acyclovir **1:** 584
ADA
    See adenosine deaminase (ADA)
Adair, Gilbert **3:** 1573
Adams, Cyril **1:** 345
Adams, Numa P. G. **2:** 1029, 1031
Adams, Roger **1:** 4, 313; **4:** 1898
Adams, W. A. **1:** 548
Adams, Walter Sydney **1:** 5
Adamson, George **1:** 7
Adamson, Joy **1:** 7
Adams's catalyst **1:** 4, 5
adaptation **4:** 2028
adaptive landscape **3:** 1338
adaptive response **3:** 1282
addiction **1:** 510, 512; **2:** 789, 790
Addison's disease **4:** 1959
additives, antiknock for gasoline **3:** 1374, 1375
adenine **1:** 427
adenohypophysis portion of the pituitary gland **3:** 1244
adenosine deaminase (ADA) deficiency **1:** 52
adenosine diphosphate (ADP) **4:** 2036
adenosine triphosphate (ATP) **3:** 1254, 1255, 1367; **4:** 2036
adenovirus **3:** 1692
adermin **2:** 1142
adiabatic demagnetization **2:** 752
ADP
    See adenosine diphosphate (ADP)
adrenal cortex **2:** 894
adrenal glands **2:** 976; **3:** 1662; **4:** 1958
adrenalectomy **2:** 976

adrenaline **1:** 601; **3:** 1244, 1266; **4:** 1947
adrenaline reversal **1:** 442
adrenergic receptors **1:** 185
adrenocorticotropic hormone (ACTH) **2:** 894, 895; **3:** 1244
Adrian, Edgar Douglas **1:** 9, 153, 257; **2:** 810; **4:** 1829
adsorption **3:** 1173; **4:** 2030, 2053, 2290
AEC
    See Atomic Energy Commission (AEC)
Aëdes aegypti mosquito **3:** 1658
aenorhabditis elegans (*C. elegans*) nematodes **1:** 250
aerial warfare **4:** 2092
aerodynamic flutter **4:** 2303
aerodynamics **2:** 980; **3:** 1610; **4:** 2216
aeronautical engineering **2:** 980, 1027
aeronautical propulsion **1:** 534
aeronautics **2:** 662, 865, 866, 980; **4:** 1922, 2184
aeropropulsion **3:** 1663
aerospace engineering **3:** 1710; **4:** 2184
aesthetics in science **2:** 939
aether
    See ether
affinities, chemical **3:** 1521, 1522
AFM
    See atomic force microscope (AFM)
African Americans, biological study of **3:** 1238, 1239
African Americans in American College of Surgeons **4:** 2259
African infantile leishmaniasis **3:** 1472
aga **1:** 444
Agassiz, Louis **3:** 1420, 1705
age of rocks and minerals **1:** 447
aging **3:** 1733
Agramonte, Aristides **3:** 1658
agriculture **1:** 325; **4:** 2088
agronomy **1:** 218, 219, 220; **4:** 1857
Ahlfors, Lars V. **1:** **10**
Ahlquist, Raymond P. **1:** 186
AI
    See artificial intelligence (AI)

A **boldface** page number refers to the full entry for the scientist

Subject Index

Subject Index

Subject Index

Subject Index

Subject Index

Subject Index

Subject Index

Subject Index

Subject Index

Subject Index